S0-ASF-719

Cases in
Strategic Management

Seventh Edition

Cases in Strategic Management

Charles W. L. Hill
University of Washington

Gareth R. Jones
Texas A&M University

Houghton Mifflin Company

Boston   New York

For my children, Elizabeth, Charlotte, and Michelle
Charles W. L. Hill

For Nicholas and Julia and Morgan and Nia
Gareth R. Jones

Vice-President and Publisher: George T. Hoffman
Senior Sponsoring Editor: Lise Johnson
Associate Editor: Julia Perez
Editorial Assistant: Amy Galvin
Senior Project Editor: Kerry Falvey
Manufacturing Manager: Karen Fawcett
Executive Marketing Manager: Steven W. Mikels
Marketing Associate: Lisa Boden

Cover image: © Medioimages/Imagestate

Copyright © 2007 by Houghton Mifflin Company. All rights reserved.

No part of this work may be reproduced or transmitted in any form or by any means, electronic or mechanical, including photocopying and recording, or by any information storage or retrieval system without the prior written permission of Houghton Mifflin Company unless such copying is expressly permitted by federal copyright law. Address inquiries to College Permissions, Houghton Mifflin Company, 222 Berkeley Street, Boston MA 02116-3764.

Library of Congress Control Number: 2005935203

ISBNs:
Instructor's Exam Copy:
ISBN-13: 978-0-618-73168-8
ISBN-10: 0-618-73168-7

For orders, use student text ISBNs:
ISBN-13: 978-0-618-64163-5
ISBN-10: 0-618-64163-7

1 2 3 4 5 6 7 8 9—DOW—10 09 08 07 06

Contents

Introduction: Analyzing a Case Study and Writing a Case Study Analysis

Cases

SECTION A: Business Level Cases: Domestic and Global

Section B: Corporate Level Cases: Domestic and Global

Preface

The significant revisions we made to the sixth edition of *Strategic Management: An Integrated Approach* have been well received by instructors and students alike. Our book has strengthened its position as the most widely used strategic management textbook on the market. This tells us that we continue to meet the expectations of existing users and attract many new users to our book. It is clear that most strategy instructors share with us a concern for currency in text and examples to ensure that cutting-edge issues and new developments in strategic management are continually addressed.

Just as in the last edition, our objective in rewriting the seventh edition has been to maintain all that was good about prior editions, while refining our approach to discussing established strategic management issues and adding new material to the text to present a more complete, clear, and current account of strategic management in the 2000s. We believe that the result is a book that is more closely aligned with the needs of today's professors and students and the realities of competition in the new global environment.

It is important to emphasize that we have overhauled the case selection. There are 34 cases in this edition, and 26 of these cases are new to this edition. The remaining cases have been updated and revised. For example, the home videogame and Nucor cases have been revised to include material through to early 2005. As always, we have used a tight screen to weed out poor-quality cases and we believe that the selection we offer is the best on the market.

The 34 cases that we have selected for this edition will appeal, we are certain, to students and professors alike, both because these cases are intrinsically interesting and because of the number of strategic management issues they illuminate. The organizations discussed in the cases range from large, well-known companies, for which students can do research in order to update the information, to small, entrepreneurial businesses that illustrate the uncertainty and challenge of the strategic management process. In addition, the selections include many international cases, and most of the other cases contain some element of global strategy.

To help students learn how to effectively analyze and write a case study, we continue to include a special section on this subject. This section includes a checklist and explanation of areas to consider, suggested research tools, and tips on financial analysis.

We feel that our entire selection is unrivaled in breadth and depth, and we are grateful to the other case authors who have contributed to this edition:

Vincent Amanor-Boadu, *Kansas State University*
Sally Baack, *San Francisco State University*
Frank C. Barnes, *University of North Carolina–Charlotte*
Christopher A. Bartlett, *Harvard Business School*
David Barton, *Kansas State University*
Mike Boland, *Kansas State University*
Lew Brown, *University of North Carolina, Greensboro*
Isaac Cohen, *San Jose State University*
Christina Darwall, *Harvard Business School California Research Center*
S.S. George, *ICFAI Center for Management Research*

Armand Gilinsky, Jr., *Sonoma State University*
Robert H. Girling, *Sonoma State University*
Debra Glassman, *University of Washington*
Jeffrey A. Krug, *Appalachian State University*
Suresh Kotha, *University of Washington*
Anne T. Lawrence, *San Jose State University*
Robert J. Mockler, *St. John's University*
Rebecca J. Morris, *University of Nebraska at Omaha*
Susan L. Peters, *Texas A&M University*
Murray Silverman, *San Francisco State University*
Beverly B. Tyler, *North Carolina State University*
Meg Wozny, *Harvard Business School*
Jie Xu, *Sonoma State University*
Pai-Ling Yin, *Harvard Business School California Research Center*
David Yoffie, *Harvard Business School California Research Center*

Teaching and Learning Aids

Taken together, the teaching and learning features of *Strategic Management* provide a package that is unsurpassed in its coverage and that supports the integrated approach that we have taken throughout the book.

For the Instructor

■ The **Instructor's Resource Manual: Cases** includes a complete list of Case Discussion Questions as well as a *comprehensive teaching note* for each case, which gives a complete analysis of case issues. It is written in a user-friendly question-and-answer format.

■ **HM ClassPrep™ with HMTesting CD** provides a variety of teaching resources in electronic format allowing for easy customization to meet specific instructional needs. Included in ClassPrep are electronic *Instructor's Resource Manual* files, Premium and Basic PowerPoint slides, Classroom Response System content, and much more. The computerized version of the Test Bank allows instructors to select, edit, and add questions, or generate randomly selected questions to produce a test master for easy duplication. Online Testing and Gradebook functions allow instructors to administer tests via their local area network or the World Wide Web, set up classes, record grades from tests or assignments, analyze grades, and produce/compile class and individual statistics.

■ The **video program** highlights many issues of interest and can be used to spark class discussion. It offers a compilation of footage from the Videos for Humanities series.

■ An extensive **website** contains many features to aid instructors including downloadable files for the text and case materials from the *Instructor's Resource Manual*, the downloadable Premium and Basic PowerPoint slides, the Video Guide, and sample syllabi. Additional materials on the student website may also be of use to instructors.

■ **Eduspace®**, powered by Blackboard®, is a course management tool that includes downloadable MP3 audio chapter summaries and quizzes, chapter outlines, visual glossaries, all questions from the textbook with suggested answers, Debate Issues, ACE self-test questions, auto-graded quizzes, Premium and Basic Power-

Point slides, Classroom Response System content, links to content on the websites, video activities, and Test Bank content. A Getting Started Guide is also available.

■ **Blackboard®/Web CT®** includes course material, downloadable MP3 audio chapter summaries and quizzes, chapter outlines, visual glossaries, all questions from the textbook with suggested answers, Premium and Basic PowerPoint slides, Classroom Response System content, links to content on the websites, video activities, and Test Bank content.

For the Student

■ The **student website** includes downloadable MP3 audio chapter summaries and quizzes, chapter overviews, Internet exercises (repeated from the textbook, with updates as necessary), ACE self-tests, links to the companies highlighted in the chapter opening and closing cases and the Strategy in Action boxed features as well as to the cases featured in the second half of the book, case discussion questions to help guide student case analysis, glossaries, visual glossaries, flashcards for studying the key terms, a section with guidelines on how to do case study analysis, and much more.

Acknowledgments

This book is the product of far more than two authors. We are grateful to Lise Johnson, our sponsor, Julia Perez, our editor, and Steve Mikels, our marketing manager, for their help in promoting and developing the book and for providing us with timely feedback and information from professors and reviewers that have allowed us to shape the book to meet the needs of its intended market. We are also grateful to Kerry Falvey, senior project editor, and Sarah Driver, editorial assistant, for their adept handling of production. We are also grateful to the case authors for allowing us to use their materials. We also want to thank the departments of management at the University of Washington and Texas A&M University for providing the setting and atmosphere in which the book could be written, and the students of these universities who reacted to and provided input for many of our ideas. In addition, the following reviewers of this and earlier editions gave us valuable suggestions for improving the manuscript from its original version to its current form:

Ken Armstrong, *Anderson University*
Kunal Banerji, *West Virginia University*
Kevin Banning, *Auburn University–Montgomery*
Glenn Bassett, *University of Bridgeport*
Thomas H. Berliner, *The University of Texas at Dallas*
Richard G. Brandenburg, *University of Vermont*
Steven Braund, *University of Hull*
Philip Bromiley, *University of Minnesota*
Geoffrey Brooks, *Western Oregon State College*
Lowell Busenitz, *University of Houston*
Charles J. Capps III, *Sam Houston State University*
Gene R. Conaster, *Golden State University*
Steven W. Congden, *University of Hartford*
Catherine M. Daily, *Ohio State University*
Robert DeFillippi, *Suffolk University Sawyer School of Management*

Helen Deresky, *SUNY–Plattsburgh*
Gerald E. Evans, *The University of Montana*
John Fahy, *Trinity College, Dublin*
Patricia Feltes, *Southwest Missouri State University*
Mark Fiegener, *Oregon State University*
Isaac Fox, *Washington State University*
Craig Galbraith, *University of North Carolina at Wilmington*
Scott R. Gallagher, *Rutgers University*
Eliezer Geisler, *Northeastern Illinois University*
Gretchen Gemeinhardt, *University of Houston*
Lynn Godkin, *Lamar University*
Robert L. Goldberg, *Northeastern University*
James Grinnell, *Merrimack College*
Todd Hostager, *University of Wisconsin–Eau Claire*
Graham L. Hubbard, *University of Minnesota*
Tammy G. Hunt, *University of North Carolina at Wilmington*
James Gaius Ibe, *Morris College*
W. Grahm Irwin, *Miami University*
Jonathan L. Johnson, *University of Arkansas Walton College of Business Administration*
Marios Katsioloudes, *St. Joseph's University*
Robert Keating, *University of North Carolina at Wilmington*
Geoffrey King, *California State University–Fullerton*
Rico Lam, *University of Oregon*
Robert J. Litschert, *Virginia Polytechnic Institute and State University*
Franz T. Lohrke, *Louisiana State University*
Paul Mallette, *Colorado State University*
Lance A. Masters, *California State University–San Bernardino*
Robert N. McGrath, *Embry-Riddle Aeronautical University*
Charles Mercer, *Drury College*
Van Miller, *University of Dayton*
Tom Morris, *University of San Diego*
Joanna Mulholland, *West Chester University of Pennsylvania*
Francine Newth, *Providence College*
Paul R. Reed, *Sam Houston State University*
Rhonda K. Reger, *Arizona State University*
Malika Richards, *Indiana University*
Stuart Rosenberg, *Dowling College*
Ronald Sanchez, *University of Illinois*
Joseph A. Schenk, *University of Dayton*
Brian Shaffer, *University of Kentucky*
Leonard Sholtis, *Eastern Michigan University*
Pradip K. Shukla, *Chapman University*
Dennis L. Smart, *University of Nebraska at Omaha*
Barbara Spencer, *Clemson University*
Lawrence Steenberg, *University of Evansville*
Kim A. Stewart, *University of Denver*
Ted Takamura, *Warner Pacific College*
Bobby Vaught, *Southwest Missouri State*

Robert P. Vichas, *Florida Atlantic University*
Edward Ward, *St. Cloud State University*
Kenneth Wendeln, *Indiana University*
Daniel L. White, *Drexel University*
Edgar L. Williams, Jr., *Norfolk State University*
Jun Zhao, *Governors State University*

Charles W. L. Hill
Gareth R. Jones

Cases in
Strategic Management

Introduction: Analyzing a Case Study and Writing a Case Study Analysis

What Is Case Study Analysis?

Case study analysis is an integral part of a course in strategic management. The purpose of a case study is to provide students with experience of the strategic management problems that actual organizations face. A case study presents an account of what happened to a business or industry over a number of years. It chronicles the events that managers had to deal with, such as changes in the competitive environment, and charts the managers' response, which usually involved changing the business- or corporate-level strategy. The cases in this book cover a wide range of issues and problems that managers have had to confront. Some cases are about finding the right business-level strategy to compete in changing conditions. Some are about companies that grew by acquisition, with little concern for the rationale behind their growth, and how growth by acquisition affected their future profitability. Each case is different because each organization is different. The underlying thread in all cases, however, is the use of strategic management techniques to solve business problems.

Cases prove valuable in a strategic management course for several reasons. First, cases provide you, the student, with experience of organizational problems that you probably have not had the opportunity to experience firsthand. In a relatively short period of time, you will have the chance to appreciate and analyze the problems faced by many different companies and to understand how managers tried to deal with them.

Second, cases illustrate the theory and content of strategic management. The meaning and implications of this information are made clearer when they are applied to case studies. The theory and concepts help reveal what is going on in the companies studied and allow you to evaluate the solutions that specific companies adopted to deal with their problems. Consequently, when you analyze cases, you will be like a detective who, with a set of conceptual tools, probes what happened and what or who was responsible and then marshals the evidence that provides the solution. Top managers enjoy the thrill of testing their problem-solving abilities in the real world. It is important to remember that no one knows what the right answer is. All that managers can do is to make the best guess. In fact, managers say repeatedly that they are happy if they are right only half the time in solving strategic problems. Strategic management is an uncertain game, and using cases to see how theory can be put into practice is one way of improving your skills of diagnostic investigation.

Third, case studies provide you with the opportunity to participate in class and to gain experience in presenting your ideas to others. Instructors may sometimes call on students as a group to identify what is going on in a case, and through classroom discussion the issues in and solutions to the case problem will reveal themselves. In such a situation, you will have to organize your views and conclusions so that you can present them to the class. Your classmates may have analyzed the issues differently from you, and they will want you to argue your points before they will accept your conclusions, so be prepared for debate. This mode of discussion is an example of the dialectical approach to decision making. This is how decisions are made in the actual business world.

Instructors also may assign an individual, but more commonly a group, to analyze the case before the whole class. The individual or group probably will be responsible for a thirty- to forty-minute presentation of the case to the class. That presentation must cover the issues posed, the problems facing the company, and a series of recommendations for resolving the problems. The discussion then will be thrown open to the class, and you will have to defend your ideas. Through such discussions and presentations, you will experience how to convey your ideas effectively to others. Remember that a great deal of managers' time is spent in these kinds of situations: presenting their ideas and engaging in discussion with other managers who have their own views about what is going on. Thus, you will experience in the classroom the actual process of strategic management, and this will serve you well in your future career.

If you work in groups to analyze case studies, you also will learn about the group process involved in working as a team. When people work in groups, it is often difficult to schedule time and allocate responsibility for the case analysis. There are always group members who shirk their responsibilities and group members who are so sure of their own ideas that they try to dominate the group's analysis. Most of the strategic management takes place in groups, however, and it is best if you learn about these problems now.

Analyzing a Case Study

The purpose of the case study is to let you apply the concepts of strategic management when you analyze the issues facing a specific company. To analyze a case study, therefore, you must examine closely the issues confronting the company. Most often you will need to read the case several times—once to grasp the overall picture of what is happening to the company and then several times more to discover and grasp the specific problems.

Generally, detailed analysis of a case study should include eight areas:

1. The history, development, and growth of the company over time

2. The identification of the company's internal strengths and weaknesses

3. The nature of the external environment surrounding the company

4. A SWOT analysis

5. The kind of corporate-level strategy that the company is pursuing

6. The nature of the company's business-level strategy

7. The company's structure and control systems and how they match its strategy

8. Recommendations

To analyze a case, you need to apply the concepts taught in this course to each of these areas. To help you further, we next offer a summary of the steps you can take to analyze the case material for each of the eight points we just noted:

1. *Analyze the company's history, development, and growth.* A convenient way to investigate how a company's past strategy and structure affect it in the present is to chart the critical incidents in its history—that is, the events that were the most unusual or the most essential for its development into the company it is today. Some of the events have to do with its founding, its initial products, how it makes new-product market decisions, and how it developed and chose functional competencies to pursue. Its entry into new businesses and shifts in its main lines of business are also important milestones to consider.

2. *Identify the company's internal strengths and weaknesses.* Once the historical profile is completed, you can begin the SWOT analysis. Use all the incidents you have charted to develop an account of the company's strengths and weaknesses as they have emerged historically. Examine each of the value creation functions of the company, and identify the functions in which the company is currently strong and currently weak. Some companies might be weak in marketing; some might be strong in research and development. Make lists of these strengths and weaknesses. The SWOT Checklist (Table 1) gives examples of what might go in these lists.

3. *Analyze the external environment.* To identify environmental opportunities and threats, apply all the concepts on industry and macroenvironments to analyze the environment the company is confronting. Of particular importance at the industry level are Porter's five forces model and the stage of the life cycle model. Which factors in the macroenvironment will appear salient depends on the specific company being analyzed. Use each factor in turn (for instance, demographic factors) to see whether it is relevant for the company in question.

   Having done this analysis, you will have generated both an analysis of the company's environment and a list of opportunities and threats. The SWOT Checklist table also lists some common environmental opportunities and threats that you may look for, but the list you generate will be specific to your company.

4. *Evaluate the SWOT analysis.* Having identified the company's external opportunities and threats as well as its internal strengths and weaknesses, consider what your findings mean. You need to balance strengths and weaknesses against opportunities and threats. Is the company in an overall strong competitive position? Can it continue to pursue its current business- or corporate-level strategy profitably? What can the company do to turn weaknesses into strengths and threats into opportunities? Can it develop new functional, business, or corporate strategies to accomplish this change? *Never merely generate the SWOT analysis and then put it aside.* Because it provides a succinct summary of the company's condition, a good SWOT analysis is the key to all the analyses that follow.

5. *Analyze corporate-level strategy.* To analyze corporate-level strategy, you first need to define the company's mission and goals. Sometimes the mission and goals are stated explicitly in the case; at other times, you will have to infer them from available information. The information you need to collect to find out the company's corporate strategy includes such factors as its lines of business and the nature of its subsidiaries and acquisitions. It is important to analyze the relationship among the company's businesses. Do they trade or exchange resources? Are there gains to be achieved from synergy? Alternatively, is the company just running a portfolio of investments? This analysis should enable you to define the corporate strategy that the company is pursuing (for example, related or unrelated diversification, or a

TABLE 1

A SWOT Checklist

Potential internal strengths	Potential internal weaknesses
Many product lines?	Obsolete, narrow product lines?
Broad market coverage?	Rising manufacturing costs?
Manufacturing competence?	Decline in R&D innovations?
Good marketing skills?	Poor marketing plan?
Good materials management systems?	Poor material management systems?
R&D skills and leadership?	Loss of customer good will?
Information system competencies?	Inadequate human resources?
Human resource competencies?	Inadequate information systems?
Brand name reputation?	Loss of brand name capital?
Portfolio management skills?	Growth without direction?
Cost of differentiation advantage?	Bad portfolio management?
New-venture management expertise?	Loss of corporate direction?
Appropriate management style?	Infighting among divisions?
Appropriate organizational structure?	Loss of corporate control?
Appropriate control systems?	Inappropriate organizational structure and control systems?
Ability to manage strategic change?	High conflict and politics?
Well-developed corporate strategy?	Poor financial management?
Good financial management?	Others?
Others?	
Potential environmental opportunities	Potential environmental threats
Expand core business(es)?	Attacks on core business(es)?
Exploit new market segments?	Increases in domestic competition?
Widen product range?	Increase in foreign competition?
Extend cost or differentiation advantage?	Change in consumer tastes?
Diversify into new growth businesses?	Fall in barriers to entry?
Expand into foreign markets?	Rise in new or substitute products?
Apply R&D skills in new areas?	Increase in industry rivalry?
Enter new related businesses?	New forms of industry competition?
Vertically integrate forward?	Potential for takeover?
Vertically integrate backward?	Existence of corporate raiders?
Enlarge corporate portfolio?	Increase in regional competition?
Overcome barriers to entry?	Changes in demographic factors?
Reduce rivalry among competitors?	Changes in economic factors?
Make profitable new acquisitions?	Downturn in economy?
Apply brand name capital in new areas?	Rising labor costs?
Seek fast market growth?	Slower market growth?
Others?	Others?

combination of both) and to conclude whether the company operates in just one core business. Then, using your SWOT analysis, debate the merits of this strategy. Is it appropriate given the environment the company is in? Could a change in corporate strategy provide the company with new opportunities or transform a weakness into a strength? For example, should the company diversify from its core business into new businesses?

Other issues should be considered as well. How and why has the company's strategy changed over time? What is the claimed rationale for any changes? Often, it is a good idea to analyze the company's businesses or products to assess its situation and identify which divisions contribute the most to or detract from its competitive advantage. It is also useful to explore how the company has built its portfolio over time. Did it acquire new businesses, or did it internally venture its own? All of these factors provide clues about the company and indicate ways of improving its future performance.

6. *Analyze business-level strategy.* Once you know the company's corporate-level strategy and have done the SWOT analysis, the next step is to identify the company's business-level strategy. If the company is a single-business company, its business-level strategy is identical to its corporate-level strategy. If the company is in many businesses, each business will have its own business-level strategy. You will need to identify the company's generic competitive strategy—differentiation, low cost, or focus—and its investment strategy, given its relative competitive position and the stage of the life cycle. The company also may market different products using different business-level strategies. For example, it may offer a low-cost product range and a line of differentiated products. Be sure to give a full account of a company's business-level strategy to show how it competes.

Identifying the functional strategies that a company pursues to build competitive advantage through superior efficiency, quality, innovation, and customer responsiveness and to achieve its business-level strategy is very important. The SWOT analysis will have provided you with information on the company's functional competencies. You should investigate its production, marketing, or research and development strategy further to gain a picture of where the company is going. For example, pursuing a low-cost or a differentiation strategy successfully requires very different sets of competencies. Has the company developed the right ones? If it has, how can it exploit them further? Can it pursue both a low-cost and a differentiation strategy simultaneously?

The SWOT analysis is especially important at this point if the industry analysis, particularly Porter's model, has revealed threats to the company from the environment. Can the company deal with these threats? How should it change its business-level strategy to counter them? To evaluate the potential of a company's business-level strategy, you must first perform a thorough SWOT analysis that captures the essence of its problems.

Once you complete this analysis, you will have a full picture of the way the company is operating and be in a position to evaluate the potential of its strategy. Thus, you will be able to make recommendations concerning the pattern of its future actions. However, first you need to consider strategy implementation, or the way the company tries to achieve its strategy.

7. *Analyze structure and control systems.* The aim of this analysis is to identify what structure and control systems the company is using to implement its strategy and to evaluate whether that structure is the appropriate one for the company. Different corporate and business strategies require different structures. You need to determine the *degree of fit between the company's strategy and structure.* For example, does the company have the right level of vertical differentiation (e.g., does it have the appropriate number of levels in the hierarchy or decentralized control?) or horizontal differentiation (does it use a functional structure when it should be using a product structure?)? Similarly, is the company using the right integration or control systems to manage its operations? Are managers being appropriately rewarded? Are the right rewards in place for encouraging cooperation among divisions? These are all issues to consider.

In some cases, there will be little information on these issues, whereas in others there will be a lot. In analyzing each case, you should gear the analysis toward its most salient issues. For example, organizational conflict, power, and politics will be important issues for some companies. Try to analyze why problems in these areas are occurring. Do they occur because of bad strategy formulation or because of bad strategy implementation?

Organizational change is an issue in many cases because the companies are attempting to alter their strategies or structures to solve strategic problems. Thus, as part of the analysis, you might suggest an action plan that the company in question could use to achieve its goals. For example, you might list in a logical sequence the steps the company would need to follow to alter its business-level strategy from differentiation to focus.

8. *Make recommendations.* The quality of your recommendations is a direct result of the thoroughness with which you prepared the case analysis. Recommendations are directed at solving whatever strategic problem the company is facing and increasing its future profitability. Your recommendations should be in line with your analysis; that is, they should follow logically from the previous discussion. For example, your recommendation generally will center on the specific ways of changing functional, business, and corporate strategies and organizational structure and control to improve business performance. The set of recommendations will be specific to each case, and so it is difficult to discuss these recommendations here. Such recommendations might include an increase in spending on specific research and development projects, the divesting of certain businesses, a change from a strategy of unrelated to related diversification, an increase in the level of integration among divisions by using task forces and teams, or a move to a different kind of structure to implement a new business-level strategy. Make sure your recommendations are mutually consistent and written in the form of an action plan. The plan might contain a timetable that sequences the actions for changing the company's strategy and a description of how changes at the corporate level will necessitate changes at the business level and subsequently at the functional level.

After following all these stages, you will have performed a thorough analysis of the case and will be in a position to join in class discussion or present your ideas to the class, depending on the format used by your professor. Remember that you must tailor your analysis to suit the specific issue discussed in your case. In some cases, you might completely omit one of the steps in the analysis because it is not relevant to the situation you are considering. You must be sensitive to the needs of the case and not apply the framework we have discussed in this section blindly. The framework is meant only as a guide, not as an outline.

Writing a Case Study Analysis

Often, as part of your course requirements, you will need to present a written case analysis. This may be an individual or a group report. Whatever the situation, there are certain guidelines to follow in writing a case analysis that will improve the evaluation your work will receive from your instructor. Before we discuss these guidelines and before you use them, make sure that they do not conflict with any directions your instructor has given you.

The structure of your written report is critical. Generally, if you follow the steps for analysis discussed in the previous section, *you already will have a good structure for your written discussion*. All reports begin with an *introduction* to the case. In it, outline briefly what the company does, how it developed historically, what problems it is experiencing, and how you are going to approach the issues in the case write-up. Do this sequentially by writing, for example, "First, we discuss the environment of Company X. . . . Third, we discuss Company X's business-level strategy. . . . Last, we provide recommendations for turning around Company X's business."

In the second part of the case write-up, the *strategic analysis* section, do the SWOT analysis, analyze and discuss the nature and problems of the company's business-level and corporate strategies, and then analyze its structure and control systems. Make sure you use plenty of headings and subheadings to structure your analysis. For example, have separate sections on any important conceptual tool you use. Thus, you might have a section on Porter's five forces model as part of your analysis of the environment. You might offer a separate section on portfolio techniques when analyzing a company's corporate strategy. Tailor the sections and subsections to the specific issues of importance in the case.

In the third part of the case write-up, present your *solutions and recommendations*. Be comprehensive, and make sure they are in line with the previous analysis so that the recommendations fit together and move logically from one to the next. The recommendations section is very revealing because your instructor will have a good idea of how much work you put into the case from the quality of your recommendations.

Following this framework will provide a good structure for most written reports, though it must be shaped to fit the individual case being considered. Some cases are about excellent companies experiencing no problems. In such instances, it is hard to write recommendations. Instead, you can focus on analyzing why the company is doing so well, using that analysis to structure the discussion. Following are some minor suggestions that can help make a good analysis even better:

1. Do not repeat in summary form large pieces of factual information from the case. The instructor has read the case and knows what is going on. Rather, use the information in the case to illustrate your statements, defend your arguments, or make salient points. Beyond the brief introduction to the company, you must avoid being *descriptive*; instead, you must be *analytical*.

2. Make sure the sections and subsections of your discussion flow logically and smoothly from one to the next. That is, try to build on what has gone before so that the analysis of the case study moves toward a climax. This is particularly important for group analysis, because there is a tendency for people in a group to split up the work and say, "I'll do the beginning, you take the middle, and I'll do the end." The result is a choppy, stilted analysis; the parts do not flow from one to the next, and it is obvious to the instructor that no real group work has been done.

3. Avoid grammatical and spelling errors. They make your work look sloppy.

4. In some instances, cases dealing with well-known companies end in 1998 or 1999 because no later information was available when the case was written. If possible, do a search for more information on what has happened to the company in subsequent years.

   Many libraries now have comprehensive web-based electronic data search facilities that offer such sources as *ABI/Inform, The Wall Street Journal Index,* the *F&S Index,* and the *Nexis-Lexis* databases. These enable you to identify any article that has been written in the business press on the company of your choice within the past few years. A number of nonelectronic data sources are also useful. For example, *F&S Predicasts* publishes an annual list of articles relating to major companies that appeared in the national and international business press. *S&P Industry Surveys* is a great source for basic industry data, and *Value Line Ratings and Reports* can contain good summaries of a firm's financial position and future prospects. You will also want to collect full financial information on the company. Again, this can be accessed from web-based electronic databases such as the Edgar database, which archives all forms that publicly quoted companies have to file with the Securities and Exchange Commission (SEC; e.g., 10-K filings can be accessed from the SEC's Edgar database). Most SEC forms for public companies can now be accessed from Internet-based financial sites, such as Yahoo's finance site (**http://finance.yahoo.com/**).

5. Sometimes instructors hand out questions for each case to help you in your analysis. Use these as a guide for writing the case analysis. They often illuminate the important issues that have to be covered in the discussion.

If you follow the guidelines in this section, you should be able to write a thorough and effective evaluation.

The Role of Financial Analysis in Case Study Analysis

An important aspect of analyzing a case study and writing a case study analysis is the role and use of financial information. A careful analysis of the company's financial condition immensely improves a case write-up. After all, financial data represent the concrete results of the company's strategy and structure. Although analyzing financial statements can be quite complex, a general idea of a company's financial position can be determined through the use of ratio analysis. Financial performance ratios can be calculated from the balance sheet and income statement. These ratios can be classified into five subgroups: profit ratios, liquidity ratios, activity ratios, leverage ratios, and shareholder-return ratios. These ratios should be compared with the industry average or the company's prior years of performance. It should be noted, however, that deviation from the average is not necessarily bad; it simply warrants further investigation. For example, young companies will have purchased assets at a different price and will likely have a different capital structure than older companies do. In addition to ratio analysis, a company's cash flow position is of critical importance and should be assessed. Cash flow shows how much actual cash a company possesses.

■ Profit Ratios

Profit ratios measure the efficiency with which the company uses its resources. The more efficient the company, the greater is its profitability. It is useful to compare a company's profitability against that of its major competitors in its industry to determine whether the company is operating more or less efficiently than its rivals. In addition, the change in a company's profit ratios over time tells whether its performance is improving or declining.

A number of different profit ratios can be used, and each of them measures a different aspect of a company's performance. Here, we look at the most commonly used profit ratios.

■ Return on Invested Capital

This ratio measures the profit earned on the capital invested in the company. It is defined as follows:

$$\text{Return on invested capital (ROIC)} = \frac{\text{Net profit}}{\text{Invested capital}}$$

Net profit is calculated by subtracting the total costs of operating the company away from its total revenues (total revenues − total costs). Total costs are the (1) costs of goods sold, (2) sales, general, and administrative expenses, (3) R&D expenses, and

(4) other expenses. Net profit can be calculated before or after taxes, although many financial analysts prefer the before-tax figure. Invested capital is the amount that is invested in the operations of a company—that is, in property, plant, equipment, inventories, and other assets. Invested capital comes from two main sources: interest-bearing debt and shareholders' equity. Interest-bearing debt is money the company borrows from banks and from those who purchase its bonds. Shareholders' equity is the money raised from selling shares to the public, *plus* earnings that have been retained by the company in prior years and are available to fund current investments. ROIC measures the effectiveness with which a company is using the capital funds that it has available for investment. As such, it is recognized to be an excellent measure of the value a company is creating.[1] Remember that a company's ROIC can be decomposed into its constituent parts.

■ **Return on Total Assets (ROA)** This ratio measures the profit earned on the employment of assets. It is defined as follows:

$$\text{Return on total assests} = \frac{\text{Net profit}}{\text{Total assets}}$$

■ **Return on Stockholders' Equity (ROE)** This ratio measures the percentage of profit earned on common stockholders' investment in the company. It is defined as follows:

$$\text{Return on stockholders' equity} = \frac{\text{Net profit}}{\text{Stockholders' equity}}$$

If a company has no debt, this will be the same as ROIC.

■ **Liquidity Ratios** A company's liquidity is a measure of its ability to meet short-term obligations. An asset is deemed liquid if it can be readily converted into cash. Liquid assets are current assets such as cash, marketable securities, accounts receivable, and so on. Two liquidity ratios are commonly used.

■ **Current Ratio** The current ratio measures the extent to which the claims of short-term creditors are covered by assets that can be quickly converted into cash. Most companies should have a ratio of at least 1, because failure to meet these commitments can lead to bankruptcy. The ratio is defined as follows:

$$\text{Current ratio} = \frac{\text{Current assets}}{\text{Current liabilities}}$$

■ **Quick Ratio** The quick ratio measures a company's ability to pay off the claims of short-term creditors without relying on selling its inventories. This is a valuable measure since in practice the sale of inventories is often difficult. It is defined as follows:

$$\text{Quick ratio} = \frac{\text{Current assets} - \text{inventory}}{\text{Current liabilities}}$$

---

[1] Tom Copeland, Tim Koller, and Jack Murrin, *Valuation: Measuring and Managing the Value of Companies* (New York: Wiley, 1996).

■ **Activity Ratios**

Activity ratios indicate how effectively a company is managing its assets. Two ratios are particularly useful.

■ **Inventory Turnover** This measures the number of times inventory is turned over. It is useful in determining whether a firm is carrying excess stock in inventory. It is defined as follows:

$$\text{Inventory turnover} = \frac{\text{Cost of goods sold}}{\text{Inventory}}$$

Cost of goods sold is a better measure of turnover than sales because it is the cost of the inventory items. Inventory is taken at the balance sheet date. Some companies choose to compute an average inventory, beginning inventory, and ending inventory, but for simplicity, use the inventory at the balance sheet date.

■ **Days Sales Outstanding (DSO) or Average Collection Period** This ratio is the average time a company has to wait to receive its cash after making a sale. It measures how effective the company's credit, billing, and collection procedures are. It is defined as follows:

$$\text{DSO} = \frac{\text{Accounts receivable}}{\text{Total sales}/360}$$

Accounts receivable is divided by average daily sales. The use of 360 is the standard number of days for most financial analysis.

■ **Leverage Ratios**

A company is said to be highly leveraged if it uses more debt than equity, including stock and retained earnings. The balance between debt and equity is called the *capital structure*. The optimal capital structure is determined by the individual company. Debt has a lower cost because creditors take less risk; they know they will get their interest and principal. However, debt can be risky to the firm because if enough profit is not made to cover the interest and principal payments, bankruptcy can result. Three leverage ratios are commonly used.

■ **Debt-to-Assets Ratio** The debt-to-assets ratio is the most direct measure of the extent to which borrowed funds have been used to finance a company's investments. It is defined as follows:

$$\text{Debt-to-assets ratio} = \frac{\text{Total debt}}{\text{Total assets}}$$

Total debt is the sum of a company's current liabilities and its long-term debt, and total assets are the sum of fixed assets and current assets.

■ **Debt-to-Equity Ratio** The debt-to-equity ratio indicates the balance between debt and equity in a company's capital structure. This is perhaps the most widely used measure of a company's leverage. It is defined as follows:

$$\text{Debt-to-equity ratio} = \frac{\text{Total debt}}{\text{Total equity}}$$

■ **Times-Covered Ratio** The times-covered ratio measures the extent to which a company's gross profit covers its annual interest payments. If this ratio declines to less than 1, the company is unable to meet its interest costs and is technically insolvent. The ratio is defined as follows:

$$\text{Times-covered ratio} = \frac{\text{Profit before interest and tax}}{\text{Total interest charges}}$$

■ **Shareholder-Return Ratios**

Shareholder-return ratios measure the return that shareholders earn from holding stock in the company. Given the goal of maximizing stockholders' wealth, providing shareholders with an adequate rate of return is a primary objective of most companies. As with profit ratios, it can be helpful to compare a company's shareholder returns against those of similar companies as a yardstick for determining how well the company is satisfying the demands of this particularly important group of organizational constituents. Four ratios are commonly used.

■ **Total Shareholder Returns** Total shareholder returns measure the returns earned by time $t + 1$ on an investment in a company's stock made at time t. (Time t is the time at which the initial investment is made.) Total shareholder returns include both dividend payments and appreciation in the value of the stock (adjusted for stock splits) and are defined as follows:

$$\text{Total shareholder returns} = \frac{\text{Stock price } (t+1) - \text{stock price } (t) + \text{sum of annual dividends per share}}{\text{Stock price } (t)}$$

If a shareholder invests $2 at time t and at time $t + 1$ the share is worth $3, while the sum of annual dividends for the period t to $t + 1$ has amounted to $0.20, total shareholder returns are equal to $(3 - 2 + 0.2)/2 = 0.6$, which is a 60 percent return on an initial investment of $2 made at time t.

■ **Price-Earnings Ratio** The price-earnings ratio measures the amount investors are willing to pay per dollar of profit. It is defined as follows:

$$\text{Price-earnings ratio} = \frac{\text{Market price per share}}{\text{Earnings per share}}$$

■ **Market-to-Book Value** Market-to-book value measures a company's expected future growth prospects. It is defined as follows:

$$\text{Market-to-book value} = \frac{\text{Market price per share}}{\text{Earnings per share}}$$

■ **Dividend Yield** The dividend yield measures the return to shareholders received in the form of dividends. It is defined as follows:

$$\text{Dividend yield} = \frac{\text{Dividend per share}}{\text{Market price per share}}$$

Market price per share can be calculated for the first of the year, in which case the dividend yield refers to the return on an investment made at the beginning of the year. Alternatively, the average share price over the year may be used. A company must decide how much of its profits to pay to stockholders and how much to reinvest in the company. Companies with strong growth prospects should have a lower dividend payout ratio than mature companies. The rationale is that shareholders can invest the money elsewhere if the company is not growing. The optimal ratio depends on the individual firm, but the key decider is whether the company can produce better returns than the investor can earn elsewhere.

■ Cash Flow

Cash flow position is cash received minus cash distributed. The net cash flow can be taken from a company's statement of cash flows. Cash flow is important for what it reveals about a company's financing needs. A strong positive cash flow enables a company to fund future investments without having to borrow money from bankers or investors. This is desirable because the company avoids paying out interest or dividends. A weak or negative cash flow means that a company has to turn to external sources to fund future investments. Generally, companies in strong-growth industries often find themselves in a poor cash flow position (because their investment needs are substantial), whereas successful companies based in mature industries generally find themselves in a strong cash flow position.

A company's internally generated cash flow is calculated by adding back its depreciation provision to profits after interest, taxes, and dividend payments. If this figure is insufficient to cover proposed new investments, the company has little choice but to borrow funds to make up the shortfall or to curtail investments. If this figure exceeds proposed new investments, the company can use the excess to build up its liquidity (that is, through investments in financial assets) or repay existing loans ahead of schedule.

Conclusion

When evaluating a case, it is important to be *systematic*. Analyze the case in a logical fashion, beginning with the identification of operating and financial strengths and weaknesses and environmental opportunities and threats. Move on to assess the value of a company's current strategies only when you are fully conversant with the SWOT analysis of the company. Ask yourself whether the company's current strategies make sense given its SWOT analysis. If they do not, what changes need to be made? What are your recommendations? Above all, link any strategic recommendations you may make to the SWOT analysis. State explicitly how the strategies you identify take advantage of the company's strengths to exploit environmental opportunities, how they rectify the company's weaknesses, and how they counter environmental threats. Also, do not forget to outline what needs to be done to implement your recommendations.

Brown-Forman Wine Estates

This case was prepared by Armand Gilinsky Jr., Professor of Business at Sonoma State University; Sally Baack, Assistant Professor of Business at San Francisco State University; Murray Silverman, Professor of Business at San Francisco State University; and Lew Brown, Associate Professor of Business at the University of North Carolina, Greensboro.

Steve Dorfman flicked his turn signal and edged his BMW to the left, merging in the congested flow of traffic onto the south entrance to the Golden Gate Bridge. As traffic crept along, Steve had the chance to glance across the Bay and enjoy a clear view of downtown San Francisco.

Dorfman's cell phone rang, and he answered, "Hello."

"Steve?"

Recognizing Keith LaVine's voice, he responded, "Yes, Keith, what's going on?"

"Where are you?"

"Just crossing the Golden Gate, headed back to the office."

"Well, sorry to bother you, but I thought you'd want to know I just learned that Tom Burnet has announced his resignation. He's going to become the

Copyright © 2004 by Armand Gilinsky Jr., Sally Baack, Murray Silverman, and Lew Brown. This case was prepared by Armand Gilinsky Jr., Sally Baack, Murray Silverman, and Lew Brown as the basis for class discussion rather than to illustrate either effective or ineffective handling of an administrative situation. Reprinted by permission of Armand Gilinsky Jr., Sally Baack, Murray Silverman, and Lew Brown. All rights reserved. This case was originally presented at the 2002 North American Case Research Association conference in Banff, Canada. The authors gratefully acknowledge a Business and International Education (BIE) grant from the U.S. Department of Education and a matching grant from the College of Business at San Francisco State University in support of this research. We also gratefully acknowledge the contributions of student researchers Scott Sissom and Kimberly Stark, whose work was underwritten by a case writing grant from the Wine Business Program at Sonoma State University. For the most recent financial results of the company discussed in this case, go to http://finance.yahoo.com, input the company's stock symbol, and download the latest company report from its homepage.

president and CEO of Southcorp, the Australian Winery," said LaVine, Dorfman's senior vice president for sales.

"That's interesting," Dorfman continued after a pause. "I'm sure he'll do a good job there, and it's a good move for him. But it sure raises some interesting questions for us. Look, I'd better keep my eyes on all this traffic. I'll stop by your office when I get back. Thanks for the call."

Dorfman served as managing director of Brown-Forman's Wine Estates (WE) division. WE was headquartered in Healdsburg, California, sixty miles north of the Golden Gate Bridge in the heart of the world-renowned Napa, Mendocino, and Sonoma wine-growing regions. WE marketed premium and ultra-premium branded wines.

One year earlier, in late July 2001, Brown-Forman Corporation (BFC), headquartered in Louisville, Kentucky, had created WE as a corporate venture group to house its portfolio of small, upscale brands, and appointed Dorfman to head the division. WE's brands included California wines from Bonterra, Bel Arbor, Jekel, Mariah, and Sonoma-Cutrer, and Australian wines from Chateau Tahbilk, Geoff Merrill Reserve, and Owen's Estate.

At the time of WE's creation, BFC had decided to keep its older wine brands, Bolla, Fetzer, Fontana Candida, Korbel, MacPherson, and Michel Picard, within its established Wine Division (WD). Thomas Burnet, as WD's president, had championed the idea of setting WE up as a separate division.

Since WE's creation, however, its sales had been flat relative to the premium wine segment's double-digit growth rates, and Dorfman felt the pressure to improve results. He knew that some of BFC's executives questioned the decision to make WE a separate division. They wanted more centralized control over all the wine brands and the implied ability to cut costs and reduce duplication. However, other executives believed that keeping the premium brands separate was important to maintaining their images and positioning and preserving the entrepreneurial spirit behind those brands.

Dorfman knew that there had been growing tension within the organization over this issue and that he needed to justify WE's existence as an entity distinct from BFC's Wine Division. Now, with Burnet's departure, he also knew that the tension would escalate.

As Dorfman turned into his parking place, he realized that he had been lost in thought, and the sixty miles since the Golden Gate seemed to have vanished. He parked and headed for Lavine's office.

Dorfman knocked on LaVine's office door, and he looked up from his work.

"Hi, Steve. Did you have a good trip?"

"Well, I was lost in thought after your call, Keith. You know I hate to see Tom leave, but his timing may be good for us. It's August now and we have the annual planning meetings coming up next month. That's when we have to present our marketing strategy for 2003–2004. I know that we're going to get pressure to justify our continued existence as a separate unit. So, obviously, even more than normal, we have to show a plan to improve the division's performance. But, and this is the interesting thought, maybe we also need to revisit the idea of BFC's having all its wine brands in one division. Could be those executives pushing for this are correct. Either way, we need to be prepared to present and defend our strategy recommendations. And looking at both sides of the argument will help us prepare and strengthen our position. Let's get to work."

Recent Trends in the U.S. Wine Industry

The U.S. wine industry was composed of approximately 1,500 wineries. However, it was highly concentrated. The top 10 wineries accounted for 70 percent (by volume) of U.S. production, according to the 1999 *Adams Wine Handbook*. California dominated the U.S. wine industry with over 800 wineries, which accounted

for more than 90 percent of the wine produced in and exported by the United States. Washington, Oregon, and Idaho had attracted approximately 200 wineries and were developing an export presence and a reputation for quality wines.

During the late 1990s three significant trends had emerged in the U.S. wine industry. These trends were (1) consolidation of the industry's "three-tier" distribution network (winery-wholesaler/distributor-retailer); (2) market segmentation due to consumers' "trading up" from inexpensive jug wines to premium-priced varietals, such as Chardonnay, Merlot, and Cabernet Sauvignon; and (3) the emergence of global markets for wines.

Distribution Channels

Wine was sold through a three-tier distribution system. Wineries (the first tier) or importers sold wine to wholesalers (the second tier), who provided legal fulfillment of wine products to local retail businesses (the third tier) within a certain state. Wine was a controlled substance, and laws in each state differed regarding how wine could be sold. Typically, wine passed through each tier of the distribution system, making direct shipping to retailers or selling wine through the Internet difficult or impossible in most states.

The third tier of the distribution system consisted of retail and nonretail outlets. Off-premises sales via supermarkets, convenience stores, club stores, mail order and Internet retailers, specialty stores, and wine clubs accounted for 78 percent of total sales volume. Supermarkets alone accounted for 52 percent of retail wine sales and were dominant in food and drink retailing, having made one-stop shopping an appealing concept for consumers. Supermarkets had therefore developed considerable bargaining leverage with wholesalers. Conversely, the role of specialty stores in wine distribution had diminished due to the increasing power of supermarkets. Specialty stores' share of retail wine sales shrank to about 30 percent by 1998. However, specialty stores were not likely to disappear soon because they provided superior customer service and extensive knowledge of wines. Specialty stores also carried specialty brands and limited production labels, attracting wine connoisseurs and enthusiasts. On-premises sales via nonretail outlets such as restaurants, hotels, and airlines accounted for the remaining 22 percent of wine volume in the United States, according to *Adams*.

Market Segmentation

"Table" wines were those with 7 to 14 percent alcohol content by volume and were traditionally consumed with food. This was in contrast to other wine products such as sparkling wines (champagnes if from France), wine coolers, and fortified wines, which were typically consumed as stand-alone beverages. Table wines that retailed at less than $3 per 750-milliliter bottle were generally considered to be "economy" or "jug" wines, whereas those selling for more than $3 per bottle were considered "premium" wines.

Premium wines generally had a vintage date on their labels. This meant that the product was made with at least 95 percent of grapes harvested, crushed, and fermented in the calendar year shown on the label and used grapes from an appellation of origin (e.g., Napa Valley, Sonoma Valley, Central Coast, etc.). Within the premium table wine category, a number of market segments emerged, based on retail price points. Subpremium wines generally fell into the $3 to $7 per bottle range, while premium wines retailed for $7 to $10 per bottle. The super premium category sold for $10 to $14 per bottle. Any retail price above $14 per bottle was considered deluxe premium.

U.S. wine market retail sales reached about $15 billion in 2002 (Exhibit 1). In retail sales, the U.S. wine market was ranked third in the world behind France and Italy, but only twelfth in the world in per capita consumption (Exhibit 2). The greatest concentration of core U.S. wine consumers was in the forty to forty-nine age bracket (Exhibit 3). About the same proportion of men and women consumed wine. While all income levels consumed wine, higher income was associated with greater wine consumption. By 1998, adults in families earning over $75,000 annually represented 18.7 percent of the population and 31.4 percent of the domestic table wine consumption

EXHIBIT 1

U.S. Table Wine Retail Sales, by Price Segment: 2001 and 2002 (Estimated)

	Retail Sales ($ millions)		
	2001	2002e	% Change
Total Economy (under $3.00)	$1,448	$1,518	4.8%
Domestic	1,442	1,512	4.9
Imported	6	6	—
Total Sub-Premium ($3.00–$6.99)	4,790	5,328	11.2
Domestic	3,310	3,562	7.6
Imported	1,480	1,766	19.3
Total Premium ($7.00–$9.99)	3,553	3,691	3.9
Domestic	1,975	1,989	0.7
Imported	1,578	1,702	7.9
Total Super-Premium ($10.00–$13.99)	2,956	3,399	15.0
Domestic	2,148	2,395	11.5
Imported	808	1,004	24.3
Total Deluxe ($14.00 and over)	1,312	1,416	7.9
Domestic	1,018	1,073	5.4
Imported	294	343	16.7
Total Table Wine	$14,059	$15,352	9.2
Domestic	9,893	10,531	6.4
Imported	4,166	4,821	15.7

Source: Data compiled from IMPACT Databank Review and Forecast, *The U.S. Wine Market,* 2003 edition, p. 360.

EXHIBIT 2

Per-Capita Wine Consumption in the United States: 1990, 1995, and 2000–2002 (Estimated)

Country	Population Year 2000	Liters Per Capita[1]					Average Annual Compound Growth Rate		Percent Change[2]		Volume Rank
		1990	1995	2000	2001	2002e	1990–1995	1995–2000	2000–2001	2001–2002e	
France	59,329,691	72.56	62.94	55.54	56.68	55.05	−2.8%	−2.5%	2.1%	−2.9%	1
Portugal	10,048,232	50.73	60.51	50.12	49.79	49.22	3.6	−3.7	−0.7	−1.1	10
Italy	57,634,691	62.07	62.13	49.89	48.87	48.16	0.0	−4.3	−2.0	−1.5	2
Spain	39,996,671	42.08	38.76	36.33	35.07	35.07	−1.6	−1.3	−3.5	0.0	5
Argentina	36,955,182	54.46	38.81	33.73	32.11	31.60	−6.6	−2.8	−4.8	−1.6	7
Germany[3]	82,797,408	20.53	22.75	23.85	23.97	23.87	2.1	0.9	0.5	−0.4	4
Australia	19,357,594	18.06	18.25	20.32	20.48	21.19	0.2	2.2	0.8	3.5	12
Romania	22,411,121	25.77	29.11	23.24	21.00	21.16	2.5	−4.4	−9.6	0.8	11
United Kingdom	59,508,382	10.95	12.38	16.32	17.36	20.87	2.5	5.7	6.4	20.2	6
Netherlands	15,892,237	16.08	14.01	19.38	19.46	19.67	−2.7	6.7	0.4	1.1	15
South Africa	43,421,021	9.93	10.31	8.99	9.03	8.79	0.8	−2.7	0.4	−2.7	13
United States	275,562,673	6.26	6.40	7.25	7.28	7.64	0.4	2.5	0.4	4.9	3
Russia[4]	146,001,176	13.53	4.22	3.99	4.01	4.04	−20.8	−1.1	0.5	0.7	9
Brazil	172,860,370	1.95	1.94	1.95	2.09	2.06	−0.1	0.1	7.2	−1.4	14
China	1,261,832,482	0.03	0.32	0.43	0.45	0.49	60.5	6.1	4.7	8.9	8
Average - Top 15		27.00	25.52	23.42	23.18	23.26	−1.1	−1.7	−1.0	0.4	
Rest of World	3,784,338,702	1.23	1.22	1.20	1.19	1.16	−0.2	−0.3	−0.8	−2.5	
World Average		4.39	3.90	3.61	3.58	3.57	−2.3	−1.5	−0.8	−0.3	

[1]Based on total population.
[2]Based on unrounded data.
[3]1990 includes West Germany only.
[4]1990 includes the entire (former) Soviet Union.

Source: Impact Databank, 2003. New York: M. Shanken Publications, p. 504.

according to the *Adams Wine Handbook.* Still, barely more than 10 percent of the adults in the United States consumed 86 percent of all wine sold according to the Wine Market Council.

EXHIBIT 3

Wine Consumer: Age Segmentation, Percent

Ages	50–59	40–49	30–39	21–29
Core Wine Consumers	23	40	21	16
Marginal Consumers	19	26	33	22
Non-Wine Drinkers	11	27	31	31

Source: Wine Market Council.

Emergence of Global Markets

By 2000, the United States had become the second largest market for exported wine and the fourth leading producer of wine in the world. In 2000, U.S. wine exports to 164 countries totaled $560 million, more than 90 percent of which came from California. Wine was produced commercially in over 60 countries with 23 percent (by volume) of the wine produced exported to international markets according to *Wines & Vines.* Leading wine producers included the "Old World" wineries in France, Italy, and Spain, which were also the leading exporters. So-called "New World" producers, such as the United States, Australia, Chile, Argentina, and South Africa, had been making both production and export inroads globally over the past few decades. Although France, Italy, and

Spain all exported more than 25 percent of the wine they produced, Australia exported over 40 percent of its production and Chile over 80 percent. Many observers attributed these higher export numbers to the small size of the respective home markets.

Until the mid-1990s, the U.S. wine market had remained largely a domestic industry, with some imports from France, Italy, and Spain competing with U.S. wineries. By 1999, however, imports had risen to 20 percent of the U.S. market, seven percentage points above 1995, according to *Wine Business Monthly*. Australian and Chilean wines had become increasingly dominant in the U.S. market: From 1995 to 1999, Australia increased the value of its exports to the United States by 243 percent and Chile by 152 percent. Since 1995, the unfavorable balance of trade for wine in the United States had increased by 78 percent. Tariffs and trade barriers, meanwhile, continued to play a pivotal role in obstructing U.S. wineries' access to export markets.

Owing to the globalization of markets and the creation of the European Union, trade barriers were beginning to fall worldwide. The worldwide consolidation trend accelerated among wineries and distributors. For example, Allied Domecq (United Kingdom), Constellation Brands (United States), Diageo PLC (United Kingdom), and BFC all courted larger premium wineries around the world. In the largest deal to date, Foster's Group of Australia had completed its friendly $1.5 billion merger with Beringer Wine Estates of California in October 2000.[1] Southcorp (Australia) and Kendall-Jackson (California) were most often rumored as takeover targets. Wine industry analysts expected further consolidation in the wine industry. Industry observers expected that large wine and alcoholic beverage companies would acquire smaller winery operations across national borders, in order to gain access to premium and ultra-premium brands, as well as access to the growing markets for those brands.

BFC's Main Competitors in the Wine Industry

The premium segment was highly fragmented, composed of hundreds of individual, small to large wine-producing operations that were all competing to produce the most acclaimed wines each year. Although larger producers held advantages in scale and capital, smaller "boutique" wineries were able to compete by consistently producing high-quality wines in limited quantities that gained critical acclaim by wine enthusiasts. Smaller wine producers, however, were at a disadvantage in the competition for grape sources. Larger better-financed competitors, such as Constellation Brands's Canandaigua division, Diageo PLC's Chateau & Estates division, E & J Gallo, Foster's Group's Beringer Blass Wine Estates division, Kendall-Jackson, and Robert Mondavi Corporation, all had extensive vineyard holdings in different wine-growing regions around the world. Larger rivals could therefore develop portfolios of brands and offer wines of many varietal types across the price spectrum of the premium, super-premium, and deluxe premium market segments.

BFC competed with two major types of large wine businesses: stand-alone wineries and conglomerates. BFC's primary stand-alone winery competitors in the United States included publicly traded Robert Mondavi and Chalone and the privately held Kendall-Jackson, E&J Gallo, and a host of medium-size wineries primarily based in Northern California, such as Sebastiani and Bonnie Doon. Selected financial data for BFC's publicly traded competitors are shown in Exhibit 4 and Exhibit 5.

BFC's major privately held competitor, E&J Gallo (Modesto, California), had been dominant in the U.S. wine industry since the end of Prohibition in 1933. E&J Gallo had been, until January 2003, the single largest wine producer in the world. E&J Gallo had a market share comprising approximately 45 percent of California wine sales. In recent years E&J Gallo, like many other jug wine producers, sought to enter the premium wine market, choosing to develop and launch new E&J Gallo brands from twenty-three hundred acres of prime vineyards in Sonoma County, acreage acquired to supply the development of new premium and ultra-premium brands. Gallo had also purchased Louis M. Martini, a premium winery based in Napa, California, in the summer of 2002.

Large conglomerate competitors included Allied Domecq, Constellation, Diageo, Fortune Brands, Foster's Group, Louis Vuitton Möet Hennesey (LVMH), and UST (formerly known as US Tobacco). These conglomerates expanded their wine portfolios through acquisitions of independent wineries and purchases of and majority interests in the beverage divisions of

---

[1] Constellation subsequently announced its $1.4 billion purchase of BRL Hardy, an Australian wine producer, in the second week of January 2003. This deal was expected to make Constellation the largest wine producer in the world, overtaking the previous industry leader, E&J Gallo.

EXHIBIT 4

Selected Financial and Operating Highlights of Publicly Traded Wine Businesses, October 2002

Company	Ticker Symbol	Recent Stock Price	P/E Ratio (x)	12 mo. Trail EPS	30 Day Price Change (%)	1 Year Price Change (%)	Beta	Yield (%)	Stk. Mkt. Capitaliz. ($ millions)	Return on Equity (%)	Pretax Margin (%)	LTD to Capital (%)
Brown-Forman Corp.	BF.B	$75.00	23x	$3.29	13%	23%	0.44	1.9	$2,963	18.3%	17.8%	2.8%
Chalone Wine Group	CHLN	8.65	62	0.14	8	−10	0.25	Nil	104	2.8	6.5	38.6
Constellation Brands	STZ	25.50	14	1.82	0	19	0.30	Nil	1,994	17.5	8.2	53.6
Diageo plc*ADS	DEO	46.14	15	2.98	−8	15	0.39	3.1	39,346	24.8	13.4	40.5
Robert Mondavi Corp.	MOND	31.86	14	2.21	6	−1	0.82	Nil	305	6.1	9.3	41.0

Source: Richard Joy, *Standard & Poor's Rankings,* through October 3, 2002.

other conglomerates (e.g., Diageo's late 2000 takeover of Seagram's drink business). In 2000 and 2001, conglomerates began divesting those satellite businesses that diverted resources from their core beverage businesses, including Allied Domecq's sale of the majority of its food operations and Diageo's sale of its Pillsbury Unit to General Mills in a $10.5 billion deal. Exhibit 6 presents a comparison of portfolios and recent strategic

EXHIBIT 5

Selected Financial and Operating Highlights of Global Alcohol and Beverage Conglomerates: 1999–2001

Company	HQ Location	Sales ($ millions) 2001	2000	1999	Net Income ($ millions) 2001	2000	1999	ROE (%) 2001	2000	ROA (%) 2001	2000
Allied-Domecq[1]	Bristol, England	$4,318	$6,154	$3,948	$516	$476	$114	117.7%	N/A	12.7%	N/A
Brown-Forman	Louisville, KY	2,180	2,009	2,134	233	202	218	19.6	20.8	19.3	19.3
Constellation Brands, Inc.	Fairport, NY	3,154	2,340	1,497	136	97	77	14.4	15.8	3.9	3.3
Diageo plc[1]	London, England	12,933	18,716	29,229	1,848	1,593	1,630	25.6	25.1	9.1	8.0
Fortune Brands	Lincolnshire, IL	5,678	5,579	5,844	385	(891)	(138)	18.9	−6.2	7.5	−2.3
Foster's Group[2]	Australia	2,244	1,874	1,656	256	236	203	12.2	18.5	9.0	12.8
Louis Vuitton Moet Hennessy (LVMH)[3]	Paris, France	1,168	8,589	10,909	10	696	680	0.2	10.3	2.0	8.4
Southcorp[2]	Australia	1,375	1,441	1,554	118	168	11	15.2	N/A	N/A	N/A
UST	Greenwich, CT	1,670	1,548	1,512	492	442	469	84.6	163.3	24.4	26.8

N/A = Not Available.
[1]Converted from British £ sterling to U.S. dollars at a rate of £1 = $1.50 U.S
[2]Converted from Australian dollars to U.S. dollars at a rate of $1 Australian = $0.55 U.S.
[3]Converted from Euros to U.S. dollars at a rate of 1€ = $0.95 U.S.

Source: Company reports, *Value Line,* and **WSRN.com**, accessed October 25, 2002.

EXHIBIT 6

Profiles of Brown-Forman's Major Wine Business Competitors: Brand Portfolios and Recent Strategic Moves

Company	Portfolio Brands—Wine	Other Portfolio Brands	Annual Wine Production	Recent Strategic Moves
Allied Domecq	Clos du Bois, Callaway Coastal, Atlas Peak, William Hill, Bodegas Balbi, Graffigna & Ste Sylvie, Montana, Marques de Arienzo, Harveys, Cockburn's, La Ina, Mumm and Perrier-Jouet.	*Spirits:* Ballantine's, Beefeater, Kahlua, Sauza, Stolichnaya, Tia Maria, Maker's Mark, Courvoisier Canadian Club *Fast-food:* Dunkin' Donuts, Baskin-Robbins and Togo's	Atlas Peak: 40,000 cases; 500 acres owned Callaway: 340,000 cases; 40 acres owned, 605 leased or controlled Clos du Bois: 1.4 million cases; 640 owned, 160 leased or controlled	Unsuccessfully bid to acquire Seagram's drinks businesses' assets in 2001.
Constellation (Canandigua)	Almaden, Arbor Mist, Franciscan Oakville Estate, Ravenswood, Simi, Estancia, Talus, Taylor, Vendange	*Spirits:* Paul Masson brandy, Corona Extra, Modelo Especial, St. Pauli Girl, Alice White, Black Velvet, Fleischmann's, Schenley, Ten High, Stowells of Chelsea,	30 million cases; 765 acres owned, 2,600 leased or controlled	Acquired Ravenswood Estates (Sonoma. CA) for $148 million in cash and assumed debt in July 2001. Announced $1.4 bill. purchase of Australia's BRL Hardy in January 2003.
Diageo (UDV Guinness NA)	Sterling Vineyards, Beaulieu Vineyards, Glen Ellen, M.G. Vallejo, Blossom Hill	*Spirits:* Captain Morgan, Crown Royal, and VO Canadian whiskeys, Guinness Stout, Harp Lager, Johnnie Walker Scotch, Tanqueray gin, Smirnoff vodka	6 million cases; 2,000 acres	Sold Pillsbury unit to General Mills for $20.5 billion in 2001; sold Guinness Book of World Records unit for $63 million in July 2001; completed spin-off of Burger King unit in 2002.
E & J Gallo	E & J Gallo (Modesto, CA): Gallo, Thunderbird, Carol Rossi, Bartles & Jaymes Gallo of Sonoma: E&J Gallo Estate, Gallo of Sonoma, Anapamu, Marcelina, Rancho Zabacho, Indigo Hills, Louis M. Martini	None	E & J Gallo (Modesto, CA): 90 million cases (est.) Gallo of Sonoma (Healdsburg, CA): 1 million cases (est.); 3,000 acres	Is world's largest wine producer and leading U.S. wine exporter, selling in 85 countries; wines also account for over 25% of all U.S. wine sales; exports one million bottles annually to the French market; plans to create first-mover advantage in the Indian wine market.
Kendall-Jackson	Kendall-Jackson, Pepi, La Crema, Edmeades Estate, Camelot, Tapiz, Villa Arceno, Calina	None	4 million cases; 12, 000 acres	Launched new Australian line, Yangarra Park in 2001; in May 2001, rejected several rumored takeover bids, including one by BFC; also lost five-year battle with Gallo over alleged theft of trade secrets.
Robert Mondavi	Robert Mondavi Winery, Robert Mondavi Coastal, Woodbridge, La Famiglia de Robert Mondavi, Byron, Arrowood, Vichon Mediterranean, Opus One, Caliterra, Luce	None	Unknown; 7,730 acres	Joint ventures with producers in France, Chile, and Italy; created a $10 million wine country attraction in 2001 at Disney's California Adventure theme park; began shift from vineyard development to production; internal grape supply expected to rise from 7% to 20% by 2004.

Source: Dow Jones Interactive on-line, Wines and Vines's *2002 Annual Buyers' Guide.*

moves by some of BFC's major publicly and privately held competitors.

BFC's History

George Brown and John Forman opened the BFC Distillery in Louisville, Kentucky, in 1870 to produce Old Forester–brand bourbon. Old Forester sold well through the end of the century, in part because of the company's innovative packaging (safety seals and quality guarantees on the bottles). When Forman died in 1901, Brown bought his interest in the company. Old Forester continued to be successful under the Brown family. BFC obtained government approval to produce alcohol for medicinal purposes during Prohibition. In 1923, it made its first acquisition, Early Times, and then went public in 1933. In the year after the repeal of Prohibition, Old Forester was reintroduced as an alcoholic beverage. During World War II, the U.S. government had greatly curtailed alcoholic beverage production, because alcohol was needed for the war effort. BFC compensated by providing alcohol for wartime rubber and gunpowder production.

In 1956, BFC purchased Lynchburg, Tennessee, based Jack Daniel's (sour-mash whiskey). The company retained the simple, black Jack Daniel's label and promoted the image of a small Tennessee distillery for the brand. BFC achieved global success by introducing Jack Daniels into new markets overseas, becoming the second largest brand of premium whiskey sold worldwide.

Subsequent to the Jack Daniels purchase, BFC continued to expand its spirits line, developing marketing relationships with Quality Importers (Ambassador Scotch, Ambassador Gin, and Old Bushmills' Irish Whisky, 1967), and Canadian Mist (blended whiskey, 1971). In 1979, BFC purchased a top-selling liqueur, Southern Comfort. BFC launched Gentleman Jack Rare Tennessee Whiskey in 1988, the first new whiskey from its Jack Daniels distillery in more than one hundred years. In 1999, BFC purchased a 33 percent interest in Tequila Orendain de Jalisco, S.A. de C.V., and 67 percent in a new company that was expected to develop Tequila Orendain products for markets outside Mexico. BFC then purchased a 45 percent stake in Tuoni & Canepa SpA of Italy, and became the exclusive marketer for that company's Tuaca liqueur. In 2000, the company bought 45 percent of Finlandia Vodka Worldwide for $83 million.

BFC also diversified into luxury consumer durables, purchasing well-known global brands. Its nonbeverage acquisitions included Lenox, a leading American maker of fine china, crystal, and gifts, in 1983; Hartmann, luggage, in 1983; Kirk Stieff, silver and pewter, in 1990; Dansk International Designs, china, crystal, and silver, in 1991; and the high-quality Gorham silver and crystal lines, in 1991. By 2002, BFC's subsidiary locations and manufacturing branches included seven production facilities in the United States, two in Italy, and one each in the U.S. Virgin Islands and Canada. Its Consumer Durables segment owned production facilities in New Jersey, North Carolina, Pennsylvania, Rhode Island, and Tennessee.

BFC's fiscal year 2002 net sales were $2.2 billion, rising 1 percent from the previous year. By contrast, in the fiscal year ending April 2001, BFC's net sales had grown 6 percent over fiscal year 2000. Operating and net incomes for 2002 were flat, dropping by 6 percent to $353 million and 2 percent to $228 million, respectively. Wine and Spirits segment sales had grown by 6 percent. Sales of the WD's Fetzer, Bolla, and Korbel brands had increased 6 percent, 3 percent, and 3 percent, respectively. Sales of the WE's brands increased 7.5 percent in fiscal 2002, after a decline of 4.6 percent the previous year. Exhibits 7–9 present company historical income statements, balance sheets, and cash flow statements, from 1998–2002. Exhibits 10 and 11 present BFC wine brand sales in 1995 and 2000–2002.

BFC's Organization

Headquartered in Louisville, Kentucky, BFC was publicly owned, though descendants of the cofounding Brown family remained in control. In 1993, Owsley Brown II succeeded his brother, Lee, as CEO. In 1999, BFC appointed the first woman, Dace Brown Stubbs, to serve on its board of directors. By 2002, members of the fifth generation of the Brown family were working in the organization, in such areas as corporate development, the spirits division, U.S. sales, international sales, and in the WE division.

BFC employed seventy-four hundred people worldwide, and 19 percent of BFC's workforce (fourteen hundred) was employed on a part-time or temporary/seasonal basis. The average age of BFC's top executives was fifty-five years. Most of its senior management had spent over thirteen years with the

EXHIBIT 7

Brown-Forman Corporation, Consolidated Income Statements
(Years ended April 30; $ millions, except share and per share amounts)

		2002	2001	2000	1999	1998
Net sales		$2,208	$2,180	$2,134	$2,009	$1,924
Excise taxes		250	256	257	254	255
Cost of sales		825	771	774	736	690
Gross profit		1,133	1,153	1,103	1,019	979
Advertising expenses		299	295	281	263	260
Selling, general, and administrative expenses		481	484	474	434	412
Operating income		353	374	348	322	307
Interest income		3	8	10	6	3
Interest expense		8	16	15	10	14
Income before income taxes		348	366	343	318	296
Taxes on income		120	133	125	116	111
Net income after tax		$228	$233	$218	$202	$185
Earnings per share:						
	Basic	$3.33	$3.40	$3.18	$2.93	$2.67
	Diluted	$3.33	$3.40	$3.18	$2.93	$2.67
Weighted average shares used to calculate earnings per share:						
	Basic	68.3	68.5	68.5	68.6	68.9
	Diluted	68.5	68.6	68.6	68.7	69.0

Source: Company reports.

company. (See Exhibit 12 for BFC's and WE's organization charts.)

BFC divided its operations into two major segments: Wine and Spirits, and Consumer Durables. The Wine and Spirits segment included the operations, manufacturing, bottling, importing, exporting, and marketing of all alcoholic beverages (whiskey, champagne, and wine). BFC distributed products in this segment domestically through state agencies or wholesale distributors. It used contracts with authorized dealers for international distributions. Consumer Durables included the manufacturing and marketing of fine china, silver, luggage, giftware, leather, and collectibles. Items within this segment were sold and distributed through retail chains, department stores, mail order, catalogs, and via the Internet.

Development of BFC's Wine Portfolio

In 1965, BFC entered the wine business through multiple marketing and distribution arrangements with Korbel champagne and brandies in California. A similar relationship with the Bolla family winery in Italy, begun in 1968, eventually led to full ownership. BFC acquired Jekel Vineyards in 1991 and Fetzer Vineyards in 1992. In 1999, BFC added four new wine brands to its portfolio. It bought an 80 percent stake in Sonoma-Cutrer Vineyards of California

EXHIBIT 8

Brown-Forman Corporation, Consolidated Balance Sheets
(Years ended April 30; $ millions, except share and per share amounts)

	2002	2001	2000	1999	1998
Assets					
Cash and cash equivalents	$116	$86	$180	$171	$78
Accounts receivable, less allowance for doubtful accounts of $10 in 1997, $11 in 1998, and $11 in 1999	280	303	294	274	265
Inventories:					
Barreled whiskey	219	219	202	191	187
Finished goods	183	216	184	189	179
Work in process	118	93	80	89	88
Raw materials and supplies	58	49	48	56	48
Total inventories	578	577	514	525	502
Current portion of deferred income taxes					
Prepaid income taxes	31	—	—	—	—
Other current assets	24	28	32	29	24
Total Current Assets	1,029	994	1,020	999	869
Investment in affiliates	127	—	—	—	—
Property, plant, and equipment, net	437	424	376	348	281
Intangible assets, less accumulated amortization of $130 in 1998 and $135 in 1999	246	263	270	264	250
Other assets	177	258	136	124	94
Total Assets	$2,016	$1,939	$1,802	$1,735	$1,494
Liabilities					
Commercial paper	$167	$204	$220	$226	$107
Accounts payable and accrued expenses	296	281	271	235	233
Current portion of long-term debt	—	—	6	18	7
Accrued taxes on income	32	45	1	0	8
Deferred income taxes	—	8	15	31	27
Total Current Liabilities	495	538	513	510	382
Long-term debt	40	40	41	53	50
Deferred income taxes	58	62	95	137	150
Accrued postretirement benefits	60	59	58	57	55
Other liabilities and deferred income	52	53	47	61	40
Total Liabilities	705	752	754	818	677
Stockholders' Equity					
Capital Stock:					
Preferred $0.40 cumulative, $10 par value; 1,177,948 authorized & outstanding shares redeemed in 1999 at $10.25 per share plus unpaid accrued dividends.	—	—	—	—	12

EXHIBIT 8

(Continued) Brown-Forman Corporation, Consolidated Balance Sheets
(Years ended April 30; $ millions, except share and per share amounts)

	2002	2001	2000	1999	1998
Class A common stock, voting, $0.15 par value; authorized shares, 30,000,000; issued shares, 28,988,091	4	4	4	4	4
Class B common stock, nonvoting, $0.15 par value; authorized shares, 60,000,000; issued shares, 40,008,147	6	6	6	6	6
Retained Earnings	1,360	1,226	1,080	945	821
Cumulative translation adjustment	(15)	(17)	(12)	(8)	(9)
Treasury stock, at cost (310,000 and 490,000 Class B common shares in 1998 and 1999, respectively)	(40)	(32)	(30)	(30)	(17)
Pension liability adjustment	(3)	—	—	—	—
Unrealized loss on cash flow hedge contracts	(1)	—	—	—	—
Common Stockholders' Equity	1,311	1,187	1,048	917	805
Total Stockholders' Equity	1,311	1,187	1,048	917	817
Total Liabilities and Stockholders' Equity	**$2,016**	**$1,939**	**$1,802**	**$1,735**	**$1,494**

Source: Company reports.

(superpremium Chardonnay); introduced two new Australian wines, McPherson Wines and Owen's Estates Wines; and purchased Mariah Wines of California. (See Exhibit 13 for a timeline of events in the creation of BFC's wine portfolio.)

Preceding the formation of the WE group was BFC's Beverages Wine Division (WD). Established in 1991, the WD was emblematic of the parent organization's new commitment to building premium wine brands. The WD's brands are listed in Exhibit 14. Since its acquisition by BFC in 1992, Fetzer had been considered to be the WD's flagship brand in the crowded popular-priced premium wine category. A good deal of the WD's reputation and clout in the wine industry had been built around Fetzer over the years, particularly in terms of relationships with its distributors.

Fetzer Vineyards

BFC acquired its second winery Fetzer Vineyards, Hopland (Mendocino County), California, in 1992. Fezer was well known in the industry for being a

certified organic grower of grapes. Since 1993, its recycling and waste diversion programs reduced the amount of material hauled to landfills by 93 percent. Fetzer led the industry in organic wine best practices. Paul Dolan, president of Fetzer Vineyards, had joined the winery in 1977 as a head winemaker. Dolan came from a generation of family winemakers, and he became president in 1992. The winery employed about 325 people.

Although Fetzer continued to be headquartered in Hopland, the California Central Coast region, which had contributed about one-third of Fetzer's cabernet sauvignon grapes in the past, was rapidly becoming its major locus of wine-growing operations. In San Luis Obispo County, Fetzer was building a 200,000-square-foot winery on North River Road, across from the San Miguel Mission. The first phase of the plant construction cost more than $7 million. Construction was expected to continue through 2004. The winery would by then employ a staff of 30 to 50, in addition to seasonal help. Fetzer was also building a 20,000-ton capacity winery, on 630 acres, to grow red grapes

EXHIBIT 9

Brown-Forman Corporation, Consolidated Statements of Cash Flow
(Years ended April 30 in $ millions)

	2002	2001	2000	1999	1998
Cash Flows from Operating Activities:					
Net income	$228	$233	$218	$202	$185
Adjustments to reconcile net income to net cash provided by (used for) operations:					
Depreciation	55	53	52	46	42
Amortization	—	11	10	9	9
Deferred income taxes	(43)	(40)	(51)	(25)	19
Other	(22)	(20)	(14)	(5)	(14)
Change in assets and liabilities, excluding the effects of business acquired or sold:					
Accounts receivable	23	(9)	(20)	(5)	(2)
Inventories	5	(63)	8	(8)	(52)
Other current assets	5	3	(3)	2	7
Accounts payable and accrued expenses	15	10	36	8	24
Accrued taxes on income	(13)	44	1	(8)	2
Accrued postretirement benefits	1	1	1	2	1
Other liabilities and deferred income	(4)	8	3	(5)	(1)
Cash provided by operating activities	$250	$231	$241	$213	$220
Cash Flows from Investing Activities:					
Additions to property, plant, and equipment	(71)	(96)	(78)	(46)	(44)
Disposals of property, plant, and equipment	—	—	—	—	13
Acquisitions of business, net of cash acquired		(114)	(27)	(54)	—
Other	(5)	(2)	(14)	(17)	(15)
Cash (used for) investing activities	$(76)	$(212)	$(119)	$(117)	$(46)
Cash Flows from Financing Activities:					
Net change in commercial paper	(37)	(16)	(6)	119	(48)
Proceeds from long-term debt	—	—	—	—	1
Reduction of long-term debt		(7)	(24)	(18)	(14)
Dividends paid	(94)	(87)	(83)	(79)	(76)
Acquisition of treasury stock	(13)	(3)		(13)	(17)
Redemption of preferred stock	—	—	—	(12)	—
Cash (used for) financing activities	(144)	(113)	(113)	(3)	(154)
Net increase in cash and cash equivalents	30	(94)	9	93	20
Cash and cash equivalents, beginning of year	86	180	171	78	58
Cash and cash equivalents, end of year	$116	$86	$180	$171	$78

Source: Company reports.

EXHIBIT 10

Brown-Forman Corporation Wine Brands, Sales by Brand, and Estimated Market Share: 1990, 1995, and 2001–2002 (Estimated)

Brand	Thousands of Nine-Liter Cases					Domestic Share, %		
	1990	1995	2000	2001	2002e	2000	2001	2002e
Bel Arbor	—	—	—	—	—	—	—	—
Bolla	925	955	1,095	1,180	1,215	7.1%	6.7%	6.2%
Bonterra	—	—	90	95	105	0.1	0.1	0.1
Chateau Tahbilk	—	—	—	—	—	—	—	—
Fetzer	1,380	1,875	2,310	2,225	2,350	1.6	1.6	1.6
Fontana Candida	285	200	205	225	235	1.3	1.3	1.2
Geoff Merrill Res.	—	—	—	—	—	—	—	—
Jekel	—	60	115	105	120	0.1	0.1	0.1
Korbel*	1,105	1,050	925	1,015	1,090	11.1	12.7	13.5
Mariah	—	—	—	—	—	—	—	—
McPherson	—	—	105	140	175	1.7	1.9	1.7
Owen's Estate	—	—	15	15	20	0.2	0.3	0.2
Picard	—	—	65	60	65	0.7	0.6	0.7
Sonoma-Cutrer	—	—	155	140	150	0.1	0.1	0.1

*Sparkling wine.

Source: Data compiled from IMPACT Databank Review and Forecast, *The U.S. Wine Market,* 2003 edition, pp. 261–301.

organically. The winery was expected to process and age red varietals grown locally. Ninety percent of these grapes were cabernet sauvignon and merlot. Once aged, the wine would be sent to the company's headquarters in Hopland for blending. Fetzer had 12,000 acres on long-term contracts with grape growers in the Paso Robles appellation. Fetzer grew 100 acres of Chardonnay grapes in the Paso Robles area that was sent to Greenfield, California, for processing by Jekel Vineyards.

The most popular Fetzer brands included Sundial Chardonnay, Valley Oaks Cabernet Sauvignon, Eagle Peak Merlot, and home Ranch Zinfandel. Fetzer also produced superpremium reserve wines such as Cabernet Sauvignon, Merlot, Pinot Noir, Chardonnay, and Zinfandel. Fetzer's critically acclaimed classic varietals included Johannisberg Riesling, Gewürztraminer, and White Zinfandel. The majority of Fetzer's sales, however, came from wines in the $6 to $7 per bottle range.

Michel Picard

Michel Picard was the second largest wine producer and the third largest vineyard (227 acres) in Burgundy. BFC entered into a joint venture with Picard *Père et Fils* in 1997 to market and sell their wines in North America and the West Indies. Among other varietals and blends, Michel Picard produced Syrah, Chardonnay, Cabernet Sauvignon, Chablis, Pouilly-Fuisse, and Chateauneuf-du-Pâpe, as well as other brands.

Thomas Burnet became the WD's group president in 1999 and chairman in 2000. Burnet had previously been involved in the start-up of the very successful NutraSweet Company and worked for it from its founding in 1981. He had served in various capacities at NutraSweet, including chief financial officer (CFO), general manager of its international business, and director of the company's new product development activities. Burnet had joined BFC as the CFO of Brown-Forman Beverage Company in 1990. In 1994, he became CFO of Brown-Forman Beverages Worldwide,

EXHIBIT 11

Sales of Brown-Forman Corporation's Leading Wine Brands: 1995 and 2000–2002 (Estimated)

Brand	Type of Wine	Thousands of Nine-Liter Cases				Growth Rate[1]	Percent Change[2]		Share of Company Portfolio[2]			
		1995	2000	2001	2002e	1995–2000	2000–2001	2001–2002e	1995	2000	2001	2002e
Fetzer	California table	1,875	2,310	2,225	2,350	4.3%	−3.7%	5.6%	39.7%	42.7%	40.3%	40.2%
Bolla	Italian table	955	1,095	1,180	1,215	2.8	7.8	3.0	20.2	20.3	21.4	20.8
Korbel	California sparkling	1,050	925	1,015	1,090	−2.5	9.7	7.4	22.2	17.1	18.4	18.6
Fontana Candida	Italian table	200	205	225	235	0.5	9.8	4.4	4.2	3.8	4.1	4.0
McPherson	Australian table	—	105	140	175	N/A	33.3	25.0	—	1.9	2.5	3.0
Total Top 5		4,080	4,640	4,785	5,065	2.6	3.1	5.9	86.4	85.8	86.8	86.6
Other brands		640	765	730	785	3.6	−4.6	7.5	13.6	14.2	13.2	13.4
Total Brown-Forman Wine[3]		4,720	5,405	5,515	5,850	2.7%	2.0%	6.1%	100.0%	100.0%	100.0%	100.0%

[1] Average annual compound growth rate.
[2] Based on unrounded data.
[3] Addition of columns may not agree due to rounding.

Source: Data compiled from IMPACT Databank Review and Forecast, *The U.S. Wine Market,* 2003 edition, p. 258.

then a newly formed global division of BFC. In the following year, Burnet accepted additional corporate financial responsibilities and was subsequently named president of the Advancing Markets Group in 1997. Burnet's major responsibility was to oversee the evolution of a loosely organized portfolio of wine brands into a more tightly knit group.

On July 20, 2001, BFC announced the formation of WE, a corporate venture that would be responsible for vineyards, production, sales, and marketing for the company's finest high-end wine brands. In a company press release, Burnet said,

> This is the natural next step in the development of our fine wine business. For the past two years, we've run our Estates Group and Sonoma-Cutrer as separate organizations. We can take better advantage of the strengths of both organizations by combining them. The goal of WE is to build our fine-wine business to be the best in the industry, and we believe that merging these two outstanding organizations will help us accomplish that mission.

Based on Fetzer's established strengths in the distribution and retail channels, Burnet hoped that WE's recently acquired brands, primarily sold to on-premises accounts such as restaurants and hotels, could be leveraged onto off-premises accounts, such as distributors and retailers.

Burnet promoted Steve Dorfman, formerly vice president of Winery Operations at BFC, to serve as managing director of WE. Dorfman, forty-one, and a native of New Jersey, graduated from the University of California at Davis, earning a bachelor's degree in winemaking, and from St. Mary's College, where he earned an MBA. Dorfman had joined Fetzer in 1983 as a winemaker, and over the next seventeen years, he had held positions of increasing responsibility. Dorfman had been involved in grower relations, vineyard management, vineyard acquisitions, and business development. Since BFC's initial purchase of Sonoma-Cutrer in 1999, Dorfman had served as the liaison between BFC and the Sonoma-Cutrer organization. Dorfman felt the key to the Sonoma-Cutrer deal was

EXHIBIT 12

Brown-Forman Corporation's Organization Chart, 2001

Source: Steve Dorfman and Brown-Forman Corporation *Annual Report, 2001.*

Sonoma-Cutrer sold 97 percent of its wine to on-premise accounts, such as restaurants. This was important to BFC because we didn't have much of a presence in on-premise wine sales. Also, Sonoma Cutrer had an incredible tracking system that enabled management to know where every one of its bottles was sold for the past 10 years. It was basically a sophisticated contact management system with 25,000 accounts and hundreds of thousands of contact transactions over 10+ years, an account history that potentially provides the Estates group the opportunity to penetrate sales of our other brands to Sonoma-Cutrer's accounts. We plan to incorporate that account management system into our other brands. There are also opportunities to expand this system, in order to obtain better knowledge of accounts than our distributors have. This should increase our power over distributors, given that they don't want to lose Sonoma-Cutrer and our other brands.

At the time of Dorfman's promotion, BFC announced that Brice Cutrer Jones, sixty-one, was leaving Sonoma-Cutrer, which he had founded in 1970, over policy disagreements regarding the decision to merge the Sonoma-Cutrer and WE organizations. After Jones departed, a senior BFC executive warned Dorfman, "We know that wine has a low ROA [return on assets], Steve. Don't screw with a tried and true system! Especially when you're just making peanuts vis-à-vis Jack Daniels!" Dorfman felt that if top executives at BFC

EXHIBIT 13

How Brown-Forman Corporation Built Its Wine Portfolio

1965	The company acquired exclusive distribution rights to Korbel's California Champagnes and Brandies.
1968	Bolla Italian Wines added to the company's portfolio.
1987	Distribution rights for Fontana Candida Italian Wines obtained.
1990	Brolio Wines, Italy, exclusive U.S. sales and marketing rights obtained.
1991	BFC Beverages Wine Division established. Jekel Vineyards's super-premium wines added to the portfolio.
1992	Fetzer of Mendocino County purchased.
1994	BFC Beverages Worldwide (BFBW) created. The new wine division was renamed BFC Beverages Worldwide Wine Group (BFBWWG).
1996	John Ash, Fetzer's culinary director, won the Julia Child Best Cookbook of the Year Award for *From the Earth to the Table*.
1997	The Wine Group entered into a joint venture with Michel Picard et Fils, to market French wines in North America and the West Indies.
	Korbel Champagne designated the "Official Champagne of the Millennium" for ten consecutive years, to serve as the exclusive champagne for all New Year's Eve Times Square celebrations until 2007.
1999	Four new brands added: Sonoma-Cutrer Chardonnay, Owen's Estates Wines, McPherson Wines, Mariah Wines.
2000	Thomas P. Burnet named president of the Wine Group, succeeding David Higgins, who retired after forty years with BFC in February 2000.
2001	Steven P. Dorfman named managing director of Brown-Forman Wine Estates (WE), a new group within BFC comprising its super-premium and ultra-premium California and Australian wine brands.
2002	Thomas P. Burnet departs to become president and CEO of Southcorp Wines (Australia).

Source: Company press releases.

really believed that brand power was all that mattered, then they should let WE build brands and do what it needed to do with a minimum of interference. In early January 2002, Dorfman recalled why he had taken the position:

> Becoming Managing Director was the third leg on my stool. For the first time, I had the abilities *and* experience to do everything on my own. I started out in the wine industry as a vintner and grower, and was now comfortable to do something on my own, because I knew the growers, sales, marketing, and distribution channels.

WE's brands are listed in Exhibit 15. Each is discussed in more detail below:

Bonterra   Bonterra was, along with Bel Arbor, created as a second label of Fetzer's. Bonterra grew Chardonnay, Merlot, Cabernet Sauvignon, and Petite Syrah on 133 acres. Bonterra also purchased the historic 378-acre organic McNab Ranch. Paul Dolan, president of Fetzer, also performed those duties for Bonterra Vineyards.

Jekel Vineyards   This winery was founded by Bill Jekel in Greenfield, California, in 1972. It was located along the ancient bed of the Arroyo Seco River. The winery produces estate-bottled wines in the superpremium category. Among them are Cabernet Sauvignon, Pinot Noir, Syrah, and Riesling in the $11 to $30 prices range. Furthermore, Chardonnay—grown on one hundred acres by Fetzer in the Paso Robles area—was being sent for processing to Jekel Vineyards. Jekel Vineyards was acquired by BFC in 1991.

EXHIBIT 14

Brown-Forman Corporation: Wine Division Portfolio Brands

Brand	Price Segment	Location	Vineyard Holdings	Facilities	Other Information
Bolla	Premium	Verona, Italy	Grower based	Bolla Verona Bolla Soave	
Fetzer	Premium Super-Premium Ultra-Premium	Mendocino County, CA	1,000 acres	Fetzer Mendocino Fetzer Paso Robles	Recognized industry leader in environmental best practices.
Fontana Candida	Premium	Italy	Grower based	Fontana Candida	
Korbel	Premium	Sonoma County, CA	Agency brand	Sonoma County	
McPherson	Ultra-Premium	McLaren Vale, Australia	Grower based	Del Farras	
Picard	Premium	Chany, France	Grower based	Chany Montpelier	2nd largest wine producer and 3rd largest vineyard (227 acres) in Burgundy.

Source: Based on personal correspondence with Steve Dorfman.

EXHIBIT 15

Brown-Forman Wine Estates: Portfolio of Brands

Brand	Price Segment	Location	Vineyard Holdings	Facilities	Other Information
Bonterra	Premium	Mendocino County, CA	325 acres	Fetzer Mendocino	Started as second label of Fetzer; certified organic.
Bel Arbor	Bulk	Mendocino County, CA	Bulk Wines	Fetzer Mendocino	Second label of Fetzer.
Ch. Tahbilk	Ultra-Premium	Golburn Valley, Australia	Agency brand	Ch, Tahbilk	
Geoff Merril Reserve	Ultra-Premium	McLaren Vale, Australia	JV trademark	Geoff Merrill Wines	
Jekel	Super-Premium Ultra-Premium	Monterey County, CA	310 acres	Jekel Monterey	Estate-bottled wines in $11–$30 per bottle range.
Mariah	Ultra-Premium	Mendocino County, CA	27 acres	Fetzer Mendocino	Produces 2,000 cases/yr of reserve Zinfandel for on-premise sales.
Owen's Estate	Ultra-Premium	McLaren Vale, Australia	Agency brand	Geoff Merrill Wines	
Sonoma-Cutrer	Ultra-Premium Luxury Premium	Sonoma County, CA	1125 acres	Sonoma-Cutrer	Mostly on-premises sales of premium Chardonnays.

Source: Based on personal correspondence with Steve Dorfman.

Mariah Wines   Acquired by BFC in 1999, Mariah produced wines in the Mendocino Ridge (Mendocino County) appellation in the ultra-premium price range. This winery produced 250 cases of Reserve Zinfandel a year from 24 acres of plantings. It sold high-end Zinfandel on-premise (restaurant) only.

Owen's Estate, Geoff Merrill Reserve, and Chateau Tahbilk   Due to deregulation in the 1990s, the Australian wine industry experienced unprecedented boom-times and record harvests, which brought about an oversupply of good quality grapes. Australia was by 2001 the fourth largest exporter of wine to the United States, following Italy, France, and Chile. BFC entered into joint ventures with these three Australian estate wineries to market their high-quality wines worldwide.

Sonoma-Cutrer Winery   Founded by Brice Jones in 1970, Sonoma-Cutrer was located in California's Sonoma Coast region. Sonoma-Cutrer used modern technology combined with Burgundian traditions (i.e., extended underground aging in proprietary French oak barrels). To obtain the best French oak possible, Sonoma-Cutrer went into the forestry business in 1994. They grew, cut, and aged the wood (for three years) in France. Barrel coopering was done locally in France. The winery used traditional cave or underground cellars with earthen floors, in order to provide natural humidity (over 90 percent) and constant cool, ambient air (at 58°F) that prevented oxidation and evaporation. Sonoma-Cutrer owned and farmed its own vineyards and did not purchase fruit from outside sources. Sonoma-Cutrer was well known in the high-end restaurant trade for its ultra-premium Chardonnay wines. Its luxury premium products, Les Pierres, The Cutrer, and The Russian River Ranches, were estate-bottled Chardonnays sold on an allocation basis to select on-premises accounts.

Given BFC's historical emphasis on achieving ROA targets in excess of 19 percent, the past year had been a disappointment. Dorfman was mindful that any projected sales of WE's brands would have to show how his group could contribute to meeting BFC's corporate targeted ROA for 2003 and beyond. Past results and internal financial projections for 2002–2004 by wine brand are shown in Exhibits

EXHIBIT 16

Brown-Forman Corporation, Actual and Projected Sales by Brand, 1998–2004 ($000s)

	Actual Sales				Projected Sales		
	1998	1999	2000	2001	2002	2003	2004
Brown-Forman Wine Estates' U.S. Brands							
Sonoma-Cutrer	$—	$—	$17,078	$18,136	$18,798	$21,302	$24,246
Bonterra—International	6,913	8,016	11,633	12,368	15,504	18,668	21,119
Bonterra—U.S.	5,503	5,823	7,885	9,006	9,779	11,740	13,329
Jekel	7,229	7,788	9,995	9,997	11,809	14,193	16,515
Mariah	—	99	405	293	414	986	1,116
Brown-Forman Wine Estates' Australian Brands							
Owen's Estates	—	—	1,364	1,699	2,514	3,119	3,849
Geoff Merrill Reserve	—	—	53	197	217	217	224
Tahbilk	—	—	60	297	790	945	1,100
Consolidated Wine Group Brands							
Fetzer—Worldwide	$156,518	$176,620	$185,744	$187,815	$224,414	$235,704	$249,541
Fetzer—U.S.	105,609	115,212	123,342	127,717	144,656	145,378	148,321
Bolla—International	26,857	49,367	46,056	43,481	56,158	62,439	67,176
Bolla—U.S.	44,119	44,949	50,399	55,358	62,438	64,583	69,530
Korbel	83,177	101,486	120,587	82,425	96,354	107,682	110,932

Source: Prepared by case writers from personal correspondence with Steve Dorfman.

EXHIBIT 17

Brown-Forman Wine Estates, Actual and Projected Brand Profit per Case, 1998–2004

	Actual Per Case				Projected Per Case		
	1998	1999	2000	2001	2002	2003	2004
Brown-Forman Wine Estates' U.S. Brands							
Sonoma-Cutrer	$ —	$ —	$11.64	$14.14	$14.64	$19.01	$24.41
Bonterra—International	9.04	1.35	12.53	11.47	13.04	16.94	19.05
Bonterra—U.S.	5.44	(4.67)	10.95	14.91	13.62	17.49	20.89
Jekel	22.86	16.36	15.52	9.30	13.90	16.89	17.69
Mariah	—	(21.13)	1.84	4.54	21.51	57.59	59.58
Australian Brands							
Owen's Estates	—	—	(7.29)	(2.75)	2.45	3.85	6.11
Geoff Merrill Reserve	—	—	8.85	18.19	13.67	31.91	32.69
Tahbilk	—	—	(13.08)	5.32	12.23	12.23	11.56
Consolidated Wine Group Brands							
Fetzer—Worldwide	$5.77	$4.97	$6.29	$7.97	$7.84	$8.07	$8.58
Fetzer—U.S.	6.75	5.64	7.79	9.99	9.84	9.62	9.70
Bolla—International	3.56	5.82	4.32	4.08	3.56	3.99	4.43
Bolla—U.S.	5.28	5.83	5.72	7.68	8.43	8.53	9.46
Korbel	2.99	6.29	4.28	1.23	6.60	5.78	5.33

Source: Prepared by case writers from personal correspondence with Steve Dorfman.

16–18. These projections include brand sales in dollars, per case income, and incremental ROAs for selected super- and ultra-premium labels.

Exhibit 19 provides BFC's internal projections out to the year 2020, showing the respective shares of its wine and spirits segments in its drinks portfolio. These projections were based on internal estimates that the growth rate in wine sales would be nearly seven times as fast as the growth rate in sales of spirits.

BFC also maintained a significant presence in export markets via its international division. In the past, this division had been primarily responsible for selling Fetzer wines into export markets. BFC's Wines International Division, headed by David Dearie, marketed Fetzer and twenty-five other brands in seventy-five countries and was expanding rapidly. Prior to assuming his position as managing director of Wines International, Dearie had worked for four years in BFC's international spirits division. BFC executives hoped that Dearie's International Division could sell WE's super- and ultra-premium wine portfolio brands into export markets. Exhibit 20 illustrates BFC's current estimated share of California

wine exports based on volume of cases sold, using 1999 shipments as a base.

BFC's Future Prospects

Over the previous ten years, sales of wine in the premium and ultra-premium segments had enjoyed double-digit growth rates. However, in summer 2002 news coming from the California wine industry indicated that growth was slowing. After modest declines in sales immediately following the September 11, 2001, terrorist attacks in New York and Washington, D.C., California wines had continued to experience a "difficult year" thus far in 2002. The U.S. wine industry as a whole was undergoing increasing consolidation as the rapid growth of the 1990s—which had enticed numerous new entrants into the wine industry—gave way to overproduction, oversupply of grapes, and inadequate growth in demand to keep up with the increasing supply. The "Two Buck Chuck" phenomenon was also contributing to lackluster growth in premium wine sales. Franzia's Charles Shaw wines (nicknamed "Two Buck Chuck") had been the greatest

EXHIBIT 18

Brown-Forman Corporation, Actual and Projected Returns on Assets (ROA) by Brand, 1998–2004

	Actual Incremental ROA				Projected Incremental ROA		
	1998	1999	2000	2001	2002	2003	2004
U.S. Brands							
Sonoma-Cutrer	—	—	5.3%	5.0%	4.4%	4.4%	4.7%
Bonterra—International	N/A	6.9	14.7	12.1	13.4	16.6	17.4
Bonterra—U.S.	8.9	6.4	18.6	19.3	17.5	22.1	24.1
Jekel	10.6	11.4	16.5	9.4	13.4	14.9	15.0
Mariah	0.0	−1.0	5.0	3.4	17.2	39.1	38.9
Australia							
Owen's Estates	—	—	−0.7	7.8	20.6	22.3	27.1
Geoff Merrill Reserve	—	—	11.2	16.7	25.1	49.8	52.6
Tahbilk	—	—	−5.1	−13.0	35.2	35.5	35.3
Consolidated Wine Group							
Fetzer—Worldwide	19.5	19.1	23.3	22.6	21.2	20.6	20.3
Fetzer—U.S.	26.8	26.0	35.0	30.9	28.8	27.4	26.3
Bolla—International	4.8	10.1	6.4	6.1	5.9	6.3	7.1
Bolla—U.S.	81.2	24.2	23.8	48.3	56.2	43.7	47.7
Korbel	78.2	96.4	107.0	84.6	172.5	164.2	153.8

Source: Prepared by case writers from personal correspondence with Steve Dorfman.

EXHIBIT 19

Projected Share of Total U.S. Wine and Spirits Revenue
for Brown-Forman Corporation

Source: Brown-Forman Wine Estates.

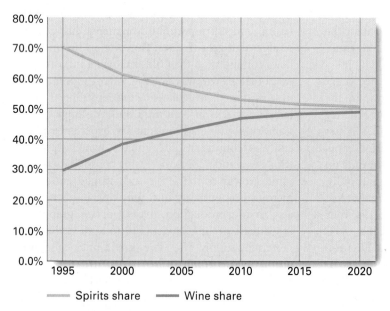

— Spirits share   — Wine share

EXHIBIT 20

Brown-Forman Wine Segment: Estimated Export Volume
as a Percentage of California Exports

Key Markets	BFC Volume (000 cases)	Total California Exports (000 cases)	BFC's Share of Total California Exports
United Kingdom	222	7,069	3%
Japan	160	5,742	3%
Canada	107	5,054	2%
Netherlands	8	2,126	—
Switzerland	41	1,290	3%
Germany	42	1,040	4%
Denmark	3	566	<1%

Source: Brown-Forman Wine Estates' estimates.

success story in the wine industry in the first half of 2002, retailing for $24 per case of twelve bottles at Trader Joe's Markets.

In this uncertain sales environment and with his champion Burnet now heading up a rival firm in Australia, Dorfman was preparing for a presentation of his annual plan back at BFC's headquarters in Kentucky. Dorfman felt sure that his preferred strategy, retaining WE as a separate "intrapreneurial" venture within the WD, would be met with skepticism. Still, WE might be spared if he were to identify how to restructure its portfolio of wine businesses, selling off poorly performing or noncore brands, as well as how to implement cost reductions across the remaining brands. However, throughout its long history BFC had never divested a business it had previously purchased. Dorfman felt that bowing to the inevitable pressure to fold the WE group back in with the WD could reduce costs but likely result in his own job as managing director being redefined or possibly eliminated entirely.

Upon his return to Healdsburg, Dorfman asked for Keith LaVine's counsel. After a long career in hotel beverages purchasing and wholesale distribution of wine, LaVine had become Sonoma-Cutrer's regional manager for the Southeast United States, just two years prior to its purchase by BFC in 1999. Since then, LaVine had been promoted to national sales manager and moved to California, becoming WE's senior vice president of sales in late July 2001.

LaVine began the meeting by saying flatly that,

It is time for us to become more flexible, Steve. Corporate is streamlining, 'trimming the fat.' This includes layoffs and spin-offs. I believe that we can meet any future challenge, but the bad news is that the wine industry isn't going to get better for the next few years. We need to be as productive as in the past, just with fewer personnel. Does keeping the our division the way it is make any sense now or should we just fold it in with the WD's brands and have a 'monster' wine division?

Dorfman reminded LaVine of the potential synergies among WE's and the WD's brands.

Well, there is going to have to be some more interaction in the future, Keith. Sales, marketing, and finance are probably where any future combinations will occur in order to avoid duplication of effort. Corporate will look for cost advantages such as vineyard purchasing, grape purchasing, glass procurement, and other things where buying in larger quantity or centralized negotiations gives us a leg up.

LaVine mentioned several rumors that had been circulating around the WD.

Steve, I hear that corporate might decide to integrate some of the high-end spirits into our division. The advantage to our division the way it is today is that we can focus more on fewer brands, which garners more attention for those brands. What do the spirits salespeople know about selling wine?

Dorfman agreed to some extent.

Keith, there is *some* potential for synergy between wines and spirits, since spirits, like wines, are sold through similar distribution channels, *if the goal is to grow price by entering premium segments*. Look, the major benefit of having BFC as our parent organization is that it provides access to capital and talent. Corporate is akin to a mutual fund or investment bank first; a marketer, second. Whatever happens, we need to maintain a symbiotic relationship with BFC. That's how we were able to hire our new CFO—we hired her from Fetzer. Corporate formerly ran Sonoma-Cutrer like a mutual fund—one organization didn't bother the other—yet this had some negative effects in that some BFC salespeople didn't know what Sonoma-Cutrer was or how to sell or position its wine. Also, corporate views distributors as its customers while Sonoma-Cutrer views each account as a customer and distributors as a necessary evil.

LaVine wasn't sure that corporate executives at BFC held all the cards.

Okay, Steve, but there is also a 'halo effect' created by small wineries such as Mariah to help consumers look at Brown-Forman as a diversified company instead of just being a 'Bourbon house.' We are in a unique position, really, because we have a parent who is cash rich. We also have an opportunity to take advantage of someone else's misfortune during the coming hard times in the wine industry and perhaps purchase new smaller wineries.

Dorfman ended the meeting with LaVine and sat down to prepare his presentation for the upcoming Beverages Division meeting in Louisville. In addition to choosing a course of action, Dorfman faced the challenge of identifying what managerial components WE needed to correct in order to implement any changes that he (with BFC approval) might want to make. He reflected on his dilemma:

Before I went into the wine industry, I wish I had known how complex this business was. You have to be able to make wine, sell it, and market it. Marketing is very difficult, and it is very competitive on the sales side. It seems to me that the cost savings of combining all wines into a centralized organization are outweighed by the differentiation in production that results from separation. This can carry through to sales and marketing,

because the decisions that each production unit [winery] makes every day allows for a unique sales story to be told out in the marketplace.

Mindful that selection of either strategic option would require BFC's approval, Dorfman decided to sit down and rethink what role his group of brands should play within BFC's conglomerate portfolio and how he would implement this role.

REFERENCES

Adams (1999). *Adams Wine Handbook*, Adams Business Media, New York.

Anonymous (1999). And Now the Numbers, *Wine & Vines*, July.

Anonymous (2001). Gallo "Expansion Project Slowed." [Online]. **www.kj.com/**.

Anonymous (2001). "Lew Platt Was Out at KJ." *Wines and Vines*, June.

Appel, T. (1995). "Deal Closed for Top Wineries Sale, Include Beringer, a Record." *Santa Rosa Press Democrat*, November 22, p. E1.

Brown-Forman Corporation (2000, 2001). *Annual Reports*.

California Wine Export Program (2000). *World Vineyard, Grape, and Wine Report, 2000*, July, 425 Market Street, Suite 1000, San Francisco, California 94105.

Correspondence to the case writers with Steve Dorfman (2001). May 8.

De Luca, J. (2002). "The Outlook for the California Wine Industry in 2002," Presentation to the North Bay Economic Outlook Conference, Rohnert Park. California, February.

Echikson, W. et al. (2001). "Wine War," *Business Week*, September 3, pp. 54–60.

Gomberg-Fredrikson (1999). *1999 Annual Wine Industry Review*, Gomberg, Fredrikson & Associates, 703 Market Street, Suite 1602, San Francisco, California 94103.

Gould, L. E. (2001). "A Golden Opportunity," Advanstar Communications.

IMPACT Databank Review and Forecast (2003). *The U.S. Wine Market*, 2003 edition. New York: M. Shanken Publications.

Interviews with Steve Dorfman, April 2001, January 2002, and April 2003.

Interviews with Keith LaVine, March and October 2003.

Love, J. M. (2000). "United States Wine Producers Face Increasing Competition." *Wine Business Monthly*, June, p. 1.

Moran, T. (2001). "California Wineries Quietly End Legal Battle." *Modesto Bee*, March 31, p. C1.

Motto Kryla Fisher. (2002). "High-end California Wine Sales Increase 10% in 2001." Unified Grape Symposium, Sacramento, California, January.

Mutual Acceptance Agreement on Oenological Practices, 2001. April 9.

Nation's Restaurant News, 35(10), March 5, 2001.

www.hoovers.com/. Hoovers Online Capsule: Diageo PLC, 2001.

www.napanews.com/. Saturday, March 10, 2001.

www.hoovers.com. Hoovers Online Capsule: Robert Mondavi Corporation, 2001.

Peterson, T. (2001). "For the Mondavis, It's a Long Way from Muscatel." *Business Week*, June 15.

Sinton, P. (1999). "California Wines Quenching the World." *San Francisco Chronicle*, January 23, p. D1.

Tagliabue, J. (2001). "Trying to Make the Wine List." *New York Times*, April 11.

U.S. Department of Commerce (2000). *2000 National Trade Data Bank*.

Wine Institute (2000). Wine Institute, 425 Market Street, Suite 1000, San Francisco, California 94105, www.wineinstitute.org.

Wines & Vines (2001). *Directory and Buyer's Guide*, vol. 81, p. 12-A (December 31, 2000), The Hiaring Company, San Rafael, California.

Case 2

Welch Foods, Inc.

This case was prepared by Vincent Amanor-Boadu, Michael Boland, and David Barton, Kansas State University.

Welch Foods Inc. (Welch's) is a wholly owned subsidiary of the National Grape Cooperative Association, Inc. (National Grape). Welch's president and CEO, Dan Dillon, says his company faces an increasingly strong challenge to remain relevant to customers and consumers. He put it this way: "At our current size, are we going to be able to remain on the radar screen of companies such as Wal-Mart? Will they want to see us if we request a meeting?" Additionally, says Dillon, it is critical for Welch's that its consumers associate grape juice with the distinctive characteristics of Concord and Niagara grapes. This question of competitive relevance and scale is critical to all food companies in the rapidly consolidating marketplace. But perhaps more important to the viability and survival of a cooperative-owned food processing company such as Welch's is its organizational system. The unique structure of the two-board of directors has to support the strategies that Welch's needs to remain relevant.

Dillon has made it his mission to maintain Welch's relevancy by strengthening relationships with key customers and suppliers, as well as providing consumers with the products they want at a price point they believe is competitive. The question of relevance was not new at Welch's or to Dillon. When a consultant advised Welch's to move away from dark juices in the early 1980s, Dillon, then a young Welch's executive,

Copyright © 2004 by Vincent Amanor-Boadu, Michael Boland, and David Barton. This case was prepared by Vincent Amanor-Boadu, Michael Boland, and David Barton, Kansas State University, as the basis for class discussion rather than to illustrate either effective or ineffective handling of an administration situation. Reprinted by permission of Michael Boland. All rights reserved.

responded sharply that that view was unacceptable. He proceeded to embark on a mission to prove that "the purple grape juice" was not only a successful product with a future but also capable of leading the entire juice category. By 2002, Welch's purple grape juice and other products claimed number one or number two spots among all noncitrus multiserve manufacturers.

Origin of National Grape Cooperative and Welch Foods

Jack Kaplan, an entrepreneur, purchased a small grape processing facility in 1933 from some investment bankers in Brocton, New York, and called his new company National Grape Corporation. To control inflation during World War II, the U.S. government instituted price control policies for most industries but exempted farmer cooperatives, allowing them to pass through their prices to the market. Kaplan decided to take advantage of this legislation by selling his company to the growers supplying grapes to his plant on the condition they formed a cooperative. The growers accepted and National Grape was born in 1945. Its membership has grown to encompass the majority of the Concord and Niagara grape growers in Michigan, New York, Ohio, Pennsylvania, Washington, and Ontario, Canada.

In 1869, Dr. Thomas Welch and his son Charles applied Louis Pasteur's theory to the processing of Concord grapes, succeeding in producing an unfermented wine for use at church services. Charles took over the business in the 1870s, producing "Dr. Welch's Unfermented Wine" on a part-time basis while running his dentistry practice. He changed the brand name to "Dr. Welch's Grape Juice" in 1890, and after a successful exhibition of the product at the Chicago World Fair in 1893, dropped the "Dr." from the label. This success at the World Fair also caused the younger Dr. Welch to quit his dentistry practice and devote his attention to the company full time, significantly growing the business and the brand. Charles successfully ran the company until his death in 1926 and the company was sold to a group of private investors from Tennessee shortly thereafter.

Welch's came up for sale in 1945, and Kaplan purchased it and became its president. Kaplan set in motion for National Grape to purchase Welch's during the early 1950s, with the objective of giving growers "complete control of their destiny, from raw fruit to finished product." But since the growers did not have the money to pay outright, Kaplan offered them a "mortgage" that allowed him to specify how the processing company was governed. In 1956, the directors of National Grape Cooperative voted to purchase Welch's stock and paid off the mortgage on the company in three years.

Over time, National Grape Cooperative Association set the vision "to be the best choice of present and future members to market their grape production." Its mission focused on being "dedicated to providing the most profitable long-term market for all of its members' quality Concord and Niagara grapes." Its ownership of Welch Foods, Inc., provided it with a vehicle to achieve the vision and accomplish the mission.

The Governance System in National Grape and Welch Foods

National Grape and Welch's each has its own board of directors, a stipulation put in place by Kaplan when he sold his processing company to the growers. Aware of the failure rate of farmer cooperatives attempting to undertake consumer products manufacturing and marketing, Kaplan stipulated a two-board system to allow the growers to govern the cooperative and a mix of growers and people knowledgeable in the packaged goods industry to govern Welch's. The two-board system turned out to provide the appropriate checks and balances required to manage the complex business of growing, processing, and marketing consumer packaged goods. "What you have is an arrangement that carefully balances the needs and concerns of the growers with the needs of the business," explained Dillon. "You have this stable system in place that care-

fully analyzes and weighs the costs and benefits of every key decision that needs to be made," Dillon continued about the two-board system.

In 2003, National Grape's governance was based on the traditional one-member, one-vote principle of cooperative representation. The key Concord and Niagara grape growing areas for National Grape were Yakima Valley in Washington State, southwestern Michigan and northern Ohio, the Lake Erie area of New York and Pennsylvania, and the Finger Lakes in New York and Ontario, Canada. These four key areas were divided into thirteen production districts and 103 geographic sections.

National Grape's board of directors was comprised of thirteen members elected from each of the production areas and was responsible for establishing policies regarding member needs and raw grape production. The board elected the officers of National Grape annually and appointed a general manager to implement board policy and oversee operations. The distribution of directors in the different areas is based on the number of grower members in the area. Areas I, II, and III each has three directors while Area IV has four directors. Because the directors are elected by area, it is possible for more than one director to come from a particular district. Each director is elected to a three-year term, and director terms are staggered into three classes, each class representing a particular year on the board. There are no term limits on directors as long as they are willing to serve and are elected by members in their area.

In addition to the board, National Grape's members annually elected thirteen delegates to represent them in each of the organization's thirteen production districts. Their responsibilities included acting as a critical communications link between members, the board, and management and chairing their district's membership meetings. Finally, the advisory committees, 103 members, are elected from the geographic sections to provide direct feedback on issues to the board and to management and to provide a gauge on the pulse of the general membership. Advisory committee members meet at the local level about four to six times per year.

There are 10 people on Welch's board; 4 representatives from the National Grape board, 4 outside directors, and 2 representatives of Welch's management, including the company's CEO (Figure 1). The 4 representatives from National Grape include the

FIGURE 1

National Grape and Welch's Two-Board System

chair of National Grape's board and 3 others elected by National Grape's board. The outside directors are appointed from a slate of candidates, and the management representatives are submitted by the nominating committee of Welch's board to the National Grape board. Membership of the Welch's board is for one year. "The fact that there are four outside directors and four growers provides the balance that has contributed to the effectiveness of this model," Dillon observed.

Dillon was very clear in his perception about the relationship between the two companies. "We look at the members of National Grape as our stockholders and we think about the National Grape board in the same way General Motors thinks about its investment bankers," he explained. "We provide them with all the information they need, but we do not ask them for a vote."

When there are major issues that could affect growers—acquisitions, divestitures, plant closings, etc.—Welch's discussed those issues with the National Grape board to ensure that there was enhanced understanding of the possible ramifications. Welch's also negotiated grape quality specifications with National Grape to ensure that Welch's products remained competitive in the consumer marketplace in terms of its value proposition and that growers received competitive compensation for their products. Once these specifications are decided, neither Welch's nor National Grape can change them without the other's consent. This arrangement has worked very well for both companies, given that the National Grape board has all the relevant information motivating decisions at Welch's.

The two-board system demanded significant effort from all concerned to work effectively. For example, Welch's staff devoted a lot of time educating new National Grape and Welch's directors to create a "common language" and facilitate communication. A. B. (Trey) Wright, Welch's CFO, explained it this way: "Outside board members have to learn the difference between proceeds and profits, and the grower-members, who tend to talk and think in terms of crop year results, have to learn to convert to fiscal year results because Welch's is run on a fiscal year basis."

The representatives of National Grape's board on Welch's board have changed more frequently than the outside directors. Consequently, they needed more training to ensure that the "common language" was maintained among Welch's board members. For example, Welch's people noted that they often have to explain to new growers on Welch's board the importance of financing assets with sufficient equity because there is a belief that since Welch's can borrow at better interest rates than producers, it should distribute all proceeds and borrow or leverage with debt to finance capital improvements. This education was not limited to just National Grape's representatives on Welch's board. Welch's made presentations to the National Grape board at almost every National Grape board meeting and answered any questions that allowed National Grape's board members to increase their understanding of the packaged goods business and industry. Welch's also provided all necessary information to the National Grape board, as any public company does. "We have to do this. It helps us operate more efficiently and create the value that is our primary objective," Dillon pointed out.

There was significant collegiality among board members, despite their different backgrounds. "The outside directors respect the growers because of their extensive agricultural knowledge and the owners respect the outside directors for their commitment and valuable input," noted Wright about the relationship among Welch's board members. "In twenty-two years of going to six board meetings a year, I can count on one hand the number of times we have ever had a vote that wasn't unanimous," Dillon added. Thus, the system works because people learn quickly to appreciate the challenges confronting the packaged goods company and their responsibilities in addressing these challenges. "Even those who get elected to the board on the promise of changing the system change their opinions once they come on the board and recognize the effort everyone is putting in to addressing the issues confronting us," Dillon noted.

Welch's board structured its management compensation incentives to be aligned with the grower-owners' rewards. For example, management was rewarded on items such as net proceeds per ton of grapes received and not on profit per case of grape juice sold. "This ties it all together," Wright pointed out. "Even though we are separate companies and we focus on the different segments of the business, the reward systems are the same and they tie the two companies together."

The governance structure at National Grape and Welch's offered two critical advantages: (1) it allowed National Grape to focus on its core functions—such as cooperative and ownership issues and the production and delivery of quality grapes; and (2) it allowed Welch's to focus on the job of product development, manufacturing, marketing, and sale of packaged goods. Since the issues facing grape producers and the packaged goods company were different, the governance system ensured that the critical issues in each facet were not overlooked or underemphasized. Dillon recognized this important benefit of the two-board system when he noted that "we are able to succeed at what we do because of the two-board system which insulates us from most of the issues occurring at the production level."

The Business of Welch Foods

Welch's saw its purpose as building long-term value in the cooperative and releasing that value back to the grower-owner over time and providing a reliable market for their grapes through excellence in product quality, customer service, market responsiveness, and consumer satisfaction. Welch's processed 50 percent of Concord grapes and 80 percent of Niagara grapes produced in the United States into juices, jellies, jams, and other products. It was the leading marketer of Concord and Niagara grape-based products in the world. The company produced a variety of other fruit-based products, including 100 percent juices and juice cocktails. The company owned the Welch's and BAMA brand names, using the latter in the marketing of its jams, jellies, and preserves in the South. Its products were available in bottled, refrigerated, single-serve, and frozen and shelf-stable formats. Additionally, it served the industrial market, supplying concentrates to further processors and other manufacturers (Figure 2).

Marketing and Promotion

Welch's was one of the first food companies to take advantage of radio and television to market products. In 1934, it began an eleven-year sponsorship of the Irene Rich radio show. It became one of television's first corporate sponsors when it found a fit between its products and its image and *The Howdy Doody Show* in 1951. Its "Memories" advertising campaign, which features young spokeschildren, enters its tenth year in 2004. Since the early days with Charles Welch, the company focused on innovative marketing and sales approaches—magazines, radio, television, the sides of trolley cars—to reach customers and consumers. For example, it advertised in magazines to explain to its customers why there were shortages of Welch's products during World War II. Welch's also introduced the long-running jelly glasses in 1953, featuring Howdy Doody as the first "star."

FIGURE 2

Product Categories at Welch Foods, Inc.

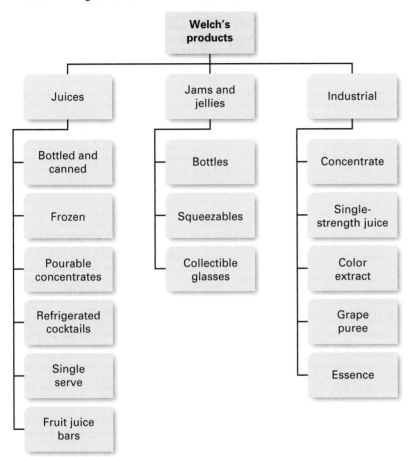

Since then the campaign has featured kids' favorite movie and cartoon characters such as Simba's Pride, Winnie the Pooh, Tom and Jerry, Looney Tunes characters, the Flintstones, Jimmy Neutron, and Dragon Tales characters.

Welch's always looked for ways to extend its strong brand image. One such opportunity was the 1999 licensing agreement with C. H. Robinson, which allowed Welch's to enter the fresh produce aisle with branded fresh grapes. The program had been very successful, generating sales of more than 16 million packages of Welch's Fresh Grapes to consumers and involving more than thirty grocery chains across the country in its first year.

Welch's was very aggressive in the increasingly competitive fruit juice market, using new product launches, well-crafted and targeted consumer promotions and advertising, and enhanced consumer communication in various media, including via the Internet. The company recently established a loyalty program with Upromise, whereby money is contributed to a child's college education fund when a consumer (with a Upromise account) purchases Welch's jelly products. The company has also collaborated with **ValuPage.com** to offer consumers the opportunity to select particular promotional products online and print associated coupons to be used in participating stores for discounts on its products.

International Activities

By 2003, Welch's was marketing its products in forty international markets, but the company's principal export markets were Canada, Japan, South Korea, and the Latin America–Caribbean area. Through an alliance arrangement, the company processed and distributed a variety of shelf-stable products in the United Kingdom, introducing seven new products in 2002 and launching an approximately $8 million marketing campaign (television ads, a public relations campaign championing the health benefits of its products, and a tactical sampling program encompassing radio promotions) to support them. The company also signed a distribution agreement with Nong Shim, a South Korean consumer products company, to improve its penetration into the Southeast Asian market. Welch's had used a similar strategic alliances approach when it entered Japan, reducing new market entry costs and enhancing its competitive advantage. Total international sales in 2003 reached $120 million compared with $100 million in 2002.

Innovations in Products and Packaging

From its early days, Welch's had continuously looked to product and packaging innovation as a competitive strategy (Figure 3). For example, it introduced the squeezable containers for jelly and jams in 1985 to improve the feasibility of kids preparing their own sandwiches and launched the shatterproof jelly jar in 1999 to minimize accidents when kids took the initiative to "take care of themselves." Welch's also focused on innovation in convenience, such as the

introduction of shelf-stable juice concentrates in 1996 which allowed juice to be mixed without waiting for it to thaw. In 2003, the company introduced three new 100 percent white grape blends into the market.

A principal driver in these efforts is the objective to have 25 percent of the company's sales come from new products (products that have been introduced within the past five years). This objective was considered essential not only in extending and growing Welch's brand, but also in answering the demands of consumers as their tastes and needs evolved. "In other words," emphasizes Dillon, "it's what the company has to do in order to remain relevant."

Research and Development

In 1997, Welch's built a new Technology Center in Billerica, Massachusetts, a short drive from the company's Concord headquarters. The forty-thousand-square-foot facility, one of the largest among cooperative organizations, employed about fifty quality control, engineering, and research and development professionals. Prior to building the Technology Center, Welch's research and development, engineering, and quality control professionals were located three hundred fifty miles away in Westfield, New York, away from the marketing, market research, and operations people with whom they needed to interact frequently. It was hoped that by bringing the marketing and

FIGURE 3

Innovation at Welch's Through the Years

Source: Developed from information on Welch Foods Inc.'s website (**www.welchs.com**).

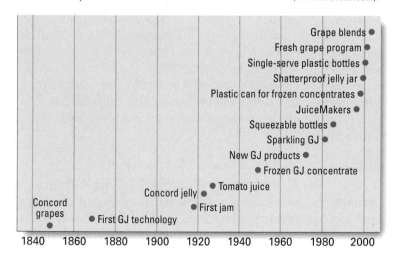

GJ = Grape juice

market research group together with the engineering, quality control, and research and development group in the same facility, ideas would flow more easily and the enhanced communication would engender more new products. It did—in the generation of both products and intellectual property. Dillon explained it this way: "In the first fifty years of the company's existence, we received two patents; in the last five years, we have filed for fourteen patents and to date have received patent awards on nine of those. It tells you what sort of company we are today compared to what we have been."

Welch's has driven its product development objective with its own internal effort as well as through collaboration with other organizations and researchers. For example, the company has contributed to funding research exploring the health benefits of grape juice made from Concord and Niagara grapes. A USDA study found that Welch's Purple 100 percent grape juice had three times more antioxidant power than other popular juices such as grapefruit, orange, tomato, and apple, and more antioxidant power than forty two other tested fruits and vegetables.[1] Other preliminary studies have suggested that the antioxidant activity of Concord grape juice may be similar to that of red wine. In 1999, *Circulation,* the journal of the American Heart Association, published a report by researchers from the University of Wisconsin Medical School indicating that the elasticity of blood vessels increased significantly and the rate at which their LDL ("bad") cholesterol oxidized decreased significantly when their subjects drank purple grape juice for two weeks.[2] Similarly, in 2002, researchers at the University of Illinois Urbana–Champaign indicated that purple grape juice fed to laboratory animals led to significant reductions in both mammary tumor mass and the number of tumors per animal.[3] In another study, researchers at University of California, Davis Medical Center, also found that

Concord grape juice flavonoids are potent antioxidants that may protect against oxidative stress and reduce the risk of free radical damage and chronic diseases.[4]

Not one to miss opportunities, Welch's recruited such celebrity personalities as Larry King and Paul Harvey to extol the health benefits of Welch's products to consumers. The company also communicated directly with medical practitioners and attended the relevant medical conventions to educate and exhibit to the professionals the role of its products in human health.

Technology and Quality

Welch's had an intense focus on protecting its brand image while listening and responding to the needs of consumers. The company's reputation for quality has been earned through sustained dedication to uniform standards. Welch's excellent quality control enabled the company to offer premium products consistently and continuously. The company also introduced new technologies, such as its three-time pasteurization process (once after harvest, once after filtering, and a final pasteurization after the bottle is filled), which, according to company reports, has increased first-pass inspection from approximately 70 percent to over 90 percent.

The company installed a web-based information system to provide up-to-date information on prices, promotion, and category information in 1998. Company officials note that not only did this improve information flow and support efficient customer service, but also it allowed Welch's to respond faster to market conditions. Although retailers were not tied into Welch's extranet information system directly, the system allowed sales representatives to get more accurate and timely information. To improve its merchandising performance, Welch's also installed software in partnership with a software development company to create orders and manage the inventories of its retail customers. This technology allowed some retailers to double the number of times they turned Welch's products. These efforts at improving efficiency of customers through effective use of information technology matched Welch's desire to strengthen customer relationships.

[1]H. Wang, C. Guohua, R. L. Prior, "Total Antioxidant Capacity of Fruits," *Journal of Agricultural and Food Chemistry* 44 (1996): 701–703.

[2]J. H. Stein, J. G. Keevil, D. A. Wiebe, S. Aeschlimann, and J. D. Folts, "Purple Grape Juice Improves Endothelial Function and Reduces the Susceptibility of LDL Cholesterol to Oxidation in Patients with Coronary Artery Disease," *Circulation* 100 (1999): 1050–1055.

[3]K. W. Singletary, M. J. Stansbury, M. Giusti, R. B. van Breemen, M. Wallig, and A. Rimando, "Inhibition of Rat Mammary Tumorigenesis by Concord Grape Juice Constituents," *Journal of Agricultural and Food Chemistry* 51 (2003): 7280–7286.

[4]D. J. O'Byrne, S. Devaraj, S. M. Grundy, and I. Jialal, "Comparison of the Antioxidant Effects of Concord Grape Juice Flavonoids and Alpha-Tocopherol on Markers of Oxidative Stress in Healthy Adults," *American Journal of Clinical Nutrition* 76 (2002): 1367–1374.

TABLE 1

Summary of Financial Indicators for Welch Foods, 1998 to 2002

(In Thousands) Operations	1998	1999	2000	2001	2002
Net Sales	509,331	526,454	550,275	535,027	553,476
Cost of Sales	319,835	327,485	350,126	347,390	346,051
Patron Cash Distribution	55,723	57,621	60,608	51,314	56,358
Patron Equity Investment	16,645	17,211	18,103	15,327	14,982
Net Proceeds	69,807	70,532	78,084	67,367	65,056
Financial Position					
Working Capital	66,173	147,025	158,008	150,063	130,602
Net Property, Plant and Equipment	08,919	111,241	118,134	119,648	122,073
Total Assets	66,841	351,269	383,155	352,647	330,472
Current Liabilities	07,641	101,472	119,205	93,783	106,580
Non-Current Liabilities	167,381	157,151	165,795	155,603	128,730
Owners' Equity	91,819	92,646	98,155	103,261	95,162

Source: National Grape Cooperative Association Inc. and Welch Foods Inc. Annual Report, various years.

Financial Performance

Common profitability measures, such as return on equity or investment, cannot be calculated and compared in the usual way to other food processing companies because net proceeds in Welch's are not equivalent to net income. Welch's operates on a pool basis, and, hence, its cost of sales does not include the cost of purchasing grapes from members. Members are not paid a market price for their grapes but receive net proceeds which include the purchase value of their grapes. The net sales and case sold equivalent data indicated that the company experienced slightly higher average unit prices for its products in 2002 compared with the two previous years (Figure 4).

Patron Financial Performance

The members of the cooperative are the residual recipients of the company's financial performance, and their payment is referred to as patronage distribution or refund. The patronage distribution or refund received by a member depended on the volume of business the member did with the cooperative. Patron proceeds have varied widely over the five years, 1998–2002. They ranged from a high of $78.7 million in 2000 to a low of $66.6 million in 2001. Although most members consider proceeds received per acre as the most important measure of their profitability, the fact that some of their acreage is nonbearing can confuse this measure. However, since proceeds per ton were based primarily on members' patronage in the particular year, it provided a good indicator of their performance, reflecting the impact of weather and other conditions in the industry. Proceeds per ton have varied from $255 in 2000 to $208 in 2002, and paralleled the average price per case even as total tons sold by members varied between about 239,529 tons in 2002 and 309,218 tons in 2000 (Figure 5).

Challenges and Options

The future presented some interesting challenges for Welch's and National Grape because of changes in the market and industry. Dillon believed that because his company offered growers premium prices and a secure market for their grapes provided quality specifications were met, National Grape's share of good Concord and Niagara grape growers would continue to increase. But access to high-quality grapes is only one side of the equation; the other side is for Welch's to remain relevant by living its ethos, by strengthening the brand, and by responding to customer needs. "If we continue to be innovative, then we can remain relevant in the marketplace," Dillon emphasized.

FIGURE 4

Case Equivalent Sales and Average Price per Case Sold
(1998–2002)

Source: National Grape Cooperative Association Inc. and Welch Foods Inc. Annual Report,
various years.

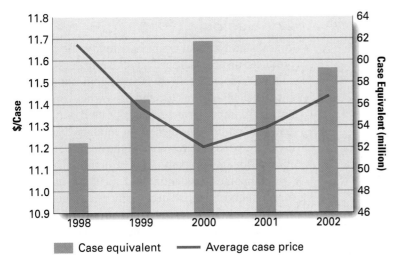

The challenges presented by well-financed competitors and private label products continued to put pressure on the cooperative. Chicago-based Information Resources Inc. reported that total category sales for bottled grape juice was $221.4 million in the 52 weeks ending December 29, 2002 and private labels accounted for almost 24 percent. However, while private label grape juice dollar sales increased by 3.6 percent compared with the year before, the total grape juice category declined by 1.7 percent. Overall, 7 of the top 14 bottled shelf-stable juice subcategories posted gains in market share, and 9 of these outperformed the subcategory as a whole in the 52 weeks ending December 29, 2002. The challenge posed by store brands was that they often offered lower prices and, when bundled with the same or higher quality and

FIGURE 5

Total Patron Tonnage Sold and Patronage per Ton (1998–2002)

Source: National Grape Cooperative Association Inc. and Welch Foods Inc. Annual Report,
various years.

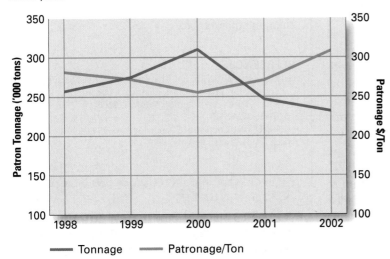

packaging presentation, they successfully seized market share away from national branded products. Other competitors to Welch's were SoBe's new Long John Lizard's Grape Grog which, although it contained only 5 percent real grape fruit, had grape seed extract and vitamin C added and was marketed to a different market segment—young and active—with an intense aggressiveness akin to the marketing strategies of its parent company, PepsiCo.

Grape juice was in direct competition with other fruit juices, especially apple juice. New research results showed the nutraceutical qualities of grape juice and other fruit juices such as cranberries, and the companies are using these results to differentiate themselves in the face of increasing competition among processors and marketers. For this reason, government regulations that provided inequitable distribution of advantages in the manufacturing process could adversely affect grape juice's competitiveness. A case in point was the changes in labeling regulations imposed by the Food and Drug Administration (FDA), which required that grape juice manufacturers who declared "grape juice" or "from grape concentrate" on their retail product labels cannot dilute those products below 16.0° brix. Processors used to dilute some grape juice products to 14.3° brix. On the other hand, apple and pear concentrates can be diluted to 11.2° brix and still qualify in labeling their products "juice" or "from concentrate." Since higher brix implied lower volume, this meant that grape manufacturers processed a lower volume of juice from the same quantity of concentrate than their apple or pear competitors. For example, a gallon of grape juice concentrate yields 5.4 gallons of reconstituted juice while a gallon of apple juice concentrate yields 8.1 gallons of reconstituted juice. While these regulations may help producers sell more grapes for processing, they do impose significant pressure on processors who are confronted with competition from other juices and beverages in the marketplace.

Finally, there were numerous mergers and consolidations in the beverage products and inputs industries leading to increased concentration. Larger companies had larger product lines to offer wholesalers and distributors who were looking to minimize their operating costs. Larger companies also tended to have lower technology costs and were more able to adopt technologies that offered supply chain benefits. Smaller companies that were unable to meet the service needs of larger customers and provide economies of size benefits to their suppliers face an increasing threat of becoming less relevant in their markets. Welch's is a unique company with control over a unique input—Concord and Niagara grapes.

Conclusion

Welch's and National Grape had done well when most producer-owned packaged goods companies and agricultural cooperatives were facing significant performance challenges. Welch's and its owner-cooperative, National Grape, have successfully used a two-board system to ensure that there is an equitable balance between the needs of growers and the needs of the packaged products company. This structure allowed the two companies to identify and focus on the critical components of their respective but related businesses.

However, the market landscape was changing rapidly, and Welch's board needed to continuously explore ways to maintain and improve the company's relevancy with its consumers, its customers, and its suppliers. For example, to expand its product portfolio, Welch's may have to adopt the traditional mergers and acquisition approach that many in the industry are using to increase market share and gain economies of size, or it may also embark on building larger strategic alliances. Either of these options may require significant capital outlay. One way to achieve the required investment is to reduce cash patronage payments and cash equity redemptions, increasing the equity investment of patrons. Dillon and Welch's need to assess the two-board system, which has worked well over the last half-century for Welch's and National Grape, will support the different strategies that they need to pursue to maintain Welch's relevance in the changing marketplace.

REFERENCES

Gale Group, Inc. "Drink up! The Shelf Stable Juice Segment Proves Fruitful for Private Label, Though Opportunities Remain in Single-Serves and Isotonics." *Private Label Buyer,* 17, no. 3 (March 2003): 31.
National Grape Cooperative. Annual reports, 1998–2002.
Welch Foods. Annual Reports, 1998–2003.

Appendix A: The U.S. Grape Juice Industry

The United States has the third largest grape output after Italy and France and the fifth largest acreage after Spain, France, Italy, and Turkey. Its acreage and production shares have averaged about 5 percent and about 10 percent, respectively, over the past four years (FAO, 2002). The USDA (2002) reported that the U.S. grape industry has consistently been, over more than a decade, the most valuable crop among nuts, fruits, and vegetables, ahead of oranges, apples, and strawberries.

Total U.S. utilized grape production, divided between processing and table grapes, increased by 52.5 percent, from 4.3 million short tons to about 6.6 million short tons between 1977 and 2001. This increase resulted from acreage increases and improved varieties. Between 1991 and 2001, processing grapes' share of total utilized grapes averaged about 86.5 percent of annual production. Table grapes' share of total U.S. grape production has declined due to imports from countries such as Chile, which accounted for about 78 percent of total U.S. imports in 2001.

These improvements in production have been accompanied by strengthening average prices in the grape production industry (Exhibit A1). The average price per ton of table grapes increased by 57 percent compared with a 151 percent increase in the average price per ton of processing grapes between 1977 and 2001. The average annual growth rate in processing grape prices was 3.8 percent over that period compared with 2 percent for table grapes.

U.S. grape production is concentrated in California, which accounts for about 90 percent of total processing grape production and utilization. New York and Washington each account for about 3 percent of total domestic grape production. Weather and soil conditions support the distribution of grape varieties because the vinifera varieties are primarily grown in California while the juice grape varieties of Concord and Niagara are primarily grown in New York and Washington.

Processed grape products are divided into four main categories: juice, canned, raisins, and alcoholic beverages (mainly wine). Wine and raisins account for about 60 percent and 30 percent, respectively, of total processing grape production in the United States. Less than 1 percent of total processing grape production goes to canned, and the remaining 9 percent is allocated to juice. Although there are eight thousand varieties of grapes, the largest proportion of juice grape acreage in the United States is planted to the native Concord and Niagara varieties.

These varieties are also the most common varieties used in juice production and are primarily produced in four states: Michigan, New York, Pennsylvania, and Washington (Exhibit A2). Total juice grape production increased from 353,250 tons in 1998 to almost 418,000 tons in 2002, an increase of about 18 percent. This was a result of both acreage and yield improvement in the industry.

There were also some significant shifts in the distribution of juice grape production within that period.

EXHIBIT A1

Nominal Price of U.S. Table and Processing Grapes in Current Dollars, 1977–2001

Source: NASS/USDA.

Production of Juice Grapes by State, 1998–2002

State	1998	1999	2000	2001	2002
			Quantity (Tons)		
Michigan	67,500	71,500	83,600	26,000	29,200
New York	87,000	152,000	111,000	107,000	109,000
Ohio	5,000	7,500	6,400	4,700	4,500
Pennsylvania	41,500	74,000	46,000	48,500	45,900
Washington	152,000	195,000	175,000	183,000	217,000
Others	250	2,050	2,250	650	2,200
U.S. Total	353,250	502,050	424,250	369,850	417,800

For example, Washington's share of juice production increased from 43 percent in 1998 to 52 percent in 2002 while Michigan's share decreased from 19 percent to 11 percent over the same period. There was little change in New York and Pennsylvania. A similar trend was observed for Niagara production. It is important to recognize the increasing production in Ontario, Canada, which is being shipped to the United States for processing and production and is not reflected in Exhibit A2.

Concord grapes are native to North America and grow well only in certain geographic regions. In New York, Pennsylvania, and Ohio, Concord grapes grow along a narrow stretch of no more than 6 miles in its widest points along a 90-mile stretch of Lake Erie, Lake Ontario, and the Finger Lakes in northwest New York. Michigan's production all occurs in a 40-mile stretch in the southwestern region of the state. Washington's Concord grape production is primarily located in the semidesert region of lower Yakima Valley, east of the Cascade Mountains, and is irrigated with water from the Cascades. The higher temperature and water availability are the major advantages that Washington has in Concord grape production.

Concord grapes have higher yields, higher sugar-acid ratios, and milder labrusca flavors than other

Juice Grape Demand, 1990–2001

Source: Economic Research Service/U.S. Department of Agriculture, 2002.

EXHIBIT A4

Grape Product Prices, 1990–2001

Source: Economic Research Service/U.S. Department of Agriculture, 2002.

grape varieties. Europe, for example, uses vinifera or wine grape strains to make grape juice, giving it a lower sugar-acid ratio, as well as a less sweet taste than the juice made from Concord and Niagara grape production. These natural production advantages allow the industry to have better control over its marketplace in comparison to other agricultural commodities. That notwithstanding, the juice grape market is subject to price volatility because of supply fluctuations due to weather and other factors, including competition among the different uses and the substitutability among different varieties.

When both quantity and price increase over time, it is indicative of product demand increasing faster than its supply. However, juice grape demand has been variable over the past ten years (Exhibit A3).

The average price per ton of wine and juice grapes was about $280 in 1990. However, the average price of wine grapes by 2001 was about twice that of juice grapes at $250 per ton (Exhibit A4). The growth of the wine industry in the last decade likely explains a significant component of the price trend for wine grapes during the same time period. The industry has seen enhanced competitiveness against traditional French and Italian products arising from increased varieties, technology, and education. The price of raisin grapes has fallen significantly over the same period, reaching about $130 per ton in 2001. The trend in juice grape prices, however, indicates

that prices have been strengthening since the mid-1990s after consistently falling between 1990 and 1995.

Appendix B: Processing Grape Juice Industry

Grape Juice processors obtain 185 to 190 gallons of single strength juice from a ton of grapes, regardless of the variety.[1] However, depending on the brix (or sugar solids) strength of the single strength juice, a ton of Concord grapes yields only 34 gallons of 68° brix concentrate. The higher the brix of the juice, the higher the volume of concentrate it produces. In general, the soil and water conditions in Washington give its Concord grapes a higher brix than Concord grapes produced in Michigan, New York, and Pennsylvania. This implies that in general Washington Concord grapes yield higher volumes of concentrate than Eastern Concord grapes. In contrast, Eastern Concord grapes have higher acids and deeper color, allowing them to be blended with concentrates from cheaper viniferous varieties without losing their taste. Processors who purchase the concentrate add water to reconstitute the original single strength or some other strength juice.

---

[1]Single strength means straight juice that is neither diluted nor concentrated. Concentrates are produced from single strength juice by evaporating water from the juice using heat and vacuum.

EXHIBIT B1

A Simplified Overview of the Grape Processing Process

Grape juice production is different from other fruit juices because it is the only fruit juice that cannot be concentrated immediately after pressing because of the presence of potassium salts, commonly called tartrates, in the juice that cannot be filtered or centrifuged out. They have to be detartrated by gravity, a process that usually takes about six weeks. Juice grapes such as Concord and Niagara are used in the manufacture of jelly, jam, straight or sparkling juice, drinks diluted 50 percent or more with water, ades diluted with up to 98 percent water and added sugar, drink bases, carbonated beverages, frozen and shelf stable concentrates that may be diluted with water, frozen bars and slush, ice cream topping, yogurt base, pie mix, powders, and crystals (Exhibit B1).

The total value of shipments for frozen fruits, juices, drinks, and cocktails was about $2.86 billion in 1997. The total value of shipments for companies producing grape juice concentrates was almost $58 million in 1997 compared with $74.2 million in 1992. This implies that the grape juice industry is a relatively small component of the fruit juice industry, and it is accounted for by very few companies. In fact, there were only seventeen companies in 1997,

EXHIBIT B2

Number of Firms, Shipment Quantity, and Value for Frozen Grape Juice Concentrate Manufacturers

	1997			1992		
Product Types	No. of Companies ($100K + Shipments)	Quantity of Shipments	Value of Shipments ($1,000)	No. of Companies ($100K + Shipments)	Quantity of Shipments	Value of Shipments ($1,000)
Frozen Concentrate grape juice (4.1 oz–7 oz), 1,000 cases of 48	4	1770.1	18057	5	1745.6	17750
Frozen Concentrate grape juice (10.1 oz–13 oz), 1,000 cases of 24	6	1994.6	24643	5	2709.1	31300
Frozen Concentrate grape juice (other sizes), 1,000# solid	7	16.9	15290	10	28.9	25150

Source: Frozen Fruit, Juice, and Vegetable Manufacturing, 1997 Manufacturing Industry Census, Washington, D.C.: U.S. Census Bureau, November 1999, p. 10.

EXHIBIT B3

Per Capita Consumption of Selected Fruit Juices (Gallons per Year Single Strength Equivalent)

Season	Apple	Grape	Pineapple	Cranberry	Prune	Total Noncitrus	Total Citrus	Total Fruit Juice
1990/91	1.72	0.28	0.50	0.14	0.04	2.68	5.21	7.89
1991/92	1.51	0.36	0.50	0.17	0.03	2.57	4.82	7.39
1992/93	1.56	0.38	0.47	0.16	0.04	2.61	5.96	8.57
1993/94	1.78	0.35	0.41	0.15	0.04	2.73	5.79	8.52
1994/95	1.77	0.29	0.35	0.19	0.04	2.64	6.16	8.80
1995/96	1.57	0.45	0.38	0.16	0.03	2.59	6.14	8.73
1996/97	1.69	0.38	0.38	0.17	0.03	2.65	6.18	8.83
1997/98	1.54	0.41	0.34	0.20	0.03	2.52	6.29	8.81
1998/99	1.79	0.27	0.29	0.21	0.03	2.59	6.00	8.59
1999/00	1.78	0.44	0.32	0.23	0.02	2.79	6.66	9.46
2000/01	1.80	0.34	0.30	0.20	0.02	2.66	5.95	8.61
2001/02	1.76	0.33	0.31	0.17	0.03	2.60	5.81	8.41

Source: Economic Research Service/U.S. Department of Agriculture, 2002.

down from twenty in 1992 (Exhibit B2).[2] It is important to note that these data do not present the whole picture of the grape juice processing industry because, as shown in Exhibit B1, there are other products being supplied by the industry besides frozen concentrates. It does, however, illuminate the challenge in the industry with respect to the general trends of consolidations and rationalization of products toward retail packs.

Grape Juice Consumption

Per capita consumption of grape juice has exhibited an upward trend since 1977, growing at about 2.2 percent per annum. It increased from 0.28 gallons per capita per annum in 1990/91 to 0.33 gallons per person per year in 2001/02 (Exhibit B3). Citrus is the only fruit increasing its share of fruit juice consumption in the United States. Between 1990/91 and 2001/02, it was estimated that citrus share of the per capita

consumption of fruit juices increased at an average annual rate of 0.45 percent. This contrasts with –0.4 percent for grape juice, –0.13 percent for apple juice, and –6.0 percent for pineapple.

Citrus was by far the fruit juice of choice in the United States, accounting for almost 70 percent of the total fruit juice consumed on a per capita basis in 2001/02. Apple juice was the second largest with a share of almost 21 percent in the same year. The remaining 9 percent is distributed among the rest of the fruit juices, with grapes and pineapple accounting for 3.9 percent and 3.7 percent, respectively, and cranberry accounting for 2 percent. The year-to-year change in per capita consumption of total fruit juice consumed has been most unstable for grape juice. For example, between 1996/97 and 1997/98, the per capita consumption of grape juice increased by 8 percent, decreased by about 34 percent the following period, and increased by 63 percent thereafter. This pattern is likely due to data collection methods, inventory, and promotional activities carried out by processors.

These appendices were written using public data from USDA and National Grape's annual reports.

[2]Companies in the census are defined as businesses with value of shipments in excess of $100,000.

The Global Automobile Industry in 2004

This case was prepared by Charles W. L. Hill, the University of Washington.

Some fifty years ago renowned management author Peter Drucker called the automobile industry the "industry of industries." In many respects his characterization is still true today. The industry makes some 60 million cars and trucks a year, employs millions of people in factories scattered around the globe, and accounts for about 10 percent of the gross domestic product in rich countries. The top ten global producers collectively sold $1.1 trillion worth of vehicles in 2003. The industry consumes nearly half the world's output of rubber, 25 percent of its glass and 15 percent of its steel.[1] Its products are responsible for almost half of the world's oil consumption and are a major source of rising carbon dioxide levels in the atmosphere, the greenhouse gas implicated in global warming. Modern cities with their attendant suburban sprawl have been designed around the automobile. The automobile has shaped our landscape, changed our atmosphere, and exerted a profound influence on the global economy. It is indeed, still the industry of industries—and today the industry of industries is going through wrenching changes.

Background

The emergence of the modern industry can be dated back to 1913 and Henry Ford's first implementation of the production technology that would revolutionize so much of industrial capitalism over the next few decades, the continuously moving assembly line. Ford quickly became the master of mass production, churning out thousands of black Model T Fords from his Highland Park plant in Michigan. Mass production dramatically lowered the costs of building cars and paved the way for the emergence of a mass consumer market. It was not Ford, however, but Alfred Sloan, the CEO of General Motors, who in the mid-1920s realized that the key to success in the industry was serving the customer by offering them "a car for every purse and purpose."[2] Under Sloan, GM segmented the market, producing a differentiate range of models to consumers. In doing so, the company seized market leadership from Ford and has not relinquished it since.

By the 1960s, General Motors, Ford, and Chrysler dominated the U.S. market; then by far the world's largest. GM at one point made over 60 percent of all automobile sales in the United States, and collectively the three companies accounted for over 90 percent of sales. Moreover, the companies were now multinationals with significant operations outside of North America, and particularly in Europe, the world's second biggest car market. This, however, was all about to change. Riding the wave of economic disruption caused by the OPEC oil price hikes of the 1970s, foreign manufacturers of fuel efficient cars began to invade the U.S. market. First there was Volkswagen, with its revolutionary VW Beatle, and then a slew of Japanese manufacturers including, most notably, Honda, Nissan, and Toyota.

It was one of these foreign invaders, Toyota, that was to usher in the next revolution in car making.

Copyright © 2005 by Charles W. L. Hill. This case was prepared by Charles W. L. Hill, the University of Washington, as the basis for class discussion rather than to illustrate either effective or ineffective handling of an administrative situation. Reprinted by permission of Charles W. L. Hill. All rights reserved.

Faced with a small and intensely competitive home market, and constrained by a lack of capital, Toyota started to tweak the mass production system first developed by Ford. Engineers tried to find ways to build cars efficiently in smaller volumes and with less capital. After years of experimentation, by the 1970s a new production system was emerging at Toyota. Later dubbed "lean production," it was based upon innovations that reduced setup times for machinery and made shorter production runs economical. When coupled with the introduction of just-in-time inventory systems, flexible work practices, an organization-wide focus on quality, and the practice of stopping the assembly line to fix defects (which was the antithesis of Ford's continually moving assembly line), the lean production system yielded significant gains in productivity and product quality. In turn, this lowered costs, improved brand equity, and gave Toyota a competitive advantage.

As was the case with mass production, Toyota's innovation of lean production was imitated, with varying degrees of success, by other volume car makers. Japanese competitors were the first to try and adopt Toyota's innovation. During the 1990s the American volume car makers jumped on the bandwagon. Despite this, Toyota still enjoys a competitive advantage in the automobile industry that is based upon production excellence. Just as significantly, the sluggish American response to Japanese and European invasions of their home market allowed the foreigners to capture ever more market share.

By the early years of the new century, America's big three (now often referred to as the Detroit Three) were rapidly losing their grip on their domestic market. Collectively, GM, Ford, and Chrysler (now part of the German-owned Daimler Chrysler Corporation) accounted for just 47.1 percent of passenger car sales in 2003. The other 52.9 percent of sales were attributed to foreign producers, up from 34 percent in 1988.[3] Moreover, in stark contrast to the situation in the 1980s when most foreign cars were imported into the United States, by 2003 most foreign nameplates were built in "transplant" factories located in North America.

What saved the Detroit Three during the 1990s were robust sales of light trucks, and particularly sports utility vehicles (SUVs). Foreign manufacturers had been caught off-guard by the American appetite for SUVs, which surged as oil prices remained low and the economy boomed. In 2003, GM, Ford, and Chrysler still accounted for 74 percent of light truck sales. This pumped up their overall market share of U.S. light vehicles to 61.8 percent in 2003. But here, too, market share was eroding (it had fallen from 66.8 percent in 2000) due to gains made by Japanese and European SUV models.[4] Making matters worse, rapidly rising oil prices during 2004 hinted at an end to the decade long boom in SUV sales. With competition in the passenger car segment intensifying, the outlook for the Detroit Three looked increasingly grim.

Competition in the U.S. Market, 2004

Demand and Supply

Total sales of passenger cars and light trucks in the United States peaked in 2000 at 17.35 million units before declining for three consecutive years to 16.64 million units in 2003 (see Exhibit 1). In total, U.S. dealers sold some $400 billion worth of vehicles in 2003. The decline between 2000 and 2003 was pronounced in the passenger car segment, where volume fell from 8.85 million units in 2000 to 7.61 million in 2003. Light truck sales, however, continued to expand from 8.5 million units to 9 million units between 2000 and 2003, driven in large part by America's continuing love affair with SUVs.[5]

The decline in overall vehicle sales was a product of the economic slowdown following the long boom of the 1990s and September 11, 2001. The sales decline has left the American industry with too much productive capacity. Estimates suggest that in 2003, the industry had the capacity to build some 18 million cars and light trucks in the United States, but actually only made 13.33 million units (the balance of sales was accounted for by imports).[6]

In large part, the excess capacity situation has been created by foreign car makers, who have made significant investments in the United States over the last twenty years. Japanese investments began in the early 1980s as a response to the threat of import controls on exports from Japan. By the early 2000s, foreign owned producers had the capacity to build some 3 million automobiles in the United States, up from zero in 1981.[7] (The figure excludes the Chrysler division of Daimler Chrysler, which is counted as one of the Detroit Three, even though it is now owned by a German firm).

The foreign investment shows no sign of slowing down. Hyundai will open its first U.S. factory in

EXHIBIT 1

Sales of Cars and Light Trucks, 1992–2003 (000s)

Source: Standard & Poor's.

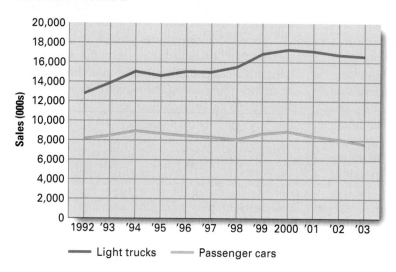

Montgomery, Alabama, in 2005, making it the first Korean car company to build in North America. Meanwhile, Toyota will open its sixth North American factory in San Antonio, Texas, in 2006. Collectively, foreign-owned auto factories accounted for 26 percent of U.S. automobile production in 2003, and that percentage seems set to rise.

Many states offered financial incentives such as tax breaks in an effort to attract inward investment by foreign producers, and the associated jobs. Estimates suggest that by 2003 the cumulative value of incentives given to attract new factories amounted to between $1.2 billion and $2 billion, which translates into an investment incentive of $1,000 for every car built by a foreign-owned factory.[8]

Price Competition

In the aftermath of September 11, 2001, sales slumped at American car dealers. Faced with excess capacity, high fixed costs, and an inability to quickly shutter capacity due to commitments made to labor unions, General Motors responded with aggressive sales incentives. These included 0 percent financing deals and cash back rebates on certain vehicles that reached as high as $3,000. Very quickly its rivals were forced to respond, and incentives became the industry norm. The size of incentives, however, varied from producers to producer. While the Detroit Three have been offering incentive packages that have

exceeded $4,000 per vehicle, the big Japanese producers, Honda, Nissan, and Toyota, have been less aggressive. Toyota, for example, offered incentives of just over $2,000 per vehicle in 2003, compared with GM's average incentive package of $4,300 a vehicle.[9]

The incentives have had the effect of making cars more affordable. In 1973, the average U.S. citizen needed 17.5 weeks of annual family earnings to purchase an average priced car. By 1994, that figure had risen to 24 weeks, but by 2003, it had declined to 20.7 weeks. The signs are that the downtrend continued in 2004.[10]

In late 2003, GM tried to cut back on incentives, only to find that sales declined as consumers bought cars from those who kept incentives in place. In part, GM noted, two years of incentives had conditioned consumers to expect them, and breaking that habit was proving difficult. By February 2004, GM had gone back to offering a full range of sales incentives—indeed, it had even boosted them slightly in an effort to shift unsold inventory that was starting to accumulate of dealers lots.[11]

One effect of sales incentives has been to get consumers to sell their used vehicles at a higher rate than would otherwise have been the case. This has hurt the price of used cars. An index of used car prices, for example, fell from 115 in 2002 to 102.4 by April 2003.[12] Ironically, falling used car prices can hurt demand for new cars as more consumers purchase

EXHIBIT 2A

Market Share of U.S. Dealer Passenger Cars (%)

Manufacturer	2000	2001	2002	2003
General Motors	28.6	27	25.5	25.7
Ford	19.1	17.8	16.4	15.4
Daimler Chrysler	7.3	6.6	6.5	6.0
Toyota	11.0	11.3	12.2	13.1
Honda	10.0	10.7	10.3	10.8
Nissan	4.8	4.9	6.1	6.6
Volkswagen	4.9	5.1	5.1	4.8

EXHIBIT 2B

Market Share of U.S. Dealer Light Trucks (%)

Manufacturer	2000	2001	2002	2003
General Motors	28.0	29.7	31.5	30.5
Ford	28.9	27.8	25.8	25.1
Daimler Chrysler	22.0	19.7	19.3	18.5
Toyota	7.6	9.0	8.8	9.6
Honda	3.3	3.5	4.7	5.9
Nissan	3.9	3.3	2.9	3.2

Source: Standard & Poor's.

used cars, trapping the car producers in something of a vicious cycle. Moreover, the fall in used car prices is of direct concern to the automobile companies, who have expanded their leasing programs in the last decade. Ford in particular took a financial hit in 2001 when it found that vehicles coming off lease were worth less than originally projected.

Market Share

The launching of incentives by GM was not sufficient to stem market share losses during the early 2000s (see Exhibit 2). Between 2000 and 2003, GM saw its share of passenger cars fall from 28.6 percent to 25.7 percent. Ford and Chrysler also experienced significant declines in passenger car share, while Toyota, Nissan, and BMW made significant gains. Toyota, in particular, captured 13.1 percent of U.S. passenger car sales in 2003, more than twice as much as Chrysler.

While GM was able to offset losses in the passenger car segment by gains in the light truck segment where it held 30.5 percent of the market in 2003, Ford and Chrysler experienced market share declines here, too. Toyota and Honda were the largest gainers. Both companies introduced new SUVs in this time period and were reaping the gains. In 2003, Toyota held a 9.6 percent share of the U.S. light truck market, up from 7.6 percent in 2000.

Quality seems to be an important factor explaining market share changes in the industry. J.D. Power Associates produces quality rankings for automobiles sold in the U.S. market. According to these rankings, Toyota and Honda consistently have the best quality rankings in the industry. In 2004, J.D. Power's Vehicle Dependability Study, which

measures quality after cars have been on the market for three years, ranked Toyota and Honda one and two, with 207 and 210 problems reported per 100 vehicles respectively, compared to an industry average of 269 (see Exhibit 3). J.D. Power's Initial Quality Study, which measures problems reported in the first 90 days after sale, similarly ranked Toyota and Honda one and two in terms of quality, with scores of 101 and 102 against an industry average of 119. GM came out best of the Detroit Three on both surveys.[13]

However, tracking of quality improvements since 1998 suggests that the Detroit Three are closing the quality gap between themselves and foreign producers and may ultimately achieve parity (see Exhibit 4). If the trend continues, differentiation on factors other than quality—such as styling, design, and technology—will come to the fore. Also of major note in Exhibit 4 are the poor performance of Korean manufacturers in 1998 and their rapid improvement over the next six years.

Profitability and Labor Productivity

The combination of falling demand, excess capacity, and incentives hurt profits, particularly for the Detroit Three, all of whom saw their profits slump in 2001, and despite a recovery, have seen their profits remain below through to 2004 (see Exhibit 5). Toyota, on the other hand, made record profits in 2003 and 2004. Indeed, in both years it made more than the Detroit Three combined.

What is not evident from Exhibit 5 is that Toyota's earnings were held back by weak conditions in Japan. In the United States, the company has been very successful in recent years. According to a 2004 study by

EXHIBIT 3

J.D. Power 2004 Vehicle Dependability Study

Source: J.D. Power Associates.

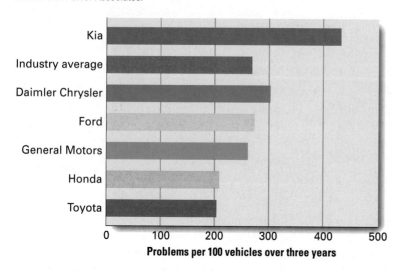

Problems per 100 vehicles over three years

Harbour & Associates, in 2003 Toyota made $1,742 in profit on every vehicle it manufactured in North America. Nissan did even better, making $2,402 on every car sold in North America, while Honda made $1,488. General Motors, in contrast, made only $178 profit per vehicle, Ford lost $48 and Daimler Chrysler lost $496 per vehicle (Ford was profitable in 2003 only due to the success of its foreign operations).[14]

As noted earlier, Toyota has the best reputation for quality in the industry. The higher quality translates into a higher value and allows Toyota to charge 5 to 10 percent higher prices than General Motors for equivalent cars. Historically, Toyota and other Japanese manufacturers also benefited from superior labor productivity in their North American plants, but according to the Harbour Report, the labor productivity gap in North American plants has narrowed significantly in recent years. In 2002, the last year for which full data are available, Nissan was the productivity leader in U.S. assembly operations,

EXHIBIT 4

J.D. Power Initial Quality Study, Trends in Quality 1998–2004

Source: J.D. Power Associates.

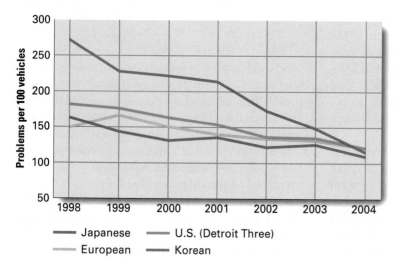

— Japanese   — U.S. (Detroit Three)
— European   — Korean

EXHIBIT 5

Net Income 2000–2004 (Millions)

Company	2000	2001	2002	2003	2004
General Motors	$4452	$601	$1736	$2862	$3990
Ford	$4823	–$5443	$284	$921	$4000
Daimler Chrysler	$3338	–$589	$5114	–$526	$2945
Toyota	$5447	$4177	$6247	$10995	$11800

taking just 17.92 employee hours to build a car. Honda took 19.78 hours, Toyota 22.53, General Motors 26.10, Ford 26.87, and Daimler Chrysler 30.82 hours.[15]

The 2004 report revealed that improvements continued across the board. Nissan's assembly plant in Tennessee led the way, building a car in 15.33 hours of labor. The most improved automaker was Daimler Chrysler, which increased labor productivity at its assembly plants by 7.8 percent over the prior year. General Motors also registered improvement in its assembly operations, and on average took 23.61 hours to build a car, down from 26.10 in 2002.[16] Since neither Honda nor Toyota fully participated in the 2004 study, data for them are no longer available. Still, the author of the Harbour Report, Ron Harbour, has noted that over the 1999–2004 period productivity gains at Japanese plants in North America have been relatively modest, and lagged the gains made by the Detroit Three. The problem for the Detroit Three, according to Harbour, is that the variance of productivity across their plants is much greater than at Japanese manufacturers.[17]

For their part, American manufacturers argue that their profitability has been hurt by huge pension burdens. General Motors, for example, has 2.4 pensioners for every current employee. The more that these companies lay off older workers, the more they add to their burden of pensions and health care costs. The collapse of the stock market in 2000–2001 didn't help matters either, since it reduced the value of company pension funds. Both Ford and GM had to issue bonds worth billions of dollars just to plug the holes in their pension funds. GM now has to pay out $1 billion a year in interest payments just to service these bonds. Moreover, the company has to pay out some $3 billion a year to cover health care costs for retirees. Just as troubling, GM may have to increase funds going into its pension plan if the fund does not earn a long-term return of 9 percent per annum.[18]

Industry Trends

In an effort to cope with the tough competitive conditions in the North American market and elsewhere, automobile companies are looking hard at additional ways to take costs out of their system or to capture more of the available demand. Among the most notable initiatives underway have been an industrywide attempt to streamline product development, offer a wider range of niche cars, work more closely with suppliers, develop systems for building cars to order, and introduce a new breed of hybrid cars.

Market Fragmentation and Product Development

Historically it took four years and cost as much as $1 billion to develop a new car model and prepare a factory for its production. To recoup those fixed costs, automobile companies needed high-volume sales, which required selling the car without a major update for four years and sometimes as long as seven years. To attain maximum economies of scale, automobile companies tried to run their plants at full capacity, producing 240,000 units a year. The ideal was to have each plant produce just one model.

In recent years the automobile market has become increasingly fragmented. Models are now updated more frequently to keep pace with changing consumer tastes and competitive pressures, shortening product life cycles. Customers have demanded more variety, and automobile companies have been willing to give it to them, bringing a wider variety of niche cars to the market. The Ford Taurus, for example, was once the best-selling passenger car in America with annual sales of around 500,000 (equivalent to two plants running at full capacity). As sales have slipped, Ford has decided to kill the Taurus, and replace it with two models, one smaller than the Taurus and one bigger.

To recoup the costs of such offerings, development and manufacturing costs have to be reduced. Automobile companies are trying to do this by using a common platform and parts in a wider range of cars. An example of the industry's new philosophy is GM's 2005 roadster, the Pontiac Solstice. Under the old economics, the Solstice would never have made it off the drawing board. The car is forecasted to sell only 25,000 units a year. With a projected sticker price of $20,000 the volume was insufficient under the old paradigm to recoup costs. To make the car economically, GM has had to revolutionize its product design philosophy. By digitalizing much of the design of the car and tools, GM was able to cut $50 million out of design costs. It used to take 12 design engineers 3 months to produce a clay model, an essential step in the design process. Now a single designer can take an idea on a computer screen to an animated video of a vehicle in three weeks. GM saved another $80 million by designing the car so that it could use existing tools at its factory. More money was saved by a decision to base the car on a common platform architecture called Kappa, which will be used for other small rear drive cars. According to GM Design Chief Bob Lutz, GM can make an almost unlimited number of bodies on the Kappa architecture, and each vehicle will be profitable with a volume of 20,000 to 25,000 a year.[19]

Using the same platform across a wide model range is fast becoming industry standard practice. As with so many other industry trends, the Japanese pioneered the practice. Honda, for example, builds its Odyssey minivan, and Pilot and Acura MDX SUVs on the same platform, and has added a pickup truck to the mix. Currently Chrysler bases its vehicle fleet on thirteen distinct platforms. The company is trying to bring this down to just four platforms, in the process reducing the product development budget from $42 billion to $30 billion. Ford and General Motors have similar aims. The Kappa platform for GM's Pontiac Solstice will also be used for its new Saturn coupe and at least one more GM car. As GM develops its next generation Chevy Silverado and GMC Sierra pickups, it plans to reuse much of the existing platform, cutting development costs in half to nearly $3 billion. Over the next eight years, Ford plans to use its Mazda 6 sedan platform (Ford owns Mazda) as the basis for ten new vehicles. The idea, according to Ford's head of operations, is to engineer it once, use it often.[20]

Another design goal is to try and use the same parts in a wider variety of car models and where appropriate use parts from old models in new cars. Detroit auto designers used to boast that new models were completely redesigned from the floor up with all new parts. Now that is seen as costly and time consuming. At General Motors the current goal is to reuse 40–60 percent of parts from one car generation to the next, thereby reducing design time and tooling costs. At Ford, the number of parts has been slashed. For example, Ford engineers now choose from just four steering wheels, instead of contemplating fourteen different designs.

As a result of all these changes, the costs and time for bringing new cars to market is shrinking. Most of GM's new development projects are now on 24-month schedules—a far cry from the late 1980s when GM engineers celebrated because they were able to bring out the Chevrolet Corsica in *just* 45 months![21] Ford has reduced its product development time by 25 percent since the late 1990s, and is still getting better by 10 percent per year.

Flexible Factories

Hand in hand with changes in design philosophy, automobile companies are retooling their factories to reduce costs and make them capable of producing several car models from the same line. By doing so, they hope to be able to reduce the break-even point for a new car model. With the Solstice, for example, GM cut design costs by using a common platform and parts. It has cut tooling and production costs by investing in flexible manufacturing technologies that can be used to produce multiple designs based on the Kappa platform from the same basic line. GM has also worked hard to get unions to agree to changes in inflexible work rules. Assembly line workers now perform several different jobs, which reduces waste and boosts productivity.

Ford hopes to have 75 percent of its production built on flexible assembly lines by 2010. If successful, its investments in flexible factories could reduce annual costs by some $2 billion a year.[22] Ford spent $400 million modernizing an eighty-year-old assembly plant in Chicago. This plant is now capable of making eight models from two different chassis.

Reengineering their plants to accommodate a wider range of models is not cheap. In 2003, GM spent some $7.3 billion on capital improvements at its automobile plants, up from an average of $5.4 billion in the early 1990s. A In the early 1990s, Ford spent some $3.5 billion annually on capital improvements. More recently its capital spending has been running at a $7.5–$8 billion annual rate. Chrysler, too, has increased its spending, while Toyota planned to spend some $9 billion upgrading its factories in 2004.[23]

Supplier Relations

At one time the American automobile companies were highly vertically integrated, producing as much as 70 percent of their component parts in-house. Those parts that were not made in-house were often purchased using an annual competitive bidding process. The last decade has seen enormous changes here. Both Ford and GM have sold off a major chunk of their in-house suppliers. GM spun out its in-house suppliers in 1999 as Delphi Automotive. Delphi took some 200,000 former GM employees with it, about one-third of the total, many of who were union members. Ford spun out its in-house suppliers the following year as Visteon Corporation. Delphi and Visteon are now the number one and two auto parts suppliers in the United States. In an effort to assert their independence, both companies are moving rapidly to build a more diverse set of customers.

The Detroit Three have also been reconfiguring their relationships with independent suppliers. The automobile companies are now expecting their Tier 1 or major suppliers to produce modules—larger vehicle parts that comprise several components such as fully assembled chassis, finished interiors, and "ready for the road" exterior trim. These modules are then bolted and welded together to make finished vehicles, rather like toy models being snapped together. For such an approach to work, the suppliers have to get involved earlier in the process of designing and developing new models and engineering assembly tools. To create an incentive for them to do so, the automobile manufacturers have been entering into longer term contracts with their Tier 1 suppliers. At the same time, Tier 1 suppliers face intense price pressures and requirements for quality improvements. If they don't meet these, the automobile companies have shown a willingness to walk away from long-term deals. In 2003,

for example, Daimler Chrysler pulled a $90 million contract from a supplier of interior products, Collins & Aikman, because of poor product quality.[24]

Another trend has been to encourage major suppliers to locate new facilities next to assembly plants. Ford's refurbished plant in Chicago has a supplier park located next door. The idea is to get suppliers to deliver inventory to the assembly line on a just-in-time basis. At the Chicago plant, the average component now needs to travel only half a mile, as opposed to 450 miles in the past. The proximity has saved suppliers transportation costs, which are passed onto Ford in the form of lower prices. In addition, Ford has reduced inventory on hand at its Chicago plant from two to three days' worth to just eight hours' worth.[25]

Dealer and Customer Relations

Once a car is built, it spends between forty and eighty days sitting in factory lots, distribution centers, and dealers' forecourts before it is actually sold. This represents a huge amount of working capital that is tied up in inventory. To make matters worse, one of the biggest problems in the automobile industry is predicting what demand will be. To a large extent, repeated rounds of price cutting (disguised as incentives) in the American automobile industry have been initiated in an attempt to move slow selling inventory sitting on dealers' lots. If automobile companies could predict demand more accurately, they might be able to reduce the mismatch between inventories and demand—and hence the need to resort to incentives.

In an effort to improve this end of the value chain, the automobile companies have been trying to reduce the time between ordering and delivery. The ultimate goal is to have cars built to order, with cars being assembled and shipped to a dealer within days of a customer placing an order. This is similar in conception to the way that Dell sells computers, with customers ordering a computer, and paying for it, online, while the machine is shipped out within days. Nissan has calculated that if it could move to a build-to-order system with a short cycle time, it could reduce costs by as much as $3,600 a vehicle.[26]

Achieving this goal, however, is easier in theory than in practice. One obvious problem is that if the flow of orders is lumpy or seasonal, so will be the output of a factory, which might result in periods where capacity is not being fully utilized. Another problem involves changing buyer behavior. In America, at least, many consumers look for instant gratification and expect to be able to purchase a car when they walk onto a dealer's lot, which is the antithesis of a build-to-order system. Still, there are some signs of a shift away from this mentality. Honda, for example, has been building its best-selling MDX SUV to order—although the delivery time is more like two months than two days. In Germany, BMW now builds some 60 percent of its cars to order, but once again the delivery time can be as long as two months. Toyota, too, is trying to build more cars to order. In late 2004, the automaker claimed that it was building about 11 percent of the cars it sold in the United States to order, with a build time of just fourteen days.[27]

New Technologies

For years automobile companies have experimented with alternative power sources, most notably fuel cells. These investments have been driven by national and local government demands for lower emissions of carbon dioxide, carbon monoxide, and nitrogen oxides. Of particular concern has been the global buildup of carbon dioxide, the greenhouse gas implicated in global warming. In Europe, the European Commission has persuaded car makers to agree to a voluntary deal to cut overall emissions across their car fleet by 25 percent by 2008, or face the imposition of strict emission rules on specific models. In California, draft regulations may require car manufacturers to reduce emissions of carbon dioxide by 30 percent, starting in 2009. In addition, California already has regulations in place that require 2 percent of a car maker's fleet to be zero emission vehicles (ZEV) by 2005 (although this requirement is proving to be a "soft" one).

The only conceivable ZEV at this juncture is a car powered by an electric motor that runs on a fuel cell. A fuel cell combines hydrogen with oxygen from the air to produce water. The process generates an electric current strong enough to power a car. For all of their promise, however, fuel cells have drawbacks. It costs about ten times more to produce a fuel cell than an internal combustion engine, the range of cars using fuel cells is still too limited for most customers, and replenishing hydrogen will require a network of hydrogen filling stations, which is currently not available.

Automakers have also been experimenting with modified internal combustion engines that use hydrogen rather than gasoline as a fuel. Here too, however, progress has been held back by the total absence of a network of hydrogen filling stations and serious technical problems associated with storing liquid hydrogen (which requires very cold temperatures).

More promising in the short to medium term are hybrid cars. In hybrid cars, at low speed the power comes from an electric motor which gets electricity from an onboard battery. At higher speed, the internal combustion engine kicks in and provides power, while simultaneously recharging the battery through a generator. When braking, energy from the slowing wheels is sent back through the electric motor to charge the batteries. The result can be substantial savings in fuel consumption, with little in the way of a performance penalty. Toyota's Prius hybrid can go from standstill to 60 mph in 10 seconds, averages 60 mpg in the city, and 51 mpg highway driving. This makes the Prius an ideal commuting car. The big drawback is that the hybrid propulsion system adds about $3,000 to $5,000 to a vehicle's sticker price, and the battery has to be replaced about every 100,000 miles at a cost of around $2,000. At an average gas price of $2 a gallon, it takes some five years for a hybrid to repay the additional investment.

Introduced in 1997, Toyota had sold some 200,000 Prius cars by mid-2004. Sales started to increase rapidly in 2003 and 2004 as higher fuel prices made consumers more concerned about fuel economy. In 2004, sales in the United States were limited only by supply constraints to 47,000 units. For 2005, Toyota is planning to sell 100,000 Prius cars in the United States and some 300,000 units worldwide. The company will introduce hybrid versions of its Lexus SUV, Highlander SUV, and Camry sedan in 2005. In addition to Toyota, Honda also had a hybrid on the market in 2002, its Honda Civic hybrid, which was expected to sell over 40,000 units in 2004. Ford introduced a hybrid version of its Escape SUV in late 2004. Priced at $27,000, the hybrid version of the Escape costs $6,000 more than the regular version. GM and Daimler Chrysler also have plans to introduce hybrids in 2006 and 2007.

J.D. Power has estimated that the U.S. market for hybrids could reach 500,000 units by 2008. A more aggressive forecast from Booze, Allen, and Hamilton suggests that hybrids could capture some 20 percent of the U.S. automobile market by 2010 (assuming that gasoline prices stay high), which would represent unit sales of about 3.4 million.[28]

International Developments

Over 80 percent of the world's cars and light trucks are sold in just three markets—North America, Europe, and Japan. Europe is a close second to North America in terms of size, with total sales estimated to be around 16 million units in 2004. The two largest automobile companies in Europe are Volkswagen and PSA Peugeot Citroen with 17.5 percent and 14.4 percent of the market, respectively, in the first half of 2004. Ford had 11.5 percent, Renault 10.4 percent, GM 9.7 percent, and Fiat 9.7 percent. Collectively the Japanese companies held 13.4 percent of the European market in the first half of 2004 (Toyota had a 5.1 percent share).[29]

In some respects, these figures understate the degree of market concentration in Europe. GM, for example, owns 20 percent of Fiat, and Renault owns some 44 percent of Nissan. The Renault/Nissan alliance is particularly close. Renault took its stake in Nissan in the late 1990s when the Japanese company was in deep financial trouble. For Renault, the move was designed to give it access to the large American market where Nissan has a significant presence. For Nissan, it was a matter of survival. Renault invested some $5 billion in Nissan, effectively stabilizing the Japanese company's balance sheet and helping to engineer a turnaround. Although the two companies are continuing to keep their separate identities, their plans call for them to share common car platforms across both companies and to reduce the number of platforms from 40 in 2000 to 10 by 2010, saving some $500 million in costs.

The competitive picture in Europe is not that different from the picture in North America. A combination of inward investment and market share gains by Japanese automakers, and slowing export sales to North America due to the strong euro, have hurt demand and helped to create an excess capacity situation. As in the United States, automakers have responded by introducing sales incentives to try and shift inventory. Consequently, profits are down across the board.

Globally, the big story has been the continued rise of Toyota, which in 2003 passed Ford to become the world's second largest automobile company after GM (see Exhibit 6). With Ford now firmly in the rear view mirror, Toyota is setting its sights on GM. Toyota's plans call for the company to capture 15 percent of the global market for automobiles in 2010, up

EXHIBIT 6

Global Sales in 2003

Company	Vehicle Units Sold (millions)
GM	8.59
Toyota	6.78
Ford	6.54
Volkswagen	5.02
Daimler Chrysler	4.36
PSA Peugeot Citroen	3.29
Hyundai	3.05
Nissan	2.97
Honda	2.91
Renault	2.39

Source: Company Reports, Automotive News.

from 10 percent in 2003. If that goal is attained, Toyota will surpass GM to become the world's largest auto company (it is already the world's most profitable auto company—see Exhibit 5).

The most rapidly growing automobile market in the world is China. Production and sales of cars in China have soared since the country joined the World Trade Organization in 2001. Some 4.1 million cars and light trucks were sold in China in 2003, a 37 percent rise over the prior year, and China seems set to surpass Japan as the world's third largest automobile market in 2004.[30] With just 8 vehicles per 1,000 residents in 2003, versus 940 in the United States and 584 in Europe, many think that China is set to continue growing for years to come, and could potentially become the world's largest automobile market by 2020.[31]

The majority of these vehicles were made locally, often by joint ventures between foreign automobile companies and Chinese enterprises. Collectively, foreign automobile companies invested some $19 billion in China between 1994 and 2003. In 2004, General Motors, Ford, Volkswagen, and Toyota all announced plans to invest in new factories in China, with some $13 billion of investment planned for 2005–2010. The largest foreign player in China in 2003 was Volkswagen. Volkswagen was the first foreign manufacturer to set up operations in China, and has reaped the benefits of its early investments. Its two joint ventures with Chinese companies accounted for about 35 percent of total sales in 2003. GM and its local joint venture partner, SAIC, were second with about 11 percent of the total market.

Investments by foreign companies should increase production capacity in China to some 5.4 million units by 2006. If the demand continues to grow at its torrid pace, this will not be enough to serve local demand—but if local demand softens, the result could be excess capacity. Some think in such circumstances, China might start to become an export base for car makers.

ENDNOTES

1. The *Economist*, A Survey of the Car Industry, "Perpetual Motion," September 4, 2004, pages 3–4.
2. The phrase first appeared in GM's 1924 Annual Report to Shareholders, and more than anything else, it captured the essence of Sloan's revolutionary marketing philosophy. For details visit GM's website at **http://www.gm.com/company/corp_info/ history/index.html.**
3. Figures from Standard & Poor's, *Industry Survey: Autos & Auto Parts*, June 24, 2004.
4. Figures from Standard & Poor's, *Industry Survey: Autos & Auto Parts*, June 24, 2004.
5. Figures from Standard & Poor's, *Industry Survey: Autos & Auto Parts*, June 24, 2004.
6. The *Economist*, A Survey of the Car Industry, "Detroit's Nine Lives," September 4, 2004, pages 6–9.
7. The *Economist*, A Survey of the Car Industry, "Detroit's Nine Lives," September 4, 2004, pages 6–9.
8. The *Economist*, A Survey of the Car Industry, "Detroit's Nine Lives," September 4, 2004, pages 6–9.
9. D. Welch, "Price Breaks Are Here to Stay," *Business Week*, February 16, 2004, page 39.
10. Figures from Standard & Poor's, *Industry Survey: Autos & Auto Parts*, June 24, 2004.
11. D. Welch, "Price Breaks Are Here to Stay," *Business Week*, February 16, 2004, page 39.
12. Figures from Standard & Poor's, *Industry Survey: Autos & Auto Parts*, June 24, 2004.
13. J.D. Power Press Release, April 28, 2004, "Korean Branded Vehicles Overtake Europeans and Domestics in Initial Quality," J.D. Press Release, June 29, 2004, "Toyota Motor Sales Capture Top Corporate Rankings in Vehicle Dependability."
14. L. Hawkins, "US Auto Makers Get Better Grades for Productivity," *Wall Street Journal*, June 11, 2004, page A3.
15. D. Winter, "Efficiency Scoreboard," *Ward's Auto World*, July 2002, page 53.
16. Harbor Consulting, "New Benchmarks Set in 2004," Harbour Report, Press Release, June 10, 2004. Available at **http://www .harbourinc.com/.**
17. L. Hawkins, "US Auto Makers Get Better Grades for Productivity," *Wall Street Journal*, June 11, 2004, page A3.
18. D. Welch, "Has GM Outrun Its Pension Problems?" *Business Week*, January 19, 2004, page 70.
19. M. Phelan, "GM Predicts Sporty Profits Even From Fewer Sales," *Knight Ridder Tribune Business News*, March 13, 2004, page 1.
20. D. Welch and K. Kerwin, "Detroit Tries It the Japanese Way," *Business Week*, January 26, 2004, page 76; A. Taylor, "Detroit Buffs Up," *Fortune*, February 9, 2004, pages 90–94.
21. D. Winter, "Shrinking Product Development Time," *Ward's Auto World*, June 2003, pages 36–40.
22. J. Muller, "The Little Car That Could," *Forbes*, December 8, 2003, page 82; *The Economist*, "The Year of the Car," January 3, 2004, page 47.
23. Standard & Poor's, *Industry Survey: Autos & Auto Parts*, June 24, 2004.
24. Standard & Poor's, *Industry Survey: Autos & Auto Parts*, June 24, 2004.
25. K. Kerwin, "Ford to Suppliers: Let's Get Cozier," *Business Week*, September 20, 2004, page 8.
26. The *Economist*, A Survey of the Car Industry, "Fighting Back," September 4, 2004, pages 14–16.
27. R. Rosmarin, "Your Custom Car Is Ready at Toyota," *Business*, 2 (October 2004): 150–151.
28. S.S. Carty, "Hybrids Could Hitt 20 Percent of Car Market by 2010," *Wall Street Journal*, October 14, 2002, page D3.
29. The *Economist*, A Survey of the Car Industry, "The New European Order," September 4, 2004, pages 9–11.
30. Standard & Poor's, *Industry Survey: Autos & Auto Parts*, June 24, 2004.
31. D. Welch, D. Roberts, and G. Edmondson, "GM: Gunning It in China," *Business Week*, June 21, 2004, pages 112–114.

Toyota: Origins, Evolution, and Current Prospects

This case was prepared by Charles W. L. Hill, the University of Washington.

The growth of Toyota has been one of the great success stories of Japanese industry during the last half century. In 1947, the company was a little-known domestic manufacturer producing around 100,000 vehicles a year. As 2004 drew to a close, Toyota stated that the company and its affiliates would produce a record 7.84 million vehicles in 2004, placing it comfortably ahead of Ford and second only to General Motors in the global industry. Moreover, the company raised its production targets for 2006 to 8.5 million vehicles following better than expected sales in both North America and Asia. If Toyota meets this goal, it could surpass GM to become the world's largest automobile company. It would also put the company ahead of schedule to achieve its stated goal of gaining a 15 percent share of the global automobile market by 2010.[1]

This case describes the rise of Toyota from an obscure Japanese automobile company into the giant of today. It explains how the revolutionary production system developed at Toyota during the quarter of a century after 1950 paved the way for the company's current success. The case closes with a look at the challenges and opportunities Toyota now faces.

Copyright © 2004 by Charles W. L. Hill. This case was prepared by Charles W. L. Hill, the University of Washington, as the basis for class discussion rather than to illustrate either effective or ineffective handling of an administrative situation. Reprinted by permission of Charles W. L. Hill. All rights reserved. For the most recent financial results of the company discussed in this case, go to http://finance.yahoo.com, input the company's stock symbol, and download the latest company report from its homepage.

The Origins of Toyota

The original idea behind the founding of the Toyota Motor Company came from the fertile mind of Toyoda Sakichi.[2] The son of a carpenter, Sakichi was an entrepreneur and inventor whose primary interest lay in the textile industry, but he had been intrigued by automobiles since a visit to the United States in 1910. Sakichi's principal achievement was the invention of an automatic loom that held out the promise of being able to lower the costs of weaving high-quality cloth. In 1926, Sakichi set up Toyoda Automatic Loom to manufacture this product. In 1930, Sakichi sold the patent rights to a British textile concern, Platt Brothers, for about 1 million yen, a considerable sum in those days. Sakichi urged his son, Toyoda Kiichiro, to use this money to study the possibility of manufacturing automobiles in Japan. A mechanical engineer with a degree from the University of Tokyo, in 1930 Kiichiro became managing director of loom production at Toyoda Automatic Loom.

Kiichiro was at first reluctant to invest in automobile production. The Japanese market was at that time dominated by Ford and General Motors, both of which imported knock-down car kits from the United States and assembled them in Japan. Given this, the board of Toyoda Automatic Loom, including Kiichiro's brother-in-law and the company's president, Kodama Risaburo, opposed the investment on the grounds that it was too risky. Kiichiro probably would not have pursued the issue further had not his father made a deathbed request in 1930 that Kiichiro explore the possibilities of automobile production. Kiichiro had to push, but in 1933, he was able to get permission to set up an automobile department within Toyoda Automatic Loom.

Kiichiro's belief was that he would be able to figure out how to manufacture automobiles by taking apart U.S.-made vehicles and examining them piece by piece. He also felt that it should be possible to adapt U.S. mass-production technology to manufacture cost efficiently at lower volumes. His confidence was based in large part upon the already considerable engineering skills and capabilities at his disposal through Toyoda Automatic Loom. Many of the precision engineering and manufacturing skills needed in automobile production were similar to the skills required to manufacture looms.

Kiichiro produced his first 20 vehicles in 1935, and in 1936, the automobile department produced 1,142 vehicles—910 trucks, 100 cars, and 132 buses. At this time, however, the production system was essentially craft-based rather than a modern assembly line. Despite some progress, the struggle might still have been uphill had not fate intervened in the form of the Japanese military. Japan had invaded Manchuria in 1931 and quickly found American-made trucks useful for moving men and equipment. As a result, the military felt that it was strategically important for Japan to have its own automobile industry. The result was the passage of an automobile manufacturing law in 1936 which required companies producing more than 3,000 vehicles per year in Japan to get a license from the government. Moreover, to get a license over 50 percent of the stock had to be owned by Japanese investors. The law also placed a duty on imported cars, including the knock-down kits that Ford and GM brought into Japan. As a direct result of this legislation, both GM and Ford exited from the Japanese market in 1939.

Once the Japanese government passed this law, Kodama Risaburo decided that the automobile venture could be profitable and switched from opposing to proactively supporting Kiichiro (in fact, Risaburo's wife, who was Kiichiro's elder sister, had been urging him to take this step for some time). The first priority was to attract the funds necessary to build a mass-production facility. In 1937, Risaburo and Kiichiro decided to incorporate the automobile department as a separate company in order to attract outside investors—which they were successful in doing. Kiichiro Toyoda was appointed president of the new company. The company was named the Toyota Motor Company. (The founding family's name, "Toyoda," means "abundant rice field" in Japanese. The new name had no meaning in Japanese.)

Upon incorporation, Risaburo and Kiichiro's vision was that Toyota should expand its passenger car production as quickly as possible. However, once again fate intervened in the form of the Japanese military. Toyota had barely begun passenger car production when war broke out; in 1939, the Japanese government, on advice from the military, prohibited passenger car production and demanded that the company specialize in the production of military trucks.

The Evolution of Toyota

After the end of World War II, Kiichiro was determined that Toyota should reestablish itself as a manufacturer of automobiles.[3] Toyota, however, faced a number of problems in doing this:

1. The Japanese domestic market was too small to support efficient-scale mass-production facilities such as those common in America by that time.

2. The Japanese economy was starved of capital, which made it difficult to raise funds to finance new investments.

3. New labor laws introduced by the American occupiers increased the bargaining power of labor and made it difficult for companies to lay off workers.

4. North America and Western Europe were full of large auto manufacturers eager to establish operations in Japan.

In response to the last point, in 1950 the new Japanese government prohibited direct foreign investment in the automobile industry and imposed high tariffs on the importation of foreign cars. This protection, however, did little to solve the other problems facing the company at this time.

Limitations of Mass Production

At this juncture a remarkable mechanical engineer entered the scene: Ohno Taiichi. More than anyone else, it was Ohno who was to work out a response to the above problems. Ohno had joined Toyoda Spinning and Weaving in 1932 as a production engineer in cotton thread manufacture and entered Toyota when the former company was absorbed into the latter in 1943. Ohno worked in auto production for two years, was promoted, and managed auto assembly and machine shops between 1945 and 1953, and in 1954, he was appointed a company director.

When Ohno Taiichi joined Toyota, the mass-production methods pioneered by Ford had become the accepted method of manufacturing automobiles. The basic philosophy behind mass production was to produce a limited product line in massive quantities to gain maximum economies of scale. The economies came from spreading the fixed costs involved in setting up the specialized equipment required to stamp body parts and manufacture components over as large a production run as possible. Since setting up much of the equipment could take a full day or more, the economies involved in long production runs were reckoned to be considerable. Thus, for example, Ford would stamp 500,000 right-hand door panels in a single production run and then store the parts in warehouses until they were needed in the assembly plant, rather than stamp just those door panels that were needed immediately and then change the settings and stamp out left-hand door panels or other body parts.

A second feature of mass production was that each assembly worker should perform only a single task, rather than a variety of tasks. The idea here was that as the worker became completely familiar with a single task, he could perform it much faster, thereby increasing labor productivity. Assembly line workers were overseen by a foreman who did not perform any assembly tasks personally, but instead ensured that the workers followed orders. In addition, a number of specialists were employed to perform nonassembly operations such as tool repair, die changes, quality inspection, and general "housecleaning."

After working in Toyota for five years and visiting Ford's U.S. plants, Ohno became convinced that the basic mass-production philosophy was flawed. He saw five problems with the mass-production system:

1. Long production runs created massive inventories that had to be stored in large warehouses. This was expensive both because of the cost of warehousing and because inventories tied up capital in unproductive uses.
2. If the initial machine settings were wrong, long production runs resulted in the production of a large number of defects.

3. The sheer monotony of assigning assembly line workers to a single task generated defects, since workers became lax about quality control. In addition, since assembly line workers were not responsible for quality control, they had little incentive to minimize defects.
4. The extreme division of labor resulted in the employment of specialists such as foremen, quality inspectors, and tooling specialists, whose jobs logically could be performed by assembly line workers.
5. The mass-production system was unable to accommodate consumer preferences for product diversity.

In addition to these flaws, Ohno knew that the small domestic market in Japan and the lack of capital for investing in mass-production facilities made the American model unsuitable for Toyota.

Reducing Setup Times

Given these flaws and the constraints that Toyota faced, Ohno decided to take a fresh look at the techniques used for automobile production. His first goal was to try to make it economical to manufacture auto body parts in small batches. To do this, he needed to reduce the time it took to set up the machines for stamping out body parts. Ohno and his engineers began to experiment with a number of techniques to speed up the time it took to change the dies in stamping equipment. This included using rollers to move dies in and out of position along with a number of simple mechanized adjustment mechanisms to fine-tune the settings. These techniques were relatively simple to master, so Ohno directed production workers to perform the die changes themselves. This in itself reduced the need for specialists and eliminated the idle time that workers previously had enjoyed while waiting for the dies to be changed.

Through a process of trial and error, Ohno succeeded in reducing the time required to change dies on stamping equipment from a full day to 15 minutes by 1962, and to as little as 3 minutes by 1971. By comparison, even in the early 1980s many American and European plants required anywhere between 2 and 6 hours to change dies on stamping equipment. As a consequence, American and European plants found it economical to manufacture in lots equivalent to 10 to 30 days' supply and to reset equipment only every other day. In contrast, since Toyota could change the dies on stamping equipment in a matter of minutes, it manufactured in lots equivalent to just one day's supply, while resetting equipment three times per day.

Not only did these innovations make small production runs economical, but they also had the added benefit of reducing inventories and improving product quality. Making small batches eliminated the need to hold large inventories, thereby reducing warehousing costs and freeing up scarce capital for investment elsewhere. Small production runs and the lack of inventory also meant that defective parts were produced only in small numbers and entered the assembly process almost immediately. This had the added effect of making those in the stamping shops far more concerned about quality. In addition, once it became economical to manufacture small batches of components, much greater variety could be included into the final product at little or no cost penalty.

Organization of the Workplace

One of Ohno's first innovations was to group the work force into teams. Each team was given a set of assembly tasks to perform, and team members were trained to perform each task that the team was responsible for. Each team had a leader who was himself an assembly line worker. In addition to coordinating the team, the team leader was expected to perform basic assembly line tasks and to fill in for any absent worker. The teams were given the job of housecleaning, minor tool repair, and quality inspection (along with the training required to perform these tasks). Time was also set aside for team members to discuss ways to improve the production process (the practice now referred to as "quality circles").

The immediate effect of this approach was to reduce the need for specialists in the workplace and to create a more flexible work force in which individual assembly line workers were not treated simply as human machines. All this resulted in increased worker productivity.

None of this would have been possible, however, had it not been for an agreement reached between management and labor after a 1950 strike. The strike was brought on by management's attempt to cut the work force by 25 percent (in response to a recession in Japan). After lengthy negotiations, Toyota and the union worked out a compromise. The work force was cut by 25 percent as originally proposed, but the remaining employees were given two guarantees, one for lifetime employment and the other for pay graded by seniority and tied to company profitability through bonus payments. In exchange for these guarantees, the employees agreed to be flexible in work assignments. In turn, this allowed for the introduction of the team concept.

Improving Quality

One of the standard practices in the mass-production automobile assembly plants was to fix any errors that occurred during assembly in a rework area at the end of the assembly line. Errors routinely occurred in most assembly plants either because bad parts were installed or because good parts were installed incorrectly. The belief was that stopping an assembly line to fix such errors would cause enormous bottlenecks in the production system. Thus it was thought to be more efficient to correct errors at the end of the line.

Ohno viewed this system as wasteful for three reasons: (1) since workers understood that any errors would be fixed at the end of the line, they had little incentive to correct errors themselves; (2) once a defective part had been embedded in a complex vehicle, an enormous amount of rework might be required to fix it; and (3) since defective parts were often not discovered until the end of the line when the finished cars were tested, a large number of cars containing the same defect may have been built before the problem was found.

In an attempt to get away from this practice, Ohno decided to look for ways to reduce the amount of rework at the end of the line. His approach involved two elements. First, he placed a cord above every workstation and instructed workers to stop the assembly line if a problem emerged that could not be fixed. It then became the responsibility of the whole team to come over and work on the problem. Second, team members were taught to trace every defect back to its ultimate cause and then to ensure that the problem was fixed so that it would not reoccur.

Initially, this system produced enormous disruption. The production line was stopping all the time, and workers became discouraged. However, as team members began to gain experience in identifying problems and tracing them back to their root cause, the number of errors began to drop dramatically and stops in the line became much rarer, so that today in most Toyota plants the line virtually never stops.

Developing the Kanban System

Once reduced setup times had made small production runs economical, Ohno began to look for ways to coordinate the flow of production within the Toyota manufacturing system so that the amount of inventory in the system could be reduced to a minimum. Toyota produced about 25 percent of its major components in-house (the rest were contracted out to independent suppliers). Ohno's initial goal was to arrange for components and/or subassemblies manufactured in-house to be delivered to the assembly floor only when they were needed, and not before (this goal was later extended to include independent suppliers).

To achieve this, in 1953 Ohno began experimenting with what came to be known as the kanban system. Under the kanban system, component parts are delivered to the assembly line in containers. As each container is emptied, it is sent back to the previous step in the manufacturing process. This then becomes the signal to make more parts. The system minimizes work in progress by increasing inventory turnover. The elimination of buffer inventories also means that defective components show up immediately in the next process. This speeds up the processes of tracing defects back to their source and facilitates correction of the problem before too many defects are made. Moreover, the elimination of buffer stocks, by removing all safety nets, makes it imperative that problems be solved before they become serious enough to jam up the production process, thereby creating a strong incentive for workers to ensure that errors are corrected as quickly as possible. In addition, by decentralizing responsibility for coordinating the manufacturing process to lower-level employees, the kanban system does away with the need for extensive centralized management to coordinate the flow of parts between the various stages of production.

After perfecting the kanban system in one of Toyota's machine shops, Ohno had a chance to apply the system broadly in 1960 when he was made general manager of the Motomachi assembly plant. Ohno already had converted the machining, body stamping, and body shops to the kanban system, but since many parts came from shops that had yet to adopt

the system, or from outside suppliers, the impact on inventories was initially minimal. However, by 1962 he had extended the kanban to forging and casting, and between 1962 and 1965, he began to bring independent suppliers into the system.

Organizing Suppliers

Assembly of components into a final vehicle accounts for only about 15 percent of the total manufacturing process in automobile manufacture. The remaining 85 percent of the process involves manufacturing more than ten thousand individual parts and assembling them into about one hundred major components, such as engines, suspension systems, transaxles, and so on. Coordinating this process so that everything comes together at the right time has always been a problem for auto manufacturers. Historically, the response at Ford and GM to this problem was massive vertical integration. The belief was that control over the supply chain would allow management to coordinate the flow of component parts into the final assembly plant. In addition, American firms held the view that vertical integration made them more efficient by reducing their dependence on other firms for materials and components and by limiting their vulnerability to opportunistic overcharging.

As a consequence of this philosophy, even as late as the mid-1990s General Motors made 68 percent of its own components in-house, while Ford made 50 percent (in the late 1990s both GM and Ford deintegrated, spinning out much of their in-house supply operations as independent enterprises). When they didn't vertically integrate, U.S. auto companies historically tried to reduce the procurement costs that remain through competitive bidding—asking a number of companies to submit contracts and giving orders to suppliers offering the lowest price.

Under the leadership of Kiichiro Toyoda during the 1930s and 1940s, Toyota followed the American model and pursued extensive vertical integration into the manufacture of component parts. In fact, Toyota had little choice in this matter, since only a handful of Japanese companies were able to make the necessary components. However, the low volume of production during this period meant that the scale of integration was relatively small. In the 1950s, however, the volume of auto production began to increase dramatically. This presented Toyota with a dilemma: Should the company increase its capacity to manufacture components in-house in line with the growth in production of autos, or should the company contract out?

In contrast to American practice, the company decided that while it should increase in-house capacity for essential subassemblies and bodies, it would do better to contract out for most components. Four reasons seemed to bolster this decision:

1. Toyota wanted to avoid the capital expenditures required to expand capacity to manufacture a wide variety of components.

2. Toyota wanted to reduce risk by maintaining a low factory capacity in case factory sales slumped.

3. Toyota wanted to take advantage of the lower wage scales in smaller firms.

4. Toyota managers realized that in-house manufacturing offered few benefits if it was possible to find stable, high-quality, and low-cost external sources of component supply.

At the same time, Toyota managers felt that the American practice of inviting competitive bids from suppliers was self-defeating. While competitive bidding might achieve the lowest short-run costs, the practice of playing suppliers off against each other did not guarantee stable supplies, high quality, or cooperation beyond existing contracts to solve design or engineering problems. Ohno and other Toyota managers believed that real efficiencies could be achieved if the company entered into long-term relationships with major suppliers. This would allow them to introduce the kanban system, thereby further reducing inventory holding costs and realizing the same kind of quality benefits that Toyota was already beginning to encounter with its in-house supply operations. In addition, Ohno wanted to bring suppliers into the design process since he believed that suppliers might be able to suggest ways of improving the design of component parts based upon their own manufacturing experience.

As it evolved during the 1950s and 1960s, Toyota's strategy toward its suppliers had several elements. The company spun off some of its own in-house supply operations into quasi-independent entities in which it took a minority stake, typically holding between 20 percent and 40 percent of the stock. It then recruited a number of independent companies with a view to establishing a long-term relationship with them for the supply of critical components. Sometimes, but not always, Toyota took a minority stake in these companies as well. All these companies were designated as "first-tier suppliers." First-tier suppliers were responsible for working with Toyota as an integral part of the new product development team. Each first tier was responsible for the formation of a "second tier" of suppliers under its direction. Companies in the second tier were given the job of fabricating individual parts. Both first- and second-tier suppliers were formed into supplier associations.

By 1986 Toyota had three regional supply organizations in Japan with 62, 135, and 25 first-tier suppliers. A major function of the supplier associations was to share information regarding new manufacturing, design, or materials management techniques among themselves. Concepts such as statistical process control, total quality control, and computer-aided design were rapidly diffused among suppliers by this means.

Toyota also worked closely with its suppliers, providing them with management expertise, engineering expertise, and sometimes capital to finance new investments. A critical feature of this relationship was the incentives that Toyota established to encourage its suppliers to focus on realizing continuous process improvements. The basic contract for a component would be for four to five years, with the price being agreed in advance. If by joint efforts the supplier and Toyota succeeded in reducing the costs of manufacturing the components, then the additional profit would be shared between the two. If the supplier by its own efforts came up with an innovation that reduced costs, the supplier would keep the additional profit that the innovation generated for the lifetime of the contract.

As a consequence of this strategy, Toyota outsourced more production than almost any other major auto manufacturer. By the late 1980s Toyota was responsible for only about 27 percent of the value going into a finished automobile, with the remainder coming from outside suppliers. In contrast, at the time General Motors was responsible for about 70 percent of the value going into a finished automobile. Other consequences included long-term improvements in productivity and quality among Toyota's suppliers that were comparable to the improvements achieved by Toyota itself. In particular, the extension of the kanban system to include suppliers, by eliminating buffer inventory stocks, in essence forced suppliers to focus more explicitly on the quality of their product.

Consequences

The consequences of Toyota's production system included a surge in labor productivity and a decline in the number of defects per car. Exhibit 1 compares the number of vehicles produced per worker at General Motors, Ford, Nissan, and Toyota between 1965 and 1983.

These figures are adjusted for the degree of vertical integration pursued by each company. As can be seen, in 1960 productivity at Toyota already outstripped that of Ford, General Motors, and its main Japanese competitor, Nissan. As Toyota refined its production system over the next eighteen years, productivity doubled. In comparison, productivity essentially stood still at General Motors and Ford during the same period (see Exhibit 2).

Exhibit 2 provides another way to assess the superiority of Toyota's production system. Here the performance of Toyota's Takaoka plant is compared with that of General Motors's Framingham plant in 1987. As can be seen, the Toyota plant was more productive, produced far fewer defects per one hundred cars, and kept far less inventory on hand.

A further aspect of Toyota's production system is that the short setup times made it economical to manufacture a much wider range of models than is feasible at a traditional mass-production assembly plant. In essence, Toyota soon found that it could supply much greater product variety than its competitors with little in the way of a cost penalty. In 1990 Toyota was offering consumers around the world roughly as

EXHIBIT 2

General Motors's Framingham Plant Versus Toyota's Takaoka Plant, 1987

	GM Framingham	Toyota Takaoka
Assembly Hours per Car	31	16
Assembly Defects per 100 Cars	135	45
Inventory of Parts	2 weeks	2 hours

Source: J. P. Womack, D. T. Jones, and D. Roos, *The Machines That Changed the World* (New York: Macmillan, 1990), Figure 4.2, p. 83.

many products as General Motors (about 150), even though Toyota was still only half GM's size. Moreover, it could do this at a lower cost than GM.

Distribution and Customer Relations

Toyota's approach to its distributors and customers as it evolved during the 1950s and 1960s was in many ways just as radical as its approach toward suppliers. In 1950, Toyota formed a subsidiary, Toyota Motor Sales, to handle distribution and sales. The new subsidiary was headed by Kaymiya Shotaro from its inception until 1975. Kaymiya's philosophy was that dealers should be treated as "equal partners" in the Toyota family. To back this up, he had Toyota Motor Sales provide a wide range of sales training and service training for dealership personnel.

Kaymiya then used the dealers to build long-term ties with Toyota's customers. The ultimate aim was to bring customers into the Toyota design and production process. To this end, through its dealers, Toyota Motor Sales assembled a huge database on customer preferences. Much of these data came from monthly or semiannual surveys conducted by dealers. These asked Toyota customers their preferences for styling, model types, colors, prices, and other features. Toyota also used these surveys to estimate the potential demand for new models. This information was then fed directly into the design process.

Kaymiya began this process in 1952 when the company was redesigning its Toyopet model. The Toyopet was primarily used by urban taxi drivers. Toyota Motor Sales surveyed taxi drivers to try to find out what type of vehicle they preferred. They

EXHIBIT 1

Vehicles Produced per Worker (Adjusted for Vertical Integration), 1965–1983

Year	General Motors	Ford	Nissan	Toyota
1965	5.0	4.4	4.3	8.0
1970	3.7	4.3	8.8	13.4
1975	4.4	4.0	9.0	15.1
1979	4.5	4.2	11.1	18.4
1980	4.1	3.7	12.2	17.8
1983	4.8	4.7	11.0	15.0

Source: M. A. Cusumano, *The Japanese Automobile Industry* (Cambridge, Mass.: Harvard University Press, 1989), Table 48, p. 197.

wanted something reliable, inexpensive, and with good city fuel mileage—which Toyota engineers then set about designing. In 1956, Kaymiya formalized this process when he created a unified department for planning and market research whose function was to coordinate the marketing strategies developed by researchers at Toyota Motor Sales with product planning by Toyota's design engineers. From this time on, marketing information played a critical role in the design of Toyota's cars and in the company's strategy. In particular, it was the research department at Toyota Motor Sales that provided the initial stimulus for Toyota to start exporting during the late 1960s after predicting, correctly, that growth in domestic sales would slow down considerably during the 1970s.

Expanding Internationally

Large-scale overseas expansion did not become feasible at Toyota until the late 1960s for one principal reason: despite the rapid improvement in productivity, Japanese cars were still not competitive.[4] In 1957, for example, the Toyota Corona sold in Japan for the equivalent of $1,694. At the same time the Volkswagen Beetle sold for $1,111 in West Germany, while Britain's Austin company was selling its basic model for the equivalent of $1,389 in Britain. Foreign companies were effectively kept out of the Japanese market, however, by a 40 percent value-added tax and shipping costs.

Despite these disadvantages, Toyota tried to enter the U.S. market in the late 1950s. The company set up a U.S. subsidiary in California in October 1957 and began to sell cars in early 1958, hoping to capture the American small car market (which at that time was poorly served by the U.S. automobile companies). The result was a disaster. Toyota's cars performed poorly in road tests on U.S. highways. The basic problem was that the engines of Toyota's cars were too small for prolonged high-speed driving and tended to overheat and burn oil, while the poorly designed chassis resulted in excessive vibration. Sales were slow, and in 1964, Toyota closed down its U.S. subsidiary and withdrew from the market.

The company was determined to learn from its U.S. experience and quickly redesigned several of its models based on feedback from American consumer surveys and U.S. road tests. As a result, by 1967 the picture had changed considerably. The quality of Toyota's cars was now sufficient to make an impact in the U.S. market, while production costs and retail prices had continued to fall and were now comparable with international competitors in the small car market.

In the late 1960s, Toyota reentered the U.S. market. Although sales were initially slow, they increased steadily. Then the OPEC-engineered fourfold increase in oil prices that followed the 1973 Israeli/Arab conflict gave Toyota an unexpected boost. U.S. consumers began to turn to small fuel-efficient cars in droves, and Toyota was one of the main beneficiaries. Driven primarily by a surge in U.S. demand, worldwide exports of Toyota cars increased from 157,882 units in 1967 to 856,352 units by 1974 and 1,800,923 units by 1984. Put another way, in 1967 exports accounted for 19 percent of Toyota's total output. By 1984, they accounted for 52.5 percent.

Success brought its own problems. By the early 1980s, political pressures and talk of local content regulations in the United States and Europe were forcing an initially reluctant Toyota to rethink its exporting strategy. Toyota already had agreed to "voluntary" import quotas with the United States in 1981. The consequence for Toyota was stagnant export growth between 1981 and 1984. Against this background, in the early 1980s Toyota began to think seriously about setting up manufacturing operations overseas.

Transplant Operations

Toyota's first overseas operation was a 50/50 joint venture with General Motors established in February 1983 under the name New United Motor Manufacturing, Inc. (NUMMI). NUMMI, which is based in Fremont, California, began producing Chevrolet Nova cars for GM in December 1984.[5] The maximum capacity of the Fremont plant is about 250,000 cars per year.

For Toyota, the joint venture provided a chance to find out whether it could build quality cars in the United States using American workers and American suppliers. It also provided Toyota with experience dealing with an American union (the United Auto Workers Union) and with a means of circumventing "voluntary" import restrictions. For General Motors, the venture provided an opportunity to observe in full detail the Japanese approach to manufacturing. While General Motors's role was marketing and distributing the plant's output, Toyota designed the product and designed, equipped, and operated the plant. At the venture's start, thirty-four executives were loaned to NUMMI by Toyota and sixteen by General Motors. The chief executive and chief operating officer were both Toyota personnel.

By the fall of 1986, the NUMMI plant was running at full capacity, and the early indications were that the NUMMI plant was achieving productivity and quality levels close to those achieved at Toyota's major Takaoka plant in Japan. For example, in 1987 it took the NUMMI plant nineteen assembly hours to build a car, compared with sixteen hours at Takaoka, while the number of defects per one hundred cars was the same at NUMMI as at Takaoka—forty-five.[6]

Encouraged by its success at NUMMI, in December 1985 Toyota announced that it would build an automobile manufacturing plant in Georgetown, Kentucky. The plant, which came on stream in May 1988, officially had the capacity to produce 200,000 Toyota Camrys a year. Such was the success of this plant, however, that by early 1990 it was producing the equivalent of 220,000 cars per year. This success was followed by an announcement in December 1990 that Toyota would build a second plant in Georgetown with a capacity to produce a further 200,000 vehicles per year.[7]

By 2001, Toyota had four vehicle assembly plants in North America with a total capacity to produce over 1 million vehicles per year. In addition, the company had two engine plants, an aluminum wheel plant, an aluminum casting plant, special parts and body parts plants, and an automatic transmission plant. In total, these factories employed more than 123,000 Americans, more than Coca-Cola, Microsoft, and Oracle combined. Some 60 percent of all Toyota vehicles sold in the United States were now locally produced, and the company had announced plans to add another U.S. plant capable of turning out an additional 250,000 vehicles a year by 2005.[8]

In addition to its North American transplant operations, Toyota moved to set up production in Europe in anticipation of the 1992 lowering of trade barriers among the twelve members of the European Economic Community. In 1989, the company announced that it would build a plant in England with the capacity to manufacture 200,000 cars per year by 1997.

In 2001, Toyota opened a second European plant in France, raising its total production capacity within the European Union to 370,000. Toyota's goal was to sell 800,000 cars a year in the EU by 2005, which would give the company a 5 percent share of the EU market.[9]

Despite Toyota's apparent commitment to expand U.S.- and European-based assembly operations, it was not all smooth sailing. One problem was building an overseas supplier network comparable to Toyota's Japanese network. For example, in a 1990 meeting of Toyota's North American supplier's association, Toyota executives informed their North American suppliers that the defect ratio for parts produced by 75 North American and European suppliers was 100 times greater than the defect ratio for parts supplied by 147 Japanese suppliers—1,000 defects per million parts versus 10 defects per million among Toyota's Japanese suppliers. Moreover, Toyota executives pointed out that parts manufactured by North American and European suppliers tend to be significantly more expensive than comparable parts manufactured in Japan.

Because of these problems, Toyota had to import many parts from Japan for its U.S. assembly operations. However, for political reasons Toyota was being pushed to increase the local content of cars assembled in North America. The company's plan was for 50 percent of the value of Toyota cars assembled in the United States to be locally produced by January 1991. By the early 2000s, the local content of cars produced in North America was over 70 percent. To improve the efficiency of its U.S.-based suppliers, Toyota embarked upon an aggressive supplier education process. In 1992, it established the Toyota Supplier Support Center to teach its suppliers the basics of the Toyota production system. By 2001, eighty-nine supplier companies had been through the center. Many have reportedly seen double- and triple-digit productivity growth as a result, as well as dramatic reductions in inventory levels.[10]

Product Strategy

Toyota's initial production was aimed at the small car/basic transportation end of the automobile market. This was true both in Japan and of its export sales to North America and Europe. During the 1980s, however, Toyota progressively moved up market and abandoned much of the lower end of the market to new entrants such as the South Koreans. Thus, the company's Camry and Corolla models, which initially were positioned toward the bottom of the market, have been constantly upgraded and now are aimed at the middle-income segments of the market. This upgrading reflects two factors: (1) the rising level of incomes in Japan and the commensurate increase in the ability of Japanese consumers to purchase midrange and luxury cars and (2) a desire to hold onto its U.S. consumers, many of whom initially purchased inexpensive Toyotas in their early twenties and who have since traded up to more expensive models.

The constant upgrading of Toyota's models reached a logical conclusion in September 1989 when the company's Lexus division began marketing luxury cars to compete with Jaguars, BMWs, and the like. Although the Lexus brand initially got off to a slow start—in large part due to an economic recession—by 2001 Toyota was selling over 200,000 Lexus models a year in the United States, making it the best-selling luxury brand in the country.

Another addition to Toyota's product range in the late 1980s was a minivan. This vehicle was aimed at the North American market, where the minivan segment had grown rapidly. Toyota first introduced a minivan in 1986, but it flopped. The company dispatched product planners and design engineers to showrooms to find out why. Among the problems they identified were that the minivans lacked an aisle down the center, the short wheelbase gave them a pitchy ride, and the engine was not easy to service. Based on this feedback, Toyota designers completely redesigned the vehicle and reintroduced it in April 1990 as the Previa minivan; sales soon exceeded expectations.[11]

Toyota in 2004

As 2004 drew to a close, Toyota was enjoying one of its best years ever. The company had overtaken Ford to become the second largest automobile company in the world, and it had its sights firmly set on General Motors. Its goal of attaining a 15 percent share of the global market seemed attainable. Toyota was now a truly international company. Its overseas operations had grown from 11 production facilities in 9 countries in 1980 to 42 production facilities in 24 countries around the world by 2004.[12] In the all important U.S. market, the world's largest, Toyota held a 13.1 percent share of passenger car sales in 2003 and a 9.6 percent share of light truck sales, up from 11 percent and 7.6 percent, respectively, in 2000.[13]

The company was very profitable. In the financial year ending March 2004, it earned $11 billion net profits on sales of $163 billion. It had more profits than General Motors, Ford, and Daimler Chrysler combined and ended the year with some $30 billion in cash and short-term investments.

According to data from J.D. Power, Toyota was still the quality leader in the U.S. market. For cars that had been on the market for over three years, Toyota led the pack with 207 problems per 100 vehicles, compared with an industry average of 269 problems per 100 vehicles. Toyota also had the best record in the industry when measured by problems reported in the first 90 days after a sale—101 problems per 100 cars versus an industry average of 119 problems per 100 cars.[14]

J.D. Power also found that Toyota led the market in Japan. An April 2004 survey found that for vehicles purchased in 2002, Toyota had 89 problems per 100 vehicles compared with an industry average of 104. Honda was next with 91 problems per 100 vehicles, followed by Nissan with 108 problems per 100 vehicles.[15]

Furthermore, Toyota seemed to be maintaining a high level of productivity. In its American assembly operations, Toyota took 20.6 employee hours to build a car in 2004. This compares with 23.6 hours at General Motors, 25.4 hours at Ford, and 26.0 hours at Daimler Chrysler. However, both Nissan and Honda had more productive factories in the United States. Indeed, Nissan took 17.32 employee hours to build a car at its North American factories.[16] On the other hand, according to J.D. Power, Toyota has the three most efficient assembly plants in the world, all of which are located in Japan.

Toyota's ability to stay on top of productivity and quality rankings can be attributed to a company-wide obsession with continuing to improve the efficiency and effectiveness of its manufacturing operations. The latest round of these was initiated in 2000 by Toyota President, Fujio Cho. Cho, who worked for a while under Toyota's legendary engineer, Taichi Ohno, introduced an initiative known as "Construction of Cost Competitiveness for the 21st Century" or CCC21. The initiative has as a goal slashing component part costs by 30 percent on all new models. Attaining this goal necessitated Toyota working closely with suppliers—something it has long done.

According to news reports, by 2004 Toyota was close to attaining its CCC21 goal. In implementing CCC21, no detail has been too small. For example, Toyota took a close look at the grip handles mounted above the doors inside most cars. By working closely with suppliers, they managed to reduce the number of parts in these handles from 34 to 5, which cut procurement costs by 40 percent and reduced the time needed for installation from 12 seconds to 3 seconds.[17]

More generally, Toyota continues to refine its lean production system. For example, in die making, by 2004 Toyota had reduced the lead time to engineer and manufacture die sets for large body panels to 1.7 months, down from 3 months in 2002. By reducing lead time, Toyota reduces the startup costs associated with producing a new model, and the development time.[18]

In welding, Toyota has developed and installed a simplified assembly process known as the "global body line" or GBL. First developed in a low-volume Vietnamese assembly plant in 1996, and introduced into its first Japanese plant in 1998, by 2004 the GBL was operating in some 20 of the company's 50 assembly plants and was scheduled to be found in all 50 by 2007. The GBL system replaced Toyota's flexible body line assembly philosophy that has been in place since 1985. The GBL system is based upon a series of programmable robotic welding tools. Under the old FBL system, each car required three pallets to hold body parts in place during the welding process, each gripping either a major body side assembly or the roof assembly. The GBL system replaces these three pallets with a single pallet that holds all three major body panels in place from the inside as welding proceeds.[19]

According to Toyota, the GLB system has the following consequences:

- 30 percent reduction in the time a vehicle spends in the body shop
- 70 percent reduction in the time required to complete a major body change
- 50 percent cut in the cost to add or switch models
- 50 percent reduction in the investment to set up a line for a new model
- 50 percent reduction in assembly line footprint

The floor space freed up by the GLB allows two assembly lines to be placed in the space traditionally required for one, effectively doubling plant capacity. Moreover, using GLB technology as many as eight different models can be produced on a single assembly line. To achieve this, Toyota has pushed for consistency in design across model ranges, particularly with regard to the "hard points" that are grasped by the single master pallet.

Meanwhile, Toyota has also been accelerating the process of moving toward fewer vehicle platforms, the goal being to build a wide range of models on a limited range of platforms that use many of the same component parts or modules. The company is reportedly working toward a goal of having just ten platforms, down from over twenty in 2000.[20]

While Toyota is undoubtedly making progress refining its manufacturing efficiency, the fact remains that the productivity and quality gap between Toyota and its global competitors has narrowed. General Motors and Ford have both made significant strides in improving their quality and productivity in recent years. Moreover, in the American market at least, Toyota has suffered from the perception that its product offerings lack design flair and are not always as well attuned to consumer tastes as they might be. Here, too, however, there are signs that Toyota is improving matters, interestingly enough, by listening more to its American designers and engineers.

A pivotal event in the changing relationship between Toyota and its American designers occurred in the late 1990s. Japanese managers had resisted their U.S. colleagues' idea that the company should produce a V8 pickup truck for the American market. To change their minds, the U.S. executives flew their Japanese counterparts over from Japan and took them to a Dallas Cowboys football game—with a pit stop in the Texas Stadium parking lot. There the Japanese saw row upon row of full-size pickups. Finally, it dawned on them that Americans see the pickup as more than a commercial vehicle, considering it primary transportation. The result of this was Toyota's best-selling V8 pickup truck, the Toyota Tundra.[21]

American designers also pushed Toyota to redesign the Prius, its hybrid car first introduced in Japan in 1997. The Americans wanted a futuristic design change so that people would notice the technology. The result, the new Prius has become a surprise hit with Toyota, forecasting global sales of 300,000 units in 2005.[22]

Toyota's Americanization runs deeper than just product design issues. On the sales front, the company now sells more cars and trucks in North America than it does in Japan, and 70–80 percent of Toyota's global profits come from North America. On the personnel front, President Cho himself made his reputation by opening Toyota's first U.S. production plant in Georgetown, Kentucky, in 1988. His likely successor, Yoshi Inaba, spent eight years in the United States and has an MBA from Northwestern University. Americans are also starting to make their way into Toyota's top ranks. Two Americans from Toyota's U.S. subsidiary now rank among Toyota's top forty-two executives, and each spends from one to two weeks a month in Japan.[23]

Another concern of Toyota has been the aging of its customer base. According to J.D. Power, the average Toyota customer is 44 years old, compared with 38 for Volkswagen and 41 for Honda. Concerned that it was loosing its cache with the younger generation, some 60 million of whom will reach driving age over the next few years, Toyota introduced a new car brand, the Scion, into America in June 2004. Currently the brand has three models, all priced in the $13,000–$17,000 range. The cars are targeted at young entry level buyers and can be purchased over the web in addition to buying through traditional Toyota dealers. Early sales results suggest that the brand is doing well. Toyota's initial sales goals for the brand were 100,000 cars in 2005, but in October 2004, it raised that target to 170,000. The average buyer in the months following launch was 31 years old.[24]

As Toyota entered 2005, the key question facing management was whether the company was doing enough to attain its goal of capturing 15 percent of the global marketplace, particularly given the renewed efforts by its global rivals to close the quality and productivity gap between themselves and Toyota.

ENDNOTES

1. J. Sapsford, "Toyota Aims to Rival GM in Production," *Wall Street Journal*, November 2, 2004, page A3.
2. This section is based primarily on the account given in M. A. Cusumano, *The Japanese Automobile Industry* (Cambridge, Mass.: Harvard University Press, 1989).
3. The material in this section is drawn from three main sources: M. A. Cusumano, *The Japanese Automobile Industry*; Ohno Taiichi, *Toyota Production System* (Cambridge, Mass.: Productivity Press, 1990; Japanese edition, 1978); J. P. Womack, D. T. Jones, and D. Roos, *The Machine That Changed the World* (New York: Macmillan, 1990).
4. The material in this section is based on M. A. Cusumano, *The Japanese Automobile Industry*.
5. Niland Powell, "U.S.-Japanese Joint Venture: New United Motor Manufacturing, Inc.," *Planning Review*, January–February 1989, pp. 40–45.
6. From J. P. Womack, D. T. Jones, and D. Roos, *The Machine That Changed the World*.
7. J. B. Treece, "Just What Detroit Needs: 200,000 More Toyotas a Year," *Business Week*, December 10, 1990, page 29.
8. C. Dawson and L. Armstrong, "The Americanization of Toyota," *Business Week*, April 15, 2002, pages 52–54.
9. W. Kimberley, "Toyota Is Building in France," *Automotive Manufacturing and Production*, December 1999, p. 38.
10. P. Strozniak, "Toyota Alters the Face of Production," *Industry Week*, August 13, 2001, pages 46–48.
11. J. Flint, "The New Number Three?" *Forbes*, June 11, 1990, pages 136–140.
12. J. Sapsford, "Toyota Aims to Rival GM Production," *Wall Street Journal*, November 2, 2004, page A3.
13. Standard & Poor's Industry Surveys, *Auto and Auto Parts*, June 24, 2004.
14. J.D. Power Press Releases, April 28, 2004, "Korean Branded Vehicles Overtake Europeans and Domestics in Initial Quality"; June 29, 2004, "Toyota Motor Sales Capture Top Corporate Rankings in Vehicle Dependability."
15. J.D. Power Press Releases, "Toyota Ranks Highest in Japan's First Long Term Vehicle Dependability Study," September 2, 2004.
16. Data reported in J. Palmer, "Can Anyone Stop Toyota?" *Barron's*, September 13, 2004, pages 25–29.
17. B. Bremner and C. Dawson, "Can Anything Stop Toyota?" *Business Week*, November 17, 2003, pages 114–117.
18. M. Hara, "Moving Target," *Automotive Industries*, June 2004, pp. 26–29.
19. B. Visnic, "Toyota Adopts New Flexible Assembly Process," *Ward's Auto World*, November 2002, pages 30–31; M. Bursa, "A Review of Flexible Automotive Manufacturing," *Just Auto*, May 2004, page 15.
20. M. Hara, "Moving Target," *Automotive Industries*, June 2004, pages 26–29.
21. C. Dawson and L. Armstrong, "The Americanization of Toyota," *Business Week*, April 15, 2002, pages 52–54.
22. A. Taylor, "Toyota's Secret Weapon," *Fortune*, August 23, 2004, pages 66–65.
23. A. Taylor, "The Americanization of Toyota," *Fortune*, December 8, 2004, page 165.
24. N. Shirouzu, "Scion Plays Hip-Hop Impresario to Impress Young Drivers," *Wall Street Journal*, October 5, 2004, page B1.

General Motors in 2005

This case was prepared by Gareth R. Jones, Texas A&M University.

General Motors (GM) is one of the largest industrial corporations in the world. In 2005, GM employed over 325,000 people globally, down from over 700,000 in 1995. Its manufacturing operations were in 32 countries, producing 9 million vehicles that are sold in 200 countries. But despite its size, GM is one of the least profitable global carmakers; its return on invested capital is a measly 1% compared with Toyota's 6%. To understand why it had performed so poorly over the last few decades, it is necessary to examine the history of the company and the car industry.

GM's Origins

The company was founded on September 16, 1908, when William C. Durant formed the General Motors Company by bringing twenty-five independent car companies, including Buick and Cadillac, together. At the beginning each company retained its own individual identity, and GM was simply a holding company, that is, a central office surrounded by its twenty-five satellites. Hundreds of models of cars were produced, principally targeted at wealthy customers who were the only individuals who could afford them at the time because the costs of manufacturing cars was so high.

GM's principal competitor at this time was the Ford Motor Car Company, and in 1908, Henry Ford announced the development of the Model T car which was to be produced by a revolutionary method—mass

Copyright © 1994, 2005 by Gareth R. Jones. This case was prepared by Gareth R. Jones, Texas A&M University, as the basis for class discussion rather than to illustrate either effective or ineffective handing of an administrative situation. Reprinted by permission of Gareth R. Jones. All rights reserved. For the most recent financial results of the company discussed in this case, go to **http://finance.yahoo.com**, input the company's stock symbol, and download the latest company report from its homepage.

production. Ford's new mass production technology was based on moving conveyor belts; the belt brought the car to be assembled by unskilled workers rather than having skilled workers work in small teams to make a car. Ford also pioneered the use of standardized auto parts that could be easily fitted together to make assembly easier and less costly. As a result of his efforts, the costs of manufacturing cars plummeted, and Ford created a mass market for the Model T. Ford became the industry leader, and GM was suddenly in a losing situation due to its production of a wide variety of expensive cars for a very small market (as opposed to Ford's single, inexpensive product targeted at the middle of the market). Ford grew rich during the period 1910–1920 while GM struggled to keep its head above water.

In 1920, Alfred P. Sloan took control of GM as chief executive officer, and he saw that major changes were necessary if GM was to be able to compete effectively with Ford. It was clear to Sloan that operating twenty-five different car companies that produced hundreds of different models was very inefficient compared with Ford's strategy of producing one model of car in large quantities. Moreover, GM's high cost–high priced cars were competing against one another for the same set of wealthy customers. In addition, GM's car companies were not learning anything from one another; they were all purchasing or making their own sets of auto components, so that economies of scale in parts manufacturing or auto assembly were not being obtained. Sloan saw that GM's very survival was at stake.

GM's New Structure

Sloan searched for a new way to organize and manage GM's different car companies to increase their competitive advantage. While he realized the need to reduce costs and increase efficiency, Sloan also saw that Ford's strategy to produce only one model of car for the whole market meant that Ford ignored the needs of other market segments—such as the luxury end that GM served. Moreover, he also realized that customers in the middle of the market might want a superior product to the standard Ford Model T and that there were a lot of opportunities to produce cars for market segments between those served by the standardized Model T or the expensive GM models.

The problem Sloan faced was how to organize GM's twenty-five different car divisions to achieve both superior efficiency and customer responsiveness. The solution he hit upon was to group the twenty-five different companies into five major self-contained operating divisions: Chevrolet, Pontiac, Oldsmobile, Buick, and Cadillac.

Each of the different divisions was given its own support services like sales, production, engineering, and finance, and each became responsible for producing a range of cars that was aimed at a specific socioeconomic market segment. Sloan's plan was that GM's divisions would market five lines of cars to customers in five different socioeconomic segments. Chevrolet, for example, would manufacture inexpensive cars for customers at the entry level of the market. Pontiac, Oldsmobile, and Buick would produce cars for progressively more prosperous market segments while Cadillac would specialize in the high-price, luxury end of the market. Sloan's goal was to be responsive to each segment of the car market by producing a car to meet each segment's specific needs. He hoped that customers would move up to the next most expensive line of GM car as they prospered, and GM carefully priced the cars of the different divisions to entice customers to move up, for example, from an Oldsmobile to a Buick, or from a Buick to a Cadillac. Realizing that customers might be confused about the number of GM models they would be choosing from, he was insistent that each division develop a range of cars that had a unique image so that the cars of the different divisions would be clearly differentiated. Thus, for example, Cadillac customers needed to believe that the Cadillac they were buying was a product that was clearly superior to a Buick, not just a more expensive car with a different name.[1]

Sloan's goal in reorganizing GM into five different car divisions was also to increase operating efficiency and car design. His plan was for each division to operate as an independent profit center that would be evaluated on its return on investment. Decision making would be decentralized to the divisions, and each division would be in control of its own strategy. Managers would be responsible for bottom line results. Sloan's idea was that this new way of organizing GM's activities would create competition between divisions that would lead them to improve their efficiency in order to receive more capital for future investment. As Sloan wrote in his autobiography, he thought the creation of independent operating divisions would "(1) increase the morale of the organization by placing each operation on its own foundation . . . assuming its own responsibility and contributing its share to the final result, (2) develop statistics correctly reflecting . . . the true measure of efficiency, (3) and enable the corporation to direct the placing of additional capital where it will result in the greatest benefit to the corporation as a whole."[2]

Sloan also recommended that interdivisional transactions of auto parts, technology, and so on should be set by a transfer pricing scheme based on cost plus some predetermined rate of return. To avoid protecting a high-cost internal supplier, however, he also recommended a number of steps involving analysis of the parts and assembly operations of outside competitors to determine the fair price. In this way he hoped to keep down the cost of GM's inputs. Sloan established a strong, professional centralized headquarters staff to determine the fair price of inputs and to establish transfer prices between divisions. The staff's primary role would be to audit divisional performance and to plan strategy for the total organization. The divisions were responsible for all product-related decisions.

The results of this change in GM's business model and strategies were dramatic. By 1925, GM became the dominant U.S. car company as it took a large share of the market from Ford which saw the demand for its Model T plummet as customers switched to GM's upscale cars. Ford was soon forced to close down his factory for seven months in order to retool the production line to imitate GM and produce new models of cars targeted at different kinds of customers.

---

[1]A.P. Sloan, *My Years at General Motors.* Garden City, New York, Doubleday, 1964.

[2]A.P. Sloan, *My Years at...* p. 50.

Demand for the Model T plummeted because customers could get an affordable, better equipped, more prestigious, or more luxurious GM car.

With its new strategy and structure in place, GM took the lead in the U.S. car market and has enjoyed the largest market share of any car manufacturer since. From 1925–1975, it embarked on a continuous program to expand its product range to include all kinds of models of cars, full-size trucks, lightweight trucks, and various forms of specialized vehicles such as vans and ambulances. As time went on, GM also began to take over its suppliers and became highly vertically integrated. For example, GM took over Fisher Body Co., which made the car bodies for GM cars. GM also internally developed many of its own car parts' manufacturing operations, such as its Delco Division which still supplies GM with most of its electrical and electronic components (it was spun off in the 2000s as discussed later). From 1925–1975, GM dominated the U.S. car market, controlling over 65 percent of domestic sales. Together, GM, Ford, and Chrysler (now DaimlerChrysler), the Big Three carmakers, controlled over 90 percent of the U.S. vehicle market.

1970s: Big Changes in the Global Car Industry

GM's preeminent position in the U.S. car market was broken in the 1970s by a combination of two factors that altered the nature of competition in the car industry forever: the oil crisis and the emergence of low-cost Japanese competition. The oil embargo of 1973 revealed the inefficiency of U.S. "gas guzzler" cars that frequently only obtained six to nine miles per gallon. U.S. customers began to demand smaller, more fuel-efficient vehicles, which the Big Three were not equipped to build. The Japanese, however, were competent in the production of small, fuel-efficient cars, and customers began to switch to their vehicles. Moreover, as U.S. customers began buying inexpensive Japanese cars, such as the Honda Accord and the Toyota Celica, they began to realize that these cars were not only inexpensive but also they were reliable. One major survey, for example, reported that while Japanese cars averaged 1.3 flaws per vehicle, Ford averaged 2, GM had 2.5, and Chrysler had almost 3.

The combination of the switch in customer demand to small, reliable cars and the ability of the Japanese to serve the small car niche precipitated a crisis for GM. Demand for its large sedans plummeted,

and divisions like Buick and Cadillac began to lay off thousands of employees because of their inability to satisfy customers' needs for smaller, more fuel-efficient cars. Moreover, growing customer awareness that the quality problems that plagued GM's cars were not present in those of Japanese carmakers helped contribute to GM's declining market share. The problem lay not in the car but the company that made the car.

GM's operating philosophy that large cars meant large profits was revealed as false as Japanese carmakers, which had been developing efficient, quality-enhancing "lean production" techniques to reduce manufacturing costs, began to make enormous profits selling their economy cars to U.S. customers. Customers flocked to the rapidly expanding Japanese car dealerships that were spreading over the United States during the 1970s. Within the space of five years, 1973–1978, not only was it revealed that the Big Three were high-cost carmakers, it was also revealed that they were low-quality car makers. In particular, GM's extensive range of large, luxurious, boxy car models had began to compare unfavorably either with the inexpensive (and boxy) Japanese models or with the sleek European luxury cars like Jaguar, Mercedes, and BMW, which also began to rapidly steal away GM's share of the luxury car market by the late 1970s. GM was being attacked both at the inexpensive and the luxury ends of the market, and its profits fell drastically as the sales of its large cars slowed to a trickle.

GM Fights Back

Reeling from the onslaught of the new competition, GM began to use its huge resources (e.g., in 1978 despite its problems GM still earned $3.5 billion on $63 billion in sales) to try to restore its competitive advantage. Under the control of a new CEO, Roger Smith, who took over in 1980, GM began several major programs to reduce costs and improve quality; by 1990 these programs had cost the company over $100 billion—enough money, analysts pointed out, to have bought Toyota and Honda given their market value at that time.

New Technology

To enhance its competitive position in cars and trucks, GM invested over $50 billion to improve and update its technology and to gain expertise in the Japanese lean-manufacturing techniques. Beginning in the early 1980s, Roger Smith started to champion the development of automated factories and robots as a way of reducing costs and raising productivity. Under his leadership, plants, such as GM's Saginaw Vanguard plant in Michigan, became heavily automated. As in Japanese factories, GM used automated equipment mold parts, robots to assemble car components, and automated vehicles to pick up and distribute parts to the robots on the assembly line. While these automated factories were impressive, they proved very expensive to operate. For example, axles made in the new factories cost twice as much as ones produced conventionally. Moreover, they were subject to frequent downtime as robots broke down and stopped the production line. By some estimates, GM's new automated factories were no more productive than those that operated conventionally. GM seemed to lack the Japanese know-how to operate automated factories successfully.

Saturn Project

A major experiment that GM began in 1982 to develop new skills in manufacturing low-cost, quality cars was the Saturn Project. Smith created a new GM division called Saturn, which was given the task of creating a Japanese-like manufacturing unit that could produce a small car at the same cost as Japanese small cars. The division was deliberately kept separate from GM's other divisions so that new skills could be developed from scratch. GM chose Spring Hill, Tennessee, as the location for the new plant. In 1987, the board approved $1.9 billion for the new factory, equipment, and tooling. Saturn became the biggest construction undertaking in GM's history. In 1990, the plant moved into full production, and Saturn cars went on sale in 1991 priced from $10,000 to $12,000 to compete with the Honda Civic and Toyota Corolla. By 1991, Saturn had built just 50,000 cars, short of its 240,000 capacity. Saturn lost $800 million in 1991.

By 1992, Saturn was selling well, and its cars were ranked in the top ten list of customer satisfaction. However, it still lost $700 million, and the skills that GM developed in lean manufacturing through its Saturn Project did not spread widely through the company as GM had hoped. Moreover, GM realized that Saturn never could match the low costs of Japanese manufacturers. The division built a high-quality product, but it never had the sales success that GM had hoped for in competing with Japanese carmakers.

Strategic Alliances

In another venture to learn Japanese techniques in lean manufacturing, in 1983 GM created a joint venture with Toyota called New United Motor Manufacturing, Inc. (NUMMI) to produce Chevrolet Novas in GM's Freemont, California, plant, which had closed in 1982 because of poor quality and bad labor-management relations. Through the venture Toyota would get the chance to see if it could make high-quality cars in the United States with American workers and suppliers, while GM would gain intimate knowledge and access to Toyota's lean manufacturing techniques. In 1984, NUMMI reopened under the control of Japanese management. By 1986, its productivity was higher than any other GM factory, and it was operating at twice the old level under GM management.

One of the primary reasons for its success was the use of flexible work teams. At the NUMMI factory, Toyota divided the work force into 350 flexible work teams consisting of 5 to 7 people plus a team leader. Each worker was trained to perform the jobs of other workers, and they all regularly rotated jobs . In addition, all workers were taught the procedures for analyzing jobs to improve work procedures. Team members designed all the team's jobs, timed each other using stopwatches, and continually attempted to find better ways to perform tasks. GM previously had employed eighty managers to perform this analysis; now not only did flexible work teams do it but also they were responsible for monitoring product quality. The role of managers in the new factory was to provide shop-floor workers with support, not to monitor or supervise their activities. From this venture GM finally learned how Toyota's lean production system worked and that work relationships are at least as important as automated factories in increasing productivity and reducing costs. From this point on, it began to implement the new system across all its hundreds of manufacturing plants although this was a slow process.

From its investment in new automated technology, its Saturn Project, and by learning Japanese lean-manufacturing techniques from its joint ventures with Toyota and other companies, by 1990 GM had been able to reduce the number of defects per car, raise quality, and reduce costs. However, Ford and Chrysler had learned the new manufacturing methods *better* than GM. For most of the 1980s and 1990s, their quality ratings were higher and their market share rose while GM's continued to fall. For example, in 1987 Ford earned higher profits than GM for the first time since 1924 because of its $3 billion investment in developing a new line of higher quality cars at lower costs. One reason for Ford's success was that it was highly centralized, which made it easier for its top managers to pursue new quality initiatives quickly. GM, with its hundreds of divisions, found it much more difficult to transfer new information and knowledge between them, and top management orders were often lost in the bureaucracy.

In sum, although GM was successful in reducing its operating costs and increasing quality during the 1980s, its competitors were more successful, and it failed to obtain a competitive edge over them. GM was still at a major disadvantage compared with its Japanese competitors, which, in the 1990s, began to open their own plants inside the United States at an accelerating pace. Toyota and Honda led the quality ranking of U.S. made cars, and by 1995 manufactured over 1.5 million cars a year in the United States.

Changing Its Structure

In the 1980s, fierce competition from the Japanese forced GM to take a hard look at its multidivisional structure and the way it impacted the company's competitive advantage. Compared with Ford, Chrysler, and Japanese companies that operated with flat, streamlined structures, GM, with its hundreds of divisions, an extensive array of internal suppliers, and a corporate headquarters with thirty thousand managers, had become a huge lumbering bureaucracy. Roger Smith and his top management team, prompted by outside critics, realized that GM's structure had reduced its competitive advantage in several ways.

First, each division performed its own research and development and engineering, and the duplication of value creation activities across divisions was costing the company billions of extra dollars. Each division also purchased its inputs independently of other divisions so that economies of purchasing and distribution were being lost, which raised costs. Moreover, as discussed earlier, divisions were not sharing their knowledge about new, more efficient methods of design and manufacturing so that quality was slow to increase.

Second, each division produced cars in its own traditional way using its own set of platforms—the basic design behind which cars are assembled and made. Each division used several different platforms,

which is very expensive because each platform requires different inputs and its own method of manufacturing, and a specific platform could not be used to produce other models of cars. Chrysler, for example, decided to use only one platform in the 1990s, the K-Platform, to build all its cars; this led to substantial savings in manufacturing costs. Another problem for GM was the sheer cost of its huge staff of corporate executives, a cost that many analysts calculated to be several billions of dollars.

Beyond reduced efficiency, GM's tall, overly bureaucratic structure also slowed innovation because it took the organization a long time to adopt new technological advances and reduced GM's ability to recognize and respond to changing customer demands. As mentioned earlier, GM was slow to see the move toward small, more nimble, fuel-efficient, high-reliability cars from the long, boxy, chrome-laden, heavyweight vehicles that had become the principal offerings of the Big Three.

On all fronts, GM's organizational structure reduced its competitive advantage. For example, whereas Toyota only had seven levels in the hierarchy in the early 1980s, there were twenty-one levels in GM's hierarchy. One consequence was that while it took GM five to six years to bring a new car to market, it took Toyota only thirty-six months—a major source of competitive advantage.

The 1984 Reorganization

To try to solve many of these problems and increase its competitiveness, in 1984 GM consolidated its five powerful, autonomous vehicle divisions into two business groups. The operations of Chevy and Pontiac would be managed together, and these divisions would concentrate on smaller cars. Buick, Oldsmobile, and Cadillac (BOC) divisions would be managed together and would focus on bigger, luxury cars. The goal behind the change was to reduce costs by centralizing R&D, engineering, and purchasing activities at the level of the business group. Also GM hoped that this reorganization would speed product development.

The 1984 reorganization added yet another layer of GM bureaucracy: In addition to corporate management and individual divisional managers, there was now the level of group manager (e.g., BOC group manager). Divisions inside a group would produce car models from a limited number of platforms, and each model would be assembled from a limited number of inputs to reduce costs. Each division would then customize its models for specific groups of customers.

The reorganization was a disaster. The result of centralizing decision making at the group level and standardizing the activities of the divisions inside a group was that by 1987 all the cars produced by a group began to look alike. Cadillac buyers did not know why they paid more for a car that looked like other less expensive GM models such as Buicks, and sales of Cadillacs plummeted. Eighty percent of Buicks, Olds, and Pontiacs only differed slightly in price and engineering, and due to the lack of a unique image, sales of those three divisions fell sharply because their cars were basically similar. Divisions had become just marketing organizations.

The basic problem was that key decisions were made by central engineering and manufacturing staffs instead of by the five divisions. Moreover, the central engineering design staff reported to top management only two layers below the CEO and not to the heads of the car divisions. Consequently, division managers had to bargain with the design staff to get the desired car styling for its unit! This new structure prevented GM from launching a range of successful new models, as Ford and the Japanese were doing, and costs were still not falling by as much as had been hoped. Even though design time had been reduced, the result was poorer, not better, customer responsiveness as GM's new models failed to attract buyers.

As Roger Smith recognized, GM's problem was that it needed to centralize many of its activities to achieve economies of scale and reduce costs, but only decentralization can provide the flexibility needed to react to changes quickly and to allow divisions to design and develop products to meet the needs of their customers. Realizing their mistake GM's top management made some moves to give control of engineering and design back to the divisions. However, the benefits of centralizing R&D and purchasing were realized, and these activities became increasingly controlled at the group level.

The 1988 Reorganization

The Cadillac division benefited the most from the new policy of decentralization. Due to centralized engineering at the group level, Cadillac's image had become tainted, and its sales had fallen. For example, due to an anticipated energy crisis in 1986, GM decided that the Cadillac Eldorado and Seville should be made smaller but increased their price. GM tried to target these cars at import buyers as well as traditional buyers, which were the over fifty age group. However, traditional customers did not like these models because the cars were built on a common platform, which made them look similar to cheaper cars; for example, the new Cadillacs looked like Buicks. As a result, 1986 sales were 51 percent less than 1985 sales which was a severe blow to GM since profit margins on luxury cars were some of the highest.

To turn around the division, Cadillac was granted its own engineering team in 1988, and they moved quickly to forge a new identity for the division. Once again in control of its decision making, Cadillac managers lengthened the cars two inches, restyled them, increased advertising, and promoted test drives of the cars through direct mail. By 1990, Cadillac had gross margins of 40 to 45 percent compared with 30 percent for the rest of GM's divisions. Cadillac had become very successful, launching redesigned models in 1991, 1992, and 1993, and their sales rose steadily over time. GM's other car divisions experienced mixed fortunes during the 1990s. In its small car business group, GM implemented a major plan to reduce the number of car platforms and to centralize purchasing of inputs to reduce costs through its GM10 program. The GM10 program was created to replace all of GM's midsize cars such as the Chevy Celebrity, Pontiac 6000, Buick Century, and Olds Cutlass Supreme. Each of these four divisions would get a coupe and a sedan. At a cost of $7 billion, GM10 was the largest new model program ever created, indicating GM's interest in obtaining economies of scale from its reorganized car operations. However, design errors resulting from its centralized design operations led to failure. None of these cars became a major seller of the order of a Ford Taurus, Honda Accord, or Toyota Camry because GM still didn't understand what customers wanted.

For example, sales in its Buick division declined from 1984 to 1988, but then Edward Mertz, who took over the division in 1986, established a major program to increase quality and began to listen to dealers, customers, and employees. Mertz insisted that Buick should be given its own engineering team to respond to its customers' needs and to listen to dealer and customer complaints. This engineering team communicated directly with plant engineers who were instructed to work with manufacturing to build quality into its cars. With its revised lineup of cars, Buick began doing fairly well in the midsize car segment.

By 1991, sales of Buick's 1991 models increased 6.6 percent at a time when total U.S. car sales decreased 8.2 percent, and its cars were recognized as among the most reliable.

The upturn in Buick's fortunes came at the expense of Oldsmobile, however. Oldsmobile's cars were similar to Buick's and targeted the same customer segment. Sales declined from 1.1 million cars in 1986 to about 560,000 cars in 1990 because of declining quality and because they lacked a distinct image. By 1992, with falling sales the future of the Oldsmobile Division was called into question; however, it was not until 2001 that GM finally announced it would close down this division's operations. Finally, even Chevrolet suffered from GM's flawed design process during the 1980s and by 1990 was desperately in need of new models.

The result was that throughout the 1980s Japanese carmakers continuously gained market share, mainly by stealing sales from GM. In 1978, American automakers had an 84 percent market share compared with 68 percent in 1989. From 1985 to 1989, GM's market share declined from about 44 percent to about 33 percent while Japan's share increased from 19 percent to 26 percent.

By the early 1990s, more changes were occurring in the global car environment. Japanese companies, which now dominated the small- to medium-size car market, decided to compete in the luxury segment. Toyota established its Lexus division, Nissan its Infinity, and Honda its Acura to compete with Cadillac and upscale European makers for luxury sales. Japan also decided to enter the profitable large truck segment dominated by Chevrolet. Of all vehicles sold in the United States, trucks are the most profitable. To fight back GM introduced sixteen new vehicles; for example, the 1992 Cadillac Seville STS was successfully launched to compete with Toyota's Lexus and Germany's Mercedes, and it redesigned its large trucks.

Diversification at GM

During the 1980s, to help reduce costs and improve quality and customer responsiveness GM also began a program of diversification and acquisition. To help its core automotive business it bought Electronic Data Systems (EDS) and Hughes Aircraft. In 1984, GM was the largest user of computers in the world. Each of its divisions used different computer systems or programs, however, so that the corporation lacked an integrated computer network. Moreover, GM saw

that many of the problems it had experienced with its advanced factories and robotically controlled manufacturing were due to its lack of programming ability in computer aided manufacturing (CAM). To quickly develop a competence in CAM that would allow it to operate its new manufacturing systems effectively, in 1984 it acquired EDS for $2.5 billion.

GM's goal was that EDS would program its manufacturing operations and integrate its computers into one network. As it turned out, however, EDS had little experience in CAM; its strengths were in data processing. EDS helps customers develop and customize computer hardware and software systems to match their needs, which is called systems integration. EDS was the leader in this field and in information technology (IT) outsourcing, which entails maintaining and upgrading a company's IT in return for a fee. Thus, while EDS was able to help GM integrate its incompatible system of computers and automated machines, it could not help it to improve its CAM skills. Many analysts wondered why GM bought EDS, rather than simply buying its skills like other companies, and thought the money could have been spent better in developing GM's core skills in car making. However, fortuitously for GM, it had bought a rising star whose revenues increased throughout the 1990s.

In 1985, GM acquired Hughes Aircraft, a large defense contractor, for $5.2 billion. GM Hughes operated in four business segments: 32 percent automotive, 18 percent telecommunications, 44 percent defense, and 6 percent commercial. GM bought Hughes to create synergies with its vehicle-making operations by using Hughes's radar and satellite technology to develop advanced electronics, such as guidance systems for future cars. However, once again analysts wondered why GM would spend so much money on such a risky venture, one in which returns were far into the future.

A New Management Team Takes Over

In 1990, GM's board chose Robert Stempel, Roger Smith's hand-picked successor, to succeed Smith on his retirement. Stempel, who had been head of the BOC group, focused on manufacturing and engineering; however, like Smith he moved slowly to downsize the corporation and was reluctant to make the huge cuts in its work force that analysts thought imperative to turn around the company. For example, even though GM's market share had declined rapidly (GM's market share declined from 50 percent in 1978 to 35 percent in 1992) it had not reduced the number of its manufacturing plants or downsized its work force in any significant way. The downsizing process was slow because Smith insisted that GM would reach a 50 percent market share again. Everyone but GM's top executives recognized that the company had at least 100,000 white-collar workers and an even larger excess of production employees, but top managers would not make drastic cuts.

In 1991, John Smale, an outside director, began looking for ways to stop GM's losses. In April 1992, the board finally took action. Robert Stempel was removed from his position as chairman of the GM board's executive committee and replaced by Smale who was a former CEO of Procter & Gamble. Stempel remained CEO and a board member. Jack Smith, the former head of GM's European operations, took over the president's position from one of Stempel's followers. Finally, by 2002 GM announced that it would lay off 80,000 workers and close 10 U.S. assembly plants by 1995; 4 engine factories and 11 parts plants would also be closed. About 54,000 of GM's 304,000 blue-collar workers would be cut through attrition, early retirement, and layoffs. A total of 26,000 white-collar workers would also be axed, and the corporate staff was to be reduced from 13,500 people to around 2,300 people.

GM's board had watched Jack Smith cut white-collar staff, freeze salaries, reduce health care benefits, and put some noncore businesses up for sale. The board decided to replace Stempel with Smith in late 1992 and also promoted younger GM executives into top positions—defying the GM tradition of top executives being in their midfifties and sixties. New CEO Jack Smith soon defined GM's future strategies to become profitable: an aggressive focus of reducing costs and improving quality, an aggressive marketing of redesigned vehicles to better satisfy customers' needs, and a new, more flexible decentralized organizational structure.

New Production Manufacturing Initiatives

Smith, who had been in charge of GM's European operations and responsible for implementing new lean production techniques there, had a clear vision of what GM needed to do to reduce its cost structure. First,

GM has learned from its failures over the last ten years, especially the importance of dropping unsuccessful products and trimming its product line to reduce costs. By 1993, GM reduced the number of models in production from 85 to 65 while introducing over 20 new cars and trucks. To do this cost-effectively, GM imitated other carmakers by reducing the number of its basic platforms from 14 to 6 by the late 1990s, such as platforms for small, medium, large cars, and trucks, and then making each different division produce similar-sized vehicles using the same basic platform but with parts customized to their individual design.

Beginning in the mid 1990s, GM began a program to improve the technology built into its cars and to reduce the cost of developing it. For example, GM formed a new powertrain division by integrating two independent divisions to cut costs. Also to implement common systems and processes and use best industry practices throughout its North American Operations, GM created a centralized vehicle launch center. Now engineers from each of the car and truck divisions work with engineers from the centralized vehicle launch center and with manufacturing to speed product development. This program was so successful that in 2000 GM announced that its North American car and truck operating groups would be consolidated into one new manufacturing group.

A major part of GM's new efficiency program was to build new state-of-the-art assembly plants and close down old, inefficient ones. In 2000, GM started to build a $1 billion new vehicle manufacturing plant in Lansing, Michigan, that utilizes the most advanced flexible manufacturing configurations and technologies to help GM raise its quality nearer to that of its Japanese competitors. The new plant consists of three buildings, covering 2.4 million square feet, and vehicle production began in 2005. GM also finally closed its Oldsmobile division in 2004.

The result of all these efforts was that GM improved its productivity more than any of its other U.S. competitors in 1991 and surpassed DaimlerChrysler's productivity in North America. GM claims that once its new plants and technology come online, it will equal both Japanese productivity and quality by 2010.

New Supply Chain

Finding more cost-effective ways to manage its supply chain has also been a major part of GM's strategy in the last decade. In developing its unsuccessful line of new models in the 1980s, GM learned the need to standardize components across models and to reduce the number of parts needed to produce a car, thereby reducing costs and speeding product development. Smith directed GM's engineers to work to reduce the number of parts used to make a car's basic metal frame by one-third, something that customers would not see.

However, GM also began to change the way it managed relationships with suppliers. In 1992, GM obtained 57 percent of its parts from its own component divisions, compared with Chrysler's 30 percent and Toyota's 5 percent. GM's car assembly divisions were locked into own "allied plant" suppliers such as Central Foundry for casting, Delco for brakes, and so on. In 1993, GM introduced a new strategy so that its in-house parts operations would no longer be protected from efficient outside suppliers.

To help suppliers reduce costs, GM followed Toyota and implemented a Purchased Input Concept Optimization with Suppliers (PICOS) strategy, where teams of GM engineers visit supplier plants and work with suppliers to reduce costs. However, with the program up and running GM, unlike Toyota, began to bargain hard with its suppliers to get lower component prices. It started to give one supplier's plans to other suppliers to get lower prices from them, essentially trading off one against the other, and made them rebid contracts year by year to try to get them to lower their bids. This angered outside suppliers, who advised GM that if it bought mainly on price they would not invest money to improve the components that GM wanted them to make and would move their business to Ford, Chrysler, and Japanese companies operating inside the United States. As a result, GM had to rethink its aggressive strategy.

GM also extended its supply chain management program globally and began to develop hundreds of alliances with overseas parts manufacturers to produce components that could be used in its cars assembled around the world. For example, GM formed a joint venture with a Hungarian company to build axles and diesel engines for assembly in cars sold under the Opel name throughout Western Europe. The next major development in the supply chain management process took place in 2000 when GM, Ford, and Daimler-Chrysler announced they would form an organization called Covisint to coordinate their purchase of standardized car components through the Internet. Billed as the world's largest virtual marketplace, Covisint

gives large carmakers considerable power over global suppliers, which essentially are forced to compete to obtain the Big Three's business. However, at the same time this presents the opportunity to create economies of scale in producing many kinds of components.

At the same time, however, Japanese carmakers established many factories inside the United States, and they also created networks of efficient high-quality component suppliers that have allowed them to maintain high productivity and quality. U.S. carmakers are still in a "catch up" position. Toyota, for example, was the first to launch a joint program with its suppliers to radically reduce the number of steps needed to make components and car parts; it saw costs fall by $2.6 billion. Toyota also created an integrated, flexible, global manufacturing system based on assembly plants from Indonesia to Argentina, which are designed both to customize cars for local markets and to shift production to quickly satisfy any increases in demand in any market worldwide. This also is a way Toyota can keep costs low because this avoids the need to build more plants—which cost over $1 billion to build today. (Recall how GM's new plants each cost over $1 billion.)

In the 2000s, GM introduced a new initiative to reduce costs, its Global Manufacturing System (GMS), which is being implemented across all GM facilities worldwide to standardize its approach to making cars. To implement its new system, GM drastically changed its hundreds of old IT legacy systems and chose a standardized platform that links all its car plants directly to its chain of global suppliers to improve the efficiency of its global supply chain management. This was one of the major reasons for the jump in its productivity in North America. Also, it explains why in 2001–2002 GM became the best-performing domestic manufacturer in initial quality by J.D. Power Associates. GM had fourteen top three performing vehicles, including three that were ranked first in their market segments.

With IT continually advancing, it is necessary for carmakers to keep up with their suppliers in the design and manufacture of car parts. The current trend in the car industry is to develop strong relationships with Tier One parts suppliers, which are able to collaborate and improve the quality and lower the cost of vehicle components or modules that are assembled into the final vehicle. As carmakers seek to lower costs and increase quantity, they are increasingly requiring their primary or first-tier suppliers to take on the cost of creating the car modules that otherwise carmakers would have to do themselves. For example, after GM spun off its auto-parts division, Delphi, to reduce costs, it outsourced assembly of car modules to suppliers like Delphi because they have the ability to make these modules cheaper than GM. If this trend of outsourcing component and module development to suppliers continues, barriers to entry will shrink as carmakers become more like car designers, and component suppliers become more and more like car manufacturers.

Structural Changes

Side-by-side with changes to its production and supply chain operations, GM also radically altered its corporate structure. Starting in 1990, GM realized the need to streamline its operations and to decentralize decision making and to integrate its design and manufacturing operations. In 1992, it consolidated its 9 engine groups into 5 and brought together its divisional engineering and manufacturing units to eliminate redundancy. Also, 5 different design and technical departments at GM's Technical Center were combined into 3 to speed product development. GM also created a new product design system to provide strong single point management of a vehicle program and to accelerate the vehicle development process. GM's goal was to achieve economies of scale through integrating and coordinating its functional activities in product development, engineering, manufacturing, and marketing around the world. In this way it could avoid unnecessary duplication of activities between divisions and facilitate the sharing and learning about cost-saving processes and quality innovations across divisions and countries. Restructuring has led to more flexible decision making, better use of resources, an increase in management accountability, and an improved ability to serve its customers.

Promoting innovation is also a key element of GM's strategy, in particular the need to improve vehicle design and engineering, develop new models to target profitable market segments, and to provide high-margin add-on vehicle accessories, such as its OnStar service, to increase the profit made on each car sale. Cooperation between the United States and Europe became vital to achieve these goals in the 1990s because GM's engineers must share resources and best practices to develop a wide range of vehicles in order to suit many different customer needs

from the six vehicle platforms GM now has. Fewer platforms significantly reduce costs as discussed earlier. In addition, the industry average development time for new cars has gone down from five years in 1990 to three years by the late 1990s, and today some companies like Toyota are able to develop a new car within eighteen months—a major competitive advantage that GM is striving to copy.

To permit such integration, GM changed its global organizational structure and adopted the global matrix structure shown in Exhibit 1. The vertical axis consists of GM's five main business units and the four world regions in which GM operates, that is, North America, Europe, Asia-Pacific, and Latin America, Africa, and the Middle East. The fifth business unit is GM's Financial Services Division which is responsible for financing the sale of GM's cars throughout the world.

On the horizontal axis are the main value chain activities required to efficiently orchestrate the global production of its cars: supply chain management, product development, production, customer experience or marketing, and business services. Where the axes intersect are found the hundreds of assembly plants and engineering facilities that belong to a specific GM car division such as Cadillac, Buick, and so on, but while each car division operates as an independent entity, at the same time it is embedded in the global value-chain organization GM needs to compete against its highly efficient global rivals.

For example, GM created a new Vehicle Engineering Center at its Warren, Michigan, Technical Center campus to harmonize product engineering across all its car divisions. The 2.2-million square foot facility houses eight thousand employees and further enhances the collaboration between the engineering, design, and manufacturing groups as they work with the car divisions and managers in its global business units to create the cars that customers want.

The Role of IT

IT plays a vital part in helping GM implement its new global organizational structure. IT provides the integration necessary to manage the enormously complex transactions required to operate global assembly and value chain activities using a matrix structure. Using software and consultancy services from IBM, GM has harmonized all its IT systems across the company. All its divisions and business activities are now seamlessly

EXHIBIT 1

GM's Global Matrix Structure

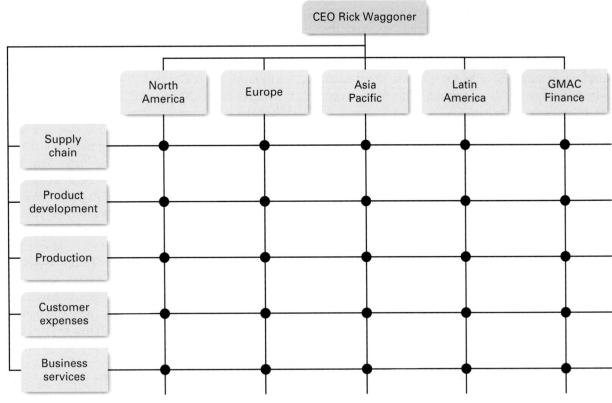

● GM assembly, design, and operating units located in countries around the world.

interconnected, and no conversion work has to be done to transmit information from one GM facility to another anywhere in the world.

IT has helped GM better implement its business model in many ways. First, it has permitted fast global coordination in design and engineering development. Engineers can share information globally real-time, and this has reduced costs and lessened the duplication of work by engineers in different research areas. Second, it has increased the efficiency of GM's supply chain operations, for example, in 2004 GM was able to cut its material costs by 3 percent in North America and by 3.5 percent in Europe. Third, GM's new Internet-enabled IT has helped it lower the costs of value creation in many ways. For example, using the new IT, GM reduced the costs associated with communicating with its thousands of U.S. car dealers by $25 million in 2000. In another initiative GM created **GMsupplypower.com** in 2001 which gives suppliers an online window into GM's future production plans and allows them to better manage inventory, overtime, and freight costs.

GM Exits Many Businesses

As discussed earlier GM bought several large companies in the 1980s to promote its efficiency and effectiveness. GM did receive some benefits from this; for example, in 1994 its Hughes Electronics Division developed the OnStar technology that has helped GM differentiate its cars, a system that today it also licenses to other carmakers. The OnStar system is an in-vehicle safety, security, and information system that provides automatic notifications of airbag releases, stolen vehicles, assistance and access to emergency service providers, and remote entry. Hughes also introduced DIRECTV—the first high-quality direct satellite TV distribution system in the United States.

However, GM recognized that it was not obtaining the synergies it had expected, and it was fortunate in that EDS and Hughes, as a result of the escalation in stock prices during the 1990s, were worth many times what it had paid for them. Consequently it began the process of selling off the companies. In 1996, EDS was officially split off from GM and later divested. In 2004, GM sold its Hughes DIRECTV operations to News Corp., the entertainment and media company. GM used the proceeds from both sales to fund its company pension plan and to invest in its new global vehicles.

During the 1990s, GM also began to sell off some of its vehicle-building assets. In 1998, signaling its intention to vertically disintegrate, GM announced that it would spin off its Delphi electronics unit through an initial public offering of Delphi stock, and the company was spun off in 1999. In 1999, GM sold its defense unit, which built light armored vehicles (LAVs) to General Dynamics Corporation. On the other hand, in 2001 GM announced it was entering the collision repair business with the introduction of the Goodwrench auto body center program, and it established a nationwide chain of body shops to take advantage of the high-profit margin repair business.

Global Expansion

In the 1990s, watching the Japanese carmakers expand into Europe and North America, GM realized it needed to take steps to bolster its global presence. Recall that GM had early expanded into Europe, Canada, and Australia to take advantage of these large markets. As discussed earlier, GM now had the goal of learning Japanese lean-manufacturing techniques. In 1996, GM formed joint ventures with Japanese companies Isuzu Motors and Suzuki to learn Japanese lean-manufacturing techniques and to establish jointly owned facilities to make specialized kinds of vehicle engines and transmissions for specific market segments, such as the European diesel engine market. GM also took a minority equity stake in these ventures. In 2000, GM also acquired a 20 percent equity stake in Fuji, the manufacturer of Subaru brand vehicles. A strategic alliance with Honda was also established.

While Japan was an important market, GM also realized the need to strengthen its presence in the rapidly developing Chinese and Eastern European markets. In 2002, GM formed an alliance with a Russian company to produce a line of low-cost Chevrolets tailored to the needs of customers in Eastern Europe. After several years of cooperation with Chinese companies, in 2001 GM's new assembly plant in Shanghai, China, began production of the Regal economy car for the Chinese market. All global makers were rushing to seize a share of this market that they hoped would prove profitable in the future.

In Europe, too, GM took steps to compete against DaimlerChrysler, BMW, and Ford which had acquired the U.K. carmaker Jaguar and Sweden's Volvo after a bidding war with GM. In 2000, GM acquired Saab, and it also bought a 20 percent stake in Fiat and an option to buy the whole company later. The Fiat alliance was ill-fated, however, because in 2005 GM had to pay $2 billion to terminate its option to buy the troubled company. Its Saab operation also proved to be an expensive acquisition and lost hundreds of millions of dollars. In the meantime, GM's established European Brands like Opel, its German subsidiary, and Vauxhall, its British unit, were also struggling to compete effectively against Ford, the largest European manufacturer; Japanese companies that now had established operations within the European Union; and Renault, which had bought a controlling interest in struggling Japanese company Nissan in 2000. However, after installing a star Renault manager to head its Japanese subsidiary, Nissan's performance soared, and the company became a major competitor in all global markets.

Watching its competitors enter China, potentially the largest market in the world, in 2000 GM also decided to acquire the car operations of Korean conglomerate Daewoo to help it enter the Asian and Chinese markets. It also opened a new car assembly complex in Brazil, utilizing state-of-the-art modular assembly techniques to produce cars for the rapidly growing South American market. Similar assembly plants were opened in Thailand and in Germany as part of its program to extend the learning it was gaining from its global matrix operations. Meanwhile, the joint venture between GM and Shanghai Automotive Industry Corporation led to its launch of the Buick Sail, the first modern family car built in China. Also, the Chevrolet Cruze developed by GM and its alliance partner Suzuki, the first GM vehicle to be built in Japan since the 1930s, was launched in 2001.

To build competitive advantage in Europe, GM built a new facility at Russelsheim, Germany, which allows its Opel division to assemble up to four different vehicle models on a three-shift, flexible line system with a total capacity of 270,000 vehicles a year. In Mexico GM's new plants led to record sales of 230,636 vehicles in 2002. Holden, GM's Australian automotive division, also announced vehicle sales in 2002 that reached an all-time record. Holden was the Australian industry's sales leader for the second straight year.

Although GM has been strengthening its global operations in these many ways, its problem is that it still has had to meet the challenge of its global competitors, and it has had mixed success. In Europe, for example, the new vehicles made by its Vauxhall and Opel divisions have had mixed success against Ford and Volkswagen's new vehicles and against upscale sedan makers such as BMW, Volvo, and Mercedes. GM has no luxury sedan to compete in this important upscale market. All global carmakers have been working to improve their efficiency and design profitable niche models, and even in China competition is intense as all major global carmakers are competing head to head, which lowers profit margins.

Brands and Marketing

Finding the right way to brand and market its cars has been one of GM's biggest problems in the last decade as global competition increased. Its problems with its Cadillac and Oldsmobile divisions were discussed earlier. Since 2000, GM has moved to focus its resources on new models of cars and trucks, and each of its car and truck divisions, including Saturn and GMC Truck, have a separate marketing strategy to differentiate its vehicles.

GM's Chevrolet division became a keystone of its plan to increase its truck sales around the world, and GM is investing hundreds of millions to promote its brand name since the cost of developing a new brand from scratch today would cost billions. The Chevrolet name has equity in many parts of the world, and GM began a big push in the 1990s to develop the trucks and SUVs that are the mainstay of Chevrolet's reputation. Today, however, these market segments are saturated and so GM plans to spend its resources producing new sedans and niche vehicles targeted toward more specific market segments.

As a part of this push, in 1999 GM signed an agreement to acquire exclusive rights to the Hummer automotive brand from AM General Corp. It also entered an agreement with XM Satellite Radio to introduce its services into its vehicles and package it

with its OnStar service, which is now standard on most GM models. OnStar had over 1 million subscribers by 2003. In 2000, GM also created a new diversity marketing and sales organization to focus on the women's market and the growing markets of African-American, Hispanic-American, and Asian-American customers in the United States to meet the needs of these niche markets.

As noted earlier, in the beginning of the 1990s GM decentralized control of product design to its Cadillac division and instructed it to reestablish its place as a luxury brand. The Cadillac division developed a bold exterior and interior Cadillac design, the CTS, a radical departure from traditional Cadillac styling, and has since introduced a series of vehicles that all possess this new style, the latest being its convertible sports car introduced in 2004. These moves have helped Cadillac become GM's most profitable car division in North America, and its sales are currently the highest they have been for a decade. However, other GM brands have not fared so well. Oldsmobile is gone. The Saturn division experienced declining sales in the 1990s because its models were aging, and the success of its new ones remains to be seen. In 2002, GM announced it would end production of its Chevrolet Camaro and Pontiac Firebird and discontinue the Camaro and Firebird models because of the loss of this market niche to competitors such as Ford, Nissan, and Toyota. In 2003, GM announced that its entire midsize car portfolio in North America would be revamped over the next three years, focusing on fewer yet stronger "nameplates" or on its premium brands. GM's strategy was to introduce ten new or restyled midsize vehicles between 2003 and 2006 to strengthen its product line. To support its efforts, GM spent $2.4 billion on intensive marketing campaigns in national media outlets in 2003 and has spent the same or more in each year since.

GM also began a major customer relations management program that led to 1.5 million more vehicles being sold in 2004 than in 2003. This program was designed to show U.S. customers cars made inside the United States are equal in quality to those that are imported, and in fact, three of its new midsize and full-size cars received top quality ratings. GM's goal was to encourage people to try out their cars, for example, by allowing them to take home one of its cars for the weekend and test drive it to experience its superior quality.

New Leadership but Same Old Problems

In 2000, GM also went through a change in leadership when Rick Wagoner became its new CEO with Jack Smith remaining as chairman of the board. Also, Gary L. Cowger was elected group vice president and president, GM North America, and he assumed control of GM's North American vehicle operations. A thirty-six-year veteran of GM, Cowger's previous assignments include president, GM de Mexico; group vice president in charge of global manufacturing; and CEO of GM's Opel division. In 2003, Rick Wagoner became chairman and CEO following the retirement of Chairman Jack Smith, and Cowger is next in line to assume control of the company.

Its new leaders all have an extensive background in global operations that has helped promote GM's rapid global revival. However, they still have to deal with GM's huge problems because of the legacies of its past. During the 1960s and 1970s, GM's high profitability and dominance of the U.S. car market meant that the company had little incentive to resist its trade unions' demands for ever higher pay and benefits. Shareholders, managers, and workers were all enjoying rising prosperity. When the Japanese put an end to this fortunate situation, GM, like Ford and Chrysler, found itself saddled with strict union rules that prevented it from laying off employees or closing down facilities quickly, as well as huge health care and pension liabilities to its former and current employees—something that has been estimated at over $45 billion. GM also pays its current work force much more than its competitors. In benefits, for example, GM pays an average of $35 for each employee's pension and medical costs compared with the $11 Toyota pays for the same benefits.

It has been estimated that the costs of paying these pensions and benefits gives Toyota and Honda, which have no such problems, a cost advantage of about $1,500 a car. However, GM cannot charge a $1,500 premium for its cars and, indeed, has to charge less than its stronger competitors, so its profit margins are extremely low, and it sells many of its vehicles at a loss. In 2004, GM's return on sales was 1.5 percent, which was considerably less than Toyota's 6.8 percent. Although Toyota's revenues are 33 percent lower than GM's, its net earnings are 60 percent higher. Toyota's ROIC was almost 6 percent in 2004, while GM's was 1 percent, Ford's .6 percent, and DaimlerChrysler was a negative .5 percent.

The principal reason why GM makes any ROIC is because of the profitability of its financing division, GMAC, which has earned the company billions and allowed it to remain profitable even though its *total* vehicle operations have been making a loss. GM makes most of its profit on financing the sale of its vehicles to customers, rather than on actually making the vehicle itself. And intense competition and the recession of the early 1990s led GM to begin its zero-percent financing program and to offer rebates to undercut competitors. However, GM's strategic move to gain market share resulted in a price war when other car companies, such as Ford and Honda, also began price discounting and special offers to match GM. Similarly, GM is in a discounting war with Volkswagen in Germany.

GM was forced into its discounting strategy because it has considerable excess capacity and makes many more cars than it can profitably sell. Indeed, it has been estimated that there is 20 percent overcapacity in the car industry as a whole, which makes price wars more likely. In order to get its cars off the lot and protect its market share, GM must discount its cars. Although the profitability of each car sale is low, GM claims that 67 percent of its customers return and buy a second GM vehicle, which is the highest loyalty rate in the industry. Therefore, if overcapacity falls and prices rise in the next decade as carmakers continue to prune and simplify their global operations this will help GM's bottom line considerably. No carmaker boasts such a large installed base of customers. GM sells 9 million vehicles annually, and each of these new vehicles represents a potential opportunity to generate future profits from maintaining customer relationships, from its OnStar system or Goodwrench repair centers.

In the 2000s, however, the bad news for GM has been that Japanese automakers have been rapidly introducing new and improved SUVs and trucks, and GM is having to fight back to maintain its sales in this area. Since this also threatens Ford, price wars may develop in this market segment, too, which would be a severe blow to GM. GM also needs to look closely at the need to introduce hybrid and fuel-efficient cars to maintain its market share and profitability given that many hybrid SUVs, sedans, and even trucks were being introduced in the mid 2000s. GM placed its bet on hydrogen fuel-cell technology, but this technology is far from practical. In the meantime, Toyota's gas/electric hybrid technology has become the industry standard, and Toyota licenses this technology to other carmakers. For example, Ford introduced vehicles using this system in 2005. This segment will only become more important in the future if the high oil prices of the mid 2000s continue.

Thus, GM's fight continues, and global carmakers are all locked in a battle to develop the right kinds of vehicles to meet changing customer needs all around the globe. U.S. carmakers are catching up, but the question is can they catch up with Japanese carmakers that have so far maintained their first mover advantage by striving to be one step ahead of their competitors.

The Comeback of Caterpillar, 1985–2002

This case was prepared by Isaac Cohen, San Jose State University.

For three consecutive years, 1982, 1983, and 1984, the Caterpillar Company lost $1 million a day. Caterpillar's major competitor was a formidable Japanese company called Komatsu. Facing a tough global challenge, the collapse of its international markets, and an overvalued dollar, Caterpillar had no choice. It had to reinvent itself, or die.

Caterpillar managed to come back as a high-tech, globally competitive, growth company. Over a period of fifteen years, and throughout the tenure of two CEOs—George Schaefer (1985–1990) and Donald Fites (1990–1999)—Caterpillar had transformed itself. George Schaefer introduced cost-cutting measures and employee involvement programs; outsourced machines, parts, and components; and began modernizing Caterpillar's plants. Donald Fites diversified Caterpillar's product line and reorganized the company structurally. He also completed Caterpillar's plant modernization program, revitalized Caterpillar's dealership network, and altered radically Caterpillar's approach to labor relations.

As Donald Fites retired in February 1999, Glen Barton was elected CEO. Barton was in an enviable position. The world's largest manufacturer of construction and mining equipment, and a Fortune 100 company, Caterpillar generated $21 billion in revenues in 1998,

the sixth consecutive record year. Leading its industry while competing globally, Caterpillar recorded a $1.5 billion profit in 1998, the second best ever.[1]

Notwithstanding Caterpillar's dramatic comeback, Barton could not count on the continual prosperity of the company because the U.S. construction industry was moving into a grinding economic downturn. At the time Barton completed his first year as CEO, on February 1, 2000, the company announced its 1999 result: sales declined by 6 percent and earnings by 37 percent. In March 2000, Caterpillar share price was trading close to its fifty-two-week low ($36 against a high of $66), and one industry analyst declared, "The stock for the foreseeable future is dead money."[2]

What should Barton do? Should Barton follow the strategies implemented by Schaefer and Fites to enhance Caterpillar's competitive position relative to its principal rivals, Komatsu, John Deere, and CNH Global? (CNH was the product of a 2000 merger between the Case Corp. and New Holland.) Should he, instead, reverse some of the policies introduced by his predecessors? Or should he, rather, undertake whole new strategies altogether?

To assess Barton's strategic choices in improving Caterpillar's results, the case looks back at the experience of his two predecessors. How precisely did both Schaefer and Fites manage to turn Caterpillar around?

This case was presented at the October 2001 meeting of the North American Case Research Association (NACRA) at Sedona, AZ. Copyright © 2001 by Isaac Cohen and NACRA. Reprinted by permission. All rights reserved. For the most recent financial results of the company discussed in this case, go to **http://finance.yahoo.com**, input the company's stock symbol, and download the latest company report from its homepage.

The Heavy Construction Equipment Industry

The heavy construction equipment industry supplied engineering firms, construction companies, and mine operators. The industry's typical product line included

EXHIBIT 1

Global Demand of Heavy Construction Equipment
by Major Categories, 1985–2005

Item	1985	1994	2000	2005*
Earthmoving Equipment	50%	49%	49%	49%
Off Highway Trucks	8%	7%	7%	7%
Construction Cranes	9%	11%	10%	10%
Mixers, Pavers, and Related Equipment	6%	6%	7%	7%
Parts and Attachments	27%	27%	27%	26%
	—	—	—	—
Total Demand (billions)	$38	$56	$72	$90

Source: Andrew Gross and David Weiss, "Industry Corner: The Global Demand for Heavy Construction Equipment," *Business Economics,* July 1996, p. 56.

*Percentages do not add up to 100 because of rounding.

earthmovers (bulldozers, loaders, and excavators), road building machines (pavers, motor graders, and mixers), mining related equipment (off-highway trucks, mining shovels), and large cranes. Most machines were offered in a broad range of sizes, and a few were available with a choice of wheels or crawler tracks. Most were used for the construction of buildings, power plants, manufacturing plants, and infra-structure projects such as roads, airports, bridges, tunnels, dams, sewage systems, and water lines. On a global basis, earthmoving equipment accounted for about half of the industry's total sales in the 1990s (Exhibit 1). Among earthmovers, hydraulic excavators accounted for 45 percent of the sales. Excavators were more productive, more versatile, and easier to use in tight spaces than either bulldozers or loaders. Off-highway trucks that hauled minerals, rocks, and dirt were another category of fast-selling equipment.[3]

Global demand for heavy construction machinery grew at a steady rate of 4.5 percent in the 1990s. The rate of growth, however, was faster among the developing nations of Asia, Africa, and Latin America than among the developed nations. In the early 2000s, North America and Europe were each expected to account for 25 percent of the industry's sales, Japan for 20 percent, and the developing nations for the remaining 30 percent.[4]

The distinction between original equipment and replacement parts was an essential feature of the industry. Replacement parts and "attachments" (work tools) made up together over a quarter of the total revenues of the heavy construction equipment industry (Exhibit 1), but accounted for a substantially larger share of the industry's earnings for two reasons: First, the sale of replacement parts was more profitable than that of whole machines; and second, the market for replacement parts was less cyclical than that for original equipment.[5] As a rule of thumb, the economic life of a heavy construction machine was 10 to 12 years, but in many cases, especially in developing countries, equipment users kept their machines in service much longer, perhaps 20 to 30 years, thus creating an ongoing stream of revenues for parts, components, and related services.[6]

Another characteristic of the industry was the need to achieve economies of scale. According to industry observers, the optimal scale of operation was about 90,000 units annually, in other words, up to a production level of 90,000 units a year. Average equipment unit cost declined as output increased, and therefore capturing a large market share was critical for benefiting from economies of scale.[7] The relatively low volume of global sales—200,000 to 300,000 earthmoving equipment units per year (1996)[8]—further intensified competition over market share among the industry's leading firms.

Successful marketing also played an important role in gaining competitive advantage. A widespread distribution and service network had always been essential for competing in the heavy construction equipment industry because "downtime" resulting from the inability to operate the equipment at a construction site was very costly. Typically, manufacturers used a worldwide network of dealerships to sell machines, provide support, and offer after-sales service. Dealerships were independent, company owned, or both, and were normally organized on an exclusive territorial basis. Since heavy construction machines operated in a tough and inhospitable environment, equipment wore out and broke down frequently, parts needed to be rebuilt or replaced often, and therefore manufacturers placed dealers in close proximity to equipment users, building a global service network that spread all over the world.

Manufacturers built alliances as well. Intense competition over market share drove the industry's top firms to form three types of cooperative agreements. The first were full-scale joint ventures to share production. Caterpillar's joint venture with Mitsubishi Heavy Industries was a notable case in point. The second were technology sharing agreements between equipment manufacturers and engine makers to ensure access to the latest engine technology. The joint venture between Komatsu and Cummins Engine, on the one hand, and the Case Corporation and Cummins, on the other, provided two examples. The third type of agreements were technology sharing alliances between major global firms and local manufacturers whereby the former gained access to new markets, and in return, supplied the latter with advanced technology. Caterpillar utilized such an arrangement with Shanghai Diesel in China, and Komatsu did so with the BEML Company in India.[9]

History of Caterpillar

At the turn of the century, farmers in California faced a serious problem. Using steam tractors to plow the fine delta land of the San Joaquin valley, California farmers fitted their tractors with large drive wheels to provide support on the moist soil; nevertheless, despite their efforts, the steamer's huge wheels— measuring up to 9 feet high—sank deeply into the soil. In 1904, Benjamin Holt, a combine maker from Stockton, California, solved the problem by replacing the wheels with a track, thereby distributing the tractor's weight on a broader surface. Holt, in addition, replaced the heavy steam engine with a gasoline engine, thus improving the tractor's mobility further by reducing its weight (a steam tractor weighed up to

20 tons). He nicknamed the tractor "Caterpillar," acquired the Caterpillar trademark, and applied it to several crawler-type machines that his company manufactured and sold. By 1915, Holt tractors were sold in twenty countries.[10]

Outside agriculture, crawler tractors were first used by the military. In 1915, the British military invented the armor tank, modeling it after Holt's machine, and during World War I, the United States and its allies in Europe utilized Holt's track-type tractors to haul artillery and supply wagons. In 1925, the Holt Company merged with another California firm, the Best Tractor Company, to form Caterpillar (Cat). Shortly thereafter, Caterpillar moved its corporate headquarters and manufacturing plants to Peoria, Illinois. The first company to introduce a diesel engine on a moving vehicle (1931), Caterpillar discontinued its combine manufacturing during the 1930s and focused instead on the production of road-building, construction, logging, and pipe laying equipment. During World War II, Caterpillar served as the primary supplier of bulldozers to the U.S. Army; its sales volume more than tripled between 1941 and 1944 to include motor graders, diesel engines, and electric generators, apart from tractors and wagons.[11]

Demand for Caterpillar products exploded in the early post war years. Cat's equipment was used to reconstruct Europe, build the U.S. interstate highway system, erect the giant dams of the Third World, and lay out the major airports of the world. The company managed to differentiate itself from its competitors by producing reliable, durable, and high-quality equipment, offering a quick after-sales service, and providing a speedy delivery of replacement parts. As a result, during the 1950s and 1960s, Caterpillar had emerged as the uncontested leader of the heavy construction equipment industry, far ahead of any rival. By 1965, Caterpillar had established foreign manufacturing subsidiaries—either wholly owned or joint ventures—in Britain, Canada, Australia, Brazil, France, Mexico, Belgium, India, and Japan. Caterpillar's fifty/fifty joint venture with Mitsubishi in Japan, established in 1963, had become one of the most successful, stable, and enduring alliances among all American-Japanese joint ventures.[12]

Caterpillar's distribution and dealership network also contributed to the company's worldwide success. From the outset, the company's marketing organization rested on a dense network of independent dealers who sold and serviced Cat equipment. Strategically located throughout the world, these dealers were self-sustaining entrepreneurs who invested their own capital in their business, derived close to 100 percent of their revenues from selling and supporting Cat equipment, and cultivated close relationships with Caterpillar customers. On average, a Caterpillar dealership had remained in the hands of the same family—or company—for over fifty years. Indeed, some dealerships, including several located overseas, pre-dated the 1925 merger that gave birth to Caterpillar.[13] In 1981, on the eve of the impending crisis, the combined net worth of Cat dealers equaled that of the company itself, and the total number of employees working for Cat dealers was slightly lower than the company's own workforce.[14]

The Crisis of the Early 1980s

Facing weak competition both at home and abroad, Caterpillar charged premium prices for its high-quality products, paid its production workers union-scale wages, offered its shareholders high rates of return on their equity, and enjoyed superior profits. Then, in 1982, following a record year of sales and profits, Caterpillar suddenly plunged into three successive years of rising losses totaling nearly $1 billion. "Quite frankly, our long years of success made us complacent, even arrogant,"[15] Pierre Guerindon, an executive vice president at Cat conceded.

The crisis of 1982–1984 stemmed from three sources: a global recession, a costly strike, and unfavorable currency exchange rates. First, the steady growth in demand for construction machinery, dating back to 1945, came to an end in 1980, as highway construction in the United States slowed down to a halt while declining oil prices depressed the worldwide market for mining, logging, and pipe laying equipment. Second, Caterpillar's efforts to freeze wages and reduce overall labor cost triggered a seven-month strike (1982–1983) among its U.S. employees. Led by the United Auto Workers (UAW) union, the strike accounted for a sizable portion of the company's three-year loss. The third element in Caterpillar's crisis was a steep rise in the value of the dollar (relative to the Yen and other currencies) that made U.S. exports more expensive abroad and U.S. imports (shipped by Caterpillar's competitors) cheaper at home. "The strong dollar is a prime factor in Caterpillar's reduced sales and earning … [and]

is undermining manufacturing industries in the United States,"[16] said Cat's annual reports for 1982 and 1984.

Taking advantage of the expensive dollar, Komatsu Limited had emerged as Caterpillar's principal rival. Komatsu ("little pine tree" in Japanese) had initially produced construction machinery for the Japanese and Asian markets, then sought to challenge Caterpillar's dominance in the markets of Latin America and Europe, and eventually penetrated the United States to rival Caterpillar in its domestic market. Attacking Caterpillar head-on, Komatsu issued a battle cry, *Maru C*, meaning "encircle Cat." Launching a massive drive to improve quality while reducing costs, Komatsu achieved a 50 percent labor productivity advantage over Caterpillar, and, in turn, underpriced Caterpillar's products by as much 30 percent. The outcome was a dramatic change in market share. Between 1979 and 1984, Komatsu global market share more than doubled to 25 percent while Caterpillar's fell by almost a quarter to 43 percent.[17]

Turnaround: George Schaefer's Caterpillar, 1985–1990

Competition with Komatsu and the crisis of 1982–1984 forced Caterpillar to reexamine its past activities. Caterpillar's new CEO (1985), George Schaefer, was a congenial manager who encouraged Cat executives to openly admit the company's past mistakes. "We have experienced a fundamental change in our business—it will never again be what it was," Schaefer said as he became CEO. "We have no choice but to respond, and respond vigorously, to the new world in which we find ourselves."[18] Under Schaefer's direction, Caterpillar devised and implemented a series of strategies that touched upon every important function of the company, including purchasing, manufacturing, marketing, personnel, and labor relations.

Global Outsourcing

Traditionally, Caterpillar functioned as a vertically integrated company that relied heavily on in-house production. To ensure product quality as well as an uninterrupted supply of parts, Cat self-produced two-thirds of its parts and components, and assembled practically all of its finished machines. Under the new policy of "shopping around the world," Caterpillar sought to purchase parts and components from low-cost suppliers who maintained high quality standards. Working closely with its suppliers, Caterpillar moved toward the goal of outsourcing 80 percent of its parts and components.[19]

An additional goal of the policy was branding, that is, the purchase of final products for resale. Through its branding program, Caterpillar sold outsourced machines under its own brand name, taking advantage of its superior marketing organization and keeping production costs down. Beginning in the mid 1980s, Cat contracted to buy lift trucks from a Norwegian company, hydraulic excavators from a West German manufacturer, paving machines from an Oklahoma corporation, off-highway trucks from a British firm, and logging equipment from a Canadian company, and resell them all under the Cat nameplate. Ordinarily, Caterpillar outsourced product manufacturing but not product design. By keeping control over the design of many of its outsourced products, Caterpillar managed to retain in-house design capability, and ensure quality control.[20]

Broader Product Line

For nearly a decade, the DC10 bulldozer had served as Caterpillar's signature item. It stood 15 feet tall, weighed 73 tons, and sold for more than $500,000 (1988). It had no competitors. But as demand for highway construction projects dwindled, Caterpillar needed to reevaluate its product mix because heavy equipment was no longer selling well. Sales of light construction equipment, on the other hand, were fast increasing. Between 1984 and 1987, accordingly, Caterpillar doubled its product line from 150 to 300 models of equipment, introducing many small machines that ranged from farm tractors to backhoe loaders (multipurpose light bulldozers), and diversified its customer base. Rather than focusing solely on large clients, that is, multinational engineering and construction firms like the Bechtel corporation—a typical user of heavy bulldozers—Cat began marketing its lightweight machines to a new category of customers: small-scale owner operators and emerging contractors. Still, the shift in Cat's product mix had a clear impact on the company's bottom line. Unlike the heavy equipment market where profit margins were wide, intense competition in the market for light products kept margins slim and pitted Caterpillar against John Deere and the Case corporation, the light equipment market leaders.[21]

Labor Relations

To compete successfully, Caterpillar also needed to repair its relationship with the union. In 1979, following the expiration of its collective bargaining agreement, Caterpillar experienced an eighty-day strike, and three years later, in 1982, contract negotiations erupted in a 205-day strike, the longest companywide work stoppage in the UAW history.[22] Named CEO in 1985, George Schaefer led the next two rounds of contract negotiations.

Schaefer's leadership style was consensual. By contrast to the autocratic style of his predecessors, Schaefer advocated the free flow of ideas between officers, managers, and production workers, and he promoted open communication at all levels of the company. A low-key CEO who often answered his own phone, Schaefer possessed exceptional people skills. Asked to evaluate Schaefer's performance, John Stark, editor of *Off Highway Ledger*, a trade journal, said, "Schaefer is probably the best manager the construction machinery industry has ever had."[23]

Schaefer's social skills led to a significant improvement in Cat's relations with the UAW. Not a single strike broke out over contract negotiations during Schaefer's tenure; on the contrary, each cycle of bargaining was settled peacefully. Under Schaefer's direction, furthermore, the union agreed to reduce the number of labor grades and job classifications and to streamline seniority provisions—a move that enhanced management flexibility in job assignment and facilitated the cross utilization of employees.[24] More important, improved labor relations contributed to the success of two programs that played a critical role in Caterpillar's turnaround strategy, namely, an employee involvement plan based on teamwork and a reengineering effort of plant modernization and automation.

Employee Involvement

An industrywide union famous for its cooperative labor-management efforts at the Saturn corporation, the NUMMI plant (a GM-Toyota joint-venture in Fremont, California), and elsewhere, the UAW lent its support to Caterpillar's employee involvement program. Called the Employee Satisfaction Process (ESP), and launched by Schaefer in 1986, the program was voluntary. ESP members were organized in work teams, met weekly with management, and offered suggestions that pertained to many critical aspects of the manufacturing process, including production management, workplace layout, and quality enhancement. Implemented in a growing number of U.S. plants, the program resulted (1990) in productivity gains, quality improvements, and increased employee satisfaction. At the Cat plant in Aurora, Illinois, for example, the local ESP chairman recalled that the ESP program "changed everything: the worker had some say over his job … [and t]op management was very receptive. We zeroed in on quality, anything to make the customer happy." Management credited the ESP teams at Aurora with a steep fall in the rate of absenteeism, a sharp decline in the number of union grievances filed, and cost savings totaling $10 million.[25] At another ESP plant, a Cat assembly-line worker told a *Fortune* reporter in 1988: "Five years ago the foreman wouldn't even listen to you, never mind the general foreman or plant supervisor. . . . Now everyone will listen." Caterpillar applied the ESP program to outside suppliers as well. Typically, ESP teams made up of Caterpillar machinists visited suppliers' plants to check and certify equipment quality. The certified vendors received preferential treatment, mostly in the form of reduced inspection, counting, and other controls. Only 0.6 percent of the parts delivered by certified suppliers were rejected by Caterpillar compared with a reject rate of 2.8 percent for noncertified suppliers.[26]

Plant with a Future

Caterpillar's employee involvement plan went hand in hand with a $1.8 billion plant modernization program launched by Schaefer in 1986.[27] Dubbed "Plant with a Future" (PWAF), the modernization program combined just-in-time inventory techniques, a factory automation scheme, a network of computerized machine tools, and a flexible manufacturing system. Several of these innovations were pioneered by Komatsu late in the 1970s. The industry's technological leader, Komatsu had been the first construction equipment manufacturer to introduce both the just-in-time inventory system and the "quick changeover tooling" technique, a flexible tooling method designed to produce a large variety of equipment models in a single plant.[28]

To challenge Komatsu, top executives at Caterpillar did not seek to merely imitate the Japanese. This was not enough. They studied, instead, the modernization efforts of several manufacturing companies, and arrived at two important conclusions: It was necessary (1) to change the layout of an entire plant, not just selected departments within a plant; and (2) to implement the program companywide, that is, on a global basis both at home and abroad. Implementing such a comprehensive program took longer than expected, however, lasting seven years: four under Schaefer's direction and three more under the direction of his successor, Donald Fites.[29]

The traditional manufacturing process at Caterpillar, known as "batch" production, was common among U.S. assembly plants in a number of industries. Under batch production, subassembly lines produced components (radiators, hydraulic tanks, etc.) in small lots. Final assembly lines put together complete models, and the entire production system required large inventories of parts and components owing to the high level of "work in process" (models being built at any one time). Under batch production, furthermore, assembly tasks were highly specialized, work was monotonous and dull, and workers grew lax and made mistakes. Correcting assembly mistakes, it should be noted, took more time than the assembly process itself because workers needed to disassemble components in order to access problem areas. Parts delivery was also problematic. Occasionally, delays in delivery of parts to the assembly areas forced workers to leave the line in order to locate a missing part. Occasionally, the early arrival of parts before they were needed created its own inefficiencies.[30]

To solve these problems, Caterpillar reconfigured the layout of its manufacturing plants into flexible work "cells." Grouped in cells, workers used computerized machine tools to perform several manufacturing steps in sequence, processing components from start to finish and sending them "just-in-time" to an assembly area, as the following example suggests. To manufacture steel tractor-tread under the batch production layout, Cat workers were required to cut, drill, and heat-treat steel beams on three distinct assembly lines. Under cellular manufacturing, by contrast, all three operations were carried out automatically in single tractor-tread cells linked together by computers.[31]

Caterpillar, in addition, reduced material handling by means of an automated electrified monorail which delivered parts to storage and assembly areas, traveling on a long aluminum track throughout the modernized plant. When parts arrived at the delivery point, a flash light alerted the assembly line workers, semiautomatic gates (operated by infrared remote

EXHIBIT 2

George Schaefer's Caterpillar: Highlights of
Financial Data, Caterpillar Versus Komatsu

	Cat		Komatsu	
	Sales ($ billion)	Income as % of Sales	Sales ($ billion)	Income as % of Sales
1985	$6.7	2.9%	*	1.8%
1986	$7.3	1.0%	*	2.8%
1987	$8.2	3.9%	$5.1	1.3%
1988	$10.4	5.9%	$6.2	0.4%
1989	$11.1	4.5%	$6.0	2.6%

Source: For Caterpillar, *Hoover's Handbook of American Business, 1995*, p. 329; for
Komatsu, *Hoover's Handbook of World Business, 1995–96*, p. 291.

*Sales are available only in Yen: 1985, 796 billion Yen; 1986, 789 billion Yen.

control) opened, and a lift lowered the components directly onto an assembly line. Don Western, a manufacturing manager at the Cat Aurora plant, observed, "Materials now [1990] arrive at the assembly point only when required—and in the order required. At most, we hold about a 4 hour supply of large parts and components on the line."[32]

Caterpillar, finally, improved product quality. Formerly, components moved down the assembly line continuously, not intermittently, and therefore workers were unable to respond quickly to quality problems. Managers alone controlled the speed of the line. Under the new assembly plan, on the other hand, components moved automatically between work areas and remained stationary during the actual assembly operation. More important, under the PWAF plan, managers empowered production workers to change the speed of the assembly line at will, granting them the flexibility necessary to resolve quality and safety problems.[33]

The PWAF program resulted in productivity and quality gains across the board in many of Caterpillar plants. At the Aurora plant in Illinois, for instance, factory workers managed to reduce the assembly process time fourfold, building and shipping a customer order in 4 rather than 16 days, and cutting product defects by one-half in 4 years (1986–1990).[34] At the Cat plant in Grenoble, France, to mention another case, workers slashed the time it took to assemble machinery parts from 20 to 8 days in 3 years

(1986–1989). Companywide changes were equally impressive: collectively, Caterpillar's 30 worldwide plants cut inventory levels by 50 percent and manufacturing space by 21 percent in 3 years.[35]

Looking back at Schaefer's five year-long tenure, Caterpillar had reemerged as a globally competitive company, lean, flexible, and technologically advanced. Caterpillar's world market share rebounded from 43 percent to 50 percent (1984–1990),[36] revenues increased by 66 percent (1985–1989), and the company was profitable once again. As Caterpillar prospered, Komatsu was retrenching. In 1989, Caterpillar's sales totaled over $11 billion or nearly twice the sales reported by Komatsu, Caterpillar's profit margins exceeded Komatsu's, and the gap between the two companies—in terms of both market share and income on sales—was growing (Exhibit 2).

The Transformation Continued: Donald Fites's Caterpillar, 1990–1999

Notwithstanding Schaefer's achievements, the transformation of Caterpillar was far from over. For one thing, the company stock lagged far behind its earnings; Cat shares underperformed the S&P 500 index by over 50 percent for five years (1987–1992).[37] For another, Caterpillar was facing an industrywide downturn in both its domestic and international markets. Partly as a result of the cyclical nature of the construction equipment industry, and also as a result of an increase in the value of the dollar (a weak dollar in the late 1980s helped Caterpillar's foreign sales), Caterpillar revenues and profits fell. During the two years following Schaefer's retirement, the company actually lost money (see Exhibit 3).

Replacing Schaefer in the winter of 1990, Donald Fites viewed Caterpillar's financial troubles as an opportunity to introduce change: "I certainly didn't count on … [a] recession … but [the recession] made it easier to accept the fact that we needed to change."[38] "It's hard to change an organization when you're making record profits."[39]

Leadership

Fites's leadership style stood in stark contrast to Schaefer's. "George was … a consensus builder" while "[Don] expects people to challenge him forcefully,"[40] one Cat executive said, and another (former Cat CEO Lee Morgan) described Fites as "one of the most determined men I've ever met."[41] Fites was a hard-line executive, feared by his subordinates, respected by his peers, and cheered by Wall Street. An imposing man standing 6 feet 5 inches, Fites led by explicit command rather than persuasion, asserted the company's "right to manage" in face of mounting union opposition, and did not hesitate to cut thousands of management and production jobs at a stroke.

The son of a subsistence corn farmer, Fites had joined Caterpillar in 1956, rising through the ranks, and spending sixteen years overseas. A career marketeer, he worked for Cat in South Africa, Germany, Switzerland, Brazil, Japan, and other countries. In 1971, Fites had earned an MBA from MIT, writing a thesis titled "Japan Inc.: Can U.S. Industry Compete?" and soon thereafter, he received an assignment in Japan, serving nearly five years as the marketing director of the Caterpillar-Mitsubishi joint venture. Fites's Japanese experience resonated throughout the remainder of his career. He was impressed, first of all, by the ways in which the Japanese trained their managers, rotating executives through functional departments in order to educate them in all aspects of the business. Returning from Japan to Peoria in the mid 1970s, Fites revamped Cat's product development process, utilizing an integrated approach based on Japanese-style functional teams. He also admired Japanese labor relations. Historically, American unions had been organized on an industrywide basis, and therefore labor relations in the United States were often adversarial. Trade unions

in Japan, by contrast, were company-based organizations, loyal, cooperative, and, in Fites's words, "deeply dedicated to the success of the [firm]."[42] Leading Caterpillar in the 1990s, Fites sought to bring Caterpillar's labor relations closer to the Japanese model.

Reorganization

A marketing manager, Fites was convinced that Caterpillar did not pay sufficient attention to customer needs because global pricing decisions were made at the company's headquarters in Peoria with little knowledge of the local market conditions around the world. In 1985, as he took charge of Cat's worldwide marketing organization, Fites delegated district offices the authority to set prices, thereby pushing responsibility down the chain of command to the lowest possible level. Promoted to president in 1989, Fites applied the same principle to Caterpillar's entire structure, developing a companywide reorganization plan under Schaefer's direction.[43]

Caterpillar's organizational structure was archaic. It was a functional structure suitable for a small company that operated just a few plants, all located within the United States. A centralized body with only four primary functions—engineering, manufacturing, marketing, and finance—the old structure served Caterpillar well until World War II, but as the company expanded globally in subsequent decades, the limitations of such a structure had become apparent. First, decisions were made at the top of each functional unit, and executives were reluctant to delegate authority to mid- or low-level managers. Second, each functional unit tended to focus on its own goal rather than the enterprise's objectives (marketing was preoccupied with market share, engineering with product safety, manufacturing with assembly problems, etc.), making it difficult for top management to coordinate functional goals.[44] And third, the bureaucratization of the decision-making process impaired effective communication. Under the old structure, Fites recalled, the flow of information upward was "so filtered with various prejudices—particularly functional prejudice[s]—that you didn't know whether you were really looking at the facts or looking at someone's opinion."[45]

To equip Caterpillar with the flexibility, speed, and agility necessary to operate in the global economy, Fites broke the company into 17 semiautonomous divisions or "profit centers"; 13 were responsible for products (tractors, engines, etc.) and 4 for services.[46]

EXHIBIT 3

Donald Fites's Caterpillar:
Employment and Sales

Year	Number of Employees	Sales ($ billion)
1990	60,000	11.4
1991	56,000	10.2
1992	52,000	10.2
1993	50,000	11.6
1994	54,000	14.3
1995	54,000	16.1
1996	57,000	16.5
1997	60,000	18.9
1998	64,000	21.0

Source: For 1990–1997: *Hoover's Handbook of American Business,*
1999, p. 329; for 1998, Caterpillar Inc. 1999 Annual Report, p. 1.

He then required each division to post a 15 percent rate of return on assets, and threatened to penalize any division that fell behind. He stood by his words. When Caterpillar's forklift division failed to improve its return on assets in 1992, Fites transferred it into an 80 percent to 20 percent joint venture controlled by Mitsubishi.[47]

Caterpillar's new divisional structure facilitated downsizing. Under the new structure, Caterpillar cut 10,000 jobs in three years, 1990–1993 (Exhibit 3). Of the 7,500 employees who lost their jobs between January 1990 and August 1992, 2,000 were salaried managers and 5,500 hourly workers.[48] As Caterpillar's sales grew from $10 billion to $15 billion in the first half of the 1990s, the number of managers employed by the company fell by 20 percent.[49] In addition, the move from a functional into a divisional structure, coupled with the drive for profit making, brought about a change in the methods of managerial compensation. Traditionally, Cat managers were paid in proportion to the size of the budget they controlled or the number of employees they supervised. Under the new plan, Caterpillar based all its incentive compensation schemes on return on assets.[50] Lastly, Caterpillar decentralized its research and development activities. With each division controlling its own product development programs and funding, R&D activities under the new plan were more customer driven than at any other period in the past.[51]

Marketing and Dealerships

Caterpillar's reorganization plan affected the company's distribution network as well. Under the new structure, dealers seeking assistance could contact any of the seventeen product and service profit centers directly, saving time and money; they no longer needed to call the General Office in their search for assistance within the company.[52] The new structure also facilitated a more frequent interaction between Caterpillar's managers and dealers, a development that resulted in "virtually everyone from the youngest design engineer to the CEO" having "contact with somebody in [a] dealer organization" (wrote Fites). Ordinarily, low-level managers at Caterpillar communicated daily with their counterparts at Cat dealerships and senior corporate executives, several times a week.[53]

Caterpillar's network of dealerships was extensive. In 1999, 207 independent dealers served Caterpillar: 63 were stationed in the United States and 144 abroad. The number of employees working for Cat dealers exceeded the company's own workforce (67,000) by nearly one-third; the combined net worth of Cat dealers surpassed Caterpillar's stockholders' equity ($5.5 billion)[54] by nearly one-quarter (Exhibit 4). Many of Caterpillar's dealerships were privately owned; a few were public companies. On average, the annual sales of a Caterpillar dealership amounted to $150 million (1996); several of the large dealerships, however, generated annual revenues of up to $1 billion.

To Caterpillar, the informal relationships between the company and its dealers were far more important than the formal contractual relations. Dealership

EXHIBIT 4

Caterpillar Dealerships, 1999

	Inside U.S.	Outside U.S.	Worldwide
Dealers	63	144	207
Branch Stores	382	1,122	1,504
Employees	34,338	54,370	88,708
Service Bays	6,638	5,529	12,167
Estimated Net Worth	$3.22 bil.	$3.54 bil.	$6.77 bil.

Source: Caterpillar Inc. 1999 Annual Report, p. 43.

agreements ran only a few pages, had no expiration date, and allowed each party to terminate the contract at will, following ninety-days' notice. Notwithstanding the open-ended nature of the contract, turnover among Cat dealerships was extremely low. Caterpillar actively encouraged its dealers to keep the business in their families, running seminars on tax issues and succession plans for dealers, holding regular conferences in Peoria for the sons and daughters of "dealer Principals" (dealership owners), and taking concrete steps to encourage a proper succession from one generation to another.[55]

While Caterpillar had always protected its dealers against failure, under Fites's direction, Caterpillar did so more aggressively than before, assisting individual dealers who were subjected to intense price competition by rival manufacturers. To help a dealer, Caterpillar sometimes offered discounted prices, sometimes helped reduce the dealer's costs, and occasionally launched a promotion campaign in the dealer's service territory, emphasizing the lower lifetime cost of a Cat machine relative to a competitor's. Caterpillar also protected dealers during recessions. Despite the company's loses during the industry slump of 1991–1992, Fites's Caterpillar helped vulnerable Cat dealers survive the downturn, stay in the business, and order equipment in advance of the 1993 upturn. Caterpillar's competitors, in contrast, saw several of their dealers go out of business during the recession.[56]

Fites's Caterpillar cooperated with dealers in other ways. During the 1990s, Caterpillar worked together with its dealers to conduct surveys among customers in order to improve customer service and parts delivery. Sending out ninety thousand survey forms annually, Cat received a response rate of nearly 40 percent. Through its "Partners in Quality" program, Caterpillar involved dealers in quality control discussions, linking personnel at Cat plants and dealerships, and sponsoring quarterly meetings. Periodically, Caterpillar invited its entire body of independent dealers to a week-long conference in Peoria to review corporate strategy, manufacturing plants, and marketing policies. A firm believer in strong personal business ties, Fites explained

> Dealers can call me or any senior corporate officer at any time, and they do. Virtually any dealer in the world is free to walk in my door. I'll know how much money he made last year and his market position. And I'll know what is happening in

his family. I consider the majority of dealers personal friends. Of course, one reason I know the dealers so well is that I rose through our distribution organization.[57]

Caterpillar's worldwide distribution system, according to Fites, was the company's single greatest advantage over its competitors. It was a strategic asset whose importance was expected to grow in the future: "Until about 2010," Fites predicted, "distribution"— that is, after-sales support, product application, and service information—" will be what separates the winners from the losers in the global economy."[58] Contrasting American and Japanese manufacturing firms, Fites elaborated

> Although many Japanese companies had the early advantage in manufacturing excellence, U.S. companies may have the edge this time around. . . . they know more about distribution than anyone else. . . . Quite frankly, distribution traditionally has not been a strength of Japanese companies. Marketing people and salespeople historically have been looked down upon in Japanese society.[59]

Information Technology

Fites's Caterpillar invested generously in expanding and upgrading Caterpillar's worldwide computer network—a system linking together factories, distribution centers, dealers, and large customers. By 1996, the network connected 1,000 locations in 160 countries across 23 time zones, providing Caterpillar with the most comprehensive and fastest part delivery system in the industry. Although Caterpillar had long guaranteed a 48-hour delivery of parts anywhere in the world, by 1996, Cat dealers supplied 80 percent of the parts a customer needed at once; the remaining 20 percent—not stocked by the dealers—were shipped by the company on the same day the parts were ordered. With 22 distribution centers spread all around the world, Caterpillar serviced a total of 500,000 different parts, keeping over 300,000 in stock, and manufacturing the remainder on demand.[60]

A critical element in Caterpillar's drive for technological leadership was an electronic alert information system the company was developing under Fites. The new system was designed to monitor machines remotely, identify parts that needed to be replaced, and replace them before they failed. Once fully operational in the mid 2000's, the new IT system was expected first to help dealers repair machines before they broke down, thereby reducing machine down-time, on the one hand, and saving repair costs, on the other; and second to provide Caterpillar and its dealers with the opportunity to slash their inventory costs. In 1995, the value of the combined inventories held by Caterpillar and its dealers amounted to $2 billion worth of parts.[61]

Diversification

Fites's Caterpillar expanded its sales into farm equipment, forest products, and compact construction machines, introducing new lines of products, one at a time. Between 1991 and 1999, Caterpillar entered a total of thirty-eight mergers and joint venture agreements, many of which contributed to the company's efforts to diversify.[62]

The growth in Caterpillar's engine sales was the company's largest. Caterpillar had traditionally produced engines for internal use only, installing them on Cat machines, but beginning in the mid 1980s, as the company was recovering from its most severe crisis, Cat embarked on a strategy of producing engines for sale to other companies. In 1999, engine sales accounted for 35 percent of Cat's revenues, up from 21 percent in 1990, and Cat engines powered about one-third of the big trucks in the United States. Apart from trucking companies, Caterpillar produced engines for a variety of other customers, including petroleum firms, electric utility companies, and shipbuilding concerns (see Exhibit 6). Only 10 percent of the diesel engines manufactured by Caterpillar in 1999 were installed on the company's own equipment.[63]

Two important acquisitions by Caterpillar helped the company compete in the engine market. In 1996, Donald Fites purchased the MaK Company—a German maker of engines for power generation. Partly because governments of developing countries were reluctant to build large power plants, and partly because the utility industry in the United States deregulated and new electrical suppliers entered the market, worldwide demand for generators was fast increasing. The rise in demand helped Caterpillar increase its sales of power generators by 20 percent annually between 1995 and 1999.[64]

Similarly, in 1998, Fites bought Britain's Perkins Engines, a manufacturer of engines for compact construction machinery, for $1.3 billion. The new acquisition contributed to Caterpillar's efforts to increase its share in the small equipment market which was growing at a rate of 10 percent a year. Perkins's best-selling engine powered the skid steer loader. A compact wheel tractor operated by one person and capable of maneuvering in tight spaces, the skid dug ditches, moved dirt, broke up asphalt, and performed a wide variety of other tasks.[65]

Labor Relations

Perhaps no other areas of management had received more attention than Caterpillar's labor relations under Fites. For nearly seven years, 1991–1998, Fites fought the UAW in what had become the longest U.S. labor dispute in the 1990s. On the one side, a union official described the UAW relationship with Fites as "the single most contentious … in the history of the union"; on the other, a Wall Street analyst called Fites "the guy who broke the union, pure and simple."[66]

In part, Fites's opposition to the UAW was ideological: It "is not so much a battle about economics as it is a battle about who's going to run the company."[67] Yet economics did matter, and Fites was determined to ensure Caterpillar's global competitiveness by cutting the company's labor cost. His principal target was a UAW "pattern" agreement, a collective bargaining contract modeled on agreements signed by the UAW and Caterpillar's domestic competitors, John Deere, the Case Corporation, and others (a pattern agreement tied separate labor contracts together so that changes in one led to similar changes in others within the same industry). Fites rejected pattern bargaining because Caterpillar was heavily dependent on the export of domestically manufactured products, selling over 50 percent of its American-made equipment in foreign markets, and thus competing head-to-head with foreign-based, global companies like Komatsu. Cat's U.S.-based competitors, by contract, exported a far smaller proportion of their domestically made goods. Because Cat's global competitors paid lower wages overseas than the wages paid by Cat's American-based competitors at home, Fites argued, Caterpillar could not afford paying the UAW pattern of wages.[68]

The first Caterpillar strike erupted in 1991, at a time when Caterpillar's 17,000 unionized employees were working under a contract. The contract was set to expire on September 30, and Fites was prepared. He had built up enough inventory to supply customers for six months, giving Cat dealers special incentives to buy and stock parts and equipment in case a strike shut down the company's U.S. plants. Caterpillar's contract offer included three principal demands: no pattern on wages, flexible work schedules, and a two-tier wage system. The union rejected the offer outright and staged a strike. About 50 percent of the strikers were within six years of retirement, and as the strike prolonged, 30 percent of the strikers crossed the picket line. Five months into the strike, Fites threatened to replace the strikers permanently if they did not return to work within a week. Shortly thereafter, the union called off the strike, the strikers went back to work "unconditionally," and Cat's unionized employees continued working without a contract under the terms of the rejected offer.[69]

One casualty of the 1991–1992 strike was Caterpillar's Employee Satisfaction Process. The strike effectively put an end to Cat's ESP program which George Schaefer had launched in 1986 and strove so painstakingly to perverse. As the climate of labor relations at Caterpillar deteriorated, the number of unresolved grievances increased. At the Aurora plant at Illinois, the number of grievances at the final stage before arbitration rose from less than twenty prior to the strike to over three hundred in the year following the end of the strike. When Cat employees began wearing their own ESP buttons to read "Employee Stop Participating," Caterpillar terminated the program altogether.[70]

During 1992–1994, Caterpillar's unionized employees continued to resist Fites's hard-line stand against the UAW. They organized shop floor disruptions ("informational picketing"), slowdowns ("work to rule"), wildcat strikes in selected plants, and picket lines at Cat's dealerships.[71] Fites, in the meantime, trained managers and office workers to operate factory machinery and reassigned many of them to the shop floor of plants undergoing short-term work stoppages. Once again, he was fully prepared for a long strike. The 1994–1995 strike broke out in June 1994, lasted seventeen months, was bitterly fought by the striking unionists, and came to an abrupt end when the UAW ordered its members to return to work "immediately and unconditionally" in order to save their jobs.[72] During the strike, Caterpillar supplemented its workforce with 5,000 reassigned white collar employees, 3,700 full-time and part-time new hires, 4,000 union members who crossed the picket line, and skilled workers borrowed from its dealerships. The company, furthermore, shifted work to nonunion plants in the South. Additionally, Caterpillar supplied the U.S. market with equipment imported from its plants in Europe, Japan, and Brazil.[73] Operating effectively all through the strike, Caterpillar avoided massive customer defection, and managed to keep up production, expand sales, increase profits, and drive up the company stock price. In 1995, the company earned record profits for the second year in a row (see Exhibit 5). During the two years following the end of the strike, the shop floor struggle between Cat management and the union resumed. Caterpillar issued strict rules of workplace conduct, limiting employees' behavior as well as speech.

EXHIBIT 5

Caterpillar's Financial Results
During the Labor Disputes of the 1990s

	Sales ($ Mil.)	Net Income ($Mil.)	Income as % of Sales	Stock Price FY Close
1991	10,182	(404)	—	10.97
1992	10.194	(2,435)	—	13.41
1993	11,615	652	5.6%	22.25
1994	14.328	955	6.7%	27.56
1995	16.072	1,136	7.1%	29.38
1996	16,522	1,361	8.2%	37.63
1997	18,925	1,665	8.8%	48.50

Source: Hoover's Handbook for American Business, 1999, p. 329.

Union activists, in response, launched a work-to-rule campaign in Cat's unionized plants. The UAW, in addition, filed numerous charges with the National Labor Relations Board (NLRB), alleging that the company committed unfair labor practices. Accepting many of these charges, the NLRB issued formal complaints.[74] Meanwhile, in 1997, Caterpillar racked up record profits for the fourth year in a row (Exhibit 5).

In February 1998, at long last Caterpillar and the union reached an agreement. The terms of the 1998 agreement clearly favored Caterpillar. First and most important, the contract allowed Caterpillar to break away from the long-standing practice of pattern bargaining. Second, the contract allowed Caterpillar to introduce a two-tier wage system and pay new employees 70 percent of the starting union scale. A third clause of the contract provided for a more flexible work schedule, allowing management to keep employees on the job longer than eight hours a day and during weekends (without paying overtime). The contract also granted management the right to hire temporary employees at certain plants without the union's approval, and reduce the number of union jobs below a certain level. Running for six years rather than the typical three years, the contract was expected to secure Caterpillar with a relatively long period of industrial peace.[75]

Several provisions of the contract were favorable to the union. The contract's key economic provisions included an immediate wage increase of 2 to 4 percent and future increases of 3 percent in 1999, 2001, and 2003; cost of living allowances; and substantial gains in pension benefits (the average tenure of the 1994–1995 strikers was twenty-four years). Another provision favorable to the UAW was a moratorium on most plant closings. But perhaps the most significant union gain was simply achieving a contract, as AFL-CIO Secretary Treasurer Rich Trumka observed: "The message to corporate America is this: Here's one of the biggest companies, and they couldn't walk away from the union."[76]

Why, then, was Fites willing to sign a contract? Why did a company that operated profitably year after year without a contract, and operated effectively during strikes, suddenly seek to reach an agreement with the UAW?

Fites's decision was influenced by two developments. First, Caterpillar's record revenues and profits during 1993–1997 came to an end in 1998–1999, as the industry was sliding into a recession. Revenues and profits were declining as a result of a strong dollar coupled with a weak demand for Cat products. Caterpillar, therefore, needed a flexible wage agreement, stable employment relations, and a more cooperative workforce in order to smooth its ride during the impending downturn. Another reason why Fites sought accommodation with the union was the need to settle some four hundred unfair labor practice charges filed by the NLRB against the company during the dispute. These charges were not only costly to adjudicate but also could have resulted in huge penalties that the company had to pay in cases where the NLRB ruled in favor of the UAW. One of Caterpillar's principal demands in the 1998 settlement— to which the UAW agreed—was dropping these unfair labor practice charges.[77]

The Future: Glen Barton's Caterpillar, 1999–

As Fites retired in February 1999, Glen Barton, a thirty-nine-year Cat veteran, assumed the company's leadership. During his first year in office, Barton lost two potential allies on the Cat Board of Directors, Glen Schaefer and Donald Fites. In January 2000, Caterpillar's Board of Directors revised the company's corporate governance guidelines to prohibit retired Cat employees from sitting on the board. The move was intended to safeguard the interests of stockholders and prevent the company's inside directors from opposing swift actions proposed by the board's outside members.[78]

Barton faced other difficulties. In 1999, Caterpillar's profits fell 37 percent to $946 million, the worst results since 1993, and its North American market, which accounted for half of Cat's sales and nearly two-thirds of its profits, was in a slump.[79]

Barton believed that the downturn in the U.S. construction market could be offset by an upturn in the international market. He thought that Caterpillar could take advantage of its global positioning to cushion the U.S. decline by increasing sales in Asia and Latin America where economies were rebounding. But being cautious, Barton also realized that he needed to ensure the future of Caterpillar in the long run. He, therefore, embarked on four growth strategies: expansion into new markets, diversification, the development of a new distribution channel, and the buildup of alliances with global competitors.

New Markets

In 1999, 80 percent of the world's population lived in developing countries, and Caterpillar's sales to developing nations accounted for only 23 percent of the total company's sales. Developing countries had limited access to water, electricity, and transportation, and therefore needed to invest in building highways, bridges, dams, and waterways. Under Barton's leadership, increased sales of Caterpillar's equipment to the developing nations of Asia, Latin America, Eastern Europe, and the Commonwealth of Independent States (the former Soviet Union) was a top strategic priority.[80]

Diversification

Just as globalization protected Caterpillar from the cyclical movements of boom and bust, so did diversification. Cat's expansion into the engine business is a case in point. In 1999, Caterpillar's overall sales fell by 6 percent, yet its engine sales rose by 5 percent. Cat's engine business itself was further diversified, with truck-engine sales making up just over one-third of all Cat's engine sales in 1999 (Exhibit 6).

Such a diversification, according to Barton, ensured the company that any future decline in truck engine sales could be offset, at least in part, by an increase in sales of non-truck engines. By 2010, Caterpillar's total engine sales were expected to double to nearly $14 billion.[81]

Of all Cat engine sales, the growth in sales of electric diesel generators—20 percent a year since 1996—had been the fastest (Exhibit 7). Caterpillar's energy business clearly benefited from the energy crisis. Large corporations, manufacturing facilities, Internet

EXHIBIT 7

Caterpillar's Sales of Power Generators

	Power Generator Sales (Billions)	Power Generator Sales as % of Total Revenues
1996	$1.2	7.3%
1997	$1.3	6.9%
1998	$1.6	7.6%
2000	$1.8	9.1%
2001	$2.3	11.4%

Source: David Barboza, "Cashing in on the World's Energy Hunger," *New York Times*, May 22, 2001.

server centers, and utility companies had installed backup diesel generators for standby or emergency use; in the nine months ending May 2001, Cat sales of mobile power modules (trailer equipped with a generator) quadrupled.[82]

The world's largest manufacturer of diesel generators, Caterpillar nevertheless faced a serious challenge in its efforts to transform itself into an ET (energy technology) company: diesel generators produced far more pollution than other sources of power. To address this problem, Barton's Caterpillar accelerated its shift toward cleaner micropower. In 2001, only 10 percent of Caterpillar's generators were powered by natural gas; in 2011, the corresponding figure was expected to climb to 50 percent.[83]

To diversify the company in still another way, Barton planned to double its farm equipment sales in five years (1999–2004).[84] In the agricultural equipment market, Caterpillar needed to compete head-to-head with the John Deere Co. and the CNH Corporation (former Case Corp. and New Holland), the leading U.S. manufacturers.

A New Distribution Channel

Under Barton's direction, Caterpillar expanded its rental equipment business, reaching a new category of customers both at home and abroad. Formerly, Caterpillar sold or rented equipment to rental centers, and these centers, in turn, rerented the equipment to end users. Rarely did Caterpillar rent directly to customers. Now Barton was making aggressive efforts to help Cat dealers diversify into rentals. Nearly half of all Cat's machines sold in North America in 2000 entered the market through the rental distribution channel, and

EXHIBIT 6

Cat Engine Sales to End Users, 1999, 2000

	1999	2000
Trucks	34%	27%
Electric Power Generators	26%	33%
Oil Drilling Equipment	20%	19%
Industrial Equipment	11%	13%
Ships and Boats	9%	8%

Source: Caterpillar Inc. 1999 Annual Report, p. 24; and 2000 Annual Report.

the fastest growing segment of the business was short-term rentals. Implemented by Barton in 1999–2000, the Cat Rental Store Program was designed to assist dealers in operating a one-stop rental shop that offered a complete line of rental equipment from heavy bulldozers and tractors, to light towers, work platforms, and hydraulic tools.[85]

Joint Ventures

Increasingly, Caterpillar had used joint ventures to expand into new markets and diversify into new products. In November 2000, Barton's Caterpillar announced a plan to form two joint ventures with DaimlerChrysler, the world's leading manufacturer of commercial vehicles. One was for building medium-duty engines; the other was for manufacturing fuel systems. The combined share of the two companies in the medium-duty engine market was only 10 percent, yet the medium-duty engine market generated worldwide sales of $10 billion annually. The sales of fuel systems were even more promising. Fuel systems were designed to increase the efficiency of diesel engines and thereby reduce diesel emissions. Participating in the two joint ventures were Cat and DaimlerChrysler plants in four U.S. states (South Carolina, Georgia, Illinois, and Michigan) and at least five other countries.[86]

EXHIBIT 8

Caterpillar: Five-Year Financial Summary

(Dollars in million except per share data)	2001	2000	1999	1998	1997
Sales and Revenues	$20,450	$20,175	19,702	20,977	18,925
Profits	$805	1,053	946	1,513	1,665
As % of Sales & Revenue	3.9%	5.2%	4.8%	7.2%	8.8%
Profits per Share	$2.35	3.04	2.66	4.17	4.44
Dividends per Share	$1,390	1.345	1,275	1.150	0.950
Return on Equity	14.4%	19.0%	17.9%	30.9%	37.9%
R&D Expenses	$898	854	814	838	700
As % of Sales & Revenue	4.4%	4.2%	4.1%	4.0%	3.7%
Wages, Salaries, & Employee Benefits	$4,272	4,029	4,044	4,146	3,773
Number of Employees	70,678	67,200	66,225	64,441	58,366
December 31					
Total assets					
Consolidated	$30,657	28,464	26,711	25,128	20,756
Machinery & Engines	$17,275	16,554	16,158	15,619	14,188
Financial Products	$15,895	14,618	12,951	11,648	7,806
Long-term debt					
Consolidated	$11,291	11,334	9,928	9,404	6,942
Machinery & Engines	$3,492	2,854	3,099	2,993	2,367
Financial Products	$7.799	8,480	6,829	6,411	4,575
Total debt					
Consolidated	$16,602	15,067	13,802	12,452	8,568
Machinery & Engines	$3,784	3,427	3,317	3,102	2,474
Financial Products	$13.021	11,957	10,796	9,562	6,338

Source: Caterpillar Inc. 2000 and 2001 Annual Reports (2000, p. 39, 2001, p. 25.)

Future Prospects

Notwithstanding their initial prospects, Barton's strategic initiatives failed to address adequately two major concerns that could have affected the company's future. One had to do with the state of labor relations, particularly Cat's employee satisfaction program, which Schaefer had introduced and Fites terminated. Implemented effectively by Schaefer, the ESP program, we have seen, contributed to increased labor productivity, improved product quality, enhanced employee satisfaction, and reduced employee absenteeism. Should Barton, then, reintroduce Cat's employee satisfaction program and thereby improve the climate of labor relations at the company's U.S. plants? Would Barton be able to cooperate closely with the local union leadership to persuade shop floor employees to join the program?

Another challenge Barton faced pertained to the impact of E-commerce. How could Caterpillar take advantage of the opportunities offered by E-commerce without undermining its distribution system? How, in other words, could Caterpillar benefit from utilizing the Internet for the marketing, distribution, and service of its products without weakening its strong dealers' networks?

ENDNOTES

1. The Caterpillar Company 1999 Annual Report, p. 39
2. Michael Arndt, "This Cat Isn't So Nimble," *Business Week*, February 21, 2000, p. 148; online, Lexis-Nexis Academic Universe; Mark Tatge, "Caterpillar's Truck-Engine Sales May Hit Some Breaking," *Wall Street Journal*, March 13, 2000.
3. Andrew Gross and David Weiss, "Industry Corner: The Global Demand for Heavy Construction Equipment," *Business Economics*, 31 no. 3 (July 1996), pp. 54–55.
4. Ibid., p. 54.
5. Ibid., p. 55.
6. Donald Fites, "Making Your Dealers Your Partners," *Harvard Business Review*, March–April 1996, p. 85.
7. U. Srinivasa Rangan, "Caterpillar Tractor Co.," in Christopher Bartlett and Sumantra Ghoshal, eds., *Transatlantic Management: Text, Cases, and Readings in Cross Border Management* (Homewood, IL.: Irwin, 1992), p. 296.
8. Fites, "Making Your Dealers Your Partners," p. 85.
9. Gross and Weiss, "Industry Corner," p. 58.
10. William L. Naumann, *The Story of Caterpillar Tractor Co.* (New York: Newcomen Society, 1977), pp. 7–9.
11. "Caterpillar Inc.," *Hoover's Handbook of American Business* 1999 (Austin: Hoover Business Press, 1999), p. 328; "The Story of Caterpillar," online, **Caterpillar.com**, accessed March 9, 2000.
12. Michael Yoshino and U. Srinivasa Rangan, *Strategic Alliances: An Entrepreneurial Approach to Globalization* (Boston: Harvard Business School Press, 1995), p. 93; Naumann, *Story of Caterpillar*, pp. 12–14; William Haycraft, *Yellow Power: The story of the Earthmoving Equipment Industry* (Urbana: University of Illinois Press, 2000), pp. 118–122, 159–167, 196–203.
13. Fites, "Making Your Dealers Your Partners," p. 94.
14. Rangan, "Caterpillar Tractor Co.," p. 304; James Risen, "Caterpillar: A Test of U.S. Trade Policy," *Los Angeles Times*, June 8, 1986, online, Lexis-Nexis, Academic Universe.
15. Cited in Kathleen Deveny, "For Caterpillar, the Metamorphosis Isn't Over," *Business Week*, August 31, 1987, p. 72.
16. Cited in Dexter Hutchins, "Caterpillar's Triple Whammy," *Fortune*, October 27, 1986, p. 91. See also Robert Eckley, "Caterpillar's Ordeal: Foreign Competition in Capital Goods," *Business Horizons*, March-April 1989, pp. 81–83.
17. James Abegglen and George Stalk, *Kaisha, the Japanese Corporation* (New York: Basic Books, 1985), pp. 62, 117–118; Yoshino and Rangan, *Strategic Alliances*, pp. 94–95; "Komatsu Ltd.," *Hoover's Handbook of World Business*, 1999, p. 320.
18. Quoted in Yoshino and Rangan, *Strategic Alliances*, p. 96.
19. Ibid., p. 97; Eckley, "Caterpillar's Ordeal," p. 84.
20. Eckley, "Caterpillar's Ordeal," p. 84; *Business Week*, August 31, 1987, p. 73; Yoshino and Rangan, *Strategic Alliances*, p. 97.
21. Ronald Henkoff, "This Cat Is Acting Like a Tiger," *Fortune*, December 19, 1988, pp. 67, 72, 76; *Business Week*, August 31, 1987, p. 73.
22. Eckley, "Caterpillar Ordeal," pp. 81, 83.
23. Quoted in *Fortune*, December 19, 1988, p. 76.
24. Eckley, "Caterpillar Ordeal," p. 84; *Fortune*, December 19, 1988, p. 76; Alex Kotlowitz, "Caterpillar Faces Shutdown with UAW," *Wall Street Journal*, March 5, 1986. Online. ABI database.
25. Barry Bearak, "The Inside Strategy: Less Work and More Play at Cat," *Los Angeles Times*, May 16, 1995. Online. Lexis-Nexis. Academic Universe.
26. *Fortune*, December 19, 1988, p. 76.
27. Brian Bremner, "Can Caterpillar Inch Its Way Back to Heftier Profits?" *Business Week*, September 25, 1989, p. 75.
28. Abegglen and Stalk, *Kaisha*, p. 118.
29. *Fortune*, December 19, 1988, pp. 72, 74; *Business Week*, September 25, 1989, p. 75.
30. Karen Auguston, "Caterpillar Slashes Lead Times from Weeks to Days," *Modern Materials Handling*, February 1990, p. 49.
31. Barbara Dutton, "Cat Climbs High with FMS," *Manufacturing Systems*, November 1989, pp. 16–22; *Business Week*, August 31, 1987, p. 73; September 25, 1989, p. 75.
32. Quoted in Auguston, "Caterpillar Slashes Lead Times," p. 49.
33. Auguston, "Caterpillar Slashes Lead Times," pp. 50–51.
34. Ibid., pp. 49, 51.
35. *Business Week*, September 25, 1989, p. 75.
36. Yoshino and Rangan, *Strategic Alliances*, p. 98.
37. Jennifer Reingold, "CEO of the Year," *Financial World*, March 28, 1995, p. 68.
38. Quoted in "An Interview with Caterpillar Inc. Chairman and CEO Donald V. Fites," *Inter-Business Issues*, December 1992, p. 32.
39. Quoted in Tracy Benson, "Caterpillar Wakes Up," *Industry Week*, May 20, 1991, p. 36.
40. Quoted in Reingold, "CEO of the Year," p. 74.
41. Quoted in Kevin Kelly, "Caterpillar's Don Fites: Why He Didn't Blink," *Business Week*, August 10, 1992, p. 56.
42. Quoted in *Business Week*, August 10, 1992, pp. 56–57.
43. *Business Week*, August 10, 1992, p. 57.
44. Quoted in Benson, "Caterpillar Wakes Up," p. 32.
45. "An Interview with Fites," *Inter Business Issues*, p. 32.
46. Benson, "Caterpillar Wakes Up," p. 33.
47. *Business Week*, August 10, 1992, p. 56.
48. J. P. Donlon, "Heavy Metal," *Chief Executive*, September 1995, p. 50.
49. Andrew Zadoks, "Managing Technology at Caterpillar," *Research Technology Management*, January 1997, pp. 49–51. Online. Lexis-Nexis. Academic Universe.
50. *Business Week*, August 10, 1992, p. 56.

51. Donlon, "Heavy Metal," p. 50.

52. Benson, "Caterpillar Wakes Up," p. 36.

53. Fites, "Make Your Dealers Your Partners," p. 93.

54. Caterpillar Inc. 1999 Annual Report, p. 34.

55. Fites, "Make Your Dealers Your Partners." pp. 89, 91–92, 94.

56. Fites, "Make Your Dealers Your Partners," pp. 92–93.

57. Quoted in Fites, "Make Your Dealers Your Partners," p. 94, but see also pp. 90, 93.

58. Quoted in Donlon. "Heavy Metals," p. 50.

59. Quoted in Fites, "Make Your Dealers You Partners," p. 86.

60. Myron Magnet, "The Productivity Payoff Arrives," *Fortune*, June 27, 1994, pp. 82–83; Benson, "Caterpillar Wakes Up," p. 36; Fites, "Making Your Dealers Your Partners," pp. 88–89.

61. Quoted in Steven Prokesch, "Making Global Connections in Caterpillar," *Harvard Business Review*, March-April 1996, p. 89, but see also p. 88; and Donlon, "Heavy Metals," p. 50.

62. "Caterpillar's Growth Strategies," Copyright 1999. Online. **Caterpillar.com.**

63. *Wall Street Journal*, March 13, 2000; David Barboza, "Aiming for Greener Pastures," *New York Times*, August 4, 1999.

64. De'Ann Weimer, "A New Cat on the Hot Seat," *Business Week*, March 9, 1998, p. 61; *Wall Street Journal*, March 13, 2000.

65. *Business Week*, March 9, 1998; *Wall Street Journal*, March 13, 2000.

66. The quotations, in order, are from Reingold, "CEO of the Year," p. 72; Carl Quintanilla, "Caterpillar Chairman Fites to Retire," *Wall Street Journal*, October 15, 1998. Online. ABI database.

67. Quoted in Reingold, "CEO of the Year," p. 72.

68. "An Interview with Fites," *Inter Business Issues*, pp. 34–35; "What's Good for Caterpillar," *Forbes*, December 7, 1992. Online. ABI database.

69. Michael Cimini, "Caterpillar's Prolonged Dispute Ends," *Compensation and Working Conditions*, Fall 1998, pp. 5–6; Kevin Kelly, "Cat May Be Trying to Bulldoze the Immovable," *Business Week*, December 2, 1991, p. 116, "Cat vs. Labor: Hardhats, Anyone?" *Business Week*, August 26, 1991, p. 48. Lexis-Nexis. Academic Universe.

70. Michael Verespej, "Bulldozing Labor Peace at Caterpillar," *Industry Week*, February 15, 1993, p. 19. Online. ABI database.

71. "Caterpillar: Union Bull," *Economist*, January 9, 1993, p. 61. Online. Lexis-Nexis. Academic Universe; Cimini "Caterpillar's Prolonged Dispute Ends," pp. 7–9.

72. Cimini, "Caterpillar's Prolonged Dispute Ends," p. 9; Robert Rose, "Caterpillar Contract with UAW May Be Tough to Sell to Workers," *Wall Street Journal*, February 17, 1998. Online. ABI database; Reingold, "CEO of the Year," p. 72.

73. Cimini, "Caterpillar's Prolonged Dispute Ends," pp. 8–9.

74. Ibid., pp. 9–10.

75. Carl Quintanilla, "Caterpillar Touts Its Gains as UAW Battle Ends," *Wall Street Journal*, March 24, 1998; Dirk Johnson, "Auto Union Backs Tentative Accord with Caterpillar," *New York Times*, February 14, 1998.

76. Quoted in Philip Dine, "Gulf Remains Wide in Caterpillar's Home," *St. Louis Post Dispatch*, March 29, 1998. Online. Lexis-Nexis. Academic Universe. See also Cimini, "Caterpillar's Prolonged Dispute Ends," p. 11.

77. "The Caterpillar Strike: Not Over Till Its Over," *Economist*, February 28, 1998.

78. *Business Week*, February 21, 2000, p. 148.

79. *Business Week*, February 21, 2000, p. 148.

80. "Growth Strategies." **www.caterpillar.com**, p. 2.

81. *Wall Street Journal*, March 13, 2000.

82. David Barboza, "Cashing in on the World's Energy Hunger," *New York Times*, May 22, 2001.

83. Ibid.; "Energy Technology: Beyond the Bubble," *Economist*, April 21, 2001.

84. Heather Landy, "Putting More Cats Down on the Farm," *Chicago Sun Times*, March 28, 1999. Online. Lexis-Nexis. Academic Universe.

85. Michael Roth, "Seeing the Light," *Rental Equipment Register*, January 2000. Online. Lexis-Nexis. Academic Universe; Nikki Tait, "Cat Sharpens Claws to Pounce Again," *Financial Times*, November 8, 2000. Online. Lexis-Nexis. Academic Universe.

86. Joseph Hallinan, "Caterpillar, DaimlerChrysler Team Up," *Wall Street Journal*, November 23, 2000.

Case 7

Huawei Technologies Co., Ltd.

This case was prepared by Jie Xu and Robert H. Girling, Sonoma State University.

Until quite recently, China was regarded exclusively as a world factory for inexpensive products. Its inexpensive exports, such as textiles, toys, and plastic merchandise, have occupied the majority of discount store shelves worldwide. As symbols of low price and durability, these "Made-in-China" products have also carried connotations of being low-tech.

But this is not the whole picture. As a result of China's recent rapid technological development, low-tech products are no longer the totality of this world factory. An avalanche of high-tech "Made-in-China" products, especially those in the information technology (IT) industry such as semiconductors and telecommunication equipment, have increasingly flooded into the world market and caught the world's eyes. These products, which boast not only Chinese-made but also Chinese-designed traits, have bit by bit seized market shares, which used to be monopolized by the top-tier firms in the developed countries.

Recently, noticing these products, the world began to pay attention to their creators: numerous Chinese high-tech companies. Just how were these companies able to take business from well-known multinational giants in the tough world market? This case study examines the emergence of one such example, a Chinese telecommunication company.

Huawei Technologies Co., Ltd. is China's biggest telecommunication equipment manufacturer and one of the fastest developing firms in China. Unlike most large companies in China, Huawei was never a state-owned enterprise, and unlike most Chinese high-tech firms, it was never a result of a joint-venture with a foreign multinational. It grew from a simple imported-product vendor, which just had about US$ 3,000[1] capital at the beginning. Now it is a leading international provider offering almost the full range of telecommunication equipment and network solutions. In 2003, Huawei earned an annual revenue of US$ 3.83 billion.

While multinational companies clamor for a share of the Chinese market, Huawei strives to "step out of China" and conquer overseas markets. It is getting the upper hand over its rivals not only by its low price but also by its innovation ("High-tech firms sharpen edge," 2004). Cisco Systems, the leading manufacturer of telecommunication equipment, has had to put Huawei's name on its competitors' list and has had to seriously concern itself with Huawei's market strategy (Angell, 2003). Other multinational giants such as IBM, 3Com, and Siemens have built partnerships with Huawei. Last year, it reaped US$ 1.05 billion from markets in more than forty countries, an evident growth of 90 percent over the previous year.

China's Telecommunication Industry Background

China's telecommunication industry lagged far behind the world during the central planning period (1949–1978). During that period, as an autarkic country, China seldom accepted foreign investments and concepts. In 1978, its telephone penetration rate was just thirty for every thousand people, less than

Copyright © 2004 by Robert H. Girling. This case was prepared by Jie Xu and Robert H. Girling, Sonoma State University, as the basis for class discussion rather than to illustrate either effective or ineffective handling of an administrative situation. Reprinted by permission of Robert H. Girling. All rights reserved.

[1]The numerical value in this paper is based on the exchange rate of 1 USD = CYN 8.27.

one-tenth of the world average, and its number of telephone subscribers equaled that of the United States at the beginning of the twentieth century (Liu, 2001). Meanwhile, China's telecommunication equipment was made solely by the state-owned enterprises, which were directly under the monopoly of the government. In that uncontested position, the government designated the production plan and directed purchases and sales, while at the same time, the restricted development of technology caused China's telecommunication products to fall behind those of the rest of the world. In the 1970s, China was barely skilled at analog technology and transmission technology, whereas the world's advanced countries were already using digital communication products, such as switching and optical products.

Beginning in 1978 with the "Open Door Policy," China started an economic reform process. The telecommunication industry, as one of the country's most important basic industries, experienced a huge change and became a notable contributor to the nation's economy. Beginning in 1995, the industry grew at three times the growth rate of the GDP ("Comprehensive overview of China's IT industry in the past 13 years," 2002). The development of the industry within this quarter century can be broken into three periods: (1) a period of preparation, (2) a period of high-speed development, and (3) a period of globalization.

Preparation Period

This first stage began in 1978 and lasted until 1989. At the beginning of China's economic reform, inefficient telecommunication restricted the development of China's economy. For example, in 1978, even in Beijing, the capital of the country, an estimated 20 percent of long-distance phone calls could not be connected, and another 15 percent were connected only after a one-hour wait ("Shi jie dian xin fa zhan shi," 2004). To break this bottleneck, the central government decided to modernize the industry by making policies to streamline it as the first priority.

To raise capital, which would assist the improvement of the inadequate telecommunication infrastructure, a policy of collecting telephone installation fees was initiated in 1979. This policy was a critical contributor to further development of industry. Between 1979 and 1995, one-third of the investment (US$ 33 billion) in the development of infrastructure came from the collection of this installation fee (Li, 2001).

In order to rapidly close the gap with the rest of world, the government decided to introduce advanced foreign equipment and technologies. In 1982, China imported its first digitally programmed switch. Two years later, a state-owned enterprise, under the Ministry of Post and Telecommunication (MPT), working with Belgium Bell Telephone Co., founded Shanghai Bell Telephone Equipment Manufacturing Co., Ltd., the first joint venture telecommunication company to research and develop the Chinese digitally programmed switches. Subsequently, to encourage the introduction of advanced equipment, the government in 1986 reduced by half the import tariff for telecommunication products ("Wo guo tong xin ling yu gai ge fa zhan da shi ji," 2001). During the same period, domestic small private telecommunication companies began to enter the industry by importing telecommunication products and serving as dealers to telecommunication companies abroad. These changes furthered preparation of the infrastructure for the next stage.

High-Speed Development Period

During the second stage, from 1990 to 2000, the central government continued a series of reform measures to speed up the development of the infrastructure, including accelerating depreciation of equipment, increasing capital input, and reorganizing the industry's management structure. Meanwhile, a sharply increased demand pushed the industry into a leapfrogging growth.

In one of its reports to the APEC (Asian-Pacific Economic Cooperation) Information and Telecommunication Work Group at the end of the 1990s, China presented the following information:

> Qualitative changes have taken place in network technology and service level, as represented by the transition from manual to automatic operation, analog to digital technology, small to large capacity and mono- to multi-service. Optical cable, digital microwave, satellite, stored and programmed control, mobile communication, data and multimedia and other advanced technologies have been widely used on telecommunication network. Long distance communication, telephone switching and mobile communication have been digitalized. Telecommunication network is migrating to a new generation of broadband multimedia information network and overall network capability and technological level are in the front rank in the world. ("Rapidly developing China's telecommunication industry")

China set up its first long distance optical cable in 1990. In 1998, it completed the "Eight Vertical, Eight Horizontal" grillwork optical backbone project, thereby shaping its own long-distance telecommunication backbone network. By 2000, the length of nationwide optical cable reached 1.25 million km, with 286,000 km of domestic long-distance cable. During this period, China also built international optical cables with Japan and America and merged its international optical network ("Wo guo tong xin ling yu gai ge fa zhan da shi ji," 2001).

In the telecommunication service area, the central government was cognizant of the disadvantages of the old structure and worked to change this position. In 1993, to break China Telecom Corporation's (China Telecom) monopoly in the service area, the government set up another state-owned telecommunication enterprise, China United Telecommunications Corporation (China Unicom), to provide telecommunication service. In the following years, China's government strengthened the force of previous reforms by separating enterprises from the government and restructuring service sectors. The purpose of service carriers was changed from merely obeying central directives to responding to customers and seeking to satisfy the continuously increasing demands for high-quality services. In 1997 and 2000, China Unicom and China Telecom went public sequentially to improve their capital structure, thereby improving their competitive

abilities and visibility to prepare for contending with international rivals in the future. At the end of 2000, China reduced the telecommunication service fees in order to stimulate demand. Meanwhile, the first joint venture telecommunication carrier, Shanghai Xintian Telecom Co., Ltd., was established. It indicated that China's telecommunication service had begun to accept foreign rivals and become more competitive.

The huge transformation built China's position in the world's telecommunication industry. The number of fixed-line telephone subscribers became the world's second largest in 1997 and in 2000 reached 200 million with a penetration rate of about 20 per hundred (see Exhibits 1 and 2). In 1994, China began to develop GSM mobile telecommunication, and at the end of 2000, the number of mobile phone subscribers grew to become the world's second largest. Also by 2000 China had over 16 million Internet users since its introduction in 1994 (Ministry of Information Industry [MII], 2001).

Telecommunication equipment manufacturing also experienced a rapid development. Numerous foreign manufacturers have come into the Chinese market. Besides introducing advanced products and setting up joint venture companies, they poured technology and advanced management skills into launching R&D centers in China. In 1994, the Chinese R&D Center of North Telecommunications, the first foreign R&D institute in China, was established (Jiang, 2004).

EXHIBIT 1

Number of China's Telephone Subscribers 1991–2004 (Unit: Thousands)

Source: 1998–2002 telecommunication industry annual report, 2003–2004 telecommunication industry monthly report from Ministry of Information Industry (MII). **www.mii.gov.cn.** Organized by Jie Xu.

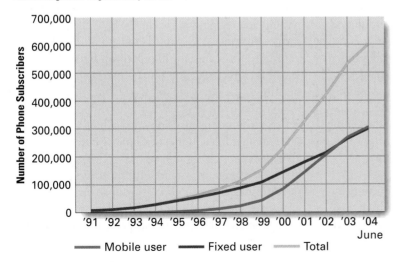

EXHIBIT 2

Telephone Penetration Rate in China from 1995–2004 June (Per hundred people)

Source: 1998–2002 telecommunication industry annual report, 2003–2004 telecommunication industry monthly report from Ministry of Information Industry (MII). **www.mii.gov.cn.** Organized by Jie Xu.

The nation's telecommunication manufacturers rapidly grew up after the first independently developed HJD-04 digitally programmed switch came out in 1991. During a short period, these manufacturers had the abilities to develop and manufacture most of the products in all telecommunication sectors, including digitally programmed switching equipment, optical cable, and mobile networks. The interaction among (a) the direct introduction of foreign telecommunication equipment and technology, (b) establishment of joint venture enterprises, and (c) the development of independent developing domestic telecommunication products catapulted China's telecommunication industry. With the maturation of domestic manufacturers, the government discontinued preferential tariffs to telecommunication equipment imports and began to encourage purchasing from domestic companies in 1996 ("Wo guo tong xin ling yu gai ge fa zhan da shi ji," 2001), which resulted in the end of China's status as an importer in the industry and gradually exportation of the equipment abroad.

Globalization Period

From 2001 to the present, China's telecommunication industry has exhibited rapid development. On December 11, 2001, China entered the WTO (World Trade Organization). According to its commitment to related WTO regulations, China has gradually opened its telecommunication provider market to other WTO members. This has included eliminating tariffs on computers, computer equipment, telecommunication equipment, semiconductors, and other high-tech products before 2005 ("WTO and opening up China's telecommunications market," 2000). To complete its legal frame for ensuring its WTO accession, in 2001, it enacted two important regulations: (1) the People's Republic of China Telecommunications Regulations and (2) the Regulations on Foreign Investment in Telecom Enterprises. It also set up provincial telecommunications administrations (PTAs) to complete its nationwide regulatory system ("The U.S. commercial service promotes U.S. exports to China," 2002).

In order to meet the competition from strong international firms, China restructured its telecommunications market. Even though China Unicom was established for a long time, the monopoly of China Telecom was not really dismantled. China Unicom's assets were just 1/260 of that of China Telecom (Li, 2001). To bring in competition in all the service segments and break the company's monopoly, the government separated China Telecom into four companies. Now, China has seven basic telecommunication carriers to carry basic telecommunication services and at least two carriers in every segment. Through optimizing the network structure and supplying all the telecommunication services, carriers have satisfied and stimulated the demands in different levels of society. As a result of these efforts, in 2001 China had the world's largest number of mobile phone users, and mobile phone users exceeded the number of fixed-line users in 2003 ("Zhong guo yi dong yong hu ju shi jie di yi," 2001). The number of Internet users in China grew to the second largest in the world (see Exhibit 3). China's telecommunications network grew to become the world's largest in 2002, and as of June 2004 had over 600 million users with a penetration rate of 47.4 percent (see Exhibits 1 and 2).

Like telecommunication service, telecommunication equipment manufacturing has also experienced an explosive development. Multinationals have adjusted their investment strategies to compete with the Chinese rivals, using methods such as acquisition and creating partnerships with indigenous companies. The domestic Chinese manufacturers have broadly introduced advanced management methods and pushed forward international cooperation, while independently developing their own products. They have strived not only to satisfy the indigenous markets but also to extend the overseas market. By the end of 2003, ten Chinese manufacturers were exporting products abroad. The total exports of digitally programmed switches reached US$ 450 million, an increase of 81.8 percent compared with the previous year. The value of handsets exports increased to US$ 738 million, 39.4 percent more than in the previous year (MII, 2004). China's telecommunication products have won a reputation of high quality and low prices in the international market and have spread to more than forty countries and regions worldwide ("Wo guo xin xi chan yie shi xian li shi xing kua yue," 2002).

Huawei Technologies Co., Ltd. Background

At the end of the 1980s, following the period of economic reform, the Chinese government encouraged the introduction of advanced foreign telecommunication equipment to change the lagging position of its telecommunication industry. An estimated 90 percent of the equipment used in Chinese telecommunication networks came from foreign companies (Angell, 2003). Huawei Technologies Co., Ltd. was founded in Shenzhen, China's first Special Economic Zone (SEZ), in 1988. During this time, with fourteen employees and about US$ 3,000 capital, it was a vendor of imported PABX (Private Automatic Branch Exchange) systems.

EXHIBIT 3

Top Ten Countries with Highest Number of Internet Users

	Country or Region	Internet Users Latest Data	% of World Usage/Users
1	United States	201,661,159	24.80%
2	China	87,000,000	10.70%
3	Japan	66,763,838	8.20%
4	Germany	47,182,668	5.80%
5	United Kingdom	34,874,469	4.30%
6	South Korea	30,670,000	3.80%
7	Italy	28,610,000	3.50%
8	France	24,352,522	3.00%
9	Canada	20,450,000	2.50%
10	Brazil	19,311,854	2.40%
	Top Ten Countries	560,876,470	69.00%
	Rest of the World	252,055,122	31.00%
	Totals	812,931,592	100.00%

Source: Internet Usage Statistics (2004). **http://www.internetworldstats.com/ top10.htm.**

By the end of 1992, responding to the growing Chinese telecommunication market, Huawei's sales revenue had grown to US$ 12 million with profits of more than US$ 1.2 million. At this juncture, Ren Zhengfei, the founder and president of Huawei, decided to reinvest all the profits into research and development for Huawei's own digitally programmed switch. It was an unusual decision. The telecommunication equipment manufacturing required a huge capital and technological input with high risk; companies seldom wanted to take this chance. But Ren Zhengfei believed this field had a potential opportunity. Through the experience of selling imported products for several years, he noticed that, due to the scarcity of telecommunication equipment in China, the imported products sold at very high prices and earned attractive margins. If Huawei could manufacture its own products, even if they were sold cheaper than imported products, it still could gain considerable profits.

In 1993, imitating international advanced technology, Huawei released its first digitally programmed switch—2,000 ports of C&C08 switch—which could provide the basic voice switching functions. It was successfully put into commercial use in a rural county of Zhejiang province. This success transformed Huawei from a vendor of imported equipment into an independent manufacturer. Subsequently, the company continued to develop the C&C08 switching system and made it its pillar product.

In the beginning years, Huawei's product was only used in the poor, rural regions of China. Its product was not yet mature, and the capacity of the product was not adequate to meet the demands of urban telecommunication carriers. Likewise, multinational companies, which had first-mover advantage in China, had already penetrated the urban markets; the good performance and stability of their products made the telecommunication carriers unable to make the switch from imported to domestic products easily. Even so, Huawei didn't give up. It adopted the suggestion from the telecommunication carriers and experts, thereby continuously developing the C&C08 switch with a view to China's particular needs. For example, due to China's vast territory, it is important that telecommunication equipment in some remote rural villages—many of which have atrocious weather and difficult geography—should have anti-lightning and power reduction functions. Huawei worked out a solution that used fiber as a connecting method. Compared with the conventional international method,

which used cable as a connecting tool, this solution greatly reduced the cost and was applicable in the country's vast rural telecommunication markets.

In the middle of the 1990s, because of the rapid development of the industry, the urban carriers needed to extend the capacity of the telecommunication network to meet increasing demands of telephone users. They were attracted by C&C08's gradually matured performance—which had gotten the praise of its rural users—and its low price—which was just 80 percent of those of imported products—and finally chose it as the cost-effective alternative to those of multinational rivals. Therefore, Huawei's products at last entered into the profitable urban markets.

C&C08's national success was a good start. Huawei gradually extended its product lines from telephone exchange equipment to the other key telecommunication technology fields, including fiber optic networks, mobile telephone technologies, data routing systems, intelligent networks, routers, and videoconferencing, and set up sales distribution in almost every province. However, Ren Zhengfei realized that as the home market grew, it would also increasingly become tougher to compete: Cheaper domestic rivals would rapidly blossom and more foreign competitors would continue to step in. Therefore, the competition would decrease profit margins. If Huawei wanted to achieve long-term success, it should turn its eyes to the global market.

In 1996, Huawei signed its first overseas sales contract with Hutchison Global Communications Limited, Hong Kong's telecommunication carrier, consequently beginning its overseas entry.[2] Its high-quality product and service received Hutchison's praise and laid the foundation for future global exploit. But the road to conquest abroad was bumpy. Because of Huawei's obscurity in the telecommunication industry, it was hard to compete with the veteran global telecommunication giants. Ren Zhengfei realized that if Huawei were to win in the global market, it must become a multinational company first, with distinctive products and an effective management structure. Understanding this, Huawei undertook a full-range reform in 1997. Domestic and international think tanks were invited to design a highly effective organizational structure. Huawei built a market-driven R&D model

---

[2]Although Hong Kong returned to China on July 1, 1997, trade between Hong Kong and mainland China is still treated as international business. Investments from Hong Kong are still looked as foreign investments. Based on this designation, in this thesis, the Hong Kong market is categorized as an international market.

EXHIBIT 4

Huawei's R&D Centers Worldwide

Source: Huawei Company Profile 2004.

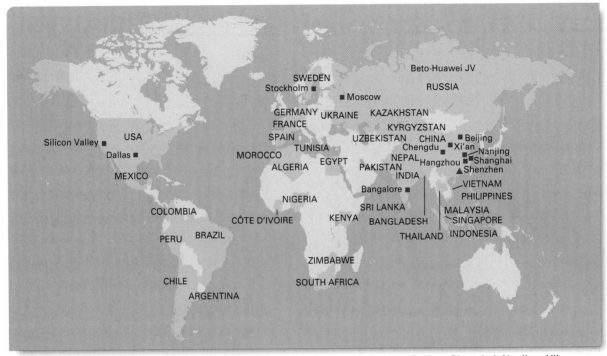

Research Institutes = ■ (The Silicon Valley, Dallas, Stockholm, Moscow, Bangalore, Beijing, Shanghai, Nanjing, Xi'an, Chengdu, Hangzhou)

Headquarters = ▲ (Shenzhen)

for developing customized products. In order to better understand customer demands and respond more quickly, it set up 40 branch offices, 8 regional headquarters, 4 R&D centers, and many customer support and training centers outside of China (see Exhibits 4 and 5). It also built joint laboratories with leading players, such as IBM, Intel, Motorola, and Texas Instruments (TI). In order to hasten the process to enter the developed markets, such as those in the United States, in 2003, Huawei joined with 3Com and incorporated a joint venture company: Huawei-3Com.

At the end of 2003, Huawei had 22,000 employees and was one of the world's major vendors with full-range telecommunication product manufacturing capability. It had a 40 percent share in the fixed-line switch market, as well as 55 percent of transmission equipment in the domestic market (Buckley, 2003). From 2001 to 2003, its sales of C&C08 remained first in the world switch market. In 2003, its broadband and optic network products ranked second in their respective markets ("Huawei's overseas strategy starts to pay off," 2004); more than 120 telecommunication carriers used its products worldwide ("Huawei undergoes international tests," 2004); and its sales revenue reached US$ 3.83 billion (see Exhibit 6), including US$ 1.05 billion from international markets that year.

Huawei's International Strategy

Huawei's development can be categorized in three stages. The first stage was from 1988 to 1992. During this time, as an imported telecommunication products vendor, Huawei gained a lot of experience: learning the advantages of foreign products and the Chinese market demands and also accumulating capital for a future changeover to make its own products.

The second stage was from 1993 to 1996. In this stage, Huawei imitated and followed world advanced technology to manufacture its own products. At the same time as being accepted by the domestic telecommunication carriers, it set the goal to go abroad. In 1996, it successfully entered the Hong Kong market.

EXHIBIT 5

Huawei's Overseas Branch Offices

Source: Huawei Company Profile 2004.

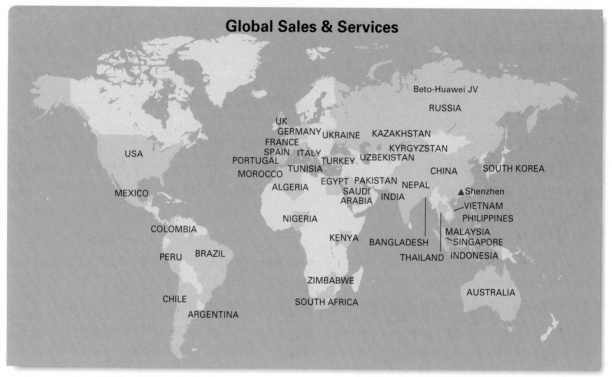

Headquarters = ▲ (Shenzhen)

The third stage was the global phase, beginning in 1997. While introducing the advanced management methods to restructure its internal process, Huawei had pushed its global strategy by establishing overseas R&D centers and branch offices. It also cooperated with leading industrial players by building joint laboratories and joint-venture companies to create a win-win situation. Its global process can be explained by Yip's (1990) "total global strategy" (see Exhibit 7). Huawei developed its core strategy by first opening home markets from the rural areas to urban areas. Then it extended this strategy to the international markets by opening the markets from the developing countries to developed countries. Finally it built its market-driven R&D model to integrate the strategy across countries. Its efforts to provide customers with high-quality products, sound service, and cost-effective solutions built its international reputation.

Since 1996, when it first stepped out of China, via the spread of its products worldwide, Huawei gradually became a major provider of telecommunication equipment in the industry. Its customers included AT&T, Brazil Telecom, British Telecom, Hutchison Telecom (Hong Kong), French Telecom, Rostelecom (Russia), Telefonica, and so on. Its international sales revenue increased from US$ 50 million in 1999 to US$ 128 million in 2000 and to US$ 1.05 billion in 2003.

Huawei thrives because of its high price-performance ratio, customized products, sound service, and unswerving tenacity in the international market, including these markets described below.

Hong Kong Market

Hong Kong, China's Special Administrative Region (SAR), is an important international financial center in the world. Because of its special history, as a

Huawei's Sales Revenue 1998–2003 (Based on Annual Signed Contract Value)

Source: Huawei Company Profile 2004.

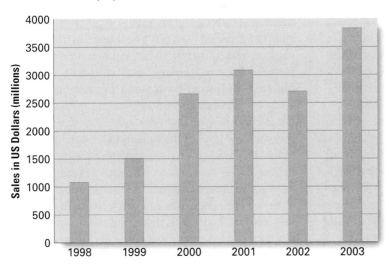

colony of the United Kingdom, this Asian city has its unique capacity for merging Eastern and Western factors. Most Mainland Chinese companies choose Hong Kong as their bridge to enter into the world market, and Huawei was no exception.

In the middle of the 1990s, as the important tool of external trade, Hong Kong's telecommunication service level and network facilities were already advanced. World famous telecommunication giants looked to Hong Kong as an important telecommunication market, and sold their latest switching products there. Telecommunication carriers competed to use the new technology, which could provide new services to attract customers.

Hutchison Global Communications Limited was a late entrant to the competitive Hong Kong telecommunication market. In 1996, it was looking for a reliable manufacturer to provide cost-effective advanced telecommunication equipment to meet its

Total Global Strategy

Source: Yip, G.S. (1995), *Total Global Strategy*, p. 4.

1. Develop core business strategy
2. Internationalize the strategy
3. Globalize the strategy

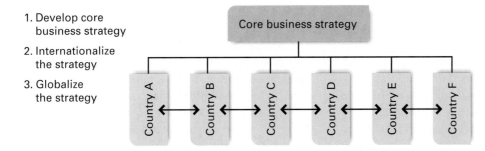

licensing requirement. After carefully comparing the numerous providers and products, it chose Huawei as its partner.

Huawei could outperform its international rivals because it not only had the ability to supply advanced cost-effective products and flexible technical support, but it also promised to support a specific workforce to provide a tailor-made solution in only half a year, which others could not. It established a technical support department in Hong Kong to respond to its customers' need and get timely feedback. To improve its service development ability, it set up a test platform there. Huawei strived to work out a solution that could help Hutchison gain the advantage in a competitive environment. After signing the contract on June 5, 1996, the first batch of equipment was delivered to Hong Kong on October 28. Two months later—on December 28—the C&C08 Switching System was applied and interconnected with the Hong Kong telecommunication network ("C&C08 EV in Hutchison IP business network," 2002).

Huawei's outstanding products made Hutchison able to support low-cost, diversified services to its customers, thereby increasing Hutchison's competitive ability and enabling it to recover its investment in only one year. Since then, Hutchison and Huawei have built a strategic partner relationship. Through several years' cooperation, Hutchison's fixed network has gradually become Hong Kong's second largest fixed network, and all the switching equipment on its network comes from Huawei ("Successful cooperation between Hutchison and Huawei," 2002). This first overseas success also built a stable foundation for further products of Huawei, such as transmission, data communication, NGN, and multimedia products, which have entered into wider telecommunication areas in Hong Kong. In 2003, the sales revenue in Hong Kong reached over US$ 56 million.

Russian Market

After successfully gaining the first foothold in Hong Kong, Huawei focused on its next target, Russia's huge potential telecommunication market. However, before the entry of Huawei, multinational giants, such as Alcatel, Lucent, and Siemens, dominated this lucrative market. At the time, the unfamiliarity of Russia to the Chinese high-tech products made Huawei's entry more difficult. When Huawei's salesmen first visited Russian telecommunication carriers, they even didn't believe China could produce switching equipment, and rejected cooperation with Huawei.

In 1997 Huawei decided to use a new method to enter the Russian market. It set up its first joint venture, Beto-Huawei, in Russia to manufacture C&C08 switches and used this joint venture (JV) platform to exploit the market. The first sales contract—US$12 million— was signed in Russia that year; however, compared with Huawei's investment in its JV, this contract was uninspiring. But Huawei didn't give up. In following years, Huawei noticed there were many different companies' switching equipment that operated in Russia's network, which made Russia's telecommunication network have a complex structure and low level of digitalization. Huawei proposed to use a LCMS (Low Cost and Multi Service) solution in its C&C08 switches to help carriers improve the network structure and get O&M (Operation & Maintenance) efficiency. Russia's carriers finally accepted this solution in 1999. It improved the network capabilities, reduced operation costs, and increased network profit. Huawei's endeavor got recognition; by 2002, the LCMS solution was used in over twenty-two administrative regions ("Network optimization application in Russia," 2002).

Coupled with rapid economic development, Russia's telecommunication industry grew quickly, thereby requiring more new services. Based on C&C08's outstanding performance, Huawei's other products were rapidly accepted by Russia's carriers and finally helped in constructing a high-end optical national "backbone." On the last day of 2002, Huawei and Rostelecom, the largest national long-haul carrier in Russia, signed a final engineering acceptance test report for the national optical "backbone" project. This project, from Moscow to Samara, had a transmission distance of up to 1021 km. It was the first time that Huawei applied its high-end optical equipment in Russia. In 2003, Huawei earned more than US$ 300 million sales revenue there ("Huawei helps Rostelecom to complete Russia's national backbone," 2003.)

West European Market

In contrast with Russia, West Europe has mature telecommunication markets. These markets have solid infrastructures and a sophisticated service structure. When the information and communication technology industry blossomed, the telecommunication carriers did not care much about costs and chose most of the products from the top telecommunication manufacturers (Bolande & Hutzler, 2002). However, at the turn of the century, the dotcom bubble collapse spread to the whole IT industry and made the industry decline. The telecommunication carriers had to be more rational and cautious when they made investments.

Besides facing the decline of the IT industry, the fixed carriers also experienced more serious tribulation than other carriers. Due to mobile communication's fast development, the number of mobile subscribers gradually exceeded that of fixed users. The decrease of fixed traffic volume resulted in a decline of revenues. The European fixed carriers, which faced the challenge of expensive operation costs and poor earnings, had to constrain their spending and needed to rebuild an effective new fixed network to cut down costs, promote broadband services, and provide customized services ("Huawei demonstrating its brand-new overall fixed network solution throughout Europe," 2004).

Emerging as a lower-cost rival to giant companies, such as Cisco System and Lucent, Huawei engaged the attention of European carriers. It responded to such changes in customers' demands rapidly and presented its SOFTX3000 IP softswitch and media gateway management systems—"21CN Fixed Line architecture." In this brand-new fixed network solution, it incorporated its latest fixed network solution, including softswitch (NGN), data communication, next generation access network (NG-AN), and IP telecommunication network. One of the big advantages of this solution was that it's a win-win strategy, not only between the telecommunication provider and carrier but also between the carrier and its customers. It lowered the operation costs, supported the full range of next-generation protocols, and formed the flexible networks, which let the customers of the carriers get cost-savings and huge capacity ("Huawei U-SYS next generation network entering into the U.K. telecommunication markets," 2004).

EEscape, one of Europe's largest telecommunication carriers and UK's first IP Network carrier, introduced this solution and used Huawei's equipment to provide the integrated voice-data-video services to its corporate and small/medium business customers in April 2004. It greatly reduces complexity and cost of operation by using MPLS (Multi Protocol Label Switching), the original infrastructure, to provide clients new voice services. Mark Lower, CEO of EEscape, claimed the cooperation with Huawei "will see new price, service and quality benchmarks for multi-sited business customers in the UK" ("EEscape deploys Huawei VOIP kit," 2004).

Huawei's International Marketing Strategy

Similar to its domestic market strategy, which occupied markets from the outlying rural areas to the central cities, Huawei's overseas market strategy was to open markets from the developing countries to the developed countries. This process also facilitated brand recognition.

Entry Strategy

Huawei first focused on entering the Asia-Pacific, Africa, East Europe, and Latin American markets. These rising markets, which had lower telephone penetration rates and lagging telecommunication infrastructure, were similar to the initial development stage of China's telecommunication industry and presented huge market potential. Huawei hoped to use its abundant experience, which it gained from China's market, to open these markets.

Although it had ambition, Huawei experienced its hardest time during the initial several years of its overseas campaign. The biggest disadvantage was that the world market knew nothing about Huawei at that time. Since a telecommunication project is an investment-style project, which involves huge capital and technology outlays, carriers could not take a risk by choosing an unknown company as a partner. Building its name recognition became a pressing affair to transform this disadvantage.

The first step was to let customers know Huawei's name. At the beginning, Huawei entered numerous international bids, even though it knew that it had no chance to get the bids. The purpose of this action was to just let the telecommunication carriers know that this Chinese company had the ability to manufacture advanced telecommunication products. Huawei's constant presence gradually got the customers' notice. But soon after connecting with customers, Huawei found another problem. The impression of China in customers' minds, which came from literature and movies, stopped several decades before, or even earlier. They thought China was still very backward in its standard of living and level of technologies. Under these conditions, it was hard to imagine that they would order several million dollars of high-tech equipment from a company from China. To change their notions, Huawei published an elaborate brochure named "Huawei in China"—a collection of China's natural scenes and modern buildings—to present China's huge transformation during economic reform. In this volume, Huawei cleverly interjected the application of its equipment in China, thereby representing its important position in China's telecommunication industry. This method renovated customers' out-of-date impressions of China and compelled them to put Huawei's name in their list of choices.

The next step was to get customers to believe Huawei's high-quality products can compete with those of the famous brands. Since 1996, Huawei began to attend international exhibitions with a high frequency. Through presenting its products with the multinationals in the same arena, Huawei let customers know about its products' advantages. Customers, who always looked down upon China's products, were astounded by Huawei's products. Those products, which used all self-designed chips, were able to carry out the similar functions to those of Western companies but were 20 to 40 percent cheaper. More important was that Huawei offered better customized solutions for its customers. Huawei's higher margins were in part attributed to its lower engineering labor cost—where one-fifth were those paid by American companies—and effective sales teams, which set up branch offices and recruited local employees worldwide. As its name became well-known, Huawei was able to enter the overseas market. In 1997, it penetrated the Russian market. In 1998, it went into the Indian market, and in 2000, it stepped into the Middle East and African markets.

Win-Win Strategy

America, dominated by the world's newer technologies, was the toughest market. Many tier-one companies, such as Cisco Systems, started up there and have absolute control there. They use enormous protocols to set a high-priced gate to enter, thereby blocking out newcomers. Ren Zhengfei realized if Huawei just depended on its own force to enter, it would be costly and problematic. A better way for Huawei would be to cooperate with an established company in possession of an established position in America and to rely on its distribution channels and well-known brand name. Thinking of this plan, Huawei attempted to form a joint venture with somebody. At the same time, 3Com, the tier-one voice and data products provider in the industry, was looking for a strategic partner that could help it complement its product lines and consolidate its position in the Asian—especially Chinese—market. These matched objectives finally let Huawei and 3Com join hands. On November 7, 2003, Huawei-3Com Co., Ltd., a joint venture of developing and manufacturing

enterprise-class networking equipment, was established in Hangzhou, China. The press release from 3Com said

> Huawei-3Com Co., Ltd., will deliver enterprise networking solutions including routers and LAN switches. 3Com has the rights to market and support the Huawei-3Com products under the 3Com brand in all countries except China and Japan. In China and Japan, Huawei-3Com will sell products sourced internally as well as from 3Com.…

> Huawei is contributing to Huawei-3Com its enterprise networking business assets, including LAN switches and routers, engineering and sales/marketing resources and personnel, and licenses to its related intellectual property. 3Com is contributing $160 million in cash, assets related to its operations in China and Japan, and licenses to certain intellectual property. In two years, 3Com has the right to acquire a majority ownership interest in Huawei-3Com. (Huawei-3Com Joint Venture Begins Operations)

This cooperation was a win-win situation. It let 3Com extend its product range by adding Huawei's enterprise-class equipment in and securing its position in China and Japan; on the other hand, it let Huawei's products be branded 3Com, and through 3Com's formidable distribution network—comprising 41,000 distribution partners in areas outside China and Japan—it sped up its entry in world markets, especially those of North America ("Step to world: Huawei-3Com established," 2003). The complementary businesses have very little overlaps in product lines and regional sales channels, thereby saving the costs of new product research and market development for both companies ("3Com, Huawei join hands behind Cisco's back," 2003).

Huawei's R&D Strategy

Admittedly, having outstanding products is an extremely important factor to achieve overseas success. To a company looking for long-term development, the most important factor is whether this company can continuously invent outstanding products to meet the customers' increasing demands. Imitators can only share and occupy the existent profit space—the more imitators, the less profit to share; only the innovator can build a new profit space center and gain huge returns from it. Ren Zhengfei realized this and set a goal to make Huawei an innovator in the industry. He believed that if Huawei were to get a high return, it should have a formidable R&D capability first, because in the telecommunication industry, the advanced level of technology decides the competition's victory or defeat.

Based on this viewpoint, Huawei spent no less than 10 percent of its sales revenue on its R&D every year to specialize in designing silicon chips and developing new products. Huawei is one of the few companies in China that can design its own chip. All of its products are based on one common platform, which is supported by its own ASIC (Application Specific Integrated Circuits) chips. This core strength allowed Huawei to lower its costs dramatically: A chip bought from the West costs more than US$ 100, but a similar one designed by Huawei and produced by an American company costs less than US$ 15. In a year, Huawei uses several million self-designed chips, which means it can save more than US$ 100 million per year ("Huawei quan mian xi hua," 2004). Also, its independence ensures that Huawei can freely pursue its own research (see Exhibit 8).

To attract the cream of the employee crop and chase the latest industry trends, Huawei created thirteen R&D centers worldwide. Seven domestic centers are scattered in Shenzhen (headquarters), Beijing, Shanghai, Nanjing, Xi'an, Hangzhou, and Chengdu to gain access to their university graduates and their established economic positions in China. Meanwhile Huawei set up four overseas centers and recruited local employees. Because of America's leading position as disseminator of first-class IT technologies, Huawei set up a center in Dallas, Texas, to do the chip design. India's reputation as "the software hothouse of Asia" encouraged Huawei to set up a software center in Bangalore. Likewise, considering that Sweden is the front end of mobile technology development and Russia is the top player in the RF (Radio Frequency) area, Huawei also built centers in Stockholm and Moscow. Now Huawei has over ten thousand employees working in R&D domestically and worldwide, which is 46 percent of its

EXHIBIT 8

Huawei's Products

Source: Huawei Company Profile 2004.

- Products are based on shared platform of technologies and self-designed ASIC chips.
- All products are TL 9000, ISO 14001 compliant as certified by DNV.

EXHIBIT 9

Huawei's Human Resources

Source: Huawei Company Profile 2004.

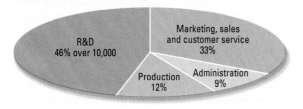

total employees (see Exhibit 9). These employees, who are part of Huawei's fortune, are not just bright and well educated but extremely curious. Their hard work guarantees the high reliability and low cost of Huawei's products.

The high capital and work force input in R&D can produce tangible profits only when directed by the correct R&D orientation. While some of the high-tech companies concentrated too much on developing tech-savvy products, Huawei drew its product roadmap based on customer needs. It believed that the direction of innovation should be market oriented; the objective of innovation should be to forecast the market, guide consumption, and satisfy the customers' demands. Otherwise an impracticable innovation is lifeless and wastes money, even causing the company to experience finance difficulties. With this realization, Huawei builds its mission statement as "Huawei is in pursuit of realizing customers' dreams in the IT sector, and becoming a business with sustainable growth" and believes that "the enhancement of customers' interest is the only reason for Huawei's existence" ("Huawei company profile," 2004). Before it explores a new technology or develops a new product, Huawei tries to find out what the customers need and then strives to meet these needs. In 2003, Huawei rebuilt its R&D organization by turning each product line into a profit center. This transformation forced the R&D system and marketing system to collaborate more effectively to respond to customers' demands. This guideline ensured that Huawei's products had the ideal functions and price-performance ratio.

As an aggressive firm, Huawei attaches importance to learning advanced ideas and processes in order to make its own R&D develop in a more orderly and active fashion. To enhance the capability in some research areas, it has partnered with Texas Instruments, Motorola, Microsoft, Intel, Sun Micro Systems, and so on to build joint laboratories. Through cooper-

ation, Huawei and its partner can license and cross-license their respective patents to each other.

Competitor Analysis

Cisco Systems

Cisco Systems, Inc., the worldwide leader of developing and manufacturing telecommunication and networking equipment, was established in 1984 in California. In 1990, it went public. During its peak time, the stock price reached US$ 82 per share after many splits. In its 2003 fiscal year, it had 34,466 employees and obtained a sales revenue of US$ 18.878 billion. Cisco made its first acquisition in 1993. As of July 2004, its total acquisitions numbered eighty-four companies. Through these acquisitions, Cisco Systems not only controlled numerous newer technologies and products, but also eliminated the threat that those small companies would be acquired by rivals or grow up to be rivals, thereby maintaining its dominant position. Its products, as a key factor of Internet infrastructure, have provided a broad range of solutions and have been used in corporations, public institutions, telecommunication companies, commercial businesses, and personal residences. It has a reputation for its high-performance products. Seventy-five percent of Cisco's sales revenues came from routers and data switch products ("Huawei ban dao si ke," 2004).

In 1994, Cisco Systems set up its first China branch office in Beijing. In the following years, it opened other branch offices in Shanghai, Guangzhou, and Chengdu. Based on the extension of its business in the Asia-Pacific area and China's important position in this area, in 1998 it established the largest Asian network lab in Beijing. Depending on its solid capability, Cisco Systems has been able to maintain a 50 percent growth rate of sales revenue in the Chinese market ("Na xie gong si she xian long duan zhai zhong guo," 2004). It has competitive advantages in the Ethernet switch and high-end router market. In 1999, its high-end router occupied a 78 percent market share in China ("Report of market research of network equipment in China," 2000). In recent years, even though China's domestic manufacturers have grown up and grabbed back some of the markets, its high-performance products still maintain a dominant position in China. In 2002, it owned a 60 percent share in China's data networking market (Angell, 2003). Although its router products' market share fell to 41.6 percent that year, it was still far more than the

EXHIBIT 10

Router Product Brand Distribution in China's Telecommunication Market (2003)

Source: CCID Telecommunication Market Report, February, 2004.

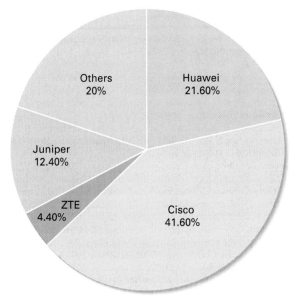

nearest Chinese rival—Huawei—which had just a 21.6 percent share (see Exhibit 10).

Zhongxing Telecom Equipment Corporation (ZTE)

ZTE Corporation was founded in 1985. Initially, it was a state-owned company and sponsored by NO. 591 Factory under former Ministry of Aerospace Industry, Changcheng Industrial Co., Ltd. and Yunxing Electronic Trading Co., Ltd. In 1997, ZTE went public. Now it is one of China's largest telecommunication equipment providers, with 17,000 employees. In 2003, its sales revenue got US$ 1.9 billion. Its products have been distributed in over forty countries, including the United States, Russia, and Zambia.

As a full-scale telecommunication equipment provider, it provides equipment for fixed, mobile, data, intelligent, optical, and next-generation networks. The main product lines include switch, access, transmission, mobile communications, PHS (Personal Handy-phone System) networks and terminals, videoconferencing, data communications, and mobile handset.

ZTE has several competitive advantages. It was the first individual manufacturer member of 3rd Generation Partnership 2 (3GPP2) in China and was an International Telecommunication Union (ITU) member ("ZTE profile," 2004). It is also a strong player in PHS.

The company seized the opportunity to develop this cheap, low-tech service's local mobile-telephone network and has become not only the leading supplier of PHS equipment, but also the big seller of PHS handsets, which sold 2.6 million in 2003 and held about 30 percent of the PHS market in China. Huawei's misstep was that it spurned involvement in this area, lost this market, and let its rivals such as ZTE get the best opportunity easily. Finally ZTE attained a sizable market share of the CDMA (Code Division Multiple Access) mobile communication system products during the past several years, as well as the reputation of "Top Chinese CDMA Brand."

The Future

Huawei has succeeded in entering into the global market as one of the world's major telecommunication manufacturers. Currently, Huawei is still developing rapidly by improving its reputation and consolidating its presence in the global market.

It is striking that Huawei never relied on the capital market. As a private company fully owned by its employees, it collected capital from issuing internal stock and getting bank loans. Its financial performance looks healthy (see Exhibit 11). However, coupled with Huawei's global extension, which continuously demands huge investments in R&D and marketing, it is important to reserve capital for potential needs. Solely depending on internal capital sources cannot satisfy these future demands. To keep its growth trend healthy for the long term, Huawei will need to raise substantial funds from an initial public offering (IPO) in the capital market. Currently, Huawei is preparing for the possibility to go public in mid-2005 ("Huawei to capitalize on international capital market," 2004).

EXHIBIT 11

Huawei's Financial Performance (2000–2003)

Year ended December 31	2000	2001	2002	2003
		(USD in millions)		
Revenue	1933	2290	2128	2694
Net Income	345	258	108	384
Cash Flow from Operations	255	204	311	385
Operating Ratio	24%	17%	10%	19%
Return on Net Assets	36%	16%	7%	20%

Source: Huawei Company Profile 2004.

To pave the way for its listing, Huawei will need to consider reorganization. Huawei may need to divide itself into several companies based on specialization. In the past sixteen years, the company grew quickly, and because of the huge structure, the company will find it difficult to respond rapidly to the dynamic market. Huawei will need to continue to offer better services to its customers to maintain its competitiveness.

Ten years ago, none of its earnings came from the overseas market. In 2003, one-third of its income was gained from the international market. By 2008, Huawei hopes to earn two-thirds of its annual revenue from the rest of the world. As the company regroups for the future, Huawei's management is considering what they would need to do to gain the confidence of foreign investors.

REFERENCES

A comprehensive overview of China's IT industry in the past 13 years. (2002, October 15). Available at: **http://web.syr.edu/~ztan/China-tel.html** (in Chinese).

Angell, M. (2003, January 29). Cisco hopes to block knock-offs produced by Chinese firm. *Investor's Business Daily*, p. A5.

Bolande, H. A., and Hutzler, C. (2002, September 24). Huawei's cost advantage spurs sales amid the telecom slump. *Wall Street Journal*, p. B7.

Buckley, C. (2003, October 6). Rapid growth of China's Huawei has its high-tech rivals on guard. *The New York Times*, p. 1.

C&C08 EV in Hutchison IP Business Network. (2002). Available at **http://www.huawei.com/products/infodetail.jsp?type=1&id=231**.

EEscape deploys Huawei VOIP kit. (2003, December 12). Available at **http://www.lightreading.com/document.asp?doc_id=44816**.

High-tech firms sharpen edge. (2004, April 14). Available at **http://0-web.lexis-nexis.com.iii1.sonoma.edu/universe/document?_m=5c101c46a289fd515636fa62624c3d8b&_docnum=2&wchp=dGLbVtz-zSkVb&_md5=4d165db124ec23379c21495343cc4cba**.

Huawei ban dao si ke. (2004). Available at **http://www.ce.cn/cysc/telecom/xwzx/gndt/200407/30/t20040730_1364341.shtml**.

Huawei C&C08 fa zhan li cheng.(2004, May 20). Available at **http://www.huawei.com.cn/news/media/1804.shtml**.

Huawei corporate profile. (2004). Available at **http://www.huawei.com/about/Corporate/Corp-Profile/index.shtml**.

Huawei demonstrating its brand-new overall fixed network solution throughout Europe. (2004, May 17). Available at **http://www.huawei.com/about/News-Events/News-Center/947.shtml**.

Huawei helps Rostelecom to complete Russia's national backbone. (2003). Available at **http://www.huawei.com/about/News-Events/News-Center/848.shtml**.

Huawei quan mian xi hua. (2004, September 13). Available at **http://telecom.chinabyte.com/NetCom/218425681439096832/20040913/1853003_1.shtml**.

Huawei's overseas strategy starts to pay off. (2004, April 29). Available at **http://0-web.lexis-nexis.com.iii1.sonoma.edu/universe/document?_m=93d92bb6ad1ab73e42ff5d039859357a&_docnum=1&wchp=dGLbVlz-zSkVb&_md5=97ab1a985227f53c0da4bbd8b809a215**.

Huawei to capitalize on international capital market. (2004, July 27). *China Internet Weekly*, p. 1.

Huawei undergoes international tests. (2004, August 17). *The Economic Observer*, p. 1.

Huawei U-SYS next generation network entering into the U.K. telecom markets. (2003). Available at **http://www.huawei.com.cn/news/newscenter/1637.shtml**.

Huawei-3Com joint venture begins operations. (2003). Available at **http://www.3com.com/corpinfo/en_US/pressbox/press_release.jsp?INFO_ID=170570**.

Jiang, J. (2004). FDI and technology transfer in China. Available at **http://www.hhs.se/NR/rdonlyres/ezbze2zdp4jsfu7d4pbvv7keslkmhvanrcpqosyrqfiiup23kn3jlyc56o766y6lr2h24hfahbypif**.

Li, J. (2001). China's telecom industry reform. Available at **http://tech.sina.com.cn/it/t/2001-12-11/95470.shtml**.

Liu, X. (2001). Dian hua chu zhuang wei zhong guo dian xin li xia han ma gong lao. Available at **http://it.sohu.com/20010714/file/0000,643,100002.html**.

Ministry of Information Industry (MII) (China). (2001). 2000 Annual statistic report of Ministry of Information Industry. Available at **http://www.mii.gov.cn/mii/hyzw/tongji/gongbao2000.htm**.

Ministry of Information Industry (MII) (China). (2004). 2003 Annual statistic report of Ministry of Information Industry. Available at **http://www.mii.gov.cn/mii/hyzw/tongji/2004-040501.htm**.

Na xie gong si she xian long duan zhai zhong guo. (2004). Available at **http://info.news.hc360.com/HTML/001/002/009/004/47794.htm**.

Network optimization application in Russia. (2002). Available at **http://www.huawei.com/products/infodetail.jsp?type=1&id=229**.

Rapidly developing China's telecommunication industry. (2000). Available at **http://www.apectelwg.org/apecdata/telwg/24tel/plenary/12POLICY%20AND%20REGULATORY%20UPDATE%20CHINA.htm**.

Report of market research of network equipment in China. (2000). Available at **http://www.china-asean.net/china_biz/marketing_report/china_report_network.html**.

Shi jie dian xin fa zhan shi. (2004, June 30). Available at **http://news.chinabyte.com/busnews/216456456113750016/20040630/1825874.shtml**.

Step to world: Huawei-3Com established. (2003). Available at **http://industry.ccidnet.com/pub/disp/Article?articleID=41242&columnID=32**.

Successful cooperation between Hutchison and Huawei. (2002). *C&C08 and HONET in Hong Kong*. Shenzhen: Huawei.

The U.S. commercial service promotes U.S. exports to China. (2002). Available at **http://www.buyusa.gov/china/en/telecommunications.html**.

Wo guo tong xin ling yu gai ge fa zhan da shi ji. (2001). Available at **http://ydqy.cnii.com.cn/20020203/ca30945.htm**.

Wo guo xin xi chan yie shi xian li shi xing kua yue. (2002, October 16). Available at **http://news.xinhuanet.com/zhengfu/2002-10/16/content_598059.htm**.

WTO and opening up China's telecommunications market. (2000). Available at **http://www.prcinvestment.com/dtt/wto.php?id=7230**.

Yip, G.S. (1995). *Total global strategy*. New Jersey: Prentice Hall.

Zhong guo yi dong yong hu ju shi jie di yi. (2001, June 21). Available at **http://www.zaobao.com/special/newspapers/2001/06/jjckb210601.html**.

ZTE portfolio. (2004) Available at **http://www.zte.com.cn/English/01about/index.jsp**.

3Com, Huawei join hands behind Cisco's back. (2003). Available at **http://siliconvalley.internet.com/news/article.php/2119621**.

Case 8

The Home Video Game Industry: From Pong to Halo 2

This case was prepared by Charles W. L. Hill, the University of Washington.

Introduction: November 2004

On November 9, 2004, Microsoft released Halo 2, the second version of its bestselling science fiction video game for the company's Xbox console. Orders for Halo 2 were closely watched in the industry. The original Halo was the game that more than any other attracted millions of users to Microsoft's Xbox. Launched in November 2001, some 18 months after rival Sony launched PlayStation 2 (PS2), Microsoft's Xbox has trailed PlayStation 2 by a wide margin. As of mid 2004, Sony had sold some 70 million PS2 consoles worldwide, compared with 14 million Xbox consoles, and 13 million units of Nintendo's Game Cub, which was also launched in 2001. Had Microsoft not had Halo, it might well have been a distant third to Nintendo.

Could Halo 2 help close the gap between Xbox and PS2? Might Microsoft be able to ride Halo 2 into a leadership position in the industry, particularly given that all participants in the industry were busy developing a new generation of super powerful video game consoles? Dramatic leadership changes had happened before in the industry. The industry was once dominated by Atari, and then by Nintendo, which in turn lost its lead to Sega, which was subsequently overtaken by Sony with its original PlayStation console. Might Microsoft be able to seize industry leadership with the next generation gaming machine?

As first day sales for Halo 2 were totaled up, executives at Sony had to be worried. Microsoft announced that Halo 2 had sales of $125 million in its first 24 hours on the market in the United States and Canada. These figures represented sales of 2.38 million units, and put Halo 2 firmly on track to be one of the biggest video games ever with a shot at surpassing Nintendo's Super Mario 64, which had sold $308 million in the United States since its September 1996 debut.

An Industry Is Born

In 1968, Nolan Bushnell, the twenty-four-year-old son of a Utah cement contractor, graduated from the University of Utah with a degree in engineering.[1] Bushnell then moved to California, where he worked briefly in the computer graphics division of Ampex. At home, Bushnell turned his daughter's bedroom into a laboratory. There, he created a simpler version of Space War, a computer game that had been invented in 1962 by an MIT graduate student, Steve Russell. Bushnell's version of Russell's game, which he called Computer Space, was made of integrated circuits connected to a nineteen-inch black-and-white television screen. Unlike a computer, Bushnell's invention could do nothing but play the game, which meant that, unlike a computer, it could be produced cheaply.

Copyright © 2004 by Charles W. L. Hill. This case was prepared by Charles W. L. Hill, the University of Washington, as the basis for class discussion rather than to illustrate either effective or ineffective handling of an administrative situation. Reprinted by permission of Charles W. L. Hill. All rights reserved. For the most recent financial results of the company discussed in this case, go to **http://finance.yahoo.com,** input the company's stock symbol, and download the latest company report from its homepage.

Bushnell envisioned video games like his standing next to pinball machines in arcades. With hopes of having his invention put into production, Bushnell left Ampex to work for a small pinball company that manufactured fifteen hundred copies of his video game. The game never sold, primarily because the player had to read a full page of directions before he or she could play the game—way too complex for an arcade game. Bushnell left the pinball company, and with a friend, Ted Dabney, put up $500 to start a company that would develop a simpler video game. They wanted to call the company Syzygy, but the name was already taken, so they settled on Atari, a Japanese word that was the equivalent of "*check* in the *go*."

In his home laboratory, Bushnell built the simplest game he could think of. People knew the rules immediately, and it could be played with one hand. The game was modeled on table tennis, and players batted a ball back and forth with paddles that could be moved up and down sides of a court by twisting knobs. He named the game "Pong" after the sonarlike sound that was emitted every time the ball connected with a paddle.

In the fall of 1972, Bushnell installed his prototype for Pong in Andy Capp's tavern in Sunnyvale, California. The only instructions were "avoid missing the ball for a high score." In the first week, 1,200 quarters were deposited in the casserole dish that served for a coin box in Bushnell's prototype. Bushnell was ecstatic; his simple game had brought in $300 in a week. The pinball machine that stood next to it averaged $35 a week.

Lacking the capital to mass-produce the game, Bushnell approached established amusement game companies, only to be repeatedly shown the door. Down but hardly out, Bushnell cut his hair, put on a suit, and talked his way into a $50,000 line of credit from a local bank. He set up a production line in an abandoned roller skating rink, and he hired people to assemble machines while Led Zeppelin and the Rolling Stones were played at full volume over the speaker system of the rink. Among his first batch of employees was a skinny seventeen-year-old named Steve Jobs, who would later found a few companies of his own, including Apple Computer, NeXT, and Pixar. Like others, Jobs had been attracted by a classified ad that read "Have Fun and Make Money."

In no time at all, Bushnell was selling all the machines that his small staff could make—about ten per day—but to grow, he needed additional capital.

While the ambience at the rink, with its mix of rock music and marijuana fumes, put off most potential investors, Don Valentine, one of the country's most astute and credible venture capitalists, was impressed with the growth story. Armed with Valentine's money, Atari began to increase production and expand their range of games. New games included Tank and Breakout; the latter was designed by Jobs and a friend of his, Steve Wozniak, who had left Hewlett-Packard to work at Atari.

By 1974, 100,000 Ponglike games were sold worldwide. Although Atari manufactured only 10 percent of the games, the company still made $3.2 million that year. With the Pong clones coming on strong, Bushnell decided to make a Pong system for the home. In fact, Magnavox had been marketing a similar game for the home since 1972, although sales had been modest.[2] Bushnell's team managed to compress Atari's coin-operated Pong game down to a few inexpensive circuits that were contained in the game console. Atari's Pong had a sharper picture and more sensitive controllers than Magnavox's machine. It also cost less. Bushnell then went on a road show, demonstrating Pong to toy buyers, but he received an indifferent response and no sales. A dejected Bushnell returned to Atari with no idea of what to do next. Then the buyer for the sporting goods department at Sears came to see Bushnell, reviewed the machine, and offered to buy every home Pong game Atari could make. With Sears's backing, Bushnell boosted production. Sears ran a major television ad campaign to sell home Pong, and Atari's sales soared, hitting $450 million in 1975. The home video game had arrived.

Boom and Bust

Nothing attracts competitors like success, and by 1976, about twenty different companies were crowding into the home video game market, including National Semiconductor, RCA, Coleco, and Fairchild. Recognizing the limitations of existing home video game designs, Fairchild came out in 1976 with a home video game system capable of playing multiple games. The Fairchild system consisted of three components—a console, controllers, and cartridges. The console was a small computer optimized for graphics processing capabilities. It was designed to receive information from the controllers, process it, and send signals to a television monitor. The controllers were handheld devices used to direct on-screen action. The cartridges contained chips encoding the instructions for a game. The cartridges were designed to be inserted into the console.

In 1976, Bushnell sold Atari to Warner Communications for $28 million. Bushnell stayed on to run Atari. Backed by Warner's capital, in 1977 Atari developed and bought out its own cartridge-based system, the Atari 2600. The 2600 system was sold for $200, and associated cartridges retailed for $25 to $30. Sales surged during the 1977 Christmas season. However, a lack of manufacturing capacity on the part of market leader Atari and a very cautious approach to inventory by Fairchild led to shortages and kept sales significantly below what they could have been. Fairchild's cautious approach was the result of prior experience in consumer electronics. A year earlier it had increased demand for its digital watches, only to accumulate a buildup of excess inventory that had caused the company to take a $24.5 million write-off.[3]

After the 1977 Christmas season, Atari claimed to have sold about 400,000 units of the 2600 VCA, about 50 percent of all cartridge-based systems in American homes. Atari had also earned more than $100 million in sales of game cartridges. By this point, second-place Fairchild sold around 250,000 units of its system. Cartridge sales for the year totaled about 1.2 million units, with an average selling price of around $20. Fresh from this success and fortified by market forecasts predicting sales of 33 million cartridges and an installed base of 16 million machines by 1980, Bushnell committed Atari to manufacturing 1 million units of the 2600 for the 1978 Christmas season. Atari estimated that total demand would reach 2 million units. Bushnell was also encouraged by signals from Fairchild that it would again be limiting production to around 200,000 units. At this point, Atari had a library of nine games. Fairchild had seventeen.[4]

Atari was not the only company to be excited by the growth forecasts. In 1978, a host of other companies, including Coleco, National Semiconductor, Magnavox, General Instrument, and a dozen other companies, entered the market with incompatible cartridge-based home systems. The multitude of choices did not seem to entice consumers, however, and the 1978 Christmas season brought unexpectedly low sales. Only Atari and Coleco survived an industry shakeout. Atari lost Bushnell, who was ousted by Warner executives. (Bushnell went on to start Chuck E. Cheese Pizza Time Theater, a restaurant chain that had 278 outlets by 1981.) Bushnell later stated that part of the problem was a disagreement over strategy. Bushnell wanted Atari to price the 2600 at cost and make money on sales of software; Warner wanted to continue making profits on hardware sales.[5]

Several important developments occurred in 1979. First, several game producers and programmers defected from Atari to set up their own firm, Activision, and to make games compatible with the Atari 2600. Their success encouraged others to follow suit. Second, Coleco developed an expansion module that allowed its machine to play Atari games. Atari and Mattel (which entered the market in 1979) did likewise. Third, the year 1979 saw the introduction of three new games to the home market—Space Invaders, Asteroids, and Pac Man. All three were adapted from popular arcade games and all three helped drive demand for players.

Demand recovered strongly in late 1979 and kept growing for the next three years. In 1981, U.S. sales of home video games and cartridges hit $1 billion. In 1982, they surged to $3 billion, with Atari accounting for half of this amount. It seemed as if Atari could do no wrong; the 2600 was everywhere. About 20 million units were sold, and by late 1982, a large number of independent companies, including Activision, Imagic, and Epyx, were now producing hundreds of games for the 2600. Second-place Coleco was also doing well, partly because of a popular arcade game, Donkey Kong, which it had licensed from a Japanese company called Nintendo.

Atari was also in contact with Nintendo. In 1982, the company very nearly licensed the rights to Nintendo's Famicom, a cartridge-based video game system machine that was a big hit in Japan. Atari's successor to the 2600, the 5200, was not selling well, and the Famicom seemed like a good substitute. The negotiations broke down, however, when Atari discovered that Nintendo had extended its Donkey Kong license to Coleco. This allowed Coleco to port a version of the game to its home computer, which was a direct competitor to Atari's 800 home computer.[6]

After a strong 1982 season, the industry hoped for continued growth in 1983. Then the bottom dropped out of the market. Sales of home video games plunged to $100 million. Atari lost $500 million in the first nine months of the year, causing the stock of parent company Warner Communications to drop by half. Part of the blame for the collapse was laid at the feet of an enormous inventory overhang of unsold games. About 15 to 20 million surplus game cartridges were left over from the 1982 Christmas season (in 1981, there were none). On top of this, around 500 new games hit the market in 1993. The average price of a cartridge plunged from $30 in 1979 to $16 in 1982, and then to $4 in 1983. As sales slowed, retailers cut back on the shelf space allocated to video games. It proved difficult for new games to make a splash in a crowded market. Atari had to dispose of 6 million ET: The Extraterrestrial games. Meanwhile, big hits from previous years, such as Pac Man, were bundled with game players and given away free to try to encourage system sales.[7]

Surveying the rubble, commentators claimed that the video game industry was dead. The era of dedicated game machines was over, they claimed. Personal computers were taking their place.[8] It seemed to be true. Mattel sold off its game business, Fairchild moved on to other things, Coleco folded, and Warner decided to break up Atari and sell its constituent pieces—at least, those pieces for which it could find a buyer. No one in America seemed to want to have anything to do with the home video game business—no one, that is, except for Minoru Arakawa, the head of Nintendo's U.S. subsidiary, Nintendo of America (NOA). Picking through the rubble of the industry, Arakawa noticed that there were people who still packed video arcades, bringing in $7 billion a year, more money than the entire movie industry. Perhaps it was not a lack of interest in home video games that had killed the industry. Perhaps it was bad business practice.

The Nintendo Monopoly

Nintendo was a century-old Japanese company that had built up a profitable business making playing cards before diversifying into the video game business. Based in Kyoto and still run by the founding Yamauchi family, the company started to diversify into the video game business in the late 1970s. The first step was to license video game technology from Magnavox. In 1977, Nintendo introduced a home video game system in Japan based on this technology that played a variation of Pong. In 1978, the company began to sell coin-operated video games. It had its first hit with Donkey Kong, designed by Sigeru Miyamoto.

The Famicom

In the early 1980s, the company's boss, Hiroshi Yamauchi, decided that Nintendo had to develop its own video game machine. He pushed the company's engineers to develop a machine that combined superior graphics-processing capabilities and low cost. Yamauchi wanted a machine that could sell for $75, less than half the price of competing machines at the time. He dubbed the machine the Family Computer, or Famicom. The machine that his engineers designed was based on the controller, console, and plug in the cartridge format pioneered by Fairchild. It contained two custom chips—an 8-bit central processing unit and a graphics-processing unit. Both chips had been scaled down to perform only essential functions. A 16-bit processor was available at the time, but to keep costs down, Yamauchi refused to use it.

Nintendo approached Ricoh, the electronics giant, which had spare semiconductor capacity. Employees at Ricoh said that the chips had to cost no more that 2,000 yen. Ricoh thought that the 2,000-yen price point was absurd. Yamauchi's response was to guarantee Ricoh a 3 million chip order within two years. Since the leading companies in Japan were selling, at most, 30,000 video games per year at the time, many within the company viewed this as an outrageous commitment, but Ricoh went for it.[9] Another feature of the machine was its memory—2,000 bytes of random access memory (RAM), compared with the 256 bytes of RAM in the Atari machine. The result was a machine with superior graphics-processing capabilities and faster action that could handle far more complex games than Atari games. Nintendo's engineers also built a new set of chips into the game cartridges. In addition to chips that held the game program, Nintendo developed memory map controller (MMC) chips that took over some of the graphics-processing work from the chips in the console and enabled the system to handle more complex games. With the addition of the MMC chips, the potential for more sophisticated and complex games had arrived. Over time, Nintendo's engineers developed more powerful MMC chips, enabling the basic 8-bit system to do things that originally seemed out of reach. The engineers also figured out a way to include a battery backup system in cartridges that allowed some games to store information independently—to keep track of where a player had left off or to track high scores.

The Games

Yamauchi recognized that great hardware would not sell itself. The key to the market, he reasoned, was great games. Yamauchi had instructed the engineers, when they were developing the hardware, to make sure that "it was appreciated by software engineers." Nintendo decided that it would become a haven for game designers. "An ordinary man," Yamauchi said, "cannot develop good games no matter how hard he tries. A handful of people in this world can develop games that everyone wants. Those are the people we want at Nintendo."[10]

Yamauchi had an advantage in the person of Sigeru Miyamoto. Miyamoto had joined Nintendo at the age of twenty-four. Yamauchi had hired Miyamoto, a graduate of Kanazawa Munici College of Industrial Arts, as a favor to his father and an old friend, although he had little idea what he would do with an artist. For three years, Miyamoto worked as Nintendo's staff artist. Then in 1980, Yamauchi called Miyamoto into his office. Nintendo had started selling coin-operated video games, but one of the new games, Radarscope, was a disaster. Could Miyamoto come up with a new game? Miyamoto was delighted. He had always spent a lot of time drawing cartoons, and as a student, he had played video games constantly. Miyamoto believed that video games could be used to bring cartoons to life.[11]

The game Miyamoto developed was nothing short of a revelation. At a time when most coin-operated video games lacked characters or depth, Miyamoto created a game around a story that had both. Most games involved battles with space invaders or heroes shooting lasers at aliens; Miyamoto's game did neither. Based loosely on *Beauty and the Beast* and *King Kong*, Miyamoto's game involved a pet ape who runs off with his master's beautiful girlfriend. His master is an ordinary carpenter called Mario, who has a bulbous nose, a bushy mustache, a pair of large pathetic eyes, and a red cap (which Miyamoto added because he was not good at hairstyles). He does not carry a laser gun. The ape runs off with the girlfriend to get back at his master, who was not especially nice to the beast. The man, of course, has to get his girlfriend back by running up ramps, climbing ladders, jumping off elevators, and the like, while the ape throws objects at the hapless carpenter. Since the main character is an ape, Miyamoto called him Kong; because the main character is as stubborn as a donkey, he called the game Donkey Kong.

Released in 1981, Donkey Kong was a sensation in the world of coin-operated video arcades and a smash hit for Nintendo. In 1984, Yamauchi again summoned Miyamoto to his office. He needed more games, this time for Famicom. Miyamoto was made the head of a new research and development (R&D) group and told to come up with the most imaginative video games ever.

Miyamoto began with Mario from Donkey Kong. A colleague had told him that Mario looked more like a plumber than a carpenter, so a plumber he became. Miyamoto gave Mario a brother, Luigi, who was as tall and thin as Mario was short and fat. They became the Super Mario Brothers. Since plumbers spend their time working on pipes, large green sewer pipes became obstacles and doorways into secret worlds. Mario and Luigi's task was to search for the captive Princess Toadstool. Mario and Luigi are endearing bumblers, unequal to their tasks yet surviving. They shoot, squash, or evade their enemies—a potpourri of inventions that include flying turtles and stinging fish, man-eating flowers and fire-breathing dragons—while they collect gold coins, blow air bubbles, and climb vines into smiling clouds.[12]

Super Mario Brothers was introduced in 1985. For Miyamoto, this was just the beginning. Between 1985 and 1991, Miyamoto produced eight Mario games. About 60 to 70 million were sold worldwide, making Miyamoto the most successful game designer in the world. After adapting Donkey Kong for Famicom, he also went on to create other top-selling games, including another classic, The Legend of Zelda. While Miyamoto drew freely from folklore, literature, and pop culture, the main source for his ideas was his own experience. The memory of being lost among a maze of sliding doors in his family's home was re-created in the labyrinths of the Zelda games. The dog that attacked him when he was a child attacks Mario in Super Mario. As a child, Miyamoto had once climbed a tree to catch a view of far-off mountains and had become stuck. Mario gets himself in a similar fix. Once Miyamoto went hiking without a map and was surprised to stumble across a lake. In the Legend of Zelda, part of the adventure is in walking into new places without a map and being confronted by surprises.

Nintendo in Japan

Nintendo introduced Famicom into the Japanese market in May 1983. Famicom was priced at $100, more than Yamauchi wanted, but significantly less than the products of competitors. When he introduced the machine, Yamauchi urged retailers to forgo profits on the hardware because it was just a tool to sell software, and that is where they would make their money. Backed by an extensive advertising campaign, 500,000 units of Famicom were sold in the first two months. Within a year, the figure stood at 1 million, and sales were still expanding rapidly. With the hardware quickly finding its way into Japanese homes, Nintendo was besieged with calls from desperate retailers frantically demanding more games.

At this point Yamauchi told Miyamoto to come up with the most imaginative games ever. However, Yamauchi also realized that Nintendo alone could not satisfy the growing thirst for new games, so he initiated a licensing program. To become a Nintendo licensee, companies had to agree to an unprecedented series of restrictions. Licensees could issue only five Nintendo games per year, and they could not write those titles for other platforms. The licensing fee was set at 20 percent of the wholesale price of each cartridge sold (game cartridges wholesaled for around $30). It typically cost $500,000 to develop a game and took around six months. Nintendo insisted that games not contain any excessively violent or sexually suggestive material and that they review every game before allowing it to be produced.[13]

Despite these restrictions, six companies (Bandai, Capcom, Konami, Namco, Taito, and Hudson) agreed to become Nintendo licensees, not least because millions of customers were now clamoring for games. Bandai was Japan's largest toy company. The others already made either coin-operated video games or computer software games. Because of these licensing agreements, they saw their sales and earnings surge. For example, Konami's earnings went from $10 million in 1987 to $300 million in 1991.

After the six licensees began selling games, reports of defective games began to reach Yamauchi. The original six licensees were allowed to manufacture their own game cartridges. Realizing that he had given away the ability to control the quality of the cartridges, Yamauchi decided to change the contract for future licensees. Future licensees were required to submit all manufacturing orders for cartridges to Nintendo. Nintendo charged licensees $14 per cartridge, required that they place a minimum order for 10,000 units (later the minimum order was raised to 30,000), and insisted on cash payment in full when the order was placed. Nintendo outsourced all manufacturing to other companies, using the volume of its orders to get rock bottom prices. The cartridges were estimated to cost Nintendo between $6 and $8 each. The licensees then picked up the cartridges from Nintendo's loading dock and were responsible for distribution. In 1985, there were seventeen licensees. By 1987, there were fifty. By this point, 90 percent of the home video game systems sold in Japan were Nintendo systems.

Nintendo in America

In 1980, Nintendo established a subsidiary in America to sell its coin-operated video games. Yamauchi's American-educated son-in-law, Minoru Arakawa, headed the subsidiary. All of the other essential employees were Americans, including Ron Judy and Al Stone. For its first two years, Nintendo of America (NOA), based originally in Seattle, struggled to sell second-rate games such as Radarscope. The subsidiary seemed on the brink of closing. NOA could not even make the rent payment on the warehouse. Then they received a large shipment from Japan: 2,000 units of a new coin-operated video game. Opening the box, they discovered Donkey Kong. After playing the game briefly, Judy proclaimed it a disaster. Stone walked out of the building, declaring that "it's over."[14] The managers were appalled. They could not imagine a game less likely to sell in video arcades. The only promising sign was that a twenty-year employee, Howard Philips, rapidly became enthralled with the machine.

Arakawa, however, knew he had little choice but to try to sell the machine. Judy persuaded the owner of the Spot Tavern near Nintendo's office to take one of the machines on a trial basis. After one night, Judy discovered $30 in the coin box, a phenomenal amount. The next night there was $35, and $36 the night after that. NOA had a hit on its hands.

By the end of 1982, NOA had sold over 60,000 copies of Donkey Kong and had booked sales in excess of $100 million. The subsidiary had outgrown its Seattle location. They moved to a new site in Redmond, a Seattle suburb, where they located next to a small but fast-growing software company run by an old school acquaintance of Howard Philips, Bill Gates.

By 1984, NOA was riding a wave of success in the coin-operated video game market. Arakawa, however, was interested in the possibilities of selling Nintendo's new Famicom system in the United States. Throughout 1984, Arakawa, Judy, and Stone met with numerous toy and department store representatives to discuss the possibilities, only to be repeatedly rebuffed. Still smarting from the 1983 debacle, the representatives wanted nothing to do with the home video game business. They also met with former managers from Atari and Caloco to gain their insights. The most common response they received was that the market collapsed because the last generation of games was awful.

Arakawa and his team decided that if they were going to sell Famicom in the United States, they would have to find a new distribution channel. The obvious choice was consumer electronics stores. Thus, Arakawa asked the R&D team in Kyoto to redesign Famicom for the U.S. market so that it looked less like a toy (Famicom was encased in red and white plastic), and more like a consumer electronics device. The redesigned machine was renamed the Nintendo Entertainment System (NES).

Arakawa's big fear was that illegal, low-quality Taiwanese games would flood the U.S. market if NES was successful. To stop counterfeit games being played on NES, Arakawa asked Nintendo's Japanese engineers to design a security system into the U.S. version of Famicom so that only Nintendo-approved games could be played on NES. The Japanese engineers responded by designing a security chip to be embedded in the game cartridges. NES would not work unless the security chips in the cartridges unlocked, or shook hands with, a chip in NES. Since the code embedded in the security chip was proprietary, the implication of this system was that no one could manufacture games for NES without Nintendo's specific approval.

To overcome the skepticism and reluctance of retailers to stock a home video game system, Arakawa decided in late 1985 to make an extraordinary commitment. Nintendo would stock stores and set up displays and windows. Retailers would not have to pay for anything they stocked for ninety days. After that, retailers could pay Nintendo for what they sold and return the rest. NES was bundled with Nintendo's best-selling game in Japan, Super Mario Brothers. It was essentially a risk-free proposition for retailers, but even with this, most were skeptical. Ultimately, thirty Nintendo personnel descended on the New York area. Referred to as the Nintendo SWAT team, they persuaded some stores to stock NES after an extraordinary blitz that involved eighteen-hour days. To support the New York product launch, Nintendo also committed itself to a $5 million advertising campaign aimed at the seven- to fourteen-year-old boys who seemed to be Nintendo's likely core audience.

By December 1985, between 500 and 600 stores in the New York area stocked Nintendo systems. Sales were moderate, about half of the 100,000 NES machines shipped from Japan were sold, but it was enough to justify going forward. The SWAT team then moved first to Los Angeles, then to Chicago, then to Dallas. As in New York, sales started at a moderate pace, but by late 1986, they started to accelerate rapidly, and Nintendo went national with NES.

In 1986, around 1 million NES units were sold in the United States. In 1987, the figure increased to 3 million. In 1988, it jumped to over 7 million. In the same year, 33 million game cartridges were sold. Nintendo mania had arrived in the United States. To expand the supply of games, Nintendo licensed the rights to produce up to five games per year to thirty-one American software companies. Nintendo continued to use a restrictive licensing agreement that gave it exclusive rights to any games, required licensees to place their orders through Nintendo, and insisted on a 30,000-unit minimum order.[15]

By 1990, the home video game market was worth $5 billion worldwide. Nintendo dominated the industry, with a 90 percent share of the market for game equipment. The parent company was, by some measures, now the most profitable company in Japan. By 1992, it was netting over $1 billion in gross profit annually, or more than $1.5 million for each employee in Japan. The company's stock market value exceeded that of Sony, Japan's premier consumer electronics firm. Indeed, the company's net profit exceeded that of all the American movie studios combined. Nintendo games, it seemed, were bigger than the movies.

As of 1991, there were over 100 licensees for Nintendo, and over 450 titles were available for NES. In the United States, Nintendo products were distributed through toy stores (30 percent of volume), mass merchandisers (40 percent of volume), and department stores (10 percent of volume). Nintendo tightly controlled the number of game titles and games that could be sold, quickly withdrawing titles as soon as interest appeared to decline. In 1988, retailers requested 110 million cartridges from Nintendo. Market surveys suggested that perhaps 45 million could have been sold, but Nintendo allowed only 33 million to be shipped.[16] Nintendo claimed that the shortage of games was in part due to a worldwide shortage of semiconductor chips.

Several companies had tried to reverse-engineer the code embedded in Nintendo's security chip, which competitors characterized as a lockout chip. Nintendo successfully sued them. The most notable was Atari Games, one of the successors of the original Atari, which in 1987 sued Nintendo of America for anticompetitive behavior. Atari claimed that the purpose of the security chip was to monopolize the market. At the same time, Atari announced that it had found a way around Nintendo's security chip and would begin to sell unlicensed games.[17] NOA responded with a countersuit. In a March 1991 ruling, Atari was found to have obtained Nintendo's security code illegally and was ordered to stop selling NES-compatible games. However, Nintendo did not always have it all its own way. In 1990, under pressure from Congress, the Department of Justice, and several lawsuits, Nintendo rescinded its exclusivity requirements, freeing up developers to write games for other platforms. However, developers faced a real problem: what platform could they write for?

Sega's Sonic Boom

Back in 1954, David Rosen, a twenty-year-old American, left the U.S. Air Force after a tour of duty in Tokyo.[18] Rosen had noticed that Japanese people needed lots of photographs for ID cards, but that local photo studios were slow and expensive. He formed a company, Rosen Enterprises, and went into the photo-booth business, which was a big success. By 1957, Rosen had established a successful nationwide chain. At this point, the Japanese economy was booming, so Rosen decided it was time to get into another business—entertainment. As his vehicle, he chose arcade games, which were unknown in Japan at the time. He picked up used games on the cheap from America and set up arcades in the same Japanese

department stores and theaters that typically housed his photo booths. Within a few years, Rosen had 200 arcades nationwide. His only competition came from another American-owned firm, Service Games (SeGa), whose original business was jukeboxes and fruit machines.

By the early 1960s, the Japanese arcade market had caught up with the U.S. market. The problem was that game makers had run out of exciting new games to offer. Rosen decided that he would have to get into the business of designing and manufacturing games, but to do that he needed manufacturing facilities. SeGa manufactured its own games, so in 1965, Rosen approached the company and suggested a merger. The result was Sega Enterprise, a Japanese company with Rosen as its CEO.

Rosen himself designed Sega's first game, Periscope, in which the objective was to sink chain-mounted cardboard ships by firing torpedoes, represented by lines of colored lights. Periscope was a big success not only in Japan, but also in the United States and Europe, and it allowed Sega to build up a respectable export business. Over the years, the company continued to invest heavily in game development, always using the latest electronic technology.

Gulf and Western (G&W), a U.S. conglomerate, acquired Sega in 1969, with Rosen running the subsidiary. In 1975, G&W took Sega public in the United States, but left Sega Japan as a G&W subsidiary. Hayao Nakayama, a former Sega distributor, was drafted as president. In the early 1980s, Nakayama pushed G&W to invest more in Sega Japan so that the company could enter the then-booming home video game market. When G&W refused, Nakayama suggested a management buyout. G&W agreed, and in 1984, for the price of just $38 million, Sega became a Japanese company once more. (Sega's Japanese revenues were around $700 million, but by now the company was barely profitable.)

Sega was caught off guard by the huge success of Nintendo's Famicom. Although it released its own 8-bit system in 1986, the machine never commanded more than 5 percent of the Japanese market. Nakayama, however, was not about to give up. From years in the arcade business, he understood that great games drove sales. Nevertheless, he also understood that more powerful technology gave game developers the tools to develop more appealing games. This philosophy underlay Nakayama's decision to develop a 16-bit game system, Genesis.

Sega took the design of its 16-bit arcade machine and adapted it for Genesis. Compared with Nintendo's 8-bit machine, the 16-bit machine featured an array of superior technological features, including high-definition graphics and animation, a full spectrum of colors, two independent scrolling backgrounds that created an impressive depth of field, and near CD quality sound. The design strategy also made it easy to port Sega's catalog of arcade hits to Genesis.

Genesis was launched in Japan in 1989 and in the United States in 1990. In the United States, the machine was priced at $199. The company hoped that sales would be boosted by the popularity of its arcade games, such as the graphically violent Altered Beast. Sega also licensed other companies to develop games for the Genesis platform. In an effort to recruit licensees, Sega asked for lower royalty rates than Nintendo, and it gave licensees the right to manufacture their own cartridges. Independent game developers were slow to climb on board, however, and the $200 price tag for the player held back sales.

One of the first independent game developers to sign up with Sega was Electronic Arts. Established by Trip Hawkins, Electronic Arts had focused on designing games for personal computers and consequently had missed the Nintendo 8-bit era. Now Hawkins was determined to get a presence in the home video game market, and aligning his company's wagon with Sega seemed to be the best option. The Nintendo playing field was already crowded, and Sega offered a far less restrictive licensing deal than Nintendo. Electronic Arts subsequently wrote several popular games for Genesis, including John Madden football and several gory combat games.[19]

Nintendo had not been ignoring the potential of the 16-bit system. Nintendo's own 16-bit system, Super NES, was ready for market introduction in 1989—at the same time as Sega's Genesis. Nintendo introduced Super NES in Japan in 1990, where it quickly established a strong market presence and beat Sega's Genesis. In the United States, however, the company decided to hold back longer to reap the full benefits of the dominance it enjoyed with the 8-bit NES system. Yamauchi was also worried about the lack of backward compatibility between Nintendo's 8-bit and 16-bit systems. (The company had tried to make the 16-bit system so that it could play 8-bit games but concluded that the cost of doing so was prohibitive.) These concerns may have led the company to delay market introduction until the 8-bit market was saturated.

Meanwhile, in the United States, the Sega bandwagon was beginning to gain momentum. One development that gave Genesis a push was the introduction of a new Sega game, Sonic the Hedgehog. Developed by an independent team that was contracted to Sega, the game featured a cute hedgehog that impatiently tapped his paw when the player took too long to act. Impatience was Sonic's central feature—he had places to go, and quickly. He zipped along, collecting brass rings when he could find them, before rolling into a ball and flying down slides with loops and underground tunnels. Sonic was Sega's Mario.

In mid 1991, in an attempt to jump-start slow sales, Tom Kalinske, head of Sega's American subsidiary, decided to bundle Sonic the Hedgehog with the game player. He also reduced the price for the bundled unit to $150, and he relaunched the system with an aggressive advertising campaign aimed at teenagers. The campaign was built around the slogan "Genesis does what Nintendon't." The shift in strategy worked, and sales accelerated sharply.

Sega's success prompted Nintendo to launch its own 16-bit system. Nintendo's Super NES was introduced at $200. However, Sega now had a two-year head start in games. By the end of 1991, about 125 game titles were available for Genesis, compared with twenty-five for Super NES. In May 1992, Nintendo reduced the price of Super NES to $150. At this time Sega was claiming a 63 percent share of the 16-bit market in the United States, and Nintendo claimed a 60 percent share. By now, Sega was cool. It began to take more chances with mass media–defined morality. When Acclaim Entertainment released its bloody Mortal Kombat game in September 1992, the Sega version let players rip off heads and tear out hearts. Reflecting Nintendo's image of their core market, its version was sanitized. The Sega version outsold Nintendo's two to one.[20] Therefore, the momentum continued to run in Sega's favor. By January 1993, there were 320 titles available for Sega Genesis and 130 for Super NES. In early 1994, independent estimates suggested that Sega had 60 percent of the U.S. market and Nintendo had 40 percent, figures Nintendo disputed.

3DO

Trip Hawkins, whose first big success was Electronic Arts, founded 3DO in 1991.[21] Hawkins's vision for 3DO was to shift the home video game business away from the existing cartridge-based format and toward a CD-ROM-based platform. The original partners in 3DO were Electronic Arts, Matsushita, Time Warner, AT&T, and the venture capital firm Kleiner Perkins. Collectively they invested over $17 million in 3DO, making it the richest start-up in the history of the home video game industry. 3DO went public in May 1993 at $15 per share. By October of that year, the stock had risen to $48 per share, making 3DO worth $1 billion—not bad for a company that had yet to generate a single dollar in revenues.

The basis for 3DO's $1 billion market cap was patented computer system architecture and a copyrighted operating system that allowed for much richer graphics and audio capabilities. The system was built around a 32-bit RISC microprocessor and proprietary graphics processor chips. Instead of a cartridge, the 3DO system stored games on a CD-ROM that was capable of holding up to 600 megabytes of content, sharply up from the 10 megabytes of content found in the typical game cartridge of the time. The slower access time of a CD-ROM compared with a cartridge was alleviated somewhat by the use of a double-speed CD-ROM drive.[22]

The belief at 3DO—a belief apparently shared by many investors—was that the superior storage and graphics-processing capabilities of the 3DO system would prove very attractive to game developers, allowing them to be far more creative. In turn, better games would attract customers away from Nintendo and Sega. Developing games that used the capabilities of a CD-ROM system altered the economics of game development. Estimates suggested that it would cost approximately $2 million to produce a game for the 3DO system and could take as long as twenty-four months to develop. However, at $2 per disc, a CD-ROM cost substantially less to produce than a cartridge.

The centerpiece of 3DO's strategy was to license its hardware technology for free. Game developers paid a royalty of $3 per disc for access to the 3DO operating code. Discs typically retailed for $40 each.

Matsushita introduced the first 3DO machine into the U.S. market in October 1993. Priced at $700, the machine was sold through electronic retailers that carried Panasonic high-end electronics products. Sega's Tom Kalinsky noted, "It's a noble effort. Some people will buy 3DO, and they'll have a wonderful experience. It's impressive, but it's a niche. We've done the research. It does not become a large

market until you go below $500. At $300, it starts to get interesting. We make no money on hardware. It's a cutthroat business. I hope Matsushita understands that."[23] CD-ROM discs for the 3DO machine retailed for around $75. The machine came bundled with Crash n Burn, a high-speed combat racing game. However, only eighteen 3DO titles were available by the crucial Christmas period, although reports suggested that 150 titles were under development.[24]

Sales of the hardware were slow, reaching only 30,000 by January 1994.[25] In the same month, AT&T and Sanyo both announced that they would begin to manufacture the 3DO machine. In March, faced with continuing sluggish sales, 3DO announced that it would give hardware manufacturers two shares of 3DO stock for every unit sold at or below a certain retail price. Matsushita dropped the price of its machine to $500. About the same time, Toshiba, LG, and Samsung all announced that they would start to produce 3DO machines.

By June 1994, cumulative sales of 3DO machines in the United States stood at 40,000 units. Matsushita announced plans to expand distribution beyond the current 3,500 outlets to include the toy and mass merchandise channels. Hawkins and his partners announced that they would invest another $37 million in 3DO. By July, there were 750 3DO software licensees, but only forty titles were available for the format. Despite these moves, sales continued at a very sluggish pace, and the supply of new software titles started to dry up.[26]

In September 1996, 3DO announced that it would either sell its hardware system business or move it into a joint venture.[27] The company announced that about 150 people, one-third of the workforce, would probably lose their jobs in the restructuring. According to Trip Hawkins, 3DO would now focus on developing software for online gaming. Hawkins stated that the Internet and Internet entertainment constituted a huge opportunity for 3DO. The stock dropped $1.375 to $6.75.

Sega's Saturn

3DO was not alone in moving to a CD-ROM-based format. Both Sega and Sony also introduced CD-ROM-based systems in the mid 1990s. Sega had in fact beaten 3DO to the market with its November 1992 introduction of the Sega CD, a $300 CD-ROM add-on for the 16-bit Genesis. Sega sold 100,000 units in its first month alone. Sales then slowed down, however, and by December 1993 were standing at just 250,000 units. One reason for the slowdown, according to critics, was a lack of strong games. Sega was also working on a 32-bit CD-ROM system, Saturn, which was targeted for a mid 1995 introduction in the United States. In January 1994, Sega announced that Microsoft would supply the operating system for Saturn.[28]

In March 1994, Sega announced the Genesis Super 32X, a $150 add-on cartridge designed to increase the performance of Genesis cartridge and CD-ROM games. The 32X contained the 32-bit Hitachi microprocessor that was to be used in Saturn. Sega called the 32X "the poor man's 32-bit machine" because it sold for a mere $149. Introduced in the fall of 1994, the 32X never lived up to its expectations. Most users appeared willing to wait for the real thing, Sega Saturn, promised for release the following year.

In early 1995, Sega informed the press and retailers that it would release Saturn on "Sega Saturn Saturday, Sept 2nd," but Sega released the 32-bit Saturn in May 1995. It was priced at $400 per unit and accompanied by the introduction of just ten games. Sega apparently believed that the world would be delighted by the May release of the Saturn. However, Saturn was released without the industry fanfare that normally greets a new game machine. Only four retail chains received the Saturn in May, while the rest were told they would have to wait until September. This move alienated retailers, who responded by dropping Sega products from their stores.[29] Sega appeared to have made a marketing blunder.[30]

Sony's PlayStation

In the fall of 1995, Sony entered the fray with the introduction of the Sony PlayStation.[31] PlayStation used a 32-bit RISC microprocessor running at 33 MHz and using a double-speed CD-ROM drive. PlayStation cost an estimated $500 million to develop. The machine had actually been under development since 1991, when Sony decided that the home video game industry was getting too big to ignore. Initially, Sony was in an alliance with Nintendo to develop the machine. Nintendo walked away from the alliance in 1992, however, after a disagreement over who owned the rights to any future CD-ROM games. Sony went alone.[32]

From the start, Sony felt that it could leverage its presence in the film and music business to build a strong position in the home video game industry. A consumer electronics giant with a position in the Hollywood movie business and the music industry (Sony owned Columbia Pictures and the Columbia record label), Sony believed that it had access to significant intellectual property that could form the basis of many popular games.

In 1991, Sony established a division in New York: Sony Electronic Publishing. The division was to serve as an umbrella organization for Sony's multimedia offerings. Headed by Iceland native Olaf Olafsson, then just twenty-eight years old, this organization ultimately took the lead role in both the market launch of PlayStation and in developing game titles.[33] In 1993, as part of this effort, Sony purchased a well-respected British game developer, Psygnosis. By the fall of 1995, this unit had twenty games ready to complement PlayStation: The Haldeman Diaries, Mickey Mania (developed in collaboration with Disney), and Johnny Mnemonic, based on the William Gibson short story. To entice independent game developers such as Electronic Arts, Namco, and Acclaim Entertainment, Olafsson used the promise of low royalty rates. The standard royalty rate was set at $9 per disc, although developers that signed on early enough were given a lower royalty rate. Sony also provided approximately four thousand game development tools to licensees in an effort to help them speed games to market.[34]

To distribute PlayStation, Sony set up a retail channel separate from Sony's consumer electronics sales force. It marketed the PlayStation as a hip and powerful alternative to the outdated Nintendo and Sega cartridge-based systems. Sony worked closely with retailers before the launch to find out how it could help them sell the PlayStation. To jump-start demand, Sony set up in-store displays to allow potential consumers to try the equipment. Just before the launch, Sony had lined up an impressive 12,000 retail outlets in the United States.[35]

Sony targeted its advertising for PlayStation at males in the eighteen- to thirty-five-year age range. The targeting was evident in the content of many of the games. One of the big hits for PlayStation was Tomb Raider, whose central character, Lara Croft, combined sex appeal with savviness and helped to recruit an older generation to PlayStation.[36] PlayStation was initially priced at $299, and games retailed for as much as $60. Sony's Tokyo-based executives had reportedly been insisting on a $350 to $400 price for PlayStation, but Olafsson pushed hard for the lower price. Because of the fallout from this internal battle, in January 1996, Olafsson resigned from Sony. By then, however, Sony was following Olafsson's script.[37]

Sony's prelaunch work was rewarded with strong early sales. By January 1996, more than 800,000 PlayStations had been sold in the United States, plus another 4 million games. In May 1996, with 1.2 million PlayStations shipped, Sony reduced the price of PlayStation to $199. Sega responded with a similar price cut for its Saturn. The prices on some of Sony's initial games were also reduced to $29.99. The weekend after the price cuts, retailers reported that PlayStation sales were up by between 350 percent and 1,000 percent over the prior week.[38] The sales surge continued through 1996. By the end of the year, sales of PlayStation and associated software amounted to $1.3 billion, out of a total for U.S. sales at $2.2 billion for all video game hardware and software. In March 1997, Sony cut the price of PlayStation again, this time to $149. It also reduced its suggested retail price for games by $10 to $49.99. By this point, Sony had sold 3.4 million units of PlayStation in the United States, compared with Saturn's 1.6 million units.[39] Worldwide, PlayStation had outsold Saturn by 13 million to 7.8 million units, and Saturn sales were slowing.[40] The momentum was clearly running in Sony's favor, but the company now had a new challenge to deal with: Nintendo's latest generation game machine, the N64.

Nintendo Strikes Back

In July 1996, Nintendo launched Nintendo 64 (N64) in the Japanese market. This release was followed by a late fall introduction in the United States. N64 is a 64-bit machine developed in conjunction with Silicon Graphics. Originally targeted for introduction a year earlier, N64 had been under development since 1993. The machine used a plug-in cartridge format rather than a CD-ROM drive. According to Nintendo, cartridges allow for faster access time and are far more durable than CD-ROMs (an important consideration with children).[41]

The most-striking feature of the N64 machine, however, was its 3D graphics capability. N64 provides fully rounded figures that can turn on their heels and rotate through 180 degrees. Advanced ray tracing techniques borrowed from military simulators and engineering workstations added to the sense of realism by providing proper highlighting, reflections, and shadows.

N64 was targeted at children and young teenagers. It was priced at $200 and launched with just four games. Despite the lack of games, initial sales were very strong. Indeed, 1997 turned out to be a banner year for both Sony and Nintendo. The overall U.S. market was strong, with sales of hardware and software combined reaching a record $5.5 billion. Estimates suggest that PlayStation accounted for 49 percent of machines and games by value. N64 captured a 41 percent share, leaving Sega trailing badly with less than 10 percent of the market. During the year, the average price for game machines had fallen to $150. By year-end there were 300 titles available for PlayStation, compared with forty for N64. Games for PlayStation retailed for $40, on average, compared with over $60 for N64.[42]

By late 1998, PlayStation was widening its lead over N64. In the crucial North American market, PlayStation was reported to be outselling N64 by a two-to-one margin, although Nintendo retained a lead in the under-twelve category. At this point, there were 115 games available for N64 versus 431 for PlayStation.[43] Worldwide, Sony had now sold close to 55 million PlayStations. The success of PlayStation had a major impact on Sony's bottom line. In fiscal 1998, PlayStation business generated revenues of $5.5 billion for Sony, 10 percent of its worldwide revenues, but accounted for $886 million, or 22.5 percent, of the company's operating income.[44]

The 128-Bit Era

When Nintendo launched its 64-bit machine in 1996, Sony and Sega didn't follow, preferring instead to focus on the development of even more powerful 128-bit machines.

Sega was the first to market a 128-bit video game console, which it launched in Japan in late 1998 and in the United States in late 1999. The Dreamcast came equipped with a 56-kilobit modem to allow for online gaming over the Internet. By late 2000, Sega had sold around 6 million Dreamcasts worldwide, accounting for about 15 percent of console sales since its launch. Sega nurtured Dreamcast sales by courting outside software developers who helped develop new games, including Crazy Taxi, Resident Evil, and Quake III Arena. The company had a goal of shipping 10 million units by March 2001, a goal it never reached.[45]

Despite its position as first mover with a 128-bit machine, and despite solid technical reviews, by late 2000, the company was struggling. Sega was handicapped first by product shortages due to constraints on the supply of component parts and then by a lack of demand as consumers waited to see whether Sony's 128-bit offering, the much anticipated PlayStation 2 (PS2), would be a more attractive machine. In September 2000, Sega responded to the impending U.S. launch of Sony's PS2 by cutting the price for its console from $199 to $149. Then in late October, Sega announced that, due to this price cut, it would probably lose over $200 million for the fiscal year ending March 2001.[46]

Sony's PlayStation 2

PlayStation 2 was launched in Japan in mid 2000 and in the United States at the end of October 2000. Initially priced at $299, PlayStation 2 is a powerful machine. At its core is a 300-megahertz graphics processing chip that was jointly developed with Toshiba and consumed about $1.3 billion in R&D. Referred to as the Emotion Engine processor, the chip allows the machine to display stunning graphic images previously found only on supercomputers. The chip made the PlayStation 2 the most powerful video game machine yet.

The machine is set up to play different CD and DVD formats, as well as proprietary game titles. As is true with the original PlayStation, PlayStation 2 can play audio CDs. The system is also compatible with the original PlayStation: any PlayStation title can be played on the PlayStation 2. To help justify the initial price tag, the unit doubled as a DVD player with picture quality as good as current players. The PlayStation 2 did not come equipped with a modem, but it did have networking capabilities and a modem could be attached using one of two USB ports.[47]

Nintendo's GameCube

Nintendo had garnered a solid position in the industry with its N64 machine by focusing on its core demographic, seven- to twelve-year-olds. In 1999, Nintendo took 33 percent of the hardware market and 28 percent of the game market. Nintendo's next generation video game machine, GameCube, packed

a modem and a powerful 400-megahertz, 128-bit processor made by IBM into a compact cube. GameCube marked a shift away from Nintendo's traditional approach of using proprietary cartridges to hold game software. Instead, software for the new player came on 8-centimeter compact disks, which are smaller than music compact disks. The disks hold 1.5 gigabytes of data each, far greater storage capacity than the old game cartridges. Players could control GameCube using wireless controllers.[48]

Nintendo tried to make the GameCube easy for developers to work with rather than focusing on raw peak performance. While developers no doubt appreciated this, by the time GameCube hit store shelves in late 2001, PlayStation 2 had been on the market for eighteen months and boasted a solid library of games. Despite its strong brand and instantly recognized intellectual property, which included Donkey Kong, Super Mario Brothers, and the Pokemon characters, Nintendo was playing catch up to Sony. Moreover, another new entrant into the industry launched its 128-bit offering at around the same time: Microsoft.

Microsoft's Xbox

Microsoft was first rumored to be developing a video game console in late 1999. In March 2000, Bill Gates made it official when he announced that Microsoft would enter the home video game market in fall 2001 with a console code named Xbox. In terms of sheer computing power, the 128-bit Xbox had the edge over competitors. Xbox has a 733-megahertz Pentium III processor, a high-powered graphics chip from Nvidia Corp, a built-in broadband cable modem to allow for online game playing and high-speed Internet browsing, 64 megabytes of memory, CD and DVD drives, and an internal hard disk drive. The operating system was a stripped-down version of its popular Windows system optimized for graphics-processing capabilities. Microsoft claimed that because the Xbox was based on familiar PC technology, it would be much easier for software developers to write games for, and it would be relatively easy to convert games from the PC to run on the Xbox.[49]

Although Microsoft was a new entrant to the video game industry, it was no stranger to games. Microsoft had long participated in the PC gaming industry and was one of the largest publishers of PC games, with hits such as Microsoft Flight Simulator and Age of Empires I and II to its credit. Sales of

Microsoft's PC games have increased 50 percent annually between 1998 and 2001, and the company now controls about 10 percent of the PC game market in 2001. Microsoft had also offered online gaming for some time, including its popular MSN Gaming Zone site. Started in 1996, by 2001 the website had become the largest online PC gaming hub on the Internet with nearly 12 million subscribers paying $9.95 a month to play premium games such as Asheron's Call or Fighter Ace. Nor is Microsoft new to hardware; its joysticks and game pads outsell all other brands and it has an important mouse business.

To build the Xbox, Microsoft chose Flextronics, a contract manufacturer that already made computer mice for Microsoft. Realizing that it would probably have to cut Xbox prices over time, Microsoft guaranteed Flextronics a profit margin, effectively agreeing to subsidize Flextronics if selling prices fell below a specified amount. By 2003, Microsoft was thought to be losing $100 on every Xbox sold. To make that back and turn a profit, Microsoft reportedly had to sell between six and nine video games per Xbox.[50]

Analysts speculated that Microsoft's entry into the home video game market was a response to a potential threat from Sony. Microsoft was worried that Internet-ready consoles like PlayStation 2 might take over many web-browsing functions from the personal computer. Some in the company described Internet-enabled video game terminals as Trojan horses in the living room. In Microsoft's calculation, it made sense to get in the market to try and keep Sony and others in check. With annual revenues in excess of $20 billion worldwide, the home video game market is huge and an important source of potential growth for Microsoft. Still, by moving away from its core market, Microsoft was taking a huge risk, particularly given the scale of investments required to develop the Xbox, reported to run as high as $1.5 billion.

Mortal Combat: Microsoft Versus Sony

The launch of Xbox and GameCube helped propel sales of video game hardware and software to a record $9.4 billion in 2001, up from $6.58 billion in 2000. Although both Xbox and Nintendo initially racked up strong sales, the momentum started to slow significantly in 2002. Microsoft in particular found it very difficult to penetrate the Japanese market. By September 2002, Sony had sold 11.2 million units of PS2 in the United States, versus 2.2 million units of Xbox and 2.7 million units of Nintendo's GameCube. Unable to hold onto market share in the wake of the new competition, Sega withdrew from the console market, announcing that henceforth it would focus just on developing games for other platforms.

In June 2002, Sony responded to the new entry by cutting the price for PS2 from $299 to $199. Microsoft quickly followed, cutting the price for Xbox from $299 to $199, while Nintendo cut its price from $299 to $149.[51] A year later, Sony cut prices again, this time to $179 a console. Again, Microsoft followed with a similar price cut, and in March 2004, it took the lead, cutting Xbox prices to $149. Snoy followed suit two months later.[52]

Microsoft's strategy, however, involved far more than just cutting prices. In November 2002, Microsoft announced that it would introduce a new service for gamers, Xbox Live. For $50 a year, Xbox Live subscribers with broadband connections would be able to play online enabled versions of Xbox games with other online subscribers. To support Xbox Live, Microsoft invested some $500 million in its own data centers to host online game playing.

Online game playing was clearly a strategic priority from the outset. Unlike the PS2 and GameCube, Xbox came with a built in broadband capability. The decision to make the Xbox broadband capable was made back in 1999 when less than 5 percent of U.S. homes were linked to the Internet with a broadband connection. Explaining the decision to build broadband capabilities into the Xbox at a time when rivals lacked them, the head of Xbox, Jay Allard, noted that "my attitude has always been to bet on the future, not against it."[53] While Sony's PS2 can be hooked up to the Internet via a broadband connection, doing so requires purchase of a special network adapter for $40.

By mid 2003, Xbox Live had some 500,000 subscribers, versus 80,000 who had registered to play PlayStation 2 games online. By this point in time there were 28 online games for Xbox, and 18 for PS2. By January 2004, the comparative figures stood at 50 for Microsoft and 32 for Sony. By mid 2004, Xbox Live reportedly had over 1 million subscribers, with Sony claiming a similar number of online players.[54] In May 2004, Microsoft struck a deal with Electronic Arts, the world's largest video game publisher, to bring EA games, including its bestselling Madden Football, to the Xbox Live platform. Until this point, EA had only produced live games for Sony's platform.

In spite of all these strategic moves, by late 2004 Xbox was still a distant second of PS2 in the video game market, having sold 14 million consoles against Sony's 70 million. While Sony was making good money from the business, Microsoft was registering significant losses. In fiscal 2004, Microsoft's home and entertainment division, of which Xbox is the major component, registered $2.45 billion in revenues but lost $1.135 billion. By way of contrast, Sony's game division had $7.5 billion of sales in fiscal 2004 and generated operating profits of $640 million.

Microsoft, however, indicated that it was in the business for the long term. The remarkable early success of Halo 2 suggested that the company was continuing to attract a strong following for its platform. More important perhaps, Microsoft was rumored to be ahead of Sony by as much as a year to bring the next generation video game console to market. Current reports suggest that Xbox 2, which is code named Xenon, will be on the market in time for the 2005 Christmas season, probably a full year ahead of Sony's PlayStation 3. Sony is rumored to be running into technical problems as it tries to develop PlayStation 3. To date the specifications for Xbox 2 have been kept under tight wraps.[55]

Microsoft is also trying to make it easier for developers to write games for Xbox and Xbox 2 by investing programming tools that automate many of the key software tasks. Currently it costs $5 to $10 million to develop a game, and this may double or even triple with the next round of games. Back in the early 1990s, Microsoft gained an edge over rival computer operating systems such as Apple's Macintosh and IBM's OS/2 because it developed its Visual Basic Programming Language that made it easier for developers to write applications for Windows. The increased supply of applications helped to secure a market leadership role for Windows. Now Microsoft is hoping that it can do the same in the video game industry by helping to reduce the costs of developing games for Xbox 2.[56]

ENDNOTES

1. A good account of the early history of Bushnell and Atari can be found in S. Cohen, *Zap! The Rise and Fall of Atari* (New York: McGraw-Hill, 1984).
2. Isaacs, R., "Video Games Race to Catch a Changing Market," *Business Week*, December 26, 1977, p. 44B.
3. Pagnano, P., "Atari's Game Plan to Overwhelm Its Competitors," *Business Week*, May 8, 1978, p. 50F.
4. Isaacs, R., "Video Games Race to Catch a Changing Market," *Business Week*, December 26, 1977, p. 44B.
5. Pagnano, P., "Atari's Game Plan to Overwhelm Its Competitors," *Business Week*, May 8, 1978, p. 50F; and Sheff, D., *Game Over* (New York: Random House, 1993).
6. Cohen, S., *Zap! The Rise and Fall of Atari* (New York: McGraw-Hill, 1984).
7. Kehoe, L., "Atari Seeks Way Out of Video Game Woes," *Financial Times*, December 14, 1983, p. 23.
8. Schrage, M., "The High Tech Dinosaurs: Video Games, Once Ascendant, Are Making Way," *Washington Post*, July 31, 1983, p. F1.
9. Sheff, D., *Game Over* (New York: Random House, 1993).
10. Quoted in Sheff, D., *Game Over* (New York: Random House, 1993), p. 38.
11. Sheff, D., *Game Over* (New York: Random House, 1993).
12. Golden, D., "In Search of Princess Toadstool," *Boston Globe*, November 20, 1988, p. 18.
13. Gross, N., and Lewis, G., "Here Come the Super Mario Bros.," *Business Week*, November 9, 1987, p. 138.
14. Sheff, D., *Game Over* (New York: Random House, 1993).
15. Golden, D., "In Search of Princess Toadstool," *Boston Globe*, November 20, 1988, p. 18.
16. Staff Reporter, "Marketer of the Year," *Adweek*, November 27, 1989, p. 15.
17. Lazzareschi, C., "No Mere Child's Play," *Los Angeles Times*, December 16, 1988, p. 1.
18. For a good summary of the early history of Sega, see Battle, J. and Johnstone, B., "The Next Level: Sega's Plans for World Domination," *Wired*, release 1.06, December 1993.
19. Sheff, D., *Game Over* (New York: Random House, 1993).
20. Battle, J., and Johnstone, B., "The Next Level: Sega's Plans for World Domination," *Wired*, release 1.06, December 1993.
21. For background details, see Flower, J., "3DO: Hip or Hype?" *Wired*, release 1.02, May/June 1993.
22. Brandt, R., "3DO's New Game Player: Awesome or Another Betamax?" *Business Week*, January 11, 1993, p. 38.
23. Flower, J., "3DO: Hip or Hype?" *Wired*, release 1.02, May/June 1993.
24. Jacobs, S., "Third Time's a Charm (They Hope)," *Wired*, release 2.01, January 1994.
25. Dunkin, A., "Video Games: The Next Generation," *Business Week*, January 31, 1994, p. 80.
26. Greenstein, J., "No Clear Winners, Though Some Losers; the Video Game Industry in 1995," *Business Week*, December 22, 1995, p. 42.
27. Staff Reporter, "3DO Says 'I Do' on Major Shift of Its Game Strategy," *Los Angeles Times*, September 17, 1996, p. 2.
28. Battle, J., and Johnstone, B., "The Next Level: Sega's Plans for World Domination," *Wired*, release 1.06, December 1993.
29. Greenstein, J., "No Clear Winners, Though Some Losers: The Video Game Industry in 1995," *Business Week*, December 22, 1995, p. 42.
30. Hamilton, D. P., "Sega Suddenly Finds Itself Embattled," *Wall Street Journal*, March 31, 1997, p. A10.
31. Taves, S., "Meet Your New Playmate," *Wired*, release 3.09, September 1995.
32. Kunni, I., "The Games Sony Plays," *Business Week*, June 15, 1998, p. 128.
33. Platt, C., "WordNerd," *Wired*, release 3.10, October 1995.
34. Kunni, I., "The Games Sony Plays," *Business Week*, June 15, 1998, p. 128.
35. Trachtenberg, J. A., "Race Quits Sony Just Before U.S. Rollout of Its PlayStation Video-Game System," *Wall Street Journal*, August 8, 1995, p. B3.
36. Beenstock, S., "Market Raider: How Sony Won the Console Game," *Marketing*, September 10, 1998, p. 26.

37. Trachtenberg, J. A., "Olafsson Calls It Quits as Chairman of Sony's Technology Strategy Group," *Wall Street Journal*, January 23, 1996, p. B6.

38. Greenstein, J., "Price Cuts Boost Saturn, PlayStation Hardware Sales," *Video Business*, May 31, 1996, p. 1.

39. Greenstein, J., "Sony Cuts Prices of PlayStation Hardware," *Video Business*, March 10, 1997, p. 1.

40. Hamilton, D., "Sega Suddenly Finds Itself Embattled," *Wall Street Journal*, March 31, 1997, p. A10.

41. Staff Reporter, "Nintendo Wakes Up," *The Economist*, August 3, 1996, pp. 55–56.

42. Takahashi, D., "Game Plan: Video Game Makers See Soaring Sales Now—And Lots of Trouble Ahead," *Wall Street Journal*, June 15, 1998, p. R10.

43. Takahashi, D., "Sony and Nintendo Battle for Kids Under 13," *Wall Street Journal*, September 24, 1998, p. B4.

44. Kunni, I., "The Games Sony Plays," *Business Week*, June 15, 1998, p. 128.

45. Guth, R. A., "Sega Cites Dreamcast Price Cuts for Loss Amid Crucial Time for Survival of Firm," *Wall Street Journal*, October 30, 2000, p. A22.

46. Guth, R. A., "Sega Cites Dreamcast Price Cuts for Loss Amid Crucial Time for Survival of Firm," *Wall Street Journal*, October 30, 2000, p. A22.

47. Oxford, T., and Steinberg, S. "Ultimate Game Machine Sony's PlayStation 2 Is Due on Shelves Oct. 26. It Brims with Potential—But at This Point Sega's Dreamcast Appears a Tough Competitor," *Atlanta Journal/Atlanta Constitution*, October 1, 2000, p. P1.

48. Guth, R. A., "New Players From Nintendo Will Link to Web," *Wall Street Journal*, August 25, 2000, p. B1.

49. Takahashi, D., "Microsoft's X-Box Impresses Game Developers," *Wall Street Journal*, March 13, 2000, p. B12.

50. Powers, K., "Showdown", *Forbes*, August 11, 2003, pp. 86–87.

51. *The Economist*, "Console Wars," June 22, 2002, p. 71.

52. Guth, R. A., "Game Gambit: Microsoft to Cut Xbox Price," *Wall Street Journal*, March 19, 2004, p. B1.

53. Powers, K., "Showdown", *Forbes*, August 11, 2003, pp. 86–87.

54. Taub, E., "No Longer a Solitary Pursuit: Video Games Move Online," *New York Times*, July 5, 2004, p. C4.

55. Greene, J., and Edwards, C., "Microsoft Plays Video Leapfrog," *Business Week*, May 10, 2004, pp. 44–45.

56. Guth. R. A., "Microsoft Bets Software Tools Will Spur Xbox," *Wall Street Journal*, March 24, 2004, p. B1.

Satellite Radio: XM Versus Sirius

This case was prepared by Charles W. L. Hill, the University of Washington.

The Birth of a Market

More than anyone else, Canadian-born David Margolese was the key player in the creation of the satellite radio business. In 1978, at the tender age of twenty, Margolese dropped out of college to create a Vancouver-based paging company. He soon turned his attention to the nascent cellular telephone business. When he tried to obtain funding to establish a cellular telephone business in Canada, he was initially rebuffed by venture capitalists who told him that the industry would never amount to much. At best, they said, cellular phones would only be used by a few CEOs and diplomats. Undeterred, Margolese persisted in his fund-raising efforts. In 1980, when cellular was still little more than a dream, he convinced Ameritech to invest in his company, Cantel.

Using these funds he acquired licenses to cellular phone rights in Canada. Along the way, he joined forces with others, including Ted Rodgers of Rodgers Communications, to create what became Rogers Wireless, which by 2001 was Canada's largest cellular telephone company. In the late 1980s, while he was still just thirty-one, Margolese sold his stake for $2 billion in cash and set himself up as a venture capitalist.

It was in that capacity that Margolese met Robert Briskman, a former NASA engineer and the operations chief at Geostar, a satellite messaging company that went bankrupt in 1991. Briskman had designed the core technology for satellite radio,

Copyright © 2007 by Charles W. L. Hill. This case was prepared by Charles W. L. Hill, the University of Washington, as the basis for class discussion rather than to illustrate either effective or ineffective handling of an administrative situation. Reprinted by permission of Charles W. L. Hill. All rights reserved. For the most recent financial results of the company discussed in this case, go to **http://finance.yahoo.com**, input the company's stock symbol, and download the latest company report from its homepage.

called the unified S-band. He and other former Geostar employees had established a company named Satellite Radio CD to commercialize the technology, but they were without funding and needed to overcome numerous regulatory hurdles.

Initially Margolese invested just $1 million in the business, whose name was changed to CD Radio, but he soon decided that this was the best business he had ever seen. What attracted Margolese was the fact that radio programs beamed from satellite, using the unified S-band technology and digital signals, could deliver nationwide coverage and CD quality sound. Established radio was local, the quality of the analog signal was often poor, and it faded quickly outside of the local area. Moreover, the local markets served by established radio businesses were too small to support niche programming, such as stations devoted to jazz, classical music, or Reggae, but this might not be the case for a radio company that could serve a nationwide market.

However, numerous hurdles stood in the way of establishing a viable satellite radio business. It would be very expensive to put satellites into space, easily several hundred million dollars. The Federal Communication Commission (FCC) had to be persuaded to allocate radio spectrum to satellite radio. Receiving the radio signal from space would require special radios, and how could potential customers be persuaded to purchase these when they already had radios in their cars and at home? Moreover, it would be difficult to get advertisers to support a service that initially had no listeners—a classic chicken and egg problem—and without the advertisers, how would the service generate revenues?

By 1994, Margolese was estimating that satellite radio would be operational by 1997 and cost some $500 million, but CD Radio faced substantial roadblocks.

Despite lobbying from Margolese, the FCC had not yet decided if it would license radio spectrum for satellite radio. Fierce opposition from the National Association of Broadcasters (NAB), which represented existing radio stations, was slowing things down. Among other things, NAB filings with the FCC argued that satellite radio would lead to the demise of local radio service, hundreds of which would close, to the detriment of local communities that relied on AM and FM radio for important local news.

It wasn't until 1997 that the FCC finally auctioned off the spectrum for satellite radio. There were four bidders for the spectrum. The FCC decided to license two providers, creating a duopoly. CD Radio and XM Radio won the auction, paying $83.3 million and $89.8 million, respectively. Established in 1992, XM Radio was a development stage company backed by American Mobile Satellite Corp, which was itself owned by Hughes Electronics (then a subsidiary of General Motors) and McCaw Cellular. With spectrum in hand, CD Radio, which in 1999 changed its name to Sirius, and XM Radio now had to deliver on their promise to establish a nationwide satellite radio service. If they did not, the FCC would not renew the licenses when they came up for review in 2007. If not renewed, the licenses would expire on February 14, 2010.

The Radio Industry

The radio industry dates back to 1921 when the first radio station was licensed. Radio involves the transmission of sound waves, which are sent from amplitude modulated (AM) or frequency modulated (FM) stations. AM radio operates on relatively low frequencies and was the earliest broadcast service. FM radio, which was first patented in 1933, operates at much higher frequencies, but was very slow to catch on because of heavy investment by stations and listeners in AM equipment.

Radios are ubiquitous, and can be found in 99 out of 100 American households. The average number of radios per household is 5.6, including radios in cars (there are approximately 150 million radios in vehicles). Some 95.4 percent of radio owners listen to the radio during any given week. The typical adult listener tunes in for 3 hours and 12 minutes every weekday, and 5 hours 30 minutes on weekends. On a typical weekday the average person of 12 years or older spends 41.7 percent of radio listening time in a car or truck, 37.3 percent while at home, and 21 percent at work or other places. On weekends car listening jumps to 47.3 percent, home listening to 40.5 percent, and listening elsewhere falls to 12.1 percent. On average, some 13 to 17 percent of airtime every hour is devoted to advertising on FM/AM radio stations.[1]

Encouraged by broadcast deregulation, the number of radio stations in the United States increased from 10,500 in 1985 to roughly 13,000 by the end of 2001.[2] In 1996, the Telecommunications Act removed limits on the number of radio stations that a company could own in a given market (a "market" is generally defined as a discrete geographic area, such as a city or county). Prior to 1996, a company could only own 2 FM and 2 AM stations in any one market, no matter how populated that market. Under the new regulations, a company may own or operate up to 8 stations in any one market, with up to 5 in one service (AM or FM). These new rules have facilitated consolidation in the industry and led to the growth of large radio broadcasting companies that own many stations. The leader among these, Clear Channel Communications, owned 1,182 U.S. radio stations at the end of 2003, reached an audience of 180 million, and generated $3.70 billion in revenues from radio advertising.[3] The next largest radio broadcasting company in terms of revenues, Infinity Broadcasting, owned 180 radio stations, which were concentrated in the most populated markets in the United States. By 2002, the ten largest broadcasters owned about 17 percent of all U.S. stations, and accounted for over 40 percent of radio industry advertising revenues (the largest broadcasters are focused on the largest markets where advertising revenues are greater). Most analysts believe that the industry will continue to consolidate over the next few years.

Due to the limited range of their signal, radio stations focus on the market in which they are located. Radio stations earn their revenues from advertising. Advertising rates are a function of a station's ability to attract an audience that has certain demographic characteristics. Stations offer programs of a specific format in order to attract the demographic that advertisers are interested in. Popular formats include news/talk radio, rock, oldies, sports, country, or jazz. The ability of radio to offer different programs that target different demographics is a big selling point, attracting advertisers pursuing narrowly defined audiences. Also important are the number of other stations and advertising media competing

EXHIBIT 1

Radio Advertising Spending ($ billion)

Source: Standard & Poor's Industry Survey, Broadcasting and Cable Industry, July 2002.

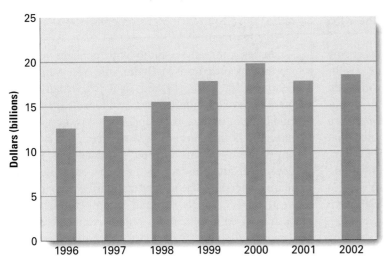

in that market. Advertising rates are normally highest during morning and evening drive-time hours.

In 2002, advertising revenues for radio stations was $18.6 billion, an increase from $12.41 billion in 1996 (see Exhibit 1). Advertising revenues dropped by almost $2 billion in 2001 compared with 2000 due to a weak national economy and the impact of September 11, 2001. The cost structure of radio broadcasters is largely fixed, making the profitability of radio stations sensitive to the overall level of advertising revenues.

The Business Plan for Satellite Radio

The Business Case

The business case for Sirius and XM was based on the argument that the number of radio stations in local markets is limited, most of these stations focus on the same five formats, and the geographic range of service is also limited with the signal fading outside of the market area. According to market data, over 48 percent of all commercial radio stations use one of only three general programming formats—country, news/talk/sports, and adult contemporary—and over 71 percent of all commercial radio stations use one of only five general formats—the same three, plus oldies and religion.[4] The small number of available

programming choices means that artists representing other niche music formats are likely to receive little or no airtime in many markets. Radio stations prefer featuring artists they believe appeal to the broadest market. Meanwhile, according to the Recording Industry Association of America, recorded music sales of niche music formats such as classical, jazz, movie and Broadway soundtracks, religious programming, new age, children's programming, and others comprised up to 27 percent of total recorded music sales in 2001.

Both Sirius and XM planned to offer around 100 channels. Sirius planned to keep 50 channels of music commercial free, while selling advertising spots on the remaining news, sports, and information channels. XM planned to have 15 to 20 channels commercial free, while limiting advertising sports to just seven minutes an hour on other channels. The channels would focus on a wide range of different music formats and news/information/talk formats. For example, XM planned to offer music channels focusing on each decade from the 1940s to the 1990s, plus contemporary music channels, several different country formats (e.g., bluegrass, Nashville), Christian rock channels, numerous news formats, information formats, and so on. Both Sirius and XM also planned to enter into agreements with established broadcasters to offer satellite radio formats of their services. These formats included MTV, VH1, CNN, the BBC, ESPN, Court TV, C-Span, and Playboy. XM also partnered with Clear Channel Communications, the largest owner of FM and AM stations in the nation, to offer Clear Channel program formats, such as the KISS pop music station, over XM Satellite radio.

To generate revenues, in addition to advertising fees both Sirius and XM decided to charge a subscription-based fee for their services that would run at around $10 to $12 per month. When it was pointed out that existing radio is offered for free to consumers, executives at Sirius and XM noted that the same is true for traditional broadcast TV, but, nevertheless, consumers have been more than willing to pay a monthly subscription fee for cable TV service and satellite TV service. Penetration data relating to cable, satellite television, and premium movie channels suggest that consumers are willing to pay for services that expand programming choice or enhance quality. There were more than 22.9 million digital cable subscribers and 22.3 million satellite television subscribers in early 2004. As of 2004, some 69 percent of TV households subscribed to basic cable television, and 20 percent of TV households subscribed to satellite television.[5]

Infrastructure

Although the technology used by Sirius and XM Radio differs in important ways, both companies followed the same basic business plan. Sirius and XM decided to place satellites in orbit to serve the United States. Sirius planned to put three satellites in elliptical orbits 23,000 miles above the earth, while XM planned to put a pair of more powerful satellites in geostationary orbits at 22,300 miles. The satellites were expected to have a useful life of up to fifteen years. Both Sirius and XM planned to keep a spare satellite in storage that could be launched quickly in the event of failure of one of their satellites. If an orbiting satellite were to fail, it would take approximately six months to get a replacement satellite into space. Service would be partially interrupted during this time. Initial plans called for Sirius to launch its satellites in 1999 and XM in 2000, with service starting soon thereafter.

The satellites broadcast a digital signal that can be converted into CD quality sound by radios fitted with the appropriate chip set and receivers that decode, decompress, and output digital signals from a satellite. The S-band signal used by both companies can be picked up by moving vehicles and will not be "weathered out" by dense cloud cover. The radios were expected to cost between $200 and $400. Since the digital signal cannot be picked up by a standard radio, this required the customer to invest in new radio equipment.

At least initially, a radio with a Sirius receiver would not pick up XM Radio, and vice versa. On February 16, 2000, XM and Sirius signed an agreement to develop a unified standard for satellite radios, enabling consumers to purchase one radio capable of receiving both Sirius and XM services. The technology relating to this unified standard was jointly developed and funded by the two companies that share ownership. The unified standard was mandated by the FCC, which required interoperability with both licensed satellite radio systems. Radios based on the unified standard started to become available at the end of 2004.

To offer truly seamless nationwide coverage, satellites alone would not be enough. To receive a satellite signal, a clear line of sight is needed. In tunnels, buildings, and the urban canyons of American cities, a clear line of sight is not available. To solve this problem, both companies had plans to build a nationwide network of terrestrial repeaters. Sirius initially planned to put up 105 repeaters in 42 cities, and XM some 1,700 repeaters in about 70 cities. Sirius could get away with fewer repeaters because the orbits of its satellites allowed for a better coverage of the United States—but to get that Sirius had to put three satellites in space, not two, placing them in figure 8 orbits that have 2 of the 3 satellites high in the sky over North America at any time during the day. In contrast, XM Radio's two satellites are in geostationary orbits. The chipsets required to pick up Sirius signals are more expensive than those for XM Radio.

In addition to satellites and repeaters, the third infrastructure element required to offer the service is recording studios. XM established three recording studios, one in Washington, D.C., one in New York City, and one in Nashville. Taken together, the three studios comprise an all digital radio complex that is one of the largest in the world with over eighty soundproof studios of different configurations. Sirius built a single studio complex in New York City.

By mid 2000, Sirius was expecting to spend $1.2 billion and XM Radio $1.1 billion to develop this infrastructure. These estimates had increased considerably from the initial estimates made in the mid 1990s, which were around $500 million. Given the infrastructure, operational, and advertising costs, the companies estimated that they needed to have 2 to 3 million subscribers each to make a profit. In 2000, forecasts by market research agencies and securities analysts suggested that in total, satellite radio could have as many as 15 million subscribers by 2006, 36 million by 2010, and around 50 million by 2014.[6]

Distribution

Both Sirius and XM believe that installation in cars and trucks was likely to drive early growth for satellite radio. In the early 2000s, 17 to 18 million new cars and light trucks were sold in the United States each year. Some 30 million car radios were sold, either embedded in new cars or in the aftermarket. In total there were over 210 million vehicles on American roads. Both companies made deals with major automobile manufacturers to have satellite radios installed in new cars as optional—and ultimately standard—equipment. The price of the radio is embedded in the price of the car, with the customer signing up for service at the time of purchase. XM has an exclusive deal with General Motors and Honda, and Sirius with Ford and DaimlerChrysler. Both companies have now entered into an agreement with the FCC under which they have agreed to refrain from making any more exclusive deals. Plans called for satellite radio to be offered as an option on certain models, with the offering to be increased to more models over time.

The exclusive deals with automobile companies do not come cheap. As part of its deal with Daimler-Chrysler, Sirius reimbursed DaimlerChrysler for some advertising expenses and hardware costs, and issued to DaimlerChrysler Corporation a warrant to purchase 4 million shares of Sirius common stock at an exercise price of $3 per share. The deal with Ford was very similar. The deal between Sirius and Daimler-Chrysler expires in October 2007, while the Ford deal expires May 2007.

The agreement between XM and General Motors requires XM to guarantee annual, fixed payment obligations to GM. However, the agreement is subject to renegotiation if General Motors does not achieve and maintain specified installation levels, starting with 1,240,000 by November 2005 and installations of 600,000 per year thereafter. The GM agreement expires

September 2013. For its part, Honda has committed to shipping 400,000 cars with XM Radios in 2005.

The companies also lined up manufacturers of aftermarket car receivers and signed retail arrangements with the Best Buy and Circuit City chains to distribute them.

Capital Requirements and Investors

Financing these two ventures was not trivial. XM Radio raised some $2.6 billion equity and debt proceeds through January 2004 from investors and strategic partners to fund its infrastructure build out and operations. The strategic investors in XM Radio included General Motors, Hughes Electronics/DIRECTV, Clear Channel Communications, American Honda, and Hearst Communications. Financial investors in XM included Columbia Capital, Madison Dearborn Partners, AEA Investors, BayStar Capital, and Eastbourne Capital. XM Radio went public in late 1999. Honda and General Motors are major investors in XM Radio, with stakes of 13 percent and 8.6 percent, respectively, in late 2004.[7] Similarly, Sirius, which went public in 1995, had raised around $2.5 billion by 2004.

Much of the funds raised went into building out the infrastructure. At the end of 2003, XM Radio reported that it had spent $470 million to put its two satellites in orbit and purchase a spare satellite, $267 million to set up a system of ground repeaters covering 60 cities, and $130 million on satellite control facilities and studios. Sirius is believed to have spent similar amounts.

Competition

Satellite radio faces competition from three main sources. Traditional AM/FM radio stations are obvious competitors. The big advantage of AM/FM radio is its local content, such as local news, sports, and weather, which listeners do want. Although AM/FM radio is predominantly local, the emergence of consolidators such as Clear Channel Communications is beginning to change this. Clear Channel has made an effort to realize scale economies by developing a nationwide branded format for radio shows, most notably its pop format that goes under the KISS brand. KISS offers standard programming developed in a national studio. Local content such as news, weather, sports, and some dialogue is spliced into KISS programming to make it seem as if the broadcast is local.[8] There are also signs that traditional AM/FM radio will ultimately move toward digital broadcasting, although doing so will require that consumers purchase radios capable of receiving a digital signal.

Internet radio is a second potential competitor. A number of FM and AM radio stations are now broadcasting digital signals over the Internet that can be accessed anywhere in the world for users with the appropriate equipment (a computer, Internet connection, and media player).

A third competitor comes in the form of satellite TV and cable TV systems. Both satellite and cable TV providers are offering digital radio services as part of a package of digital services, with the radio being bundled with TV service, typically at no additional cost to the consumer.

Launching the Services

Initially Sirius was thought to have the lead over XM Radio, but this changed when technical problems with the chip sets to go in the radio receivers delayed the launch of Sirius's service for two years (the receivers, which were built by Lucent, did a poor job of picking up the digital signal and had to be redesigned).

XM Radio also had some delays due to problems with the Boeing rockets that were to launch its satellites, but was able to launch its two satellites—named "Rock" and "Roll" in early 2001, more than a year behind its initial schedule. XM started offering national service in November 2001 for a monthly fee of $9.95. XM Radio's launch was supported by an advertising campaign that was in excess of $100 million.

Beset by technical problems, Sirius did not launch its final satellite until early 2002 and did not start offering service until July 2002. Sirius charged $12.95 a month, justifying its price premium over XM by the fact that all of Sirius's 60 music channels run without commercials. XM has limited commercials of about two minutes per hour on 35 of its 70 music channels (see Exhibit 2 for a comparison between XM and Sirius). Sirius has stated that it will depend upon subscriptions for about 85 percent of its revenue. XM initially expected to rely somewhat more on advertising revenues.

By the end of 2003, Sirius had 133 terrestrial repeaters in 92 urban markets where high buildings interfere with line of sight. XM had some 800 repeaters in 60 markets.

The nine-month lead that XM gained as a result of Sirius's technical problems proved to be invaluable. By the end of 2002, XM had 347,000 subscribers,

while Sirius had just 30,000. XM passed the 500,000 subscriber milestone in April 2003 and was projecting that it would end 2003 with over 1 million subscribers. This rapid subscriber accrual helped XM Radio sell faster than CD and DVD players did in their first year on the market.[9] Sirius, meanwhile, was aiming to end 2003 with some 300,000 subscribers and had just over 100,000 by midyear. Both companies were now estimating that they needed 2 to 3 million subscribers to break even, with XM predicting that it would be cash flow positive by late 2004.

In addition to XM's nine-month lead in the market, analysts attribute much of the company's early gains to an aggressive push by General Motors. GM rolled out XM's satellite radio as optional factory installed equipment in 25 of its 57 car, light truck, and sport's utility models, including the entire Cadillac line. GM planned to increase that figure to 44 models for the 2004 model year, and the company expected to sell some 800,000 cars autos with XM's radio installed during 2004, and 1.1 million during 2005. The GM-installed radio, which is built by GM supplier Delphi, costs $325 and is bundled into the price of the vehicle. In addition to being a shareholder of XM, GM is believed to get about $100 from XM for every radio it installs.

In early 2003, Honda stated that it planned to include XM radios as standard equipment in the 2004 Acura RL, and as factory-installed options in the 2004 Accord. In September 2003, Honda announced that XM radios would be installed as standard equipment in certain Honda Accord models. An XM Satellite Radio spokesman said that between the Accord, Pilot, and S2000 models, Honda will release about 200,000 automobiles that have the XM radio as a factory-installed feature during the 2004 model year and 400,000 during the 2005 model year.[10] In addition to GM and Honda, XM radios are now available as dealer-installed options on certain offerings from Toyota, Volkswagen, and Audi, among others.

In contrast, Sirius's main partners are not as far along putting Sirius radios into their vehicles. Daimler and BMW offer Sirius radios as a dealer-installed option, as opposed to factory installed, meaning that a buyer has to request that the dealer install the equipment. In 2004, Daimler committed to factory install 550,000 radios by mid 2007. Ford reportedly planned to offer factory-installed radios in select models for the 2004 model year, but that did

EXHIBIT 2

XM Versus Sirius in 2003

	XM Satellite	Sirius
Monthly Cost	$9.99	$12.95
Radio Cost	$325 factory installed radio, $400–$500 for dealer installed $200–$299 for home radio	$400–$500 for dealer installed radio No home radio
Programming	101 channels 70 music 30 talk, sports, news 1 premium channel (Playboy)	100 channels 60 music 40 sports, talk, news
Commercials	None on 35 music channels Limited commercials on rest (about 2 minutes per hour)	None on music channels
Key Formats	Classic (3 channels) Pop (10 channels) Jazz/Blues (7 channels) Country (6 channels) Rock (12 channels) Latin (5 channels) Frank's Place The Joint (Reggae) Broadway Old Time Radio Classics	Classic (3 channels) Pop (9 channels) Jazz/standards (5 channels) Hip Hop (5 channels) Country (5 channels) Dance (6 channels) R&B (4 channels) Rock (13 channels) Broadway Radio Classics
News	Fox, CNN, CNBC, ESPN, Others	Fox, CNN, CNBC, ESPN, Others
Automotive Partners	GM, Honda	Ford, DaimlerChrysler, BMW
Subscribers as of Mid 2003	692,253	105,186

not transpire. Now Ford has announced that it will begin factory installing Sirius radios in the 2006 model year, and will be factory installing Sirius radios in twenty of its twenty-one car lines by 2007.[11]

The wild card in the industry may be Toyota, which had not aligned itself with either XM or Sirius by late 2004, although Toyota did offer XM Radio as a dealer-installed option on some models. Nissan, too, has not aligned itself with either company, but the company again offers either XM or Sirius radios as a dealer-installed option.

Both XM and Sirius are also starting to offer an array of satellite radios for home use. The best selling of these in 2002 and 2003 was the Delphi XM SkyFi radio, which is made by Delphi for XM and sold through major consumer electronics chains for between $199 and $230 a unit. By mid 2003, some 80,000 Delphi XM SkyFi units had been sold, and Wal-Mart, the nation's largest retailer, now stocked the item. The SkyFi radio could be used both at home, where it slots into an audio player, and adapted to fit into a car (see Exhibit 3). In late 2004, XM Radio and Delphi announced that they would start selling a handheld portable radio, the Delphi MyFi, in December 2004.

Early surveys suggest high customer satisfaction with satellite radio. Surveys carried out by GM reported a 90 percent satisfaction rate among customers

EXHIBIT 3

Delphi XM SkiFi Radio Receiver in a Car[12]

Source: Reprinted courtesy of XM Satellite Radio, Inc.

who chose satellite radio as an option, with 70 to 75 percent saying that they are likely to order satellite radio for their next vehicle.[13] Several consumer products reporters have also given satellite strong reviews although some have complained that the sound quality is not quite CD quality.[14]

Sirius's late entry into the market and relatively low traction has left it in a very shaky financial condition (see Exhibit 4 for Sirius's financial data). In October 2001, CEO David Margolese abruptly resigned, presumably a casualty of the company's failure to launch its service on time. Margolese continues as non–executive chairman of Sirius. The delay in the launch of its service resulted in Sirius running down its cash reserves, and by mid 2002, it looked almost certain that the company would default on debt payments and have to file for chapter 11 bankruptcy protection. However, at the last minute in October 2002 Sirius was able to pull off something of a coup, converting $700 million in debt and $525 million in preferred stock into common equity. In addition, three of the original investors in Sirius agreed to supply the company with another $200 million in cash. As a result of the recapitalization plan, the existing holders of the company's common stock ended up owning just 8 percent of the recapi-

talized company. It remains to be seen whether these funds will be sufficient to see the company through to profitability.

XM Radio also returned to the capital markets in early 2003, lining up an additional $475 million in funding (see Exhibit 5 for financial data from XM). Of the $475 million, $225 million came from new investors, and the remainder from General Motors in the form of deferred payments and credit facilities. Critical to the deal's success was the agreement by more than 90 percent of the holders of $325 million in XM bonds to swap them for newly issued debt that pays no interest until 2006.

Although XM did launch on schedule, it, too, has experienced some technological problems that do represent a potential cloud on the horizon. XM's two satellites, "Rock" and "Roll," are experiencing unexpected degradation of their solar power panels. The degradation has prompted XM to cut their useful life to 2008 from 2015. However, XM believes that it will be able to launch additional satellites by the time the degradation impacts signal strength. XM believes that its current insurance policies cover this problem and that it will be able to claim sufficient funds from insurance to be able to launch additional satellites.

EXHIBIT 4

Selected Consolidated Financial Data for Sirius[15]

Sirius Satellite Radio Inc. and Subsidiary

Consolidated Statements of Operations (in Thousands, Except per Share Amounts)

	For the Years Ended December 31,		
	2003	2002	2001
Revenue:			
Subscriber revenue, including effects of mail-in rebates	$12,615	$623	$
Advertising revenue, net of agency fees	116	146	—
Equipment revenue	61	—	—
Other revenue	80	36	—
Total Revenue	**12,872**	**805**	**—**
Operating Expenses:			
Cost of services (excludes depreciation expense shown separately below):			
Satellite and transmission	32,604	39,308	31,056
Programming and content	30,398	22,728	9,836
Customer service and billing	23,657	7,862	6,572
Cost of equipment	115	—	—
Sales and marketing	121,216	87,347	21,566
Subscriber acquisition costs	74,860	21,038	—
General and administrative	36,211	30,682	28,536
Research and development	24,534	30,087	47,794
Depreciation expense	95,353	82,747	9,052
Non-cash stock compensation expense (benefit) (1)	11,454	(7,867)	14,044
Total Operating Expenses:	**450,402**	**313,932**	**168,456**
Loss from operations	(437,530)	(313,127)	(168,456)
Other Income (Expense):			
Debt restructuring	256,538	(8,448)	—
Gain on extinguishment of debt	—	—	5,313
Interest and investment income	5,287	5,257	17,066
Interest expense, net of amounts capitalized	(50,510)	(106,163)	(89,686)
Total Other Income (Expense):	**211,315**	**(109,354)**	**(67,307)**
Net loss	(226,215)	(422,481)	(235,763)
Preferred Stock Dividends	(8,574)	(45,300)	(41,476)
Preferred Stock Deemed Dividends	(79,634)	(685)	(680)
Net Loss Applicable to Common Stockholders	$(314,423)	$(468,466)	$(277,919)
Net Loss per Share Applicable to Common Stockholders (Basic and Diluted)	$ (0.38)	$ (6.13)	$ (5.30)
Weighted Average Common Shares Outstanding (Basic and Diluted)	827,186	76,394	52,427

(continued)

EXHIBIT 4 (*continued*)

Sirius Satellite Radio Inc. and Subsidiary

Consolidated Balance Sheets (in Thousands, Except Share and per Share Amounts)

Period Ending	31-Dec-03	31-Dec-02	31-Dec-01
Assets			
Current Assets			
Cash and Cash Equivalents	520,979	18,375	4,726
Short Term Investments	30,901	155,327	326,216
Net Receivables	—	—	—
Inventory	—	—	—
Other Current Assets	27,784	25,907	12,303
Total Current Assets	**579,664**	**199,609**	**343,245**
Long-Term Investments	6,750	7,200	—
Property Plant and Equipment	941,052	1,032,874	1,082,915
Goodwill	—	—	—
Intangible Assets	83,654	83,654	83,654
Accumulated Amortization	—	—	—
Other Assets	493	17,603	17,791
Deferred Long Term Asset Charges	5,704	—	—
Total Assets	**1,617,317**	**1,340,940**	**1,527,605**
Liabilities			
Current Liabilities			
Accounts Payable	67,268	48,320	45,313
Short/Current Long-Term Debt	—	—	15,000
Other Current Liabilities	14,735	—	—
Total Current Liabilities	**82,003**	**48,320**	**60,313**
Long-Term Debt	194,803	670,357	589,990
Other Liabilities	11,593	54,264	47
Deferred Long-Term Liability Charges	3,724	—	69,438
Minority Interest	—	—	—
Negative Goodwill	—	—	—
Total Liabilities	**292,123**	**1,304,094**	**1,204,956**
Stockholders' Equity			
Misc. Stock Options Warrants	—	531,153	485,168
Redeemable Preferred Stock	—	—	—
Preferred Stock	—	—	—
Common Stock	1,138	77	57
Retained Earnings	(1,153,694)	(927,479)	(504,998)
Treasury Stock	—	—	—
Capital Surplus	2,525,135	963,335	827,590
Other Stockholder Equity	(47,385)	913	—
Total Stockholder Equity	**1,325,194**	**36,846**	**322,649**
Net Tangible Assets	**$1,241,540**	**($46,808)**	**$238,995**

EXHIBIT 5

Selected Financial Data for XM Radio[16]

XM Satellite Radio Holdings Inc. and Subsidiaries
Consolidated Statements of Operations Years Ended December 31, 2003, 2002, and 2001

	2003	2002	2001
	(in thousands except share amounts)		
Revenue:			
Subscription revenue	$78,275	$ 16,344	$ 238
Activation revenue	1,868	484	8
Equipment revenue	6,692	757	—
Net ad sales revenue	4,065	2,333	251
Other	881	263	36
Total revenue	91,781	20,181	533
Operating Expenses:			
Cost of revenue (excludes depreciation & amortization, shown below):			
Revenue share & royalties	26,440	12,790	1,739
Customer care & billing	25,945	16,069	5,724
Cost of equipment	9,797	1,679	—
Ad sales	3,257	1,870	2,243
Satellite & terrestrial	39,692	44,818	62,641
Broadcast & operations	19,712	19,851	21,960
Programming & content	23,109	25,379	17,649
Total cost of revenue	147,952	122,456	111,956
Research & development (excludes depreciation and amortization, shown below)	12,285	10,843	13,689
General & administrative (excludes depreciation and amortization, shown below)	27,418	26,448	20,250
Marketing (excludes depreciation and amortization, shown below)	200,267	169,165	93,584
Impairment of goodwill	—	11,461	—
Depreciation & amortization	158,317	118,588	42,660
Total operating expenses	546,239	458,961	282,139
Operating Loss	(454,458)	(438,780)	(281,606)
Other Income (Expense):			
Interest income	3,066	5,111	15,198
Interest expense	(110,349)	(63,573)	(18,131)
Other income (expense)	(22,794)	2,230	160
Net loss	(584,535)	(495,012)	(284,379)
8.25% Series B Preferred Stock Dividend Requirement	(2,471)	(3,766)	(3,766)
8.25% Series B Preferred Stock Retirement Gain	8,761	—	—
8.25% Series C Preferred Stock Dividend Requirement	(15,098)	(17,093)	(19,387)
8.25% Series C Preferred Stock Retirement Loss	(11,537)	—	—
Net loss attributable to common stockholders	$ (604,880)	$ (515,871)	$ (307,532)
Net Loss Per Share:			
Basic and diluted	$ (4.83)	$ (5.95)	$ (5.13)
Weighted Average Shares Used in Computing Net Loss per Share-Basic and Diluted	125,176,320	86,735,257	59,920,196

(*continued*)

EXHIBIT 5 (continued)

XM Satellite Radio Holdings Inc. and Subsidiaries
Consolidated Balance Sheets December 31, 2003 and 2002

ASSETS	2003	2002
	(in thousands except share data)	
Current Assets:		
Cash and cash equivalents	$418,307	$32,818
Short-term investments	—	9,997
Restricted investments	116	25,014
Accounts receivable, net of allowance for doubtful accounts of $796 and $241	13,160	3,756
Due from related parties	5,176	1,478
Related party prepaid expenses	22,261	—
Prepaid and other current assets	19,542	10,362
Total current assets	478,562	83,425
Restricted investments, net of current portion	4,035	4,728
System under construction	92,577	55,016
Property and equipment, net of accumulated depreciation and amortization of $315,063 and $158,266	709,501	847,936
DARS license	141,200	144,042
Intangibles, net of accumulated amortization of $4,433 and $3,172	8,429	9,690
Deferred financing fees, net of accumulated amortization of $10,561 and $3,898	43,999	13,276
Related party prepaid expenses, net of current portion	44,521	—
Prepaid and other assets, net of current portion	3,958	2,167
Total assets	$1,526,782	$1,160,280
Liabilities and Stockholders' Equity		
Current Liabilities:		
Accounts payable	$35,773	$40,006
Accrued expenses	57,293	46,924
Accrued network optimization expenses	4,136	2,201
Current portion of long-term debt	38,686	3,845
Due to related parties	2,103	13,410
Accrued interest	5,427	16,651
Deferred revenue	39,722	9,925
Total current liabilities	183,140	132,962
Related party long-term debt, net of current portion	141,891	—
Long-term debt, net of current portion	601,363	412,540
Due to related parties, net of current portion	23,921	10,618
Deferred revenue, net of current portion	14,162	2,372
Other non-current liabilities	29,417	9,477
Total liabilities	993,894	567,969

(continued)

EXHIBIT 5   (*continued*)

XM Satellite Radio Holdings Inc. and Subsidiaries
Consolidated balance sheets December 31, 2003 and 2002

ASSETS	2003	2002
	(in thousands except share data)	
Stockholders' Equity:		
Series A convertible preferred stock, par value $0.01 (liquidation preference of $102,739 at December 31, 2003, and December 31, 2002); 15,000,000 shares authorized, 10,786,504 shares issued and outstanding at December 31, 2003 and December 31, 2002	108	108
Series B convertible redeemable preferred stock, par value $0.01 (liquidation preference of $23,714 and $43,364 at December 31, 2003 and December 31, 2002, respectively); 3,000,000 shares authorized, 474,289 and 867,289 shares issued and outstanding at December 31, 2003 and December 31, 2002, respectively	5	9
Series C convertible redeemable preferred stock, par value $0.01 (liquidation preference of $153,605 and $239,508 at December 31, 2003, and December 31, 2002, respectively); 250,000 shares authorized, 120,000 and 200,000 shares issued and outstanding at December 31, 2003 and December 31, 2002, respectively	1	2
Series D convertible redeemable preferred stock, par value $0.01 (liquidation preference of $0 at December 31, 2003 and December 31, 2002); 250,000 authorized; no shares issued and outstanding at December 31, 2003 and December 31, 2002, respectively	—	—
Class A common stock, par value $0.01; 600,000,000 and 225,000,000 shares authorized, 160,665,194 and 91,706,056 shares issued and outstanding at December 31, 2003 and December 31, 2002, respectively	1,607	917
Class C common stock, par value $0.01; 15,000,000 shares authorized, no shares issued and outstanding at December 31, 2003 and December 31, 2002, respectively	—	—
Additional paid-in capital	2,001,688	1,477,261
Accumulated deficit	(1,470,521)	(885,986)
Total stockholders' equity	532,888	592,311
Commitments and contingencies		
Total liabilities and stockholders' equity	$1,526,782	$1,160,280

By mid 2003, some analysts remained very bullish about the potential of XM Radio, although the future of Sirius was somewhat hazy. A May 2002 study by the Yankee Group projected satellite radio would achieve 15 million subscribers by 2006. Other market studies conducted for XM Radio project that as many as 50 million people may subscribe to satellite radio by 2012. More conservative investment analysts were suggesting that satellite radio might garner 4 to 5 million subscribers by mid-decade, and that the ultimate total may be closer to 40 to 50 million. According to some projections made in early 2003, if XM hits 10 million subscribers in 2007 it could earn $500 million, or $1.50 a share. If XM Radio were ultimately to garner 30 million subscribers, it could earn $7 or more a share.[17]

EXHIBIT 6

Forecasted Subscriber Growth (millions)

Source: Salmon Smith Barney Estimates. 2003 figures are actual figures.

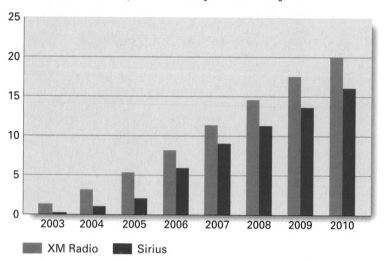

XM Radio ▪ Sirius

Significant Developments in 2004

As 2004 drew to a close, subscription data suggested that XM Radio was continuing to capitalize on its early lead over Sirius in the industry. Analysts were now expecting XM to end 2004 with 3.11 million subscribers versus around 1 million for Sirius (see Exhibit 6). During 2004, XM Radio's net subscriber additions (gross additions less cancellations) were 1.75 million, versus 0.76 million for Sirius. XM was forecasted to have 5.31 million subscribers in 2005, versus 2.14 million for Sirius.

Sirius had tried to differentiate itself by aggressively signing valuable branded content. In December 2003, Sirius signed a seven-year exclusive deal with the NFL to broadcast football games, beginning with the 2005–2006 season. The deal cost Sirius $188 million in cash over the course of the contract, plus $32 million in warrants. In early October 2004, Sirius signed up "shock jock" Howard Stern to an exclusive five-year deal for $500 million, which would start to air on January 1, 2006. The branded content was used by Sirius to justify the premium subscription price of its service.

XM Radio has responded to these moves with deals of its own. In October 2004, XM signed an eleven-year $650 million deal with Major League Baseball (MBL), giving XM exclusive rights to the satellite broadcast of MLB games beginning in 2005, including the World Series. Also in October 2004, XM launched a premium channel dedicated to shock jocks Opie and Anthony, who had previously been removed from the air due to profanity. The Opie and Anthony channel will cost subscribers an additional $1.99 a month.

By late 2004, the business models at XM Radio and Sirius were starting to crystallize. It was now clear that earlier statements regarding breakeven subscription levels were too low. A detailed research report on XM Radio by Salmon Smith Barney suggested that the company would not start to generate positive earnings before interest, tax, depreciation and amortization (EBITDA) until 2007, when the subscriber base was forecasted to be around 11 million (see Exhibit 7).[18] On the same basis, Sirius was not expected to start generating a positive EBITDA until 2008.

The key variables in analysts' estimation of breakeven volume were subscription revenues, fixed costs, variable costs, customer acquisition costs, and customer churn rates. For 2004, Smith Barney estimated that XM Radio would have revenues of $243 million, with only $6 million of those being attributed to advertising revenues. Fixed costs—which included costs related to equipment, broadcasting,

EXHIBIT 7

EXHIBIT 7

Financial Performance and Forecasts for XM Radio

$(million)	2003	2004E	2005E	2006E	2007E
Revenue	$91.8	$243.5	$469.7	$790	$1,183.2
Variable Costs	($52.4)	($96.5)	($150.9)	($231.5)	($324.3)
Fixed Costs	($143.1)	($175.9)	($248.7)	($281.1)	($299.6)
Customer Acquisition Costs	($192.4)	($279.9)	($347.4)	($412.5)	($508.1)
EBITDA	($296.1)	($308.8)	($277.2)	($135.7)	$51.1

Source: Company Reports and Salmon Smith Barney.

programming and content, and customer support—were estimated to be around $175 million. Variable costs—including revenue sharing with partners such as GM, royalties paid for the right to broadcast songs, and customer care costs—amounted to $96.5 million. The average cost of acquiring a customer—including advertising, marketing, and subsidies given to equipment suppliers—was pegged at $130 per customer, and forecasted to hit $279.9 million in 2004. In its 2003 10K, XM Radio estimated that 1.3 percent of its paying customers left the service every month. However, if nonpaying customers who get the service on a trial basis through automobile companies are counted in, the churn rate rises to 3.5 percent a month.

Sirius had a similar revenue and cost structure to XM Radio, although accounting differences make a direct comparison difficult (see Exhibit 8). The largest difference was that Sirius still charged a premium price for subscriptions, but was also committed to paying higher fees for content on an annualized basis. In 2006, for example, forecasts suggest that programming costs per subscriber will be $3.88 at Sirius and $1.31 at XM Radio.[19] Sirius also had a larger customer churn rate than XM Radio in 2004, around 1.7 percent a month, and larger customer acquisitions costs, which were forecasted to be around $247 a customer in 2005. The higher customer acquisition costs, relative to XM Radio, were because Sirius paid a larger subsidy to equipment manufacturers, and it had a small base over which to spread its marketing costs. In Exhibit 8, customer acquisition costs are bundled in with marketing expenses.

EXHIBIT 8

Financial Performance and Forecasts for Sirius

$(million)	2003	2004	2005	2006	2007
Revenue	$12.9	$68.2	$186.7	$520.7	$1383.4
Non-Marketing Operating Expense	($160.9)	($224.7)	($258.3)	($469.6)	($614.4)
Marketing Expenses	($194.1)	($294.4)	($339.8)	($542.5)	($489.5)
EBITDA	($342.2)	($450.9)	($411.3)	($513.7)	$154.2

Source: Company Reports and Salmon Smith Barney.

REFERENCES

K. Bachman. "The next wave." *Mediaweek*, April 12, 1999, pages 26–31.

K. Bachman. "Reaching for the stars." *Mediaweek*, March 25, 2002, pages 22–28.

A. Barry. "A sound idea." *Barrons*, February 17, 2003, pages 17–19.

A. Barry. "Interference." *Barrons*, April 21, 2003, pages 13–14.

A. Cosper. "Sirius competition." *Satellite Broadband*, March 2002, pages 24–29.

P. Lewis. "Satellite Radio." *Fortune*, October 15, 2001, pages 253–256.

P. Lewis. "Sirius competition." *Fortune*, June 23, 2003, pages 130–132.

A. W. Mathews. "From a distance." *Wall Street Journal*, February 25, 2002, page A1.

B. McLean. "Satellite killed the radio star." *Fortune*, January 22, 2001, pages 94–99.

E. Rathbun. "Radio flyer." *Broadcasting & Cable*, June 5, 2000, pages 18–23.

A. Rodgers. "A little space music." *Newsweek*, November 12, 2001, pages 67–69.

Salmon Smith Barney. XM Satellite Radio Holdings. October 26, 2004.

Sirius Radio 2002 and 2003 10K Form.

Standard & Poor's *Industry Survey*. Broadcasting and Cable, July 25, 2002.

XM Radio 2002 and 2003 10K Form.

ENDNOTES

1. Statistics from Standard & Poor's *Industry Survey*, Broadcasting and Cable, July 25, 2002.

2. Standard & Poor's *Industry Survey*, Broadcasting and Cable, July 25, 2002.

3. Clear Channel Communications 2002 10K Form.

4. XM Radio 2003 10K Form.

5. National Cable Television Association website and **skyreport.com** website.

6. XM Radio 2002 10K Form. Smith Barney, *XM Satellite Radio Holdings*, October 26, 2004.

7. Smith Barney, *XM Satellite Radio Holdings*, October 26, 2004.

8. A. W. Mathews, "From a distance," *Wall Street Journal*, February 25, 2002, page A1.

9. Anonymous, "Outstanding subscriber growth for XM," *Dealerscope*, June 2003, page 5.

10. Anonymous, "XM Satellite Radio to be standard equipment on Honda Accord models," Dow Jones News Wire, September 9, 2003.

11. Smith Barney, *XM Satellite Radio Holdings*, October 26, 2004.

12. Image Gallery XM radio at **http://www.xmradio.com/newsroom/photo_gallery_sub.jsp?cat=Facilities**.

13. A. Barry. "A sound idea," *Barrons*, February 17, 2003, pages 17–19.

14. K. Bachman, "Reaching for the stars," *Mediaweek*, March 25, 2003, pages 22–30.

15. Sirius Satellite Radio 2003 10K Form.

16. XM Radio 2003 10K Form.

17. A. Barry, "A sound idea," *Barrons*, February 17, 2003, pages 17–19.

18. Smith Barney, *XM Satellite Radio Holdings*, October 26, 2004.

19. Smith Barney, *Sirius Satellite Radio*, October 26, 2004.

Case 10

Strategic Inflection: TiVo in 2003

This case was prepared by Professors David Yoffie and Pai-Ling Yin, and Christina Darwall of the HBS California Research Center.

Mike Ramsay, chief executive officer of TiVo Inc., looked out at the Santa Cruz Mountains, not far from the company's headquarters in San Jose, California. Midway through 2003, he felt buoyed by TiVo's strong first-quarter increase in subscribers and steadily rising stock price, but he was pensive about the company's next steps.

TiVo was a leading provider of digital video recorder (DVR) technology and services, selling directly to consumers as well as through original equipment manufacturers (OEMs) and licensees. (See Exhibit 1.) DVRs—an emerging consumer electronics (CE) category—were similar to videocassette recorders (VCRs) except that TV recordings were made to hard disks rather than to cassette tapes. Also referred to as personal video recorders (PVRs), DVRs could change the way consumers experienced television. A user could pause live TV, fast-forward through commercials, and run instant replay during his or her favorite sporting event. Along with many other features, TiVo would even suggest and record programs that the consumer might like.

Copyright © 2003 Harvard Business School Publishing. This case was prepared by Professors David Yoffie and Pai-Ling Yin, and Christina Darwall of the HBS California Research Center. HBS cases are developed solely as the basis for class discussion. Cases are not intended to serve as endorsements, sources of primary data, or illustrations of effective or ineffective management. Reprinted by permission of Harvard Business School Publishing. All rights reserved. For the most recent financial results of the company discussed in this case, go to **http://finance.yahoo.com**, input the company's stock symbol, and download the latest company report from its homepage.

Despite having the strongest brand, the most differentiated product in terms of features, and one of the largest installed bases, TiVo would be at an inflection point in 2003, Ramsay knew. TiVo's competition had increased from just one competitor in 1998 to more than a dozen. Moreover, the cable TV industry was in the midst of a massive transition from analog to digital set-top boxes. If TiVo did not participate during this transition, it would become much more difficult to enter the market. At the same time, TiVo had suffered $500 million in operating losses since it was founded, and the company was just turning the financial corner. Ramsay had to balance long-term strategy with the company's short-term finances. While financial discipline had been relatively less important in the early days of the Internet bubble, Ramsay and his management team knew that the future of the company depended on avoiding the excesses of the past. As Ramsay told the casewriters:

> From day one, I've had a strong conviction that we're going to change the way people relate to home entertainment. Starting with DVR isn't bad—in fact it's a killer app. Our users tell us, "TiVo's changed my life," so we can see that the service is important to them. But in the long run we want TiVo to be the portal to entertainment services in the home. People think our competitors are other DVR manufacturers, but we aren't really in the "DVR" business—we're in the user interface and entertainment services business.

EXHIBIT 1

Glossary of Terms

CPU	The central processing unit was the "brains" of a computer.
DVD	DVD stood for digital video disc or digital versatile disc and was a type of optical disc-storage medium that could store a full-length feature film.
DVD-DVR	DVD-DVR was a consumer electronics device that combined a digital video disc player with a digital video recorder.
DVR	DVR stood for digital video recorder. A DVR was similar to a VCR (video cassette recorder) except that it recorded digitally onto a hard drive instead of onto video-cassette tape. This meant that it could store dozens of hours of programming and perform many functions that a VCR could not, such as pausing and rewinding live TV. DVRs were sometimes referred to as PVRs (see below).
EPG	EPGs, or electronic programming guides, were available on most cable and satellite services as well as most DVRs. EPGs allowed consumers to see from three to 14 days of programming in advance and, in the case of DVRs, to click on a show to record it or double click to record it every time the show was shown. Stand-alone DVRs required a connection to a phone line to download the EPG each evening. EPGs were also referred to as IPGs (see below).
GB	Gigabyte was a unit used to measure the capacity of hard drives.
IPG	IPG was an abbreviation for interactive programming guide. (See EPG above.) IPGs could have more advanced features than EPGs.
IR Blaster	A feature of most DVRs but usually lacking in DVD-DVRs, an IR (infrared) blaster was a small bulb on a wire that acted like a remote control to change channels on cable or satellite set-top boxes. Without an IR blaster, consumers had to set the recording device to the correct channel before recording.
MPEG	MPEG, a digital compression standard, stood for motion picture experts group.
MSO	MSO, an abbreviation for multiple services operator—meaning a cable operator with more than one network—was a term commonly used for all cable operators.
PVR	PVR stood for personal video recorder. Also referred to as DVR (see above).
STB	STB was an abbreviation for set-top box, which meant any piece of hardware (generally in the shape of a VCR) that was placed on top of (or beside or beneath) the television.
SVOD	SVOD stood for subscription video on demand, which provided consumers with continuous access to certain content (e.g., HBO shows) for a monthly fee.
VOD	VOD stood for video on demand, a service that allowed consumers to pay for a movie or other content and watch it on their cable or satellite TV at their convenience.

Source: Casewriter research, adapted from Webopedia web site, **<http://www.webopedia.com>**, and The Online ITV Dictionary, **<http://itvdictionary.com/broadband.html>**, accessed May 7, 2003.

The big issue we are facing today is whether, given our long-term goals, we should go all out to "mass market" TiVo and speed consumer adoption, or whether we should strive for increased levels of innovation and differentiation to maintain the substantial distance between ourselves and the increasing number of knockoffs.

What Is TiVo?

Former Silicon Graphics, Inc. executives Ramsay and Jim Barton—who had been working on a joint venture with Time Warner to create the first large-scale interactive TV system—founded TiVo in 1997. At its simplest, the TiVo product was a hard disk-based replacement for the VCR.[1] TiVo enabled consumers to

[1]There were over 500 million VCRs in the world in 2003. While introduced to allow consumers to watch TV shows they had previously recorded, the worldwide installed base of VCRs grew from fewer than 10 million in 1980 to over 200 million in 1990 as consumers began using their VCRs to watch prerecorded movies—with adult movies the first killer app. Jimmy Schaeffler, "Ten Trends in Consumer Electronics," *Satellite News*, Vol. 26, No. 13, March 31, 2003; David Backus and Luis Cabral, "Betamax and VHS," NYU Stern School Case, November 26, 2001, p. 2; and Peter Sealey, Ph.D., "Commercial Television: Rest in Peace," speech to the 2003 Association of National Advertisers, March 13, 2003.

record and play back TV shows, to pause "live" TV, to record shows based on general preferences (by using TiVo's WishList feature to input a favorite actor, director, sport, hobby, or whatever), and to "time-shift" their television viewing watching shows whenever they wanted. In fact, many users preferred to watch prerecorded shows even if they were home when the show was shown live. It was easier for a TiVo user to control the viewing experience, and users could fast-forward through the commercials. TiVo users could access two weeks' worth of electronic program guide (EPG) information, recording shows the "old-fashioned way"—by noting the date and time of the show they wanted to record—or simply by telling the TiVo device to record an entire season's worth of a favorite show (TiVo's "Season Pass" feature). The TiVo product even had a suggestion engine, similar to the technology found on Amazon.com. Based on consumers' viewing habits and their ability to give shows a positive or negative rating, TiVo would record programs that might be enjoyed by the consumer.

TiVo helped the consumer solve two problems. One was that, due to conflicts, consumers were sometimes unable to watch their favorite TV shows when they were broadcast. TiVo, as well as other DVRs, allowed users to record shows when they were broadcast, storing them for playback in the future. The other problem was that—with the advent of cable and satellite TV—sifting through hundreds of channels to find the most interesting shows had become a daunting task.

After purchasing a TiVo machine with 40 to 80 hours of recording time for between $249 and $349, the consumer had to install the machine and activate the service, which cost $12.95 per month or a one-time up-front fee of $299. Installing the TiVo was not as easy as plugging in an appliance and turning it on. The TiVo not only needed to connect to the TV but also to a phone jack or the Internet.[2] There were up to six cables that needed to be connected,[3] and most users needed help from the customer service desk during installation.[4] However, once the TiVo unit

had been set up and activated, it was very easy to operate, generally getting high marks from consumers for its user interface and ease of use. (See Exhibit 2.)

In early 2002, TiVo launched its second-generation product, the TiVo Series2, which featured a more robust processor and increased memory, creating an opportunity to offer new premium services such as digital music and broadband VOD (video on demand). TiVo and DirecTV—the largest U.S. satellite TV operator—then launched an integrated DirecTV/DVR set-top box based on TiVo's Series2 technology and announced that DirecTV would both market to and service the accounts.[5] (TiVo would have no ongoing costs associated with DirecTV subscribers.) DirecTV offered a DVR subscription price of $4.95 per month with free service to subscribers to DirecTV's premium package; the hardware was priced at $199.[6] DirecTV paid a monthly fee per household to TiVo. The average monthly fee to TiVo was $3 in mid-2003, but TiVo expected a lower average fee in the future.

In the spring of 2003, TiVo shipped its first premium service application—the Home Media Option (HMO)—which enabled users to view digital photos, listen to and catalog digital music, and schedule programs to be recorded. TiVo Series2 subscribers could purchase HMO for a one-time fee of $99, with an additional $49 fee for each additional machine. Once the HMO software was downloaded via broadband or telephone line and activated at the TiVo web site, the TiVo DVR was capable of linking over wired or wireless (802.11b) networks with either Apple or Windows PCs. Users with HMO could do remote scheduling over the Internet and use their TVs to view digital photos or listen to digital music. In addition, households with more than one TiVo unit could record programs on one TiVo and then transfer the programs to another for viewing. In theory, HMO also created an opportunity for new services such as broadband VOD, where content could be streamed directly to TVs. Broadband to the home was growing more rapidly than pay television services, either

---

[2]Almost all DVRs included automatic access to an EPG; in order to update the EPG daily, DVRs either had an internal modem that allowed them to dial out on a phone line or used an Internet, cable, or satellite connection to access the EPG.

[3]Dawn C. Chmielewski, "The Number of Cables Needed for TiVo Should Have Been a Clue," *The San Jose Mercury News*, June 19, 2003, p. 1E.

[4]TiVo outsourced call center operations to be a big call center operator. Customer service costs varied, primarily with new subscribers.

[5]iVo had had a partnership with DirecTV since 1999, and under terms of the earlier agreement, TiVo had shouldered most of the marketing and operations costs and received a high proportion of the monthly subscriber fees generated.

[6]Richard Shim, "DirecTV Cuts Fee for TiVo Service," CNET News.com Web site, September 3, 2002 <**http://news.com.com/2100-1040-956384. html**>, accessed July 2, 2003.

EXHIBIT 2

TiVo Subscriber History

For Quarter Ended	Net New Additions			Total Cumulative Subscriptions			Percent of TiVo Service Cumulative Subscriptions Paying Recurring Fees
	TiVo Svc	DirecTV	Total	TiVo Svc	DirecTV	Total	
1999 June			1,000			1,000	
1999 September			1,500			2,500	
1999 December			15,500			18,000	
2000 March			14,000			32,000	
2000 June			16,000			48,000	
2000 September			25,000			73,000	
2000 December			63,000			136,000	
2001 January			18,000			154,000	
2001 April	22,000	13,000	35,000	160,000	29,000	189,000	36
2001 July	22,000	18,000	40,000	182,000	47,000	229,000	37
2001 October	24,000	27,000	51,000	206,000	74,000	280,000	39
2002 January	40,000	60,000	100,000	246,000	134,000	380,000	41
2002 April	24,000	18,000	42,000	270,000	152,000	422,000	34
2002 July	21,000	21,000	42,000	291,000	173,000	464,000	33
2002 October	30,000	16,000	46,000	321,000	189,000	510,000	34
2003 January	74,000	40,000	114,000	396,000	228,000	624,000	34
2003 April	37,000	42,000	79,000	433,000	270,000	703,000	34
2003 July	34,000	56,000	90,000	467,000	326,000	793,000	34
2003 October	59,000	150,000	209,000	526,000	476,000	1,002,000	35

Note 1: The "Percent of TiVo Service Cumulative Subscriptions Paying Recurring Fees" excludes DirecTV subscribers.

Note 2: TiVo changed its fiscal year-end from December 31 to January 31 to better capture the holiday sales season in its fourth quarter. Due to this change, the month ending January 31, 2001 was accounted for separately and not in conjunction with any fiscal year.

Note 3: By mid-2003, approximately 45% of new subscribers were choosing to pay the up-front lifetime fee, whereas 55% were opting to pay the monthly fee.

Source: Casewriter research, adapted from company reports and press releases, TiVo Web site, **<http://www.tivo.com>**, accessed February, 2004.

digital cable or satellite, with multiple services operator (MSO, i.e., cable company) broadband providers enjoying greater growth and a larger share than digital-subscriber line (DSL) broadband providers. Estimated at more than 2 million at the end of 2002, the number of home-based wireless networks was projected to grow to nearly 20 million by the end of 2006.[7] However, an obstacle to streaming content was obtaining the digital rights from content providers.

TiVo also sold services to advertisers and networks. TiVo's "Showcases" were long-form (four to six minutes) commercials that were designed to be very entertaining, as TiVo subscribers had to choose to "opt in" to watch them. TiVo helped advertisers develop interactive ads which would allow viewers to solicit more information on a product or record a pilot program by responding to a prompt during a commercial for a new show. TiVo's audience-measurement services allowed buyers to analyze viewer behavior, for example, whether commercials or shows did

[7]Marc van Impe, "20 Million U.S. Households to Go 802.11 by 2006," Nordic Wireless Watch Web site, July 13, 2002, <http://www.nordicwirelesswatch.com/wireless/story.html?story_id=1939>, accessed July 7, 2003.

better at certain times or in certain markets. TiVo's deal with DirecTV allowed TiVo to collect and share data on audience viewing habits, and if TiVo sold advertising to DirecTV customers, it also shared those revenues.

TiVo Technology

The TiVo DVR was essentially a computer with a large hard disk, read-write MPEG digital video chips for encoding and decoding, a modem, and other components. The product was designed to keep costs low and manufacturing relatively easy since the unit was outsourced. The biggest portion of the bill of materials was the hard disk at 33%, with the MPEG components also expensive. The TiVo DVR ran on an MIPS CPU core with the Linux operating system.

TiVo took security and privacy very seriously. The TiVo DVR's microprocessor, containing cryptography software, was soldered into the box. This made TiVo very difficult to hack. The DVRs would call in—usually through the public switched telephone network—for EPG information and/or any software updates. Although TiVo was able to download data to the DVRs, TiVo was not able to upload all data residing on the DVR. In effect, every night TiVo would upload anonymous batch files that would be aggregated across the TiVo user base, allowing the company to analyze viewing habits at a very granular level. Showcases were distributed to the TiVo DVRs via broadcast whenever possible. Each night TiVo bought 30 minutes of very early morning broadcast time on the Discovery Channel. TiVos that had access to the Discovery Channel would automatically record any Showcases, giving TiVo an inexpensive method for transferring large files to the DVRs.

David Courtney, TiVo's CFO and executive vice president for operations and administration, explained that broadcast center costs "scaled with subscriber volume fairly logarithmically" and in 2003 "cost pennies per day per subscriber." Broadcast center costs consisted primarily of annual fees for program guide content (less than 10 cents per subscriber per month), local Internet access service charges (about 15 to 20 cents per month per subscriber), and the capital and maintenance costs of maintaining big server farms. Ultimately, TiVo could scale to 100 million users without changing the underlying infrastructure.

TiVo management believed strongly that TiVo should be a platform technology where third parties could add value. At the same time, TiVo would never operate like a PC, where software providers would write software directly to TiVo's operating system. Barton, a company cofounder whose role was chief technical officer and senior vice president of research and development, elaborated, "Our future lies not with APIs [application program interfaces] but with protocols. For example, we now have a music protocol that allows TiVo to play digital music on your television. In the future, other services will interact with, but not sit on top of, the DVR." One of the company's bigger challenges with regard to its technology platform was that TiVo was not originally built to be an extensible system that could be easily adapted to different hardware and software environments. In mid-2003, the TiVo platform could only handle the English language, which ultimately limited the number of subscribers. In addition, TiVo was not modular; additional engineering work and therefore significant costs were required whenever TiVo wanted to extend its technology to a new OEM or CE device.

Having filed for patents early in the company's life, TiVo management received three major patents in 2001: one for personal video recording software and hardware design, and two for core DVR functions and home networking capabilities. Several aspects of TiVo's system were patent protected including the scheduling and optimization of disk space—for example, what was recorded when—and resolving recording conflicts—for example, when a subscriber wanted to tape two shows whose broadcast times overlapped, the TiVo DVR "knew" that there was a conflict and tried to resolve it by finding another time when one of the shows would be broadcast. In 2003, TiVo sued a major competitor (EchoStar) for the first time for violating one of its approximately 50 patents.

TiVo Manufacturing and Licensees

Initially, TiVo management decided to focus on software. In order to entice brand-name CE firms to manufacture and distribute the TiVo DVR, the company had to subsidize CE manufacturers up to $200 per TiVo unit shipped. After TiVo discontinued CE subsidies in 2002 in an effort to conserve cash, management discovered that there was not enough profit in the TiVo Series2 box for CE manufacturers to make their required margins. As one TiVo executive commented, "We had a difficult time in 2002—we had no manufacturers, and therefore no retail relationships, and not much money." To correct the situation, TiVo management set out to produce the product more cheaply than the CE firms had done. By reducing the number of parts and outsourcing to a very efficient contracting firm, TiVo was indeed able to lower the cost of the box. In TiVo's fiscal year ending January 2003, TiVo manufactured 55% of all TiVo-enabled DVRs.[8] The great majority of the TiVo-manufactured DVRs (81%) were sold through national CE retailers such as Best Buy and Circuit City, major regional retailers such as The Good Guys, and online retailer Amazon.com, with about one-fifth sold directly to consumers through TiVo's own Web site. TiVo's agreement with Best Buy stipulated that TiVo would share a portion of the TiVo service revenue generated from the TiVo-manufactured DVRs sold by Best Buy. CE retailers such as Best Buy had product margins ranging from 15% to 30%, with those margins tending toward the lower end during recessions.[9]

In mid-2003, TiVo signed up two new Japan-based brand-name licensees (Toshiba and Pioneer) with TiVo's new "basic service" option. The basic service option allowed licensees to include "entry-level" DVR functionality—with no monthly fee—in high-end integrated CE devices such as a combination DVD player with a built-in DVR. This version of the TiVo service used the TiVo interface and allowed consumers to pause live TV and record from the three days of EPG or manually using date and time, but it would not have access to popular TiVo features such as WishList and Season Pass. TiVo planned to offer consumers a 45-day free trial for the full service at the time of installation, hoping to spur adoption of TiVo's $12.95 monthly service. When a company licensed TiVo's DVR technology, it generally paid an up-front license fee of several million dollars, with annual maintenance fees set at about 15% to 20% of the up-front license fee. TiVo devoted engineering resources to then make TiVo's technology compatible with the CE company's product.

Buy TiVo!

End Users: Consumers

The market for TVs, TV-related devices, and TV services in the United States was a large one, with around 105 million households owning a TV in 2003. While cable and satellite services and devices such as VCRs and DVD players had made significant inroads into most households, DVR penetration remained low, around 2% to 4%. (See Exhibit 3.) Some industry observers believed that the price of DVR devices needed to fall below $200 before growth would accelerate, citing adoption patterns for consumer devices such as DVD players.[10] (See Exhibits 4 and 5.)

To build awareness of the TiVo brand and educate consumers about TiVo's "personal TV service" during calendar years 2000 and 2001, TiVo spent over $250 million on sales and marketing, including advertising campaigns.[11] (See Exhibit 6.) The company initially tried to enumerate all of TiVo's features and benefits in one 30-second ad, which proved difficult to do; eventually the ads focused on how TiVo could help consumers overcome a specific TV-related problem.[12] Despite a big spike in brand recognition following the advertising, TiVo management found that consumers were still confused about what a DVR did and did not do—and in particular, what the TiVo product could and could not do. Even the name of the device was not settled—half the manufacturers and market analysts used "PVR" for "personal video recorder," while the other half used "DVR." TiVo had done research that showed that the term "personal video recorder" caused consumers to conjure up images of a small, personal electronic device rather than the actual set-top box product. In addition, TiVo had found that consumers were still somewhat confused about the fact that they first had to purchase the product in a retail store and then subsequently pay a monthly service fee.

Although the average consumer was not yet clear about the DVR concept, TiVo users were rabid fans. Almost all (97%) TiVo users were very satisfied—saying

---

[8]Half of TiVo's 248 employees were in engineering, with one-fourth in general and administrative and the remainder split about evenly between service operations and sales and marketing. About 10% worked on hardware design and management.

[9]Joseph Palenchar, "Microsoft: See SPOT Run Despite Past Wristwatch-Pager Failures," TWICE Web site, March 10, 2003, <http://www.twice.com>, accessed April 30, 2003.

[10]David Farina, Mary O'Toole, and Ralph Schackart, "TiVo Inc.," William Blair & Company, March 17, 2003, p. 10.

[11]Through its IPO, the sale of convertible preferred stock, and subsequent stock offerings, TiVo raised approximately $280 million in capital during the 1999 to 2000 time frame.

[12]Om Malik, "Ta-Ta TiVo," Red Herring Web site, January 29, 2003, <http://www.redherring.com/investor/2003/01/tivo012903.html>, accessed June 16, 2003.

EXHIBIT 3

Projected DVR Demand by Type of DVR (households, millions)

	Actual 2000	Actual 2001	Estimated 2002	Forecast 2003	Forecast 2004	Forecast 2005
Satellite DVR/STB	0.1	0.7	1.36	2.4	4.2	6.4
Satellite gateway	0	0	0	0.1	0.2	1.1
Satellite stand-alone	0.09	0.1	0.26	0.6	0.9	1.2
Cable DVR/STB	0	0	0.05	0.3	0.8	1.3
Cable gateway	0	0	0.02	0.1	0.5	1.9
Cable stand-alone	0.05	0.08	0.21	0.7	2.7	5.6
Other stand-alone	0.01	0.02	0.05	0.1	0.1	0.2
Total DVR	**0.25**	**0.9**	**1.95**	**4.3**	**9.6**	**17.8**
Stand-alone DVRs	0.15	0.2	0.52	1.4	3.7	7.0
DVRs sold through satellite companies	0.1	0.7	1.36	2.5	4.4	7.5
DVRs sold through cable companies	0	0	0.07	0.4	1.3	3.2

Note: A "gateway" is a node on a network that acts as the entrance to another network. In homes, the Internet service provider (ISP) was traditionally considered the gateway since it connected the consumer to the Internet. "Gateway" or "media gateway" eventually came to refer to a means to connect multiple media paths and to traverse a converged network. A home media gateway could connect several different sorts of networks from the public switched telephone network to an Internet protocol (IP) network.

Source: Casewriter research, adapted from Josh Bernoff, "Will Ad-Skipping Kill Television?" Forrester Research, Inc., November 2002.

they would recommend TiVo to a friend—and many spoke gushingly about how TiVo had changed their life. Numerous celebrities sang the praises of TiVo, including Oprah Winfrey—who often spoke about "TiVo-ing" a favorite show—and Michael Powell, head of the Federal Communications Commission, who called TiVo "God's machine." TiVo had found

EXHIBIT 4

Example of CE Device Adoption Rates

CE Device	Number of Years to Reach Adoption by 30% of U.S. Households
Color TV	17
VCR	13
Cell phone	12
Personal computer	10
CD player	8
DVD	5

Source: Casewriter research, adapted from David Farina, Mary O'Toole, and Ralph Schackart, "TiVo Inc.," William Blair & Company, March 17, 2003.

that its core consumer segment was "discriminating enthusiasts," people comfortable with technology, but not necessarily "techies," whose lives revolved around their passions. The typical discriminating enthusiast was married, between 25 and 45 years old, and had a household income of $70,000–$100,000. Families with young children were particularly found of TiVo, not only because of its "TV on demand" aspect but the parental controls as well. Susan Cashen, TiVo's vice president of marketing, spoke about other consumer research findings:

We're a bit nervous about saying "you can love your TV," but over three-fourths of our subscribers agree that "TiVo has made my life better." When we ask what that means, they say, "We don't fight with our kids, we have dinner as a family, I can go out with my husband in the evening and then he can watch the game when we get home."

Among nonusers, TiVo is viewed differently. Somebody else has it and loves it, but they're not sure why. Cable customers with some DVR capability say, "It's free and it gets me into digital recording, but it's not TiVo and my friends love TiVo." This is because when you buy a DVR it allows you to pause live TV and time-shift what

EXHIBIT 5

Price and Units Shipped for DVDs and DVRs (1998–2002)

	DVD Players		DVRs			
Year	Average Price/Unit ($)	Units Shipped (millions)	Average Price/Unit ($)	Average Monthly Charge ($)	Lifetime Subscription Fee	Units Shipped (millions)
1998	504	0.9	N/A	N/A	N/A	N/A
1999	353	3.6	499	10	199	0.04
2000	247	9.9	311	10	199	0.25
2001	173	16.7	300	7	199	0.90
2002	129	25.1	250	9	250	1.95

Note 1: Not all DVRs had a monthly subscription fee. The average monthly subscription fee for DVRs that charged a fee is TiVo's fee in 1999 and 2000 and casewriter's estimate for 2001–2002.
Note 2: The 1999 DVR price per unit reflects TiVo's pricing, whereas the 2000–2002 price per unit indicates the average price per unit for all units shipped.

Source: Casewriter research, adapted from David Farina, Mary O'Toole, and Ralph Schackart, "TiVo Inc.," William Blair & Company, March 17, 2003; and Greg Tori, "'02 Digital Gains to Offset Analog Video Sales Declines," This Week in Consumer Electronics Web site, January, 28, 2002, **<http://www.twice.com/ index.asp?layout=story_stocks & articleid=CA193456>,** accessed June 13, 2003.

you watch—but ultimately, you *love* it for other reasons. Systems such as EchoStar's and Time Warner's provide the basic DVR functions, but they don't have the features that make users passionate about the product and service. One of the things that will help us the most is getting the cost of our product low enough that we can sell the product for $199.

We like to think of ourselves as the Google of TV. As more and more people get premium TV programming, we can help people manage their TV better—and with HMO [Home Media Option], we can take it beyond that to managing all the digital content in the home. With HMO, we're targeting TiVo users who have home networks and broadband.

Market research on consumer willingness to pay a monthly fee for DVR devices was conflicting. On the one hand, one study showed that while one-fourth of consumers were interested in getting television programs whenever they wanted them, just 5% said they were willing to pay a monthly fee for a DVR product.[13] On the other hand, another study showed that consumers were willing to pay cable operators

between $5 and $10 a month for DVR service and that there was high satisfaction with the service.[14] Once consumers subscribed to TiVo, they seemed to believe the service was worth continuing. TiVo's churn rate—the rate at which customers gave up their subscriptions—was extremely low. At less than 1% per month and about 10% per year, it was lower than churn rates for other subscription services such as cell phone service (about 33% per year), cable TV service (about 30% per year), and DirecTV (about 18% per year).[15]

The confusion about what drove consumer purchases and the differences between TiVo fanatics and uninformed potential DVR customers made it hard to position TiVo clearly in the market. Management was clearly comforted by the uptick in consumer adoption in 2003 and the projected growth in DirectTV subscribers, but TiVo was still not exploding. If TiVo was going to reach its full potential, Ramsay and the management team had to find additional ways to increase TiVo subscribers and/or sell additional services.

[13]"Research Notes 3Q 2002," Leichtman Research Group, Inc., p. 1.

[14]David Farina, Mary O'Toole, and Ralph Schackart, "TiVo Inc.," William Blair & Company, March 17, 2003, p. 13.
[15]Ibid., p. 25; and Bob Parks, "Where the Customer Service Rep Is King," *Business 2.0*, June 2003, <http://www.business2.com/articles/ mag/print/0,1643,49462,00.html>, accessed July 1, 2003.

EXHIBIT 6

TiVo Income Statements and Selected Balance Sheet Items ($000s)

	Year Ended 12/31/1999	Year Ended 12/31/2000	1 Mo. Ended 1/31/2001	Year Ended 1/31/2002	Year Ended 1/31/2003	9 Mos. Ended 10/31/2002	9 Mos. Ended 10/31/2003
Revenues							
Service revenues	223	3,782	989	19,297	39,261	27,911	42,477
Technology revenues	0	0	0	100	20,909	18,544	13,671
Hardware revenues	0	0	0	0	45,620	31,109	47,345
Rebates and other payments to channel	−667	−5,029	−630	0	−9,780	−4,568	−5,045
Net Revenues	−444	−1,247	359	19,397	96,010	72,996	98,448
Costs and Expenses							
Cost of service revenues	4,183	18,734	1,719	19,825	17,119	12,399	12,453
Cost of technology revenues	0	0	0	62	8,033	5,924	11,113
Cost of hardware revenues	0	0	0	0	44,647	30,599	48,149
Research and development	10,158	25,070	2,544	27,205	20,714	14,395	16,693
Sales and marketing	39,183	151,658	13,946	104,897	48,117	44,152	14,205
General and administrative	7,834	15,537	1,395	18,875	14,465	11,100	11,788
Other operating expense, net	7,210	0	0	0	0	0	0
Loss from operations	−69,012	−212,246	19,245	−151,494	−57,085	−45,573	−15,953
Interest income/expense and other	2,447	7,406	655	−5,211	−23,086	−2,232	−3,552
Provision for income taxes	0	0	0	−1,000	−425	−261	−152
Net loss	−66,565	−204,840	−18,590	−157,705	−80,596	−48,066	−19,657
Net loss after Series A expenses	−66,565	−206,354	−19,013	−160,723	82,261	−49,731	−19,657
Net cash on hand (unrestricted)	139,687	106,096	124,474	52,327	44,201	40,593	61,807
Current assets	148,781	214,646	189,619	124,391	63,811	66,324	97,371
Long-term assets	4,061	21,672	21,924	22,543	18,509	21,474	14,546
Current liabilities	18,454	91,673	100,783	77,007	62,676	60,716	72,913
Long-term liabilities	1,141	12,806	13,868	56,316	44,341	46,784	47,613
Accumulated shareholders' deficit	−76,881	−283,235	−302,248	−462,971	−545,232	−512,702	−564,889
Total shareholders' deficit	133,247	34,849	50,337	−29,944	−24,697	−19,702	−8,609

Note 1: TiVo changed its fiscal year-end from December 31 to January 31 to better capture the holiday sales season in its fourth quarter. Due to this change the month ending January 31, 2001 was accounted for separately and not in conjunction with any fiscal year.

Note 2: Service revenues include customer subscription fees, showcases, and audience-measurement revenues; technology revenues include license fees and engineering service fees. Technology revenues were particularly high in FY 2003 due to a one-time payment from Sony of approximately $10 million as part of the sale of TiVo source code to Sony for use in Japan.

Source: Casewriter research, adapted from TiVo Inc. 10-K for the year ended January 31, 2003, published April 2003; and TiVo financial press releases, 2000–2003.

Advertisers

Although advertising had been in a lull given the U.S. economic recession, TV advertising remained significant, with advertising expenditures for broadcast and cable TV totaling over $57 billion in 2002 and total advertising in the United States representing 2% of the gross domestic product.[16] TV advertising was relatively much more important for broadcast networks than for cable operators because TV stations typically received about 90% of their revenues from advertising, while cable system operators received from 65% to 70% of their revenues from subscriber fees.[17] In addition, cable operators generated revenue from such things as installation charges and sales of VOD movies and events. About one-third of cable advertising revenues went to the cable operators and two-thirds to the cable networks, content generators such as Nickelodeon.

Some analysts believed that advertising was shifting away from traditional 30-second commercials and away from broadcast TV as the anchor medium. Advertising was instead moving toward such things as 1) "minimovies," which were in essence very entertaining commercials, often shown on the advertiser's (e.g., Anheuser Busch's) Web site; 2) creating TV series where product placement was integral (e.g., the reality TV series "Survivor" and MTV's "Surf Girl" series for young girls, which featured Roxy clothing); 3) commercial-free programming (the WB network was in the process of developing such a show, which would have two paid sponsors mentioned briefly at the beginning and end of the show); and 4) reallocation of some advertising dollars from TV to the Internet.[18] (In 2003, approximately $6 billion in advertising was spent on the Internet.) Overall, the trends signaled a move to more "opt-in" advertising, where the consumer chose which commercials he or she wanted to view.

TiVo's "Showcase" service, dubbed "advertainment" by some, fit in with this trend. Showcases provided specialized digital content meant to entertain subscribers while promoting an advertiser's product, such as a new movie or automobile. Subscribers could choose whether to "opt in" and could be given other choices as well, for example, to enter a contest or receive a free product or brochure. These types of interactive features had to be written specifically for the TiVo platform. TiVo frequently sold Showcases in combination with another service aimed at networks and advertisers, TiVo's audience-measurement service. This service allowed second-by-second analysis of viewing patterns within TV programs or ads. Networks and advertisers could analyze such things as what percentage of viewers opted to watch a Showcase and how many times they watched it. Courtney explained, "TiVo charges a few hundred thousand dollars to place content over three to six months, although we're moving towards charging a cost per viewer fee so that revenues would reflect the size of the subscriber base." Showcase and audience-research revenues were relatively small, although Showcase revenues were projected to reach several million dollars in fiscal-year 2004. (See Exhibit 7.)

TiVo's Ecosystem

TiVo operated in a complex ecosystem, which required the company to manage a wide array of potential competitors, partners, and complementors. (See Exhibit 8.) The most important players for TiVo included content aggregators, such as the major networks, content providers, including the big entertainment companies, advertisers, consumer electronics companies, and content distributors, especially the MSOs (cable companies) and satellite operators.

Content Aggregators and Distributors

The three major types of TV distributors were the terrestrial TV stations, the cable operators, and the satellite companies. The Big Three broadcasters' (ABC, CBS, and NBC) share of the prime-time television audience had declined for several decades. Cable had grown to have the lion's share of U.S. TV households, while satellite's share was the fastest growing. The cable operators and the satellite companies were both potential DVR customers and potential DVR competitors.

Believing that it was important to have the blessing of at least some of the major TV networks and cable operators, TiVo management had pursued the networks and MSOs when searching for major equity investors early in the company's life. One-fourth of the company was owned by industry-related firms such as AOL Time Warner (10%), DirecTV (6%),

[16]"Industry Survey: Broadcasting and Cable," Standard & Poor's report, July 25, 2002, p. 1.

[17]Ibid., p. 12.

[18]Dr. Peter Sealey, "Commercial Television: Rest in Peace," speech to the 2003 Meeting of the Association of National Advertisers, March 13, 2003.

EXHIBIT 7

Types of Revenue Generated by TiVo's Lines of Business

Product or Service	Customer	Types of Revenue Generated
TiVo DVR	Consumers	*Hardware revenues* *Services revenues* (either a lifetime fee amortized over 48 months or a recurring monthly fee)
Showcases (advertising services)	Networks/studios/advertisers	*Services revenues* (the company intended to use a CPM-like model to charge for advertising services revenues)
Audience research services	Networks/advertisers	*Services revenues* (research services)
DVR technology	OEMs and CE manufacturer licensees	*Technology revenues,* which included 1) license fees—both up-front fees, which ranged from several million dollars for object code and up to $10 million for source code; 2) per unit license fees; and 3) engineering service fees, which were charged by the man-hour for the engineering services necessary to help OEMs and licensees adapt the TiVo technology to the licensees/OEMs' hardware. *Service revenues,* whenever TiVo received a percentage of the monthly fees paid by consumers to the CE or OEM; e.g., DirecTV paid TiVo a monthly per subscriber fee for each of DirecTV's DVR subscribers.

Source: TiVo Inc.

EXHIBIT 8

Home Entertainment Ecosystem

Source: Casewriters.

EXHIBIT 9

U.S. Satellite, Cable, and Broadband Subscribers and Monthly Revenue
(Q1 2003)

Company	Number of Subscribers	Net Adds, Q1 2003	Average Revenue per Customer per Month	Churn
DirecTV—satellite	11,420,000	245,000	$59.00	1.60%
EchoStar—satellite	8,530,000	350,000	$51.48	
Total Satellite	19,950,000	595,000		
Digital Cable subscribers	21,500,000	691,000	$60.00	
Analog (Basic) Cable subscribers	46,500,000	44,000	$40.57	2.50%
Broadband Internet—Top MSOs	12,304,779	1,250,831		
Broadband Internet—Top DSL Providers	6,806,000	651,918		
Total Broadband Internet	19,110,779	1,902,749	~$42	

Note 1: "Churn" is defined as the average monthly rate of loss of subscribers. Net new subscriber additions take churn into account.

Note 2: The top 10 MSOs represent approximately 90% of all cable subscribers.

Note 3: "Top MSOs" and "Top DSL Providers" represent approximately 98% of all broadband Internet subscribers.

Source: Casewriter research, adapted from TiVo financial statements; "US Premium Cable Subscription Market, 2002–2007," *eMarketer* report, May 1, 2003, Chase Carey (News Corp. board member), "Keynote speech at 2003 Spring SkyFORUM," May 20, 2003, **<http://www.newscorp.com/news>**, accessed July 3, 2003; David Lieberman, "Tolls Stack Up On Info Superhighway," *USA Today,* June 2, 2002, **<http://www.usatoday.com/tech/news>**, accessed July 3, 2003; "Research Notes 1Q 2003," Leichtman Research Group, Inc. report, p. 1; "Research Notes 2Q 2003," Leichtman Research Group, Inc. report, p. 9; David Farina, Mary O'Toole, and Ralph Schackart, "TiVo Inc.," William Blair & Company Research report, March 17, 2003, p. 25; Jed Kolko, with James L. McQuivey, Jennifer Gordon, and Charles Q. Strohm, "The Big Picture: Today's Consumer Approaches Technology with a Purpose," Forrester Research report, June 2003, p. 40.

Sony (5%), General Electric and its NBC subsidiary (4% combined), and Discovery Communications (1%). The chairman and CEO of Discovery, the president of NBC Cable, and the president of DirecTV Global Digital Media joined TiVo's board of directors.

The battle between cable and satellite had important implications for TiVo. The MSOs were at a critical juncture in their history. In 2002, basic cable had lost subscribers, while satellite gained several million new customers.[19] The MSOs had spent billions of dollars in the past decade upgrading their systems to carry digital signals. Over the next several years, the cable industry was projected to go through a massive change, as millions of subscribers switched their analog set-top boxes for new digital boxes. Cable operators averaged around $40 per analog subscriber per month and $60 per digital subscriber, providing a big incentive for using consumers to make the switch. (See Exhibit 9.)

The MSOs had been very slow to adopt DVRs, with some, such as Comcast, urging the cable industry to adopt VOD instead of DVR. (See Exhibit 10.) Taken to an extreme, if all content were available "on demand," consumers would have no need for DVR products. AOL Time Warner was developing a large VOD system set to debut in mid-2005. Dubbed "Mystro TV," the system would store programming

[19]Chase Carey (News Corp. board member and industry consultant), "Keynote Speech at 2003 Spring SkyFORUM," May 20, 2003, **<http://www.newscorp.com/news/news_191.html>**, accessed July 2, 2003.

EXHIBIT 10

Cable Operators' VOD and DVR Activity (mid-2003)

Cable Operator	Millions of Subscribers Basic/Digital	Broadband	Current VOD Activity Deployment	Tests	Pricing	Current DVR Activity Deployment	Tests	Pricing	Comments
Comcast/AT&T	21.3/6.8	3.3	30 markets (movie-based VOD) 2 markets (3-pronged VOD—see Note 2)	N/A	$3.95 for new releases $2.95 for library titles	None	2 markets Plan trials in 2003 with Ucentric and with Motorola DCT 6000 DVR-enabled set-top boxes	N/A	"Most bullish on VOD" (EVP, Marketing) 5%–6% VOD usage overall 25% usage in one market with 3-pronged VOD offered
Time Warner Cable	11.0/3.9	2.3	33 markets	N/A	N/A	14 markets (more than 100,000 in the field)	Plan trial in one market with Microsoft's DVR-capable IPG software	$4.95–$9.95 per month	"SVOD substantially reduces churn" by as much as 40% (EVP, Marketing)
Charter Communications	6.7/2.7	1.1	18 markets	SVOD being tested in 2 markets	$3.99 for new releases $2.99 for library titles	None	1 market Have ordered 100,000 DVR-enabled set-top boxes	N/A	"Not sure DVR and VOD need to coexist" (VP, Marketing)
Cox	6.3/2.7	1.3	4 markets	2 markets	$3.95 for most movies. Some content is free SVOD pricing will be $6.95 a month for HBO, Showtime, etc.	2 markets	None	$9.95 per month for 80GB storage plus set-top lease fee	"We're very encouraged by what we see with DVR" (VP, video product management)
Adelphia (in bankruptcy)	5.3/1.7	0.6	2 limited deployments	None	$3.99 for new releases $2.99 for library titles SVOD will be $5.95 per month for HBO, Showtime	None	None	N/A	
Cablevision	2.9/0.4	0.7	3 markets	None	$4.95 for new releases $2.95 for library titles $8.95 for adult titles	None	None	N/A	

Note 1: SVOD refers to subscription video on demand, which provided consumers with continuous access to certain content for a monthly fee.

Note 2: Comcast was experimenting with three types of VOD: (1) movie based; (2) an SVOD offering that provided access to Showtime content anytime; and (3) free VOD, which offered about 750 hours a month of programming that could be accessed anytime, free of charge.

Source: "US Cable Subscriber Statistics," *eMarketer* report, April 1, 2003; "Deploy and Conquer," *Cable World*, April 7, 2003, **<http://www.seachangeinternational.com/news-events/articles/2003/Cable_World_April_7_2003.pdf>,** accessed July 20, 2003; Shirley Brady, "Mystro Wants to Play," *Cable World*, July 2, 2003, **<http://cableworld.com/microsites>,** accessed July 23, 2003; and "4Q 2002 Research Notes," Leichtman Research Group, Inc. report, p. 5.

in the central "hubs" of cable networks, allowing the networks to control the features (e.g., there would be no ability to skip ads). The two largest roadblocks to developing the service were that cable hubs would need significant centralized storage capacity—compared to the TiVo system, where capacity was decentralized—and licensing agreements with studios and networks would be necessary.

The cable industry was highly fragmented, and cable set-top boxes could vary slightly from locale to locale. Most MSOs sold their DVR-capable set-top boxes directly through their local subsidiary. Both the Time Warner and Cox cable operations had begun using Scientific Atlanta's Explorer 8000—the first integrated set-top box for the cable industry—in local market experiments. Some of these experiments were proving very successful. The Time Warner cable operator in Rochester, New York, for example, had more than 12% of its subscribers sign up in the first six months.[20] TiVo management estimated that Time Warner had 100,000 DVR-capable boxes in place. Those cable companies offering DVR-capable receivers generally did not charge for the receiver/DVR set-top box (or charged a nominal monthly lease fee of $5), but they did charge a DVR subscription fee ranging from $5 to $10 a month. DVR was viewed by some as having the potential to help push consumers from analog cable to digital cable—or to satellite TV. One consulting firm's report highlighted DVR as one of two features that cable companies should use to gain and keep subscribers, recommending that MSOs offer DVR as a subscription-based service integrated with the cable EPG, with the DVR service priced at $4.99 per month to maximize revenue.[21]

Both U.S. satellite operators provided DVR capabilities. DirecTV utilized TiVo's DVR technology, and EchoStar offered DVR capability based on OpenTV's technology. Both satellite providers had been experiencing healthy growth rates. EchoStar's Dish Network was estimated to be one of the leading providers of DVR devices, with approximately 550,000 subscribers.[22] EchoStar initially offered DVRs for $100 with no service fee, but in the spring of 2003 it announced that new DVR customers would be charged a monthly fee of $9.99 per month for "Top 100" subscribers, $4.98 per month for "Top 150" subscribers, and no fee for premium-package subscribers.[23] However, EchoStar once again introduced an aggressive offer in the summer of 2003 when it began promoting "free DVR" for new customers who purchased the "Top 50" programming package (a $24.99 monthly fee) for a minimum of 12 months.

DirecTV had become a very successful channel for TiVo. However, the future of the DirecTV relationship was murky in 2003. In the late 1990s, TiVo had sold its first-generation product to BSkyB, a satellite operator in the United Kingdom. Rupert Murdoch, the CEO of News Corp. and the majority owner of BSkyB, discontinued TiVo, replacing it with a DVR product developed in-house using another technology. Because it had acquired Hughes Electronics, News Corp. was scheduled to take control of DirecTV in 2003—and given Murdoch's mercurial reputation, no one was certain about his plans for his new satellite company. Nonetheless, 200 man-years of engineering time had been dedicated by TiVo and DirecTV to make the integrated set-top box a success. Moreover, DirecTV announced publicly that it expected more than three-quarters of a million customers with integrated TiVo boxes in their homes by the end of 2003.

Relative to satellite and cable offerings, TiVo remained a highly differentiated product. The cable and satellite DVR products lacked the features that TiVo fans valued most (e.g., WishList, Season Pass, the ability to handle programming conflicts intelligently, and the suggestion engine), but MSO products as well as the EchoStar (Dish Network) DVRs were lower priced, with the hardware sometimes "leased" for free, and the service price ranging from free to $9.98 a month. In addition, DVR solutions that featured an integrated receiver/DVR set-top box helped ensure DVR accuracy and quality. A common problem for TiVo and other stand-alone DVRs was that they controlled nonintegrated set-top boxes indirectly via an infrared "blaster." Since the set-top box manufacturers had no incentives to help TiVo or other stand-alone DVRs interconnect with their products, such DVRs might fail to tune to the correct channel. Finally, when using an integrated

[20]Lance Williams, "Time Warner Launches DVR Service," *The Business Courier*, April 14, 2003 <**http://boston.bizjournals.com/cincinnati/ stories/2003/04/14/story4.html**>, accessed July 15, 2003.
[21]Leszek Izdebski, "Path to Profitability: How Cable Companies Can Achieve Attractive Returns from iTV Services," an Accenture report, 2001, p. 6.
[22]"EchoStar/DISH US Subscriber Statistics, Q1 2003," *eMarketer*, April 1, 2003.

[23]Ellen Cheng, "EchoStar to Charge for Digital Video Recorder Functions," *Dow Jones Newswire*, July 30, 2003.

receiver/DVR set-top box, consumers did not have to have an extra set-top box on top of their television.

Content Providers

Filmed-entertainment content providers had become more concentrated following several acquisitions and mergers in the late 1990s and early 2000s. The industry's top nine companies owned a variety of entertainment assets ranging from Hollywood studios to television networks to theme parks. The four major U.S. TV broadcast networks, which attracted about 40% of prime-time viewers, were each owned by one of these top entertainment companies. Seven of the top nine companies also owned cable TV operations.

The TV and movie content providers were somewhat conflicted regarding DVR technology. On the one hand, several Hollywood studios sued TiVo competitor ReplayTV over its "send show" feature, which allowed consumers to record and then send shows to others, and its "commercial advance" feature, which allowed consumers to skip commercials with the push of a button. On the other hand, several large players had significant ownership positions in DVR companies—for example, AOL retained a large share of TiVo's equity; News Corp., which sold its own DVR product in the United Kingdom, was acquiring a controlling interest in Hughes Electronics, which owned DirecTV with its TiVo-powered DVR offering; and Sony manufactured and sold DVRs in Japan and in the United States. Some smaller players such as Liberty Media, which had a controlling interest of OpenTV, were also involved with DVR technologies.

In 2003, filmed-entertainment content providers were concerned about preserving their rights and not falling into the trap that music producers had fallen into when MP3 technology appeared. The widespread downloading of music over the Internet—without compensation—struck the music industry like a tidal wave, and although some players (such as Apple Computer) had introduced mechanisms to enable consumers to pay for downloads, the long-term outcome for the music industry was still unclear.

Equipment and Technology Competitors

In addition to cable and satellite DVR offerings, there were several other types of DVR competitors. (See Exhibits 11 and 12.) These included stand-alone DVR providers, technology-component (e.g., software and chips) suppliers, and PC manufacturers. ReplayTV was the only major competitor in the stand-alone DVR product category. Founded at about the same time as TiVo, ReplayTV sold the DVRs most often compared with TiVo's, with some reviewers preferring TiVo's features and some preferring ReplayTV's. However, ReplayTV, unlike TiVo, antagonized the TV and movie industry with some of its operational features and had not enjoyed the relative success of TiVo.

Initially ReplayTV did not charge a monthly service fee, instead charging more for the DVR unit, which included lifetime service. In 2002 Replay began charging a monthly service fee—$9.95—for the first time. Management said that although they and consumers believed that paying one price for the hardware and the service up front was much simpler, CE retailers wanted the DVR unit priced lower, and the only way to do that was to charge a separate service fee.

In part because the DVR was more like a computer than the typical CE device, there were several DVR component suppliers, with some selling to CE manufacturers and PC makers and others selling to consumers. Scientific Atlanta's combination cable receiver/DVR set-top boxes were powered by MetaByte Networks software and Keen Personal Media software. Keen received 80 cents per DVR. OpenTV's middleware platform was used by dozens of large and small set-top box manufacturers. Consumers could purchase one of several DVR hardware components or software packages, but these were for the more adventurous, as generally several components—costing several hundred dollars—were needed to make the PC a functional DVR. Some software packages required a monthly subscription fee of about $5 a month in order to receive an EPG, while in other cases, programming guide information was included for free. Almost all DVR component companies were experiencing financial difficulties, losing money and/or suffering a decline in revenues.

Consumers could also purchase PCs that included DVR technology. PCs that used Microsoft's Windows XP Media Center were the best example. HP and Gateway made such Media Center PCs, priced from about $1,400 to $2,000. The Sony Vaio also included DVR capability.

The Debate Over Future Strategies

The DVR industry was in a rapid state of change; each month brought an announcement of a new product or approach. TiVo management knew that

EXHIBIT 11

DVR Competitors (excludes pure DVR technology providers, as of June 2003)

Product	Company	Parent Company	DVR Technology Used	Box Manufacturer	Hard-Drive Capacity	Comments on Features	Price of Hardware	Subscription Fee	Total Estimated DVR Units Sold to Date
Stand-alone DVRs									
TiVo Series2	TiVo	N/A	TiVo	TiVo (contract mfr.) Sony	40GB–80GB 80GB		$249–$349 $449 (80GB)	$12.95 or $299 lifetime	433,000 (plus 270,000 DirecTV, see below)
ReplayTV	ReplayTV	D&M Holdings	ReplayTV	Various	40GB		$249 (40GB)	$9.95 or $250 lifetime	~120,000 (Replay TV '02 revenue was about $22mm)
Stand-alone DVD-DVRs									
DMR-HS2 (DVD-R-DVR)	Panasonic	Matsushita	N/A	Self	40GB	No EPG; no IR blaster	$999	None	
Scenium DRS70000N (DVD-DVR)	RCA	N/A	N/A	Thomson	40GB	Only 2½ days of EPG; no IR blaster	$599	None	
Satellite and Cable Integrated Set-top Boxes									
HDVR2	DirecTV (satellite)	Hughes Electronics	TiVo	Hughes, Samsung, RCA, Philips	40GB		$199	$4.95; free to premium subscribers	270,000
DishPVR508 and 721	Dish Network (satellite)	EchoStar Communications	OpenTV	N/A	40GB–120GB		$199 to $549 with rebate	$4.98–$9.99; free to premium subscribers	550,000+
Digital Video Recorder	Time Warner Cable	AOL Time Warner	Scientific Atlanta 8000 with Keen and MetaByte Networks technology	Scientific Atlanta	40GB–80GB (2 tuners)		$650 list (free to digital subscribers)	$10	100,000+
PCs w/DRV software									
Media Center PC	Microsoft	N/A	Microsoft (Ultimate TV)	Various (e.g., Hewlett Packard)	30GB–90GB (75% of total storage)		$1,399–$1,999	None	300,000+ (~180,000 used as DVRs)

Source: Casewriter research, adapted from company Web sites (<http://www.tivo.com>, <http://www.directv.com>, <http://www.dishnetwork.com>, <http://www.digitalnetworksna.com/replaytv>, <http://www.rca.com>, <http://www.panasonic.com>, <http://www.microsoft.com>), accessed July 14, 2003; "Interdependence Day," a CED In-depth report, July 2002; David Farina, Mary O'Toole, and Ralph Schackart, "TiVo Inc.," William Blair & Company, March 17, 2003, p. 13; "WinHec 2003 New Orleans," Jon Peddie research, May 9, 2003, <http://www.jonpeddie.com/dispatches/WinHec2003>, accessed August 6, 2003.

EXHIBIT 12

Product Features of Selected DVR Products

	TiVo Basic	TiVo Series2	TiVo S2 with Home Media	ReplayTV 4000	ReplayTV 5000	DirecTV with TiVo	EchoStar's Dish PVR 508	EchoStar's Dish PVR 721	Example Cable: Time Warner Scientific Atlanta 8000	Example DVD/DVR: Panasonic
Pricing—Hardware	Varies by CE manufacturer, but integrated DVD/DVRs will cost ~$500-$600	$249–40GB $349–80GB	N/A	$249	$349–$449 after rebate	$199	$199 with rebate	Bundled with a premium set-top box	Equipment leased free of charge (cost to cable company $300)	$500+
Pricing—Service	None	$12.95/mo. or $299 lifetime	$99 one-time fee per box to upgrade	$9.95/mo. or $250 lifetime	$9.95/mo. or $250 lifetime	$4.95/mo. Free to premium subscribers	$4.98–$9.99/mo. Free to premium subscribers	$4.98–$9.99/mo. Free to premium subscribers	$9.95/mo.	None
Hard-disk recording, VCR style (e.g., by date, time)	x	x	x	x	x	x	x	x	x	x
Record from EPG	x	x	x	x	x	x	x	x	x	No
Amount of program guide data	3 days	14 days	14 days	12 days	12 days	14 days	7 days	7 days	7 days	N/A
Skip forward 30 seconds	x	x	x	x	x	x	x	x	x	x
Two tuners	No	No	N/A	No	No	x	No	x	x	No
Storage capacity (GB)	Varies	40–80	N/A	Up to 320	Up to 160	Up to 35	Up to 60	Up to 90	80	80
Ability to "suggest" shows to user based on user's viewing habits	No	x	x	No	No	x	No	No	No	No
Ability to let DVR know the types of shows the user is interested in by theme or person (e.g., gardening)	No	x	x	x (personal channels)	x (personal channels)	x	x (themes list)	x (themes list)	No	No
DVR is integrated into cable or satellite receiver	No	No	N/A	No	No	x	x	x	x	No
Ability to display digital photos	No	No	x	x	x	x	No	No	No	No
Ability to play digital music (MP3 files)	No	No	x	No	No	No	No	No	No	No
Source of DVR technology	TiVo	TiVo	TiVo	ReplayTV	ReplayTV	TiVo	OpenTV	OpenTV	MetaByte Networks & Keen Personal Media DVR software	MetaByte Networks & Keen Personal Media DVR software

Note: Two tuners enabled a user to record two live programs at once, record live while watching live, or record two programs live while watching one prerecorded.

Source: Casewriter research, adapted from "Dish Network PVR Brochures," Dish Network Web site, <**http://www.pvrcmpare.com/featurechart.html**>, accessed July 9, 2003; TiVo Web site, <**http://www.tivo.com/2.0asp**>, accessed July 7, 2003; TiVo Inc. Form 10-K for years ended January 31, 2003, May 1, 2003, pp. 11–12.

the industry was likely to remain unsettled for the foreseeable future, making it even harder to predict which strategy had the best odds of succeeding. In mid-2003 TiVo management was debating many possible strategic options.

One option being debated was the possibility of **manufacturing and selling a TiVo Basic DVR** that would have no monthly fee. This was seen as having more upside and more risk than licensing CE manufacturers to include TiVo Basic functionality in high-end CE devices. On the upside, TiVo could sell a TiVo Basic DVR at a price point lower than bundled units offering basic functionality, plus engineering resources could be conserved. On the other hand, TiVo would receive no monthly revenues until buyers began upgrading to the full TiVo service, yet the company would incur some monthly costs for EPG content and transmission. Edward Lichty, TiVo's vice president of business development, pointed out that the cost to build a TiVo Basic DVR would not differ significantly from the cost to build a regular DVR given that the product needed to be automatically capable of being upgraded. "The two main issues we have to grapple with are how much we would cannibalize our current revenue stream, and whether the buyers of the TiVo basic product would upgrade," commented Lichty. Added Stuart West, the vice president of finance:

> There's a tension between making the TiVo Basic service good enough to sell a machine, but not so good that consumers won't want to upgrade to the full service. The key is how many customers will convert. Somewhere around 20% the model doesn't work, but at 50 to 60% or higher, it's fantastic. Predicting how many would convert is critical—but obviously not possible. We have to be comfortable with uncertainty to take that step.

Another more radical option was **manufacturing and selling a DVR "white box" to CE retailers,** allowing the retailers to sell their own branded DVR device. Jeff Klugman, the vice president of the licensing group, believed that most CE companies had relatively high cost structures, in part because they had been slow to move their manufacturing operations offshore and in part because they had to amortize large R&D budgets. "One example of a company that used offshore manufacturing to their big advantage is Apex, who went from number ten to number one in DVD market share in a very short time," explained

Klugman. Apex sourced its products from multiple Chinese manufacturers and had a three- to six-month design cycle, compared with the Japanese DVD manufacturers' two-year cycle.[24] Many TiVo executives were uncomfortable with the "white box" option. Echoing the thoughts of others, Klugman commented, "We don't want to be Lexus, and it's OK to be Toyota, but we don't want to be Hyundai."

Another option being debated was exploring ways to lower the price of TiVo-enabled units at retail. Cashen believed this was important because there were certain market segments that were very interested in purchasing TiVo but could not quite afford it. One way in which this could be done was by **lowering the license fee TiVo charged CE manufacturers.** Lowering the per unit license fee by $1.00 decreased the retail price by $1.50, to $1.75, and lowering the up-front license fee lowered the amount of amortized license fee per unit sold. This was one way in which TiVo could help reduce the retail price of its CE licensees' products, thus helping spur demand. In addition, this might help TiVo expand its pool of CE partners. Klugman explained, "We want consumers to see TiVo associated with many different brands at retail—and I think that DVD-Rs [units that could record as well as play DVDs] will be the driving force that pulls DVR." The obvious downside to lowering fees associated with licensing was that the company was on the cusp of breaking even, a goal viewed as very important to investors.

Given the large number of cable TV households and the shift from analog to digital cable boxes under way, TiVo management often discussed **entering into a major partnership with a cable company.** Clearly, the biggest upside in terms of TV homes lay in the cable market. Klugman emphasized the need to move quickly in the DVR market, saying, "We need to swing for the fences. Losing a cable household today to a digital cable/DVR box means you lose them for at least five years." And several executives believed that TiVo had a compelling story for the cable operators, whose promises to Wall Street about VOD generating large profits had not yet materialized. Marty Yudkovitz,

---

[24]Russ Arensman, "Watch Out Sony: Apex Is Taking Aim at TVs," *Electronic Business,* May 1, 2002, <**http://www.e-insite.net/eb-mag**>, accessed July 20, 2003.

TiVo's president, believed that TiVo could make an appealing offer:

> We can offer cable—and satellite—a stream of enhanced advertising revenue and other premium-service revenue that they hadn't planned on if they use TiVo's Showcases. Since this additional revenue would come without additional capital investment, or operational headache or risk, it would be a great demonstration to Wall Street of the leverage the MSO can get from having built the new digital plant. And we've found from our satellite and stand-alone business that TiVo subscribers use their DVRs far more than any other DVR service, an issue of importance to cable and satellite distributors. The technology is great, but the economic impact of TiVo is what can really make a difference to distributors.

Despite the importance of the cable market, entering into a substantive partnership with a cable company presented several challenges. West elaborated, "One obvious challenge is whether the cable companies will settle on a 'good enough' solution from their current set-top box suppliers—Scientific Atlanta and Motorola—or whether they will want to go with a new provider that can offer a better product and enhanced revenue potential." The second challenge was whether, given the market-by-market monopsony into which cable market suppliers sold, TiVo would be able to build a profitable business in the cable market. One of the major economic negotiating points for TiVo management was the company's goal of receiving recurring fees, as was the case with TiVo's DirecTV partnership in the satellite industry. The goal of receiving ongoing fees conflicted with the cable industry's custom of paying up-front fees for hardware (set-top boxes) and not sharing any of the ongoing subscriber revenues. TiVo management was well aware of the many cable industry suppliers that had been very successful in terms of volumes of units sold to the industry—but very unsuccessful in terms of making a profit. Yet another challenge was that TiVo would probably have to integrate into one of the standard industry set-top boxes. TiVo could become a software application that operated on a Scientific Atlanta or Motorola box. Despite these challenges, the possibility of a major cable partnership remained a widely discussed alternative.

Some executives argued that, while continuing to push for mass deployment in the DVR market was important, **expanding efforts to grow TiVo's services for advertisers** was equally important. The advertising market was enormous, and the TV audience-measurement research market was also large, with Nielsen—the largest supplier in the audience-research market—having an estimated $800 million in revenues. In addition, although Nielsen measured TV program ratings, no one currently measured the ratings of ads.

Yudkovitz believed strongly that TiVo should be a television services company. Prior to joining TiVo in the spring of 2003, he had been an executive at NBC, where for 20 years he was involved with most of NBC's new business initiatives—including programming, cable, and Internet. He shared his point of view:

> Our customers will be media companies—programmers, broadcasters, networks, satellite and cable distributors, and advertisers—as well as consumers for consumer-facing services. We can deepen the media companies' connection with the customer, allow the consumer to interact and become more involved with the advertising and programming, and measure all of it in a way that no other service does. This is exactly what interactive TV tried to do for so long without success—the difference is that we've actually done it in the marketplace. Two-thirds of our viewers opt in to one of our Showcases each month and spend an average of four minutes viewing it.
>
> For an advertiser to be able to enhance their ads with interaction and measurement is key. To track the effectiveness of ad viewing in various programming in various parts of the country is a major step forward for advertisers. The fact that we can offer a better financial proposition—for example, offering ad enhancement and other premium services that drive revenue up, and costs and churn down—is what will make the difference. We can change the way that advertising is bought and sold on television, and in the war between the networks and advertisers, I want to be the arms dealer.

Cashen agreed and shared her belief that the company had proven that Showcases could work well for advertisers:

> Our Showcases are very compelling. Even our worst performing Showcase attracted 35% of our subscribers for about two to three minutes. Our most successful Showcase attracted over two-thirds of our subscribers for an average of four to six minutes each, with many subscribers watching that Showcase—which featured Mike Myers talking about the movie *Austin Powers in Goldmember*—multiple times.

The last major strategic option being discussed was **focusing resources on developing new DVR and home entertainment capabilities.** Several executives believed that pursuing this option was important to the company's future. Barton expanded on the dilemma faced by engineering:

> Our engineering work for OEMs and licensees provides us with revenues and some margin, and we use the opportunity to enhance aspects of our system architecture. Nevertheless, there are some costs, as we're not able to work as much on other projects. The types of things we would spend more time on if we could include software portability, improving Showcase authoring capabilities to make Showcases more dynamic, developing the ability to work with another EPG supplier, and continuing to upgrade the user interface. Our next big development opportunities are making the platform more advertiser friendly and continuing to make the TiVo DVR cheaper.

Lichty believed that DVR technology was fast becoming a commodity and that therefore TiVo needed to become a platform for delivering distinctive value-added services such as the HMO. "The only way to keep your pricing up is to have unique offerings," he said. Brodie Keast, TiVo's senior vice president and general manager of TiVo service, agreed, adding that, along with developing new not-yet-announced services for the TiVo platform, the company should develop tiered pricing for different levels and types of service.

The View from TiVo

Ramsay worried that if the consumer adoption rate remained relatively slow, it would give competitors time to catch up. This meant that TiVo was truly at an inflection point. Should the company aggressively pursue mass deployment? Or should the company focus its limited resources on product development and differentiation? Ramsay understood that it was in TiVo's best interest for both the industry and TiVo to grow rapidly. The fact that millions of households still had analog cable service convinced him that there was still much room to maneuver—but again, TiVo had to move quickly to convert these consumers to TiVo users before the cable operators upgraded the consumers to new digital receivers using another company's DVR technology. Yudkovitz believed that there were no longer any obstacles to mass deployment, sharing that "it's now obvious that DVRs will be mass deployed, and even the cable and media folks accept that." Yet Ramsay also believed that DVR providers that did not charge a monthly service fee would eventually see the error of their ways. "My prediction is that people who give it away will realize that it's expensive to do—and they will eventually go back and do it right," he said. And finally, he was convinced that TiVo needed to maintain its position as the value-added DVR leader able to charge premium pricing if the company was to keep from falling into the trap that so many DVR providers had—charging very little for their products and hoping to "make it up in volume." Given TiVo management's emphasis on cash flow break-even, he knew that the company would have to focus primarily on just one of the many options being debated. The company simply did not have the luxury of pursuing them all.

Case 11

The Music Industry in the Age of the Internet: From Napster to Apple's iPod

This case was prepared by Charles W. L. Hill, the University of Washington.

Sometime in the fall of 1998, an indifferent eighteen-year-old student at Northeastern University in Boston had an epiphany. Wouldn't it be great, he thought, if people could share their music with each other over the Internet.[1] The student's name was Shawn Fanning, and the service that grew out of his epiphany, Napster, would shake the very foundations of the music recording industry. By 2000, Napster had taken center stage in a pivotal struggle for the future of the industry. On one side was the Recording Industry Association of America (RIAA), the big five music recording labels, and several high-profile recording artists, all of whom argued that Napster was violating copyright laws, facilitating the illegal copying and distribution of copyrighted music, and should be shut down. On the other was a small company with less than fifty employees and limited funds, but which had 30 million users. In the middle was the U.S. judicial system.

By 2001, the RIAA had won the first round of the struggle. Napster had been effectively put out of business by judicial decree. But the genie that Napster sprung out of the Internet bottle would not go back in.

Copyright © 2004 by Charles W. L. Hill. This case was prepared by Charles W. L. Hill, the University of Washington, as the basis for class discussion rather than to illustrate either effective or ineffective handling of an administrative situation. Reprinted by permission of Charles W. L. Hill. All rights reserved. For the most recent financial results of the company discussed in this case, go to http://finance.yahoo.com, input the company's stock symbol, and download the latest company report from its homepage.

New file sharing technologies based on peer-to-peer computing such as Kazaa had sprung up and were diffusing rapidly through the Internet. Unlike Napster, these new technologies were proving to be more difficult to stop. To complicate matters further, the music recording labels knew that even if they could shut down Kazaa and its ilk for copyright violations, the digital distribution of music over the Internet was here to stay and might potentially revolutionize the industry value chain. Consequently, in the wake of Napster's decline they decided to set up their own Internet-based distribution services. But demand for these services was slow to develop, and they were soon eclipsed by the rapid rise of Apple's iPod digital music player and iTunes online music service. From a standing start in 2001, Apple generated over $1 billion in sales from the iPod and iTunes service in 2004. In 2000, industry observers were fretting over the possibility that Napster might revolutionize the music industry—now it looked as if Apple was doing just that.

The Music Recording Industry

The music recording industry grew at a robust rate throughout the 1990s, registering global sales of $38.5 billion in 1999. The largest markets were the United States (37 percent), Japan (16.7 percent), the United Kingdom (7.6 percent), Germany (7.4 percent), France (5.2 percent), and Canada (2.3 percent). The growth was helped by the introduction of a new technology in the late 1980s, CDs, and significant replacement demand as consumers replaced their favorite vinyl records with CDs. By 2003, CD sales dominated the U.S. market for record sales, accounting for $11.2 billion out of an $11.85 billion total. Cassette tapes accounted for $108 million in sales, and vinyl records just $21 million. A relatively new product category, DVD videos, accounted for some $369 million of sales in 2003, up from $80 million in 2000.[2]

The years of strong growth came to an end in 2000, when global sales fell 5 percent. They fell for the next three years, hitting a low of $32 billion in 2003. Despite the fall in sales, the International Federation of the Phonographic Industry (IFPI) claimed that demand for music was higher than ever, but that the decline in sales reflected the fact that "the commercial value of music is being widely devalued by mass copying and piracy."[3] According to the IFPI, 40 percent of all CDs and cassettes around the globe were illegally produced and sold in 2003, suggesting that piracy cost the industry over $12 billion per annum.[4] Although historically illegal plants in Asia have been the source of many pirated CDs and tapes, by the early 2000s the IFPI was increasingly concerned about consumers "burning" songs downloaded over the Internet onto CDs. In Germany, 18 percent of 10,000 consumers surveyed in 2001 said burning CDs resulted in them buying less music. In the United States in 2001, nearly 70 percent of people who downloaded music burned the songs onto a CD-R disc, while 35 percent of people downloading more than twenty songs per month said they purchased less music as a result.[5]

Industry Structure

In 2003, the industry was dominated by five large recording companies that collectively accounted for around 75 percent of global recorded music sales (see Exhibit 1 for market share figures). The five were Sony Music, Universal Music Group (which was owned by Vivendi, a French media conglomerate), EMI, Warner Music Group, and Bertelsmann Music Group or BMG (owned by Bertelsmann, a large German media conglomerate). The industry concentration was due in large part to mergers between majors and acquisitions of independent record labels by the majors during the 1990s.

The last big merger between majors occurred in the late 1990s, when Universal acquired PolyGram NV for $10.5 billion. In 2000, Warner Music Group and EMI had attempted to merge their activities, but were prohibited from doing so by antitrust authorities in the European Union (EU), who believed that the merger would put too much market power in the hands of a small number of recording labels. At the time, Warner was owned by the media conglomerate AOL Time Warner. Having failed in their attempt to merge with EMI, Time Warner subsequently spun off Warner to a group of independent investors led by Edgar Bronfman for $2.6 billion. Bronfman was at one time CEO of Seagram, which owned Universal Music. Bronfman had sold Seagram to Vivendi for $30 billion in 2000. In explaining his reentry into the industry, Bronfman argued that despite several years of declining revenues, demand could improve in the future as illegal Internet-based distribution services were replaced with legal services such as Apple's iTunes.[6]

In 2004, Sony made a bid to acquire BMG. Many thought that once again, the EU antitrust authorities would stand in the way of a deal. But in a closed door session before the EU's competition commission, the companies argued that the rise of Internet-based music distribution services were hurting the big labels, and the merger was necessary to reduce costs and respond to this new competitive threat. This time the EU bought the argument, and the merger was cleared both by EU regulators, and then by regulators in the United States. In August 2004, the deal was completed. The new

EXHIBIT 1

Global Market Share Figures, 2002 and 2003

Year	BMG	EMI	Sony	Universal	Warner	Independents
2002	9.6%	12.2%	13.8%	25.4%	11.8%	27.1%
2003	11.9%	13.4%	13.2%	23.5%	12.7%	25.3%

Source: IFPI, "IFPI publishes global market shares." IFPI Press Release, June 16, 2004.

company, known as Sony BMG Music Entertainment, rivaled Universal in market share. After the merger, Sony BMG stated that it would lay off 20 percent of the combined workforce as part of a plan to achieve annual cost savings of $350 million.[7]

The Hit Making Machine

Music recording companies sign artists in return for royalties on units sold, which generally run between 12 percent and 16 percent of net revenues. The typical contract specifies that in return for royalties on future sales, the copyright of the artists' creations become the property of the music company. Most contracts also bind recording artists to multi-album deals with the recording company—a constraint that many successful artists try to break (the artist formally known as Prince being a prime example).

The music company bears the costs of recording and producing the music, pressing the CDs, marketing, and distribution. Production costs for a typical album are around $125,000, but they can reach $1 million. Marketing expenses range from $100,000 to over $500,000 per album for a major artist. Music videos are now an essential additional marketing tool for many artists, and production costs for those can run anywhere from $100,000 to $250,000. Thus, it can cost from $350,000 to $2 million to launch an artist.[8] Under standard royalty contracts, these upfront costs are normally deducted from the artists' royalties. Moreover, under an industry practice know as cross-collateralization, if an artist does not cover product and marketing costs on their first album, the deficit is then applied to the second album, and so on, making it very difficult for some artists to ever make a return from their work.

The hit rate in the music business is very low. Although there are rare cases of instant hits where an album will sell over a million copies, the vast majority of new CDs are never profitable. Each year the major music recording companies issue about 7,000 new CDs (and minor "independent" labels issue another 20,000). Most never recover the upfront recording and marketing costs. In the end, less than 10 percent are profitable. Music recording companies make most of their returns from a handful of "gold" albums that sell over 500,000 copies a year. In 2001, of some 6,455 new albums released by major labels, only 112 sold at least that many.[9]

A *Wall Street Journal* article reported one example of how difficult it is to produce a hit album. In 2001, MCA, which is part of the Universal Music Group, spent some $2.2 million to produce and promote an eighteen-year-old artist from Ireland, Carly Hennessy. MCA hoped that Hennessy would be the next teen diva. She had a very strong singing voice, good looks, and stage presence. Her album, *Ultimate High*, was produced by Gregg Alexander, who had produced albums for The Spice Girls. The single from the album, "I'm Going to Blow Your Mind," was accompanied by a video that cost $250,000 to make. The reviews were solid. Carly Hennessy went on a four-week promotional tour, which cost a further $150,000, and involved Hennessy singing at malls and radio-sponsored concerts. MCA also spent some $200,000 to hire independent promoters, who visited radio producers to try and secure airplay. It was all to no avail. Three months after the release of the album, it had sold just 378 copies, generating $4,900 in revenues, and Ms. Hennessy disappeared from public view.[10]

Record industry executives claim that producing a new hit album has become ever harder due to industry trends. Most new acts first get heard on radio, but deregulation of the radio industry in 1996 ushered in a wave of consolidation, with companies like Clear Channel Communications purchasing rival radio stations. Under increased pressures to maximize audience ratings, radio stations now quickly pull songs that are not instant nationwide hits. The growing importance of music videos also makes it more difficult to succeed, since there are only a limited number of TV stations that play music videos, such as MTV and VH1, and they, too, quickly pull videos that are not instant hits.

In the 1950s and 1960s, the industry would pay radio station deejays to play records. The practice, know as "payola," caused a major scandal when it was exposed in the 1960s, and is now illegal. Under current law, broadcasters are prohibited from taking cash or anything of value in return for playing a specific song, unless they disclose the transaction to listeners. But in a practice that is common in the industry, major record labels hire independent promoters, who in turn pay radio stations annual fees, which range from $20,000 to $300,000, not to play specific records, but to get advanced access to a stations' play lists. The promoters then bill the record labels for each new song that is played. In echoes of the 1960s payola scandals, in late 2004, New York Attorney General Elliot Spitzer announced his intention to investigate the practice of using independent promoters for possible antitrust violations. For their part, radio stations argue that the use of independent promoters hasn't affected their airplay decisions. In 2003, in an attempt to avoid the appearance of pay for play, Clear Channel Communications, the nation's largest radio chain, ended its deals with promoters.[11]

Distribution

Historically, the other big players in the music industry have been retailers. In 2003, 86 percent of sales of recorded music in the United States were still made through retail stores. However, the nature of distribution was changing, with discount stores such as Wal-Mart beginning to account for a larger proportion of total CD sales as opposed to traditional music retailers. In 1994, traditional music stores accounted for 53.3 percent of record sales, but only 33.2 percent in 2003. Sales over the Internet were still small in 2003, amounting to just 5 percent of the total, but they had grown from just 1 percent in 1998.[12] Amazon.com, in particular, was emerging as an important distributor of CDs over the Internet, while Apple's iTunes business accounted for around 1 percent of total sales in 2003, but it was growing very fast. In addition, experiments by the big five music companies in the online distribution of music were causing tensions with retailers, who started to fear that they might be cut out of the equation.

Industry Pricing Trends

Since CDs were first introduced in 1983, their average price in real terms has fallen significantly. Between 1983 and 1996, the average price of a CD fell by more than 40 percent, while the consumer price index rose by nearly 60 percent. Despite the price fall, antitrust authorities on both sides of the Atlantic have investigated the music recording industry for alleged price fixing. In May 2000, the big five companies settled a suit with the United States Federal Trade Commission, agreeing to end a requirement that retail stores adhere to minimum prices in advertisements.[13] The agreement was expected to open the way for more price discounting of CDs in retail stores.[14] In August 2001, the EU ended a similar investigation after three major recording companies agreed to end minimum price requirements.

In September 2003, Universal rocked the music industry when it announced its intention to significantly cut prices for CDs. The company stated that it would drop its wholesale price by just over $3 from $12.12 to $9.09, and lower the suggested retail price by $6 from $18.98 to $12.98. In addition, Universal said that it would end cooperative advertising payments, discounting programs, and other mechanisms that gave retailers an incentive to sell CDs at a lower price. None of Universal's major rivals followed suit.[15]

For this initiative to work, Universal reportedly had to see sales volume rise by 21 percent to offset the lower wholesale price. However, in the first nine months of the initiative the company reportedly only saw volume increases in the 8 percent to 13 percent range. In part, this was because discount retailers such as Wal-Mart and Best Buy were already offering CDs at a low price to drive traffic into their stores. As for traditional music retailers, such as Tower Records, many of them simply refused to follow the suggested retail price. Indeed, they stated that if Universal placed a sticker with the recommended retail price on a CD, which was the company's original plan, they would cover it up with a sticker of their own charging a higher price. By late 2004, it appeared as if Universal was retreating from its price initiative, and was nudging wholesale prices back up.[16]

Intellectual Property Rights, Technology, and Piracy

Music recordings are copyrighted material. In the United States, the rights given to copyright holders are based on the Copyright Act on 1976 (similar legislation exists in other nations, and intellectual property is protected under World Trade Organization agreements, which over 120 countries have signed). Under the 1976 act, copyright holders have the exclusive right to control the reproduction, modification, distribution, public performance, and public displays of their copyrighted material. This set of rights can be violated in three ways:[17]

1. **Direct copyright infringement:** The direct infringer violated any of the copyright holder's exclusive rights. For example, producing and selling a CD without obtaining permission from the copyright holder.

2. **Vicarious copyright infringement:** The vicarious infringer had the right and ability to control the direct infringer's actions and reaped financial benefits from those actions. For example, the courts have held that swap meet organizers vicariously infringed if they knowingly created and administered a market in which bootleg music is bought and sold and are paid a fee for admission.

3. **Contributory copyright infringement:** The infringer knowingly induced or caused the directly infringing conduct. For example, an electronic bulletin board service was found liable when it encouraged subscribers to upload *Playboy* pictures so that other subscribers could download them.

Historically the music industry had always been concerned about the potential for piracy of copyrighted material. New technology has often facilitated the low-cost copying and distribution of music. In the 1960s and 1970s, the advent of the audio cassette tape led to widespread illegal copying and distribution of music. In the early 1990s, the industry was deeply concerned about attempts by Sony to commercialize its digital audio tape (DAT) technology, which they felt would facilitate high fidelity copying of recorded music and thus lead to greater piracy. Although the RIAA initially opposed Sony, they switched to supporting the technology once Sony agreed to incorporate software that would make it difficult to use DAT technology to make multiple copies of a music recording. In addition, in 1992 the Audio Home Recording Act required DAT manufacturers to pay a royalty on each blank tape they sold to compensate music companies for the piracy that would take place through DAT. In any event, DAT technology was not accepted by consumers, but it was clear the underlying copyright issues would not go away.

Another technology that raised the specter of copyright infringement was MP3. Originally developed in the 1980s, MP3 is a software technology for creating compressed digital music files which could be downloaded for free from the Internet. MP3 music files were created through a process knowing as "ripping," in which computer owners copy a CD into MP3's digital format that is about one-twelfth the size of the original file. This compression was achieved by eliminating overlapping sound waves and digital audio signals that fell outside of human hearing range. The great virtue of compressed MP3 files is that they take up less space on a hard drive, and can be transferred more easily over the Internet. Until the late 1990s, however, the speed of most Internet connections was so slow that there was little online demand for MP3 music files. Three things changed that: the emergence of high-speed Internet connections, especially on college campuses; the growth of websites such as MP3.com, which archived MP3 files; and the introduction of portable MP3 players.

In November 1997, MP3.com launched its site. MP3.com had purchased thousands of CDs and converted their contents into MP3 files which were stored on its web servers, where subscribers to MP3.com's service could access and download them. In an attempt to protect itself from legal problems, MP3.com required users to demonstrate that they owned the CD for which they were downloading MP3 files by inserting a copy of the CD into their computer's CD-ROM drive for a few seconds, where it could be detected by software MP3.com used. In the same year, Diamond Multimedia introduced the Rio, a small portable device that could play up to two hours of MP3s.

The music industry immediately saw the threat—consumers could use high-speed Internet connections to download MP3 files over the Internet and store them on their Rios, circumventing copyright in the process. The RIAA filed a temporary restraining order against Diamond in October 1998, but the U.S. Court of Appeals ruled that converting the digital content of a CD to other formats for personal use was protected by the so called *fair use* doctrine contained in the 1976 Copyright Act (the fair use doctrine allows individuals to make copies from copyrighted material they have purchased for their personal use—i.e., not for resale or distribution).

Having failed to halt the sale of the Rio, Universal Music Group (UMG) immediately went after websites from which MP3 files could be downloaded. MP3.com was the obvious first target. In May 2000, the U.S. District Court ruled that MP3.com had directly infringed on music companies' copyrights, noting that in actuality MP3.com was "replaying for the subscribers converted versions of the recordings it copied, without authorization, from plaintiffs' copyrighted CDs."[18] On September 6, Judge Jed Rakoff delivered his ruling that MP3.com would have to pay the music companies $25,000 for each of the CDs it had copied to stream to consumers who also owned those discs. It looked as if MP3.com would have to pay UMG between $118 million and $250 million. In making his judgment, Rakoff stated that "some companies operating in the area of the Internet seemed to believe that because their technology is somewhat novel, they are somehow immune from the ordinary application of the law."[19] Around the same time, the

RIAA was also trying to shut down another Internet music service, Napster.

In addition to seeking legal recourse against copyright violators, the music industry also tried to develop technology that would protect digital audio recordings from piracy and counterfeiting. The RIAA recruited Leonard Chiariglione, inventor of the MP3 format, to head up the effort. Chiariglione pulled together a consortium of 180 firms, including record companies and consumer electronics and software firms, in an attempt to create the Security Digital Music Initiative (SDMI), a set of technological guidelines that was intended to reduce the risk of copyright infringements of digital audio media. The SDMI tried to develop guidelines for two types of security measures: (1) digital watermarks would be embedded in digital music, which then could only be played on SDMI compliant music players, and (2) digital rights management technology would embed digital music within an encrypted digital package that would limit the number of times a CD could be copied. Unfortunately, the SDMI made little progress, reportedly because there were too many competing voices, all with veto power. Apparently, different sides in the industry kept vetoing each other's schemes for copyright protection.[20]

Blindsided: The Rise of Napster

While the music industry was struggling with the SDMI, Shawn Fanning was giving birth to its biggest challenge yet, Napster. There was nothing remarkable about Fanning that would lead one to believe that he would spawn a potentially world-shattering idea.[21] One of five children, he grew up in Brockton, Massachusetts, a small town some twenty miles south of Boston. His family was solidly working class with one exception, his uncle, John Fanning, was a computer industry entrepreneur who ran a company called NetGames. During summers at high school, Shawn worked at John's company where he picked up programming skills from other interns who were studying computer science at Carnegie Mellon. It was at this time that he also became a regular visitor to Internet chat rooms, and particularly Internet Rely Chat, or IRC, which had become a de facto meeting place in cyberspace for hackers, traders of copied software and music, and so on. To enter IRC rooms, Fanning had to give a user name, so he chose his nickname from high school, Napster.

Although Fanning tried to get into Carnegie Mellon, he had to settle for Northeastern. As luck would have it, one of Fanning's roommates was obsessed with MP3 technology, which he used to download music from Internet sites and play on his computer. What caught Fanning's interest was not so much the ability to trade music files over the Internet using MP3 technology, as his roommate's constant complaints about the process. Internet music sites were not always easy to find, they were unreliable, the links were often broken, and the indices listing music on a site were more often than not out of date. At the time, Fanning was disenchanted with his courses at Northeastern, which he found to be pretty basic, and was looking around for something to do. Solving his roommate's problems seemed to fit the bill.

As it developed, Fanning's approach to fixing this problem was relatively straightforward. He envisioned an index managed by a central server that would list all of the MP3 music files that people had on their hard drives and were willing to share, along with the embedded web addresses of their location. The list could be created if people downloaded a piece of "client" software onto their PCs. This software would update the central list every time someone logged onto the Internet, or logged off. The MP3 files themselves would continue to reside on the hard drives of individual PCs. To download a file, a user simply had to click on the title of the song, and so long as the PC where the title was located was logged on, the file would be transferred from one PC to the other over the Internet.

In essence, Fanning was proposing to create a peer-to-peer network of personal computers, coordinated by a central server that managed the index of MP3 files. First of all, however, Fanning had to get the program written, and he needed some help. Fanning roped in two friends, Jordan Ritter and Sean Parker, that he had met through an online hacker group called w00w00. Together they would develop the core of Napster. As Ritter later commented, "At that stage, Napster was really just Shawn and a bunch of friends trying to help out. There were no venture capitalists, no uncles on the scene and no shady hangers on."[22] What drove Fanning on, according to another friend, was that people kept telling him it wouldn't work. They said that people would not be willing to share their music files. According to this friend, Fanning was "driven more by the desire to prove to everyone that he was right than he was by any realization or recognition of a potential revolution."[23]

By early 1999, Shawn Fanning had dropped out of Northeastern and was working around the clock writing code for the server and client. To prove his doubters wrong, he decided to try out an early version of his software, which he had christened Napster, giving out the client software to around thirty friends. He asked them not to pass it on, an instruction that several ignored, and within a few days, the software had been downloaded by about three to four thousand people. Many of these early adopters proved to be an invaluable resource, providing feedback that helped Fanning to improve the software.

It was around this time that Shawn Fanning told his uncle, thirty-six-year-old John Fanning, what he was up to. John quickly saw the commercial potential of Napster. In May 1999, he incorporated Napster as a company and went looking for investors. According to *Business Week*, when the company was incorporated John took 70 percent of the equity and Shawn 30 percent.[24] One insider reportedly commented that "I am told that this was done without Shawn Fanning's immediate knowledge or involvement. Newspapers have accurately reported the morally deplorable distribution of equity."[25]

Digital Boom

The embryonic company clearly had a number of problems to solve. First, it needed capital; second, it had to develop a business model that would enable it to profit from the service; and third, it needed to prepare itself for the inevitable challenge from the RIAA. Early on, John Fanning began to explore the legal ramifications of Napster's business. Among others, he consulted with the law firm of Wilson, Sonsini, Goodrich & Rosati, which had successfully defended Diamond Multimedia against the RIAA. The conversations reportedly gave John the confidence to push the business forward, and the belief that if Napster were sued, the company would have a good shot of winning in court.[26] John seemed to think that because Napster did not actually copy and distribute MP3 files, but simply put people who wanted to swap files in touch with each other, it was not breaking the law.

In the summer of 1999, John Fanning started to get initial funding for Napster. His first calls were to high–net worth individuals whom he knew personally. A friend, Yosi Amram, kicked in $250,000, and another added $100,000. By the end of the summer,

John had raised enough capital to keep Napster going through to year end. Napster moved to Silicon Valley in the fall of 1999, primarily on John's suggestion that being in the Valley would help in the quest to raise more capital. Shawn and his friends (now all Napster employees) were working long stints writing code—sixteen- to twenty-hour days—while John was out looking for more venture capital.

In September, realizing that the company needed a CEO who could develop a business model, Eileen Richardson, who had ten years' experience in the venture capital world—but had never run a company—was hired. Richardson's main claim to fame was that she had led an investment in Firefly, an Internet service that recommends music that was subsequently purchased by Microsoft. Her task was to help secure additional funding, develop a business model, and then hand off the job to her replacement. In October 1999, Napster had raised $2 million in series B venture capital funding from a number of wealthy Silicon Valley executives, including Angel Investors founding partner, Ron Conway, and Joe Kraus, founder of *Excite@Home*. What helped to secure the funds for the fledgling company was the extraordinary growth of Napster over the previous few months.

Formally launched in June 1999, the program spread with unprecedented speed. There was no marketing or advertising to sell the service, which was given away for free. The service spread through word of mouth. The early adopters were students on university campuses with access to personal computers and high bandwidth Internet connections. In the fall of 1999, there was a feature on Napster on the website download.com. This helped to raise the service to new heights. In July 1999, the Napster community was estimated at 4.9 million. By October 2000, it was 32 million, and the site was growing by a million users a week, with some 800,000 logged on at any one time.

Among the first to take notice were the administrators of university computing and communications resources. The utilization of their networks was skyrocketing as students used them to transfer MP3 files. By October 1999, Napster was already occupying 10 percent of the Internet bandwidth capacity at Oregon State University, which became the first to ban the service. At Florida State University Napster was taking up 20 to 30 percent of bandwidth, and at the University of Illinois, the figures at times soared to seventy-five to eighty percent. Soon, university after university banned Napster. In almost all cases, the primary motive was not the protection of copyright, but a desire to protect scarce computing resources from being soaked up by Napster. By February 2000, for example, the popularity of Napster had pushed network utilization at New York University to 98 percent, slowing down access and impeding its value as an academic tool. Once Napster was banned, network utilization dropped immediately to 60 percent of capacity.[27] Not all universities banned Napster, however. Several Ivy League universities, including MIT and Harvard, continued to allow students to use the service, citing their commitment to providing Internet access for all of their community, and noting that they did not regulate or monitor a user's choice of sites to visit. Moreover, in many universities that did ban Napster, students fought back using 1960s style rhetoric to claim that a ban on Napster amounted to "censorship" and a violation of free speech.

Why was Napster so attractive? The obvious appeal was that users could download music for free. Why pay $17.95 for a CD that contained ten tracks—only three of which you wanted—when you could download the best three from the Internet for free and leave out the junk? Others cited the immediacy of the technology. To get new music, you didn't have to go down to a music store. You just booted up your computer, logged onto the service, and quickly downloaded what you wanted. Many also found it interesting to browse through the play lists of other users, finding music that they would not otherwise listen to. And you could find music on Napster that you could not find in a retail store: old music recordings, esoteric music, unpopular noncommercial music, and so on. Napster also seemed to go hand in hand with two other developments: the spread of portable MP3 players and new technology that allowed PC users to burn or create customized CDs. In both cases, users could create personal collections or play lists of music tracks from Napster downloads.

According to an RIAA survey of 1,015 music consumers on the attractions of peer to peer file sharing services, having access to a large selection and variety of artists ranked highest (87 percent), followed by the capability to download files quickly (84 percent), the ability to download individual songs (83 percent), a convenient search feature (81 percent), and the ability to get music for free (79 percent). Ability to

access songs not commercially available ranked lowest (64 percent).[28]

Collision Course

It was soon apparent that Napster was on a collision course with the music industry. The core of the problem, according to the RIAA, was that Napster's service was violating copyright, facilitating massive piracy of intellectual property, and consequently stealing. The RIAA, along with executives from several music companies, started informal discussions with Napster during the late summer of 1999. Record industry executives insist that the talks were a sincere attempt to find some common ground. One idea being floated at the time was to sell a minority stake in Napster to the record companies, and allow Napster to license a host of content. On the other hand, many Napster insiders believed that the record industry executives were never serious about negotiating a deal, and they were just biding time. Whatever the truth, many observers do agree that Napster's new CEO, Eileen Richardson, did nothing to help matters. By all reports, Richardson had an abrasive and combative manner in her dealings with the record companies and RIAA, which only served to distance the two sides.[29] For example, the following exchange apparently occurred in a CNN online chat room:

> *RIAA*: While there are many legitimate uses of MP3s, don't you feel that your service will be primarily used by music pirates?
> *Eileen Richardson*: We are about enabling amateur and unknown artists to share their music on this new medium. Our job is not to stop pirating, that is your job.[30]

According to other sources, Eileen Richardson was once heard yelling on the phone to Frank Creighton, the head of the RIAA's antipiracy group. Richardson also had face-to-face meetings with Hilary Rosen, the RIAA's president, that apparently did not go too well. One observer noted that "Eileen got into fights with Hilary. . . . Eileen was fairly arrogant and thought what they were doing was right."[31]

Whatever the truth, on December 7, 1999, with talks between Napster and the RIAA at an impasse, the RIAA filed suit against Napster on behalf of eighteen record companies, citing copyright infringement. Several songwriters filed suit a few days later, and others were to follow. The RIAA alleged that Napster was vicariously infringing copyright and that it contributed to the direct infringement of copyright held by members of the music industry. The RIAA claimed damages of $100,000 for each copyrighted musical work that was copied as a result of Napster's software. For its part, Napster contended that its users did not infringe copyright because they only made personal copies and used the service in a way that amounted to sampling. The "fair use" section of the 1976 Copyright Protection Act stated, "The fair use of a copyrighted work, including such use by reproduction in copies or phonorecords or by any other means specified by that section, for purposes such as criticism, comment, news reporting, teaching (including multiple copies for class room use), scholarship, or research, is not an infringement of copyright."[32]

One of the most high-profile suits filed by songwriters was by the music group Metallica. Metallica had protested that Napster's users were engaged in the unauthorized copying and distribution of copyrighted material. Napster responded that if Metallicca could identify users that were violating copyright law, it would remove them from the service. In April 2000, the band's attorney, Howard King, filed suit against Napster and several universities that allowed the service to continue, alleging that Napster and the universities were violating the Racketeering Influenced and Corrupt Organizations Act, legislation that was originally aimed at organized crime. King and the band's drummer, Lars Ulrich, also turned up at Napster's headquarters with thirteen boxes of computer printouts that contained the names of 335,435 Napster users who had swapped Metallica MP3 files and asked Napster to take them off the service. According to Ulrich, their complaint was that "Napster hijacked our music without asking . . . my band authored the music which is Napster's lifeblood. We should decide what happens to it, not Napster—a company with no rights in our recordings, which has never invested a penny in Metallica's music or had anything to do with its creation."[33] Shawn Fanning, a Metallica fan himself, was somewhat disturbed at the criticism made by one of his heroes. Thereafter, he would frequently appear in public wearing a Metallica T-shirt, most notably, at the MTV Music Awards, where Ulrich sat in the audience.

One of the defenses of Napster often voiced at this time was that far from hurting CD sales, Napster actually encouraged them. The basic argument was that Napster was dispensing free samples. When something was appealing enough as a sound file on a

EXHIBIT 2

Reactions to Napster

Lou Reed (Artist): *"Artists, like anyone else, should be paid for their work."*[34]

Alanis Morissette (Artist): *"Napster presents huge problems for the artists. It raises the questions— which is positive— of where and how artists are compensated. But I don't agree with the model they have set up. The artist should be the person who's ultimately in a position to decide when, and how something should be shared with whomever they choose to share it."*[35]

Eminem (Artist): *"Whoever put my s**t on the Internet, I want to meet that mother****** and beat the s**t out of him."*[36]

Ted Cohen (Record Industry Executive): *"I think it (Napster) is one of the coolest things to come around. I also thought the moment I saw it 'My God!' This could destroy the whole business."*[37]

Shawn Fanning (Napster Founder) on hearing that the rock group Metallica had filed suit against Napster: *"Napster respects the role of artists and is very interested in working with Metallica and the music industry to develop a workable model that is fair to everyone while unleashing the power of the Internet to build enthusiasm for music."*[38]

Steven Wendell Isaacs (Independent Artist): *"I believe that Napster is a powerful promotional tool for the many artists and bands that want to reach large numbers of listeners but have not been able to get, or are disappointed by, the support provided by large recording labels."*[39]

James Breyer (Venture Capitalist): *"Napster is truly revolutionary—and it will be a precursor of some of the most important Web applications over the next several years."*[40]

home computer, people would go out to a record store and buy the entire CD, just as they would if they had heard the song on the radio.[41] In early 2000, N Sync, Britney Spears, and Eminem each had huge hits. In the weeks before their records came out, these were the three most heavily trafficked artists on Napster's services, causing some to wonder if marketing departments at their respective labels had seeded Napster with prerelease copies of their music as a promotional tool.[42] In contrast to Metallica, some musicians also supported Napster. Smashing Pumpkins broke with its label, Virgin, and gave away the group's final album for free via Napster, a move that met with a massive response. Even some senior record industry executives seemed to exhibit a degree of schizophrenia. Thomas Middelhoff, the CEO of Bertelsmann, owner of BMG, noted, "Let's be honest, despite all the dangers, Napster is pretty cool." He thought that file sharing as a system was a great idea, but that Fanning's mistake was "not having developed a complementary system for the protection of intellectual property rights and combining the two."[43]

Roadblock

By late spring Napster had its back against the wall. Not only was the company the object of several lawsuits, but it was also fast running out of cash. Into the breach stepped Hummer Winblad, a high-profile Silicon Valley venture capital firm. On May 21, Hummer Winblad announced that it would invest $15 million in Napster. A Hummer Winblad partner, Hank Barry, was brought in as CEO, replacing Richardson, while Hummer cofounder, John Hummer, joined Napster's board. Hank Barry was an interesting choice for CEO. A former lawyer with a strong background in intellectual property law, he promised to build a working business model for the company and to solve its legal problems. One of Barry's first actions was to bring in David Boies, who had led the Justice Department to victory in the Microsoft antitrust case, to defend Napster against the RIAA. He also hired two seasoned record industry executives to round out the senior management team.

However, Barry had little breathing room. The pace of the legal assault against Napster was quickening. On June 12, 2000, the RIAA filed for a preliminary injunction that would shut down Napster pending trial, citing ongoing and widespread copyright infringement that was causing the industry great harm. On July 26, 2000, Napster had its day in court. Inside Napster, there seemed to be a strong belief that the company would triumph. John Fanning sent around an internal e-mail stating, "If the motion is granted, the order will be stayed pending appeal to the Ninth Circuit, where the motion will be decided . . . and if they rule against us, which I view as a 10% chance, we would be appealing to the Supreme Court, where the future of the world will be hanging in the balance."[44] It was not to be. After a two-hour hearing and a brief fifteen-minute recess, the presiding judge dismissed virtually every argument that Boies could muster for Napster, and granted the injunction. In making her ruling, Judge Marilyn Patel noted that there was a big difference between making copies for friends, which might be protected by the fair use section of the 1976 act, and making copies available via Napster, where a music file could be downloaded by millions of anonymous users.[45]

With the injunction granted, and the service shut down, Barry scrambled to develop a business model that would make sense and would facilitate an alliance with Napster's opponents, the music labels. With the cash burn rate running in excess of $500,000 a month, Barry realized that he needed to move as expeditiously as possible. One idea floated was for the music labels to take a minority stake in Napster, and split subscription, sponsorship, and advertising revenues. The economics seemed compelling; if 20 million users (half of Napster's total in mid 2000) paid $100 a year for subscriptions that would allow for unlimited downloads, that would be $2 billion a year for Napster and the record labels. One survey found that 68 percent of Napster users would be prepared to pay a $15 monthly subscription for the service. Barry himself was reportedly contemplating a subscription of $4.95 a month.[46]

In the interim, Napster continued to hope that it would ultimately win out in court but that hope was dashed when on February 12, 2001, a three-judge panel from the Ninth Circuit Court of Appeals issued its ruling. The Appeals Court upheld Patel's injunction and determined that Napster should be held liable for copyright infringement. The judges stated that using Napster to "get something for free they would ordinarily have to buy" was a commercial use, and thus copyright infringement. Although the Appeals Court did send the injunction back to Patel for clarification, it was clear that Napster would get little relief from the courts. The service stayed shut.

BMG Attempts a Rescue

While the court drama was unfolding, on October 31, 2000, Bertelsmann (owner of BMG) broke ranks with the other major labels and announced that it was forming an alliance with Napster to develop a subscription based music distribution service based on Napster's peer-to-peer technology. As part of the alliance, Bertelsmann provided Napster with a $60 million loan, buying the service much needed time. In explaining the decision, Bertelsmann's CEO Thomas Middelhoff indicated that the genie was already out of the bottle with file swapping technology. Indeed, with two other Napster alternatives, Gnutella and FreeNet, already making an appearance, Middelhoff suggested that the industry needed to embrace the technology, not rail against it in the courts.

Middelhoff's goal was that BMG and Napster would introduce a paid subscription service by mid 2001. However, progress was slow. In November 2001, with no subscription service in sight, and Napster's service now shut down, Bertelsmann kicked in an additional $25 million loan to help the company. By early 2002, Bertelsmann was contemplating a bid to buyout Napster for $15 million.[47] However, the bid was derailed by internal strife at Napster. On March 25, board member John Fanning filed a lawsuit against two fellow directors, John Hummer and Hank Barry, claiming that the two venture capitalists were no longer directors because they were voted out on March 24, 2002. Napster's new CEO, the third, Konrad Hilbers, issued a statement calling the lawsuit "legally groundless." Observers speculated that the reason for the lawsuit was that Napster was running out of cash, and might have to file for bankruptcy, leaving John Fanning (and very possibly Shawn Fanning) with no return from Napster. On April 12, Napster announced that it would lay off 30 percent of its workforce, and this followed a 10 percent reduction in the previous month.[48]

In mid May, CEO Hilbers resigned after Napster's board formally rejected a buyout offer from BMG. Most of the management team resigned at the same time, including company cofounder Shawn Fanning. With no service to offer, no business model, and no cash in hand, it was only a matter of time. On September 4, 2002, Napster announced its liquidation.

The Revolution Continues

With Napster on a death watch, the major record labels continued to push ahead with plans to introduce their own online music service. In early 2002, the big five companies launched two services. Both services sold monthly subscriptions that allow users to listen to songs without downloading by using streaming audio technology. Alternatively, subscribers could download versions of songs that in most cases could not be burned onto a CD or transferred to a portable device. Each service only offered songs from certain labels.

MusicNet, which offered songs from Warner Music, BMG, and EMI, had one subscription plan—$9.85 a month for 100 streams and 100 downloads. After 30 days, downloads expired and couldn't be played.

Pressplay, which offered music from Sony, Universal, and EMI, had 4 subscription plans, from $9.95 to $24.95 a month, for up to 1,000 streams and 100 downloads. The higher subscription fee service from Pressplay let users burn up to 20 songs a month onto CDs that would not expire, but no more than two songs could be burned from any one artist.[49]

Second Generation Peer to Peer Networks

The introduction of legal services for downloading music over the Internet did little to stop online piracy. In very short order after Napster's service was shut down, a number of new file sharing services started to rapidly gain users. Foremost among these were Kazaa, Grokster, and Morpheus. By mid 2002, these three networks had some 70 million active users between them, more than twice the users Napster had at its peak.[50] These services were all peer to peer networks, but, unlike Napster, they did not rely upon a central registry or central server to track and control the transfer of files between users. These second generation networks were truly distributed and decentralized. All one needed to do was download the software from a central site, and you were ready to go. The software would reach out over the net and link up with other users of that software, scanning their play lists to find the song you were looking for. No central institution mediated, controlled, or tracked the transfer of a file from one computer to another. They were true peer to peer networks.

The music industry responded as it had with Napster, filing lawsuits in an attempt to shut down the services for copyright violation. But in this case it was more difficult to prove infringement. The software had legal uses, too—for example, file sharing within an organization—and its makers claimed that they could not control how it was used. The music industry filed its first suit against several second generation peer to peer networks in October 2001. In April 2003, the court ruled that the creators of Internet file sharing software should be allowed to stay in business, despite piracy by users of their programs. According to the court, the makers of such software were not violating copyright by simply making software available that allows users to trade files. The industry immediately appealed, and the case wound up at the Ninth Circuit Court of Appeals in San Francisco—the very same court that had shut down Napster. The appeal was to no avail, however, for in August 2004 the higher court upheld the lower court's ruling.

The Big Chill

By this juncture, however, the industry had decided on a different approach to the copyright problem—to go after users. In 2003, the industry won a landmark case against Verizon, which runs a broadband Internet service, forcing the company to release the names of subscribers who were believed to be infringing copyright. The RIAA then sent subpoenas to Internet Service Providers, seeking to have them identify and contact customers who were potential copyright infringers. Armed with names, between September and December 2003 the RIAA sued some 382 individuals for copyright infringement. All of these individuals had made over 1,000 unique copyrighted files available for distribution to millions of other users of peer to peer networks. The law allowed the RIAA to collect up to $150,000 per violation. Many of those identified quickly settled out-of-court, reportedly for amounts ranging from $2,500 to $10,000, although some individuals elected to fight in court, arguing that their privacy rights had been invaded.[51]

According to comScore Media Matrix, an online tracking service, the effect was immediate. In the four months following the RIAA announcement that it would sue individuals for copyright violation, the percentage of Americans who downloaded music over the Internet dropped by half from 29 percent of Internet users to just 18 percent. Moreover, on an average day during early 2003, some 4 percent of Internet users surveyed said they downloaded music files. The same survey in late 2003 found that only 1 percent admitted to downloading music files. comScore also found that the user base for peer-to-peer applications fell between 9 percent and 59 percent from November 2002 to November 2003 depending on the network. Mirroring this decline was a rapid rise in usage of legal online music services, such as Apple's iTunes.[52]

In a spring 2004 survey, comScore found that the number of people actively running second generation peer to peer networks continued to decline, with 5 million fewer people running the largest network, which is based on software from Kazaa. Moreover, the same data indicated that in March more than 11 million U.S. Internet users visited six major paid online music services.[53]

Throughout 2004, the RIAA kept up its legal assault against people who use peer to peer networks to illegally download music. In the first three months of 2004 alone, it filed almost 1,600 lawsuits, roughly 530 a month. Those targeted were sharing an average of 837 songs. In March the RIAA targeted users at twenty-one universities around the country. The RIAA also sent letters to several universities detailing massive illegal uploading of digital music files through their networks. The universities responded by taking steps to stop downloading. Virginia State University put in firewalls that block known sites for illegal music, and updated the firewalls as new sites emerged. Columbia University placed limits on outgoing bandwidth usage, and simultaneously disseminated material to students informing them that it is illegal to share copyrighted material over the Internet. The University of Florida developed its own software to detect illegal downloading from peer to peer networks. Students who do so are cut off from the Internet—fifteen minutes for the first offense and five days for the second offense. To regain access they have to read a presentation about copyright law. Third time offenders are cut off for 30 days and a notice is placed in their academic files. In the first 10 months of operation, the University caught 4,000 first time violators, 400 second time violators, and just 7 third time violators. There have been no fourth time violators.[54]

Apple's iTunes and iPod

Apple's entry into the music downloading business was born out of an oversight—in the late 1990s, when students were starting to burn their favorite CDs, Macs did not have a CD burner or software to manage their digital music collections. Realizing the mistake, CEO Steven Jobs ordered Apple's software developers to create the iTunes program to help Mac users manage their growing digital music collections. The first iTunes program led to the concept of the iPod. If people were going to maintain the bulk of their music collection on a computer, they needed a portable device to take music with them—a Sony Walkman for the digital age. While there were such devices on the market already, they could only hold a few dozen songs each.

To run the iPod, Apple licensed software from PortalPlayer. Apple also learnt that Toshiba was building a tiny 1.8 inch hard drive that could hold over one thousand songs. Apple quickly cut a deal with Toshiba, giving it exclusive rights to the drive for eighteen months. Meanwhile, Apple's engineers focused on designing the user interface, the exterior styling, and the synchronization software to make it work with the Mac.

The iPod was unveiled in October 2001 to mixed reviews. The price of $399 was significantly above that of competing devices, and since the iPod only worked with Apple computers, it seemed destined to be a niche product. However, initial sales were strong. It turned out that consumers were willing to pay a premium price for the iPod's huge storage capacity. Moreover, Jobs made the call to develop a version of the iPod that would be compatible with Windows. After it was introduced in mid 2002, sales surged.

By this times Jobs was dealing with a bigger strategic issue—how to persuade the music companies to make their music available for legal downloads. By all accounts, it was here that Steve Job's legendary selling ability came into play. With a prototype for an online iTunes store in hand, Jobs met with executives from the major labels. He persuaded them that it was in their best interest to support a legal music download business. People would pay to download music over the Internet, he argued. Although all of the labels were setting up their own online businesses, Jobs felt that since they were limited to selling music owned by the parent companies, demand would be limited too. What was needed was a reputable, independent online music retailer, and Apple fit the bill. If it was going to work, however, all of the labels needed to get on board. Under Jobs's scheme, iTunes files would be downloaded for 99 cents each. The only portable digital player that the files could be stored and played on was an iPod. Jobs's pitch was that this closed world made it easier to protect copyrighted material from unauthorized distribution.

Jobs also met with twenty of the world's top recording artists, including U2's Bono, Sheryl Crow, and Mick Jagger. His pitch to them—digital distribution is going to happen, and the best way to protect your interests is to support a legal online music distribution business. Wooed by Jobs, these powerful stakeholders encouraged the music recording companies to take Apple's proposal seriously.

By early 2003, Jobs had all of the major labels onboard. Launched in April 2003, within days it was clear that Apple had a major hit on its hands. A million songs were sold in the first week. In mid 2004, iTunes passed the 100 million download mark and sales kept accelerating, hitting the 150 million download market in October 2004. At that point, customers were downloading over 4 million songs per week, which represented a run rate of more than 200 million a year. However, Jobs has admitted that Apple does not make much money from iTune downloads, probably only 10 cents a song, but it does make good margins on

sales of the iPod—and sales of the iPod ballooned in late 2004. By September 2004, Apple had sold 5.7 million iPods, some 2 million in the third quarter alone, netting over $500 million in revenues. iTunes revenues for the third quarter were close to $100 million. Apple had 61 percent of the total digital audio player market at that point and more than 90 percent of the market for high-capacity players.[55]

As 2004 drew to a close, the pace of expansion in Apple's legal digital music business did not seem to be slowing down. In mid 2004, Apple inked a deal with Hewlett Packard under which HP would install iTunes software on its PCs and sell iPods under its brand name. In October 2004, Apple opened iTunes stores to serve Europe and Canada, and Japan was reportedly next in line.

The Emerging Competitive Battle

As 2004 drew to a close, there were signs that the competitive battle to dominate the legal music download business was heating up. A host of other device makers were offering powerful portable digital audio players, although none worked with iTunes. RealNetworks had entered the online music business in 2002 and now had some 1 million subscribers who paid $9.95 a month to listen to music streamed to their PC through Real Player. They could choose from a playlist that included some 700,000 titles. Although the streamed media could not be downloaded onto PCs or portable devices, Real had also set up a Real Player online music store. This sold downloads that could be played on a wide range of portable devices, including the iPod. In August 2004, Real started to sell music downloads at 49 cents each—far below the 89 cents Real had to pay the music companies for the titles. The sales promotion was scheduled to last for just three weeks, but some observers wondered if it was the first shot in a price war.[56] Wal-Mart was also offering music downloads from its website at 89 cents each.

In the fall of 2004, Microsoft entered the fray. The company announced that the new version of Windows Media Player would synchronize with legal online music stores and with a wide range of mobile devices. Using Media Player, users could browse different stores, download music onto their PC, and transfer it onto a portable device, all while staying with Media Player.

Napster also resurfaced in 2003, this time as a legal streaming media and music downloading service owned by Roxio, which made its name selling CD burning software. Roxio had purchased the rights to the defunct company's brand name for $6.1 million in November 2002. The company then purchased PressPlay from Sony and Universal in March 2003 for some $39 million. Roxio also persuaded Samsung to create a portable music player designed to work with the new service. Launched in October 2003, the service, dubbed Napster 2.0, offers downloads for 99 cents each and the ability to stream songs to a PC for $9.95 a month. In September 2004, Napster raised the competitive stakes when it introduced a service, called Napster to Go, which enables consumers to download an unlimited number of songs for a subscription price of just $14.95 a month.[57]

Yahoo also entered the market in late 2004 when it purchased Musicmatch, a software company whose jukebox software to digitalize CDs had been preinstalled on Dell PCs for several years. Musicmatch had set up an online store for downloading music that by late 2004 was selling 1.5 to 2 million downloads per month, roughly similar to estimates of the monthly download rate at Napster and Real Networks. Apple, in contrast, was estimated to be selling some 16 million downloads per month.[58]

ENDNOTES

1. Trevor Merriden, *Irresistible Forces* (Oxford, UK: Capstone Books, 2001).
2. Recording Industry Association of America, 2003 Year End Statistics, archived at **www.riaa.com**.
3. IFPI news release, "Global Music Sales Down 5% in 2001," **www.ifpi.org**.
4. International Federation of the Phonographic Industry, Commercial Piracy Report 2004, **www.ifpi.org**.
5. IFPI News release, "Global Music Sales Down 5% in 2001," **www.ifpi.org**.
6. J.R. Laing, "Bronfman's Return," *Barron's*, December 1, 2003, page 13.
7. B. Mitchener, "Sony, Bertelsmann Deal Defended," *Wall Street Journal*, June 10, 2004, page B4.
8. RIAA, "How Much Does It Cost to Make a CD?" **www.riaa.org**.
9. J. Ordonez, "Behind the Music," *Wall Street Journal*, February 26, 2002, page A1.
10. Ibid.
11. E. Smith, "Spitzer Probes How Music Labels Get Radio Airplay," *Wall Street Journal*, October 22, 2004, page A2.
12. Recording Industry Association of America, 2003 Consumer Profile, at **www.riaa.com**.
13. J.R. Wilke, "Music Firms, U.S. Hold Settlement Talks." *Wall Street Journal*, December 16, 1999, page A3.
14. J.R. Wilke, "FTC Move Expected to Bring Lower CD Prices," *Wall Street Journal*, May 10, 2000, page A3.
15. E. Smith, "Universal's CD Price Cuts Will Squeeze Music Retailers," *Wall Street Journal*, September 18, 2003, page B1.
16. E. Smith, "Harsh Feedback," *Wall Street Journal*, June 4, 2004, page A1.
17. D. Kiron, C.E. Bagley, and M.J. Roberts, Napster, Harvard Business School Case # 801-219, March 29, 2001.
18. UMG Recordings v MP3.com Inc., 92 F. Supp. 2d 349 (S.D.N.Y. 2000).
19. John Alderman, *Sonic Boom* (Cambridge, MA: Perseus Publishing, 2001), page 143.
20. Ibid., page 91.
21. Ibid.
22. Merriden, *Irresistible Forces*, page 6.
23. Ibid., page 7.
24. S.P. Ante, S.V. Brull., D.K. Berman, and M. France, "How the Music Sharing Phenomenon Began, Where It Went Wrong, and What Happens Next," *Business Week*, August 14, 2000, pages 112–120.
25. Merriden, *Irresistible Forces*, page 9.
26. Ante, Brull, Berman, and France, "How the Music Sharing Phenomenon Began," pages 112–120.
27. Ibid.
28. RIAA, Market Data, **www.riaa.org**.
29. Ante, Brull, Berman, and France, "How the Music Sharing Phenomenon Began," pages 112–120.
30. Cited in D. Kiron, C.E. Bagley, and M.J. Roberts, Napster, Harvard Business School Case # 801-219, March 29, 2001.
31. Ante, Brull, Berman, and France, "How the Music Sharing Phenomenon Began," pages 112–120.
32. Section 107 on the Copyright Act of 1976.
33. **Salon.com** magazine, May 1, 2000.
34. Merriden, *Irresistible Forces*, page 45.
35. Ibid.
36. Alderman, *Sonic Boom*, page 114.
37. Ibid., page 116.
38. Ibid., page 10.
39. Merriden, *Irresistible Forces*, page 26.
40. Ante, Brull, Berman, and France, "How the Music Sharing Phenomenon Began," page 114.
41. J. Selvin, "Did Napster Help Boost Record Sales?" *San Francisco Chronicle*, August 5, 2001.
42. Alderman, *Sonic Boom*, page 117.
43. Ibid., page 116.
44. Quoted in Ante, Brull., Berman and France, "How the Music Sharing Phenomenon Began," pages 112–120.
45. Anonymous, "Rewired for Sound," *The Economist*, August 5, 2000, pages 59–60.
46. S. Ante, "Napster: Tune In, Turn on, Pay Up," *Business Week*, November 13, 2000, page 52.
47. L. Himelstein and T. Lowry, "The Sound at Napster: Tick, Tick, Tick," *Business Week*, April 8, 2002, page 73.
48. N. Wingfield, "Napster Lays Off 30% of Workers," *Wall Street Journal*, April 12, 2002, page A 16.
49. W.S. Mossberg, "Record Labels Launch Two Feeble Services to Replace Napster," *Wall Street Journal*, February 7, 2002, page B1.
50. M. Warner, "The New Napsters," *Fortune*, August 12, 2002, pages 115–117.
51. N. Wingfield and S. McBride, "Green Light for Grokster," *Wall Street Journal*, August 20, 2004, page B1.
52. comScore Matrix, "Sharp Decline in Music File Swapping," Press Release, January 4, 2004, archived at **comscore.com**.
53. comScore Matrix, "One in Seven Internet Users Say They No Longer Download Music Files," Press Release, April 26, 2004, archived at **comscore.com**.
54. S. McBride, "Stop the Music!" *Wall Street Journal*, August 23, 2004, page B1.
55. N. Wingfield and E. Smith, "U2's Gig: Help Apple Sell iPods," *Wall Street Journal*, October 20, 2004, page D5; Apple Computer Press Release, "iTunes Music Store Downloads Top 150 Million Songs," October 14, 2004.
56. N. Wingfield, "Price War in Online Music," *Wall Street Journal*, August 17, 2004, page D1.
57. P. Burrows, "Napster Lives Again," *Business Week*, October 20, 2003, page 66; "Napster to Go," *Wall Street Journal*, September 2, page 1.
58. K.J. Delaney, "Yahoo Agrees to Buy Musicmatch," *Wall Street Journal*, September 15, 2004, page B10.

Case 12

Staples

This case was prepared by Charles W. L. Hill, the University of Washington.

Introduction

It was 1985, and a thirty-six-year-old retailer called Tom Stemberg was being interviewed by the CEO of the Dutch-based warehouse club, Makro, for the top job at Makro's nascent U.S. operation. Stemberg didn't think Makro's concept would work in the United States, but he was struck by one thing as he toured Makro's first U.S. store in Langhorne, Pennsylvania: office supplies were flying off the shelves. "It was obvious that this merchandise was moving very fast," he later recalled. "That aisle (where the office supplies were located) was just devastated."[1] Stemberg began to wonder whether an office supplies supermarket would be a viable concept. He thought it might be possible that a supermarket selling just office supplies could do to the office supplies business what Toys "R" Us had done to the fragmented toy retailing industry; that is, consolidate it and create enormous economic value in the process.

Within a year Stemberg had founded Staples, the first office supplies supermarket. Less than two decades later, Staples was a leading retailer in the office supplies business with 1,088 stores in the United States, 212 in Canada, and 188 in Europe. Its revenues for 2003 exceeded $13 billion, net profit was over $540 million, and the company had earned a return on invested capital of between 12.5 percent and 14 percent for the last six years, which was considered high for retailing.[2]

Tom Stemberg

Despite his young age, by 1985 Stemberg had assembled an impressive resume in retailing. Stemberg had been born in Los Angeles but spent much of his teens in Austria, where his parents were originally from. He moved back to the United States to enter Harvard University, ultimately graduating with an MBA from Harvard Business School in 1973. Stemberg was hired out of Harvard by the Jewel Corporation, which put him to work at Star Market, the company's supermarket grocery division in the Boston area.

Henry Nasella, Stemberg's first boss at Jewel, who would later work for Stemberg at Staples, remembers meeting Stemberg on his first day at Jewel: "He came in 15 minutes late, his hair too long, his tie over his shoulder, his shirt hanging out over the back of his pants. I thought, what in the world do I have here?"[3] (Stemberg is still known for his disheveled appearance.) What he had was a man who started out on the store floor, bagging groceries, stocking the aisle, and ringing up sales at the checkout counter. Stemberg rose rapidly, however, and by the time he was twenty-eight, he had been named vice president of sales and marketing at Star Market, the youngest vice president in the history of the Jewel Corporation.

At Jewel, Stemberg became known as an aggressive marketer, competing vigorously on price and introducing generic brands (Stemberg developed and launched the first line of "generic" foods sold in the country).[4] According to Stemberg, "It was a nutso thing we were trying to do, and the fact that it

Copyright © 2004 by Charles W. L. Hill. This case was prepared by Charles W. L. Hill, the University of Washington, as the basis for class discussion rather than to illustrate either effective or ineffective handling of an administrative situation. Reprinted by permission of Charles W. L. Hill. All rights reserved. For the most recent financial results of the company discussed in this case, go to **http://finance .yahoo.com,** input the company's stock symbol, and download the latest company report from its homepage.

worked out well was a miracle. We opened all these big stores, and we were trying to take market share away from people who were much better financed than we were. They retaliated and lowered prices. . . . I learnt to experience the challenges of rapid growth. There was no better experience to have been through. It taught me the necessity of having infrastructure and putting it in place."[5]

One of the supermarkets that Stemberg found himself battling with was Heartland Food Warehouse, the first successful deep discount warehouse supermarket in the country. Heartland was run by Leo Kahn, one of the country's leading supermarket retailers. Kahn had started the Purity Supreme supermarket chain in the late 1940s, making him one of the founding fathers of the supermarket business. Stemberg and Kahn fought relentless marketing battles with each other. In a typical example of their tussles, at one point Kahn ran ads guaranteeing that his customers would get the best price on Thanksgiving turkeys. Stemberg responded with his own ads promising that Star would match the lowest advertised price on turkeys. Technically that made Kahn's claim incorrect, a point that Stemberg made to the Massachusetts attorney general's office, who told Kahn to pull his ad.

In 1982, Stemberg left Jewel to run the grocery division of another retailer, First National Supermarkets Inc. To build market share, he decided to take the company into the warehouse food business, imitating Leo Kahn's Heartland chain. Stemberg soon came into conflict with the CEO at First National. As he later admitted, "I probably didn't do a very good job, in a corporate political sense, of making sure he understood the risks in what we were trying to do. The situation was very stressful."[6] In January 1985, things came to a head and Stemberg was fired. It was probably the best thing that ever happened to him.

When Kahn heard that Stemberg had been fired, he quickly got in touch with him. Kahn had just sold his own business for $80 million, and he was looking for investment opportunities. He had developed a great respect for his old adversary, and wanted to back him in a new retailing venture. As Stemberg paraphrases it, Kahn said "I want to back you in a business kid, what have you got in mind?"[7] Kahn agreed to put up $500,000 in seed money to help Stemberg develop a new venture opportunity. He also took on the role of mentor, evaluating Stemberg's ideas.

Initially Kahn and Stemberg looked at the business they both knew best, supermarket grocery retailing.

But they were put off by the intense competition now raging in the business, and the high price they would have to pay for properties. At this juncture, Bob Nakasone, then president of Toys "R" Us, stepped into the picture. Nakasone had worked at Jewel alongside Stemberg before moving to Toys "R" Us. It was Nakasone who urged Stemberg to "think outside of the food box." Nakasone told Stemberg that there were more similarities than differences across product categories, and that profit margins were much better outside of the grocery business.

While mulling over possible entrepreneurial opportunities, Stemberg continued to explore other options, including working for an established retailer. It was this parallel search that took him down to Makro for a job interview, and it was there that he suddenly realized there was a possible opportunity to be had in starting the Toys "R" Us of office supplies.

The Founding of Staples

Hot on the heels of his trip to Makro, Stemberg started to think about his idea. The first thing was to get a handle on the nature of the market. Stemberg started by asking people if they knew how much they spent on office supplies. In his words:

> "There was this lawyer I knew in Hartford, which is where I lived then. If ever there was a cheap bastard in this world, he was a cheap bastard. And I said, 'Gee, how much do you spend on office supplies?' He said, "Oh I don't know, I guess about a couple of hundred bucks a person, 40 people in the office, I bet you we spend ten grand.' I said, 'Do me a favor will you? You've got good records. Go through your records and tell me exactly how much you spend': he calls me up the next day. 'Son of a bitch, I spend $1,000 apiece! But I'm getting a discount, I'm paying 10% off list': I said, 'Toys "R" Us' is paying 60% off list': He says, 'Are you kidding me? You mean I could save like half? I could save like twelve grand?' In his mind, this is the payment on his new Jaguar."[8]

Stemberg began to think that this idea had some potential. He reasoned that people want to save money, and in this case the money they could save might be substantial, but they didn't even know they were paying too much. Small businesses in particular, he thought, might be a viable target market. While working on the idea, the printer ribbon on his printer ran out. It was a weekend. He drove down to the local office supply store in Hartford, and it was closed. Went to another, but that was also closed. He ended up going to BJ's Wholesale Club, a deep discount warehouse club. BJ's was open, they sold office supplies at low prices, but the selection was limited and they didn't carry the type of ribbon Stemberg wanted. Stemberg immediately saw the opportunity.

Around the same time, Stemberg went to see another mentor of his, Walter Salmon, who taught retailing at Harvard Business School. Over lunch they discussed the supermarket business and Stemberg's quest. Salmon asked Stemberg if he had thought of applying his retailing skills to a product category that was growing faster than the grocery business and was not well served by modern retailers. Stemberg replied that he had been thinking about office supplies. Salmon's response, "Gee, this is a really big idea."

Scoping Out the Opportunity

Stemberg ended up hiring a former teaching assistant of Salmon's for $20,000 to do some basic market research on the industry and validate the market. As he tells the story: "I never forget the night I went to her house and we went through the slide deck. I always want to jump ahead. And she puts her hand on my hand and says, 'Wait, we will walk though it.' She's teasing us! Finally she said it was a $45 billion market growing at 15% per year. And it turns out she was lying. That was actually at the manufacturer level. It was actually more than $100 billion already if you looked at retail. She confirmed that the pricing umbrellas were as big as we thought they were, and that small businesses were getting raped the way we had said they were. I was pretty damn excited during the long drive home."[9]

The market growth, it turned out, was being driven by some favorable demographic trends. The U.S. economy was recovering from the recessions of the late 1970s and early 1980s, and underlying economic growth was strong. A wave of new technology was finding its way into American businesses, including personal computers, printers, faxes, and small copiers, and this was driving demand for office supplies including basic equipment along with consumables from paper and printer ink to diskettes and copy toner.

The wave of downsizing that had swept corporate America in the early 1980s also had a beneficial side effect—unemployed people were starting their own businesses. The rate of new business formation was the highest in years. There were 11 million small businesses in the country—Stemberg's proposed target market, the vast majority of which had less than twenty employees. This sector was the engine of job growth in the economy—between 1980 and 1986, small enterprises had been responsible for a net increase of 10.5 million jobs. Many of these new jobs were in the service sector, which was a big consumer of office supplies. Each new white-collar job meant another $1,000 a year in office supplies.

Stemberg's research started to uncover an industry that was highly fragmented at the retail level, but had some huge participants. Upstream in the value chain were the manufacturers. This was a very diverse collection of companies including paper manufacturers such as Boise Cascade; office furniture makers; manufacturers of pencils, pens, and markers such as the Bic Corporation; companies like 3M that supplied Post-it Notes, and a whole lot more besides, such as office equipment companies from Xerox and Canon (manufacturers of copiers and consumables) to manufacturers of personal computers, printers, and faxes such as Apple, Compaq, and Hewlett Packard.

Then there were the wholesalers, some of which were very large such as United Stationers and McKesson. The wholesalers bought in bulk and sold to business clients and smaller retail establishments, either directly or through a network of dealers. The dealers often visited businesses to collect orders and arrange for delivery. The dealers themselves ranged in scale from small one person enterprises to large firms that sold through central warehouses. Some dealers also had a retail presence, while others did not. Manufacturers and wholesalers would also sell directly to large businesses through catalogs or a direct sales presence.

The retailers fell into two main categories. There were the local office supply retailers, generally small businesses themselves, and there were the general merchandise discounters, such as BJ's Wholesale and Wal-Mart. The smaller retailers had an intrinsically high-cost structure. They were full service retailers who purchased in small lots and delivered in trucks or sold out of the store. The general merchandise discounters purchased from wholesalers, or direct from manufacturers, and their prices were much lower, but they did not carry a wide range of product.

On the consumer side, most large businesses had dedicated personnel for purchasing office supplies. They either bought from dealers, who purchased directly from manufacturers or through wholesalers, or bought direct from the manufacturer themselves. Large firms were able to negotiate on price and received discounts that could be as large as 80 percent of the list price on some items. Businesses of fewer than one hundred people did not generally have someone dedicated to managing office supplies, and they tended to rely primarily on dealers. For these companies, product availability, not price, was viewed as key. In even smaller firms, it was the convenience of being able to get office supplies that seemed to matter more than anything else.

Consistent with his initial insight, Stemberg found that smaller firms were ignored by the big dealers. To verify this he called Boise Cascade, which operated as both a dealer and a manufacturer, to see what service they might offer. First he called on behalf of Ivy Satellite Network, a small company that Stemberg owned that broadcast events of Ivy League schools to alumni around the world. Boise couldn't even be bothered to send a catalog to this company. Then he called Boise back, this time representing the one hundred–person office of a friend of his who was a food broker. This time Boise was happy to send a representative to the food broker. The representative offered the broker deep discounts. A Bic pen from Boise that cost Ivy $3.68 from the local stationary store was offered for just 85 cents. More generally, Stemberg found that while an office manager in a company with more than one thousand employees could often obtain discounts averaging 50 percent from dealers, small businesses with fewer than twenty employees were lucky to get a 10 percent discount, and often had to pay full price.[10]

Stemberg also found a study produced by researchers at the Wharton School that seemed to confirm his suspicions. "Essentially they first asked dealers. 'What does the customer want?' Ninety percent of the dealers said, 'Better service' and 10% said, 'other.' Then they asked customers, and 90% of the customers said what they really wanted was lower prices. Ha! The dealers were totally out of touch. They were making 40% to 50%, the wholesalers were making 30%, and the manufacturers were making huge margins. Everybody's rich, fat, and happy, and they're all going what's wrong with this?"[11]

Creating the Company

Stemberg knew from experience that for Staples to succeed it would have to execute well, and to do that, it needed experienced management. Stemberg turned to people he knew, managers who like him had risen quickly through the ranks at the Jewel Corporation or other Boston area retailers. From Jewel came Myra Hart, who was to become the Staples group vice president for growth and development; Todd Krasnow, who became vice president for marketing; Paul Korian, the Staples vice president of merchandising; and Henry Nasella, Stemberg's mentor at Star market who subsequently became president of Staples. The CFO was Bob Leombruno, who had bought Mammoth Mart, a failed retail operation, out of bankruptcy for a group of investors. Stemberg took on the CEO role, while Kahn became chairman. Most of these people started working full time on January 1, 1986. They gave up secure jobs, high salaries, and annual bonuses for a salary cut, loss of bonuses, and fourteen-hour days.

According to Stemberg, the pitch to prospective managers was this: "I'm going to give you a big chunk of stock in this thing. This is your chance. We're all going to work our tails off. We're going to work crazy hours. But here you'll be part of a retailing revolution. If you own 2% of the company and it gets to be worth $100 million, you're going to make $2 million."[12] In the end, each member of the top management team got a 2.5 percent stake in the company.

By now Stemberg had a name for this nascent company, Staples. Reflecting on how it came about years later, he noted that "I'm driving between Hartford and Boston. I'm thinking about names. Pencils? Pens? 8 1/2 by 11? Staples? Staples! Staples the Office Superstore. That was it. The bad thing about the name was that when we started out, we had to explain to everybody what it was. Office Depot basically copied Home Depot and put the 'office' in front. It was Home Depot for the office, and it lived off the Home Depot name. Office Club was a Price Club for the office. It lived off the Price Club name. In the early days ours was actually a problem. But those other names aren't a brand. Ours is a brand."[13]

With the management team in place, the next steps were to refine the concept and raise capital. The concept itself was relatively straightforward, implementing it would not be. The plan was to offer a wide selection of merchandise in a warehouse type setting with prices deeply discounted from those found in mom-and-pop retailers. Because it was to be a supermarket, the idea was to move from full-service to a self-service format. At the same time, the management team recognized the staff would need to be trained in office supplies so that they could provide advice when asked.

To make the concept viable, a number of issues had to be dealt with. They had to decide where to locate the stores. How big a population base would be needed to support a store? What kind of selection was required? How many stock keeping units (SKUs) should the store offer? There was the problem of educating the customer. If potential customers currently didn't know that they were paying excessive prices for office supplies, and consistently underestimated how much they spent on the category, what could Staples do to change this?

To get low prices, Staples would need to cut costs to the bone and be managed very efficiently. They would have to get manufacturers or wholesalers to deliver directly to Staples. How could this be done? Wouldn't wholesalers and manufacturers create channel conflict with dealers and established retailers by delivering straight to Staples? How was this to be resolved? Staples also needed to minimize its inventory, thereby reducing its working capital needs. Management knew that if they could turn inventory over twelve times a year, and delay payment to vendors for thirty days, then vendors would essentially finance Staples's inventory. Pulling that off would require state-of-the-art information systems, and the state of the art at the time in office supplies did not include bar coding on individual items. How was Staples to deal with this?

There was also the potential competition to worry about. Stemberg was sure that once Staples unveiled its concept, others would follow quickly. To preempt competitors, the plan called for rapid rollout of the concept, with sales ramping up from nothing to $42 million after three years. This would require a lot of capital. It also required that the concept be very easy to replicate so that once the first store was opened, others could be opened in quick succession. This meant that the systems that were put in place for the first store had to be the right ones, and able to support rapid expansion. There wasn't much room for error here.

As the management team refined the concept, they came to the realization that the information systems were one of the keys to the entire venture. With the right information systems in place, Staples could track sales and inventory closely at the level of individual items and figure out its gross profit on each item sold, adjusting its merchandising mix accordingly. This would be a departure from existing retailers, the majority of whom lacked the ability to calculate profit on each item sold, and could only calculate the average gross profit across a range of items. The right information systems could also be used to collect data on customers at the point of sales, and this would assist greatly in market research and direct marketing to customers.

On the other hand, raising capital proved to be easier than they thought. Stemberg valued Staples, which was still little more than a concept, a management team, and a business plan full of unanswered questions, at $8 million. He went looking for $4 million, which he would exchange for 50 percent of the company. The venture capitalists were initially reluctant. They seemed to hold back, waiting to see who would commit first. They also valued Staples at $6 million, and wanted a 67 percent stake for the $4 million in first round financing. Stemberg balked at that, and instead focused his efforts on one firm that seemed more willing to break away from the pack. The firm was Bain Venture Capital, whose managing general partner, Matt Romney, later observed, "A lot of retailing startups come by, but a lot of them are a twist on an old theme, or a better presentation. . . . Stemberg wasn't proposing just a chain of stores, but an entirely new retailing category. That really captures your attention. It slaps you in the face with the idea that this could be big."[14]

To validate the business concept, Romney's firm surveyed one hundred small businesses after being urged to do so by Stemberg. Auditing invoices from these companies for office supplies, Romney discovered what Stemberg already knew—the companies were spending about twice what they estimated. Romney then ran the numbers on his own company and found that his firm would save $117,000 a year by purchasing supplies at the discount that Stemberg promised. That was enough for Romney, and he committed to investing. Others followed, and Staples raised $4.5 million in its first round of financing, which closed on January 23, 1986. This gave the company enough capital to go ahead with the first store. In return for the financing, Staples had to give the VCs a 54 percent stake in the company. To get the money, however, Staples had to commit to opening its first store on May 1, 1986, and to meet a plan for rolling out additional stores as quickly as possible.

The First Store

With just four months to open their first store, the management team went into overdrive. They would meet every morning at about seven A.M. in a session that could run from thirty minutes to two hours. Someone would rush out to get sandwiches for lunch, and they would keep working. The workday came to a close at nine or ten P.M. Not only was there no template for what they were doing, but also they knew they had to put a system in place that would allow them to quickly roll out additional stores.

One of the most difficult tasks fell on the shoulders of Leombruno, the CFO. In addition to setting up an accounting system, he was put in charge of installing the entire information system for Staples. The system had to be able to track customer purchases so that Staples could reorder products. The cash registers, which were to be connected individually to the system, had to be easy to operate so that there would be no congestion at the checkout stands. Stemberg himself was adamant that the register receipts indicate the list price of each item, as well as a much lower Staples price, and an even lower price for customers who became Staples members. He also wanted the system to collect detailed demographics on each customer.

Leombruno insisted that the system be able to do two things: First, calculate the gross profit margin Staples made on each item sold. Most retailers at the time could only calculate the average profit margin across the mix of inventory. Second, Leombruno wanted to make sure that inventory turned over at least twelve times a year, and good information systems were the key to that. With most vendors requiring payment in thirty days, an inventory turnover of greater than twelve would allow Staples to cut its working capital requirements.

As the wish list for the information systems grew, it soon became apparent that it would not be possible to do everything in the allotted time span. No existing software package did what the management team wanted, and they had to hire consultants to customize existing packages. In the end, several proposed features were dropped. However, at Stemberg's insistence the three-way price requirements remained. To track sales and inventory levels, Staples assigned a six-digit look up code for each item. While entering the codes was a slower process than scanning items, most manufacturers in the office supplies business were still not marking their products with bar codes, which meant scanning was not feasible.

Another problem was to get suppliers to ship products to the first Staples store. The company was asking suppliers to bypass the existing distribution system, and risk alienating long-time customers in the established channel of distribution. To get suppliers on board, Staples used a number of tactics. One was a visionary pitch. The company told suppliers that they were out to revolutionize the retail end of the industry. Staples would be very big, they said, and it was in the best interests of the suppliers to back the startup. Stemberg's punch line was simple: "I'm going to be very loyal to those who stick their necks out for us. But it's going to cost you a lot more to get in later."[15] Connections also helped to get suppliers to deliver to Staples. One of the VC backers of Staples, Bessemer Venture Partners, also owned a paper manufacturer, Ampad. Bessemer told Ampad to start selling to Staples, which they did, even though existing distributors complained bitterly about the arrangement.

Finding real estate also presented a problem. As an enterprise with no proven track record, Staples found it difficult to rent decent real estate large enough to stock and display the five thousand SKUs that it was planning for its first store, and to do so at a decent price. Most landlords wanted sky high rent from Staples. In the end, the best that Staples could do was a site in Brighton, Massachusetts, that was within site of a housing project and had failed as a site for several different retailers. There was one redeeming feature of the site—it was smack in the middle of a high concentration of small businesses.

Despite all of the problems, Staples was able to open its first store on May 1, 1986. The opening day was busy, but only because everybody who worked at Staples had invited everybody they knew. On the second day just sixteen people came through the store. On the third day, it was the same number. A few weeks of this, and Staples would have to shut its doors. Desperate, Krasnow decided to bribe customers to get them into the store. The company sent $25 to each of thirty-five office managers, inviting them to shop in the store and pass along their reactions. According to Krasnow, "A week later we called them back. They had all taken the money, but none of them had come into the store. I was apoplectic."[16] In the end, nine of them finally came in, and they gave Staples rave reviews. Slowly the momentum started to build, and by August lines were starting to form at the cash registers at lunch time.

The 1990s: Growth, Competition, and Consolidation

Growth

Staples had set of target of $4 million in first year sales from its Brighton Store, but within a few months, the numbers were tracking up toward a $6 million annual run rate. The concept was starting to work. The number of customers coming through the door every month was growing, but it was not only customers that were coming. One day Joe Antonini, the CEO of Kmart, was spotted walking around the Staples store. Around the same time, Stemberg heard from contacts that Staples had been mentioned at a Wal-Mart board meeting. He realized that if other discount retailers were noticing Staples when it had just one store, competition could not be far behind.

Within five months of the opening of the first Staples store, a clone had appeared in the Southeast: Office Depot. Needing money fast to fund expansion and lock in Staples territory, Stemberg went back to the venture capitalists. While the initial backers were only willing to value Staples at $15 million, Stemberg held out for and got a valuation of $22 million, raising another $14 million. He pulled off this trick by finding institutional investors who were willing to invest on a valuation of $22 million. He then went back to the original VCs and told them that the deal was closing fast, which persuaded them to commit.

By May 1987, Staples had 3 stores open and planned to increase the number to 20 by the end of 1988 (in the event it opened 22). Sales were running at anywhere from $300 to $800 per square foot. In contrast, high-volume discount stores were lucky to get $300 per square foot. By mid 1989, three years after its first store opened, Staples had 27 stores open in the northeast and an annual sales run rate of $120 million, way above the original three-year target of $42 million. The stores now average 15,000 square feet and stocked 5,000 items.

Explaining the success, Stemberg noted, "From a value perspective, I think there is no question that we have been a friend to the entrepreneur. If you look at the average small town merchant, we've lowered the costs of his office products—where he was once paying say $4,000 to $5,000 a year, now he's paying $2,000 or $3,000. We've made him more efficient."[17]

Helping to drive sales growth was the development of a direct marketing pitch. Every time Staples opened a store, it purchased a list of small businesses within fifteen minutes' driving distance. Then a group of telemarketers would go to work calling up the buyer of office supplies at the businesses. The telemarketers would tell them Staples was opening up a store like Toys "R" Us for office supplies, ask them how much they spent on office supplies every year (often they did not know), cite typical cost savings at small businesses, and sent them a coupon for a free item such as copy paper. At first the customers would come in slowly, but momentum would build up as customers realized the scale of the savings they were getting.

Every time a customer redeemed a coupon at a store, they were given a free Staples Card. This "membership" card entitled cardholders to even deeper discounts on select items. The card quickly became the lynchpin of Staples's direct marketing effort. From the card application, Staples gathered information about the customer—what type of business they were in, how many employees they had, where they were located. This information was entered into a customer database, and every time a card member used that card, the card number and purchases were logged into the database via the cash register. This gave Staples up-to-date information about what was being purchased and by whom. This information then allowed Staples to target promotions at certain customer groups—for example, card members who were not making purchases. The goal was to get existing customers to spend more at Staples, a goal that over time was attained.

Because Staples started to reach so many of its customers through direct marketing (about 80 percent of its sales were made to cardholders), it was able to spend less on media ads—in some areas it dropped media advertising altogether, saving on costs. This was an important source of cost savings in the Northeast where the media is expensive.

A problem that continued to bedevil Staples as it expanded was the shortage of good real estate locations that could be rented at a reasonable price, particularly in the Northeast. Finding a good site in the early days required flexibility; at various times Staples converted anything and everything from restaurants to massage parlors into Staples stores. As the company grew, its real estate strategy started to take a defensive aspect, with Staples bidding for prime sites in order to preempt competitors.

The high cost of real estate in the Northeast led Staples to establish its first distribution center in 1987.

This decision was hotly debated within the company and opposed by some of the investors who thought that the capital should be used to build more stores, but Stemberg prevailed. The distribution center was located off an interstate highway in an area of rural Connecticut where land was cheap. The facility cost $6 million to build, and tied up a total of $10 million in working capital, almost 29 cents out of every dollar that the company had raised to that point. But Stemberg saw this as a necessary step. The inventory storage capacity at the distribution center enabled the company to operate with smaller stores than many of its rivals, but still offer the same variety of goods. By 1989, the average Staples store was 35 percent smaller than the Office Depot outlets that were then opening up all over the Southeast, saving on real estate costs. The distribution center also helped save labor costs, since wages are lower in rural areas. Equally important, inventory storage at the distribution centers allowed the stores to remain fully stocked. A Stemberg noted, "In competition with the clones, it will come down to who has the lowest costs and the best in stock position."[18]

The expansion strategy at Staples was very methodical. Stores were clustered together in a region, even to the extent that they cannibalized each other on the margin, so that Staples could become the dominant supplier in that market. The early focus was on major metropolitan areas such as Boston, New York, Philadelphia, and Los Angeles. Although high real estate and labor costs in these areas were a disadvantage, strong demand from local businesses helped compensate, as did the distribution centers. In 1990, Staples open its second distribution center in California to support expansion there.

The expansion at Staples was fueled by the proceeds from a 1989 Initial Public Offering, which raised $61.7 million of capital—enough for Staples to accelerate its store openings. By mid 1991, Staples store count passed over one hundred.

Competition

A rash of imitators to Staples soon appeared on the market. The first of these was Office Depot, which was focused on the Southeast. By the end of 1988, Office Depot had 26 stores, Office Club had opened 15, Biz Mart had established 10, and Office Max around a dozen. More than a dozen other office supplies superstores had sprung up. Some of these businesses were financed by venture capitalists looking to

repeat the success with Staples, others were financed by established retailers, or even started by them. For example, Ben Franklin started Office Station in 1987, but shut it down in 1989 as it failed to gain traction.

Initially, most of the competitors focused in unique regions—Office Depot on the Southeast, Office Club on California, Office Max on the Midwest, BizMart on the Southwest—but as the number of entrants increased, head-to-head competition started to become more frequent. Stemberg's belief had always been that competition was inevitable, and that the winners in the competitive race would not necessarily be those that grew the fastest but those that executed best. It was this philosophy that underpinned Stemberg's insistence that the company should grow by focusing on key urban areas and achieving a critical mass of stores served by a central distribution system.

Not everyone agreed with this recipe for success. Office Depot did the opposite—the company grew as fast as possible, entering towns quickly to preempt competitors. Office Depot lacked the centralized distribution systems, but made up for that by locating in less expensive areas than Staples, persuading suppliers to ship directly to stores and keeping more backup inventory on the premises. Although this meant larger stores, the lower rental costs in Office Depot's markets offset this.

What soon became apparent is that the rash of entrants included a number of companies that simply could not execute. Very quickly a handful of competitors emerged in the forefront of the industry—Staples, Office Depot, Office Max, and Office Club. As the market leaders grew, they increasingly came into contact with each other. The result was price wars. These first broke out in California. Staples entered the market in 1990 and initially focused on pricing not against Office Club, but against Price Club. Although Price Club was a warehouse store selling food and general merchandise, it still had the largest share of the office supplies market in California. Staples positioned itself as having the same low prices as Price Club, but a wider selection of office supplies and no membership fee.

Todd Krasnow, the executive vice president of marketing at Staples, describes what happened next: "What we failed to realize was that Price Club was very worried about Office Club—and was pricing against Office Club. So when we went and matched Price Club, we were matching Office Club. And Office Club was saying: 'We are not going to let anybody have the same prices as us.'"[19] Office Club lowered its prices, causing Price Club to lower prices, and Staples followed. Not willing to be beat, Office Club cut prices again, and so they continued the spiral down. The price war drove profit margins down by as much as 8 percent.

Ultimately Krasnow noted, "We realized that by engaging in this price war, we were focusing on our competitors, not our customers. Our customers weren't paying attention to this spat. So we raised our prices a little. You feel like you're just doing absolutely the wrong thing, because your whole position is: We have the lowest price."[20] Be that as it may, Office Club and Price Club followed suit, and prices started to rise again. Ultimately the three companies carved out different price niches, each unwilling to be undercut on about twenty or so top-selling items, but in general, they were not the same items.

What happened in California also occurred elsewhere. When Office Max entered the Boston market in 1992, for example, a price war broke out again. There was an unanticipated effect this time because the price cuts apparently broadened the market by making buying from Staples attractive to customers with between twenty-five and one hundred employees, who previously bought directly from mail order and retail stationers.[21]

Ultimately Krasnow noted that price wars such as those that started to break out in California and Boston started to moderate. "We finally realized that it's not in any company's self-interest to have a price war because you can get lots of market share without having a price war. And having a price war among low priced competitors doesn't get you more market share. It doesn't serve any purpose."[22] Other factors that may have contributed toward more rational pricing behavior in the market were the strong economy of the 1990s and industry consolidation.

Industry Consolidation

At its peak in 1991, there were twenty-five chains in the office supply industry.[23] Industry consolidation started when some of the clones began to fall by the wayside, filing for bankruptcy. U.S. Office Supply, itself the result of a merger between two office supplies chains, filed for bankruptcy in 1991, as did Office Stop. Consolidation was also hastened by acquisitions. In 1991, Office Depot acquired Office Club, giving the primary rival of Staples more than twice the number of stores. For its part, Staples acquired HQ Office Supplies Warehouse in 1991, and in 1992, it purchased another smaller chain, Workplace.[24]

As these trends continued, by the mid 1990s it was apparent that three players were rising to dominance in the industry: Office Depot, Staples, and Office Max. By mid 1996, Office Depot led the industry with 539 stores, followed by Staples with 517 and Office Max with around 500 stores. In terms of revenues, Office Depot had a clear lead with $5.3 billion in 1996, Staples was second with $3.07 billion, and Office Max third with $2.6 billion. Staples remained concentrated in the Northeast and California, with a large number of stores in dense urban areas. Office Depot's stores were concentrated in the South, and the company continued to stay clear of congested cities. Office Max was still strongest in the Midwest.[25]

The consolidation phase peaked in September 1996 when Staples announced an agreement to purchase its larger rival, Office Depot, for $3.36 billion. The executives of the two companies had apparently been talking about merger possibilities for years, while continuing to pursue their own independent-growth strategies. If the merger went through, Tom Stemberg would step into the CEO role. The two companies sold the merger to the investment community on the basis of cost savings. The combined firm would have almost eleven hundred stores and revenues of $8.5 billion. The combination, Stemberg argued, would attain terrific economies of scale that would allow it to significantly lower costs, saving an estimated $4.9 billion over five years, including $2.2 billion in product cost savings.

In a move to preempt a possible investigation by the Federal Trade Commission (FTC), the companies claimed that since their stores focused on different territories, the combination would not reduce competition. They also noted that Staples still faced intense competition not only from Office Max, but also from the likes of Wal-Mart, Circuit City, and mail order outlets. Indeed, Stemberg claimed that the combined company would still only account for 5 percent of the total sales of office supplies in the United States.[26]

The FTC didn't buy the arguments, quickly started an investigation, and in May 1997 sought an injunction to block the deal. The FTC claimed that the deal would stifle competition and raise prices for office supplies, especially in those markets where the two firms competed head to head. To buttress its case, the FTC released a report of pricing data that showed that nondurable office supplies such as paper were 10 percent to 15 percent higher in markets where Staples faced no direct rivals. Staples claimed that the FTC's pricing surveys were done selectively and were biased.

In July 1997, a federal judge granted the FTC's request for an injunction to halt the merger. Staples realized that it was in a losing fight, and pulled its bid for Office Depot. But the failure had a silver lining—not anticipating much interference from the FTC, Office Depot had put most of its expansion plans on hold, opening just two stores in eight months. In comparison, Staples opened forty-three, allowing the company to close the gap between itself and its larger rival.

Staples's Evolving Strategy

Moving Into Small Towns

Stemberg has described Staples's initial strategy to deal with the high costs of doing business in the Northeast as follows: "Establish superstores that were smaller than most, save on rent and operating costs, cluster them in densely populated areas to justify paying for expensive advertisements, and stock the stores from a distribution center."[27] The drawback with this strategy, in retrospect, was that Staples ignored a lot of potentially lucrative markets in smaller towns. While Office Depot was barnstorming into towns with populations of just seventy-five thousand, Staples could not see how they made it pay. Surely towns of that size were just too small to support an office supplies superstore?

As it turned out, they were not. The mistake Staples made was to assume that a store would serve customers within a ten- to fifteen-minute drive. But in smaller cities, customers would drive much farther to get good prices. The revelation did not hit home until Staples opened its first store in Portland, Maine. With a population of two hundred thousand, the town was smaller than most areas focused on by Staples, but within a few months, the store was doing very well. To test the hypothesis, in 1992 and 1993 Staples opened stores in a number of smaller towns. The results were surprising. Many of the stores actually generated higher sales per square foot that those located in large cities. Sales were helped by the fact that in many of these small towns the only competitors were small "mom and pop" stationers, and that many small towns also lacked supermarket electronic retailers, such as Circuit City, selling low priced office equipment, allowing Staples to pick up a much larger

share of that business. Moreover, the lower rent, labor costs, advertising costs, and shrinkage made these stores significantly more profitable.

From that point on, Staples moved into small towns and suburban locations, where the same economics apply. Stemberg has described not moving into small towns earlier as "one of the dumbest mistakes I made." In 1994, some 10 percent of Staples stores were in small towns; by 1998, that figure had risen to 28 percent, and some of the most profitable stores in the Staples network were located in small towns.[28]

Selling Direct

Established as a retailer, Staples initially turned its back on customer requests for delivery and mail or telephone order service. The reason for doing this was simple: Staples saw itself as a low cost retailer, and a delivery service would probably raise costs. However, Staples competitors started to offer mail order and delivery service, and customers continued to ask for the service, so in 1988, Staples began to experiment with this.

Initially the experimentation was halfhearted. Store managers were not enthusiastic about supporting a delivery service that they believed decreased store sales, and Staples discouraged delivery by tacking a 5 percent delivery charge onto the order price. Moreover, the company questioned whether it could generate the volume of business to cover the costs of a delivery service and make a decent return on capital.

What changed this was a study undertaken for Staples by a management consulting firm. The study found that the customers who purchased via a catalog and required delivery were not always the same ones who brought directly from the store. While there was a lot of cross shopping, the mail order customers tended to be bigger and somewhat more interested in service, whereas those buying from the store were often buying for home offices. Staples also could not help but notice that its major rivals were offering a delivery service, and that business seemed to be thriving.

In 1991, Staples set up an independent business unit within the company to handle the mail/telephone order and delivery service, known as Contract and Commercial. The guts of this business unit was a division know as Staples Direct (it is now called Staples Business Delivery). The man put in charge of this business, Ronald Sargent, would ultimately replace Stemberg as CEO of Staples in 2003.

One issue that had to be dealt with was the potential conflict between Staples Direct and the stores. The stores didn't want to push business the way of Staples Direct because they would not get credit for the sale. As Sargent commented later, "We were like the bad guys inside Staples, because the feeling was that if customers got products delivered they wouldn't shop inside our stores."[29] To align incentives, Staples changed the compensation systems so that (a) the store would get credit if a delivery order was placed through the store, and (b) the annual bonus of store employees was partly based on how well they meet goals for generating delivery sales.

As Staples Direct started to grow, the company also discovered that the delivery infra-structure they put in place could be used to serve clients in addition to the company's established small business customers, which typically had less than 50 employees. Increasingly, medium-sized business (with 50 to 100 employees) and larger businesses with more than 100 employees started to utilize Staples Direct. To support this new business, Staples started to grow by acquisition, purchasing a number of regional stationary companies with established customers and delivery systems. Typically Staples kept the owners of these businesses on as Staples employees, often because they had long-established relationships with key accounts in large organizations such as Xerox, Ford, and Pepsi Cola. Staples, however, established a consistent product line, brand image, and computer and accounting systems across all of the acquisitions.

Between 1991 and 1996, Staples Direct grew from a $30 million business to almost $1 billion. As sales volume ramped up, Staples was able to get greater efficiencies out of its distribution network, which helped to drive down the costs of doing business through this channel. Staples used a network of regional distribution centers to hold an inventory of some 15,000 SKUs for delivery, compared with 8,000 SKUs in a typical store. In 1998, a web-based element was added to Staples Direct, Staples.com. Through the web or a catalog, Staples customers could get access to some 130,000 SKUs, many of which were shipped directly from manufacturers with Staples acting as an intermediary and consolidator.

To continue building the direct business, in 1988, Staples acquired Quill Corporation for $685 million in Staples stock. Established in 1956, Quill is a direct mail catalog business with a targeted approach to servicing the business products needs of around a million small- and medium-sized businesses in the United States. Quill differentiated itself through excellent customer service. Staples decided to let Quill keep its own organization, setting it up as a separate division within the Contract and Commercial business unit, but integrated Quill's purchasing with those of the rest of Staples to gain economies of the input side. Quill now operates under two brands—Staples National Advantage, which focuses on large multiregional businesses, and Staples Business advantage, which focuses on large- and medium-sized regional companies, and has the flexibility to handle smaller accounts (although these are mostly handled via Staples Direct). In justifying the acquisition of Quill, Stemberg noted that the direct business amounted to a $60 billion a year industry, but it was highly fragmented with the top eight players accounting for less than 20 percent of the market.[30]

By 2002, the combined delivery business had grown to become a $3.4 billion enterprise in its own right.

Going International

Staples's first foray into international markets occurred in the early 1990s when the company was approached by a Canadian retailer, Jack Bingleman, who wanted to start a Staples type chain north of the border. Bingleman also approached Office Depot and Office Max, but had a preference for Staples because of the close geographic proximity. Board members at Staples initially opposed any expansion into Canada, arguing that scarce resources should be dedicated toward growth in the much larger United States, but Stemberg liked Bingleman's vision, and pushed the idea. Ultimately, in 1991 Staples agreed to invest $2 million in Bingleman's startup for a 16 percent equity stake.

Known as Business Depot, the Canadian venture expanded rapidly, modeling itself after Staples. Between 1991 and 1994, the number of Canadian Business Depot stores expanded to 30 stores, and the enterprise turned profitable in 1993. In 1994, Staples announced an agreement to purchase Business Depot outright for $32 million.[31] By 2003, there were 215 stores in Canada.

The Canadian venture was soon followed by investments in Europe. Staples entered the U.K. market in 1992, partnering with Kingfisher PLC, a large U.K. retailer that operated home improvement and consumer electronics stores among other things. The Canadian venture had taught Staples that a local partner was extremely valuable. As one Staples executive noted later: "You absolutely cannot do it yourself. There are too many cultural impediments for you to know where the booby traps lie. In a retail startup, the most important task is to generate locations. There's no way a U.S. national can go into any country and generate the real estate it needs. That person will be chasing his tail for a long time."[32]

On the heels of entry into the United Kingdom, Staples purchased MAXI-Papier, a German company that was attempting to copy what Staples had done in the United States. This was followed by entry into the Netherlands and Portugal. By early 2003, Staples had 188 stores in Europe, 83 in the United Kingdom, 56 in Germany, 37 in the Netherlands, and 12 in Portugal. By 2002, the European operations were generating over a billion dollars in revenues, primarily through retail sales. In late 2002, Staples purchased the mail order business of a French company, Guilbert, for nearly $800 million, which boosted delivery sales in Europe from $50 million a year to $450 million a year almost overnight.[33]

Staples in 2003

In February 2002, Tom Stemberg announced that he was stepping down as CEO, and passing the baton on to Ron Sargent. Stemberg would remain on as chairman. Upon taking over as CEO, Sargent put the breaks on store expansion, declaring that Staples would open no more than 75 new stores a year, down from over 130 in 2000. He used the slowdown to refocus attention upon internal operating efficiencies. The product line within stores was rationalized, with Staples cutting back on the stocking of low margin items such as personal computers. He also set up a task force to look for ways to take every excess cent out of the cost structure. As a result, operating margins at Staples stores came in at 5.9 percent of sales in 2002, the best in the industry, and up from 4.5 percent in 2000.

Going forward, Sargent's task is to grow the top line. With the retail market for office supplies superstores now approaching saturation in the United States, Sargent has turned his attention to the business where he made his name, the direct delivery business. He points out that although the number of independent office supplies dealers is down to 6,000 from 15,000 a decade ago, the delivery market is still highly fragmented and very large. Ultimately Sargent believes that direct delivery from warehouses can be as big a business as Staples office supplies stores. He also sees huge potential for growth in Europe, which is the second largest office supplies market in the world and still years behind the United States in terms of consolidation.

At the same time, Staples continues to face strategic challenges. The retail market in the United States is now consolidated, and additional expansion by Staples is likely to bring it increasingly into head-to-head contact with Office Depot or Office Max. To compound matters, in mid 2003 Boise Cascade, the large wood and paper products company which has long had its own direct delivery business, purchased Office Max for $1.2 billion. Prior to the purchase, Office Max had 2002 sales of $4.8 billion against Staples's sales of $11.6 billion, and Office Depot's sales of $11.4 billion. The merger boosts the combined office supplies sales of the new company to $8.3 billion.

ENDNOTES

1. Stephen D. Solomon, "Born to Be Big," *Inc.* (June 1989): 94.
2. Value Line. Value Line Investment Survey, Staples, October 17, 2003.
3. Solomon, "Born to Be Big", page 96.
4. Tom Stemberg, *Staples for Success* (Santa Monica, CA: Knowledge Exchange, 1996).
5. Michael Barrier, "Tom Stemberg Calls the Office," *Nation's Business* (July 1990): 42.
6. Ibid., page 44.
7. Ibid., page 44.
8. Tom Stemberg and David Whiteford, "Putting a Stop to Mom and Pop," *Fortune Small Business* (October 2002): 39.
9. Ibid., page 40.
10. Stemberg, *Staples for Success*.
11. Stemberg and Whiteford, "Putting a Stop to Mom and Pop," page 40.
12. Stemberg, *Staples for Success*, page 17.
13. Stemberg and Whiteford, "Putting a Stop to Mom and Pop," page 41.
14. Solomon, "Born to Be Big," pages 94 and 95.
15. Stemberg, *Staples for Success*, page 24.
16. Ibid., page 27.
17. Stemberg and Whiteford, "Putting a Stop to Mom and Pop," page 40.
18. Solomon, "Born to Be Big," page 100.
19. Stemberg, *Staples for Success*, page 97.
20. Ibid.
21. Norm Alster, "Penney Wise," *Forbes*, February 1, 1993, pages 48–51.
22. Stemberg, *Staples for Success*, page 97.
23. Renee Covion Rouland, "And Then There Were Three," *Discount Merchandiser* (December 1994): 27.

24. Leland Montgomery. "Staples: Buy the Laggard," *Financial World*, November 9, 1993, page 22; Anonymous, "The New Plateau in Office Supplies," *Discount Merchandiser* (November 1991): 50–54.

25. James S. Hirsch and Eleena de Lisser, "Staples to Acquire Archrival Office Depot," *Wall Street Journal*, September 5, 1996, page A3.

26. Joseph Pereira and John Wilke, "Staples Faces FTC in Antitrust Showdown on Merger," *Wall Street Journal*, May 19, 1997, page B4.

27. Stemberg, *Staples for Success*, page 128.

28. William M. Bulkeley, "Office Supplies Superstores Find Bounty in the Boonies," *Wall Street Journal*, September 1, 1998, page B1.

29. William C. Symonds, "Thinking Outside the Big Box," *Business Week*, August 11, 2003, page 62.

30. William M. Bulkeley, "Staples, Moving Beyond Superstores, Will Buy Quill for $685 Million in Stock," *Wall Street Journal*, April 8, 1998, page A1.

31. Steff Gelston, "Staples Goes on Buying Spree to Acquire Business Depot, National Office Supply Company," *Boston Herald*, January 25, 1994, page 24.

32. Stemberg, *Staples for Success*, page 90.

33. Symonds, "Thinking Outside the Big Box," pages 62–64.

Gap International: A Specialty Apparel Retailer

This case was prepared by Robert J. Mockler, St. John's University.

Introduction

On September 26, 2002, Gap Inc. announced that Paul Pressler, fifteen-year veteran of The Walt Disney Company and chairman of its global theme park and resorts division, had been named president and chief executive officer of the company. Pressler succeeded outgoing CEO Millard Drexler, who had announced in May his plans to retire as soon as his replacement was hired [Kaiser, 2002]. Earlier that month, Gary Muto, former president of Banana Republic division, was appointed the new president of the Gap division of Gap Inc. They were both faced with the inevitable task of developing an effective differentiating enterprise-wide strategy if Gap was to survive and prosper against aggressive competition over the intermediate and long-term future.

Gap Inc. sold its private label clothing in its own retail stores only and to no other retailer, wholesaler, or independent distributor. The three main brands/ divisions were Banana Republic, Gap, and Old Navy, as shown in Figure 1.

The three divisions had a presence in Japan, United Kingdom, France, Canada, and Germany, but the majority of the stores were based in the United States. Each brand targeted a different type of customer with

Copyright © 2003 by Robert J. Mockler. This case was prepared by Robert J. Mockler, St. John's University, as the basis for class discussion rather than to illustrate either effective or ineffective handling of an administrative situation. Reprinted by permission of Robert J. Mockler. All rights reserved. For the most recent financial results of the company discussed in this case, go to http://finance.yahoo.com, input the company's stock symbol, and download the latest company report from its homepage.

varying income level and lifestyle. Each division was an independent strategic business unit. Gap Inc. had had major problems for more than two years after an ill-fated foray into trendy clothes in early 2000 that had alienated its traditional customers. In September 2002, it reported its twenty-eighth straight month of declines in sales at stores open at least one year. The company's problems were reflected in its stock price. The stock reached its highest price of $51.68 on February 4, 2000. On October 8, 2002, the stock closed at $9.59, as shown in Figure 2.

All three divisions were having problems, but the Gap division was in the worst condition. For the past two years, since 2000, it had been struggling with problems resulting from overexpansion and misjudgment of fashion trends. The Gap division's stores went from casual to trendy, with bold colors, low-cut jeans, and teeny tops. New product lines were no longer appealing to regular customers, and they did not attract new ones. Overexpansion added to the "wrong-merchandise problem" by creating the effect of cannibalism of sales; individual stores sold less and less with operating costs going up.

Gap was no exception in its industry. According to the U.S. Department of Commerce, sales at specialty apparel stores rose only 0.7 percent in 2001. Family clothing stores had the best performance, with sales up 1.6 percent. Sales at women's apparel stores fell 2.5 percent, and those at men's stores declined 1.8 percent [Standard & Poor's, 2002A].

In light of all the problems, Muto and Pressler had to come up with a future strategy for the Gap division, including especially decisions in the areas of product

FIGURE 1

Brands/Divisions of Gap Inc.

mix, including colors, fabrics, fashions, and quality. Gap also had to identify its customer base. For example, decisions such as staying with the same customer base or expanding to the plus sizes or extended plus-sizes market had to be made. The main question to be resolved was how to differentiate Gap from its competition and to achieve a winning edge over competitors within intensely competitive, rapidly changing immediate, intermediate, and long-term time frames.

Industry and Competitive Market: Retail

Retailing includes all business activities that involve the sale of goods and services to consumers for personal, family, or household use. It is largely a high-volume, low-margin business. It can be divided into two main categories: general retail and specialty retail, as shown in Figure 3. General retail includes department stores and general merchandisers, and specialty retail includes home furnishing stores, building supplies stores, office supplies stores, consumer electronics stores, miscellaneous goods stores, and apparel stores.

The year 2001 was challenging for retailers. The difficulties had their roots in the confluence of three trends. First, U.S. consumers had a wide choice of stores competing for their business, so the industry remained highly competitive. Second, consumer spending was growing slowly due to the economic slowdown. Consumers were able to choose among

FIGURE 2

Gap Inc.'s Five-Year Stock History

Source: CBS Market Watch (2002), [Online], **http://cbs.marketwatch.com/tools/quotes/intchart.asp?symb=gps&siteid=mktw&dist=mktwqn**, accessed October 9.

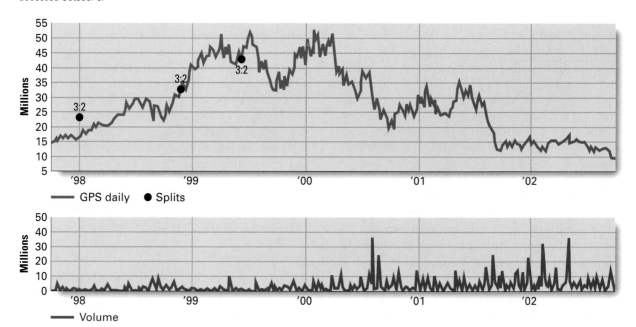

FIGURE 3

The Retail Industry

more places to shop than ever before, but at the same time had less interest in shopping. Finally, value had become crucial. Consumers moved to shopping at lower-priced, value-driven retailers, which resulted in most department store chains suffering [Standard & Poor's, 2002A].

Retail: General

General retailers included department stores and general merchandisers.

Department Stores The U.S. government defines department stores as establishments selling the following lines of merchandise: furniture, home furnishings, appliances, and radio and television sets; a general line of apparel for the family; and household linens and dry goods [Standard & Poor's, 2002A]. Most department stores, however, stopped offering certain categories of merchandise, including major appliances, electronics, toys, sporting goods, furniture, and photographic supplies, as margins on those lines had declined. In addition, such items took up large amounts of floor space, tied up capital in inventory costs, or required more aggressive pricing than department store retailing allowed. Meanwhile, selections of women's apparel, accessories, cosmetics, and fragrances, which typically generate higher margins and have a more upscale image, have been greatly expanded.

General merchandisers have taken over the department store's old role as purveyors of everything. Department stores' market share continued to erode as consumers shopped more at discount stores (general merchandisers). According to the Department of Commerce, in 1992, department stores accounted for 50 percent of general merchandise, apparel, and furniture sales. By 2001, department stores' share of those sales had fallen to 37 percent, while general merchandise stores share reached 32 percent, up from 25 percent in 1992 [Standard & Poor's, 2002A]. Department stores learned their lesson. Inventory levels were being reduced and expenses were being cut. Managers were examining the business with a more careful eye toward demographic changes and remerchandising departments accordingly, appealing to a young customer and focusing on the fast growing junior market. Major department stores included Macy's (Federated Department Stores), J.C. Penney (Penney Co.), Sears, and Nordstrom.

General Merchandisers The term "general merchandiser" applies to stores carrying a much broader assortment of merchandise than most department stores. They strive to be all things to all people by carrying broad assortments of merchandise, catering to a value-conscious consumer who demands low prices every day. The term applies mainly to discounters such as Target, Wal-Mart, or Kmart. In times of recession, such as in 2002, many customers were willing to sacrifice brand names and even quality for lower prices. As value became increasingly important for many customers, discounters became competition for department stores and specialty retailers [Standard & Poor's, 2002A].

Retail: Specialty

The specialty retailing industry was comprised of merchants that sold a single category of merchandise, as well as those carrying a few closely related categories of products. Retail specialty stores included home furnishing stores, building supplies stores, office supplies stores, electronics stores, miscellaneous goods stores (including sporting goods, pets, books, and toys), and apparel stores.

Home Furnishing Stores Retail home furnishing stores were divided into two categories: large-sized superstores and small specialty stores. Superstores carried a broad assortment of merchandise for living rooms, bedrooms, dining rooms, kitchens, and bathrooms. The main competitors included Bed Bath and Beyond, Linens and Things, Pier 1 Imports, and IKEA. Smaller specialty stores carried a limited assortment of goods within a specified niche, and were usually more expensive than the big competitors. This segment of the market was highly influenced by the housing market and interest rates. In a low interest–rate environment, consumers were more likely to buy new homes and spend money on furniture, new appliances, and home improvement.

Building Supplies Stores The building supply segment was dominated by a few large warehouse stores that allowed customers to buy products for their homes at a discount from the prices found at traditional hardware stores. Two main competitors in this segment were Home Depot and Lowes.

Office Supplies Stores Office supplies stores consisted of stores that sold office supplies and equipment that served the needs of businesses and individuals. Main competitors in this segment included Staples and Office Depot.

Consumer Electronics Stores Consumer electronic stores sold home electronic goods such as televisions, stereos, or videocassette recorders. The market was becoming saturated. In 2001, the popularity of digital videodisk (DVD) players, digital cameras, and home theater systems were boosting the sales of those stores. Main competitors included Best Buy, Circuit City, and Radio Shack.

Miscellaneous Goods Stores Miscellaneous stores included toy stores, sporting goods stores, pet stores, and bookstores.

Toy Stores Toy stores included Toys "R" Us, K-B Toys, and FAO Schwarz. The market for toys has been gradually changing. Specialty stores have been losing their market shares to discounters such as Target or Wal-Mart that offered a wide assortment of toys at highly competitive prices.

Sporting Goods Stores Sporting goods stores consisted of stores that sold products to amateur athletes. The assortment of goods included football, baseball, golf, tennis, ski, fishing, and camping equipment. The main competitors included The Sports Authority and Dick's Sporting Goods. As with toy stores, sporting goods have also been facing increasing competition from the discount stores.

Pet Stores Pet stores sold not only pets, but also food and other supplies for pets. PETsMART and Petco Animal Supplies dominated this segment. Both chains also offered services, such as training programs or veterinary services. As the pet population was increasing, both chains were adding more stores.

Bookstores Bookstores were being heavily influenced by e-commerce. The main competitors included Barnes & Noble and Borders Group. They faced strong competition not only from Internet retailers such as Amazon, but also from discounters such as Target or Wal-Mart.

Apparel Stores Apparel stores included retailers that sold clothing and accessories. The main competitors included Gap Inc., Limited Brands, Abercrombie and Fitch Co., Hennes & Mauritz (H&M), and American Eagle Outfitters. Besides competing against each other, they also faced competition from department stores and general merchandise discounters.

Apparel specialty retailers are the focus of this study, and are discussed in detail in the following sections.

Industry and Competitive Market: Specialty Apparel Retail

For specialty apparel retailers, the beginning of the twenty-first century was a difficult time. According to the Department of Commerce, sales rose only 0.7 percent in 2001. Although consumers bought more of their apparel from specialty stores (23 percent of annual spending on clothes) than from any other type of retail establishment (18 percent department stores, and 14 percent for general merchandisers), their sales were still rather weak. Apparel purchases accounted for almost 3.2 percent of disposable income in 2001, down from 3.5 percent in 1991, and

3.7 percent in 1981. In addition, prices had fallen in each of the prior three years. Therefore, stores had to sell more items just to stay even with the total sales dollars of the prior year. Many retailers suffered from overexpansion and misjudgment of fashion trends. Throughout the segment the same-store sales and margins were declining [Standard & Poor's, 2002B].

How the Industry Segment Works: The Essence of the Business Process

The industry under study sells a variety of clothing, accessories, and body care products to individual customers of all genders, ages, sizes, and income levels, as shown in Figure 4. Their decisions to buy are influenced by a number of different factors such as price, style, quality of the fabric, and color.

Products are sold through retail stores, catalogs, and companies' websites. All customer groups have different preferences as to where they like to buy. A number of factors influence that decision. For some, convenience or speed may be important; others like to spend time doing their shopping and enjoy the experience.

Retailers have a choice of manufacturing their goods in-house or outsourcing the production to outside vendors. All firms in the segment use a number of ways of advertising their products, from TV and radio commercials, to outdoor billboards, newspapers and magazines, to advertisements on the Internet. The industry takes advantage of the available technology in different ways both to reach the consumer and to improve operating efficiency. This is a fiercely competitive market domestically as well as internationally.

According to a recent study by the America's Research Group of South Carolina, about 73 percent of consumers surveyed said they believed that stores within the same retail category tend to look alike. In addition, the product mix from store to store was virtually identical [Standards & Poor's, 2002B]. As a result most simple expansion strategies, such as adding new store locations, could no longer guarantee sustainable revenue growth for a company. Rather, sales growth has become contingent upon connecting with target customers and building a distinct image. Specialty retailers that built strong brand names—such as Gap, Limited Brands Inc., or Abercrombie & Fitch—were likely to take away market share from those that did not. Those that concentrated on strong brand management were also likely to reap the rewards of increased customer loyalty, thus improving long-term growth prospects. If a company was able to build its retail store name into a brand, it would also usually be able to leverage that name into other categories. Gap and Limited were good examples.

The participants in the industry included specialty retailers, such as Gap, Limited, H&M, American Eagle Outfitters, and Abercrombie and Fitch. They compete not only with each other but also with department stores, such as Macy's and J.C. Penney, and general merchandise discounters, such as Target and Wal-Mart.

Products

Specialty apparel retailers sold a wide variety of clothing, accessories, and body care products.

Clothing Clothing sold at specialty stores included loungewear, sleepwear, underwear, activewear, jeans, dressy wear, and casual wear.

> *Loungewear and sleepwear.* Loungewear and sleepwear included pajamas, robes, pants, hooded sweatshirts, and T-shirts.

FIGURE 4

Specialty Apparel Retail Segment Business Model

Underwear. Underwear included tank tops, t-shirts, briefs, boxers, panties, and bras.

Activewear. Activewear included jackets, hooded sweatshirts, sweatshirts, sweatpants, t-shirts, and tank tops.

Jeans. Jeans were available in many styles and colors.

Dressy wear. Dressy wear included coats, jackets, blazers, pants, dresses, shirts, blouses, and skirts.

Casual wear. Casual wear, or weekend wear as some sources referred to it, included shirts, pants, blouses, sweaters, jackets, skirts, capri pants, and skirts.

Accessories Accessories included shoes, socks, bags, handbags, backpacks, belts, wallets, jewelry, hats, scarves, gloves, and mittens.

Body Care Products Many apparel retailers added body care products to their product mix. They included lotions, body mists, fragrances, soaps, shower gels, and makeup lines, to name few.

In addition to having a strong brand image, having "the right merchandise, in the right place, at the right time" was a major success factor. It meant not only right fashions but also right colors, high quality, and durable fabrics. Although buildings, property, and equipment usually exceeded inventory value in dollar terms, merchandise inventories were a retailer's most important asset. Inventory generated sales were the key determinant of a retailer's success or failure, profitability, or loss. Although consumer buying decisions were influenced by a variety of retailing variables, such as price, location, and service, it's primarily the merchandise in the store that drove consumers to shop there and that built customer loyalty over time.

Companies needed to keep adequate inventories of merchandise. When a retailer correctly anticipated the next hot fashion trend, the merchandise sold quickly. It was very important that a store had enough of the popular product. When "wrong" merchandise, which did not appeal to customers, occupied shelf space, sales plummeted. In that case the retailer had to mark its price down to make room for new—and hopefully more salable—items. Low-turnover products could not occupy the valuable shelf space for too long. Merchants always planned for some sales, but excess markdowns eroded profitability.

It was also important for the companies to have good customer service via more appealing product displays, improved customer-friendly, understandable signage, and highly trained employees able to provide any requested information regarding the products sold in the stores.

Customers

Specialty apparel retailers catered to women and men of all ages, sizes, and income levels. For specialty retailers, as noted earlier, stores had to be stocked with goods that appealed to those customers. To build an appropriate business strategy, retailers had to anticipate changes in customers' needs and desires over time. Even more important than the number of people was the composition of that population—especially for specialty retailers, which often targeted a specific age group for their products.

Gender Apparel retailers catered to both women and men.

Women. Women accounted for 80 percent of household spending and 83 percent of all purchases [Reyes, 2002]. Approximately 72 percent of American women worked full time, which for apparel retailers was good news because it meant more income at the disposal of the most important customer [Stein, 2000]. It also meant that they needed to buy a new wardrobe suitable for their work. Women bought not only clothes for themselves, but also for their kids. In addition, they had a great influence on what their husbands were buying. Quality and affordability were important. Also women were driving the Internet sales. In 1999, the percentage of online shoppers who were women had jumped to 38 percent from 29 percent, and was continually rising [Tedeschi, 1999].

Men. Men were increasingly purchasing casual clothes. They were spending a growing percentage of their apparel money on casual wear, because of the changes in the dressing codes for many white-collar workers. For men the important issues were quality and durability of the products, as well as reliable customer service and product information. Return policies of the stores were also very important, a success factor in dealing with all types of customers.

Age For analysis purposes, customers can be divided into five major age groups: seniors, the baby boomers, Generation X, Generation Y, and little emperors [Standard & Poor's, 2002B].

Seniors. Seniors were comprised of individuals sixty-five-years old and older. They accounted for more than 12 percent of the U.S. population. When the baby boomers would begin turning sixty-five, the number of senior citizens was expected to swell, and was assumed to comprise nearly 15 percent of the U.S. population by 2015, as shown in Figure 5. Companies had to take the aging of the population into consideration. Successful store designs had to include features that catered to the demands and needs of an aging population, such as brighter lighting, larger letters on labels and signs, and better security. Loungewear, sleepwear, underwear, activewear, and casual wear were popular with seniors. They also bought accessories and body care products.

Baby Boomers. The baby boom generation, comprising individuals born between 1946 and 1964, constituted some 77 million Americans. They accounted for about 23 percent of the population. As the baby boomers moved into adulthood and formed households, they fueled much of the boom in retail sales in the 1970s and 1980s. Over

time, their spending habits have affected various retail categories. The boomers were in their forties and fifties in the early 2000s. Their priorities have shifted to tuition payments for children, saving for retirement, and caring for elderly parents. Although people in this age group continued to spend on furnishings and accessories for their homes, fashion had become less important. Baby boomers spent money on loungewear, sleepwear, underwear, activewear, dressy wear, casual wear, accessories, and body care products.

Generation X was comprised of approximately 45 million people born between 1965 and 1976. They accounted for about 15 percent of the U.S. population. These individuals began reaching adulthood in the mid 1980s. Although they have remained single longer than previous generations, they were beginning to form families. Home improvement and home furnishing retailers were likely to target this group. Members of this generation bought sleepwear, underwear, activewear, dressy wear, casual wear, jeans, accessories, and body care products.

FIGURE 5

U.S. Population Projections

Age Group	2002 Number (Thous.)	2002 % of Total	2010 Number (Thous.)	2010 % of Total	2015 Number (Thous.)	2015 % of Total
Under 5 yrs.	18,944	6.8	20,099	6.7	21,179	6.8
5 to 14 yrs.	39,938	14.2	39,345	13.1	40,549	13.0
15 to 19 yrs.	20,163	7.2	21,668	7.2	20,892	6.7
20 to 24 yrs.	19,438	6.9	21,151	7.1	21,748	7.0
25 to 29 yrs.	17,386	6.2	19,849	6.6	20,765	6.6
30 to 34 yrs.	19,536	7.0	19,002	6.3	20,484	6.6
35 to 39 yrs.	21,236	7.6	19,039	6.3	19,442	6.2
40 to 44 yrs.	22,988	8.2	20,404	6.8	19,346	6.2
45 to 49 yrs.	21,021	7.5	22,227	7.4	20,057	6.4
50 to 54 yrs.	18,240	6.5	21,934	7.3	21,929	7.0
55 to 64 yrs.	26,113	9.3	35,429	11.8	39,919	12.8
65 yrs. & over	35,303	12.6	39,715	13.2	45,959	14.7
All ages	280,306	100.0	299,862	100.0	312,268	100.0

Source: Standard & Poor's (2002A), "Retailing: General," [Online], **http://www.netadvantage.standardpoor.com/**, accessed September 26.

Generation Y. According to the Census Bureau, about 72 million Americans were born between 1977 and 1994, representing about 25 percent of the population. Members of this group were becoming young adults and teenagers. This group is known as Generation Y. Their numbers were good news for retailers. Teenagers typically did much of the household shopping and had influence on spending by their parents. Teens decided for themselves where to spend their money. Much of their spending, over $200 billion in 2001, went toward clothing items, such as jeans, activewear, dressy wear, casual wear, and accessories. They also bought body care products [Standard & Poor's, 2002B].

For a retailer to be successful with members of Generation X and Generation Y, it had to adopt the changes in fashion trends quickly.

Little Emperors. According to the Census Bureau, the population of children younger than five years of age reached 18.9 million in 2001, up from 16.3 million in 1980, and was expected to keep climbing over the next decade. To tap into this growing customer base, well-known specialty retailers have extended their product lines into infant and children's clothing. For example, Gap sold to these markets via its GapKids and Baby-Gap outlets; the Talbots Inc. operated Talbots Kids and added infants' clothing as well [Standard & Poor's, 2002B].

Size The customers in the specialty apparel market were divided into three main groups. Sizes 0 to 14, sizes 16 to 26, also called plus sizes, and sizes 28 to 34, called extended plus sizes. The first section of the market was already highly saturated, but plus sizes and extended plus sizes presented an opportunity for the competitors in that segment. Customers were looking for comfortable, stylish, and durable clothes. No successful company could afford to miss that opportunity. Even as concerns were growing about the health consequences of rising obesity in the United States, it still was a very large and potentially highly lucrative market [Ellison, 2002].

Income Specialty apparel stores targeted all income levels. Consumers were divided into three groups: high income, middle income, and lower income [DeNavas-Walt, 2002].

High-income. Twenty percent of all households that had the highest income of at least $83,500 during 2001 tended to be family households that included two or more earners, lived in the suburbs of a large city, and had a working householder between 35 and 54 years old [DeNavas-Walt, 2002]. For those consumers quality, brand name, customer service, and convenience of shopping mattered the most. Since most of those customers worked full time, time was also personally important. Consumers seemed more strapped for time than ever, and shopping became less of a fun pastime than it was in the 1980s. Research indicated that consumers were attempting to limit the time they spent shopping and looked to buy what they needed as quickly as possible, rather than scanning the mall in search of the perfect item. To satisfy consumer demand for convenience, retailers had to provide a full range of merchandise, speedy checkout, and generally good customer service which included sufficient number of sales representatives being able to answer questions about product selection, quality, prices, and availability. For specially retailers, the upside of this trend was that shoppers were spending more money per visit to the store, as their time constraints made their shopping ventures more purposeful. This was, however, true for all income levels.

Middle-income. Sixty percent of American households belonged to the middle-income group. Most of them lived in metropolitan areas; more than 70 percent were family households with either one or two earners [DeNavas-Walt, 2002]. High quality and affordability were the most important for these customers. In addition, the keys to success mentioned in the high-income customers' section applied to middle-income customers as well.

Lower-income. Twenty percent of all households had the lowest income of around $18,000 during 2001, and tended to be living in a city. Many included an elderly householder who lived alone and did not work [DeNavas-Walt, 2002]. These consumers were extremely price conscious. Sales and seasonal price reductions were important to them.

A successful company in this retail segment had to offer competitive prices. "Value," a subjective term that often connoted low prices, became increasingly important. This was distinctly different from the attitudes of the 1980s when high prices seemed synonymous with high quality. In the twenty-first century, the shopper who bought expensive jewelry at Tiffany & Co. was just as likely to purchase commodity goods at a BJ's Wholesale Club. This change in spending habits appeared to be a permanent shift in behavior. Another change was that more consumers tended to wait for sales before making their purchases [Standard & Poor's, 2002A].

Another very important trend for the specialty retailers was the increasing popularity of store credit cards. The ease of obtaining credit was driving sales for most retailers. In addition, many retailers offered their own credit cards. Consumer debt levels had continued to rise. According to the Federal Reserve, U.S. household debt at the end of the fourth quarter of 2001 represented 14.3 percent of disposable personal income, including 7.93 percent in consumer loans and 6.37 percent in mortgage payments, as shown in Figure 6. Successful companies had to take advantage of this trend by providing valuable customers with store credit cards.

Consumers were spending a growing percentage of their apparel money on casual wear, particularly in the United States where more than half of the country's white-collar workers were wearing casual clothing to work on a daily basis. While this trend has been troublesome for department stores and men's specialty stores, which have watched their sales of men's suits plummet, it has been a boon of sorts for casual-apparel specialty outlets such as The Gap, Abercrombie & Fitch, and American Eagle Outfitters.

Sales/Distribution

Specialty apparel retailers sold their products through retail stores, catalogs, and websites.

Retail Stores   The ability to obtain prime store locations was key to any specialty retailer's success. Retailers had two choices: lease stores (as most did) or opt to own the real estate. The decision about whether to buy or lease was made only after a careful financial analysis of all the options. When a company bought real estate, it had to have the capital to pay the purchase price. Such purchases were financed either by obtaining a loan or by using currently available funds. In the case of leasing, the retailer paid a yearly rental fee. Both leasing and ownership had their pros and cons. Leasing could be restrictive in regard to subleases, store expansion, and the ability to close unprofitable stores. On the plus side, leases eventually expired and thus gave retailers the flexibility to relocate or close units. To finance a real estate purchase, a company had to be in good financial

FIGURE 6

Household Debt

Source: Board of Governors of the Federal Reserve System (2002), "Monetary Policy Report to the Congress," July 16, [Online], **http://www.federalreserve.gov/boarddocs/ hh/2002/July/FullReport.pfd/**, accessed October 8.

shape, with cash on its balance sheet and ample borrowing power.

Specialty retailers used both stand-alone stores and shopping mall locations. According to a recent study by *Management Horizons*, the number of trips to the mall has decreased 50 percent since the early 1990s. In 1980, mall visits were 4.6 per month, but dropped to 1.6 per month as early as 1995. The number of stores visited per trip had dropped from seven to three. According to Kurt Salmon Associates, more than half of consumers surveyed said that they shop less often and that shopping is a "hassle." One of the main reasons for this decline was the time pressure faced by Americans. Americans were going to the mall less. When they shopped, they were generally looking for a specific item [Barta et al., 1999].

Successful specialty retailers used information about customer shopping habits to improve store layout and design, even to the point of "market basket analysis," which involved identifying product pairs or groups that tend to be purchased together, and then stocking those items next to each other in the store. Goods displays and use of mannequins to provide the customers with inspiration about how they could match and combine available products was also important.

Merchandise shipping and receiving were a crucial part of the retail industry's operations. Carefully managing the way inventory was ordered, transported, received, distributed, reordered—and generally monitored—was a driving factor in lowering costs. Retailers generally operated one or more distribution centers that served stores in a particular region. Localization of the centers was very important. As a retailer expanded into new regions, additional distribution facilities were needed. In efficient distribution centers, merchandise was scanned via bar coding equipment; this process was almost totally automated. Throughout the distribution center, automated conveyance systems allowed for the flow of merchandise. Merchandise was stored until it was picked up for distribution and sent to stores. This automation helped to minimize the retailer's overall inventory levels while maintaining optimal in-stock positions at the store level.

Customer service was very important for specialty retailers. As a result, all competitors paid considerable attention to the training of their store employees. Sales representatives were trained not only in how to assist customers, but they also had to learn everything there was to know about the products. They learned about the selection, the quality, the fabrics, the availability of items, the sizes available, and the like. They were trained to talk to the customers in a way that would help them get to know the customer, so they could offer him/her the right product.

Catalogs Many specialty retailers used catalogs to sell their products. The key here was to get to know the customers through the data gathering, so the catalogs were sent to those customers likely to make a purchase. It was also important that the process of ordering the products was simple. Speedy delivery of the products was also important. Another crucial factor was low shipping and handling fees. Many customers got discouraged by high costs of shipping and handling and ended up not buying the products for that reason. This was also true for online shoppers.

Websites Due to the Internet, the majority of specialty retailers were able to make their products available to a wider range of customers 24/7. Websites were not only another way for the consumers to make a purchase. It was also a way for the company to get to know the customer. Safety and simplicity of online shopping were very important. Many companies allowed their customers to return the items ordered online in their retail stores. The option of picking up items ordered online in the stores was, however, not frequent.

A study by the National Retail Federation found that 68 percent of any particular company's catalog shoppers had also shopped at the company's stores. Among a retailer's online shoppers, 59 percent had also made purchases in the store, and 43 percent shopped from the retailer's catalog [Lipke, 2000]. Successful specialty retailers transformed themselves into multichannel retailers. It was very important that the customers felt that the three channels were part of one big entity [Hansell, 2002]. The information about the customers gathered in any of those channels should be used wherever the customer was making a purchase. Integrated data-collection efforts were a key. New analytic systems, such as Customer-Centric from SPSS Inc. or MerchantReach from IBM, made the integration possible. Using a process called ETLM (Extract, Transport, Load, Manage), which extracted, transported, loaded, and managed company's existing data stores into a single, comprehensive data warehouse, these systems provided a full view of a customer. When a customer's credit card was run through the system, their past purchases from the store, the website, or company's catalog were analyzed, and a sales suggestion would appear on the register's screen [Lipke, 2000].

Manufacturing

Retailers could choose between manufacturing the products they sold or outsourcing the production to vendors.

In-House Due to the high cost of manufacturing in-house, virtually all specialty retailers outsourced the production of their products. In most cases, the retailers provided the designs for the products themselves.

Outsourcing Due to the high costs of manufacturing in-house, most retailers outsourced the production of their products.

Retailers were dependent on suppliers to provide a steady and reliable supply of product. Disruptions in supply, including those due to manufacturers' product quality, which could differ from the quality agreed on when the retailer was ordering the items, or any other issues, could have a disastrous effect on the retailers' sales. Higher than expected demand could also place a strain on retailers. It was crucial for a retailer to have established high standards when selecting vendors. Close and continuous monitoring of vendors was also very important. Most retailers had a separate department within the company that dealt with vendors. Employees of the retailer would evaluate and monitor vendors' facilities on a daily basis. They conducted health and safety inspections, checked sewing machines for required features and safety guards, reviewed payroll records, and interviewed workers.

Advertising/Promotion

Specialty retailers have been using all means of advertising their products to reach the customers. Companies have used television, print, outdoor, and the Internet.

Television Most specialty retailers advertised on television. It was a very important channel of promotion because for many people it was the main, if not only, source of information. Through television ads retailers not only promoted their products but also built their brand names. Selection of highly watched network channels was important. Also crucial was the time that the commercial would appear and the type of show during which it would be shown. The financial situation of a retailer was a key to success here since this was the most expensive channel of advertising.

Print Specialty retailers used a number of magazines to advertise their brands in. Depending on what type of customer they wanted to reach, they would turn to the type of magazine the target customers would typically read. Retailers also advertised in daily newspapers, but those ads were used more to inform about sales and other events than to help build the brand name.

Outdoor Outdoor posters and billboards were used by many specialty retailers to promote sales and new products, announce new store locations, or help build a strong brand name. Location was a key. To be effective, billboards were located in areas of high traffic or close to the new store location announced by the billboard.

Internet As the Internet became more popular, the need to use it as a means of advertising became clear. Internet ads were used to promote new products or to announce a sale or other event. The main use of the Internet for the specialty retailers was, however, branding. It was achieved through a variety of means, such as banners or pop-up ads. People browsing the Internet often stared at a screen for several seconds while a page downloaded, so an ad that appeared at the top of the page, or in a window covering the page, could have had a significant impact on a viewer [Murray, 2001]. The key was to select the right web pages to advertise on. Getting to know the potential customer and that customer's interests was also a key success factor.

Successful specialty retailers realized how information about their customers could be used to compete. Establishing one-to-one relationships with customers so a retailer was able to cater to their needs and desires and thus build customer loyalty was very important. Customer-driven marketing initiatives, or data-mining efforts, served to boost customer loyalty in the tightening retail market. Retailers gathered information about their customers in different ways, varying from data collection at the cash register to development of customer-loyalty programs that tracked spending habits through the use of sign-in forms on their e-commerce sites. Credit cards, warranty registrations, or gift registries were also an opportunity to collect customer data. Website users were asked about their age, gender, household income, hobbies, names of stores they liked to shop in, marital status, and other demographic information. The information gathered was used in a variety of ways. As specialty retailers gained a clearer understanding of their customers' needs, they were able to avoid development of low-demand products and step up production and orders for items that held better promise. It was, however, very important to effectively utilize the information and feedback from the customers.

Regardless of the channel used, one of the most important tasks that retailers were facing when advertising was communicating a clear message. Advertisements needed to be clear and understandable, so that the message they conveyed would not confuse customers in any way.

Strong brand was very important for specialty retailers. According to Richard S. Tedlow, a professor of business administration at the Harvard Business School, brand is a "promise" of a relationship between the product and the user [Hazel, 1999]. A strong brand promised that customers would be happy with the product they bought. As a result, high quality of product was essential. Unique design of the stores was also very important. Many companies improved their image, and built their brand names through charitable activities. By doing so, they made the customers familiar with the brand names. Competitors were sponsoring cultural and sports events. They were also helping to fund many organizations committed to different issues, such as the environment, education, health, and helping underprivileged kids.

Geographic Region

Specialty apparel retailers operated in domestic and international markets. Most large competitors had some kind of presence abroad.

Domestic Domestically, specialty retailers have to be present in major U.S. cities. Overexpansion, however, had to be avoided, because as the experience of Limited or Gap showed it could lead to cannibalism of sales. It was also important for the retailers to be present in densely populated suburbs, where the potential shopping traffic was high. It was, however, crucial for any specialty retailer to carefully select malls in which to locate their outlets. Presence in a poor quality mall could damage the brand name of a retailer.

International In light of the mature and oversaturated markets in the most developed countries of the world and the accompanying competitive pressures, the majority of specialty retailers operating in more saturated markets such as the United States, Canada, Europe, and Japan were pursuing expansion in faster-growing international markets. Expanding information technologies enabled retailers to manage globally. Improved economic efficiency, increased competition, economic growth, and increased consumer purchasing power have made emerging markets such as China, Latin America, or Central Europe attractive for the retailers. International expansion allowed specialty retailers to reduce their dependency on regional economies by spreading risks across economic areas, and further provided specialized products and targeted untapped niche markets throughout the world.

Global expansion was not possible without significant investment; therefore, a solid financial situation and ability to attract investors were crucial.

Problems associated with entering new markets included the potential for misunderstanding local consumers, their tastes and needs as far as service and quality were concerned, having to compete against unfamiliar companies, and dealing with the different labor laws and work ethics of different countries. Specialty retailer The Home Depot, for example, which has been expanding quickly in Latin American and South American countries, has run into serious challenges in promoting its customer-service culture among local workers, who are not accustomed to the level of service that their employers were demanding from them. Thorough research of any potential market was unavoidable. Potential customers and their tastes, potential and existing competitors, the economic situation, and the legal environment had to be analyzed and incorporated in all planning and operations.

Even expanding from the United States to the European Union or other developed markets could pose challenges for a retailer. A U.S.-based retailer might find it difficult to export its domestic retail concept to other markets and might have to purchase a local retailer who was more attuned to local preferences and tastes to make inroads into the market.

Technology

Technology used by specialty apparel retailers included e-tailing, interactive kiosks, bar coding, and electronic data interchange.

E-tailing E-commerce offered many opportunities to specialty retailers worldwide. In addition to allowing them to target customers in previously untapped markets—without building new stores—it also removed physical barriers that were present in brick-and-mortar retailing. Small and regional businesses could immediately become global players through e-commerce. Online retailers have struggled with a variety of challenges, including orders' fulfillment, heavy competition, underdeveloped business plans, and slowing demand. These difficulties have been particularly hard-hitting for pure Internet companies, which have struggled with capital shortages. With years of retail experience, the traditional outlets had numerous advantages over the pure e-tailers, including brand-name recognition, preexisting supply chain and system infrastructure, economies of scale, and experience in dealing with seasonal peaks.

Internet usage continued to gain consumers' confidence. E-commerce sales in 2001 totaled U.S.$ 32.6 billion, up 19.3 percent from 2000, which was well above the 3.4 percent gain in overall retail sales in 2001 [Standard & Poor's, 2002A]. Increasingly, the traditional retailers were capturing a larger and larger share of these online sales. Virtually all major retailers have developed e-commerce strategies, and retailers with international operations were also developing separate websites for the global customers.

For the bricks-and-clicks operations to be successful, a retailer had to have brand recognition. Customers bought a product online if they were familiar with the company and brand name. Selection and convenience were very important. Clear and easy return policies, for example, the possibility of returning an item bought online in a physical retail store, were also crucial. As far as the website itself was concerned, content, reliability, and accurate and speedy delivery were crucial success factors. The success of companies that used the Internet for sales was highly dependent on order fulfillment. The time it took to receive orders after they had been placed was critical. It also was crucial to ensure consumers that the transaction they made over the Internet was secure.

Interactive Kiosks A growing number of specialty retailers were placing interactive kiosks in their stores to attract traffic to their retail outlets and their websites and to offer other services or information. Kiosks were used to tie retailers' stores to their Internet strategies in an effort to develop true "clicks-and-bricks" operations. Kiosks offered information about retailers' products and store availability—and even offered recommendations, in some cases. Consumers could also walk over to a kiosk and order an item online that was out of stock. Some apparel retailers, such as Gap Inc., had pulled the kiosks out of their stores because customers did not want to spend time online when they were in a store and were able to touch and feel the clothes. Even if that was the case, kiosks could still have been useful. Instead of making customers use them by themselves, sales representatives could use them while helping customers pick the right product, order an item not available in the store, or locate a store carrying a certain item.

Bar Coding and Electronic Data Interchange Among the more ubiquitous technologies for inventory management by specialty retailers worldwide was the practice of bar coding via universal product codes, or UPCs. The bar code provided a universal language, with an alphabet composed of alternating black and white parallel lines, which encoded product information and was read by laser scanners. Having this efficient system in place was very important. Bar codes conveyed a great deal of useful information for retailers, including the identities of items sold, their sizes and colors, and their manufacturers. When retailers received products, they would feed bar-code data into their databases, which also held detailed information about price and inventory count. This system allowed companies to change prices more efficiently via computers versus manually marking down price tags on individual products. Another significant use of that technology was in the point-of-sale (POS) systems. POS scanning equipment at the checkout counter, which was linked to a computer, was able to read the universal product code (UPC) labels on products, instantly providing the retailer with detailed sales data. This allowed the retailer to follow customers' demands, gauge emerging merchandise trends, and meet inventory replenishment requirements. POS scanners also reduced labor costs, by eliminating the need to mark items individually, and enhanced price accuracy. From the customer's perspective, scanners reduced checkout time and generated a receipt that detailed the type and price of each item purchased.

Given the need to maximize efficiency in distribution and turnover, retailers had embraced electronic data interchange (EDI) as a source for quick and accurate transactions. EDI helped companies manage inventories during slower or quicker sales cycles. It was based upon direct, electronic communication with suppliers and distributors. EDI technology had been around, in one form or another, for at least three decades, and new forms were constantly emerging. One recent development to influence EDI was satellite technology. Retailers used EDI to transmit information on a timely basis from stores to headquarters or other central locations. Successful specialty retailers demanded sophisticated planning and technology so that decisions could be made on the basis of information rather than intuition. Those systems helped maintain lean inventories and avoid overstocking, while ensuring that retailers have on hand the merchandise that customers want to buy when they want to buy it. Under this program, retailer and manufacturers were linked via EDI, which allowed the transfer of information from one computer to another. By notifying vendors immediately when new merchandise had to be ordered, EDI made quicker replenishment cycles possible. As packages were received and their bar code labels were scanned, the system knew exactly which store to route it to. The merchandise spent only a few hours at the warehouse, instead of a few days.

As the age of technology offered opportunities for cost savings in the supply chain, retailers were increasingly teaming up to maximize efficiencies in merchandise ordering and delivery. In an evolving practice known as business-to-business (B2B) e-commerce, companies were transacting sales between themselves via the Internet. B2B provided a communication medium for retailers to view products, share information, and place orders across multiple manufacturers' product lines. B2B gave rise to an improved purchasing process that could minimize inventory, reduce delivery cycle times, and increase productivity. It also gave firms the ability to connect internationally without major infrastructure investments. More important, it was expected to level the playing field for smaller retailers, who could consolidate orders with other retailers to obtain discounts from manufacturers. One of the B2Bs serving specialty retailers, DirectSource .com (a product of DirectSource Global Purchasing) focused on serving small- and medium-sized retailers looking to import products from Asia by giving them access to online catalogs of goods. Larger retailers could make online purchases directly from about five thousand suppliers in Hong Kong, Taiwan, China, and other Asian countries.

The potential of other technologies being developed was also expected to have a major impact in retailing. For example, Wal-Mart, working with MIT, was in October 2001 testing a new wireless tool (initially called "Radio Frequency ID Tags") that could be printed or painted onto or attached to individual products (and/or by extension clothing or even skin) which would enable tracking the location and usage of a product through this radio/wireless device and which could be directly linked to a computer. For instance, it would substantially reduce instore theft, enable producers to know just how long an individual consumer took to use a product, such as a tube of toothpaste, an item of clothing, and generally produce a wide range of detailed market information [Downes, 2001; Rendon, 2002]. The tests were begun when the cost of this technology was predicted to drop to only one cent per individual product. The implications of this technology were enormous, extending beyond business to finding lost or stolen autos or helicopter parts (the government is developing a radio frequency system for this), tracking the location of children and other people, and the like. At the same time, all of this potential also raised many questions about invasion of privacy [Konicki, 2001].

Competition

Retailing was a fiercely competitive industry. Besides competing with each other, specialty retailers also faced competition from department stores and discount stores (general merchandisers).

Specialty Retailers Limited Brands, Abercrombie and Fitch (A&F), and Hennes & Mauritz (H&M) were the main competition in the Gap market. They offered high-quality products, which in most cases appealed to the customers. Most stores offered an alternative way of shopping, some through the Internet, some through catalogs. Specialty stores had a good and reliable customer service. The store personnel were trained to answer customers' questions regarding product mix. In most cases seasonal price reductions and sales were offered. All the stores outsourced the manufacturing of their products. One of the main strengths of those stores was the ability to establish one-on-one relationships with the customer.

Stores gathered the information about their customers and studied their spending habits. Most of those retailers was available in major U.S. cities and densely populated suburbs. Specialty retailers did not offer products in plus or extended plus sizes. Most of them did not offer an extensive product line that went beyond clothing. One of the most important weaknesses, however, was the inability to remove the low-turnover products from the stores. These products occupied the shelves for too long, costing those retailers money, and even more importantly customers.

Limited Brands After a disagreement with his father in 1963 over the operation of the family store (Leslie's), Leslie Wexner, then twenty-six, opened the first Limited store in Columbus, Ohio. When The Limited went public in 1969, it had only five stores, but the rapid development of large, covered malls spurred growth to one hundred stores by 1976. Two years later The Limited acquired Mast Industries, an international apparel purchasing and importing company. The company opened Express in 1980 to serve the teen market.

The Limited grew with acquisitions, including the 1982 purchases of Lane Bryant (large sizes) and Victoria's Secret (lingerie). That year it formed the Brylane fashion catalog division and acquired Roaman's, a bricks-and-mortar and catalog merchandiser. Wexner bought The Lerner Stores (budget women's apparel) and Henri Bendel (high fashion) in 1985, sportswear retailer Abercrombie & Fitch (A&F) in 1988, and London-based perfumer Penhaligon's in 1990 (sold in 1997). The Limited introduced several in-store shops, including Cacique (French lingerie) in 1988 and Limited Too (girls' fashions), which were expanded into stand-alone stores. It also launched Structure (men's sportswear) in 1989 and Bath & Body Works shops in 1990. All of these stores were in malls, often strategically clustered together.

The Limited in 1993 closed many of The Limited and Lerner stores and sold 60 percent of its Brylane catalog unit to Freeman Spogli (taking it public in 1997). It opened four Bath & Body Works stores in the United Kingdom (its first non-U.S. stores) to compete with British rival The Body Shop. In 1994, The Limited bought Galyan's Trading Co., a chain of sporting goods superstores.

The company began spinning off its businesses while keeping controlling stakes; it spun off Intimate Brands (Victoria's Secret, Cacique, and Bath & Body Works) in 1995 and A&F in 1996. The Limited sold its remaining 84 percent in A&F in 1998. In 1997, the company closed more than one hundred of its women's apparel stores; the next year it closed nearly three hundred more companywide (excluding the Intimate Brands chains) and all but one of its Henri Bendel stores. Also in 1997, Intimate Brands closed the Cacique chain. In 1998, White Barn Candle Co. (candle and home fragrance stores) was launched. The following year the company spun off Limited Too, its most successful chain, as Too, Inc., and reduced its interest in Galyan's to 40 percent. Galyan's management and the buyout firm Freeman Spogli owned 60 percent of the sporting goods chain. The Limited (as well as Intimate Brands) declared a two-for-one stock split in 2000.

To boost profits, in 2001 The Limited folded the Structure brand into the Express unit and spun off its Galyan's and Alliance Data Systems subsidiaries, retaining 22 percent and 20 percent, respectively. The Limited sold its Lane Bryant unit to Charming Shoppers for $335 million that year.

The Columbus, Ohio, based retailer operated about forty-six hundred U.S. stores that sold a variety of apparel and personal care products in late 2002. Its apparel store names included The Limited, Express, Lerner New York, Henri Bendel, and Structure (which the company was rebranding as Express Men's). Its stores under its Intimate Brands subsidiary included Victoria's Secret, Bath & Body Works, and White Barn Candle Co. [Hoover's Online, 2002].

Limited Brands offered its products through fully owned retail stores. It did not, however, sell its products through the Internet (except for Victoria's Secret). Although Limited once owned a brand selling large sizes (Lane Bryant), it was sold on August 16, 2001. Since then the company did not offer plus or extended plus-sizes. Limited Brands' products were high quality. All brands allowed the customers to make returns easily. Stores often offered seasonal price reduction. The layout and design of the stores was strategic. Products often bought together were placed close to each other. Stores were frequently using mannequins to inspire customers. Limited outsourced its manufacturing. Like other specialty retailers, Limited had problems with inventory management. In many cases unpopular, low-turnover products occupied shelf space for too long.

Abercrombie and Fitch (A&F) Scotsman David Abercrombie began selling camping equipment in lower Manhattan in 1892. Joined by lawyer Ezra Fitch, Abercrombie & Fitch (A&F) soon established itself as the purveyor of outdoors equipment for the very rich. A&F supplied Theodore Roosevelt and Ernest Hemingway for safaris and provided gear for polar explorer Richard Byrd.

A&F thrived through the 1960s. However, by the 1970s the number of A&F's core customers was falling. Hunting was no longer popular and the company struggled to find new markets. In 1977, A&F filed for bankruptcy. A year later sports retailer Oshman's bought the company and expanded the number of stores while providing an eclectic assortment of goods. In 1988, clothing retailer The Limited bought A&F, then with about twenty-five stores, and shifted the company's emphasis to apparel. Michael Jeffries took over in 1992 and transformed the unprofitable chain into an outfitter for college students. In 1995, A&F returned to profitability. The company went public in 1996 with more than 110 stores. In 1998, The Limited spun off its remaining 84 percent stake. Also that year A&F sued rival American Eagle Outfitters, claiming it illegally copied A&F's clothing (the suit was dismissed in 1999). In 1999, the SEC launched an investigation after A&F leaked sales figures to an analyst before they were made available to the public. In 2000, A&F launched its new teen store concept called Hollister Co.

Through about 490 stores nationwide (mostly in malls), New Albany, Ohio, based A&F sold upscale, casual apparel for men, women, and kids. Its clothing included shirts, khakis, jeans, underwear, and outerwear. Most items were emblazoned with the A&F logo. The company also sold merchandise through its subscription catalog, A&F Quarterly, and its website.

Though college students were the company's main target market, A&F sold its products to adults, teens, and kids as well. Its children's stores were called Abercrombie, and the teen stores concept was called Hollister Co. The company's carefully selected college-age sales staff and photos of twenty-something models adorning the walls imbued its main stores with an upscale fraternity house feel.

A&F was no stranger to controversy. In the last four years, various marketing techniques and product choices (including sexually suggestive ads and children's thong underwear) have drawn complaints and criticism from conservative politicians, family advocacy groups, cultural groups, Mothers Against Drunk Driving and other women's groups [Hoover's Online, 2002].

The company offered products of good quality, which appealed to its target market. A&F sold its goods in retail stores, through catalogs, and through the Internet. As other specialty apparel retailers, the company had problems with removing low turnover products from shelf space to make space for new product lines. Compared with other retailers A&F's products were also quite pricey. Like the majority of competitors A&F did not offer their products in plus and extended plus-sizes. Stores allowed their customers to return the products. It was also possible to return an item bought online into a physical retail store. One of the weaknesses of A&F when compared with other specialty retailers was the store layout. Stores rarely used mannequins, and the display of the products needed improvement.

Hennes and Mauritz (H&M) In 1947, Erling Persson opened his first Hennes (Swedish for "hers," because it only sold women's apparel) store in Västerås, Sweden. The company expanded, opening its first foreign stores in Norway in 1964 and Denmark in 1967. As it grew and increased volume, the retailer was able to offer lower prices. The company bought hunting and men's clothing shop Mauritz Widforss in 1968 and began offering men's clothing in Mauritz stores.

In 1974, the company went public. H&M Hennes & Mauritz introduced cosmetics in 1975 and began opening stores in London the following year. Also in 1976, the company introduced its teenage clothing stores under the Impulse banner. By the end of the 1970s, the company had moved into Switzerland (1978) and Germany (1980) and introduced baby clothes. In 1980, H&M also purchased mail-order company Rowell.

Stefan Persson took over as CEO from his father, Erling, in 1982. He expanded throughout northern Europe, and H&M boasted two hundred stores in 1985. By 1988, the company was experiencing annual sales growth rates of 25 to 30 percent. The firm's European expansion continued, and by 1998, H&M had entered six more countries, including France, Austria, Finland, and the Benelux countries. By this time the company had also consolidated its men's, women's, children's, and teens' stores under the H&M

banner. Stefan gave up his CEO position and became executive chairman of the board in 1998. The company's purchasing director, Fabian Månsson, succeeded him as CEO. In 1998 and 1999, H&M began selling online, first in Sweden, then in Denmark and Finland.

The company moved into the United States and Spain in 2000. The openings, considered a success by H&M, put a strain on earnings, which sent the stock into a dive. In a move the company said was unrelated, Månsson resigned and was replaced by Danish subsidiary CEO Rolf Eriksen.

H&M designed cheap but chic clothing, mainly for men and women ages eighteen to forty-five, children's apparel, and its own brands of cosmetics. H&M operated some eight hundred stores in fourteen countries with direct sales operations in selected areas. Half of its clothing was made in Europe, the rest mostly in Asia.

More than 85 percent of sales come from outside of H&M's home country, and the company was continuing to expand, planning to open nearly one hundred stores per year, including in new markets in Europe and the United States. H&M has slowed its plans to have up to eighty-five stores in the United States by 2003. Women's clothing accounted for 60 percent of sales; private-label brands included Hennes, L.O.G.G. (Label of Graded Goods), and BiB (Big is Beautiful).

H&M was controlled by the family of Chairman Stefan Persson (the son of founder Erling Persson); they owned about 33 percent of the company's stock [Hoover's Online, 2002].

H&M's most important strength and advantage over competitors was its competitive pricing. Stores were strategically designed. Mannequins were often used, and products were attractively displayed. Items often purchased together were placed close to each other. The quality of the products, although still good, was lower than of other specialty apparel retailer's products. The company was fairly new on the U.S. market. It was not yet present in major U.S. cities or in suburbs. H&M did not offer its products through catalogs or the Internet in the United States, although it planned to in the future. The company did not offer store credit cards for its customers.

Department Stores   Specialty retailers also competed with department stores. The main competitors included Macy's and J.C. Penney. Department stores offered extensive product lines of good quality. They attracted customers with seasonal price reductions and sales, and most of them offered store credit cards. Their strengths also included a wide domestic presence, both in major U.S. cities and in densely populated suburbs. They offered clothes in sizes 1 through 14, and limited selections of clothes in plus sizes. The main weakness of those stores was a lack of strong customer service. Although trained staff was present, in most department stores it was hard to find the right person able to provide the information about offered products. Another problem in department stores was long checkout time, at times long enough for customers to feel discouraged and leave the store without making a purchase.

General Merchandisers   In times when consumers became increasingly price conscious, discounters such as Wal-Mart, Kmart, or Target were posing a huge threat to both specialty retailers and department stores. The ability to price products competitively and a wide product line were the main strengths of those merchandisers. Those stores also targeted the market for plus, and extended plus sizes, which was ignored by department stores and most specialty retailers. The weakness of those stores was in customer service and product quality areas. Although the product line was extensive, many products were of poor quality. The styles, colors, and fabrics of clothes often did not appeal to customers. Although returns were possible, the staff often lacked information about the products that were offered in the store. These stores did not try to establish more personal relationships with the customers. Unlike most specialty retailers, the majority of discounters did not work on building their own brands.

The Company

History

Donald Fisher and his wife, Doris, opened a small store in 1969 near what is now San Francisco State University. The couple named their store The Gap (after "the generation gap") and concentrated on selling Levi's jeans. The couple opened a second store in San Jose, California, eight months later, and by the end of 1970, there were six Gap stores. The Gap went public six years later.

In the beginning, the Fishers catered almost exclusively to teenagers, but in the 1970s, they expanded into active wear that would appeal to a larger spectrum of customers. Nevertheless, by the early 1980s The Gap—which had grown to about five hundred stores—was still dependent on its large teenage customer base. However, it was less dependent on Levi's (about 35 percent of sales), due to its growing private labels.

In a 1983 effort to revamp the company's image, Fisher hired Mickey Drexler, a former president of AnnTaylor with a very successful apparel industry track record, as The Gap's new president. Drexler immediately overhauled the motley clothing lines to concentrate on sturdy, brightly colored cotton clothing. He also consolidated the stores' many private clothing labels into the Gap brand. As a final touch, Drexler replaced circular clothing racks with white shelving so that clothes could be neatly stacked and displayed. Also in 1983, The Gap bought Banana Republic, a unique chain of jungle-themed stores that sold safari clothing. The company expanded the chain, which enjoyed tremendous success in the mid 1980s but slumped after the novelty of the stores wore off late in the decade. In response, Drexler introduced a broader range of clothes (including higher-priced leather items) and dumped the safari lines in 1988. By 1990, Banana Republic was again profitable, and in 1995, it opened its first two stores outside the United States, both in Canada.

The first GapKids store opened in 1985 after Drexler couldn't find clothing that he liked for his son. In 1990, Gap Inc. introduced babyGap in twenty-five GapKids stores, featuring miniature versions of its GapKids line. The Gap announced in 1991 that it would no longer sell Levi's (which had fallen to less than 2 percent of total sales) and would sell nothing but private-label items.

In 1994, The Old Navy Clothing Co. was launched, named after a bar Drexler saw in Paris.

Robert Fisher (the founders' son) became the president of the Gap division (including babyGap and GapKids) in 1997 and was charged with reversing the segment's sales decline. The company refocused its Gap chain on basics (jeans, T-shirts, and khakis) and helped boost its performance with a high-profile advertising campaign focusing on those wares. Later in 1997, the Gap opened an online Gap store. In 1998, the retailer opened its first GapBody stores and introduced its only catalog (for Banana Republic). In late 1999, amid sluggish Gap division sales, Robert resigned, and CEO Drexler took over his duties. Beginning in 2000, Gap Inc. started to report its store count based on the number of concepts for Gap brand. This meant that any Gap Adult, GapKids, babyGap, or GapBody meeting a certain square footage threshold was counted as a separate store even when residing within a single physical location. GapMaternity was a part of babyGap, but it did not have separate stores. Gap concepts are shown in Figure 7.

In 2000, Gap misjudged fashion trends, which resulted in disappointing earnings. In May 2002, Drexler announced that he wanted to retire, and that he would do so as soon as a replacement was found. On September 26, 2002, Paul Pressler was named president and chief executive officer of Gap Inc. In September 2002, the company reported its twenty-eighth straight month of declines in sales at stores open at least one year [Gap Inc. Company Website, 2002].

The focus of this case study is on one of the three divisions of Gap Inc., namely, The Gap.

FIGURE 7

Gap Store Concepts

FIGURE 8

The Gap Division of Gap, Inc.

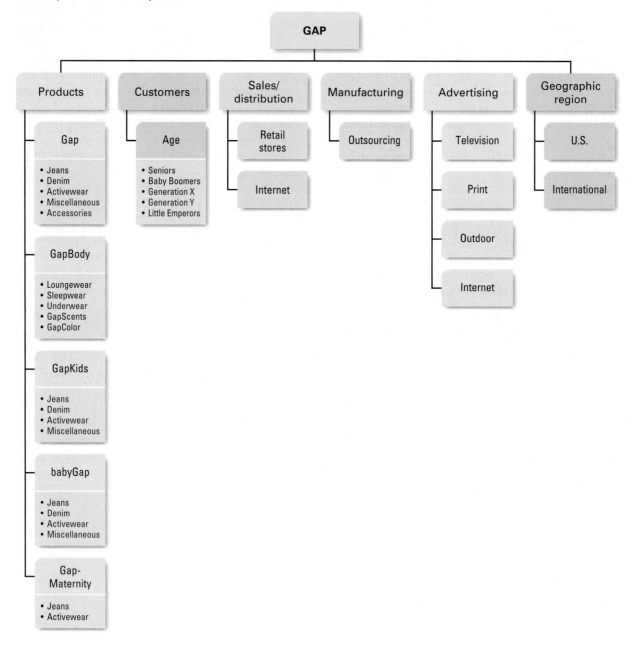

Products

The Gap brand name can be divided into five concepts. Each of them offered different products for different customers.

The Gap The Gap, or Gap Adult as some sources referred to it, offered activewear, denim products, accessories, jeans, and miscellaneous products to both men and women. They all came in a variety of fits, colors and washes, and fabrics.

Jeans and Pants. This is what made Gap famous. Gap offers a variety of jeans and pants. They came in a variety of styles, fabrics, and colors. Women's jeans included boot cut, long and lean, low-rise boot cut, flare, modern boot cut, classic, loose fit, square pocket, utility, sidewinder, carpenter, and patch pocket. They were available in dark faded, light faded, stretch brown tinted, stretch faded, stretch black, stretch rinsed, stretch sandblasted, sandblasted, stonewashed, khaki, dark khaki, dark cement, and black. The men's selection included boot fit, easy fit, standard fit, relaxed fit, loose fit, wide leg, carpenter, worker, and straight fit. They came in vintage, faded, antiqued, brown tinted, rustic, black tinted, stonewashed, rinsed, black, dark blasted, black blasted, dark sandblasted, tinted rinsed, and black.

Denim. Denim products included shirts, blouses, jackets, skirts, dresses, accessories, and shoes.

Activewear. Activewear included sweatshirts, hooded sweatshirts, fleece sweatshirts, sweatpants, T-shirts, and tops.

Miscellaneous. Miscellaneous products included sweaters, turtlenecks, vee-necks, blouses, shirts, dresses, jackets, coats, pea coats, trench coats, vests, tops, T-shirts, and polos.

Accessories. Accessories included bags, handbags, backpacks, tote bags, belts, hats, scarves, gloves, mittens, socks, shoes, flip-flops, and slides.

GapBody With a focus on everyday essentials, GapBody offered loungewear, sleepwear, underwear, GapScents, and Gap Color.

Loungewear, Sleepwear, and Underwear. GapBody offered loungewear, sleepwear, women's bras and panties, and men's underwear. One of the most popular products was the GapBody Seamless style, T-shirts, tanks, and camisoles with no seams or bulky edges. They were created on a cylinder, which made it possible to eliminate side seams.

GapScents. Body lotions, body mists, and eau de toilette were available in "So Pink," "Dream," and "Heaven" fragrances. Gap also introduced "G," a men's fragrance composed of crisp white cotton, juniper, and musk. There were "G" eau de toilette, aftershave balm, hair and body wash, body lotion, soap on a rope, and gift sets available. Gap also introduced "Simply White," a new women's fragrance with floral top notes of honeysuckle and jasmine and warm, woodsy bottom notes. There were eau de toilette, shower gel, moisturizing soap, body mist, body lotion, intensified fragrance lotion, shimmer lotion, and gift sets available in this fragrance line.

GapColor. GapBody introduced GapColor, a new line of wearable, high-quality cosmetics that were offered in a range of versatile colors for lips, eyes, face, and nails. Some of the products included lip glaze, lip gloss in 10 shades, lip color in 25 shades, lipstick in 10 shades, lip care in 4 shades, lip liners in 5 shades, nail color in 12 shades, eye color in 20 shades, face powder in 8 shades, and 5 kinds of brushes.

GapKids GapKids's products included activewear styles, jackets, sweaters, pants, and jeans. As always, the emphasis on quality was shown in the details: from embellished denim for girls and knit tops for boys, to expanded washes in jeans and bright, simple colors across the assortment. Highlights for girls included flare, bootcut, and classic jeans; embellished jeans were also available—glitter flares, glitter patch pocket, charm and heart styles. Other offerings included polos, cotton cardigans, yoga pants, zip hoodies, velour or tricot track suits, boots, clogs, and slip-ons. Some highlights for boys included jeans (basic five-pocket jeans, carpenter, cargo, all in stonewash blast, antique blast, dark sandblast, and whisker antique), basic tops, polos, Oxford shirts, tracksuits, hooded sweatshirts, sneakers, and slip-ons. GapKids also offered bags, small backpacks for younger kids, premier backpacks for older students, and messenger-style bags.

babyGap babyGap offered products for the little kids, from newborns up to age five. Products included bodysuits, playwear, overalls, tops, cardigans, sweaters, socks, and shoes, all in denim and cozy fabrics.

GapMaternity GapMaternity did not have its own separate stores. It was a section of babyGap stores. The products for moms-to-be included jeans and activewear. According to Rachel DiCarlo, vice president of fashion public relations for Gap, "These are the same jeans women wear when they're not pregnant" [Gap Inc. Company's Website, 2002]. The favorite items from Gap were translated into maternity wear so women could maintain their sense of style throughout their pregnancy. A wide range of fits and washes was available; maternity jeans took on a modern look in different styles. Jeans included stretch patch pocket, a worker-inspired jean with front patch pockets, the sandblasted stretch long and lean that fits slim through the leg and has a demi-belly panel that sits slightly lower at the waist, and stretch boot cut. The stretch fabric in all of the jeans styles improved fit, maximized comfort, and provided ease of movement. GapMaternity also offered activewear, which included stretch hoods, pants, and jackets. Stores carried sizes from XS to XL. Styles have been designed for comfort throughout the pregnancy, with stretch fabrics and special features such as four comfortable belly panels (the new demi-panel, no panel, side panel, and full panel) to ensure that jeans fit perfectly at every stage.

Overall, Gap had a strong brand name. Its products were high quality. The fashions and colors appealed to the customers. Products were attractively displayed on white shelving. Products' labels were clear and understandable and they provided sufficient product information. Gap often marked down the prices of different products. The company had some problems with inventory management, low-turnover products occupied shelf space for too long, and there were cases of inadequate inventory of high turnover items.

Customers

Gap catered to women and men of almost all ages. Different Gap brands targeted different age groups. Gap paid close attention to the age distribution and priorities of potential customers in its markets.

Gap targeted women and men through all its store concepts. *Women* accounted for 80 percent of household spending and 83 percent of all purchases [Reyes, 2002]. Most women worked full time, which for apparel retailers such as Gap was good news because it meant not only more income at the disposal of the most important customer, but also a need to buy a new wardrobe suitable for their work. Women bought not only clothes for themselves, but also for their kids. In addition, they had a great influence on what their husbands were buying. *Men* were spending a growing percentage of their apparel money on casual wear, because of the changes in the dressing codes for many white-collar workers. This was a good change for specialty retailers such as Gap that specialized in casual clothing.

Seniors Seniors are comprised of individuals sixty-five years old and older. They accounted for more than 12 percent of the U.S. population. By 2015, they are expected to comprise nearly 15 percent of the U.S. population. Gap and GapBody targeted seniors.

Baby Boomers The baby boom generation, comprising individuals born between 1946 and 1964, constituted some 77 million Americans. The boomers were then in their forties and fifties. Gap and GapBody targeted those consumers.

Generation X Generation X was comprised of approximately 45 million people born between 1965 and 1976. These individuals had reached adulthood in the mid 1980s, and were then in their twenties and thirties. Products from Gap, GapBody, and GapMaternity were targeting this group.

Generation Y The Generation Y group included individuals born between 1977 and 1994, representing about 25 percent of the population. Gap, GapBody, and GapKids targeted this segment.

The Little Emperors The little emperors included a population of children younger than five years of age. Gap sold to these markets via its GapKids and babyGap outlets.

Gap sold high-quality products at competitive price levels. Consumers were able to shop whenever it was convenient for them, by either going to a physical store or to the Gap websites. It also offered a store credit card for its customers. Gap offered products in sizes 0 to 14, a limited selection of products in plus-sizes, but no extended plus-sizes. Another important strength of Gap was the customer service the company provided. Company stores had bright lighting, and products were attractively displayed on shelves. A sufficient number of cash registers provided speedy checkout for the customers. Sales associates and other store personnel were trained to answer customers' questions about fabric, fit, and fashion, and to help them select merchandise that would be perfect for them.

Sales and Distribution

Gap was headquartered in the San Francisco Bay Area, its product development offices were in New York City, and distribution operations and offices coordinating sourcing activities were located around the globe. Third-party manufacturers shipped merchandise to distribution centers, which sorted and redistributed it to the stores. Strategically placed throughout the United States, Canada, the United Kingdom, the Netherlands, and Japan, the distribution centers were the backbone of Gap Inc.'s worldwide operations. The company used bar coding and electronic data interchange systems in inventory management. The company operated all its stores, it did not franchise or enter into joint ventures, and it did not wholesale its products or serve as a supplier to other companies.

Retail Stores Gap's retail stores were attractively located. Gap used stand-alone stores and mall locations. Gap leased most of its store premises. Store layout and design were strategic, and products often bought together were placed in close proximity. Products were attractively displayed on white shelving, and mannequins provided ideas and inspiration for customers. Sales associates and other store personnel were trained to answer customers' questions about fabric, fit, and fashion, and to help them select merchandise that would be perfect for them.

Internet Gap products were available through the website that included gap.com, gapbody.com, gapkids.com, and babygap.com. Shopping on those websites was safe, quick, and simple. Customers were able to return products bought online to the company's retail stores. Ordered products were sent to the customer directly from one of the distribution centers. However, customers were not able to pick up their online orders in retail stores.

Manufacturing

Gap Inc.'s goods were produced in approximately thirty-six hundred factories in more than fifty countries. It did not manufacture any of the goods itself; it neither owned nor operated any garment factories. Instead, it was almost always one of a manufacturer's many customers. Gap was a designer and marketer.

Gap Inc. developed a set of principles and operating standards for garment manufacturers that reflected its values, beliefs, and business ethics. These standards were set out in its Code of Vendor Conduct, which was first written in the early 1990s and updated in 1996. The Code focused on compliance with local labor laws, working conditions, and the natural environment. It also spelled out to vendors Gap's expectations regarding wages, child labor, health, and safety issues, respecting the right of workers to unionize and much more. It was written in order to help vendors understand and apply these standards to their day-to-day operations, and adopt them as "company policy." Few factories, if any, in the United States or anywhere else were in total compliance all of the time.

Gap Inc.'s Global Compliance department was comprised of over ninety full-time employees dedicated exclusively to working with potential and current vendors to help them understand and achieve compliance with the Code. Before Gap approved or placed an order with a vendor, the Global Compliance team was involved. First, before any orders were placed, a manufacturer and the factories it intended to use were subjected to a comprehensive approval process to make sure they could operate under the Code of Vendor Conduct. Second, if a garment factory was eventually approved, the Compliance team monitored compliance on an ongoing basis. In addition, other Gap employees visited factories—from quality assurance and production experts to employees who determined if a vendor was capable of producing a specific kind of garment.

Advertising/Promotion

Gap advertised its products in a number of ways. Each of the three main brands, including Gap, has its own marketing team headquartered in the San Francisco Bay Area. In-house marketing teams created everything from hangtags and in-store posters to billboards and TV commercials. A more recent campaign was titled "For Every Generation." The global campaign was comprised of television, print, outdoor, and online initiatives.

Television Gap TV spots were aired in the United States, United Kingdom, Canada, and Japan. TV spots in the United States were shown during prime-time programs, including *Friends, Will & Grace, West Wing, Law & Order, Ed, Scrubs,* and *ER* on NBC; *Alias, The Practice* and *My Wife & Kids* on ABC; *CSI* and *Survivor* on CBS; and *Malcolm in the Middle* and *Boston Public* on Fox [Howard, 2002A]. In those TV spots, Gap has turned to celebrities such as Lauren Hutton or Bridget Hall for help [Brown, 2002].

Print Print ads appeared in more than forty international magazines, which included *Vogue, Harper's Bazaar, Marie Claire, InStyle, Details, Vanity Fair, W, ESPN, GQ, Spin, Sports Illustrated, Rolling Stone,* and *Interview.* They also appeared in major newspapers.

Outdoor Major market outdoor billboards were used by Gap. Billboards, walls, and transit posters appeared in high-visibility markets throughout the United States, Canada, Europe, and Japan.

Internet Gap pop-up ads and banners appeared on various popular web pages, such as aol.com or yahoo.com. Those ads were used not only to promote Gap brand name but also to announce new product lines and sales.

Although Gap took advantage of various channels of promotion, some customers complained that the message of the advertisements was sometimes unclear and confusing. This highlighted another problem in the company; it took a long time for Gap to react to the negative feedback and reaction of the customers.

Gap worked hard to earn a good reputation and establish a strong brand name. To enhance and exceed the expectations of every customer, Gap store designers were constantly evolving everything that touches the customers—from store signage and merchandise displays, to dressing rooms and inventory systems. Their goal was to create a relaxed shopping environment that intensifies Gap's bold brand expression and enhances the sales associates' ability to provide outstanding service. Going forward, these design changes were originated to help support Gap's growth and future vision, and make the customers' experiences the best of any retailer. Gap wanted its customers to know that when they visited one of their stores, they're not just walking into a store, they're walking into a brand.

High-quality products, good customer service, and a distinct shopping environment ensure a good reputation, but it often is not enough. In 1977, Gap Inc. established its charitable arm—Gap Foundation. In order to make a name for itself Gap, through Gap Foundation, engaged in a number of partnerships. It funded two national organizations that share the commitment to helping underserved youth. Boys & Girls Clubs of America and the Lorraine Monroe Leadership Institute aimed to help students develop self-esteem, stay in school, and succeed academically so they can lead more rewarding and fulfilling lives. To help teens make sound educational decisions, explore career opportunities, and prepare for the workforce, Gap was funding a career exploration and mentoring program for more than twenty-six hundred Boys & Girls Clubs nationwide. Gap Inc. employees were also in charge of workshops, conducted Career Day sessions at their local Boys & Girls Clubs, and provided job-shadowing opportunities for youth at headquarters and store locations. Dr. Lorraine Monroe acknowledges the challenges of education in underserved urban areas. By embracing these challenges—adding a mix of first-rate teachers, a creative but disciplined environment, and the expectation of perfection—Dr. Monroe has helped transform the future of public urban education. This is the premise of the Lorraine Monroe Leadership Institute, which is focused on developing leaders for public schools who are committed to educating underserved youth. Through funding from Gap Foundation, the Institute created Demonstration Schools to train teachers and administrators in Dr. Monroe's extraordinary leadership principles. In addition to the major partnerships with Boys & Girls Clubs of America and the Lorraine Monroe Leadership Institute, Gap Inc. supported nonprofit organizations serving kids in local communities around the world. Although it focused primarily on education and youth development, Gap, Banana Republic and Old Navy supported many other organizations in areas such as health and human services, civics and arts, and the environment [Gap Inc. Company Website, 2002].

Geographic Region

Gap stores were located in five countries outside the United States—the United Kingdom, Canada, France, Japan, and Germany, as shown in Figure 9. The company was successful in expanding into international markets. It was not present in any emerging markets, such as Eastern and Central Europe, as well as Asian or South American countries.

Because it was a sole owner of all its subsidiaries, and it operated its stores by itself, it was able to avoid any problems associated with loss of control. Because it did not enter into joint ventures or franchises, the expansion was slower than it could have been.

Gap operated 2,323 store concepts domestically, 235 in the United Kingdom, 192 in Canada, 155 in Japan, 54 in France, and 20 in Germany, as shown in Figure 9. The actual number of stores was less because in some instances "concepts" were located in a single store.

FIGURE 9

Gap Division Stores in Operation as of August 3, 2002.*

Gap Domestic	2,323
Gap Adult	1,024
GapKids	819
babyGap	193
GapBody	154
Gap Outlet	133
Gap International	**656**
Canada	192
United Kingdom	235
France	54
Japan	155
Germany	20
Total	**2,979**

*For the past two years, Gap Inc. has reported store count based on the number of concepts for Gap brand. This means that any Gap Adult, GapKids, babyGap or GapBody meeting a certain square footage threshold is counted as a separate store even when residing within a single physical location.

Source: Gap Inc. Company Website (2002), [Online], **http://www.gapinc.com**, accessed September 26.

Although Gap was present in all states of the United States, it concentrated mostly on highly populated areas, such as in California, Florida, New York, and Texas, as shown in Figure 10.

Financials

Gap Inc. was in a reasonably good financial condition. In 2001, because of its decreased current liabilities, liquidity of the company had increased. However, as a result of various problems in the company, as well as decreasing sales, Gap Inc. was forced to increase its long-term debts, as shown in Figure 11. The debt to equity ratio grew from 1.32 in 2000 to 1.52 in 2002.

Due to misjudgment of fashion trends in 2000 and 2001, Gap's revenue grew slower than the cost of goods sold, as shown in Figure 12. Between January 2001 and January 2002, revenues grew less than 2 percent. At the same time, costs of goods sold grew more than 10 percent. As a result gross profit margin fell from more than 41 percent to 35.8 percent, as shown in Figure 12.

Comparable store sales by division for the second quarter of 2002 were as follows: Gap Domestic reported negative 13 percent versus a negative 8 percent in 2001; Gap International reported negative 12 percent versus a negative 6 percent in 2001.

Total sales by division for the second quarter of 2002 were as follows: Gap Domestic reported $1.1 billion versus $1.2 billion in 2001, Gap International reported $374 million versus $388 million in 2001.

Comparable store sales by division for year-to-date were as follows: Gap Domestic reported negative 17 percent versus a negative 6 percent in 2001, Gap International reported negative 15 percent versus a negative 7 percent in 2001.

Total sales by division for the year-to-date (2002) were as follows: Gap Domestic reported $2.1 billion versus $2.4 billion last year, Gap International reported $692 million versus $765 million last year, as shown in Figure 13.

Comprehensive earnings included net earnings and other comprehensive earnings (losses). Other comprehensive earnings (losses) included foreign currency translation adjustments and fluctuations in the fair market value of certain derivative financial instruments. Figure 14 presents comprehensive earnings for the thirteen and twenty-six weeks ended August 3, 2002, and August 4, 2001, respectively.

Although Gap was still able to raise capital, the worsening situation has made it more expensive. On February 14, 2002, Moody's reduced Gap's long- and short-term senior unsecured credit ratings from Baa3 to Ba2 and from Prime-3 to Not Prime, respectively, with a negative outlook on long-term ratings. Standard & Poor's reduced the long- and short-term credit ratings from BBB+ to BB+ and from A-2 to B, respectively, with a stable outlook on long-term ratings. On February 27, 2002, Moody's reduced the long-term senior unsecured credit ratings from Ba2 to Ba3 and stated that its outlook on the long-term ratings was stable. On May 9, 2002, and May 24, 2002, the outlook on Gap's credit ratings was changed from stable to negative by Standard & Poor's and Moody's, respectively.

As a result of the downgrades in the long-term credit ratings, effective June 15, 2002, the interest rates payable by Gap on $700 million of outstanding notes increased by 175 basis points to 9.9 percent per

FIGURE 10

Gap Division U.S. Store Concepts in Operation as of August 3, 2002

State	Number of Concepts	State	Number of Concepts	State	Number of Concepts
Alaska	29	Louisiana	35	Ohio	89
Arkansas	20	Massachusetts	105	Oklahoma	27
Arizona	35	Maryland	39	Oregon	27
California	235	Maine	12	Pennsylvania	132
Colorado	36	Michigan	51	Puerto Rico	12
Connecticut	50	Minnesota	39	Rhode Island	18
District of Columbia	5	Missouri	37	South Carolina	25
		Mississippi	14	South Dakota	5
Delaware	8	Montana	6	Tennessee	38
Florida	145	North Carolina	51	Texas	179
Georgia	61	North Dakota	4	Utah	31
Hawaii	16	Nebraska	11	Virginia	47
Iowa	31	New Hampshire	17	Vermont	6
Idaho	8	New Jersey	86	Washington	40
Illinois	97	New Mexico	14	Wisconsin	31
Indiana	34	Nevada	19	West Virginia	10
Kansas	23	New York	212	Wyoming	1
Kentucky	20				
Total of 2,323					

Source: Gap Inc. Company Website (2002), [Online], **http://www.gapinc.com**, accessed September 26.

annum on $200 million of outstanding notes due in 2005, and to 10.55 percent per annum on $500 million of outstanding notes due in 2008. The interest rates payable on these notes would be decreased only upon upgrades of long-term credit ratings by these rating agencies. Any further downgrades of those ratings by these rating agencies would result in further increases in the interest rates payable on the notes.

As a result of the downgrades in the short-term credit ratings, Gap Inc. no longer had meaningful access to the commercial paper market. In addition, it was expected that both the recent, and any future, lowering of the ratings on Gap Inc.'s debt would result in reduced access to the capital markets and higher interest costs on future financing. The increase in interest expense in the second quarter and first half of fiscal 2002 as compared with the same periods in fiscal 2001 was primarily due to an increase

in long-term borrowings and higher interest rates on new debt issuance. Long-term debt (in $000) as of August 3, 2002, was equal to 2,873,132, up 126 percent from 1,961,397 on August 4, 2001 [Gap Inc., 2002].

Management and Strategy

Gap Inc.'s management has demonstrated that they are very proactive, especially when it comes to looking for opportunities for growth. For example, in 1983 the company seemed to have become stagnant so Mickey Drexler was brought in as president. Since then Gap Inc. has grown tremendously, the store's image has been changed, and new store concepts have been started, such as GapKids, babyGap, and Old Navy. The firm also expanded with the acquisition of Banana Republic in 1983.

Gap Inc. opened 663 new stores between October 1999 and October 2000 but had slowed new-store openings in 2001 and 2002, as it continued to be

FIGURE 11

Gap Inc. Balance Sheet

Balance Sheet	Jan 02	Jan 01	Jan 00
Cash	1,035.7	408.8	450.4
Net Receivables	0.0	0.0	0.0
Inventories	1,677.1	1,904.2	1,462.0
Other Current Assets	331.7	335.1	285.4
Total Current Assets	3,044.6	2,648.1	2,197.8
Net Fixed Assets	4,161.3	4,007.7	2,715.3
Other Noncurrent Assets	385.5	357.2	275.7
Total Assets	**7,591.3**	**7,012.9**	**5,188.8**
Accounts Payable	1,105.1	1,067.2	805.9
Short-term Debt	41.9	1,029.9	169.0
Other Current Liabilities	909.2	702.0	778.0
Total Current Liabilities	2,056.2	2,799.1	1,752.9
Long-term Debt	1,961.4	780.2	784.9
Other Noncurrent Liabilities	564.1	505.3	417.9
Total Liabilities	4,581.7	4,084.6	2,955.7
Preferred Stock Equity	0.0	0.0	0.0
Common Stock Equity	3,009.6	2,928.2	2,233.0
Shares Outstanding (mil.)	865.7	854.0	850.5
Total Equity	3,009.6	2,928.2	2,233.0
Total Liabilities and Shareholders' Equity	**7,591.3**	**7,012.9**	**5,188.8**

Source: Gap Inc. (2001). Annual Report.

plagued by the merchandising, marketing, and logistical problems that have wreaked havoc since spring 2000. Long accustomed to spectacular growth and flashy television advertising, Gap Inc. revamped its strategies in 2001, as competition in the apparel industry continued to increase, and the absence of new merchandise offerings and new trends turned up the heat even more.

Gap Inc. pursued a hybrid strategy containing elements of both cost leadership and differentiation, as defined by Porter. It relied on strong brand differentiation and had made considerable investment in brand image, as well as customer service. At the same time, the strategy also contained several characteristics affiliated with the cost leadership approach, including economies of scale and scope, simple product designs, and low-cost distribution.

Because of all the problems, which referred mainly to the Gap division, changes in management have been made. On August 8, 2002, Gap Inc. announced that Gary Muto, President, Banana Republic, had been named president of Gap U.S. On September 26, 2002, it was announced that Paul Pressler had been named president and chief executive officer of Gap Inc., effective immediately [Day, 2002].

Looking Toward the Future

Although Gap had strong and well-established brand recognition in the specialty apparel retailers market, the mistakes that were made within the company, the increasing competition, and changing consumer groups and tastes all added pressure on this division to reevaluate its strategies in order to

FIGURE 12

FIGURE 12

Gap Inc. Income Statement

Income Statement All amounts in millions of U.S. dollars except per share amounts.	Jan 02	Jan 01	Jan 00
Revenue	13,847.9	13,673.5	11,635.4
Cost of Goods Sold	8,893.9	8,009.1	6,339.1
Gross Profit	4,954.0	5,664.4	5,296.3
Gross Profit Margin	35.8%	41.4%	45.5%
SG&A Expense*	3,806.0	3,629.3	3,043.4
Depreciation & Amortization	810.5	590.4	436.2
Operating Income	337.5	1,444.7	1,816.7
Operating Margin	2.4%	10.6%	15.6%
Nonoperating Income	13.3	12.0	0.0
Nonoperating Expenses	109.2	74.9	31.8
Income Before Taxes	241.6	1,381.8	1,784.9
Income Taxes	249.4	504.4	657.9
Net Income After Taxes	(7.8)	877.4	1,127.0
Net Profit Margin	—	6.4%	9.7%
Diluted Net Earnings (loss) Per Share	(0.01)	1.00	1.26
Dividends per Share	0.09	0.09	0.09

*Selling, General, and Administrative Expenses include all salaries, indirect production, marketing, and general corporate expenses.

Source: Gap Inc. (2001). Annual Report.

FIGURE 13

Store Sales for Gap Domestic and Gap International

	Gap Domestic	Gap International
Comparable Store Sales for Second Quarter of 2002 (Second Quarter of 2001)	−13% (−8%)	−12% (−6%)
Total Sales for Second Quarter of 2002 (2001)	$1.1 billion ($1.2 billion)	$347 million ($388 million)
Comparable Store Sales for Year-to-Date for 2002 (2001)	−17% (−6%)	−15% (−7%)
Total Sales for Year-to-Date for 2002 (2001)	$2.1 billion ($2.4 billion)	$692 million ($765 million)

Source: Gap Inc. (2002). Form 10-Q.

FIGURE 14

Gap Inc.'s Comprehensive Earnings

($000)	Thirteen Weeks Ended		Twenty-six Weeks Ended	
	August 3, 2002	August 4, 2001	August 3, 2002	August 4, 2001
Net earnings	56,780	89,751	93,458	205,231
Other comprehensive earnings (losses)	18,664	(7,488)	25,433	(19,647)
Comprehensive earnings	75,444	82,263	118,891	185,584

Source: Gap Inc. (2002). Form 10-Q.

remain competitive. The new CEO of Gap Inc., Paul Pressler, and the new president of Gap U.S., Gary Muto, were faced with various alternatives in order to put the company ahead of competition. Both alternatives focused on customers and the mix of products offered to them. Both maintained that changes were needed. Each one, however, had a different view on what exactly needed to be done.

The first alternative considered was to extend the customer base. It proposed that Gap would target the plus sizes (sizes 16 to 26) and extended plus sizes (sizes 28 to 34) markets. In a sense Gap would offer the same mix of products, such as clothing, accessories, and body care products, to an expanded customer base.

The *benefit* of this alternative was that Gap would get into major unsaturated markets with substantial growth opportunities.

The alternative was *feasible* because of the brand recognition Gap had in the market, which could be extended into new customer groups. It was also feasible because of the widely recognized high quality of Gap products.

This alternative could *win against competition*, because Gap had good relationships with its vendors, and would be able to produce the goods in the new sizes, which would not differ from existing ones as far as quality and the fabrics of the products were concerned. Gap monitored its vendors closely, and had high standards when choosing new ones. This could also be a winning strategy for Gap because the competition present in that market, including H&M, some discounters, such as Wal-Mart or Target, and department stores, such as Macy's, offered only a limited selection of those products, often of poor quality and styles, while Gap was known for classic and comfortable styles and high-quality, durable fabrics. Gap was also better than the competition because among those offering plus sizes it was the only one having a widely recognized, strong brand name, while others were either just beginning to build a brand name, such as H&M, or did not sell products under private labels, such as department stores or discounters.

The *drawback* within this alternative was that creating clothes in extended plus sizes was difficult. The same trajectory of sizing up could not be continued; it required drawing new patterns, because necks, for example, don't get larger above a certain weight, but backs, thighs, or tummies do.

A way around this drawback was to utilize the good relationships with the vendors and pay extra attention to the new designs by hiring designers with experience in this area. With good designs prepared by Gap employees, and close monitoring by the Compliance Department, the quality could be achieved.

The second alternative was to maintain the same customer base and to extend the product line offered to them. Besides jeans, casual wear, activewear, loungewear, sleepwear, underwear, accessories, and body care products, Gap would also offer various home goods, such as picture frames, throw rugs, pillows, sheets, pillowcases, comforters, and towels.

The *benefit* of this alternative was that Gap would be stretching the brand that was widely known and identified with quality.

This alternative is *feasible* because Gap could use the experiences of its sister division Banana Republic to better plan and execute this strategy. It was also feasible because through Banana Republic, Gap would also have access to already tested and reliable vendors that were selected using high standards, and then monitored by the Compliance Department.

Gap would be able to *win against the competition* because the company would be able to offer a broader range of products than most of its competitors. The only competitors that offered a substantially wider product range were discounters and department stores. The goods offered by discounters, such as Target or Wal-Mart, often lacked the quality that Gap was able to provide. Gap was also better than most department stores, such as J.C. Penney or Macy's, because through extensive data gathering it was able to establish a one-to-one relationship with its customers and offer them reliable customer service and product information. Through their efforts to get to know their customers, Gap was able to develop customer loyalty, which would help persuade the customers that the new product lines offered by Gap were as good as the ones they already were used to and trusted. Gap would also be using a recognized brand name and image to market the products, while competitors, such as H&M, were only beginning to build their brand names.

The *drawback* of this alternative was the fact that creating a new product line could stretch the brand too much and diminish the quality brand image that Gap had worked hard to create. It also might use valuable store space now given to apparel. Or the store size needed to be expanded, something that is not always possible.

The way around this drawback was to continue using the highest quality materials and designs, using the same high standards when choosing the vendors, as with other Gap products, and using close monitoring by the Compliance Department.

Both alternatives seemed to make sense. They both seemed to have advantages and disadvantages. Both presented views about how to achieve the same results of maintaining and increasing the market share and getting ahead of the competitors. Muto and Pressler decided to study both alternatives further, especially within present financial situations, as well as other alternatives in other strategic areas, in order to decide which would be most appropriate. The only sure thing at this point in time was that if Gap was to stay competitive, immediate action needed to be taken.

REFERENCES

Barta, S., Jason, M., Frye, J., and Woods, M. (1999). "Trends in Retail Trade." Oklahoma State University, November. [Online], **http://www.agweb.okstate.edu/pearl/agecon/resource/wf-565.pdf**, accessed December 2, 2002.

Board of Governors of the Federal Reserve System (2002). "Monetary Policy Report to the Congress." July 16. [Online], **http://www.federalreserve.gov/boarddocs/hh/2002/July/FullReport.pfd/**, accessed October 8.

Brown, S. (2002). "Gap Customers Get Reassurance; Ads Emphasize Store's Classic Style." *Denver Post*, August 22, p. F01.

Day, S. (2002). "The Gap Chooses Next Chief." *New York Times*, September 27.

DeNavas-Walt, C. and R. Cleveland (2002). "Money Income in the United States: 2001." *Current Population Reports, U.S. Census Bureau*, September.

Downes, L. (2001). "Perpetual Strategy: Building an Information Supply Chain." *Presentation, Foresight on the Future: An Executive Form, New York: Business Objects and IBM DB2*, October 3.

Ellison, S. (2002). "Obese America: Retailer Bets Super-Size Women Will Buy Clothes That Fit—Catherine's Expands Plus Line for Those Who Need a 28 or 34; Studying How Body Gets Larger." *Wall Street Journal*, June 21, p. B1.

Gap Inc. (2000). Annual Report.

Gap Inc. (2001). Annual Report.

Gap Inc. (2002). Form 10-Q.

Gap Inc. Company Website (2002). [Online], **http://www.gapinc.com/**, accessed September 26.

Hansell, S. (2002). "A Retailing Mix: On Internet, in Paint and in Store." *New York Times*, December 14, p. C1.

Hazel, D. (1999). "Is Branding Working? Developers Hope the Name Game Will Pay Off." *Shopping Centers Today*, September 1. [Online], **http://www.icsc.org/srch/sct/current/sct9909/02.html**, accessed October 20.

Hoover's Online (2002). "Company Profiles." [Online], **http://hoovers.com/**, accessed October 20.

Howard, T. (2002A). "Gap Counts on Known, New Stars; Chain Puts Fresh Face on Classic Clothing." *USA Today*, August 8, p. B02.

Howard, T. (2002B). "Gap Goes Back to Basics; Turnaround Plan Is About a Lot More Than Fashion." *USA Today*, August 8, p. B01.

Huff, L. (2002). "Apparel Specialty Stores: A Year to Forget." *Chain Store Age*, 78 no. 8 (August): A14–A15.

Kaiser, E. (2002). "Interview—New Gap CEO Starting at the Bottom." *CBS Market Watch*. [Online], **http://cbs.marketwatch.com/**, accessed September 26.

Konicki, S. (2001). "Sophisticated Supply." *InformationWeek*, December 10.

Lee, L. (2002). "Buried Alive in Khakis." *Business Week*, 3747 no. 40, (July 9): 40.

Lipke, D. (2000). "Mystery Shoppers." *American Demographics*, December, pp. 41–43.

Murray, S. (2001). "The Second Coming." *American Demographics*, April, pp. 28–30.

Rendon, J. (2002). "The Supply Chain's RFID Gambit." *Mbusiness*, March.

Reyes, S. (2002). "Tapping Girl Power." *Brandweek*, 43 no. 16 (April 22): 26–30.

Standard & Poor's (2002A). "Retailing: General." [Online], **http://www.netadvantage.standardpoor.com/**, accessed September 26.

Standard & Poor's (2002B). "Retailing: Specialty." [Online], **http://www.netadvantage.standardpoor.com/**, accessed September 26.

Stein, A. (2000). "The Money in the Middle: Step Right Up to the Roaring 2000s." *American Demographics*, April 01.

Strasburg, J. (2002). "Gap Gets Ready to Try on a New Leadership Style." *San Francisco Chronicle*, August 11, p. G1.

Tedeschi, B. (1999). "As Women Start to Use Internet More for Shopping, the Prospects Sharply Improve for On-line Retailers." *New York Times*, July 12, p. 4.

Valkin, V. (2002). "Gap Taps Ex-Disney Executive as CEO." *Financial Times*, September 26.

Waters, J. (2002). "Gap Finds a New Leader From Disney." *CBS MarketWatch*. [Online], **http://cbs.marketwatch.com/**, accessed September 26.

Charles Schwab

This case was prepared by Charles W. L. Hill, the University of Washington.

Introduction

In 1971, Charles Schwab, who was thirty-two years old at the time, set up his own stock brokerage concern, First Commander. Later he would change the name to Charles Schwab & Company, Inc. In 1975, when the Securities and Exchange Commission abolished mandatory fixed commissions on stock trades, Schwab moved rapidly into the discount brokerage business, offering rates that were as much as 60 percent below those offered by full commission brokers. Over the next twenty-five years, the company experienced strong growth, fueled by a customer-centric focus, savvy investments in information technology, and a number of product innovations, including a bold move into online trading in 1996.

By 2000, the company was widely regarded as one of the great success stories of the era. Revenues had grown to $5.7 billion and net income to $718 million, up from $1.1 billion and $124 million, respectively, in 1993. Online trading had grown to account for 84 percent of all stock trades made through Schwab, up from nothing in 1995. The company's stock price had appreciated by more than that of Microsoft over the prior ten years. In 1999, the market value of Schwab eclipsed that of Merrill Lynch, the country's largest full service broker, despite Schwab's revenues being more than 60% lower.

Copyright © 2004 by Charles W. L. Hill. This case was prepared by Charles W. L. Hill, the University of Washington, as the basis for class discussion rather than to illustrate either effective or ineffective handling of an administrative situation. Reprinted by permission of Charles W. L. Hill. All rights reserved. For the most recent financial results of the company discussed in this case, go to **http://finance.yahoo.com**, input the company's stock symbol, and download the latest company report from its homepage.

However, 2000 proved to be a high-water mark. Between March 2000 and mid 2003, share prices in the United States tumbled, with the technology heavy NASDAQ index losing 80 percent of its value from peak to trough. The volume of online trading at Schwab slumped from an average of 204,000 trades a day in 2000 to 112,000 trades a day in 2002. Revenues fell to $4.14 billion, net income to $109 million, and the stock price fell from a high of $51.70 a share in 1999 to a low of $6.30 in early 2003. By mid 2003, the key question facing Charles Schwab and his co-CEO David Pottruck was how to reverse the decline, revitalize growth, and attain the company's goal of 20 percent a year revenue growth and a profit margin greater than 12 percent?

The Securities Brokerage Industry[1]

A security refers to financial instruments, such as stocks, bonds, commodity contracts, stock option contracts, and foreign exchange contracts. The securities brokerage industry is concerned with the issuance and trading of financial securities, as well as a number of related activities. A broker's clients may be individuals, corporations, or government bodies. Brokers undertake one or more of the following functions: assist corporations to raise capital by offering stocks and bonds, help governments raise capital through bond issues, give advice to businesses on their foreign currency needs, assist corporations with mergers and acquisitions, help individuals plan their financial future and trade financial securities, and provide detailed investment research to individuals and institutions so that they can make more informed investment decisions.

Industry Background

In 2002, there were more than 8,000 broker-dealers registered in the United States, down from 9,515 in 1987. The industry is highly concentrated with some 261 firms that are members of the New York Stock Exchange (NYSE) accounting for 81 percent of the assets of all broker-dealers, and 70 percent of the revenue and capital. The ten largest NYSE firms accounted for 59 percent of the gross revenue in the industry in 2001, up from 48 percent in 1998. The consolidation of the industry has been driven in part by deregulation, which is discussed in more detail below.

Broker-dealers make their money in a number of ways. They earn *commissions* (or fees) for executing a customer's order to buy or sell a given security (stocks, bonds, option contracts, etc). They earn *trading income,* which is the realized and unrealized gains and losses on securities held and traded by the brokerage firm. They earn money from *underwriting fees,* which are the fees charged to corporate and government clients for managing an issue of stocks or bonds on their behalf. They earn *asset management fees,* which represent income from the sale of mutual fund securities, from account supervision fees, or from investment advisory or administrative service fees. They earn *margin interest,* which is the interest that customers pay to the brokerage when they borrow against the value of their securities to finance purchases. They earn *other securities related revenue* which comes from subscription fees for research services, charges for advisory work on proposed mergers and acquisitions, and so on. Finally, many brokerages earn *non-securities revenue* from other financial services, such as credit card operations or mortgage services. Exhibit 1 illus-

trates the breakdown between the various income sources for brokers in 2002.

Industry Groups

Brokerage firms can be segmented into five groups. First, there are *national full line firms,* which are the largest full-service brokers with extensive branch systems. They provide virtually every financial service and product that a brokerage can offer to both households (retail customers) and institutions (corporations, governments, and other nonprofit organizations such as universities). Examples of such firms include Merrill Lynch, Salmon Smith Barney, and A.G. Edwards. Most of these firms are headquartered in New York. For retail customers, national full line firms provide access to a personal financial consultant, traditional brokerage services, securities research reports, asset management services, financial planning advice, and a range of other services such as margin loans, mortgage loans, and credit cards. For institutional clients, these firms will also arrange and underwrite the issuance of financial securities, manage their financial assets, provide advice on mergers and acquisitions, and provide more detailed research reports than those normally provided to retail customers, often for a fee.

Large investment banks are a second group. This group includes Bear Stearns, Goldman Sachs, and Morgan Stanley. These banks have a limited branch network and focus primarily on institutional clients, although they also may have a retail business focused on high net worth individuals (typically individuals with more than $1 million to invest).

A third group are *regional brokers,* which are full service brokerage operations with a branch network in certain regions of the country. Regional brokers typically focus on retail customers, although some have an institutional presence.

Fourth, there are a number of *New York City–based* brokers, who conduct a broad array of financial services, including brokerage, investment banking, traditional money management, and so on.

Finally, there are the *discounters,* who are primarily involved in the discount brokerage business and focus on executing orders to buy and sell stocks for retail customers. Commissions are their main source of business revenue. They charge lower commissions than full service brokers, but do not offer the same infrastructure such as personal financial consultants and detailed research reports. The discounters provide trading and execution services at deep discounts

EXHIBIT 1

Brokers' Line of Business, as a Percentage of Revenues, 2002

Source: Securities Industry Association.

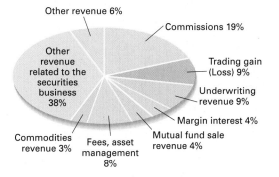

- Other revenue 6%
- Commissions 19%
- Other revenue related to the securities business 38%
- Trading gain (Loss) 9%
- Underwriting revenue 9%
- Margin interest 4%
- Mutual fund sale revenue 4%
- Commodities revenue 3%
- Fees, asset management 8%

online via the Web. Many discounters, such as Ameritrade and E*Trade, do not maintain branch offices. Schwab, which was one of the first discounters, and remains the largest, has a network of brick and mortar offices, as well as a leading online presence.

Earnings Trends

Industry revenues and earnings are volatile, being driven by variations in the volume of trading activity (and commissions), underwriting, and merger and acquisition activity. All of these tend to be highly correlated with changes in the value of interest rates and the stock market. In general, when interest rates fall, the cost of borrowing declines so corporations and governments tend to issue more securities, which increases underwriting income. Also, low interest rates tend to stimulate economic growth which leads to higher corporate profits, and thus higher stock values. When interest rates decline, individuals typically move some of their money out of low interest bearing cash accounts or low yielding bonds, and into stocks, in an attempt to earn higher returns. This drives up trading volume and hence commissions. Low interest rates, by reducing the cost of borrowing, can also increase merger and acquisition activity. Moreover, in a rising stock market, corporations often use their stock as currency with which to make acquisitions of other companies. This drives up merger and acquisition activity, and the fees brokerages earn from such activity.

The 1990s was characterized by one of the strongest stock market advances in history (see Exhibit 2, which shows the value of the Standard & Poor's 500 stock market index between January 1990 and October 2003). This was driven by a favorable economic environment, including falling interest rates, new information technology, productivity gains in American industry, and steady economic expansion, all of which translated into growing corporate profits and rising stock prices.

Also feeding the stock market's advance were favorable demographic trends. During the 1990s American baby boomers started to save for retirement, pumping significant assets into equity funds. In 1989, some 32.5 percent of U.S. households owned equities. By 2002, the figure had risen to 49.5 percent. In 1975, some 45 percent of the liquid financial assets of American households were in financial securities, including stocks, bonds, mutual funds, and money market funds. By 2002, this figure had increased to 75 percent. The total value of household liquid financial assets increased from $1.7 trillion to $15 trillion over the same period.[2] Adding fuel to the fire, by the late 1990s stock market mania had taken hold. Stock prices rose to speculative highs rarely seen before as "irrationally exuberant" retail investors who seemed to believe that stock prices could only go up made increasingly risky and speculative "investments" in richly valued equities.[3]

The long stock market boom drove an expansion of industry revenues, which, for brokerages that were members of the NYSE, grew from $54 billion in 1990

EXHIBIT 2

The S&P 500 Index, January 1990 to October 2003

EXHIBIT 3

Total Revenue for the Brokerage Industry, 1990–2002

Source: Securities Industry Association.

to $245 billion in 2000 (see Exhibit 3). As the bubble burst and the stock market slumped in 2001 and 2002, so brokerage revenues plummeted to $149 billion, forcing brokerages to cut expenses.

The expense structure of the brokerage industry is dominated by two big items—interest expenses and compensation expenses (see Exhibit 4), which together account for about three-quarters of industry expenses. Interest expenses reflect the interest rate paid on cash deposits at brokerages, and rise or fall with the size of deposits and interest rates. As such, they are generally not regarded as a controllable expense (since the interest rate is ultimately set by the U.S. Federal Reserve and market forces).

Compensation expenses reflect both employee headcount and bonuses. For some brokerage firms, particularly those dealing with institutional clients, bonuses can be enormous, with multimillion dollar

EXHIBIT 4

Expense Structure of Brokerages, 1990–2002

Source: Securities Industry Association.

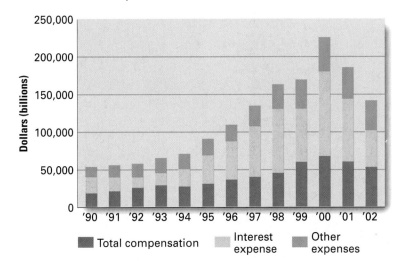

bonuses being awarded to productive employees. Compensation expenses and employee headcount tend to grow during bull markets, only to be rapidly curtailed once a bear market sets in.

The bursting of the 1990s stock market bubble brought a fall in profitability for brokerage firms. However, the fall was not as bad as many expected because it was accompanied by a sharp drop in interest rates to historic lows, by quick reductions in employee headcounts, and by a drop in bonuses. Pretax profit margins for the NYSE members dropped from 15.6 percent in 1999 to 6.9 percent in 2002. The drop was most significant among discounters, who saw their pretax profit margin fall from 20.1 percent in 2000 to 1.5 percent in 2001. By comparison, the pretax profit margin of national full line brokers fell from 14.1 percent in 2000 to 6.1 percent in 2001.

Exhibit 5 provides more detail on industry profitability, comparing the profitability, measured by return on invested capital, of five firms for 1993–2002. These firms were the national full line firms Merrill Lynch and A.G. Edwards, the investment banks Bears Stearns and Legg Mason, and the largest discounter, Charles Schwab. The exhibit shows Schwab's premier performance during the 1990s, but also shows that Schwab suffered a rapid decline in profitability during 2000–2002. Significantly though, Schwab still outperformed all but Legg Mason in 2002.

Deregulation

The industry has been progressively deregulated since May 1, 1975, when a fixed commission structure on securities trades was dismantled. This development allowed for the emergence of discount brokers such as Charles Schwab. Until the mid 1980s, however, the financial services industry was highly segmented due to a 1933 act of Congress known as the Glass-Steagall Act. This act, which was passed in the wake of widespread bank failures following the stock market crash of 1929, erected regulatory barriers between different sectors of the financial services industry, such as commercial banking, insurance, saving and loans, and investment services (including brokerages). Most significantly, Section 20 of the act erected a wall between commercial banking and investment services, barring commercial banks from investing in shares of stocks, limiting them to buying and selling securities as an agent, prohibiting them from underwriting and dealing in securities, and from being affiliated with any organization that did so.

In 1987, Section 20 was relaxed to allow banks to earn up to 5 percent of their revenue from securities underwriting. The limit was raised to 10 percent in 1989 and 25 percent in 1996. In 1999, the Gramm-Leach-Bliley (GLB) Act was past, which finalized the repeal of the Glass-Steagall Act. By removing the walls between commercial banks, broker-dealers, and

EXHIBIT 5

Return on Invested Capital (%), 1993–2002

Source: Value Line Investment Survey.

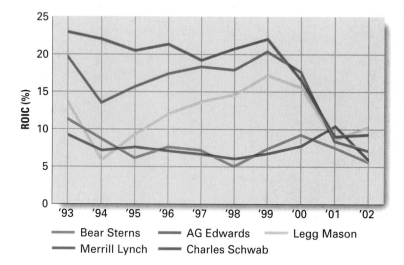

insurance companies, many predicted that the GLB Act would lead to massive industry consolidation, with commercial banks purchasing brokers and insurance companies. The rationale was that such diversified financial services firms would become one-stop financial supermarkets, cross-selling products to their expanded client base. For example, a financial supermarket might sell insurance to brokerage customers, or brokerage services to commercial bank customers. The leader in this process was Citigroup, which was formed in 1998 by a merger between Citicorp, a commercial bank, and Traveler's, an insurance company. Since Traveler's had already acquired Salmon Smith Barney, a major brokerage firm, the new Citigroup seemed to signal a new wave of consolidation in the industry. The passage of the GLB Act allowed Citigroup to start cross-selling products.

However, industry reports suggest that cross-selling is easier in theory than practice, in part because customers were not ready for the development.[4] In an apparent admission that this was the case, in 2002 Citigroup announced that it would spin off Traveler's Insurance as a separate company. At the same time, the fact remains that the GLB Act has made it easier for commercial banks to get into the brokerage business, and there have been several acquisitions to this effect. The most significant entry by commercial banks so far has been into the securities underwriting business.

The Growth of Schwab

The son of an assistant district attorney in California, Charles Schwab started to exhibit an entrepreneurial streak from an early age. As a boy he picked walnuts and bagged them for $5 per 100-pound sack. He raised chickens in his backyard, sold the eggs door to door, killed and plucked the fryers for market, and peddled the manure as fertilizer. Schwab called it "my first fully integrated businesses."[5]

As a child, Schwab had to struggle with a severe case of dyslexia, a disorder that makes it difficult to process written information. To keep up with his classes, he had to resort to Cliffs Notes and Classics Illustrated comic books. Schwab believes, however, that his dyslexia was ultimately a motivator, spurring him on to overcome the disability and excel. Schwab excelled enough to gain admission to Stanford, where he received a degree in economics, which was followed by an MBA from Stanford Business School.

Fresh out of Stanford in the 1960s, Schwab embarked upon his first entrepreneurial effort, an investment advisory newsletter, which grew to include a mutual fund with $20 million under management. However, after the stock market fell sharply in 1969, the State of Texas ordered Schwab to stop accepting investments through the mail from its citizens because the fund was not registered to do business in the state. Schwab went to court and lost. Ultimately, he had to close his business, leaving him with $100,000 in debt and a marriage that had collapsed under the emotional strain.

The Early Days

Schwab soon bounced back. Capitalized by $100,000 that he borrowed from his uncle Bill, who had a successful industrial company of his own called Commander Corp, in 1971 Schwab started a new company, First Commander. Based in San Francisco, a world away from Wall Street, First Commander was a conventional brokerage that charged clients fixed commissions for securities trades. The name was changed to Charles Schwab the following year.

In 1974, at the suggestion of a friend, Schwab joined a pilot test of discount brokerage being conducted by the Securities and Exchange Commission. The discount brokerage idea instantly appealed to Schwab. He personally hated selling, particularly cold calling, the constant calling on actual or prospective customers to encourage them to make a stock trade. Moreover, Schwab was deeply disturbed by the conflict of interest that seemed everywhere in the brokerage world, with stock brokers encouraging customers to make questionable trades in order to boost commissions. Schwab also questioned the worth of the investment advice brokers gave clients, feeling that it reflected the inherent conflict of interest in the brokerage business and did not empower customers.

Schwab used the pilot test to finetune his model for a discount brokerage. When the SEC abolished mandatory fixed commission the following year, Schwab quickly moved into the business. His basic thrust was to empower investors by giving them the information and tools required to make their own decisions about securities investments, while keeping Schwab's costs low so that this service could be offered at a deep discount to the commissions charged by full-service brokers. Driving down costs meant that unlike full-service brokers, Schwab did not employ financial analysts and researchers who developed proprietary investment research for the firm's clients. Instead, Schwab focused on providing clients with third-party investment research. These "reports" evolved to include a company's financial history, a smatter of comments from securities analysts at other brokerage firms that had appeared in the news, and a tabulation of buy and sell recommendations from full commission brokerage houses. The reports were sold to Schwab's customers at cost (in 1992, this was $9.50 for each report plus $4.75 for each additional report).[6]

A founding principle of the company was a desire to be the most useful and ethical provider of financial services. Underpinning this move was Schwab's own belief in the inherent conflict of interest between brokers at full-service firms and their clients. The desire to avoid a conflict of interest caused Schwab to rethink the traditional commission-based pay structure. As an alternative to commission-based pay, Schwab paid all of its employees, including its brokers, a salary plus a bonus that was tied to attracting and satisfying customers and achieving productivity and efficiency targets. Commissions were taken out of the compensation equation.

The chief promoter of Schwab's approach to business, and marker of the Schwab brand, was none other than Charles Schwab himself. In 1977, Schwab started to use pictures of Charles Schwab in its advertisements, a practice it still follows today.

The customer centric focus of the company led Schwab to think of ways to make the company accessible to customers. In 1975, Schwab became the first discount broker to open a branch office and to offer access twenty-four hours a day seven days a week. Interestingly, however, the decision to open a branch was not something that Charles Schwab initially embraced. He wanted to keep costs low and thought it would be better if everything could be managed by way of a telephone. However, Charles Schwab was forced to ask his uncle Bill for more capital to get his nascent discount brokerage off the ground. Uncle Bill agreed to invest $300,000 in the company, but on one condition: He insisted that Schwab open a branch office in Sacramento and employee uncle Bill's son-in-law as manager![7] Reluctantly Charles Schwab agreed to Uncle Bill's demand for a show of nepotism, hoping that the branch would not be too much of a drain on the company's business.

What happened next was a surprise; there was an immediate and dramatic increase in activity at Schwab, most of it from Sacramento. Customer inquiries, the number of trades per day, and the number of new accounts, all spiked upward. Yet there was also a puzzle here, for the increase was not linked to an increase in foot traffic in the branch. Intrigued, Schwab opened several more branches over the next year, and each time noticed the same pattern. For example, when Schwab opened its first branch in Denver it had three hundred customers. It added another seventeen hundred new accounts in the months following the opening of the branch, and yet there was not a big spike up in foot traffic at the Denver branch.

What Schwab began to realize is that the branches served a powerful psychological purpose—they gave customers a sense of security that Schwab was a real company. Customers were reassured by seeing a branch with people in it. In practice, many clients would rarely visit a branch. They would open an account, and execute trades over the telephone (or later, via the Internet). But the branch helped them to make that first commitment. Far from being a drain, Schwab realized that the branches were a marketing tool. People wanted to be "perceptually close to their money," and the branches satisfied that deep psychological need. From one branch in 1975, Schwab grew to have 52 branches in 1982, 175 by 1992, and 430 in 2002.

By the mid 1980s, customers could access Schwab in person at a branch during office hours, by phone day or night, by a telephone voice recognition quote and trading service known as TeleBroker, and by an innovative proprietary online network. To encourage customers to use TeleBroker or its online trading network, Schwab reduced commissions on transactions executed this way by 10 percent, but it saved much more than that because doing business via computers was cheaper. By 1995, Telebroker was handling 80 million calls and 10 million trades a year, 75 percent of Schwab's annual volume. To service this system, in the mid 1980s Schwab invested $20 million in four regional customer call centers, routing all calls to them rather than branches. Today these call centers have four thousand employees.

Schwab was the first to establish a PC-based online trading system in 1986, with the introduction of its Equalizer service. The system had 15,000 customers in 1987, and 30,000 by the end of 1988. The online system, which required a PC with a modem, allowed investors to check current stock prices, place orders, and check their portfolios. In addition, an "offline" program for PCs enabled investors to do fundamental and technical analysis on securities. To encourage customers to start using the system, there was no additional charge for using the online system after a $99 sign-up fee. In contrast, other discount brokers with PC-based online systems, such as Quick and Riley's (which had a service known as "Quick Way") or Fidelity's (whose service was called "Fidelity Express") charged users between 10 cents and 44 cents a minute for online access depending on the time of day.[8]

Schwab's pioneering move into online trading was in many ways just an evolution of the company's early utilization of technology. In 1979, Schwab spent $2 million, an amount equivalent to the company's entire net worth at the time, to purchase a used IBM System 360 computer, plus software, that was leftover from CBS's 1976 election coverage. At the time, brokerages generated and had to process massive amounts of paper to execute buy and sell orders. The computer gave Schwab a capability that no other brokerage had at the time: take a buy or sell order that came in over the phone, edit it on a computer screen, and then submit the order for processing without generating paper. Not only did the software provide for instant execution of orders, but it also offered what were then sophisticated quality controls, checking a customer's account to see if funds were available before executing a transaction. As a result of this system Schwab's costs plummeted as it took paper out of the system. Moreover, the cancel and rebill rate—a measure of the accuracy of trade executions—dropped from an average of 4 percent to 0.1 percent.[9] Schwab soon found it could handle twice the transaction volume of other brokers, at less cost, and with much greater accuracy. Within two years, every other broker in the nation had developed similar systems, but Schwab's early investment had given it an edge and underpinned the company's belief in the value of technology to reduce costs and empower customers.

By 1982, the technology at Schwab was well ahead of that used by most full-service brokers. It was this commitment to technology that allowed Schwab to offer a product that was similar in conception to Merrill Lynch's revolutionary Cash Management Account (CMA), which was introduced in 1980. The CMA account automatically sweeps idle cash into money market funds and allows customers to draw on their money by check or credit card. Schwab's system, know as the Schwab One Account, was introduced in 1982. It went beyond Merrill's in that it allowed brokers to execute orders instantly through Schwab's computer link to the exchange floor.

In 1984, Schwab moved into the mutual fund business, not by offering its own mutual funds, but by launching a mutual fund marketplace, which allowed customers to invest in some 140 no-load mutual funds (a "no-load" fund has no sales commission). By 1990, the number of funds in the market place was four hundred, and the total assets involved exceeded $2 billion. For the mutual fund companies, the mutual fund marketplace offered distribution to Schwab's growing customer base. For its part, Schwab kept a small portion of the revenue stream that flowed to the fund companies from Schwab clients.

In 1986, Schwab made a gutsy move to eliminate the fees for managing individual retirement accounts (IRAs). IRAs allow customers to deposit money in an account where it accumulates interest tax free until withdrawal at retirement. The legislation establishing IRAs had been passed by Congress in 1982. At the time, estimates suggest that IRA accounts could attract as much as $50 billion in assets within ten years. In actual fact, the figure turned out to be $725 billion!

Initially Schwab followed industry practice and collected a small fee for each IRA. By 1986, the fees amounted to $9 million a year, not a trivial amount for Schwab in those days. After looking at the issue, Charles Schwab himself made the call to scrap the fee, commenting, "It's a nuisance, and we'll get it back."[10] He was right; Schwab's No-Annual Fee IRA immediately exceeded the company's most optimistic projections.

Despite technological and product innovations, by 1983 Schwab was scrapped for capital to fund expansion. To raise funds, he sold the company to Bank of America for $55 million in stock and a seat on the bank's board of directors. The marriage did not last long. By 1987, the bank was reeling under loan losses, and the entrepreneurially minded Schwab was frustrated by banking regulations that inhibited his desire to introduce new products. Using a mixture of loans, his own money, and contributions from other managers, friends, and family, Schwab led a management buyout of the company for $324 million in cash and securities.

Six months later on September 22, 1987, Schwab went public with an IPO that raised some $440 million, enabling the company to pay down debt and leaving it with capital to fund an aggressive expansion. At the time, Schwab had 1.6 million customers, revenues of $308 million, and a pretax profit margin of 21 percent. Schwab announced plans to increase its branch network by 30 percent to around 120 offices over the next year. Then on Monday, October 19, 1987, the U.S. stock market crashed, dropping over 22 percent, the biggest one-day decline in history.

October 1987–1995

After a strong run up over the year, on Friday, October 16, the stock market dropped 4.6 percent. During the weekend, nervous investors jammed the call centers and branch offices, not just at Schwab, but at many other brokerages, as they tried to place sell orders. At Schwab, 99 percent of the orders taken over the weekend for Monday morning were sell orders. As the market opened on Monday morning, it went into free fall. At Schwab, the computers were overwhelmed by eight A.M. The toll free number to the call centers was also totally overwhelmed. All the customers got when they called were busy signals. When the dust had settled, Schwab announced that it had lost $22 million in the fourth quarter of 1987, $15 million of which came from a single customer who had been unable to meet margin calls.

The loss, which amounted to 13 percent of the company's capital, effectively wiped out the company's profit for the year. Moreover, the inability of customers to execute trades during the crash damaged Schwab's hard-earned reputation for customer service. Schwab responded by posting a two-page ad in the *Wall Street Journal* on October 28, 1987. On one page there was a message from Charles Schwab thanking customers for their patience, on the other an ad thanking employees for their dedication.

In the aftermath of the October 1987 crash, trading volume fell by 15 percent as customers, spooked by the volatility of the market, sat on cash balances. The slowdown prompted Schwab to cut back on its expansion plans. Ironically, however, Schwab added a significant number of new accounts in the aftermath of the crash as people looked for cheaper ways to invest.[11]

Beset by weak trading volume through the next eighteen months and reluctant to lay off employees, Schwab sought ways to boost activity. One strategy started out as a compliance issue within Schwab. A compliance officer in the company noticed a disturbing pattern: A number of people had given other people limited power of attorney over their accounts. This in itself was not unusual—for example, the middle-aged children of an elderly individual might have power of attorney over their account—but what the Schwab officer noticed was that some individuals had power of attorney over dozens, if not hundreds, of accounts.

Further investigation turned up the reason—Schwab had been serving an entirely unknown set of customers, independent financial advisors who were managing the financial assets of their clients using Schwab accounts. In early 1989, there were some five hundred financial advisors who managed assets totaling $1.5 billion at Schwab, about 8 percent of all assets at Schwab.

The advisors were attracted to Schwab for a number of reasons, including cost and the company's commitment not to give advice, which was the business of the advisors. When Charles Schwab heard about this, he immediately saw an opportunity. Financial advisors, he reasoned, represented a powerful way to acquire customers. In 1989, the company rolled out a program to aggressively court this group. Schwab hired a marketing team and told them to focus explicitly on financial planners, set apart a dedicated trading desk for them, and gave discounts of as much as 15 percent on commissions to financial planners with significant assets under management at Schwab accounts. Schwab also established a Financial Advisors Service, which provided its clients with a list of financial planners who were willing to work solely for a fee, and had no incentive to push the products of a particular client. At the same time, the company stated that it wasn't endorsing the planners' advice, which would run contrary to the company's commitment to offer no advice. Within a year, financial advisors had some $3 billion of clients' assets under management at Schwab.

Schwab also continued to expand its branch network during this period, at a time while many brokerages, still stunned by the October 1987 debacle, were retrenching. Between 1987 and 1989, Schwab's branch network increased by just five, from 106 to 111, but in 1990, it opened up an additional 29 branches and another 28 in 1991.

By the 1990s, Schwab's positioning in the industry had become clear. Although a discounter, Schwab was by no means the lowest price discount broker in

EXHIBIT 6

Commission Structure in 1990

Type of Broker	Average Commission Price on 20 Trades Averaging $8,975 Each
Deep Discount Brokers	$54
Average Discounters	$73
Banks	$88
Schwab, Fidelity, and Quick & Reilly	$92
Full Service Brokers	$206

Source: E. C. Gottschalk, "Schwab Forges Ahead as Other Brokers Hesitate," *Wall Street Journal*, May 11, 1990, page C1.

the country. Its average commission structure was similar to that of Fidelity, the Boston-based mutual fund company that had moved into the discount brokerage business, and Quick & Reilly, a major national competitor (see Exhibit 6). While significantly below that of full-service brokers, the fee structure was also above that of deep discount brokers. Schwab differentiated itself from the deep discount brokers, however, by its branch network, technology, and the information (not advice) that it gave to investors.

In 1992, Schwab rolled out another strategy aimed at acquiring assets—OneSource, the first mutual fund "supermarket." OneSource was created to take advantage of America's growing appetite for mutual funds. By the early 1990s, there were more mutual funds than individual equities. On some days Fidelity, the largest mutual fund company, accounted for 10 percent of the trading volume on the New York Stock Exchange. As American baby boomers aged, they seemed to have an insatiable appetite for mutual funds. But the process of buying and selling mutual finds had never been easy. As Charles Schwab explained in 1996:

> In the days before the supermarkets, to buy a mutual fund you had to write or call the fund distributor. On Day Six, you'd get a prospectus. On Day Seven or Eight you call up and they say you've got to put your money in. If you're lucky, by Day Ten you've bought it. . . . It was even more cumbersome when you redeemed. You had to send a notarized redemption form.[12]

OneSource took the hassle out of owning funds. With a single visit to a branch office, telephone call, or PC-based computer transaction, a Schwab client could buy and sell mutual funds. Schwab imposed no fee at all on investors for the service. Rather, in return for shelf space in Schwab's distribution channel and access to the more than 2 million accounts at Schwab, Schwab charged the fund companies a fee amounting to 0.35 percent of the assets under management. By inserting itself between the fund managers and customers, Schwab changed the balance of power in the mutual fund industry. When Schwab sold a fund through OneSource, it passed along the assets to the fund managers, but not the customers' names. Many fund managers did not like this, because it limited their ability to build a direct relationship with customers, but they had little choice if they wanted access to Schwab's customer base.

OneSource quickly propelled Schwab to the number three position in direct mutual fund distribution, behind the fund companies Fidelity and Vanguard. By 1997, Schwab customers could choose from nearly fourteen hundred funds offered by two hundred different fund families, and Schwab customers had nearly $56 billion in assets invested through OneSource.

1996–2000: eSchwab

In 1994, as access to the World Wide Web began to diffuse rapidly throughout America, a two-year-old start-up run by Bill Porter, a physicist and inventor, launched its first dedicated website for online trading. The company's name was E*Trade. E*Trade announced a flat $14.95 commission on stock trades, significantly below Schwab's average commission, which at the time was $65. It was clear from the outset that E*Trade and other online brokers, such as Ameritrade, offered a direct threat to Schwab. Not only were their commission rates considerably below those of Schwab, but also the ease, speed, and flexibility of trading stocks over the Web suddenly made Schwab's proprietary online trading software, Street Smart, seem limited. (Street Smart was the Windows-based successor to Schwab's DOS-based Equalizer program.) To compound matters, talented people started to leave Schwab for E*Trade and its brethren, which they saw as the wave of the future.

At the time, deep within Schwab, William Pearson, a young software specialist who had worked on the development of Street Smart, quickly saw the transformational power of the Web and believed that it would make proprietary systems like Street Smart obsolete. Pearson believed that Schwab needed to develop its own Web-based software, and quickly. Try as he might, though, Pearson could not get the attention of his supervisor. He tried a number of other executives, but found support hard to come by. Eventually he approached Anne Hennegar, a former Schwab manager that he knew who now worked as a consultant to the company. Hennegar suggested that Pearson meet with Tom Seip, an executive vice president at Schwab who was known for his ability to think outside of the box. Hennegar approached Seip on Pearson's behalf, and Seip responded positively, asking her to set up a meeting. Hennegar and Pearson turned up expecting to meet just Seip, but to their surprise in walked Charles Schwab; his chief operating officer, David Pottruck; and the vice presidents in charge of strategic planning and the electronic brokerage arena.

As the group watched Pearson's demo of how a Web-based system would look and work, they became increasingly excited. It was clear to those in the room that a Web-based system based on real-time information, personalization, customization, and interactivity all advanced Schwab's commitment to empowering customers. By the end of the meeting, Pearson had received a green light to start work on the project.

It soon transpired that several other groups within Schwab had been working on projects that were similar to Pearson's. These were all pulled together under the control of Dawn Lepore, Schwab's chief information officer, who headed up the effort to develop the Web-based service that would ultimately become eSchwab. Meanwhile, significant strategic issues were now beginning to preoccupy Charles Schwab and David Pottruck. They realized that Schwab's established brokerage and a Web-based brokerage business were based on very different revenue and cost models. The Web-based business would probably cannibalize business from Schwab's established brokerage operations, and that might lead people in Schwab to slow down or even derail the Web-based initiative. As Pottruck later put it:

> The new enterprise was going to use a different model for making money than our traditional business, and we didn't want the comparisons to form the basis for a measurement of success or failure. For example, eSchwab's per trade revenue would be less than half that of the mainstream of the company, and that could be seen as a drain on resources rather than a response to what customers would be using in the future.[13]

Pottruck and Schwab understood that unless eSchwab was placed in its own organization, isolated and protected from the established business, it might never get off the ground. They also knew that if they did not cannibalize their own business with eSchwab, someone would do it for them. Thus they decided to set up a separate organization to develop eSchwab. The unit was headed up by Beth Sawi, a highly regarded marketing manager at Schwab who had very good relations with other managers in the company. Sawi set up the development center in a unit physically separated from other Schwab facilities.

eSchwab was launched in May 1996, but without the normal publicity that accompanied most new products at Schwab. Schwab abandoned its sliding scale commission for a flat rate commission of $39 (which was quickly dropped to $29.95) for any stock trade up to 1,000 shares. Within two weeks, 25,000 people had opened eSchwab accounts. By the end of 1997, the figure would soar to 1.2 million, bringing in assets of about $81 billion, or ten times the assets of E*Trade.

Schwab initially kept the two businesses segmented. Schwab's traditional customers were still paying an average of $65 a trade while eSchwab customers were paying $29.95. While Schwab's traditional customers could make toll-free calls to Schwab brokers, eSchwab clients could not. Moreover, Schwab's regular customers couldn't access eSchwab at all. The segmentation soon gave rise to problems. Schwab's branch employees were placed in the uncomfortable position of telling customers that they couldn't set up eSchwab accounts. Some eSchwab customers started to set up traditional Schwab accounts with small sums of money so that they could access Schwab's brokers and Schwab's information services, while continuing to trade via eSchwab. Clearly the segmentation was not sustainable.

Schwab began to analyze the situation. The company's leaders realized that the cleanest way to deal with the problem would be to give every Schwab customer online access, adopt a commission of $29.95 on trading across all channels, and maintain existing levels of customer service at the branch level, and on the phone. However, internal estimates suggested that the cut in commission rates would reduce revenues by $125 million, which would hit Schwab's stock. The problem was compounded by two factors: First, employees owned 40 percent of Schwab's stock, so they would be hurt by any fall in stock price, and second, employees were worried that going to the Web would result in a decline in business at the branch level, and hence a loss of jobs there.

An internal debate ranged within the company for much of 1997, a year when Schwab's revenues surged 24 percent to $2.3 billion. The online trading business grew by more than 90 percent during the year, with online trades accounting for 37 percent of all Schwab trades during 1997, and the trend was up throughout the year.

Looking at these figures, Pottruck, the COO, knew that Schwab had to bite the bullet and give all Schwab customers access to eSchwab (Pottruck was now running the day-to-day operations of Schwab, leaving Charles Schwab to focus on his corporate marketing and PR role). His first task was to enroll the support of the company's largest shareholder, Charles Schwab. With 52 million shares, Charles Schwab would take the biggest hit from any share price decline. According to a *Fortune* article, the conversation between Schwab and Pottruck went something like this:[14]

Pottruck: We don't know exactly what will happen. The budget is shaky. We'll be winging it.

Schwab: We can always adjust our costs.

Pottruck: Yes, but we don't have to do this now. The whole year could be lousy. And the stock!

Schwab: This isn't that hard a decision, because we really have no choice. It's just a question of when, and it will be harder later.

Having secured the agreement of Schwab's founder, Pottruck formed a task force to look at how best to implement the decision. The plan that emerged was to merge all of the company's electronic services into Schwab.com, which would then coordinate Schwab's online and off line business. The base commission rate would be $29.95 whatever channel was used to make a trade—online, branch, or the telephone. The role of the branches would change, and they would start to focus more on customer support. This required a change in incentive systems. Branch employees had been paid bonuses on the basis of the assets they accrued to their branches, but now they would be paid bonuses on assets that came in via the branch or the Web. They would be rewarded for directing clients to the Web.

Schwab implemented the change of strategy on January 15, 1998. Revenues dropped 3 percent in the first quarter as the average commission declined from $63 to $57. Earnings also came in short of expectations

by some $6 million. The company's stock had lost 20 percent of its value by August 1998. However, over much of 1998 new money poured into Schwab. Total accounts surged, with Schwab gaining a million new customers in 1998, a 20 percent increase, while assets grew by 32 percent. As the year progressed, trading volume grew, doubling by year end. By the third quarter, Schwab's revenues and earnings were surging past analysts' expectations. The company ultimately achieved record revenues and earnings in 1998. Net income ended up 29 percent over the prior year, despite falling commission rates, aided by surging trading volume and the lower cost of executing trades over the Web. By the end of the year, 61 percent of all trades at Schwab were made over the Web. After its summer lows, the stock price recovered, ending the year up 130 percent, pushing Schwab's market capitalization past that of Merrill Lynch.[15]

2000–2003: After the Boom

The end of the long stock market boom of the 1990s hit Schwab hard (see Exhibit 7 for selected financial and operating data) as the average number of trades made per day through Schwab fell from 300 million to 190 million between 2000 and 2002. Reflecting this, revenues slumped from $5.79 billion to $4.14 billion and net income from $718 million to $109 million. To cope with the decline, Schwab was forced to cut back on its employee headcount, which fell from a peak of nearly 26,000 employees in 2000 to just over 16,000 in late 2003.

Schwab's strategic reaction to the sea change in market conditions was already taking form as the market implosion began. In January 2000, Schwab acquired U.S. Trust for $2.7 billion. U.S. Trust is a 149-year-old investment advisement business that manages money for high–net worth individuals whose invested assets exceed $2 million. When acquired, U.S. Trust had 7,000 customers and assets of $84 billion, compared with 6.4 million customers and assets of $725 billion at Schwab.[16]

Schwab made the acquisition because it discovered that high–net worth individuals were starting to defect from Schwab for money managers like U.S. Trust. The main reason was that as Schwab's clients got older and richer they started to need institutions that specialized in services that Schwab didn't offer, including personal trusts, estate planning, tax services, and private banking. With baby boomers starting to enter middle to late middle age, and their average net worth projected

EXHIBIT 7

Selected Financial and Operating Data (in Millions, Except per Share Amounts, Ratios, Number of Offices, Average Revenue per Revenue Trade, and as Noted)

| | Growth Rates | | | | | | |
	Compounded 5-Year 1997–2002	Annual 1-Year 2001–2002	2002	2001	2000	1999	1998
Operating Results							
✔Revenues	9%	(5%)	$4,135	$4,353	$5,788	$4,486	$3,178
Expenses excluding interest	13%	(6%)	$3,967	$4,218	$4,557	$3,387	$2,500
Net income	(19%)	(45%)	$109	$199	$718	$666	$410
Basic earnings per share[1]	(20%)	(43%)	$.08	$.14	$.53	$.51	$.32
Diluted earnings per share[1]	(20%)	(43%)	$.08	$.14	$.51	$.49	$.31
Adjusted operating income[2]	3%	(3%)	$396	$407	$849	$666	$410
Dividends declared per common share[3]	7%		$.0440	$.0440	$.0407	$.0373	$.0360
Weighted-average common shares outstanding—diluted			1,375	1,399	1,404	1,373	1,343
Non-trading revenues as a percentage of revenues[4]			66%	63%	51%	47%	49%
Trading revenues as a percentage of revenues[4]			34%	37%	49%	53%	51%
Effective income tax rate			42.6%	44.1%	41.7%	39.4%	39.5%
Capital expenditures—cash purchases of equipment, office facilities, property, and internal-use software development costs, net	1%	(47%)	$160	$301	$705	$370	$199
Capital expenditures as a percentage of revenues			3.9%	6.9%	12.2%	8.3%	6.3%
Performance Measures							
Revenue growth (decline)			(5%)	(25%)	29%	41%	19%
Pre-tax profit margin—reported			4.6%	8.2%	21.3%	24.5%	21.3%
After-tax profit margin—reported			2.6%	4.6%	12.4%	14.9%	12.9%
After-tax profit margin—operating[2]			9.6%	9.4%	14.7%	14.9%	12.9%
Return on stockholders' equity			3%	5%	21%	31%	27%
Financial Condition (at year end)							
Total assets	14%	(2%)	$39,705	$40,464	$38,154	$34,322	$26,407
Long-term debt	8%	(12%)	$642	$730	$770	$518	$419
Stockholders' equity	24%	(4%)	$4,011	$4,163	$4,230	$2,576	$1,673
Assets to stockholders' equity ratio			10	10	9	13	16
Long-term debt to total financial capital (long-term debt plus stockholders' equity)			14%	15%	15%	17%	20%
Client Information (at year end)							
Active client accounts[5]	11%	3%	8.0	7.8	7.5	6.6	5.6
Client assets (in billions)	12%	(10%)	$764.8	$845.9	$871.7	$846.0	$594.3

EXHIBIT 7 (*continued*)

Selected Financial and Operating Data (in Millions, Except per Share Amounts, Ratios, Number of Offices, Average Revenue per Revenue Trade, and as Noted)

| | Growth Rates | | | | | | |
	Compounded 5-Year 1997–2002	Annual 1-Year 2001–2002	2002	2001	2000	1999	1998
Total mutual fund assets (in billions)	14%	(6%)	$323.8	$342.8	$330.3	$294.0	$218.1
Active independent investment advisors (in thousands)	2%	2%	5.9	5.8	5.7	5.8	5.4
Independent investment advisor client accounts (in thousands)	17%	9%	1,182.4	1,081.7	986.5	848.3	689.9
Independent investment advisor client assets (in billions)	16%	(5%)	$222.4	$235.0	$231.3	$213.1	$146.4
Number of Schwab domestic branch offices	7%	(2%)	388	395	384	340	291
Number of U.S. Trust offices	12%		34	34	31	28	24
Employee Information							
Full-time equivalent employees (at year end, in thousands)	3%	(15%)	16.7	19.6	26.3	20.1	15.1
Revenues per average full-time equivalent employee (in thousands)	2%	15%	$220	$192	$239	$249	$214
Compensation and benefits expense as a percentage of revenues			44.8%	43.1%	41.7%	42.1%	43.3%
Clients' Daily Average Trading Volume (in thousands)							
Daily average revenue trades	13%	(16%)	134.1	159.7	242.0	163.1	97.2
Mutual Fund OneSource and other asset-based trades	10%	4%	56.1	54.0	58.1	45.6	40.3
Daily average trades	12%	(11%)	190.2	213.7	300.1	208.7	137.5
Average Revenue per Revenue Trade	(10%)	8%	$37.78	$35.02	$37.38	$45.55	$53.44

[1]Both basic and diluted earnings per share include an extraordinary gain of $.01 per share in 2002 and $.08 per share in 2001.

[2]Represents a non-GAAP income measure, which in 2002 excludes an extraordinary gain, restructuring charges, goodwill and other impairment charges, and merger- and acquisition-related costs totaling $287 million after-tax. In 2001, excludes an extraordinary gain, non-operating revenue (which primarily consists of a gain on the sale of an investment), restructuring and other charges, and merger- and acquisition-related costs totaling $208 million after-tax. In 2000, excludes merger- and acquisition-related costs totaling $131 million after-tax.

[3]Dividends declared per common share do not include dividends declared by USTC prior to the completion of the merger in 2000.

[4]Non-trading revenues include asset management and administration fees, net interest revenue, and other revenues. Trading revenues include commission and principal transaction revenues.

[5]Effective in 1998, active accounts are defined as accounts with balances or activity within the preceding eight months instead of twelve months as previously defined. This change in definition had the effect of decreasing the number of active accounts in 1998 by approximately 200,000.

to rise, Schwab decided that it needed to get into this business or lose high–net worth clients.

The decision, though, started to bring Schwab into conflict with the network of six thousand or so independent financial advisors that the company had long fostered through the Schwab Advisers Network, and who funneled customers and assets into Schwab accounts. Some advisors felt that Schwab was starting to move in on their turf, and they were not too happy about it.

In May 2002, Schwab made another move in this direction when it announced that it would launch a new service targeted at clients with more than $500,000 in assets. Known as Schwab Private Client, and developed with the help of U.S. Trust employees, for a fee of 0.6 percent of assets Private Client customers can meet face to face with a financial consultant to work out an investment plan and return to the same consultant for further advice. Schwab stressed that the consultant would not tell clients what to buy and sell—that is still left to the client. Nor will clients get the legal, tax, and estate planning advice offered by U.S. Trust and independent financial advisors. Rather, they get a financial plan and consultation regarding industry and market conditions.[17]

To add power to this strategy, Schwab also announced that it would start a new stock rating system. The stock rating system is not the result of the work of financial analysts. Rather, it is the product of a computer model, developed at Schwab, that analyzes more than 3,000 stocks on twenty-four basic measures, such as free cash flow, sales growth, insider trades, and so on, and then assigns grades. The top 10 percent get an A, the next 20 percent a B, the middle 40 percent a C, the next 20 percent a D, and the lowest 10 percent an F. Schwab claims that the new system is "a systematic approach with nothing but objectivity, not influenced by corporate relationships, investment banking, or any of the above."[18]

Critics of this strategy were quick to point out that many of Schwab's branch employees lacked the qualifications and expertise to give financial advice. At the time the service was announced, Schwab had some 150 qualified financial advisors in place, and planned to have 300 by early 2003. These elite employees will of course demand a higher salary than the traditional Schwab branch employees, who in many respects were little more than order takers and providers of prepackaged information.

The Schwab Private Client service also caused further grumbling among the private financial advisors affiliated with Schwab. In 2002, there were 5,900 of these. In total their clients amounted to $222 billion of Schwab's $765 billion in client assets. Several stated that they would no longer keep clients' money at Schwab. However, Schwab stated that it would use the Private Client Service as a device for referring people who wanted more sophisticated advice than Schwab

could offer to its network of registered financial advisors, and particularly an inner circle of 330 advisors who have an average of $500 million in assets under management and seventeen years of experience.[19] According to one member of this group, "Schwab is not a threat to us. Most people realize the hand holding it takes to do that kind of work and Schwab wants us to do it. There's just more money behind the Schwab Advisors Network. The dead wood is gone, and firms like ours stand to benefit from even more additional leads."[20]

Also in May 2002, Schwab announced that it would be raising commission rates for broker assisted trades from $39 to $54.95 on June 1, 2002. The fee for trading via the automated telephone service went from $29.95 to $49.95, and a $3 "handling fee" was tacked onto the basic $29.95 online commission rate.

ENDNOTES

1. Material for this section is drawn from two main sources: (a) *Securities Industry 2002 Fact Book*, Securities Industry Association, New York, 2002; and (b) *Standard & Poor's Industry Survey*, Investment Services, May 1, 2003.
2. Securities Industry Association, *Key Trends in the Securities Industry*, November 7, 2002.
3. Robert E. Shiller, *Irrational Exuberance* (Princeton, NJ: Princeton University Press, 2002).
4. Anthony O'Donnell, "New Thinking on Convergence," *Wall Street & Technology*, May 2002, pages 16–18.
5. Terence P. Pare, "How Schwab Wins Investors," *Fortune*, June 1, 1992, pages 52–59.
6. Ibid.
7. John Kador, *Charles Schwab: How One Company Beat Wall Street and Reinvented the Brokerage Industry* (New York: John Wiley & Sons, 2002).
8. Earl C. Gottschalk, "Computerized Investment Systems Thrive as People Seek Control over Portfolios," *Wall Street Journal*, September 27, 1988, page 1.
9. Kador, *Charles Schwab*.
10. Ibid., page 73.
11. G. C. Hill, "Schwab to Curb Expansion, Tighten Belt Because of Post Crash Trading Decline," *Wall Street Journal*, December 7, 1987, page 1.
12. Kador, *Charles Schwab*, page 185.
13. Ibid., page 217.
14. Erick Schonfeld, "Schwab Puts It All Online," *Fortune*, December 7, 1998, pages 94–99.
15. Anonymous, "Schwab's e-Gambit," *Business Week*, January 11, 1999, page 61.
16. Amy Kover, "Schwab Makes a Grand Play for the Rich," *Fortune*, February 7, 2000, page 32.
17. Louise Lee and Emily Thornton, "Schwab v Wall Street," *Business Week*, June 3, 2002, pages 64–70.
18. Quoted in Lee and Thornton, "Schwab v Wall Street," pages 64–70.
19. Erin E. Arvedlund, "Schwab Trades Up," *Barron's*, May 27, 2002, pages 19–20.
20. Ibid., page 20.

Li & Fung—The Global Value Chain Configurator

This case was prepared by S.S. George, ICFAI Center for Management Research.

In an age when the Internet is supposedly going to eliminate the middle-man, here's a middleman, an old Asian trading company that has made itself indispensable.[1]

—*An Article in* Forbes

We deliver a new type of value added, truly global product that has never been seen before. We're pulling apart the value chain and optimising each step— and we're doing it globally.[2]

—*Victor Fung, Chairman, Li & Fung, in June 2000*

Strengthening Its Fort

In January 2004, Li & Fung Limited (Li & Fung), a Hong Kong–based global consumer goods trading giant, announced that Li & Fung Trading (Shanghai), its wholly owned subsidiary, had been granted an export company license by the Ministry of Commerce of the People's Republic of China (China). After receiving the license, Li & Fung Trading (Shanghai) became the first wholly owned foreign trading company to be offered direct export rights in China. The company was authorized to export China-sourced goods directly to customers worldwide and import raw materials for manufacturing in China. Li & Fung was until then dependent on its Chinese partners for exporting from China.

Copyright © 2007 by S.S. George. This case was prepared by S.S. George, ICFAI Center for Management Research, as the basis for class discussion rather than to illustrate either effective or ineffective handling of an administrative situation. Reprinted by permission of S. S. George. All rights reserved. For the most recent financial results of the company discussed in this case, go to http://finance.yahoo.com, input the company's stock symbol, and download the latest company report from its homepage.

According to William Fung (William), managing director, Li & Fung, the license freed the group companies (see Exhibit 1) from the many trading restrictions in China. It would enhance the company's competitiveness and increase its share in the global market. William said, "With the ability to directly export products from China to our customers worldwide, Li & Fung is now able to offer an even more complete supply chain service."[3]

After China joined the World Trade Organization (WTO) in 2001, it emerged as the world's largest exporter of textile and clothing. The country also consolidated its position as one of the world's largest and fastest growing manufacturing economies. According to the U.S. International Textiles Association, export of textiles and clothing from China to the United States

[1]"Stitches in Time," www.forbes.com, June 9, 1999.
[2]"Winning at a Global Game: Part Five of an Eleven Part Series," www.asiabusinesstoday.org, June 10, 2000.
[3]"First Hong Kong Trading Firm to Gain China Licence," www.hktrader.net, February 2004.

EXHIBIT 1

Li & Fung's Major Subsidiaries and Associated Companies

Held Directly	Place of Incorporation and Operation	Issued and Fully Paid Share Capital	Principal Activities
Li & Fung (B.V.I.) Limited	British Virgin Islands	US$ 400,010	Marketing services and investment holding
Basic & More Fashion Limited	Hong Kong	HK$ 1,000,000	Export trading
Black Cat Fireworks Limited	England	GBP 1,200,000	Wholesaling
Camberley Enterprises Limited	Hong Kong	HK$ 250,000	Apparel exporting
Civati Limited	Hong Kong	US$ 450,000	Export trading
Colby International Limited	Hong Kong	HK$ 1,500,000	Exporting of garments and sundry goods
Colby Tekstil ve Dis Ticaret Limited Sirketi	Turkey	TL 50,000,000,000	Export trading
CS International Limited	Hong Kong	HK$ 1,000,000	Provision of export assistance service
Dodwell (Mauritius) Limited	Hong Kong	HK$ 500,000	Export trading
Golden Gate Fireworks Inc.	U.S.A.	US$ 600,000	Commission agent and investment holding
GSCM (HK) Limited	Hong Kong	HK$ 140,000	Export trading
Hillung Enterprises Limited	Hong Kong	HK$ 300,000	Export trading
International Sourcing Group, LLC	U.S.A.	US$ 300,000	Trading of apparel
Janco Overseas Limited	Hong Kong	HK$ 760,000	Buying agent
Kariya Industries Limited	Hong Kong	HK$ 1,000,000	Manufacturing and trading
LF Maclaine (Thailand) Limited	Thailand	Baht 4,000,000	Export trading
Li & Fung Agencia De Compras em Portugal, Limitada	Portugal	PTE 20,000,000	Export trading
Li & Fung (Exports) Limited	Hong Kong	HK$ 8,610,000	Export trading
Li & Fung (Fashion Accessories) Limited	Hong Kong	HK$ 600,000	Export trading
Li & Fung (India)	India	Rupees 64,000,200	Export trading
Li & Fung (Italia) S.r.l.	Italy	Lire 90,000,000	Export trading
Li & Fung (Korea) Limited	Korea	Won 200,000,000	Export trading
Li & Fung (Korea) Limited	Mauritius	Rupees 1,250,000	Export trading
Li & Fung Mumes sillik, Pazarlama Limited	Turkey	TL 25,000,000,000	Export trading
Li & Fung (Phillippines) Inc.	The Philippines	Peso 500,000	Export trading
Li & Fung (Properties) Limited	Hong Kong	HK$ 1,000,000	Property investment
Li & Fung Taiwan Holdings Limited	Taiwan	NT$ 287,996,000	Investment holding
Li & Fung Taiwan Investments Limited	British Virgin Islands	US$ 4,912,180	Investment holding
Li & Fung (Taiwan) Limited	Taiwan	NT$ 63,000,000	Export trading
Li & Fung (Thailand) Limited	Thailand	Baht 6,000,000	Export trading

EXHIBIT 1 (*continued*)

Li & Fung's Major Subsidiaries and Associated Companies

Held Directly	Place of Incorporation and Operation	Issued and Fully Paid Share Capital	Principal Activities
Li & Fung (Trading) Limited	Hong Kong	HK$ 10,000,200	Export trading and investment holding
Li & Fung Trading (Shanghai) Limited	The People's Republic of China	RMB 50,000,000	Export trading
Li & Fung (Zhanjiang) Limited	The People's Republic of China	US$ 1,999,055	Packaging
Livring Limited	Mauritius	Rs 250,000	Export trading
Lloyd Textile Trading Limited	Hong Kong	HK$ 1,000,000	Export trading
Maclaine Limited	Hong Kong	HK$ 5,570,150	Export trading
Perfect Trading Inc.	Egypt	LE 2,480,000	Export trading
Shiu Fung Fireworks Company Limited	Hong Kong	HK$ 1,200,000	Export trading
The Millwork Trading Co., Ltd	U.S.A.	US$ 1,331,000	Distribution and wholesaling
Toy Island Manufacturing Company Limited	Hong Kong	HK$ 62,000,000	Design and marketing
Verity Enterprises Limited	Hong Kong	HK$ 2,000,000	Export trading
W S Trading Limited	Hong Kong	HK$ 1,000,000	Export trading

Notes:
(1) Li & Fung (B.V.I.) Limited provides the subsidiaries with promotional and marketing services outside Hong Kong.
(2) Subsidiaries not audited by PricewaterhouseCoopers, Hong Kong. The aggregate net assets of subsidiaries not audited by PricewaterhouseCoopers, Hong Kong amounted to approximately 5 percent of the Group's total net assets.

Exhibit 1 lists out the principal subsidiaries of the company as of December 31, 2003, which, in the opinion of the directors, principally affected the results for the year or form a substantial portion of the net assets of the Group. To give details of other subsidiaries would, in the opinion of the directors, result in particulars of excessive length.

Source: Li & Fung Annual Report, 2003.

doubled from US$ 6.5 billion in 2001 to US$ 11.6 bn in 2003. With export quotas among WTO members proposed to be eliminated from January 2005, China would be free of restrictions on quantity of exports to the United States, enabling further growth.

In this light, analysts felt Li & Fung stood to benefit significantly from its new license as it was one of the world's leading textile export traders, and the largest to the United States. The company was well placed to leverage China's leadership position in textile manufacturing and exports, as that country was the company's largest manufacturing hub, from where it sourced over US$ 2 bn worth of products annually. Li & Fung had sixteen offices in China, which it planned to take to thirty-six by 2007. The downside was that in early 2004, Li & Fung faced many challenges such as a slowdown in its overall revenues and net profit growth, overdependence on the U.S. market, declining share of revenues from the European market, and negligible growth in revenues from the rapidly growing Asian markets.

Background Note

The history of Li & Fung goes back to the early 1900s, making it the oldest trading company in Hong Kong. The company was founded in 1906 by Fung Pak-Liu (Pak-Liu) and Li To-ming (To-ming) in Guangzhou (South China) and was one of the first Chinese-owned export companies. Trade in China at that time was controlled by foreign commercial houses. Li & Fung began operations by exporting porcelain and silk, mainly to the United States. It later expanded its product portfolio to include bamboo, jade, ivory, rattan ware, fireworks, and handicrafts.

During the early 1900s, since U.S. buyers did not know Chinese and Chinese sellers did not know English, traders who could speak both languages became essential mediators between buyers and sellers. Therefore, Li & Fung prospered, earning commissions as high as 15 percent on each export deal. Li & Fung was formally established in Hong Kong as a limited company in 1937.

World War II disrupted trading in the early 1940s, forcing Li & Fung to cease trading for some years. In 1943, Pak-Liu passed away. Shortly after the end of the war, To-ming, who had been a silent partner, retired and sold his stake to Pak-Liu's family. With this, the Fung family became the sole owners of Li & Fung.

In 1949, Pak-Liu's son, Fung Hon-chu (Hon-chu), restarted trading operations in Hong Kong, which had come under British control. Hon-chu was instrumental in leading Li & Fung into the new era. The trading business picked up momentum in Hong Kong during the mid 1900s, driven by the influx of refugees, which transformed China into a manufacturing economy that exported labor intensive consumer products. Li & Fung began exporting consumer products such as garments, electronics, plastic flowers, and toys and was soon Hong Kong's biggest exporter.

By the early 1970s, the trading business in Hong Kong began to struggle owing to stiff competition from other manufacturing economies in Asia such as Taiwan and Singapore. Trading margins also went down significantly to 3 percent, as buyers and sellers became comfortable dealing directly with each other, doing away with intermediaries.

Under these circumstances, Hon-chu called his sons—William and Victor Fung (Victor)—back home from the United States. Victor was teaching at the Harvard Business School, and William had just finished his MBA from the same business school. Despite their friends' warning that trading would die out in a decade, the two brothers returned to Hong Kong to join their family firm.

Victor and William worked hard to modernize and rebuild Li & Fung into a well-structured organization, professionally managed at all levels. In 1973, the company went public and was listed on the Hong Kong Stock Exchange. Li & Fung's initial public offering was oversubscribed 113 times—a record that stood for fourteen years.

With the opening up of the Chinese economy in 1979, many manufacturers in Hong Kong relocated their factories to southern China, which was more cost effective thanks to low labor costs. The rapid industrialization of underdeveloped Asian countries widened the choice of supply sources. Li & Fung realized that there was a huge potential for the trading business. To benefit, the company established a regional network of sourcing offices in Asian countries such as Taiwan, Singapore, and Korea in the 1980s. It emerged as a major regional trading company in Asia.

In 1989, with trading margins decreasing further, Victor and William realized the need for drastic changes to safeguard the company's business. As a result, in that year, Li & Fung was again made a private company, in one of the first management buyouts in Hong Kong. The company was then restructured into a diversified group with export trading and retail as its core businesses. In 1992, the firm's export trading business, Li & Fung (Trading) Pvt. Limited., was relisted on the Hong Kong Stock Exchange.

As Li & Fung expanded its business, it understood that sourcing could no longer be restricted to a few countries but a vast network of sourcing offices to sustain trading business was required. Thus, the company established sourcing offices across the world, mainly around its major markets, the United States and Europe. Li & Fung also went in for acquisitions to strengthen its sourcing and distribution networks and expand its product lines and customer networks. It pursued an active information technology (IT) and Internet strategy to enhance the efficiency and effectiveness of its internal and external communications.

By the turn of the twentieth century, Li & Fung was a premier global trading company, with more than 95 percent of its revenues coming from North America and Europe. East Asia and the South Hemisphere accounted for the rest. In the fiscal year 2002, North America and Europe accounted for 76 percent and 19 percent of the group's total revenues, while East Asia and the South Hemisphere were placed at 3 percent and 2 percent, respectively (see Table 1 for Li & Fung's revenues by geographic segments in percentage terms).

The group's major product segments were both soft and hard goods. While soft goods included garments, hard goods constituted product lines such as fashion accessories, footwear, gifts, and furnishings (see Table 2 for Li & Fung's major product lines). Soft

TABLE 1

Revenues by Geographic Segments (1999–2003) (in percentage terms)

Geographic Regions	1999	2000	2001	2002	2003
North America	69%	70%	75%	76%	75%
Europe	27%	26%	21%	19%	19%
East Asia	1%	1%	1%	3%	3%
South Hemisphere	3%	3%	3%	2%	2%
Total (%)	100%	100%	100%	100%	100%
Total Revenues (in HK$ bn)	16.298	24.992	32.941	37.281	42.631

Source: Li & Fung Annual Report 2003.

goods contributed to a majority of the group's revenues. In 2002, this segment accounted for 68 percent of Li & Fung's total revenues, while hard goods generated the remaining 32 percent (see Table 3 for Li & Fung's revenues by product segments in percentage terms).

In 2002, export trading remained Li & Fung's major business, but it also actively operated in the retailing and distribution business through its privately held companies. The retailing business was confined to China and the Asian market, where it operated as a regional license holder for Toys "R" Us, the biggest US toy products chain and was the franchisee for the

TABLE 2

Li & Fung's Product Lines

Soft Goods	Hard Goods
Garments	Fashion Accessories
	Footwear
	Furnishings
	Gifts
	Handicrafts
	Home Products
	Promotional Merchandise
	Toys
	Stationery
	Sporting Goods
	Travel Goods

Source: **www.lifung.com**.

Hong Kong–based Circle K convenience store chain. The distribution business, too, was confined to China and the Asian region. Li & Fung was also involved in other businesses such as venture capital, investment holding, and property investment.

In the fiscal 2002, Li & Fung registered revenues of HK$ 37.3 bn, a 13 percent increase over HK$ 32.94 bn revenues in 2001. The company recorded a net profit of HK$ 1.08 bn in 2002, an increase of 38 percent over the figure of HK$ 782 mn in 2001. The company's largest customer in the United States was Kohl's Department Store Chain, accounting for nearly 13 percent of Li & Fung's total revenues in 2002. Other major clients included Abercrombie & Fitch, Ann Taylor, Disney, American Eagle Outfitters, Guess, Laura Ashley Jeans, Levi Strauss & Company (Levi's), Reebok, The Limited Inc., and Warner Brothers.

By this time, Li & Fung had successfully positioned itself as a cutting edge sourcing company in the world, with a well-established sourcing network of 68 offices across 40 countries and over 4,500 employees. In 2002, Li & Fung was reportedly one of the best professionally run companies in Hong Kong. The company's commitment to excellence and high standards in corporate governance practices earned it many awards and recognitions. Li & Fung was named one of Hong Kong's best companies, by *Euromoney* magazine, in the category "Asia's Best Company 2002." The same year, Li & Fung was named the "Best Managed Company 2002" and "Company Most Committed to Corporate Governance" by *Finance Asia* magazine (see Figure 1 for the corporate governance structure of Li & Fung).

TABLE 3

Revenues by Product Segments (1999–2003) (in percentage terms)

Product Segments	1999	2000	2001	2002	2003
Soft Goods	75%	78%	72%	68%	67%
Hard Goods	25%	22%	28%	32%	33%
Total (%)	100%	100%	100%	100%	100%
Total Revenues (in HK$ bn)	16.298	24.992	32.941	37.281	42.631

Source: Li & Fung Annual Report 2003.

Analysts credited the growth and success of Li & Fung to the visionary leadership and managerial capabilities of Victor and William. Since the early 1970s, the duo had led Li & Fung through a series of transformations in line with changes in the external environment. The major factors that helped Li & Fung evolve into a major global export trading company were the focus on efficiently managing the supply chain of its clients, a unique customer-centric organizational structure, leveraging IT and the Internet and global expansion strategies.

Managing the Global Supply Chain

Li & Fung's evolution into a supply chain manager took place in three stages, driven by significant changes in the global retailing industry, customer and retailer preferences, and economic trends across Asia through the early 1970s.

In the first stage (during the 1970–1978 period), Li & Fung acted as a regional sourcing agent. The company extended its geographic reach by establishing sourcing offices in Singapore, Korea, and Taiwan. Li & Fung's knowledge and reach in the Asian region held value for customers. This was because many big buyers could manage their own sourcing if they needed to deal only in Hong Kong. Dealing with the whole region was far more complex, and buyers did not have the necessary resources. Commenting on the complexity of sourcing from the region, in an interview to *Harvard Business Review*, Victor said that as quotas governed world trade in the textiles industry, knowledge on which quotas had been used up in Hong Kong and which was the next best place to source textiles from, where quotas had not been

FIGURE 1

Li & Fung's Corporate Governance Structure
Source: Li & Fung Annual Report, 2003.

exhausted, enabled Li & Fung to provide customers with a complete product package.

In the second stage (1979–1982), Li & Fung evolved from a sourcing agent into a manager and deliverer of production programs. When a customer came up with an idea of a product and gave specifications such as look, color, and quality, the company developed a detailed manufacturing program for that product. In other words, the firm created an entire manufacturing program for its customers for a particular fashion season. The program involved all tasks from specifying the product mix to scheduling the manufacturing process and delivery time. Li & Fung worked with factories to plan and monitor the manufacturing process and to ensure quality and on-time delivery.

This strategy worked well for Li & Fung. Yet, the 1980s brought a new challenge. This led to its third stage of evolution (1983 to the present period). Other countries in Asia such as Korea, Taiwan, and Thailand had by then emerged as labor-intensive manufacturing hubs, while Hong Kong had become an expensive and noncompetitive place to manufacture. The Chinese economy was being liberalized, and the company soon took the advantage by moving the labor-intensive portion of production to southern China.

Dispersed Manufacturing

Li & Fung broke the value chain into parts that it called "dispersed manufacturing." Under this, the company performed all high-end value-added activities such as design and quality control in Hong Kong and outsourced low-end activities like manufacturing to the best possible locations across the world. For every order, the company aimed at customizing the supply chain to meet the client's specific requirements. For example, when Li & Fung got an order for transistor radios, it created little kits (plastic bags) filled with all the components necessary to build a radio and shipped the kits to China, where they were assembled. The assembled radios were then shipped back to Hong Kong, where they underwent final testing and inspection.

Similarly, to fulfill an order for baby dolls, Li & Fung designed them in Hong Kong, produced molds for the dolls using sophisticated machinery, and then shipped the molds to China, where plastic was injected into the molds, the dolls were assembled, their fingers were painted, and their clothes were tailored. After the completion of such labor-intensive work in China, the dolls were shipped back to Hong Kong for final testing, inspection, packaging, transportation and distribution. So, while the front and back ends of the value chain were taken care of in Hong Kong, the middle portion was performed in China.

Once Li & Fung understood the benefits of dispersed manufacturing and gained expertise in it, the company extended its network beyond southern China. It moved into the inner parts of China, where wages were even lower. Li & Fung also began searching for other labor-intensive and potential sources of supply outside China and established a strong global network of suppliers by the late 1990s. Soon, the concept of dispersed manufacturing spread to other industries in Hong Kong, which led to the transformation of Hong Kong from a manufacturing economy into a service economy. By 1997, 84 percent of Hong Kong's gross domestic product[4] came from services (see Exhibits 2 and 3).

Meanwhile, owing to maturing markets, intense competition and changing consumer trends, many companies in the Western countries were compelled to outsource not only their manufacturing but also the entire supply chain management (SCM) to reap time and cost benefits. Li & Fung, with its extensive sourcing depth and network, grew from a deliverer of production programs into a potential manager of supply chains for companies looking for optimum SCM.

Li & Fung described SCM as "tackling the soft $3" in the structure—that is, if the price of a consumer product when it leaves a factory in China was $1, it would end up on retail shelves at $4. The company felt there was very little companies could do to further reduce production costs, as they had already exhausted all possible ways. It would be easier to cut on costs that were spread across distribution channels—that is, the $3 (difference between the product price on retail shelves and price when it left the factory).

Li & Fung took its dispersed manufacturing technique further, dissecting the entire value chain and optimizing every step of the chain, from product design and development, raw material sourcing, production planning, conducting quality assurance and factory inspections, managing production and logistics of

---

[4]GDP is used to measure the growth and health of an economy and is defined as the total market value of all final goods and services produced in a country in a given year, equal to total customer, investment, and government spending, plus the value of the total exports, minus the value of total imports.

EXHIBIT 2

Exports and Imports of Services in Hong Kong (2000–2002)

Major Service Group	Year	Exports of Services			Imports of Services			Net Exports of Services
		HK$ mn	Share (%)	Year-on-Year % Change	HK$ mn	Share (%)	Year-on-Year % Change	HK$ mn
Transportation	2000	99,513	33.0	11.5	48,628	25.4	23.9	50,885
	2001	93,675	30.4	−5.9	50,916	26.5	4.7	42,759
	2002	103,751	30.9	10.8	48,518	24.3	−4.7	55,233
Travel	2000	46,019	15.2	7.4	97,402	50.9	−4.4	−51,383
	2001	46,362	15.1	0.7	96,057	49.9	−1.4	−49,695
	2002	58,855	17.5	26.9	96,846	48.5	0.8	−37,991
Insurance services	2000	3,452	1.1	12.6	4,111	2.1	−17.4	−659
	2001	3,556	1.2	3.0	4,028	2.1	−2.0	−472
	2002	3,421	1.0	−3.8	4,618	2.3	14.6	−1,197
Financial services	2000	20,859	6.9	8.6	5,536	2.9	−3.4	15,323
	2001	21,823	7.1	4.6	5,242	2.7	−5.3	16,581
	2002	19,564	5.8	−10.4	4,876	2.4	−7.0	14,688
Merchanting and other trade-related services	2000	97,616	32.3	19.7	11,170	5.8	6.3	86,446
	2001	106,447	34.6	9.0	11,802	6.1	5.7	94,645
	2002	115,996	34.6	9.0	14,660	7.3	24.2	101,336
Other services	2000	34,355	11.4	15.8	24,695	12.9	13.7	9,660
	2001	35,794	11.6	4.2	24,408	12.7	−1.2	11,386
	2002	33,826	10.1	−5.5	30,158	15.1	23.6	101,336
All services	2000	301,813	100.0	13.7	191,543	100.0	4.1	110,270
	2001	307,657	100.0	1.9	192,453	100.0	0.5	115,204
	2002	335,412	100.0	9.0	199,676	100.0	3.8	135,736

Notes:
(1) Figures for exports of travel services have incorporated the new data released by the Hong Kong Tourism Board in November 2003 on destination consumption expenditure of incoming visitors and travelers. For details, please refer to the feature article "Statistics on Inbound Tourism" in the December 2003 issue of the *Hong Kong Monthly Digest of Statistics*.
(2) The sum of individual items and the corresponding total shown in the table may not tally because of rounding.

Source: **www.info.gov.hk.**

exporting, timely delivery, and complying with import and export quota restrictions, imposed by the buyer and seller countries, respectively. The company became a much broader intermediary by connecting and coordinating many links in the supply chain. It made its services more valuable by delivering a better product, which translated into better price and margins for customers (see Exhibit 4).

Global Supplier Network

When Li & Fung got an order from a customer, it sifted through its global supplier network (see Exhibit 5) to find the right manufacturer for the specific product and the most attractive combination of cost and quality. The company broke up its supply chain to disperse different production processes to manufacturers in various countries, based on factors

EXHIBIT 3

Hong Kong's External Trade Performance

	2003 (HK$ Mn)	2004 Jan–May (HK$ Mn)	% Change	
			03/02	J–M 04/03
Overall				
- Domestic Exports	121,687	44,668	−7	1
- Re-exports	1,620,749	713,531	13	16
- Imports	1,805,770	816,918	12	19
- Total Trade	3,548,206	1,575,117	12	17
Balance	−63,334	−58,719	8	99
Total Exports—Major Markets				
All Markets	1,742,436	758,199	12	15
- China	742,544	334,450	21	18
- U.S.A.	324,215	122,950	−3	5
- E.U.	231,033	98,469	12	13
- Japan	94,003	41,241	12	13
- Singapore	35,704	16,866	13	27
- Taiwan	42,269	20,334	22	23
- Rep. of Korea	35,526	18,054	17	29
Total Exports—Major Products				
All Products	1,742,436	758,199	12	15
- Electronics #	732,653	332,023	20	23
- Clothing	180,357	65,408	3	5
- Electrical Products #	192,485	88,524	13	21
- Textile Yarn & Fabrics	101,923	45,067	5	9
- Toys & Games	75,008	22,538	1	−3
- Footwear	44,755	17,874	−1	−3
- Watches and Clocks	41,903	17,237	9	8
- Travel Goods & Handbags	32,070	14,333	*	12
- Plastic Articles	23,872	9,309	−8	−6
- Food	15,404	5,597	−8	−7
- Jewelry	22,231	9,794	17	21
Re-exports—with China				
Total Re-exports	1,620,749	713,531	13	16
- To China	705,787	321,126	23	19
- Of China Origin	967,104	418,816	12	16
Imports—End-use Categories				
Total Imports	1,805,770	816,918	12	19
- Foodstuffs	53,439	22,747	−3	8
- Consumer Goods	573,926	235,109	5	9
- Raw Materials	654,452	319,439	17	27
- Fuels	35,398	18,026	13	28
- Capital Goods	481,081	218,494	12	18

Overlap with other products

*Insignificant

Source: **http://stat.tdctrade.com**.

EXHIBIT 4

Li & Fung's Supply Chain

Source: Li & Fung Annual Report, 2003.

such as labor costs, quality, trade barriers, transportation costs, and so on. The company coordinated all processes in the value chain, managing the logistics and arranging the shipment of the finished order to the client. Li & Fung also ensured that suppliers complied with rules and regulations pertaining to environmental standards, child labor, and so on in the importing countries (see Exhibit 6).

For instance, when Li & Fung got an order from Levi's, a leading retail clothes chain in the United States, with garment designs for the next fashion season, the company took the basic product concepts and researched the market to find the right kind of raw materials such as yarn, dye, and buttons. The company then assembled the raw materials to create a prototype, which was sent to Levi's for inspection. Once the prototype was approved, Levi's placed an order for the garments with Li & Fung, asking for delivery within six weeks.

Li & Fung immediately went to work; it distributed various tasks of the overall manufacturing process to different producers based on their capabilities and costs. It decided to purchase yarn from a Korean supplier but have it woven and dyed in Taiwan. The yarn was picked up from Korea and

shipped to Taiwan. As the Japanese offered best quality zippers and buttons, which they got manufactured in China, Li & Fung approached the leading zipper manufacturer in Japan to order the right zippers from Chinese factories. Li & Fung decided to manufacture the final garments in Thailand, based on factors like quota availability and favorable labor conditions. It moved all the materials to Thailand. Since the order had to be fulfilled within six weeks, the order was divided across five factories in Thailand. Li & Fung ensured that within the scheduled date of delivery, the finished products, all looking as if they came from one factory, arrived at Levi's retail stores.

Efficient SCM also addressed the problem of obsolete inventory, a major area of concern for fast-moving consumer goods (FMCG) companies, which were consumer driven. FMCG companies preferred buying closer to the market as it shortened the buying cycle and gave them more time to get a better sense of the changing needs and preferences of consumers. Such quick changes led to shorter product cycles, and the problem of obsolete inventories went up significantly. This was where Li & Fung's global SCM expertise was useful, as it aimed at buying the right things at the right place, at the right cost and quality.

EXHIBIT 5

Li & Fung's Global Sourcing Network

EUROPE & THE MEDITERRANEAN	THE AMERICAS	NORTH ASIA
Amsterdam	Boston	Beijing
Bucharest	Guadalajara	Dalian
Cairo	Guatemala City	Dongguan
Denizli	Managua	Guangzhou
Florence	Mexico City	Hepu
Huddersfield	New York City	Hong Kong
Istanbul	San Francisco	Huizhu
Izmir	San Pedro Sula	Liuyang
London	Santo Domingo	Longhua
Oporto	**SOUTHEAST ASIA**	Macau
Tunis	Bangkok	Nanjing
Turin	Hanoi	Ningbo
SOUTH ASIA	Ho Chi Minh City	Qingdao
Amman	Jakarta	Seoul
Bahrain	Makati	Shanghai
Bangalore	Phnom Penh	Shantou
Chennai	Saipan	Shenzhen
Colombo	Shan Alam	Taipei
Delhi	Singapore	Tokyo
Dhaka	**SOUTH AFRICA**	Zhanjiang
Karachi	Durban	Zhongshan
Lahore	Madgascar	
Mumbai	Mauritius	
Sharjah		

Source: Li & Fung Annual Report, 2003.

The SCM Strategy

To ensure shorter product delivery cycles, Li & Fung managed the whole supply chain of its customers. To shrink the delivery cycle, the company reached upstream to organize production and ensure small production runs, which resulted in improved response time for retailers, enabling them to alter production in tandem with market trends. For instance, Li & Fung got to know that Levi's would order 1 million pieces of garments, but did not have specific details of style or colors. This would be disclosed only four weeks before delivery was due. Under these circumstances, based on trust and its strong relationship with suppliers, Li & Fung reserved undyed yarn and locked up capacity at mills for weaving and dying. It told suppliers that they would receive an order for a specific size and colors six days before delivery. Then the company contacted the factory owners, stating that it did not know product specifications yet, but it had organized the colors, fabric, and trim for them, and they should deliver the order on a specific date, say two weeks from the arrival of raw materials at their factories.

Having a vast network of suppliers enabled Li & Fung to configure activities as if they were modules in a process. For instance, a South Korean yarn

EXHIBIT 6

Li & Fung's Code of Conduct for Suppliers

Li & Fung (Trading) Limited Code of Conduct ("Code of Conduct") outlines the basic requirements on working conditions that must be satisfied by all vendors ("Vendors") to principals of Li & Fung (Trading) Limited ("Li & Fung"). Li & Fung and its principals can supplement these requirements at any time.

Child Labour: Vendors shall not use child labour. A "Child" is defined as a person who is not older than the local age for completing compulsory education, but in no event is less than 15 years old. Vendors must verify the age of their workers and maintain copies of proof of age. Vendors must follow all applicable laws and regulations regarding working hours and conditions for minors.

Involuntary Labour: Vendor shall not use involuntary labour. "Involuntary Labour" is defined as work or service extracted from any person under threat or penalty for its non-performance, and for which the worker does not offer himself or herself voluntarily. It includes prison, bonded, indentured and forced labour.

Disciplinary Practices: Vendors shall not use corporal punishment, any form of physical or psychological coercion or intimidation against workers.

Non-discrimination: Vendors shall employ workers solely on the basis of their ability to do the job. They shall not discriminate on the basis of age, gender, racial characteristics, maternity or marital status, nationality or cultural, religious or personal beliefs in relation to hiring, wages, benefits, termination or retirement.

Health and Safety: Vendors shall maintain a clean, safe and healthy workplace in compliance with applicable laws and regulations. They shall ensure that workers have access to clean drinking water, sanitary washing facilities and adequate number of toilets, fire-extinguishers and fire exits. Workplaces should provide adequate lighting and ventilation. Vendors shall ensure that these standards are also met in any canteen and/or dormitory provided for workers.

Environmental Protection: Vendors shall comply with all applicable laws and regulations to protect the environment and maintain procedures for notifying the local authorities in the event of an environmental accident resulting from the vendors' operations.

Wages and Benefits: Vendors shall provide wages and benefits that comply with all applicable laws and regulations or match prevailing local manufacturing or industry rates, whichever is higher. Overtime pay shall be calculated at the legally required rate, regardless of whether workers are compensated hourly or by piece rate.

Working Hours: Vendors shall not require workers to work, including overtime, more than 60 hours per week or more than the maximum number of hours per week set by applicable laws and regulations, whichever is less. Vendors shall guarantee that workers receive at least one day off during each seven-day period.

Freedom of Association: Vendors shall respect the right of workers to associate, organize and bargain collectively in a legal and peaceful manner.

Familiarization and Display of this Code of Conduct: Vendors shall familiarize workers with this Code of Conduct and display it, translated in the local language, at each of their facilities in a place readily visible and accessible to workers.

Legal Requirements: Vendors shall comply with all legal requirements applicable to the conduct of their businesses, including those set out above.

Contractors and Suppliers: Vendors shall ensure that their contractors and suppliers adhere to this Code of Conduct.

Monitoring of Compliance: Vendors authorize Li & Fung and its principals to conduct scheduled and unscheduled inspections of vendors' facilities for ensuring compliance with the Code of Conduct. During these inspections, Li & Fung and its principals have the right to review all employee-related books and records maintained by vendors and to interview workers.

Corrective Action: When violations are found, Li & Fung and the vendor concerned will agree on a corrective action plan that eliminates the problem in a timely manner. If it is determined that a vendor is knowingly and/or repeatedly in violation of this Code of Conduct, Li & Fung and its principals shall take appropriate corrective action. This may include cancellation of orders and/or termination of business with that vendor.

Source: **www.lifung.com**.

provider might be appropriate for a product line, but an Indonesian supplier who used different raw materials and production technology might be a better choice for the needs and preferences of a specific customer. Li & Fung assembled the right modules for each job, customizing value chain solutions for its clients. Such flexible modules also meant that the company could quickly change its plans if there were unforeseen problems at the manufacturing site. The company could tap its worldwide network and send the order to another company to avoid delays in order fulfillment. For example, Li & Fung quickly shifted production from high-risk countries to lower risk countries following the September 11, 2001, terrorist attacks in the United States.

A major supplier management strategy of Li & Fung was to utilize anywhere from 30 percent to 70 percent of factory capacity of suppliers, ensuring that at such a capacity, the company would be one of their important customers. Most times, Li & Fung would be their largest customer. Li & Fung also ensured that it did not use up the entire capacity of any manufacturer to give itself flexibility. It did not want manufacturers to be completely dependent on the company. This strategy also enabled the company to gain exposure to new suppliers.

To improve suppliers' performance, Li & Fung managers, based on their interactions with them, provided a detailed performance feedback to each supplier, mentioning strengths and weaknesses. Faltering suppliers were dropped from a project or from the company's network if they failed to improve. According to analysts, as Li & Fung offered many economic incentives to suppliers, they willingly customized their own operations to fit Li & Fung's supply chain strategy. The major benefits to suppliers were substantial and steady business from Li & Fung and the opportunity to improve their performance, as the company set detailed benchmarks across its entire process network and gave all partners valuable insights into their specific strengths and weaknesses. It also helped them address performance gaps.

To further strengthen its supplier network, Li & Fung constantly looked out for new suppliers. The company evaluated the experience and skills of each prospect to determine whether its operational standards could be met. By the early 2000s, Li & Fung had an extensive network of over seventy-five hundred regular suppliers; each on an average had about two hundred employees. Li & Fung described itself as

a smokeless factory. Though it did not own any manufacturing concern, it was involved in various functions that qualified it as a manufacturer.

Customer-Centric Organizational Structure

Li & Fung had an organizational structure that masked its size. In line with the transformation of the company's business strategy during the 1980s, Li & Fung revamped its organizational structure to manage its global sourcing network better and meet customer needs. The company discarded its traditional structure of geographic division as it found inefficiencies in this. During this period, all large trading companies in the world with vast supplier networks were organized geographically with country units as profit centers. Such a structure made it tough for the companies to optimize the value chains for their customers, as the country units competed against each other for business. The lack of cooperation and coordination among country units also resulted in loss of customers, affecting a company's business.

To eliminate this, Li & Fung adopted a new customer-centric structure, where it organized itself into various small customer-centric divisions.[5] Under the new structure, an entire division focused on serving a big customer such as The Limited, Levi's, Kohl's, and Abercrombie & Fitch. A single division aimed at fulfilling the needs of a group of smaller customers, with similar needs. For example, the company's theme-store division served a group of customers like Warner Brothers stores chain and Rainforest Café. According to company sources, this new model assisted them in creating a customized value chain for each customer order.

As part of its customer-centric strategy, Li & Fung created small divisions dedicated to serving one customer, and a person managing the unit as if it was his/her own company. Li & Fung hired people who were entrepreneurial in nature and whose ultimate aim was to run their own business. Thus, each division was run by a lead entrepreneur, designated as division manager, who was responsible for understanding customers' needs and fulfilling them by mobilizing resources from the group's sourcing and process network. For instance, the Gymboree division, which served

---

[5]In 2002, Li & Fung had about 120 business divisions across forty countries.

Gymboree, a leading U.S.-based clothing store, was headquartered in a separate office within the Li & Fung building in Hong Kong. It had forty plus employees focused on meeting Gymboree's needs. The division was further broken up into specialized teams in areas such as technical support, raw material purchase, quality assurance, merchandising, and shipping. Apart from the employees at its head office, the division also had dedicated sourcing teams across the branch offices of Li & Fung in China, Indonesia, and Philippines, the countries from where the division purchased in high volumes.

These divisions also promoted knowledge sharing during their interactions with customers, which benefited customers. Commenting on this, Frank Leong (Leong), CFO and head of the Operation Support Group (OSG), Li & Fung, said, "Our people sit down to share with them the latest information from the production side—what sort of material is hot, what new colours are available, where a product can be produced."[6] Such discussions not only expanded the fashion retailers' knowledge, but also gave them scope for more creativity and financial liberty in designing garments for a season. If required, the divisions also offered trade financing services to customers, through Letters of Credit (L/C).[7]

To preserve the entrepreneurial spirit, Li & Fung kept each division relatively small, with average revenues ranging between HK$ 30 million and HK$ 50 million. The company allowed each division to act as an independent unit with its own customers and profit and loss accounts. Li & Fung gave considerable freedom to division managers to run their divisions, as it believed that autonomy would encourage a free spirit. To further ensure the commitment of division managers, Li & Fung tied up their compensation to their division's bottom line. To motivate them to achieve their division's targets, the company gave out substantial financial incentives. Reportedly, Li & Fung did not fix any ceilings on bonuses. The company followed the same policy of performance based compensation and incentives for other employees, too.

Li & Fung provided the divisions with all necessary financial resources and administrative support, mainly through the OSG, which provided back-end support to the entire group operations. The OSG supplied all divisions with personal computers and network connections, at a charge per PC, which covered the entire network, including order processing, production tracking, and e-mail communication. These charges were paid from the division's revenues.

The OSG also acted as an in-house HR provider, as it supplied recruitment services by internally matching staff from across various divisions, to meet some specific requirements of clients, and training them. It also acted as the divisions' chief banker as all divisional revenues finally went to the OSG. According to company sources, the divisions could take loans from the OSG at an interest rate cheaper than the market rate.

The OSG's performance was measured against its profit and loss account as was the case of any other division in the group. According to Leong, such a performance measurement strategy ensured that the OSG provided advanced high-quality services to its customers (other divisions) and at the same time optimized its costs.

The logic behind such an organizational structure was to allow each division to function like an independent company without worrying about back-end needs. Such a model provided the group with the flexibility of a small company, while having the strengths of a large, global company. As Leong said, "We're marrying the strength of being small and big together. Big companies tend to get bureaucratic, while small companies can do specialized products. Our small business units act extremely fast, but at the back-end, they get the level of service of a huge company."[8]

However, while Li & Fung believed in flexibility in some things, the company was highly conservative when it came to financial control and operating procedures. These were centralized and tightly managed. Li & Fung also maintained tight control over its working capital. All cash flows were centrally managed through headquarters in Hong Kong. For instance, L/Cs from all divisions came to headquarters for approval and were then reissued. The company

---

[6]"Asset Lite," **www.cfoasia.com**, April 2002.

[7]A document, consisting of specific instructions by the buyer of goods, that is issued by a bank to the seller who is authorized to draw a specified sum of money under certain conditions, that is, the receipt by the bank of certain documents within a given time. A confirmed L/C is one issued by a foreign bank, which is validated or guaranteed by a Hong Kong bank for a Hong Kong exporter in the case of default by the foreign buyer or bank.

[8]"Asset Lite," **www.cfoasia.com**, April 2002.

also had a standardized and fully computerized order executing and tracking system used by all divisions.

Leveraging IT and the Internet

To leverage the potential of IT, Li & Fung took many initiatives through the mid 1990s. It tied up its global network of offices with intranet[9] since 1995, to enable free information flow. In 1998, the company began creating dedicated extranet[10] sites for major customers. These sites enabled the company to interact with customers, track their orders, help in product development, and perform many other tasks in a cost-efficient manner. The extranet also enabled customers to track their orders and gain access to related information through Li & Fung's Electronic Trading System, known as XTS, which was linked to Li & Fung's global network of offices.

The major benefits of a dedicated extranet site can be understood from the following example. In the late 1990s, Coca-Cola, the leading soft drinks company, and many of its independent bottlers worldwide, largely relied on merchandize tied to sporting events to promote the company's core brand, Coca-Cola. As Coca-Cola was mainly a beverage company, with no exposure to manufacturing, the company found managing the manufacturing activity (for its merchandise) expensive and outside its area of core expertise. The company also feared that its manufacturing process might be too slow to respond to sporting and entertainment events. As a result, in March 2001, the company turned to Li & Fung for managing its manufacturing activities. Li & Fung designed and built an extranet site, called Kodimsum.com (KO for Coke's stock symbol, and dimsum for a Hong Kong food delicacy), enabling Coca-Cola's executives and bottlers to place online orders. The extranet also allowed bottlers to check orders placed by other bottlers of the company, enabling them to place a similar order if they found that the product would be useful in their own markets.

With the emergence of the Internet as a major communication medium, industry observers felt it would make trading companies like Li & Fung redundant. Li & Fung opposed this view, stating that the key to its business was not hardware but information and its application to the management of client supply chains. The company believed that instead of being a threat, the Internet and e-commerce would offer more opportunities by helping it drive supply chain costs down and integrating management of supply chain via IT. Analysts, too, felt that this was true. They said that the real value of Li & Fung's business model lay not just in its ability to link suppliers and buyers, but in its power to influence suppliers and manufacturers, with whom the company had a strong relationship of trust.

Thus, Li & Fung used the Internet as a tool to make supply chains more transparent. When Li & Fung received an order from a customer, it used extranet sites and the Internet to fine-tune specifications. It then took instructions from the customer and fed the information on to its intranet to find the right raw material suppliers and right factory or factories to assemble the product. The Web also aided customers in quickly assessing shifting consumer demands. Thus, as an order moved through different phases of production, customers could make last-minute changes through Li and Fung's website, which hosted real-time information on the entire production process.

This real-time tracking by customers was not possible until the mid-1990s, when Li & Fung began using phone and fax. For instance, when a customer ordered 50,000 khaki cargo pants, the company delivered the pants five months later, leaving the customer with little chance of altering their orders in line with changing market trends. By the early 2000s, once the Web-based communication system was established, customers could cancel their order until the time the material was woven, change the color until the fabric was dyed, and alter design or size until the fabric was cut.

In March 2000, Li & Fung announced its Internet strategy to enter the e-commerce market, through its Business-to-Business (B2B) initiatives. Li & Fung aimed at creating economies of scale and scope for small- and medium-sized enterprises by bundling their orders for the same products and then customizing the mass-produced product to meet the requirements of each customer.

---

[9]An intranet is a restricted-access network that works like the Internet. Usually owned and managed by a corporation, an intranet enables an organization to provide content and services to its employees across its various divisions, without allowing external people to view it.

[10]An extranet is an Internet site that is offered to a select group of people such as customers, suppliers, and business partners, usually to provide or share nonpublic information.

Commenting on this, William said

Li & Fung has done private-label manufacturing for a long time. We can only do this if the customers are very large and they have the scale, since you need intensive interaction when you do private-label work. To capture economies of scale, we need large customers, not small ones.... What the Internet does is allow us to reach the small and midsize guys we could never reach before. What do they want? What the big guys have—a private label, their own differentiated line, and at the same price as the big guys.... The Internet allows us to reach those people—without intensive interaction—and to aggregate their orders. We can allow you different styles, limited customisation using American yarn, knitted in China, assembled in Bangladesh. And we can allow you to put in your own label, embroidery, colours, packages, boxes. We can reap the economics of mass production, but with enough customisation.[11]

As part of Li & Fung's Internet strategy, StudioDirect Inc. was formed in April 2000 as an e-commerce subsidiary of the company (57 percent controlling stake) with an investment of US$19 million. StudioDirect's website, **www.studiodirect.com**, launched in March 2001, allowed placement of highly individualized orders from small- and medium-sized retailers, enabling them to choose from a wide variety of fabrics, colors, and accessories such as cuffs, pockets, buttons, and embroidery. According to Li & Fung sources, StudioDirect had customization options that could satisfy 90 percent of the smaller retailers.

StudioDirect aggregated all orders placed on its website and put them on to Li & Fung's manufacturers, resulting in a series of private-label lines ready for delivery. To handle the logistics needed to deliver finished goods to retailers across the world, StudioDirect tied up with Danzas AEI Intercontinental, a business division of the Danzas Group, which specialized in logistics services and had already worked with Li & Fung.

StudioDirect was reportedly capable of beginning production within six hours of receiving an order from a client over the Internet. For marketing its B2B initiative, the company chose the strategy of direct mailing. Through this, the company aimed at reaching about one thousand small- and medium-sized retailers in the first year and expected to do business of $2 million with each of them, in the next five years. The initiative was launched in the United States in early 2001.

Analysts felt that Li & Fung, with its sound global sourcing network and strong financials (US$ 270 million in cash reserves) was poised to establish itself as a strong player in the B2B market place. Commenting on what Li & Fung could provide small- and medium-sized customers with, Barnett, a Goldman Sachs's analyst, said, "A large company that uses Li & Fung typically pays 4% to 12% of the value of the order [because of economies of scale]. It's about 30% for a small company. Those costs come down to 4% to 12% if clients use the studiodirect.com Internet site."[12]

In the early 2000s, Li & Fung maintained Internet-based communication with all its major customers worldwide. About 75 percent of them were large retailers in the United States, who reaped significant benefits from the transparent SCM attained due to the use of IT and the Internet.[13] Laurence H. Alberts, managing partner, Mercer Management Consulting (Asia), said, "They [Li and Fung] are the leaders in Asia in providing this full solution of sourcing and supply-chain management. They've built up a very considerable barrier to anyone else trying to replicate it."[14]

Global Expansion

During the late 1990s, with the growing popularity of private label brands, shortening product life cycles, and acute competition in the retailing industry, companies had to focus on their supply chain processes. As many companies did not have expertise in SCM and outsourcing was a cost-efficient alternative, the demand for companies that offered SCM services increased. Li & Fung, which already had an impressive sourcing network and SCM expertise, increased efforts to position itself as a global consumer goods trading company. The company devised an acquisition strategy to strengthen its position in the global trading market. The strategy aimed at expanding the sourcing network, product lines, and customer base.

---

[11]"A Different Kind of B2B Play in China?" **www.businessweek.com**, May 8, 2000.

[12]"Picking Asian Winners in the Internet Age," **www.asiaweek.com**, 2000.

[13]However, in countries such as China, Bangladesh, Philippines, Africa, and the Caribbean, where communication systems are still underdeveloped, Li & Fung relied on personal visits, phones, faxes, and couriers to communicate information and manage operations.

[14]"Middleman Becomes Master," **www.chiefexecutive.net**, October 2002.

In 1995, Li & Fung acquired Inchcape Buying Services (also known as Dodwell) from Inchcape Pacific, a leading British trading conglomerate. That company had an established network of offices in South Asia, the Mediterranean, and Caribbean regions, where Li & Fung had little or no presence. The acquisition nearly doubled the size and geographic reach of Li & Fung and brought with it a vast European customer base that complemented Li & Fung's strength in North America. The acquisition also contributed significantly to the company's success in achieving its three-year plan (1995–1998) target of doubling its profits from HK$ 225 million in 1995 to HK$ 455 million in 1998.

As a part of its proximity strategy, which aimed at producing products closer to the customer market (North America and Europe), Li & Fung began establishing and expanding its sourcing networks in regions such as the Mediterranean, Eastern Europe, North Africa, South Africa, and Central America in the late 1990s.

In December 1999, Li & Fung acquired Swire & Maclaine and Camberley Enterprises, the trading businesses of the Hong Kong–based group, Swire Pacific, for HK$ 450 million. While Swire & Maclaine was a major provider of product sourcing and quality assurance services in Hong Kong, Camberley Enterprises made high-quality ladies sportswear, ready-to-wear garments, and home accessories. These acquisitions offered Li & Fung design process expertise and helped it further strengthen its customer base in the United States and Europe, by adding some major customers such as Laura Ashley and Ann Taylor. As Swire & Maclaine had been a major competitor of Li & Fung in Hong Kong, its acquisition helped Li & Fung further consolidate its business in Hong Kong and strengthened its position as one of the world's leading sourcing and supply chain management companies.

In November 2000, Li & Fung announced the acquisition of Colby Group Holdings Limited; a Hong Kong–based leading consumer goods trading company, for HK$ 2.2 billion to consolidate its global competitive position further and helped it emerge as the largest consumer goods export trading groups in Hong Kong. Commenting on the rationale behind the acquisition, William said, "Colby has strong brand recognition, especially among US department stores. Its seasoned staff and diversified sourcing capabilities will complement our existing business. With this acquisition, we will be able to expand our

customer base and further penetrate what is an important new market segment."[15] Even after the acquisition, Colby continued to operate under its own company name as a subsidiary of Li & Fung.

In the early 2000s, Li & Fung focused its acquisition strategy on hard goods companies. In mid 2002, Li & Fung acquired Janco Overseas, a Hong Kong–based buying agent, specializing in hard goods, for HK$ 249.6 million. According to company sources, the acquisition was expected to increase Li & Fung's turnover by HK$ 1.4 billion. Reportedly, Janco's strengths in the hard goods segment and focus on large food retailers, who were rapidly expanding their nonfood offerings, was expected to strengthen Li & Fung's position in the hard goods segment. It was also expected to open up new customer segments and opportunities on account of expansion in its hard goods product portfolio.

In the fiscal year 2002, the hard goods segment accounted for 32 percent of Li & Fung's revenues compared with 28 percent in 2001. The segment registered a 29 percent increase in revenues and 70 percent in operating profits over 2001. Li & Fung sources said the acquisition of Janco was a major factor that contributed to such a significant growth in its hard goods business.

In August 2003, Li & Fung announced plans to purchase the remaining one-third stake in the group's New York–based garment importer unit, International Sourcing Group (ISG), for US$ 5.22 million, from ISG's chief executive, Alan Chartash, who owned that stake. The acquisition was expected to increase Li & Fung's profitability. Victor said, "By further leveraging the group's financial resources, management strength and entrepreneurial corporate culture, it is envisaged that a more comprehensive service will be provided to ISG's customers."[16]

During the early 2000s, Li & Fung focused on expanding its customer base in non-U.S. markets to balance the group's overall revenue portfolio, which was highly skewed toward the United States. It concentrated on the fast developing economies in Asia and the Southern Hemisphere, where more and more companies were outsourcing manufacturing and SCM on account of increasing globalization and resulting competitive pressures that were forcing companies to optimize resources.

[15]"Li & Fung to Acquire Colby," **www.irasia.com**, November 9, 2000.
[16]"Li & Fung to Buy Out Last Stake of US Unit," Hong Kong iMail (China), August 20, 2003.

EXHIBIT 7

Li & Fung's Five-Year Stock Price Chart (August 1999–July 2004)
(Price in HK$, Volume in mns)

Source: **www.prophet.net**.

Li & Fung identified Japan as a potential market, where the fashion retailing business was booming. In October 2003, Li & Fung entered into an alliance with Nichimen Corporation (Nichimen), a leading general trading firm in Japan, to offer higher value for Japanese retailers. This was possible due to the integration of Li & Fung's global sourcing network with Nichimen's customer servicing capabilities.

In December 2003, Li & Fung acquired the sourcing business of the Hong Kong–based Firstworld Garments Limited and the U.S.-based International Porcelain Inc. for US$ 27 million. These two companies would together operate under the name "International Sources." They were expected to strengthen Li & Fung's presence in the hard goods business and enable it to reach out to Mexico.

The Challenges

By the end of 2003, Li & Fung emerged as one of the few global consumer goods trading companies with geographic flexibility and depth of expertise required for success in the fiercely competitive business environment of the early twenty-first century. In the fiscal year ending December 31, 2003, the group's revenues amounted to HK$ 42.6 billion, a 14.3 percent

rise over HK$ 37.3 billion in 2002. Net profits amounted to HK$ 1.22 billion in fiscal 2003, a 13.2 percent increase over the HK$ 1.08 billion in fiscal 2002. In December 2003, the share price of Li & Fung was quoting around HK$ 13 (see Exhibit 7).

However, according to company sources, revenues and profits were below expectations. The Iraq War,[17] the SARS epidemic,[18] and poor business

[17]The U.S. government believed that the Osama Bin Laden led terrorist organization, Al-Qaida, which was responsible for the September 11, 2001, terrorist attacks on the World Trade Center in the United States, may obtain weapons of mass destruction (WMD) from Iraq. As Iraq was ruled by Saddam Hussein (Hussein), who was openly hostile to the United States, the U.S. officials considered it a severe threat to the country's security, and felt the need for preemptive war against Iraq to prevent further damage from occurring in the United States. In March 2003, the United States declared war against Iraq (the second war, the first being in January 1991), called "Operation Iraqi Freedom." In May 2003, the U.S. Army captured Tikrit, the birthplace of Saddam Hussein. Saddam himself was captured in December 2003.

[18]According to **www.cdc.gov**, Severe Acute Respiratory Syndrome (SARS) is a viral respiratory illness caused by a corona virus called the SARS associated corona virus (SARS–CoV). The first case of SARS was reported in Asia in February 2003. Within a few months, the illness spread to more than twenty-four countries throughout the world. The outbreak of SARS in the Asian region severely damaged its economic performance—the hardest-hit business was the region's tourism industry.

performance in the holiday season of some major customers were cited as reasons. The drop in the group's nontrading income also had an unfavorable effect on overall financial results. Reportedly, the net loss from Li & Fung's venture capital business amounted to HK$ 8 million in the fiscal 2003.

That year, the soft goods segment accounted for 67 percent of Li & Fung's total revenues, while hard goods accounted for the remaining 33 percent. Geographically, North America continued to be the company's largest export market, accounting for 75 percent of its total revenues. It was followed by Europe (19 percent), East Asia (3 percent), and the Southern Hemisphere (3 percent). As part of achieving its three-year plan (2001–2004) goal of doubling profits by the fiscal 2004, Li & Fung announced that it would continue its aggressive acquisition drive, focused at non-U.S. companies, and new product lines that could open up more revenue opportunities.

In August 2003, Li & Fung finalized a licensing agreement with Levi's, under which the former would design, manufacture, and market clothing under the latter's Levi Strauss Signature label. According to company sources, these products would be marketed in the United States by late 2004. In early 2004, Li & Fung also signed similar licensing deals with Official Pillowtex LLC, a U.S.-based company that owned the Royal Velvet linen brand. Commenting on these deals, William said, "Leveraging our strong position in the supply chain, we are building a higher-margin business model of licensing well-known brand names. This new business model will augment our core sourcing business and will be an important growth driver for the group in our next three-year plan for 2005–2007."[19]

By mid 2004, Li & Fung had an extensive network of over 65 offices in 40 countries worldwide, managed by a dedicated employee base of over 6,000. Reportedly, the company faced very little competition, which analysts attributed to its unique positioning as a supply chain manager for its clients and its focused acquisition strategy. William E. Connor & Associates (WEC&A), an American-owned, Hong Kong–based trading company, was the closest competitor to Li & Fung in Hong Kong as textiles was WEC&A's major product line. But, as WEC&A focused on large department store customers and

Li & Fung concentrated on specialty store chains, analysts felt that competition between them was not intense (see Exhibit 8).

While Li & Fung's business model might seem error free and its future bright, analysts were quick to point out that every business had its negative side, and Li & Fung also had made miscalculations. They said the company's much hyped B2B initiative "StudioDirect," had failed to get the expected response, forcing Li & Fung to restructure its operations. In 2002, Li & Fung converted StudioDirect from a full-service e-commerce company into a private label golf-wear specialist, offering services to customers through the Internet. The company also reduced its stake in StudioDirect from 57 percent to 15 percent. Li & Fung attributed this restructuring to changes in market conditions in the United States, which were not conducive to the growth of StudioDirect's business. It stated that it was still committed to e-commerce, and its aim was to reach smaller and midsized retailers. However, even by early 2004, StudioDirect had failed to make major progress on this front.

The continuous fall in the annual growth of revenues and profitability through the early 2000s was also perceived as an area of concern by many analysts (see Exhibit 9). While Li & Fung registered a high growth in revenues and profit after taxation of 53.35 percent and 49 percent, respectively, for the fiscal year ending December 31, 2000, the growth in revenues and profit after taxation came down to 14.35 percent and 12.06 percent, respectively, by the fiscal 2003. Analysts felt that the sharp decline in the share of overall revenues derived from European markets, during the early 2000s, was not a good sign for the company. They felt the company had failed to come up with effective strategies to increase revenue share from the European market, which, next to the United States, had immense potential for fashion goods, especially garments, Li & Fung's major business. They criticized Li & Fung for failing to build on the opportunities provided by its acquisition of Inchcape Buying Services, which had a strong presence in Europe.

Analysts also felt that Li & Fung's high dependence on large retailers, especially in the United States and Europe, might prove a threat for the company in the long run, given the uncertainties in the retailing industry. They pointed out that a major consolidation in the North American retailing industry, Li & Fung's largest export market, might severely affect the company's business. For instance, if a retailing giant such as Wal-Mart,

[19]"Hong Kong Li & Fung Posts 13% Net Profit Rise on Sales Growth," www.prophet.net, March 24, 2004.

EXHIBIT 8

A Note on Hong Kong's Export Trade Industry

The Export Trade Industry:

Hong Kong has always been one of the world's major export trade centres. Until the 1970s, Hong Kong was a manufacturing economy, supplying the world with textiles, handbags, toys, plastic flowers, watches and footwear. Most of its exports were to the US and Europe. After the Chinese economy was liberalized in 1979 (initially only some coastal regions were opened up for foreign investors) many companies across all the major industrial segments and trading companies in Hong Kong moved the labour-intensive part of manufacturing to China.

The rapid industrialization of Asian countries from the 1980s resulted in expansion of production capabilities in the manufacturing sector and related supporting services especially in other low cost countries like Taiwan and Korea. This in turn led to trading companies expanding their sourcing reach beyond China to optimise sourcing costs for their clients. By the late 1990s, Hong-Kong emerged as a service economy with 84% of GDP derived from services. According to a survey by the Hong Kong Trade Development Council (TDC) in 1998, 64% of international buyers sourced China-made products through trading companies in Hong Kong. The country's strategic location, good physical infrastructure, expertise in international trade and well-established legal framework made trading reliable, simple and convenient. By the turn of the 20th century, Hong Kong became one of the world's largest export trade countries.

In 2001, Hong Kong earned HK$ 106 bn from exporting trade-related services, accounting for 32.7% of total services exports. In 2002, one in five employed persons in Hong Kong were engaged in the import-export trade. The sector produced a net output of HK$ 249 bn and accounted for 21% of Hong Kong's GDP. In 2002, there were more than 1,133 companies involved in the wholesale, retail and import and export trade businesses.

In the early 2000s, off shore export trading was increasing rapidly on account of many factors. The use of advanced technology, sophisticated production processes and on-site inspections by trading firms eliminated the need for further processing of products like final assembly, packaging and imposing quality control procedures. At the same time, the increased availability of cost-effective and reliable transport services contributed to the rise in off shore export trade. Some expected changes in the regional trade regimes including the China-ASEAN Free Trade Agreement and the Closer Economic Partnership Arrangement (CEPA) between Hong Kong and mainland China were expected to further boost the trading industry in Hong Kong.

In 2003, Hong Kong was the world's freest and 10th largest trading economy. It was a major trading centre with total merchandise trade amounting to US$ 457 bn, equivalent to 289% of GDP for that year. Major exports included clothing, electrical machinery, apparatus, textiles, jewelry, insurance services, financial services, transportation and travel services. In 2003, Hong Kong earned US$ 287.9 bn from exporting goods and services. Major export trading partners included mainland China (39.3%), US (21.3%), Japan (5.4%) and the UK (3.5%). With trading volumes of such magnitude, Hong Kong became a leading sourcing hub in the Asia-Pacific region in the early 21st century.

Export Trading Firms in Hong Kong:

Export trading firms in Hong Kong can be divided into three categories:

Left hand–right hand traders: Traditional trading firms that matched sellers and buyers but did not add significant value. These firms identified goods produced in Hong Kong or neighbouring countries and shipped them to their customers.

Traders with some value-added services: These firms, apart from sourcing raw material for their customers, offered some additional value such as providing trade finance and freight forwarding services.

Traders with sophisticated value-added services: These exporting firms went beyond traditional trading services. Additional services included product designing and development, manufacturing prototypes, offering supply chain management services, undertaking distribution and delivery of finished goods.

Hong Kong's export trading firms source garments, toys, electronic items and other manufactured goods. The sourcing activities are of three types:

- Sourcing goods produced in Hong Kong.
- Sourcing goods from the Asian region for re-export from Hong Kong.
- Sourcing goods from one country for direct shipping to another country, without touching Hong Kong. This is called offshore trade.

Trading firms in Hong Kong usually specialize in one product. In most cases, they offer shipping services to customers and manage their own warehousing facilities. Such facilities enable exporters of durable goods to offer better customer service, as a certain quantity of stock is always readily available for shipment. For goods like textiles, trading firms use temporary storage, with emphasis placed on prompt dispatch for shipping.

EXHIBIT 8   (*continued*)

A Note on Hong Kong's Export Trade Industry

Most export trading firms in Hong Kong are closely involved in manufacturing activities, though indirectly, as actual production is usually sub-contracted. Short production cycles, a preference for smaller quantities of more product lines and keeping tight deadlines ensured that companies met customer needs. They provided supplier factories with advanced production techniques and know-how and helped solve production bottlenecks.

Profile of William E. Conner & Associates (Li & Fung's Major Competitor):
William E. Conner & Associates (WEC&A) was founded in 1949 in Tokyo and moved to Hong Kong in 1985. It is one of the major export trade companies in Hong Kong in the early 21st century and the closest competitor to the market leader, Li & Fung, in the consumer goods trading market. WEC&A optimised the supply chain for its clients by managing every aspect of sourcing, right from product design & development to distribution and delivery of the finished product. The company's products included apparel, fabrics, fashion accessories, footwear, decorative accessories, textiles, housewares, furniture, lighting, office products, stationery and fashion-related products.

In the early 2000s, WEC&A had a global network of 35 offices in 20 countries. With an employee base of over 1,400, the company fulfilled the requirements of over 70 customers, which included leading department stores, specialty stores, catalogue companies, e-commerce retailers and importers, mainly in North America, Australia, Europe, Latin America and Japan. In 2002, WEC&A's net worth amounted to US$ 850 mn.

Sources: **www.tdc.trade.com** and **www.weconnor.com**.

EXHIBIT 9

Li & Fung—Consolidated Statements of Income (1997–2003)

Year Ending December 31	2003 HK$'000	2002 HK$'000	2001 HK$'000	2000 HK$'000	1999 HK$'000	1998 HK$'000	1997 HK$'000
Continuing operations	42,630,510	37,281,360	32,941,392	24,992,227	16,297,501	14,312,618	13,345,722
Discontinued operations	—	—	87,183	791	—	—	—
Total Turnover	**42,630,510**	**37,281,360**	**33,028,575**	**24,993,018**	**16,297,501**	**14,312,618**	**13,345,772**
Counting operations	1,285,952	1,134,605	904,520	830,223	592,885	469,501	361,289
Discontinued operations	—	—	(237,955)	(39,375)	—	—	—
Gross Profit	**1,285,952**	**1,134,605**	**666,565**	**790,848**	**592,885**	**469,501**	**361,289**
Interest income	38,373	49,581	112,837	140,330	43,830	56,093	37,772
Interest expenses	(9,813)	(8,987)	(12,464)	(20,585)	(32,243)	(61,346)	(6,270)
Share of profit less losses of associated companies	2,015	393	1,443	13,677	9,389	6,850	6,666
Profit before taxation	1,316,527	1,175,592	768,381	924,270	613,861	471,098	399,457
Taxation	(105,513)	(94,896)	(55,637)	(64,178)	(36,638)	(16,425)	(25,326)
Profit after taxation	1,211,014	1,080,696	712,744	860,092	577,223	454,673	374,131
Minority interests	12,104	(228)	69,567	10,296	(2,585)	495	974
Continuing operations	1,223,118	1,080,468	951,307	893,118	574,638	455,168	375,105
Discontinued operations	—	—	(168,996)	(22,730)	—	—	—
Net Profit	**1,223,118**	**1,080,468**	**782,311**	**870,388**	**574,638**	**455,168**	**375,105**

Source: Li & Fung Annual Report, 2003.

which rarely outsourced its manufacturing activities, acquired other major American retailers, or put them out of business, it could lead to an 8 percent to 10 percent cut in margins for Li & Fung. Such consolidation might also result in only a few large retailing giants surviving (with other companies either having been acquired or forced to quit) in the market, which might also have severe implications on Li & Fung's revenues. This was because the company mainly derived its revenues from a large base of companies in the United States, with revenues of over US$ 100 million.

Analysts further added that Li & Fung's hopes of benefiting from increased manufacturing activity in China to strengthen its competitive position in the United States, after the removal of the quota system in January 2005, might fail. They were of the view that according to WTO rules, the United States and Europe were entitled to impose "antisurge" quotas until the end of 2008, in case they felt any threat to domestic industry from exports. Antisurge quotas restricted annual growth of imports from a country to 7.5 percent per product category. Analysts also said that it was very likely that the antisurge quotas would come into existence in 2005.

Despite these challenges, industry observers felt that with Li & Fung focusing on expanding its customer base outside the United States, especially in Asia, in the years to come the company could reduce its dependence on the United States, its largest market. Meanwhile, Li & Fung had already achieved considerable success in lessening its dependence on soft goods over the years, reducing some risks in its business.

Media reports expressed optimism for Li & Fung's future. They wrote that the company, powered by its depth of sourcing knowledge and positioning as an efficient manager of global supply chains, was well poised for growth, in the light of increasing globalization. An *Economist* article had quoted in 2001, "Li & Fung appears to have as bright a future as globalisation itself."[20]

---

[20]"Li & Fung: Optimising Supply Chain for Other Companies," *The Economist*, May 31, 2001.

Case 16

Starbucks Corporation: Competing in a Global Market

This case was prepared by Suresh Kotha and Debra Glassman, the University of Washington.

Starbucks Corporation is a Seattle, Washington, based coffee company. It buys, roasts, and sells whole bean specialty coffees and coffee drinks through an international chain of retail outlets. From its beginnings as a seller of packaged, premium specialty coffees, Starbucks has evolved into a firm known for its coffeehouses, where people can purchase beverages and food items as well as packaged whole bean and ground coffee. Starbucks is credited with changing the way Americans—and people around the world—view and consume coffee, and its success has attracted global attention.

Starbucks has consistently been one of the fastest growing companies in the United States. Over a ten-year period starting in 1992, the company's net revenues increased at a compounded annual growth rate of 20 percent to $3.3 billion in fiscal 2002. Net earnings have grown at an annual compounded growth rate of 30 percent to $218 million in fiscal 2002, which is the highest reported net earnings figure in the company's history (see Exhibit 1). As *Business Week* tells it:

On Wall Street, Starbucks is the last great growth story. Its stock, including four splits, has soared more than 2,200% over the past decade, surpassing Wal-Mart, General Electric, PepsiCo, Coca-Cola, Microsoft, and IBM in total return. Now at $21 [September 2002], it is hovering near its all-time high of $23 in July [2002], before the overall market drop.[1]

To continue this rapid pace of growth, the firm's senior executives are looking to expand internationally. Specifically, they are interested in further expansion in Europe (including the Middle East), Asia Pacific (including Australia and New Zealand), and Latin America. Expanding in these three continents represents both a challenge and an opportunity to Starbucks. While the opportunity of increased revenues from further expansion is readily apparent to the company's top management, what is not clear is how to deal with growing "antiglobalization" sentiment around the world.

This case looks at issues that are arising as Starbucks seeks to dominate specialty coffee markets around the world and explores what changes in strategy might be required.

Background

In 1971, three Seattle entrepreneurs—Jerry Baldwin, Zev Siegl, and Gordon Bowker—started selling whole-bean coffee in Seattle's Pike Place Market. They named

This case was written by Professors Suresh Kotha and Debra Glassman, both of the University of Washington, as the basis for class discussion rather than to illustrate either effective or ineffective handling of an administrative situation. Some of the facts provided in the case have been disguised to protect confidentiality. Copyright © Kotha & Glassman 2003. All rights reserved. For the most recent financial results of the company discussed in this case, go to **http://finance.yahoo.com**, input the company's stock symbol, and download the latest company report from its homepage.

[1]Planet Starbucks, *Business Week*, September 9, 2002, pp. 100–110.

EXHIBIT 1

Selected Financial and Store Data
(in Thousands, Except Earnings per Share and Store Operating Data)

As of and for the Fiscal Year Ended (1)	Sept 29, 2002 (52 Wks)	Sept 30, 2001 (52 Wks)	Oct 1, 2000 (52 Wks)	Oct 3, 1999 (53 Wks)	Sept 27, 1998 (52 Wks)
Results of Operations Data					
Net revenues:					
Retail	$2,792,904	$2,229,594	$1,823,607	$1,423,389	$1,102,574
Specialty	496,004	419,386	354,007	263,439	206,128
Total net revenues	3,288,908	2,648,980	2,177,614	1,686,828	1,308,702
Merger expenses (2)	—	—	—	—	8,930
Operating income	318,725	281,094	212,252	156,711	109,216
Internet-related investment losses	—	2,940	58,792	—	—
Gain on sale of investment	13,361	—	—	—	—
Net earnings	$215,073	$181,210	$94,564	$101,693	$68,372
Net earnings per common share—diluted	$0.54	$0.46	$0.24	$0.27	$0.19
Balance Sheet Data					
Working capital	$310,048	$148,661	$146,568	$135,303	$157,805
Total assets	2,292,736	1,846,519	1,491,546	1,252,514	992,755
Long-term debt (including current portion)	5,786	6,483	7,168	7,691	1,803
Shareholders' equity	1,726,638	1,375,927	1,148,399	961,013	794,297
Store Operating Data					
Percentage change in comparable store sales (3)					
North America	7%	5%	9%	6%	5%
International	(3)%	2%	23%	20%	28%
Consolidated	6%	5%	9%	6%	5%
Systemwide retail store sales (4)	$3,796,000	$2,950,000	$2,250,000	$1,633,000	$1,190,000
Systemwide stores opened during the year: (5)	1,177	1,208	1,003	612	474
Systemwide stores open at year end:					
Continental North America					
Company-operated stores	3,496	2,971	2,446	2,038	1,622
Licensed stores	1,078	809	530	179	133
International					
Company-operated stores	384	295	173	97	66
Licensed stores	928	634	352	184	65
Total	5,886	4,709	3,501	2,498	1,886

(1) The company's fiscal year ends on the Sunday closest to September 30. All fiscal years presented include 52 weeks, except fiscal 1999, which includes 53 weeks.
(2) Merger expenses relate to the business combination with Seattle Coffee Holdings Limited.
(3) Includes only company-operated stores open 13 months or longer.
(4) Systemwide retail store sales include sales at company-operated and licensed stores and are believed by management to measure global penetration of Starbucks retail stores.
(5) Systemwide store openings are reported net of closures.

their store Starbucks, after the first mate in *Moby Dick*.[2] By 1982, the business had grown to five stores, a small roasting facility, and a wholesale business selling coffee to local restaurants. At the same time, Howard Schultz had been working as Vice President of U.S. operations for Hammarplast, a Swedish house wares company in New York, marketing coffee makers to a number of retailers, including Starbucks. Through selling to Starbucks, Schultz was introduced to the three founders, who then recruited him to bring marketing savvy to their company. Schultz, twenty-nine and recently married, was eager to leave New York. He joined Starbucks as manager of retail sales and marketing.

A year later, Schultz visited Italy for the first time on a buying trip. He noticed that coffee is an integral part of the culture in Italy; Italians start their day at an espresso bar and later in the day return with their friends. There are 200,000 coffee bars in Italy, and about 1,500 in Milan alone. Schultz believed that, given the chance, Americans would pay good money for a premium cup of coffee and a stylish place to enjoy it. Enthusiastic about his idea, Schultz returned to tell Starbucks's owners of his plan for a national chain of cafés styled on the Italian coffee bar. The owners, however, did not want to be in the restaurant business. Undaunted, Schultz wrote a business plan and began looking for investors. By April 1985, he had opened his first coffee bar, Il Giornale (named after the Italian newspaper), where he served Starbucks coffee. Following Il Giornale's immediate success, he expanded to three stores. In 1987, the owners of Starbucks agreed to sell the firm to Schultz for $4 million. The Il Giornale coffee bars took on the name of Starbucks.

Convinced that Starbucks would one day be in every neighborhood in America, Schultz focused on growth. At first, the company's losses almost doubled (to $1.2 million in fiscal 1990), as overhead and operating expenses ballooned with the expansion. Starbucks lost money for three years running, and the stress was hard on Schultz, but he stuck to his conviction not to "sacrifice long-term integrity and values for short-term profit."[3] In 1991, sales shot up 84 percent, and the company turned profitable. In 1992, Schultz took the firm public at $17 a share.

Believing that market share and name recognition are critical to the company's success, Schultz continued to expand the business aggressively. Schultz observes, "There is no secret sauce here. Anyone can do it." From the beginning, Schultz has professed a strict growth policy. Although many other coffeehouses or espresso bars are franchised, Starbucks owns all of its North American stores outright, with the exception of license agreements in airports. Further, rather than trying to capture all the potential markets as soon as possible, Starbucks goes into a geographic market and tries to completely dominate it before setting its sights on further expansion. Using this strategy, Starbucks has grown from 17 coffee shops in 1987 to 5,688 outlets in 28 countries by the end of fiscal 2002 (see Exhibit 2). It also employed over 60,000 individuals, including approximately 50,000 in retail stores at the end of 2002.

Starbucks Corporation is organized into two business units that correspond to the company's operating segments: North American and International. In 1995, Starbucks Coffee International, a wholly owned subsidiary of Starbucks Coffee Company, was set up to build Starbucks's businesses outside North America, including opening company-owned, licensed, and joint-venture-based retail stores worldwide.

A recent article in *Business Week* notes:

Starbucks also has a well-seasoned management team. Schultz, 49, stepped down as chief executive in 2000 to become chairman and chief global strategist. Orin Smith, 60, the company's numbers-cruncher, is now CEO and in charge of day-to-day operations. The head of North American operations is Howard Behar, 57, a retailing expert who returned last September, two years after retiring. The management trio is known as H2O, for Howard, Howard, and Orin.[4]

Exhibit 3 provides a partial list of Starbucks top management, and Appendix A provides a timeline and history of Starbucks.

[2]According to *Business Week* (September 9, 2002, p. 103), "The name came about when the original owners looked to Seattle history for inspiration and chose the moniker of an old mining camp: Starbo. Further refinement led to Starbucks, after the first mate in *Moby Dick*, which they felt evoked the seafaring romance of the early coffee traders (hence the mermaid logo).

[3]*Success*, April 1993.
[4]Planet Starbucks, *Business Week*, September 9, 2002, pp. 100–110.

EXHIBIT 2

Starbucks Store Locations (as of November 2002)

Source: Starbucks Corporation.

The Starbucks Model

Howard Schultz's goal is to: "Establish Starbucks as the premier purveyor of the finest coffee in the world while maintaining uncompromising principles as we grow." The company's twenty-five-year goal is to "become an enduring, great company with the most recognized and respected brand in the world, known for inspiring and nurturing the human spirit." The company's mission statement articulates several guiding principles to measure the appropriateness of the firm's decisions (see Exhibit 4). In describing Starbucks's unique approach to competition, *Fortune* notes

> The strategy is simple: Blanket an area completely, even if the stores cannibalize one another's business. A new store will often capture about 30% of the sales of a nearby Starbucks, but the company considers that a good thing: The Starbucks-everywhere approach cuts down on delivery and management costs, shortens customer lines at individual stores, and increases foot traffic for all the stores in an area. Last week 20 million people bought a cup of coffee at a Starbucks. A typical customer stops by 18 times a month; no American retailer has a higher frequency of customer visits. Sales have climbed an average of 20% a year since the company went public. Even in a down economy, when other retailers have taken a beating, Starbucks store traffic has risen between 6% and 8% a year. Perhaps

even more notable is the fact that Starbucks has managed to generate those kinds of numbers with virtually no marketing, spending just 1% of its annual revenues on advertising. (Retailers usually spend 10% or so of revenues on ads.)[5]

Business Week adds

> Clustering stores increases total revenue and market share, [CEO] Orin Smith argues, even when individual stores poach on each other's sales. The strategy works, he says, because of Starbucks size. It is large enough to absorb losses at existing stores as new ones open up, and soon overall sales grow beyond what they would have with just one store. Meanwhile, it's cheaper to deliver to and manage stores located close together. And by clustering, Starbucks can quickly dominate a local market.[6]

And Schultz points out:

> The market is much larger than we originally thought. . . . In most cases local competitors benefit from our arrival because of the expansion of the marketplace. Our strategy is never to eliminate or hurt the competition. We never underprice our coffee and it's clear that we position ourselves so as not to undercut the pricing structure in the marketplace.

[5]Mr. Coffee. *Fortune*, March 30, 2003.
[6]Planet Starbucks, *Business Week*, September 9, 2002, p. 103.

EXHIBIT 3

Starbucks Top Management Team

Howard Schultz is the founder of the company and has been chairman of the board since its inception in 1985. Mr. Schultz served as chief executive officer from 1985 until June 2000, when he transitioned into the role of chief global strategist. From 1985 to June 1994, Mr. Schultz was also the company's president. From September 1982 to December 1985, Mr. Schultz was the director of Retail Operations and Marketing for Starbucks Coffee Company, a predecessor to the company; and from January 1986 to July 1987, he was the chairman of the board, chief executive officer and president of Il Giornale Coffee Company, a predecessor to the company.

Orin C. Smith joined Starbucks Corporation in 1990 and has served as president and chief executive officer of the company since June 2000. From June 1994 to June 2000, Mr. Smith served as the company's president and chief operating officer. Prior to June 1994, Mr. Smith served as the company's vice president and chief financial officer and later, as its executive vice president and chief financial officer.

Peter Maslen joined Starbucks in August 1999 as president, Starbucks Coffee International, Inc. Prior to joining Starbucks, Mr. Maslen served in various executive positions within Asia Pacific and Europe with Mars Inc., PepsiCo, Inc. and Tricon Global Restaurants. From 1992 to 1999, as senior vice president with Tricon, he served as president of its German, Swiss, Austrian and Central Europe divisions.

Jim Donald joined Starbucks in November 2002 as president, Starbucks North America. He is responsible for managing Starbucks North America company-owned and licensed stores, business alliances (food service, grocery, club channels of distribution, joint venture partnerships with Pepsi-Cola Company and Dreyer's Grand Ice Cream)—in the United States and Canada, store development, retail systems, administration and retail partner resources. Jim brings 32 years of experience in the retail and food industry. Prior to joining Starbucks, he was chairman, president and chief executive officer at Pathmark Stores, Inc. since 1996. In addition, he has held several senior leadership positions at top-tier retail companies including Safeway, Wal-Mart and Albertson's.

Michael Casey joined Starbucks in August 1995 as senior vice president and chief financial officer and was promoted to executive vice president, chief financial officer and chief administrative officer in September 1997. Prior to joining Starbucks, Mr. Casey served as executive vice president and chief financial officer of Family Restaurants, Inc. from its inception in 1986. During his tenure there, he also served as a director from 1986 to 1993, and as president and chief executive officer of its El Torito Restaurants, Inc. subsidiary from 1988 to 1993.

Eduardo R. (Ted) Garcia joined Starbucks in April 1995 as senior vice president, Supply Chain Operations and was promoted to executive vice president, Supply Chain and Coffee Operations in September 1997. From May 1993 to April 1995, Mr. Garcia was an executive for Gemini Consulting. From January 1990 until May 1993, he was the vice president of Operations Strategy for Grand Metropolitan PLC, Food Sector.

Source: Starbucks Corporation, November 2002.

Schultz observes that the company is still in its early days of growth worldwide. "We are opening three or four stores every day," he notes. "We feel strongly that the driver of the equity of the brand is directly linked to the retail experience we create in our stores. Our commitment to the growth of the company is significant and will continue to be based on the long-term growth potential of our retail format."

Securing the Finest Raw Materials

Starbucks's coffee quality begins with the purchase of high-quality *arabica* coffee beans. Although many Americans were raised on a commodity-like coffee made from lower quality *robusta* beans (or arabica beans mixed with less-expensive filler beans), Starbucks

coffee is strictly *arabica*, and the company ensures that only the highest quality beans are used. Dave Olsen, the company's then senior vice president and then chief coffee procurer, scoured mountain trails in Indonesia, Kenya, Guatemala, and elsewhere in search of Starbucks's premium bean. His standards were demanding, and he conducted exacting experiments in order to get the proper balance of flavor, body, and acidity.

From the company's inception, it has worked on developing relationships with the countries from which it buys coffee beans. Traditionally, Europeans and Japanese bought most of the premium coffee beans. Olsen sometimes had to convince coffee growers to sell to Starbucks—especially since American

EXHIBIT 4

Starbucks Mission Statements and Guiding Principles

Mission Statement

Establish Starbucks as the premier purveyor of the finest coffee in the world while maintaining our uncompromising principles while we grow.

The following six guiding principles will help us measure the appropriateness of our decisions:

- Provide a great work environment and treat each other with respect and dignity.
- Embrace diversity as an essential component in the way we do business.
- Apply the highest standards of excellence to the purchasing, roasting and fresh delivery of our coffee.
- Develop enthusiastically satisfied customers all of the time.
- Contribute positively to our communities and our environment.
- Recognize that profitability is essential to our future success.

Environmental Mission Statement

Starbucks is committed to a role of environmental leadership in all facets of our business.

We fulfill this mission by a commitment to:

- Understanding of environmental issues and sharing information with our partners.
- Developing innovative and flexible solutions to bring about change.
- Striving to buy, sell and use environmentally friendly products.
- Recognizing that fiscal responsibility is essential to our environmental future.
- Instilling environmental responsibility as a corporate value.
- Measuring and monitoring our progress for each project.
- Encouraging all partners to share in our mission.

coffee buyers are notorious purchasers of the "dregs" of the coffee beans. In 1992, Starbucks set a new precedent by outbidding European buyers for the exclusive Narino Supremo Bean crop.[7] Starbucks collaborated with a mill in the tiny town of Pasto, located on the side of the Volcano Galero. There they set up a special operation to single out the particular Narino Supremo bean, and Starbucks guaranteed to purchase the entire yield. This enabled Starbucks to be the exclusive purveyor of Narino Supremo, purportedly one of the best coffees in the world.[8]

Vertical Integration

Roasting the coffee bean is close to an art form at Starbucks. Starbucks currently operates multiple roasting and distribution facilities. Roasters are promoted from within the company and trained for over a year, and it is considered quite an honor to be chosen. The coffee is roasted in a powerful gas-fired drum roaster for twelve to fifteen minutes while roasters use sight, smell, hearing, and computers to judge when beans are perfectly done. The color of the beans is even tested in an Agtron blood-cell analyzer, with the whole batch being discarded if the sample is not deemed perfect.

---

[7]This Colombian coffee bean crop is very small and grows only in the high regions of the Cordillera mountain range. For years, the Narino beans were guarded zealously by Western Europeans, who prized their colorful and complex flavor. It was usually used for upgrading blends. Starbucks was determined to make them available for the first time as a pure varietal. This required breaking Western Europe's monopoly over the beans by convincing the Colombian growers that it intended to use "the best beans for a higher purpose."

[8]The *Canada Newswire*, March 1, 1993.

The Starbucks Experience

According to Schultz, "We're not just selling a cup of coffee, we are providing an experience." In order to create American coffee enthusiasts with the dedication of their Italian counterparts, Starbucks provides a seductive atmosphere in which to imbibe. Its stores are distinctive and sleek, yet comfortable. Though the sizes of the stores and their formats vary, most are modeled after the Italian coffee bars where regulars sit and drink espresso with their friends.

Starbucks stores tend to be located in high-traffic locations such as malls, busy street corners, and even grocery stores. They are well lighted and feature plenty of light cherry wood and artwork. The people who prepare the coffee are referred to as "baristas," Italian for bartender. Jazz or opera music plays softly in the background. The stores range from 200 to 4,000 square feet, with new units tending to range from 1,500 to 1,700 square feet. In 2003, the average cost of opening a new store (including equipment, inventory and leasehold improvements) is in the neighborhood of $350,000; a "flagship" store costs much more.

Building a Unique Culture

While Starbucks enforces almost fanatical standards about coffee quality and service, the policy at Starbucks toward employees is laid back and supportive. They are encouraged to think of themselves as partners in the business. Schultz believes that happy employees are the key to competitiveness and growth.

> We can't achieve our strategic objectives without a work force of people who are immersed in the same commitment as management. Our only sustainable advantage is the quality of our work force. We're building a national retail company by creating pride in—and stake in—the outcome of our labor.[9]

On a practical level, Starbucks promotes an empowered employee culture through generous benefits programs, an employee stock ownership plan, and thorough employee training. Each employee must have at least twenty-four hours of training. Classes cover everything from coffee history to a seven-hour

workshop called "Brewing the Perfect Cup at Home." This workshop is one of five classes that all employees must complete during their first six weeks with the company. Reports *Fortune*:

> It's silly, soft-headed stuff, though basically, of course, it's true. Maybe some of it sinks in. Starbucks is a smashing success, thanks in large part to the people who come out of these therapy-like training programs. Annual barista turnover at the company is 60% compared with 140% for hourly workers in the fast-food business.[10]

Starbucks offers its benefits package to both part-time and full-time employees. The package includes medical, dental, vision, and short-term disability insurance, as well as paid vacation, paid holidays, mental health/chemical dependency benefits, an employee assistance program, a 401k savings plan, and a stock option plan. They also offer dependent coverage that includes same-sex partners.[11] Schultz believes that without these benefits, people do not feel financially or spiritually tied to their jobs. He argues that stock options and the complete benefits package increase employee loyalty and encourage attentive service to the customer.[12]

Employee turnover is also discouraged by Starbucks's stock option plan known as the Bean Stock Plan. Implemented in August 1991, the plan made Starbucks the only private company to offer stock options unilaterally to all employees.

Starbucks's concern for employee welfare extends beyond its retail outlets to coffee producers. The company's guidelines call for overseas suppliers to pay wages and benefits that "address the basic needs of workers and their families" and to allow child labor only when it does not interrupt required education.[13] This move has set a precedent for other importers of agricultural commodities.

---

[9] *Inc.*, January 1993.

[10] *Fortune*, December 9, 1996.

[11] The decision to offer benefits even to part-time employees (who represent roughly two-thirds of Starbucks's 10,000 employees) has gained a great deal of attention in the press. According to a Hewitt Associates L.L.C. survey of more than 500 employers, only 25 percent of employers offer medical coverage to employees working less than 20 hours a week. It was difficult to get insurers to sign Starbucks up since they did not understand why Starbucks would want to cover part-timers.

[12] *Inc.*, January, 1993.

[13] *Wall Street Journal*, October 23, 1995.

Leveraging the Brand

Multiple Channels of Distribution Besides its stand-alone stores, Starbucks has set up cafés and carts in hospitals, banks, office buildings, supermarkets, and shopping centers. Other distribution agreements have included office coffee suppliers, hotels, and airlines. Office coffee is a large segment of the coffee market. Associated Services (an office coffee supplier) provides Starbucks coffee exclusively to thousands of businesses around the United States. Starbucks has deals with airlines, such as an agreement with United Airlines to provide Starbucks coffee to United's nearly 75 million passengers a year. Starbucks, through a licensing agreement with Kraft Foods Inc., offers its coffee in grocery stores across the United States.

Brand Extensions In 1995, Starbucks launched a line of packaged and prepared teas in response to growing demand for teahouses and packaged tea. Tea is a highly profitable beverage for restaurants to sell, costing only 2 cents to 4 cents a cup to produce.[14] As its tea line became increasingly popular, in January 1999 it acquired Tazo, a Portland, Oregon, based tea company.

Starbucks coffee is also making its way onto grocery shelves via a carefully planned series of joint ventures.[15] An agreement with PepsiCo Inc. brought a bottled version of Starbucks Frappuccino (a cold, sweetened coffee drink) to store shelves in August 1996. In another fifty-fifty partnership, Dreyers' Grand Ice Cream Inc. distributes seven quart-products and two bar-products of Starbucks coffee ice cream.

Other partnerships by the company are designed to form new product associations with coffee. For instance, the company's music subsidiary, Hear Music, regularly releases CDs, some in collaboration with major record labels, that are then sold through Starbucks retail stores.

While Starbucks is the largest and best known of the coffeehouse chains and its presence is very apparent in metropolitan areas, the firm's estimates indicate that only a small percentage (about 7 percent) of the U.S. population has tried its products. Through distribution agreements and the new product partnerships, Starbucks hopes to capture more of the U.S. market.

International Expansion

For many years analysts have observed that the U.S. coffee-bar market may be reaching saturation. They point to market consolidation, as bigger players snap up some of the smaller coffee bar competitors.[16] Further, they note that Starbucks's store base is also maturing, leading to a slowdown in the growth of unit volume and firm profitability. In response, some argue, Starbucks has turned its attention to foreign markets for continued growth. For instance *Business Week* notes

> To duplicate the staggering returns of its first decade, Starbucks has no choice but to export its concept aggressively. Indeed, some analysts give Starbucks only two years at most before it saturates the U.S. market. The chain now [in August 2002] operates 1,200 international outlets, from Beijing to Bristol. That leaves plenty of room to grow. Indeed, about 400 of its planned 1,200 new stores this year will be built overseas, representing a 35% increase in its foreign base. Starbucks expects to double the number of its stores worldwide, to 10,000 in three years.[17]

However, of the predicted three or four stores that will open each day, the majority will continue to be in the United States.

Early Expansion

In 1995, the firm established a subsidiary called Starbucks Coffee International Inc. At that time, the subsidiary consisted of twelve managers located in Seattle. Today this subsidiary is led by Australian expatriate Peter Maslen and is staffed with about one hundred eighty experienced multinational and

---

[14]*Nations Restaurant News*, July 10, 1995.

[15]The Specialty Coffee Association of America notes that supermarkets account for over 60 percent of all coffee sold in America, followed by gourmet stores (14 percent), mass market (11 percent), mail order (8 percent), and other.

[16]The *Washington Post*, August 1, 1995.

[17]Planet Starbucks, *Business Week*, September 9, 2002, p. 102. However, Schultz firmly believes that Starbucks growth is far from saturation both in the United States and overseas: "We have less than 7% of the coffee-consuming opportunities in North America. People are still drinking bad coffee."

multilingual managers located in Seattle and three regional offices around the world. This group is responsible for all Starbucks business development outside North America, including developing new businesses, financing and planning stores, managing operations and logistics, merchandising, and training and developing Starbucks's international managers.

Starbucks's first non–North American store was opened in 1996 in Tokyo. In reflecting on this early step in internationalizing the chain, Schultz notes

> Two years prior to opening up in Japan, we hired this blue-chip consulting firm to guide us to succeed here. Basically, they said we would not succeed in Japan. There were a number of things they told us to change. [They said] we had to have smoking, but that was a non-starter for us. They also said no Japanese would ever lose face by drinking from a cup in the street. And third, they said that given the [high] rent, stores couldn't be larger than 500 square feet.... Well, our no smoking policy made us an oasis in Japan. As for our to-go business, you can't walk down a street in Tokyo today and not see someone holding a cup of Starbucks coffee. And our store size in Japan is identical to our store size in the U.S., about 1,200 to 1,500 square feet. It just shows the power of believing in what you do. And also that Starbucks is as relevant in Tokyo, Madrid, or Berlin as it is in Seattle.[18]

The Starbucks Way

According to *US News and World Report*:

> When venturing overseas, there is a Starbucks way. The company finds local business partners in most foreign markets.... It tests each country with a handful of stores in trendy districts, using experienced Starbucks managers. It sends local baristas to Seattle for 13 weeks of training. Then it starts opening stores by the dozen. Its coffee lineup doesn't vary, but Starbucks does adapt its food to local tastes. In Britain, it won an award for its mince pie. In Asia, Starbucks offers curry puffs and meat buns. The company also fits its interior

décor to the local architecture, especially in historic buildings. "We don't stamp these things out cookie-cutter style," says Peter Maslen, president of Starbucks Coffee International.[19]

Although Starbucks is committed to owning its North American stores, it has sought partners for much of its overseas expansion. As Kathy Lindemann, senior vice president of operations for Starbucks International, describes it:

> Our approach to international expansion is to focus on the *partnership first, country second*. We rely on the local connection to get everything up and working. The key is finding the right local partners to negotiate local regulations and other issues. We look for partners who share our values, culture, and goals about community development. We are primarily interested in partners who can guide us through the process of starting up in a foreign location. We look for firms with: (1) similar philosophy to ours in terms of shared values, corporate citizenship, and commitment to be in the business for the long haul, (2) multi-unit restaurant experience, (3) financial resources to expand the Starbucks concept rapidly to prevent imitators, (4) strong real-estate experience with knowledge about how to pick prime real estate locations, (5) knowledge of the retail market, and (6) the availability of the people to commit to our project.

In an international joint venture, it is the partner that chooses store sites. These are submitted for approval to Starbucks, but the partner does all the preparatory and selection work. Cydnie Horwat, vice president for international assets development systems and infrastructure, explains how a Starbucks market entry plan starts with brand building, which then facilitates rapid further expansion in a country:

> When first entering a market, we're looking for different things in the first one to three years than later on. During these early years, we're building our brand. Our stores are the biggest source of advertising, since we do not do a lot of separate advertising. So we have a higher investment in stores in the first three years. About 60–70% of stores opened in these first three years are our high brand-builders.

---

[18]Online Extra: Q&A with Starbucks' Howard Schultz, *Business Week*, September 9, 2002.

[19]*US World and News Report*, February 19, 2001.

Adds Horwat:

First, we look for extremely visible sites in well-trafficked areas and focus on three major factors: demographics, branding potential, and financials. Second, we categorize sites on an A to D scale. "A" sites are "signature" sites that are qualitatively superior to all other sites within the trade area [an area within which Starbucks chooses to locate one store]. We rarely take a "C" or "D" store.[20] Third, we ask our international market business unit[21] (MBU) to send in the "site" submittal package with quantitative and qualitative measures, such as how the site meets Starbucks' established criteria and the partner's agreed-upon criteria. This package is reviewed by a number of functional units—operations, finance, and real estate—within the International Group. Fourth, we move into the design phase, which is done in Seattle using information provided by the partner. Next we negotiate the lease with landlord and initiate the construction when the appropriate permits are obtained. Finally, we turn over the store to operations. The whole process takes about 13–16 weeks from start to finish.

Establishing Starbucks as a Global Brand

Based on the success in Japan and other locations, Schultz's goal is for Starbucks to have a ubiquitous image as one of the most respected brands in the world. He notes

Whenever we see the reception we're getting in markets in places such as China, the Philippines, Malaysia, the U.K., and most recently Spain and Germany, we recognize that the growth potential for the company [overseas] is very significant. We want to accelerate that growth, maintain our leadership position, and, ultimately, become one of the most respected brands in the world.[22]

Since its early foray into the Japanese market, the pace of international expansion has picked up significantly. In 1998, Starbucks acquired Seattle Coffee Company in the United Kingdom, a chain with more than thirty-eight retail locations. That same year, it opened stores in Taiwan, Thailand, New Zealand, and Malaysia. In 1999, Starbucks opened in China (Beijing), Kuwait, South Korea, and Lebanon. In 2000, it entered another seven markets (China—Hong Kong and Shanghai, Dubai, Australia, Qatar, Saudi Arabia, and Bahrain). It added three markets in 2001 (Switzerland, Israel, and Austria). Last year, another nine markets were opened (Oman, Spain, Indonesia, Germany, Southern China—Macau and Shenzhen, Mexico, Puerto Rico, and Greece). Exhibit 5 highlights the growth of international stores, and Exhibit 6 provides the list of countries where Starbucks has a presence.

Schultz says that this expansion is only beginning and confidently predicts more to come:

Ten years ago, we had 125 stores and 2000 employees. Today we have 62,000 people working in 30 countries outside of North America, serving approximately 22 million customers a week. Our core customer is coming in about 18 times a month. With the majority of adults around the world drinking two cups of coffee a day and with Starbucks having less than 7% share of total coffee consumption in the U.S. and less than 1% worldwide, these are the early days for the growth and development of the company. We've got a model that has been well tested from market to market.

Starbucks is well on its way to becoming a global brand. According to *Business Week*:

The Starbucks name and image connect with millions of consumers around the globe. It was one of the fastest-growing brands in a *Business Week* survey of the top 100 global brands published August 5 [2002]. At a time when one corporate star after another has crashed to earth, brought down by revelations of earnings

---

[20]The difference between an "A" store and a "D" store can be substantial. A "D" store is expected to have about 50–60 percent lower sales. Starbucks classifies a store as "A" if the store location is the focal point of the area, has great visibility, has readily available parking, has excellent access to and from the site, cannot be out-positioned by competitors, and fits with Starbucks's desire to build a distinctive image.
[21]Starbucks's international businesses are typically joint ventures in which Starbucks holds various levels of equity (ranging from 5 percent to 100 percent). These ventures are referred to as market business units (MBUs). Regardless of the level of equity Starbucks holds, it supports all of its MBUs in an "ownership blind" manner by providing all MBUs with the same level of support.

[22]Online Extra: Q&A with Starbucks' Howard Schultz, *Business Week*, September 9, 2002.

EXHIBIT 5

Growth of International Stores 1996–2002

Source: Starbucks International Group.

In a box/map: **FY 2002...1,312 stores in 30 countries**

misstatements, executive greed, or worse, Starbucks hasn't faltered.[23]

But becoming a global company is not without risks. As *Business Week* points out:

> Global expansion poses huge risks for Starbucks. For one thing, it makes less money on each overseas store because most of them are operated with local partners. While that makes it easier to start up on foreign turf, it reduces the company's share of the profits to only 20% to 50%.[24]

In addition, the firm is becoming a target for antiglobalization activists around the world.

Perils of Globalization

As Starbucks establishes a global presence, its growing ubiquity has not gone unnoticed by antiglobalization activists. A clear manifestation of this came in November 1999, as tens of thousands of protesters took to the streets of downtown Seattle when the World Trade Organization (WTO) held its third ministerial conference there. Although non-governmental organizations (NGOs) and activists had gathered to oppose the WTO, some activists deliberately targeted multinationals like Starbucks, Nike, and McDonalds.[25]

[25]The protesters claim that international organizations like the WTO and International Monetary Fund (IMF) are tools of multinational corporations. Since Seattle, violent protests have been the norm at events such as the annual meetings of the IMF and World Bank, G-8 summits, and the World Economic Forum.

[23]*Business Week*, "Planet Starbucks," September 9, 2002, p. 102
[24]Ibid.

EXHIBIT 6

Licensed Starbucks International Stores (as of September 2002)

Asia-Pacific		Europe/Middle East/Africa		Latin America	
Japan	397	United Arab Emirates	23	Hawaii	30
Taiwan	99	Saudi Arabia	22	Mexico	1
China	88	Kuwait	16	Puerto Rico	1
South Korea	53	Switzerland	12		
Philippines	49	Lebanon	11		
New Zealand	34	Israel	6		
Singapore	32	Austria	5		
Malaysia	26	Spain	5		
Indonesia	5	Germany	4		
		Qatar	3		
		Bahrain	2		
		Greece	2		
		Oman	2		
Total	783		113		32

Product sales to, and royalty and license fee revenues from, licensed international retail stores accounted for approximately 17 percent of specialty revenues in fiscal 2002. *These figures do not include company operated stores.*

Source: Starbucks 10-K report.

A small, but vocal, percentage of these protestors garnered international press coverage by committing acts of vandalism against carefully chosen targets. As a report in *Business Week* recalls

> Protesters flooded Seattle's streets, and among their targets was Starbucks, a symbol, to them, of free-market capitalism run amok, another multinational out to blanket the earth. Amid the crowds of protesters and riot police were black-masked anarchists who trashed the store, leaving its windows smashed and its tasteful green-and-white decor smelling of tear gas instead of espresso.[26]

Recalling this incident against his firm Schultz says: "It's hurtful. I think people are ill-informed. It's very difficult to protest against a can of Coke, a bottle of Pepsi, or a can of Folgers. Starbucks is both a ubiquitous brand and a place where you can go and break a window. You can't break a can of Coke."

Antiglobalization protesters target recognizable global brands because they are convenient symbols. The following excerpt from "The Ruckus Society's Action Planning Manual and Media Manual"[27] illustrates the close ties between global brands and the principles of direct action against them:

> First, [we] use direct action to reduce the issues to symbols. These symbols must be carefully chosen for their utility in illustrating a conflict: an oil company vs. an indigenous community, a government policy vs. the public interest. Then we work to place these symbols in the public eye, in order to identify the evildoer, detail the wrongdoing and, if possible, point to a more responsible option.

[26]*Business Week*, "Planet Starbucks," September 9, 2002.

[27]The Ruckus Society website, **http://ruckus.org/man/action_planning.html** (site visited 3/14/03).

The message that activists want to communicate focuses on the overseas activities of corporations. They accuse multinationals of paying less than a living wage to workers in the Third World, of engaging in labor and environmental practices that would be outlawed in their home countries, of driving local competitors out of business, and of furthering "cultural imperialism." As one Global Trade Watch field organizer describes it:

> The rules by which trade is governed need to have more to do with the interests of citizens than with the back pockets and cash wads of a couple corporate CEOs. And we want to make sure that there is a balance consideration. Obviously people are always going to be concerned with their profits—it's business, we understand that, we accept that. But we think that needs to be balanced with concern for the rights of workers, basic human rights, [and] protecting the environment.[28]

Critics further accuse international organizations such as the WTO, World Bank, and IMF of promoting corporate globalization by supporting trade liberalization, by promoting export-based economic development, and by facilitating foreign direct investment. According to an organization that bills itself as Mobilization for Global Justice:

> Most of the world's most impoverished countries have suffered under IMF/World Bank programs for two decades: they've seen debt levels rise, unemployment skyrocket, poverty increase, and environments devastated. Urged to export, they focus on cash crops like coffee instead of food for their own people, and allow foreign governments to build sweatshops—which also puts pressure on jobs in the US.[29]

When Starbucks opened its first store in Mexico in September 2002, it chose a site in the Sheraton Hotel on Reforma Boulevard in Mexico City. This was Starbucks's first store in Latin America and its first in an "origin country," that is, a coffee-producing country. An article on the Organic Consumers Association website describes Starbucks' Mexican flagship store:

The new Starbucks on Reforma features soft lighting and an aromatic ambiance…. Behind the counter, well-groomed employees whip out the signature Frappuccinos and lattes. Indeed, the only jarring note is the 36 pesos ($3.60) the young woman at the register wants for a double latte, 10 times the price Indian farmers are getting for a pound of their product in Chiapas, Oaxaca, and other coffee-rich states of southern Mexico…. There is no starker contrast in the economics of coffee these days than between the cushy comforts and gourmet blends of the Starbucks "Experiencia" and the grim, daily existence of 360,000 mostly Indian coffee farmers who work small plots carved from the jungle mountains of southern Mexico.[30]

Multinational corporations and their supporters respond that the effects of—and solutions for—globalization are more complicated than the critics contend. They note that multinationals create jobs, pay better prices and wages than domestic firms, and conform to *local* labor and environmental regulations.

> The skeptics are right to be disturbed by sweatshops, child labour, bonded labour and the other gross abuses that go on in many poor countries (and in the darkest corners of rich ones, too). But what makes people vulnerable to these practices is poverty. . . . The more thoroughly these companies [multinationals] penetrate the markets of the third world, the faster they introduce their capital and working practices, the sooner poverty will retreat and the harder it will be for such abuses to persist.[31]

Moreover, multinationals argue, they have responded to the criticism of profit-driven behavior by developing corporate codes of conduct, corporate social responsibility programs, and partnerships with nongovernmental organizations.[32] They point out, however, that

---

[28]Interview with Alesha Daughtrey, Global Trade Watch field organizer, August 17, 2000; archived in the WTO History Project, University of Washington Center for Labor Studies, **http://depts.washington.edu/ wtohist/Interviews/Interviews.htm**.

[29]From the website of Mobilization for Global Justice, **http://sept .globalizethis.org** (site visited 3/14/03).

[30]John Ross, "The Unloving Cup," December 12, 2002, Organic Consumers Association website, **www.organicconsumers.org/starbucks**.
[31]"Grinding the Poor," *The Economist*, November 6, 1997.
[32]For example, Starbucks's *Commitment to Origins*™ is a four-part Corporate Social Responsibility Program that includes offering Fair Trade certified coffee, organic certified coffee, Farm Direct (single-origin coffees purchased directly from the farmer), and Conservation coffees (emphasizing shade-grown in partnership with the NGO Conservation International). See **www.starbucks.com/aboutus/ cto_coffees.asp**.

they are in a no-win situation vis-à-vis their critics, because they can always be criticized for not doing enough.

Starbucks has found that global concerns often get mixed up with and intertwined with local issues. Even the mere act of opening a Starbucks retail store in a neighborhood can result in local activism and community "push-back" against the Starbucks brand. For example, when Starbucks opened a store in Cambridge, Massachusetts, in 1998, picketers carrying signs that read "Don't Let Corporate Greed Destroy Our Neighborhood" greeted it. A lawyer who helps communities keep national chains out, says, "It's part of the growing tension in the world between the mass-market economy and people's desire to retain self-control and some local culture. . . . If you've got a beef with Starbucks, you've got a beef with capitalism."[33]

Starbucks has faced a variety of "community push back" situations around the world. Soon Beng Yeap, one of Starbucks's International brand reputation managers, notes, "This [community push-back] is a live issue and Starbucks manages each push-back incident case-by-case. In some markets [we] have gone in and in some [we] have pulled out." He cites two recent examples, one in London, where Starbucks decided to withdraw its efforts to open a store after local activists actively campaigned against the firm, and the other in Beijing, where the firm opened a store in an historic district, and, following subsequent and significant adverse comment reported in local and international media, decided to stay put.

Primrose Hill and Starbucks's Decision to Withdraw

In 2002, Starbucks made plans to open a store in Primrose Hill, a London suburb. Located in North West London, Primrose Hill is a well-known historical and picturesque area comprised of a public park, a shopping "village" area, and attractive Victorian residential housing. Residents of Primrose Hill— many of whom are writers, photographers, actors, and musicians—take great pride in the area and are

protective of their local environment, acting to ensure that no chain stores operate in the area.[34]

In early 2002, Starbucks selected Primrose Hill as a potential site for a store, and in April 2002 submitted an application to the local council. When this information was published in the local papers, it received considerable negative feedback from the residents, in particular from the Primrose Hill Conservation Area Advisory Committee. This committee claimed that litter, noise, and disruption from deliveries to a Starbucks store in Primrose Hill would ruin the village ambience and contribute to the "homogenization of the high street." The opposition surprised Starbucks because Primrose Hill residents, associations (including the Primrose Hill Conservation Area Advisory Committee), and businesses had been contacted as part of the consultation period for the potential site. Although the objections to Starbucks's entry focused on local planning issues, there was an antiglobalization element as well. One critic was quoted as saying that Starbucks was "renowned for not paying proper money to coffee growers."[35]

In response to the critics, Starbucks offered to arrange meetings between the planning committee, local councilors, and its representatives to discuss the issue and hear their concerns. Despite Starbucks's efforts, no meeting offers were accepted, and minimal responses were received.

In the meantime, the Primrose Hill Conservation Area Advisory Committee began to campaign strongly against Starbucks. They collected more than one thousand three hundred letters of objection, which they then presented to the local council. Many celebrities, such as the actor Jude Law, National Theater Director Nicholas Hytner, broadcaster Joan Bakewell, singer Neneh Cherry, author Jeanette Winterson, and artist Patrick Caufield, lent their support by opposing the Starbucks application. Media coverage that was initially local became national when celebrities became involved. According to Horwat:

---

[33]Edward McMahon, quoted in "Brewing a Tempest in a Coffee Cup," *Christian Science Monitor*, February 25, 1998.

[34]This desire for protection dates back to 1841 when the residents actively campaigned against the area being opened up to the general public. Such actions discouraged further building developments, thus enabling the residents to retain the look and feel of their neighborhood.

[35]From "Stars v Starbucks: Not a Bean for the Coffee Shop Giant," *Independent on Sunday* (London), June 2, 2002.

Primrose Hill was an "A" site. A very affluent neighborhood, little or no competition and we knew it would be a winner. Everyone [at Starbucks International] loved it. The real estate people, the finance people and others signed off on the deal. Opposition came only when city council was about to approve [our application]. The opposition claimed that our entry would raise rents in the community. So we went back to city council to argue our case. But activists brought in movie stars and got local and national media attention.

In early June 2002, when it was apparent that Starbucks was not welcome in Primrose Hill, the company decided against opening the store. Reflecting on their decision to withdraw, Horwat explained

We care about the views of the communities of which we are a part. We try to have our stores be part of a community. We had hoped to make a positive contribution for people to get together in Primrose Hill. If the community does not welcome us, it's not someplace we want to be.

Adds Soon Beng Yeap:

You have to understand the bigger picture in the UK to appreciate what was going on locally at that time—Starbucks was seen as an American chain coming into the British market and the British media tend to be very cynical. The specialty coffee market was becoming crowded and extremely competitive with several other chains such as Café Nero, Coffee Republic and Costa Coffee making a strong push for market share. The Starbucks team reviewed all the factors involved as well as listened carefully to the community concerns. At the end of the day, we decided to withdraw our application.

Beijing and Starbucks's Decision to Stay

Starbucks opened its first outlet in Beijing in January 1999 and has over one hundred stores in the country today. However, Starbucks touched a nationalist nerve in 2000 when it opened a small coffee shop in Beijing's Forbidden City.[36] In highlighting this particular store, the *New York Times* noted

If ever there was an emblem of the extremes to which globalization has reached, this is it: mass-market American coffee culture in China's most hallowed historic place. Even a McDonald's in the Kremlin would not come as close. Starbucks opened its Forbidden City shop a month ago [September 2000] with a signature menu board advertising the usual Americano and decaf latte coffee and a glass display case filled with fresh glazed donuts, cinnamon rings and banana walnut muffins.

Starbucks, for its part, had taken extraordinary care to ensure that its presence was unobtrusive. To avoid ruining the atmosphere of the Forbidden City, the signs and brand images were placed inside for this store. This small store (barely a closet according to some reports) had only two small tables and few chairs. It was located on the edge of the Forbidden City, among fifty other retailers, including some selling souvenirs and trinkets. Despite such a low-key presence, this store ignited controversy. Dozens of Chinese newspapers reported on reactions to the shop. According to one such report in the *People's Daily*:

The reason for the uproar is due to the café's location: the Forbidden City, the world's largest imperial palace.... First constructed in 1406, the Forbidden City is China's best-preserved ancient architecture encircled by a rampart of three kilometers. The cafe, named Starbucks, is situated in the southeastern corner of the Hall of Preserving Harmony (Baohedian), one of the three most impressive buildings on the palace ground. The hall used to be the venue to hold feasts by emperors and nobles of ethnic groups on New Year's Eve of China's lunar calendar.... Debates over the mini-cafe took place first on the web. A survey by Sina.com showed that over 70 percent of nearly 60,000 people surveyed were opposed to the cafe's entry into the Forbidden City, the main reason being the damaging effects to Chinese cultural heritage and its atmosphere.[37]

The administrators of the Forbidden Palace and other government officials took note of the controversy but were supportive of Starbucks. Chen, a spokesperson for the Forbidden City Museum, maintained that

[36] *The Economist*, "Coffee With Your Tea?" October 4, 2001.

[37] "Starbucks Cafe in Forbidden City Under Fire," *People's Daily*, November 24, 2000.

allowing Starbucks into the Forbidden City was part of their efforts to improve services in the area. Moreover, Chen added, "The reaction has been very intense. Some people say this is a gem of Chinese culture and that foreign brands should not be allowed in.... We can't give up eating for the fear of choking."[38]

According to Horwat:

> The Forbidden City location was a "C" site at best. But definitely not a "D" site, because there was still the benefit of brand presence. But the government said, "We think you should come in," and it was difficult to say no. There was no local community, only tourists.

Following the flurry of articles in the Chinese media, CNN began to run news clips of this story in the United States. Watching this unfold in the U.S. media, some senior managers at Starbucks became alarmed at the negative publicity. According to Soon Beng Yeap:

> The immediate reaction was to "close the store!" due to the relentless negative coverage generated by the international media. After serious discussion among the senior executives, we felt as guests in a foreign country, we should be respectful of our hosts—the Forbidden City officials—who invited us to be there in the first place. We decided to not pull out because it was the international media that stirred up the whole controversy. Unlike the Primrose Hill case, there was no real local community "push-back." It was all media-driven. A few reporters got hold of the story and ran with it, all citing the same survey by Sina.com. We were very disappointed by the negative media coverage, which created a false sense of "cultural imperialism" about our intentions in opening the store, especially when we worked very hard to be culturally sensitive and listen to the local community.

The controversy has since died down, as a recent report (February 2003) in *The Straits Times* (Singapore) indicates: "[Today] if anything, the tourists were more upset than the Beijing residents about the presence of Starbucks in the Forbidden City, complaining that it was out of place in a historical site.... Asked what were the hottest issues of the day for or-dinary citizens, taxi driver Liu Zhiming said: 'Cars, apartments and making money. What else?'"[39]

Entering Rio de Janeiro, Brazil

Peter Maslen, president of Starbucks International, hurriedly convened a meeting of his key executives in Starbucks International, including Julio Gutierrez, his president for Latin America. Starbucks's entry into Brazil was in jeopardy, because certain activists opposing Starbucks's presence in the country were gaining momentum.

Brazil is the largest coffee-producing country in the world, and this was Starbucks's second foray into Latin America (after Mexico). The company chose not to seek a joint venture partner to enter Brazil. Since many copycat chains had sprung up in Rio de Janeiro, some imitating Starbucks to the last detail, Peter felt that his team had to move quickly before any particular group established itself as the premier chain. After several years of work by Julio's Latin America team, no suitable joint venture partner had been identified, and Peter was considering establishing a 100 percent Starbucks-owned MBU (as it had already done in the United Kingdom, Australia, and Thailand).

The business development group, with Julio's team, had picked a site in the Ipanema area of Rio de Janeiro. They proposed that a flagship store be opened on this neighborhood's main commercial street—Rua Visconde de Pirajá (see Figure 1). Many of Rio's most traditional boutiques started in Ipanema, later to be exported to the malls and other parts of town. Many world-renowned brands such as Cartier, Louis Vuitton, and Polo Ralph Lauren had stores on the Rua Visconde de Pirajá. It is often said that news in Ipanema makes headlines all over Brazil.

Starbucks had also chosen other sites, four to be specific, where the company could open stores immediately following the opening of the flagship Ipanema store. One of these stores was to be located in the posh neighborhood of Barra de Tijuca; another was slated for Leblon, and two others for shopping malls located in affluent residential neighborhoods in the city. The real estate group was ready to sign the lease with the agents of the Ipanema property owner,

[38]Quoted in "Globalization Puts a Starbucks into the Forbidden City in Beijing," *New York Times*, November 25, 2000.

[39]"Capitalism Runs Amok," *The Straits Times*, February 16, 2003.

FIGURE 1

Map of the Ipanema Area, Rio de Janeiro, Brazil

Source: **www.ipanema.com**

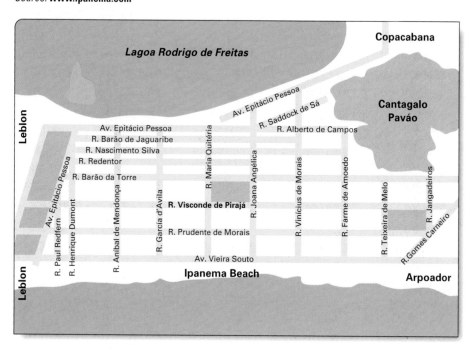

but was awaiting a formal response from the city council members.

The business development group, let by Troy Alstead, senior vice president of finance and business development at Starbucks International, was confident that the Ipanema location was an "A" category site. "The demographics of this area are just right for a flagship store. They are affluent, young and love American brands." The business development group's financial projections indicated that the Ipanema Starbucks store would be profitable in a short time, and Alstead believed that this was a conservative figure. Further, he pointed out:

> Based on the company's experiences of opening flagship stores in similar, high traffic posh neighborhoods in other cites around the world—our store in Ginza, Japan comes to mind—we believe the Ipanema store would be viable for Starbucks. We estimate meeting store level ROI targets in aggregate for the first five stores within two years.

Exhibit 7 provides the finance group's forecast for the Ipanema and the other four stores in Brazil for the first five years of operations.

But Peter had some concerns. He was troubled by reports of rising levels of violence and street crime in Rio and São Paulo. In response to this growing violence, some of the most fashionable retailers were relocating themselves in shopping malls. He also questioned whether the timing for Starbucks was off. Current world events had generated anti-American feeling in many countries.

Following the standard practice, Starbucks had been working with the local chamber of commerce since January 2003, and with the local city council for the required permits. The members of the city council and local chamber of commerce were positive about granting Starbucks permission to begin construction. While the formal voting had yet to be undertaken, it looked certain that, barring anything unusual, permission would be granted.

But nongovernmental organizations like the Organic Consumers Association and Global Exchange were mobilizing faster than expected to oppose Starbucks's entry into Brazil. They found out about Starbucks's intent to enter Brazil when the Ipanema district chamber of commerce newsletter proudly

EXHIBIT 7

Financial Analysis for the First 5 Brazilian Stores

Projected P&L for Ipanema Store (US $)					
	Year 1	Year 2	Year 3	Year 4	Year 5
Net Sales (1)	$1,000,000	$1,100,000	$1,210,000	1,270,500	1,334,025
Cost of Goods Sold (2)	$350,000	$330,000	$326,700	$343,035	$360,187
Gross Profit	$650,000	$770,000	$883,300	$927,465	$973,838
Staff Costs	$200,000	$225,000	$250,000	250,000	250,000
Marketing (3)	$75,000	$50,000	$50,000	50,000	50,000
Other Costs	$75,000	$100,000	$125,000	125,000	125,000
Occupancy Costs	$175,000	$175,000	$175,000	175,000	175,000
Total Costs	$525,000	$550,000	$600,000	$600,000	$600,000
Operating Cash Flow	$125,000	$220,000	$283,300	$327,465	$373,838
Depreciation (4)	$54,200	$54,200	$54,200	$54,200	$54,200
Store Pretax Profit	$70,800	$165,800	$229,100	$273,265	$319,638
Construction Costs (5)	$400,000				
Key Money (6)	$1,000,000				

Projected P&L for a "Typical" Store in Locations Outside the Ipanema Area (US $)*					
	Year 1	Year 2	Year 3	Year 4	Year 5
Net Sales (1)	$625,000	$650,000	$700,000	$735,000	$771,750
Cost of Goods Sold (2)	$218,750	$195,000	$189,000	$198,450	$208,373
Gross Profit	$406,250	$455,000	$511,000	$536,550	$563,378
Staff Costs	$100,000	$115,000	$135,000	$135,000	$135,000
Marketing (3)	$45,000	$30,000	$30,000	$30,000	$30,000
Other Costs	$60,000	$75,000	$75,000	$75,000	$75,000
Occupancy Costs	$70,000	$70,000	$70,000	$70,000	$70,000
Operating Cash Flow	$131,250	$165,000	$201,000	$226,550	$253,378
Depreciation (4)	$25,000	$25,000	$25,000	$25,000	$25,000
Store Pretax Profit	$106,250	$140,000	$176,000	$201,550	$228,378
Construction Costs (5)	$215,000				
Key Money (6)	$400,000				

*Starbucks intends to open four such stores in Rio, in addition to the one in Ipanema.

Notes:
(1) Net sales are projected to grow at 10 percent for years 1 and 2, and at 5 percent thereafter.
(2) Due to increases in efficiency, the cost of goods sold are estimated at 35 percent for year 1, 30 percent for year 2, and 27 percent thereafter.
(3) Marketing costs are higher for year 1.
(4) Straight-line ten-year depreciation for construction and equipment costs.
(5) These represent initial design and construction costs.
(6) Monies paid to the landlord to secure the site.

announced "We are extremely pleased to welcome Starbucks into the fashionable district of Ipanema. By opening a store in our neighborhood, they will join other global brands and help enhance further our district's image as *the* place to be in Rio."

The NGOs were recruiting local activists and had informed Starbucks that they would oppose its entry into Brazil by petitioning the local council to reject its application. They also threatened to start picketing in front of the store once construction was initiated. The "brand" group at Starbucks was concerned about the turn of events. Soon Beng elaborated:

> People in Latin America know the brand because of their proximity to the US. Potential partners are always contacting us about coming in. Before we go into a place like Brazil, what is the due diligence we have to do? It's an origin country for us [i.e., coffee producing country]. It's a very vocal place, and there is a love-hate relationship with the United States. Finance people always want to say yes to a store when the numbers look good. Today some in Starbucks, at least in our group, say that maintaining and protecting our strong "brand" reputation is equally important. Others counter: if our brand is strong then why worry about it? This is a discussion we have here every day in the company. While the "push-back" is not totally unexpected, it is hard to gauge to the severity of the situation and its likely impact on our brand.

Peter asked Troy's business development group to work with Julio's Latin American team to estimate how the picketing in front of the store might impact the financial projections his group had prepared. Their answer:

> Our financial estimates for the Ipanema store are based on comparables from other flagship stores in locations similar to Rio in other parts of the world. Our financial models are sensitive to the demographics of the area. We project that demand could fall from 5 to 25%, because of people picketing in front of the store. We acknowledge it is much harder to guess what the impact on our entire system in Brazil might be as we open new stores. It all depends upon the type of media coverage the activists are able to muster and the issues the media choose to highlight.

Volunteered Soon Beng:

> The tide of public opinion is unpredictable. We review each "push–back" incident the best we can, and we have a reasonable track record of predicting outcomes. But, every time we walk into a potential site somewhere in the world, we potentially face this ['push-back']. It would be great to have a foolproof tool or system to help us evaluate these sorts of issues and make the appropriate decisions.

Peter had to leave Seattle to attend an important meeting in Europe the following day. He called together his key managers and said

> Look, we've experienced a variety of "push-backs" and protests before. What lessons have we learned? We've been deciding whether to go into sites or pull out on a case-by-case basis. If we're going to grow to 25,000 stores, we cannot keep taking an ad-hoc approach. We need a systematic method to respond to push-back—to decide whether we stay with a site or pull out. I want you to come up with a way to help me decide whether to go into Rio at all. And it's got to be a system or decision process that would work equally well in London or Beijing or anyplace else that we want to open. Let's meet again when I get back to town in a couple days.

The managers of Starbucks International had their work cut out for them. But they looked forward to tackling the issues raised by Peter.

APPENDIX A

Starbucks Timeline and History

1971

Starbucks opens its first location in Seattle's Pike Place Market.

1982

Howard Schultz joins Starbucks as director of retail operations and marketing. Starbucks begins providing coffee to fine restaurants and espresso bars.

1983

Schultz travels to Italy, where he's impressed with the popularity of espresso bars in Milan. He sees the potential in Seattle to develop a similar coffee bar culture.

1984

Schultz convinces the founders of Starbucks to test the coffee bar concept in a new location in downtown Seattle. This successful experiment is the genesis for a company that Schultz founds in 1985.

1985

Schultz founds Il Giornale, offering brewed coffee and espresso beverages made from Starbucks coffee beans.

1987

With the backing of local investors, Il Giornale acquires Starbucks assets and changes its name to Starbucks Corporation.

Opens in Chicago and Vancouver, B.C.

Starbucks location total = 17

1988

Starbucks introduces mail order catalog with service to all fifty states.

Starbucks location total = 33

1989

Opens in Portland, Oregon.

Starbucks location total = 55

1990

Starbucks expands headquarters in Seattle and builds a new roasting point.

Starbucks location total = 84

1991

Establishes a relationship with CARE, the international relief and development organization, and introduces the CARE coffee sampler.

Becomes the first U.S. privately owned company to offer a stock option program that includes part-time employees.

Opens first licensed airport location with HMS Host at Sea-Tac International Airport.

Opens in Los Angeles.

Starbucks location total = 116

1992

Completes initial public offering with Common Stock being traded on the Nasdaq National Market under the trading symbol "SBUX."

Opens in San Francisco; San Diego; Orange County, California; and Denver.

Starbucks location total = 165

1993

Begins Barnes & Noble, Inc. relationship.

Opens in Washington, D.C.

Starbucks location total = 272

1994

Awarded ITT/Sheraton (now Starwood Hotel) account.

Opens in Minneapolis; Boston; New York; Atlanta; Dallas; and Houston.

Starbucks location total = 425

1995

Based on an extremely popular in-house music program, Starbucks begins selling compact discs.

Awarded United Airlines account.

Begins serving Frappuccino® blended beverages, a line of low-fat, creamy, iced coffee beverages.

Forms alliance with Canadian bookstore Chapters Inc.

Starbucks Coffee International forms joint venture with SAZABY Inc., to develop Starbucks coffeehouses in Japan.

Opens in Philadelphia; Pittsburgh; Las Vegas; Cincinnati; Baltimore; San Antonio; and Austin, Texas.

Starbucks location total = 676

1996

Starbucks Coffee International opens locations in Japan, Hawaii, and Singapore.

Awarded Westin (now Starwood Hotel) account.

Starbucks and Dreyer's Grand Ice Cream, Inc. introduce Starbucks® Ice Cream and Starbucks Ice Cream bars. Starbucks Ice Cream quickly becomes the number one brand of coffee ice cream in the United States.

North American Coffee Partnership (Starbucks and Pepsi-Cola Company business venture) begins selling a bottled version of Starbucks Frappuccino® blended beverage.

Opens in Rhode Island; Idaho; North Carolina; Arizona; Utah; and Ontario, Canada.

Starbucks location total = 1,015

1997

Starbucks Coffee International opens locations in the Philippines.

Awarded Canadian Airlines account.

Forms alliance with eight companies to enable the gift of more than 320,000 new books for children through the All Books for Children first annual book drive.

Establishes the Starbucks Foundation, benefiting local literacy programs in communities where Starbucks has coffeehouses.

Opens in Florida, Michigan, and Wisconsin.

Starbucks location total = 1,412

1998

Starbucks Coffee International opens locations in Taiwan, Thailand, New Zealand, and Malaysia.

Introduces Tiazzi® blended juice tea, a refreshing mixture of tea, fruit juice, and ice.

Acquires Seattle Coffee Company in the United Kingdom with more than sixty retail locations.

Acquires Pasqua Inc., a San Francisco–based coffee retailer.

Forms Urban Coffee Opportunities, a joint venture with Earvin "Magic" Johnson's Johnson Development Corp., to develop Starbucks Coffee locations in underserved, urban neighborhoods throughout the United States.

Signs a licensing agreement with Kraft Foods Inc. to extend the Starbucks brand into grocery channels across the United States.

Launches Starbucks.com.

Opens two new coffeehouse concepts, Cafe Starbucks in Seattle and Circadia® Coffee House in San Francisco.

Opens in New Orleans; St. Louis; Kansas City, Missouri; and Portland, Maine.

Starbucks location total = 1,886

1999

Starbucks Coffee International opens locations in China, Kuwait, Korea, and Lebanon.

Acquires Tazo®, a Portland, Oregon, based tea company.

Partners with Conservation International to promote environmentally sound methods of growing coffee.

Introduces Shade Grown Mexico Coffee.

Acquires Hear Music, a San Francisco–based music company.

Enters agreement with Albertson's, Inc. to open more than one hundred Starbucks locations in their supermarkets in the year 2000.

Opens in Memphis and Nashville, Tennessee; and Saskatchewan, Canada.

Starbucks location total = 2,135

2000

Enters into licensing agreement with TransFair USA to market and sell Fair Trade Certified^{SM} coffee.

Introduces a Commitment to Origin™ coffee category that includes shade grown, organic, and Fair Trade Certified selections.

Expands contribution to Conservation International to establish conservation efforts in five new sites.

Enters agreement with Host Marriott International to open locations in select properties. Starbucks Coffee International opens in Dubai, Hong Kong, Shanghai, Qatar, Bahrain, Saudi Arabia, and Australia.

Starbucks location total = 3,501

2001

Introduces coffee sourcing guidelines developed in partnership with the Center for Environmental Leadership in Business, a division of Conservation International.

Commits to the purchase of 1 million pounds of Fair Trade Certified^{SM} coffee.

Offers $1 million in financial support to coffee farmers through Calvert Community Investments.

Begins to offer high-speed wireless Internet access in stores.

The Starbucks Foundation awards more than 450 grants totaling $4.2 million to literacy, schools, and community-based organizations across North America.

Begins offering the Starbucks Card, a stored value card for customers to use and reload.

Enters agreement with Hyatt Hotels Corp.

Starbucks Coffee Japan introduces a stock option program for eligible full- and part-time partners and successfully implements IPO.

Starbucks and international business partners seed Starbucks Cares Fund with $1.2 million contribution to benefit September 11th Fund. Customers and partners contribute more than $1.4 million to Starbucks Cares.

Starbucks opens 300th location in Japan and celebrates fifth year of business in Japan.

Starbucks Coffee International opens in Switzerland, Israel, and Austria.

Starbucks location total = 4,709

2002

Signs memorandum of understanding with Fair Trade Labelling Organizations International (FLO) that enables the company to enter into licensing agreements with national Fair Trade organizations to sell Fair Trade certified coffee in the countries where Starbucks does business.

Publishes its first Corporate Social Responsibility Annual Report.

Celebrates ten-year anniversary of Starbucks IPO.

Introduces Starbucks DoubleShot™ to the ready-to-drink coffee category.

Signs licensing agreement with TransFair Canada to bring Fair Trade Certified™ coffee to more than 270 retail locations in Canada.

Starbucks Coffee International opens in Oman, Indonesia, Germany, and Spain.

Current location total = 5,688

Kentucky Fried Chicken and the Global Fast-Food Industry

This case was prepared by Jeffrey A. Krug, Appalachian State University.

Kentucky Fried Chicken Corporation (KFC) was the world's largest chicken restaurant chain and third largest fast-food chain in 2004. It held more than 51 percent of the U.S. market in terms of sales and operated more than 12,200 restaurants in 99 countries. KFC was one of the first fast-food chains to go international in the late 1950s and is one of the world's most recognizable brands. KFC's early international strategy was to grow its company and franchise restaurant base throughout the world. By early 2004, however, KFC had refocused its international strategy on several high growth markets that included China, Canada, the United Kingdom, Australia, South Africa, Malaysia, Thailand, Mexico, Korea, and Indonesia. KFC planned to base much of its growth in these markets on company-owned restaurants, which gave KFC greater control over product quality, service, and restaurant cleanliness. In other international markets, KFC planned to grow primarily through franchises, which were operated by local business people who understood the local market better than KFC. Franchises enabled KFC to more rapidly expand into smaller countries that could only support a small number of restaurants. KFC planned to more aggressively expand its company-owned restaurants into other major international markets in Europe and Latin America in the future. Latin America was an appealing area for investment because of the size of its markets and geographic proximity to the United States. Mexico was of particular interest because of the North American Free Trade Agreement (NAFTA), a free trade zone between Canada, the United States, and Mexico that went into effect in 1994. McDonald's, Burger King, and Wendy's, however, were rapidly expanding into other countries in Latin America such as Argentina, Chile, Brazil, and Venezuela. KFC's task in Latin America was to develop an effective strategy for further penetrating the Latin American market.

Company History

Fast-food franchising was still in its infancy in 1952 when Harland Sanders began his travels across the United States to speak with prospective franchisees about his "Colonel Sanders Recipe Kentucky Fried Chicken." By 1960, "Colonel" Sanders had granted KFC franchises to more than two hundred take-home retail outlets and restaurants across the United States. He had also established a number of franchises in Canada. By 1963, the number of KFC franchises had risen to more than three hundred and revenues

Copyright © 2003 by Jeffrey A. Krug. This case was prepared by Jeffrey A. Krug, as the basis for class discussion rather than to illustrate either effective or ineffective handling of an administrative situation. Reprinted by permission of Jeffrey A. Krug. All rights reserved. For the most recent financial results of the company discussed in this case, go to **http://finance.yahoo.com,** input the company's stock symbol, and download the latest company report from its homepage.

topped $500 million. The Colonel celebrated his seventy-fourth birthday the following year and was eager to lessen the load of running the day-to-day operations of his business. He sold his business to two Louisville businessmen—Jack Massey and John Young Brown Jr.—for $2 million. The Colonel stayed on as a public relations man and goodwill ambassador for the company. During the next five years, Massey and Brown concentrated on growing KFC's franchise system across the United States. In 1966, they took KFC public, and the company was listed on the New York Stock Exchange. By the late 1960s, a strong foothold had been established in the United States. Massey and Brown then turned their attention to international markets. In 1969, a joint venture was signed with Mitsuoishi Shoji Kaisha, Ltd. in Japan, and the rights to operate franchises in England were acquired. Subsidiaries were later established in Hong Kong, South Africa, Australia, New Zealand, and Mexico. By 1971, KFC had established 2,450 franchises and 600 company-owned restaurants in 48 countries.

Heublein, Inc

In 1971, KFC entered into negotiations with Heublein, Inc. to discuss a possible merger. The decision to pursue a merger was partially driven by Brown's desire to pursue other interests that included a political career (Brown was elected governor of Kentucky in 1977). Several months later, Heublein acquired KFC. Heublein was in the business of producing vodka, mixed cocktails, dry gin, cordials, beer, and other alcoholic beverages. It had little experience, however, in the restaurant business. Conflicts quickly erupted between Colonel Sanders and Heublein management. In particular, Colonel Sanders was distraught over poor quality control and restaurant cleanliness. By 1977, new restaurant openings had slowed to only twenty a year. Few restaurants were being remodeled, and service quality had declined. To combat these problems, Heublein sent in a new management team to redirect KFC's strategy. A "back-to-the-basics" strategy was implemented, and new restaurant construction was halted until existing restaurants could be upgraded and operating problems eliminated. A program for remodeling existing restaurants was implemented, an emphasis was placed on cleanliness and service, marginal products were eliminated, and product consistency was reestablished. This strategy enabled KFC to gain better control of its operations, and it was soon again aggressively building new restaurants.

R.J. Reynolds Industries, Inc.

In 1982, R.J. Reynolds Industries, Inc. (RJR) acquired Heublein and merged it into a wholly owned subsidiary. The acquisition of Heublein was part of RJR's corporate strategy of diversifying into unrelated businesses such as energy, transportation, food, and restaurants to reduce its dependence on the tobacco industry. Tobacco had driven RJR's sales since its founding in North Carolina in 1875. Sales of cigarettes and tobacco products, however, while profitable, were declining as consumption continued to fall in the United States. Reduced consumption was largely the result of increased awareness among Americans of the negative health consequences of smoking.

RJR, however, had a little more experience in the restaurant business than did Heublein when it acquired KFC eleven years earlier. In contrast to Heublein, which tried to actively manage KFC using its own managers, RJR allowed KFC to operate autonomously. RJR believed that KFC's executives were better qualified to operate the business than its own managers; therefore, KFC's top management team was left largely intact. In doing so, RJR avoided many of the operating problems that plagued Heublein during its ownership of KFC. In 1985, RJR acquired Nabisco Corporation for $4.9 billion. The acquisition of Nabisco was an attempt to redefine RJR as a world leader in the consumer foods industry. Nabisco sold a variety of well-known food products such as Oreo cookies, Ritz crackers, Planters peanuts, Lifesavers, and Milk-Bone dog biscuits. RJR subsequently divested many of its nonconsumer food businesses. It sold KFC to PepsiCo, Inc. one year later.

PepsiCo, Inc.

PepsiCo, Inc. was formed in 1965 with the merger of the Pepsi-Cola Co. and Frito-Lay Inc. The merger created one of the largest consumer products companies in the United States. Pepsi-Cola's traditional business was the sale of soft drink concentrates to licensed independent and company-owned bottlers that manufactured, sold, and distributed Pepsi-Cola soft drinks. Pepsi-Cola's best known trademarks were Pepsi-Cola, Diet Pepsi, and Mountain Dew. Frito-Lay manufactured and sold a variety of leading snack foods such as Lay's Potato Chips, Doritos Tortilla Chips, Tostitos Tortilla Chips, and Ruffles Potato Chips.

PepsiCo believed the restaurant business complemented its consumer product orientation. The marketing of fast-food followed many of the same patterns as soft drinks and snack foods. Pepsi-Cola and Lay's Potato Chips, for example, could be marketed in the same television and radio segments, which provided higher returns for each advertising dollar. Restaurant chains also provided an additional outlet for the sale of Pepsi soft drinks. PepsiCo believed it could take advantage of numerous synergies by operating the three businesses under the same corporate umbrella. PepsiCo also believed that its management skills could be transferred among the three businesses. This practice was compatible with PepsiCo's policy of frequently moving managers among its business units as a means of developing future executives. PepsiCo's acquisition of KFC in 1986 followed earlier acquisitions of Pizza Hut and Taco Bell. The three restaurant chains were the market leaders in the chicken, pizza, and Mexican categories.

Following the acquisition of KFC, PepsiCo initiated sweeping changes. It announced that the franchise contract would be changed to give PepsiCo greater control over KFC franchisees and to make it easier to close poorly performing restaurants. Staff at KFC was reduced to cut costs, and many KFC managers were replaced with PepsiCo managers. Soon after the acquisition, KFC's new personnel manager, who had just relocated from PepsiCo's New York headquarters, was overheard in the KFC cafeteria saying, "There will be no more home grown tomatoes in this organization." Rumors spread quickly among KFC employees about their opportunities for advancement within KFC and PepsiCo. Harsh comments by PepsiCo managers about KFC, its people, and its traditions; several restructurings that led to layoffs throughout KFC; the replacement of KFC managers with PepsiCo managers; and conflicts between KFC and PepsiCo's corporate cultures created a morale problem within KFC. KFC's culture was built largely on Colonel Sanders' laid-back approach to management. Employees enjoyed good job security and stability. A strong loyalty had been created over the years as a result of the Colonel's efforts to provide for his employees' benefits, pension, and other nonincome needs. In addition, the Southern environment in Louisville resulted in a friendly, relaxed atmosphere at KFC's corporate offices.

PepsiCo's culture, in contrast, was characterized by a strong emphasis on performance. Top performers expected to move up through the ranks quickly. PepsiCo used its KFC, Pizza Hut, Taco Bell, Frito Lay, and Pepsi-Cola divisions as training grounds for its executives, rotating its best managers through the five divisions on average every two years. This practice created pressure on managers to demonstrate their management skills within short periods to maximize their potential for promotion. This practice reinforced feelings among KFC managers that they had few opportunities for advancement within the new company. One PepsiCo manager commented, "You may have performed well last year, but if you don't perform well this year, you're gone, and there are 100 ambitious guys with Ivy League MBAs at PepsiCo's headquarters in New York who would love to have your job." An unwanted effect of this performance driven culture was that employee loyalty was lost, and turnover was higher than in other companies.

Kyle Craig, president of KFC's U.S. operations, commented on PepsiCo's relationship with KFC:

The KFC culture is an interesting one because it was dominated by a lot of KFC folks, many who have been around since the days of the Colonel. Many of those people were very intimidated by the PepsiCo culture, which is a very high performance, high accountability, highly driven culture. People were concerned about whether they would succeed in the new culture. Like many companies, we have had a couple of downsizings which further made people nervous. Today, there are fewer old KFC people around and I think to some degree people have seen that the PepsiCo culture can drive some pretty positive results. I also think the PepsiCo people who have worked with KFC have modified their cultural values somewhat and they can see that there were a lot of benefits in the old KFC culture.

PepsiCo pushes their companies to perform strongly, but whenever there is a slip in performance, it increases the culture gap between PepsiCo and KFC. I have been involved in two downsizings over which I have been the chief architect. They have been probably the two most gut-wrenching experiences of my career. Because you know you're dealing with peoples' lives and their families, these changes can be emotional if you care about the people in your organization. However, I do fundamentally believe that your first obligation is to the entire organization.

A second problem for PepsiCo was its poor relationship with KFC franchisees. A month after becoming president and chief executive officer in 1989, John Cranor addressed KFC's franchisees in Louisville to explain the details of the new franchise contract. This was the first contract change in thirteen years. It gave PepsiCo greater power to take over weak franchises, relocate restaurants, and make changes in existing restaurants. In addition, restaurants would no longer be protected from competition from new KFC units, and PepsiCo would have the right to raise royalty fees on existing restaurants as contracts came up for renewal. After Cranor finished his address, there was an uproar among the attending franchisees, who jumped to their feet to protest the changes. KFC's franchise association later sued PepsiCo over the new contract. The contract remained unresolved until 1996, when the most objectionable parts of the contract were removed by KFC's new president and CEO, David Novak. A new contract was ratified by KFC's franchisees in 1997.

PepsiCo's divestiture of KFC, Pizza Hut, and Taco Bell PepsiCo's strategy of diversifying into three distinct but related markets—soft drinks, snack foods, and fast-food restaurants—created one of the world's largest food companies and a portfolio of some of the world's most recognizable brands. Between 1990 and 1996, PepsiCo's sales grew at an annual rate of more than 10 percent, surpassing $31 billion in 1996. PepsiCo's growth, however, masked troubles in its fast-food businesses. Operating margins (profit after tax as a percent of sales) at Pepsi-Cola and Frito Lay averaged 12 and 17 percent, respectively. During the same period, margins at KFC, Pizza Hut, and Taco Bell fell from an average of more than 8 percent in 1990 to a little more than 4 percent in 1996. Declining margins in the fast-food chains reflected increasing maturity in the U.S. fast-food industry, intense competition, and the aging of KFC and Pizza Hut's restaurant bases. As a result, PepsiCo's restaurant chains absorbed nearly one-half of PepsiCo's annual capital spending during the 1990s but generated less than one-third of PepsiCo's cash flows. This meant that cash had to be diverted from PepsiCo's soft drink and snack food businesses to its restaurant businesses. This reduced PepsiCo's corporate return on assets, made it more difficult to compete effectively with Coca-Cola, and hurt its stock price. In 1997, PepsiCo decided to spin off its restaurant businesses into a new company called Tricon Global Restaurants, Inc.

The new company was based in KFC's headquarters in Louisville, Kentucky.

PepsiCo's objective was to reposition itself as a beverage and snack food company, strengthen its balance sheet, and create more consistent earning growth. PepsiCo received a one-time distribution from Tricon of $4.7 billion, $3.7 billion of which was used to pay off short-term debt. The balance was earmarked for stock repurchases. In 1998, PepsiCo acquired Tropicana Products, which controlled more than 40 percent of the U.S. chilled orange juice market. Because of the divestiture of KFC, Pizza Hut, and Taco Bell, PepsiCo sales fell by $11.3 billion, and assets fell by $7.0 billion. Profitability, however, soared. Operating margins rose from 11 percent in 1997 to 14 percent in 1999, and ROA rose from 11 percent in 1997 to 16 percent in 1999. By focusing on high cash flow market leaders, PepsiCo raised profitability while decreasing its asset base. In 2001, PepsiCo acquired The Quaker Oats Company, which included Gatorade. Gatorade and Tropicana were moved into a separate division to increase efficiencies. By 2003, PepsiCo sales exceeded $25 billion annually.

Yum! Brands, Inc.

The spin-off created a new, independent, publicly held company called Tricon Global Restaurants, Inc. The new company managed the KFC, Pizza Hut, and Taco Bell franchise systems. David Novak became Tricon's new CEO and moved quickly to create a new culture within the company. One of his primary objectives was to reverse the long-standing friction between management and franchisees that was created under PepsiCo ownership. Novak announced that PepsiCo's top-down management system would be replaced by a new management emphasis on providing support to the firm's franchise base. Franchises would have greater independence, resources, and technical support. Novak symbolically changed the name on the corporate headquarters' building in Louisville to "KFC Support Center" to drive home his new philosophy.

In 2002, Tricon announced the acquisition of Long John Silver's and A&W All-American Food Restaurants. The acquisition increased Tricon's worldwide system to 32,500 restaurants. The acquisition signaled Tricon's decision to aggressively promote a multibranding strategy that combined two brands in one restaurant and attracted a larger consumer base by offering them a broader menu selection in one location. One week after it announced the acquisition, shareholders approved a

EXHIBIT 1

Yum! Brands, Inc. Organizational Chart (2004)

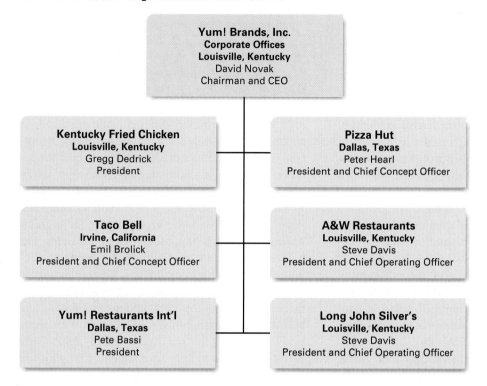

Yum! Brands, Inc.
Corporate Offices
Louisville, Kentucky
David Novak
Chairman and CEO

Kentucky Fried Chicken
Louisville, Kentucky
Gregg Dedrick
President

Pizza Hut
Dallas, Texas
Peter Hearl
President and Chief Concept Officer

Taco Bell
Irvine, California
Emil Brolick
President and Chief Concept Officer

A&W Restaurants
Louisville, Kentucky
Steve Davis
President and Chief Operating Officer

Yum! Restaurants Int'l
Dallas, Texas
Pete Bassi
President

Long John Silver's
Louisville, Kentucky
Steve Davis
President and Chief Operating Officer

corporate name change to Yum! Brands, Inc. The new name reflected the company's expanding portfolio of fast-food brands (see Exhibit 1). In 2003, Novak announced the acquisition of Pasta Bravo, a made-to-order pasta and salad concept based in California. The acquisition followed several months of test marketing of the multibranding of Pasta Bravo and Pizza Hut.

Novak also initiated a plan to reduce the company-owned restaurant base by either closing poorly performing restaurants or selling company restaurants to individual franchisees. In 1997, 38 percent of the restaurant base (KFC, Pizza Hut, and Taco Bell) was company owned. By early 2004, company-owned restaurants had declined to 23 percent of the total. The long-term goal was to reduce the company base to 20 percent. The firm's new emphasis on supporting individual franchisees had an immediate effect on morale. In 1997, the year of the divestiture, the company recorded a loss of $111 million in net income. In 2003, net income was estimated at $585 million on estimated sales of $8.3 billion, a return on sales of about 7.0 percent.

Fast-Food Industry

The National Restaurant Association (NRA) estimated that U.S. food service sales increased by 4.3 percent to $408 billion in 2002. More than 858,000 restaurants made up the U.S. restaurant industry and employed almost 12 million people. Sales were highest in the full-service, sit-down sector, which grew 4.5 percent to $147 billion. Fast-food sales grew at a slower rate, rising about 3.7 percent to $115 billion. The fast-food sector was increasingly viewed as a mature market. As U.S. incomes rose during the late 1990s and early 2000s, more consumers frequented sit-down restaurants that offered better service and a more comfortable dining experience. Together, the full-service and fast-food segments made up about 64 percent of all U.S. food service sales.

Major Fast-Food Segments

Eight major segments made up the fast-food segment of the restaurant industry: sandwich chains, pizza chains, family restaurants, grill buffet chains, dinner houses, chicken chains, non-dinner concepts, and other chains. Sales data for the leading restaurant chains in each segment are shown in Exhibit 2. Most striking is the dominance of McDonald's, which had sales of more than $20 billion in 2002. McDonald's accounted for 13 percent of the sales of the top 100 chains. To put McDonald's dominance in perspective, the second largest chain—Burger King—held less than 6 percent of the market.

Sandwich chains made up the largest segment of the fast-food market. McDonald's controlled 33 percent of the sandwich segment, while Burger King ran a distant second with a 14 percent market share. Sandwich chains, however, were struggling because of continued price discounting that lowered profits. The threat of obesity lawsuits and increased customer demand for more healthy food items and better service lowered demand for the traditional hamburger, fries, and soft drink combinations. Per store sales declined most at Hardee's, Carl's Jr., McDonald's, and Jack in the Box, the segment's best-known hamburger chains. In contrast, per store sales increased sharply at Quiznos, Taco Bell, Schlotsky's, Subway, and Wendy's. These chains made in-roads by offering more healthy food items. Wendy's promoted its leadership in gourmet salads, while Subway heavily advertised its low-fat sandwiches. Taco Bell rolled out a new "fresco" menu that replaced cheese and sour cream on most menu items with fat-free salsa. To meet health trends, McDonald's introduced premium salads, and Burger King introduced a new line of low-fat, grilled chicken sandwiches. In contrast, Hardee's introduced a new "Thickburger" menu that included 1/3-, 1/2-, and 2/3-pound Angus burgers in an attempt to distinguish itself from other hamburger chains.

Dinner houses made up the second largest and fastest growing fast-food segment. Sales in the dinner house segment increased by more than 9 percent in 2002, surpassing the average increase of 4 percent among other segments. Much of the growth in dinner houses came from new unit construction, a marked contrast with the other fast-food segments, which have slowed U.S. construction because of market saturation. Much of the new unit construction took place in new suburban markets and small towns. Applebee's, Red Lobster, Outback Steakhouse, and Chili's Grill & Bar dominated the dinner house segment. Each chain generated sales of more than $2 billion in 2002. The fastest growing dinner houses, however, were chains generating less than $600 million in sales, such as

Texas Road House, P.F. Chang's China Bistro, and The Cheesecake Factory. Each of these chains increased sales by more than 20 percent.

Increased growth among dinner houses came at the expense of sandwich chains, pizza and chicken chains, grilled buffet chains, and family restaurants. "Too many restaurants chasing the same customers" was responsible for much of the slower growth in these other fast-food categories. Sales growth within each segment, however, differed from one chain to another. In the family segment, for example, Denny's (the segment leader) and Shoney's continued to shut down poorly performing restaurants while IHOP, Bob Evans, and Cracker Barrel expanded their bases. In the pizza segment, Pizza Hut, Little Caesars, and Papa John's closed underperforming restaurants while Chuck E. Cheese's added more restaurants. The hardest hit segment was grilled buffet chains. Declining sales caused both Sizzlin' and Western Sizzlin' to drop out of the list of Top 100 chains, leaving only three chains in the Top 100 (Golden Grill, Ryan's, and Ponderosa). Dinner houses, because of their more upscale atmosphere and higher ticket items, were better positioned to take advantage of the aging and wealthier U.S. population. Even dinner houses, however, faced the prospect of market saturation and increased competition in the near future.

Chicken Segment

KFC continued to dominate the chicken segment with sales of $4.8 billion in 2002 and estimated sales of $5.0 billion in 2003 (see Exhibit 3). Its nearest competitor, Chick-fil-A, ran a distant second with sales of $1.4 billion. KFC's leadership in the U.S. market was so extensive that it had fewer opportunities to expand its U.S. restaurant base, which was only growing at about one percent per year. Despite its dominance, KFC was slowly losing market share as other chicken chains increased sales at a faster rate. KFC's share of chicken segment sales fell from 64 percent in 1993 to less than 51 percent in 2003, a ten-year drop of 14 percent (see Exhibit 4). During the same period, Chick-fil-A and Boston Market increased their combined market share by 11 percent. In the 1990s, many industry analysts predicted that Boston Market would challenge KFC for market leadership. Boston Market was a new chain that emphasized roasted rather than fried chicken. It successfully created the image of an upscale deli offering healthy, "home-style" alternatives to fried chicken.

EXHIBIT 2

Top U.S. Fast-Food Restaurants (Ranked by 2002 Sales, $ 000s)

Rank	Sandwich Chains	Sales	Share	Rank	Dinner Houses	Sales	Share
1	McDonald's	20,306	33.3%	9	Applebee's	3,183	15.2%
2	Burger King	8,350	13.7	14	Red Lobster	2,360	11.3
3	Wendy's	6,953	11.4	15	Outback Steakhouse	2,271	10.9
5	Subway	5,230	8.6	16	Chili's Grill & Bar	2,240	10.7
6	Taco Bell	5,200	8.5	21	Olive Garden	1,940	9.3
12	Arby's	2,695	4.4	23	T.G.I. Friday's	1,746	8.3
17	Jack in the Box	2,240	3.7	33	Ruby Tuesday	1,255	6.0
18	Sonic Drive-In	2,205	3.6	55	Bennigan's	681	3.3
19	Dairy Queen	2,190	3.6	62	Romano's Mac. Grill	639	3.1
24	Hardee's	1,700	2.8	63	Hooters	629	3.0
	Other Chains	3,980	6.5		Other Chains	3,985	19.0
	Total Segment	61,049	100.0%		Total Segment	20,928	100.0%

Rank	Pizza Chains	Sales	Share	Rank	Chicken Chains	Sales	Share
7	Pizza Hut	5,100	43.4%	8	KFC	4,800	50.7%
10	Domino's	2,927	24.9	31	Chick-fil-A	1,373	14.5
22	Papa John's	1,749	14.9	34	Popeyes	1,215	12.8
37	Little Caesars	1,150	9.8	51	Church's	720	7.6
80	Chuck E. Cheese's	460	3.9	61	Boston Market	641	6.8
95	Round Table Pizza	374	3.2	97	El Pollo Loco	364	3.8
	Total Segment	11,761	100.0%	99	Bojangles'	347	3.7
					Total Segment	9,460	100.0%

Rank	Family Restaurants	Sales	Share	Rank	Other Dinner Chains	Sales	Share
20	Denny's	2,120	22.2%	49	Long John Silver's	756	23.5%
27	IHOP	1,461	15.3	52	Disney Theme Parks	705	21.9
29	Cracker Barrel	1,406	14.7	54	Panera Bread Co.	688	21.4
43	Bob Evans	876	9.2	67	Old Country Buffet	574	17.8
46	Perkins	798	8.3	74	Captain D's Seafood	497	15.4
48	Waffle House	768	8.0		Total Segment	3,219	100.0%
	Other Chains	2,133	22.3				
	Total Segment	9,561	100.0%	Rank	Non-Dinner Concepts	Sales	Share

Rank	Grill Buffet Chains	Sales	Share	Rank	Non-Dinner Concepts	Sales	Share
				11	Dunkin' Donuts	2,700	34.6%
				13	Starbuck's	2,478	31.7
36	Golden Corral	1,157	46.3%	32	7-Eleven	1,335	17.1
44	Ryan's	812	32.5	47	Krispy Kreme	772	9.9
71	Ponderosa	532	21.3	72	Baskin-Robbins	523	6.7
	Total Segment	2,501	100.0%		Total Segment	7,808	100.0%

Source: Nation's Restaurant News. Sales rankings for contract and hotel chains not included.

To distinguish itself from more traditional fast-food, it refused to construct drive-thrus and established most of its units outside of shopping malls rather than at major city intersections.

On the surface, it appeared that Boston Market and Chick-fil-A's market share gains were achieved by taking customers away from KFC. Another look at the data, however, reveals that KFC's sales have grown at a

EXHIBIT 3

Top Chicken Chains

	1997	1998	1999	2000	2001	2002	Growth Rate
Sales ($ Millions)							
KFC	4,000	4,200	4,300	4,400	4,700	4,800	4%
Chick-fil-A	643	764	943	1,082	1,242	1,373	16%
Popeyes	720	843	986	1,077	1,179	1,215	11%
Church's	574	620	705	699	721	720	5%
Boston Market	1,197	929	855	685	640	641	−12%
El Pollo Loco	235	245	275	305	339	364	9%
Bojangles'	229	250	270	298	333	347	9%
Total	7,598	7,851	8,334	8,546	9,154	9,460	5%
U.S. Restaurants							
KFC	5,092	5,105	5,231	5,364	5,399	5,472	1%
Chick-fil-A	749	812	897	958	1,014	1,074	8%
Popeyes	945	1,066	1,165	1,248	1,327	1,380	8%
Church's	1,070	1,105	1,178	1,217	1,242	1,232	3%
Boston Market	1,166	889	858	712	657	653	−11%
El Pollo Loco	243	261	270	279	293	306	5%
Bojangles'	258	255	265	278	280	292	3%
Total	9,551	9,493	9,864	10,056	10.212	10.409	2%
Sales per Unit ($ 000s)							
KFC	781	823	822	820	871	877	2%
Chick-fil-A	859	941	1,051	1,130	1,225	1,278	8%
Popeyes	762	790	847	863	889	880	3%
Church's	536	561	598	574	581	584	2%
Boston Market	1,027	1,045	997	962	974	982	−1%
El Pollo Loco	967	939	1,019	1,094	1,157	1,190	4%
Bojangles'	888	980	1,020	1,072	1,189	1,188	6%
Total	796	827	845	850	896	909	3%

Source: Nation's Restaurant News.

stable rate during the last ten years. Boston Market, rather than drawing customers away from KFC, appealed to new consumers who did not regularly frequent KFC and wanted non–fried chicken alternatives. Boston Market was able to expand the chicken segment beyond its traditional emphasis on fried chicken by offering non–fried chicken products that appealed to this new consumer group. After aggressively growing its restaurant base through 1997, however, Boston Market fell on hard times as it was unable to handle mounting debt problems. It soon entered bankruptcy proceedings. McDonald's acquired Boston Market in 2000. The acquisition followed earlier acquisitions of Donatos Pizza in 1999 and Chipotle Mexican Grill in 1998. McDonald's hoped the acquisitions would help it expand its U.S. restaurant base as there were few opportunities to expand the McDonald's concept. Chick-fil-A's early strategy was to establish sit-down restaurants in shopping malls. As more malls added food courts, however, malls became less enthusiastic about allocating separate store space to restaurants. As a result, Chick-fil-A began to open smaller units

EXHIBIT 4

Top Chicken Chains—Market Share (%, Based on Annual Sales)

	KFC	Chick-fil-A	Popeyes	Church's	Market	Loco	Bojangles'	Total
1993	64.2	7.5	10.7	8.3	2.9	3.2	3.2	100.0
1994	60.7	7.8	10.6	8.0	6.6	3.1	3.2	100.0
1995	56.6	7.7	10.1	7.7	11.6	3.0	3.3	100.0
1996	54.2	7.9	9.3	7.3	15.3	3.0	3.0	100.0
1997	52.5	8.5	9.5	7.6	15.8	3.1	3.0	100.0
1998	53.4	9.7	10.7	7.9	11.8	3.1	3.2	100.0
1999	51.6	11.3	11.8	8.5	10.3	3.3	3.2	100.0
2000	51.4	12.7	12.6	8.2	8.0	3.6	3.5	100.0
2001	51.3	13.6	12.9	7.9	7.0	3.7	3.6	100.0
2002	50.8	14.5	12.8	7.6	6.8	3.8	3.7	100.0
10-Year Change (%)								
	−13.4	7.0	2.1	−0.7	3.9	0.6	0.5	0.0
5-Year Compounded Annual Growth Rate (CAGR %)								
	−2.6	7.6	2.1	−1.0	10.0	2.1	1.5	0.0

in shopping mall food courts and to build freestanding restaurants that competed head-to-head with existing chicken chains. Despite market share gains by Boston Market and Chick-fil-A, however, KFC's customer base has remained loyal to the KFC brand because of its unique taste.

The maturation of the U.S. fast-food industry increased the intensity of competition within the chicken segment. While Chick-fil-A and Popeyes continued to grow new restaurants at a fast pace, other chains focused their strategies on new product introductions, product launches beyond fried chicken, and intensive marketing campaigns. All chains attempted to differentiate themselves based on unique product and customer characteristics. KFC used animated images of the "Colonel" to drive home its homestyle image. Recent product introductions included popcorn chicken, honey BBQ chicken, and spicy BBQ wings. Popeyes continued to reimage its restaurants with its "Heritage" design which included a balcony over the drive-thru, Cajun-style murals, and new signage. It recently introduced a Chicken Strip Po' Boy sandwich to expand its New Orleans–style menu of spicy chicken, jambalaya, etouffée, and gumbo. Bojangles' also promoted a Cajun décor but focused more heavily on core chicken products such as its Cajun fried chicken, Cajun filet sandwich, and Buffalo bites.

El Pollo Loco served marinated, flame-broiled chicken and other Mexican food entrees such as chicken burritos, tostada salads, and chicken nachos. Church's emphasized its "made-from-scratch," Southern-style fried chicken and side dishes such as corn-on-the-cob, fried okra, and macaroni and cheese. It was testing new products such as batter-fried fish, fried thigh filets, and fried fruit pies that would be introduced later in 2004. Chick-fil-A continued to focus on its pressure-cooked and char-grilled skinless chicken breast sandwiches. It focused on introducing salads and more portable menu items such as the recently introduced Cool Wrap Chicken Sandwich.

Trends in the Restaurant Industry

A number of demographic and societal trends influenced the demand for food eaten outside of the home. During the last two decades, rising incomes, greater affluence among a greater percentage of American households, higher divorce rates, and the fact that people married later in life contributed to the rising number of single households and the demand for fastfood. More than 50 percent of women worked outside of the home, a dramatic increase since 1970. This number was expected to rise to 65 percent by 2010. Doubleincome households contributed to rising household incomes and increased the number of times families ate out. Less time to prepare meals inside the home added to this trend. Countering these trends, however, was a slower growth rate of the U.S. population and an overpopulation of fast-food chains that increased consumer alternatives and intensified competition.

Baby Boomers 35 to 50 years of age constituted the largest consumer group for fast-food restaurants. Generation X'ers (ages 25 to 34) and the "Mature" category (ages 51 to 64) made up the second and third largest groups. As consumers aged, they became less enamored with fast-food and were more likely to trade up to more expensive restaurants such as dinner houses and full-service restaurants. Sales of many Mexican restaurants, which were extremely popular during the 1980s, began to slow as Japanese, Indian, and Vietnamese restaurants became more fashionable. Ethnic foods were rising in popularity as U.S. immigrants, who constituted 13 percent of the U.S. population in early 2004, looked for establishments that sold their native foods.

Labor was the top operational challenge of U.S. restaurant chains. Restaurants relied heavily on teenagers and college age workers. Twenty percent of all employed teenagers worked in food service, compared with only 4 percent of all employed men over the age of eighteen and 6 percent of all employed women. As the U.S. population aged, fewer young workers were available to fill food service jobs. The short supply of high school and college students also meant they had greater opportunities outside of food service. Turnover rates were notoriously high. The National Restaurant Association estimated that about 96 percent of all fast-food workers quit within a year, compared with about 84 percent of employees in full-service restaurants.

Labor costs made up about 30 percent of the fast-food chain's total costs, second only to food and beverage costs. To deal with the decreased supply of employees in the sixteen to twenty-four age category, many restaurants were forced to hire lower quality workers, which affected service and restaurant cleanliness. To improve quality and service, restaurants increasingly hired elderly employees who were interested in returning to the work force. To attract more workers, especially the elderly, restaurants offered health insurance, noncontributory pension plans, and profit-sharing benefits that were generally not given only ten years before. To combat high turnover rates, restaurants also turned to better training programs and mentoring systems, which paired new employees with more experienced ones. Mentoring systems were particularly helpful in increasing the learning curve of new workers and providing better camaraderie among employees.

Intense competition in the mature restaurant industry made it difficult for restaurants to increase prices sufficiently to cover the increased cost of labor. Consumers made decisions about where to eat partially based on price. As a result, profit margins were squeezed. To reduce costs, restaurants eliminated low-margin food items, increased portion sizes, and improved product value to offset price increases. Restaurants also attempted to increase consumer traffic through discounting, by accepting coupons from competitors, by offering two-for-one specials, and by making limited-time offerings.

Technology was increasingly used to lower costs and improve efficiencies. According to the National Restaurant Association, restaurant operators viewed computers as their number one tool for improving efficiency. Computers were used to improve labor scheduling, accounting, payroll, sales analysis, and inventory control. Most restaurant chains also used point-of-sale systems that recorded the selected menu items and gave the cashier a breakdown of food items and the ticket price. These systems reduced serving times and cashier accuracy. Other chains like McDonald's and Carl's Jr. converted to new food preparation systems that allowed them to prepare food more accurately and a variety of sandwiches using the same process.

Higher costs and poor availability of prime real estate was another trend that negatively affected profitability. A plot of land suitable for a freestanding restaurant cost between $1.5 and $2.5 million. Leasing was a less costly alternative to buying. Nevertheless, market saturation decreased per store sales as newer units cannibalized sales from existing units. As a result, most food chains began to expand their U.S. restaurant bases into alternative distribution channels in hospitals, airports, colleges, highway rest areas, gas stations, shopping mall food courts, and large retail stores or by dual branding with other fast-food concepts.

The Global Fast-Food Industry

As the U.S. market matured, more restaurants turned to international markets to expand sales. Foreign markets were attractive because of their large customer bases and comparatively little competition. McDonald's, for example, operated 46 restaurants for every 1 million U.S. residents. Outside of the United States, it operated only one restaurant for every 3 million residents. McDonald's, KFC, Burger King, and Pizza Hut were the earliest and most aggressive chains to expand abroad beginning in the 1960s. By early 2004, at least 35 chains had expanded into a least one foreign country. McDonald's operated more than 13,000 U.S. units and 17,000 foreign units in the 119 countries. With the acquisition of A&W and Long John Silver's, however, Yum! Brands became the world's largest restaurant chain in 2003. It operated more than 21,000 U.S. and close to 33,000 non-U.S. KFC, Pizza Hut, Taco Bell, A&W, and Long John Silver's restaurants in 88 countries. Because of their early expansion abroad, McDonald's, KFC, Burger King, and Pizza Hut had all developed strong brand names and managerial expertise operating in international markets. This made them formidable competitors for fast-food chains investing abroad for the first time. Subway, TCBY, and Domino's were more recent global competitors but were expanding more aggressively than McDonald's or KFC. By 2003, each was operating in more than 65 countries.

Exhibit 5 lists the world's thirty-five largest restaurant chains. The global fast-food industry had a distinctly American flavor. Twenty-eight chains (80 percent of the total) were headquartered in the United States. U.S. chains had the advantage of a large domestic market and ready acceptance by the American consumer. European firms had less success developing the fast-food concept because Europeans were more inclined to frequent midscale restaurants, where they spent several hours enjoying multicourse meals in a formal setting. KFC had trouble breaking into the German market during the 1970s and 1980s because Germans were not accustomed to buying take-out or ordering food over the counter. McDonald's had greater success penetrating the German market because it made a number of changes to its menu and operating procedures to appeal to German tastes. German beer, for example, was served in all of McDonald's restaurants in Germany. In France, McDonald's used a different sauce on its Big Mac sandwich that appealed to the French palate. KFC had more success in Asia and Latin America, where chicken was a traditional dish.

Aside from cultural factors, international business carried risks not present in the domestic market. Long distances between headquarters and foreign franchises made it more difficult to control the quality of individual restaurants. Large distances also caused servicing and support problems. Transportation and other resource costs were higher than in the domestic market. In addition, time, cultural, and language differences increased communication and operational problems. As a result, most restaurant chains limited expansion to their domestic market as long as they were able to meet profit and growth objectives. As companies gained greater expertise abroad, they turned to profitable international markets as a means of expanding restaurant bases and increasing sales, profits, and market share. Worldwide demand for fast-food was expected to grow rapidly during the next two decades as rising per capita incomes worldwide made eating out more affordable for greater numbers of consumers. In addition, the development of the Internet was quickly breaking down communication and language barriers. Greater numbers of children were growing up with computers in their homes and schools. As a result, teenagers in Germany, Brazil, Japan, and the United States were equally likely to be able to converse about the Internet. The Internet also exposed more teenagers to the same companies and products, which enabled firms to quickly develop global brands and a worldwide consumer base.

Kentucky Fried Chicken Corporation

Marketing Strategy

Many of KFC's problems during the 1980s and 1990s surrounded its limited menu and inability to quickly bring new products to market. The popularity of its Original Recipe Chicken allowed KFC to expand through the 1980s without significant competition from other chicken chains. As a result, new product introductions were not a critical part of KFC's business strategy. KFC suffered one of its most serious setbacks in 1989 as it prepared to introduce a chicken sandwich to its menu. KFC was still experimenting with the chicken sandwich concept when McDonald's rolled out its McChicken sandwich. By beating KFC to the market, McDonald's developed strong consumer awareness for its sandwich. This significantly increased KFC's cost of developing awareness for its own sandwich,

EXHIBIT 5

The World's 35 Largest Fast-Food Chains in 2004[1]

	Franchise	Corporate Headquarters	Home Country	Countries
1.	McDonald's	Oakbrook, Illinois	U.S.A.	121
2.	KFC	Louisville, Kentucky	U.S.A.	99
3.	Pizza Hut	Dallas, Texas	U.S.A.	92
4.	Subway Sandwiches	Milford, Connecticut	U.S.A.	74
5.	TCBY	Little Rock, Arkansas	U.S.A.	67
6.	Domino's Pizza	Ann Arbor, Michigan	U.S.A.	65
7.	Burger King	Miami, Florida	U.S.A.	58
8.	T.G.I. Friday's	Dallas, Texas	U.S.A.	53
9.	Baskin Robbins	Glendale, California	U.S.A.	52
10.	Dunkin' Donuts	Randolph, Massachusetts	U.S.A.	40
11.	Wendy's	Dublin, Ohio	U.S.A.	34
12.	Chili's Grill & Bar	Dallas, Texas	U.S.A.	22
13.	Dairy Queen	Edina, Michigan	U.S.A.	22
14.	Little Caesar's Pizza	Detroit, Michigan	U.S.A.	22
15.	Popeyes	Atlanta, Georgia	U.S.A.	22
16.	Outback Steakhouse	Tampa, Florida	U.S.A.	20
17.	A&W Restaurants	Lexington, Kentucky	U.S.A.	17
18.	PizzaExpress	London, England	U.K.	16
19.	Carl's Jr.	Anaheim, California	U.S.A.	14
20.	Church's Chicken	Atlanta, Georgia	U.S.A.	12
21.	Taco Bell	Irvine, California	U.S.A.	12
22.	Hardee's	Rocky Mt., North Carolina	U.S.A.	11
23.	Applebee's	Overland Park, Kansas	U.S.A.	9
24.	Sizzler	Los Angeles, California	U.S.A.	9
25.	Arby's	Ft. Lauderdale, Florida	U.S.A.	7
26.	Denny's	Spartanburg, South Carolina	U.S.A.	7
27.	Skylark	Tokyo	Japan	7
28.	Lotteria	Seoul	Korea	5
29.	Taco Time	Eugene, Oregon	U.S.A.	5
30.	Mos Burger	Tokyo	Japan	4
31.	Orange Julius	Edina, Minnesota	U.S.A.	4
32.	Yoshinoya	Tokyo	Japan	4
33.	IHOP	Glendale, California	U.S.A.	3
34.	Quick Restaurants	Brussels	Belgium	3
35.	Red Lobster	Orlando, Florida	U.S.A.	3

[1]Case writer research.

which KFC introduced several months later. KFC eventually withdrew the sandwich because of low sales. Today, about 95 percent of chicken sandwiches are sold through traditional hamburger chains.

KFC's focus on fried chicken ("chicken-on-the-bone") became a serious problem by the 1990s as the U.S. fast-food industry matured. In order to expand sales, restaurant chains began to diversify their menus to include non-core products, thereby cutting into the business of other fast-food segments. For example, hamburger and pizza chains, family restaurants, and dinner houses all introduced a variety of chicken items such as chicken sandwiches and chicken wings to expand their consumer base. This made it difficult for KFC to increase per-unit sales. By 2003, McDonald's boasted a menu that included hamburgers, chicken sandwiches, fish sandwiches, burritos, a full line of breakfast items, ice cream, and milkshakes. By diversifying its menu, McDonald's was able to raise annual sales to $1.5 million per restaurant. This compared with KFC's average restaurant sales of $883,000. In 2003, Yum! Brands conducted market research showing that customers preferred multiple menu offerings over single-concept menus like chicken or pizza by a six-to-one margin.

KFC's short-term strategy was to diversify its menu. It rolled out a buffet that included over thirty dinner, salad, and dessert items. The buffet was most successful in rural locations and suburbs but less successful in urban areas where restaurant space was limited. It then introduced Colonel's Crispy Strips and a line of chicken sandwiches that complimented its core fried chicken products. More recent product innovations include popcorn chicken, chunky chicken pot pie, and twisters (a flour tortilla filled with chunks of chicken). To increase brand awareness for these new products, KFC introduced a new television campaign featuring a cartoon caricature of Colonel Sanders stating "I'm a Chicken Genius!" It also featured Jason Alexander from the television sitcom *Seinfeld* promoting popcorn chicken using the slogan "There's fast food, then there's KFC." Sandwiches and other non-core items, however, cannibalized sales of KFC's core chicken products. Most important, it did little to address the consumer's desire for greater menu variety beyond chicken.

Multibrand Strategy

By 2000, the company began to open "2-in-1" units that sold both KFC and Taco Bell or KFC and Pizza Hut in the same location. Most of KFC's sales (64 percent) and Pizza Hut's sales (61 percent) were driven by dinner, while most of Taco Bell's sales (50 percent) were driven by lunch (50 percent). The combination of KFC and Taco Bell was a natural success because it increased per unit sales simply by filling up counter space left empty by KFC at lunch or Taco Bell at dinner. It became increasingly apparent, however, that the real value of combining restaurant concepts was in attracting greater numbers of consumers who wanted more menu variety. The acquisition of A&W and Long John Silver's in 2002 provided additional opportunities to create a variety of combinations of five highly differentiated fast-food category leaders. By 2003, Yum! Brands had opened 1,975 multibrand restaurants worldwide that included KFC/Taco Bell, KFC/A&W, Taco Bell/Pizza Hut, and A&W/Long John Silver's. The company believed there was potential for opening thirteen thousand multibrand restaurants in the United States alone. The increase in per unit sales that resulted from multibranding meant that new restaurants could be opened in more expensive locations and lower population areas than were profitable with stand-alone restaurants.

International Operations

KFC's early experience operating abroad put it in a strong position to take advantage of the growing trend toward global expansion. By early 2004, 56 percent of KFC's restaurants were located outside of the United States. KFC was the most global of the five brands managed by Yum! Brands, Inc. The other brands had a significantly smaller percentage of their restaurant base outside of the United States—Pizza Hut (37 percent), Taco Bell (4 percent), Long John Silver's (2 percent), and A&W (22 percent). Historically, franchises made up a large portion of KFC's international restaurant base because franchises were owned and operated by local entrepreneurs who had a deeper understanding of local language, culture, customs, law, financial markets, and marketing characteristics. Franchising was also a good strategy for establishing a presence in smaller countries such as Grenada, Bermuda, and Suriname, whose small populations could only support a single restaurant. The costs of operating company-owned restaurants were prohibitively high in these smaller markets. Of the seven thousand KFC restaurants located outside of the United States, 77 percent were franchises, licensed restaurants, or joint ventures. In larger markets such as Mexico, China, Canada, Australia, Puerto Rico, Korea, Thailand, and the United Kingdom, there was a stronger emphasis on building company-owned restaurants. By coordinating purchasing, recruiting, training, financing, and advertising in these larger markets, fixed costs could be spread over a larger restaurant base. KFC could also maintain tighter control over product quality and customer service.

Latin American Strategy

KFC operated 650 restaurants in Latin America in 2003 (Exhibit 6). Its primary presence was in Mexico, Puerto Rico, and the Caribbean. KFC established subsidiaries in Mexico and Puerto Rico in the late 1960s and expanded through company-owned restaurants. Franchises were used to penetrate countries in the Caribbean whose market size prevented KFC from profitably operating company-owned restaurants.

Subsidiaries were later established in the Virgin Islands, Venezuela, and Brazil. KFC had planned to expand into these regions using company-owned restaurants. The Venezuelan subsidiary, however, was later closed because of the high costs of operating the small subsidiary. KFC had opened eight restaurants in Brazil but closed them by 2000 because it lacked the cash flow needed to support an expansion program in that market. Franchises were opened in other markets that had good growth potential such as Chile, Ecuador, and Peru. In 2003, KFC signed a joint venture agreement with a Brazilian partner that had a deeper understanding of the Brazilian market. KFC hoped the joint venture would help it reestablish a presence in Brazil.

KFC's early entry into Latin America gave it a leadership position over McDonald's in Mexico and the Caribbean. It also had an edge in Ecuador and

EXHIBIT 6

Latin America Restaurant Count in 2003: McDonald's, Burger King, Wendy's, and KFC

	McDonald's	Burger King	Wendy's	KFC
Mexico	261	154	16	274
Puerto Rico	112	163	46	97
Caribbean Islands	29	55	20	134
Central America	99	104	38	32
Subtotal	501	476	120	537
% Total	31%	82%	68%	83%
Colombia	25	0	3	9
Ecuador	10	13	0	39
Peru	10	12	0	25
Venezuela	129	20	33	5
Other Andean	45	6	0	5
Andean Region	219	51	36	83
% Total	14%	9%	25%	13%
Argentina	203	25	21	0
Brazil	584	0	0	0
Chile	70	23	0	30
Paraguay + Uruguay	28	6	0	0
Southern Cone	885	54	21	30
% Total	55%	9%	15%	5%
Latin America	1,605	581	143	650
% Total	100%	100%	100%	100%

Peru. KFC's Latin America strategy represented a classic internationalization strategy. It first expanded into Mexico and Puerto Rico because of their geographic proximity, as well as political and economic ties to the United States. KFC then expanded its franchise system throughout the Caribbean, gradually moving away from its U.S. base as its experience in Latin America grew. Only after it had established a leadership position in Mexico and the Caribbean did it venture into South America. McDonald's pursued a different strategy. It was late to expand into the region. Despite a rapid restaurant construction program in Mexico during the 1990s, McDonald's still lagged behind KFC. Therefore, McDonald's initiated a first mover strategy in Brazil and Argentina, large markets where KFC had no presence. By 2003, 55 percent of McDonald's restaurants in Latin America were located in the two countries. Wendy's pursued a different strategy. It first expanded into Puerto Rico, the Caribbean, and Central America because of their geographic proximity to the United States. Wendy's late entry into Latin America, however, made it difficult to penetrate Mexico, where KFC, McDonald's, and Burger King had already established strong positions. Wendy's announced plans to build one hundred Wendy's restaurants in Mexico by 2010; however, its primary objective was to establish strong positions in Venezuela and Argentina, where most U.S. fast-food chains had not yet been established.

Country Risk Assessment in Latin America

Latin America comprised some fifty countries, island nations, and principalities that were settled primarily by the Spanish, Portuguese, French, Dutch, and British during the 1500s and 1600s. Spanish was spoken in most countries, the most notable exception being Brazil where the official language is Portuguese. Catholicism was the major religion, though Methodist missionaries successfully exported Protestantism into many regions of Latin America in the 1800s, most notably on the coast of Brazil. Despite commonalities in language, religion, and history, however, political and economic policies differed significantly from one country to another. Frequent changes in governments and economic instability increased the uncertainty of doing business in the region.

Most U.S. and Canadian companies realized that they could not overlook the region. Geographic proximity made communications and travel easier, and the North American Trade Agreement (NAFTA) eliminated tariffs on goods shipped between Canada, Mexico, and the United States. A customs union agreement signed in 1991 (Mercosur) between Argentina, Paraguay, Uruguay, and Brazil eliminated tariffs on trade among those four countries. Other countries such as Chile had also established free trade policies that were stimulating strong growth. The primary task for companies investing in the region was to accurately assess the different risks of doing business in Latin America and to select the proper countries for investment. Miller (1992) developed a framework for analyzing country risk that was a useful tool for evaluating different countries for future investment. He argued that firms must examine country, industry, and firm factors to fully assess country risk.

Country factors addressed the risks associated with changes in the country's political and economic environment that potentially affected the firm's ability to conduct business. They included

1. *Political risk* (e.g., war, revolution, changes in government, price controls, tariffs and other trade restrictions, appropriation of assets, government regulations, and restrictions on the repatriation of profits)

2. *Economic risk* (e.g., inflation, high interest rates, foreign exchange rate volatility, balance of trade movements, social unrest, riots, and terrorism)

3. *Natural risk* (e.g., rainfall, hurricanes, earthquakes, and volcanic activity)

Industry factors addressed changes in industry structure that inhibited the firm's ability to successfully compete in its industry. They included

1. *Supplier risk* (e.g., changes in quality, shifts in supply, and changes in supplier power)

2. *Product market risk* (e.g., consumer tastes and availability of substitute products)

3. *Competitive risk* (e.g., rivalry among competitors, new market entrants, and new product innovations)

Firm factors examined the firm's ability to control its internal operations. They included

1. *Labor risk* (e.g., labor unrest, absenteeism, employee turnover, and labor strikes)

2. *Supplier risk* (e.g., raw material shortages and unpredictable price changes)

3. *Trade secret risk* (e.g., protection of trade secrets and intangible assets)

4. *Credit risk* (e.g., problems collecting receivables)

5. *Behavioral risk* (e.g., control over franchise operations, product quality and consistency, service quality, and restaurant cleanliness)

Mexico

Many U.S. companies considered Mexico to be one of the most attractive investment locations in Latin America. Mexico's population of 105 million exceeded one-third of that of the United States. It was three times larger than Canada's 32 million. Prior to 1994, Mexico levied high tariffs on many goods imported from the United States. Other goods were regulated by quotas and licensing requirements that made Mexican goods more expensive. As a result, many U.S. consumers purchased less expensive products from Asia or Europe. In 1994, the long-awaited NAFTA agreement between Canada, the United States, and Mexico went into effect. NAFTA eliminated tariffs on goods traded among the three countries and created a trading bloc with a larger population and gross domestic product than the European Union. The elimination of tariffs led to an immediate increase in trade between Mexico and the United States. In 1995, only one year after NAFTA was signed, Mexico posted its first balance of trade surplus in six years. A large part of that surplus was attributed to greater exports to the United States. By 2003, almost 85 percent of Mexico's exports were purchased by U.S. consumers. In turn, about 68 percent of Mexico's total imports came from the United States.

U.S. investment in Mexico also increased significantly after NAFTA was signed, largely in the Maquiladoras located along the U.S.-Mexican border. With the elimination of import tariffs, U.S. firms could produce or assemble goods and transport them back into the United States more quickly and at significantly less cost than they could transport goods from Asia or Europe. Mexico's largest exports to the United States were automobiles, automobile parts, crude oil, petroleum products, and natural gas. A large portion of Mexico's automobile and auto part production was produced in U.S.-owned plants. The cost of transporting automobiles back into the United States was more than offset by the lower cost of labor in Mexico. Today, twenty-six hundred U.S. firms operate in Mexico and account for 60 percent of all foreign direct investment in that country.

Despite the benefits, many Mexican farmers and unskilled workers strongly opposed NAFTA and U.S. investment. The day after NAFTA went into effect, rebels rioted in the southern Mexican province of Chiapas on the Guatemalan border. After four days of fighting, Mexican troops drove the rebels out of several towns the rebels had earlier seized. Around 150 people were killed. The Mexican government negotiated a cease-fire with the rebels; however, armed clashes between rebel groups protesting poverty and lack of land rights continued to be a problem. Another protest followed the signing of NAFTA when 30 to 40 masked men attacked a McDonald's restaurant in the tourist section of Mexico City. The men threw cash registers to the floor, smashed windows, overturned tables, and spray-painted "No to Fascism" and "Yankee Go Home" on the walls.

Most Mexicans (70 percent) lived in urban areas such as Mexico City, Guadalajara, and Monterrey. Mexico City's population of 18 million made it one of the most populated areas in Latin America. Many U.S. firms had operations in or around Mexico City. The fast-food industry was well developed in Mexico's cities. The leading U.S. fast-food chains already had significant restaurant bases in Mexico: KFC (274 restaurants), McDonald's (261), Pizza Hut (174), Burger King (154), and Subway (71). Mexican consumers readily accepted the fast-food concept. Chicken was also a staple product in Mexico and helped explain KFC's wide popularity. Mexico's large population and ready acceptance of fast-food represented a significant opportunity for fast-food chains. Competition, however, was intense.

Despite Mexico's relative economic stability during the late 1990s and early 2000s, Mexico had a history of high inflation, foreign exchange controls, and government regulations. These often affected foreign firms' ability to make a profit. In 1989, President Salinas attempted to reduce high inflation by controlling the peso-dollar exchange rate, allowing the peso to depreciate by only one peso per day against the dollar. He also instituted price and wage controls. Firms like KFC were unable to raise prices and were closely monitored by Mexican authorities. However, smaller firms that supplied KFC and other U.S. firms with raw materials continued to charge higher prices to compensate for inflation. KFC was soon operating at a loss, setting off heated debate in PepsiCo's headquarters. PepsiCo's finance group wanted to halt further restaurant construction in Mexico until economic stability improved. PepsiCo's marketing group wanted to continue expansion despite losses to protect its leading market share in Mexico. PepsiCo's marketing group eventually won the debate, and KFC continued to build new restaurants in Mexico during the period.

When Ernesto Zedillo became Mexico's president in December 1994, one of his objectives was to continue the stability of prices, wages, and exchange rates achieved by ex-president Carlos Salinas. This stability, however, was achieved primarily on the basis of price, wage, and foreign exchange controls. While giving the appearance of stability, an overvalued peso continued to encourage imports that exacerbated Mexico's balance of trade deficit. At the same time, Mexican exports became less competitive on world markets. Anticipating a devaluation of the peso, investors began to move capital into U.S. dollar investments. On December 19, 1994, Zedillo announced that the peso would be allowed to depreciate by an additional 15 percent per year against the dollar. Within two days, continued pressure on the peso forced Zedillo to allow the peso to float freely against the dollar.

By mid-January 1995, the peso had lost 35 percent of its value against the dollar, and the Mexican stock market had plunged 20 percent. By the end of the year, the peso had depreciated from 3.1 pesos per dollar to 7.6 pesos per dollar. In order to thwart a possible default by Mexico, the U.S. government, International Monetary Fund, and World Bank pledged $25 billion in emergency loans. Shortly thereafter, Zedillo announced an emergency economic package called the "pacto" that included lower government spending, the sale of government-run businesses, and a wage freeze. By 2000, there were signs that Mexico's economy had stabilized. Interest rates and inflation, however, remained higher than in the United States, putting continuous pressure on the peso. This led to higher import prices and exacerbated inflation. In sum, optimism about future prospects for trade and investment in Mexico was tempered by concern about continued economic stability.

Brazil

Mexico's geographic proximity and membership in NAFTA partially explained why many U.S. firms with little experience in Latin America expanded to Mexico first. Mexico's close proximity to the United States minimized travel and communication problems, and NAFTA reduced the complexity of establishing production in Mexico and importing goods back into the United States. Many firms overlooked the potential of Brazil. Brazil, with a population of 182 million, was the largest country in Latin America and fifth largest country in the world. Its land base was as large as the United States and bordered ten countries. It was the world's largest coffee producer and largest exporter of sugar and tobacco. In addition to its abundant natural resources and strong export position in agriculture, Brazil was a strong industrial power. Its major exports were airplanes, automobiles, and chemicals. Its gross domestic product of $1.3 trillion was larger than Mexico's and the largest in Latin America (see Exhibit 7). Some firms did view Brazil as one of the most important emerging markets, along with China and India.

In 1990, U.S. President George Bush initiated negotiations on a Free Trade Area of the Americas (FTAA) that would eliminate tariffs on trade within North, Central, and South America. The FTAA would create the world's largest free trade area with a combined gross domestic product of $13 trillion and 800 million consumers. In 1994, the presidents of thirty-three countries met with President Bush to negotiate details of the free trade agreement to go into effect by 2005. Many Brazilians opposed the FTAA because they feared Brazilian companies could not compete with more efficient U.S. firms. Brazil imposed high tariffs of between 10 and 35 percent on a variety of goods imported from the United States such as automobiles, automobile parts, computers, computer parts, engines, and soybeans. Other Brazilian firms, however, stood to gain substantially. To protect U.S. producers from lower cost Brazilian goods, the United States imposed tariffs of between 10 and 350 percent on imported Brazilian sugar cane, tobacco, orange juice concentrate, soybean oil, and women's leather footwear. The FTAA would eliminate these tariffs. This would give U.S. consumers the opportunity to buy Brazilian products at significantly lower prices.

EXHIBIT 7

Latin America—Selected Economic and Demographic Data

	U.S.A.	Canada	Mexico	Colombia	Venezuela	Peru	Brazil	Argentina	Chile
Population (millions)	290.3	32.2	104.9	41.7	24.7	28.4	182.0	38.7	15.7
Growth Rate	0.9%	0.9%	1.4%	1.6%	1.5%	1.6%	1.5%	1.1%	1.1%
Population Data: Origin									
European (non-French origin)	65.1%	43.0%	9.0%	20.0%	21.0%	15.0%	55.0%	97.0%	95.0%
European (French origin)		23.0%							
African	12.9%			4.0%	10.0%		6.0%		
Mixed African & European				14.0%		37.0%	38.0%		
Latin American (Hispanic)	12.0%								
Asian	4.2%	6.0%							
Amerindian or Alaskan native	1.5%	2.0%	30.0%	1.0%	2.0%	45.0%			3.0%
Mixed Amerindian & Spanish			60.0%	58.0%	67.0%				
Mixed African & Amerindian				3.0%					
Other	4.3%	26.0%	1.0%			3.0%	1.0%	3.0%	2.0%
Total	100.0%	100.0%	100.0%	100.0%	100.0%	100.0%	100.0%	100.0%	100.0%
GDP ($ billion)	$10,400	$923	$900	$268	$133	$132	$1,340	$391	$151
Per Capita Income ($U.S.)	$37,600	$29,400	$9,000	$6,500	$5,500	$4,800	$7,600	$10,200	$10,000
Real GDP Growth Rate	2.5%	3.4%	1.0%	2.0%	−8.9%	4.8%	1.0%	−14.7%	1.8%
Inflation Rate	1.6%	2.2%	6.4%	6.2%	31.2%	0.2%	8.3%	41.0%	2.5%
Unemployment Rate	5.8%	7.6%	3.0%	17.4%	17.0%	9.4%	6.4%	21.5%	9.2%
Literacy Rate	97.0%	97.0%	92.2%	92.5%	93.4%	90.9%	86.4%	97.0%	96.2%

Source: U.S. Central Intelligence Agency, *The World Factbook.* Demographic data are 2003 estimate; economic data as of year-end 2002.

Brazil played a leading role in negotiating trade and investment arrangements with other countries in Latin America. In 1991, Brazil, Argentina, Uruguay, and Paraguay signed an agreement to form a common market (Mercosur) that eliminated internal tariffs on goods traded among member countries and established a common external tariff. By 1995, 90 percent of trade among member countries was free from trade restrictions. Member countries were allowed to impose tariffs on a limited number of products considered to be a threat to sensitive domestic industries. The hope was to expand Mercosur to include other countries in the region. Chile and Bolivia, for example, were offered associate memberships. Chile, however, later withdrew because it wanted to negotiate future membership in NAFTA. Like NAFTA, the signing of Mercosur had a dramatic effect on trade among its members. Argentina quickly became Brazil's second-largest trading partner after the United States, while Brazil became Argentina's largest trading partner. Brazilian officials made it clear that making Mercosur successful was their highest priority and that the Free Trade Area of the Americas might have to wait. Many believed Brazil was the major stumbling block to establishing FTAA by 2005.

Historically, the Brazilian government used a variety of tariffs and other restrictions on imports to encourage foreign investment in Brazil. The most highly visible example was automobiles that were taxed at rates up to 100 percent during the 1980s and 1990s. By 2003, almost all global automobile companies, including General Motors, Mercedes-Benz, Toyota, Volkswagen, Honda, Fiat, and Peugeot, were producing cars in Brazil for the Brazilian market. During the 1980s, the Brazilian government attempted to stimulate domestic production in a number of technology industries like computers through an outright prohibition on imports. An example was Texas Instruments (TI), a major computer manufacturer with semiconductor operations in São Paulo. TI was prohibited from using its own computers in its Brazilian production facilities. Instead, it was forced to use slower, less efficient Brazilian computers. The Brazilian government later eliminated such restrictions after it became clear that Brazilian computer firms were unable to compete head-to-head with global computer firms. Strong government regulations and the tendency of the Brazilian government to change regulations from year to year eventually caused TI to withdraw from Brazil, even though its plant was profitable.

During the 1980s and early 1990s, Brazil battled sustained cycles of high inflation and currency instability. Between 1980 and 1993, inflation averaged more than 400 percent per year. Brazil's government attempted to reduce inflation through a variety of new currency programs, price and wage controls, and the policy of indexation, which adjusted wages and contracts based on the inflation rate. In 1994, President Cardoso introduced the Real Plan, which restructured Brazil's currency system. The cruzeiro was eliminated and replaced with a new currency called the real. The real was pegged to the U.S. dollar in an attempt to break the practice of indexation. By 1997, inflation had dropped to under 7 percent. Brazil's ability to successfully peg the real against the dollar was made possible in large part by the large foreign investment flows into Brazil during this period. The inflow of dollars boosted Brazil's dollar reserves, which could be used to buy the real on currency markets, thereby stabilizing the value of the real against the dollar.

By 1998, however, investors began to pull investments out of Brazil. Many investors were increasingly concerned about Brazil's growing budget deficit and pension system crisis. Pension benefits represented almost 10 percent of Brazil's gross domestic product. Almost half of Brazil's retirement payments went to retired civil servants who made up only 5 percent of all retired Brazilians. The heavy demand on public funds for pension benefits diminished Brazil's ability to use fiscal and monetary policy to support economic development and promote stability. The Brazilian Central Bank attempted to reduce the outflow of investment capital by raising interest rates; however, dwindling dollar reserves finally reached a crisis in 1999, when Brazil abandoned its policy of pegging the real. The real was subsequently allowed to float against the dollar. The real depreciated by almost 50 percent against the dollar in 1999.

The fast-food industry in Brazil was less developed than in Mexico or the Caribbean. This was partly the result of the structure of the fast-food industry that was dominated by U.S. restaurant chains. U.S. chains expanded further away from their home base as they gained experience operating in Latin America. As firms gained a foothold in Mexico and Central America, it was a natural progression to move into South America. McDonald's understood the importance of the Brazilian market and was early to expand there. By 2003, it was operating 584 restaurants. Many restaurant chains such as Burger King,

Pizza Hut, and KFC built restaurants in Brazil in the early to mid-1990s but eventually closed them because of poor sales. In one example, Pizza Hut opened a restaurant in a popular restaurant section of Goiânia, a city of more than 1 million people about a two-hour drive from Brasìlia, Brazil's capital. When the restaurant opened, long lines of Brazilian customers wrapped around the block waiting to try Pizza Hut for the first time. Within a few weeks, the lines were gone. Pizza Hut had opened a freestanding restaurant identical to those it operated in the United States. U.S. consumers were accustomed to waiting until a table was opened, sitting down and eating their meal, and leaving. Brazilian consumers did not mind waiting. However, they were accustomed to sitting outside with friends, socializing with a drink and hors d'oeuvres until a table was ready. Pizza Hut restaurants didn't accommodate this facet of Brazilian culture. Rather than change the structure of its operations, Pizza Hut sold the restaurant to Habib's, a popular Brazilian restaurant chain that sold Arab food.

Another problem was eating customs. Brazilians normally ate their big meal in the early afternoon. This could last two hours. It normally included salad, meat, rice and beans, dessert, fruit, and coffee. In the evening, it was customary to have a light meal such as a soup or small plate of pasta. Brazilians rarely ate food with their hands, preferring to eat with a knife and fork. This included food like pizza, which Americans typically ate with their hands. They also were not accustomed to eating sandwiches. If they did eat sandwiches, they wrapped the sandwich in a napkin. U.S. fast-food chains catered to a different kind of customer, one who wanted more than soup but less than a full sit-down meal. U.S. fast-food chains such as McDonald's were more popular in larger cities such as São Paulo and Rio de Janeiro, where business people were in a hurry. In smaller cities, however, traditional customs of eating were still popular. Food courts were well developed in Brazil's shopping malls. They included a variety of sit-down restaurants, fast-food restaurants, and kiosks. In the United States, in contrast, food courts consisted primarily of fast-food restaurants. U.S. restaurant chains were, therefore, faced with a daunting task of changing Brazilians' eating habits—or convincing Brazilians of the attractiveness of fast-food, American style. The risk of not penetrating the Brazilian market, however, was significant given the size of Brazil's economy and McDonald's already significant presence.

Risks and Opportunities

KFC faced difficult decisions surrounding the design and implementation of an effective Latin American strategy over the next twenty years. It wanted to sustain its leadership position in Mexico and the Caribbean but also looked to strengthen its position in other regions in South America, particularly in Brazil. Limited resources and cash flow limited KFC's ability to aggressively expand in all countries simultaneously. KFC also faced the task of adapting its entry strategy to overcome barriers to entry in countries where it had little presence such as Argentina, Paraguay, Uruguay, and Venezuela. In Brazil, KFC hoped a joint venture partner would help overcome cultural barriers that forced it to withdraw in 2000. How should KFC expand its restaurant base in Latin America given differences in consumer acceptance of the fast-food concept, intensity of competition, and culture? Should KFC open company-owned restaurants or rely on franchises to grow its restaurant base? In which markets should KFC approach joint venture partners as a means of more effectively developing the KFC concept? Could KFC approach markets like Brazil and Argentina cautiously in light of McDonald's and Wendy's aggressive first mover advantages in those countries, or should KFC proceed more aggressively? Last, in which countries should KFC establish subsidiaries that actively managed multiple restaurants in order to exploit synergies in purchasing, operations, and advertising? A country subsidiary that was supported by resources from KFC headquarters in Louisville could only be justified if KFC had a large restaurant base in the targeted country. KFC's Latin American strategy required considerable analysis and thought about how to most efficiently use its resources. It also required an in-depth analysis of country risk and selection of the right country portfolio.

REFERENCES

General References

Direction of Trade Statistics, International Monetary Fund, Washington, DC.

International Financial Statistics, International Monetary Fund, Washington, DC.

Miller, Kent D., "A Framework for Integrated Risk Management in International Business," *Journal of International Business Studies* 23, no. 2 (1992): pages 311–331.

Quickservice Restaurant Trends, National Restaurant Association, Washington, DC.

Standard & Poor's Industry Surveys, Standard & Poor's Corporation, New York, NY.

The World Factbook, U.S. Central Intelligence Agency, Washington, D.C.

Periodicals

FIU Hospitality Review, FIU Hospitality Review, Inc., Miami, FL.

IFMA Word, International Foodservice Manufacturers Association, Chicago, IL.

Independent Restaurant, EIP, Madison, WI.

Journal of Nutrition in Recipe & Menu Development, Food Product Press, Binghamton, NY.

Nation's Restaurant News, Lebhar-Friedman, Inc., New York, NY (**http:// www.nrn.com**).

Restaurants & Institutions, Cahners Publishing Co., New York, NY (**http:// www.restaurantsandinstitutions.com**).

Restaurant Business, Bill Communications Inc., New York, NY (**http:// www.restaurant.biz.com**).

Restaurants USA, National Restaurant Association, Washington, DC. (**http://www.restaurant.org**).

Associations

International Franchise Association, 1350 New York Ave. NW, Suite 900, Washington, DC 20005-4709, (202) 628-8000, **http:// www.franchise.org.**

National Restaurant Association, 1200 17th St. NW, Washington, DC 20036-3097, (202) 331-5900, **http://www.restaurant.org.**

Books

Dave's Way: A New Approach to Old-Fashioned Success, by R. David Thomas (founder of Wendy's), Berkley Publishing Group, 1992.

The Globalization Reader, by Frank Lechner and John Boli (eds.), Blackwell Publishing, 2000.

Golden Arches East: McDonald's in East Asia, by James L. Watson (ed.), Stanford University Press, Palo Alto, CA, 1998.

Grinding It Out: The Making of McDonald's, by Ray Kroc (founder of McDonald's) and Robert Anderson, St. Martin's, 1990.

I'd Like the World to Buy a Coke: The Life and Leadership of Roberto Goizueta, by David Greising, John Wiley & Sons, 1999.

It's Easier to Succeed Than to Fail, by S. Truett Cathy (founder of Chick-fil-A), Oliver-Nelson Books, Nashville, TN, 1989.

Kentucky Fried Chicken Japan Ltd.: International Competitive Benchmarks and Financial Gap Analysis, by Icon Group Ltd., 2000.

Kentucky Fried Chicken Japan Ltd.: Labor Productivity Benchmarks and International Gap Analysis, by Icon Group Ltd., 2000.

McDonaldization Revisited, by Mark Alfino, John S. Caputo, and Robin Wynyard (eds.), Greenwood Publishing Group, 1998.

The McDonaldization of Society: An Investigation into the Changing Character of Contemporary Social Life, by George Ritzer, Pine Forge Press, 1995.

McDonald's Behind the Arches, by John F. Love, Bantam Books, 1986, 1995, 1999.

The McDonald's Thesis: Explorations and Extensions, by George Ritzer, Sage Publications, 1998.

Selling 'Em by the Sack: White Castle and the Creation of American Food, by David Gerard Hogan, New York University Press, 1999.

Taco Titan: The Glen Bell Story, by Debra Lee Baldwin, Summit Publishing Group, 1999.

Web Pages

Bojangles' (**http://www.bojangles.com**).

Boston Market Corporation (**http://www.bostonmarket.com**).

Burger King Corporation (**http://www.burgerking.com**).

Chick-fil-A (**http://www.chickfila.com**).

Churchs Chicken (**http://www.churchs.com**).

McDonald's Corporation (**http://www.mcdonalds.com**).

Popeyes Chicken & Biscuits (**http://www.popeyes.com**).

Yum! Brands, Inc. (**http://www.yum.com**).

Wendy's International Incorporated (**http://www.wendys.com**).

Nucor in 2005

This case was prepared by Frank C. Barnes, University of North Carolina-Charlotte, and Beverly B. Tyler, North Carolina State University.

Nucor Corporation took first place in the 2005 *Business Week* 50 list of the best performers of the S&P 500 companies. Not bad for a company in an industry often considered unexciting and low tech! In 2004, sales were up 82%, from $6 to $12 billion, and earnings went from $.40 to $7.02 per share. In a little over a year, the stock price tripled. Long-time employees with $300,000 in their retirement stock saw it rise to over $1 million. The tons shipped increased 9%, with the average selling price up 66%. However, scrap prices were up 74%. At the beginning of 2005, prices seemed to be holding up because of the mergers in the United States and the state control of supply in China. And Nucor expected the first quarter of 2005 to double its 2004 results. This was a reasonable expectation, since Nucor began the year with 70% of its flat-rolled steel output for all of 2005 sold, compared to just 25% a year earlier. Furthermore, in 2005 Nucor had two joint ventures with global partners to find alternatives to the use of scrap steel. In Brazil they were working on an environmentally friendly way to produce pig iron. With Mitsubishi and the Chinese steelmaker they were building a facility in Western Australia to use the new Hismelt process to produce iron from iron ore fines and cold fines with less energy and pollution.

The previous three years had been among the worst down cycle in the steel industry's history. During those years Nucor acquired failing competitors, increased its steel capacity, and achieved a profit in every quarter. The world economy and demand had improved recently as prices went from $300 a ton to $640 a ton. Thus, Nucor expected profits to continue to grow for a while. While bankruptcies had eliminated some excess capacity in the United States and state-controlled China could hold back capacity to maintain prices, global competitors were consolidating, suppliers were raising their prices on iron ore and scrap, and buyers were considering alternatives to steel. Nucor, and its new president Dan DiMicco, faced a challenge in continuing Nucor's reputation for excellence.

Background

Nucor could be traced back to the company that manufactured the first Oldsmobile in 1897 and became the Reo Truck Company. As the company declined into bankruptcy in the postwar years, a 1955 merger created Nuclear Corp. of America. Following the "conglomerate" trend of the period, Nuclear acquired various "high-tech" businesses, such as radiation sensors, semiconductors, rare earths, and air-conditioning equipment. However, the company lost money continually, and a fourth reorganization in 1966 put forty-year-old Ken Iverson in charge. The building of Nucor had begun.

Ken Iverson had joined the Navy after high school in 1943 and had been transferred from officer training school to Cornell's Aeronautical Engineering Program. On graduation he selected mechanical engineering/metallurgy for a master's degree to avoid

Copyright © 2005 by Frank C. Barnes and Beverly B. Tyler. This case was prepared by Frank C. Barnes and Beverly B. Tyler as the basis for class discussion rather than to illustrate either effective or ineffective handling of an administrative situation. Reprinted by permission of Frank C. Barnes and Beverly B. Tyler. All rights reserved. For the most recent financial results of the company discussed in this case, go to **http://finance.yahoo.com,** input the company's stock symbol, and download the latest company report from its homepage.

the long drafting apprenticeship in aeronautical engineering. His college work with an electron microscope earned him a job with International Harvester. After five years in their lab, his boss, and mentor, prodded him to expand his vision by going with a smaller company.

Over the next ten years, Iverson worked for four small metals companies, gaining technical knowledge and increasing his exposure to other business functions. He enjoyed working with the presidents of these small companies and admired their ability to achieve outstanding results. Nuclear Corp., after failing to buy the company Iverson worked for, hired him as a consultant to find them another metals business to buy. In 1962, the firm bought a small joist plant in South Carolina that Iverson found, on the condition that he run it.

Over the next four years, Iverson built up the Vulcraft division as Nuclear Corporation struggled. The president, David Thomas, was described as a great promoter and salesman but a weak manager. A partner with Bear Stearns actually made a personal loan to the company to keep it going. In 1966, when the company was on the edge of bankruptcy, Iverson, who headed the only successful division, was named president and moved the headquarters to Charlotte, North Carolina, where he focused the company business first on the joist industry and soon moved into steel production.

He immediately began getting rid of the esoteric, but unprofitable, high-tech divisions and concentrated on the steel joist business he found successful. They built more joist plants and in 1968 began building their first steel mill in South Carolina to "make steel cheaper than they were buying from importers." By 1984, Nucor had six joist plants and four steel mills, using the new "minimill" technology.

From the beginning, Iverson had the people running the various plants, called divisions, make all the major decisions about how to build and run Nucor. The original board was composed of Iverson; Sam Siegel, his financial chief; and Dave Aycock, who had been with the South Carolina joist company before Nuclear acquired it. Siegel had joined Nuclear as an accountant in 1961. He had quit Nuclear but in their crisis agreed to return as treasurer if Iverson were named president. Aycock and Siegel were named vice presidents at the time Iverson was named president.

Dave Aycock had been very impressed with the original owner of Vulcraft, Sanborn Chase. Aycock had started his career as a welder there. He described

him as "the best person I've ever known" and as "a scientific genius." He said he was a man of great compassion, who understood the atmosphere necessary for people to self-motivate. Chase, an engineer by training, invented a number of things in diverse fields. He also established the incentive programs for which Nucor later became known. With only one plant, he was still able to operate with a "decentralized" manner. Before his death in 1960, while still in his forties, the company was studying the building of a steel mill using newly developed minimill technology. His widow ran the company until it was sold to Nucor in 1962.

Aycock met Ken Iverson when Nuclear purchased Vulcraft, and they worked together closely for the next year and a half. Located in Phoenix at the corporate headquarters, he was responsible to Iverson for all the joist operations and was given the task of planning and building a new joist plant in Texas. In late 1963, he was transferred to Norfolk, where he lived for the next thirteen years and managed a number of Nucor's joist plants. Then in 1977 he was named the manager of the Darlington South Carolina steel plant. In 1984, Aycock became Nucor's President and Chief Operating Officer, while Iverson became Chairman and Chief Executive Officer.

Aycock had this to say about Iverson: "Ken was a very good leader, with an entrepreneurial spirit. He is easy to work with and has the courage to do things, to take lots of risks. Many things didn't work, but some worked very well." There is the old saying "failure to take risk is failure." This saying epitomizes a cultural value personified by the company's founder and reinforced by Iverson during his time at the helm. Nucor was very innovative in steel and joists. Their plant was years ahead in wire rod welding at Norfolk. In the late 1960s, they had one of the first computer inventory management systems and design/engineering programs. They were very sophisticated in purchasing, sales, and managing, and they beat their competition often by the speed of their design efforts.

Between 1964 and 1984 the bankrupt conglomerate became a leading steel company in America. It was a fairytale story. Tom Peters used Nucor's management style as an example of "Excellence" while the barons of old steel ruled over creeping ghettos. NBC featured Nucor on television and *New Yorker* magazine serialized a book about how a relatively small American steel company built a team, which led the whole world into a new era of steelmaking. As the NBC program asked, "If Japan Can, Why Can't We?" Nucor had! Iverson was rich, owning $10 million in stock, but with a salary that rarely reached $1 million, compared with some U.S. executive's $50 or $100 million. The forty-year-old manager of the South Carolina Vulcraft plant had become a millionaire. Stockholders chuckled and ununionized hourly workers, who had never seen a layoff in the twenty years, earned more than the unionized workers of old steel and more than 85 percent of the people in the states where they worked. Many employees were financially quite secure.

Nucor owed much of its success to its benchmark organizational style and the empowered division managers. There were two basic lines of business, the first being the six steel joist plants that made the steel frames seen in many buildings. The second line included four steel mills that utilized the innovative minimill technology to supply the joist plants at first and later outside customers. Nucor was still only the seventh largest steel company in America. Over its second twenty years, Nucor was to rise to become the second-largest U.S. steel company. A number of significant challenges were to be met and overcome to get there, and once that horizon was reached even greater challenges would arise. Below are described the systems Nucor built and its organization, divisions, management, and incentive system.

Nucor's Organization

In the early 1990s, Nucor's twenty-two divisions (up to thirty by 2005), one for every plant, had a general manager, who was also a vice president of the corporation. The divisions were of three basic types, joist plants, steel mills, and miscellaneous plants. The corporate staff consisted of less than forty-five people (twenty-five in the 1990s). In the beginning Iverson had chosen Charlotte "as the new home base for what he had envisioned as a small cadre of executives who would guide a decentralized operation with liberal authority delegated to managers in the field," according to *South* magazine.

Iverson gave his views on keeping a lean organization:

> Each division is a profit center and the division manager has control over the day-to-day decisions that make that particular division profitable or not profitable. We expect the division to provide contribution, which is earnings before corporate expenses. We do not allocate our corporate expenses, because we do not think there is any way to do this reasonably and fairly. We do focus on earnings. And we expect a division to earn 25 percent return on total assets employed, before corporate expenses, taxes, interest or profit sharing. And we have a saying in the company—if a manager doesn't provide that for a number of years, we are either going to get rid of the division or get rid of the general manager, and it's generally the division manager.

A joist division manager commented on being in an organization with only four levels:

> I've been a division manager four years now and at times I'm still awed by it: the opportunity I was given to be a Fortune 500 vice-president. . . . I think we are successful because it is our style to pay more attention to our business than our competitors. . . . We are kind of a "no nonsense" company.

The divisions did their own manufacturing, selling, accounting, engineering, and personnel management. A steel division manager, when questioned about Florida Steel, which had a large plant 90 miles away, commented, "I expect they do have more of the hierarchy. I think they have central purchasing, centralized sales, centralized credit collections, centralized engineering, and most of the major functions."

Nucor strengthened its position by developing strong alliances with outside parties. It did no internal research and development. Instead, they monitored other's work worldwide and attracted investors who brought them new technical applications at the earliest possible dates. Though Nucor was known for constructing new facilities at the lowest possible costs; their engineering and construction team consists of only three individuals. They did not attempt to specify exact equipment parameters, but asked the equipment supplier to provide this information and then held the manufacturer accountable. They had alliances with selected construction companies around the country who knew the kind of work Nucor wanted. Nucor bought 95 percent of its scrap steel from an independent broker who followed the market and made recommendations regarding scrap purchases. They did not have a corporate advertising department, corporate public relations department, or a corporate legal or environmental department. They had long-term relationships with outsiders to provide these services.

The steel industry had established a pattern of absorbing the cost of shipment so, regardless of the distance from the mill, all users paid the same delivered price. Nucor broke with this tradition and stopped equalizing freight. It offered all customers the same sales terms. Nucor also gave no volume discounts, feeling that with modern computer systems there was no justification. Customers located next to the plant guaranteed themselves the lowest possible costs for steel purchases. Two tube manufacturers, two steel service centers, and a cold rolling facility had located adjacent to the Arkansas plant. These facilities accounted for 60 percent of the shipments from the mill. The plants were linked electronically to each other's production schedules, allowing them to function in a just-in-time inventory mode. All new mills were built on large enough tracks of land to accommodate collaborating businesses.

Iverson didn't feel greater centralization would be good for Nucor. Hamilton Lott, a Vulcraft plant manager, commented in 1997, "We're truly autonomous; we can duplicate efforts made in other parts of Nucor. We might develop the same computer program six times. But the advantages of local autonomy make it worth it." Joe Rutkowski, manager at Darlington steel, agreed, "We're not constrained; headquarters doesn't restrict what I spend. I just have to make my profit contribution at the end of year."

South magazine observed that Iverson had established a characteristic organizational style described as "stripped down" and "no nonsense." "Jack Benny would like this company," observed Roland Underhill, an analyst with Crowell, Weedon and Co. of Los Angeles, "so would Peter Drucker." Underhill pointed out that Nucor's thriftiness doesn't end with its "spartan" office staff or modest offices. "There are no corporate perquisites," he recited. "No company planes, No country club memberships. No company cars."

Fortune noted, "'Iverson takes the subway when he is in New York,' a Wall Street analyst reports in a voice that suggests both admiration and amazement." The general managers reflected this style in the operation of their individual divisions. Their offices were more like plant offices or the offices of private companies built around manufacturing rather than for public appeal. They were simple, routine, and businesslike.

Division Managers

The corporate personnel manager described management relations as informal, trusting, and not "bureaucratic." He felt there was a minimum of paperwork, that a phone call was more common than memos, and that no confirming memo was thought to be necessary.

A Vulcraft manager commented, "We have what I would call a very friendly spirit of competition from one plant to the next. And of course all of the vice-presidents and general managers share the same bonus systems so we are in this together as a team even though we operate our divisions individually." He added, "When I came to this plant four years ago, I saw we had too many people, too much overhead. We had 410 people at the plant and I could see, from my experience at the Nebraska plant, we had many more than we needed. Now with 55 fewer men, we are still capable of producing the same number of tons as four years ago."

The divisions managed their activities with a minimum of contact with the corporate staff. Each day disbursements were reported to the corporate office. Payments flowed into regional lock-boxes. On a weekly basis, joist divisions reported total quotes, sales cancellations, backlog, and production. Steel mills reported tons rolled, outside shipments, orders, cancellations, and backlog.

Each month the divisions completed a two-page (11″ x 17″) "Operations Analysis" which was sent to all the managers. Its three main purposes were (1) financial consolidation, (2) sharing information among the divisions, and (3) corporate management examination. The summarized information and the performance statistics for all the divisions were then returned to the managers.

The general managers met three times a year. In late October they presented preliminary budgets and capital requests. In late February they met to finalize budgets and treat miscellaneous matters. Then, at a meeting in May, they handled personnel matters, such as wage increases and changes of policies or benefits. The general managers as a group considered the raises for the department heads, the next lower level of management for all the plants.

Vulcraft—The Joist Divisions

One of Nucor's major businesses was the manufacture and sale of open web steel joists and joist girders at seven Vulcraft divisions located in Florence, South Carolina; Norfolk, Nebraska; Ft. Payne, Alabama; Grapeland, Texas; St. Joe, Indiana; Brigham City, Utah; and Chemung, New York. Open web joists, in contrast

FIGURE 1

Illustration of Joists

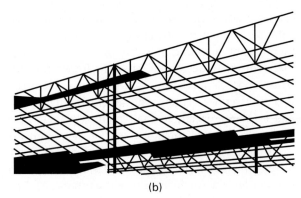

(a)   (b)

to solid joists, were made of steel angle iron separated by round bars or smaller angle iron (Figure 1). These joists cost less, were of greater strength for many applications, and were used primarily as the roof support systems in larger buildings, such as warehouses and shopping malls.

The joist industry was characterized by high competition among many manufacturers for many small customers. With an estimated 40 percent of the market, Nucor was the largest supplier in the United States. It utilized national advertising campaigns and prepared competitive bids on 80 percent to 90 percent of the buildings using joists. Competition was based on price and delivery performance. Nucor had developed computer programs to prepare designs for customers and to compute bids based on current prices and labor standards. In addition, each Vulcraft plant maintained its own Engineering Department to help customers with design problems or specifications. The Florence manager commented, "Here on the East Coast we have six or seven major competitors; of course none of them are as large as we are. The competition for any order will be heavy, and we will see six or seven different prices." He added, "I think we have a strong selling force in the market place. It has been said to us by some of our competitors that in this particular industry we have the finest selling organization in the country."

Nucor aggressively sought to be the lowest-cost producer in the industry. Materials and freight were two important elements of cost. Nucor maintained its own fleet of almost one hundred fifty trucks to ensure on-time delivery to all of the states, although most business was regional due to transportation costs. Plants were located in rural areas near the markets they served. Nucor's move into steel production was a move to lower the cost of steel used by the joist business.

Joist Production

On the basic assembly line used at the joist divisions, three or four of which might make up any one plant, about six tons of joists per hour would be assembled. In the first stage, 8 people cut the angles to the right lengths or bend the round bars to the desired form. These were moved on a roller conveyer to 6-man assembly stations, where the component parts would be tacked together for the next stage, welding. Drilling and miscellaneous work were done by 3 people between the lines. The 9-man welding station completed the welds before passing the joists on roller conveyers to 2-man inspection teams. The last step before shipment was the painting.

The workers had control over and responsibility for quality. There was an independent quality control inspector who had the authority to reject the run of joists and cause them to be reworked. The quality control people were not under the incentive system and reported to the engineering department.

Daily production might vary widely, since each joist was made for a specific job. The wide range of joists made control of the workload at each station difficult; bottlenecks might arise anywhere along the line. Each workstation was responsible for identifying such bottlenecks so that the foreman could reassign people promptly to maintain productivity. Since workers knew most of the jobs on the line, including the more skilled welding job, they could be shifted as needed. Work on the line was described by one general manager as "not machine type but mostly physical labor." He said the important thing was to avoid bottlenecks.

There were four lines of about twenty-eight people, each on two shifts, at the Florence division. The jobs on the line were rated on responsibility and assigned a base wage, from $11 to $13 per hour. In addition, a weekly bonus was paid on the total output of each line. Each worker received the same percent bonus on his base wage. The Texas plant was typical with the bonus running 225 percent, giving a wage of $27 an hour in 1999.

The amount of time required to make a joist had been established as a result of experience; the general manager had seen no time studies in his fifteen years with the company. As a job was bid, the cost of each joist was determined through the computer program. The time required depended on the length, number of panels, and depth of the joist. At the time of production, the labor value of production, the standard, was determined in a similar manner. The South Carolina general manager stated, "In the last nine or ten years we have not changed a standard."

The Grapeland plant maintained a time chart, which was used to estimate the labor required on a job. The plant teams were measured against this time for bonus. The chart was based on the historical time required on the jobs. Every few years the time chart was updated. Because some of the changes in performance were due to equipment changes, generally the chart would be increased by half the change, and the employee would benefit in pay from the other half. The last change, two years ago, saw some departments' pay increased by as much as 10 percent. The production manager at Grapeland considered himself an example for the Nucor policy—"the sky is the limit." He had started in an entry position and risen to the head of this plant of two hundred people.

Table 1 below shows the productivity of the South Carolina plant in tons per man-hour for a number of years. The year 1999 set a record for overall tonnage,

TABLE 1

Tons per Man-Hour

1977	0.163	1982	0.208	1987	0.218
1978	0.179	1983	0.215	1988	0.249
1979	0.192	1984	0.214	1999	0.251
1980	0.195	1985	0.228	2000	0.241
1981	0.194	1986	0.225	2004	0.222

before a downturn which bottomed in 2002 but had begun to rise again by 2004.

Steel Divisions

Nucor moved into the steel business in 1968 to provide raw material for the Vulcraft plants. Iverson said, "We got into the steel business because we wanted to build a mill that could make steel as cheaply as we were buying it from foreign importers or from offshore mills." Thus, they entered the industry using the new minimill technology after they took a task force of four people around the world to investigate new technological advancements. A case writer from Harvard recounted the development of the steel divisions:

By 1967 about 60% of each Vulcraft sales dollar was spent on materials, primarily steel. Thus, the goal of keeping costs low made it imperative to obtain steel economically. In addition, in 1967 Vulcraft bought about 60% of its steel from foreign sources. As the Vulcraft Division grew, Nucor became concerned about its ability to obtain an adequate economical supply of steel and in 1968 began construction of its first steel mill in Darlington, South Carolina. By 1972 the Florence, South Carolina, joist plant was purchasing over 90% of its steel from this mill. The Fort Payne, Alabama plant bought about 50% of its steel from Florence. Since the mill had excess capacity, Nucor began to market its steel products to outside customers. In 1972, 75% of the shipments of Nucor steel was to Vulcraft and 25% was to other customers.

Between 1973 and 1981, they constructed three more bar mills and their accompanying rolling mills to convert the billits into bars, flats, rounds, channels, and other products. Iverson explained in 1984:

In constructing these mills we have experimented with new processes and new manufacturing techniques. We serve as our own general contractor and design and build much of our own equipment. In one or more of our mills we have built our own continuous casting unit, reheat furnaces, cooling beds and in Utah even our own mill stands. All of these to date have cost under $125 per ton of annual capacity—compared with projected costs for large integrated mills of $1,200—1,500 per ton of annual capacity, ten times our cost. Our mills have high productivity. We currently use less than four man hours to produce a ton of steel. Our total employment costs are less than $60 per ton compared with the average employment costs of the seven largest U.S. steel companies of close to $130 per ton. Our total labor costs are less than 20% of our sales price.

In 1987, Nucor was the first steel company in the world to begin to build a minimill to manufacture steel sheet, the raw material for the auto industry and other major manufacturers. This project opened up another 50 percent of the total steel market. The first plant in Crawfordsville, Indiana, was successful, and three additional sheet mills were constructed between 1989 and 1990. Through the years these steel plants were significantly modernized and expanded until the total capacity was 3 million tons per year at a capital cost of less than $170 dollars per ton by 1999. Nucor's total steel production capacity was 5.9 million tons per year at a cost of $300 per ton of annual capacity. The eight mills sold 80 percent of their output to outside customers and the balance to other Nucor divisions.

By 2005, Nucor had sixteen steel facilities producing three times as much as in 1999. The number of bar mills had grown to nine mills with capacity of 6 million tons by the addition of Birmingham's four mills with 2 million tons and Auburn's 400,000 tons. The sheet mills grew to four and increased capacity one-third with the acquisition of Trico. Nucor-Yamato's structural steel capacity was increased by half a million tons from the South Carolina plant. The new million ton plate mill opened in North Carolina in 2000. Ninety-three percent of production was sold to outside customers.

All four of the original "bar mills" were actually two mills operating side by side. One mill concentrated on the larger bar products, which had separate production and customer demands, while the other mill concentrated on smaller diameter bar stock. Throughout Nucor each operation was housed in its own separate building with its own staff. Nucor designed its processes to limit work-in-process inventory, to limit space, to utilize a pull approach to material usage, and to increase flexibility.

The Steel Making Process

A steel mill's work is divided into two phases, preparation of steel of the proper "chemistry" and the forming of the steel into the desired products. The typical minimill utilized scrap steel, such as junk auto parts, instead of the iron ore, which would be used in larger, integrated steel mills. The typical bar minimill had an annual capacity of 200–600 thousand tons, compared with the 7 million tons of Bethlehem Steel's Sparrow's Point, Maryland, integrated plant.

In the bar mills a charging bucket fed loads of scrap steel into electric arc furnaces. The melted load, called a heat, was poured into a ladle to be carried by an overhead crane to the casting machine. In the casting machine, the liquid steel was extruded as a continuous red-hot solid bar of steel and cut into lengths weighing some 900 pounds called "billets." In the typical plant, the billet, about 4 inches in cross section and about 20 feet long, was held temporarily in a pit where it cooled to normal temperatures. Periodically billets were carried to the rolling mill and placed in a reheat oven to bring them up to 2000°F at which temperature they would be malleable. In the rolling mill, presses and dies progressively converted the billet into the desired round bars, angles, channels, flats, and other products. After cutting to standard lengths, they were moved to the warehouse.

Nucor's first steel mill, which employed more than five hundred people, was located in Darlington, South Carolina. The mill, with its three electric arc furnaces, operated 24 hours per day, 5 1/2 days per week. Nucor had made a number of improvements in the melting and casting operations. The general manager of the Darlington plant developed a system that involved preheating the ladles, allowing for the faster flow of steel into the caster and resulting in better control of the steel characteristics. Thus, less time and lower capital investment were required at Darlington than other minimills at the time of its construction. The casting machines were "continuous casters," as opposed to the old batch method. The objective in the "front" of the mill was to keep the casters working. At the time the Darlington plant was also perhaps the only mill in the country that regularly avoided the reheating of billets. This saved $10–12 per ton in fuel usage and losses due to oxidation of the steel. The cost of developing this process had been $12 million. All research projects had not been successful. The company spent approximately $2 million in an unsuccessful effort to utilize resistance heating. They lost even more on an effort at induction melting. As Iverson told *Metal Producing*, "That costs us a lot of money. Time wise it was very expensive. But you have got to make mistakes and we've had lots of failures."

The Darlington design became the basis for plants in Nebraska, Texas, and Utah. The Texas plant had cost under $80 per ton of annual capacity. Whereas the typical minimill at the time cost approximately $250 per ton, the average cost of Nucor's four mills was under $135. An integrated mill was expected to cost between $1,200 and $1,500 per ton.

The Darlington plant was organized into twelve natural groups for the purpose of incentive pay. Two mills each had two shifts with three groups—melting and casting, rolling mill, and finishing. In melting and casting, there were three or four different standards, depending on the material, established by the department manager years ago based on historical performance. The general manager stated, "We don't change the standards." The caster, key to the operation, was used at a 92 percent level—one greater than the claims of the manufacturer. For every good ton of billet above the standard hourly rate for the week, workers in the group received a 4 percent bonus. For example, with a common standard of 10 tons per run hour and an actual rate for the week of 28 tons per hour, the workers would receive a bonus of 72 percent of their base rate in the week's paycheck. In the rolling mill, there were more than one hundred products, each with a different historical standard. Workers received a 4 percent to 6 percent bonus for every good ton sheared per hour for the week over the computed standard. A manager stated, "Melt-shop employees don't ask me how much it costs Chaparral or LTV to make a billet. They want to know what it costs Darlington, Norfolk, Jewitt to put a billet on the ground—scrap costs, alloy costs, electrical costs, refractory, gas, etc. Everybody from Charlotte to Plymouth watches the nickels and dimes."

Management Philosophy

Aycock, while still the Darlington manager, stated,

> The key to making a profit when selling a product with no aesthetic value, or a product that you really can't differentiate from your competitors, is cost. I don't look at us as a fantastic marketing organization, even though I think we are pretty good; but we don't try to overcome unreasonable costs by mass marketing. We maintain low costs by keeping the employee force at the level it should be, not doing things that aren't necessary to achieve our goals, and allowing people to function on their own and by judging them on their results.

> To keep a cooperative and productive workforce you need, number one, to be completely honest about everything; number two, to allow each employee as much as possible to make decisions about that employee's work, to find easier and more productive ways to perform duties; and number three, to be as fair as possible to all employees. Most of the changes we make in work procedures and in equipment come from the employees. They really know the problems of their jobs better than anyone else.

> To communicate with my employees, I try to spend time in the plant and at intervals have meetings with the employees. Usually if they have a question they just visit me. Recently a small group visited me in my office to discuss our vacation policy. They had some suggestions and, after listening to them, I had to agree that the ideas were good.

In discussing his philosophy for dealing with the work force, the Florence manager stated,

> I believe very strongly in the incentive system we have. We are a non-union shop and we all feel that the way to stay so is to take care of our people and show them we care. I think that's easily done because of our fewer layers of management. . . . I spend a good part of my time in the plant, maybe an hour or so a day. If a man wants to know anything, for example an insurance question, I'm there and they walk right up to me and ask me questions, which I'll answer the best I know how.

> We don't lay our people off and we make a point of telling our people this. In the slowdown of 1994, we scheduled our line for four days, but the men were allowed to come in the fifth day for maintenance work at base pay. The men in the plant on an average running bonus might make $17 to $19 an hour. If their base pay is half that, on Friday they would only get $8–$9 an hour. Surprisingly, many of the men did not want to come in on Friday. They felt comfortable with just working four days a week. They are happy to have that extra day off. About 20% of the people took the 5th day at base rate, but still no one had been laid off, in an industry with a strong business cycle.

In an earlier business cycle, the executive committee decided in view of economic conditions that a pay freeze was necessary. The employees normally received an increase in their base pay the first of June. The decision was made at that time to freeze wages. The officers of the company, as a show of good faith, accepted a 5 percent pay cut. In addition to announcing this to the workers with a stuffer in their pay envelopes, meetings were held. Each production line, or incentive group of workers, met in the plant conference room with all supervision—foreman, plant production manager, and division manager. The economic crisis the company was facing was explained to the employees by the production manager, and all of their questions were answered.

The Personnel and Incentive Systems

The foremost characteristic of Nucor's personnel system was its incentive plan. Another major personnel policy was providing job security. Also all employees at Nucor received the same fringe benefits. There was only one group insurance plan. Holidays and vacations did not differ by job. Every child of every Nucor employee received up to $1,200 a year for four years if they chose to go on to higher education, including technical schools. The company had no executive dining rooms or restrooms, no fishing lodges, company cars, or reserved parking places.

Jim Coblin, Nucor's vice president of human resources, described Nucor's systems for *HRMagazine* in a 1994 article, "No-frills HR at Nucor: A Lean, Bottom-Line Approach at This Steel Company Empowers Employees." Coblin, as benefits administrator, received part-time help from one of the corporate secretaries in the corporate office. The plants typically used someone from their finance department to handle compensation issues, although two plants had personnel generalists. Nucor plants did not have job descriptions, finding they caused more problems than they solved, given the flexible work force and nonunion status of Nucor employees. Surprisingly, Coblin found performance appraisal a waste of time. If an employee was not performing well, the problem would be dealt with directly. He had observed that when promotional opportunities became available, the performance appraisals were not much help filling the position. So he saw both of these as just more paperwork. The key, he believed, was not to put a maximum on what employees could earn and pay them directly for productivity. Iverson firmly believed that the bonus should be direct and involve no discretion on part of a manager.

Employees were kept informed about the company. Charts showing the division's results in return-on-assets and bonus payoff were posted in prominent places in the plant. The personnel manager commented that as he traveled around to all the plants, he found everyone in the company could tell him the level of profits in their division. The general managers held dinners at least once but usually twice a year with each of their employees. The dinners were held with fifty or sixty employees at a time, resulting in as many as twenty dinners per year. After introductory remarks the floor was open for discussion of any work-related problems. There was a new employee orientation program and an employee handbook that contained personnel policies and rules. The corporate office sent all news releases to each division where they were posted on bulletin boards. Each employee in the company also received a copy of the annual report. For the last several years the cover of the annual report had contained the names of all Nucor employees.

Absenteeism and tardiness were not problems at Nucor. Each employee had four days of absences before pay was reduced. In addition to these, missing work was allowed for jury duty, military leave, or the death of close relatives. After this, a day's absence cost them bonus pay for that week, and lateness of more than a half-hour meant the loss of bonus for that day.

Safety was a concern of Nucor's critics. With ten fatalities in the 1980s, Nucor was committed to doing better. Safety administrators had been appointed in each plant, and safety had improved in the 1990s. The company also had a formal grievance procedure, although the Darlington manager couldn't recall the last grievance he had processed.

The company had conducted attitude surveys every three years for over two decades. These provided management insight into employee attitudes on twenty issues and allowed comparisons across plants and divisions. There were some concerns and differences but most employees appeared very satisfied with Nucor as an employer. The surveys suggested that pay was not the only thing the workers liked about Nucor. The personnel manager said that an NBC interviewer, working on the documentary "If Japan Can, Why Can't We," often heard employees say, "I enjoy working for Nucor because Nucor is the best, the most productive, and the most profitable company that I know of."

The average hourly worker's pay was over twice the average earnings paid by other manufacturing companies in the states where Nucor's plants were located. In many rural communities where Nucor had located, they provided better wages than most other manufacturers. The new plant in Hertford County illustrated this point as reported in a June 21, 1998, article in *The Charlotte Observer*, entitled "Hope on the Horizon: In Hertford County, Poverty Reigns and Jobs Are Scarce." Here the author wrote, "In North Carolina's forgotten northeastern corner, where poverty rates run more than twice the state average, Nucor's $300 million steel mill is a dream realized." The plant on the banks of the Chowan River in North Carolina's banks coastal district would have their employees earning a rumored $60,000 a year, three times the local average manufacturing wage upon completion. Nucor had recently begun developing its plant sites with the expectation of other companies co-locating to save shipping costs. Four companies have announced plans to locate close to Nucor's property, adding another one to two hundred jobs. People couldn't believe such wages, but calls to the plant's chief financial officer got "we don't like to promise too much, but $60,000 might be a little low." The average wage for these jobs at Darlington was $70,000. The plant's CFO added that Nucor didn't try to set pay "a buck over Wal-Mart" but went for the best workers. The article noted that steel work is hot and often dangerous, and that turnover at the plant may be high as people adjust to this and Nucor's hard-driving team system. He added, "Slackers don't last." The state of North Carolina had given $155 million in tax credits over twenty-five years. The local preacher said, "In 15 years, Baron (a local child) will be making $75,000 a year at Nucor, not in jail. I have a place now I can hold in front of him and say 'Look, right here. This is for you.'"

The Incentive System

There were four incentive programs at Nucor, one each for (1) production workers, (2) department heads, (3) staff people such as accountants, secretaries, or engineers, and (4) senior management, which included the division managers. All these programs were based on group performance.

Within the production program, groups ranged in size from twenty-five to thirty people and had definable and measurable operations. The company believed that a program should be simple and that bonuses should be paid promptly. "We don't have any discretionary bonuses—zero. It is all based on performance. Now we don't want anyone to sit in judgment, because it never is fair," said Iverson. The personnel manager stated, "Their bonus is based on roughly 90% of historical time it takes to make a particular joist. If during a week they make joists at 60% less than the standard time, they receive a 60% bonus." This was paid with the regular pay the following week. The complete pay check amount, including overtime, was multiplied by the bonus factor. A bonus was not paid when equipment was not operating. "We have the philosophy that when equipment is not operating everybody suffers and the bonus for downtime is zero." The foremen are also part of the group and received the same bonus as the employees they supervised.

The second incentive program was for department heads in the various divisions. The incentive pay here was based on division contribution, defined as the division earnings before corporate expenses and profit sharing are determined. Bonuses were reported to run between 0 and 90 percent (average 35 to 50 percent) of a person's base salary. The base salaries at this level were set at 75 percent of industry norms.

There was a third plan for people who were not production workers, department managers, or senior managers. Their bonus was based on either the division return-on-assets or the corporate return-on-assets depending on the unit they were a part of. Bonuses were typically 30 percent or more of a person's base salary for corporate positions.

The fourth program was for the senior officers. The senior officers had no employment contracts, pension or retirement plans, or other perquisites. Their base salaries were set at about 75 percent of what an individual doing similar work in other companies would receive. Once return-on-equity reached 9 percent, slightly below the average for manufacturing firms, 5 percent of net earnings before taxes went into a pool, which was divided among the officers based on their salaries. "Now if return-on-equity for the company reaches, say 20%, which it has, then we can wind up with as much as 190% of our base salaries and 115% on top of that in stock. We get both." Half the bonus was paid in cash, and half was deferred. Individual bonuses ranged from zero to several hundred percent, averaging 75 to 150 percent.

However, the opposite was true as well. In 1982, the return was 8 percent, and the executives received no bonus. Iverson's pay in 1981 was approximately $300,000 but dropped the next year to $110,000. "I think that ranked by total compensation I was the lowest paid CEO in the Fortune 500. I was kind of proud of that, too." In his 1997 book, *Plain Talk: Lessons From a Business Maverick*, Iverson said, "Can management expect employees to be loyal if we lay them all off at every dip of the economy, while we go on padding our own pockets." Even so by 1986, Iverson's stock was worth over $10 million, and the once Vulcraft manager was a millionaire.

In lieu of a retirement plan, the company had a profit sharing plan with a deferred trust. Each year 10 percent of pretax earnings was put into profit sharing for all people below officer level. Twenty percent of this was set aside to be paid to employees in the following March as a cash bonus, and the remainder was put into trust for each employee on the basis of the percentage of their earnings as a percentage of total wages paid within the corporation. The employee was vested after the first year. Employees received a quarterly statement of their balance in profit sharing.

The company had an Employer Monthly Stock Investment Plan to which Nucor added 10 percent to the amount the employee contributed on the purchase of any Nucor stock and paid the commission. After each five years of service with the company, the employee received a service award consisting of five shares of Nucor stock. Moreover, if profits were good, extraordinary bonus payments would be made to the employees. For example, in December 1998 each employee received an $800 payment.

According to Iverson:

> I think the first obligation of the company is to the stockholder and to its employees. I find in this country too many cases where employees are underpaid and corporate management is making huge social donations for self-fulfillment. We regularly give donations, but we have a very interesting corporate policy. First, we give donations where our employees are. Second, we give donations that will benefit our employees, such as to the YMCA. It is a difficult area and it requires a lot of thought. There is certainly a strong social responsibility for a company, but it cannot be at the expense of the employees or the stockholders.

Having welcomed a parade of visitors over the years, Iverson had become concerned with the pattern apparent at other companies' steel plants: "They only do one or two of the things we do. It's not just incentives or the scholarship program; it's all those things put together that results in a unified philosophy for the company."

Building on Their Success

Throughout the 1980s and 1990s, Nucor continued to take the initiative and be the prime mover in steel and the industries vertically related to steel. For example, in 1984 Nucor broke with the industry pattern of basing the price of an order of steel on the quantity ordered. Iverson noted, "Some time ago we began to realize that with computer order entry and billing, the extra charge for smaller orders was not cost justified." In a seemingly risky move in 1986, Nucor began construction of a $25 million plant in Indiana to manufacture steel fasteners. Imports had grown to 90 percent of this market as U.S. companies failed to compete. Iverson said, "We're going to bring that business back; we can make bolts as cheaply as foreign producers." A second plant, in 1995, gave Nucor 20 percent of the U.S. market for steel fasteners. Nucor also acquired a steel bearings manufacturer in 1986, which Iverson called "a good fit with our business, our policies and our people."

In early 1986, Iverson announced plans for a revolutionary plant at Crawfordsville, Indiana, which would be the first minimill in the world to manufacture flat-rolled or sheet steel, the last bastion of the integrated manufacturers. This market alone was twice the size of the existing market for minimill products. It would be a quarter of a billion dollar gamble on a new technology. The plant was expected to halve the integrated manufacturer's $3 of labor per ton and save $50 to $75 on a $400 a ton selling price. If it worked, the profit from this plant alone would come close to the profit of the whole corporation. *Forbes* commented, "If any mini-mill can meet the challenge, it's Nucor. But expect the going to be tougher this time around." If successful, Nucor had the licensing rights to the next two plants built in the world with this technology.

Nucor had spent millions trying to develop the process when it heard of some promising developments at a German company. In the spring of 1986, Aycock flew to Germany to see the pilot machine at SMS Schloemann-Siemag AG. In December the Germans came to Charlotte for the first of what they thought would be many meetings to hammer out a deal with Nucor. Iverson shocked them when he announced Nucor was ready to proceed to build the first plant of its kind.

Keith Busse was given the job of building the Crawfordsville, Indiana, steel sheet plant. The process of bringing this plant online was so exciting it became the basis for a bestselling book by Robert Preston, which was serialized in *New Yorker* magazine. Preston reported on a conversation at dinner during construction between Iverson and Busse. Thinking about the future, Busse was worried that Nucor might someday become like Big Steel. He asked, "How do we allow Nucor to grow without expanding the bureaucracy?" He commented on the vice presidents stacked on vice presidents, research departments, assistants to assistants, and so on. Iverson agreed. Busse seriously suggested, "Maybe we're going to need group vice presidents." Iverson's heated response was, "Do you want to ruin the company? That's the old Harvard Business School thinking. They would only get in the way, slow us down." He said the company could at least double, to $2 billion, before it added a new level of management. "I hope that by the time we have group vice presidents I'll be collecting Social Security."

The gamble on the new plant paid off, and Busse, the general manager of the plant, became a key man within Nucor. The new mill began operations in August of 1989 and reached 15 percent of capacity by the end of the year. In June of 1990, it had its first profitable month, and Nucor announced the construction of a second plant in Arkansas.

In December 1992, Nucor signed a letter of intent with Oregon Steel Mills to build a sheet mill on the West Coast to begin in 1994. This project was later canceled. The supply and cost of scrap steel to feed the minimills was an important future concern to Iverson. So at the beginning of 1993 Nucor announced the construction of a plant in Trinidad to supply its mills with iron carbide pellets. The innovative plant would cost $60 million and take a year and a half to complete. In 1994, the two existing sheet mills were expanded, and a new $500 million, 1.8 million ton sheet mill in South Carolina was announced, to begin operation in early 1997.

In what the *New York Times* called their "most ambitious project yet," in 1987 Nucor began a joint venture with Yamato Kogyo, Ltd. to make structural steel products in a mill on the Mississippi River in a direct challenge to the Big Three integrated steel companies. He put John Correnti in charge of the operation. Correnti built and then became the general manager of Nucor-Yamato when it started up in 1988. In 1991, he surprised many people by deciding to double Nucor-Yamato's capacity by 1994. It became Nucor's largest division and the largest wide flange

producer in the United States. By 1995, Bethlehem Steel was the only other wide flange producer of structural steel products left and had plans to leave the business.

Nucor started up its first facility to produce metal buildings in 1987. A second metal buildings facility began operations in late 1996 in South Carolina and a new steel deck facility, in Alabama, was announced for 1997. At the end of 1997, the Arkansas sheet mill was undergoing a $120 million expansion to include a galvanizing facility.

In 1995, Nucor became involved in its first international venture, an ambitious project with Brazil's Companhia Siderurgica National to build a $700 million steel mill in the state of Ceara. While other minimills were cutting deals to buy and sell abroad, Nucor was planning to ship iron from Brazil and process it in Trinidad.

Nucor set records for sales and net earnings in 1997. In the spring of 1998, as Iverson approached his seventy-third birthday, he was commenting, "People ask me when I'm going to retire. I tell them our mandatory retirement age is 95, but I may change that when I get there." It surprised the world when, in October 1998, Ken Iverson left the board. He retired as chairman at the end the year. Although sales for 1998 decreased 1 percent and net earnings were down 10 percent, the management made a number of long-term investments and closed draining investments. Start-up began at the new South Carolina steam mill and at the Arkansas sheet mill expansion. The plans for a North Carolina steel plate mill in Hertford were announced. This would bring Nucor's total steel production capacity to 12 million tons per year. Moreover, the plant in Trinidad, which had proven much more expensive than was originally expected, was deemed unsuccessful and closed. Finally, directors approved the repurchase of up to 5 million shares of Nucor stock.

Still, the downward trends at Nucor continued. Sales and earnings were down 3 percent and 7 percent, respectively, for 1999 (see Appendix 1 for financial reports and Appendix 2 for financial ratios). However, these trends did not seem to affect the company's investments. Expansions were underway in the steel mills, and a third building systems facility was under construction in Texas. Nucor was actively searching for a site for a joist plant in the northeast. A letter of intent was signed with Australian and Japanese companies to form a joint venture to commercialize the strip casting technology. To understand the challenges facing Nucor, industry, technology, and environmental trends in the 1980s and 1990s must be considered.

The U.S. Steel Industry in the 1980s

The early 1980s had been the worst years in decades for the steel industry. Data from the American Iron and Steel Institute showed shipments falling from 100 million tons in 1979 to the mid-eighty levels in 1980 and 1981. A slackening in the economy, particularly in auto sales, led the decline. In 1986, when industry capacity was at 130 million tons, the outlook was for a continued decline in per-capita consumption and movement toward capacity in the 90–100 million ton range. The chairman of Armco saw "millions of tons chasing a market that's not there: excess capacity that must be eliminated."

The large, integrated steel firms, such as U.S. Steel and Armco, which made up the major part of the industry, were the hardest hit. *The Wall Street Journal* stated, "The decline has resulted from such problems as high labor and energy costs in mining and processing iron ore, a lack of profits and capital to modernize plants, and conservative management that has hesitated to take risks."

These companies produced a wide range of steels, primarily from ore processed in blast furnaces. They had found it difficult to compete with imports, usually from Japan, and had given market share to imports. They sought the protection of import quotas. Imported steel accounted for 20 percent of the U.S. steel consumption, up from 12 percent in the early 1970s. The U.S. share of world production of raw steel declined from 19 percent to 14 percent over the period. Imports of light bar products accounted for less that 9 percent of the U.S. consumption of those products in 1981, according to the U.S. Commerce Department, while imports of wire rod totaled 23 percent of U.S. consumption.

Iron Age stated that exports, as a percent of shipments in 1985, were 34 percent for Nippon, 26 percent for British Steel, 30 percent for Krupp, 49 percent for USINOR of France, and less than 1 percent for every American producer on the list. The consensus of steel experts was that imports would average 23 percent of the market in the last half of the 1980s.

Iverson was one of the very few in the steel industry to oppose import restrictions. He saw an outdated U.S. steel industry that had to change.

We Americans have been conditioned to believe in our technical superiority. For many generations a continuing stream of new inventions and manufacturing techniques allowed us to far outpace the rest of the world in both volume and efficiency of production. In many areas this is no longer true and particularly in the steel industry. In the last three decades, almost all the major developments in steel making were made outside the U.S. I would be negligent if I did not recognize the significant contribution that the government has made toward the technological deterioration of the steel industry. Unrealistic depreciation schedules, high corporate taxes, excessive regulation and jaw-boning for lower steel prices have make it difficult for the U.S. steel industry to borrow or generate the huge quantities of capital required for modernization.

By the mid 1980s, the integrated mills were moving fast to get back into the game: They were restructuring, cutting capacity, dropping unprofitable lines, focusing products, and trying to become responsive to the market. The industry made a pronounced move toward segmentation. Integrated producers focused on mostly flat-rolled and structural grades, reorganized steel companies focused on a limited range of products, minimills dominated the bar and light structural product areas, and specialty steel firms sought niches. There was an accelerated shutdown of older plants, elimination of products by some firms, and the installation of new product lines with new technologies by others. High-tonnage mills restructured to handle sheets, plates, structural beams, high-quality bars, and large pipe and tubular products which allowed resurgence of specialized mills: cold-finished bar manufacturers, independent strip mills, and minimills.

The road for the integrated mills was not easy. As *Purchasing* pointed out, tax laws and accounting rules slowed the closing of inefficient plants. Shutting down a ten thousand-person plant could require a firm to hold a cash reserve of $100 million to fund health, pension, and insurance liabilities. The chairman of Armco commented, "Liabilities associated with a planned shutdown are so large that they can quickly devastate a company's balance sheet."

Joint ventures had arisen to produce steel for a specific market or region. The chairman of USX called them "an important new wrinkle in steel's fight for survival" and stated, "If there had been more joint ventures like these two decades ago, the U.S. steel industry might have built only half of the dozen or so hot-strip mills it put up in that time and avoided today's over-capacity."

The American Iron and Steel Institute reported steel production in 1988 of 99.3 million tons, up from 89.2 in 1987, and the highest in seven years. As a result of modernization programs, 60.9 percent of production was from continuous casters. Exports for steel increased and imports fell. Some steel experts believed the United States was now cost competitive with Japan. However, 1989 proved to be a year of "waiting for the other shoe to drop," according to *Metal Center News*. U.S. steel production was hampered by a new recession, the expiration of the voluntary import restraints, and labor negotiations in several companies. Declines in car production and consumer goods hit flat-rolled hard. AUJ Consultants told MCN, "The U.S. steel market has peaked. Steel consumption is tending down. By 1990, we expect total domestic demand to dip under 90 million tons."

The U.S. Steel Industry in the 1990s

The economic slowdown of the early 1990s did lead to a decline in the demand for steel through early 1993, but by 1995, America was in its best steel market in twenty years and many companies were building new flat-roll minimills. A *Business Week* article at the time described it as "the race of the Nucor look-alikes." Six years after Nucor pioneered the low-cost German technology in Crawfordsville, Indiana, the competition was finally gearing up to compete. Ten new projects were expected to add 20 million tons per year of the flat-rolled steel, raising U.S. capacity by as much as 40 percent by 1998. These mills opened in 1997 just as the industry was expected to move into a cyclical slump. It was no surprise that worldwide competition increased, and companies that had previously focused on their home markets began a race to become global powerhouses. The foreign push was new for U.S. firms who had focused on defending their home markets. U.S. minimills focused their international expansion primarily in Asia and South America.

Meanwhile in 1994, U.S. Steel, North America's largest integrated steel producer, began a major business process reengineering project to improve order fulfillment performance and customer satisfaction on the heels of a decade of restructuring. According to *Steel Times International*, "US Steel had to completely change the way it did business. Cutting labor costs, and increasing reliability and productivity took the company a long way towards improving profitability and competitiveness. However, it became clear that this leaner organization still had to implement new technologies and business processes if it was to maintain a competitive advantage." The goals of the business process reengineering project included a sharp reduction in cycle time, greatly decreased levels of inventory, shorter order lead times, and the ability to offer real-time promise dates to customers. In 1995, the company successfully installed integrated planning/production/order fulfillment software and results were very positive. U.S. Steel believed that the reengineering project had positioned it for a future of increased competition, tighter markets, and raised customer expectations.

In late 1997 and again in 1998, the decline in demand prompted Nucor and other U.S. companies to slash prices in order to compete with the unprecedented surge of imports. By the last quarter of 1998, these imports had led to the filing of unfair trade complaints with U.S. trade regulators, causing steel prices in the spot market to drop sharply in August and September before they stabilized. A press release by the U.S. secretary of commerce, William Daley, stated "I will not stand by and allow U.S. workers, communities and companies to bear the brunt of other nations' problematic policies and practices. We are the most open economy of the world. But we are not the world's dumpster." In early 1999, American Iron and Steel Institute reported in its Opinion section of its web page the following quotes by Andy Sharkey and Hank Barnette. Sharkey said, "With many of the world's economies in recession, and no signs of recovery on the horizon, it should come as no surprise that the United States is now seen as the only reliable market for manufactured goods. This can be seen in the dramatic surge of imports." Barnette noted, "While there are different ways to gauge the impact of the Asian crisis, believe me, it has already hit. Just ask the 163,000 employees of the U.S. steel industry."

The Commerce Department concluded in March 1999 that six countries had illegally dumped stainless steel in the United States at prices below production costs or home market prices. The Commerce Department found that Canada, South Korea, and Taiwan were guilty only of dumping, while Belgium, Italy, and South Africa also gave producers unfair subsidies that effectively lowered prices. However, on June 23, 1999, *The Wall Street Journal* reported that the Senate decisively shut off an attempt to restrict U.S. imports of steel despite industry complaints that a flood of cheap imports were driving them out of business. Advisors of President Clinton were reported to have said the president would likely veto the bill if it passed. Administrative officials opposed the bill because it would violate international trade law and leave the United States open to retaliation.

The American Iron and Steel Institute reported that in May 1999, U.S. steel mills shipped 8,330,000 net tons, a decrease of 6.7 percent from the 8,927,000 net tons shipped in May 1998. They also stated that for the first five months of 1999 shipments were 41,205,000 net tons, down 10 percent from the same period in 1998. AISI President and CEO Andrew Sharkey III said, "Once again, the May data show clearly that America's steel trade crisis continues. U.S. steel companies and employees continue to be injured by high levels of dumping and subsidized imports. . . . In addition, steel inventory levels remain excessive, and steel operating rates continue to be very low."

As the 1990s ended, Nucor was the second-largest steel producer in the United States, behind USX. The company's market capitalization was about two times that of the next smaller competitor. Even in a tight industry, someone can win. Nucor was in the best position because the industry was very fragmented, and there were many marginal competitors.

Steel Technology and the Minimill

A new type of mill, the "minimill," had emerged in the United States during the 1970s to compete with the integrated mill. The minimill used electric arc furnaces initially to manufacture a narrow product line from scrap steel. The leading U.S. minimills in the 1980s were Nucor, Florida Steel, Georgetown Steel, North Star Steel, and Chaparral. Between the late 1970s and 1980s, the integrated mills' market share fell from about 90 percent to about 60 percent, with the integrated steel companies averaging a 7 percent return on equity, the minimills averaging 14 percent, and some, such as Nucor, achieving about 25 percent. In the 1990s, minimills tripled their output to capture 17 percent of domestic shipments. Moreover, integrated mills' market share fell to around 40 percent, while minimills' share rose to 23 percent, reconstructed

mills increased their share from 11 percent to 28 percent, and specialized mills increased their share from 1 percent to 6 percent.

Some experts believed that a relatively new technology, the twin shell electric arc furnace, would help minimills increase production and lower costs and take market share. According to the *Pittsburgh Business Times*, "With a twin shell furnace, one shell—the chamber holding the scrap to be melted—is filled and heated. During the heating of the first shell, the second shell is filled. When the heating is finished on the first shell, the electrodes move to the second. The first shell is emptied and refilled before the second gets hot." This increased the production by 60 percent. Twin shell production had been widely adopted in the last few years. For example, Nucor Steel began running a twin shell furnace in November 1996 in Berkeley, South Carolina, and installed another in Norfolk, Nebraska, which began operations in 1997. "Everyone accepts twin shells as a good concept because there's a lot of flexibility of operation," said Rodney Mott, vice president and general manager of Nucor-Berkeley. However, this move toward twin shell furnaces could mean trouble in the area of scrap availability. According to an October 1997 quote in *Pittsburgh Business Times* by Ralph Smaller, vice president of process technology at Kvaerner, "Innovations that feed the electric furnaces' production of flat-rolled (steel) will increase the demand on high quality scrap and alternatives. The technological changes are just beginning and will accelerate over the next few years."

According to a September 1997 *Industry Week* article, steelmakers around the world were now closely monitoring the development of continuous "strip casting" technology, which may prove to be the next leap forward for the industry. "The objective of strip casting is to produce thin strips of steel (in the 1-mm to 4-mm range) as liquid steel flows from a tundish—the stationary vessel which received molten steel from the ladle. It would eliminate the slab-casting stage and all of the rolling that now takes place in a hot mill." Strip casting was reported to have some difficult technological challenges, but companies in Germany, France, Japan, Australia, Italy, and Canada had strip-casting projects under way. In fact, all of the significant development work in strip casting was taking place outside the United States.

Larry Kavanaph, American Iron and Steel Institute vice president for manufacturing and technology, said, "Steel is a very high-tech industry, but nobody knows it." Today's most productive steel-making facilities incorporated advanced metallurgical practices, sophisticated process-control sensors, state-of-the-art computer controls, and the latest refinements in continuous casting and rolling mill technology. Michael Shot, vice president–manufacturing at Carpenter Technology Corp., Reading, Pennsylvania, a specialty steels and premium-grade alloys producer, said, "You don't survive in this industry unless you have the technology to make the best products in the world in the most efficient manner."

Environmental and Political Issues

Not all stakeholders were happy with the way Nucor did business. In June 1998, *Waste News* reported that Nucor's mill in Crawfordsville, Indiana, was cited by the United States Environmental Protection Agency for alleged violations of federal and state clean-air rules. The Pamlico-Tar River Foundation, the NC Coastal Federation, and the Environmental Defense Fund had concerns about the state's decision to allow the company to start building the plant before the environmental review was completed. According to the *News & Observer* website, "The environmental groups charge that the mill will discharge 6,720 tons of pollutants into the air each year."

Moreover, there were other concerns about the fast-track approval of the facility being built in Hertford County. First, this plant was located on the banks of one of the most important and sensitive stretches of the Chowan, a principle tributary to the national treasure Albemarle Sound and the last bastion of the state's once vibrant river-herring fishery. North Carolina passed a law in 1997 that required the restoration of this fishery through a combination of measures designed to prevent overfishing, restore spawning and nursery habitats, and improve water quality in the Chowan. "New federal law requires extra care in protecting essential habitat for the herring, which spawn upstream," according to an article in the *Business Journal.* Second were the concerns regarding the excessive incentives the state gave to convince Nucor to build a $300 million steel mill in North Carolina. Some questioned whether the promise of three hundred well-paying jobs in Hertford County was worth the $155 million in tax breaks the state was giving Nucor to locate there.

Management Evolution

As Nucor opened new plants, each was made a division and given a general manager with complete responsibility for all aspects of the business. The corporate office did not involve itself in the routine functioning of the divisions. There was no centralized purchasing, or hiring and firing, or division accounting. The total corporate staff was still less than twenty-five people, including clerical staff when 1999 began.

In 1984, Dave Aycock moved into the corporate office as president. Ken Iverson was chief executive officer and chairman. Iverson, Aycock, and Sam Siegel operated as an executive board, providing overall direction to the corporation. By 1990, Aycock, who had invested his money wisely, owned over six hundred thousand shares of Nucor stock, five hotels and farms in three states, and was ready to retire. He was 60, five years younger than Iverson, and was concerned that if he waited, he and Iverson might be leaving the company at the same time. Two people stood out as candidates for the presidency, Keith Busse and John Correnti. In November, Iverson called Correnti to the Charlotte airport and offered him the job. Aycock commented, "Keith Busse was my choice, but I got outvoted." In June 1991, Aycock retired, and Keith Busse left Nucor to build an independent sheet mill in Indiana for a group of investors.

Thus Iverson, Correnti, and Siegel led the company. In 1993, Iverson had heart problems and major surgery. Correnti was given the CEO role in 1996. The Board of Directors had always been small, consisting of the executive team and one or two past Nucor vice presidents. Several organizations with large blocks of Nucor stock had been pressing Nucor to diversify its board membership and add outside directors. In 1996, Jim Hlavacek, head of a small consulting firm and friend of Iverson, was added to the board.

Only five, not six, members of the board were in attendance during the Board of Directors meeting in the fall of 1998, due to the death of Jim Cunningham. Near its end, Aycock read a motion, drafted by Siegel, that Ken Iverson be removed as chairman. It was seconded by Hlavacek and passed. It was announced in October that Iverson would be a chairman emeritus and a director, but after disagreements Iverson left the company completely. It was agreed Iverson would receive $500,000 a year for five years. Aycock left retirement to become chairman.

The details of Iverson's leaving did not become known until June of 1999 when John Correnti resigned after disagreements with the board and Aycock took his place. All of this was a complete surprise to investors and brought the stock price down 10 percent. Siegel commented that "the board felt Correnti was not the right person to lead Nucor into the 21st century." Aycock assured everyone he would be happy to move back into retirement as soon as replacements could be found.

In December 1999, Correnti became chairman of rival Birmingham Steel, with an astounding corporate staff of 156 people. With Nucor's organizational changes, he predicted more overhead staff and questioned their ability to move as fast in the future: "Nucor's trying to centralize and do more mentoring. That's not what grew the company to what it is today."

Aycock moved ahead with adding outside directors to the board. He appointed Harvey Gantt, principal in his own architectural firm and former mayor of Charlotte, Victoria Haynes, formally BF Goodrich's chief technology officer, and Peter Browning, chief executive of Sonoco (biographical sketches of board members and executive management are provided in Appendices 3 and 4). Then he moved to increase the corporate office staff by adding a level of executive vice presidents over four areas of business and adding two specialist jobs in strategic planning and steel technology. When Siegel retired, Aycock promoted Terry Lisenby to CFO and treasurer, and hired a director of IT to report to Lisenby (Figures 2 and 3 show the organization chart in 2000 and 2004, respectively).

Jim Coblin, vice president of human resources, believed the additions to management were necessary: "It's not bad to get a little more like other companies." He noted that the various divisions did their business cards and plant signs differently; some did not even want a Nucor sign. Sometimes six different Nucor salesmen would call on the same customer. "There is no

FIGURE 2

Nucor Organization Chart 2000

FIGURE 3

Nucor Organization Chart: Executive Management 2004

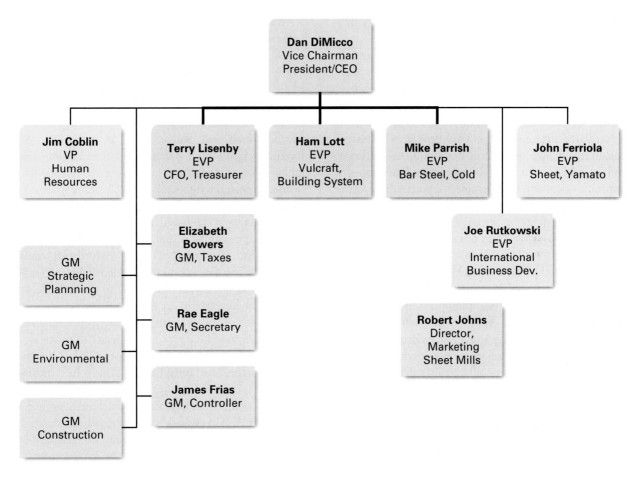

manager of human resources in the plants, so at least we needed to give additional training to the person who does most of that work at the plant," he stated. With these new additions there would be a director of information technology and two important committees, one for environmental issues and the second for audit.

He believed the old span of control of twenty might have worked well when there was less competition. Aycock considered it "ridiculous." "It was not possible to properly manage, to know what was going on. The top managers have totally lost contact with the company." Coblin was optimistic that the use of executive vice presidents would improve management. The three meetings of the general managers had slowly increased from about 1 1/2 days to about 2 1/2 days and become more focused. The new EVP

positions would bring a perspective above the level of the individual plants. Instead of fifteen individual detailed presentations, each general manager would give a short, five-minute briefing, and then there would be an in-depth presentation on the group, with team participation. After some training by Lisenby, the divisions had recently done a pretty good job with a SWOT analysis. Coblin thought these changes would make Nucor a stronger global player.

To Jeff Kemp, the new general manager of strategic planning and business development, the big issue was how to sustain earnings growth. In the U.S. steel industry, there were too many marginal competitors. The U.S. government had recently added to the problem by giving almost a billion dollars to nine mills, which simply allowed them to limp along and weaken the industry. He was looking for Nucor's opportunities within the steel industry. He asked why Nucor had bought a bearing company. His experience in the chemical industry suggested a need for Nucor to establish a position of superiority and grow globally, driving industry competition rather than reacting. He argued that a company should protect its overall market position, which could mean sacrifices for individual plants. Aycock liked Kemp's background in law and accounting and had specifically sought someone from outside the steel industry to head up Nucor's strategic planning. By June 2000, Kemp had conducted studies of other industries in the U.S. market and developed a working document that identified opportunities worthy of further analysis.

"Every company hits a plateau," Aycock observed. "You can't just go out and build plants to grow. How do you step up to the next level? I wouldn't say it's a turning point but we have to get our strategic vision and strategic plans." He stated, "We are beginning Nucor's first ever strategic planning sessions, it was not necessary before." His conclusions were partly the result of an Imaging Study Nucor had conducted.

In early 2000, Nucor had an outside consulting firm conduct a survey of the company's image as seen by the top ten to fifteen managers, including the corporate office. They also gathered the views of a few analysts and media personnel. In looking at the survey, one saw that the managers still agreed that Nucor valued risk taking, innovation, and a lean management structure with aggressive, hardworking employees who accepted the responsibility of failure along with the opportunity for success. They seemed to see Nucor as a way of doing business—not just a way of making steel—in terms of values and personality, not just business terms. When asked to associate Nucor's persona with a public figure, John Wayne was the clear choice.

The managers in the field seemed to believe the new layer of management was needed, and were not concerned about a loss of decentralization. They liked the new management team and the changes so far, particularly the improved communications with the corporate office. However, the corporate managers thought the company was changing much faster than the division managers. They also held a more positive view of the company on such things as how good the company was in their community or with the environment.

The people from the media had positive views of Nucor as hardworking and committed to its employees, an innovative risk-taking economic powerhouse.

Some—those most familiar with the company—believed the company needed to do a better job of communicating its vision during a period of transition.

Aycock believed Nucor needed to be quick to recognize developing technology in all production areas. He noted the joint venture to develop a new "strip caster," which would cast the current flat-rolled material in a more finished form. The impact could be "explosive," allowing Nucor to build smaller plants closer to markets. This would be particularly helpful on the West Coast. Nucor would own the U.S. and Brazilian rights, their partners the rest. He was also looking forward to the next generation of steel mills and wanted to own the rights this time. He praised Iverson's skill at seeing technology and committing to it.

He was very interested in acquisitions, but "they must fit strategically." A bar mill in the upper central Midwest and a flat-rolled plant in the Northeast would be good. A significant opportunity existed in preengineered buildings. Aycock intended to concentrate on steel for the next five to six years, achieving an average growth rate of 15 percent per year. In about seven years, he would like to see Nucor ready to move into other areas. He said Nucor had already "picked the low hanging grapes" and must be careful in its next moves.

Daniel DiMicco assumed the role of Nucor's president and chief executive officer in September 2000 when David Aycock stepped down as planned. Peter Browning was elected chairman of the Board of Directors. Aycock retired from the board a year later.

Sales for 2000 increased 14 percent over 1999 to reach a record level. Earnings were also at record levels, 27 percent over 1999. The year had begun on a strong footing but had turned weak by the years' end. While Nucor remained profitable, other steel companies faced bankruptcy. A Vulcraft plant was under construction in New York. It was their first northeastern operation and expanded the geographical coverage into a new region. They were also attempting a breakthrough technological step in strip casting at Crawfordsville, the Castrip process. They sold their Grinding Ball process and the Bearing Products operation because they were not a part of their core business.

In the company's annual report, DiMicco laid out their plans for 2000 and beyond:

> Our targets are to deliver an average annual earnings growth of 10–15 percent over the next ten years, to deliver a return well in excess of our cost of capital, to maintain a minimum average return on equity of 14 percent and to deliver a return on sales

of 8–10 percent. Our strategy will focus on Nucor becoming a "Market Leader" in every product group and business in which we compete. This calls for significant increases in market share for many of our core products and the maintenance of market share where we currently enjoy a leadership position.

While pointing out that it would be impossible to obtain this success through the previous strategy of greenfield construction, he added, "There will now be a heavy focus on growth through acquisitions. We will also continue growing through the commercialization of new disruptive and leapfrog technologies."

Steel and Nucor in the Twenty-First Century

In early 2001, *The Wall Street Journal* predicted that all but two of the United States's biggest steel makers would post fourth quarter losses. AK Steel Holding Corp. and Nucor Corp. were expected to have profits for the quarter of 2000, while U.S. Steel Group, a unit of USX Corp., was expected to post a profit for the year but not the fourth quarter. By October 1, more than twenty steel companies in the United States, including Bethlehem Steel Corp. and LTV Corp., the nation's third and fourth largest U.S. steel producers, respectively, had filed for bankruptcy protection. Over a dozen producers were operating under Chapter 11 bankruptcy-law protection, which allowed them to maintain market share by selling steel cheaper than non-Chapter 11 steelmakers. On October 20, *The Economist* noted that of the fourteen steel companies followed by Standard & Poor's, only Nucor was indisputably healthy. In the fall of 2001, 25 percent of domestic steel companies were in bankruptcy proceedings, although the United States was the largest importer of steel in the world. Experts believed that close to half of the U.S. steel industry might be forced to close before conditions improved.

The world steel industry found itself in the middle of one of its most unprofitable and volatile periods ever, in part due to a glut of steel that had sent prices to twenty-year lows. While domestic steel producers found themselves mired in red ink, many foreign steel makers desperately needed to continue to sell in the relatively open U.S. market to stay profitable. The industry was hovering around 75 percent capacity utilization, a level too low to be profitable for many companies. Three European companies—France's Usinor SA, Luxembourg's Arbed SA, and Spain's Aceralia

Corp.—merged to form the world's largest steel company. Two Japanese companies—NKK Corp. and Kawasaki Steel Corp.—merged to form the world's second-biggest steel maker. These new mega-steelmakers could outmuscle U.S. competitors, which were less efficient, smaller, and financially weaker than their competitors in Asia and Europe. At this time the largest U.S. steelmaker, USX-U.S. Steel Group, was only the eleventh largest producer in the world, and continued consolidation in the industry was expected.

In addition to cheap imports, U.S. steel producers faced higher energy prices, weakening demand by customer industries, increasingly tough environmental rules, and a changing cost structure among producers. With the declining economy, energy prices began to drop. However, so did demand for construction, automobiles, and farm equipment. Environmental rules led to costly modifications and closings of old plants, which produced coke along with vast clouds of ash and acrid green smoke. In 1990, minimills accounted for 36 percent of the domestic steel market, but by 2000, the more efficient minimill had seized 50 percent of the market and the resulting competition had driven prices lower.

The year 2001 turned out to be one of the worst years ever for steel. There was 9/11, a recession, and a surge of imports. DiMicco broke with Nucor's traditional opposition to government intervention to make a major push for protective tariffs. He stated, "The need to enforce trade rules is similar to the need to enforce any other law. If two merchants have stores side by side, but one sells stolen merchandise at a vast discount, we know that it's time for the police to step in." In March 2002, President Bush, after an investigation and recommendation by the ITC, imposed antidumping tariffs under Section 201 of the Trade Act of 1974. This restricted some imports of steel and placed quotas of up to 30 percent on others. The move was opposed by many, including steel users. Columnist George Will in his editorial on March 10, 2002, criticized Bush for abandoning free trade and pointed out the protection would hamper the necessary actions to restructure the steel industry in America by reducing excess capacity. The European Union immediately threatened reprisals and appealed to the WTO. In December, China imposed its own three-year program of import duties. Steel prices rose 40 percent in 2002 after the tariffs. Within a year hot-rolled steel prices increased 50 percent to $260 per ton over the twenty-year low of $210 during 2002. The price had been $361 in 1980. In November 2003, the WTO ruled against the tariffs, and, under increasing pressure of retaliation, Bush withdrew the tariffs.

While many steel companies floundered, Nucor was able to take advantage of the weakened conditions. In March 2001, Nucor made its first acquisition in ten years, purchasing a minimill in New York from Sumitomo Corp. Nucor had hired about five people to help plan for future acquisitions. DiMicco commented, "It's taken us three years before our team has felt this is the right thing to do and get started making acquisitions." In the challenged industry, he argued it would be cheaper to buy than build plants. They purchased the assets of Auburn Steel, which gave them a merchant bar presence in the Northeast and helped the new Vulcraft facility in New York. They acquired ITEC Steel, a leader in the emerging load-bearing light-gauge steel framing market, and saw an opportunity to aggressively broaden its market. Nucor increased its sheet capacity by roughly one-third when it acquired the assets of Trico Steel Co. in Alabama for $120 million. In early 2002, they acquired the assets of Birmingham Steel Corp. The $650 million purchase of four minimills was the largest acquisition in Nucor's history. In addition to making acquisitions to efficiently increase their market share and capacity, Nucor was actively working on new production processes that would provide them with technological advantages. They acquired the U.S. and Brazilian rights to the promising Castrip process for strip casting, the process of directly casting thin sheet steel. After development work on the process in Indiana they began full-time production in May 2002 and produced 7,000 tons in the last 10 months of 2002.

Moreover, in April Nucor entered into a joint venture with a Brazilian mining company, CVRD, the world's largest producer of iron-ore pellets, to jointly develop low-cost iron-based products. Success with this effort would give them the ability to make steel from scratch by combining iron ore and coke rather than using scrap steel.

As the year ended they were encouraged by the decrease in total steel capacity and what appeared to be a recovery in prices from record lows and expected slight improvement for 2002.

However, 2002 proved to be a difficult year for Nucor. Revenue increased 11 percent and earnings improved 43 percent over weak 2001, but the other financial goals were not met. They did increase their steel-making capacity by more than 25 percent. Looking

ahead to 2003, they anticipated a challenging year. However, they commented, "Nucor has a long-standing tradition of successfully emerging from industry downturns stronger than ever. It will be no different this time."

During 2003, prices of steel rose in the United States and Asia as global demand outpaced supply in some areas. China, with its booming economy, drove the market. An article in *The Wall Street Journal*, October 15, quoted Guy Dolle, chief executive of Arcelor SA of Luxembourg, the world's largest steelmaker in terms of steel product shipped, as saying, "China is the wild card in the balance between supply and demand." World prices did not soar dangerously because the steel industry continued to be plagued by overcapacity. Still steel-hungry China and other fast-growing nations added to their steel capacity.

Imports of steel commodities into the United States fell in August 2003 by 22 percent. A weakened dollar, the growing demand from China, and tariffs imposed in 2002 by Bush drove away imports. Domestic capacity declined, increasing capacity utilization from 77.2 percent to 93.4 percent as producers consolidated, idled plants, or went out of business. Prices for iron ore and energy rose, affecting integrated producers. Minimills saw their costs rise as worldwide demand for scrap prices rose. Thus, U.S. steelmakers boosted their prices. By February 2004, a growing coalition of U.S. steel producers and consumers were considering whether to petition to limit soaring exports of scrap steel from the United States, the world's largest producer of steel scrap. The United States had exported an estimated 12 million metric tons of steel scrap in 2003, a 21 percent increase from 2002. Moreover, the price of scrap steel was up 83 percent from a year earlier to $255 a ton. At the same time, the price of hot-rolled sheet steel rose 30 percent to $360 a ton. One result was that the International Steel Group (ISG) replaced Nucor as the most profitable U.S. steel producer. ISG was created when investor Wilbur Ross began acquiring the failing traditional steel producers in America, including LTV, Bethlehem, and Weirton. These mills used iron ore rather than scrap steel.

When 2003 ended, Nucor struck a positive note by reminding their investors that they had been profitable every single quarter since beginning operations in 1966. But while Nucor set records for both steel production and steel shipments, net earnings declined 61 percent. While the steel industry struggled through one of its deepest down cycles with weak prices and bankruptcies throughout the industry, Nucor increased its market share and held on to profitability. They worked on expanding their business with the automotive industry, continued their joint venture in Brazil to produce pig iron, and pursued a joint venture with the Japanese and Chinese to make iron without the usual raw materials. In February 2004 they were "optimistic about the prospects for obtaining commercialization" of their promising Castrip process for strip casting in the U.S. and Brazil. Moreover, Nucor was optimistic because the administration was using its trade laws to curtail import dumping and Nucor expected higher margins.

Global competition continued. Nucor has good reason to be proactive. According to the *Wall Street Journal*, Posco steelworks in Pohang, South Korea enjoyed the highest profits in the global steel industry as of 2004. Moreover, *Business Week* reported that the company had developed a new technology called Finex, which turns coal and iron ore into iron without coking and sintering, and which was expected to cut production costs by nearly a fifth and harmful emissions by 90%. They had also expanded their 80 Korean plants by investing in 14 Chinese joint ventures. By December 2004, demand in China had slowed and it had become a net steel exporter, sparking concerns of global oversupply.

Global consolidation continued. In October 2004, London's Mittal family announced that they would merge their Ispat International NV with LNM Group and ISG, to create the world's largest steel maker, with estimated annual revenues of $31.5 billion and output of 57 million tons. This would open a new chapter for the industry's consolidation, which had been mostly regional. Although the world's steel industry remains largely fragmented, with the world's top 10 steelmakers supplying less than 30% of global production, Mittal Steel will have about 40% of the U.S. market in flat-rolled steel. Moreover, Mittal, which had a history of using its scale to buy lower-cost raw materials and import modern management techniques into previously inefficient state-run mills, was buying ISG, a U.S. company which already owned the lowest-cost, highest profit mills in the United States. In January 2005, Mittal announced plans to buy 37% of China's Hunan Valin Iron & Steel Group Co.

With output of around 20 million metric tons each, U.S. Steel and Nucor face an uncertain environment as the industry consolidates. Some argue that if they didn't grow quickly, they might be taken over by foreign makers trying to gain entry into the United States. According to *Business Week*, Karlis Kirsis, managing partner of World Steel Dynamics, Inc., an information service, said "everybody's in play these days" in the wake of Mittal's planned merger with ISG. Even as they made bids of their own, South Korea's Posco and Belgium's Arcelor might snap them up.

APPENDIX 1

Financial Report
Balance Sheet 2000–2004 (in millions of USD)

As of:	12/31/2004	12/31/2003	12/31/2002	12/31/2001	12/31/2000
Assets					
Cash	779.05	350.33	219	462.35	490.58
Marketable Securities	n/a	n/a	n/a	n/a	n/a
Receivables	962.76	572.48	483.61	330.86	350.18
Total Inventories	1,239.89	560.4	588.99	466.69	461.15
Other Current Assets	193.26	137.35	157.34	133.8	79.53
Total Current Assets	3,174.95	1,620.56	1,448.94	1,393.69	1,381.45
Property, Plant & Equipment, Net	2,818.31	2,817.14	2,932.06	2,365.66	2,329.42
Property, Plant & Equipment, Gross	2,818.31	2,817.14	2,932.06	2,365.66	2,329.42
Deposits & Other Assets	139.95	54.66	n/a	n/a	n/a
Total Assets	6,133.21	4,492.35	4,381.00	3,759.35	3,710.87

(continued)

Financial Report
Balance Sheet 2000–2004 (in millions of USD)

As of:	12/31/2004	12/31/2003	12/31/2002	12/31/2001	12/31/2000
Liabilities					
Accounts Payable	471.55	329.86	247.23	189.24	203.33
Curr. Long-Term Debt	n/a	n/a	n/a	n/a	n/a
Accrued Expense	565.28	299.73	319.36	294.92	354.73
Income Taxes	28.96	n/a	8.95	n/a	n/a
Other Current Liabilities	n/a	n/a	n/a	n/a	n/a
Total Current Liabilities	1,065.79	629.6	591.54	484.16	558.07
Deferred Charges/Inc.	514.57	439.85	371.27	329.39	260.05
Long-Term Debt	923.55	903.55	878.55	460.45	460.45
Other Long-Term Liab.	n/a	n/a	n/a	n/a	n/a
Total Liabilities	2,503.91	1,973.00	1,841.36	1,274.00	1,278.57
Shareholder Equity					
Minority Interest	173.31	177.28	216.65	283.89	301.34
Preferred Stock	n/a	n/a	n/a	n/a	n/a
Common Stock	73.75	36.43	36.27	36.13	36.04
Capital Surplus	147.21	117.4	99.4	81.19	71.49
Retained Earnings	3,688.56	2,641.71	2,641.58	2,538.88	2,478.79
Treasury Stock	451.96	453.46	454.26	454.74	455.37
Total Shareholders Equity	3,455.99	2,342.08	2,322.99	2,201.46	2,130.95
Total Liab.& Shdr Equity	6,133.21	4,492.35	4,381.00	3,759.35	3,710.87

Income Statement 2000–2004 (in millions of USD)

Period Ended	12/31/2004	12/31/2003	12/31/2002	12/31/2001	12/31/2000
Net Sales	11,376.83	6,265.82	4,801.78	4,333.71	4,756.52
Cost of Goods Sold	9,128.87	5,996.55	4,332.28	3,914.28	3,929.18
Gross Profit	2,247.96	269.28	469.5	419.43	827.34
R & D Expenditure	n/a	n/a	n/a	n/a	n/a
Selling, General & Admin Exps	415.03	165.37	175.59	150.67	183.18
Depreciation & Amort.	n/a	n/a	n/a	n/a	n/a
Non-Operating Income	−79.3	−12.4	−49.57	−82.87	−150.65
Interest Expense	22.35	24.63	14.29	6.53	n/a
Income Before Taxes	1,731.28	66.88	230.05	179.37	493.52
Prov. For Inc. Taxes	609.79	4.1	67.97	66.41	182.61
Minority Interest	n/a	n/a	n/a	n/a	n/a
Realized Investment (Gain/Loss)	n/a	n/a	n/a	n/a	n/a
Other Income	n/a	n/a	n/a	n/a	n/a
Net Income Before Extra Items	1,121.49	62.78	162.08	112.96	310.91
Extra Items & Disc. Ops.	n/a	n/a	n/a	n/a	n/a
Net Income	1,121.49	62.78	162.08	112.96	310.91

Source: Data by Thomson Financial, Nucor webpage.

Financial Ratios
Nucor Valuation Ratios 2004

P/E (TTM)	7.38
Per Share Ratios	
Dividend per Share	0.47
Book Value per Share	21.54
EPS Fully Diluted	7.02
Revenue per Share	71.21
Profit Margins	
Operating Margin	16.23
Net Profit Margin	9.86
Gross Profit Margin	19.88
Dividends	
Dividend Yield	1.13
Dividend Yield - 5 Yr. Avg.	1.28
Dividend per Share (TTM)	0.52
Dividend Payout Ratio	6.66
Growth (%)	
5 Year Annual Growth	35.6
Revenue - 5 Year Growth	23.19
Div/Share - 5 Yr Growth	12.57
EPS - 5 Year Growth	32.58
Financial Strength	
Quick Ratio	1.63
Current Ratio	2.98
LT Debt to Equity	26.72
Total Debt to Equity	26.72
Return on Equity (ROE) per Share	38.57
Return on Assets (ROA)	25.4
Return on Invested Capital (ROIC)	33.33
Assets	
Asset Turnover	1.85
Inventory Turnover	9.7

Source: Data by Thomson Financial, Nucor webpage.

Board of Directors and Executive Management
In 1990
Board: Iverson, Aycock, Cunningham, Siegel, Vandekieft

Executive Office: Iverson, Aycock, Siegel

1991 to 1994
Board: Iverson, Aycock, Siegel, Cunningham, Correnti

Executive Office: Iverson, Siegel, Correnti, Lisenby, Prichard

1995 to 1996
Board: Iverson, Aycock, Siegel, Cunningham, Correnti, Hlavacek

Executive Office: Iverson, Siegel, Correnti, Doherty, Prichard

In 1997
Board: Iverson, Aycock, Siegel, Cunningham, Correnti, Hlavacek

Executive Office: Iverson, Siegel, Correnti, Lisenby, Prichard

In 1998
Board: Aycock, Siegel, Correnti, Hlavacek, Browning, Gantt, Haynes

Executive Office: Aycock, Siegel, Correnti, Parrish, Rutowski, Lisenby, Prichard

1999 to 2000
Board: Aycock, Siegel, Hlavacek, Browning, Gantt, Haynes

Executive Office: Aycock, Lisenby, DiMicco, Lott, Parrish, Rutowski, Coblin, Prichard

2002 to 2003
Board: Browning, Daley, DiMicco, Gantt, Haynes, Hlavacek, Milchovich, Waltermire

Executive Office: DiMicco, Lisenby, Ferriola, Lott, Parrish, Rutkowski, Coblin, Bowers, Frias, Johns, Laxton, Maero, Rowlan, Eagle (new 2003)

Biographies of Selected Board Members
and Executive Managers

Peter C. Browning has been the president and chief executive officer of Sonoco Products Company and was senior officer in 1993. He was previously the president, chairman, and chief executive officer of National Gypsum Company. He was elected chairman of Nucor's Board of Directors in September 2000 and became the nonexecutive chairman of Nucor when David Aycock retired from the board in 2001.

Daniel R. Dimicco was executive vice president of Nucor–Yamato Steel, Nucor Steel Hertford (plate division), and Nucor Building Systems before becoming president. He graduated from Brown University in 1972 with a bachelor of science in engineering, metallurgy and materials science. He received a master's in metallurgy from the University of Pennsylvania in 1975. He was with Republic Steel in Cleveland as a research metallurgy and project leader until he joined Nucor in 1982 as plant metallurgist and manager of quality control for Nucor Steel in Utah. In 1988, he became melting and castings manager. In 1991, he became general manager of Nucor–Yamato and a vice president in 1992. In September 2000, he was elected president and chief executive officer of Nucor. In 2001, when Aycock retired, he became vice chairman, president, and chief executive officer of Nucor.

Harvey B. Gantt was a partner in Gantt Huberman Architects for more than twenty-five years. He also served as mayor of the City of Charlotte, North Carolina, and was active in civic affairs. He was the first African-American graduate of Clemson University. He joined Nucor's Board of Directors in 1998.

Victoria F. Haynes is the president of Research Triangle Institute in Chapel Hill, North Carolina. Until 2000, she was the chief technical officer of the B. F. Goodrich Co. and vice president of its advanced technology group. She started with Goodrich in 1992 as vice president of research and development. She joined Nucor's Board of Directors in 1998.

James D. Hlavacek is the managing director of market driven management. Hlavacek was a neighbor and long-term friend of Iverson. He joined Nucor's Board of Directors in 1995.

Terry S. Lisenby is chief financial officer and an executive vice president. He graduated from the University of North Carolina at Charlotte in 1976 with a bachelor of science in accounting. Mr. Lisenby held accounting and management positions with Seidman and Seidman, Harper Corporation of America, and Concept Development, Inc. He joined Nucor in September 1985 as manager of financial accounting. He became vice president and corporate controller in 1991 and assumed the role of chief financial officer on January 1, 2000.

Hamilton Lott Jr. is executive vice president over the Vulcraft operations, cold-finished operations in Nebraska, and the Utah grinding ball plant. He graduated from the University of South Carolina in 1972 with a bachelor of science in engineering and then served in the United States Navy. He joined Nucor in 1975 as a design engineer at Florence. He later served as engineering manager and as sales manager at Nucor's Vulcraft division in Indiana. He was general manager of the Vulcraft division in Texas from 1987 to 1993 and the general manager in Florence from 1993 to 1999. He became a vice president in 1988 and joined the executive office in 1999.

D. Michael Parrish is executive vice president for the four steel plants and Nucor Fastener. He graduated from the University of Toledo in 1975 with a bachelor of science degree in civil engineering. He joined Nucor in September 1975 as a design engineer for Vulcraft and became engineering manager at Vulcraft in 1981. In 1986, he moved to Alabama as manufacturing manager, and in 1989, he returned to Utah as vice president and general manager. In 1991, he took the top job with Nucor Steel Texas and in 1995 at Nucor Steel Arkansas. In January 1999, he moved into corporate offices as executive vice president.

Joseph A. Rutkowski is executive vice president of Nucor Steel in Indiana, Arkansas, Berkeley, South Carolina, and Nucor Bearing Products. He graduated from Johns Hopkins University in 1976 with a bachelor of science in materials science engineering. He held metallurgical and management positions with Korf Lurgi Steeltec, North American Refractories, Georgetown Steel, and Bethlehem Steel. He joined Nucor in 1989 as manager of cold finish in Nebraska and became melting and casting manager in Utah before becoming vice president and general manager of Nucor Steel in Darlington in 1992. In 1998, he moved to Hertford as vice president, general manager to oversee the building of the new plate mill.

3M in the New Millennium

This case was prepared by Charles W. L. Hill, the University of Washington.

Established in 1902, by 2002 3M was one of the largest technology-driven enterprises in the United States with annual sales of $16.4 billion, 55 percent of which were outside the United States. Throughout its history 3M's researchers had driven much of the company's growth. In 2002, the company sold some fifty thousand products, including Post-it Notes, Flex Circuits, Scotch tape, abrasives, specialty chemicals, Thinsulate insulation products, Nexcare bandage, optical films, fiber optic connectors, drug delivery systems, and much more. One-third of the company's products in 2002 didn't even exist in 1997. Around 7,000 of the company's 68,000 employees were technical employees. 3M's annual R&D budget exceeded $1 billion. The company had garnered over six thousand patents since 1990, with more than six hundred new patents awarded in 2002 alone. 3M was organized into forty different business units in a wide range of sectors, including consumer and office products; display and graphics; electronics and telecommunications; health care; industrial; safety, security, and protection services; and transportation (see Exhibit 1 for more details).

The company's 100-year anniversary was a time for celebration, but also one for strategic reflection. During the prior decade, 3M had grown profits and sales by between 6 to 7 percent per annum, a respectable figure but one that lagged behind the growth rates achieved by some other technology-based enterprises and diversified industrial enterprises such as General Electric. In 2001, 3M took a step away from its past when the company hired the first outsider to become CEO, James McNerney Jr. McNerney, who joined 3M after heading up GE's fast growing medical equipment business (and losing out in the race to replace legendary GE CEO, Jack Welch), was quick to signal that he wanted 3M to accelerate its growth rate. McNerney set an ambitious target for 3M to grow sales by 11 percent per annum and profits by 12 percent per annum. The question was how to achieve this without damaging the innovation engine that had propelled 3M to its current stature?

The History of 3M: Building Innovative Capabilities

The 3M story goes back to 1902 when five Minnesota businessmen established the Minnesota Mining and Manufacturing Company to mine a mineral that they thought was corundum, which is ideal for making sandpaper. The mineral, however, turned out to be low-grade anorthosite, nowhere near as suitable for making sandpaper, and the company nearly failed. To try and salvage the business, 3M turned to making the sandpaper itself using materials purchased from another source.

In 1907, 3M hired a twenty-year-old business student, William McKnight, as assistant bookkeeper. This turned out to be a pivotal move in the history of the company. The hardworking McKnight soon made his mark. By 1929, he was CEO of the company, and in 1949, he became chairman of 3M's Board of Directors, a position that he held until 1966.

Copyright © 2004 by Charles W. L. Hill. This case was prepared by Charles W. L. Hill, the University of Washington, as the basis for class discussion rather than to illustrate either effective or ineffective handling of an administrative situation. Reprinted by permission of Charles W. L. Hill. All rights reserved. For the most recent financial results of the company discussed in this case, go to http://finance.yahoo.com, input the company's stock symbol, and download the latest company report from its homepage.

EXHIBIT 1

3M Facts: Year-end 2002

3M is one of thirty companies in the Dow Jones Industrial Average and also is a component of the Standard & Poor's 500 Index.

Sales

Worldwide	$16.332 billion
International	$8.906 billion
55% of company's total	

Net Income*

Net income—reported	$1.974 billion
Percent to sales	12.1%
Earnings per share—diluted—reported	$4.99

*Includes non-recurring net loss of $108 million ($0.27 per share) principally related to 3M's restructuring plan.

Taxes

Income tax expense	$966 million

Dividends

(Paid every quarter since 1916)

Cash dividends per share	$2.48
One original share, if held, is now	1,536 shares

R&D and Related Expenditures

For 2002	$1.070 billion
Total for last five years	$5.339 billion

Capital Spending

For 2002	$763 million
Total for last five years	$5.361 billion

Employees

Worldwide	68,774
United States	35,024
International	33,750

Common Stock Data

Price at 12/31/02	$123.30
52-Week Range	$100.00–131.55
Market Capitalization	$48 billion
Indicated Annual Dividend	$2.48
Dividend Yield	2.0%
Year End	December 31
Ticker Symbol (NYSE)	MMM

Organization

- More than 40 business units, organized into seven businesses:
  - Health Care
  - Industrial
  - Consumer and Office
  - Display and Graphics
  - Electro and Communications
  - Safety, Security, and Protection Services
  - Transportation
- Operations in more than 60 countries—29 international companies with manufacturing operations, 32 with laboratories.
- In the United States, operations in 24 states.

Contributions

From 3M and 3M Foundation

U.S. cash and gifts-in-kind	more than $43 million

U.S. Patents Awarded 2002　　608

3M Values

- Provide investors an attractive return through sustained, quality growth
- Satisfy customers with superior quality, value, and service
- Respect our social and physical environment
- Be a company employees are proud to be part of

3M Performance Initiatives

- Six Sigma
- 3M Acceleration
- eProductivity
- Sourcing Effectiveness
- Indirect Cost Control

As part of our everyday business processes, these initiatives will drive improvements in productivity and efficiency, and help us focus even more strongly on customer solutions and growth.

Source: 3M website.

From Sandpaper to Post-it Notes

It was McKnight, then 3M's president, who hired the company's first scientist, Richard Carlton, in 1921. Around the same time, McKnight's interest had been piqued by an odd request from a Philadelphia printer by the name of Francis Okie for samples of every sandpaper grit size that 3M made. McKnight dispatched 3M's East Coast sales manager to find out what Okie was up to. The sales manager discovered that Okie had invented a new kind of sandpaper that he had patented. It was waterproof sandpaper that could be used with water or oil to reduce dust and decrease the friction that marred auto finishes. In addition, the lack of dust reduced the poisoning associated with inhaling the dust of paint that had a high lead content. Okie had a problem though: He had no financial backers to commercialize the sandpaper. 3M quickly stepped into the breach, purchasing the rights to Okie's Wetordry waterproof sandpaper, and hiring the young printer to come and join Richard Carlton in 3M's lab. Wetordry sandpaper went on to revolutionize the sandpaper industry, and was the driver of significant growth at 3M.

Another key player in the company's history, Richard Drew, also joined 3M in 1921. Hired straight out of the University of Minnesota, Drew would round out the trio of scientists, Carlton, Okie and Drew, who, under McKnight's leadership, would do much to shape 3M's innovative organization.

McKnight charged the newly hired Drew with developing a stronger adhesive to better bind the grit for sandpaper to paper backing. While experimenting with adhesives, Drew accidentally developed a weak adhesive that had an interesting quality—if placed on the back of a strip of paper and stuck to a surface, the strip of paper could be peeled off the surface it was adhered to without leaving any adhesive residue on that surface. This discovery gave Drew an epiphany. He had been visiting autobody paint shops to see how 3M's Wetordry sandpaper was used, and he noticed that there was a problem with paint running. His epiphany was to cover the back of a strip of paper with his weak adhesive, and use it as "masking tape" to cover parts of the auto body that were not to be painted. An excited Drew took his idea to McKnight, and explained how masking tape might create an entirely new business for 3M. McKnight reminded Drew that he had been hired to fix a specific problem, and pointedly suggested that he concentrate on doing just that.

Chastised, Drew went back to his lab, but he could not get the idea out of his mind, so he continued to work on it at night, long after everyone else had gone home. Drew succeeded in perfecting the masking tape product, and then went to visit several autobody shops to show them his innovation. He quickly received several commitments for orders. Drew then went to see McKnight again. He told him that he had continued to work on the masking tape idea on his own time, had perfected the product, and got several customers interested in purchasing it. This time it was McKnight's turn to be chastised. Realizing that he had almost killed a good business idea, McKnight reversed his original position, and gave Drew the go ahead to pursue the idea.[1]

Introduced into the market in 1925, Drew's invention of masking tape represented the first significant product diversification at 3M. Company legend has it that this incident was also the genesis for 3M's famous 15 percent rule. Reflecting on Drew's work, both McKnight and Carlton agreed that technical people could disagree with management, and should be allowed to go and do some experimentation on their own. The company then established a norm that technical people could spend up to 15 percent of their own workweek on projects that might benefit the consumer, without having to justify the project to their manager.

Drew himself was not finished. In the late 1920s he was working with cellophane, a product that had been invented by DuPont, when lightning struck for a second time. Why, Drew wondered, couldn't cellophane be coated with an adhesive and used as a sealing tape? The result was Scotch Cellophane Tape. The first batch was delivered to a customer in September 1930, and Scotch Tape went on to become one of 3M's best selling products. Years later, Drew noted, "Would there have been any masking or cellophane tape if it hadn't been for earlier 3M research on adhesive binders for 3M™ Wetordry™ Abrasive Paper? Probably not!"[2]

Over the years, other scientists followed Drew's footsteps at 3M, creating a wide range of innovative products by leveraging existing technology and applying it to new areas. Two famous examples illustrate how many of these innovations occurred—the invention of Scotch Guard and the development of the ubiquitous Post-it Notes.

The genesis of Scotch Guard was in 1953 when a 3M scientist named Patsy Sherman was working on a new kind of rubber for jet aircraft fuel lines. Some of the latex mixture splashed onto a pair of canvas tennis shoes. Over time, the spot stayed clean while the rest of the canvas soiled. Sherman enlisted the help of fellow chemist Sam Smith. Together they began to investigate polymers, and it didn't take long for them to realize that they were onto something. They discovered an oil and water repellent substance, based on the fluorocarbon fluid used in air conditioners, with enormous potential for protecting fabrics from stains. It took several years before the team perfected a means to apply the treatment using water as the carrier, thereby making it economically feasible for use as a finish in textile plants.

Three years after the accidental spill, the first rain and stain repellent for use on wool was announced. Experience and time revealed that one product could not, however, effectively protect all fabrics, so 3M continued working, producing a wide range of Scotch Guard products that could be used to protect all kinds of fabrics.[3]

The story of Post-it Notes began with Spencer Silver, a senior scientist studying adhesives.[4] In 1968, Silver had developed an adhesive with properties like no other; it was a pressure sensitive adhesive that would adhere to a surface, but was weak enough to easily peel off the surface and leave no residue. Silver spent several years shopping his adhesive around 3M, to no avail. It was a classic case of a technology in search of a product. Then one day in 1973, Art Fry, a new product development researcher who had attended one of Silver's seminars, was singing in his church choir. He was frustrated that his bookmarks kept falling out of his hymn book, when he had a "Eureka" moment. Fry realized that Silver's adhesive could be used to make a wonderfully reliable bookmark.

Fry went to work next day, and using 15 percent time, started to develop the bookmark. When he started using samples to write notes to his boss, Fry suddenly realized that he had stumbled on a much bigger potential use for the product. Before the product could be commercialized, however, Fry had to solve a host of technical and manufacturing problems. With the support of his boss, Fry persisted, and after eighteen months, the product development effort moved from 15 percent time to a formal development effort funded by 3M's own seed capital.

The first Post-it Notes were test marketed in 1977 in four major cities, but customers were lukewarm at best. This did not gel with the experience within 3M,

where people in Fry's division were using samples all the time to write messages to each other. Further research revealed that the test marketing effort, which focused on ads and brochures, didn't resonate well with consumers, who didn't seem to value Post-it Notes until they had the actual product in their hands. In 1978, 3M tried again, this time descending on Boise, Idaho, and handing out samples. Follow-up research revealed that 90 percent of consumers who tried the product said they would buy it. Armed with this knowledge, 3M rolled out the national launch of Post-it Notes in 1980. The product subsequently went on to become a bestseller.

Institutionalizing Innovation

Early on McKnight set an ambitious target for 3M— a 10 percent annual increase in sales and 25 percent profit target. He also indicated how he thought that should be achieved with a commitment to plow 5 percent of sales back into R&D every year. The question though was how to ensure that 3M would continue to produce new products.

The answer was not apparent all at once, but rather evolved over the years from experience. A prime example was the 15 percent rule, which came out of McKnight's experience with Drew. In addition to the 15 percent rule and the continued commitment to push money back into R&D, a number of other mechanisms evolved at 3M to spur innovation.

Initially research took place in the business units that made and sold products, but by the 1930s, 3M had already diversified into several different fields, thanks in large part to the efforts of Drew and others. McKnight and Carlton realized that there was a need for a central research function. In 1937, they established a central research laboratory that was charged with supplementing the work of product divisions and undertaking long-run basic research. From the outset, the researchers at the lab were multidisciplinary, with people from different scientific disciplines often working next to each other on research benches.

As the company continued to grow, it became clear that there was a need for some mechanism to knit together the company's increasingly diverse business operations. This led to the establishment of the 3M Technical Forum in 1951. The goal of the Technical Forum was to foster idea sharing, discussion, and problem solving between technical employees located in different divisions and the central research laboratory. The Technical Forum sponsored "problem solving sessions" at which businesses would present their most recent technical nightmares in the hope that somebody might be able to suggest a solution—and that often was the case. The forum also established an annual event in which each division put up a booth to show off its latest technologies. Chapters were also created to focus on specific disciplines, such as polymer chemistry or coating processes.

During the 1970s, the Technical Forum cloned itself, establishing forums in Australia and England. By 2001, the forum had grown to 9,500 members in 8 U.S. locations and 19 other countries, becoming an international network of researchers who could share ideas, solve problems, and leverage technology.

According to Marlyee Paulson, who coordinated the Technical Forum from 1979 to 1992, the great virtue of the Technical Forum is to cross pollinate ideas. To quote:

3M has lots of polymer chemists. They may be in tape; they may be medical or several other divisions. The forum pulls them across 3M to share what they know. It's a simple but amazingly effective way to bring like minds together.[5]

In 1999, 3M created another unit within the company, 3M Innovative Properties (3M, IPC) to leverage technical know-how. 3M IPC is explicitly charged with protecting and leveraging 3M's intellectual property around the world. At 3M there has been a long tradition that while divisions "own" their products, the company as a whole "owns" the underlying technology, or intellectual property. One task of 3M IPC is to find ways in which 3M technology can be applied across business units to produce unique marketable products. Historically, the company has been remarkably successful at leveraging company technology to produce new product ideas (see Exhibit 2 for some recent examples).

EXHIBIT 2

Recent Examples of Leveraging Technology at 3M[6]

Richard Miller, a corporate scientist in 3M Pharmaceuticals, began experimental development of an antiherpes medicinal cream in 1982. After several years of development, his research team found that the interferon-based materials they were working with could be applied to any skin-based virus. The innovative chemistry they were working with was applied topically and was more effective than other compounds on the market. They found that the cream was particularly effective at interfering with the growth mechanism of genital warts. Competitive materials on the market at the time were caustic and tended to be painful. Miller's team obtained FDA approval for its Aldara (imiquimod) line of topical patient-applied creams in 1997.

Miller then applied the same Aldara-based chemical mechanism to basal cell carcinomas and found that here, too, it was particularly effective at restricting the growth of the skin cancer. "The patient benefit is quite remarkable," says Miller. New results in efficacy have been presented for treating skin cancers. His team recently completed phase III clinical testing and expects to apply later this year for FDA approval for this disease preventative. This material is already FDA approved for use in the treatment of genital warts. Doctors are free to choose to use it to treat those patients with skin cancers.

Andrew Ouderkirk is a corporate scientist in 3M's Film & Light Management Technology Center. 3M has been working in light management materials applied to polymer-based films since the 1930s, according to Ouderkirk. Every decade since then 3M has introduced some unique thin film structure for a specific customer application from high-performance safety reflectors for street signs to polarized lighting products. And every decade, 3M's technology base has become more specialized and more sophisticated. Their technology has now reached the point where they can produce multiple-layer interference films to 100-nm thicknesses each and hold the tolerances on each layer to within $+/-3$ nm. "Our laminated films are now starting to compete with vacuum-coated films in some applications," says Ouderkirk.

Rick Weiss is technical director of 3M's Microreplication Technology Center, one of 3M's twelve core technology centers. The basic microreplication technology was discovered in the early 1960s when 3M researchers were developing the fresnel lenses for overhead projectors. 3M scientists have expanded upon this technology to a wide variety of applications, including optical reflectors for solar collectors and adhesive coatings with air bleed ribs that allow large area films to be applied without having the characteristic "bubbles" appear. Weiss is currently working on development of dimensionally precise barrier ribs that can be applied to separate the individual "gas" cells on the new high-resolution large screen commercial plasma displays. Other applications include fluid management where capillary action can be used in biological testing systems to split a drop of blood into a large number of parts.

Another key to institutionalizing innovation at 3M has been the principle of "patient money." The basic idea is that producing revolutionary new products requires substantial long-term investments, and often repeated failure, before a major payoff occurs. The principle can be traced back to 3M's early days. It took the company twelve years before its initial sandpaper business started to show a profit, a fact that drove home the importance of taking the long view. Throughout the company's history, similar examples can be found. Scotchlite reflective sheeting, now widely used on road signs, didn't show much profit for ten years. The same was true of flurochemicals and duplicating products. Patient money doesn't mean substantial funding for long periods of time, however. Rather, it might imply that a small group of five researchers is supported for ten years while they work on a technology.

More generally, if researchers create a new technology or idea, they can begin working on it using 15 percent time. If the idea shows promise, they may request seed capital from their business unit managers to develop it further. If that funding is denied, which can occur, they are free to take the idea to any other 3M business unit. Unlike the case in many other companies, requests for seed capital do not require that researchers draft detailed business plans that are reviewed by top management. That comes later in the process. As one former senior technology manager has noted:

> In the early stages of a new product or technology, it shouldn't be overly managed. If we start asking for business plans too early and insist on tight financial evaluations, we'll kill an idea or surely slow it down.[7]

Explaining the patient money philosophy, Ron Baukol, a former executive vice president of 3M's international operations, and a manager who started as a researcher, has noted that

> You just know that some things are going to be worth working on, and that requires technological patience. . . . you don't put too much money into the investigation, but you keep one to five people working on it for twenty years if you have to. You do that because you know that, once you have cracked the code, it's going to be big.[8]

An internal review of 3M's innovation process in the early 1980s concluded that despite the liberal process for funding new product ideas, some promising ideas did not receive funding from business units or the central research budget. This led to the establishment in 1985 of Genesis Grants, which provide up to $100,000 in seed capital to fund projects that do not get funded through 3M's regular channels. About a dozen of these grants are given every year. One of the recipients of these grants, a project that focused on creating a multilayered reflective film, has subsequently produced a breakthrough reflective technology that may have applications in a wide range of businesses, from better reflective strips on road signs to computer displays and the reflective linings in light fixtures. Company estimates in 2002 suggest that the commercialization of this technology might ultimately generate $1 billion in sales for 3M.

Underlying the patient money philosophy is recognition that innovation is a very risky business. 3M has long acknowledged that failure is an accepted and essential part of the new product development process. As former 3M CEO Lew Lehr once noted:

> We estimate that 60% of our formal new product development programs never make it. When this happens, the important thing is to not punish the people involved.[9]

In an effort to reduce the probability of failure, in the 1960s 3M started to establish a process for auditing the product development efforts ongoing in the company's business units. The idea has been to provide a peer review, or technical audit, of major development projects taking place in the company. A typical technical audit team is composed of ten to fifteen business and technical people, including technical directors and senior scientists from other divisions. The audit team looks at the strengths and weaknesses of a development program, and its probability of success, both from a technical standpoint and a business standpoint. The team then makes nonbinding recommendations, but they are normally taken very seriously by the managers of a project. For example, if an audit team concludes that a project has enormous potential, but is terribly underfunded, managers of the unit would often increase the funding level. Of course, the converse can also happen, and in many instances, the audit team can provide useful feedback and technical ideas that can help a development team to improve their project's chance of success.

By the 1990s, the continuing growth of 3M had produced a company that was simultaneously pursuing a vast array of new product ideas. This was a natural outcome of 3M's decentralized and bottom up approach to innovation, but it was problematic in one crucial respect: the company's R&D resources were being spread too thinly over a wide range of opportunities, resulting in potentially major projects being underfunded.

To try and channel R&D resources into projects that had blockbuster potential, in 1994 3M introduced what was known as the Pacing Plus Program.

The program asked business to select a small number of programs that would receive priority funding, but 3M's senior executives made the final decision on which programs were to be selected for the Pacing Plus Program. An earlier attempt to do this in 1990 had met with limited success because each sector in 3M submitted as many as 200 programs. The Pacing Plus Program narrowed the list down to 25 key programs that by 1996 were receiving some 20 percent of 3M's entire R&D funds (by the early 2000s the number of projects funded under the Pacing Plus Program had grown to 60). The focus was on "leapfrog technologies," revolutionary ideas that might change the basis of competition and led to entirely new technology platforms that might, in typical 3M fashion, spawn an entire range of new products.

To further foster a culture of entrepreneurial innovation and risk taking, over the years 3M established a number of reward and recognition programs to honor employees who make significant contributions to the company. These include the Carton Society Award, which honors employees for outstanding career scientific achievements, and the Circle of Technical Excellence and Innovation Award, which recognizes people who have made exceptional contributions to 3M's technical capabilities.

Another key component of 3M's innovative culture has been an emphasis on duel career tracks. Right from its early days, many of the key players in 3M's history, people like Richard Drew, chose to stay in research, turning down opportunities to go into the management side of the business. Over the years, this became formalized in a dual career path. Today, technical employees can choose to follow a technical career path or a management career path, with equal advancement opportunities. The idea is to let researchers develop their technical professional interests, without being penalized financially for not going into management.

Although 3M's innovative culture emphasizes the role of technical employees in producing innovations,

the company also has a strong tradition of emphasizing that new product ideas often come from watching customers at work. Richard Drew's original idea for masking tape, for example, came from watching workers use 3M Wetordry sandpaper in autobody shops. As with much else at 3M, the tone was set by McKnight who insisted that salespeople needed to "get behind the smokestacks" of 3M customers, going onto the factory floor, talking to workers, and finding out what their problems were. Over the years this theme has become ingrained in 3M's culture, with salespeople often requesting time to watch customers work, and then bringing their insights about customer problems back into their organization.

By the mid 1990s, McKnight's notion of getting behind the smokestacks had evolved into the idea that 3M could learn a tremendous amount from what were termed "lead users," who were customers working in very demanding conditions. Over the years, 3M had observed that in many cases, customers themselves can be innovators, developing new products to solve problems that they face in their work setting. This was most likely to occur for customers working in very demanding conditions. To take advantage of this process, 3M has instituted a lead user process in the company in which cross functional teams from a business unit go and observe how customers work in demanding situations.

For example, 3M has a $100 million business selling surgical drapes, which are drapes backed with adhesives that are used to cover parts of a body during surgery and help prevent infection. As an aid to new product development, 3M's surgical drapes business formed a cross functional team that went to observe surgeons at work in very demanding situations—including on the battlefield, hospitals in developing nations, and in vets' offices. The result was a new set of product ideas, including low-cost surgical drapes that were affordable in developing nations and devices for coating a patient's skin and surgical instruments with antimicrobial substances that would reduce the chance of infection during surgery.[10]

Driving the entire innovation machine at 3M has been a series of stretch goals set by top managers. The goals date back to 3M's early days and McKnight's ambitious growth targets. In 1977, the company established "Challenge 81," which called for 25 percent of sales to come from products that had been on the market for less than five years by 1981. By the 1990s, the goal had been raised to the requirement that

30 percent of sales should come from products that had been on the market less than four years.

The flip side of these goals was that over the years, many products and businesses that had been 3M staples were phased out. More than twenty of the businesses that were 3M mainstays in 1980, for example, had been phased out by 2000. Analysts estimate that sales from mature products at 3M generally fall by 3 to 4 percent per annum. The company has a long history of inventing businesses, leading the market for long periods of time, and then shutting those businesses down, or selling them off, when they can no longer meet 3M's own demanding growth targets. Notable examples include the duplicating business, a business 3M invented with Thermo Fax copiers (which were ultimately made obsolete by Xerox's patented technology), and the video and audio magnetic tape business. The former division was sold off in 1985, and then later in 1995. In both cases the company exited these areas because they had become low-growth commodity businesses that could not generate the kind of top line growth that 3M was looking for.

Still, 3M was by no means invulnerable in the realm of innovation and on occasion squandered huge opportunities. A case in point was the document copying business. 3M invented this business in 1951 when it introduced the world's first commercially successful Thermo Fax copier (which used specially coated 3M paper to copy original typed documents). 3M dominated the world copier business until 1970, when Xerox overtook the company with its revolutionary xerographic technology that used plain paper to make copies. 3M saw Xerox coming, but rather than try and develop their own plain paper copier, the company invested funds in trying to improve its (increasingly obsolete) copying technology. It was not until 1975 that 3M introduced its own plain paper copier, and by then it was too late. Ironically, 3M turned down the chance to acquire Xerox's technology twenty years earlier, when the company's founders had approached 3M.

Building the Organization

McKnight, a strong believer in decentralization, organized the company into product divisions in 1948 making 3M one of the early adopters of this organizational form. Each division was set up as an individual profit center that had the power, autonomy, and resources to run independently. At the same time, certain functions remained centralized, including significant R&D, human resources, and finance.

McKnight wanted to keep the divisions small enough that people had a chance to be entrepreneurial, and focused on the customer. A key philosophy of McKnight's was "divide and grow." Put simply, when a division became too big, some of its embryonic businesses were spun off into a new division. Not only did this new division then typically attain higher growth rates, but also the original division had to find new drivers of growth to make up for the contribution of the businesses that had gained independence. This drove the search for further innovations.

At 3M the process of organic diversification by splitting divisions became known as "renewal." The examples of renewal within 3M are legion. A copying machine project for Thermo-Fax copiers grew to become the Office Products Division. When Magnetic Recording Materials was spun off from the Electrical Products Division, it grew to become its own division, and then in turn spawned a spate of divisions.

However, this organic process was not without its downside. By the early 1990s, some of 3M's key customers were frustrated that they had to do business with a large number of different 3M divisions. In some cases, there could be representatives from ten to twenty 3M divisions calling on the same customer. To cope with this problem, in 1992 3M started to assign key account representatives to sell 3M products directly to major customers. These representatives typically worked across divisional lines. Implementing the strategy required many of 3M's general managers to give up some of their autonomy and power, but the solution seemed to work well, particularly for 3M's consumer and office divisions.

Underpinning the organization that McKnight put in place was his own management philosophy. As explained in a 1948 document, his basic management philosophy consisted of the following values:[11]

> As our business grows, it becomes increasingly necessary to delegate responsibility and to encourage men and women to exercise their initiative. This requires considerable tolerance. Those men and women to whom we delegate authority and responsibility, if they are good people, are going to want to do their jobs in their own way.
>
> Mistakes will be made. But if a person is essentially right, the mistakes he or she makes are not as serious in the long run as the mistakes management

will make if it undertakes to tell those in authority exactly how they must do their jobs.

Management that is destructively critical when mistakes are made kills initiative. And it's essential that we have many people with initiative if we are to continue to grow.

At just 3 percent per annum, employee turnover rate at 3M has long been among the lowest in corporate America, a fact that is often attributed to the tolerant, empowering, and familylike corporate culture that McKnight helped to establish. Reinforcing this culture has been a progressive approach toward employee compensation and retention. In the depths of the Great Depression, 3M was able to avoid laying off employees while many others did because the company's innovation engine was able to keep building new businesses even through the worst of times.

In many ways, 3M was ahead of its time in management philosophy and human resource practices. The company introduced its first profit sharing plan in 1916, and McKnight instituted a pension plan in 1930 and an employee stock purchase plan in 1950. McKnight himself was convinced that people would be much more likely to be loyal in a company if they had a stake in it. 3M also developed a policy of promoting from within and of giving its employees a plethora of career opportunities within the company.

Going International

The first steps abroad occurred in the 1920s. There were some limited sales of Wetordry sandpaper in Europe during the early 1920s. These increased after 1929 when 3M joined the Durex Corporation, a joint venture for international abrasive product sales in which 3M was involved along with eight other U.S. companies. In 1950, however, the Department of Justice alleged that the Durex Corporation was a mechanism for achieving collusion among U.S. abrasives manufacturers, and a judge ordered that the corporation be broken up. After the Durex Corporation was dissolved in 1951, 3M was left with a sandpaper factory in Britain, a small plant in France, a sales office in Germany, and a tape factory in Brazil. International sales at this point amounted to no more than 5 percent of 3M's total revenues.

Although 3M opposed the dissolution of the Durex Corporation, in retrospect it turned out to be one of the most important events in the company's history, for it forced the corporation to build its own

international operations. By 2002, international sales amounted to 55 percent of total revenues.

In 1952, Clarence Sampair was put in charge of 3M's international operations and charged with getting them off the ground. He was given considerable strategic and operational independence. Sampair and his successor, Maynard Patterson, worked hard to protect the international operations from getting caught up in the red tape of a major corporation. For example, Patterson recounts how

I asked Em Monteiro to start a small company in Colombia. I told him to pick a key person he wanted to take with him. "Go start a company," I said, "and no one from St. Paul is going to visit you unless you ask for them. We'll stay out of your way, and if someone sticks his nose in your business you call me."[12]

The international businesses were grouped into an International Division that Sampair headed. From the get-go the company insisted that foreign ventures pay their own way. In addition, 3M's international companies were expected to pay a 5 to 10 percent royalty to the corporate head office. Starved of working capital, 3M's International Division relied heavily on local borrowing to fund local operations, a fact that forced those operations to quickly pay their own way.

The international growth at 3M typically occurred in stages. The company would start by exporting to a country and working through sales subsidiaries. In that way, it began to understand the country, the local marketplace, and the local business environment. Next 3M established warehouses in each nation, and stocked those with goods paid for in local currency. The next phase involved converting products to the sizes and packaging forms that the local market conditions, customs, and culture dictated. 3M would ship jumbo rolls of products from the United States, which were then broken up and repackaged for each country. The next stage was designing and building plants, buying machinery, and getting everything up and running. Over the years, R&D functions were often added, and by the 1980s, considerable R&D was being done outside of the United States.

Both Sampair and Patterson set an innovative, entrepreneurial framework that, according to the company, still guides 3M's international operations today. The philosophy can be reduced to several key and simple commitments: (1) Get in early (within the company, the strategy is known as FIDO—"First in Defeats Others");

(2) hire talented and motivated local people; (3) become a good corporate citizen of the country; (4) grow with the local economy; (5) American products are not one size fits all around the world—tailor products to fit local needs; and (6) enforce patents in local countries.

As 3M stepped into the international market vacuum, foreign sales surged from less than 5 percent in 1951 to 42 percent by 1979. By the end of the 1970s, 3M was beginning to understand how important it was to integrate the international operations more closely with the U.S. operations and to build innovative capabilities overseas. It expanded the company's international R&D presence (there are now more than twenty-two hundred technical employees outside the United States), built closer ties between the United States and foreign research organizations, and started to transfer more managerial and technical employees between businesses in different countries.

In 1978, the company started the Pathfinder Program to encourage new product and new business initiatives born outside the United States. By 1983, products developed under the initiative were generating sales of over $150 million a year. 3M Brazil invented a low-cost, hot melt adhesive from local raw materials. 3M Germany teamed up with Sumitomo 3M of Japan (a joint venture with Sumitomo) to develop electronic connectors with new features for the worldwide electronics industry, and 3M Philippines developed a Scotch-Brite cleaning pad shaped like a foot after learning that Filipinos polished floors with their feet, and so on. On the back of such developments, in 1992 international operations exceeded 50 percent for the first time in the company's history.

By the 1990s, 3M started to shift away from a country-by-country management structure to more regional management. Drivers behind this development included the fall of trade barriers, the rise of trading blocks such as the European Union and NAFTA, and the need to drive down costs in the face of intense global competition. The first European Business Center (EBC) was created in 1991 to manage 3M's chemical business across Europe. The EBC was charged with product development, manufacturing, sales and marketing for Europe, but also with paying attention to local country requirements. Other EBCs soon followed, such as EBCs for disposable products and pharmaceuticals.

As the millennium ended, 3M seemed set on transforming the company into a transnational organization characterized by an integrated network of businesses that spanned the globe. The goal was to get the right mix of global scale to deal with competitive pressures while at the same time maintaining 3M's traditional focus on local market differences and decentralized R&D capabilities.

The New Era
The DeSimone Years

In 1991, Desi DeSimone became CEO of 3M. A long-time 3M employee, the Canadian born DeSimone was the epitome of a twenty-first century manager—he had made his name by building 3M's Brazilian business, and he spoke five languages fluently. Unlike most prior 3M CEOs, DeSimone came from the manufacturing side of the business, rather than the technical side. He soon received praise for managing 3M through the recession of the early 1990s. By the late 1990s, however, his leadership had come under fire from both inside and outside the company.

In 1998 and 1999, the company missed its earnings targets, and the stock price fell as disappointed investors sold. Sales were flat, profit margins fell, and earnings slumped by 50 percent. The stock had underperformed the widely tracked S&P 500 stock index for most of the 1980s and 1990s.

One cause of the earnings slump in the late 1990s was 3M's sluggish response to the 1997 Asian crisis. During the Asian crisis, the value of several Asian currencies fell by as much as 80 percent against the U.S. dollar in a matter of months. 3M generated a quarter of its sales from Asia, but it was slow to cut costs there in the face of slumping demand following the collapse of currency values. At the same time, a flood of cheap Asian products cut into 3M's market share in the United States and Europe as lower currency values made Asian products much cheaper.

Another problem was that for all of its vaunted innovative capabilities, 3M had not produced a new blockbuster product since Post-it Notes. Most of the new products produced during the 1990s were just improvements over existing products, not truly new products.

DeSimone was also blamed for not pushing 3M hard enough earlier in the decade to reduce costs. An example was the company's supply chain excellence program. Back in 1995, 3M's inventory was turning over just 3.5 times a year, subpar for manufacturing. An internal study suggested that every half point increase in inventory turnover could reduce 3M's working capital needs by $700 million and boost its return on invested capital. But by 1998, 3M had made no progress on this front.[13]

By 1998, there was also evidence of internal concerns. Anonymous letters from 3M employees were sent to the Board of Directors, claiming that DeSimone was not committed to research as he should have been. Some letters complained that DeSimone was not funding important projects for future growth, others that he had not moved boldly enough to cut costs, and still others that the company's dual career track was not being implemented well and that technical people were underpaid. Critics argued that he was a slow and cautious decision maker in a time that required decisive strategic decisions. For example, in August 1998 DeSimone announced a restructuring plan that included a commitment to cut forty-five hundred jobs, but reports suggest that other senior managers wanted ten thousand job cuts, and DeSimone had watered down the proposals.[14]

Despite the criticism, 3M's board, which included four previous 3M CEOs among its members, stood behind DeSimone until he retired in 2001. However, the board began a search for a new top executive in February 2000 and signaled that it was looking for an outsider. In December 2000, the company announced that it had found the person they wanted, Jim McNerney, a fifty-one-year-old General Electric veteran who ran GE's medical equipment businesses, and before that GE's Asian operations. McNerney was one of the front runners in the race to succeed Jack Welsh as CEO of General Electric, but lost out to Jeffrey Immelt. One week after that announcement, 3M hired him.

McNerney's Plan for 3M

In his first public statement days after being appointed, McNerney said that his focus would be on getting to know 3M's people and culture and its diverse lines of business:

> I think getting to know some of those businesses and bringing some of GE here to overlay on top of 3M's strong culture of innovation will be particularly important.[15]

It soon became apparent that McNerney's game plan was exactly that: to bring the GE play book to 3M and use it to try and boost 3M's results, while simultaneously not destroying the innovative culture that had produced the company's portfolio of fifty thousand products.

The first move came in April 2001 when 3M announced that the company would cut five thousand jobs, or about 7 percent of the work force, in a restructuring effort that would zero in on struggling businesses. To cover severance and other costs of restructuring, 3M announced that it would take a $600 million charge against earnings. The job cuts were expected to save $500 million a year. In another effort to save costs, the company streamlined its purchasing processes, for example, by reducing the number of packaging suppliers on a global basis from fifty to five, saving another $100 million a year in the process.

Next, McNerney introduced the Six-Sigma process, a rigorous statistically based quality control process that was one of the drivers of process improvement and cost savings at General Electric. At heart, Six Sigma is a management philosophy, accompanied by a set of tools, that is rooted in identifying and prioritizing customers and their needs, reducing variation in all business processes, and selecting and grading all projects based on their impact on financial results. Six Sigma breaks every task (process) in an organization down into increments to be measured against a perfect model.

McNerney called for Six Sigma to be rolled out across 3M's global operations. He also introduced a 3M-like performance evaluation system at 3M under which managers were asked to rank every single employee who reported to them.

In addition to boosting performance from existing business, McNerney quickly signaled that he wanted to play a more active role in allocating resources between new business opportunities. At any given time, 3M has around fifteen hundred products in the development pipeline. McNerney thinks that is too many, and he has stated that he wants to funnel more cash to the most promising ideas, those with a potential market of $100 million a year or more, while cutting funding to weaker looking development projects.

In the same vein, he signaled that he wanted to play a more active role in resource allocation than had traditionally been the case for a 3M CEO, using cash from mature businesses to fund growth opportunities elsewhere. He scrapped the requirement that each division get 30 percent of its sales from products introduced in the past four years, noting that:

> To make that number, some managers were resorting to some rather dubious innovations, such as pink Post it Notes. It became a game, what could you do to get a new SKU?[16]

Some long time 3M watchers, however, worried that by changing resource allocation practices McNerney might harm 3M's innovative culture. If the company's history proves anything, they say, it's that it is hard to tell which of today's tiny products will become tomorrow's home runs. No one predicted that Scotch Guard or Post-it Notes would earn millions. They began as little experiments that evolved without planning into big hits. McNerney's innovations all sound fine in theory, they say, but there is a risk that he will transform 3M into "3E" and lose what is valuable in 3M in the process.

In general though, securities analysts greeted McNerney's moves favorably. One noted that "McNerney is all about speed" and that there will be "no more Tower of Babel—everyone speaks one language." This "one company" vision was meant to replace the program under which 3M systematically spun off successful new products into new business centers. The problem with this approach, according to the analyst, was that there was no leveraging of best practices across businesses.[17]

McNerney also signaled that he would reform 3M's regional management structure, replacing it with a global business unit structure that will be defined by either products or markets.

Fall 2003

At a meeting for investment analysts, held on September 30, 2003, McNerney summarized a number of achievements to date.[18] At the time, the early indications seemed to suggest that McNerney was helping to revitalize 3M. Profitability, measured by return on invested capital, had risen from 17.6 percent in 2001 to 21.6 percent in the first half of 2003, and 3M's stock price had risen from $42 just before McNerney was hired to $73 in October 2003.

Like his former boss, Jack Welsh at GE, McNerney seemed to place significant value on internal executive education programs as a way of shifting to a performance-oriented culture. McNerney noted that some twenty thousand employees had been through Six-Sigma training by the third quarter of 2003. Almost four hundred higher level managers had been through an Advanced Leadership Development Program set up by McNerney, and offered by 3M's own internal executive education institute. Some 40 percent of participants had been promoted on graduating. All of the company's top managers had graduated from an Executive Leadership Program offered by 3M.

McNerney also emphasized the value of five initiatives that he has put in place at 3M; indirect cost control, global sourcing, e-productivity, Six Sigma, and the 3M Acceleration Program. With regard to indirect cost control, some $800 million had been taken out of 3M's cost structure since 2001, primarily by reducing employee numbers, introducing more efficient processes that boost productivity, benchmarking operations internally, and leveraging best practices. According to McNerney, internal benchmarking highlighted another $200 to $400 million in potential cost savings over the next few years.

On global sourcing, McNerney noted that more than $500 million had been saved since 2000 by consolidating purchasing, reducing the number of suppliers, switching to lower cost suppliers in developing nations, and introducing dual sourcing policies to keep price increases under control.

The e-productivity program at 3M embraces the entire organization and all functions. It involves the digitalization of a wide range of processes, from customer ordering and payment, through supply chain management and inventory control, to managing employee processes. The central goal is to boost productivity by using information technology to more effectively manage information within the company, and between the company and its customers and suppliers. McNerney cites some $100 million in annual cost savings from this process to date.

The Six-Sigma program overlays the entire organization, and focuses on improving processes to boost cash flow, lower costs (through productivity enhancements), and boost growth rates. By late 2003, there were some seven thousand Six-Sigma projects in process at 3M. By using working capital more efficiently, Six-Sigma programs had helped to generate some $800 million in cash, with the total expected to rise to $1.5 billion by the end of 2004. 3M has applied the Six-Sigma process to the company's R&D process, enabling researchers to engage customer information in the initial stages of a design discussion, which, according to Jay Inlenfeld, the vice president of R&D, Six-Sigma tools, "allow us to be more closely connected to the market and give us a much higher probability of success in our new product designs."[19]

Finally, the 3M Acceleration program is aimed to boost the growth rate from new products through better resource allocation, particularly by shifting resources from slower growing to faster growing markets. As McNerney noted,

> 3M has always had extremely strong competitive positions, but not in markets that are growing fast enough. The issue has been to shift emphasis into markets that are growing faster.[20]

Part of this program is a tool termed 2X/3X. 2X is an objective for two times the number of new products that were introduced in the past, and 3X is a business objective for three times as many winning products as there were in the past (see Exhibit 3). 2X focuses on generating more "major" product initiatives, and 3X on improving the commercialization of those initiatives. The process illustrated in Exhibit 3 is 3M's "stage gate" process, where each gate represents a major decision point in the development of a new product, from idea generation to postlaunch.

Other initiatives aimed at boosting 3M's organization growth rate through innovation include the Six-Sigma process, leadership development programs, and technology leadership (see Exhibit 4). The purpose of these initiatives is to help implement the 2X/3X strategy.

As a further step in the Acceleration Program, 3M has decided to centralize its corporate R&D effort. Prior to the arrival of McNerney, there were 12 technology centers staffed by 900 scientists that focused on core technology development. The company is replacing these with one central research lab, staffed by 500 scientists, some 120 of whom will be located outside the United States. The remaining 400 scientists will be relocated to R&D centers in the business units. The goal of this new corporate research lab is to focus on developing new technology that might fill high growth "white spaces," which are areas where the company currently has no presence, but where the long-term market potential is great. An example is research on fuel cells, which is currently a big research project within 3M.

Responding to critics' charges that changes such as these might impact on 3M's innovative culture, Vice President of R&D Inlenfeld notes that:

> We are not going to change the basic culture of innovation at 3M. There is a lot of culture in 3M, but we are going to introduce more systematic, more productive tools that allow our researchers to be more successful.[23]

For example, Inlenfeld has repeatedly emphasized that the company remains committed to basic 3M principles, such as the 15 percent rule and leveraging technology across businesses.

By late 2003, McNerney noted that some six hundred new product ideas were under development and that, collectively, they were expected to reach the

EXHIBIT 3

The New Product Development Process at 3M[21]

2X/3X Strategy: 2X Idea Velocity/3X Winning Products Out

| Ideas | Concept | Feasibility | Development | Scale-up | Launch | Post-launch |

New product development process

Gates 1 2 3 4 5 6

2X New opportunities   3X Market success

Identification 2X

Development

Commercialization 3X

EXHIBIT 4

R&D's Role in Organic Growth[22]

market and generate some $5 billion in new revenues between 2003 and 2006, up from $3.5 billion eighteen months earlier. Some $1 billion of these gains were expected to come in 2003.

The Acceleration Program was helping to increase 3M's organic growth rate in earnings per share, which hit an annual rate of 3.6 percent in the first half of 2003, up from 1 percent a year earlier and a decline in 2001. To complement internally generated growth, McNerney signaled that he would make selected acquisitions in business that 3M already had a presence in.

REFERENCES

J.C. Collins and J.I. Porras. *Built to Last.* New York: Harper Business, 1994.

Michelle Conlin. "Too Much Doodle?" *Forbes*, October 19, 1998, pages 54–56.

M. Dickson. "Back to the Future." *Financial Times*, May 30, 1994, page 7.

Joseph Hallinan. "3M's Next Chief Plans to Fortify Results With Discipline He Learned at GE Unit." *Wall Street Journal*, December 6, 2000, page B17.

Eric von Hippel et al. "Creating Breakthroughs at 3M." *Harvard Business Review* (September–October 1999).

Rick Mullin. "Analysts Rate 3M's New Culture." *Chemical Week*, September 26, 2001, pages 39–40.

Tim Studt. "3M—Where Innovation Rules," *R&D Magazine* 45 (April 2003): pages 20–24.

3M. "A Century of Innovation, the 3M Story." 3M, 2002. Available at http://www.3m.com/about3m/century/index.jhtml.

3M Investor Meeting, September 30, 2003, archived at http:// www.corporate-ir.net/ireye/ir_site.zhtml?ticker=MMM&script= 2100.

Jerry Useem. "(Tape) + (Light bulb) = ?" *Fortune*, August 12, 2002, pages 127–131.

De'Ann Weimer. "3M: The Heat Is on the Boss." *Business Week*, March 15, 1999, pages 82–83.

ENDNOTES

1. M. Dickson, "Back to the Future," *Financial Times*, May 30, 1994, page 7, http://www.3m.com/profile/looking/mcknight.jhtml.
2. http://www.3m.com/about3M/pioneers/drew2.jhtml.
3. http://www.3m.com/about3M/innovation/scotchgard50/index.jhtml.

4. "3M. A Century of Innovation, the 3M Story." 3M, 2002. Available at **http://www.3m.com/about3m/century/index.jhtml.**

5. Ibid., page 33.

6. Tim Studt, "3M—Where Innovation Rules," *R&D Magazine* 45 (April 2003): pages 20–24.

7. "3M. A Century of Innovation," page 78.

8. Ibid.

9. Ibid., page 42.

10. Eric Von Hippel et al., "Creating Breakthroughs at 3M," *Harvard Business Review* (September–October 1999).

11. From 3M website at **http://www.3m.com/about3M/history/mcknight.jhtml.**

12. "3M. A Century of Innovation," pages 143–144.

13. Michelle Conlin, "Too Much Doodle?" *Forbes*, October 19, 1998, pages 54–56.

14. De'Ann Weimer, "3M: The Heat Is on the Boss," *Business Week*, March 15, 1999, pages 82–83.

15. Joseph Hallinan, "3M's Next Chief Plans to Fortify Results With Discipline He Learned at GE Unit," *Wall Street Journal*, December 6, 2000, page B17.

16. Jerry Useem, "(Tape) + (Light bulb) = ?" *Fortune*, August 12, 2002, pages 127–131.

17. Rick Mullin, "Analysts Rate 3M's New Culture," *Chemical Week*, September 26, 2001, pages 39–40.

18. 3M Investor Meeting, September 30, 2003, archived at **http://www. corporate-ir.net/ireye/ir_site.zhtml?ticker=MMM&script= 2100.**

19. Studt, "3M—Where Innovation Rules," page 22.

20. 3M Investor Meeting, September 30, 2003.

21. Adapted from presentation by Jay Inlenfeld, 3M Investor Meeting, September 30, 2003, archived at **http://www.corporate-ir.net/ireye/ ir_site.zhtml?ticker=MMM&script=2100.**

22. Ibid.

23. Studt, "3M—Where Innovation Rules," page 21.

The Rise of IBM

This case was prepared by Gareth R. Jones and Susan L. Peters, Texas A&M University.

In 1900 Charles Flint, a financier and arms merchant, owned among many other businesses two business machine manufacturers: the International Time Recording Co. (ITR), a clock manufacturer, and Computing Scale Co. of America, a weighing scale and food slicing machine manufacturer. In the search for new markets for its products, ITR began to produce new kinds of time-measuring machines that, among other things, permitted the rapidly expanding Bell telephone company to time its customers' long-distance calls. By 1910 ITR had become the leader in the time-recording industry with sales over $1 million. Computing Scale's main product was a scale that weighed items and calculated the cost per unit; the company also sold meat and cheese slicers to retail stores.

Toward the end of the nineteenth century, engineer Herman Hollerith invented a tabulating machine that sorted cards by punching holes. Any kind of data could be recorded by punching holes in cards according to a standard procedure and then the data could be analyzed statistically to provide a picture of the overall results. Potential customers for this device were organizations that needed a way of managing and manipulating large amounts of information, such as government agencies, railroads, and retail establishments. The U.S. Census Bureau, for example, saw the potential of this device for handling its national

data collection efforts and Hollerith was awarded a contract for managing the data processing of the 1890 census. Holes were punched in cards to represent different census attributes like age, sex, and national origin. The cards were then sorted by these punched holes and Hollerith's tabulating machine would then supply the requested data such as the statistics for the percentage of people in a certain age group in a certain state.

The punch card machine required a huge number of punched cards—in the census, one for every family unit—that could be used only once, so each machine sale provided card revenue. Nevertheless, the potential uses of the machine were limitless since any kind of data could be recorded on these cards. James Powers, an employee of the U.S. Census Bureau, immediately saw the potential of the tabulating machine and from his experience with Hollerith's machines at the Census Bureau he understood its strengths and weaknesses. Using this information, Powers invented an improved tabulating machine. Using his contacts at the Census Bureau, he managed to secure the contract for the 1910 census beating out Hollerith.

Hollerith was now in a difficult position because he had lost his principal customer and lacked the resources to improve his machine and to find new customers. He approached Flint to get Flint to invest in the business. Flint, seeing the opportunity to broaden his company's line of business machines, decided instead to acquire Hollerith's Tabulating Machine Company. In 1911 Flint merged it with ITR and Computing Scale to form the Computing Tabulating & Recording Company (CTR).

In operating his business, Hollerith had developed the practice of leasing, rather than selling, his machines to customers. He had opted for leasing

Copyright © 1993 by Gareth R. Jones. This case was prepared by Gareth R. Jones and Susan L. Peters, Texas A&M University, as the basis for class discussion rather than to illustrate either effective or ineffective handling of an administrative situation. Reprinted by permission of Gareth R. Jones. All rights reserved. For the most recent financial results of the company discussed in this case, go to **http://finance.yahoo.com**, input the company's stock symbol, and download the latest company report from its homepage.

because his machines were prone to breaking down, and they needed frequent repair as their mechanical components tended to break down with repeated use. By leasing his machines and backing them with an efficient repair service, Hollerith kept his customers happy. Moreover, customers liked the arrangement because it lowered their costs. Using CTR's resources, the Hollerith tabulating machines were continually improved over time, and as new machines were developed, they were leased to customers and replaced the old machines. These leases provided CTR with a continuing source of revenue, but more important, each of CTR's customers was required to buy punch cards from CTR. Seventy-five percent of tabulating revenues and most of the profit came from the sale of the punched cards, while only 25 percent came from the lease of the actual machine itself. In 1912 CTR's profits were $541,000 with 66 percent of this total coming from ITR, its time machine division. By 1913, however, profits rose to $613,000 with most of the increase traceable to revenues from punch cards and tabulators. The revenue produced by its new tabulator business proved very important to CTR because the next year, 1914, profits plunged to $490,000 due to a decline in the time clock sector. Only the tabulating business kept the company afloat.

The Impact of Thomas Watson

In 1914, to build CTR's business, Flint agreed to hire Thomas Watson as the general manager of CTR. Watson was a former employee of National Cash Register (NCR), another major business machine company, which he had joined in 1895 when he was 21 years old. Watson had a passion for selling and began selling pianos, sewing machines, and organs when he was 18. The opportunity to earn large commissions eventually led him to NCR where a mentor took an interest in his career and helped him develop his selling skills to the point where he became the star salesman at NCR within three years. Watson became an NCR branch manager in 1899.

To exploit Watson's talents, NCR assigned him to create an independent company using NCR funds. It was called Watson's Cash Register and Second Hand Exchange and was designed to beat NCR's competitors in the used cash register market. Just as NCR had a virtual monopoly over the sale of new cash registers, so Watson set out to monopolize the used cash register market by deliberately undercutting competitors'

prices. With their businesses failing, NCR would then acquire its competitors. This practice was blatantly illegal, and in 1912, Watson along with 29 other NCR managers were indicted for violation of antitrust laws. Watson was fined and sentenced to one year in jail; however, he won on appeal, and having quarreled with the head of NCR he decided to leave the company. Watson had other offers in the boat, auto, and retail industries, but because he wanted to use his knowledge of business machines, he accepted Flint's offer at CTR.

Watson's experience at NCR was significant for CTR because he implemented many of NCR's sales practices at CTR. Although NCR's competitors had higher-quality cash registers than NCR, NCR consistently beat the competition because of the way it organized and rewarded its sales force. NCR had developed the practice of granting salespeople exclusive rights to a territory and then paying them on commission. Salespeople would pursue all sales opportunities in their territories aggressively and they would call continually on customers in order to build strong, personal relationships with them. This sales strategy had been developed by the leader of NCR, John Patterson, who believed that a product was worthless until it was sold and that salespeople were the key to selling the product. Patterson insisted that NCR salespeople answer repair calls immediately and instilled in them the notion that they were selling a service, not just a product. NCR created a training school in 1894 to train its salespeople; it also established the NCR "Hundred Point Club" which recognized and rewarded salespeople who exceeded their quotas. Members of the club received bonuses and trips to conventions in big cities, coverage in the company newspaper, and personal congratulations from Patterson. Watson took full advantage of his knowledge of NCR's sales practices and transferred them to CTR. He also took full advantage of his entrepreneurial ability to sense unmet customer needs; he was fascinated by the potential of the punch card tabulating machine.

In 1904 Watson saw a friend at Eastman Kodak using a Hollerith punch card tabulating machine to monitor salespeople. Each time a sale was completed, all the data were stored onto a card, which was sorted and tabulated monthly to generate reports indicating what each person sold, which products were selling best in which regions, and so on. The cards were permanent records that could be filed, accumulated, and printed automatically. The punch card system eliminated boring jobs such as copying ledger entries and writing bills. Furthermore, the machines were relatively inexpensive (compared to employing clerks to keep records), dependable, and fast. Thus, as head of CTR, Watson became most interested in the tabulating machine side of the business even though ITR's time measurement business generated the highest sales and profits at the time.

When Watson became president of CTR in 1915 he convinced Flint that CTR should devote most of its resources to developing the tabulator side of the business. Watson implemented a plan to develop new tabulators, recorders, and printers to print the output of the tabulating machine. To achieve this new plan, the company funded the development of a research laboratory to improve the tabulating machines and established a facility to train salespeople. His goal was to create a sales force like NCR's sales force and to make better tabulating machines than CTR's competitors. To help provide the revenue to achieve this, Watson licensed foreign companies to produce and sell the tabulators in foreign markets. The licensees paid a royalty to CTR based on sales. This was the beginning of CTR's international strategy. Within two years, CTR's research laboratory created a new line of tabulators that were easier to use than competitors' models and that were priced below its competitors and offered for lease on favorable terms.

Powers was still CTR's major competitor at this time. To compete with Powers, which had tabulators as good as CTR's, Watson used the strategy that NCR had developed in the cash register business: sell a service, not just a product. Watson, like Patterson, emphasized that the salesperson's role was to provide good quality customer service, not merely to lease and install a machine. What CTR was selling was a way to handle information. This new philosophy was to guide the company's future mission.

Watson established the "100 Percent Club" to reward his best salespeople, and employees were paid generous commissions for meeting and exceeding their quotas. Those who met quotas and joined the 100 Percent Club were honored at conventions and received special status in the organization; 80 percent of employees made the club. In addition, employees received a premium salary and good benefits. The company's policy of internal promotion made it possible for hard-working employees to advance quickly in the organization. These employment practices made it easy for CTR to attract and retain good salespeople and to gain the commitment of its work force which was famous for championing the company's products.

By 1917 CTR's sales had increased to $8.3 million from $4.2 million in 1914. All three of its divisions were doing well. Computing Scale's products were now used throughout the United States in places such as shipyards and factories to measure the quantity of products such as nuts and bolts. CTR had record sales during World War I. CTR had 1,400 tabulators on lease by the end of the war.

Virtually all big insurance companies, railroads, and government agencies used CTR's tabulators. In addition to the leased machines, the sales of punch cards were increasing and contributing to company revenues. In 1919, CTR launched a new printer that displayed the data collected and analyzed in the Hollerith tabulators and card sorters. The printer was priced below the machine made by Powers and was so successful that CTR had a backorder for the printers and Watson planned to build a new production plant to meet the high demand.

The large expenditures on research and development and on developing and training a skilled national sales force put a severe strain on CTR's resources. The strain was so severe that when sales revenues dropped from a record of $16 million in 1920 to $10.6 million in 1921, due to a slump in the national economy, CTR had to seek outside funds to survive. Fortunately for the company, Guaranty Trust Bank lent CTR the money it needed to meet current liabilities, and in 1922 sales revenues rebounded and the company made a profit. However, the company had to cut costs in every area, including sales and R&D, and CTR learned not to let cash balances go too low and implemented policies of low dividends, high revenues, and careful cost controls. In addition, the company intentionally refrained from introducing its new products until a mass market had developed for its new range of tabulating machines.

Watson became chairman of CTR in 1924 and renamed the company International Business Machines (IBM). This new name not only presented an integrated image of the company's three main product lines but also indicated the direction Watson planned for the company—the company's business was to provide advanced business machines for both the domestic and foreign markets.

IBM's strategy from the 1920s on was to produce and lease business machines that collect, process, and present large amounts of data. From 1924 to 1941, IBM's primary business was the production and lease of punched card tabulating machines and the sale of punch cards; punched cards still contributed most to the revenues of the company. As the technology of punch card tabulators became more advanced, they were able to sort 400 cards a minute and could print paychecks and address labels. Tabulating machines were used increasingly by large companies to keep records on their employees and suppliers and to keep track of their customer accounts. Companies usually leased IBM's machines and IBM would develop a specific punch card system to meet the needs of each individual customer. For example, IBM would help the customer design a coding system appropriate to each client's information processing needs.

The potential of punch card tabulating machines had been recognized by other companies as well. While the Powers Accounting Machine Corp. had long been IBM's competitor, new computers included Burroughs, National Cash Register, Remington Rand, and Underwood Elliot Fisher. Underwood, which was created in 1927, ruled the typewriter industry with its Model 5 and had a sales force as good as IBM's, while Burroughs was the leader in adding machines. At this time, IBM was not interested in mass producing machines like typewriters and adding machines unless such machines could be made part of the tabulating system. Its strategy was to lease its machines and then support the machines with trained service representatives who were available to handle a customer's problems and to make suggestions for improving a customer's information processing as the individual business changed.

Leasing gave IBM several competitive advantages over Burroughs, NCR, and Remington Rand, which all sold their machines to customers. First, it allowed the company to retain control over outdated technology which could not be resold in the used market (a problem NCR had encountered which reduced its profits). Second, leasing made it easier for the customer because they were not committed to a large capital outlay or the threat of purchasing a machine that would be outmoded quickly by technological change. Third, leasing provided IBM with a steady cash flow. Fourth, and very important, by leasing its machine IBM was also able to force customers to purchase the thousands of punch cards they used each month from IBM.

IBM's practice of requiring customers to buy its cards led to an antitrust suit in 1936, and the Supreme Court ruled that IBM should discontinue requiring customers to buy cards from it alone. This ruling had little impact on IBM because IBM was the most convenient supplier of cards and its sales force serviced the machines and made sure that customers were kept happy.

During the 1920s and 1930s IBM also began to develop specialized tabulators to handle specific types of information processing needs for customers. For example, IBM developed a proofing machine to be used by banks that could sort and add checks, a very labor-intensive process. This proof machine, called the IBM 405, was launched in 1932 and became IBM's most profitable product at the time. The 405 consisted of a punch, sorter, and accounting machine. Operators punched holes in cards to represent data; the sorter then put the cards in the appropriate bins; the cards were then taken out of the bins and run through the accounting machines, which generated printouts of the data and which also could print checks. Some customers rented verifiers which attached to the punch to ensure the cards were prepared properly. IBM trained its customers' employees on how to use the 405 machines at no cost to promote customer loyalty and to ensure a demand for its products.

By 1939 IBM was the biggest and most powerful business machine company in the United States. IBM owned about 80 percent of the keypunches, sorters, and accounting machines used for tabulating purposes. By this time Remington Rand and Burroughs were minor competitors and the Powers company had disappeared, unable to match IBM's strengths in sales and research and development.

Also by 1939 Watson had reorganized the company's business divisions to meet the needs to IBM's new focus on tabulating machines. The punch card tabulating division became the center of the company business, and the company's other products were now oriented around this division. For example, Watson decided to keep ITR, which sold time clocks among other things, because customers purchased many time cards that were similar to punch cards. He sold off the largest part of the scale division because it no longer fit the company's new direction. He bought Electromatic Typewriter Co. because it was working on keypunch consoles. This purchase proved very significant; by 1945 IBM had developed this company into the U.S. leader in electric typewriters, which were sold by IBM's large, well-trained sales force.

In 1939 total revenues were $34.8 million and profits were $9.1 million. Sales of punch cards were about $5 million of this and had higher profit margins than any other product. The start of World War II accelerated the demand for IBM's tabulating machines and sales rose to $143.3 million by 1943. However, profits were only $9.7 million due to the wartime excess profits tax. IBM achieved higher sales with mobile punch card units that followed supply controllers across war zones so that bookkeeping could be done on the battlefield. For example, a mobile unit would go to a Pacific Island and compute the soldiers' payroll. The tabulators also recorded bombing results, casualties, prisoners, displaced persons, and supplies. A punch card record was maintained on every man drafted and followed him until he was discharged from the military.

By 1945 IBM had begun aggressively to pursue the idea that just producing business machines was not enough; supplying customers with a way to manage their information processing needs was even more important. This change in focus was very significant; IBM now saw its role as developing new and different kinds of products to suit its customers' needs, rather than in finding new ways to use and improve existing machines. This change in operating philosophy proved very important with the development of the first working computer.

The Computer Age

Toward the end of World War II, a research team at the University of Pennsylvania constructed a computer to solve math problems for the Army; the machine, called the ENIAC, could compute ballistic tables to accurately aim and fire the big guns of World War II. In 1946 the ENIAC was the only working computer in the world. This computer was the size of a small house and had 18,000 vacuum tubes, which were apt to burn out. The machine cost $3 million to build, took a long time to set up, and was very difficult to use. The inventors of the computer, J. Presper Eckert and John Mauchley, realized that computers could perform the same function as punch card tabulating machines only much more quickly because they processed information electronically rather than mechanically. They realized that their computer eventually could replace tabulating machines in business, so they created a company to develop and manufacture their computer for commercial use. Their machine and company was called Univac. In 1948 they received an order from the U.S. Census Bureau for their computer, just as Hollerith 60 years before had received an order for his tabulating machine. In the same year Prudential Insurance also ordered a Univac. These organizations were two of IBM's largest customers and so IBM took notice of the new technology and became interested in the Univac computer. In 1950 Remington Rand, which also sold typewriters, tabulators, filing cabinets, and electric shavers, forestalled IBM and bought Eckert and Mauchley's company to gain entry into the new computer market. Just as Watson had realized the potential of the punch card machine, so Remington Rand realized the potential of the computer. The race was on between IBM and Remington Rand to become the company that would dominate the next generation of business machines: computers.

IBM's Race to Catch Up

IBM had not ignored technical developments in the tabulating industry. By 1948 it had developed an electromechanical machine called the MARK I that was 51 feet long by 8 feet high and cost $1 million. This machine was more advanced than a punch card machine, but it was still not a true computer because it did not use vacuum tubes, and it was slower than the Univac. The company was still not committed to the new technology, however, and it took the arrival of Tom Watson, Sr.'s two sons, Tom Jr. and Arthur ("Dick") who joined IBM at the end of the war to bring IBM up to speed.

Tom Watson, Jr., convinced his father that IBM would lose everything if it did not embrace the new technology and enter the computer age. He pointed out that large IBM customers such as the Prudential and Metropolitan Life insurance companies had been complaining for a long time that the punch card system required too much storage space and was becoming too slow and cumbersome to handle the volume of information these companies were generating. Under Tom Jr.'s leadership IBM began to check into new kinds of storage systems, such as magnetic tapes, and to look at the machine that used the new electronic circuits to sort data and handle calculations: the computer. After studying the ENIAC computer, Tom Jr. encouraged IBM's research laboratory managers to recruit more electronic specialists. He prodded IBM to incorporate electronic circuits in punch card machines because a primitive electronic circuit could perform 5,000 additions per second compared to 4 per second for the fastest mechanism in a punch card machine.

Working quickly, and with access to the company's large resource base, in 1946 IBM developed a new machine, the 603 Electronic Multiplier, that could compute payroll in one-tenth the time a mechanical punch card machine could do it. The machine was upgraded to the 604 which had electronic circuits that also allowed the machine to divide. The 604 was not a true computer because numbers were still processed from punch cards rather than from signals recorded in the machine's memory circuits. Nevertheless, when it was introduced in mid 1948 it sold by the thousands. Both machines matched IBM's existing punch card equipment which made it easy for IBM customers to upgrade to the new machines. The machine's success convinced Tom Jr. and Sr. that electronics would grow even faster; from this time on, the company committed its resources to the new technology and to the development of an advanced new computer system.

IBM began working on its first family of electronic computers, called the 701 series, in 1949. Tom Jr. became president of domestic IBM in 1952, the same year the 701 was launched. The 701 was a scientific computer for use in laboratories, but it was not as advanced as the Univac. However, although Remington Rand was ahead in technology, the company lacked IBM's vision and Rand would not permit punch card salespeople to sell Univacs. Tom Jr., however, placed IBM's sales force behind its computer and required both senior executives and engineers to help its sales force in operating the new machine. By 1953 IBM had installed 32 701 computers and had 164 on order compared to Remington Rand's 33 installations and 24 orders.

The 702, a commercial computer for general accounting applications, was launched in 1954. This machine was faster than the Univac and with this machine IBM took the technological lead. By 1956 IBM had 87 computers installed at various businesses and 190 on order, compared to all other competitors' combined installations of 41 and combined orders of 40 computers.

Because all its machines were leased, it was easy for IBM to upgrade its customers to its new advanced machines. When the 705 was developed to replace the 702, and the 704 to replace the 701, IBM retained and increased its market share. Between 1950 and 1956, IBM's revenues tripled from $214.9 million to $743.3 million. The average growth rate of the company from 1946 to 1955 was 22 percent. Watson decided to expand IBM's product line as fast as the market would allow.

IBM's technological success was due to the way Tom Watson, Jr., had totally changed the company's research and development thrust. IBM's research laboratory had been dominated by mechanical engineers because its punch card machines operated on mechanical principles. None of its engineers really understood electronics. So Tom Jr. hired a new laboratory director and increased the size of the R&D staff from 500 mechanical engineers and technicians in 1950 to over 4,000 electrical engineers by 1956. Tom Jr. also created a smaller lab in California to specialize in developing advanced information storage devices; in less than three years the laboratory developed a computer disk that stored data on magnetic tape rather than punch cards, a storage system that became the backbone of IBM's future computer systems and a major source of its competitive advantage.

Tom Watson, Jr., also led the development of the IBM 650 in 1956. It provided enough data processing power for most general commercial applications. The 650 was less powerful than the 700 series but it was much cheaper. The 650 introduced thousands of punch card customers to computers. It was designed to work with ordinary punch card equipment but to make the punch card system much more powerful and versatile. For example, life insurance companies compute insurance premiums from actuarial tables based on age, sex, and other customer factors. Using a 650, these actuarial tables could be loaded into the computer memory, and when the punch card containing information of a particular customer was loaded into the machine the computer did the calculations and furnished the total premium. Previously a clerk had to figure the totals and record the information on a punch card for recording purposes.

IBM put its huge sales force behind the 650 machine; as a result of its efforts, within a year almost 1,000 machines were sold. Most computers were used in administrative offices and in factories where the computer was used to control the manufacturing process. By the end of the 1950s, IBM had a 75 percent market share. The remaining market was divided among Remington Rand, Honeywell Electronics, NCR, and a few others. Although Underwood Typewriter and NCR attempted to launch small computers, they were unable to produce as good a performer as the 650.

The Transistor

In 1956 the transistor, which weighed 100 times less than the vacuum tube, was developed by William Shockley at Bell Labs. Compared to a vacuum tube, the transistor required less electrical power, had the potential to miniaturize computing systems, and, most important, could perform calculations at a much faster rate. The transistor made the design of a more complex and powerful computer feasible; it also made it possible to sell the computer at a price that most large companies could afford.

IBM's electronic researchers had been successfully using the vacuum tube, and as the mechanical engineers before them, they were reluctant to change to new technology: a transistor-based computer technology. So Tom Watson, Jr., sent a memo to R&D personnel stating that no more IBM machines would be designed using vacuum tubes. This memo started a whole new thrust in IBM's research efforts that led to the 7000 computer series, IBM's first computer based on transistors rather than vacuum tubes. However, IBM's scientists had a major problem in wiring transistors together to produce the new advanced computer until the integrated circuit was invented in 1959 by a Fairchild Semiconductor engineer. With the arrival of the integrated circuit, thousands of transistors could be joined together on a circuit board the size of a fingernail. In turn, thousands of integrated circuits could be joined together to make the first modern computer. By the early 1960s, IBM computers guided Polaris missiles and Air Force jets. When integrated circuits were mass produced, their cost fell from $1,000 per circuit in 1960 to a few cents per circuit by 1970, and IBM developed successive generations of more powerful machines to exploit the new technology.

Redefining the Industry

As a result of this succession of technological developments, by 1960 IBM's computer division was disorganized and had a product line consisting of eight newer transistor-based computers and several older vacuum tube machines. This mixed product line caused several problems for IBM's customers and its sales force because the computers were not compatible and could not work together. For example, if a customer expanded and wanted to upgrade to a larger or newer computer, the customer had to lease a whole new range of equipment and rewrite all the programs to make the computer work. The disjointed product line also caused problems for IBM's personnel.

Because IBM's product line had grown so large, Watson decided to split the Data Processing Division into two units: one for the newer machines that rented for over the average price of $10,000 a month and one for older, less-powerful machines that rented for less than $10,000 a month. This decision caused competition between managers of the different product lines, each of whom fought to obtain resources to develop and improve their particular product line. It also led to a duplication of research and development efforts.

The diverse range of computers IBM now leased also made it more difficult for IBM's sales force to learn the characteristics of the different systems associated with each computer and to inform customers about the suitability of a given system for the particular business involved. IBM's technological thrust had outpaced the ability of the company to service its products adequately. Its attempt to dominate the industry by being the first mover in technology had resulted in the development of a fragmented product line that was confusing its customers and its employees. The company needed a new strategy to grow.

Watson's answer was that IBM needed to build a new line of computers that would cover the needs of the whole computer market. The project was called the System/360, representing the 360 degrees in a circle, because IBM wanted to meet the needs of every user in both the scientific and business community. The 360 was intended to make all other computers, both IBM's and its competitors, obsolete. All the 360 computers would be compatible with one another. Moreover, they would all use the same operating language, software, disk drives, printers, and so on. The goal of the new design was to lock in customers to IBM's computer systems and to make it very difficult for customers to change to competitors' products— both because of superior product quality and because their incentive would be to upgrade to a more powerful machine that was compatible with their old machines. The other goal of the system was to make better use of IBM's research and development resources and to make it easier for its sales force to sell an integrated package of products to customers.

The project was challenging because hardware and software had to be developed and coordinated across the whole of its product line. This meant that all of the different parts of the mainframe system—storage devices, central processors, terminals, and printers—had to be compatible, as did the components used in the various parts of the system. To ensure the compatibility of the new system, and the supply and quality of the component parts, IBM began producing many of its own electronic components itself. From this point on IBM became involved in all aspects of the mainframe computer business—it would design and manufacture almost all of the components that would be used in its mainframe computers, it would manufacture its mainframes in its own factories, and it would distribute and sell its mainframes itself. IBM opened six new plants around the world to manufacture the System/360 computers. Over a four-year period, $5 billion was invested and 50,000 new employees were hired as part of IBM's ambitious expansion plan.

The System/360 mainframe computer was launched in 1964 and captured 70 percent of the market. The project was an immense success and put IBM way ahead of its competitors. Although before the 360, competitors such as RCA, Burroughs, Honeywell, Univac, and GE sold machines that performed much better than IBM computers for the same price, the compatible design and the power of the System/360 beat all competitors. Moreover, marketing played as large a role in the success of the project as technology. While all its competitors had access to integrated circuits and could produce an advanced computer, only IBM had the capacity to provide a customer a complete information processing service—the machine itself, installation and maintenance, and the quality personalized service that allowed it to retain and tie up its customers.

Due to the technical superiority of the System/360 mainframes and the reputation for quality service established by IBM's sales force, IBM dominated the computer industry. The 360 spurred growth in the whole industry. In 1963 there were only 11,700 computers in the United States; this figure doubled in 1965 and redoubled in 1969. By 1969 IBM leased over 50,000 computer systems which generated sales revenues of $7.196 billion and earnings of $934 million, a staggering figure for the time. A large part of these revenues was generated from IBM's international operations.

Global Development

IBM's movement into global markets began in 1908 when Herman Hollerith made a licensing agreement with the British Tabulating Company (BTC) to produce and sell Hollerith tabulators throughout the British Empire. Tom Watson, Sr., continued with Hollerith's vision of IBM as an international company and established IBM's foreign department. After World War I, he began to build small manufacturing plants in Germany, France, and Great Britain to evade the tariffs these countries levied on foreign imports. Sales and marketing agencies were created throughout Europe, Latin America, and parts of Asia. The branches were called Watson Business Machines and their function, as in the United States, was to provide the high level of customer service that supported IBM's business machines. In 1935 foreign revenue was $1.6 million, with punch cards once again being the biggest contributor. By 1939 over 12 percent of IBM's revenues came from foreign operations.

During World War II, IBM's plants in Europe and Japan were seized. However, even though IBM's German plant, which contributed 50 percent of the foreign department's revenue, was in ruins, by 1945 foreign revenues were almost $2 million. After the war, IBM's British plant became the largest facility outside North America, and in 1949 IBM renegotiated the 1908 agreement with the BTC whereby BTC would receive a free, nonexclusive license on all current IBM products in exchange for letting IBM sell its new products through its own sales organization. This agreement resulted in the creation of a new subsidiary called IBM U.K. which, selling IBM's new advanced computers, soon came to dominate the British and European markets.

In 1949 Dick Watson, who spoke German, French, Italian, and Spanish, was put in charge of IBM's international operations, and in 1950 the foreign department was renamed IBM World Trade Division and became an independent subsidiary that would receive product and financial support from IBM's Domestic Division but would operate on its own. By 1950 the World Trade Division had 10 factories producing machines and over 20 facilities making cards throughout the world. World Trade operated in 58 countries through subsidiaries such as IBM Deutschland, IBM France, and many smaller units in Latin America and Africa.

Of World Trade's 16,000 employees in 1954, only 200 were Americans, because Dick Watson believed that most success would be achieved if each subsidiary was responsive to the needs of its own region or country. Dick Watson set high standards for World Trade, hired good people as country managers, and was responsive to local customs.

By 1967 foreign revenues were $1.6 billion and net earnings were $209 million. World Trade sales were equal to IBM's Domestic Division sales. Although IBM operated in 130 countries, Europe accounted for two-thirds of foreign revenue. In 1970 Dick Watson resigned from IBM to become the U.S. ambassador to France. With his departure, the World Trade Division was further divided into world regions: Europe, the Middle East, Africa, the Americas, and the Far East. By 1970 foreign revenues had increased to $3.5 billion and once again accounted for almost 50 percent of IBM's total revenues.

IBM's Structure

IBM's Domestic Division, which was led by Tom Watson, Jr., was responsible for research and development and for financing the operations of the entire global company. By 1950 not only was IBM Domestic designing and manufacturing a large number of different models of computer, it was also designing and manufacturing many of the component and peripheral parts used in the computers such as disk drives, transistors, printers, and file storage and servers. Many of these products were produced throughout the world and distributed by IBM's international division. The increase in the range of IBM's activities, both domestically and internationally, put considerable strain on IBM's organization structure, which began to cause it many problems.

IBM was run largely by Tom Watson, Sr., until he retired in 1955. Watson oversaw all of IBM's operations, and a line of top managers was always waiting to see him. No formal organizational chart existed in IBM because Watson believed that people should be interested in all aspects of IBM's activities rather than focusing on specific jobs. The company had no clear chain of command, no policy of decentralization which gave lower-level managers the right to make independent decisions, and no formal planning process or business policies. Knowledge was simply in employees' heads and strategy emerged gradually over time from discussion and negotiations between Watson and his top management team.

After Tom Watson, Sr.'s retirement, Tom Watson, Jr., and Al Williams, IBM's president at this time,

decided to construct an organizational chart to see who had reported to Watson and found that 38 to 40 top managers reported directly to him. It was obvious that this highly centralized management style could not continue if the rapidly growing company was to stay on top of the computer industry. Already unmade decisions were accumulating because managers lacked the authority to make decisions, and now they looked to Tom Watson, Jr., to take the lead.

Tom Jr. wanted to break with his father's centralized, autocratic style of management in order to speed communication and decision making, so he and Al Williams reorganized IBM's operating structure to decentralize control to managers who were given the responsibility of managing the different functional areas of the company. The organizational chart they devised put Red Lamotte in charge of sales and R&D and Al Williams in charge of finance, while Tom Jr. would take control of the company's strategy. Unfortunately, this reorganization simply divided the chaos among three people instead of one. There were still far too many managers reporting to the three top managers, and they were unable to control IBM's operations adequately. So in 1956 IBM was reorganized along divisional lines.

IBM Domestic was broken up into five separate divisions: the Field Engineering Division, which primarily served commercial customers; the Federal Systems Division, which primarily served government customers; the Systems Manufacturing Division, which manufactured the computers; the Component Manufacturing Division, which manufactured the components; and the Research Division, which performed the basic research and design activities. In each division a general manager was given the responsibility of making decisions for the division and developing its strategy. The World Trade Division would continue to operate separately from IBM Domestic.

This multidivisional structure ensured that each general manager had a clearly defined task. At the top of the organization, Tom Jr. created a top management team of six people, consisting of himself and the heads of the five divisions, to oversee the company's strategy. Each of the five general managers was responsible for a major part of IBM, and Tom Jr. was to oversee the entire company. He claimed that his ability to choose and retain an intelligent top management team was his greatest contribution to IBM.

Watson also created a corporate staff of experts in sales and marketing, finance, manufacturing, personnel, and communications to advise him and to oversee the activities of the divisions. The corporate staff was seen as staff or advisory managers to the general managers of the division who were the line managers with responsibility for bottom-line operating results. It was the line manager's job (the general manager and other divisional managers) to meet production targets, beat sales quotas, and increase market share. The staff manager's job was to give advice to line managers—the heads of the divisions who were their superiors, to convey policy from corporate headquarters to the operating divisions, and to ensure that the proper objectives were in place and being met. Each line manager would be evaluated solely on his or her unit's results, and each staff manager would be rated on his or her effort in making IBM a world leader.

IBM's divisional structure produced many tensions between corporate (staff) and divisional (line) personnel. For example, as a part of their role, staff managers often would identify problems that needed to be addressed in the divisions and would write memos to line managers suggesting how to solve them. Line managers, however, viewed these moves as interference and an intrusion into their area of operations. They began to guard their territories from corporate personnel who had no direct authority over general managers in IBM's structure.

To resolve these tensions, Williams created a check and balance system in IBM called *contention management.* This system forced both staff and line managers to meet and encouraged them to debate the merits of an idea. However, no operating plan became final without staff approval. When line and staff managers could not agree, the problem would be sent to the corporate management committee—the top six executives—to resolve the problem. Over time, an increasing number of issues were sent to the top of the organization to resolve because line and staff managers could not agree on priorities and future policy. This slowed communication and decision making; eventually, it became accepted that the top management committee would resolve important strategic issues.

Thus, despite Watson's claimed policy of decentralizing authority to divisional managers and their subordinates, much of IBM's decision making remained centralized at the top of the organization, and managers from IBM's mainframe division—its chief revenue earner—had the most power in shaping corporate decision making.

The IBM Culture

The centralized approach that was developing at IBM had important implications for IBM's culture and the values that guided the company. Because IBM's managers began to rely on their superiors to make important policy decisions, they became very conservative in their approach and became increasingly afraid to take risks and to go out on their own. IBM developed many bureaucratic rules and operating procedures that specified how decisions were to be made and how to resolve disputes. Slowly but surely the entrepreneurial values that had allowed the company to capitalize quickly on new technologies changed to emphasize values of conforming to the IBM way: commitment and loyalty to the company and respect and obedience to superiors.

IBM's conservative culture was reinforced by its policy of long-term employment. The company became known throughout the industry for its job security and good pay. With IBM's high rate of growth, internal promotion was easy to come by, and employees rose rapidly through the corporate ranks. In 1955 employee stock options were offered for the first time. In 1966 managers were required to attend an in-house IBM manager school, where they were trained in IBM's philosophy on communications, sales and service efforts, meetings, and employee treatment such as visiting workers with sick spouses. This policy taught employees the IBM way and helped to cement IBM's corporate culture and its style of doing business.

New Management and New Challenges

In 1970 Dick Watson resigned to become the U.S. ambassador to France and Tom Watson, Jr., suffered a heart attack which resulted in his retirement in 1971. When Tom Watson, Jr., appointed T. V. Learson as CEO in 1971 the period of the Watson family's control over IBM came to an end. IBM was the largest, most successful computer company in the world and had complete domination over the global mainframe computer industry. Each year, its revenues and profit reached record levels; the company plowed back over 10 percent of its revenue to fund future research and development to allow it to maintain its dominance in the mainframe market.

Despite its impressive performance, however, all was not well with the company. Although the situation was masked by increasing revenues from World

Trade, by 1970 IBM was starting to slow down. While the company had grown at an annual rate of 22 percent from 1946 to 1955, its growth was only 16 percent per year from 1955 to 1970. Indeed, its stock price actually declined in 1970 despite record sales. Why? IBM was beginning to face increased competition from other companies in the mainframe computer market and from companies that began to produce computers for other segments of the computer market. The challenge for Learson was to use IBM's vast resources to exploit a computer market that was growing by leaps and bounds. How could the company exploit its privileged position to dominate the computer market of the future? The answers were not long in coming.

REFERENCES

Mercer, David. *The Global IBM*. New York: Dodd, Mead, 1988.

Sober, Robert. *IBM: Colossus in Transition*. New York: Times Books, 1981.

Watson, Thomas, Jr., and Peter Petre. *Father and Son & Co.: My Life at IBM and Beyond*. New York: Bantam Books, 1990.

"The Intimate Tale of IBM's First Family." *Fortune*, June 14, 1990, pp. 92–131.

This case was prepared by Gareth R. Jones and Susan L. Peters, Texas A&M University.

T. V. Learson took over as CEO of IBM from Tom Watson, Jr., in 1971 and became the head of a company that had a 75 percent share of the world market for mainframe computers—computers powerful enough to manage the information processing needs of an entire company. Learson had made a major personal contribution to IBM's emergence as the dominant global mainframe manufacturer when he led the development of IBM's highly successful 360 mainframe series, the series that led to the rapid rise in the company's fortunes. IBM's 360 mainframes fully automated a company's manual information processing systems, such as payroll and accounting or customer recordkeeping, and made the punch card obsolete. As the former head of the 360 program, Learson understood the critical importance of research and development in maintaining and defending IBM's preeminent position in the mainframe market, and so he initiated and oversaw the development of IBM's new, more powerful System/370 computer series.[1]

Technical advances lowered the System/370's price per calculation to 60 percent below that of the System/360s, and the 370 had a larger information storage system as well. The 370s still used the software of the 360s, however, so they were primarily an upgrade rather than a replacement of the 360. Nevertheless, the 370 machines became the backbone of IBM's mainframe product line from the early 1970s on. Most of the advances that IBM made to its mainframe computers from this time on were designed primarily to improve the 370 machines' processing power or the performance of the various components of the 370 series, such as its software, printers, and especially its storage capacity. The 370 series became the industry standard that IBM's competitors tried to match and outperform.

Under Learson's control and then under the control of Frank Cary, who became CEO when Learson retired in 1973, IBM continued to enjoy its domination of the mainframe market. By 1980 IBM had a market value of $26 billion, four times its size in 1971.

Increasing Competition

Although IBM's continued domination of the mainframe market produced record increases in revenues and profits every year, its performance masked some major problems that were developing during the 1970s and 1980s. The first major problem, which Cary had recognized as early as 1970, was that the mainframe computer market was starting to mature. Almost every large U.S. business company possessed a mainframe computer, as had most scientific and higher education institutions. IBM also had saturated the international market. As a result, IBM's rate of growth was falling; even though its revenues were increasing, they were increasing at a decreasing rate. In the mature mainframe market, competition was increasing from companies that were trying to find ways to attract IBM's customers and share in the huge revenues in the

Copyright © 1994 by Gareth R. Jones. This case was prepared by Gareth R. Jones and Susan L. Peters, Texas A&M University, as the basis for class discussion rather than to illustrate either effective or ineffective handling of an administrative situation. Reprinted by permission of Gareth R. Jones. All rights reserved. For the most recent financial results of the company discussed in this case, go to http://finance.yahoo.com, input the company's stock symbol, and download the latest company report from its homepage.

[1]D. Mercer, *The Global IBM* (New York: Dodd, Mead, 1988), p. 58.

mainframe computer market. Its major competitors at the time were Amdahl, Honeywell, Burroughs, Univac, NCR, and Control Data.

Many of these companies began offering IBM's customers mainframe systems at a lower cost than the expensive IBM systems. Initially, IBM faced competition only from companies selling IBM-compatible peripheral equipment such as disk drives, storage devices, and printers at lower prices than IBM's products. Its sales force had been able to ward off such threats. Now, however, the nature of competition was changing. IBM's competitors began selling cheaper, higher performing, and IBM-compatible central processing units (CPUs), the brain of the computer and the source of its processing power. For the first time they were offering a low-price alternative to the IBM mainframe while IBM was still pursuing its high-priced leased strategy backed by excellent customer service. Another emerging low-price threat came from leasing companies that would buy old 360s from IBM and lease them on better terms than IBM offered, attracting price-conscious IBM customers. While these competitive threats were small, they nevertheless gave IBM cause for concern.

From 1970 on IBM became concerned about the threat of low-cost foreign competition in the mainframe computer market after witnessing the decline in several U.S. industries, including automobiles, due to the entry of low-cost Japanese competitors. The price of integrated circuits, the heart of a mainframe computer, was plummeting at this time, and Japanese companies had the technical capability to build a powerful computer that could match or exceed the IBM 370. The existence of a low-cost global competitor was a major threat to IBM's domination both of the U.S. market and the global market.

To respond to the threat of low-cost competition, Cary announced that IBM would spend $10 billion to build new automated plants to produce low-cost computers over a six-year period. In this way IBM would be able to meet the challenge of low-priced computers should the threat materialize and its customers start to switch to low-cost competitors. John Opel, who became IBM's CEO in 1981, also was concerned about competition from Japan and he carried on with Cary's low-cost producer strategy. Under his control IBM spent $32 billion from 1980 to 1985 to find ways to reduce manufacturing costs.

IBM's push to reduce manufacturing costs did not fit well with its strategy of offering excellent-quality customer service using its very expensive sales force to sell and service its machines. It was unlikely that IBM would ever be able to compete on price with its competitors because its customer service and support activities raised its costs so much. Moreover, competing on price had never been a part of its strategy; IBM always had competed on its unique ability to provide customers with an integrated full-line computer service. Analysts wondered whether Opel was spending too much to lower manufacturing costs and whether the $32 billion could not be better spent in some other way.

Changes in Technology

Changes in mainframe technology also caused a change in IBM's strategy during the 1970s. As a result of technological innovations, particularly the plunging costs of integrated circuits, the life span of a mainframe computer—the time it could be used until it was technologically outdated—was shortening rapidly and development costs were increasing. Formerly, customers would use the same IBM mainframe for several years, but now IBM was forced to replace its leased computers every two or three years, making it difficult to recoup development costs and obtain the premium price on its machines that it was accustomed to.

Because a computer's life span was getting shorter, and because of the growth of low-cost competition, IBM under Cary and then Opel decided to phase out IBM's system of leasing its machines to customers and instead to begin selling them—a major change in IBM's strategy. Although this move increased revenue in the short term, it had major repercussions for the company in the long term. First, the leasing system had tied IBM to its customers and ensured that when customers upgraded and expanded their computer systems they would look first at IBM machines. Moreover, leasing facilitated IBM's strategy of providing customers with excellent customer service and guaranteed the company a steady cash flow and control of the used machine market. With the end of leasing, IBM would be more susceptible to fluctuations in the demand for its products because its customers would be able to shop around.

From 1980 on, IBM began to face major competition from 370 clone manufacturers, large companies like Amdahl (which had a faster 370 processor than IBM), and Hitachi Data Systems (whose low-price machine generated record sales throughout the 1980s). IBM's customers began to feel more comfortable about buying 370 clones from companies that also promised quality support and service at low cost.[2] IBM's sales growth for its biggest mainframe dropped from 12 percent annually in 1984 to 5 percent annually in 1990 as a result of the increased competition. Increased mainframe competition with Amdahl and Hitachi Data Systems also led to price discounting despite the fact that IBM attempted to offer its customers a unique package that included software and services in addition to hardware. The days when IBM could demand whatever price it wanted for its machines were over.

The end of its leasing program also led to increased competition from independent computer leasing companies which would buy older mainframes and then sell the older processors at a price that was frequently only 10 percent of IBM's newest machine. These companies also disassembled mainframes in order to make smaller computers; for example, they could make two smaller machines out of one larger machine. In response to this price competition, IBM was forced to reduce the price of its machines.

The end of leasing, combined with a growth in low-cost competition, changed the nature of industry competition in ways that the company did not expect. IBM's strategy was now to protect its mainframe market from competitors and to hang on to its customers at all costs. IBM devoted most of its huge resources to developing technically superior mainframe products, to lowering their cost of production, and to supporting its very expensive but very successful sales force.

IBM's focus on protecting its mainframe market blinded it to threats from the emergence of new kinds of computers. Even when it did recognize the competitive threat, IBM's operating structure and culture, shaped by its preeminent position as the world's leading mainframe computer company, made it difficult for IBM's managers to see emerging problems in its environment and to react quickly to the changes that technology was bringing about in the computer industry. The way IBM handled the emerging threat from new kinds of computers such as minicomputers, personal computers, and workstations illustrates many of the problems it experienced

[2]John Verity, "A Slimmer IBM May Still Be Overweight," *Business Week*, December 18, 1989, pp. 197–208.

as a result of a corporate mindset that "mainframes were king."

The Minicomputer Market

One of the new computer markets that emerged in the 1970s was the minicomputer market. Minicomputers are smaller and significantly cheaper than mainframe computers and are priced anywhere from $12,000 to $700,000. The readily falling price of integrated circuits during the 1960s and 1970s made it feasible to build a minicomputer that could be afforded by small businesses or used in specialized technical or scientific applications. IBM had ignored this new market segment, preferring to focus its resources on developing and improving its profitable 360 and 370 series of computers.

It was left to two MIT researchers to pioneer the development of a smaller, powerful computer, and they founded the Digital Equipment Corporation (DEC) which in 1965 launched the PDP-8, a computer that could handle the smaller information processing needs and tasks of companies like small businesses, offices, factories, and laboratories. The venture was very successful, and by 1968 DEC's sales reached $57 million and earnings were $6.8 million. DEC's computer competed with the lower end of the 360 range. The computer sold well in research facilities, but it did not do as well in business because IBM dominated this market with its powerful sales force. DEC had plans to develop a more powerful machine, however, and as it grew it was quickly expanding its own national service network, imitating IBM's.

To meet DEC's challenge, which was still seen as a minor issue, Cary formed the General Systems Division in 1969 to produce the System/3 which was to be IBM's small, powerful minicomputer. IBM did not, however, rethink its technology or invest resources to develop a new minicomputer technology to make a product to suit this new market segment. Rather, IBM tried to adapt its existing mainframe technology to the minicomputer market.

IBM's top managers had risen up the ranks of IBM from the mainframe division, and they were conditioned by the idea that the level of computing power was everything. "The bigger the better" was the philosophy of these managers. Moreover, big machines meant big revenues. IBM's mainframe managers saw the potential earning power of the minicomputer as insignificant when compared to the huge revenues generated by its mainframes. More fundamentally, however, IBM's top managers did not want competition from a new computer division inside the company which would absorb large amounts of the company's resources and might change the company's future direction and strategy.

The result was that when the System/3s were developed they were too big and expensive to compete with DEC's machine and too small to compete with IBM's own mainframes, so they failed to make much inroad into what was becoming a very big market segment. As the minicomputer segment of the market continued to grow rapidly in the 1970s, Cary tried to increase the importance of the minicomputer group inside IBM's corporate hierarchy by reorganizing IBM's Data Processing Division and splitting it into two units: General Systems to make small minicomputers and Data Systems to make the mainframes. He hoped that this change would force IBM managers to change their mindset and support the company's move into the new markets.

So strong was the entrenched position of mainframe managers that Cary's change of structure created huge divisional rivalry between mainframe and minicomputer managers. The mainframe division saw itself as in direct competition for resources with the minicomputer division, and managers in both units failed to cooperate and to share technological resources to develop the new range of machines. When General Systems finally produced a smaller minicomputer called the 8100, it did not have a technological edge over the DEC machine. Nevertheless, it was successful, as many IBM customers had large sums of money tied up in IBM mainframes and were reluctant to switch suppliers. Moreover, IBM's powerful sales force (although at first reluctant to push minicomputers for fear of reducing their commissions) could service the needs of the minicomputer users. By the end of 1980, over 100,000 minicomputers had been sold. IBM and DEC were the industry leaders; the new companies that had sprung up, such as Hewlett-Packard and Wang, were also increasing their market share.

In 1986 DEC introduced its new VAX 9000 minicomputer which shocked IBM's mainframe managers because it had the same speed and capacity as IBM's largest 370 mainframe, the 3090, but cost only 25 percent as much. For the first time, mainframe managers were forced to accept the fact that minicomputers might be feasible substitutes for mainframes in many applications. Although DEC gained the business of some large financial service companies and corporate data processing centers with its new machine, market segments previously dominated solely by IBM, it still could not seize many of IBM's loyal customers who were locked into IBM systems. Nevertheless, DEC's share of the minicomputer market grew from 19 percent in 1984 to 25 percent in 1988, while IBM's share dropped from 24 percent to 16 percent in the same period.

Finally, in 1988 IBM brought out a minicomputer, the AS/400 series, that was superior to DEC's VAX. The AS/400 series was based on RISC (reduced instruction set computing) technology and fast RISC chips that could equal and exceed the speed of large mainframes, including IBM's own mainframes.[3] Many large companies that had a great deal of money invested in IBM mainframes now moved to adopt the IBM minicomputer system because it was compatible with their IBM mainframe systems. As a result of the success of its new minicomputers, IBM increased its market share from about 16 percent in 1988 to 28 percent in 1992 while DEC's fell.[4] DEC now plans to produce machines based on RISC, but in the interim, it has introduced new machines to compete with IBM's AS/400s on price.[5] IBM now has a $14 billion business in minicomputers, which have gross margins of 56 percent.

The Personal Computer

Another technological breakthrough, the microprocessor or "computer on a chip," sparked the development of the personal computer. The personal computer was developed in 1977 by Steven Jobs and Stephen Wozniak who founded Apple Computer. By 1980 Apple's sales had grown to $117 million.[6] Once again, IBM stood by and watched as a new market segment was created. This time, recognizing the mistakes it had made in the microcomputer market by not moving quickly enough to develop a machine to compete with the industry leader, it decided to move quickly to create its own machine to compete with Apple's.

[3]John Verity, "The New IBM," *Business Week*, December 16, 1991, pp. 112–118.
[4]John Verity, "IBM's Major Triumph in Minis," *Business Week*, March 16, 1992, p. 111.
[5]Gary McWilliams, "Can DEC Squeeze One Last Blast from VAX?" *Business Week*, October 28, 1991, p. 134.
[6]Deidre Depke and Richard Brandt, "PCs: What the Future Holds," *Business Week*, August 12, 1991, pp. 58–64.

In the mainframe market, IBM made its own chips, circuit boards, disk drives, terminals, tape drives, and printers; wrote its own proprietary software for its machines; and helped to develop software to meet the needs of its customers. As a result, its machines were not compatible with those of its rivals which used their own proprietary hardware and software. The machines of different manufacturers would not work together. In 1981, however, in an effort to enter the PC market quickly, IBM outsourced and bought the inputs it needed to make its personal computer from other companies. For example, Intel supplied the 8088 microchip that was the heart of the IBM machine and Microsoft delivered MS-DOS, its programming language and software applications for the new machine. Finally, computer stores, not the IBM sales force, were used to sell the new IBM PCs to get the machines to individual customers quickly.

IBM's first PC was introduced at a price of $1,565 in 1981 and was more powerful than the first Apple computer. Intel's 8088 chip had more main memory and was more powerful than the chip used in the Apple II computer, and Microsoft's operating system, MS-DOS, was better than the current industry standard. These features, combined with the power of the IBM brand name, made the IBM PC an immediate success, and it quickly became the industry standard for all other PCs.[7] Backed by IBM's legendary service, business users turned to the machines in the thousands. By 1984 IBM had seized 40 percent of the personal computer market, but the IBM PC still could not be produced or distributed fast enough to meet the enormous customer demand.[8]

Even the runaway success of the IBM PC became a threat to the company because its competitors rapidly imitated the IBM PC; soon clone manufacturers were selling IBM-compatible personal computers as powerful or more powerful than IBM's own machines. For example, Compaq, founded in 1981, began to clone IBMs and produced a high-powered machine that seized a large share of the high-price business market. In 1986 Compaq beat IBM to the market with a machine using Intel's new powerful 386 chip. At the same time, other clone makers like Zenith and Packard Bell attacked the low-price segment of the computer market and began producing PCs that undercut IBM's.

IBM, threatened both in the high-price and the low-price end of the PC market, fought back with the PS/2 which had a proprietary hardware channel that IBM made sure could not be imitated, as its first personal computer had been. However, customers resisted buying the new PS/2 because they did not want to become locked into a new IBM system that was not compatible with IBM's old system and that was not compatible with their other software or hardware investments. In the face of hostility from its customers, and losing market share, IBM was forced to back down and in 1988 began producing PS/2s that were compatible with the existing industry standard—its own older standard.

It was suddenly clear to IBM that it no longer controlled the rules of the competitive game in the personal computer industry. Nonetheless, it was still slow to change its strategy. Despite the fact that its cheaper rivals had machines that were as powerful as its own, IBM still attempted to charge a premium price for its product and so its customers went elsewhere. IBM's share of U.S. PC sales dropped from about 37 percent in 1985 to 24 percent in 1988. Clone makers continued to improve IBM's older standard, and IBM's market share declined to 16.5 percent in 1990.[9]

In 1991 a major price war broke out in the PC market, brought on in large part because of the steadily dropping price of computer hardware such as Intel's microprocessors. IBM reduced prices three times to compete, and prices of the PS/2 were cut as much as 25 percent.[10] Partly due to price competition, a typical 386 PC which had cost $3,500 in early 1991 cost $1,600 in late 1991 and only $1,200 in early 1992. Also in 1992 IBM introduced new low-priced lines of computers like the PS/Value Point targeted at the fastest-growing segment of the computer market, the home market, and to business customers who do not need all the features of the high-end PS/2. These new models have been very successful and are in great demand. Nonetheless, IBM does not hold a dominant position in the PC market; in 1992 its market share was 12 percent, the same as its rival Apple and about twice that of rivals like Dell, Compaq, and NEC.

The PC price wars continued into 1993. In February 1993, Dell Computer, a rapidly growing clone maker, introduced price cuts of 5 percent to 22 percent across

[7]Ibid.
[8]Mercer, pp. 106–111.

[9]Depke and Brandt.
[10]Ibid.

its entire product line. In response, IBM cut prices as much as 16 percent on some models including PS/Value Point.[11] Apple cut prices five times in 1993 for a reduction of up to 33 percent on its three highest-priced computers in an effort to increase U.S. sales.[12] PC makers also battled over distribution and the offering of extras such as warranties. PCs currently range from $500 clones to $2,000 laptops to $25,000 network hubs.[13] PCs dominate the computer industry with world sales of $93 billion in 1993 compared to mainframe sales of $50 billion.[14] The laptop segment of the PC market alone reached $5.67 billion in 1990. IBM, however, did not have a product for this market segment until 1991 and it faces tough competition from the market leader Toshiba and from Apple.[15]

By 1992 it was clear to IBM and to industry analysts that IBM was just one more competitor in a very competitive market. Since 1990 IBM's PC division has yet to show a profit because of the intense price competition and because IBM's costs are above its competitors like Compaq, which moved quickly to slash costs in 1990 when the price of PCs began tumbling.

IBM's response to competition in the personal computer industry throughout the 1980s clearly was affected by its "mainframe mindset." Even though it was clear that new segments of the computer market were developing and that new uses for computers were being found, IBM managers still discounted the potential threat to mainframes from either the minicomputer or the personal computer. IBM was not alone in being unable to sense the significance of changes in the environment. Kenneth Olsen, one of the founders of DEC, the minicomputer maker, went on record saying that "personal computers are just toys" in discounting the challenge of PCs to minicomputers, just as IBM had discounted the threat of minicomputers to mainframes ten years before. The Olsen philosophy blinded IBM's top management to the prospect that powerful PCs could become a threat to IBM's main line of business, mainframes. This predicament was somewhat surprising given that the computer industry always had been dominated by technological change, and IBM's success was itself the result of it moving quickly and decisively to exploit the opportunities of new technology—the punch card machine, the transistor, and the integrated circuit.

Throughout the 1980s, IBM's personal computer division (which is the biggest personal computer operation in the world) could not respond quickly to the price-cutting moves of its rivals and could not introduce new kinds of personal computers as a result of its centralized decision-making style. Whenever a competitor reduced prices, managers of the personal computer division had to get approval from the corporate management committee to cut prices, a process that sometimes took months. As a result, the PC division was never able to forestall its rivals. Moreover, just as in the case of minicomputers, rivalry between PC and mainframe managers hampered efforts to exploit quickly the potential of the powerful new microprocessors.

IBM's competitors moved quickly to increase the power of their PCs by exploiting the power of the new generation of microprocessors. They also encouraged the development of powerful new netware software that could link PCs together and to a more powerful computer, such as a minicomputer or workstation, so that a network of PCs could work as effectively as a mainframe—but more conveniently and at only a fraction of the cost.

Workstations

Workstations are the fourth wave of computers following mainframes, minicomputers, and PCs. While PCs are designed for individual jobs like word processing and financial analysis, workstations essentially are very powerful PCs designed to be connected to each other and to a mainframe through software. Workstations can analyze financial results and track inventories much faster than PCs and much more cheaply than minicomputers or mainframes. A network of workstations can also be linked to an even more powerful workstation (or minicomputer) called a file server, which contains a company's files and database which can retrieve them from a company's mainframe computer. Workstations, usually priced from $5,000 to $100,000, were first developed for sci-

[11]Richard Hudson and Laurence Hooper, "IBM Slashes PC Prices in the U.S., Europe, Moving Swiftly to Counter Rivals' Cuts," *The Wall Street Journal*, February 12, 1993, p. B6.

[12]Bill Richards, "Apple Computer Cuts Its PC Prices Fifth Time in 1993," *The Wall Street Journal*, August 12, 1993, p. B1.

[13]Depke and Brandt.

[14]Ibid.

[15]John Bryne, Deidre Depke, and John Verity, "IBM: As Markets and Technology Change, Can Big Blue Remake Its Culture?" *Business Week*, June 17, 1991, pp. 24–32.

entists and engineers but increasingly are utilized by business professionals. New network software links workstations so that many people can work together simultaneously on the same project. These desktop machines have "user-friendly" graphic displays and allow people at different machines to share data and software. By 1988, the workstation market was $4.7 billion.[16] Workstations have a 45 percent profit margin compared to 58 percent for minicomputers.[17]

Prior to 1989 IBM was a small player in this segment. Underestimating the potential power of personal computers and slow to develop powerful minicomputers (its AS/400 series was introduced only in 1988), IBM managers once again failed to see the potential of an emerging market. IBM had only a 3.9 percent market share in 1987 compared to Sun Microsystems's 29 percent and Apollo's 21 percent, the two upstart companies that innovated the workstation. Once they realized the importance of this market segment, both IBM and DEC introduced workstations based on RISC (reduced instruction set computing) processors which make machines two to three times faster by eliminating all insignificant instructions. IBM introduced the IBM RT PC workstation in 1986, but the machine failed due to an underpowered microprocessor. Notwithstanding its problems, IBM launched the RS/6000 workstation in 1989 and captured 18 percent of the market by the end of 1991.[18]

Competition in the workstation market is increasing as a result of market growth. This segment was growing 27 percent annually by 1992, compared to 5 percent for the whole computer industry. As the price of workstations falls, more and more small businesses, which could not afford to use mainframe or minicomputers, can afford workstations. The workstation market also is very important to large computer makers because workstations can be used in networks with larger mainframe computers. Thus controlling the workstation market protects a company's mainframe market. By the end of 1991, the workstation market was $11.3 billion, and IBM was facing severe competition from DEC, Sun, Apollo, and Hewlett-Packard, all of which sell RISC workstations.

[16]Stuart Gannes, "IBM and DEC Take on the Little Guys," *Fortune*, October 10, 1988, pp. 108–114.
[17]Leslie Helm, "DEC Discovers It Can't Live by VAX Alone," *Business Week*, November 21, 1988, pp. 104–105.
[18]Carol Loomis and David Kirkpatrick, "The Hunt for Mr. X: Who Can Run IBM?" *Fortune*, February 22, 1993, pp. 68–72.

Software and Services

Designing software, the instructions that allow computers to perform tasks, and providing customer service, particularly assistance in the design of programs to manage company-specific databases and systems, have been a rapidly expanding segment of the computer industry for the past 20 years. IBM always has realized the importance of developing proprietary software that can link and join its mainframes, minicomputers, workstations, and personal computers to provide customers with a totally integrated computer package. It failed, however, to recognize the developing market for more general operating language and software applications.

By 1981, 33 percent of total computer industry revenue came from software and services, a figure which had risen to an estimated 50 percent in 1993. Although software and services accounted for 33 percent of IBM's total revenues by 1990, 68 percent of this revenue came from supporting customers' IBM mainframe computer systems, which represent a declining share of the computer market. Thus IBM, tied to software that supports mainframes, is not in a strong position to compete in the new software and services market.

IBM's failure to realize the potential for software seems surprising given that it had outsourced the operating language for its personal computer to Microsoft, and saw the success of the MS-DOS operating system. IBM's focus on mainframes and its continuing belief that its own proprietary hardware and software would become the industry standard seems to have been the source of its reluctance to enlarge and expand its software operations. In 1980, when IBM had the opportunity to indirectly control the software market by purchasing a large chunk of Microsoft stock at a low price, it declined to do so.

IBM soon found that developing new applications software was a difficult business to be in. First, IBM had a hard time recruiting talented programmers who were not attracted to IBM's bureaucratic and conservative corporate culture in which centralized decision making limited their opportunities to be creative and to take risks. Second, talented software programmers found they could make more money if they were in business for themselves; any programmer who could develop a new system generally started his or her own company. Microsoft recognized this problem early on; consequently,

Bill Gates, Microsoft's chairman, gives his top programmers large stock options to encourage their best performance. Many of them have become millionaires as a result.

In today's computer market developing better and more advanced software is crucial to selling more hardware, or computers of all kinds. So, late as usual, IBM embarked on a program to forge alliances with many small independent software companies to develop software for IBM machines quickly—mainframes, minis, workstations, and PCs. One of IBM's goals is to rejuvenate sales of its mainframe by encouraging software companies to write programs that make mainframes the key part of a computer network that links personal computers and workstations.[19] IBM spent $100 million in 1989 to acquire equity stakes in twelve software developers, including Interactive Images for Graphics, Inc., Polygen Corporation for scientific software, and American Management Systems, Inc., for mainframe software. Marketing agreements were made with several other firms. IBM loans software developers up to $50,000 for start-up costs and takes a seat on the developer's board.[20] For example, IBM is working on a project called Systems Application Architecture (SAA), which is a set of rules for links between programs and computers. SAA will facilitate the creation of networks with all types of machines, including mainframes and PCs.[21]

In 1988 IBM created a new unit to launch applications software and established a position called "complementary resource marketing manager," with responsibility for connecting software "business partners" with IBM customers. Salespeople are expected to sell the products of these software partners as well as IBM products.[22] Although most of the programs are for mainframes, many can be adapted to work with networks based on PCs.[23] Software and services accounted for 40 percent of IBM's revenue in 1992, and IBM wants to get 50 percent of revenues from software and services by the year 2000.[24]

[19]Walecia Konrad, "Information Processing: Survival of the Biggest," *Business Week*, April 2, 1990, pp. 66, 68.
[20]Deidre Depke, "Suddenly, Software Houses Have a Big Blue Buddy," *Business Week*, August 7, 1989, pp. 68–69.
[21]Ibid.
[22]Ibid.
[23]Loomis and Kirkpatrick.
[24]IBM 1992 Annual Report, p. 40.

Systems Integration and Outsourcing

Traditionally, IBM limited its service activities to providing support for its own proprietary software and hardware. It did not use its skills to analyze various aspects of a customer's business, such as its inventory control or warehousing operations, and then custom design and install an appropriate mix of hardware and software to meet the customer's needs, a service known as systems integration.[25] Moreover, it had not recognized the developing market for outsourcing data processing whereby one company agrees to take over and manage all aspects of the data processing function for another company in return for a fee. By 1992, however, the systems integration and outsourcing market generated more revenues than the mainframe market.

IBM's failure to see the developing market segment for systems integration and outsourcing had not been lost on one of IBM's star salesmen, Ross Perot. When IBM capped the amount of money that Perot could earn from commissions in selling computers, and when it ignored his plan to start an IBM division whose function would be to provide data management services to customers to advise them on ways to manage their data files and systems, Perot left IBM and started Electronic Data Services (EDS).

The systems integration market and outsourcing market is now growing at 19 percent annually. IBM's failure to enter this market segment early allowed its competitors—principally EDS and Andersen Consulting, the accounting firm which early established a computer consulting division—to gain a first mover advantage and to dominate the market. Currently, EDS has 50 percent of the outsourcing business of managing a company's data storage and management needs, compared to IBM's 6 percent, while Andersen dominates the market for advising companies on their software and hardware needs. IBM leads primarily in the market for government contracts.

To develop a presence in this lucrative market quickly, IBM began developing alliances with various organizations. It formed a joint venture with Coopers & Lybrand to provide management consulting in selected industries. IBM also teamed with AT&T to make IBM's mainframes work better with AT&T's network management systems.[26] IBM established the

[25]Lewis, *Business Week*, February 14, 1988, pp. 92–98.
[26]John Verity, *Business Week*, April 8, 1991, pp. 83–84.

Integrated Systems Solutions Corporation subsidiary in 1991 to provide a platform for IBM to enter the data processing outsourcing market. Its business is increasing; for example, in 1992 it received a 10-year $3 billion agreement to run computer systems for McDonnell Douglas Corporation. The subsidiary does outsourcing for 30 companies, including Continental Bank. IBM will run all of a client company's systems from mainframes and workstations to voice and data telecommunications.[27] It is aggressively advertising its strengths and services in this area.

The New Computer Industry

By 1990 IBM received about 50 percent of its gross profit from mainframe hardware, software, peripherals, and maintenance; 6 percent from minicomputers; 18.5 percent from PCs and workstations; and 12.4 percent from non-maintenance software and services.[28] However, the future revenue-generating potential of each of these market segments is uncertain as the boundaries between the segments grow less clear. Will workstations replace minicomputers? Will workstations and minicomputers replace mainframes? Will a network of PCs linked by advanced software to a mainframe eliminate the need for minicomputers or workstations? Obviously, IBM has the most to gain from making mainframes the center of a computer network, but its competitors have as much to gain from making minicomputers and powerful workstations the way of the future.

By 1990 IBM was facing stiff competition in all the developing segments of the computer market from companies that were mainly specialized in one market niche, like Microsoft in the software segment or Sun Computer in the workstation niche. IBM was fighting to increase its market share in each market segment but was suffering because of tough competition from strong competitors that had developed their own loyal customer following.

Moreover, the market for mainframe computers, its principal source of revenue, was declining as machines such as PCs and workstations were able to perform mainframe tasks at a lower cost. It had been estimated that, while 80 percent of 1986 computer industry profits were attributable to mainframe computer sales, by 1991 sales of mainframe computer

systems accounted for only 20 percent of industry profits. The PC revolution had reduced costs and allowed customers to buy much cheaper computer systems to do the work previously performed by expensive mainframes and minicomputers.

As a result of this shift, suppliers of computer components such as chips and software have been the winners as their share of industry profits rose from 20 percent in 1986 to 31 percent in 1991. Thus, for example, the share prices of Microsoft and Intel, which control the software and microprocessor markets, respectively, have soared, as have the share prices of Conner, Quantum, and Seagate which dominate disk drives and Andersen Consulting and EDS which are the leaders in system integration. IBM's, however, has fallen dramatically from a high of $160 in 1987 to less than $50 in 1992.

To fight the trend toward PCs and workstations, IBM attempted to make its 370 computer the central component of a network of computers that link individual users to the mainframe. However, it did not succeed, as sales growth for its biggest mainframe, the 370, dropped from 4 percent a year in 1990 to less than 2 percent a year in 1992. Even many of IBM's 370 users began switching to IBM AS/400 minicomputers because they can perform the same task more easily and cheaply. The mainframe market is now the third largest market behind PCs and minicomputers.

IBM Fights Back: Restructuring

In 1985 John Akers became CEO and was charged with the task of using IBM's vast resources to make it the market leader in the new lucrative market segments of the computer industry and to reduce IBM's dependence on mainframes. He took over a company where managers were still arrogant and complacent and believed completely in IBM's preeminence despite all the warning signs that it had lost its competitive edge. Its top management committee, staffed primarily of managers from its mainframe division, seemed unable to make the kind of innovative decisions that would allow IBM to respond quickly to the rapidly changing computer environment. The result was the failure to develop products fast enough and a mistaken commitment to the mainframe computer. Even its renowned salespeople had become a problem for the company. Committed to the IBM product, they had become oriented to selling and

[27]James Hyatt, "IBM Signs Pact to Offer Service to McDonnell," *The Wall Street Journal*, December 30, 1992, p. A3.
[28]Byrne, Depke, and Verity.

servicing the mainframe; they were not oriented toward satisfying customer needs, which might be for a minicomputer or a workstation.

Akers launched a year of the customer in 1987 to refocus the sales force on meeting the needs of the customer rather than on the needs of the mainframe. Most important, Akers realized the need to restructure the company and to change IBM's highly centralized style of decision making if IBM was to be able to innovate the next generation of products and emerge as a market leader in the new market segments. Akers recognized that the biggest problem for IBM was its highly bureaucratic organizational structure which slowed decision making and continually frustrated attempts to be innovative and entrepreneurial.

The 1988 Restructuring

To speed decision making, in January 1988 Akers reorganized IBM into seven divisions based on the main product market segments in which the company was competing: personal computer systems, mid-range systems, mainframes, information systems and communications, technology development (such as microchips), programming, and software. The idea behind the reorganization was to demolish the mainframe mindset by giving the managers of each division the autonomy and responsibility for developing new products for their respective markets. No longer would mainframe managers be able to stifle the pace of change and discourage the development of products that threatened the dominance of the mainframe. The sales force, however, was to remain a separate entity whose job would still be to sell the whole line of IBM products. The logic for this was that the sales force could sell customers an integrated IBM computer system—a network of PCs, file servers, and mainframe—and provide the computer software, service, and systems consulting to tailor the system to the customers' individual needs.

The disadvantage of the single sales force was that each division would not be able to devise a sales strategy specific to its own competitive environment and salespeople would not be able to focus on a single product line. IBM felt that the economies of scale and scope provided by a unified sales force outweighed these disadvantages. Twenty-thousand employees were transferred from staff and lab positions to the sales force and the commission system was revamped so that salespeople were now

evaluated on total revenue, not on the number of units rented or sold.[29]

IBM's Contention System

If the first purpose of the reorganization was to focus IBM's activities more closely on the main segments of the computer market, the second purpose was to shorten the product development cycle and to speed products to market. Since the early 1970s, IBM had taken advantage of its dominance in the market to use a "contention" system to control new product development. In this system, two or more project teams designed competing product prototypes and a series of committees at both the divisional level and the corporate level met over a period of months to debate the merits of each project. A project would be approved after six committee members rated the two processes, which could take months or years; then the committee met to finalize the product plan. During this process if any committee member said, "I non-concur," meaning that he or she disagreed with the project, it would be sent back for further review or scrapped.

The result of the contention system was that the projects that were approved were generally successful. However, the time frame associated with making the decision was generally so long that products were late to market, putting IBM at a competitive disadvantage. For example, the small, independent team charged with the development of the first IBM PC launched the product in one year. However, once the PC group was put into the Information Systems & Communications Division and decision making became constrained by IBM's contention system, the speed of the development process slowed significantly. For example, the PS/2 was not introduced until 1987 instead of the 1985 target. This delay allowed clone makers of the older PCs to gain 33 percent of the market share in PCs. Other symptoms of IBM's overly bureaucratic approach to decision making included its failure to enter new market segments quickly. For example, IBM entered the PC market four years late; it was also a laggard in workstations. Similarly, IBM's top managers refused to recognize the importance of the growth of minicomputers and were hesitant to launch products that would compete with the mainframes.

---

[29]John Verity, *Business Week*, May 29, 1989, pp. 72–78.

The reorganization was designed to shorten the time it took to get a product to market and to overcome the hurdles to product development.[30] In the 1980s IBM no longer had the luxury of taking a long time to make competitive decisions, as smaller and more agile competitors were forging ahead and the product life cycle of computers was shortening.

In an attempt to cut costs, increase profitability, get close to the customers, and reduce bureaucracy, Akers embarked on a major campaign to downsize the organization. The 1985 work force of 405,000 was reduced to 389,300 in 1988 through early retirement and attrition. In addition, overtime and temporary employees, equivalent to 12,500 full-time employees, were cut.[31] Despite the facts that IBM closed plants, cut spending, and reduced capital outlays, costs grew faster than revenues during most of the reorganization. Moreover, analysts could not discern any noticeable change in IBM's strategy or the way it made decisions. Products were still late to market.

The 1988 reorganization was a failure. Although each division was supposed to become more autonomous, in reality most decisions still required approval by IBM's corporate headquarters managers— managers who had risen through the ranks from the powerful mainframe computer division. Products that might have cannibalized the sale of mainframes were still discouraged by corporate managers, who having achieved their success during the mainframe era were hesitant to introduce products to compete with mainframes. One example of the mainframe mindset involved the PC unit's push to get into the laptop market in 1989 by pricing the laptop competitively at $4,995. Corporate headquarters insisted on a price of $5,995 to meet corporate profit margin targets. As a result, many competitors were able to price their products lower than IBM's machines. Even though IBM later priced the machine lower, it never regained lost market share.[32]

To allow the personal computer division to respond faster to the quickly changing PC market, Akers decided to place the PC business in a separate operating unit. In 1991 Akers formed the IBM Personal Computer Co. and gave it control over the design, production, distribution, and marketing of IBM PCs. Prior to this change, distribution was performed by IBM's large sales and marketing division, but 1,200 former marketing and sales employees were transferred to the new PC unit, which also was to handle telephone sales. The corporate sales force was to continue to sell to big corporate customers.[33] In decentralizing authority to managers in the PC division, Akers was showing managers his plans for the IBM of the future.

The 1991 Restructuring

IBM announced another restructuring at the end of 1991 to try to decentralize decision-making authority to the divisions and to reduce the role of IBM corporate headquarters in setting divisional strategy.[34] Akers divided IBM into thirteen separate divisions: nine divisions were based on the company's main product lines and four divisions were to be marketing and service operations organized geographically. The nine manufacturing divisions were to supply the four marketing divisions. The goal of the restructuring effort was to make the divisions independent units operating under a broad IBM umbrella to free the divisions from corporate control.

Aker's plan was that each division would be an autonomous operating unit that could freely negotiate transfer prices of inputs with other divisions and, if a division wanted to, could buy from and sell to outside companies. The divisions were to treat each other the same as they would outside companies, and no favorable prices were to be granted to IBM divisions. Moreover, the performance of each division would be reported separately and each division would be accountable for its individual profits and losses. The heads of the divisions were responsible for developing annual business plans and were to guarantee IBM a certain return on money invested in their division. In the past, most managers did not know the details of an individual division's financial performance such as profit and loss statements.[35] Each divisional manager signed a contract to meet

[30]Lewis.

[31]Aaron Bernstein, "How IBM Cut 16,200 Employees without an Ax," *Business Week*, February 15, 1988, p. 98.

[32]Verity, "The New IBM."

[33]Laurence Hooper, "IBM Set to Unveil Restyled PC Business That Could Operate as a Separate Unit," *The Wall Street Journal*, September 3, 1992, p. A3.

[34]Verity, "The New IBM."

[35]Ibid.

objectives in revenue growth, profit, ROA (return on assets), cash flow, customer satisfaction, quality, and morale.[36] If the divisional heads were successful, they would get a share of the profits; however, if they failed, their jobs were on the line. Financial results for all thirteen units were to be made public by 1994.[37]

The goal of this restructuring was to free up IBM's powerful resources and to make it more competitive. Division heads will have control over long-term development and business-level strategy. For example, the Personal Systems Division's manager can decide how PCs and workstations are produced and designed, and the PC division's research and development function will not compete directly with the mainframe division for resources. The hope is that the divisions will be able to compete with their smaller, more entrepreneurial rivals once they are freed from corporate bureaucracy.

The sales divisions will still be responsible for selling the whole range of IBM products, however, and control over sales will be centralized at corporate headquarters. The logic, once again, is that customers want a sales force that can handle their entire computer needs and that there are synergies from having one sales force provide a full set of products and services. IBM's traditional focus on service is still a strong competitive advantage. Analysts are, however, skeptical of having only one sales force, especially one in which representatives are still biased toward mainframes.[38] Many analysts feel that one sales force is a mistake and that giving each division its own sales force would be a better source of competitive advantage. Moreover, the huge costs of operating the sales force could be hard to allocate between divisions, causing rivalry among them.[39]

To demonstrate to IBM's thirteen operating divisions top management's commitment to IBM's more autonomous and more entrepreneurial approach to doing business, IBM's PC division was given total control over its own sales and named an independent unit in 1992. James Cannavino, the head of the PC unit, took total control over the PC division's strategy and organized the PC division around products instead of functions. The five product groups of the PC division are the low-cost Value-Points; PS/2; PS-1, aimed at home and small business users; portable products; and Ambra, a line of PCs built by an Asian contractor and sold in Europe. Each product group is in charge of its own brand development, manufacturing, pricing, and marketing.[40] This change was designed to allow the product groups to respond much more quickly to changes in the PC market, where products may have a life span of only six months to a year. In addition, Cannavino met with thirty-two CEOs of Silicon Valley start-ups and told them that he wanted to form alliances with them to speed the development of new hardware and software products such as multimedia and CD-ROM products. The IBM PC division is the world's largest PC company.

New Management and New Plans

Despite the 1991 organization, IBM's profits and revenues continued to decline; 1991 revenues fell 5 percent from 1990, the first decline since 1946. The company's 1991 loss of $2.8 billion was the first loss in IBM's history. In 1992 IBM's losses increased to $5 billion on $65 billion in revenues. In January 1993 the stock went below $46, the lowest price in 17 years, and pressure for change at the top was increasing.

Under pressure from investors and the public, John Akers resigned in January 1993. Although Akers reorganized and restructured, critics claimed that he never went far enough in implementing the reforms that would really turn around IBM. For example, despite the facts that between 1986 to 1990 a total of 100,000 IBM workers were cut mainly through early retirement and that Akers had removed the whole of IBM's former top management team to try to rid IBM of the "mainframe mindset," critics claimed that Akers had avoided initiating the major layoffs that were needed to restore profitability.[41]

In 1993 the board of directors searched for a replacement for Akers and shunning an insider, for fear that he could not bring a fresh perspective to IBM's problems, chose an outsider to be CEO of IBM, the first time an outsider had occupied the top job.

[36]David Kirkpatrick, "Breaking up IBM," *Fortune*, July 27, 1992, pp. 44–58.
[37]Ibid.
[38]Verity, "The New IBM."
[39]John Verity and Arnst, December 21, 1992, p. 32.

[40]Catherine Arnst and Bart Ziegler, "A Freewheeling Youngster Named IBM," *Business Week*, May 3, 1993, pp. 134–138.
[41]Catherine Arnst and Weber, *Fortune*, February 8, 1993, pp. 22–24.

The Rebirth of IBM

This case was prepared by Gareth R. Jones, Texas A&M University.

Today, IBM has a market capitalization of over $155 billion and employs over 319,000 people worldwide who operate in over 150 countries. It is also one of the most profitable global computer companies because by 2004 it had become the leader in the global business computer services and consulting industry, surpassing competitors such as EDS, Accenture, Cap Gemini, and HP. What changes in its business model and strategies have allowed IBM to achieve such a dramatic turnaround in performance given its disastrous performance in the 1980s? To answer this question, it is necessary to look at the way changes in IBM's top management and the business model its new CEOs Louis Gerstner, and then Sam Palmisano, crafted have transformed the company over the last decade.

Akers's Last Stand

As discussed in "The Fall of IBM," John Akers's vision of IBM's future was for the corporation to be broken up into thirteen different companies that would be spun off to operate independently—essentially that the IBM empire should be dissolved. While IBM's top managers considered how to go about the mammoth task of dismantling the company, Akers still faced the problem of how to keep it afloat in the short run. In his final desperate attempt to keep IBM viable, Akers continued to make drastic cost reductions, and

Copyright © 2005 by Gareth R. Jones. This case was prepared by Gareth R. Jones, Texas A&M University, as the basis for class discussion rather than to illustrate either effective or ineffective handling of an administrative situation. Reprinted by permission of Gareth R. Jones. All rights reserved. For the most recent financial results of the company discussed in this case, go to **http://finance.yahoo.com**, input the company's stock symbol, and download the latest company report from its homepage.

between 1991 and 1993, an additional eighty thousand employees were laid off as IBM sought to lower its cost structure—it now had less than half the work force that it had at its peak. The restructuring charges associated with these layoffs and the closing of many of its factories and offices resulted in record losses of over $15 billion for IBM, and its stock price plunged to record lows as investors decided the future lay not in mainframe computers but in networks of servers and client PCs. Moreover, by this time its personal systems group that manufactured its PCs and the small size servers it was developing had become a liability. This was because such competitors as Dell, Gateway, and Sun now had gained a major cost advantage—amounting to hundreds of dollars a computer—over IBM's PCs, and the PC division was losing money.

Another major problem IBM encountered in the early 1990s was the result of a major change in business-level strategy it made during the 1980s in the attempt to prop up its revenues and profits. As discussed in the earlier cases, IBM traditionally offered a complete service to its clients who typically rented its computer hardware and software on a multi-year basis, and then their IT system was maintained and upgraded by IBM service specialists. To boost revenues in the face of growing competition from servers, IBM decided to focus on selling, rather than renting, its computers, and it began offering special deals to its clients to encourage them to buy them.

While this boosted its performance in the short run, by the 1990s, however, the result was that IBM lost its special relationship with clients who now were looking to upgrade their computer systems. Given the rapid advances in IT, they now became more likely to buy the products of other computer companies, especially because servers and PCs seemed to offer considerable cost savings over mainframes.

By the 1990s, sales of network computers were rocketing while sales of mainframes were plunging, and IBM's strategy had inadvertently reduced its clients switching costs. By 1990, sales of computer hardware and software accounted for over 80 percent of IBM's sales and revenues because revenues from its service operations had declined significantly as clients began to build their own IT departments.

In 1993, when the company's performance showed no sign of improving despite his best efforts, CEO Akers resigned and IBM's Board of Directors looked for a successor who could somehow find the right business model to turnaround the ailing company. The person they selected to be IBM's new CEO was Louis Gerstner, an ex-management consultant who, as president of American Express and CEO of Nabisco, had engineered a major turnaround in the performance of these companies. Gerstner had no background in the computing industry, however, and his appointment was viewed by many analysts—and by many of IBM's powerful top managers—as an enormous mistake, and IBM's stock dropped to a new low when Gerstner took over. How could an outsider, with no knowledge of the way IBM operated, know how to compete against its rivals in the rapidly changing computer sector?

Gerstner's Immediate Moves

IBM's board had chosen Gerstner, however, because they wanted a new leader who could take a fresh perspective on the company's problems and one who had not been a part of IBM's slow-moving bureaucratic culture in which slow, centralized decision making and power struggles between divisions had dominated its strategic thinking. Gerstner's task was to decide what the right business model was for IBM. What kinds of products, customers, and distinctive competencies should IBM invest in and pursue in the future or should the company be broken up? In the meantime he also faced the problem of stemming IBM's losses and keeping it afloat.

The major argument Akers had made in support of breaking up IBM into thirteen different and independent companies was that each new company would then be free to decide how best to compete against rivals in its particular industry, PC or storage or particular software application, for example. By doing this, each former IBM division would become more efficient because its newly independent managers would have greater incentive to make tough decisions and find the best way to compete. Before making this decision, Gerstner decided to closely study IBM's different business divisions and search out their strengths and weaknesses. Also, he wanted to examine the fit between IBM's different businesses—what was the rationale for keeping IBM as a whole versus breaking it up?

Gerstner has a reputation for hands on management that involves frequent visits to all a company's divisions to talk to managers at all levels. He spent his first months as CEO on a whistle stop tour interviewing IBM's divisional managers, searching out those who seemed to have special insight into its problems and analyzing its portfolio of businesses. He also visited many of IBM's largest corporate clients to get a sense of what they wanted from IBM and what they saw to be its future.

Gerstner soon publicly announced that his decision was that IBM should remain as one single united company; the real problem was to find a better way to integrate the products and activities of its different divisions to create more value from its businesses for clients. His strategic analysis led him to conclude that it was IBM's ability to provide clients with a complete and comprehensive collection of computer hardware, software, and services, including business consultancy that could be customized to each client's particular needs that would be the source of its future competitive advantage—just as it had been in the past when it dominated mainframe computing. In his view, what IBM needed to do was to work toward offering clients a complete computer package that suited the realities of the new computing environment, which now had strong competitors in all industries in the computer sector.

Having made the decision to keep IBM intact, Gerstner saw the main challenge as how to speed innovation and decision making both within and across IBM's many divisions. He soon found that IBM's top managers, inured as they were in its slow-moving culture based on consensus decision making, could not respond at the pace he was expecting. One IBM manager described the old IBM's decision-making process as being like "wading through a jar of peanut butter." Gerstner announced that IBM's managers "just didn't have what it takes," and he began to replace many senior IBM executives with managers from lower down in the ranks. He also continued to lay off large numbers of employees in product areas that he felt could not compete successfully in the new advanced IT environment to further reduce IBM's cost structure. He also decided to totally change the way decisions were made.

In the past, meetings to discuss important new product or strategy decisions, which were held at IBM's Armonk, New York, skyscraper headquarters, had often lasted many hours or days. Gerstner issued new rules requiring senior managers to distribute short, ten-page reports that outlined all significant strategy issues to other senior managers in advance of the meeting. Now, with all managers informed of the major issues involved, meetings could focus on the critical issues. Also, the managers championing a new product or project were now aware that they would be facing the probing questions of other managers, including Gerstner, who has a reputation for a blunt, confrontational style of management—one far removed from IBM's old consensus decision making. All managers came to meetings much better prepared and ready to defend or challenge new proposals for new products or services. Gerstner's new rules dramatically shortened meeting time, and unlike previous CEOs he often moved during or even before meetings to unilaterally approve or disapprove of new proposals regardless of the views of other managers. He knew IBM needed an autocratic, hands-on style of governance to challenge managers, to develop better strategies, and to speed decision making.

Finally, to change IBM's culture and decision making Gerstner decided to build a new campus-style IBM headquarters to replace its high-rise office building. In the old building, the more senior managers were, the higher the floor they had their offices on, and this had helped create IBM's centralized, hierarchical culture. In the new building top managers would be located on the same floor next to all the other managers in their operating group to encourage faster communication. Also, it would be easier for managers in different divisions to collaborate and discuss ways to harmonize their products and services and discover new product opportunities. The old headquarters was sold off—one more way Gerstner told his managers the old ways were gone.

Gerstner's New Business Model

Between 1993–1996, Gerstner and his top management team spent their time identifying IBM's core set of distinctive competences and deciding how they could nurture and build these competences to provide a foundation for IBM's future business model. When Gerstner found a product line or division that did not seem to meet IBM's future needs, it was either sold off to another company or closed down, which resulted in still more employee layoffs. But Gerstner's goal was to invest IBM's remaining resources in businesses where they could create the most value—and in so doing save the company. But what was Gerstner's vision for the rebirth of IBM?

His business model was that IBM should (1) provide a complete package of state-of-the-art computing solutions (hardware, software, services, and consultancy) that could be customized to a particular client's needs, and (2) to take advantage of the possibilities created by the Internet to create new markets for IBM's products and services. The whole focus of Gerstner's efforts was to make IBM a customer-driven company by which he meant that every manager and employee had the responsibility to make or provide those products or services that could best meet the needs of IBM's clients. Given that PCs, and even servers, were becoming commodity products with low-profit margins, what IBM had to do was to provide something unique so that customers would be willing to pay a premium price for its products and services. The challenge facing IBM was to learn how to customize products to the needs of customers if it was to be able to succeed in the new highly competitive computing environment.

Changes in Computer Hardware

Gerstner instructed his top managers to begin initiatives in all computer divisions to meet clients' changing IT needs. In its traditional hardware business, it faced two major problems. First, as noted earlier, mainframe sales were declining due to the growing popularity of network servers and PCs. To stem the decline Gerstner instructed the mainframe division, in conjunction with IBM's semiconductor division, to find ways to reduce the costs of mainframe computing, and to increase the scalability of its computers. Scalability means that a computer can be customized and designed and built to suit the needs of any size of company or any size computing task, from managing global databases to operating a small chain of restaurants. IBM began to position its smaller mainframes as "enterprise servers," and sales representatives were told to emphasize to clients that they could be made at a size and price to suit their unique needs, but that a large powerful mainframe computer was still needed at the hub of any company's IT system no matter what its size. Sales representatives were also told to emphasize that managing huge amounts of data and enormous databases on a more powerful enterprise server was not much higher than a network server, and that the enterprise server could satisfy the needs of a growing company. Also, IBM wanted to sell its clients its software and services such as maintenance so that it deliberately set prices of its hardware (enterprise servers) low, knowing that it could make money later on new software and services.

IBM quickly succeeded in lowering the costs of mainframe computing and had a clear cost advantage over competitors in this market. Another bright spot in its PC division was the popularity of IBM's sophisticated problem-solving ThinkPad computing devices among corporate customers. But Gerstner and his managers continued to struggle to develop strategies to increase the efficiency of IBM's server and PC division that was losing even more money as companies like Dell found new ways to slow down the learning curve. Although this division continued to lose money, however, it was difficult for IBM to leave this business because of its desire to offer its clients a complete hardware solution for their computing needs.

Another major change Gerstner made on the hardware side of the business was to take advantage of IBM's acknowledged skills in the development of new and advanced microprocessor chips. Before 1993, IBM only made chips for use in its own high-powered computers to protect its proprietary mainframe technology. Gerstner now instructed the chip division's managers to market these chips to other computer makers and to vigorously solicit contracts to build customized chips to suit the needs of other original equipment manufacturers (OEMs). In this way the division would learn how to build customized chips to suit the needs of clients in a particular industry, for example, which had a particular kind of need from a chip. This change in strategy proved very successful, and revenues from chips sales surged over time.

Changes in Computer Software

The rapid pace of change in the computer software industry resulted in a major challenge for Gerstner and his managers. Before IBM made the mistake of allowing Microsoft to provide the MS-DOS operating system for its own PC, it had been the largest seller of computer software (principally for mainframes and mainframe applications) in the world. Now Microsoft had usurped its position, but there were many other challenges as well from makers of specialized applications software such as companies like Oracle, which is the market leader in database management software, and SAP the German company whose Enterprise Resource Planning (ERP) software was soaring in popularity throughout the 1980s and 1990s. ERP software allows a company to link its value-chain activities and connects mainframes to servers and servers to PCs. It gives a company's managers at all levels extensive real-time information about a company's activities; ERP software has become the backbone of most large companies' IT systems. IBM had little to offer clients in these software applications areas; these companies had gained a first-mover advantage that was difficult for IBM to challenge.

Gerstner instructed the software division to focus its efforts on developing networking software designed to link IBM's new scalable enterprise (mainframe) servers to smaller servers and PCs. To catch up quickly, Gerstner began to buy companies that possessed unique network software that could provide clients with valuable new applications that would allow them to make better use of their computer network—and thus give IBM a competitive advantage. One of the companies IBM acquired at a cost of over $3 billion in 1995 was Lotus, which had developed the popular Lotus Notes collaborative software that essentially created a corporate intranet, an information network inside a company that allows managers at all levels to share information quickly both inside their own department and division and between divisions.

Gerstner early on saw another important way in which IBM could use its resources to develop software that would meet its clients' changing needs. This was to begin the push to develop "middleware" software that links the hardware and software provided by *any* computer company across *all* the levels of computing. In other words, middleware software provides customers with a "seamless" solution to their computing needs regardless of their legacy system. A legacy system is a company's current IT system at any point in time. Clearly, if IBM could develop middleware that could link any kind of computer products now and in the future, it would be in a good position to serve any client that wished to change or upgrade their current legacy system to take advantage of new and advanced IT applications offered by any company. This revolutionary approach was part of Gerstner's "open standards" strategy designed both to make IBM's own services available to all kinds of customers and to lessen the dominance of Microsoft.

Changes in Services and Consulting

Gerstner's drive to focus the efforts of all IBM employees on satisfying the needs of clients had been strongly influenced by the continued success of IBM's computer services group which in 1995 contributed around 20 percent to IBM's revenues. IBM's entry into the computer services business had arisen via the need of the U.S. government to employ the recognized global IT leader to run its major computing systems, such as those involved in national defense and space exploration. Recognizing that many large businesses had a similar need for expert help to install, maintain, and upgrade their computer systems—most of which then ran on IBM mainframes—the company established the Integrated Systems Solution Corporation (ISSC), which was a self-contained division separate from IBM's corporate headquarters and whose employees were service and customer oriented. Their job was to search for new clients and then to contract to manage their IT systems for a period of several years. Essentially this group provided the first computer outsourcing service that had been imitated by such growing competitors as Electronic Data Systems (EDS) and Accenture (which previously had been the consulting division of defunct Arthur Anderson) that had become the leading competitors in the IT outsourcing and services industry.

Gerstner recognized that this division possessed the customer-focused business model that IBM needed to grow its revenues in the future, especially if sales of its hardware and software declined. Moreover, Gerstner was familiar with the business model that Jack Welsh, former CEO of GE, had developed for his company. This was that GE would sell a product such as a turbine or aircraft or diesel engine at a relatively low price to increase sales because each sale would result in a profitable stream of future income from servicing and maintaining the complex equipment it sold. Gerstner recognized this same model was viable in the new IT environment; he also

recognized that in the IT sector clients need expert help to decide which kind of computer solution best meets their current and future business needs. Once again companies like EDS and Accenture were the leaders here and earned huge profits by providing companies with such expert help. And the market was only getting bigger; for example, SAP could not satisfy the demand of large global clients to install its ERP software in its clients companies, and clients were paying billions of dollars to consulting companies like Accenture and Cap Gemini for their expert help.

In 1996, Gerstner renamed the services division Global Services and charged it with the task of spearheading IBM's push into the outsourcing and value-chain management business to go head-to-head with competitors like EDS and Accenture. Gerstner's business model was now that global services would offer clients an outsourcing and business consultancy service based on assessing a customer's current legacy system and its future computing needs. IBM consultants would then design, plan, implement, maintain, and upgrade the client's IT system over time to help reduce the client's cost structure, improve its products, and build its competitive advantage.

Gerstner also hoped that providing such expert services would once again build up switching costs and keep IBM's clients loyal on a long-term basis because of its ability to show them how its comprehensive, customized computing solution could help increase their profitability over time.

Global services experienced continuing success throughout the 1990s, and it established hundreds of outsourcing deals with large corporate clients through the 1990s.

The New Global Services Division

Throughout the 1990s Gerstner continued to invest a large proportion of IBM's capital to strengthen the global services division, which was led by Sam Palmisano, because he believed this was the new foundation on which IBM's future success lay. His business model for IBM was that the company would build such a broad and sophisticated range of computer hardware and software, backed by the best consulting and service competencies in the industry, that it would overwhelm its competitors in the future. EDS and Accenture provide consultancy and service, for example, and HP, Dell, Sun, Oracle, and Microsoft produce computer hardware and software, but none of them had the capability to match the breadth and depth of IBM's growing computer offerings. By the late 1990s the ability to bundle products together was becoming a major advantage to clients seeking a seamless and cost-effective way of managing their IT—it has only become more important since.

In implementing this business model Gerstner recognized that in many specific computer hardware and software product areas IBM was no longer the industry leader. So he and Palmisano embarked on a the strategy of offering IBM's clients the "leading edge" products currently available, such as SAP's ERP software or Peoplesoft's HRM software or Sun's servers and Dell's PCs when they were either clearly better or lower priced than those supplied by IBM's own divisions. Then, and crucially, IBM's consultants, as a result of its focus on developing expertise in middleware that links any computer products together, were able to guarantee clients that they could install, maintain, and integrate them so that they work together seamlessly.

In adopting this strategy IBM was strengthening its commitment to "open standards" in the computer industry by announcing publicly that in the future it would continue to work to make all the *future* software and hardware of all producers—its competitors—compatible by strengthening its expertise in middleware. In doing so, Gerstner and IBM were also assuring clients that when they used IBM's computer consulting services this would not result in them becoming locked into its own proprietary hardware and software—so no switching costs would arise from this source. However, Gerstner hoped at the same time that clients would be so impressed by IBM's ability to provide such a complete service that they would become "locked in" because of the high quality of the service that it could provide.

An additional advantage of the open standards approach was that as IBM's consultants went from client to client assessing their needs they were able to provide detailed feedback to IBM's other divisions about whether their products were adequately meeting clients' needs. So, if a consultant decided that a competitor's software was more appropriate than that offered by IBM's, the division making the software could now clearly recognize why its product was not meeting customer needs—and what was necessary to improve its software to make it the "best of breed" or leading-edge product. Thus, Gerstner's strong focus on being close to clients had the additional advantage of spurring innovation throughout the organization;

managers had a clear goal to achieve, and they knew that Gerstner and his top management team were watching their performance. So, if a division did not meet customer needs its managers might lose their jobs or it might be sold off or shut down.

E-Business at IBM

Another indicator of how well Gerstner was attuned to the changing IT environment was his early recognition that the growth of the Internet and e-commerce would become a dominant force in the direction of computing in the future. IBM coined the term "e-business," and Gerstner established an Internet division in IBM in 1995 before most other computer companies. Its early awareness of the future possibilities of e-business in commerce also allowed it to adapt its software and hardware to serve Internet-related value-chain transactions before its competitors. Once again, being close to its clients helped it to understand their changing needs and built its competitive advantage. Also, its acquisition of Lotus helped IBM understand the potential of the Internet. Lotus Notes was a company-specific or internal software collaboration application, while the Internet provided a major channel for collaboration between different companies. It was by chance that IBM's acquisition of Lotus revealed how the power of the Internet would shape supply chain transactions between companies and their suppliers and distributors, and the Lotus collaborative software provided a model for making IBM middleware software Internet compatible.

IBM embarked on its e-business initiative in 1996 with a global marketing campaign aimed at showing companies how value-chain transactions with other companies and clients could be carried out online. Soon companies recognized that its competency in e-business gave it a competitive advantage over companies such as SAP, Oracle, and HP, which now raced to catch up. As a result, it attracted a growing number of e-business clients that resulted in a major increase in its computer service revenues. First in line to adopt IBM's e-business software were large corporations that needed to manage transactions with hundreds or even thousands of suppliers and distributors. Companies such as Wal-Mart and Goodyear formed contracts with IBM to use its immense computing resources to manage their huge volume of online transactions.

IBM, however, also recognized that small and medium businesses (SMBs) were another important kind of business opportunity to sell its service offerings—especially as it now had computer hardware and software that was scaleable so that it could be sold at a price to meet their needs. IBM had developed less expensive software targeted at the needs of SMB clients, and it now worked with the thousands of new dot.com startups, such as Internet web-design and hosting companies, to teach these companies how to install and maintain its software in SMBs. IBM hoped that once SMBs had made the connection with IBM they would start to buy other kinds of its software, for example, to manage their databases and functional, value-chain tasks such as bookkeeping and inventory control. In 1999, Gerstner announced that IBM had a goal of reaching two million SMB clients by 2001.

A last advantage of IBM's early move to the Internet was that it also helped with its own cost-cutting efforts. IBM claimed to have saved billions of dollars by selling its own computer hardware and software directly to customers online, and billions more by using e-business to purchase the components it uses to make its own products.

Gerstner Transfers Power to Palmisano

By 2000, IBM had replaced EDS as the global leader in computer services; it had a backlog of outsourcing contracts worth over $100 billion. Until he retired as CEO of IBM in February 2002, Gerstner continued to work to strengthen his new services-driven business model across all IBM's U.S. and global operations. To encourage managers, consultants, and salespeople to focus on the customer, Gerstner introduced a new pay-for-performance evaluation system that rewarded employees at all levels based upon their ability to meet the goals and objectives in the business model. In addition, Gerstner imitated EDS and Accenture in making stock options a part of IBM's incentive structure to encourage top managers to pursue IBM's new business model and forget the old IBM ways. In the old IBM, with the exception of its salespeople who had always been paid according to performance, managers and employees had been rewarded based on their time in the company or the level to which they had been promoted. Now, a manager's own performance drove promotions and rewards—and poor performance and the inability to meet goals resulted in termination. In this way, too, Gerstner changed IBM's culture; from being conservative, hierarchical, and product oriented, it now became entrepreneurial, collaborative, and customer oriented.

Sam Palmisano, the executive in charge of global services, became Gerstner's hand-picked successor. A lifelong IBM employee, Palmisano had joined the company straight from college and was known as a "street fighter" who had worked his way up global services' hierarchy. And global services had the entrepreneurial, customer-based culture that Gerstner wished to propagate throughout IBM. Together, Gerstner and Palmisano worked to hasten IBM's transition from primarily a hardware company to one whose growth would be propelled by services and software (see Exhibit 1).

EXHIBIT 1

IBM's Organizational Structure

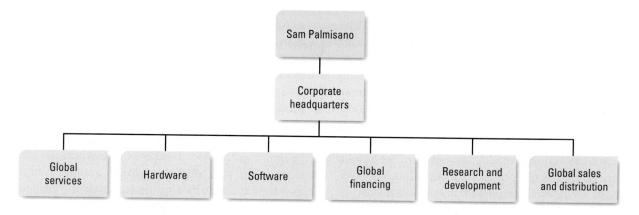

As IBM enjoyed increasing success with its e-business initiative, it became increasingly clear that clients in different industries faced different sets of e-business problems and issues and that increasingly industry-customized solutions were necessary. Also the problems facing large and SMB clients were often quite different. As a result, in 2002 Gerstner and Palmisano decided that a major overhaul of IBM's operating structure was necessary to support its new services-driven business model. At the same time, they wished to strengthen the ability of the software division to produce the kind of software that different industry customers needed. Global Services's intimate knowledge of the software capabilities of competitor's software and hardware provided IBM's software divisions with vital information that could help them improve their products. Gerstner and Palmisano wanted to increase the links between services and software to achieve more synergies. In addition, its consultant's knowledge of competitors' products provided the competitive information that helped top managers select the acquisition targets that would do the most to strengthen IBM's service and software offerings. IBM steadily acquired software and service companies throughout the 1990s to accomplish this goal, and since 2000, IBM has spent over $7 billion on over twenty acquisitions.

IBM's New Operating Structure

To pursue its business model and strategies, Gerstner and Palmisano decided to create a new operating structure to make it easier for its different divisions to cooperate to provide customized solutions to industry customers. First, they decided to divide IBM's clients into six major groups to better cater to their industry-specific needs. These groups are financial services, public, industrial, distribution, communication, and small and medium-size businesses (SMBs). As Exhibit 2 shows, the industries or types of client in each group share a need for a similar kind of computing solution. Second, they grouped IBM's many different individual divisions into six major operating groups or divisions that were instructed to cooperate to serve the needs of each of these client groups. The four main operating groups are global services, hardware and semiconductors, software, and global financing. The two principal functional support divisions are research and development, which provides assistance to the operating groups, and global sales

EXHIBIT 2

IBM's Clients by Sector and Industry

Sector	Industries
Financial Services	Banking
	Financial Markets
	Insurance
Public	Education
	Government
	Health care
	Life Sciences
Industrial	Aerospace
	Automotive
	Defense
	Chemical and Petroleum
	Electronics
Distribution	Consumer Products
	Retail
	Travel
	Transportation
Communications	Energy and Utilities
	Media and Entertainment
	Telecommunications
Small & Medium Business	The majority of businesses in this sector have fewer than 1,000 employees

and distribution, which links the client groups with the operating groups, especially to global services.

Sales and distribution is comprised of a network of internal and external routes-to-market which includes IBM's thousands of salespeople located all around the world, ibm.com, and a staff of experts who help to train and provide support for IBM's army of independent software vendors. IBM's sales force is also grouped into industry-specific global units that specialize in a certain type of client. Typically the sales force discovers a client, meets their immediate needs, but then passes the client on to global services which offers the client its services to analyze its legacy system and the way this legacy system can be improved to meet the client's future business objectives. The sales force also provides another avenue to integrate across IBM's different operating groups, for it provides information that allows the global services, hardware, and software groups to cooperate to provide a customer-specific solution.

IBM's research and semiconductor division has been one of its principal sources of competitive advantage that has allowed the company to differentiate itself from its rivals. In fact, IBM has been awarded more U.S. patents that any other company each year for the last eleven years. IBM spends about $5 billion annually on R&D and concentrates on developing new software, such as e-business, open-source, and middleware software, and new hardware such as advanced storage and memory devices, semiconductors, and autonomic computing. IBM's research and semiconductor group was also instructed to focus on projects that would have the most payoff for the company's clients, especially new projects that would be applicable across the different client groups to increase the return from the capital IBM invests in R&D. It was also charged with finding ways to shorten the time it takes to get new hardware and software to the market to maintain IBM's advantage over competitors.

Recent Developments in the Operating Groups

In the 2000s, IBM has continued to make many changes to its operating groups to strengthen its business model. Many of these changes have also resulted in its competitors altering their business models in order to compete more effectively with IBM. For example, HP's merger with Compaq in 2003 and Oracle's merger with Peoplesoft in 2005 were brought about because these companies perceived the need to offer a wider range of hardware, software, and services to compete effectively with IBM.

Global Services

Today, global services is the lynchpin, the central and most powerful operating group in the new IBM, and since 1992, services revenue has risen steadily to surpass IBM's hardware revenue. Today it is the biggest contributor to revenues and profit (see Exhibit 3). Today, the other operating groups support its activities as it works with clients to deliver solutions that use a complete lineup of IBM software and hardware. However, it still continues to offer clients the "best of breed" hardware and software from its competitors if the solution requires it and they have superior software or hardware such as Peoplesoft's HRM software and SAP's ERP software. In addition, global services has continued to champion IBM's push into open standards software, and like the other divisions, it promotes the use of the Linux open standards software for use by clients especially in linked network server and mainframe applications.

Indeed, in the early 2000s IBM invested over $3 billion to develop Linux-based operating and applications software to reduce Microsoft's hold on the server-PC software market that it dominates. In 2005, it was estimated that 30 percent of servers now run on the Linux platform. In developing countries in Asia such as India and China, IBM's global subsidiaries are strongly promoting IBM's own Linux-based software as an inexpensive alternative to Microsoft's expensive Windows platform. In 2004, Microsoft was forced to respond to this threat by offering customers in Asia stripped-down, low-cost versions of its software to retain its control of the global server-PC market, but clearly global services will promote IBM's own Linux software whenever possible.

As the company's business model continues to evolve, Palmisano's expectation is that global services

EXHIBIT 3

Changes in Percentage Revenues by Operating Group

% of Revenue/Segment	2003	2002	2001	2000	1999	1998	1992
Global Services	48%	45%	42%	43%	43%	44%	23%
Hardware	32%	34%	37%	38%	37%	35%	53%
Software	16%	16%	16%	14%	14%	15%	17%
Global Financing	3%	4%	4%	4%	4%	4%	7%
Other	1%	1%	1%	2%	2%	2%	2%
Total Revenue	100%	100%	100%	100%	100%	100%	100%

will play a larger role interfacing with IBM's customers, perhaps even IBM's sales force will be merged into global services. Global services has three main lines of business: (1) strategic outsourcing services (SO) provides customers with competitive cost advantages by outsourcing customers' processes and operations; (2) integrated technology services (ITS) designs, implements, and maintains customers' technology infrastructures; and (3) business consulting services (BCS) which deliver value to customers through business process innovation, application enablement, and integration services.

SO and ITS allow clients to outsource many different kinds of value chain activities or to outsource management of their entire IT system to IBM. Some contracts with SMB clients may only last for a few years, but contracts with large corporations and in the public client group, such as those with U.S. government agencies, may last for ten years and then be renewed. IBM had over $100 billion of long-term outsourcing deals by the end of 2002—one major reason that explains why it took the lead from EDS. BCS offers six main kinds of business and consulting and service activities for the six different client groups (Exhibit 4). *Strategic change solutions* involve analyzing a client's legacy system from the standpoint of competitive advantage, such as advising how changes in IT can increase efficiency or intraorganizational collaboration. *Customer relationship management* (CRM) is a rapidly expanding software application that provides the information companies need to accurately assess their customers' needs and to alter their products or services to respond to those needs appropriately. *Supply chain and operations solutions* are those typically involved in helping companies better manage relationships with suppliers and distributors, especially when they outsource manufacturing to companies abroad. Frequently, this involves the implementation of ERP systems that help clients collect, process, and analyze more information about their companies' operations so that they can formulate better strategies to increase their profitability.

The final three kinds of solutions IBM offers clients are *financial management, human capital management* or HRM software, such as that provided by Peoplesoft or SAP's HRM module from its ERP package, and *e-business integration*. E-business integration involves showing clients how to move and manage their value-chain activities online. Such e-business integration is often accompanied by one or more of the other solutions IBM offers, for its goal is to get its clients to utilize more and more of its hardware and software in their legacy systems. So, for example, outsourcing and supply chain management are frequently a part of the process of e-business integration.

A major coup for Palmisano occurred in 2002 when IBM was able to acquire PriceWaterhouseCoopers, a leading global business consulting services company, for $2.3 billion. This added more than twelve hundred business consultants to its ranks and gave the BCS group the expertise it needed to better serve the needs of its different industry client groups. Moreover, the

EXHIBIT 4

Global Services Solutions and Clients

BCS Solution Areas	Client Sectors					
	Communication	Distribution	Financial Services	Industrial	Public	SMB
Strategic Change Solutions						
Customer Relationship Management (CRM)						
Supply Chain and Operations Solutions						
Financial Management						
Human Capital Management						
E-Business Integration						

twelve hundred new consultants are also globally based, and this allowed global services to provide an integrated range of solutions for clients in regions around the world. Indeed, one of Gerstner's major goals was for IBM to be able to offer the same complete IBM solution to a client anywhere in the world.

Revenues from abroad account for more than 40 percent of global services total revenues. Global services is broadly divided into three world regions: the United States, Europe, and Asia. In each of these regions, its consultants may be based in one country, such as India or France, but they are always ready to travel to a client in their world region or another should their expert services be required. The goal is always that IBM should offer the best customized solution for a specific client in a specific industry. Of course, today IBM makes full use of its own expertise in global intranet and Internet applications such as online collaboration and global teleconferencing to promote collaboration between its consultants and clients anywhere in the world. Clients are also able to use ibm.com to easily access information on its products so that they can also make informed choices.

Hardware

In 2003, IBM reorganized the divisions in its hardware group to shorten product development time and ensure they offered a seamless computing solution for its different types of clients. The two main hardware segments are the Systems and Technology Group, which deals with large enterprise clients, and the Personal Systems Group, which has been undergoing a major transformation.

Systems and Technology Group

The systems and technology group provides customized hardware solutions to global services for their clients; it also provides the collection of products that IBM's salespeople sell directly to any client to meet their business needs. A large percentage of hardware is also sold directly online through ibm.com to clients that already understand their needs. The main types of hardware are servers such as enterprise (mainframe), midmarket, web, or network servers and large storage systems that manage and store vast amounts of database information. IBM has been devoting considerable resources to find ways to reduce the costs of its large servers by running them on Linux-based software to reduce their long-term maintenance and operating cost. It has been increasingly pressured by Sun and Dell, which are offering low-cost servers, or in Sun's case, complete midsize network solutions that can be rented rather than bought—the old IBM model.

The systems group comprises eServer and Storage products. eServers are based upon IBM operating systems, as well as UNIX and the Microsoft Windows operating system. All these server lines have the capability to run Linux, a key open standard operating system. Data storage products include disk, tape, and storage area networks. The systems group provides integrated business solutions to customers. Approximately half of the group's sales transactions are through business partners and approximately 40 percent direct to customers, over 20 percent of which take place through the Internet at ibm.com. In addition, the systems group also creates the hardware used internally in support of IBM Global Services offerings and contracts, such as managing clients' IT systems or outsourcing operations.

The Technology Group primarily consists of IBM's Microelectronics Division, which provides leading semiconductor technology, customized solutions, and engineering technology services to original equipment manufacturers (OEM), other computer companies and to the Systems Group. The Microelectronics Division develops and manufactures products in three general categories. First, the technology group manufactures and tests customized semiconductor products for customers. The customers design these customized product solutions using IBM's suite of design tools and portfolio of intellectual property (IP), resulting in faster speeds to market for the customers.

Second, semiconductor customers provide IBM with their product designs based upon the customer's product IP. Using the customer's design, IBM provides a full suite of semiconductor manufacturing and integrated supply chain services to deliver the product to the customer. The technology division is in the business of producing the advanced microelectronic chips both for IBM's own hardware but also for any company that wants a customized chip to support its own product applications. For example, in 2003 IBM signed a contract with Sony to design the new microprocessor that will become the heart of

Sony's new PlayStation 3 when it debuts in 2006. This chip has state-of-the-art graphic and sound capabilities and will permit a seamless integration of the user with other game players on the Internet. The chip will also become the hub of Sony's new wireless home media center whereby a user will be able to control all electronic devices such as televisions, computers, and printers using the chip and its associated operating system.

The technology group makes semiconductors designed primarily for use in IBM's own Power PC platform used in its servers and PCs. In addition, the Technology Group launched in 2002 its new Engineering and Technology Services Division that provides system and component design services, strategic outsourcing of customers' design teams, and technology and manufacturing consulting services.

Personal Systems Group

In 2003, the Personal Systems Group included the company's lines of PCs, printers, and point-of-sale terminals used in retail stores and fast-food restaurants, and IBM's Thinkpad devices. However, in the 1990s the PC business became characterized by a high degree of commoditization, short product life cycles, and intense price competition. As noted earlier, IBM's cost disadvantage compared with companies like Dell, Hitachi, and Samsung, which specialize in manufacturing low-cost computer components, increased dramatically. Despite the personal systems division's attempt to reduce costs, it could not match those of its efficient competitors so major changes have been made to the personal systems group in the 2000s. In 2001, IBM sold its hard drive unit to Hitachi, and then in 2002, it announced that it would sign a three-year outsourcing agreement to allow Sanmina-SCI to make IBM's PCs and low-range servers that would be sold under the IBM name. However, it also said it would continue to design and sell server and PC software.

In 2005, however, despite its outsourcing of production, the division was still losing money and pulling down IBM's profits, and IBM announced that it had sold its computer business to Chinese assembler Lenovo, formerly the Legend Group. Lenovo will pay Big Blue $1.25 billion, with $650 million in cash, and IBM will retain an 18.9 percent stake in the joint venture. Lenovo will be IBM's preferred supplier and retains the right to use the brand for five years. IBM will continue to provide software and technical support for the product lines for the next ten years. Its stake in the joint venture may allow it to benefit significantly from cost reductions that Lenovo hopes to make that will make its PCs competitive with those offered by Dell and Gateway.

As Exhibit 3 shows, IBM's hardware sales have largely remained steady over the last several years, and the fact that they have not declined more is the result of Gerstner's focus on making IBM's mainframe or enterprise servers and storage devices scaleable and compatible with the needs of its global clients, as well as his focus on taking advantage of IBM's expertise in semiconductors and other specialized hardware where operating margins are high. Profit margins are high in these specialized product areas, unlike in PCs which have become largely a commodity product where margins are low and only the huge buying power of companies like Dell and their vast global sales make these companies profitable. A generalist like IBM can never compete against a specialist like Dell in a specific area—and this was Gerstner's insight that led him to promote IBM's ability to provide a complete range of computer products and solutions.

In the 2000s, Dell has also recognized the need to expand its product offerings, and it began to make or sell small servers, printers, computer peripherals, and then electronics in general, such as digital cameras, PDAs, and so on, to provide its customers with a more comprehensive solution. Dell also began to offer computer services such as installation and maintenance and has been trying to develop a consultancy group to meet the needs of small companies that need advice and a customized solution. It has watched IBM and learned how profitable such a customized service can be.

Software

Despite Gerstner's hope that IBM would obtain 2 million SMB clients by 2001, this did not come to pass. The recession of the early 2000s discouraged many SMBs from investing in expensive software that had uncertain returns. Nevertheless, IBM has made increasing SMB accounts a major goal for the future in a vast market currently dominated by BEA systems. Indeed, the software division has been rapidly working to develop the open source middleware solutions that can be scaled to the needs of SMBs.

Other companies such as Oracle, SAP, and Microsoft have followed IBM's lead, recognizing the huge potential revenues from this untapped client area, and have also launched their own software and service packages aimed at this sector. Once the U.S. economy rebounds, the strength of each company's relative product offerings will become clear.

Once again, to strengthen its competencies in applications software IBM has made many strategic acquisitions. After the success of its Lotus acquisition, it followed up by acquiring companies like Tivoli Systems and Rational Software in 2003 for $2.1 billion. Rational provides software tools that allow independent software vendors (ISVs) to effectively capture and analyze requirements to create designs for software applications, test applications, and manage the software development process. Rational's software development tools can be used to develop and upgrade any other company's software products, so this acquisition was a critical part of IBM's open standard strategy.

Throughout the 2000s, the software division has focused on developing two main kinds of operating and middleware software: first, a software that seamlessly connects computers at all levels with all kinds of peripheral devices such as printers and storage devices regardless of which company makes the hardware. IBM backs Linux because it believes the highest returns are achieved when customization of open source software is possible. Second, IBM has focused on extending its rage of customized software packages for different kinds of industry clients. As noted earlier, middleware software integrates IBM's clients' IT systems end-to-end and builds a base for ISVs to install and maintain industry-specific applications that allow IBM to differentiate its products. IBM's middleware brands include WebSphere, which facilitates customers' ability to manage a wide variety of business processes through the Web; data management such as DB2 Database software; Tivoli, which enables customers to centrally manage and efficiently utilize their network and storage; and Lotus, which increases customers' ability to communicate, collaborate, and learn in an effective way. As Exhibit 3 shows, sales of IBM's own software have also held constant over the last decade because sales of mainframe software have been replaced with sales of its middleware, and this operating group contributes significantly to its revenues and profits. IBM hopes that when the economy recovers sales of software will increase dramatically.

Global Financing

IBM's global financing division allows it to provide its clients with the financing they need to purchase its computer products and services, and this division is a major source of IBM's profitability. Indeed, IBM is currently the largest IT financier in the world. Although not a major contributor to total profits, financing is a very profitable operation with high gross margins.

Research and Development

Finally, IBM has an operating division devoted to advanced research. The research division's focus is to contribute to IBM's success by balancing projects that have an immediate impact with those that are long-term investments. Thus, it will help to develop innovations that support customized industry-specific solutions, but it also focuses on emerging technologies like nanotechnologies and autonomic computing that may pay off decades in the future.

E-Business on Demand

Under Palmisano the pace of change at IBM has accelerated as the company works to achieve a sustainable competitive advantage over its rivals. IBM's acquisitions since 2001 to improve its capabilities in software and services are listed in Exhibit 5. The acquisition of PWC was supported by the acquisition of specialized companies such as Mainspring. As noted earlier, Rational Software was a significant acquisition because of its expertise in middleware; it was also an important acquisition because it fit well with Palmisano's new "e-business on demand initiative."

After becoming CEO in 2002, Palmisano faced immediate problems because of the poor economic conditions of the early 2000s. IBM's revenues, like those of all other IT companies, plunged and so did its stock price as its existing and potential clients slashed their IT budgets. With lower IT budgets, all companies worked hard to identify the types of computer hardware and software that would have the biggest impact on their company's profitability in the future. Convincing a potential client to spend millions to buy new kinds of software and hardware, or billions of dollars on outsourcing contracts, was a daunting task facing IBM's sales force and that of any other IT supplier.

Looking ahead, Palmisano searched for new IT business solutions and applications IBM could develop

EXHIBIT 5

IBM's Acquisitions in the 2000s

Year	Company
2005	Corio
	SRD
2004	KeyMRO
	Liberty Insurance Services
	Systemcorp
	Venetica
	Alphablox Corporation
	Cyanea
	Candle Corporation
	Trigo Technologies
2003	Green Pasture Software
	Productivity Solutions Inc.
	CrossAccess Technology
	Think Dynamics
	Rational Software
2002	Tarian Software
	EADS Matra Datavision
	PWC Consulting
	Holosofx
	Access360
	TrelliSoft Metamerge
	CrossWorlds Software
2001	Database Assets of Informix Corporation
	Mainspring

using its growing set of core competencies. He and his top management team identified four major business objectives companies wish to achieve from advanced IT applications: to further innovation, to significantly reduce their cost structure, to integrate activities across a company's value chain, and to more accurately forecast potential return on investment from capital expenditures on new products or projects.

To help clients obtain these goals, Palmisano pioneered "on-demand business," a customized IT platform based on IBM hardware and software that allows clients to (1) be quickly responsive to any and all opportunities, threats, or demands from their customers or from the environment in general, (2) completely integrate their company's value-chain activities, and (3) integrate with external strategic partners, suppliers, and distributors. Palmisano announced that companies that adopted IBM's new on-demand IT would

obtain millions or billions of dollars in savings in operating costs—something very appealing to companies trying to make their IT budgets go as far as possible. Also their companies would be strategically positioned better to meet future business challenges.

To promote on-demand business, IBM told its clients to think of information and computing power as a "fluid" like water that is contained in the hundreds or thousands of computers that are the "reservoirs" or "lakes" of a large company's IT system. This water flows between enterprise and network servers and PCs in a company's IT system through the fiber-optic cables that connect them. Thus, computing power, like water, can be moved between computers both inside and between companies, providing that computer hardware and software are linked seamlessly together and so do not create information "logjams" that disrupt the flow of information and computing power.

IBM's research and software engineers worked together to develop new e-business software to allow computers both inside and between companies to work seamlessly together. Among other things, this software allows computer operators at some remote location to monitor hundreds of different computers at the same time and shift work from one machine to another to distribute a company's computing power to wherever it is most needed. This has several cost saving advantages. First, it allows companies to run their computers close to capacity, which greatly improves IT productivity and reduces operating costs. Second, to ensure that there was never any possibility of its clients experiencing a "drought" IBM proposed to use its own vast mainframe computer capacity as a kind of bank or reservoir that clients could tap into whenever their own systems might become overloaded. For example, IBM's e-business software allows companies to shift any excess workload from their network to IBM's computers which means they do not have to invest tens of millions of dollars in extra computers—a huge cost saving. Third, when a company's computers are seamlessly networked they can function as a "supercomputer," a computer with immense information processing power that can easily cost upward of $50 million to purchase as a stand-alone computer and tens of millions more dollars to maintain.

To show clients the cost saving potential of its new e-business products, IBM decided it would be the first company to use it. Previously, IBM allowed its hundreds of different divisions to choose whatever software they liked to manage their own purchasing and supply chain activities. In 2003, Palmisano appointed star manager Linda Stanford to overhaul IBM's company-wide supply chain—which purchases inputs worth $44 billion a year! Stanford was made responsible for developing software to seamlessly link all IBM's divisions into a single integrated computer network. When implemented in 2004, the new software resulted in a 5 percent gain in productivity, which IBM expects to repeat for the next five to ten years—this will result in cost savings of over $2 billion a year. IBM was quick to tell its clients that they can expect to see similar savings if they purchase its e-business software.

IBM's new e-business system also has many other performance-enhancing benefits. Its thousands of IT consultants are experts in particular industries such as the car, financial services, or retail industries. They have a deep understanding of the particular problems facing companies in those industries and how to improve their business models. Palmisano told IBM's consultants to work closely with software engineers to find ways to incorporate their knowledge into advanced software that can be implanted into a customer's IT system to better manage its business model.

IBM is developing seventeen "expert systems" that are industry-specific, problem-solving software solutions clients can use to make better business decisions as well as reduce operating costs. One of these expert systems is being developed in the pharmaceutical industry, for example. Using IBM's new pharmaceutical expert system, a company's computer network will function as a supercomputer able to simulate and model the potential success of the many new drugs it has under development. Currently, only 5 to 10 percent of new drugs make it to the market. IBM believes its new expert system could raise that rate to over 50 percent which would result in billions of dollars in cost savings for drug companies.

The Future

By 2005, as companies began to increase their IT budgets IBM was working hard to promote its new customized on-demand hardware and software offerings. Palmisano believes all the pieces are in place for IBM to consolidate its leading position over the next decade. However, while IBM has been forging ahead with its new computer services initiative its rivals have also woken up to the advantages of IBM's new business model and the threats it posed to them unless they also adopted a similar business model.

The need to expand its range of computer products and services prompted the merger between HP and Compaq in 2003, which led it to claim in 2004 that it had a range of products and services that equaled those of IBM. As noted earlier Dell has also been working to increase its product range and offer a low-cost alternative to IBM's hardware and software. Sun, too, abandoned its sales model and adopted a fee-based rental model for its servers and software to try to seize a larger share of the network market. SAP in the meantime had transformed its software so that it was also e-business compatible and made it scaleable so that it could suit the needs of SMB clients. Moreover, SAP had greatly increased the number of its own consultants and was working with EDS and Accenture to train their consultants to better analyze clients' legacy systems and to install and customize its software to better meet the needs of individual clients in order to compete with IBM's business consulting group.

The threat of IBM led many analysts to believe that a wave of future mergers in the computer sector was likely as it was becoming clear clients liked the ability to deal with just only one major computer company, rather than to have to deal with several different ones, to obtain a seamless and cost-effective solution to their IT needs. A merger between Microsoft and SAP would have been a major threat to IBM, but this did not materialize in 2004 as the companies decided that the threat of antitrust regulations and their own quite different corporate cultures would make such an alliance untenable. In 2004, it appeared that HP offered the only real challenge to IBM in its ability to offer a complete computer solution although it lagged behind IBM in the sophistication of its consultancy operations and in its experience of offering customers a seamless open standards computer package. In February 2005, however, HP's failure to realize synergies between its hardware, software, and consulting groups, and the continuing problems with its PC division led its Board of Directors to oust its CEO Carly Fiorina. It was not clear in the spring of 2005 what changes would now occur in HP's business model. Some analysts wanted the company broken up—just as they had wanted to break up IBM in the 1980s; others believe the problem is just to find a better way to execute HP's business model so it can compete effectively with IBM.

As companies jockey for competitive advantage IBM will not find the future easygoing. SAP is potentially a major threat given that its software is the backbone of most large companies' IT systems, and advances in computing power that continually reduce the cost of computer hardware will work in its favor. Similarly, the lucrative SMB segment is becoming increasingly competitive as IBM, SAP, Microsoft, and Oracle compete to become the leader in this area. Nevertheless, thanks to its new CEOs, IBM now has the opportunity and ability to sustain its leading position, and Palmisano is determined that the reborn IBM will never again repeat the mistakes of the past where its success bred the complacency that led to its collapse.

Case 23

Hewlett Packard: The Merger with the Compaq Corporation

This case was prepared by Isaac Cohen, San Jose State University.

On September 4, 2001, Hewlett Packard (HP) CEO Carleton (Carly) Fiorina and Compaq CEO Michael Capellas met in New York City to announce what was expected to become the largest merger ever undertaken in the computer industry: HP offered to buy its arch-rival, the Compaq Corporation, in a stock deal valued at $25 billion. While the announcement sent shock waves throughout the industry, and while Compaq's Board of Directors readily approved the deal, the merger soon became highly contentious. HP board member Walter Hewlett, other members of the Hewlett family, and the HP Foundation opposed the merger, and, as a result, an unusual fight erupted between the HP board and the cofounding family. Assisted by the majority of the HP board members, Carly Fiorina embarked on an extensive six-month campaign to convince investors to vote yes on the deal. Subsequently, in March 2002, HP shareholders had narrowly approved the merger, and two months later, HP and Compaq closed the deal officially. Valued at about $19 billion on the day of its closing, the merger ended a twenty-year-long rivalry between the two companies.

This case was presented at the October 2004 meeting of the North American Case Research Association (NACRA) at Sedona, Arizona. Copyright © 2004 by Isaac Cohen and NACRA. Reprinted by permission of Isaac Cohen and NACRA. All rights reserved. For the most recent financial results of the company discussed in this case, go to http://finance.yahoo.com, input the company's stock symbol, and download the latest company report from its homepage.

To Capellas and Compaq's Board of Directors, the deal with HP represented an attractive offer. With Compaq losing market share in two product groups—low-end home personal computers (PCs) and high-end servers—and with both product groups undergoing a steady decline in profits, Compaq was struggling. Subject to a price war launched by Dell Computer in the PC market (home computers and PC servers), and unable to compete successfully with IBM on the supply of information technology (IT) services, Compaq's future existence was precarious. To survive, Compaq needed to either exist in both the home PC market and the high-end computer business or to merge with other firms. Capellas, therefore, was faced with a difficult dilemma: Should Compaq sell its declining businesses and continue operating as a smaller company? Should it buy other firms, or should it merge with a leading computer company to create a global technology leader equal in size and complexity to IBM? Clearly the uncertain prospects of selling its declining businesses and continuing operating on a smaller scale, coupled with Compaq's recent failure to execute successful mergers with Tandem Computers and the Digital Equipment Corporation (DEC), persuaded its Board of Directors to sell the company to HP. "We wanted to be the next IBM," Capellas recalled, noting that the alliance with HP was "intuitively obvious" to all Compaq directors. Following the acquisition, Capellas became HP's president.[1]

To Fiorina and the HP board, the acquisition of Compaq also represented an opportunity. To begin with, Compaq's products and services complemented HP's. HP built up a strong business in Unix-based servers where the market was stagnant, but was weak in the production and sales of window servers where the growth prospects were promising. HP, in addition, built a healthy business in home PCs where competition with Dell was fierce, but lagged far behind Dell in its ability to sell PCs directly to consumers. Compaq, by contrast, was highly competitive in the production of cheap, standard-designed window servers on the one hand, and in selling build-to-order PCs directly to consumers on the other. Compaq was also competitive in making data storage devices—another expanding market where HP sought growth.[2]

Fiorina, furthermore, articulated a strategy that was expected to turn HP into an IT services company comparable to IBM: Combining Compaq's $7 billion IT services revenues with HP's $7 billion was projected to vault HP from a distant competitor into the industry's number four spot behind IBM, Electronic Data System (EDS), and Fujitsu. Additionally, a consulting firm hired by Fiorina and the HP board estimated that by 2004 the merger was expected to save the consolidated company at least $2.5 billion in operating costs, phasing out duplicated products and services.[3] Following the approval of the merger, Fiorina continued serving as HP's CEO.

Although HP's Board of Directors studied the implications of the merger thoroughly, Fiorina's decision amounted to a strategic gamble. Critics of the merger contended that no large-scale merger in the computer/telecom/IT industries had ever resulted in a success;[4] that most of Compaq and HP's IT revenues took the form of low-level support and maintenance services, not high-level consulting and outsourcing, the typical services sought by large corporate customers;[5] and that the new HP was unlikely to compete successfully with Dell—the cost leader of the industry. They predicted, instead, that the merger would undermine HP's worldwide competitive position relative to IBM and Dell Computer, its two main rivals, and result in a failure to integrate the two companies together.

Were the critics right? The present case looks at the merger two years later in an attempt to assess its overall impact on HP's performance.

Compaq and the Computer Industry

The success of IBM's PC gave rise to Compaq. IBM developed its first PC in 1980, brought it to market in 1981, and captured a 50 percent share in PC revenues three years later. As sales of IBM's PCs exploded, three Texas Instruments engineers started their own company: Compaq was founded in 1982 to manufacture and sell IBM portable computers. Unlike other manufacturers of PCs, Compaq's founders imitated IBM very closely, offering their customers a computer that ran all important IBM PC software programs. Examining an IBM PC at a Houston trade show, the three founders drew a blueprint sketch of the IBM machine on a paper placemat in a local restaurant, and used the sketch later to design Compaq's first portable computer.[6]

Compaq's founders raised an initial venture capital investment of $1.5 million, and subsequently, the company expanded at a remarkable pace. In 1983, its first full year, Compaq recorded $111 million in sales, an unprecedented growth figure for any start-up company; in 1986, its third full year, Compaq became the first company to achieve a Fortune 500 ranking in less than four years; and between 1986 and 1989, Compaq's revenues jumped fivefold to $3 billion.[7]

Compaq's rapid growth may be explained by a combination of several elements. First, focusing on excellence in engineering, Compaq had quickly become the industry's most competent designer and producer of PCs. Second, Compaq managed to develop, manufacture, and market its products faster than any of its competitors; in 1986, for example, Compaq delivered a new PC based on Intel's 386 chip one year before IBM. In addition Compaq built a superior distribution system. While all other manufacturers used direct sales forces, Compaq relied exclusively on an extensive network of dealerships. Never competing directly with its own dealers, and always granting dealers generous profit margins, Compaq provided its dealers with a strong incentive to increase sales.[8]

Compaq's rapid growth was further sustained by global expansion. In 1984, Compaq was one of the earliest American companies to market PCs in Europe, and five years later, it had become the second largest supplier of PCs to the European market. Compaq expanded global sales outside Europe as well. By 1990—a record year of sales ($3.6 billion) and profits ($455 million)—Compaq generated over half of its total revenues abroad, relying on a network of nearly four thousand authorized dealers stationed in 152 countries.[9]

Compaq's first crisis unfolded shortly thereafter. Partly as a result of a worldwide economic recession, and also as a consequence of increased competition with start-up companies such as Dell Computer and AST Research, Compaq experienced its first ever quarterly loss in 1991.[10] The Board of Directors acted swiftly. It fired Compaq cofounder Rod Canion as CEO and replaced him with Eckhard Pfeiffer, the company's chief operation officer and former head of Compaq's European division.

Under Pfeiffer's leadership, Compaq's top management introduced three strategic initiatives that helped turn the company around. First, Compaq launched a ferocious price war against IBM, Dell, and other PC vendors, slashing its profit margins by more than half while increasing revenues threefold in three years, 1991–1994. In 1994, Compaq passed IBM as the world's leading supplier of PCs. Next, Compaq introduced mass merchandising as well as direct sales, thus abandoning its long-standing policy of relying solely on authorized dealers. By 1992, Compaq sold its products in six hundred U.S. outlets, and in 1994, Compaq began building PCs to order, following the Dell model.[11] A third initiative introduced by Pfeiffer was corporate reorganization. Compaq sold its first server (a powerful computer that "served" data to corporate networks and internet sites) in 1989, but sales were disappointing. To revitalize Compaq's languishing services unit and diversify further into servers, Pfeiffer revamped Compaq's functional structure (manufacturing, sales, engineering) and reorganized the company along three product groups that together made up Compaq's new divisional structure: servers, desktop and portable computers, and network products. By 1996, Compaq had become the world's leading seller of "PC servers."[12]

A year later Compaq posted its largest profits to date: $1.9 billion on $25 billion in sales (Exhibit 1). Using a "Wintel" technology—a combination of Microsoft's operating system and Intel's microprocessors—Compaq managed to keep its research expenses far below its competitors, spending on research just 3.5 percent of sales in 1997 (the corresponding figures for Sun Microsystems and HP were 9.6 percent and 7.2 percent). The largest customer of both Microsoft and Intel, Compaq, in addition, benefited from economies of scale, receiving the best prices, fastest deliveries, and earliest information on product development from its two primary suppliers. In 1997, consequently, *Forbes* magazine selected Compaq as its Company of the Year.[13]

EXHIBIT 1

Compaq: Sales, Net Income, and Stock Prices, 1991–2000

	Sales ($Bil.)	Net Income ($Bil.)	Stock Price FY Close ($)
1991	3.3	0.1	1.76
1992	4.1	0.2	3.25
1993	7.2	0.5	4.92
1994	10.9	0.9	7.90
1995	14.8	0.8	9.60
1996	18.1	1.3	14.88
1997	24.6	1.9	28.25
1998	31.2	(2.7)	42.00
1999	38.5	0.6	27.06
2000	42.4	0.6	15.05

Source: "Compaq," Hoover's Handbook of American Business, 2000. p. 399.

Compaq's second and final crisis erupted in 1998. The crisis stemmed first and foremost from Compaq's acquisition of Digital Equipment for $8.4 billion. Under Pfeiffer's direction, Compaq bought Digital in 1998 in order to expand its customer base and offer corporate clients a full range of computer software programs, hardware products, and global IT services. But the merger backfired. In 1998, Compaq lost $2.7 billion (see Exhibit 1) as a result of high restructuring costs related to the merger. Cutting seventeen thousand jobs, dismantling plants, and closing down office buildings, Compaq's losses mounted while revenue growth stalled (Exhibit 2). As it became apparent that integrating the two companies together was getting harder and harder—some two hundred integration committees grappled with the process—Pfeiffer was forced to resign.[14]

Compaq's Board of Directors selected Michael Capellas, a newcomer who had joined the company in 1998, to replace Pfeiffer as president and CEO in 2000. Capellas moved quickly. Infusing Compaq with a true sense of urgency, Capellas introduced two strategic initiatives, the first aimed at focusing "Everything [on] the Internet" and the second sought to speed up Compaq's drive at global services. To facilitate the implementation of both strategies, Capellas reorganized the company around three market-driven "profit centers,"

EXHIBIT 2

Market Share and Year/Year Growth of
Worldwide Sales of Wintel Portable, Desktop,
and Server Computers, Third Quarter, 1998

	Market Share	Year/Year Growth
Compaq	14.4%	6%
Dell	9.2%	68%
IBM	9.2%	25%
HP	6.6%	26%

Source: Eric Nee, "Defending the Desktop," *Forbes*, December 28, 1998, p. 54.

the most dynamic of which was "enterprise solutions and services."[15]

Still, Compaq continued to drift. On the eve of the HP-Compaq merger announcement in the summer of 2001, Compaq reported its third successive quarterly decline in sales and profits. In spring 2001, Dell passed Compaq as the world's leading vendor of PCs, capturing 13 percent of the global PC market (compared with Compaq's 12 percent). And in July 2001, Compaq's stock price dropped to $15 a share, down from $35 a year earlier, while its market value sank to $26 billion, its lowest valuation in years.[16] Selling the company had become now a viable option.

The Evolution of HP

Unlike Compaq, HP was an old established company dating back to the Franklin D. Roosevelt era. Founded in 1939 by William Hewlett and David Packard, two electrical engineers and recent Stanford University graduates, HP specialized in the production of test and measurement instruments. HP's first product was an electronic sound equipment test instrument called an audio oscillator, and its first large customer was the Disney movie studios. Assembled by the two partners in a Palo Alto, California, garage, the oscillator was used by Walt Disney Studios to develop a new sound track for the movie *Fantasia*.[17]

As demand for electronic test instruments exploded during World War II, the two partners hired dozens of employees, broadened their product line, and expanded their sales. HP's revenues jumped from $34,000 in 1940 to $2 million in 1950 and $30 million in 1958. In 1957, HP went public, and a few years later, HP diversified into the production

of medical and analytical instruments, acquiring the Sanborn Company, a manufacturer of medical equipment, in 1961, and the F&M Scientific Corporation in 1966.[18]

Diversification went hand in hand with international expansion. HP established its European headquarters in Switzerland in 1959, opening a manufacturing plant in Germany and building an extensive marketing organization that served the European Community. In the 1960s, HP formed a joint venture with a Japanese partner to facilitate the manufacture and sales of HP products in Japan. By 1975, foreign sales accounted for 51 percent of HP's revenues, and in 1995, HP generated 44 percent of its sales at home, 36 percent in Europe, and 20 percent in Asia, Canada, and Latin America.[19]

HP's entry into the computer industry radically changed the nature of the company. In 1965, 87 percent of HP's revenues were derived from the sales of test and measuring instruments, 11 percent from the sales of medical and analytical equipment, and just 1 percent from computer-related products ("data products"). In 1977, computer-related products accounted for 42 percent of HP's revenues, and in 1995, 80 percent of HP's revenues were generated by computers, peripherals, and related products.[20]

HP's original interest in computing stemmed from its need to improve the performance of test and measurement instruments. In the 1960s, as high-end instruments required more and more computing power, HP embarked on the manufacture of electronic calculators—desktop computers that performed scientific functions. One of HP's most profitable and bestselling products was a handheld scientific calculator, the HP 35. Introduced in 1972 and known as the "electronic slide rule," the pocket size calculator was so successful that it persuaded Hewlett and Packard to enter, at long last, the computing business, a field dominated at the time by two large companies, IBM and the Digital Equipment Corporation.[21]

The founders selected John Young to lead HP's diversification into computers. Young was named CEO in 1978, following the retirement of Hewlett and Packard from active management. During Young's first five years at HP's helm, sales tripled, reaching $4.3 billion in 1982. Young introduced several lines of PCs and workstations in the early 1980s, and was responsible for the development of HP's most successful product, the laser jet printer (introduced in 1984). In 1983, Young launched the Spectrum project, a $500 million drive to build a new family of desktop mainframe computers based in Reduced Instruction Set Computing (RISC) architecture which allowed programs to run faster by eliminating routine instructions. To ensure the success of the project, Young restructured HP's computer business, building centralized R&D and marketing organizations that cut across divisional boundaries. Under Young's direction, furthermore, HP purchased Apollo Computers in 1989, a pioneer designer and manufacturer of engineering workstations, in a $500 million deal.[22]

By the late 1980s, however, HP was losing ground. Revenue growth shrank, and HP's stock declined by 50 percent in three years (1987–1990). The Spectrum computer was introduced in 1987, yet initial sales were disappointing as the $60,000 machine failed to compete favorably with a comparable $50,000 workstation offered by Sun Microsystems. HP's merger with Apollo, moreover, resulted in a $750 million loss in new business, as the integration of the two companies proved more difficult than expected. The founders were alarmed. Serving as board members—they owned together one-third of the company stock—William Hewlett and David Packard were convinced that Young's recent restructuring was responsible for HP's underperformance, at least in part. They urged Young to reverse course and decentralize. Young, in turn, disbanded dozens of committees, and empowered executives, once again, to exercise control over their divisions. But he did not keep his job. In 1992, HP's Board of Directors announced the retirement of John Young and his replacement by Lewis Platt.[23]

Initially, HP prospered under Platt's leadership. During Platt's first three years as CEO, 1992 to 1995, HP's revenues doubled from $16 billion to $32 billion, and its rate of return on sales climbed from 3.3 percent to 7.7 percent.[24] Running HP as a collection of autonomous businesses, Platt streamlined the decision-making process, shortened the design cycle of new products, and introduced thousands of new products. By 1996, HP made more than twenty-four thousand products, including PCs, workstations, printers, Unix and NT Window servers, network products, software, and testing and analyzing instruments. HP's growth was fueled by a phenomenal rise in sales of desktop printers and PCs. In 1996, HP generated about one-third of its revenues from the printer business, and the company had clearly become the dominant firm in the industry—HP's global market share ranged from 76 percent of all laser printer sales to 61 percent of all ink-jet printer sales.[25] Under Platt's leadership, furthermore, HP had become a major player in the PC market, deriving over 19 percent of its revenues from PC sales in 1998, up from less than 6 percent in 1992.[26] Other segments of the HP computer business—most notably, Unix workstations and servers—contributed to the growth in revenues and profits as well. In 1993, HP had surpassed Digital as the second largest computer maker in the United States behind IBM.[27]

Still, HP's computer business experienced a slowdown during Platt's last three years in office (1996–1999). One reason for the slowdown was Platt's failure to embrace the Internet. In a stark contrast to IBM, Sun Microsystems, and Microsoft, HP was slow to respond to opportunities offered by the Internet, and had remained a second-tier Web player throughout Platt's tenure. Another source of HP's difficulties was the rise of Dell Computer. Over time, HP had become increasingly dependent on the sales of PCs and printers, but such commodity-like products were subject to fierce competition that drove prices and profits down. Because HP's cost of manufacturing PCs was sharply higher than Dell's, HP's rate of return on PC sales was lower, amounting to 3 percent in 1998 against Dell's 11 percent—hence the decline in HP's market value. In 1998, both Dell and Sun passed HP in stock market valuation, yet each of these two companies generated less than half of HP's revenues.[28]

Platt responded to the crisis with a bold decision that was intended to create a "single identity" for the company and thereby sharpen its competitive focus. He split HP into two: an $8 billion company selling test, measurement, and medical products and services and a $40 billion company selling computers, printers, and IT services.[29] In May 1999, HP announced the spilt and renamed the spun-off segment Agilent Technologies. Key board members, in the meantime, pressured Platt to step down and retire,[30] and sought to replace him with a new chief executive who would embrace the Internet and bring change. For the first time in HP's sixty-year history, the board would consider CEO candidates who had never worked for HP.

Fiorina's HP

Carleton Fiorina was the HP board's first choice. The Board of Director's search committee looked at three hundred candidates, four of whom were selected as finalists. The search committee members were looking for candidates with excellent management and communication skills, the ability to conceptualize complex strategies, the capacity to deliver financial results, and the power to inject a sense of urgency throughout the company. Each of the top four candidates possessed all these qualities. Three of the four were "insiders" working for major Silicon Valley firms, namely, Oracle, Sun Microsystems, and Intel. Fiorina was the outsider. A gifted salesperson with a college degree in medieval history and philosophy, Fiorina rose to become president of Lucent Technologies, an AT&T spun-off telephone equipment company located in New Jersey. In the end, only Fiorina won the unanimous support of HP's board members.[31]

Unlike Platt, Fiorina was a decisive and deliberate leader whose management style combined command and persuasion rather than consensus—the hallmark of HP's decision-making process known as "The HP Way." Not bringing with her a single executive from Lucent, Fiorina relied entirely on her ability to win over HP's employees. Seeking high visibility from the outset, Fiorina traveled from one HP facility to another all around the world, meeting employees in "coffee talks"—an HP practice first introduced by the founders decades earlier—and publicizing the content of these talks in an in-house sheet called "Travels with Carly." Making sure her speeches were posted regularly on HP's website, Fiorina told *Forbes* magazine in 1999, "Leadership is a performance."[32]

Unlike Platt, Fiorina hired managers from rival firms. Throughout Platt's six-year tenure, managers were almost always promoted from the firm's own workforce, and employee turnover rate remained under 5 percent. During Fiorina's early tenure, by contrast, the employee turnover rate more than doubled to 10 percent, and many of HP's top executives were recruited from other technology firms, most notably Motorola, Xerox, and Netscape.[33]

To motivate HP employees, Fiorina restructured HP's compensation system early on. First, across all divisions Fiorina modified the financial incentives paid to HP employees, replacing the company's profit sharing plan with a more rigorous scheme of merit pay that tied compensation directly to company performance. Second, Fiorina revamped HP's sales commission system. In the past, HP paid commissions once a year, and such commissions were often tied to orders rather than sales. To drive HP's sales force harder, Fiorina cut the period over which commis-

sions were paid from one year to six months, and tied all commissions to actual sales. "You can feel the stress her changes are causing," one executive doing business with HP commented in 1999. "These guys know they have to perform."[34] Third, Fiorina altered the financial incentive paid to researchers. In the 1990s, merit pay received by HP engineers was tied to the number of inventions they introduced, not the number of patents they filed. Consequently, engineers had little incentive to work on projects that were likely to result in new products; instead, they strove to produce incremental improvements to existing products. Fiorina, in response, restructured the R&D pay scheme to award engineers a generous bonus for each patent they filed. As a result, the number of patents filed by HP doubled from 1,500 in 2000 to 3,000 in 2001.[35]

To revamp HP's decentralized structure, Fiorina launched a sweeping corporate reorganization in 2000.

William Hewlett and David Packard had originally organized HP as a confederation of independent businesses, each responsible for the engineering, manufacturing, marketing, and sales of its own line of products. A highly decentralized structure, the founders believed, would promote flexibility, encourage entrepreneurship and innovation, and speed up the decision-making process.[36] Notwithstanding John Young's move to centralize control over HP computer business in the 1980s, the founders, as noted, managed to restore HP's highly decentralized structure in the early 1990s. By the time Fiorina took charge of the company in 1999, HP had evolved into a collection of eighty-three vertically integrated, semi-independent, and loosely coordinated divisions.

Because HP's structure was highly decentralized and divisions were vertically integrated, the company experienced difficulties in coordinating product design, pricing, and marketing strategies. Fiorina, a former HP customer at Lucent, experienced the frustration of dealing with HP personally. At the time Lucent was seeking integrated solutions, HP offered the company stand-alone products and services only. Other corporate customers—the Ford Motor Company, Boeing, and the Best Buy Company—also encountered similar difficulties in dealing with HP. In case after case reported by representatives of these companies, dozens of HP salespersons would converge on a single facility and compete against one another over the supply of narrowly designed product lines rather than address the company's overall needs.[37]

Fiorina, consequently, consolidated the company's eighty-three divisions into four large groups or "quadrants" made up of two types of units: a "front end" unit responsible for marketing and sales and a "back end" unit responsible for manufacturing and services. The front end unit was divided, in turn, into two large groups, one dealing with corporate customers, the other with consumers. The back end unit too was made up of two large groups, the first supplied customers with printing and imaging equipment and services, and the second provided clients with a whole range of computer products and services.[38]

Implemented in 2000, Fiorina's reorganization initiative produced mixed results. On the one hand, the new marketing strategy enhanced customer satisfaction. Corporate customers were no longer dealing with competing sales teams but with a single person. Front end marketers were authorized to sign agreements that took into account the total value of the customer's projected needs, granting sales representatives the flexibility to sell some products at lower prices than others and thus maximizing HP's profits over the life of the contract. The new structure, likewise, empowered marketers to authorize discounts to clients who signed long-term consulting contracts.[39]

On the other hand, the new structure undermined accountability, diffused responsibility, and weakened financial controls. Under the new structure, profit and loss responsibilities were shared by both front and back end groups, and as a result, assigning financial responsibilities to individual managers had become nearly impossible. Under the new system, similarly, allocating costs between front and back end organizations had become exceedingly difficult, and consequently, some of the sales authorized by front end sales representatives turned out later to be unprofitable.[40]

Following a two-year experience with the front/back end system, Fiorina eventually acknowledged that her original plan was flawed. Subsequently, in late 2001, she granted executives greater profit and loss responsibilities over their product lines, and replaced the new quadrant structure with a hybrid version that combined product divisions with front/back end groups.[41]

The Fight Over the Merger

Ever since Fiorina had taken charge of the Hewlett Packard Company, the Board of Directors debated the strategy of undertaking a major acquisition. In discussing HP's options with the new CEO, members of the board concluded that IBM was the only company that competed with HP in all markets, and that IBM's most profitable and fastest growing business was the supply of IT services to large corporate clients. An acquisition of a large IT services company by HP, Fiorina and the board members agreed, was therefore likely to improve HP's worldwide competitive position versus IBM.

In early September 2000, accordingly, Fiorina and her team began discussing the purchase of PricewaterhouseCoopers (PwC) consulting division—a unit employing thirty-one thousand consultants who offered a wide range of computer services to large corporate customers—with PwC top executives. Soon thereafter, the *Sunday Times* of London disclosed the merger talks, reporting that PwC set the asking price at $18 billion. Commenting on the merger, industry analysts considered the price too high and wondered whether key PwC consultants would stay with HP throughout the merger or leave to work for other consulting firms, taking with them their lucrative businesses. In the meantime, opposition to the merger was growing among PwC executives. In November 2000, finally, Fiorina backed away from the deal telling investors: "In hindsight I let the PwC opportunity linger far too long."[42]

The Compaq opportunity unfolded next. Since 1999, Fiorina and Capellas had been discussing, off and on, the possibility of an HP-Compaq merger, and following the PwC setback, Fiorina informed HP directors that Compaq was interested in combining forces with HP. The acquisition of Compaq, Fiorina pointed out, was likely to strengthen HP across the board and thereby contribute to its competitive advantage relative to both IBM and Dell. On July 19, 2001, consequently, Fiorina brought the issue before the Board of Directors for discussion and vote. All eight directors present in the meeting supported the deal and instructed Fiorina to proceed with the merger talks. Absent from the meeting was Walter Hewlett, son of the cofounder, and an HP director. He opposed the merger.[43]

HP and Compaq went ahead and announced the merger on September 4, 2001. Following the merger announcement, HP shares fell 22 percent from $23 to $18.[44] Neither Fiorina nor any other HP directors expected Walter Hewlett to oppose the deal publicly, yet within a few weeks he launched a public relations campaign against the merger, declaring, "This isn't what my father would have wanted done with the company."[45] He thought that the merger was likely to hurt HP's profitable printing business and weaken HP's healthy PC business. He scored a major victory on December 7 when the Packard Foundation—HP's largest shareholder—voted unanimously to oppose the merger. Owning 10.2 percent of all shares outstanding, the David and Lucille Packard Foundation unified the heirs in opposition to the deal.[46]

Notwithstanding the Foundation's vote, HP directors continued supporting the merger enthusiastically, empowering Fiorina to proceed with the merger's preapproval preparations. Walter Hewlett fought back, spending $36 million during a proxy battle that raged over three months. Outspending W. Hewlett by more than two to one, the Hewlett Packard Company scored an important victory when the Institutional Shareholder Services (ISS)—a major consulting firm advising institutional investors on proxy votes— recommended a shareholder approval of the deal. The proxy vote was cast on March 19, 2002, and was close: 51.2 percent of the shares were voted in favor of the merger, and 48.6 percent against it.[47]

Walter Hewlett was not ready to concede defeat, however, but sued HP, charging the company with "fraud and misinformation." HP directors decided, in response, to remove Walter Hewlett from the board. The trial was brief, attracted a great deal of media attention, and ended in another victory on behalf of Fiorina and the company directors. A day after the judge issued his ruling, Walter Hewlett's lawyers, speaking for their client, announced that they would no longer challenge the proxy vote.[48]

Integration of the Merged Companies

The fight over the merger and the plan to integrate the two companies together were interrelated. Just as the long contest with Walter Hewlett gave HP ample time to implement the integration plan effectively, so did the company's integration plan help HP win the proxy vote. Consider the following statement. In its decision to recommend an approval of the merger, the ISS, the nation's leading proxy advisory firm, concluded:

> HP and Compaq . . . appear to have done pioneering work in thinking about and planning cultural integration of the two companies. It appears that management has done everything it can to maximize the chance that integration will be a success. . . .

It is hard to remain unimpressed in the face of such enthusiastic attention paid to the integration efforts. Half a million man-hours of work have thus far been devoted to integration planning, which surely makes the HP-Compaq one of the most exhaustively planned combinations ever.[49]

Long before the approval of the merger, HP board members were involved in devising plans to ensure the success of the deal. Two board members, Boeing CEO Philip Condit and Vodafone former Chairman Sam Ginn, had managed mega mergers themselves and did so effectively—Condit directed the 1998 Boeing acquisition of McDonnell Douglas, and Ginn executed the 1999 combination of Vodafone and Air Touch Communication. Drawing upon their experiences, Condit and Ginn helped develop the blueprints of the HP-Compaq integration plan. Working together with other board members, they set cost reduction goals for each of the combined businesses of the two companies.[50]

While HP board members were preoccupied with the broad outline of the integration plan, HP and Compaq executives were busy drafting the plan's details. In August 2001, a few weeks before the merger was even announced, Fiorina and Capellas each selected a senior executive to oversee the integration plan. Representing HP, on the one side, and Compaq, on the other, the two selected officers recruited a thirty-person integration team and directed its members to study and analyze data from hundreds of mergers in dozens of industries. Team members examined relevant articles published by the *Harvard Business Review* and pertinent documents supplied by McKinsey & Co., a consulting firm contracted by Fiorina to help HP execute the merger properly. Team members, furthermore, interviewed a large number of executives who worked for companies that underwent recent mergers.[51] Lessons were drawn from mistaken deals as well as successful mergers, from failing acquisitions as well as effective combinations.

Among the deals studied by the HP-Compaq integration team were two oil industry mergers that produced distinctly different outcomes. A 1984 merger between the Chevron Corp. and the Gulf Oil Company resulted in long integration delays that led to demoralization among the employees of the combined company and to confusion among customers: new managerial jobs in the combined company remained unfilled for months. Chevron's 2001 merger with Texaco, by contrast, resulted in effective integration efforts that were facilitated by preplanning and speed: key managerial positions in the new Chevron were filled in days. The 2001 merger of Time Warner and America On Line (AOL), to mention another case studied by the team, failed to produce the expected results, and brought about a steep decline in the combined company's stock market valuation. Cultural differences between the two companies created deep divisions among the employees of the combined company, the HP-Compaq team concluded, and added that each company—Time Warner and AOL—was not sufficiently familiar with the business of the other.[52]

Next, the integration team moved on to examine past mergers undertaken by Compaq and HP. During the 1998 Compaq-Digital integration process, the team found out, many employees as well as managers continued occupying overlapping jobs for months, and some products, designed to be phased out, were never discontinued. More important, the combined (Compaq-Digital) company lost many of its customers owing to serious communication problems stemming from the failure of top management to prepare customers for the transition to a new product roadmap. The team, then, turned to HP's 1989 takeover of Apollo Computers, and discovered that Apollo's integration planning did not begin until after the acquisition was approved, a delay that led to both customer defection and a substantial loss in new business. Last, the team examined HP's 1999 spin off of Agilent Technologies, concluding that the move was successful for two reasons: Lewis Platt preplanned the diversification scheme carefully, and he executed the spin off quickly and deliberately.[53] Taken together, these deals, and many others studied by the integration team, offered an additional lesson: To retain key executives throughout the transition period, top management needed to grant these executives generous retention bonuses.

Initially, before the merger was announced, the compensation committees of both boards—HP and Compaq—set aside $55 million for the purpose of paying executives rich retention bonuses and thereby persuading them to stay with the combined company throughout the merger. The bonus plan was later expanded to cover about six thousand HP and Compaq employees, each receiving a bonus of approximately $50,000.[54]

Additionally, in summer 2001 the two CEOs—Fiorina and Capellas—commissioned a large-scale study of HP and Compaq corporate cultures. Based on interviews conducted with 127 executives and 135 focus groups (made up of 1,500 managers and employees) in 22 countries around the world, the study sought to compare and contrast cultural perceptions held by HP and Compaq employees. Subsequently, the two CEOs authorized the creation of a team for the specific goal of uncovering cultural differences among employees of the two companies. The team found, for example, that HP employees used voice mail while their Compaq counterparts used e-mail to communicate, and that HP employees viewed their Compaq counterparts as "cowboys" whereas Compaq employees viewed their HP counterparts as "bureaucrats." To bridge such differences and forge a unified culture, top management created a task force of 650 part-time "cultural consultants" who continued working in their regular jobs in the combined company while tracking the progress of the HP-Compaq integration plan across all business units.[55]

To ensure a smooth and easy integration process, top management filled managerial positions quickly. Before the merger closed, HP appointed its top three levels of executives as well as 150 senior managers. Once the deal closed in May 2002, HP named its highest ranking sales managers—account leaders serving the company's top 200 customers—in addition to 800 other managers. During the summer and fall of 2002, HP continued announcing wave after wave of new appointments, a practice that expedited the integration process and brought it into completion ahead of schedule.[56]

Integrating the product lines of the two companies was another challenge faced by management. During the premerger planning phase, members of the HP-Compaq's integration team inspected the product lines of the two companies, pitting comparable products against each other and choosing the superior product in nearly every product group. Once the selection process was over, integration team members met with each business unit to devise an exit strategy for products designed to be phased out. Executives monitored the exit progress of each product weekly, using color-coded charts. For example, in the handheld PC business, HP selected the Compaq iPAQ PC over the HP Jornada handheld PC. Renaming the Compaq product HP iPAQ, Hewlett Packard phased out its Jornada product line within a year. In the low-end server business, to take another example, the integration team decided to retire HP Netserver and adopt Compaq's ProLiant product instead. The Compaq product performed better than the HP one, benefited from worldwide brand recognition, and held the largest market share in the industry standard server market for about a decade (1992–2001).[57]

HP phased out the Netserver swiftly. It stopped accepting new orders for the Netserver in September 2002. It laid off 50 percent of Netserver's personnel in May 2002, serving the remaining three hundred employees with future dismissal or relocation notices. And it launched a promotion program whereby HP executives traveled around the world offering Netserver customers the better performing Compaq machine.[58]

HP phased out related products as well. The combined company reduced its offering from 33 to 27 business computer product lines during the first year of the merger, and was expected to discontinue 6 more business computer product lines by the end of 2004.[59]

Discontinuing redundant products contributed handsomely to cost saving. During the first year of the merger (May 2002 to May 2003), HP reduced its costs by over $3 billion, well above its expected merger related cost savings of $2.5 billion. During the same period, HP's closed plants, office buildings, and other facilities, cutting nearly seventeen thousand jobs related to the merger.[60]

Last, the successful integration of the two companies was facilitated by the protracted high-tech recession and by HP's effective use of the Internet. First, the long recession of 2000–2003 provided the combined company with sufficient time to complete the merger integration before the economy turned around and before customers were ready to increase their investments in IT products and services. Second, the key to successful planning and communication was the use of the Internet. The Internet furnished the combined company with the means to plan the merger integration extensively, as well as communicate the details of the integration plan, step by step, to employees as well as customers.[61]

The Results of the Merger: Achievements and Opportunities

Upon the completion of the merger, Fiorina took firm command of the combined company. Assuming the title of president, Michael Capellas had become increasingly invisible as Fiorina exercised day-to-day control over HP's operational divisions, instructing department heads to report directly to her. Six

months after the merger closed, in November 2002, Capellas left HP to become the CEO of World Com. His departure precipitated a decline of more than 10 percent in HP stock.[62] Following Capellas's resignation, Fiorina decided not to replace him with another executive but run the company herself without a second in command.

Under Fiorina's leadership, HP's financial performance during the first two years of the merger had improved. In 2002—the year in which the merger closed—HP lost nearly $1 billion as a result of restructuring charges related to the merger, on the one hand, and slow sales stemming from the deepening recession, on the other. A year later, in 2003, the combined company generated $2.5 billion in net income. Similarly, the combined company recorded a loss of 31 cents per share during 2002 as opposed to a gain of 83 cents per share during 2003, the first full year of the merger. Between 2002 and 2003, furthermore, the new HP experienced a modest increase in sales (Exhibit 3).

Evaluating the results of the merger, it is useful to examine each product group separately. Of HP's four postmerger product groups, Imaging and Printing had remained the company's fastest growing and most profitable one. In 2003, HP's Printing and Imaging generated $22.6 billion in sales and nearly $3.6 billion in operating income, as shown in Exhibit 4. Seeking to expand its printer business, HP diversified into copiers, introducing in 2003 a multifunction printer—a printer that operated as both a printer

EXHIBIT 3

Highlights of HP's Financial Data Before the Merger with Compaq (1999–2001) and After the Merger (2002–2003)

	Before the Merger			After the Merger	
	1999	2000	2001	2002	2003
Sales (bil.)	42	49	45	72	73
Net Income (Loss) (bil.)	3.5	3.7	0.4	(0.9)	2.5
Income as % of Sales	8.2%	7.6%	0.9%	—	3.4%
Earnings per Share (Loss)	1.68	1.80	0.21	(0.31)	0.83

Source: For 1999–2001, *Hoover's Handbook of American Business, 2003,* p. 713; for 2002–2003, HP Annual Report, 2003, p. 17.

EXHIBIT 4

Highlights of HP's Financial Data, 2003—The Combined Company's First Full Year, Broken Down by Product Groups

	Imaging & Printing	PCs	Servers	Services
Sales (mil.)	$22,623	$21,228	$15,397	$12,305
Operating Income (mil.)	3,570	19	(54)	1,372

Source: HP Annual Report, 2003, pp. 3–7.

and a copier. To build up a strong distribution network for the new product, HP formed an alliance with IKON Office Solution, an office equipment supplier. To persuade corporate customers to purchase the new machine, HP guaranteed clients substantial savings in printing costs.[63]

Hewlett Packard's second most profitable product was HP Services (see Exhibit 4). The merger with Compaq vaulted HP to the industry number four position, and, as such, turned the combined company into a real contender over lucrative IT services contracts. In 2002, HP signed a $1.3 billion outsourcing deal with the Canadian Imperial Bank of Commerce, and a year later, Hewlett Packard signed large-scale IT consulting deals with the Bank of Ireland, the Ericsson Corporation, and the U.S. Department of Agriculture. Competing successfully against both IBM and EDS, HP was awarded a landmark $3 billion ten-year IT services contract by the Procter & Gamble Corporation in 2003.[64]

While HP Services Group posted a respectable rate of return on sales, the combined company's servers unit ("Enterprise Systems Group") recorded a loss of $54 million in 2003 (see Exhibit 4). To help the struggling unit improve its financial performance, HP announced in December 2003 a reorganization move that was intended to combine its services organization with its servers unit and thereby create a new Technology Solution Group. Because corporate customers were looking for solutions, and because HP's hardware sales had increasingly been driven by its consulting services (an HP executive explained), combining the two together in one unit was likely to sharpen the company's customer focus.[65]

HP's fourth product group was responsible for the manufacture of PCs. In 2003, corporate customers accounted for 60 percent of HP's PC sales and consumers for 40 percent. The second largest product group in terms of revenues, HP's PC unit (Personal Systems Group) had improved its financial performance in 2003, recording a small profit of $19 million (see Exhibit 4) that followed an operating loss in 2002. In 2002, HP held the worldwide leading position in PC sales, delivering 22 million PC units or 1 million units more than the number delivered by its main rival, Dell Computer. In the five quarters ending August 2003, the PC market's top spot switched back and forth four times between HP and Dell.[66]

The Results of the Merger: Disappointments and Concerns

HP's two arch rivals were IBM and Dell. HP competed with IBM over the worldwide supply of servers and services, and with Dell over the global sales of PCs and servers. In 2002, Dell announced plans to enter the IT services industry, on the one side, and the printer business on the other, hence challenging HP's dominance in each of the combined firm's four postmerger product groups.[67] Two years later, in 2004, most industry analysts concluded that the new HP had lost its direction and was being squeezed by its two main rivals, IBM and Dell; HP was unable to compete successfully with either. HP's difficulties were reflected in the company's stock prices. In August 2004, the value of HP shares was lower than their value on the day the merger closed, as well as the day before the merger was announced.[68]

In 2002, HP trailed IBM in the worldwide sales of servers, and a year later, the gap between the market shares of the two companies widened (Exhibit 5).

EXHIBIT 5

Worldwide Server Market Share by Revenues, 2002–2003

	2002	2003
IBM	30%	32%
HP	27%	27%
SUN	15%	12%
DELL	7%	9%

Source: Robert Guth and Don Clark, "Behind Secret Settlement Talks: New Power of Tech Customers," *Wall Street Journal,* April 5, 2004.

A 2002 Merrill Lynch survey of chief information officers employed by large corporations found that HP's technical support for open standard-based servers lagged far behind IBM's. In 2002, for example, Home Depot selected IBM over HP as its long-term supplier of servers,[69] and in 2003, NetCreation Inc., a New York e-mail marketing firm, decided to replace its HP servers with IBM equivalents. Not only did the IBM machine cost $100,000 less than the HP one, but IBM offered its new customer superior product support. "HP did try to coax us to stay with them," a NetCreation executive explained, "but we never got to speak with any decision makers beyond a certain sales level."[70]

HP trailed IBM in the global supply of IT services too, generating just $12 billion in revenues in 2002 compared with IBM's $36 billion and EDS's $22 billion. Unlike IBM, moreover, most HP consulting services offered customers low-end technical support such as the maintenance and repair of the customer's IT system, not high-end outsourcing—that is, the planning, designing, implementing, and running of the client's entire IT system. Only about one-eighth of HP's services revenues came from outsourcing in 2002, yet according to a 2003 estimate, outsourcing was expected to grow at a rate of 8 percent annually whereas the demand for low-end support services was projected to increase at a 3 percent rate.[71]

IBM had one other advantage over HP. In an attempt to expand and diversify its global services division, IBM acquired in 2002 the Pricewaterhouse-Coopers consulting firm, paying $3.5 billion or less than a fifth of PwC's asking price two years earlier, at the time Fiorina considered purchasing the firm. IBM's takeover of PwC helped Big Blue add some 30,000 new services professionals to its global services work force of 150,000 consultants, bringing the total up to about 180,000. Hewlett Packard, by contrast, employed 65,000 IT consultants, most of whom were not nearly as experienced as the consultants working for IBM/PwC.[72]

While IBM waged war on HP Services, Dell battled HP for shares in the low-end server and desktop PC markets. For one thing, during the two-year period 2002–2003, Dell's share in the worldwide server market grew from 7 percent to 9 percent while HP's share stagnated (see Exhibit 5). For another, in 2003, Dell's PC sales produced a healthy rate of return of about 8.5 percent, whereas HP's PC unit generated a profit rate of less than 1 percent (see Exhibit 4).[73]

EXHIBIT 6

Spending on Research and Development as a Percentage of Sales, 2002

	IBM	HP*	DELL
R&D	5.9%	5.4%	1.3%
Sales (bil.)	$81.5	$72.3	$35.4

*Including Compaq.

Sources: For IBM and Dell, John Markoff, "Innovation at Hewlett Packard Tries to Evade the Ax," *New York Times*, May 5, 2003; for HP, HP Form 10K for 2002, p. 33.

Dell's higher rate of return may be explained by its lower costs. In the second quarter of 2003, Dell spent 10 cents on overhead for every dollar the company generated in PC sales; the comparable figure for HP was 21 cents per revenue dollar. One reason why Dell's costs were lower than HP's was Dell's smaller R&D budget. In 2002, Dell spent less than $0.5 billion or 1.3 percent of its revenues on R&D compared with HP's $3.9 billion or 5.4 percent of revenues (Exhibit 6). Another was Dell's overwhelming reliance on direct sales to customers and HP's heavy reliance on dealers and retailers for its PC sales: while Dell sold directly to customers nearly every machine it shipped in 2003, HP sold directly just 13 to 27 percent of the PC units it delivered.[74]

The Future

Attacked by both IBM and Dell, the new HP was fighting back, seeking to compete simultaneously with both IBM and Dell. Fiorina portrayed Dell as a "low tech, low cost" company, IBM as a "high tech, high cost" company, and HP as a "high tech, low cost" company, asserting that the new HP represented a combination of the best qualities of its two arch rivals.[75] By contrast to IBM as well as Dell, Fiorina pointed out HP was at one and the same time a leading producer of desktop PCs, a leading provider of IT services, and the dominant vendor of printers, and the three were interrelated: Selling desktop PCs to corporate clients was expected to encourage such clients to purchase HP services and printers, and vice versa, and providing corporate customers with IT services was likely to encourage such customers to buy HP printers and PCs too. "We think the PC business is strategic," Fiorina said in May 2004, noting that the company was willing to sell PCs at a very modest profit rate, or sometimes at a loss, in order to gain large corporate customers for its more profitable printers and IT services.[76]

Would Fiorina's strategy work?

Despite HP's 2004 difficulties, Fiorina had not reversed course but remained steadfast. It was still too early to tell whether her long-term strategy would eventually work.

ENDNOTES

1. Quoted in George Anders, *Perfect Enough: Carly Fiorina and the Reinvention of Hewlett Packard* (New York: Portfolio, 2003), p. 117, but see also pp. 126, 133, and Andrew Park, "Can Compaq Survive as a Solo Act?" *Business Week*, December 24, 2001, p. 71.

2. Peter Burrows, "Carly's Last Stand," *Business Week*, December 24, 2001, p. 64; Anders, *Perfect Enough*, pp. 96, 126.

3. Benjamin Pimentel, "Pumped by Big Blue; Strengthened by the Merger with Compaq, HP Prepares to Battle IBM," *San Francisco Chronicle*, August 2, 2002. Online. Lexis Nexis. Academic Universe; "Hewlett Packard," *Hoover's Handbook of American Business, 2003* (Austin, TX: Hoover Business Press, 2003), p. 713; *Business Week*, December 24, 2001, pp. 64, 71.

4. David Yoffie and Mary Kwak, "Manager's Journal: HP and Compaq Should Return to Their Roots," *Wall Street Journal*, December 17, 2001. Online. ABI database.

5. Wendy Zellner and Mike France, "HP's Beachhead in High-Tech Services," *Business Week*, April 28, 2003, p. 40.

6. Charles Ferguson and Charles Morris, *Computer Wars: How the West Can Win in a Post IBM World* (New York: Random House, 1993), pp. 51–52.

7. Ibid., pp. 52–53; "Hewlett Packard Company," *International Directory of Company Histories*, Vol. 50 (New York: St. James Press, 2003), p. 225.

8. Lois Therrien, "Compaq: How It Made Its Impressive Move Out of the Doldrums," *Business Week*, November 1992, p. 147; Julie Pitta, "Identity Crisis," *Forbes*, May 25, 1992, p. 82; Simon Caulkin, "Compaq's Compact," *Management Today*, May 1985, p. 94.

9. "Hewlett Packard," *International Directory of Company Histories*, pp. 225–226; "Compaq," *Hoover's Handbook of American Business, 2002*, p. 398, but see also Robert Heller, "The Compaq Comeback," *Management Today* (December 1994): 66.

10. *Business Week*, November 2, 1992, p. 147.

11. Ibid., pp. 146, 150; "Compaq," *Hoover's Handbook of American Business, 2002*, p. 398.

12. Eric Nee, "Compaq Computer Corp.," *Forbes*, January 12, 1998, pp. 2–3; David Kirkpatrick, "Fast Times at Compaq," *Fortune*, April 1, 1996, pp. 91–92.

13. *Forbes*, January 12, 1998, pp. 93–94.

14. *Wall Street Journal*, December 17, 2001; David Kirkpatrick, "Eckhard's Gone but the PC Rocks On," *Fortune*, May 24, 1999, p. 154.

15. Michael Gelfand, "Can a CIO Turned CEO Save Compaq?" *Chief Executive* (February 2000): 38, 40.

16. Bill Alpert, "Beating the PC Blues," *Barron's*, July 16, 2001, pp. 20–21.

17. Deone Zell, *Changing by Design: Organizational Innovation at Hewlett Packard* (Ithaca, NY: Cornell University Press, 1997), p. 35.

18. "Hewlett Packard," *Hoover's Handbook of American Business, 2003*, p. 712; "Hewlett Packard," *International Directory of Company Histories*, pp. 222–223.

19. Sara Beckman and David Mowery, "Corporate Change and Competitiveness: The Hewlett Packard Company," Working Paper 95/12, Haas School of Business, University of California, Berkeley, pp. 4, 7; Anders, *Perfect Enough*, p. 17.

20. Beckman and Mowery, "Corporate Change and Competitiveness," p. 4.

21. Anders, *Perfect Enough*, p. 20; Peter Burrows, *Backfire; Carly Fiorina's High Stakes Battle for the Soul of Hewlett Packard* (New York: John Wiley, 2003), pp. 72–73; "Hewlett Packard," *International Directory of Company Histories*, p. 223.

22. Anders, *Perfect Enough*, pp. 20–21; Burrows, *Backfire*, p. 74; David Packard, *The HP Way* (New York: Harper, 1995), ch. 8; Julia Pitta, "It Had to Be Done and We Did It," *Forbes*, April 26, 1993, pp. 151–152; "Hewlett Packard," *International Directory of Company Histories*, p. 223.

23. *Forbes*, April 26, 1993, p. 152; Anders, *Perfect Enough*, pp. 22–24; "Hewlett Packard," *Hoover's Handbook of American Business, 2003*, p. 712; Robert Hof, "Suddenly Hewlett Packard Is Doing Everything Right," *Business Week*, March 23, 1992, p. 88.

24. "Hewlett Packard," *Hoover's Handbook of American Business, 2003*, p. 713.

25. Eric Savitz, "Hewlett Packard's Money Machine," *Barron's*, August 28, 1996. Online. ABI database. Start page 25; John Sheridan, "Lew Platt: Creating a Culture for Innovation," *Industry Week*, December 19, 1994, pp. 26, 28; Alan Deutschman, "How HP Continues to Grow and Grow," *Fortune*, May 2, 1994, pp. 90–92, 96.

26. *International Directory of Company History*, p. 227.

27. *Fortune*, May 2, 1994, pp. 90–92.

28. Robert Hof, "Hewlett Packard Made a Tough Decision, but the Right One," *Business Week*, March 15, 1999, p. 32; Eric Nee, "Defending the Desktop," *Forbes*, December 28, 1998, pp. 53–54; Anders, *Perfect Enough*, pp. 39–40.

29. Eric Nee, "Lew Platt: Why I Dismember HP?" *Fortune*, May 29, 1999, p. 167; *Business Week*, March 15, 1999, p. 32; David Hamilton and Scott Thurm, "HP to Spin Off Its Measurement Operations," *Wall Street Journal*, March 3, 1999. Online. ABI database.

30. Anders, *Perfect Enough*, pp. 42–43.

31. Peter Burrows, "The Boss: Carly Fiorina's Challenge Will Be to Propel Staid Hewlett Packard Into the Internet Age," *Business Week*, August 2, 1999, pp. 76, 78; Anders, *Perfect Enough*, ch. 3.

32. Adam Lashinsky, "Now for the Hard Part: Carly Fiorina Sold Investors on the HP Merger," *Fortune*, November 18, 2002, p. 104; Quentin Hardy, "All Carly All the Time," *Forbes*, December 13, 1999, p. 135, but see also pp. 140–144.

33. Anders, *Perfect Enough*, p. 76.

34. Peter Burrows, "The Radical: Carly Fiorina's Bold Management Experiment at HP," *Business Week*, February 19, 2001, p. 78, but see also December 24, 2001, p. 66.

35. *Business Week*, February 19, 2001, p. 78; December 24, 2001, pp. 67–69.

36. Zell, *Changing by Design*, pp. 35–36.

37. Anders, *Perfect Enough*, p. 75; *Business Week*, February 19, 2001, p. 78; August 2, 1999, p. 80.

38. Anders, *Perfect Enough*, p. 75.

39. *Business Week*, February 19, 2001, p. 78.

40. Anders, *Perfect Enough*, pp. 75–76; *Business Week*, February 19, 2001, pp. 73, 78.

41. Anders, *Perfect Enough*, p. 76.

42. Ibid., pp. 93–94; Burrows, *Backfire*, pp. 168–169.

43. Burrows, *Backfire*, ch. 9; Anders, *Perfect Enough*, p. 95 and ch. 7.

44. *Business Week*, December 24, 2001, p. 67.

45. Quoted in Anders, *Perfect Enough*, p. 144.

46. Burrows, *Backfire*, ch. 10; *Business Week*, December 24, 2001, p. 67.

47. Anders, *Perfect Enough*, chs. 9, 10; Burrows, *Backfire*, ch. 11.

48. Burrows, *Backfire*, ch. 12; Anders, *Perfect Enough*, ch. 11.

49. "ISS Recommends HP Shareholders Vote for Merger," Press Release, Palo Alto, California, March 5, 2002. HP.com.

50. Carly Fiorina, "The Case for Merger," a speech delivered at the Goldman Sachs Technology Conference, Palm Springs, California, February 4, 2002, HP.com; *Business Week*, December 24, 2001, p. 66.

51. Pui-Wing Tam, "Merger by Numbers: An Elaborate Plan Forces HP Union to Stay on Target," *Wall Street Journal*, April 28, 2003; Carly Fiorina, "Remarks," a speech delivered in the Information Processing Interagency Conference, Orlando, Florida, March 3, 2003, HP.com; *Business Week*, December 24, 2001, p. 66.

52. *Wall Street Journal*, April 28, 2003; *Business Week*, December 24, 2001, p. 66.

53. Fiorina, "Remarks," December 24, 2001; *Wall Street Journal*, April 28, 2003.

54. Burrows, *Backfire*, p. 228; *Business Week*, December 24, 2001, p. 66.

55. Fiorina, "Remarks," December 24, 2001; *Wall Street Journal*, April 28, 2003.

56. "HP Announces Latest Merger Integration Milestone With Naming 150 Senior Managers," Press Release, Palo Alto, California, April 3, 2002; Fiorina, "Remarks," December 24, 2001; *Wall Street Journal*, April 28, 2003.

57. "HP White Paper: Hewlett Packard Product Roadmaps," press release, undated; *Wall Street Journal*, April 28, 2003.

58. *Wall Street Journal*, April 28, 2003.

59. Ibid.

60. Matthew Fordahl, "Hewlett Packard to Cut More Workers," *Chicago Sun Times*, May 21, 2003. Online, ABI database; *Wall Street Journal*, April 28, 2003.

61. Fiorina, "The Case for Merger," February 4, 2002; Fiorina, "Remarks," December 24, 2001; "Merger Mystery: HP and Compaq," *The Economist*, November 16, 2002, p. 7.

62. Cliff Edwards, "Why Capellas Flew the Coop," *Business Week*, December 23, 2002, pp. 52–53; Anders, *Perfect Enough*, pp. 215–216.

63. Steve Lohr, "Hewlett Now Wants to Be Your Copier Company, Too," *New York Times*, November 18, 2003.

64. *Business Week*, April 28, 2003, p. 40; Bob Keefe, "HP-Compaq Merger So Far a Success," *Palm Beach Post*, May 11, 2003. Online. ABI database; Bill Breen, "The Big Score," *Fast Company*, September 1, 2003.

65. David Bank and Gary McWilliams, "HP to Reorganize Operating Units," *Wall Street Journal*, December 9, 2003.

66. Terril Yue Jones, "Commitment to PC Market Hurts HP's Bottom Line," *Los Angeles Times*, August 25, 2003. Online. Lexis Nexis, Academic Universe.

67. Dell's impending entry into both the IT services market and the printer business posed a potential threat to HP's future earnings. On the one hand, Dell planned to supply small- and medium-size customers with low-end IT services for a price as low as $200. On the other, Dell decided to form an alliance with Lexmark, the former IBM printer company, in order to compete with HP over the supply of small size printers in the short run, and ink and laser printer cartridges in the long run. Cliff Edwards, "The New HP: How's It Doing?" *Business Week*, December 23, 2002, p. 54; Anders, *Perfect Enough*, p. 217.

68. "Losing the HP Way: Hewlett Packard," *The Economist*, August 21, 2004, p. 58.

69. Cliff Edwards, "The New HP: How's It Doing?" *Business Week*, December 23, 2002, p. 54.

70. Cited in Pui Wing Tam, "HP Launches a New Tech Strategy," *Wall Street Journal*, May 6, 2003.

71. *Business Week*, April 28, 2003, p. 40.

72. Anders, *Perfect Enough*, p. 217; Benjamin Pimental, "Pumped for Big Blue: Strengthened by Its Merger with Compaq, HP Prepares to Battle IBM for IT Customers," *San Francisco Chronicle*, August 2, 2002. Online. Lexis Nexis, Academic Universe.

73. *Los Angeles Times*, August 25, 2003.

74. A massive reliance on direct sales allowed, in turn, for greater pricing flexibility. By contrast to HP, Dell could adjust prices daily and thereby launch price wars against its competitors. In August 2003, for instance, Dell announced price reductions that ranged from 6 percent on desktop PCs to 22 percent on network servers. HP was able to adjust prices quickly on the proportion of PCs that it sold directly to customers, but it was unable to do so on the PCs it sold indirectly because it needed to set prices up to six weeks in advance in order to provide dealers and retailers with sufficient time to both advertise and replenish their inventories. Gary McWilliams and Pui Wing Tam, "Dell Price Cuts Put a Squeeze on Rival HP," *Wall Street Journal*, August 21, 2003; Scott Morrison, "Dell Delivers a Salutary Slap in the Face to HP," *Financial Times*, August 22, 2003. Online. ABI database.

75. *The Economist*, August 21, 2004.

76. David Bank and Gary McWilliams, "Picking a Big Fight with Dell, HP Cuts Profits Razor Thin," *Wall Street Journal*, May 12, 2004.

Hewlett Packard Ousts Carly Fiorina

This case was prepared by Gareth R. Jones, Texas A&M University.

On February 7, 2005, Hewlett Packard (HP) announced that Carly Fiorina, the person its Board of Directors had handpicked to be the company's new CEO in 1999, would be leaving the company with a severance package of over $20 million. The board, which named Chief Financial Officer Robert P. Wayman, a thirty-six-year veteran, as interim CEO, began the search for a new CEO who could develop a business model that would allow the company to compete with arch rivals IBM and Dell—a CEO who could perform the same miracle that Louis Gerstner accomplished for IBM. One person who may be a likely candidate is former Compaq CEO Michael A. Capellas, who served briefly as Fiorina's second in command after the Compaq-HP merger before he left to become the CEO of troubled telecommunication company MCI.

Clearly, HP's board and major stockholders felt that the merger had not achieved the results Fiorina had predicted. HP's performance has been mixed in the two years since it took place. While the immediate integration of the two companies produced cost savings faster and larger than anticipated and silenced her critics, by late 2003 some analysts began to feel the merger had not done much to improve HP's

Copyright © 2005 by Gareth R. Jones. This case was prepared by Gareth R. Jones, Texas A&M University, as the basis for class discussion rather than to illustrate either effective or ineffective handling of an administrative situation. Reprinted by permission of Gareth R. Jones. All rights reserved. For the most recent financial results of the company discussed in this case, go to http://finance.yahoo.com, input the company's stock symbol, and download the latest company report from its homepage.

ebbing position against key competitors IBM and Dell. However, other analysts felt the company would be worse off in 2005 if the merger had not taken place because its main profit generator is its printer division, which has been under attack from such low-cost competitors as Lexmark, Canon, and Dell, and its uncompetitive PC division might be making much larger losses if the merger had not taken place.

On the news of Fiorina's dismissal, HP's stock jumped 7 percent because investors hoped that the company would spin off its unprofitable PC and network computer operations, and even its money losing software division, to focus on strengthening its highly profitable Printing & Imaging Division. Yet despite Fiorina's dismissal, the board reiterated its support for her business model that is based on offering customers a complete line of computer hardware, software, services, and consultancy. Fiorina had argued that the board was simply not giving her enough time to make her business model work. After all, it took Gerstner over a decade to really turn around IBM's performance and transform that company. However, the board obviously felt the way she was implementing her business model was not resulting either in the lower costs or improved computer solutions that would raise the company's revenues and profits.

Of particular concern to analysts was a series of missed chances and botched implementation efforts that had hurt the company's image and performance. HP's software division lost over $100 million on $900 million in sales in 2004, and Fiorina moved too slowly to acquire a profitable company called Veritas Software, which made enterprise software, that might have been a perfect complement with HP's software division. It was eventually snapped up by Symantec, a major competitor. In its other divisions too, directors were concerned that she was too slow to either acquire companies or change the company's internal operating procedures to improve its competitive position, and when she did, she had made mistakes.

In sales, for example, it was widely acknowledged that HP lagged far behind both Dell and IBM. HP's direct selling model was inferior to Dell's and too little was being done to improve it. HP's marketing and sales operations were also a major problem. Its sales force found it very difficult to offer customers a complete solution, similar to IBM, because there was little coordination between sales and different operating groups. When Fiorina reorganized sales so that each operating division had its own sales force, this led to enormous problems of coordinating between operating groups so the system was changed again. In the third quarter of 2004, the company missed its profit targets because of serious glitches in a new internal order procurement system created to integrate between the different operating groups in their efforts to provide customers an integrated solution. This sign of HP's worsening performance apparently led

the board to start questioning Fiorina's ability to control the company and her failure to create a strong top management team that might have forestalled such problems. So, even if her overall business model and strategies for HP were the right ones, they were failing because of poor implementation and control over organizational structure. Indeed, HP's organizational structure and culture had changed dramatically by 2005; the old culture based on values and norms, emphasizing the importance of research and development, was slowing down her attempts to create a customer-focused culture. The clash of cultures was contributing to the problems of integrating between the various operating divisions.

In any event, the jury is out on HP's future; only time will tell what business model its new CEO will choose for the company, that is, if HP's board will allow the new CEO to radically change its current model or find ways to better implement it. The jury is even out on whether the merger will be regarded as a success or failure in the years to come. What is clear is that HP is in a major struggle with its competitors in the computer sector and that more changes are ahead as technology changes and as companies fight to reduce their cost structures to increase their efficiency and effectiveness.

Michael Eisner's Walt Disney Company: Part One

This case was prepared by Gareth R. Jones, Texas A&M University.

It was early 1991, and Michael Eisner, chairman and CEO of the Walt Disney Company, was sitting down with Frank Wells, president and chief operating officer, and Gary Wilson, executive vice president and chief financial officer, to discuss Disney's prospects for the new year. These men were still basking in the glow generated by another record revenue- and profit-breaking year in Disney's history. Disney's businesses were performing at an unprecedented level, and confidence was high. The problem facing the trio who had engineered Disney's turnaround was how to maintain Disney's explosive growth rate and its return-on-investment goal of increasing earnings per share by 20 percent over any five-year period to achieve a 20 percent annual return on equity. Paradoxically, the very success of their strategy, which had originated to protect an underperforming Disney from the rampages of corporate raiders and the threat of takeover, was causing the opposite problem: how to maintain the company's explosive growth in a business environment where attractive opportunities for expansion were becoming increasingly scarce. The men were reflecting on how to develop a five-year plan that would cement the strategy that had led to their present enviable situation and make the 1990s the "Disney Decade."

Copyright © 1996, 1997, 2005 by Gareth R. Jones. This case was prepared by Gareth R. Jones, Texas A&M University, as the basis for class discussion rather than to illustrate either effective or ineffective handling of an administrative situation. Reprinted by permission of Gareth R. Jones. All rights reserved. For the most recent financial results of the company discussed in this case, go to http://finance.yahoo.com, input the company's stock symbol, and download the latest company report from its homepage.

Disney Before Eisner

When Walt Disney died in 1966, he left a company that was experiencing record revenues and profits. Disney was at its creative peak and forging ahead at full steam on the many ideas generated by Walt Disney's creative genius. However, by the early 1980s all the drive in the Disney Company had evaporated. Although revenues were increasing somewhat, net income and profit were dropping drastically. While top executives believed they were following what "Walt would have wanted," the vision that was uniquely Walt Disney's was gone. Table 1 charts the net income of the Walt Disney Company from 1980 to 1990. How did this situation come about? To understand it, we need to look at the way in which Walt Disney built his company and try to find the pattern in his creative endeavors.

Walt Disney's Company

Walt Elias Disney was born in 1901. Raised on a farm, he early developed an interest in art and drawing, and his ambition was to be a cartoonist. His interest in static cartoons soon waned, however, with the beginning of animated cartoons in movie theaters. At the time, these were extremely crude; the figures bounced rather than moved gracefully around, they were silent, and they were in black and white. He immediately saw the potential for developing high-quality, graphic art cartoons that moved and set about marshaling resources to produce his product.

After a series of early setbacks, Disney had success with a character called Oswald the Rabbit, perhaps the forerunner of Roger the Rabbit. The carefully drawn cartoons were very popular with movie audiences and

TABLE 1

Selected Financial Data (in millions, except per share and other data)

	1989	1988	1987	1986	1985
Statement of Income Data					
Revenues	$4,594.3	$3,438.2	$2,876.8	$2,165.8	$1,700.1
Operating income	1,229.0	884.8	776.8	527.7	345.7
Interest expense	23.9	5.8	29.1	44.1	54.6
Income from continuing operations	703.3	522.0	392.3	213.2	132.3
Net income	703.3	522.0	444.7	247.3	173.5
Balance Sheet Data					
Total assets	$6,657.2	$5,108.9	$3,806.3	$3,121.0	$2,897.3
Borrowing	860.6	435.5	584.5	547.2	823.1
Stockholders' equity	3,044.0	2,359.3	1,845.4	1,418.7	1,184.9
Statement of Cash Flow Data					
Cash flow	$1,275.6	$1,075.4[*]	$830.6	$668.4	$518.8
Investments					
Theme parks, resorts, and other property, net	749.6	595.7	280.1	174.1	179.8
Film costs	426.7	225.7	178.3	203.7	149.9
Acquisitions	237.3	221.7			
Per Share Data					
Net income					
Continuing operations	$5.10	$3.80	$2.85	$1.57	$.98
Total	5.10	3.80	3.23	1.82	1.29
Cash dividends	.46	.38	.32	.315	.30
Other Data					
Stockholders at close of year	143,000	124,000	101,000	77,000	58,000
Employees at close of year	47,000	39,000	31,000	30,000	30,000

[*]Excludes $722.6 million unearned royalty advances.

Source: The Walt Disney Company, *Annual Report,* 1989.

provided Disney with the money he needed to expand his operations and to hire additional artists and animators. However, after battles about money and profits, Disney lost control of the Oswald character to Charles Mintz, the cartoon's distributor, which taught him an important lesson. From then on, he would retain all the rights to his characters, to the films produced using these characters, and to the distribution end of the film business. This was the start of Disney's fortune.

With the experience gained from Oswald the Rabbit, Disney set about finding a new character to hang his fortunes to. He came up with the idea of a mouse, and in 1928 he created Mickey Mouse. He was the voice, but the cartoons were drawn by Ubbe (Ub) Iwerks, an artist and animator who had worked closely with Disney from the beginning. The Mickey Mouse cartoons were immensely popular, and their success provided Walt Disney with the resources to expand his repertoire of characters and improve his animation techniques. He and his company then, and now, were always at the forefront of technological developments. The next decade saw the emergence of Disney's now familiar cast of characters: Donald

Duck, Goofy, and the Three Little Pigs, a cartoon for which Disney won an Oscar. At the same time, Disney became involved in making cartoons in color. Using technicolor's new three-color process, he produced these cartoons in color and won his first Oscar for color in 1932.[1] It was this ability to meld technical developments with his emerging cast of cartoon characters that was the source of Disney's distinctive strength. None of his competitors was able to take this advantage away; although other studios established animation departments, none had the same success.

Full-Length Movies

By the late 1930s, Disney's experience in short cartoons had now developed his studio's skills in the three techniques needed for quality animation and cartoon making: art and drawing, perspective and sound, and color. He had learned the value of using a large number of drawings per second to provide his characters with realistic movements, even though this dramatically increased costs. He had seen the value of color as a way of making his characters more true to life (since one of the virtues of cartoons is that they can extend and amplify reality). Lastly, he had developed a technique that gave depth to the previously flat cartoons. This was the famous Multiplane technique, which involved the use of a camera that could focus in and out of three planes of celluloid drawings: the foreground, the characters themselves, and the background. By photographing these planes at an angle, an impression of depth was achieved in the cartoon that gave the characters life. This technique resulted in another Oscar for Disney.

Taking these techniques, Walt Disney set about advancing his long-term dream: a full-length cartoon motion picture. He was careful in his selection of a subject. From the beginning, he believed that his subjects should be characters that were widely accepted by the public so that little learning by the public was involved. It was with his characteristic genius that he chose Snow White and the Seven Dwarfs as his subject in 1937. *Snow White* cost a fortune to make, but it went on to make animation history as it also grossed a fortune at the box office. It also provided the capital that precipitated Disney into the ranks of the big studios. The money from *Snow White* allowed Disney to build his studio at Burbank and financed the animated films *Pinocchio* and *Bambi*, which were also very successful. Then, in 1940, departing from

his own maxim of only choosing "brand-name characters," he made *Fantasia*. Despite being an artistic success, the film was a commercial disaster, which, coinciding with the unpopularity of cartoons during World War II, plunged Walt Disney Productions into debt. When the banks restricted the amount they were willing to provide to fund the company, Walt Disney offered stock to the public for the first time. In 1940 Walt Disney Productions issued 155,000 shares at $25 a share, raising $3,500,000 in working capital.

More Walt Disney Magic

With the end of the war, the public was once again receptive to fun and fantasy. The boom years after the war produced an audience with money in their pockets who were in search of excitement, and Walt Disney was determined to provide them with it. He began the search for new projects to exercise the talents of the Disney studios. By 1950 he had come up with new directions for the Disney studios.

Motion Pictures

Disney realized that animation was not the only way of bringing the public's favorite fantasy characters to the screen. Many popular heroes such as Robin Hood could be depicted in live-action movies. So, Disney took popular fictional characters and turned them into movies. A string of hits resulted as Disney studios came out with *Treasure Island, The Swiss Family Robinson, The Story of Robin Hood and His Merry Men, Kidnapped, 20,000 Leagues Under the Sea*, and a host of films starring such people as Hayley Mills and Maurice Chevalier. He then also decided to create new characters and developed scripts for such projects as *The Shaggy Dog, The Absent Minded Professor, Son of Flubber*, and *The Parent Trap*. Side by side with these developments, Disney embarked on a series of nature or wildlife projects. Between 1950 and 1960, films such as *Water Birds, The Alaskan Eskimo, Bear Country*, and the *White Wilderness* were produced for enthusiastic audiences. These films are still popular today.

At the same time his interest in animation did not lapse and was a major moneymaker for the studio in the 1950s. *Cinderella* was a smash hit as was *101 Dalmatians, Peter Pan, Lady and the Tramp*, and *The Jungle Book*. Moreover, by 1960 he was experimenting with combining animation and live action, and one result was *Mary Poppins*, which was an all-time revenue winner for Disney, one of the greatest hits in the history of motion pictures, and which won five Academy Awards.

Television

Another move that helped Disney studios at this time was Walt's decision to take his products to the television screen. While other movie studios were worrying that television would cut into their profits and reduce their audiences, Walt realized the prospective synergies between the television and movie businesses for Disney. Disney was already producing a wide range of family-oriented entertainment: cartoons, full-length animation, live action, and wildlife. What could be more logical than taking its characters and developing its products to fit into a television format? Not only would this be the source of additional revenues for Disney and allow it to exploit its resources and people to the full, but it would also provide advertising for the Walt Disney name and its future product offerings. The result was that in 1954 Disney brought *The Wonderful World of Disney* to the screen. In 1955 the *Mickey Mouse Club* was introduced, and the Disney name became part of popular American culture as for the next twenty years Walt Disney television became a weekly event for the viewing public.

Theme Parks

Walt Disney had another reason for entering the television market. By itself, television was not a great money spinner for Disney. It would provide some free advertising and permit a more efficient utilization of the Disney resources, but animation was expensive compared to live action. What Walt Disney principally saw in television was a way to promote an idea that had been on his mind for years: a permanent amusement park that could exploit the Disney characters' popularity and which would offer a family a fun-filled day of Disney fantasy. Rather than passively watching a movie, amusement park goers would become a part of the movie; they would become actors in a live Disney entertainment. Television would show viewers how to take part in this experience; it would also show them what they could expect. Disney realized that the combination of theme park, television, and movies would feed on each other, and each would promote the other. He was right. The theme park idea was wildly successful,

and since its opening Disneyland became the backbone of the Disney empire.

After deliberation, Disney chose the Anaheim site in California for the opening of his first theme park. Disneyland opened in July 1955. Anaheim was chosen because of the huge population base of southern California and because with less than 5 inches of rain a year, it could be operated all year round with little threat from the weather. Immense planning went into the creation of the Disney experience and still does. Every ride and attraction was crafted to highlight the Disney theme; all its movies and characters are represented by different kinds of amusements and, of course, by the personal appearances of its characters, too. The number of attractions has grown from seventeen in 1955 to sixty-two now, and exhibits are constantly improved and updated to take advantage of the latest technological developments. Attractions are often connected with a corporate sponsor that buys into a Disney theme and leases an exhibit. For example, AT&T, Sony, and Kodak are some of the many sponsors of Disney's exhibits. The park is divided into seven major areas: Adventureland, Tomorrowland, Fantasyland, Frontierland, Mainstreet, Bearcountry, and New Orleans Square.

Then, in 1965 Walt Disney announced yet another part of his grand plan, the development of Disney World including the EPCOT (Experimental Prototype Community of Tomorrow) Center in Orlando, Florida. As originally imagined by Disney, part of Disney World would include a Magic Kingdom similar to the one already established in Anaheim. However, the EPCOT Center he envisaged was a "living laboratory" where 20,000 to 30,000 people would permanently live, experimenting with advanced technology and literally providing the world with examples of future life on Earth. He did not live to see either dream realized; Walt Disney died in December 1966.

Disney After Walt

When Walt Disney died, he left his company at the pinnacle of its success up to that date. There were new films ready to distribute, plans for Disney World, steadily rising attendance at Disneyland, and a secure television audience. However, nothing seemed to go as well as before in the Disney organization. In the years from 1966 to 1984, when Michael Eisner took over, the company seemed to just be spinning its wheels.

The problem was that nobody emerged to wear Walt Disney's crown; nobody could provide the creative vision to lead a company whose mission was to provide fun and fantasy. There was a void in the organization, and little was accomplished by the company that did not already have Walt Disney's stamp of approval on it.

Walt's brother Roy took over management of the company and supervised the building of Disney World. Most of the advance planning for Disney World had been carried out by Walt. The first step in that plan had been to purchase a huge tract of land outside Orlando, Florida, to hold Disney World. Disney had never liked the situation that had developed outside Anaheim after the opening of Disneyland. Disney only owns the area on which the theme park and its car park is built. As a result, development around the park proceeded unchecked, and the surrounding area became full of motels and hotels that Walt Disney felt detracted from the Disney image. Moreover, on a financial level, the profits being earned by businesses in the vicinity of the park were vastly more than the revenues Disney received from park attendance. Because Walt Disney was determined that this should not happen in Orlando, he arranged, through subsidiary companies, the purchase of 28,000 acres of undeveloped land, an area the size of 34 square miles, enough to hold any number of hotels and amusement parks. Then, when Disney made the announcement of the park in 1965, the value of the land increased dramatically overnight.

The Magic Kingdom was the first part of Disney World to be built, and it opened in 1971 with thirty-five attractions; now there are more than fifty. Just as corporate sponsorship was important in financing the development of the Magic Kingdom, it was also very important in providing the financing for the EPCOT Center, with large corporations paying $25 million for the right to sponsor an attraction. Nevertheless, the plans for EPCOT changed dramatically after Walt's death. The company realized that development costs would be enormous, and the venture as devised by Walt was not commercially feasible. Instead, the company changed EPCOT's mission to provide a showcase of modern technology and of international culture. In essence, EPCOT became a kind of permanent World's Fair when it opened in 1982. It is composed of two main areas. The first,

World Showcase, consists of pavilions sponsored by many different countries demonstrating their national culture and products and offering a wide variety of different kinds of national foods. The second area is Future World, which, in the spirit of Walt Disney's original plan, showcases future developments that can be expected in all areas of human commerce and endeavor. Attractions include the Living Seas, sponsored by United Technologies; a future farming exhibit sponsored by Kraft; and, recently, a journey through the human body highlighting advances in medical knowledge. EPCOT was the first Walt Disney exhibit specifically designed to appeal to adults, although Walt Disney always said everything Disney does is designed for the child in everybody.

The development of EPCOT and Disney World was Disney's principal priority during these years, and the opening of EPCOT attracted record crowds. However, despite high attendance, the profit margin of Disney World was lower than that of Disneyland, and both revenues and profits were disappointing, given Disney's huge investment of $1.5 billion. Moreover, by 1984 attendance at Disney World and Disneyland dropped off from its previous record high, further reducing revenues. Clearly, Disney had problems with its theme parks, but management did not know what to do.

Another problem Disney experienced was that while it had developed three large hotels with more than 2,000 rooms at the theme park to exploit the hotel market that they had missed at Anaheim, luxury hotels chains such as the Hyatt and Hilton were opening new luxury hotels at the park's borders. The result was that Disney was losing potential Disney revenues to these hotel chains, and the situation that had happened at Disneyland was in danger of happening again.

The other areas of Disney's business were also not doing well. Planning for the Disney Channel had begun in the late 1970s, and it came on line in 1983 with 532,000 subscribers. The channel was a natural complement to Disney's other activities because it was an additional vehicle through which the company could exploit its skills and characters. However, the start-up costs of the Disney Channel were enormous, and even though it had more than 1 million subscribers by 1984, it was still losing more than $10 million a year. This was another drain on the company's dwindling resources and a threat to its profit margins.

Home Video and Consumer Products

One bright spot for Disney was its entry into the home video market. It began selling videocassettes of some of its movie hits in 1983. Some of these were contemporary hits from its new Touchstone label, such as *Splash*. However, it also began marketing its old classics, first selecting those that, while popular, were not its greatest hits to see customers' reaction and to protect its rerun movie revenues. *Dumbo* and *Alice in Wonderland* were released in 1983 to enthusiastic demand, and Disney, realizing the revenue potential from video sales was enormous, soon orchestrated the gradual release of all its classics on videotape.[2]

The sale of consumer products bearing Disney's logo had long been one of Disney's major lines of business. However, many analysts felt that Disney was not exploiting the potential of this market and that their strategy of franchising rights to the use of Disney's name and characters to other companies was bringing Disney some money, but making far more money for the actual producers and distributors of Disney's products than for the company itself. They felt the potential market for Disney's books, comics, records, clothing, and all kinds of Disney souvenirs had yet to be exploited.

Moviemaking

Since Walt's death, Disney's movie operations suffered because they failed to find good scripts and projects. The performance of Disney's film business had been lackluster throughout the 1970s, and although the film division accounted for more than 20 percent of Disney's profits in 1979, by 1982 it was losing money. The situation became so bad that Disney's CEO, E. Cardon (Card) Walker, who had taken over after Roy Disney's death in 1971, was talking about closing it down! The division that had been Disney's core business and the source of its success was now in danger. How had this come about? First, Disney was relying on reruns of its classic movies and living on its past glory rather than on the proceeds of its present activities. Reruns were contributing more than 50 percent of the revenues of the film division because Disney was having little commercial success with its new ventures. Although receiving good reviews, animated movies, such as the *Secret of Nimb*, *Watership Down*, and the *Black Hole*, were not big money spinners, and the live-action films Disney had been producing, such as *Something Wicked This Way Comes* and *Condorman*, lost money; these two, for example, lost more than $20 million each.

Moreover, analysts were claiming that Disney was not making the best use of its film library, which contained more than 700 different titles. They felt that Disney could be making a much more creative use of this resource, and, in part as a response to this pressure to exploit this resource, the company drew up plans for the Disney Channel, its pay-TV channel. Meanwhile, industry analysts did not like Card Walker's attitude toward the film division. They felt a turnaround in this division rather than liquidation was the answer, and in 1983 Ronald Miller became chief executive to implement this turnaround strategy. His answer to the problem was to create a new film division, Touchstone Films, to produce movies that were unsuitable for the family-oriented Disney label. He saw the problem as one of being straight-jacketed by Disney's conservative, family image, which had not allowed filmmakers to exploit the opportunities in the market for new kinds of movies. Touchstone brought out *Splash* in 1983; it was a huge hit and the beginning of a turnaround of the film division. Nevertheless, Disney's top management was worried that Walt would not have liked it, and they actively sought to isolate the Touchstone division from the Disney organization. This conflict over Disney's future was the start of infighting between Disney's managers and stockholders over the best way to manage the company.

Roy Disney II, the nephew of Walt Disney, in particular lost confidence in the management team. He felt it lacked the Disney vision and the skills to exploit the Disney resources; in essence, he felt that it was destroying the legacy Walt had left behind. These open conflicts brought Disney to the attention of corporate raiders, and by 1984 there was an increasing possibility of an unfriendly takeover of the Disney organization. To prevent such a takeover, the Disney family sided with new investors, the Bass family, to oust the old, conservative, management team. The Disney family then set out to recruit somebody who could return Disney to a preeminent position in the entertainment industry. The person they fixed on was Michael Eisner, previously vice chairman of Paramount, and widely regarded as the originator of a massive turnaround in the fortunes of that corporation, due to his ability to find and act on new trends in the marketplace. In September 1984, Michael Eisner took control of

Disney and a new era began. Finally, someone had emerged who could wear Walt's crown.

Michael Eisner's Walt Disney Company

It was December 1984, and Michael Eisner was sitting down with Frank Wells, the person he had recruited to help him turn the Disney Company around, and Roy Disney, the nephew of the founder who had been instrumental in Eisner's appointment to plan Disney's future. They were looking over Disney's resources and the activities of its divisions and subsidiaries, and both Eisner and Wells were amazed at the extent and diversity of Disney's resources. Eisner decided that Disney's strengths were in its three principal business segments:

- *Entertainment and recreation,* which included all its theme parks and hotel businesses, together with shopping centers, conference centers, and golf courses

- *Motion pictures and home videos,* which included the Disney studios; Buena Vista Productions, which had the Touchstone label; and Buena Vista Distribution, which distributed Disney's films at home and abroad

- *Consumer products,* which was the licensing arm of Disney and licensed its characters; literary properties; and songs and music to various manufacturers, retailers, printers, and publishers as well

Why were these businesses underperforming, and what could be done about it? It did not take Eisner and Wells long to realize that the problem was that the potential of these businesses was not being exploited. In none of these business segments was management following any clearly defined strategy to exploit the Disney resources or a vision of what use these resources could be put to in the future. Each division was drifting aimlessly along. For example, despite Disney's raw filmmaking talent, the movie business was losing money. Similarly, due to inaction, Disney had lost its television presence outside its own movie channel.

Moreover, it was apparent that while Disney was not taking advantage of its opportunities, other people were. For every dollar Disney was collecting in revenues from its characters and theme parks, those manufacturers who were licensing Disney's products

or those hotel chains housing and feeding Disney customers at the theme parks were getting five. Disney was stagnating, and new ways had to be found to exploit its revenue-generating potential and regain "Disney dollars." First, however, they realized the need to recruit some exceptional executives to provide leadership in the financial planning areas of the company to back up the creative end, which they would lead. Eisner had to find the money to finance his expansion plans and to develop new business ventures. In 1985 he hired Gary L. Wilson as executive vice president and chief financial officer of Disney and made him a director. Wilson, a project finance specialist, had previously performed the same role for the Marriot Corporation, the hotel chain, and had participated in the enormous growth of that corporation. According to Eisner, his responsibility would be to "plan and implement the company's expansion programs, including internal development and acquisitions."[3] With the team set, Eisner began to change Disney.

Entertainment and Recreation

Eisner began to take a long hard look at the theme park business. This was Disney's biggest money spinner, but revenue growth had been slow. How could he revitalize this division's strategy? He started by looking at the customer groups and segments Disney was serving. Was Disney targeting the right segment? What kind of product was Disney really offering? He soon discovered that 70 percent of theme park attendance was repeat business, and that more than anything else what brought people back time after time was the existence of new attractions and new novelties, not the price of the attractions. However, developing new attractions was expensive; it cost millions to develop a new ride, which was why corporate sponsorship was so important. Could he increase the price of attendance to provide the revenue to finance the new attractions and business ventures, or would this drive customers away? Going against the conventional wisdom that higher prices would reduce attendance, Eisner raised admission prices substantially. The result was only a small falloff in attendance and a huge increase in revenues. Essentially, he had discovered that Disney's theme parks had a captive audience. When he raised the entry price again (prices had now risen 45 percent in two years), revenues again dramatically increased with little falloff in attendance. In fact, the increase in theme park prices caused a 59 percent growth in company revenues and accounted for fully 94 percent of earnings growth in 1986. Pretax profits of Disneyland and Disney World rose by 38 percent by September 1985 to $266.4 million from $192.7 million a year earlier. This provided some much needed cash for expansion of Disney's attractions and for its hotel developments and was the source of the turnaround in Disney profits.

Eisner set about revamping the theme park concept to find ways of increasing Disney's revenues and regaining "Disney dollars" from other firms. On the theme park side, Eisner realized that what was needed was first, more kinds of attractions and more rides inside existing theme parks and second, additional theme parks, or "gates," which are new collections of attractions. Moreover, competition was developing at Orlando as other entertainment companies opened attractions to capitalize on tourists' presence. For example, a major water park attraction had been opened called Wet and Wild, which offered a wide variety of water rides. Also, Sea World had opened an Orlando theme park. The popularity of active, physically oriented attractions was accelerating, and Disney, recognizing the possibilities of such an attraction, planned Typhoon Lagoon to recapture revenue. This opened in 1989 to major success. It provided one reason to stay an extra day in a Disney hotel.

Disney sought new "gate" ideas to capture tourists' imagination. In this effort, it was helped by a rival, MCA, which announced that it would build a Universal Studio Tours theme park, similar to the one it already operated in southern California, near Orlando. Eisner, never slow to recognize opportunity, rushed to come out with an alternative. The result was a joint announcement by Disney and MGM that they would build a Disney-MGM Studio theme park on the Orlando site, which would open in 1989. It opened to enthusiastic crowds on time, ahead of Universal's, which was not planned to open until 1990. So popular was the studio tour attraction that Disney announced it would double its size by 1992.

The company began actively searching for a fourth gate at Disney World, and there was speculation that this might take the form of a zoological park. Disney did not ignore shopping and night-time entertainment at Disney World, in an effort to wrest tourists' dollars from the Orlando competition. At night, many of its guests were leaving Disney World to eat and play in the entertainment district of Church Street Station in Orlando. To keep patrons on the site, Disney built Pleasure Island, a huge complex of shops, bars, restaurants, discos, and nightclubs on its land to attract its guests. This has also been very successful and has provided a new dimension to the Disney experience.

Finally, the company looked at the food concession business. At Disney World and Disneyland, food concessions had previously been licensed to other companies that provided the food and paid Disney a percentage of the proceeds. Eisner realized that this was also a source of revenue loss, and as leases and agreements expired, Disney began to take over all the food operations at the theme parks. Not wanting to get into the soft drink business or photography business, however, Eisner was content to make lucrative deals with Coca-Cola and Kodak that they would be the sole suppliers of soft drinks and film products at Disney's theme parks.

Meanwhile, Eisner was not ignoring either the Magic Kingdom or the EPCOT Center at Orlando. New attractions were being constantly announced. For example, Captain EO, a $17 million 3-D music video starring Michael Jackson, was developed for the EPCOT Center at Disney World. Also, the Living Seas exhibit, sponsored by United Technologies, and the Wonders of Life, sponsored by Metropolitan Life, had been opened. Similarly, with George Lucas a new $32 million spaceship ride, Star Tours, was developed for the Disney-MGM Studios theme park. Production of a ride based on the exploits of Indiana Jones was also planned. At Anaheim, too, attractions were coming thick and fast. In 1985 Eisner announced a collaboration with George Lucas of Star Wars fame for a Star Wars attraction at Disneyland, and many additional Lucas attractions followed. In 1988 the company announced plans for Splash mountain at Disneyland, an attraction in which passengers ride replicas of hollowed out logs down huge slides populated with Disney characters. Moreover, in 1989 the company also bought Henson Associates Inc., the originators of the muppet characters, and the Muppet Theater opened at the Disney-MGM Studios to show the exploits of Kermit the Frog and Miss Piggy in glorious 3-D. Under Eisner, the repertoire of Disney's cast of characters constantly increases at its theme parks.

The Imagineering Unit At the source of the new developments in attractions and theme park development is Disney's Imagineering unit. Started by Walt Disney to actualize his ideas, the unit became responsible for all technical advances involving the design and building of Disney's new rides. However, as the company was experiencing problems in the early 1980s, consideration had even been given to closing down this unit to save money. Under Eisner, this unit's budget has been increased dramatically, and it is the source of new adventures and attractions at the theme parks. It was this unit that cooperated with George Lucas to develop the Star Wars attractions at the theme parks. It was also this unit that planned EPCOT Center, the Disney-MGM Studio tours attraction, the rides developed for Tokyo Disneyland, and the new EuroDisneyland outside Paris. Disney is selling the skills of this division to other interested parties. For example, Disney agreed to build a $40 million exhibit on the history of space flight for the Johnson Space Center in Houston, Texas.

Hotel Developments In developing new attractions, Eisner and his team had another moneymaking venture in mind. Disney's guests (it calls its visitors guests) would need somewhere to stay; moreover, if there were many attractions to see, they would need to stay for several days. Here was an opportunity to take advantage of. Disney should get into the hotel business in a big way and build luxury hotels to meet their guests' needs. At Anaheim, but principally in Orlando, this new strategy went into operation. At Disney World, Eisner got his team together to discuss expansion plans for exploiting the vast untapped land and resources in its Orlando site. Eisner realized that Disney was offering far more than eight hours of live entertainment. It could offer a total package of Disney fun whereby its guests could live inside Disney World—eating, sleeping, and breathing Disney. In the years since Disney World had been built, several luxury hotels and convention facilities had been built on the boundaries of Disney, such as the Grand Hyatt Regency Cypress Hotel and the Hilton. Eisner and Wilson planned to steal back the hotel and food dollars for Disney.

They embarked on an ambitious campaign that involved Disney's building not one but many luxury hotels on the Orlando site, each of which would offer a different kind of experience to Disney's guests. Then, each time guests returned, they could stay at a new Disney hotel location and never leave Disney World. In quick succession they opened hotels such

as the Grand Floridian Hotel and the Caribbean Beach Club and Resort, both of which, like the other Disney hotels, enjoyed occupancy rates of more than 90 percent, well above the industry average of 65 percent. They also built budget hotels such as Musicland and Sportsland. Moreover, Disney built major new convention centers and hotels to reclaim the convention trade it had let the Hyatt and Hilton corporations seize. Near EPCOT Center Disney opened four new luxury hotels, including the Dolphin Convention Hotel and the Swan Hotel, which together have more than 2,350 rooms and 200,000 square feet of convention space.

Using Wilson's skills, Disney has found the ideal formula for building hotels without putting a financial debt burden on the company. As with its films, it arranges limited partnerships to finance its hotel building program and then often brings in the large hotel chains to actually run the hotels themselves. For example, a partnership formed by Tischman Realty and Construction Company, Metropolitan Life Insurance Company, and Aoki Corporation financed these hotels. The Dolphin was run by the Sheraton Corporation, while the Swan was run by the Westin Company. Disney puts up the land and its name, and continuing this investment strategy it expected to develop 10,000 more hotel rooms by 1992. The proximity of the hotels and convention centers to Disney World and the Magic Kingdom gives the Disney operations a major advantage over its competitors. To get patrons to use Disney's hotels for longer periods, it was logical that Disney should find new ways of entertaining them, and this is just what Eisner did in finding new "gates" and attractions for his theme parks.

At Disneyland, Eisner's hotel and attraction development strategy was hampered by the fact that Disney did not own much of the land surrounding the park. It owned a small undeveloped tract of land at Disneyland, but this was just barely big enough to contain a new "gate" or hotel complex. Even if there was no room to build hotels, maybe Disney could acquire some. Under the old management team's operating philosophy, Disney had previously licensed the rights to use the Disney name for a hotel. The result was the Disneyland Hotel owned by the Wrather Corporation, a California entertainment corporation. Disney first acquired a large stake in the Wrather Corporation and then finally took over the whole operation in 1989. It then revamped the hotel to upgrade it to the luxury class, carrying on the Orlando strategy.

As a part of this deal, however, Disney also gained control of the Wrather Corporation's Long Beach entertainment complex, which consisted of the liner the Queen Mary, run as a hotel, together with Howard Hughes's Spruce Goose Aeroplane, the largest ever built, and an entertainment village. Disney revamped the liner as a luxury hotel complex, and then Eisner realized that maybe this complex could become Disney's second California "gate," one that tourists could stop at on their way to or from Disneyland. Moreover, there was all the revenue currently going to Sea World and Knottsberry Farm to compete for. In 1990 Disney announced a proposal to develop the Long Beach site as the center for a Disney Sea theme park which would be a water-based attraction. It would contain the largest aquarium in the world, a glass cage in which tourists could go down among the sharks, and many other water-oriented rides and attractions such as Captain Nemo's submarine from *20,000 Leagues Under the Sea,* another Imagineering unit project.

Eisner also began to consider ideas for new theme parks abroad. Disney already had participated in the planning of a Disneyland outside Tokyo, Japan. This had opened in April 1983 and had been wildly successful. However, in this venture Disney has taken no financial stake and, pursuing its old strategy, had licensed its name to a group of Japanese investors in return for 10 percent of the gate receipts and 5 percent of other proceeds. This had cost Disney much loss in profit. Now Eisner was actively considering the idea for a Disney theme park somewhere in Europe to capture the vast European market. After much planning and upfront negotiations with several European countries, in December 1985 Eisner announced the decision to build what became a $2.1 billion EuroDisney theme park and resort complex, modeled on the Disney World concept, about 20 miles east of Paris in a suburb called Marne-La-Vallee. This opened in 1991. Disney owns 49 percent of the park, the other 51 percent being held by a company consisting of French and European investors. Disney receives fees for operating the park and royalties on admissions, rides, food, and other operations, but the French company controls the entire project. Plans were for a Disney World kind of complex where, along with the Magic Kingdom, there will be Disney hotels, shopping centers, golf courses,

and convention facilities to ensure that Disney is capturing all the dollars in related entertainment activities. In short, the whole successful Eisner formula.

The result of these developments on Disney theme park revenues can be seen in Table 2. At the same time as Eisner and his team were revamping their theme park strategy, he was working on plans for a turnaround of the motion picture and television business.

Competition in the Theme Park Industry Disney is by far the biggest of the theme park companies and the most profitable. However, as it has been expanding its "gates" and attractions, it has run into the competition. The new Disney Sea attraction is a prime rival for Sea World, and in California and Florida Sea World will have to compete against an expanding Disney presence into water-related entertainments. The opening of Typhoon Lagoon hurt Sea World's Orlando operation, for example. In addition, Disney has been having a running battle with MCA, the owner of the Universal Studio Tours. Sidney Sheinberg, the president of MCA, claims that his company was the originator of the idea of the Orlando studio tours attraction but that Disney took the idea and ran with it. Competition between the Disney-MGM Studio tour and the Universal will heat up in the coming years. Moreover, after announcing that Disney would build a studio tour on its EuroDisney site, MCA announced that it, too, would open one in Paris or London. Other companies in the industry are those such as Six Flags and Busch Gardens, and Disney's new Orlando "gate" might bring it into direct competition with them. Moreover, Disney's huge expansion into hotels had brought it up against the major hotel companies, and competition could be expected to be fierce there if ever there was a falloff in demand for hotel rooms.

Motion Pictures and Television

When Eisner took over Disney in 1984, Disney executives were just apologizing for the success of their new smash hit movie *Splash,* because even though it was produced by their separate Touchstone label, it was not in the tradition of Walt Disney family entertainment. Eisner had no such problems recognizing that times had changed and that the family of 1985 was not the family of 1965. As head of children's entertainment at ABC, he had recognized the

TABLE 2

Consolidated Statement of Income (in millions, except per share data)

Year Ended September 30	1989	1988	1987
Revenues			
Theme parks and resorts	$2,595.4	$2,042.0	$1,834.2
Filmed entertainment	1,587.6	1,149.2	875.6
Consumer products	411.3	247.0	167.0
	4,594.3	**3,438.2**	**2,876.8**
Costs and Expenses			
Theme parks and resorts	1,810.0	1,477.2	1,285.3
Filmed entertainment	1,331.1	962.9	745.0
Consumer products	224.2	113.3	69.7
	3,365.3	**2,553.4**	**2,100.0**
Operating Income			
Theme parks and resorts	785.4	564.8	548.9
Filmed entertainment	256.5	186.3	130.6
Consumer products	187.1	133.7	97.3
	1,229.0	**884.8**	**776.8**
Corporate Expenses (Income)			
General and administrative	119.6	96.0	70.3
Interest expense	23.9	5.8	29.1
Investment and interest income	(67.4)	(58.9)	(49.0)
	76.1	**42.9**	**50.4**
Income From Continuing Operations Before Income Taxes	1,152.9	841.9	726.4
Income taxes	449.6	319.9	334.1
Income From Continuing Operations	**703.3**	**522.0**	**392.3**
Discontinued operations, net			52.4
Net Income	**$703.3**	**$522.0**	**$444.7**
Earnings per Share			
Continuing operations	$5.10	$3.80	$2.85
Discontinued operations			.38
	$5.10	**$3.80**	**$3.23**
Average number of common and common equivalent shares outstanding	138.0	137.4	137.8

Source: The Walt Disney Company, *Annual Report,* 1989.

changing trends in viewing habits and had understood that new definitions of family entertainment were possible in the 1980s. Later, at Paramount, he had been involved in many of that studio's huge successes. It was he who had seen the possibility for projects such as *Raiders of the Lost Ark, Airplane,* and *Terms of Endearment,* all of which became blockbuster movies.[4]

At Disney, Eisner used this experience and with Jeff Katzenberg, the creative head of Disney's movie division, began to fashion Disney's new strategy. Katzenberg was also a Paramount veteran, where he was known as the "golden retriever" for his ability to sniff out just the right scripts.[5] He also is a workaholic who makes hundreds of two-minute phone calls a week to producers, directors, and so forth. At Paramount he was attributed with the phrase, "If you don't come in on Saturday, don't bother to come in on Sunday."[6]

By 1984 Disney had only a 4 percent share of box office revenues for its movies. Its movie division was losing money and had become a drain on the company's resources. The problem facing the two men was how to turn around the division. On the financial side, to lessen the burden on Disney and to reduce the fear of failure, Eisner negotiated an agreement to raise money to finance Touchstone's movie productions with Silver Screens Management Inc. The idea was that Silver Screens would sell limited partnerships to outside investors that would put up the money to finance Disney's movies. In return, investors would receive a percentage of the movie's subsequent revenues. By 1985, $193 million had been raised to finance fourteen new movies.

With the financing in place, Eisner and Katzenberg moved to change Disney's strategy. Luring talented people away from Paramount, Eisner quickly approved *Down and Out in Beverly Hills,* which grossed an impressive $62 million. He then focused on signing stars who were then not box office draw, such as Bette Midler and Richard Dreyfus, in order to keep costs low, and he added films to the production schedule that were vehicles for their talents. Disney boasts that while other studios spend $16 million per movie, it spends about $11 million; low cost is the hallmark of Eisner's strategy. Such films as *Stakeout* and *Outrageous Fortune* were the result. By 1987 Disney had captured 14 percent of the $4.2 billion movie market, and the turnaround was clear as its film operations became the fastest-growing part of its operations. By 1987 Disney had turned the $10 million loss in 1984 into a huge profit.

He then turned to the next part of his movie strategy, which involved deals for distribution of the movies to television and videocassette sales. Disney had always distributed its own movies to movie theater chains through its distribution company, a subsidiary called Buena Vista Distributions,

and had in this way captured the profit rather than give it to distributors. In 1985 the company formed a new television division and hired yet another Paramount executive to orchestrate the sale of movies to television networks and to handle video-cassette sales.[7] In 1986 Viacom's Showtime movie channel signed an exclusive agreement to buy cable television rights for movies produced through the Touchstone division through 1990.[8] The deal started with *Down and Out in Beverly Hills* and involved more than fifty movies. Although very expensive for the movie channel, Disney was reported to have received $3 million to $5 million per film when the deal was signed, and both parties have benefited from it. Eisner also went ahead with the videocassette sales. He decided to release one classic a year, and in 1986, for example, 1 million copies of *Sleeping Beauty* were sold. Small wonder Disney's stock price increased by five times between 1983 and 1986. Disney is also vigorously expanding foreign sales of videocassettes.

On the television front, Disney also went through a major turnaround. Eisner moved quickly to exploit Disney's resources. He arranged for syndication of the twenty-nine years of the Wonderful World of Disney material, cartoons, and feature films on the new networks emerging with the advent of cable television. Three packages of material were put up for sale in 1987, which helped to double film revenues. This market had previously been ignored. He also moved to make more product for the small screen. For the adult audience, the hit series *Golden Girls* was developed; he also arranged for a new format for *Siskel & Ebert at the Movies.* Eisner then brought back the Disney Sunday Movie, introducing it himself, and arranged for the development of *Duck Tales, Gummie Bears,* and *The Little Mermaid* new animation series to take advantage of Disney's animation skills. These cartoons shown on afternoon television and then the Disney Channel have proved immensely popular. There were failures, however. For example, two series introduced in 1986, *The Ellen Burstyn Show* and *Sidekicks,* were quickly abandoned. Meanwhile, under the new management, the Disney Channel was doing somewhat better. Competition for subscribers is fierce in the pay-TV industry, but Disney had made some headway. Its subscriber base grew 27 percent to almost 3.2 million by 1986 and 4 million by 1988.

Then, in 1989 came another move in the television market. Disney acquired KHU-TV, a Los Angeles television station, and renamed it KCAL-TV. This takeover gave it a wholly owned distribution outlet for the products of its studios, so it can capture some of the value that is currently being earned by its end users. It had previously tried, but failed, to acquire the 360 screen Mann theater chain bought by Gulf & Western and a New York television station that MCA bought. So expansion into the television station market and movie theater market appears possible. They also approached CBS to buy CBS Records but were spurned by the board, which eventually sold it to the Sony Corporation. As Eisner said, "We are going to be awfully conservative in what we go after, but if there was something out there that could add value to this company, we're going to go for it."[9] The search for new assets is part of Eisner's strategy to reduce its heavy dependence on theme parks and movies for its operating revenues in the future.

By 1987 Walt Disney was number two in share of box office revenues, with 14 percent of revenues after Paramount. Twenty-two of the twenty-three films produced by Disney have made a profit, far higher than the industry ratio of about three in ten. Then came such hits as *Three Men and a Baby,* which grossed more than $160 million; *Good Morning Vietnam,* with $110 million; and *Cocktail,* with Tom Cruise. It also introduced two more animation movies, *Who Framed Roger Rabbit?* which cost $38 million, thus departing from the Disney formula of keeping costs low; and *Oliver and Company.* As a result of these films, Disney took the box office lead from Paramount in 1988 with 22 percent of revenues through Labor Day, the end of the summer film season.

At the beginning of 1989, Walt Disney established a third motion picture company, called Hollywood Pictures, to continue the success story established by Touchstone. It gave charge of this company to Ricardo Mestres, former president of production at Touchstone, and a mega performer in his own right. To finance the intended twenty-four to twenty-eight movies a year, another silver screen partnership was established, which raised $600 million to fund future Disney films. Clearly, Disney was expecting big things from its three divisions. By the end of 1989, expectations were fulfilled; Disney was the market leader with almost 20 percent of box office revenues as a result of more successes such as *The Little Mermaid* and *Oliver and Company.* The change in the revenues and profits of the movie division is given in Table 3.

TABLE 3

Consolidated Balance Sheet (in millions)

September 30	1989	1988
Assets		
Cash	$380.8	$428.0
Marketable securities	662.3	668.6
Receivables	908.5	561.5
Merchandise inventories	224.3	159.9
Film costs	443.3	211.0
Theme parks, resorts, and other property, at cost		
Attractions, buildings and equipment	4,143.3	3,322.5
Accumulated depreciation	(1,217.3)	(1,065.2)
	2,926.0	2,257.3
Projects in progress	407.4	511.1
Land	63.9	53.3
	3,397.3	2,821.7
Other assets	640.7	258.2
	$6,657.2	$5,108.9
Liabilities and Stockholders' Equity		
Accounts payable and other accrued liabilities	$1,011.4	$698.7
Income taxes payable	250.9	204.3
Borrowings	860.6	435.5
Unearned royalty and other advances	912.7	823.3
Deferred income taxes	577.6	587.8
Stockholders' equity		
Common stock, $.10 par value		
Authorized—300.00 million shares		
Outstanding—135.3 million shares and 133.2 million shares	392.8	349.6
Retained earnings	2,651.2	2,009.7
	3,044.0	2,359.3
	$6,657.2	$5,108.9

Source: The Walt Disney Company, *Annual Report,* 1989.

Consumer Products Division

The final area that Eisner turned his attention to was improving revenues from the licensing of the Disney brand name to firms that wished to manufacture and sell products using the Disney characters. Eisner's intention might be summed up as saying he would like to see a mouse or duck on every T-shirt, every wrist, and every toy or piece of baby equipment in every home in every country in the world. He started by developing deals with major manufacturers and retailers, signing an agreement with Mattel, the biggest U.S. toy manufacturer, to sell Disney-brand infant and preschool toys worldwide. In 1987 Disney signed a ten-year agreement with Sears to develop clothing and toys using certain Disney characters. By 1988 Disney had negotiated more than 3,000 agreements with companies to manufacture more than 14,000 Disney-licensed products.

Meanwhile, in 1987 the company announced plans for a large-scale expansion into retailing stores that will sell nothing but Disney products. The Disney stores will market products produced by Disney's manufacturers, so that as in the case of Disney's entry into the television station market, Disney will reap the rewards from selling its own products. These stores sell videotapes of Disney's films, children's clothing, toys, and the whole Disney paraphernalia at premium prices. Given the ability to charge a premium price, each store is proving very profitable, and malls are fighting to attract a store.[10]

In 1988 Disney paid $52 million to buy Childcraft Education Corporation, which sells educational toys and play equipment through direct mail. This move complements Disney's mail-order, catalog sales operation, which sends out more than 6 million catalogs a year and has expanded product offerings by more than 50 percent. Given its move into mail-order and store operations, it seems as if Disney is looking to become the Sears of the entertainment business. One more benefit to Disney from these store and catalog sales is the intangible brand-name loyalty it creates for other Disney ventures. The stores are a marketing vehicle for Disney; they open up the Disney Company to the public and invite attendance at its theme parks and hotels.[11]

International sales of Disney products are extremely important to the company. For example, every year Japanese consumers buy more than $1 billion worth of Disney-brand products. In Italy the Mickey Mouse comic book, *Topolino*, sells 70,000 copies a month, and when Disney took over publishing the comic itself, it made an extra $15 million a year in profits. Videocassette sales and records are major revenue earners for Disney worldwide. In 1989 Eisner pointed to the internationalization of all Disney franchises as the source of the massive gains in the revenues of the consumer products and home video operations.[12]

Another expanding dimension of Disney's business is publishing. While Disney licenses Mickey Mouse Tales and Duck Tales to Welch Publishing, it is planning the publication of *Disney Adventure Digest* to be the official magazine of *Disney Afternoon,* two hours each weekday afternoon of syndicated programming scheduled for the fall of 1990. This has a planned circulation of 100,000. Many more magazine opportunities are being explored, as are books to accompany Disney's movies. For example, many books were planned around Disney's successful *Dick Tracy* movie in 1990, and publishing provides new opportunities for Disney to exploit the linkages between its products. This division will also mastermind international publication and sales of Disney's books and magazines, a market that is likely to increase with the opening of EuroDisney. In 1990 Disney sold more than 500 million books and comics worldwide.[13]

Another venture for Disney involves selling its organizational culture, which is centered on providing high-quality customer service. Disney University in Orlando puts all new recruits through a three-day program designed to bring them into the Disney way of doing things. They learn the history of Disney, its mission, and its emphasis on courtesy to customers to maximize visitors' satisfaction. This is very important to Disney, given that more than 70 percent of visitors are repeats. New employees learn the Disney language in which employees are known as cast members, visitors as guests, and employees are said to be on stage when they are working and off stage when they are not. Now Disney is selling its expertise and its techniques to major companies. So far, more than 3,000 executives from more than 1,200 companies have attended the two-day seminar Disney offers called Traditions in order to learn Disney's techniques so that they can increase the quality of customer service in their own companies. One of the central features of the Disney approach is to empower employees so that they try to solve problems themselves as and when they occur rather than turn for help.[14] According to Disney, the secret to Disney's success is "pixie dust," which is a combination of training, communication, and care.

Disney's Future

As a result of these developments, by 1989 sales had jumped from $1.46 billion in 1984 to $4.59 billion. Net profit rose from $97.8 million to $703.3 million, and earnings per share increased more than ten times during the same period. Everything Disney is doing is designed to capitalize on the incredible progress that it has made. While the annual increase in profit was 46 percent in the 1980s Eisner and Wells have vowed to increase profits by an average of 20 percent a year in the 1990s. To do so, they are constantly expanding the range and scope of Disney's activities as well as building on the base they have established. A new Disneyland theme park somewhere in Asia is in preparation, and a new studio tours park next to the EuroDisneyland is planned, as well as a new theme park in southern California. More new attractions based on its more recent successes are planned, including one designed around Dick Tracy. Similarly, Eisner has announced that Disney will have thirty hotels with more than 26,000 rooms by 1995.

Industry analysts wonder whether or not Eisner and his team can maintain the same growth rate and even whether the company may be headed for a fall. Because most of Disney's revenue comes first from its theme parks and second from its film operations, they wonder whether the pace can be maintained. For example, they point out that a recession or an increase in the price of gas could rapidly affect theme park attendance, since the price of airplane seats and auto travel would increase. They also point out that historically no movie studio has been able to maintain an unbroken string of successes, and they wonder whether the movie division might be in for a rough ride in the future.

They also wonder about the wisdom of Disney's current projects and the direction Michael Eisner's Disney company is taking. After the incredible successes Eisner and his team have achieved, critics claim that the conceit of Disney executives is huge and that they believe they can do no wrong. Eisner has been called an egomaniac, albeit by his archcritic Sidney Sheinberg, the president of rival MCA, and is said to be in search of ever greater opportunities for the expansion of Disney's empire. Already the largest entertainment company in the world, it is now exercising its muscle as it seeks to enlarge its share of the television station market. However, critics wonder whether such expansion is wise.

Since Disney can already sell its existing film products to the networks, does it need the added burden of owning television stations? In 1990 Eisner was looking around for new acquisitions to add to its Los Angeles station, and CBS was mentioned as a possible takeover target. Critics ask whether this would add value to Disney or to CBS.

In 1990 Disney announced that it would open a new record division, called Hollywood Records, to produce records for the general public, not just the Disney audience. This move will bring it into direct competition with huge record companies such as CBS Records, which Disney bid for but lost in the very competitive record business. The huge expansion into the hotel business is justified if occupancy rates stay more than 90 percent, but is the resort market becoming saturated with too many luxury hotels and conference centers being built? Any downturn in the vacation market for whatever cause might put severe pressure on hotel operations. Against opposition from his own team, Eisner also embarked on the concept of a Disney fast-food restaurant. Offering a wide array of food, they would seek to exploit the Disney cartoon characters in a restaurant format. However, this is a relatively new business for Disney. Although Disney operates restaurants in its own theme parks, it would be entering the highly competitive $65 billion fast-food industry currently dominated by big chains such as McDonald's and Burger King. Does Disney have the core skills to compete in this market?

Moreover, while guests may like to eat, sleep, and breathe Disney on their vacations, do they want to do so 365 days a year? Is there a danger of overexposure as children wear Disney clothes, read Disney books, watch Disney television programs, go to sleep in Disney beds playing with Disney toys, and then eat Disney food, too? Will there be a reaction as people turn from Disney to new forms of excitement and fantasy? However, where would they go? Disney has co-opted George Lucas and his characters; bought the muppets; and, in films such as *Dick Tracy,* captured more characters. Is there a place for people to run? For now, it seems that Michael Eisner can force the golden goose to keep on laying golden eggs, but if the environment changes, if the film division falls on hard times, or if his new projects fail to meet expectations, the supply of eggs might stop.

ENDNOTES

1. L. Gartley and E. Leebron, *Walt Disney: A Guide to References and Resources* (Boston: G. K. Hall, 1979).
2. Walt Disney Productions' 1983 Annual Report.
3. *Wall Street Journal*, August 9, 1985, p. 14.
4. "Michael Eisner's Hit Parade," *Business Week*, February 1, 1988.
5. "Disney's Magic," *Business Week*, March 9, 1987.
6. *Time*, April 25, 1988.
7. *Wall Street Journal*, March 16, 1985.
8. *Wall Street Journal*, April 25, 1986.
9. *Business Week*, March 9, 1987.
10. *Wall Street Journal*, December 23, 1987.
11. *Advertising Age*, November 28, 1988, p. 46.
12. Walt Disney Company's 1989 Annual Report.
13. *Folio*, April 1990, p. 57.
14. *Marketing News*, January 8, 1990.

The Walt Disney Company, 1995–2005: Part Two

This case was prepared by Gareth R. Jones, Texas A&M University.

After a long struggle with analysts and board members who were increasingly critical of his performance as CEO of Disney during the last decade, and a bitter fight with Roy Disney, a major shareholder, Michael Eisner announced he would step down as its CEO in 2006 when his contract expired. While the board searched for a successor in 2005, one candidate being his hand-picked successor Robert Iger, president and chief operating officer of Disney, Eisner pondered the events that had first brought him to popular acclaim as one of the most successful CEOs in America, but who was now regarded by many as a "lame duck" CEO whose reign was coming to an end.

Disney's Growing Entertainment Empire

Michael Eisner, with his then top management team of Frank Wells and Gary Wilson, began the 1990s with the same strategy they had previously developed—to build Disney's core strengths in the three areas of entertainment and recreation, motion pictures, and video and consumer products in order to increase the value of Disney's franchises and brand

Copyright © 2005 by Gareth R. Jones. This case was prepared by Gareth R. Jones, Texas A&M University, as the basis for class discussion rather than to illustrate either effective or ineffective handling of an administrative situation. Reprinted by permission of Gareth R. Jones. All rights reserved. For the most recent financial results of the company discussed in this case, go to **http://finance.yahoo.com**, input the company's stock symbol, and download the latest company report from its homepage.

name. As a reward for all these efforts, the Walt Disney Company made Michael Eisner one of the highest-paid executives in history. In 1993 alone Disney paid Michael Eisner $203,010,590 in salary and stock options as a reward for taking Disney's market value from $2.2 billion in 1984, when Eisner took over, to $22.7 billion in 1993. This huge salary was more than any other CEO of a public corporation had made in a single year at that time, and for many CEOs in an entire career.

Entertainment and Recreation

In the entertainment area, Disney's top managers began by enlarging the size and variety of its theme parks and other entertainment properties. The number of attractions offered by its three Orlando properties—Disney World, EPCOT, and Disney MGM—was increased to seventy-eight in the 1990s. Moreover, three water parks were now in operation together with the Disney Vacation Club, Discovery Island, and the Disney Boardwalk. These properties extended Disney's hotel, restaurant, and shopping empire.

In July 1995, Disney finally announced that it would build a $500 million zoological park as its fourth property in Orlando, but it would be a zoo with a difference. Called Disney's Wild Animal Kingdom, the five hundred-acre park is larger than any of Disney's parks around the world. It has three main areas, showcasing animals that are live, extinct, and mythical. For example, the live animal section of the park features large herds of African animals such as elephants and giraffes in a natural setting; the extinct section of the park features Disney's famous moving models (animatronics) of creatures such as dinosaurs and flying lizards; and the mythical section will feature creatures such as dragons and unicorns. Eisner hoped that the new property would attract both new and repeat visitors to its parks. Repeat visitors now have another reason to return to Orlando. When both new and repeat visitors do come, they now have a reason to spend an extra day in the Disney empire, increasing the revenues that Disney receives from its hotels, catering, and shopping businesses.

The EuroDisney Disaster Some of Disney's entertainment ventures proved less than successful, however. EuroDisney, which opened in April 1992, proved to be a financial disaster through the 1990s. By 1996, Disney, which owns a 39 percent equity interest in the park, had lost more than $500 million on the venture. There were many reasons for EuroDisney's failure. First, Eisner and his team did not explore European customers' needs in enough detail, particularly the needs of its French customers. Modeling EuroDisney on its Orlando property, Disney built six theme hotels with a total of fifty-two hundred rooms and a huge entertainment center offering a full complement of shops and restaurants around its European park. However, it found that Europeans do not have the free-spending ways of their American counterparts and like to make their vacation dollars go much further. Europeans did not like Disney's high prices; they stayed fewer days in the hotels, tried to find less expensive accommodations farther away, and even bought less food and Disney merchandise. Also, fewer visitors came to the park than expected, and, in particular, French citizens did not provide the stream of revenues that Disney expected. Moreover, many Europeans found it not much more expensive to vacation in Orlando than in France; British and German tourists, in particular, flocked to Florida to enjoy its warm climate. Many critics said that Disney would have done better to locate its park in Spain, somewhere on the Costa Del Sol, where the climate is much more temperate than in France, where it becomes cold and wet in the winter.

EuroDisney's stock price plunged in 1993 and 1994 as investors fled. In 1994, Eisner authorized emergency financing to keep the park afloat. In 1995, a Saudi Arabian prince purchased a large stake in the park and, together with Disney, injected some much needed funding. By 1996, the park was showing a small profit after it had adjusted its prices and policies to match the tastes of its European customers.

One entertainment venture that Disney finalized was a revitalization of West 42nd Street in New York City. The ambitious venture turned a near red-light district into a huge entertainment complex full of games, theaters, hotels, shops, and restaurants to attract tourists to New York, which provided $35 million in financing to condemn and clear the buildings so that Disney and other entertainment companies such as Viacom could create a state-of-the-art entertainment complex. (Disney's cost was over $350 million.)

Movies

Disney's movie division also started off the 1990s in full swing. Its Walt Disney Pictures, Touchstone Pictures, Hollywood Pictures, and Buena Vista Pictures movie divisions all began producing a full array of pictures for distribution. Disney also acquired Miramax Pictures, a small company known for its production of high-quality, adult-oriented pictures, for about $60 million. While much of Miramax's movie output is critically acclaimed, Disney received considerable flack when Miramax began to make controversial films such as *Priest*, whose content has nothing in common with traditional Disney themes.

One blockbuster movie put out by Walt Disney Pictures in the early 1990s was *The Lion King*, Disney's highest-grossing animated movie ever. The success of this movie extended into the videocassette market where it sold more than 60 million copies, and then on into the consumer product areas, where Lion King games, clothing, books, and so on generated record profits for Disney. A Lion King attraction was also opened at Disneyland to take advantage of the movie's success and a Lion King theater production has been touring the United States and Europe ever since with great success.

The success of *The Lion King* convinced Disney's executives that they needed to release one new animated movie each year to keep the revenues flowing into the movie division (and eventually into the consumer products division, too). In 1995 Disney released *Pocahontas*, and in 1996, it released *The Hunchback of Notre Dame*, both accompanied by a flood of movie-related Disney merchandise to capitalize on the anticipated popularity of these movies. These movies did not have the blockbuster appeal of *Little Simba*, however, and have not generated the huge stream of revenues that have kept the movie division's profits surging.

In fact, by 1996 Disney's movie division as a whole had run into hard times. Touchstone and Hollywood Pictures produced a string of failures including *White Squall* and *Before and After*, and Eisner announced in 1996 that Disney would close Hollywood Pictures to consolidate movie production in the other divisions. As other movie studios have discovered, Disney learned that repeating major successes year after year is difficult. Also, in common with other studios, Disney has experienced cost increases, as major stars such as Tom Cruise and Jim Carrey demand $20 million a picture. As a result, Disney's former low-cost strength in movie production largely disappeared.

In fact, by 1996 most movie studios were beginning to learn that, collectively, they were making too many movies per year to be profitable. It became increasingly clear that two kinds of movies were usually the most successful: expensive blockbuster movies backed by advertising campaigns amounting to $20 million to $40 million, which could generate $200 million to $500 million in theater revenues worldwide, and inexpensive movies costing about $13 million to $15 million, backed by modest $3 million to $5 million advertising budgets that could find a niche and be profitable. What was costing Disney and the other studios a fortune was the stuck-in-the-middle movies in the $30 million to $40 million range, which often lacked true star appeal and still required a $10 million to $20 million advertising effort. When these movies flopped, as they often did, they ate up the profits from the blockbuster movies, which each studio desperately needed at least one of every year to remain profitable.

Disney, as with other movie companies, announced in 1996 that it would produce fewer movies per year in the future and focus more on the production of the two successful kinds of movie previously described. It also announced a return to its cost-cutting ways and expressed renewed support for Miramax, which specialized in finding and producing the low-budget, niche movies that often prove to be very profitable.

Home Video

Inspired by the early success of its home video releases, throughout the 1990s Disney has forged ahead with promoting this division's business. In 1995, Disney's domestic home video division reached phenomenal sales of $2 billion in revenues, up from just $1 billion in revenues in 1992. Contributing to this increase was *The Lion King*, which sold 30 million copies in 1995 alone. Even *Snow White* sold 25 million copies. Disney then started to release from its library more movies, such as *Sleeping Beauty* or *Dumbo*, that are perennial favorites. In 1996, the introduction of the new DVD digital movie format opened up a new revenue channel for Disney because customers now had to buy their favorite movies in the new format if they wished to obtain the unsurpassed picture and sound quality that the new DVD players provide.

By 1995, the Disney Channel had become the second most popular pay movie channel in the United States after HBO. Increasingly, Disney used the channel to advertise its new movie offerings, such as *The Hunchback of Notre Dame*, and all the new happenings at its theme parks.

Consumer Products

Disney's shopping empire also expanded rapidly in the 1990s. By 1995, Disney had opened 429 specialty Disney Stores worldwide (including 26 in Europe and 15 in the Asia-Pacific area). It also opened a chain of Disney boutiques called the Walt Disney Gallery, which sold high-priced, premium products such as cartoon lithographs or $1,000 reproduction Disney characters to wealthy customers. These boutiques were to be attached to existing Disney stores. Disney also started a catalog mail-order business to reach customers that are not served by Disney stores (which tend to be located only in large, prestigious malls in major cities). These catalogs offer a representative set of its merchandise and also allow customers to book complete Disney vacation packages, often at a discount.

Disney's publishing interests also increased sharply, and it now published more than 500 million books a year worldwide through its Mouse Books, Disney Press, and Hyperion Books titles. These books were intended to publicize its new features, attractions, and movies, which extends the popularity of the traditional cast of Disney characters.

Management Issues

The top management team that has been building Disney's entertainment empire changed significantly during the 1990s. In the spring of 1994, Frank Wells, Michael Eisner's trusted president, was killed in a helicopter accident. This was a major blow to Eisner, well known for the direct, hands-on way he managed the Disney empire and holds his top managers to account. Because of his trust in Wells, Eisner had been able to leave many aspects of Disney's business in Wells's hands. Now he had to manage the whole empire. To compound the matter, Eisner's move to centralize decision making came at a time when he was diagnosed with heart problems, and in 1994, he entered the hospital for quadruple bypass heart surgery.

Although successful, many analysts began to wonder how long Eisner could remain in control at Disney, especially after one executive, Jeffrey Katzenberg, launched a major move in 1994 to obtain more power at Disney. Katzenberg was the creative force behind Disney's major animated movies. It was he who had orchestrated the success of *Aladdin* and *The Lion King*, and he had major input into other movies such as *Beauty and the Beast* and *Pocahontas*. Katzenberg lobbied strongly for Eisner to name him president of the Disney Company, a position from which he could hope to become its CEO if and when Eisner departed. Eisner would not name him to this position, not wanting a powerful rival in his weakened state, some analysts said, and not believing Katzenberg was the right person to head a company such as Disney, others said. A major rift between the two men occurred, and Katzenberg resigned from Disney in 1994, leaving a major gap in Disney's creative leadership. Many other executives followed, including Richard Frank, the head of Disney's television operations.

Katzenberg then joined with David Geffen, a charismatic Hollywood mogul, and Steven Spielberg, the well-known movie producer, to form a new movie studio, Dream Works, which with $2 billion in cash began to produce a whole series of movies (live action and animated) to compete with Disney and the other major studios. Katzenberg recruited several top Disney animators and other executives for his new studio with the intention that Dream Works would become a major competitor to Disney in the years ahead. In 1996, after several rounds of failed negotiations, Katzenberg launched a $300 million lawsuit against Disney, arguing that this was the money he was due under his contract with Disney, which specified that he was to receive a percentage of the royalties associated with each of the creative efforts he was involved with, such as *The Lion King*. Katzenberg finally won his lawsuit and reportedly received a settlement of around the $300 million figure.

Recovering from surgery and under intense pressure to find someone to help him manage the Disney empire, Eisner focused on Michael Ovitz, the head of Creative Arts Agency, the agency that handled the careers of many major stars, such as Tom Cruise and Barbra Streisand, as well as sports figures, such as famous basketball and tennis players. Ovitz had a huge reputation in Hollywood as a consummate deal maker and the person that everybody had to know. In 1995, Eisner made him a lucrative offer to join Disney as its president (an offer that included over $1 million in stock options in Disney and a severance package worth over $100 million), more or less assuring Ovitz that he would be picked as Disney's next CEO. Eisner put Ovitz in charge of overseeing Disney's many divisions, in particular the movie division, and Disney's biggest money spinner. Together with a senior executive vice president and chief financial officer, Stephen F. Bollenbach (who left to become CEO of Hilton in 1996) spent 1995 analyzing all aspects of the Disney Company's operations to create a new blueprint of the company's future. Together they planned a strategy that was to take Disney to the top of the entertainment world: the acquisition of Capital Cities/ABC Inc.

The Disney-Capital Cities/ABC Merger

On July 31, 1995, Michael Eisner astonished the entertainment world when, together with Capital Cities/ABC Inc.'s CEO, Thomas S. Murphy, he announced that Disney would acquire that company for $19 billion in order to make Disney "the world's premier entertainment company, to protect and build upon the Disney name and franchise, and to preserve and foster quality, imagination and guest service." Capital Cities/ABC owned one of the three biggest television networks in the United States, owns 10 television stations that reach 25 percent of the U.S. viewing public, has 224 affiliated television stations, owns 22 radio stations in large cities, and has a network of 344 radio stations. It also owned 80 percent of ESPN and ESPN2, 37.5 percent of A&E television network, 50 percent of Lifetime television—all well-known "branded channels." Furthermore, it had interests in several international television companies, owned 6 newspapers, and had extensive publishing interests, including weekly newspapers and shopping guides.

EXHIBIT 1

Walt Disney's Revenue Breakdown, 1995

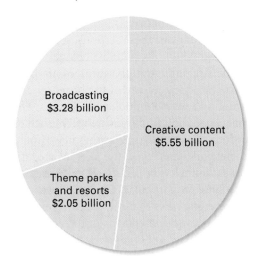

After the acquisition, Disney redefined its three main areas of business as creative content (which includes all its movie and television production operations, all licensing activities involving the Disney name and characters, and consumer products), theme parks and resorts, and broadcasting. The revenues that Disney derived from each of these three areas in 1995 in relation to each other are shown in Exhibit 1.

Using its new business area breakdown, 1995 broadcasting revenues were at $3.28 billion, which exceeded the contributions of Disney's theme parks and resorts (making it less dependent on this area) but were still only half of what it obtained from its creative content business area. Moreover, for 1995 operating income for the creative content group was down 37 percent to $262 million, while operating income for broadcasting was flat at $198 million, and income from theme parks rose significantly by 11 percent to $182 million because of good attendance. The reason for the decline in profit of the creative content group was the disappointing sales of *Pocahontas* videotapes compared with *The Lion King* in the year before; several movie flops such as *White Squall, Before and After,* and *Mr. Wrong;* and major write-offs in film development for failed or abandoned ongoing projects.

In championing the merger, Eisner and Ovitz spoke enthusiastically about the synergies that could be obtained. For example, in the future, Disney television programming would be offered primarily through its own network and then subsequently rerun on the Disney Channel. Moreover, Disney would have a secure outlet for all its new television productions, even marginal ones, in an environment in which major networks had an increasing number of content providers from which to choose. In addition, Disney could feature its new movies on television specials, similar to the one that aired on ABC in 1996 showing the making of *The Hunchback of Notre Dame.* Given the high costs of advertising new movies, the possession of its own network would allow it to publicize its movies at less cost than other studios, cost savings that would be substantial in the years ahead. Finally, Disney's movie library could be shown at low cost over the years on ABC television, and the resources of the new company could even be combined to create new digital cable television channels to strengthen the package of television channels that Disney already owned (such as the Disney Channel, ESPN, and A&E).

As in the case of the other major mergers that occurred between entertainment giants Viacom and Paramount, and Time Warner and Turner, the claimed rational for the merger was that it linked entertainment production with the means of its distribution (by television, videocassette, and so forth). By 1995, he and other top entertainment executives were arguing that in the future companies needed to be involved in both of these sides of the business. Disney's top managers claimed that by acquiring Capital Cities/ABC they had secured Disney's future as the entertainment leader and given it the platform from which it could dominate the industry.

Many critics of the merger existed, however. Some industry analysts questioned the price tag of $19 billion that Disney had paid. They pointed out that Capital Cities/ABC was at the peak of its profitability when Disney made its offer because it was enjoying record advertising revenues (which are the main source of profitability of television and radio broadcasting). Its CEO, Tom Murphy, recognizing the premium that Disney was offering for the network, was therefore happy to jump at the Disney offer. Other critics also argued that the synergies Eisner claimed would result from the merger could easily have been achieved through a strategic alliance between the two companies over such issues as programming content and advertising revenues. In other words, the two companies could just as easily have entered into a written contract with each other to achieve these gains from cooperation. For example, Disney formed an alliance with Coca-Cola to promote that company's soft drinks in its operations and in 1996 formed an alliance with McDonald's under which the latter would be given the rights for ten years to use new Disney movies to promote foods in its restaurants. Disney did not have to merge with these companies to obtain synergies.

Critics even argued that the merger was unnecessary and would lock Disney into an unprofitable situation because the Big Three television networks only attracted 40 percent of the viewing audience by 1996 and this figure was falling because of the proliferation of new cable television channels and the increasing popularity of the Internet as a media resource. Disney's executives responded that by providing their new network with innovative Disney programming they would be able to increase its viewing audience. Moreover, as discussed previously, Disney could create new digital cable channels, opening up another major source of revenue. Finally some critics argued that Eisner was driven by ego, the desire to become the head of the world's biggest entertainment company at a time when other large entertainment companies, such as Viacom and Time Warner, were expanding their empires. Disney would be able to continue to grow its revenues at a fast pace as a result of the merger, they argued, but would its profits also be growing?

Events at ABC

Whatever the merits of each side of the argument, in 1995 the ABC network saw a precipitous drop in its share of the viewing audience as its prime-time ratings plunged. These ratings are vital because they determine how much the ABC network and its owned and affiliated television stations can charge advertisers. Eisner bought ABC when its ratings were very high, so that its advertising revenues were also high. The ratings had now fallen to a new low, and NBC, owned by General Electric, had become the new industry leader.

Another factor reducing the profitability of ABC was that Rupert Murdoch, the owner of the Fox Broadcasting network, had begun a battle with the Big Three networks to convince their television station affiliates to turn their allegiance to him and to switch to the Fox channel in return for large cash payments. Traditionally, the large networks had paid their affiliates nothing, expecting them to get their

revenue from local advertising linked to local news shows and syndications of rerun series. To stop their local television affiliates from jumping ship, ABC and the other Big Three networks had to make large cash payments to many of these stations, something that also drained ABC's profitability. Finally, ABC was under intense industry pressures of its own because of the changing nature of the broadcasting industry brought about by technological changes. The rapid rise in competition from new networks such as Rupert Murdoch's Fox network, Viacom's new United Paramount network, and even the new Microsoft/NBC 24 news channel were all emerging threats to ABC in the 1990s. In particular, since ABC was the most popular evening news channel, the emergence of alternative news channels posed a major threat.

Disney After the Merger

ABC's poor performance in the year following the merger brought its top management team under intense scrutiny from Eisner and Ovitz. Although before the merger it appeared that both organizations had similar cultures (both being managed by a strong CEO who had a hands-on approach), after the merger it became apparent that the two companies were very different. Eisner uses a very centralized management style and expects all his top managers to craft a five-year and ten-year plan for their business divisions to guide their future growth. He then evaluates them on the success with which they reach their division's performance goals, and with a plan to look at he can quickly intervene to take control if a division does not perform up to expectations. Thus, Disney's top managers know they are under constant scrutiny, and it is clear that Eisner is the person in charge of Disney's future strategy.

At ABC, however, the situation had been very different. In the television business, events change rapidly because a network's success depends on how well its shows are received on a week-by-week and month-by-month basis. For example, in 1992 ABC was the most successful of the Big Three networks and NBC was the least successful. Just three years later ABC's fall 1995 new show lineup bombed, while NBC's was a hit; their positions reversed. A television network's success rises and falls rapidly, unlike in the more stable movie business, where major movies may take three years to arrive at movie theaters from their initial conception.

Because of their shorter time horizon, ABC's executives typically used a one-year plan to guide their choices for the next year's programming. This conflicted with Eisner's desire for a longer strategic plan, and in 1996, it became clear that all was not going well between Disney's top management team and the team of managers in charge of ABC. As ABC's performance deteriorated in the fall of 1995, ABC executives came under even closer scrutiny, and they were forced to defend their every move to Disney's managers. As a result, several senior managers left ABC during this time as ABC's stressed-out managers tried to formulate a strategy to turn the division's fortunes around.

Major Problems for Eisner and Disney

It was July 1996, and Eisner and had just finished reading a *Wall Street Journal* article that was highly critical of the way they had handled top executives at ABC. The article argued that their close, hands-on management style resulted in conflict with key ABC executives that had caused their departures, thus delaying the process of obtaining the much needed synergies from the merger between the two companies. Moreover, industry analysts were still questioning whether the merger should have taken place at all.

Eisner was quick to sense that something needed to be done and done soon, and suddenly Eisner decided to oust Ovitz as president. Apparently, at least two of Disney's top managers refused to report to him, rather than Eisner, and he and Eisner had a major falling out over their respective roles at the top of the organization. The contract he had signed with Disney resulted in Ovitz receiving over $40 million in his severance package, and analysts and shareholders were astounded at what had happened. All of a sudden things seemed to have gone from bad to worse at Disney.

In fact, after his first decade of incredible success at Disney, Eisner's next decade as CEO was characterized by a major decrease in its performance and a plunging share price (until it recovered somewhat after 2003). The main reason for this was that Disney's entertainment assets, now organized into four major operating groups—media networks, studio entertainment, consumer products, and parks and resorts—began to perform poorly (see Exhibit 2). This was partly due to poor strategic decision making and partly due to changes in the environment that hurt the company's ability to realize value from its assets.

Problems in Media Networks

Disney's problems in its media properties, particularly its ABC network, continued to worsen over time

---

EXHIBIT 2

Walt Disney's Organizational Structure

and reached a low point in the summer of 2002, as did its share price. As analysts had expected, hundreds of new cable channels that were established throughout the 1990s further reduced the size of ABC's viewing audience, and the constant screening of Disney's programming on the ABC network was no longer attractive to today's viewing audience. Disney also continued to find it hard to develop hit shows, and it was not until 2004 with the introduction of hit shows such as *Desperate Housewives* and *Lost* that ABC's fortunes began to look up. In addition, the massive increase in the use of the Internet and growing access to broadband further cut into the time people spent viewing television programming. In particular, men between the age of eighteen to thirty-five, a critical audience for advertisers, were reducing the time they spent watching TV. The result was that reality programming grew in popularity, and ABC had its share of hits.

Disney, like all other media companies, was also hurt badly by the recession that occurred in the early 2000s that caused many consumer products companies to reduce their TV advertising budgets. Add to this the unpopularity of its ABC network—a falling, lower viewing audience reduces the amount Disney can charge TV advertisers— its advertising revenues fell by over 10 percent between 2000–2002, which drained its bottom line profitability and sunk its share price. By 2004, as the economy recovered and its evening lineup now contained hit shows, Disney's advertising revenues rose once again, and from its low, Disney's price almost doubled by 2005, although this was still well below its peak price.

In fact the brightest spot in Disney's media networks was its ESPN sports channels, because sports programming was one of the few areas in the 2000s where the TV viewing audience was increasing as the range of different kinds of sports being televised soared, along with the price of tickets to sporting events. Disney was able to charge cable TV companies higher fees to carry its ESPN and associated networks, and its ESPN sports channels largely escaped the problem of the overall decline in advertising revenues. By 2003, ESPN was a major contributor to Disney's profits and to the turnaround in its performance that began in late 2002.

In addition, like other media companies such as Viacom and Fox, Disney worked hard throughout the 1990s to build new cable channels to attract the specialized viewing audiences that advertisers increasingly targeted, such as the ESPN male viewing audience that is a major buyer of cars, pickups, home-delivered pizza, beer, fast food, and so on. Today ESPN is broadcast in over eighteen different languages in over 165 countries; its franchise is booming as the global popularity of many different kinds of sports programming is increasing.

In 2005, ESPN and Electronic Arts (EA), the home video game maker, announced a long-term agreement for the development and integrated marketing of EA SPORTS games containing ESPN content. The relationship will include established EA SPORTS franchises—which will be enhanced by ESPN telecast, print, and online content—as well as new sports games to be published by EA based on ESPN media properties. The agreement gives EA access to ESPN programming, personalities, and integrated marketing opportunities on ESPN television programming and other ESPN properties. The ESPN integration will appear in EA SPORTS console, handheld, PC, and wireless games beginning in 2006.

In sum, the continuing poor performance of the media division from 1995–2002 was a major factor contributing to the company's poor performance in the last decade, although problems also existed in Disney's other operating groups. At the company's annual meeting in February 2005, Disney CEO Michael Eisner and President Bob Iger told investors that Disney's management team is focused on producing world-class creative content across the company to drive growth over the long term in order to increase return on invested capital.

Problems in Studio Entertainment

During the last decade Disney also has experienced major problems in its studio entertainment group, which contains its major movie studios Walt Disney, Touchstone, and Miramax. The profitability of Disney's movies has continued to fall, and for a variety of reasons, it does not seem likely that this division will be a major source of growth in the future.

First, in its core animation movie business, its Disney Studios continued to experience major problems to create new popular animated movies that could be released each year to drive up revenues. *Pocahontas* was a success compared with subsequent movies like *Hercules* (1997), *Fantasia 2000, 102 Dalmatians* (2000), *Treasure Planet* (2002), and *Brother Bear* (2003), and these releases did little to help its bottom line. In response, Disney turned to releasing regular movies through this studio, such as *Pirates of the Caribbean*, its first PG-13 movie in 2003, and *Hidalgo*, its second PG-13 release in 2004.

Second, the shift to produce animated movies using computer-based digital technology accelerated in the 1990s, and Pixar and DreamWorks became the leaders in this movie genre. Disney had been fortunate to secure its contract with Pixar to distribute its films before the obvious advantages of digital technology became apparent. Its revenues from distributing Pixar movies such as *Toy Story* (1995), *Toy Story 2* (1999), *Monsters Inc.* (2001), *Finding Nemo* (2003), and the hugely successful *The Incredibles* (2004) became the biggest single source of the profits of the studio entertainment operating group. However, the Pixar contract was to expire in 2005, and Steve Jobs, Pixar's CEO, was reluctant to renew the contract with Disney. One major reason was apparently the hostile relationship between him and Eisner that had developed over time. Another reason was Disney's announcement in 2004 that in the future it would only make animated movies using the new computer-based technology, and the company began to layoff hundreds of the animators who had created its past successes. Disney's first digital movie, *Chicken Little*, was due to be released in the spring of 2005.

In early 2005, it was still unclear if Jobs, who had been offering the Pixar franchise to other movie distributors, would renew the contract with Disney. However, it appears that Jobs might be waiting until Eisner's successor had been named. The loss of Pixar's movies would be a major blow for Disney because analysts estimate that over 40 percent or about $1 billion of the operating income of its movie studios have come from its successes with Pixar. The final movie in process, *Cars*, was due to be released in 2005, and like *The Incredibles*, it took over two years to develop and bring to the screen.

Disney also continued to experience poor success with many of its regular feature film releases. For example, in 2003 and 2004 a string of flops, including movies such as *The Alamo*, *Miracle*, *Home on the Range*, and *Around the World in Eighty Days*, drained its movie studio's profits. In its own studios, the brightest spot was Miramax Pictures whose high-quality, but relatively low-budget movies continued to enjoy enormous commercial success and reaped many

Oscars for the studio. In 2005, however, the Weinstein brothers, who have been attributed with producing its successful movies, also decided to leave the studio they founded after major disputes with Eisner and Disney over increasing studio operating costs. So the future success of this studio was uncertain in 2005.

Problems in Consumer Products

Several major developments also led to problems in Disney's consumer products group, which, although not a major contributor to its revenues (see Exhibit 3), helped to significantly reduce its profit margins. First, Disney's success with its ESPN sports networks prompted Eisner to purchase two major sports team franchises, the Mighty Ducks of Anaheim hockey team and the Anaheim Angels baseball team. However, Disney had no experience operating sports franchises, and both these ventures began to lose money. In response, in 2004 Eisner decided to reverse course and find a buyer for these assets; by 2005, only the Anaheim Angels had been divested.

Second, one of the drivers of Disney's profits in Eisner's early years was the decision to release its classic movies on videotape. However, that meant by 2000 Disney was no longer able to rerelease these movies in movie theaters, and with millions of Disney videos and DVDs in circulation, and movie video piracy rampant, its revenues from this source fell sharply. Moreover, its lack of a string of new hit movies that

EXHIBIT 3

Financial Highlights, 2004 ($ in millions)

Operating Group	2004		
	Revenue	Operating Income	Operating Profit Margin %
Media Networks	$11,778	$2,169	18.4
Parks and Resorts	7,750	1,123	14.4
Studio Entertainment	8,713	662	7.6
Consumer Products	2,511	534	2.1
Total	**$30,752**	**$4,488**	**14.6**

could be profitably released on DVD also did nothing to help its consumer product revenues at a time when DVD sales were exploding because consumers, attracted by the falling price of DVDs, began to build their own movie collections. In fact, movie and music digital piracy has reduced the revenues of most major media companies, which is why Disney agreed in 2004 to join the Blu-Ray consortium and use its new digital media encryption technology that is intended to make such activity impossible in the future.

By 2000, it was clear that Eisner's decision to open the Disney Store chain to sell its Disney merchandise at premium prices was also a disastrous investment decision as these stores began to lose more and more money. Disney's management had not understood the specific competitive problems that exist in the retail store industry, such as intense price competition and high inventory holding and store maintenance costs that make profit margins thin. Disney began to search for a buyer for its stores, and in 2004, it finally found a buyer in the Children's Place retail store chain which agreed to buy Disney's 335 stores and the right to sell Disney's merchandise in these stores. The Children's Place hopes that by operating Disney stores in conjunction with its other store chain it will be able to cut operating expenses and so make a profit. Disney will continue to receive a percentage of revenues from the sale of its products in these stores. A better strategy for Disney from the beginning would have been to distribute an exclusive line of its products through one or more specialized retailers like Toys "R" Us, which would have helped the bottom lines of both of these companies.

In sum, while promoting sales of Disney's consumer products had been seen in the 1990s as a way to leverage its resources and reap synergies from its theme parks and movie assets, in practice the way Disney implemented this strategy has proved to be a major liability and hurt its performance in the 2000s. The issue today is which businesses the company should compete in and how to market and distribute its products in a way that will maximize the profitability of sales.

Problems in Theme Parks and Resorts

Disney's theme parks have also turned in mixed performance over the last several years for a variety of reasons. Faced with increasing competition from other theme park companies such as MGM Studios, Six Flags, and the plethora of attractions that have opened up in Orlando, Disney was forced to spend billions of dollars to build new rides and modernize its Anaheim and Orlando properties to protect its famous franchise. However, just after it had spent $5 billion to enhance these franchises in the early 2000s, disasters such as the September 11 tragedy and the SARS epidemic that started in Asia occurred. These events, combined with the general world recession that started in the early 2000s, significantly reduced the volume of world air travel and the number of domestic and overseas visitors to Disney's parks, once again eroding profit margins.

However, Disney's attention to improving the quality of its properties while keeping costs in check started to pay off in 2004 as the number of visitors increased sharply and profit margins once again rose by 2003 as Exhibit 3 shows. Certainly, Disney World, with its four theme parks, remains the number one tourist attraction in the world and is one of its most important assets.

The performance of Disney's overseas theme parks has also been erratic. The Japanese Disney park continues to prosper, but the company only receives a small percentage of the profits of that enterprise. The French theme park has continued to perform poorly, so poorly in fact that Disney has allowed the park to forgo its yearly royalties to the Disney Company to keep the park viable in the hope that it will prosper once the global economy regains momentum. The park is Europe's number one tourist destination, but European vacationers spend less than the tourists that visit its U.S. parks and resorts. Disney's newest theme park is slated to open in Hong Kong. In 2005, Disney and the Hong Kong SAR Government announced that Hong Kong Disneyland is expected to welcome its first guests on September 12, 2005, earlier than originally projected. The world-class theme park and resort, located on Lantau Island, will be Disney's first theme park in China, offering the typical Disney magical experiences and signature attractions such as fireworks and parades. Disney has a significant stake in this venture, and if it enjoys the success of the Japanese park, which seems likely given the rate at which Asian economies are developing and prospering, this will increase the profitability of this operating group in the years ahead.

Finally, Disney's decision to enter the cruise line industry also proved to be a major financial disappointment. Once again the costs of operating a handful of cruise ships are much greater than the cost of operating hundreds, as Carnival Cruise Line does, because of the lack of economies of scale. So, despite Disney's ability to charge customers a premium price for the Disney experience at sea, that venture also did little or nothing to help the company's profitability. However, this operating group is also unlikely to be a driver of the kind of revenue growth that propels a company's value, although it has been and should continue to be a generator of cash for investment that Disney needs to make much better use of in the years ahead.

Governance Problems at Disney

Although it was unlikely that Eisner or any CEO could hope to maintain the rapid growth in revenues and profits that the company experienced in the first decade of his leadership, its relatively poor performance in the last decade has caused many analysts to question the soundness of Eisner's strategy for the company. The debacle over the departure of two seconds in command, Jeffrey Katzenberg and Steven Ovitz; the charge that Eisner's micromanagement of the company has reduced the level of innovation in the company; top management's inability so far to realize real synergies from the ABC/Capital Cities merger; the failure of the many ventures into new industries; and the growing competition from rivals such as Viacom, Fox, and Dream Works has all led to increasing criticism of Eisner. The company is lucky it acquired the ESPN networks as a part of the ABC merger for this seems to be the main source of its current growth in revenues and profits.

Eisner's decision to close down the animation studio in favor of computer animation also brought him into conflict with Roy Disney, who had been the head of that division which he championed because of its links to the past. Roy Disney, with the support of some other major disgruntled investors, began to publicly challenge Eisner's leadership of the company and began a campaign to oust Eisner as CEO. The dispute between Eisner and his opponents became very bitter as the performance of the company continued to suffer in the 2000s, and in February 2004, 43 percent of Disney stockholders supported a vote of no confidence in Eisner's leadership that led him to resign as chairman although he remained CEO.

In the midst of this dissent, Comcast, one of the two largest cable TV providers in the United States, took advantage of Disney's apparent weakness to launch a hostile takeover bid for the company, which Comcast valued at $66 billion. After several months it became clear that investors thought this bid was inadequate, and as noted earlier, Disney's performance began to recover in 2003–2004. So both these events lifted its stock price, and Comcast withdrew its offer for the company although some analysts expect it to try again at some point.

In the meantime, however, Eisner had not been able to escape from the criticism that he was no longer the right person to lead the company. Led by Roy Disney, many investors began to question corporate governance at Disney. As noted earlier, Eisner has always had a hands-on approach to running the business: He wants to be involved in every major business decision, and he keeps a tight reign on his managers. He has been criticized because although past sixty years old he would not publicly lay out a succession plan indicating which managers will assume the top roles in Disney after he steps down.

In addition, Eisner has been criticized for creating a weak or captive Board of Directors that has been unable or unwilling to scrutinize and question his business decisions over the last decade. In the last twenty years, Eisner had created a sixteen-member Board of Directors in the company, at least eight of whom had strong personal ties to him. Over that same period, Eisner has received more than a billion in salary, stock options, and so on from the company and enjoyed all the lavish perks that most CEOs of large companies receive today.

So in 2004 the new chairman of the board of the company began the process of reorganizing its Board of Directors to reduce Eisner's influence over it. For example, two new special outside directors were appointed, one of whom chairs two board meetings a year that Eisner—who used to chair these meetings—is not permitted to attend. While Disney's board now has more freedom to assess Eisner's performance, many analysts claim these changes were still not enough because the majority of the board is still beholden to him and he controls all Disney's important committees. Nevertheless, to avoid another major fight with Roy Disney and his supporters in the fall of 2004, Eisner announced that he would not seek another term as CEO when his contract expired in 2006, as noted earlier.

In the spring of 2005, no successor had been named as the new CEO of Disney, despite an earlier feeling that one should be named before Eisner would be forced to resign as CEO when his contract expired in 2006. His handpicked successor, Robert Iger, is waiting in the wings, and of course should he be appointed, it is very possible that Eisner will turn over the reins to him and become Disney's new chairman. In this case he would continue to have enormous influence over Disney's future strategy. In February 2005, Disney's twelve directors received a vote of support at its annual meeting, and the doubling of its stock price over the past two years has made many investors more receptive to Eisner. However, it seems likely that more fireworks are ahead in the battle over who will become Disney's new CEO and chairman—fireworks that may make Disney's nightly display in its Orlando EPCOT center pale in comparison.

Case 27

First Greyhound, Then Greyhound Dial, Then Dial, Now Henkel-Dial

This case was prepared by Gareth R. Jones, Texas A&M University.

It was the end of 2003, and Herbert Baum, Dial's CEO, was reflecting on the performance of the company since he had been brought in to engineer a turnaround in 2000. He had sold off underperforming product lines and invested heavily in building Dial's core products like Dial soap. By April 2002, he had been happy to report a rebound in Dial's earnings, which sent its share soaring from the lows it had reached in April 2001, when its earnings plunged by 69 percent due to the poor strategic decisions of his predecessor. Now the question was what to do? Should he continue to build Dial's portfolio of brand name products and strive to keep the company independent? Or should he sell off the company, either as a whole or in parts, to other companies that would now be prepared to pay a high price for its strong brand name products? While pondering this question, Baum thought that the history of the company, which had started out as Greyhound, might provide him with some important clues.

Greyhound's Early History and Growth

Greyhound was founded in Hibbing, Minnesota, in 1914. Its first business was providing bus transportation to carry miners to work at the Mesabi Iron Range.

Copyright © 2005 by Gareth R. Jones. This case was prepared by Gareth R. Jones, Texas A&M University, as the basis for class discussion rather than to illustrate either effective or ineffective handling of an administrative situation. Reprinted by permission of Gareth R. Jones. All rights reserved. For the most recent financial results of the company discussed in this case, go to **http://finance.yahoo.com**, input the company's stock symbol, and download the latest company report from its homepage.

Because Greyhound was the sole provider of bus service for these workers, it was immediately successful. In its very first year, the new corporation started expanding its routes and acquiring interests in bus companies operating near Chicago. For the next sixteen years, the young company continued purchasing interests in bus companies, extending its route structure from New York to Kansas City. In 1930, the name *Greyhound Corporation* was adopted, and the now-familiar running-dog logo was painted on the buses.

For the next twenty-seven years, Greyhound continued to acquire bus interests in order to consolidate its routes and link its various bus operations. Growth proceeded sometimes by purchase, sometimes by stock swaps, and sometimes by merger. However, the result was always the same to the traveling public: It saw more and more of the familiar running dog. By 1960, Greyhound had substantially achieved its objective of operating a bus system that could carry passengers to most destinations in the continental United States and Canada.

By 1962, however, Greyhound was facing the prospect of increasingly limited opportunities to expand its route system; in the company's favor was the fact that bus operations were generating large sums of excess cash, which could fund expansion into new businesses. So Greyhound's Board of Directors decided to diversify into operations outside the bus transportation industry.

In that same year, Greyhound began the program of acquisition that turned it into a conglomerate. It solidified its bus-manufacturing operations into Motor

Coach Industries, which became the foundation of Greyhound Dial's transportation manufacturing operating division. Also in 1962, the corporation acquired Boothe Leasing Company, an enterprise that specialized in equipment leasing. Boothe Leasing was renamed Greyhound Leasing and became the core business around which Greyhound's financial services division was to be built. Thus, by the end of 1963, Greyhound Corporation was operating in three major businesses: bus transportation, bus manufacturing, and financial services. Bus manufacturing supplied buses to bus transportation as well as to other bus companies.

Acquisitions Between 1966 and 1970

Gerry Trautman was appointed CEO in 1966, and he wasted no time in accelerating Greyhound's new strategy for expansion and growth. From Trautman's installation as CEO until 1970, Greyhound acquired more than thirty widely different companies and formed a new operating division—services—that specialized in managing transportation-related businesses, such as Border Brokerage Company, which operated two duty-free shops at the Canadian border, and Florida Export Group, which also handled duty-free commerce. In addition, the services division included Manncraft Exhibitors, a company that specialized in building displays for major exhibitions; Nassau Air Dispatch, a Caribbean shipping company; and Freeport Flight Services, a Bahamian aircraft-servicing business. Trautman also brought in a line of cruise ships in the Caribbean, the Bahama Cruise Line Company. Then he added companies as diverse as Ford Van Lines of Lincoln, Nebraska, a company specializing in furniture moving; Red Top Sedan Service, a Florida limousine service; two regional intercity bus lines; Washington Airport Transport, a commuter carrier from the Washington, D.C., suburbs to Dulles Airport; and Gray Line New York Tours Corporation, a sightseeing bus line. Furthermore, he added Hausman Bus Parts to the bus-manufacturing unit.

Not all the companies that Trautman acquired proved to be as profitable or as manageable as he had hoped. What he was looking for was value, as well as some synergy with Greyhound's existing transportation activities. However, as the acquisition process continued, synergy became a secondary objective. When Trautman became dissatisfied with an acquisition, he would divest it as quickly as he had acquired it, and many companies were spun off. Near the end of his tenure as CEO, Trautman would boast that Greyhound had achieved "diversification within diversification." What he meant was that in his view the operating groups had become diversified, so that each individually was recession-proof and all were enhancing the financial strength of the holding company.

Trautman's boldest maneuver and biggest acquisition came in 1970. He acquired Armour & Co., another large conglomerate that had many diverse business interests in food and consumer products. Trautman paid $400 million in cash, notes, and stock to take over Armour, which was primarily a large meat-packing company with more than $2 billion of sales in marginally profitable businesses. However, Armour also had interests in pharmaceuticals, cosmetics, and consumer products such as soap through its very profitable Dial division. Trautman knew that it appeared as though he had overpaid for Armour-Dial. However, he soon reduced the price of the acquisition by selling off, for some $225 million, a number of Armour's divisions that he considered to be peripheral to Armour's core food and consumer businesses. In 1977, he sold off Armour's pharmaceutical division for $87 million, reducing Greyhound's net investment to $88 million. What remained after the divestitures were Armour's food operations and Armour's Dial division, from which would emerge Greyhound Dial's consumer products operating division.

Trautman hoped that his new acquisition would be more recession-proof than the bus business, if not countercyclical to it. However, the Armour acquisition brought to Greyhound new businesses that had management problems of their own in areas in which Greyhound had no experience, such as the price of pork bellies, cycles for meat packers' contracts, and foreign competition.

Trautman's Acquisitions and Divestitures Between 1970 and 1978

For the next eight years, Greyhound under Trautman continued buying businesses and increasing the size of the operating divisions in its corporate portfolio. By 1978, Greyhound's holding company consisted of five operating divisions: transportation, bus manufacturing, food and consumer products, financial, and services/food service. Each of these operating divisions acquired many new businesses, so that Greyhound was still undergoing "diversification within diversification." Many of the new acquisitions, however, were failures. Businesses as diverse as a chicken hatchery, a European acquisition to expand the financial services group, and various transportation businesses (Caribbean Gray Cruise Line, Ltd., VAVO Greyhound N.V. of Schoonhoven, Netherlands, Shannon-Greyhound Coaches, and Hausman Bus Parts) proved unprofitable.

Greyhound's portfolio of businesses kept changing during this period, and Trautman continued to feel that he was shaping a diversified company that would have a powerful base in many lines of business. He was willing to take the risk of acquiring some companies that would be failures as long as the overall health of the company was strengthened. However, Greyhound became more and more distant from its core business—bus transportation.

In April 1978, Trautman engineered another major acquisition by acquiring 97 percent of the stock of Verex Corporation, the largest private insurer of residential mortgages in the United States. The Verex acquisition was intended to strengthen the operations of Greyhound's financial operating division. Verex insured first mortgages on residential real estate generally having loan-to-value ratios in excess of 80 percent.

By 1978, Greyhound had grown nearly as large as it would grow under Trautman's leadership. The collection of businesses that he had assembled—some by acquisition, some by internal growth, and some by selling off pieces of larger businesses—was designed to make Greyhound more resistant to economic downturns. The activities of Greyhound's five major operating divisions are summarized below.

■ *Transportation.* This operating division comprised the intercity services division and the travel services division. Transportation operated regularly scheduled passenger bus service between most metropolitan areas in North America and engaged in related operations, such as package shipping, sightseeing services, airport ground transportation, and deluxe tour and charter bus services.

■ *Bus manufacturing.* The largest maker of intercity buses in North America, the bus-manufacturing division had operations that were vertically integrated to fabricate bus shells of intercity design, assemble buses, and manufacture bus parts for final assembly. In addition, this operating division

warehoused and distributed replacement parts to meet its own requirements and the larger requirements of the bus industry. Greyhound bus manufacturing was the principal U.S. supplier of buses to charter operators and sightseeing companies.

■ *Food and consumer products.* The companies in this operating group manufactured and marketed products to independent retailers under private-label arrangements and distributed several products under their own trademarks. These trademarks included Dial, Tone, and Pure & Natural soaps, Armour Star and Armour Tree canned meat and meat food products, Dial antiperspirants and shampoos, Appian Way pizza mixes, Parsons' ammonia, Bruce floor care products, Magic sizing and prewash, and Malina handknitting yarns and needle products.

■ *Services/food service.* Companies in this operating division provided a broad range of services directed primarily to business markets, although duty-free shops located at airports and on cruise ships were targeted toward the consumer market. Greyhound convention services (GCS) specialized in designing, fabricating, warehousing, shipping, and setting up exhibits for trade shows, conventions, and exhibitions. GCS also served as a decorating contractor at conventions and trade show sites. The food service division, generally known as Greyhound food management (GFM), served approximately twenty-four hundred locations in industrial plants, bus terminals, airports, office buildings, schools, colleges, and other facilities.

■ *Financial.* This operating division consisted of Greyhound Computer Corporation, a company specializing in computer leasing and sales in the United States, Canada, Mexico, and Europe; Greyhound Leasing and Financial Corporation, a company specializing in worldwide industrial equipment leasing; Pine Top Insurance, an entity that reinsured commercial property and provided excess casualty insurance for large policyholders; and Verex Corporation, the leading private insurer of highly leveraged residential mortgages for primary lenders. Travelers Express Company, Inc., another company in the financial division, specialized in providing travelers' checks and check-cashing services in thirty-two thousand retail establishments and financial institutions in the mainland United States and Puerto Rico.

Together, those five operating divisions were generating combined revenues of nearly $4.5 billion. Trautman had accomplished his objective of using profits from the bus operations to move Greyhound into other businesses.

Trautman Selects Teets to Take over Greyhound

Serious problems became apparent at Armour when the food and consumer products operating division went from a profit of $22 million in 1979 to a loss of $1.7 million in 1980. Armour's problems came at a very inconvenient time for Trautman because he had planned to retire in 1980. Trautman wanted to solve Armour's difficulties while he kept business rolling at Greyhound's other groups and prepared a successor to take over the collection of companies that he had assembled. That successor was to be John Teets.

Teets was very different from Trautman. His background did not include Harvard Business School or law practice. Instead, Teets had learned to be an effective hands-on manager by staying as close to the action as possible. He had worked for his father's construction company but decided that he wanted to operate a restaurant. He borrowed money, started his own restaurant, and quickly made it successful. However, soon after he had paid back his loan money and his restaurant was earning a profit, it burned to the ground. In search of a new business opportunity, Teets answered a newspaper advertisement about a position managing a Greyhound food service concession stand at the New York World's Fair in 1964.

After joining the services/food service operating group, Teets quickly distinguished himself as a tight-fisted cost cutter who could make money on a miserly budget. He seemed to have a talent for squeezing every last penny out of everything he managed. Teets moved up quickly, gaining a reputation as an extremely effective manager. By 1975, he was put in charge of the food service group, which primarily operated a conglomeration of marginally profitable, obscure, franchised restaurants. His aggressive management style produced quick results, and in 1980, he was named the outstanding executive in the food industry. Also in 1980, in addition to Teets's responsibilities as CEO of the food service group, Trautman named Teets to head Armour and turn around the division's performance.

In 1981, Armour's major problem, as Teets saw it, was that it was paying 30 to 50 percent more in wages and fringe benefits than its competitors. Teets asked Armour's unions for immediate wage concessions. He told the unions that if he failed to get the concessions, he would have to start closing plants. After a bitter strike, wage concessions in excess of 15 percent were obtained. Given these concessions, the cost cutting from plant closings, and more efficient operating procedures, it looked as though Armour had bought itself some time.

With Armour running more efficiently, the bus business cruising along on excess profits because of the recession and energy crunch in 1979–1980, and high profits in its financial operating division generated by high interest rates in the early 1980s, it seemed that the stage was set for Trautman's retirement. In fact, all that remained was to formally select a successor. It was not difficult for Trautman to make up his mind about who that should be. He was impressed with Teets's successes in managing the services/food service group and also with the way in which Teets had dominated Armour's labor unions.

Teets Seeks Solutions

In 1981, John Teets succeeded Gerry Trautman as the chief executive officer of the Greyhound Corporation. The challenge facing Teets was to manage Greyhound's diverse businesses so that he would be able to achieve at least a 15 percent return on equity. However, many problems on the horizon might hinder the achievement of this goal. Some were the direct consequence of Trautman's ambitious expansion and diversification efforts. Others resulted from changes in environmental factors and consumer preferences. Still others stemmed from internal inefficiencies that Teets hoped he would be able to remedy.

Two challenges in particular caused Teets to feel uneasy about the corporation's overall profit picture. The first problem was Armour's high production costs, which made it a weak competitor. The second was the challenge faced by Greyhound Bus Lines: the need to compete in a newly deregulated bus transportation market. He knew that if he did not find solutions for these two problems, they would seriously diminish the Greyhound Corporation's earnings. The contribution of each operating division to Greyhound's total sales revenues in 1981 is presented in Figure 1.

FIGURE 1

Greyhound in 1981

Source: Data from Greyhound Dial Corporation, Annual Report, 1990.

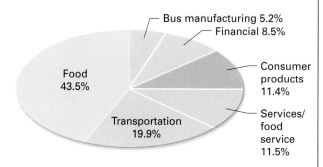

business would be based not on the extensiveness of Greyhound's route system or its fifty years of experience in operating in a regulated industry but on its ability to make money by charging competitive fares.

With the beginning of deregulated competition in the intercity bus business and declining passenger revenues resulting from the end of the energy crunch, Greyhound found itself paying wages and benefits that were 30 to 50 percent higher than those paid by its competitors. Furthermore, its chief competitor, Trailways, having negotiated significant wage concessions from the Amalgamated Transit Union, had immediately passed the savings on to customers in the form of lower fares. Trailways's action was a frontal assault on Greyhound's most lucrative routes in an attempt to gain market share. Greyhound's response was to match every one of Trailways's price cuts. Although Greyhound preserved its market share, it lost millions of dollars.

For Greyhound Bus Lines, the legacy of deregulation was a total inability to be a low-cost provider of bus transportation. Deregulation had brought about the emergence of lower-cost competitors in regional markets, competitors that were able to be responsive and flexible in pricing and in reacting to Greyhound's actions. As a result, Greyhound lost its competitive edge. In 1986, in an effort to save the bus lines, Teets converted 120 company-owned terminals to commission agencies, trimming a huge overhead burden. He also created four stand-alone regional bus companies and a new travel and charter company. Finally, he franchised several of Greyhound's least profitable routes to independent operators, licensing them to use the Greyhound logo and trademark.

However, the one factor that Teets could not control was winning a new labor contract. In February 1986, an offer to freeze wages was rejected by the union. In October, in a deteriorating market, a second offer involving concessions was presented with the understanding that its rejection would prompt the sale of the company. The offer was subsequently rejected, and fifteen days later Teets announced the sale of Greyhound Bus Lines for approximately $350 million to an investor group headquartered in Dallas. Teets claimed that the actions taken by management in an effort to salvage the bus business were exactly the ones that made it an attractive acquisition for the Currey Group in Dallas.

The sale of Greyhound Bus Lines brought in $290 million in cash and equivalents, including a

Dealing With Armour's High Production Costs

Having been president of Armour, Teets was very familiar with the division's problems: its high production costs, the reluctance of union leadership and rank-and-file workers to agree with Greyhound's assessment of Armour's problems, and its utter inability to successfully change its marketing orientation to compete effectively. In addition, Teets was concerned about Armour's inefficient plants and the volatility of hog and pork-belly prices, which cyclically depressed Armour's 1981 profit of $9 million and represented a profit margin of less than 0.39 percent on sales of more than $2.3 billion. Teets sensed that it was not going to be easy to make Armour a low-cost leader. Thus, he decided to divest Armour.

In preparation for the sale, he separated the Armour Food Company from Armour-Dial. On December 18, 1983, the food company was sold to ConAgra, Inc., for $166 million. With the Armour sale, Teets was chopping off nearly half of Greyhound's business. Nevertheless, even with Greyhound's revenues dropping from $5 billion in 1982 to less than $3 billion in 1984 without Armour, the sale gave Teets the opportunity to put Greyhound in better shape than it had been in years.

The Bus Line Divestiture

Teets was also concerned about the 1981 passage of House bill H.R. 3663, which deregulated the intercity bus business. Greyhound Bus Lines had based its route system on the competitive conditions that had existed in the earlier business environment. Teets, however, sensed that future success in the bus

22.5 percent interest in a new holding company established by the Dallas investor group.

Divestitures in the Financial Operating Division

Besides selling Greyhound Bus Lines in 1987, Teets also sold Greyhound Capital Corporation (GCC). The decision to sell GCC reportedly reflected Teets's conviction that "some businesses just fit better into Greyhound's plans than others." What this statement really meant was that GCC had become an underperformer in the face of lowered interest rates and changes in the tax laws that disallowed investment tax credits. GCC was sold for $140 million, realizing a one-time gain of $79.7 million for Greyhound.

In early 1987, Greyhound announced its intention to sell Verex. The timing of the acquisition had been a disaster, given the recession in the real estate market caused by the oil bust in the early 1980s. Verex suffered huge losses generated by insurance claims from business generated before 1985. These claims were originating in states where severe downturns in farming, auto production, and oil drilling had led to a widespread inability to keep up with mortgage payments.

Not surprisingly, Teets could not find a buyer for Verex. In January 1988, Greyhound announced that it had stopped taking applications for new mortgage insurance and that it was discontinuing its mortgage insurance business. It also announced that 1987 results would reflect a one-time aftertax charge of $45 million as a result of reclassifying Verex as a discontinued operation; then Greyhound would manage Verex's existing portfolio to minimize continuing losses from the company's operations. Management hoped the remnants of Verex would not be a drain on corporate resources.

With the sale of Greyhound Bus Lines, Greyhound Capital Corporation, and Armour, and with the discontinuation of Verex, Teets announced that he was near the end of his mammoth task of restructuring Greyhound and shedding businesses that seemed to lack sufficient growth potential. By late 1987, Greyhound Corporation was primarily a consumer products and services company. Figure 2 summarizes the contribution of the different operating groups to total revenues in 1988. Compare the Greyhound Corporation that Teets structured (Figure 2) with the corporation he inherited in 1982 (Figure 1).

FIGURE 2

Total Revenues: $3.3 Billion

Source: Data from Greyhound Dial Corporation, Annual Report, 1990.

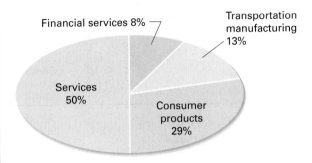

With the restructuring in place, Wall Street looked for an improvement in Greyhound's performance. However, it soon became obvious that the stack of businesses created by Teets was not proving much more profitable than the ones he had divested. There was only an 8.8 percent return on equity in 1987, and net income after nonrecurring losses was $25.1 million, the lowest for many years. Revenue was $2.5 billion. Teets maintained that the problems with Greyhound's various divisions could not have been foreseen as the restructuring was taking place but that Greyhound was set for "substantial profits in the future." Teets began a program of acquisitions and new product developments to strengthen Greyhound's presence in the four business areas identified in Figure 2 and to begin the turnaround process.

Consumer Products

In the midst of the divestiture of Armour and Greyhound Bus Lines, Teets had made one major acquisition. On February 21, 1985, he announced the purchase of Purex Industries and its thirty household cleaning products for $264 million. Teets's aim with this acquisition was to boost profits in Greyhound's Consumer Products operating division (principally composed of the old Dial division) by using the Dial sales force and marketing expertise to sell Purex products—Purex bleach, Brillo soap pads, Old Dutch cleanser, and Sweetheart and Fels-Naptha soap, among others.

The Purex acquisition drew mixed reviews from Wall Street. It did not meet Teets's goal of a 15 percent return, but Teets believed that it would by 1988. Analysts were also unimpressed with the purchase because Greyhound had not been successful in managing Armour. Teets responded that Dial was capable of marketing consumer products, although it had not been successful at developing its own lines. He cited as evidence the fact that Dial was marketing the number one deodorant soap in its Dial brand. Analysts did concede that Teets should be able to realize increased profitability by using the same sales force to sell Purex and Dial products. Along with Purex's household cleaners, Greyhound also got Elio's Pizza as part of the Purex acquisition. Teets was enthusiastic about expanding this frozen pizza business nationwide from its East Coast base. This was to be done by means of the Dial sales force.

The Dial operating division, as it was now known, became the center of Teets's attention and the flagship of the Greyhound Corporation. In the past Dial had not had much success in launching new products, but Teets was determined to change the situation, recognizing that growth in revenue had to come from the manufacture and marketing of new products. The first product introduced by the Dial division was Lunch Buckets, a range of microwavable meals with a stable shelf life of two years. This was a new market segment. Previously all microwavable meals had been frozen. Lunch Buckets meals were very successful and surpassed early expectations by a wide margin. By 1988, they had national distribution. By 1990, they had seized a 30 percent market share, becoming the market leader. In 1990, Dial announced new low-calorie Lunch Buckets.

Another new product introduced in 1987 was Liquid Dial antibacterial soap. This product, too, was very successful, and by 1990, it had achieved a 20 percent market share and was the second best-selling liquid soap in the market, after Procter & Gamble's Ivory liquid. Another successful new product was Mountain Fresh Dial, a highly scented version of Dial's deodorant soap. Additional developments were liquid Purex detergent and other cleaning products.

In 1988, Teets acquired the household products and industrial specialties businesses of the 20 Mule Team division of United States Borax and Chemical Corporation. Teets announced a new advertising campaign to reestablish the market presence of Borax bleaches and cleaning powders. Teets's formula for increasing the Dial division's market share called for

further extensions of the Dial brand, further extensions of the Purex brand name, and Parsons' ammonia.

Greyhound Dial, Then Dial

On June 4, 1990, Teets learned that Greyhound Bus lines, the bus transportation company that he had sold in 1987, had declared bankruptcy and Greyhound's stake was now valueless. To distance his "new" company from Greyhound, he changed the company's name to Greyhound Dial in February 1990, and the next year it became simply Dial. The name change also marked the company's new focus on its consumer products division. However, the price of Dial's stock, which had been more or less unchanged for the last six years, started to plunge in 1990 after Dial reported a loss. Analysts wondered whether Teets would ever be able to improve the company's profitability.

In September 1990, another consumer products acquisition was announced: Breck hair care products. Breck had 1989 revenues of $60 million. Teets announced that integrating Breck into Dial would result in annual sales of more than $1 billion for the Dial division. Teets said that "Breck has been a household name for 60 years. It's a perfect fit with our other Dial products and under Dial management the power of the Breck name will flourish." Under its previous owners, Breck had languished. Teets hoped to turn the product around by applying Dial's marketing skills.

From the changes he had orchestrated, Teets was hoping for sizable revenue growth and profit from the Dial division, and in March 1991, as an indication of the company's future strategy, the company's name was again changed, to the Dial Corporation.

Services

By 1987, the restaurant food services division was contributing the most to total revenues. It was natural, therefore, that Teets should seek to strengthen food operations. In 1987, Dial purchased the nation's second biggest airline catering and airline retailing business. The new operation had three units: Dobbs International Services, the nation's second largest provider of in-flight meals for airlines; Dobbs Houses, the operator of restaurants at many airports; and Carson International, which operated the food and beverage concession at Chicago's O'Hare Airport.

In 1990, Teets announced that Dobbs had had a record year—the company had served sixty scheduled airlines in forty cities. Moreover, it had added five new accounts, including Houston International Airport.

Teets strengthened Dial's Travelers Express money order business with the purchase of Republic Money Orders, Inc., of Dallas. This acquisition made Dial the leader in the money order business, ahead of the U.S. Postal Service. Teets had returned to the cruise ship industry in 1984 with the takeover of Premier Cruise Lines. In 1986, he negotiated an agreement with the Walt Disney Company that made Dial's Premier Cruise Line Disney's exclusive cruise ship line, with three- and four-day sailing to the Bahamas from Cape Canaveral in Florida. The cruise line business enjoyed record sales, and in 1989, another line was added.

The New Look of the Dial Corporation

The new look of Dial's businesses after the acquisitions and divestitures is shown in Table 1. Teets acknowledged the wide diversity of businesses in the company's portfolio. However, he contended that the businesses did fit together. In his words, "We are a multiservice business. We operate in niches and were number one or two in most of these niches. From a recession standpoint, I think we're going to feel it less than most major companies." Teets argued that Dial was making acquisitions to strengthen its presence in existing niches. By concentrating on a niche, the corporation avoided going head-to-head with major competitors. Moreover, the niches were recession-proof, small-ticket items such as Lunch Buckets and soap, not refrigerators and cars. Teets argued that Dial was positioned for growth and that management expected revenues to increase steadily over the next few years. See Table 2.

Some analysts, however, felt that the organization was still a hodgepodge of different businesses in need of rationalization. They pointed to the lack of fit between a cruise ship line and hotel operations in Glacier National Park and contract catering, saying that Dial was still a collection of companies with no real connection. They also argued that Greyhound Dial's breakup value was more than $60 a share, while its stock price had been in the range of $25 to $35 for years. Teets agreed that some minor divestitures were

necessary, but he believed that the best way to proceed was to stay in the same niches and manage the existing businesses more efficiently.

Dial, 1990–1996

Finally it appeared that, at last, things were going Dial's way. Dial's share price, which had plummeted to less than $10 a share at the end of 1990, rose to almost $25 a share by the end of 1992. This turn-around occurred for several reasons. First, Dial had finally spun off its loss-making financial services group to stockholders so that the liabilities no longer affected its balance sheet. Second, its consumer products group, and in particular the Dial soap division, was performing strongly. Dial had become the number one selling deodorant soap in the United States, with more than 20 percent of the market. Third, Teets had orchestrated a major downsizing, or what he had called "rightsizing," reducing the number of corporate managers from four hundred to three hundred. Also, all of Dial's different businesses were subjected to close scrutiny to try to reduce costs, and employment was reduced across the board, even in the successful Dial division. Teets also reduced corporate debt from a high of $850 million to $550 million through the sales of certain assets such as Dobbs House, its airport catering company. Analysts hoped that all these events were the first signs of a turnaround in the company's performance.

These hopes were doomed, however, by a series of problems that emerged in Dial's various businesses. In the 1990s, businesses in Dial's transportation manufacturing unit began to perform poorly, draining the company's profits. In 1993, Teets decided to dispose of it. Also, its Purex bleach business was doing poorly and losing money. It began to seem that just when Dial was making strides in one of its businesses, problems in another were wiping out the effects of the improvement. Investors began to wonder again about Teets's claims for his recession-proof niche strategy.

By 1995, major problems were affecting many areas of the company, including the pivotal Dial division. Teets, desperate to increase the company's return on equity and stock price, which had been flat since its high in 1992, began again to slash costs. One way he did this was by reducing the advertising budget for Dial soap products from $8.7 million to $4.9 million. However, this was something that no niche player could afford to do when battling such industry giants as Procter & Gamble and Unilever,

TABLE 1

Greyhound's Businesses

Consumer Products	Services	Transportation Manufacturing	Financial Services

The Dial Corporation
  Food
  Personal care
  Laundry and
  household
	Brewster Transport Company, Ltd.
	Consultants and Designers, Inc.
	Carson International, Inc.
	Dobbs Houses, Inc.
	Dobbs International Services, Inc.
		Motor Coach Industries (MCI)
		Transportation Manufacturing Corporation (TMC)
		■ Custom Coach
			Greyhound Financial Corporation
			Greyhound Financial and Leasing
			Greyhound Financial Services, Ltd.
			Greyhound Bank PLC

Greyhound Airport Services Companies

Greyhound Exhibitgroup Inc.

Greyhound Exposition Services, Inc.

Greyhound Food Management, Inc.
■ Faber Enterprises, Inc.
■ Glacier Park, Inc.
■ GFM Engineering and Design Group
■ GFM Fast Food Division
■ GFM Public Service Division
■ GFM Truckstop Systems
■ Restaura
■ Restaura, S.A.

Greyhound International Travel, Inc. (GITI)

Greyhound Leisure Services, Inc. (GLSI)
■ Florida Export Warehouse
■ International Cruise Shops
■ Greyhound Leisure Services Duty-Free Shops
■ Premier Cruise Lines, Ltd.

Greyhound Lines of Canada, Ltd.

Travelers Express Company, Inc.
■ Republic Money Orders, Inc.

Universal Coach Parts, Inc.

Source: Greyhound Dial Corporation, Annual Report, 1990.

whose new soap Lever 2000 made major inroads into sales of Dial soap. Dial soap's market share dropped to 17.6 percent from 19.7 percent of the market in 1995, which was a severe blow to the Dial Corporation's most important product line and a disaster for the company.

The Purex division also was not performing well. The Purex bleach line was phased out in 1995 because of mounting losses. Late in 1995, Purex detergent, the low-priced detergent that had been selling well, came under intense pressure from Procter & Gamble, which introduced a competing low-priced brand, Ultra Bonus, which was aimed directly at Purex. Dial was forced to slash the price of Purex by 10 percent to compete, further cutting into the company's profits. Furthermore, Dial's successful Lunch Buckets, the line of microwave products, had generated a host of imitators from major food companies that quickly introduced their own competing products. Having lost this niche and no longer able to compete, Dial phased out Lunch Buckets in 1995. It began to seem to Dial's managers that even when they found a winning strategy their larger competitors just stole the idea away from them.

TABLE 2

The Dial Corporation: Consolidated Balance Sheet
(000 omitted, except per-share data)

	Year-ended December 31		
	1995	**1994**	**1993**
Revenues	$3,575,070	$3,546,847	$3,000,342
Costs and expenses			
Costs of sales and services	$3,271,151	$3,216,627	$2,725,049
Restructuring charges and asset write downs	191,100		
Unallocated corporate expense and other items, net	43,194	43,938	42,734
Interest expense	75,994	61,195	57,292
Minority interests	4,346	3,392	3,618
	$3,585,785	$3,325,152	$2,828,693
Income (loss) before income taxes	$(10,715)	$221,695	$171,649
Income taxes (benefit)	(11,852)	81,384	61,376
Income from Continuing Operations	**$1,137**	**$140,311**	**$110,273**
Income from discontinued operations			32,120
Income before extraordinary charge and cumulative effect of change in accounting principle	$1,137	$140,311	$142,393
Extraordinary charge for early retirement of debt net of tax benefit of $11,833			(21,908)
Cumulative effect net of tax benefit of $7,544 to January 1, 1995, of initial application of SFAS No. 121, "Accounting for the Impairment of Long-Lived Assets and for Long-Lived Assets to Be Disposed Of"			(17,696)
Net income (loss)	$(16,559)	$140,311	$120,485
Income (Loss) per Common Share			
Continuing operations	$0.00	$1.61	$1.28
Discontinued operations			
Income before extraordinary charge and cumulative effect of change in accounting principle	$0.00	$1.61	$1.66
Extraordinary charge			(0.26)
Cumulative effect, to January 1, 1995, of initial application of SFAS No. 121	(0.20)		
Net income (loss) per common share	$(0.20)	$1.61	$1.40

Source: Greyhound Dial Corporation, Annual Report, 1990.

Dial's other businesses were also suffering problems. Its cruise ship line, Premier Cruise Lines, which had formed an agreement with the Walt Disney Company to operate Disney's theme cruises on the Big Red Boat, lost its license in 1995 when Disney decided that it would launch its own cruise line. With four aging ships, and lacking any differentiated appeal in the increasingly competitive cruise ship industry in the 1990s, the company put its ships up for sale and withdrew from the cruise ship business—one more recession-proof niche gone.

Then, Dial's airline food business began to suffer in the 1990s when, to cut down on costs in an increasingly competitive airline industry, the major airlines cut back on the quality of the food they offered their customers. Airlines that had offered full meals began to offer snacks, and airlines such as Southwest offered passengers nothing. In airports, too, there had been a move to allow fast-food chains to set up their franchises on-site to increase the variety of foods offered to customers. All this hurt Dial's catering businesses.

It was becoming increasingly obvious to industry analysts that Dial was nothing more than a hodge-podge of different businesses that had nothing in common, were not recession-proof, and did not even have a secure niche.

Dial, 1996–2002

With its profits flat or eroding and no turnaround in sight, the question became how to create new value from Dial's different businesses. The movement of many diversified companies to break up their operations and let individual businesses go it alone in the early 1990s gave Teets his answer. He would split apart Dial's consumer products and services operations— thus dismantling the empire he had built since 1984— into two different companies. One, which would still be known as the Dial Corp., would consist of all its consumer product interests and would have revenues of about $1.3 billion. The other, to be called Viad Corp., would manage its remaining financial, catering, and exhibition businesses and have revenues of about $2.2 billion.

Initially, analysts thought that the breakup would allow the two new companies to realize more value. For example, since they operated separately, a downturn in the business of one division would no longer hurt the performance of the other. Moreover, after the breakup managers would be able to make decisions that could promote their own businesses, not corporate interests. However, analysts later came to realize that in the future there would be two sets of managers who would have to be paid to manage the two companies and two sets of overhead costs. Moreover, the question arose as to whether there was any value to be created by the breakups, because all of Dial's businesses were under threats from more efficient and aggressive competitors such as Procter & Gamble, Colgate-Palmolive, and Unilever. Analysts came to believe increasingly that more value could be made for shareholders if the company dismantled itself and sold off its assets separately to the highest bidder. A bidder could then merge a particular Dial business into its own operations and thus reduce manufacturing, distribution, or marketing costs or

even use its skills to increase the division's differentiation advantage.

In July 1996, John Teets's plan came under increasing attack from Michael Price, president of Heine Securities Corp. Price was the advisor to Mutual Series Funds, a large mutual fund company that owned 9.9 percent of Dial's stock. Price, along with other analysts, however, argued that Teet's plan would reduce, not increase, value for shareholders and that what Teets should do was to divest Dial's many different businesses and return the proceeds to shareholders. Of course, the sell off would mean that many of Dial's managers might find themselves out of well-paying jobs, including Teets, who had earned many millions of dollars over the years. On the other hand, these managers had not created much value for their shareholders.

In 1996, Teets answered his critics with half-page ads in the *Wall Street Journal* arguing that his strategy was a "strategy for empowered growth" that would allow each of the two new companies to "aggressively pursue acquisition opportunities without worry about upsetting the balance in Dial's existing mix of business." However, he did not explain how new value would be created by the two companies or how the proposed acquisitions might create value. Since Teets's acquisition strategy had met with little success for the last twelve years, what reason would shareholders have to suppose it would improve in the future?

This question remained unanswered, but in 1996, Viad was spun off to stockholders, Teets stepped down as CEO, and a new CEO, Malcolm Jozoff, was appointed to head what was now a consumer products company, albeit one that sold canned beef and shampoo. Jozoff was recruited from Procter & Gamble because Dial's board believed that a P&G veteran would understand how to fashion a business model to promote the profitability of a soap and detergent maker. What they forgot was that P&G is a differentiator whose claim to fame is developing new and improved products and marketing them successfully to consumers. While it is true that Dial, the bestselling antibacterial soap, was their flagship differentiated product, Dial's other main products, such as Purex detergent, Breck Shampoo, and even Armour corned beef, were not bought for their differentiated qualities but because of their low price. Even Dial soap did not command much of a premium price compared with P&G's and Unilever's brands; it sold because of the advertising expenditures used to promote its brand name.

Jozoff, however, given his immersion in P&G's "differentiation" culture, saw Dial's problems as the lack of a differentiated appeal of its products, not the fact that its high-cost structure was eroding the profitability of a low-price cost leadership strategy. Jozoff's efforts were thus directed toward increasing customer demand by differentiating Dial's brands. To promote Purex washing powder, he entered into a joint venture with Germany's Henkel group to use that company's expertise in stain removal to boost Purex's cleaning power (not its strong point); he proposed to call the new powder "Purex Advanced" and to recoup the extra costs it would cost a few dollars more a pack. He felt these moves would position it against Tide, the leading brand. Knowing that P&G was entering the home dry-cleaning market, he introduced a new Purex home dry-cleaning kit, and also knowing that P&G and Unilever were introducing washing powder in tablet form, he put in motion Purex Tablets. To push Dial into higher-end personal care products, he bought two companies, Sarah Michaels and Freeman Cosmetics, that specialized in producing upscale soaps, bath powders, and oils for gift boxes, although he did not propose to sell these under the Dial name. Also, knowing that rivals were developing new kinds of anti-bacterial soap with more fragrant scents and better foaming qualities, he reformulated Dial soap to position it against tough future competition. Jozoff also agreed to acquire the Plusbelle brand hair care business from Revlon for $46.5 million. Plusbelle was the leader in the Argentinean market. These acquisitions cost over $300 million and pushed up Dial's debt to over $550 million. Teets had left Dial saddled with a $300 million debt during the Viad spinoff, whereas Viad emerged virtually debt free.

In changing Dial's business-level strategy, Jozoff plunged the company into a whole new set of problems. First, the movement to a differentiation strategy raised Dial's cost structure, especially because of the extra debt it had to assume, so he was betting the company's future on consumers' acceptance of Dial's new products and higher-pricing structure. At the same time, Jozoff brought the company into more direct competition with such rivals as P&G and Unilever that had much more money to spend on the expensive business of promoting new brand products. For example, it was estimated that in 1994 it would cost $5 million in fees to retailers to promote a new consumer product in the greater New York area; that figure

had risen to $25 million by 1999 because of increasing competition for shelf space caused by the consolidation both of consumer product companies and of retailers and supermarkets such as Kroger's.

When Dial's new products started to be manufactured and introduced in 1998 and 1999, at first things looked good; sales increased by 12 percent in 1998 and by 13 percent in 1999 to $1.7 billion, and operating profits grew 13 percent in 1998 and 17 percent in 1999. However, it turned out that things were not as good as they seemed. While sales did increase in 1998, largely as the result of a big increase in marketing expenditures to sell the new, wider product range, by 1999 consumers were turning away from Dial's brands. By the middle of 1999, Dial's top managers knew there were problems, but to disguise the issue from the board, the company's sales team was instructed to boost the end-of-year sales figures by "stuffing the channel" with Dial products; that is, sending huge inventories of products, particularly Dial soap, to retailers that counted as sales in the company's books, and by offering retailers big promotions to sell its products at discounted prices to move them off the shelves.

Major errors were also made. First, expecting customers to stock up on canned goods because of Y2K glitches, the company loaded up stores with extra Armor Star Vienna Sausage and then raised prices hoping its competitors would follow. When there was no Y2K panic and competitors didn't raise prices, most of this product was left unsold and was either returned or sold at cost. Second, although it seemed to Jozoff that the Sarah Michaels and Freeman Cosmetics acquisitions were natural, albeit "upmarket," extensions to Dial's product line, Dial was not prepared for the huge manufacturing challenges involved in custom-packing gift boxes and matching them to the needs of the customers. As Baum (see next section) later said, upmarket products such as scented lotions, bath oils, and aromatherapy products are "fashion products," whereas Dial's business was "bread-and-butter" products where low-cost production and distribution were vital. Third, it turned out that the market for home dry-cleaning was far smaller than anticipated, and Dial's dry-cleaning product was simply left on the shelf because of its rivals' higher advertising budgets.

Even in the vital soap business, problems arose. Because Dial had stuffed the channels with its old soap product, when its new improved scented moisturizing soap came out in late 1999, retailers would not sell it until they had sold the old soap product. This gave a leg up to P&G and Unilever, which had also introduced a new range of soap to compete with Dial. Finally, Dial discovered that customers didn't understand the properties of the new improved Purex washing powder or why they should spend a lot more for it. As Baum later commented, he pleaded with Jozoff to introduce it under another upmarket name to differentiate it, but this was not done, and the powder was left stuck in the middle—not differentiated and not low cost.

Dial Gets a New CEO

As a result of all these problems, estimates for Dial's 2000 operating profits dropped from $73 million to $60 million in the summer of 2000, wiping out all its previous gains. The board became increasingly aware of the problems that had been taking place, and in August 2000, they ousted Jozoff as CEO and replaced him with a vocal board member, Herbert M. Baum. Baum, a former Campbell Soup executive and CEO of Quaker State (which he had sold to Pennzoil) and then the COO of Hasbro, the toy maker, was surprised to be asked to take over yet one more turnaround effort at Dial, but he accepted the challenge. Since his experience was with bread-and-butter products—canned soups and oil—he was familiar with the problems of managing a company's cost structure to get the most value out of its products. He also recognized the importance of finding the right strategy to compete against rivals like P&G and powerful retail chains like Kroger and Wal-Mart, both of which were launching private-label low-price washing powders and soaps at the low end of the market. The problem was that he had to move fast because Dial's performance and stock price were collapsing.

Baum took a close look at how Dial's brands were managed internally. He reorganized them into a product structure with five product groups—personal cleansing, washing powders, air fresheners, food products, and Dial International. For the first time, Baum made the product line managers accountable for their own inventory management and profit-and-loss figures. Previously, these had been spread across brands so that each line's relative performance had been hidden. Now it was possible to identify specific underperforming brands and decide what to do about

them—turn them around, sell them off, or close them down.

Baum then turned his attention to the various problems that emerged in launching Dial's new products. Recognizing the importance of protecting Dial soap's market share, he pumped money into advertising its improved products to regain their momentum and build their profitability. With Purex, he decided to go ahead with the introduction of Purex tablets, but ended the joint venture with Henkel and went back to the old low-cost strategy. He also decided to sell off the Sarah Michaels and Freeman upscale lines, which had only resulted in losses, and he used the money to reduce Dial's debt. He also withdrew from the home dry-cleaning market and took Purex's product off the shelf. The savings in operating costs from abandoning these product lines provided money to fund Dial's core soap, Purex, and Renuzit air freshener products and lowered its cost structure.

In September 2001, Baum announced that, given the increasing competitive pressures in all its brand categories from companies like P&G and Unilever, he and the board felt that it would be better if Dial were part of a larger enterprise. Various possible acquirers came forward to look at the company's books in the next months, but it appeared that none of them wanted to buy the whole company. In the meantime, Baum's business model and strategies began to pay off for Dial. Its inventory stocking and manufacturing problems were gone; brand managers were squeezing out costs now that they were directly responsible for their brand's performance; and top managers were not distracted by searching for elusive new product opportunities but were focusing, perhaps for the first time, on managing all aspects of the value chain to reduce costs. With its well-known products, sold at the right price, there was no reason why Dial should not be able to increase revenues and profits and build cash flow.

In fact, the company astounded analysts when in April 2002, only six months after it put itself up for sale, it raised its first-quarter earnings estimates, citing stronger-than-expected domestic sales. Dial's share reached $20, up from just $12 only a year before. Baum also announced in April that Dial itself, to strengthen and protect its core businesses, would be looking to make acquisitions in the coming year. Baum emphasized that Dial would be buying brands, not companies—those with high sales volumes and those that used the same sales channels as Dial so it could make better use of the company's resources.

Dial Is Bought by Henkel

By the end of 2002, under Baum's turnaround strategy, Dial reported that it had turned an operating loss of $132 million in 2001 into a profit of $16 million for 2002. Baum's strategy to build Dial's strengths in its core washing powder, soap, and foods brands was apparently working. The company's stock price shot up as investors either hoped for continued operating improvements or a takeover by another company. By the end of 2003, Dial's stock price had doubled since Baum became its CEO.

In 2003, however, it became clear that Dial's worries were not over. In the retail industry, many retailers who were struggling to compete with Wal-Mart began to demand lower prices for products from their suppliers. At the same time, Dial's sales of its products to discount operations such as Sam's and Costco, which expected low prices, were accounting for an increasingly bigger part of its sales. By 2003, Wal-Mart, for example, accounted for 28 percent of Dial's sales, and it was putting pressure on Dial for cost reductions to allow it to maintain its price advantage over retail competitors.

At the same time, Dial was still struggling to compete with its much larger rivals Procter & Gamble and Unilever in an industry increasingly dominated by a few global giants who had the broad product range and financial resources to compete successfully against Dial. Indeed, using its marketing muscle, P&G had now become the leading seller of liquid soap and Dial was in second place. In addition, there had been a major change in customer taste for soap because demand for bar soap had dropped significantly as customers increasingly turned to milder body wash products. Once again P&G and Unilever with their brands such as Dove and Oil of Olay had begun to dominate the market although Baum fought back by introducing and promoting Dial's own Dial, Coast, and Tone body washes.

In this increasingly competitive industry environment, Baum continued to search for a potential takeover partner even as he strengthened the company's core products lines. In 2003, Baum was also successful in rejuvenating Dial's money-losing food

products such as its Armor and Armor Star canned meats, chili, hash, and meat spreads. As a part of this strategy, Dial began to manufacture meat products for third parties under their own private brand labels, and this accounted for 28 percent of their business in 2003 so that with Armor's own 20 percent market share Dial had close to half of the U.S. canned meats business.

With all these ongoing improvements, in December 2003 Henkel—the German company that Dial had previously entered into an alliance with to develop advanced washing powders and dry-cleaning products—announced that it would takeover Dial in a deal worth $2.9 billion or for $28.75 a share which represented an 11 percent premium over Dial's stock price. This merger would bring together two small global players who, even combined, would be dwarfed by P&G and Unilever. However, for Henkel the acquisition of Dial would bring it broader global reach and allow it to enter the profitable U.S. market. Despite the marketing mistakes with Advanced Purex that had hurt Dial's performance, Henkel saw many opportunities for using its expertise in chemicals to innovate new and improved products.

To fund the acquisition, Henkel announced it planned to sell its 29.7 percent stake in Clorox, the profitable U.S. maker of bleach and other household products; however, it would also take over some of Clorox's brands. In May 2004, the merger proceeded as planned, and Dial became an operating unit of Henkel although Henkel has gained Herbert Baum's commitment to stay on as its CEO for the next two years to guide the transition as Henkel integrates its new U.S. operations.

Baum's actions left the Dial unit in a strong position. In 2004, he was able to avoid layoffs and increase sales volume of its Purex laundry detergent to make it No. 2 nationwide. Indeed, although Wal-Mart pressured Dial for lower costs, Baum was able to reduce Dial's cost structure so that it could still maintain good profit margins from its sales of Purex to Wal-Mart.

Henkel has also benefited from the turnaround of its new Dial Unit. In 2005, it reported that its fourth quarter earnings rose nearly 13 percent, beating analyst forecasts, as the strong performance of the Dial unit compensated for slow sales in the European market for toiletries and cosmetics. It also plans to expand the presence of its European brands such as Persil in the U.S. market to better compete with giant Procter & Gamble, which announced in 2005 that it wanted to merge with Gillette to create the biggest consumer products company in the world.

REFERENCES

Moody's Transportation Manual, 1987.

A. Stuart, "Greyhound Gets Ready for a New Driver," *Fortune,* March 3, 1966, pp. 34–38.

Greyhound Corporation, Annual Reports, 1966–1990.

Dial Corporation, Annual Reports and 10K Reports, 1971–2002.

"Greyhound: A Big Sell-off Leaves It Built for Better Speed," *Business Week,* July 25, 1983, pp. 88–90.

"Greyhound's New Strategy: Slimmed Down and Decentralized, It's After More Market Share, 15% on Equity," *Dun's Business Month,* February 1984, pp. 66–68.

S. Toy and J. H. Dobrzynski, "Will More Soap Help Greyhound Shine?" *Business Week,* March 11, 1985, pp. 73–78.

"The Greyhound Corporation," *Wall Street Journal Transcript,* February 5, 1990, pp. 96, 204.

"Dial Corp.: Firm's Loss of $26.2 Million Is Due to Special Charges," *Wall Street Journal,* October 25, 2000, p. B8.

Jack Neff and Kate MacArthur, "Beleaguered Dial Cuts Product Lines," *Advertising Age,* September 25, 2000, p. 128.

"Dial Corp.: Loss of $7.5 Million Posted, Partly from a Restructuring," *Wall Street Journal,* January 25, 2001, p. B5.

Rebecca Flass, "Dial Shifts Direction," *Adweek,* May 21, 2001, p. 8.

"Dial Agrees to Buy Plusbelle," *Wall Street Journal,* March 30, 2000, p. C14.

Steven Lipin and Anna W. Mathews, "Dial Board, Hit by New Profit Shortfall, Ousts Top Executives and Turns to Baum," *Wall Street Journal,* August 8, 2000, p. A3.

Arlene Weintraub and Christopher Palameri, "Wish Everyone Used Dial? Dial Does," *Business Week,* September 25, 2000, pp. 132–134.

Kerri Walsh, "Dial Raises First-Quarter Earnings Estimates; Eyes Brand Acquisitions," *Chemical Week,* April 17, 2002, p. 36.

"Dial Jettisons Underperforming Unit," *SPC Soap, Perfumery, and Cosmetics,* London, September, 2001, p. 4.

Brent Shearer, "Under Competitive Pressures, Dial Puts Itself Up for Sale," *Mergers and Acquisitions,* October 2001, p. 23.

"Dial Corp.: Earnings Forecast Climbs Again to as Much as 25 Cents a Share," *Wall Street Journal,* April 10, 2002, p. A8.

Jack Neff, "Clorox, Dial Exit Dry Cleaning Biz," *Advertising Age,* September 10, 2001, p. 4.

Kerri Walsh, "Dial May Be Broken Up," *Chemical Week,* August 15, 2001, p. 25.

"Dial Puts Itself Up for Sale Despite Portfolio, Analysts Say Company Could Fetch $2 Billion," *Chemical Market Reporter,* August 13, 2001, p. 3.

"Dial Corp.: Quarterly Earnings Surge, Outlook for Year Is Raised," *Wall Street Journal,* July 26, 2001.

Gene G. Marcial, "With Dial, Clorox Could Clean Up," *Business Week,* October 4, 1999, p. 247.

"Dial Corp.: Laundry-Products Venture to Tap Henkel Technology," *Wall Street Journal,* April 21, 1999.

Hanson PLC (A): The Acquisition Machine

This case was prepared by Charles W. L. Hill, the University of Washington.

Introduction

Hanson PLC is one of the ten biggest companies in Britain, and its U.S. arm, Hanson Industries, is one of America's sixty largest industrial concerns. A conglomerate with more than 150 different businesses in its portfolio, Hanson PLC has grown primarily by making acquisitions. By the end of 1989, the company had recorded twenty-six years of uninterrupted profit growth, cumulating in 1989 operating income of $1.61 billion on revenues of $11.3 billion and assets of $12.03 billion. The company's shareholders have been major beneficiaries of this growth. Between 1974 and 1989, the price of the company's shares on the London Stock Exchange increased eightyfold, compared with an average increase of fifteenfold for all companies quoted on the London Stock Exchange during this period.[1] Along the way, Hanson has gained a reputation for being one of the most successful takeover machines in the world. Its acquisitions during the 1980s included three American conglomerates (U.S. Industries, SCM Corporation, and Kidde) and three major British companies (London Brick, the Imperial Group, and Consolidated Gold Fields). So high is Hanson's profile that Oliver Stone, in his film *Wall Street*, reportedly used Sir Gordon White, head of Hanson Industries, as the model for the

Copyright © 2007 by Charles W. L. Hill. This case was prepared by Charles W. L. Hill, the University of Washington, as the basis for class discussion rather than to illustrate either effective or ineffective handling of an administrative situation. Reprinted by permission of Charles W. L. Hill. All rights reserved. For the most recent financial results of the company discussed in this case, go to **http://finance.yahoo.com**, input the company's stock symbol, and download the latest company report from its homepage.

British corporate raider (the one who outmaneuvered the evil Gordon Gekko).

Despite this impressive track record, as Hanson enters the 1990s analysts increasingly wonder about the strategy of the company. There is speculation that the company may be on the verge of breaking itself up and returning the gains to shareholders. The age of the company's founders is fueling this speculation. The two men who built and still run the conglomerate, Lord Hanson and Sir Gordon White, are in their late sixties, and both have promised to consider retiring when they are seventy. As one insider put it, "The guys that started it off will finish it off."[2] Another factor is that Hanson is now so big that it would take some spectacular deals to continue its historic growth rate. According to many, including Harvard Business School strategy guru Michael Porter, there simply are not that many obvious companies for Hanson to buy. Thus, "even Hanson will be faced with poorer and poorer odds of maintaining its record."[3] On the other hand, at the end of 1989 Hanson had $8.5 billion in cash on its balance sheet. That, along with the billions it could borrow if need be (the company reportedly has a borrowing capacity of $20 billion), suggests that if Hanson and White should so wish, they could undertake an acquisition that would rival the RJR-Nabisco deal in size.

Other commentators question the long-term viability of the company. Some claim that Hanson PLC is little more than an asset stripper that in the long run will drive the companies it manages into the ground. According to one investment banker, "I'm not convinced that Hanson runs companies any better than anyone else. But I certainly know it squeezes them for cash, sucking the life from them."[4] Similarly, one former executive noted that "some of the incentive programs that they write for managers actually keep the company from growing. . . . They become so concerned with profit today that they don't re-invest for tomorrow."[5] The company disagrees. Sir Gordon White clearly sees Hanson PLC as reducing inefficiencies in the companies it acquires, not stripping assets. If anything is stripped away from acquisitions, according to White, it is unnecessary corporate bureaucracy, overstaffed head offices, and top-management perks, not assets. He steadfastly maintains that the company treats all acquired businesses as if it were going to keep them.[6]

With these issues in mind, in this case we consider the growth and development of Hanson PLC. We review the administrative systems that the company uses to manage its ongoing businesses, and we look at two acquisitions and their aftermath in depth: the 1987 acquisitions of SCM Corporation and the Imperial Group.

History

The origins of Hanson PLC go back to the port city of Hull in Yorkshire, England, in the 1950s.[7] At that time, James Hanson was learning his family's transportation business (the family operated a fleet of passenger coaches), and Gordon White was selling advertising for Welbecson Limited, a magazine printing company owned by his father. James Hanson's brother, Bill, was White's closest friend, and when Bill died of cancer at twenty-nine, James and Gordon became close friends. In the late 1950s, Hanson and White decided to team up in business. They formed Hanson White Ltd., a greeting card company. Although the company did well, the two soon became bored with the limited challenges and potential that the greeting card business offered, and in 1963 they sold out and began to look for acquisition opportunities.

Their first buy was Oswald Tillotson Ltd., a vehicle distribution company. This company was subsequently acquired by Wiles Group Ltd., a Yorkshire-based manufacturer of agricultural sacks and fertilizers. As part of the takeover deal, Hanson and White were given a substantial ownership position in the Wiles Group. Hanson and White soon gained management control of the Wiles Group, and in 1969, after deciding that James Hanson's name had a nicer ring to it than Gordon White's, they changed the name to Hanson Trust.

Because of a series of small acquisitions, by the end of 1973 Hanson Trust owned twenty-four companies with combined sales of $120 million.

By 1973, however, the British economy was in deep trouble. The stock market had collapsed; the country was paralyzed by labor disputes; inflation was increasing rapidly, as was unemployment; and Prime Minister Edward Heath of the supposedly probusiness Conservative party had blasted conglomerate companies such as Hanson Trust as representing "the unacceptable face of capitalism." All of this prompted Gordon White to rethink his future. As White put it,

> I was disgusted with England at the time. Disgusted with socialism and unions and excessive, antibusiness government, disgusted with the way initiative was being taxed out of existence. . . . I'd done a lot of thinking. I told James (Hanson) that maybe we should just call it a day. I thought I'd try America.[8]

Hanson replied that there was no need to split up, and they agreed that Hanson would run the British operations while White tried to build operations in America.

White arrived in New York in the fall of 1973 in possession of a round-trip ticket, a one-year work visa, and $3,000 in traveler's checks, which was the most that British currency controls permitted a U.K. citizen to take abroad at that time. Moreover, because of British exchange controls, White could not gain access to Hanson's ample treasury without substantial penalties, and he had to struggle to convince banks that he was creditworthy. Despite this, in 1974 White managed to borrow $32 million from Chemical Bank to finance his first major U.S. acquisition, a friendly takeover of J. Howard Smith Company, a New Jersey-based processor of edible oils and animal feed that was later renamed Seacoast Products. The CEO of J. Howard Smith was David Clarke, whose family business it was. Clarke subsequently became White's right-hand man. He is now president of Hanson Industries and the most senior executive in the United States after White.

Over the next ten years, White made another six major U.S. acquisitions, all of them friendly (see Table 1). Then, in 1984, White was ready for his first hostile takeover, the $532-million purchase of U.S. Industries (USI). USI was a conglomerate that had grown by acquisitions during the 1960s and 1970s. White became interested in the company when he read in a newspaper that management was putting together a

TABLE 1

U.S. Acquisitions, 1974–1990

Date	Acquisition	Cost (millions)	Businesses
1974	Seacost	$32	Fish processing, pet food
1975	Carisbrook	36	Textile manufacturing
1976	Hygrade	32	Castings and casing units
1977	Old Salt Seafood	2	Prepared foods
1978	Interstate United	30	Food service management
1978	Templon	7	Textile manufacturing
1981	McDonough	185	Cement, concrete
1984	U.S. Industries	532	33-company conglomerate
1986	SCM	930	22-company conglomerate
1987	Kaiser Cement	250	Cement plants
1988	Kidde	1,700	108-company conglomerate
1990	Peabody	1,230	Coal mining

Source: Adapted from Gordon White, "How I Turned $3,000 into $10 Billion," *Fortune*, November 7, 1988, pp. 80–89; and "Hanson PLC," *Value Line*, July 20, 1990, p. 832.

leveraged buyout at $20 a share for a total purchase price of $445 million. He suspected that the company was worth more than that and quickly worked out how big a loan Hanson Industries could handle, using USI's projected cash flow to cover interest charges. To USI's pretax earnings of $67 million he added $40 million generated by depreciation and $24 million in savings that he thought Hanson could effect by removing USI's corporate headquarters. That yielded a total cash flow of $131 million, or more than $70 million after taxes. With interest rates running at 13 percent, white figured that Hanson Industries could afford a loan of $544 million. In what was to become standard White thinking, he also reckoned that even with a worse-case scenario, he could recoup his investment by selling off the disparate pieces of the company.

Hanson Industries began to buy USI shares and by April 1984 held 5 percent of the company. Hanson then made a $19 per share bid for the company, which was quickly rebuffed by USI management. Three days later White increased Hanson's bid to $22 per share. USI's management, which had yet to raise the financing for its own proposed leveraged buyout, responded by increasing the purchase price to $24 per share. Hanson responded by initiating a tender offer of $23 per share in cash. For stockholders, cash in hand at $23 per share was far more attractive than management's promise of $24 per share if financing could be arranged, and Hanson's bid quickly won the day.

After the acquisition was completed, Hanson Industries President David Clarke spent six months at USI's corporate headquarters reviewing operations. At the end of this period USI's corporate headquarters was closed down, the staff was laid off, and financial control was centralized at Hanson Industries' small headquarters. However, most of the operating managers in charge of USI's constituent companies stayed on, lured by Hanson's incentive pay scheme and the promise that they could run their own shows. In what was also typical Hanson fashion, nine of USI's operating companies were subsequently sold off to outside investors for a price of $225 million.

The acquisition of USI was followed by three other hostile takeover bids in the United States: for SCM Corporation, Kaiser Cement, and Kidde. Of these, the SCM bid was by far the most acrimonious. SCM took a poison pill and tried to protect its position through the law courts before Hanson finally won control over the company. (The SCM takeover is discussed in detail later in this case.)

While White was making these U.S. acquisitions, Hanson was not sitting idle in Britain. During the 1980s

TABLE 2

U.K. Acquisitions During the 1980s

Date	Acquisition	Cost (millions)	Businesses
1981	Ever Ready	£95	Dry cell batteries
1983	UDS	£250	Retail operations
1984	London Brick	£247	Brick manufacturer
1984	Powell Duffryn	£150	Engineering, shipping, fuel
1986	Imperial Group	£2,360	Tobacco, brewing, food
1989	Consolidated Gold Fields	£3,610	Gold mining, building aggregates

Source: Various press reports.

the company made a series of acquisitions in the United Kingdom. These are summarized in Table 2. The most notable were the 1984 acquisition of London Brick, Britain's largest brick manufacturer, against vigorous opposition from London Brick's incumbent management; the £2.36-billion acquisition of Imperial, the largest tobacco company in Britain and the third largest in the world; and the £3.61-billion acquisition of Consolidated Gold Fields, the second largest gold-mining business in the world. The acquisitions of Imperial and Consolidated Gold Fields were the two largest takeovers ever undertaken in Britain. (The Imperial takeover is discussed in detail later in this case.)

Acquisitions Philosophy

Hanson PLC's acquisitions on both sides of the Atlantic are primarily overseen by Sir Gordon White. Lord Hanson is primarily responsible for the ongoing administration of the company. As Lord Hanson says of White, "He's the one with the gift for takeovers."[9] In turn, White says of Hanson, "James is a brilliant administrator and really knows how to run a company."[10] White claims that many of his acquisition ideas, including the USI deal, come from the newspapers. Others are suggested to him by contacts in the investment banking community, particularly Bob Pirie, president of the Rothschild investment bank, with whom white has lunch once a week.

Whenever possible, White avoids working at the office, opting instead to work from one of his four

houses. Unlike corporate raiders such as Saul Steinberg and Carl Icahn, White rarely reads annual reports or detailed stock reports on a target company, claiming that he can get all of the financial information that he needs from Standard & Poor's two-page summaries. In addition, his three-person takeover staff distills reams of financial data on a target and provides him with a short memo on the target company. Says White, "I'm like Churchill, tell me everything you can tell me. On one page."[11]

Under White's leadership, one of the things that has distinguished Hanson PLC from many other acquisitive conglomerates is its distinctive acquisitions philosophy (which is, in essence, White's philosophy). This philosophy appears to be based on a number of consistent factors that are found to underlie most of Hanson's acquisitions.[12]

1. *Target characteristics.* Hanson looks for companies based in mature, low-technology industries that have a less-than-inspiring record but show potential for improving performance. Normally, the objective has been to identify a poorly performing target where the incumbent management team has gone some way toward improving the underlying performance but whose efforts have not yet been reflected in either the profit-and-loss account or, more importantly, the target's stock price.

2. *Research.* Although White claims that he does little reading on takeover targets, his takeover staff does undertake detailed research into the potential of target companies before any bid is made. The staff routinely investigates companies undertaking leveraged buyouts.

3. *Risk assessment.* One of White's most often quoted edicts is "watch the downside." What this means is that instead of considering the potential benefits of a deal, give consideration to what can go wrong and the likely consequences of a worst-case scenario. White will purchase a company only if he thinks that in a worst-case scenario he will be able to recover the purchase price by breaking the target up and selling off its constituent parts.

4. *Funding.* White was one of the early pioneers of the highly leveraged takeover deal. All of the U.S. acquisitions have been financed by nonrecourse debt, secured on the assets of the target. This

enabled White to engineer substantial acquisitions when Hanson Industries itself had a very small capital base. The British acquisitions have been funded by a mix of cash, equity, convertible securities, and loan stock.

5. *Disposals to reduce debt.* After an acquisition has been completed, Hanson sends some of its own managers along with a group of external accountants to go through and audit the acquired businesses. After a thorough review, Hanson typically sells off the parts of the acquired company that cannot reach Hanson's stringent profitability targets. In the process, Hanson is able to reduce the debt taken on to fund the acquisition. The most outstanding example followed the purchase of SCM for $930 million. After the takeover, Hanson sold off SCM's real estate, pulp and paper, and food holdings for a price of $964 million while holding on to SCM's typewriter and chemicals business, which in effect had been acquired for nothing. Thus, within six months of the takeover's being completed, Hanson was able to eliminate the debt taken on to finance the SCM acquisition. Similar, although less spectacular, disposals have characterized almost all of Hanson's major acquisitions on both sides of the Atlantic.

6. *Elimination of excess overhead.* Another objective of Hanson's housecleaning of acquired companies is to eliminate any excess overhead. This typically involves closing down the corporate headquarters of the acquired company, eliminating some of the staff, and sending other staff down to the operating level. Before Hanson took over, SCM had 230 people in its corporate office, USI had 180, Kidde had 200, and Hanson itself had 30. Today the total headquarters staff for all four is 120.

Hanson also disposes of any management perks found either at the corporate or the operating level of an acquired company. For example, one of Kidde's operating companies had a collection of art and antiques, a hunting lodge, and three corporate jets. Hanson kept one jet and disposed of the rest, including the man at the top who had spent the money.

7. *The creation of incentives.* Hanson tries to create strong incentives for the management of acquired operating companies to improve performance. This is achieved by (a) decentralization designed to give operating managers full autonomy for the running of their businesses, (b) motivating operating managers by setting profit targets that, if achieved, will result in significant profit enhancements, and (c) motivating managers by giving them large pay bonuses if they hit or exceed Hanson's profit targets.

Organization and Management Philosophy

In addition to its acquisitions philosophy, Hanson is also renowned for its ongoing management of operating companies, of which there are more than 150 in the corporate portfolio. Although Hanson does have some interests elsewhere, the strategic development of the group has centered on the United States and Britain, where a broad balance has tended to exist in recent years. Hanson PLC looks after the British operations, and Hanson Industries, the U.S. subsidiary, manages the U.S. operations. Each of these two units is operated on an entirely autonomous basis. Only one director sits on the board of both companies. Hanson PLC is headed by Hanson; Hanson Industries is headed by White.[13]

There are two corporate headquarters, one in the United States and one in Britain. At both locations there is a small central staff responsible for monitoring the performance of operating companies, selecting and motivating operating management, the treasury function (including acting as a central bank for the operating units), acquisitions and disposals, and professional services such as legal and taxation.

Below each headquarters are a number of divisions (see Figure 1). These are not operating companies. Rather, they are groupings of operating companies. In 1988 there were four U.S. divisions (consumer, building products, industrial, and food) and four British divisions (again, consumer, building products, industrial, and food). There are no personnel at the divisional level with the exception of a divisional CEO. Below the divisions are the operating companies. Each operating company has its own CEO who reports to the divisional CEO. The divisional CEOs in Britain are responsible to Lord Hanson; those in the United States are responsible to David Clarke, White's right-hand man. White himself is primarily concerned with acquisitions and leaves most issues of control to David Clarke. Indeed, White claims that he has never visited Hanson Industries' U.S. corporate

FIGURE 1

Hanson PLC Organizational Structure

Source: Hanson Industries, Annual Report, 1986.

headquarters and as a matter of policy never visits operating companies.[14]

The following principles seem to characterize Hanson's management philosophy.

- *Decentralization.* All day-to-day operating decisions are decentralized to operating company managers. The corporate center does not offer suggestions about how to manufacture or market a product. Thus, within the limits set by centrally approved operating budgets and capital expenditures, operating management has unlimited autonomy. As a consequence, operating managers are responsible for the return on capital that they employ.

- *Tight financial control.* Financial control is achieved through two devices: (1) operating budgets and (2) capital expenditure policies. In a bottom-up process, operating budgets are submitted annually to the corporate center by operating company managers. The budgets include detailed performance targets, particularly with regard to return on capital employed (ROK). Corporate staff reviews

the budgets and, after consultation with operating management, approves a budget for the coming year. Once agreed upon, the operating budget becomes gospel. The performance of an operating company is compared against budget on a monthly basis, and any variance is investigated by the corporate center. If an operating company betters its projected ROK, the figure used as the base for the next year's budget is the actual ROK, not the budgeted figure.

Any cash generated by an operating company is viewed as belonging to the corporate center, not to the operating company. Capital expenditures are extremely closely monitored. All cash expenditures in excess of $3,000 (£1,000 in Britain) have to be agreed upon by corporate headquarters. Capital expenditure requests are frequently challenged by headquarters staff. For example, a manager who contends that an investment in more efficient machinery will cut labor costs must even provide the names of the employees that he or she expects to lay off to achieve the savings.

According to company insiders, when justifying a request for capital expenditure, a manager must explain every possibility. In general, Hanson looks for a pretax payback on expenditures of three years. The quicker the payback, the more likely it is that an expenditure will be approved.

■ *Incentive systems.* A major element of the pay of operating managers is linked directly to operating company performance. A manager can earn up to 60 percent of his or her base salary if the operating company exceeds the ROK target detailed in its annual budget. Bonuses are based strictly on bottom-line performance. As White puts it, "There are no bonuses for being a nice chap."[15] In addition, there is a share option scheme for the most senior operating company and corporate managers. More than 600 managers are members of the option scheme. The options are not exercisable for at least three years after they have been granted.

■ *Board structure.* No operating company managers are ever appointed to the board of either Hanson PLC or Hanson Industries. The idea is to eliminate any conflicts of interest that might arise over budgets and capital expenditures.

■ *De-emphasizing operating synergy.* In contrast to many diversified companies, Hanson has no interest in trying to realize operating synergy. For example, two of Hanson PLC's subsidiaries, Imperial Tobacco and Elizabeth Shaw (a chocolate firm), are based in Bristol, England, and both deliver goods to news agents and corner shops around Britain. However, Hanson prohibits them from sharing distribution because it reckons that any economies of scale that result would be outweighed by the inefficiencies that would arise if each operating company could blame the other for distribution problems.

The SCM Acquisition

SCM was a diversified manufacturer of consumer and industrial products. SCM had twenty-two operating companies based in five industries: chemicals, coatings and resins, paper and pulp, foods, and typewriters.[16] Among other things, SCM was the world's leading manufacturer of portable typewriters (Smith-Corona typewriters), the world's third largest producer of titanium dioxide (a white inorganic pigment widely used in the manufacture of paint, paper, plastic, and rubber products), the sixth largest paint manufacturer in the world through its Glidden Paints subsidiary, and a major force in the U.S. food industry through its Durkee Famous Foods group (see Table 3).

Attractions to Hanson

The SCM group was first brought to White's attention by Bob Pirie, president of Rothschild Inc. in New York. Pirie thought, and Hanson's research team soon confirmed, that SCM had a number of characteristics that made it a perfect Hanson buy.

1. *Poor financial performance.* Summary financial data for SCM are given in Table 4. Pretax profit had declined from a peak of $83.2 million in 1980 to $54.1 million in 1985. The 1985 return on equity of 7.7 percent was very poor by Hanson's standards, and earnings per share had declined by 19 percent since 1980.

TABLE 3

SCM Divisional Results for the Year Ended June 1985

Division	Revenues		Profits	
	$m	Percentage of Change from 1984	$m	Percentage of Change from 1984
Chemicals	$539.0	+49%	$73.7	−100%
Coatings and resins	687.0	+5%	49.9	−3%
Paper and pulp	362.0	+3%	23.1	+10%
Foods	422.0	+7%	23.0	+35%
Typewriters	176.0	−11%	(47.4)*	−200%

*Loss after a $35 million charge for restructuring.

Source: Data from Hanson Industries, Annual Report, 1986.

TABLE 4

Financial Data for SCM

	1980	1981	1982	1983	1984	1985
Net sales ($m)	$1,745.0	$1,761.0	$1,703.0	$1,663.0	$1,963.0	$2,175.0
Pretax profits ($m)	83.2	72.6	35.3	37.8	64.8	54.1
Earnings per share ($)—fully diluted	$4.76	$5.01	$3.20	$2.63	$4.05	$3.85
Return on equity	12.40%	12.00%	5.80%	4.90%	8.00%	7.70%

Source: Data from Hanson Industries, Annual Report, 1986.

2. *Beginnings of a turnaround.* There were signs that incumbent management was coming to grips with SCM's problems, particularly in the troubled typewriter operation, where the 1985 loss was due to a one-time charge of $39 million for restructuring. Financial performance had improved since the low point in 1983, but the benefits of this improvement were not yet reflected in the company's stock price.

3. *Mature businesses.* SCM's presence in mature, proven markets that were technologically stable fit White's preferences.

4. *Low risk.* Some 50 percent of SCM's turnover covered products well known to the U.S. consumer (for example, Smith-Corona typewriters, Glidden paint, Durkee foods). White felt that there would be a ready market for such highly branded businesses if Hanson decided to dispose of any companies that did not meet its stringent ROK requirements.

5. *Titanium dioxide.* Titanium dioxide was dominated by a global oligopoly. Hanson was aware of two favorable trends in the industry that made high returns likely: (a) worldwide demand was forecasted to exceed supply for the next few years, and (b) input costs were declining because of the currency weakness of the major raw material source, Australia.

6. *Corporate overhead.* A corporate staff of 230 indicated to White that SCM was "a lumbering old top-heavy conglomerate with a huge corporate overhead that was draining earnings."[17] He envisioned substantial savings from the elimination of this overhead.

The Takeover Battle

After reviewing the situation, in early August White decided to acquire SCM. He began to buy stock, and on August 21 Hanson Industries formally made a $60 per share tender offer for SCM, valuing the company at $740 million. SCM's top management team responded on August 30 with its own offer to shareholders in the form of a proposed leveraged buyout of SCM. SCM's management had arranged financing from its investment banker Merrill Lynch and offered shareholders $70 per share. On September 4 White responded by raising Hanson's offer to $72 per share.

SCM's management responded to White's second offer by increasing its own offer to $74 per share. To discourage White from making another bid, SCM's management gave Merrill Lynch a "lock-up" option to buy Durkee Famous Foods and SCM Chemicals (the titanium dioxide division) at a substantial discount should Hanson or another outsider gain control. In effect, SCM's management had agreed to give its crown jewels to Merrill Lynch for less than their market value if Hanson won the bidding war.

White's next move was to apparently throw in the towel by announcing withdrawal of Hanson's tender offer. However, in contrast to normal practice on Wall Street, White went into the market and quickly purchased some 25 percent of SCM's stock at a fixed price of $73.5 per share, taking Hanson's stake to 27 percent. Furious at this break with convention, SCM's lawyers drafted a lawsuit against Hanson charging that White's tactics violated tender-offer regulations and demanding a restraining order prohibiting Hanson from making any further market purchases. Hanson quickly filed a countersuit, claiming that Merrill Lynch's lock-up option to buy the two SCM divisions illegally prevented the shareholders from getting the best price.

Hanson lost both suits in federal court in New York. White immediately appealed and on September 30 a U.S. court of appeals ruled in Hanson's favor. This, however, was not to be the end of the matter. On

October 7 Hanson spent another $40 million to increase its stake in SCM to 33 percent, thereby effectively stalling the leveraged buyout plan, which needed approval by two-thirds of the shareholders. The following day Hanson revised its tender offer to an all-cash $75 per share offer, subject to SCM's dropping the "lock-up" option because the option had been triggered by Hanson's acquiring 33 percent of SCM.

Hanson's next move, on October 10, was to file a suit to prevent Merrill Lynch from exercising the right to buy SCM's crown jewels. On October 15 it followed this with a second suit against Merrill Lynch for conspiracy. A U.S. district court ruled on November 26 that the lock-up was legal and that Hanson had triggered its exercise by the size of its stake. Once again Hanson appealed to a higher court. On January 6, 1986, a U.S. court of appeals overturned the lower court ruling, granting to Hanson an injunction that prevented SCM from exercising the lock-up option. The following day Hanson Industries won control over SCM after further market purchases. The final purchase price was $930 million, which represented a price/earnings multiple of 11.5.

After the Acquisition

Having gained control of SCM, Hanson immediately set about trying to realize SCM's potential. Within three months, 250 employees were laid off, mostly headquarters staff, and the former SCM headquarters in New York was sold for $36 million in cash. At the same time, White and his team were using their new position as owners to thoroughly audit the affairs of SCM's operating companies. Their objective was to identify those businesses whose returns were adequate or could be improved upon and those businesses for which the outlook was such that they were unlikely to achieve Hanson's stringent ROK requirements.

At the end of this process, four businesses were sold off in as many months for a total amount that recouped for Hanson the original purchase price and left Hanson with the two best businesses in SCM's portfolio: Smith-Corona typewriters and the titanium dioxide business. In May 1986, SCM's paper and pulp operations were sold to Boise Cascade for $160 million in cash, a price that represented a price/earnings multiple of 29 and was 3 times book value. Hanson felt that the outlook for those operations was not good because of a depression in paper and pulp prices. Boise Cascade obviously thought

otherwise. Shortly afterward, Sylvachem, part of SCM's chemicals division, was sold for $30 million, representing a price/earnings multiple of 18.5.

In August 1986 Glidden Paints was sold to the British chemical giant and Europe's largest paint manufacturer, Imperial Chemical Industries PLC (ICI) for $580 million. This represented a price/earnings multiple of 17.5 and was 2.5 times book value. The purchase of this operation enabled ICI to become the world's largest paint manufacturer. A few days later Durkee Famous Foods was sold to another British firm, Reckitt & Colman PLC, for $120 million in cash and the assumption of $20 million in debt. This represented a price/earnings multiple of 17 and was 3 times book value. This disposal served to withdraw Hanson from an area that was subject to uncontrollable and volatile commodity price movements. For Reckitt & Colman, however, which was already one of the largest manufacturers of branded food products outside the United States, it represented an important strategic addition.

The four disposals amounted to $926 million and were accomplished at an average price/earnings multiple of 19.5. Having recovered 100 percent of the purchase price paid for SCM within eight months, Hanson had effectively acquired for nothing a number of businesses that were projected to contribute around $140 million to net pretax profit for their first full year under Hanson's control.

Hanson retained the titanium dioxide business for two main reasons. First, with the industry operating at close to 100 percent capacity and with projections indicating an increase in demand through to 1989, prices and margins were expected to increase substantially. Although several companies had plans to expand global capacity, given the three- to four-year time lag in bringing new capacity on stream, this sellers' market was likely to persist for a while. Nor did it look as if the additional capacity would outstrip the projected rise in demand. Second, two-thirds of world production of titanium dioxide is in the hands of global producers. SCM's business is ranked third with 12 percent of world capacity, behind Du Pont and Tioxide PLC. Given this oligopoly, orderly pricing in world markets seemed likely to continue.

Hanson also decided to retain SCM's typewriter business, despite the fact that in recent years it had been the worst-performing unit in SCM's portfolio. Hanson quickly realized that SCM management had in effect just completed a drastic overhaul of the

TABLE 5

Imperial Divisional Results for the Year Ended October 1985

| Division | Revenues | | Profits | |
	£m	Percentage of Change from 1984	£m	Percentage of Change from 1984
Tobacco	£2,641	+7%	£123.1	+11%
Brewing and leisure	974	+8%	97.0	+20%
Foods	719	+4%	33.0	+5%
Howard Johnson	617	+11%	11.1	−40%

Source: Data from Hanson Industries, Annual Report, 1986.

typewriter businesses and that a dramatic turnaround was likely. In the two years prior to Hanson's acquisition, SCM's management had undertaken the following steps:

1. A new line of electronic typewriters had been introduced to match the increasingly sophisticated Japanese models.

2. Capacity had been reduced by 50 percent, and six U.S. production facilities had been consolidated into a single assembly plant and distribution center in New York to manufacture all electronic models.

3. As a result of automation, economies of scale, and labor agreements, productivity at the New York plant had increased fourfold since 1984, and unit labor costs had declined by 60 percent.

4. The manufacture of electric models had been moved offshore to a low-cost facility in Singapore.

5. Smith-Corona had just introduced the first personal word processor for use with a portable electronic typewriter, and it retailed at slightly less than $500.

As a result of these improvements, the Smith-Corona business seemed ready to become a major profit producer. Hanson forecasted profits of $30 million for this business during 1986–1987, compared with an operating loss of $47.4 million in financial year 1985.

The Imperial Acquisition

On December 6, 1985, while still engaged in the SCM acquisition, Hanson opened another takeover battle in Britain by announcing an offer of £1.5 billion for Imperial Group PLC.[18] Imperial Group was one of the ten largest firms in Britain. Imperial was Britain's leading tobacco manufacturer and the third largest tobacco company in the world. Its Courage Brewing subsidiary was one of the "big six" beer companies in Britain. Its leisure operations included 1,371 public houses (taverns), 120-plus restaurants, and more than 750 specialized retail shops. Imperial manufactured more than 1,000 branded food products. (See Table 5 for a breakdown of Imperial's divisional results.) In September 1985 Imperial had sold its fourth business, the U.S. motel chain Howard Johnson, to Marriott. Howard Johnson had been purchased in 1980 and was widely regarded as one of the worst acquisitions ever made by a major British company.

Attractions to Hanson

Hanson's interest in Imperial was prompted by the news on December 2, 1985, of a planned merger between Imperial and United Biscuits PLC, a major manufacturer of branded food products. The financial press perceived this measure as a defensive move by Imperial. However, despite its well-documented problems with Howard Johnson, Imperial's financial performance was reasonably strong (see Table 6). What factors made Imperial an attractive takeover target to Hanson? The following seem to have been important.

■ *Mature business.* Like SCM's businesses, most of Imperial's businesses were based in mature, low-technology industries. There is little prospect of radically changing fashions or technological change in the tobacco, brewing, and food industries.

■ *Low risk.* Most of Imperial's products had a high brand recognition within Britain. Thus, Hanson could easily dispose of those that did not stand up to Hanson's demanding ROK targets.

TABLE 6

Financial Data for Imperial

	1981	1982	1983	1984	1985
Revenues (£m)	£4,526	£4,614	£4,381	£4,593	£4,918
Pretax profits (£m)	106	154	195	221	236
Earnings per share (pence)	12.8	16.4	18.0	20.3	22.4
Return on capital (%)	12.7%	17.9%	20.4%	21.1%	18.1%

Source: Data from Hanson Industries, Annual Report, 1986.

■ *Tobacco cash flow.* Imperial's tobacco business was a classic cash cow. The company had 45 percent of the tobacco market and seven of the ten best-selling brands in 1985. Although tobacco sales are declining in Britain because of a combination of health concerns and punitive taxation, the decline has been gradual, amounting to 29 percent since the peak year of 1973. Given Hanson's emphasis on ROK and cash flow, this made Imperial particularly attractive to Hanson. Imperial had arguably squandered much of this cash flow by using it to underwrite unprofitable growth opportunities, particularly Howard Johnson.

■ *Failure of Imperial's diversification strategy.* Imperial's recent track record with respect to diversification was poor. In 1978 it bought a construction company, J. B. Eastward, for £40 million. After four years of trading losses, Eastward was sold in 1982 for a total loss of £54 million. In 1979 Imperial paid $640 million for Howard Johnson, the U.S. motel and restaurant chain. In 1985, after six years of declining profits, this business was sold for $341 million. These losses suggested a fundamental weakness in Imperial's top management in an area in which Hanson was strong: diversification strategy. Moreover, the failure of Imperial's diversification strategy probably resulted in Imperial's shares being discounted by the stock market.

■ *Inadequate returns in brewing and leisure.* Imperial's brewing and leisure operations earned an ROK of 9 percent in 1985. This return was considered very low for the brewing industry, which was characterized by strong demand and was dominated by a mature oligopoly that had engineered high prices and margins. Hanson thought that this return could be significantly improved.

The Takeover Battle

The planned merger between Imperial and United Biscuits PLC (UB), announced on December 2, 1985, gave rise to considerable concern among Imperial's already disgruntled shareholders. Under the terms of the proposed merger, UB, although contributing just 21 percent of net assets, would end up with a 42 percent interest in the enlarged group. The implication was that Imperial's shareholders would experience significant earnings dilution. In addition, it was proposed that the corporate management of the enlarged group would primarily come from UB personnel. These factors prompted a reverse takeover by UB of the much larger Imperial group. See Table 7.

Hanson's interest was sparked by this controversy. Hanson's corporate staff had been tracking Imperial for some time, so when the for-sale sign was raised over Imperial, Hanson was able to move quickly. On December 6, 1985, Hanson made a 250-pence per share offer for Imperial, valuing the group at £1.9 billion. This offer was rejected out of hand by Imperial's management.

The next major development came on February 12, 1986, when the British secretary of state of trade and industry referred the proposed Imperial/UB merger to the Monopolies and Mergers Commission for consideration. Britain's Monopolies and Mergers Commission has the authority to prohibit any merger that might create a monopoly. The referral was due to the recognition that an Imperial/UB group would command more than 40 percent of the British snack-food market.

On February 17, Hanson took advantage of the uncertainty created by the referral to unveil a revised offer 24 percent higher than its original offer, valuing Imperial at £2.35 billion. On the same day,

TABLE 7

Hanson PLC—Financial Data

Income Data (million $)*										
Year Ended Sept. 30	**Revs.**	**Oper. Inc.**	**% Oper. Inc. of Revs.**	**Cap. Exp.**	**Depr.**	**Int. Exp.**	**Net Bef. Taxes**	**Eff. Tax Rate**	**Net‡ Inc.**	**% Net Inc. of Revs.**
1989§	$11,302	$1,609	14.2%	$2,141	$200	$533	$1,718†	23.6%	1,313	11.6%
1988§	12,507	1,561	12.5%	724	215	485	1,488†	23.2%	1,143	9.1%
1987‖	10,975	1,230	11.2%	522	172	493	1,217†	22.8%	939	8.6%
1986‖	6,196	713	11.5%	848	105	359	667	22.5%	517	8.3%
1985	3,771	477	12.7%	84	74	172	356	23.5%	272	7.2%
1984	2,930	303	10.3%	61	55	119	208	25.7%	154	5.3%
1983	2,226	207	9.3%	59	47	81	137	30.2%	94	4.2%
1982	1,952	NA	NA	NA	NA	NA	NA	NA	72	3.7%
1981	1,549	NA	NA	NA	NA	NA	NA	NA	62	4.0%

Balance Sheet Data (million $)*												
Sept. 30	**Cash**	**Assets**	**Curr. Liab.**	**Ratio**	**Total Assets**	**% Ret. on Assets**	**Long-Term Debt**	**Common Equity**	**Total Inv. Capital**	**% LT Debt. of Cap.**	**% Ret. on Equity**
1989	$8,574	$12,038	$5,278	2.3	$17,482	8.5%	$8,028	$1,689	$10,683	75.1%	47.6%
1988	6,527	10,413	4,165	2.5	13,210	9.4%	3,592	3,707	7,878	45.6%	33.5%
1987	5,025	8,236	3,422	2.4	10,471	9.3%	2,837	2,841	6,151	46.1%	37.5%
1986	2,509	7,977	3,572	2.2	9,577	7.6%	2,834	2,068	5,252	54.0%	29.1%
1985	1,659	2,908	1,277	2.3	4,021	7.7%	903	1,376	2,563	35.2%	27.7%
1984	641	1,775	925	1.9	2,638	9.0%	981	505	1,540	63.7%	36.7%

*Data as originally reported; prior to 1986 data as reported in the 1985 Annual Report (prior to 1984, data are from the listing application of November 3, 1986), conversion to U.S. dollars at year-end exchange rates.
†Includes equity in earnings of nonconsolidated subsidiaries.
‡Before specific item(s) in 1989, 1988, 1986.
§Excludes discount operations and reflects merger or acquisition.
‖Reflects merger or acquisition.

Source: Standard & Poor's, *Standard & Poor's NYSE Stock Reports*, Vol. 57, No. 54, Sec. 12, p. 1096. Reprinted by permission of Standard & Poor's, a division of The McGraw-Hill Companies, Inc.

UB announced a bid of £2.5 billion for Imperial and indicated that, if the offer was successful, Imperial's snack-food businesses would be sold, thus eliminating the need for a Monopolies and Mergers Commission investigation. Imperial's board duly recommended the UB offer to shareholders for acceptance.

Many of Imperial's shareholders, however, were in no mood to accept Imperial's recommendation. Under British stock market regulations, once the Imperial board accepted UB's offer, Imperial's shareholders had two months in which to indicate their acceptance or rejection of it. If the offer was rejected, then the shareholders were free to consider the hostile bid from Hanson. What followed was an increasingly acrimonious war of words between Hanson and Imperial. Hanson charged Imperial with mismanagement. Imperial responded by trying to depict Hanson as an asset stripper with no real interest in generating internal growth from the companies it owned. In the words of one Imperial executive during this period, Lord Hanson "buys and sells companies well, but he manages them jolly badly. He buys, squeezes and goes on to the next one. The only way to grow is by bigger and bigger acquisitions. Like all great conglomerate builders of the past, he's over the hill."[19]

Imperial's management failed to win the war of words. By April 17, UB had secured acceptances for only 34 percent of Imperial's shares, including 14.9 percent held by UB associates. The UB offer lapsed, leaving the way clear for Hanson. On April 18 Hanson secured acceptances for more than 50 percent of Imperial's shares, and its offer went unconditional. At £2.5 billion, the takeover was the largest in British history; it implied a price/earnings multiple of 12.3 on Imperial's prospective earnings.

After the Acquisition

After the acquisition Hanson moved quickly to realize potential from Imperial. Of the 300 staff at Imperial's headquarters, 260 were laid off, and most of the remainder were sent back to the operating level. In July Imperial's hotels and restaurants were sold to Trusthouse Forte for £190 million in cash, representing a price/earnings multiple of 24 on prospective earnings and amounting to 1.7 times book value. That sale was followed in September 1986 by the sale of the Courage Brewing operations, along with a wine and spirits wholesaler and an "off-license" chain (liquor stores) to Elders IXL, an Australian brewing company, for £1.4 billion in cash. The price/earnings multiple for that deal amounted to 17.5 times prospective earnings and represented a premium of £150 million over book value. It was quickly followed by the sale of Imperial's Golden Wonder snack-food business to Dalgety PLC, a British food concern, for £87 million in cash, representing a price/earnings multiple of 13.5 over prospective earnings.

As a result of these moves, by the autumn of 1986 Hanson had raised £1.7 billion from the sale of Imperial's businesses. Effectively, Hanson recouped 66 percent of the total cost of its acquisition by selling companies that contributed slightly more than 45 percent of Imperial's net profit forecasted for the year to October 1986. The net cost of Imperial on this basis had fallen to £850 million, with a consequent decline in the price/earnings multiple on prospective earnings from 12.3 to 7.6.

This was followed in 1988 by the sale of Imperial's food businesses for £534 million, along with the

sale of various other smaller interests for £56 million. By the end of 1988, therefore, Hanson had raised £2.26 billion from the sale of Imperial's assets. It still retained Imperial Tobacco, by far the largest business in Imperial's portfolio, which it had in effect gained for a net cost of £240 million—this for a business that in 1988 generated £150 million in operating profit.

Later Developments

Following the SCM and Imperial acquisitions, in 1987 Hanson acquired Kidde, a 108-company U.S. conglomerate, for $1.7 billion. Kidde seemed set for the "Hanson treatment." Its headquarters was closed within three months of the takeover, and a series of disposals was arranged. These were followed in 1988 by continuing disposals of operations acquired in the Imperial and Kidde acquisitions. In total, they amounted to $1.5 billion.

In mid 1989 Hanson embarked on its biggest takeover ever, the £3.61 billion ($4.8 billion) acquisition of Consolidated Gold Field PLC (CGF). In addition to being the second largest gold-mining operation in the world, CGF also owns a large stone and gravel operation, ARC Ltd., with major holdings in Britain. CGF came to Hanson's attention following an abortive takeover bid for the company from South African-controlled Minorco.

Hanson bought Minorco's 29.9 percent minority stake in CGF and launched its own takeover bid in July 1989. After raising its bid, Hanson won control of CGF in August. CGF also seemed set to be broken up. About half of CGF's value consists of minority stakes in publicly quoted mining companies in the United States, South Africa, and Australia. These stakes range from 38 to 49 percent, enough to hold the key to control in many of the companies. Thus, Hanson should be able to extract a premium price for them. Initial estimates suggest that Hanson should be able to raise $2.5 billion from the sale of CGF's minority holdings.[20] Indeed, by February 1990 Hanson had reportedly recouped about one-third of the purchase price of CGF through disposals and was looking to sell additional operations while gold prices remained high.[21]

The CGF deal led directly to the June 1990 acquisition of Peabody Holdings Co., the largest U.S. coal producer, for a total cost of $1.23 billion in cash. CGF had a 49 percent stake in Newmont Mining Corp., the biggest U.S. gold-mining concern. In turn,

Newmont owned 55 percent of Peabody. In April 1990 Hanson purchased the 45 percent of Peabody not owned by Newmont from three minority owners. Then in June it outbid AMAX Corporation for Newmont's stake in Peabody.

The attraction of Peabody to Hanson lies in two factors: (1) the company owns large deposits of low-sulfur coal, which is increasingly in demand because of environmental concerns; (2) the company has recently invested heavily to upgrade its plant. As a result, in the past four years labor productivity has increased 50 percent.[22] In addition, analysts speculate that the deals, by improving Newmont's financial position (Newmont has used the cash to reduce its debt), may make it possible for Hanson to sell off its 49 percent stake in Newmont for a reasonable premium.

ENDNOTES

1. "The Conglomerate as Antique Dealer," *Economist*, March 11, 1989, pp. 71–73.
2. Quoted in ibid.
3. Quoted in John Byrne and Mark Maremont, "Hanson: The Dangers of Living by Takeover Alone," *Business Week*, August 15, 1988, pp. 62–64.
4. Quoted in Andrew Marton, "The Buccaneer from Britain," *Mergers and Acquisitions* (February 1987), pp. 141–146.
5. Quoted in Byrne and Maremont, "Hanson: The Dangers."
6. Gordon White, "How I Turned $3,000 into $10 Billion," *Fortune*, November 7, 1988, pp. 80–89.
7. The material in this section is based on the following sources: White, "How I Turned," pp. 80–89; Marton, "The Buccaneer from Britain," pp. 141–146; and Hope Lampert, "Britons on the Prowl," *New York Times Magazine*, November 29, 1987, pp. 22–24, 36, 38, 42.
8. White, "How I Turned," p. 81.
9. Quoted in Lampert, "Britons on the Prowl," p. 36.
10. Quoted in White, "How I Turned," p. 81.
11. Quoted in Lampert, "Britons on the Prowl," p. 24.
12. The material in this section is based on the following sources: White, "How I Turned," pp. 80–89; Lampert, "Britons on the Prowl," pp. 22–24, 36, 38, 42; and Mark Cusack, *Hanson Trust: A Review of the Company and Its Prospects* (London: Hoare Govett Limited, 1987).
13. The material in this section is based on the following sources: Cusack, *Hanson Trust*; "The Conglomerate as Antique Dealer," pp. 71–73; Byrne and Maremont, "Hanson: The Dangers," pp. 62–64; and Gordon White, "Nothing Hurts More Than a Bogus Bonus," *Wall Street Journal*, July 20, 1987, p. 18.
14. White, "How I Turned," p. 81.
15. White, "Nothing Hurts More," p. 18.
16. Most of the detail in this section is drawn from two sources: Cusack, *Hanson Trust*; and Lampert, "Britons on the Prowl," pp. 22–24, 36, 38, 42.
17. White, "How I Turned," p. 84.
18. The material in this section is based on the following sources: Cusack, *Hanson Trust*; and Lampert, "Britons on the Prowl," pp. 22–24, 36, 38, 42.
19. Quoted in Philip Revzin, "U.K.'s Hanson Trust Aims for Big Leagues in Takeovers," *Wall Street Journal*, February 25, 1986, p. 30.
20. Mark Maremont and Chuck Hawkins, "Is Consgold Just an Appetizer for Hanson?" *Business Week*, July 10, 1989, pp. 41–42.
21. Joann Lubin, "Hanson to Buy Peabody Stake for $504 Million," *Wall Street Journal*, February 16, 1990, p. A4.
22. "Hanson PLC," *Value Line*, July 20, 1990, p. 832.

Hanson PLC (B): Breaking It Up

This case was prepared by Charles W. L. Hill, the University of Washington.

Introduction

During the 1970s and 1980s, Hanson PLC put together one of the most impressive growth stories of any industrial company in the world. Under the leadership of James Hanson and Gordon White, Hanson PLC made its name by acquiring poorly run conglomerate companies in both Britain and America at prices that were often below their book value. In quick order Hanson would then change the senior management of the acquired company, sell many of the company's assets to other enterprises, typically for a considerable profit, and impose tight financial controls on what remained in order to maximize profitability and cash flow. The locus classicus was Hanson's 1986 acquisition of the Imperial Group, a diversified British tobacco, brewing, and food conglomerate, where some £2.4 billion of the £2.5 billion purchase price was recouped from asset disposals, leaving Hanson with the cash-generating tobacco business intact. The results of this strategy were nothing short of stunning. Between 1973 and 1991, Hanson put together twenty-nine years of uninterrupted profit growth to build a diversified company with revenues of £7.69 billion ($12.3 billion) and operating income of £1.33 billion ($2.13 billion). Hanson's stock price appreciation was also spectacular, increasing more than a hundredfold between 1973 and 1991.

Copyright © 2007 by Charles W. L. Hill. This case was prepared by Charles W. L. Hill, the University of Washington, as the basis for class discussion rather than to illustrate either effective or ineffective handling of an administrative situation. Reprinted by permission of Charles W. L. Hill. All rights reserved. For the most recent financial results of the company discussed in this case, go to **http://finance.yahoo.com**, input the company's stock symbol, and download the latest company report from its homepage.

However, 1991 may have been the high-water mark of Hanson's growth story. In 1990 Hanson took a 2.9 percent stake in the British chemical and pharmaceutical company, Imperial Chemical Industries (ICI). Many saw this as a prelude to yet another Hanson acquisition, but ICI was not about to be taken over. After a bitter public relations battle during which ICI characterized Hanson's management as having a short-term orientation and criticized them for failure to add value to the companies they acquired, Hanson sold its stake in May 1991. While the stake was sold for a profit of £45 million ($70 million), the public relations battle damaged Hanson's image. A year later Hanson was outbid for a British food company, RHM, by a smaller conglomerate run by a former Hanson manager. These two failures raised questions as to whether Hanson's two founders, who were now both in their seventies, were still up to the rough game of hostile takeovers. To compound matters further, for the year ending in September 1993, with many of its cyclical businesses suffering from the effects of a recession in both Britain and America, Hanson reported a 33 percent decline in after-tax profits to $1.5 billion, the first such decline in its history. Reflecting these problems, Hanson's stock price peaked in early 1991 and remained flat over the next few years, while the equity markets in Britain and America boomed.

A New Direction?

In 1992 the leadership mantle at Hanson started to pass from the company's charismatic founders, the now ennobled (Lord) Hanson and White, to Derek Bonham and David Clarke, who were then forty-eight and fifty, respectively. Bonham took over as CEO with primary responsibilities for Hanson's

British-based operations, while Clarke succeeded White as president of Hanson's substantial American operation. Lord Hanson remained on in the chairman's role, while White continued as the company's senior person in charge of mergers and acquisitions. (White died in 1995.)

Although both long-time Hanson employees, Bonham and Clarke clearly lacked the predatory thirst that had driven Hanson and White. Early in his tenure Bonham admitted that Hanson had become "too much of a mishmash" and stated that he hoped to correct that by focusing management's attention on improving the performance of its core businesses in building materials, chemicals, tobacco, and natural resources (primarily timber and coal). While this might require "bolt on acquisitions," Bonham seemed to be signaling that the swashbuckling days of hostile acquisitions and quick asset disposals to pay down debt were over.[1]

Another signal of a shift in management's philosophy came in May 1994, when Hanson announced that it would lengthen the payback period required of new capital investments from three or four years to five or six years. The company stated that it had lengthened the required payback period to take advantage of low interest rates and continuing low inflation. However, many also saw the shift as an attempt to allay fears in the financial community that Hanson's management style was too focused on the short term. Moreover, the move seemed to be consistent with Bonham's stated goal of increasing internal investments as a way of generating growth.[2] The growth that Bonham was talking about, however, was a far cry from the 20 percent annual rate achieved under the leadership of Hanson and White. According to Bonham, "The reality is that we are living in a low growth, low inflation climate. To suggest that you can continue to grow by 20 percent is out of line."[3]

Both Bonham and Clarke repeatedly stated that they saw Hanson growing at about twice the rate of inflation during the 1990s, which suggested a growth rate of around 6 percent, given British and American inflation rates.

Acquiring Quantum

The first significant strategic move under Bonham occurred on June 31, 1993, when Hanson announced that it had reached an agreement to purchase Quantum Chemical Corp., the largest U.S. producer of polyethylene

plastics, in a stock swap that valued Quantum at $20 per share, or $720 million. The purchase price represented a premium of 60 percent over Quantum's closing price of $12.50 on June 30. Hanson also stated that it would assume all of Quantum's $2.5 billion in debt. The acquisition added to Hanson's U.S. chemical operations, which included SCM Chemicals, the world's third largest producer of titanium dioxide.

According to observers, the acquisition represented a strategic bet by Hanson that a protracted cyclical downturn in the polyethylene business was nearing an end. At the peak of the last plastics cycle in 1988, Quantum earned $760 million. However, Quantum had saddled itself with the $2.5 billion debt load in a 1989 restructuring, undertaken while plastics prices were at their previous cyclical peak. Massive debt service requirements and a slump in polyethylene prices had left Quantum with a 1992 loss before accounting charges of $118.4 million, or $3.98 per share. One immediate financial benefit of the acquisition was that Hanson was able to use its superior credit rating to refinance Quantum's debt (much of which was in the form of junk bonds with an average yield of more than 10 percent) at rates closer to Hanson's 5 percent borrowing costs. This move alone cut Quantum's $240 million annual interest bill in half.[4]

In retrospect the Quantum acquisition turned out to be particularly well timed. Prices for low density polyethylene bottomed out in the summer of 1993 at $28 per gallon. By the end of 1994 they had risen to $33 per gallon.[5] Quantum's profits turned out to be highly leveraged to prices. As a result of this leverage and lower interest payments, Quantum's chemical operations earned almost $200 million in fiscal 1994, more than $300 million ahead of its 1992 results. Quantum's results helped Hanson to rebound from its poor showing in 1993. For 1994 it reported a 32 percent rise in pretax profits and a record operating profit of £1.23 billion ($1.92 billion).[6]

1993–1994 Disposals

Throughout 1993 and 1994, Hanson proceeded with a series of relatively minor asset disposals. The objectives of these disposals were twofold: first, to focus the company on its core businesses and, second, to help pay down Hanson's enormous debt load, the legacy of its acquisitions including Quantum. In fiscal 1993 Hanson's long-term debt stood at £7.22 billion ($11.5 billion), and its debt to equity ratio was 1.83

TABLE 1

Hanson PLC—Financial Data

Year Ended Sept. 30	($) Per Pound[†]	Revs.	Oper. Inc.	% Oper. Inc. of Revs.	Cap. Exp.	Depr.	Int. Exp.	Net Bef. Taxes	Eff. Tax Rate	Net Inc.[ǁ]	% Net Inc. of Revs.	Cash Flow
							Income Data (million £)*					
1994	1.509	11,199	1,633	14.6	293	401	545	1,346	20.9%	1,065	9.5	1,466
1993	1.523	9,760	1,288	13.2	301	310	600	1,016	27.8%	734	7.5	1,044
1992	1.822	8,798	1,322	15.0	279	254	777	1,286	15.3%	1,089	12.4	1,343
1991[‡]	1.820	7,691	1,327	17.3	266	216	741	1,319	21.5%	1,035	13.5	1,251
1990[‡]	1.700	7,153	1,236	17.3	247	180	638	1,285	24.4%	971	13.6	NA
1989[‡]	1.690	6,998	996	14.2	192	124	330	1,064	23.6%	813	11.6	NA
1988[‡]	1.770	7,396	923	12.5	198	127	287	880	23.2%	676	9.1	NA
1987[§]	1.560	6,682	749	11.2	151	105	300	741	22.8%	572	9.6	NA

Sept. 30	($) Per Pound[†]	Cash	Curr. Assets	Curr. Liab.	Ratio	Total Assets	% Ret. on Assets	Long-Term Debt	Common Equity	Total Inv. Cap.	% LT Debt of Cap.	% Ret. on Equity
						Balance Sheet Data (million £)*						
1994	1.566	6,815	9,933	6,704	1.5	21,536	4.7	5,038	4,598	9,768	51.6	24.9
1993	1.525	8,067	11,636	7,065	1.6	24,057	3.3	7,221	3,953	11,266	64.1	18.0
1992	1.779	8,445	11,204	6,386	1.8	20,541	5.9	5,069	4,224	9,430	53.8	28.9
1991	1.750	7,771	9,955	4,751	2.1	16,583	6.6	4,880	3,325	8,351	58.4	33.6
1990	1.870	6,883	8,993	4,226	2.1	14,754	7.6	4,258	2,834	7,222	59.0	50.1
1989	1.620	5,309	7,454	3,269	2.3	10,825	8.7	4,971	1,046	6,133	81.1	50.1
1988	1.690	3,860	6,158	2,463	2.5	7,812	9.5	2,124	2,192	4,659	45.6	34.1
1987	1.630	3,059	5,014	2,083	2.4	6,375	8.8	1,727	1,730	3,745	46.1	35.5

*Data as originally reported; prior to 1988 as reported in 1987 Annual Report. Based on UK GAAP.
[†]Average exchange rates for income data; fiscal year-end exchange rates for balance sheet.
[‡]Excludes discretionary operations and reflects merger or acquisition.
[§]Reflects merger or acquisition.
[ǁ]Before special items.

(see Table 1). This debt load was beginning to trouble the financial community, who were starting to question the ability of Hanson to maintain its historically high dividend. In a previous era Hanson had quickly paid down debt from acquisitions by raising cash through asset disposals, but there had been little movement in this direction since the late 1980s.

Between January 1993 and August 1994, Hanson sold more than fifteen companies for a total of £815 million ($1.3 billion). These disposals included its Beazer home building operations in both the United States and the United Kingdom; an office supply business; and Axelson, an oil industry equipment group.[7]

Spinning off U.S. Industries

The next big strategic move occurred in February 1995, when Hanson announced that it would spin off thirty-four of its smaller American-based companies into a new entity called U.S. Industries under the leadership of David Clarke. Hanson would retain ownership over several of its larger U.S. operations, including Quantum Chemical and Peabody Coal. The new company was to include such well-known brand names as Jacuzzi whirlpools, Farberware cookware, Ames garden tools, Rexair vacuum cleaners, and Tommy Armour golf clubs. In 1994 the thirty-four companies had sales of $3 billion and operating profits of $252 million.

The company was to be responsible for $1.4 billion of Hanson's debt. According to one analyst,

> For Hanson, it achieves a one shot divestiture of a number of companies they may have struggled to sell independently, not because the individual assets are unattractive, but because it's messy to sell so many of them. They are able to divest in a tax efficient way and at the same time take a lot of cash out, leaving them with the ability to buy something else.[8]

The spinoff was completed on June 1, 1995. At the time, David Clarke stated that the new company's first objective would be to reduce its debt load, primarily by selling off a number of companies valued at $600 million.[9]

Acquiring Eastern Group

Only July 31, 1995, Hanson announced that it would acquire Eastern Group, one of Britain's major electric utilities, for £2 billion ($3.2 billion). Eastern, which was privatized in 1990, has a customer base of 3 million and is responsible for 15 percent of the electricity produced in Britain, primarily for natural gas-fired generating facilities. Eastern is also the seventh largest natural gas supplier in the country. In the year ending March 31, 1995, Eastern's earnings were up 15 percent to £203 million ($324 billion) on revenues of £2.06 billion ($3.2 billion).[10]

Hanson stated that it was attracted to Eastern by its steady earnings growth. However, critics noted that the deal yet again stretched Hanson's balance sheet, which once more had begun to look solid after the U.S. Industries spinoff. The debt-financed purchase of Eastern caused Hanson's debt-to-equity ratio to shoot up from 37 percent to 130 percent, once more raising concerns that Hanson might not be able to service its historically high dividends. A partial response to these concerns came in December 1995, when the company announced plans to dispose of two additional U.S. subsidiaries—Suburban Propane and Cavenham Forest Industries—for £1.5 billion ($2.4 billion). The proceeds were to be used to pay down Hanson's debt load. Analysts calculated that the cash raised from these spinoffs would reduce Hanson's debt-to-equity ratio to around 90 percent.[11]

The Demerger

By late 1995 it was becoming increasingly clear within Hanson's senior management team that drastic action would be required to boost the company's lagging share price.[12] As the British and American economies continued in their long recovery from recession, Hanson's cyclical business staged a significant performance improvement, with operating profits increasing by 44 percent for the fiscal year that ended in September 1995. Despite this performance, the company's share price had been essentially flat since the early 1990s (see Figure 1). Over the same period both the London and New York stock markets had increased substantially. By the end of 1995 the price-to-earnings ratio of Hanson's shares was 30 percent below that of the average stock on the London exchange, while Hanson's dividend yield at over 6.5 percent was among the highest offered by any company. It seemed that nothing could move the stock price, not the strong profit performance, not the spinoff of U.S. Industries, not the Eastern acquisition, and not the recently announced disposals.

It was against this background that Hanson stunned both London and Wall Street with its January 29 announcement that it would divide the company up into four independent businesses, effectively dismantling the conglomerate assembled by Hanson and White. Hanson stated that it would split into a chemicals business, an energy company, a tobacco company, and a building materials enterprise. Imperial Tobacco would be the largest company, with sales of £3.57 billion ($5.37 billion). The energy business, which would include Hanson's coal and electric businesses, would have sales of £3.5 billion ($5.27 billion). The chemicals business would have sales of £2 billion ($3.04 billion), while the building materials group would have sales of £2.3 billion ($3.48 billion).[13] Bonham was to run the energy business, while Hanson was to take over the building materials group until his retirement. The company estimated that the demerger would be completed by early 1997.

Hanson's stock price initially surged 7 percent on the news, but it fell later the same day and ended up less than 0.5 percent. The lack of a sustained positive reaction from the stock markets on both sides of the Atlantic puzzled Hanson's managers. Over the last few years, a number of diversified companies had announced demergers—including ITT, AT&T, and Sears—and their stock prices had almost always responded in a very positive fashion. In Hanson's case, however, this did not occur.

One possible explanation for the lack of a favorable reaction came from Moody's Investor Service,

FIGURE 1

Hanson PLC

Lord Hanson

Derek Bonham

which put Hanson's debt under review for a possible downgrade one day after the breakup was announced. Moody's noted that "this is a highly complex sequence of transactions which are at an early stage and which will require various approvals."[14] Among the concerns expressed were that the demerger might raise Hanson's borrowing costs. The tax consequences of the demerger were also not immediately apparent, although there were some indications that there might be some one-time capital gains tax charges. Moreover, several stock analysts commented that the demerged Hanson units might not be able or willing to maintain Hanson's historically high level of dividends. One influential London-based stock analyst also noted that unlike most conglomerates that were demerging, there were few if any hidden assets at Hanson. This analyst calculated that Hanson's constituent parts should be valued at 194 pence, which was below the 212 pence price that Hanson's stock closed at on January 30, 1996.[15]

As a further prelude to the demerger, in March 1996 Hanson announced the sale of its remaining U.S. timberland operations to Willamette Industries for $1.59 billion. This sale followed Hanson's disposal of Cavenham Forest Industries in December 1995, and it completed Hanson's exit from the timber business. The cash generated from the sale was to be used to pay down Hanson's debt.[16]

ENDNOTES

1. R. A. Melcher, "Can This Predator Change Its Stripes?" *Business Week*, June 22, 1992, p. 38; J. Guyon, "Hanson Crosses the Atlantic to Woo Investors," *Wall Street Journal*, December 6, 1983, p. 7D.
2. R. Rudd, "Hanson Increases Investment Payback Time," *Financial Times*, May 16, 1994, p. 15.
3. P. Dwyer and J. Weber, "Hanson Looks for a Hat Trick," *Business Week*, March 14, 1994. pp. 68–69.
4. S. McMurray, "UK's Hanson to Buy Maker of Polyethylene," *Wall Street Journal*, July 1, 1993, p. A3.
5. D. Wighton, "Conglomerate's $3.2 Billion Gamble Pays Off," *Financial Times*, December 2, 1994, p. 23.
6. "Hanson Posts 32% Rise in Pre Tax Profits," *Wall Street Journal*, December 2, 1994, p. B3.
7. P. Taylor, "Hanson Lifted by Quantum Chemical," *Financial Times*, August 17, 1994, p. 13.
8. R. W. Stevenson, "Hanson Plans to Spin Off 34 U.S. Companies," *New York Times*, February 23, 1995, p. C1.
9. L. L. Brownless and J. R. Dorfman, "Birth of U.S. Industries Isn't Without Complications," *Wall Street Journal*, May 18, 1995, p. B4.
10. D. Wighton, "Hanson Plugs into New Current," *Financial Times*, July 31, 1995, p. 15.
11. D. Wighton, "Hanson Seeks £1.5 Billion from U.S. Disposals," *Financial Times*, December 21, 1995, p. 13.
12. "Widow Hanson's Children Leave Home," *Economist*, February 3, 1996, pp. 51–52.
13. R. Bonte-Friedheim and J. Guyon, "Hanson to Divide into Four Businesses," *Wall Street Journal*, January 31, 1996, p. A3.
14. Bonte-Friedheim and Guyon, "Hanson to Divide into Four Businesses."
15. D. Wighton, "Centrifugal Forces That Pulled Hanson Apart," *Financial Times*, January 31, 1996, p. 18.
16. "Hanson to Sell Mills," *Wall Street Journal: Money & Investing Update*, March 12, 1996.

Case 30

Philips Versus Matsushita: A New Century, a New Round

This case was prepared by Christopher A. Bartlett, Harvard Business School.

Throughout their long histories, N.V. Philips (Netherlands) and Matsushita Electric (Japan) had followed very different strategies and emerged with very different organizational capabilities. Philips built its success on a worldwide portfolio of responsive national organizations while Matsushita based its global competitiveness on its centralized, highly efficient operations in Japan.

During the 1990s, both companies experienced major challenges to their historic competitive positions and organizational models, and at the end of the decade, both companies were struggling to reestablish their competitiveness. At the turn of the millennium, new CEOs at both companies were implementing yet another round of strategic initiatives and organizational restructurings. Observers wondered how the changes would affect their long-running competitive battle.

Philips: Background

In 1892, Gerard Philips and his father opened a small light-bulb factory in Eindhoven, Holland. When their venture almost failed, they recruited Gerard's

Copyright © by Harvard Business School Publishing. This case was prepared by Christopher A. Bartlett. HBS cases are developed solely as the basis for class discussion. Cases are not intended to serve as endorsements, sources of primary data, or illustrations of effective or ineffective management. Reprinted by permission of Harvard Business School Publishing. All rights reserved. For the most recent financial results of the company discussed in this case, go to **http://finance .yahoo.com**, input the company's stock symbol, and download the latest company report from its homepage.

brother, Anton, an excellent salesman and manager. By 1900, Philips was the third largest light-bulb producer in Europe.

From its founding, Philips developed a tradition of caring for workers. In Eindhoven it built company houses, bolstered education, and paid its employees so well that other local employers complained. When Philips incorporated in 1912, it set aside 10% of profits for employees.

Technological Competence and Geographic Expansion

While larger electrical products companies were racing to diversify, Philips made only light-bulbs. This one-product focus and Gerard's technological prowess enabled the company to create significant innovations. Company policy was to scrap old plants and use new machines or factories whenever advances were made in new production technology. Anton wrote down assets rapidly and set aside substantial reserves for replacing outdated equipment. Philips also became a leader in industrial research, creating physics and chemistry labs to address production problems as well as more abstract scientific ones. The labs developed a tungsten metal filament bulb that was a great commercial success and gave Philips the financial strength to compete against its giant rivals.

Holland's small size soon forced Philips to look beyond its Dutch borders for enough volume to mass produce. In 1899, Anton hired the company's first export manager, and soon the company was selling into such diverse markets as Japan, Australia, Canada,

Brazil, and Russia. In 1912, as the electric lamp industry began to show signs of overcapacity, Philips started building sales organizations in the United States, Canada, and France. All other functions remained highly centralized in Eindhoven. In many foreign countries Philips created local joint ventures to gain market acceptance.

In 1919, Philips entered into the Principal Agreement with General Electric, giving each company the use of the other's patents. The agreement also divided the world into "three spheres of influence": General Electric would control North America; Philips would control Holland; but both companies agreed to compete freely in the rest of the world. (General Electric also took a 20% stake in Philips.) After this time, Philips began evolving from a highly centralized company, whose sales were conducted through third parties, to a decentralized sales organization with autonomous marketing companies in 14 European countries, China, Brazil, and Australia.

During this period, the company also broadened its product line significantly. In 1918, it began producing electronic vacuum tubes; eight years later its first radios appeared, capturing a 20% world market share within a decade; and during the 1930s, Philips began producing X-ray tubes. The Great Depression brought with it trade barriers and high tariffs, and Philips was forced to build local production facilities to protect its foreign sales of these products.

Philips: Organizational Development

One of the earliest traditions at Philips was a shared but competitive leadership by the commercial and technical functions. Gerard, an engineer, and Anton, a businessman, began a subtle competition where Gerard would try to produce more than Anton could sell and vice versa. Nevertheless, the two agreed that strong research was vital to Philips' survival.

During the late 1930s, in anticipation of the impending war, Philips transferred its overseas assets to two trusts, British Philips and the North American Philips Corporation; it also moved most of its vital research laboratories to Redhill in Surrey, England, and its top management to the United States. Supported by the assets and resources transferred abroad, and isolated from their parent, the individual country organizations became more independent during the war.

Because waves of Allied and German bombing had pummeled most of Philips' industrial plant in the Netherlands, the management board decided to build the postwar organization on the strengths of the national organizations (NOs). Their greatly increased self-sufficiency during the war had allowed most to become adept at responding to country-specific market conditions—a capability that became a valuable asset in the postwar era. For example, when international wrangling precluded any agreement on three competing television transmission standards (PAL, SECAM, and NTSC), each nation decided which to adopt. Furthermore, consumer preferences and economic conditions varied: in some countries, rich, furniture-encased TV sets were the norm; in others, sleek, contemporary models dominated the market. In the United Kingdom, the only way to penetrate the market was to establish a rental business; in richer countries, a major marketing challenge was overcoming elitist prejudice against television. In this environment, the independent NOs had a great advantage in being able to sense and respond to the differences.

Eventually, responsiveness extended beyond adaptive marketing. As NOs built their own technical capabilities, product development often became a function of local market conditions. For example, Philips of Canada created the company's first color TV; Philips of Australia created the first stereo TV; and Philips of the United Kingdom created the first TVs with teletext.

While NOs took major responsibility for financial, legal, and administrative matters, fourteen product divisions (PDs), located in Eindhoven, were formally responsible for development, production, and global distribution. (In reality, the NOs' control of assets and the PDs' distance from the operations often undercut this formal role.) The research function remained independent and, with continued strong funding, set up eight separate laboratories in Europe and the United States.

While the formal corporate-level structure was represented as a type of geographic/product matrix, it was clear that NOs had the real power. NOs reported directly to the management board, which Philips enlarged from 4 members to 10 to ensure that top management remained in contact with and control of the highly autonomous NOs. Each NO also regularly sent envoys to Eindhoven to represent its interests. Top management, most of whom had careers that included multiple foreign tours of duty, made frequent overseas visits to the NOs. In 1954, the board established the International Concern Council to formalize regular meetings with the heads of all major NOs.

Within the NOs, the management structure mimicked the legendary joint technical and commercial leadership of the two Philips brothers. Most were led by a technical manager and a commercial manager. In some locations, a finance manager filled out the top management triad that typically reached key decisions collectively. This cross-functional coordination capability was reflected down through the NOs in front-line product teams, product-group-level management teams, and at the senior management committee of the NOs' top commercial, technical, and financial managers.

The overwhelming importance of foreign operations to Philips, the commensurate status of the NOs within the corporate hierarchy, and even the cosmopolitan appeal of many of the offshore subsidiaries' locations encouraged many Philips managers to take extended foreign tours of duty, working in a series of two- or three-year posts. This elite group of expatriate managers identified strongly with each other and with the NOs as a group and had no difficulty representing their strong, country-oriented views to corporate management.

Philips: Attempts at Reorganization

In the late 1960s, the creation of the Common Market eroded trade barriers within Europe and diluted the rationale for maintaining independent, country-level subsidiaries. New transistor- and printed circuit-based technologies demanded larger production runs than most national plants could justify, and many of Philips' competitors were moving production of electronics to new facilities in low-wage areas in East Asia and Central and South America. Despite its many technological innovations, Philips' ability to bring products to market began to falter. In the 1960s, the company invented the audiocassette but let its Japanese competitors capture the mass market. A decade later, its R&D group developed the V2000 videocassette format—superior technically to Sony's Beta or Matsushita's VHS—but was forced to abandon it when North American Philips decided to outsource, brand, and sell a VHS product which it manufactured under license from Matsushita.

Over three decades, seven chairmen experimented with reorganizing the company to deal with its growing problems. Yet, entering the new millennium, Philips' financial performance remained poor and its global competitiveness was still in question. (See Exhibits 1 and 2.)

Van Riemsdijk and Rodenburg Reorganizations, 1970s

Concerned about what one magazine described as "continued profitless progress," newly appointed CEO Hendrick van Riemsdijk created an organization committee to prepare a policy paper on the division of responsibilities between the PDs and the NOs. Their report, dubbed the "Yellow Booklet," outlined the disadvantages of Philips' matrix organization in 1971:

> Without an agreement [defining the relationship between national organizations and product divisions], it is impossible to determine in any given situation which of the two parties is responsible. . . . As operations become increasingly complex, an organizational form of this type will only lower the speed of reaction of an enterprise.

On the basis of this report, van Riemsdijk proposed rebalancing the managerial relationships between PDs and NOs—"tilting the matrix" in his words—to allow Philips to decrease the number of products marketed, build scale by concentrating production, and increase the flow of goods among national organizations. He proposed closing the least efficient local plants and converting the best into International Production Centers (IPCs), each supplying many NOs. In so doing, van Riemsdijk hoped that PD managers would gain control over manufacturing operations. Due to the political and organizational difficulty of closing local plants, however, implementation was slow.

In the late 1970s, his successor CEO, Dr. Rodenburg, continued this thrust. Several IPCs were established, but the NOs seemed as powerful and independent as ever. He furthered matrix simplification by replacing the dual commercial and technical leadership with single management at both the corporate and national organizational levels. Yet the power struggles continued.

Wisse Dekker Reorganization, 1982

Unsatisfied with the company's slow response and concerned by its slumping financial performance, upon becoming CEO in 1982, Wisse Dekker outlined

EXHIBIT 1

Philips Group Summary Financial Data, 1970–2000 (millions of guilders unless otherwise stated)

	2000	1995	1990	1985	1980	1975	1970
Net sales	F83,437	F64,462	F55,764	F60,045	F36,536	F27,115	F15,070
Income from operations (excluding restructuring)	NA	4,090	2,260	3,075	1,577	1,201	1,280
Income from operations (including restructuring)	9,434	4,044	−2,389	N/A	N/A	N/A	N/A
As a percentage of net sales	11.3%	6.3%	−4.3%	5.1%	4.3%	4.5%	8.5%
Income after taxes	12,559	2,889	F−4,447	F1,025	F532	F341	F446
Net income from normal business operations	NA	2,684	−4,526	n/a	328	347	435
Stockholders' equity (common)	49,473	14,055	11,165	16,151	12,996	10,047	6,324
Return on stockholders' equity	42.8%	20.2%	−30.2%	5.6%	2.7%	3.6%	7.3%
Distribution per common share, par value F10 (in guilders)	F2.64	F1.60	F0.0	F2.00	F1.80	F1.40	F1.70
Total assets	86,114	54,683	51,595	52,883	39,647	30,040	19,088
Inventories as a percentage of net sales	13.9%	18.2%	20.7%	23.2%	32.8%	32.9%	35.2%
Outstanding trade receivables in month's sales	1.5	1.6	1.6	2.0	3.0	3.0	2.8
Current ratio	1.2		1.4	1.6	1.7	1.8	1.7
Employees at year-end (in thousands)	219	265	273	346	373	397	359
Wages, salaries and other related costs	NA	NA	F17,582	F21,491	F15,339	F11,212	F5,890
Exchange rate (period end; guilder/$)	2.34	1.60	1.69	2.75	2.15	2.69	3.62
Selected Data in Millions of Dollars:							
Sales	$35,253	$40,039	$33,018	$21,802	$16,993	$10,098	$4,163
Operating profit	3,986	2,512	1,247	988	734	464	NA
Pretax income	5,837	2,083	−2,380	658	364	256	NA
Net income	5,306	1,667	−2,510	334	153	95	120
Total assets	35,885	32,651	30,549	19,202	18,440	11,186	5,273
Shareholders' equity (common)	20,238	8,784	6,611	5,864	6,044	3,741	1,747

Note: Exchange rate 12/31/00 was Euro/US$: 1.074.

Source: Annual reports; Standard & Poors' *Compustat*; Moody's Industrial and International Manuals.

a new initiative. Aware of the cost advantage of Philips' Japanese counterparts, he closed inefficient operations— particularly in Europe where 40 of the company's more than 200 plants were shut. He focused on core operations by selling some businesses (for example, welding, energy cables, and furniture) while acquiring an interest in Grundig and Westinghouse's North American lamp activities. Dekker also supported technology-sharing agreements and entered alliances in offshore manufacturing.

To deal with the slow-moving bureaucracy, he continued his predecessor's initiative to replace dual leadership with single general managers. He also continued to "tilt the matrix" by giving PDs formal product management responsibility, but leaving NOs responsible for local profits. And, he energized the management board by reducing its size, bringing on directors with strong operating experience, and creating subcommittees to deal with difficult issues. Finally, Dekker redefined the product planning process incorporating input from the NOs, but giving global PDs the final decision on long-range direction. Still sales declined and profits stagnated.

Van der Klugt Reorganization, 1987

When Cor van der Klugt succeeded Dekker as chairman in 1987, Philips had lost its long-held consumer electronics leadership position to Matsushita, and was

EXHIBIT 2

Philips Group, Sales by Product and Geographic Segment, 1985–2000 (millions of guilders)

	2000		1995		1990		1985	
Net Sales by Product Segment:								
Lighting	F11,133	13%	F 8,353	13%	F 7,026	13%	F 7,976	12%
Consumer electronics	32,357	39	22,027	34	25,400	46	16,906	26
Domestic appliances	4,643	6	—				6,644	10
Professional products/Systems	—	—	11,562	18	13,059	23	17,850	28
Components/Semiconductors	23,009	28	10,714	17	8,161	15	11,620	18
Software/Services	—	—	9,425	15	—	—	—	—
Medical systems	6,679	8	—	—	—	—	—	—
Origin	1,580	2	—	—	—	—	—	—
Miscellaneous	4,035	5	2,381	4	2,118	4	3,272	5
Total	**83,437**	**100%**	**64,462**	**100%**	**F55,764**	**100%**	**F 64,266**	**100%**
Operating Income by Sector:								
Lighting	1,472	16%	983	24%	419	18%	F 910	30%
Consumer electronics	824	9	167	4	1,499	66	34	1
Domestic appliances	632	7	—	—	—	—	397	13
Professional products/Systems	—	—	157	4	189	8	1,484	48
Components/Semiconductors	4,220	45	2,233	55	−43	−2	44	1
Software/Services	—	—	886	22	—	—	—	—
Medical systems	372	4	—	—	—	—	—	—
Origin	2,343	25	—	—	—	—	—	—
Miscellaneous	−249	−3	423	10	218	10	200	7
Increase not attributable to a sector	−181	−2	(805)	(20)	−22	−1	6	0
Total	**9,434**	**100%**	**4,044**	**100%**	**2,260**	**100%**	**F 3,075**	**100%**

Notes:
Conversion rate (12/31/00): 1 Euro: 2.20371 Dutch Guilders
Totals may not add due to rounding.
Product sector sales after 1988 are external sales only; therefore, no eliminations are made; sector sales before 1988 include sales to other sectors; therefore, eliminations are made.
Data are not comparable to consolidated financial summary due to restating.
Source: Annual reports.

one of only two non-Japanese companies in the world's top ten. Its net profit margins of 1% to 2% not only lagged behind General Electric's 9%, but even its highly aggressive Japanese competitors' slim 4%. Van der Klugt set a profit objective of 3% to 4% and made beating the Japanese companies a top priority.

As van der Klugt reviewed Philips' strategy, he designated various businesses as core (those that shared related technologies, had strategic importance, or were technical leaders) and non-core (stand-alone businesses that were not targets for world leadership and could

eventually be sold if required). Of the four businesses defined as core, three were strategically linked: components, consumer electronics, and telecommunications and data systems. The fourth, lighting, was regarded as strategically vital because its cash flow funded development. The non-core businesses included domestic appliances and medical systems which van der Klugt spun off into joint ventures with Whirlpool and GE, respectively.

In continuing efforts to strengthen the PDs relative to the NOs, van der Klugt restructured Philips around the four core global divisions rather than the former 14 PDs. This allowed him to trim the management board, appointing the displaced board members to a new policy-making Group Management Committee. Consisting primarily of PD heads and functional chiefs, this body replaced the old NO-dominated International Concern Council. Finally, he sharply reduced the 3,000-strong headquarters staff, reallocating many of them to the PDs.

To link PDs more directly to markets, van der Klugt dispatched many experienced product-line managers to Philips' most competitive markets. For example, management of the digital audio tape and electric-shaver product lines were relocated to Japan, while the medical technology and domestic appliances lines were moved to the United States.

Such moves, along with continued efforts at globalizing product development and production efforts, required that the parent company gain firmer control over NOs, especially the giant North American Philips Corp. (NAPC). Although Philips had obtained a majority equity interest after World War II, it was not always able to make the U.S. company respond to directives from the center, as the V2000 VCR incident showed. To prevent replays of such experiences, in 1987 van der Klugt repurchased publicly owned NAPC shares for $700 million.

Reflecting the growing sentiment among some managers that R&D was not market oriented enough, van der Klugt halved spending on basic research to about 10% of total R&D. To manage what he described as "R&D's tendency to ponder the fundamental laws of nature," he made R&D the direct responsibility of the businesses being supported by the research. This required that each research lab become focused on specific business areas (see Exhibit 3).

Finally, van der Klugt continued the effort to build efficient, specialized, multi-market production facilities by closing 75 of the company's 420 remaining plants worldwide. He also eliminated 38,000 of its 344,000 employees—21,000 through divesting businesses, shaking up the myth of lifetime employment at the company. He anticipated that all these restructurings would lead to a financial recovery by 1990. Unanticipated losses for that year, however—more than 4.5 billion Dutch guilders ($2.5 billion)—provoked a class-action law suit by angry American investors, who alleged that positive projections by the company had been misleading. In a surprise move, on May 14, 1990, van der Klugt and half of the management board were replaced.

EXHIBIT 3

Philips Research Labs by Location and Specialty, 1987

Location	Size (staff)	Specialty
Eindhoven, The Netherlands	2,000	Basic research, electronics, manufacturing technology
Redhill, Surrey, England	450	Microelectronics, television, defense
Hamburg, Germany	350	Communications, office equipment, medical imaging
Aachen, W. Germany	250	Fiber optics, X-ray systems
Paris, France	350	Microprocessors, chip materials, design
Brussels	50	Artificial intelligence
Briarcliff Manor, New York	35	Optical systems, television, superconductivity, defense
Sunnyvale, California	150	Integrated circuits

Source: Philips, in *Business Week*, March 21, 1988, p. 156.

Timmer Reorganization, 1990

The new president, Jan Timmer, had spent most of his 35-year Philips career turning around unprofitable businesses. With rumors of a takeover or a government bailout swirling, he met with his top 100 managers and distributed a hypothetical—but fact-based—release announcing that Philips was bankrupt. "So what action can you take this weekend?" he challenged them.

Under "Operation Centurion," headcount was reduced by 68,000 or 22% over the next 18 months, earning Timmer the nickname "The Butcher of Eindhoven." Because European laws required substantial compensation for layoffs—Eindhoven workers received 15 months' pay, for example—the first round of 10,000 layoffs alone cost Philips $700 million. To spread the burden around the globe and to speed the process, Timmer asked his PD managers to negotiate cuts with NO managers. According to one report, however, country managers were "digging in their heels to save local jobs." But the cuts came—many from overseas operations. In addition to the job cuts, Timmer vowed to "change the way we work." He established new performance rules and asked hundreds of top managers to sign contracts that committed them to specific financial goals. Those who broke those contracts were replaced—often with outsiders.

To focus resources further, Timmer sold off various businesses including integrated circuits to Matsushita, minicomputers to Digital, defense electronics to Thomson and the remaining 53% of appliances to Whirlpool. Yet profitability was still well below the modest 4% on sales he promised. In particular, consumer electronics lagged with slow growth in a price-competitive market. The core problem was identified by a 1994 McKinsey study that estimated that value added per hour in Japanese consumer electronic factories was still 68% above that of European plants. In this environment, most NO managers kept their heads down, using their distance from Eindhoven as their defense against the ongoing rationalization.

After three years of cost-cutting, in early 1994, Timmer finally presented a new growth strategy to the board. His plan was to expand software, services, and multimedia to become 40% of revenues by 2000. He was betting on Philips' legendary innovative capability to restart the growth engines. Earlier, he had recruited Frank Carrubba, Hewlett-Packard's director of research, and encouraged him to focus on developing 15 core technologies. The list, which included interactive compact disc (CD-i), digital compact cassettes (DCC), high definition television (HDTV), and multimedia software, was soon dubbed "the president's projects." But his earlier divestment of some of Philips' truly high-tech businesses and a 37% cut in R&D personnel left the company with few who understood the technology of the new priority businesses.

By 1996, it was clear that Philips' HDTV technology would not become industry standard, that its DCC gamble had lost out to Sony's Minidisc, and that CD-i was a marketing failure. While costs were lower, so too was morale, particularly among middle management. Critics claimed that the company's drive for cost-cutting and standardization had led it to ignore new worldwide market demands for more segmented products and higher consumer service.

Boonstra Reorganization, 1996

When Timmer stepped down in October 1996, the board replaced him with a radical choice for Philips—an outsider whose expertise was in marketing and Asia rather than technology and Europe. Cor Boonstra was a 58-year-old Dutchman whose years as CEO of Sara Lee, the U.S. consumer products firm,

had earned him a reputation as a hard-driving marketing genius. Joining Philips in 1994, he headed the Asia Pacific region and the lighting division before being tapped as CEO.

Unencumbered by tradition, he immediately announced strategic sweeping changes designed to reach his target of increasing return on net assets from 17% to 24% by 1999. "There are no taboos, no sacred cows," he said. "The bleeders must be turned around, sold, or closed." Within three years, he had sold off 40 of Philips' 120 major businesses—including such well known units as Polygram and Grundig. He also initiated a major worldwide restructuring, promising to transform a structure he described as "a plate of spaghetti" into "a neat row of asparagus." He said:

> How can we compete with the Koreans? They don't have 350 companies all over the world. Their factory in Ireland covers Europe and their manufacturing facility in Mexico serves North America. We need a more structured and simpler manufacturing and marketing organization to achieve a cost pattern in line with those who do not have our heritage. This is still one of the biggest issues facing Philips.

Within a year, 3,100 jobs were eliminated in North America and 3,000 employees were added in Asia Pacific, emphasizing Boonstra's determination to shift production to low-wage countries and his broader commitment to Asia. And after three years, he had closed 100 of the company's 356 factories worldwide. At the same time, he replaced the company's 21 PDs with 7 divisions, but shifted day-to-day operating responsibility to 100 business units, each responsible for its profits worldwide. It was a move designed to finally eliminate the old PD/NO matrix. Finally, in a move that shocked most employees, he announced that the 100-year-old Eindhoven headquarters would be relocated to Amsterdam with only 400 of the 3,000 corporate positions remaining.

By early 1998, he was ready to announce his new strategy. Despite early speculation that he might abandon consumer electronics, he proclaimed it as the center of Philips' future. Betting on the "digital revolution," he planned to focus on established technologies such as cellular phones (through a joint venture with Lucent), digital TV, digital videodisc, and web TV. Furthermore, he committed major resources to marketing, including a 40% increase in advertising to raise awareness and image of the Philips brand and de-emphasize most of the 150 other brands it supported worldwide—from Magnavox TVs to Norelco shavers to Marantz stereos.

While not everything succeeded (the Lucent cell phone JV collapsed after nine months, for example), overall performance improved significantly in the late 1990s. By 1999, Boonstra was able to announce that he had achieved his objective of a 24% return on net assets.

Kleisterlee Reorganization, 2001

In May 2001, Boonstra passed the CEO's mantle to Gerard Kleisterlee, a 54-year-old engineer (and career Philips man) whose turnaround of the components business had earned him a board seat only a year earlier. Believing that Philips had finally turned around, the board challenged Kleisterlee to grow sales by 10% annually and earnings 15%, while increasing return on assets to 30%.

Despite its stock trading at a steep discount to its breakup value, Philips governance structure and Dutch legislation made a hostile raid all but impossible. Nonetheless, Kleisterlee described the difference as "a management discount" and vowed to eliminate it. The first sign of restructuring came within weeks, when mobile phone production was outsourced to CEC of China. Then, in August, Kleisterlee announced an agreement with Japan's Funai Electric to take over production of its VCRs, resulting in the immediate closure of the European production center in Austria and the loss of 1,000 jobs. The CEO then acknowledged that he was seeking partners to take over the manufacturing of some of its other mass-produced items such as television sets.

In mid 2001, a slowing economy resulted in the company's first quarterly loss since 1996 and a reversal of the prior year's strong positive cash flow. Many felt that these growing financial pressures—and shareholders' growing impatience—were finally leading Philips to recognize that its best hope of survival was to outsource even more of its basic manufacturing and become a technology developer and global marketer. They believed it was time to recognize that its 30-year quest to build efficiency into its global operations had failed.

Matsushita: Background

In 1918, Konosuke Matsushita (or "KM" as he was affectionately known), a 23-year-old inspector with the Osaka Electric Light Company, invested ¥100 to start production of double-ended sockets in his modest home. The company grew rapidly, expanding into battery-powered lamps, electric irons, and radios. On May 5, 1932, Matsushita's 14th anniversary, KM announced to his 162 employees a 250-year corporate plan broken into 25-year sections, each to be carried out by successive generations. His plan was codified in a company creed and in the "Seven Spirits of Matsushita" (see Exhibit 4), which, along with the company song, continued to be woven into morning assemblies worldwide and provided the basis of the "cultural and spiritual training" all new employees received during their first seven months with the company.

EXHIBIT 4

Matsushita Creed and Philosophy (Excerpts)

Creed

Through our industrial activities, we strive to foster progress, to promote the general welfare of society, and to devote ourselves to furthering the development of world culture.

Seven Spirits of Matsushita

Service through Industry
Fairness
Harmony and Cooperation
Struggle for Progress
Courtesy and Humility
Adjustment and Assimilation
Gratitude

KM's Business Philosophy (Selected Quotations)

"The purpose of an enterprise is to contribute to society by supplying goods of high quality at low prices in ample quantity."

"Profit comes in compensation for contribution to society. . . . [It] is a result rather than a goal."

"The responsibility of the manufacturer cannot be relieved until its product is disposed of by the end user."

"Unsuccessful business employs a wrong management. You should not find its causes in bad fortune, unfavorable surroundings or wrong timing."

"Business appetite has no self-restraining mechanism. . . . When you notice you have gone too far, you must have the courage to come back."

Source: "Matsushita Electric Industrial (MEI) in 1987," Harvard Business School Case No. 388-144.

In the post-war boom, Matsushita introduced a flood of new products: TV sets in 1952; transistor radios in 1958; color TVs, dishwashers, and electric ovens in 1960. Capitalizing on its broad line of 5,000 products (Sony produced 80), the company opened 25,000 domestic retail outlets. With more than six times the outlets of rival Sony, the ubiquitous "National Shops" represented 40% of appliance stores in Japan in the late 1960s. These not only provided assured sales volume, but also gave the company direct access to market trends and consumer reaction. When post-war growth slowed, however, Matsushita had to look beyond its expanding product line and excellent distribution system for growth. After trying many tactics to boost sales—even sending assembly line workers out as door-to-door salesmen—the company eventually focused on export markets.

The Organization's Foundation: Divisional Structure

Plagued by ill health, KM wished to delegate more authority than was typical in Japanese companies. In 1933, Matsushita became the first Japanese company to adopt the divisional structure, giving each division clearly defined profit responsibility for its product. In addition to creating a "small business" environment, the product division structure generated internal competition that spurred each business to drive growth by leveraging its technology to develop new products. After the innovating division had earned substantial profits on its new product, however, company policy was to spin it off as a new division to maintain the "hungry spirit."

Under the "one-product-one-division" system, corporate management provided each largely self-sufficient division with initial funds to establish its own development, production, and marketing capabilities. Corporate treasury operated like a commercial bank, reviewing divisions' loan requests for which it charged slightly higher-than-market interest, and accepting deposits on their excess funds. Divisional profitability was determined after deductions for central services such as corporate R&D and interest on internal borrowings. Each division paid 60% of earnings to headquarters and financed all additional working capital and fixed asset requirements from the retained 40%. Transfer prices were based on the market and settled through the treasury on normal commercial terms. KM expected uniform performance across the company's 36 divisions, and division managers whose operating profits fell below 4% of sales for two successive years were replaced.

While basic technology was developed in a central research laboratory (CRL), product development and engineering occurred in each of the product divisions. Matsushita intentionally under-funded the CRL, forcing it to compete for additional funding from the divisions. Annually, the CRL publicized its major research projects to the product divisions, which then provided funding in exchange for technology for marketable applications. While it was rarely the innovator, Matsushita was usually very fast to market—earning it the nickname "Manishita," or copycat.

Matsushita: Internationalization

Although the establishment of overseas markets was a major thrust of the second 25 years in the 250-year plan, in an overseas trip in 1951 KM had been unable to find any American company willing to collaborate with Matsushita. The best he could do was a technology exchange and licensing agreement with Philips. Nonetheless, the push to internationalize continued.

Expanding Through Color TV

In the 1950s and 1960s, trade liberalization and lower shipping rates made possible a healthy export business built on black and white TV sets. In 1953, the company opened its first overseas branch office—the Matsushita Electric Corporation of America (MECA). With neither a distribution network nor a strong brand, the company could not access traditional retailers, and had to resort to selling its products under their private brands through mass merchandisers and discounters.

During the 1960s, pressure from national governments in developing countries led Matsushita to open plants in several countries in Southeast Asia and Central and South America. As manufacturing costs in Japan rose, Matsushita shifted more basic production to these low-wage countries, but almost all high-value components and subassemblies were still made in its scale-intensive Japanese plants. By the 1970s, protectionist sentiments in the West forced the company to establish assembly operations in the Americas and Europe. In 1972, it opened a plant in Canada; in 1974, it bought Motorola's TV business and started manufacturing its Quasar brand in the United States; and in 1976, it built a plant in Cardiff, Wales, to supply the Common Market.

Building Global Leadership Through VCRs

The birth of the videocassette recorder (VCR) propelled Matsushita into first place in the consumer electronics industry during the 1980s. Recognizing the potential mass-market appeal of the VCR—developed by Californian broadcasting company, Ampex, in 1956—engineers at Matsushita began developing VCR technology. After six years of development work, Matsushita launched its commercial broadcast video recorder in 1964, and introduced a consumer version two years later.

In 1975, Sony introduced the technically superior "Betamax" format, and the next year JVC launched a competing "VHS" format. Under pressure from MITI, the government's industrial planning ministry, Matsushita agreed to give up its own format and adopt the established VHS standard. During Matsushita's 20 years of VCR product development, various members of the VCR research team spent most of their careers working together, moving from central labs to the product divisions' development labs and eventually to the plant.

The company quickly built production to meet its own needs as well as those of OEM customers like GE, RCA, and Zenith, who decided to forego self-manufacture and outsource to the low-cost Japanese. Between 1977 and 1985, capacity increased 33-fold to 6.8 million units. (In parallel, the company aggressively licensed the VHS format to other manufacturers, including Hitachi, Sharp, Mitsubishi and, eventually, Philips.) Increased volume enabled Matsushita to slash prices 50% within five years of product launch, while simultaneously improving quality. By the mid-1980s, VCRs accounted for 30% of total sales—over 40% of overseas revenues—and provided 45% of profits.

Changing Systems and Controls

In the mid-1980s, Matsushita's growing number of overseas companies reported to the parent in one of two ways: wholly owned, single-product global plants reported directly to the appropriate product division, while overseas sales and marketing subsidiaries and overseas companies producing a broad product line for local markets reported to Matsushita Electric Trading Company (METC), a separate legal entity. (See Exhibit 5 for METC's organization.)

Throughout the 1970s, the central product divisions maintained strong operating control over their offshore production units. Overseas operations used plant and equipment designed by the parent company, followed manufacturing procedures dictated by the center, and used materials from Matsushita's domestic plants. Growing trends toward local sourcing, however, gradually weakened the divisions' direct control. By the 1980s, instead of controlling inputs, they began to monitor measures of output (for example, quality, productivity, inventory levels).

About the same time, product divisions began receiving the globally consolidated return on sales reports that had previously been consolidated in METC statements. By the mid-1980s, as worldwide planning was introduced for the first time, corporate management required all its product divisions to prepare global product strategies.

Headquarters-Subsidiary Relations

Although METC and the product divisions set detailed sales and profits targets for their overseas subsidiaries, local managers were told they had autonomy on how to achieve the targets. "Mike" Matsuoko, president of the company's largest European production subsidiary in Cardiff, Wales, however, emphasized that failure to meet targets forfeited freedom: "Losses show bad health and invite many doctors from Japan who provide advice and support."

In the mid-1980s, Matsushita had over 700 expatriate Japanese managers and technicians on foreign assignment for four to eight years, but defended that high number by describing their pivotal role. "This vital communication role," said one manager, "almost always requires a manager from the parent company. Even if a local manager speaks Japanese, he would not have the long experience that is needed to build relationships and understand our management processes."

Expatriate managers were located throughout foreign subsidiaries, but there were a few positions that were almost always reserved for them. The most visible were subsidiary general mangers whose main role was to translate Matsushita philosophy abroad. Expatriate accounting managers were expected to "mercilessly expose the truth" to corporate headquarters; and Japanese technical managers were sent to transfer product and process technologies and provide headquarters with local market information. These expatriates maintained relationships with senior colleagues at headquarters, who acted as career mentors, evaluated performance (with some input

EXHIBIT 5

Organization of METC, 1985

Note: ( ) = number of people.

Source: Harvard Business School Case No. 388-144.

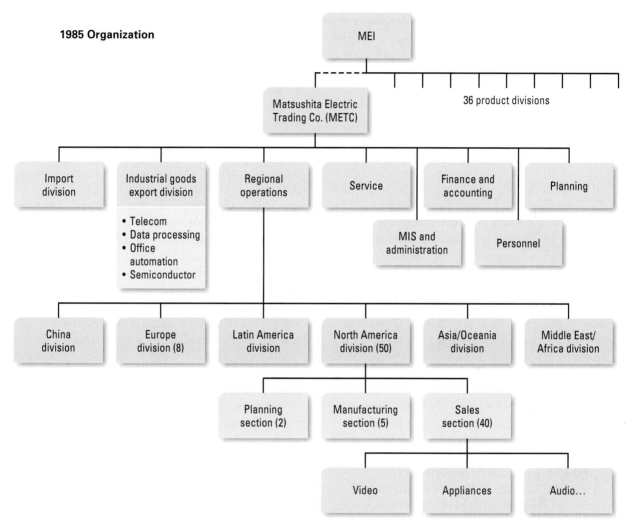

from local managers), and provided expatriates with information about parent company developments.

General managers of foreign subsidiaries visited Osaka headquarters at least two or three times each year—some as often as every month. Corporate managers reciprocated these visits, and on average, major operations hosted at least one headquarters manager each day of the year. Face-to-face meetings were considered vital: "Figures are important," said one manager, "but the meetings are necessary to develop judgment." Daily faxes and nightly phone calls between headquarters and expatriate colleagues were a vital management link.

Yamashita's Operation Localization

Although international sales kept rising, as early as 1982 growing host country pressures caused concern about the company's highly centralized operations. In that year, newly appointed company President Toshihiko Yamashita launched "Operation Localization" to boost offshore production from less than 10% of value-added to 25%, or half of overseas sales, by 1990. To support the target, he set out a program of four localizations—personnel, technology, material, and capital.

Over the next few years, Matsushita increased the number of local nationals in key positions. In the United States, for example, U.S. nationals became the presidents of three of the six local companies, while in Taiwan the majority of production divisions were replaced by Chinese managers. In each case, however, local national managers were still supported by senior Japanese advisors, who maintained a direct link with the parent company. To localize technology and materials, the company developed its national subsidiaries' expertise to source equipment locally, modify designs to meet local requirements, incorporate local components, and adapt corporate processes and technologies to accommodate these changes. And by the mid-1980s, offshore production subsidiaries were free to buy minor parts from local vendors as long as quality could be assured, but still had to buy key components from internal sources.

One of the most successful innovations was to give overseas sales subsidiaries more choice over the products they sold. Each year the company held a two-week internal merchandising show and product planning meeting where product divisions exhibited the new lines. Here, overseas sales subsidiary managers described their local market needs and negotiated for change in features, quantities, and even prices of the products they wanted to buy. Product division managers, however, could overrule the sales subsidiary if they thought introduction of a particular product was of strategic importance.

President Yamashita's hope was that Operation Localization would help Matsushita's overseas companies develop the innovative capability and entrepreneurial initiatives that he had long admired in the national organizations of rival Philips. (Past efforts to develop such capabilities abroad had failed. For example, when Matsushita acquired Motorola's TV business in the United States, its highly innovative technology group atrophied as American engineers resigned in response to what they felt to be excessive control from Japan's highly centralized R&D operations.) Yet despite his four localizations, overseas companies continued to act primarily as the implementation arms of central product divisions. In an unusual act for a Japanese CEO, Yamashita publicly expressed his unhappiness with the lack of initiative at the TV plant in Cardiff. Despite the transfer of

substantial resources and the delegation of many responsibilities, he felt that the plant remained too dependent on the center.

Tanii's Integration and Expansion

Yamashita's successor, Akio Tanii, expanded on his predecessor's initiatives. In 1986, feeling that Matsushita's product divisions were not giving sufficient attention to international development—in part because they received only 3% royalties for foreign production against at least 10% return on sales for exports from Japan—he brought all foreign subsidiaries under the control of METC. Tanii then merged METC into the parent company in an effort to fully integrate domestic and overseas operations. Then, to shift operational control nearer to local markets, he relocated major regional headquarters functions from Japan to North America, Europe, and Southeast Asia. Yet still he was frustrated that the overseas subsidiary companies acted as little more than the implementing agents of the Osaka-based product divisions.

Through all these changes, however, Matsushita's worldwide growth continued generating huge reserves. With $17.5 billion in liquid financial assets at the end of 1989, the company was referred to as the "Matsushita Bank," and several top executives began proposing that if they could not develop innovative overseas companies, they should buy them. Flush with cash and international success, in early 1991 the company acquired MCA, the U.S. entertainment giant, for $6.1 billion with the objective of obtaining a media software source for its hardware. Within a year, however, Japan's bubble economy had burst, plunging the economy into recession. Almost overnight, Tanii had to shift the company's focus from expansion to cost containment. Despite his best efforts to cut costs, the problems ran too deep. With 1992 profits less than half their 1991 level, the board took the unusual move of forcing Tanii to resign in February 1993.

Morishita's Challenge and Response

At 56, Yoichi Morishita was the most junior of the company's executive vice presidents when he was tapped as the new president. Under the slogan "simple, small, speedy and strategic," he committed to cutting headquarters staff and decentralizing responsibility. Over the next 18 months, he moved 6,000 staff to operating jobs. In a major strategic reversal, he also sold 80% of MCA to Seagram, booking a $1.2 billion loss on the transaction.

Yet the company continued to struggle. Japan's domestic market for consumer electronics collapsed—from $42 billion in 1989 to $21 billion in 1999. Excess capacity drove down prices and profits evaporated. And although offshore markets were growing, the rise of new competition—first from Korea, then China—created a global glut of consumer electronics, and prices collapsed.

With a strong yen making exports from Japan uncompetitive, Matsushita's product divisions rapidly shifted production offshore during the 1990s, mostly to low-cost Asian countries like China and Malaysia. By the end of the decade, its 160 factories outside Japan employed 140,000 people—about the same number of employees as in its 133 plants in Japan. Yet, despite the excess capacity and strong yen, management seemed unwilling to radically restructure its increasingly inefficient portfolio of production facilities.

In the closing years of the decade, Morishita began emphasizing the need to develop more of its technology

EXHIBIT 6

Matsushita, Summary Financial Data, 1970–2000[a]

	2000	1995	1990	1985	1980	1975	1970
In billions of yen and percent:							
Sales	¥7,299	¥6,948	¥6,003	¥5,291	¥2,916	¥1,385	¥932
Income before tax	219	232	572	723	324	83	147
As % of sales	3.0%	3.3%	9.5%	13.7%	11.1%	6.0%	15.8%
Net income	¥100	¥90	¥236	¥216	¥125	¥32	¥70
As % of sales	1.4%	1.3%	3.9%	4.1%	4.3%	2.3%	7.6%
Cash dividends (per share)	¥14.00	¥13.50	¥10.00	¥9.52	¥7.51	¥6.82	¥6.21
Total assets	7,955	8,202	7,851	5,076	2,479	1,274	735
Stockholders' equity	3,684	3,255	3,201	2,084	1,092	573	324
Capital investment	355	316	355	288	NA	NA	NA
Depreciation	343	296	238	227	65	28	23
R&D	526	378	346	248	102	51	NA
Employees (units)	290,448	265,397	198,299	175,828	107,057	82,869	78,924
Overseas employees	143,773	112,314	59,216	38,380	NA	NA	NA
As % of total employees	50%	42%	30%	22%	NA	NA	NA
Exchange rate (fiscal period end: ¥/$)	103	89	159	213	213	303	360
In millions of dollars:							
Sales	$68,862	$78,069	$37,753	$24,890	$13,690	$4,572	$2,588
Operating income before depreciation	4,944	6,250	4,343	3,682	1,606	317	NA
Operating income after depreciation	1,501	2,609	2,847	2,764	1,301	224	NA
Pretax income	2,224	2,678	3,667	3,396	1,520	273	408
Net income	941	1,017	1,482	1,214	584	105	195
Total assets	77,233	92,159	49,379	21,499	11,636	4,206	2,042
Total equity	35,767	36,575	20,131	10,153	5,129	1,890	900

[a]Data prior to 1987 are for the fiscal year ending November 20; data 1988 and after are for the fiscal year ending March 31.

Source: Annual reports; Standard & Poors' *Compustat;* Moody's Industrial and International Manuals.

and innovation offshore. Concerned that only 250 of the company's 3,000 R&D scientists and engineers were located outside Japan, he began investing in R&D partnerships and technical exchanges, particularly in fast emerging fields. For example, in 1998 he signed a joint R&D agreement with the Chinese Academy of Sciences, China's leading research organization. Later that year, he announced the establishment of the Panasonic Digital Concepts Center in California. Its mission was to act as a venture fund and an incubation center for the new ideas and technologies emerging in Silicon Valley. To some it was an indication that Matsushita had given up trying to generate new technology and business initiatives from its own overseas companies.

Nakamura's Initiatives

In April 2000, Morishita became chairman and Kunio Nakamura replaced him as president. Profitability was at 2.2% of sales, with consumer electronics at only 0.4%, including losses generated by one-time cash cows, the TV and VCR divisions. (Exhibit 6 and 7 provide the financial history for Matsushita and key product lines.) The new CEO vowed to raise this to 5% by 2004. Key to his plan was to move Matsushita beyond its roots as a "super manufacturer of products" and begin "to meet customer needs through systems and services." He planned to flatten the hierarchy and empower employees to respond to customer needs, and as part of the implementation, all key headquarters functions relating to international operations were transferred to overseas regional offices.

But the biggest shock came in November, when Nakamura announced a program of "destruction and creation," in which he disbanded the product division structure that KM had created as Matsushita's basic organization building block 67 years earlier. Plants, previously controlled by individual product divisions, would now be integrated into multi-product production centers. In Japan alone 30 of the 133 factories were to be consolidated or closed. And marketing would shift to two corporate marketing entities, one for Panasonic brands (consumer electronics, information and communications products) and one for National branded products (mostly home appliances).

They were radical moves, but in a company that even in Japan was being talked about as a takeover target, observers wondered if they were sufficient to restore its global competitiveness.

EXHIBIT 7

Matsushita, Sales by Product and Geographic Segment, 1985–2000 (billion yen)

	2000		1995		FY 1990		FY 1985	
By Product Segment:								
Video and audio equipment	¥1,706	23%	¥1,827	26%	¥2,159	36%	¥2,517	48%
Home appliances and household equipment	1,306	18	—	—	—	—	—	—
Home appliances	—	—	916	13	802	13	763	14
Communication and industrial equipment	—	—	1,797	26	1,375	23	849	16
Electronic components	—	—	893	13	781	13	573	11
Batteries and kitchen-related equipment	—	—	374	4	312	5	217	4
Information and communications equipment	2,175	28	—	—	—	—	—	—
Industrial equipment	817	11	—	—	—	—	—	—
Components	1,618	21	—	—	—	—	—	—
Others	—	—	530	8	573	10	372	7
Total	**¥7,682**	**100%**	**¥6,948**	**100%**	**¥6,003**	**100%**	**¥5,291**	**100%**
By Geographic Segment:								
Domestic	¥3,698	51%	¥3,455	50%	¥3,382	56%	¥2,659	50%
Overseas	3,601	49	3,493	50	2,621	44	2,632	50

Note: Total may not add due to rounding.

Source: Annual reports.

GE's Two-Decade Transformation: Jack Welch's Leadership

This case was prepared by Christopher A. Bartlett and Meg Wozny, Harvard Business School.

Jack Welch glowed with pride at General Electric's Annual Meeting in March 1999. For the first time, GE's revenues exceeded $100 billion, operating margins were at an all-time high of 16.7%, and earnings per share had increased 14% over 1997's record level. In recognition of this outstanding performance and the company's transformation over the previous two decades, the *Fortune* poll of U.S. corporate executives had voted GE the country's "Most Admired Company" for the second year running, and the *Financial Times* had named it the "Most Respected Company in the World."

While the mood at the annual meeting was clearly upbeat, some shareholders worried about Welch's intention to retire at the end of 2000. The company he would hand over to his successor was radically different from the GE he took over in 1981. The question on many minds was whether anyone could sustain the blistering pace of change and growth characteristic of the Welch era. It would be a tough act to follow. (See Exhibit 1 for financial summary of Welch's era at GE.)

Copyright © Harvard Business School Publishing. This case was prepared by Christopher A. Bartlett and Meg Wozny, Harvard Business School. HBS cases are developed solely as the basis for class discussion. Cases are not intended to serve as endorsements, sources of primary data, or illustrations of effective or ineffective management. Reprinted by permission of Harvard Business School Publishing. All rights reserved. For the most recent financial results of the company discussed in this case, go to http://finance.yahoo.com, input the company's stock symbol, and download the latest company report from its homepage.

The GE Heritage

Founded in 1878 by Thomas Edison, General Electric grew from its early focus on the generation, distribution, and use of electric power to become, a hundred years later, one of the world's leading diversified industrial companies. In addition to its core businesses in power generation, household appliances, and lighting, by 1978 the company was also engaged in businesses as diverse as aircraft engines, medical systems, and diesel locomotives.

Long regarded as a bellwether of American management practices, GE was constantly undergoing change. In the 1930s, it was a model of the era's highly centralized, tightly controlled corporate form. By the 1950s, GE had delegated responsibility to hundreds of department managers, leading a trend towards greater decentralization. But a subsequent period of "profitless growth" in the 1960s caused the company to strengthen its corporate staffs and develop sophisticated strategic planning systems. Again, GE found itself at the leading edge of management practice.

When Reg Jones, Welch's predecessor, became CEO in 1973, he inherited the company that had just completed a major reorganization. Overlaying its 10 groups, 46 divisions, and 190 departments were 43 strategic business units designed to support the strategic planning that was so central to GE's management process. Jones raised strategic planning to an art form, and GE again became the benchmark for hundreds of companies that imitated its SBU-based structure and its sophisticated planning processes. Soon, however, Jones was unable to keep up with

EXHIBIT 1

Selected Financial Data ($ millions)

General Electric Company and Consolidated Affiliates

	1998	1997	1996	1995	1994	1993	1992	1991	1990	1986	1981
Revenues	$100,469	$90,840	$79,179	$70,028	$60,109	$55,701	$53,051	$51,283	$49,696	$36,725	$27,240
Earnings from continuing operations	9,296	8,203	7,280	6,573	5,915	4,184	4,137	3,943	3,920	3,689	N/A
Loss from discontinued operations	—	—	—	—	−1,189	993	588	492	383	N/A	N/A
Net earnings	9,296	8,203	7,280	6,573	4,726	4,315	4,725	2,636	4,303	2,492	1,652
Dividends declared	4,081	3,535	3,138	2,838	2,546	2,229	1,985	1,808	1,696	1,081	715
Earned on average share owners' equity	25.7%	25.0%	24.0%	23.5%	18.1%	17.5%	20.9%	12.2%	20.2%	17.3%	19.1%
Per share											
Net earnings	2.84	2.50	2.20	1.95	1.38	3.03	2.75	2.55	2.42	2.73	N/A
Net earnings—diluted	2.80	2.46	2.16	1.93	1.37	2.52	2.75	1.51	2.42	N/A	N/A
Dividends declared	1.25	1.08	0.95	0.845	0.745	1.31	1.16	1.04	0.96	1.18	N/A
Stock price range (1)	103.9–69	76.6–47.9	53.1–34.7	36.6–24	27.4–22.5	26.7–20.2	87.5–72.7	78.1–53	75.5–50	44.4–33.2	69.9–51.1
Total assets of continuing operations	355,935	304,012	272,402	228,035	185,871	251,506	192,876	166,508	152,000	84,818	20,942
Long-term borrowings	59,663	46,603	49,246	51,027	36,979	28,194	25,298	22,602	20,886	100,001	1,059
Shares outstanding— average (in thousands)	3,268,998	3,274,692	3,307,394	3,367,624	3,417,476	1,707,979	1,714,396	1,737,863	1,775,104	912,594	227,528
Employees at year end											
United States	163,000	165,000	155,000	150,000	156,000	157,000	168,000	173,000	183,000	302,000	N/A
Other countries	130,000	111,000	84,000	72,000	60,000	59,000	58,000	62,000	62,000	71,000	N/A
Discontinued operations (primarily U.S.)	—	—	—	—	5,000	6,000	42,000	49,000	53,000	N/A	N/A
Total employees	293,000	276,000	239,000	222,000	221,000	222,000	268,000	284,000	298,000	373,000	404,000

(1) Price unadjusted for four 2-for-1 stock splits during the period.

reviewing and approving the massive volumes of information generated by 43 strategic plans. Explaining that "the review burden had to be carried on more shoulders," in 1977 he capped GE's departments, divisions, groups, and SBUs with a new organizational layer of "sectors," representing macrobusiness agglomerations such as consumer products, power systems, or technical products.

In addition to his focus on strategic planning, Jones spent a great deal of time on government relations, becoming the country's leading business statesman. During the 1970s, he was voted CEO of the Year three times by his peers, with one leading business journal dubbing him CEO of the Decade in 1979. When he retired in 1981, *The Wall Street Journal* proclaimed Jones a "management legend," adding that by handing the reins to Welch, GE had "replaced a legend with a live wire."

Welch's Early Priorities: GE's Restructuring

When the 45-year-old Welch became CEO in April 1981, the U.S. economy was in a recession. High interest rates and a strong dollar exacerbated the problem resulting in the country's highest unemployment rates since the Depression. To leverage performance in GE's diverse portfolio of businesses, the new CEO challenged each to be "better than the best" and set in motion a series of changes that were to radically restructure the company over the next five years.

#1 or #2: Fix, Sell, or Close

Soon after taking charge, Welch set the standard for each business to become the #1 or #2 competitor in its industry—or to disengage. Asked whether this simple notion represented GE's strategy, Welch responded, "You can't set an overall theme or a single strategy for a corporation as broad as GE." By 1983, however, Welch had elaborated this general "#1 or #2" objective into a "three circle concept" of his vision for GE. (See Exhibit 2.) Businesses were categorized as core (with the priority of "reinvesting in productivity and quality"), high-technology (challenged to "stay on the leading edge" by investing in R&D), and services (required to "add outstanding people and make

EXHIBIT 2

The Three-Circle Vision for GE, 1982

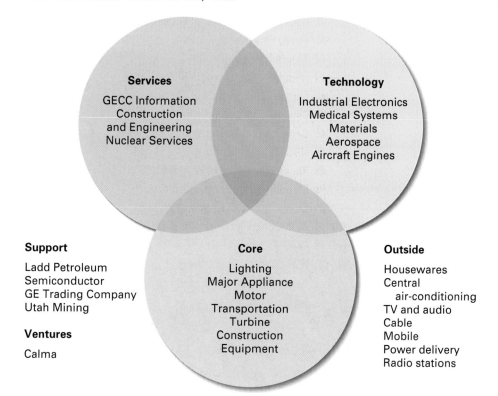

Support
Ladd Petroleum
Semiconductor
GE Trading Company
Utah Mining

Ventures
Calma

Services
GECC Information
Construction
and Engineering
Nuclear Services

Technology
Industrial Electronics
Medical Systems
Materials
Aerospace
Aircraft Engines

Core
Lighting
Major Appliance
Motor
Transportation
Turbine
Construction
Equipment

Outside
Housewares
Central
  air-conditioning
TV and audio
Cable
Mobile
Power delivery
Radio stations

contiguous acquisitions"). To a question about what he hoped to build at GE, Welch replied:

> A decade from now, I would like General Electric to be perceived as a unique, high-spirited, entrepreneurial enterprise.... the most profitable, highly diversified company on earth, with world quality leadership in every one of its product lines.[i]

But as GE managers struggled to build #1 or #2 positions in a recessionary environment and under attack from global—often, Japanese—competitors, Welch's admonition to "fix, sell, or close" uncompetitive businesses frequently led to the latter options. Scores of businesses were sold, including central air-conditioning, housewares, coal mining, and, eventually, even GE's well-known consumer electronics business. Between 1981 and 1990, GE freed up over $11 billion of capital by selling off more than 200 businesses, which had accounted for 25% of 1980 sales. In that same time frame, the company made over 370 acquisitions, investing more than $21 billion in such major purchases as Westinghouse's lighting business, Employers Reinsurance, RCA, Kidder Peabody, and Thomson/ CGR, the French medical imaging company. (See Exhibit 3.)

Internally, Welch's insistence that GE become more "lean and agile" resulted in a highly disciplined destaffing process aimed at all large headquarters

---

EXHIBIT 3

Changes in the GE Business Portfolio

Major Acquisitions ($21 Billion Total)	Major Divestitures ($11 Billion Total)
■ Calma (CAD/CAM equipment)	■ Central Air Conditioning
■ Intersil (semiconductors)	■ Pathfinder Mines
■ Employers Reinsurance Corp.	■ Broadcasting Properties (non-RCA TV & radio stations)
■ Decimus (computer leasing)	■ Utah International (mining)
■ RCA (NBC Television, aerospace, electronics)	■ Housewares (small appliances)
■ Kidder, Peabody (investment banking)	■ Family Financial Services
■ Polaris (aircraft leasing)	■ RCA Records
■ Genstar (container leasing)	■ Nacolah Life Insurance (RCA's)
■ Thomson/CGR (medical equipment)	■ Coronet Carpets (RCA's)
■ Gelco (portable building leasing)	■ Consumer Electronics (TV sets)
■ Borg-Warner Chemicals (plastics)	■ Carboloy (industrial cutting tools)
■ Montgomery Ward Credit (credit cards)	■ NBC Radio Networks
■ Roper (appliances)	■ Roper Outdoor Lawn Equipment
■ Penske Leasing (truck leasing)	■ GE Solid State (semiconductors)
■ Financial Guaranty Insurance Co.	■ Calma (CAD/CAM equipment)
■ Thungsram (light bulbs)	■ RCA Globcomm (international telex)
■ Burton Group Financial Services	■ Ladd Petroleum (oil exploration & refining)
■ Travelers Mortgage (mortgage services)	■ RCA Columbia Home Video
■ Thorn Lighting (light bulbs)	■ Auto Auctions (auctions of used cars)
■ Financial News Network (cable network)	
■ Chase Manhattan Leasing	
■ Itel Containers (container leasing)	
■ Harrods/House of Fraser Credit Cards	

Source: The Business Engine.

groups, including a highly symbolic 50% reduction in the 200-person strategic planning staff. Welch described his motivation:

> We don't need the questioners and checkers, the nitpickers who bog down the process.... Today, each staff person has to ask, "How do I add value? How do I make people on the line more effective and competitive?"[ii]

As he continued to chip away at bureaucracy, Welch next scrapped GE's laborious strategic planning system—and with it, the remaining corporate planning staff. He replaced it with "real time planning" built around a five-page strategy playbook, which Welch and his 14 key business heads discussed in shirtsleeves sessions "unencumbered by staff." Each business's playbook provided simple one-page answers to five questions concerning current market dynamics, the competitors' key recent activities, the GE business response, the greatest competitive threat over the next three years, and the GE business's planned response.

The budgeting process was equally radically redefined. Rather than documenting internally focused comparisons with past performance, results were now evaluated against external competitively based criteria: Do sales show increases in market share, for example? Do margins indicate a cost advantage compared with competition?

In 1985, Welch eliminated the sector level, previously the powerful center of strategic control. (See Exhibits 4a and 4b.) By reducing the number of hierarchical levels from nine to as few as four, Welch ensured that all businesses reported directly to him. He said:

> We used to have department managers, sector managers, subsector managers, unit mangers, supervisors. We're driving those titles out… We used to go from the CEO to sectors to groups to businesses. Now we go from the CEO to businesses. There is nothing else. Zero.[iii]

Through downsizing, destaffing, and delayering, GE eliminated 59,290 salaried and 64,160 hourly positions between 1981 and 1988; divestiture eliminated an additional 122,700. Even when offset by the acquisitions, the number of employees at GE declined from 404,000 in 1980 to 330,000 by 1984 and 292,000 by 1989. Between 1981 and 1985, revenues increased modestly from $27.2 billion to $29.2 billion, but operating profits rose dramatically from

$1.6 billion to $2.4 billion. This set the base for strong increases in both sales and earnings in the second half of the decade (see Exhibit 5).

This drastic restructuring in the early- and mid-1980s earned Welch the nickname "Neutron Jack," a term that gained currency even among GE managers when the CEO replaced 12 of his 14 business heads in August 1986. Welch's new "varsity team" consisted of managers with a strong commitment to the new management values, a willingness to break with the old GE culture, and most of all, an ability to take charge and bring about change. Despite his great dislike for a nickname he felt he did not deserve, Welch kept pushing the organization for more change. The further into the restructuring he got, the more convinced he became of the need for bold action:

> For me, the idea is to shun the incremental and go for the leap... How does an institution know when the pace is about right? I hope you won't think I'm being melodramatic if I say that the institution ought to stretch itself, ought to reach, to the point where it almost comes unglued… Remember the theory that a manager should have no more than 6 or 7 direct reports? I say the right number is closer to 10 or 15.[iv]

The Late 1980s: Second Stage of the Rocket

By the late 1980s, most of GE's business restructuring was complete, but the organization was still reeling from culture shock and management exhaustion. Welch was as eager as anyone in GE to move past the "Neutron-Jack" stage and begin rebuilding the company on its more solid foundations.

The "Software" Initiatives: Work-Out and Best Practices

Years after launching GE's massive restructuring effort, Welch concluded, "By mid-1988 the hardware was basically in place. We liked our businesses. Now it was time to focus on the organization's software." He also acknowledged that his priorities were shifting: "A company can boost productivity by restructuring, removing bureaucracy and downsizing, but it cannot sustain high productivity without cultural change."

In 1989, Welch articulated the management style he hoped to make GE's norm—an approach based on openness, candor, and facing reality. Simultaneously, he refined the core elements of the organizational

C486

EXHIBIT 4A

GE Organization in 1981

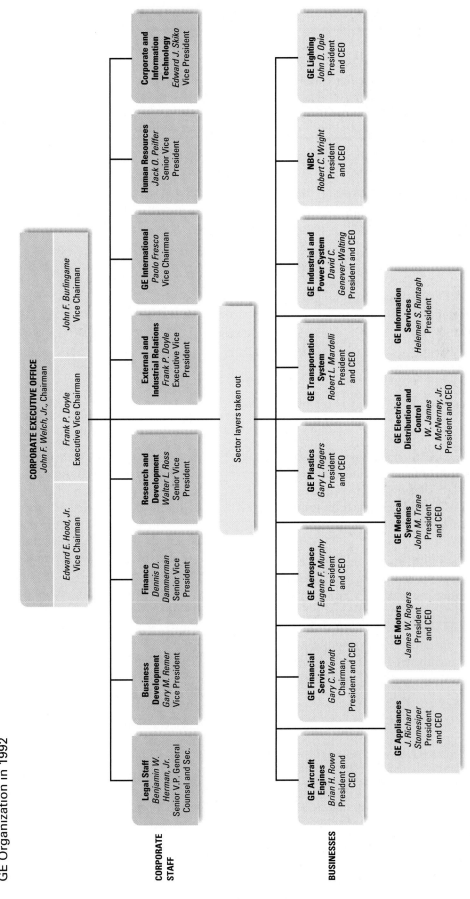

EXHIBIT 4B

GE Organization in 1992

CORPORATE STAFF

CORPORATE EXECUTIVE OFFICE
John F. Welch, Jr., Chairman

Edward E. Hood, Jr.
Vice Chairman

Frank P. Doyle
Executive Vice Chairman

John F. Burlingame
Vice Chairman

Legal Staff
Benjamin W. Herman, Jr.
Senior V.P. General Counsel and Sec.

Business Development
Gary M. Reiner
Vice President

Finance
Dennis D. Dammerman
Senior Vice President

Research and Development
Walter L. Ross
Senior Vice President

External and Industrial Relations
Frank P. Doyle
Executive Vice President

GE International
Paolo Fresco
Vice Chairman

Human Resources
Jack O. Peiffer
Senior Vice President

Corporate and Information Technology
Edward J. Skiko
Vice President

Sector layers taken out

BUSINESSES

GE Aircraft Engines
Brian H. Rowe
President and CEO

GE Financial Services
Gary C. Wendt
Chairman, President and CEO

GE Aerospace
Eugene F. Murphy
President and CEO

GE Plastics
Gary L. Rogers
President and CEO

GE Transportation System
Robert L. Mardelli
President and CEO

GE Industrial and Power System
David C. Genever-Watling
President and CEO

NBC
Robert C. Wright
President and CEO

GE Lighting
John D. Opie
President and CEO

GE Appliances
J. Richard Stonesiper
President and CEO

GE Motors
James W. Rogers
President and CEO

GE Medical Systems
John M. Trane
President and CEO

GE Electrical Distribution and Control
W. James C. McNerney, Jr.
President and CEO

GE Information Services
Helemen S. Runtagh
President

EXHIBIT 5

General Electric's Performance in Three Eras (millions of dollars)

	Borch		Jones		Welch		
	1961	1970	1971	1980	1981	1990	1998
Sales	4,666.6	8,726.7	9,557.0	24,950.0	27,240.0	52,619.0	100,469.0
Operating profit	431.8	548.9	737.0	2,243.0	2,447.0	6,616.0	13,477.0
Net earnings	238.4	328.5	510.0	1,514.0	1,652.0	4,303.0	9,296.0
ROS	5.1%	3.8%	5.3%	6.1%	6.1%	8.2%	10.8%
ROE	14.8%	12.6%	17.2%	19.5%	18.1%	19.8%	25.4%
Stock market capitalization	6,283.7	7,026.7	10,870.5	12,173.4	13,073.4	50,344.9	334,236.9
S&P 500 Stock Price Index—Composite	65.7	83.0	97.9	119.4	126.4	330.2	1,095.4
Employees	279,547	396,583	402,000	366,000	404,000	298,000	293,000
U.S. GNP ($ billion)	523.0	982.0	1,063.0	2,626.0	2,708.0	5,524.5	8,508.9

Source: GE Annual Reports, Survey of Current Business, Datastream.

culture he wanted to create—one characterized by speed, simplicity, and self-confidence.[1] Over the next few years, he launched two closely linked initiatives— dubbed Work-Out and Best Practices—aimed at creating the desired culture and management approach.

Work-Out In late 1988, during one of Welch's regular visits to teach in the company's Management Development Institute, he engaged a group of GE managers in a particularly outspoken session about the difficulty they were having implementing change back at their operations. In a subsequent discussion with James Baughman, GE's director of management development, Welch wondered how to replicate this type of honest, energetic interaction throughout the company. His objective was to create the culture of a small company—a place where all felt engaged and everyone had voice. Together, they developed the idea of a forum where employees could not only speak their minds about how their business might be run more effectively, but also get immediate responses to their ideas and proposals. By the time their helicopter touched down at GE's headquarters, Welch and Baughman had sketched out a major change initiative they called "Work-Out"—a process designed to get unnecessary bureaucratic work out of the system while providing a forum in which employees and their bosses could work out new ways of dealing with each other.

At Welch's request, Baughman formed a small implementation team and, with the help of two dozen outside consultants, led the company-wide program rollout. Assigned to one of GE's businesses, each consultant facilitated a series of off-site meetings patterned after the open-forum style of New England town meetings. Groups of 40 to 100 employees were invited to share views about their business and how it might be improved. The three-day sessions usually began with a talk by the unit boss, who presented a challenge and a broad agenda. Then,

---

[1]Interestingly, Welch's first attempts at articulating and communicating GE's new cultural values were awkward. For example, in 1986 he defined 10 desirable cultural "attitudes and policies" which few in GE could remember, let alone practice. Furthermore, he communicated his new organizational model as the GE Business Engine, a concept that many found depersonalizing since it seemed to depict people as inputs into a financial machine. Gradually, Welch became more comfortable articulating cultural values which he continued to refine into what he termed "GE's social architecture." Eventually his concept of The Business Engine evolved to become The Human Engine.

the boss was asked to leave, allowing employees aided by facilitators to list their problems, debate solutions, and prepare presentations. On the final day, the bosses returned and were asked to listen to their employees' analyses and recommendations. The rules of the process required managers to make instant, on-the-spot decisions about each proposal, in front of everyone. About 80% of proposals got immediate yes-or-no decisions; if the manager needed more information, he or she had to charter a team to get it by an agreed-upon decision date.

Armand Lauzon, a manager at a GE Aircraft Engine factory, described to *Fortune* how he felt as his employees presented him with their suggestions in a room where they had carefully arranged the seating so his boss was behind him. "I was wringing wet within half an hour," he said. "They had 108 proposals; I had about a minute to say yes or no to each one. And I couldn't make eye contact with my boss without turning around, which would show everyone in the room I was chickenshit." In total, Lauzon supported all but eight of the 108 proposals.

By mid-1992, over 200,000 GE employees—well over two-thirds of the workforce—had participated in Work-Out, although the exact number was hard to determine, since Welch insisted that none of the meetings be documented. "You're just going to end up with more bureaucracy," he said. What was clear, however, was that productivity increases, which had been growing at an average annual rate of 2% between 1981 and 1987, doubled to a 4% annual rate between 1988 and 1992.[2]

Best Practices As Work-Out was getting started, Welch's relentless pursuit of ideas to increase productivity resulted in the birth of a related movement called Best Practices. In the summer of 1988, Welch gave Michael Frazier of GE's Business Development department a simple challenge: How can we learn from other companies that are achieving higher productivity growth than GE? Frazier selected nine companies, including Ford, Hewlett Packard, Xerox, and Toshiba, with different best practices to study. In addition to specific tools and practices, Frazier's team also identified several characteristics common to the successful companies: they focused more on developing effective processes than controlling individual activities; customer satisfaction was their main gauge of performance; they treated their suppliers as partners; and they emphasized the need for a constant stream of high-quality new products designed for efficient manufacturing.

On reviewing Frazier's report, Welch became an instant convert and committed to a major new training program to introduce Best Practices thinking throughout the organization, integrating it into the ongoing agenda of Work-Out teams. As a result of the Best Practices program, many GE managers began to realize they were managing and measuring the wrong things. (Said one, "We should have focused more on *how* things get done than on just *what* got done.") Subsequently, several units began radically revising their whole work approach. For example, the head of the corporate audit staff explained: "When I started 10 years ago, the first thing I did was count the $5,000 in the petty cash box. Today, we look at the $5 million in inventory on the floor, searching for process improvements that will bring it down."

Going Global

During the early- and mid-1980s, internationalization had remained a back-burner issue at GE, but strong advocates of globalization such as Paolo Fresco, the Italian-born president of GE Europe, understood why Welch had to concentrate his early efforts on the rationalization of the U.S. operations. "It's very difficult to jump into the world arena if you don't have a solid base at home," said Fresco, "but once the solid base was created, we really took the jump."

The first rumblings of the emerging globalization priority came in Welch's challenges to his Corporate Executive Council meetings during 1986. Reflecting his own early experience in GE Plastics, he did not try to impose a corporate globalization strategy, preferring to let each business take responsibility for implementing a plan appropriate to its particular needs:

> When I was 29 years old I bought land in Holland and built the plants there. That was "my land" for "my business." I was never interested in the global GE, just the global Plastics business. The idea of a company being global is nonsense. Businesses are global, not companies.[v]

---

[2]In GE, productivity was defined by the following calculation: Productivity = Real Revenue (net of price increases) / Real Costs (net of inflationary increases).

This did not mean, however, that Welch was uninvolved in his business managers' globalization plans. In 1987, he focused their attention by raising the bar on GE's well-known performance standard: from now on, "#1 or #2" was to be evaluated on *world* market position. As if to underline his seriousness, a few months later he announced a major deal with Thomson S.A., in which GE agreed to exchange its struggling consumer electronics business for the large French electronics company's medical imaging business, a business in which GE had a leading global position.

To provide continuing momentum to the internationalization effort, in 1989, Welch appointed Paolo Fresco as head of International Operations and in 1992 made him a vice-chairman and member of his four-man corporate executive office. Fresco, a key negotiator on the Thomson swap, continued to broker numerous international deals: a joint venture with German-based Robert Bosch, a partnership with Toshiba, and the acquisition of Sovac, the French consumer credit company. As Eastern Europe opened, he initiated a major thrust into the former Communist bloc, spearheaded by the purchase of a majority share in the Hungarian lighting company, Tungsram. Fresco became the locator and champion of new opportunities. "I fill vacuums," he said. "All these assignments are temporary—once they are complete, I get out of the way."

Like subsequent strategic initiatives, globalization was not a one-time effort, but an ongoing theme that Welch doggedly pursued over the years. Taking advantage of Europe's economic downturn, GE invested $17.5 billion in the region between 1989 and 1995, half on new plants and facilities and half to finance 50 or so acquisitions. Then in 1995, after the Mexican peso collapsed, the company again saw the economic uncertainty as a great buying opportunity. Within six months GE had acquired 16 companies, positioning it to participate in the country's surprisingly rapid recovery. And as Asia slipped into crisis in 1997–1998, Welch urged his managers to view it as a buying opportunity rather than a problem. In Japan alone the company spent $15 billion on acquisitions in six months.

By 1998, international revenues were $42.8 billion, almost double the level just five years earlier. The company expected to do almost half its business outside the United States by 2000, compared with only 20% in 1985, the year before the first international push. More important, global revenues were growing at almost three times the rate of domestic sales. (See Exhibit 6.)

EXHIBIT 6

Growth Through Globalization

Source: GE Annual Report, 1998.

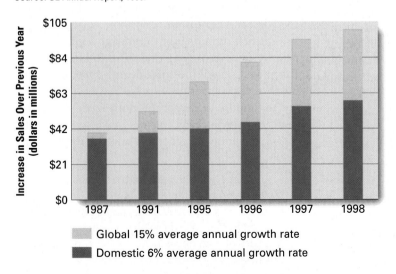

Global 15% average annual growth rate
Domestic 6% average annual growth rate

Developing Leaders

While the global thrust and the new cultural initiatives were being implemented, Welch was also focusing on the huge task of realigning the skill sets—and, more important, the mindsets—of the company's 290,000 employees with GE's new strategic and organizational imperatives. Amidst the grumbling of those who felt overworked in the new demanding environment and the residual distrust left over from the layoffs of the 1980s, he recognized his challenge was nothing short of redefining the implicit contract that GE had with its employees:

> Like many other large companies in the U.S., Europe and Japan, GE has had an implicit psychological contract based on perceived lifetime employment. This produced a paternal, feudal, fuzzy kind of loyalty. That kind of loyalty tends to focus people inward. But in today's environment, people's emotional energy must be focused outward on a competitive world... The new psychological contract, if there is such a thing, is that jobs at GE are the best in the world for people willing to compete. We have the best training and development resources and an environment committed to providing opportunities for personal and professional growth.[vi]

Like all GE managers, Welch grew up in an organization deeply committed to developing its people. He wanted to harness that tradition and use it to translate his broad cultural changes down to the individual level. This would mean adapting GE's well-established human resource systems to his goals. For example, for as long as he could remember, the company's top executives had committed substantial amounts of time to the rigorous management appraisal, development, and succession planning reviews known as Session C. He began using this process to help achieve his objectives, predictably adding his own intense personal style to its implementation.

Starting in April and lasting through May each year, Welch and three of his senior executives visited each of his businesses to review the progress of the company's top 3,000 executives. Welch kept particularly close tabs on the upper 500, all of whom had been appointed with his personal approval. In these multi-day meetings, Welch wanted to be exposed to high-potential managers presenting results on major projects. In an exhaustive 10- to 12-hour review in each business, Welch asked the top executive to identify the future leaders, outline planned training and development plans, and detail succession plans for all key jobs. The exercise reflected his strong belief that good people were GE's key assets and had to be managed as a company resource. "I own the people," he told his business heads. "You just rent them."

As these reviews rolled out through GE, all professional-level employees expected honest feedback about where they were professionally, reasonable expectations about future positions they could hold, and the specific skills required to get there. Managers at every level used these discussions as the basis for coaching and developing their staff. (As a role model, Welch estimated he spent at least 70% of his time on people issues, most of that teaching and developing others.)

A strong believer in incentives, Welch also radically overhauled GE's compensation package. From a system driven by narrow-range increases in base salary supplemented by bonuses based on one's business performance, he implemented a model in which stock options became the primary component of management compensation. He expanded the number of options recipients from 300 to 30,000 and began making much more aggressive bonus awards and options allocations strongly tied to the individual's performance on the current program priority (globalization, for example, or best practices initiatives).

Through all of these human resource tools and processes, Welch's major effort was increasingly focused on creating an environment in which people could be their best. Entering the 1990s, he described his objective for GE in these terms:

> Ten years from now, we want magazines to write about GE as a place where people have the freedom to be creative, a place that brings out the best in everybody. An open, fair place where people have a sense that what they do matters, and where that sense of accomplishment is rewarded in the pocketbook and the soul. That will be our report card.

A key institution that Welch harnessed to bring about this cultural change was GE's Crotonville management development facility. Welch wanted to convert Crotonville from its management training focus and its role as a reward or a consolation prize for those who missed out on a promotion to a powerful engine of change in his transformation effort. In the

EXHIBIT 7

Welch at GE's Crotonville Center

A typical note Welch sent to 30 participants to prepare for his session of GE's Executive Development Course (EDC):

Dear EDC Participants,

I'm looking forward to an exciting time with you tomorrow. I've included here a few thoughts for you to think about prior to our session:

As a group—

Situation: Tomorrow you are appointed CEO of GE.

- What would you do in first 30 days?
- Do you have a current "vision" of what to do?
- How would you go about developing one?
- Present your best shot at a vision.
- How would you go about "selling" the vision?
- What foundations would you build on?
- What current practices would you jettison?

Individually—

1. Please be prepared to describe a leadership dilemma that you have faced in the past 12 months, i.e., plant closing, work transfer, HR, buy or sell a business, etc.
2. Think about what you would recommend to accelerate the Quality drive across the company.
3. I'll be talking about "A, B & C" players. What are your thoughts on just what makes up such a player?
4. I'll also be talking about energy/energizing/edge as key characteristics of today's leaders. Do you agree? Would you broaden this? How?

I'm looking forward to a fun time, and I know I'll leave a lot smarter than when I arrived.

—Jack

Source: The Leadership Engine.

mid-1980s, when he was cutting costs almost everywhere else, he spent $45 million on new buildings and improvements at Crotonville. He also hired some experienced academics—Jim Baughman from Harvard and Noel Tichy from Michigan—to revolutionize Crotonville's activities.

Under Welch's direct control and with his personal involvement, Crotonville's priority became to develop a generation of leaders aligned to GE's new vision and cultural norms. Increasingly, it evolved from a training center to a place where teams of managers worked together on real priority issues and decided on results-oriented action. And this led to the gradual replacement of outside faculty by GE insiders acting as discussion leaders. Leading the

change was Welch, who twice a month traveled to Crotonville to teach and interact with GE employees. ("Haven't missed a session yet," he boasted in the late 1990s.) (See Exhibit 7.) It was during one of these sessions that the idea for Work-Out emerged, and it was at Crotonville that many of the Best Practices sessions were held.

Despite all the individual development and the corporate initiatives, not all managers were able to achieve Welch's ideal leadership profile. (See Exhibit 8.) Of greatest concern to the CEO were those who seemed unwilling or unable to embrace the open, participative values he was espousing. In 1991, he addressed the problem and the seriousness of its consequences:

In our view, leaders, whether on the shop floor or at the top of our businesses, can be characterized in at least four ways. The first is one who delivers on commitments—financial or otherwise—and shares the values of our company. His or her future is an easy call. Onward and upward. The second type of leader is one who does not meet commitments and does not share our values. Not as pleasant a call, but equally easy. The third is one who misses commitments but shares the values. He or she usually gets a second chance, preferably in a different environment.

Then there's the fourth type—the most difficult for many of us to deal with. That leader delivers on commitments, makes all the numbers, but doesn't share the values we must have. This is the individual who typically forces performance out of people rather than inspires it: the autocrat, the big shot, the tyrant. Too often all of us have looked the other way and tolerated these "Type 4" managers because "they always deliver"—at least in the short term.[vii]

To reinforce his intention to identify and weed out Type 4 managers, Welch began rating GE top-level managers not only on their performance against quantifiable targets but also on the extent to which they "lived" GE values. Subsequently, many of GE's 500 officers started using a similar two-dimensional grid to evaluate and coach their own direct reports. And when coaching failed, Welch was prepared to take action on the type 4s. "People are removed for having the wrong values," he insisted. "We don't even talk about the numbers."

To back up this commitment to the new leadership criteria, a few years later GE introduced a 360° feedback process. Every employee was graded by his or her manager, peers and all subordinates on a 1 to 5 scale in areas such as teambuilding, quality focus, and vision. Welch described it as a powerful tool for detecting and changing those who "smile up and kick down." Tied into the evaluation process and linked to the Session C human resource planning exercise, the 360° feedback became the means for identifying training needs, coaching opportunities, and, eventually, career planning—whether that be up, sideways, or out.

Into the 1990s: The Third Wave

Entering the 1990s, Welch felt that GE's new foundation had been laid. Despite the slowdown in the industrial sector in the first few years of the new decade, he was committed to the task of rebuilding the company at an even more urgent pace. The new initiatives rolled on.

Boundaryless Behavior

Moving beyond the earlier initiatives aimed at strengthening GE's individual businesses, Welch began to focus on creating what he called "integrated diversity." He articulated his vision for GE in the 1990s as a "boundaryless" company, one characterized by an "open, anti-parochial environment friendly toward

---

EXHIBIT 8

GE Leadership Capabilities

- Create a clear, simple, reality-based, customer-focused vision and are able to communicate it straightforwardly to all constituencies.
- Understand accountability and commitment and are decisive ... set and meet aggressive targets ... always with unyielding integrity.
- Have the self-confidence to empower others and behave in a boundaryless fashion... believe in and are committed to Work-Out as a means of empowerment ... be open to ideas from anywhere.

- Have a passion for excellence ... hate bureaucracy and all the nonsense that comes with it.
- Have, or have the capacity to develop global brains and global sensitivity and are comfortable building diverse global teams.
- Stimulate and relish change ... are not frightened or paralyzed by it. See change as opportunity, not just a threat.
- Have enormous energy and the ability to energize and invigorate others. Understand speed as a competitive advantage and see the total organizational benefits that can be derived from a focus on speed.

Source: 1992 Annual Report.

the seeking and sharing of new ideas, regardless of their origins"—in many ways an institutionalization of the openness "Work-Out" had initiated and "best practices" transfers had reinforced. Describing his barrier-free vision for GE, Welch wrote:

> The boundaryless company we envision will remove the barriers among engineering, manufacturing, marketing, sales, and customer service; it will recognize no distinctions between domestic and foreign operations—we'll be as comfortable doing business in Budapest and Seoul as we are in Louisville and Schenectady. A boundaryless organization will ignore or erase group labels such as "management," "salaried" or "hourly," which get in the way of people working together.[viii]

One of Welch's most repeated stories of how best practices could be leveraged by boundaryless behavior described how managers from Canadian GE identified a small New Zealand appliance maker, Fisher & Paykel, producing a broad range of products very efficiently in its small, low-volume plant. When the Canadians used the flexible job-shop techniques to increase productivity in their high-volume factory, the U.S. appliance business became interested. More than 200 managers and employees from the Louisville plant went to Montreal to study the accomplishments, and soon a Quick Response program had cut the U.S. production cycle in half and reduced inventory costs by 20%. Not surprisingly, GE's Appliance Park in Louisville became a "must see" destination for many other businesses, and within a year, the program had been adapted for businesses as diverse as locomotives and jet engines.

The CEO gave the abstract concept of boundarylessness teeth not only by repeating such success stories but also by emphasizing that there was no place at GE for the adherents of the old culture: "We take people who aren't boundaryless out of jobs… If you're turf-oriented, self-centered, don't share with people and aren't searching for ideas, you don't belong here," he said. He also changed the criteria for bonuses and options awards to reward idea-seeking and sharing, not just idea creation. Five years later, Welch had a list of boundarylessness success stories:

> We quickly began to learn from each other: productivity solutions from Lighting; "quick response" asset management from Appliances; transaction effectiveness from GE Capital; cost-reduction techniques from Aircraft Engines; and global account management from Plastics.[ix]

One of the most impressive examples of the way ideas and expertise spread throughout GE was the company's "integration model." Developed on the lessons drawn from literally hundreds of post-acquisition reviews, the model guided the actions of managers in any part of the company responsible for integrating a newly acquired operation: from taking control of the accounts to realigning the organization, and from identifying and removing "blockers" to implementing GE tools and programs. By the late 1990s, GE's integration programs were completed in about 100 days.

Stretch: Achieving the Impossible

To reinforce his rising managerial expectations, in the early 1990s Welch made a new assault on GE's cultural norms. He introduced the notions of "stretch" to set performance targets and described it as "using dreams to set business targets, with no real idea of how to get there."[x] His objective was to change the way targets were set and performance was measured by creating an atmosphere that asked of everyone, "How good can you be?"

Stretch targets did not replace traditional forecasting and objective-setting processes. Managers still had to hit basic targets—adjusted to recognize the world as it turned out to be, not some rigid plan negotiated a year earlier. But during the budget cycle they were also required to set higher, "stretch" goals for their businesses. While managers were not held accountable for these goals, those who achieved them were rewarded with substantial bonuses or stock options. Said Welch: "Rigorous budgeting alone is nonsense. I think in terms of . . . what is the best you can do. You soon begin to see what comes out of a trusting, open environment."

Within a year of introducing the concept of stretch, Welch was reporting progress:

> We used to timidly nudge the peanut along, setting goals of moving from, say, 4.73 in inventory turns to 4.91, or from 8.53% operating margin to 8.92%; and then indulge in time-consuming high-level, bureaucratic negotiations to move the number a few hundredths one way or the other… We don't do that anymore. In a boundaryless organization with a bias for speed, decimal points are a bore. They inspire or challenge no one, capture no imaginations. We're aiming at 10 inventory turns, at 15% operating margins.[xi]

By the mid-1990s, stretch goals were an established part of GE's culture. A senior executive explained: "People like problem solving. They want to go to that next level. That's becoming a bigger driver for the company than Work-Out." But the introduction of stretch targets did not come without implementation difficulties. According to Steve Kerr, the head of Crotonville, "You absolutely have to honor the don't-punish-failure concept; stretch targets become a disaster without that." Unless properly managed, he explained, stretch could easily degenerate into a justification for forcing people to work 60-hour weeks to achieve impossible goals. "It's not the number per se, especially because it's a made-up number. It's the process you're trying to stimulate. You're trying to get people to think of fundamentally better ways of performing their work."[xii]

In early 1996, Welch acknowledged that GE did not meet two of its four-year corporate stretch targets: to increase operating margins from their 1991 level of 10% to 15% by 1995, and inventory turns from 5 to 10 times. However, after decades of single-digit operating margins and inventory turns of 4 or 5, GE did achieve an operating margin of 14.4% and inventory turns of almost 7 in 1995. "In stretching for these 'impossible' targets," said Welch, "we learned to do things faster than we would have going after 'doable' goals, and we have enough confidence now to set new stretch targets of at least 16% operating margin and more than 10 turns by 1998."[xiii]

Service Businesses

In 1994, Welch launched a new strategic initiative designed to reinforce one of his earliest goals: to reduce GE's dependence on its traditional industrial products. In the early 1980s, he had initiated the initial tilt towards service businesses through the acquisition of financial service companies such as Employers Reinsurance and Kidder, Peabody. "Nearly 60% of GE's profits now comes from services," said Welch in 1995. "Up from 16.4% in 1980. I wish it were 80%."[xiv]

To fulfill that wish, Welch began moving to the next stage—a push for product services. During his annual strategic reviews with senior managers, Welch began to challenge his managers "to participate in more of the food chain." While customers would always need high-quality hardware, Welch argued that GE's future challenge would be to offset slowing growth for its products by supplementing them with added-value services. Describing it as one of "the biggest growth opportunities in [GE's] history," he named a cadre of rising executives to focus on the

issue. At the same time, he asked Vice Chairman Paolo Fresco to set up a Services Council through which top managers could exchange ideas.

Soon, all GE's businesses were exploring new service-based growth opportunities. The medical business, for example, developed a concept called "In Site." This involved placing diagnostic sensors and communications capability into their installed base of CT scanners, MRI equipment, and other GE medical devices. The system linked the equipment directly to GE's on-line service center, continuously diagnosing its operating condition in real time. Soon, GE was offering its remote diagnostics and other services to all medical equipment—including non-GE products.

Like other internal "best practice" service examples, the "In Site" story was shared in the Services Council, and soon online diagnostic technology was being transferred to other GE businesses. In Aircraft Engines, critical operating parameters of GE jet engines were monitored by GE Service experts while the engines were in flight, providing the company with a major value-added benefit for its customers. The same real-time diagnostic concepts were also applied in GE's power systems business, and other businesses had plans to develop remote diagnostic capability as well.

According to Welch, the opportunity for growth in product services was unlimited. With an advantage unique in the world—an installed base of some 9,000 GE commercial jet engines, 10,000 turbines, 13,000 locomotives, and 84,000 major pieces of medical diagnostic imaging equipment—he felt GE had an incredibly strong platform on which to build. Commented Lewis Edelheit, GE's senior VP for Corporate Research and Development:

> A few years ago, businesses were seen as a pyramid, with the base as the product and the other elements—services, manufacturing processes and information—resting on that base. We are now looking at turning the pyramid upside down. The product will become just one piece of the picture—the tip of that inverted pyramid. The biggest growth opportunities may come from providing services to the customer: providing the customer with ways to become more productive—and with information so valuable the customer will pay for it.[xv]

By 1996, GE had built an $8 billion equipment services business, which was growing much faster than the underlying product businesses. Equally important, in Welch's view, it was changing internal mindsets from selling products to "helping our customers to win." GE's product services were to be aimed at making customers' existing assets—power plants, locomotives, airplanes, factories, hospital equipment and the like—more productive. Yet while GE was helping its customers reduce their capital outlays, its managers were also shifting demand from low-margin products to their newer high-profit services with margins almost twice the company average.

This initiative led to a new round of acquisitions. In 1997 alone, GE made 20 service-related acquisitions and joint ventures, including a $1.5 billion acquisition of a jet engine service business and the $600 million purchase of a global power generation equipment service company. GE's radical business shift over two decades led Welch to claim, "We have changed the very nature of what we do for a living. Today, services account for two-thirds of our revenues." (See Exhibit 9.)

Closing Out the Decade: Welch's Final Chapter

As he entered the last half of the decade, Welch was aware that he would reach GE's mandatory retirement age in 2001. Yet his commitment to keep building GE was undiminished, despite critics who continued to question if the company could keep adding value to such a highly diversified business portfolio. In the 1995 Annual Report, he tackled the issue head on:

> The hottest trend in business is the rush toward breaking up multi-business companies. The obvious question to GE, the world's largest multi-business company, was, "When are you going to do it?" The short answer is that we're not…. We are a company intent on getting bigger, not smaller. Our only answer to the trendy question "What do you intend to spin off?" is "Cash—and lots of it."

Despite hospitalization for triple bypass surgery in 1995, he showed no signs of slowing down. Indeed, many felt he gained new energy in his post-operative state as the pressure for performance and new initiatives continued.

Six Sigma Quality Initiative

When a 1995 company survey showed that GE employees were dissatisfied with the quality of its products and processes, Welch met with Lawrence Bossidy, an old friend who had left GE in 1991 to become CEO of AlliedSignal Inc. Welch learned how the Six Sigma

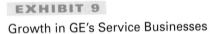

EXHIBIT 9

Growth in GE's Service Businesses

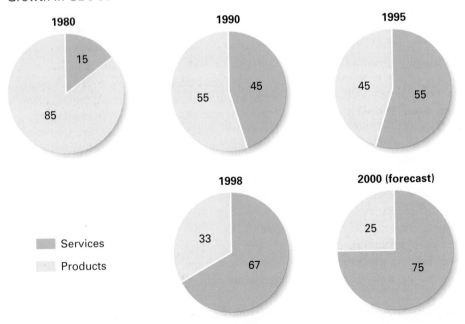

quality program Bossidy had borrowed from Motorola Inc. had helped AlliedSignal dramatically improve quality, lower costs, and increase productivity. Immediately, he invited Bossidy to GE's next Corporate Executive Council meeting. His presentation of the AlliedSignal program won universal rave reviews.

After the meeting, Welch asked Gary Reiner, vice president for Business Development, to lead a quality initiative for GE. Reiner undertook a detailed study of the impact of quality programs at companies like Motorola and AlliedSignal. His analysis concluded that GE was operating at error rates ten thousand times the Six Sigma quality level of 3.4 defects per million operations. Furthermore, he estimated that the gap was costing the company between $8 billion and $12 billion a year in inefficiencies and lost productivity. On the basis of Reiner's findings, at GE's 1996 annual gathering of its 500 top managers in Boca Raton, Welch announced a goal of reaching Six Sigma quality levels company-wide by the year 2000, describing the program as "the biggest opportunity for growth, increased profitability, and individual employee satisfaction in the history of our company."

Like all initiatives announced in Boca (services, globalization, etc.), Six Sigma quality was more than a slogan: it was a well-developed program, with a detailed plan for its implementation. Furthermore, it would be monitored throughout the year in a carefully linked series of management meetings that Welch started to refer to as GE's "operating system"—the series of planning, resource allocation, review, and communication meetings that were at the heart of its management process. The Boca initiative announcement was followed up by a first progress report at the two-day March CEC meeting; then in the April Session C reviews, Welch would check how key human resources had been deployed against the target; the July strategic review sessions would review the impact of the initiative on each business's three-year outlook; October's Officers Meeting tracked progress and showcased best practice; and the November operating plan reviews would fold the impact into the following year's forecasts. (See Exhibit 10.) Said Welch, "We are relentless."

Six Sigma participation was not optional, and Welch tied 40% of bonus to an individual's Six Sigma objectives. To provide managers the skills, Reiner designed a massive training of thousands of managers to create a cadre of "Green Belts," "Black Belts," and "Master Black Belts" in Six Sigma quality. "Green

Belt" training took about four weeks, followed by implementation of a five-month project aimed at improving quality. Black Belts required six weeks of instruction in statistics, data analysis, and other Six Sigma tools which prepared the candidate to undertake three major quality projects that resulted in measurable performance increases. Master Black Belts—full-time Six Sigma instructors—mentored the Black Belt candidates through the two-year process.

At the January 1998 Boca Raton meeting, speakers from across the company and around the world presented Six Sigma best practice and achievements. Managers from Medical Systems described how Six Sigma designs produced a tenfold increase in the life of CT scanner X-ray tubes; the railcar leasing business described a 62% reduction in turnaround time at its repair shops, making it two to three times faster than its nearest rival; and a team from the plastics business described how the Six Sigma process added 300 million pounds of new capacity, equivalent to a "free plant." In all, 30,000 Six Sigma projects had been initiated in the prior year.

At the April 1999 Annual Meeting, Welch announced that in the first two years of Six Sigma, GE had invested $500 million to train the entire professional workforce of 85,000. In addition, 5,000 managers had been appointed to work on the program full-time as Black Belts and Master Black Belts, leading Welch to claim "they have begun to change the DNA of GE to one whose central strand is quality." Returns of $750 million over the investment exceeded expectations, and the company was forecasting additional returns of $1.5 billion in 1999 (Exhibit 11). Clearly delighted by the program, Welch stated, "In nearly four decades with GE, I have never seen a company initiative move so willingly and so rapidly in pursuit of a big idea."

"A Players" with "Four E's"

The closer he got to his planned retirement date, the more Welch seemed to focus on the quality of the organization he would leave to his successor. While he felt he had assembled a first-class team of leaders at the top of the company, he wanted to continue upgrading quality deep in the organization. This implied not only raising the bar on new hires but also weeding out those who did not meet GE's high standards. Modifying his earlier language of four management types, he began describing GE as a company that wanted only "A Players"—individuals with vision,

EXHIBIT 10

The GE Management System

Core Business Processes

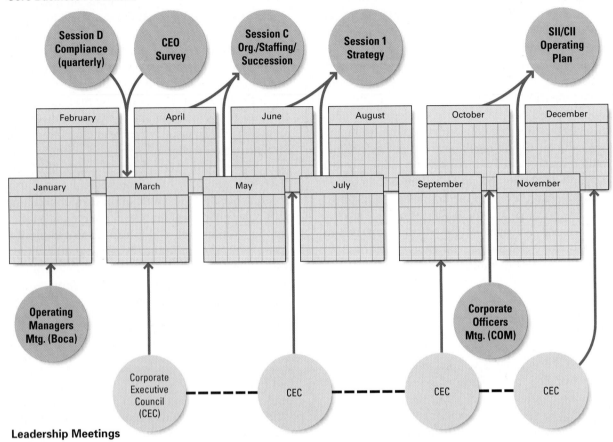

Management System Drives Resource Allocation (People and $) and Accelerates Consistent Best Practice Implementation.

leadership, energy, and courage. He described what he was trying to achieve:

> The GE leader sees this company for what it truly is: the largest petri dish of business innovation in the world. We have roughly 350 business segments. We see them as 350 laboratories whose ideas are there to be shared, learned, and spread as fast as we can. The leader sees that sharing and spreading near the top of his or her responsibilities.

"A Players" were characterized by what Welch described as the 4E's—energy ("excited by ideas and attracted to turbulence because of the opportunity it brings"), ability to energize others ("infecting everyone with their enthusiasm for an idea and having everyone dreaming the same big dreams"), edge ("the ability to make tough calls") and execution ("the consistent ability to turn vision into results").

To meet the company's need for exceptional leadership talent, Welch insisted that GE move to phase three of its globalization initiative. Beyond focusing on global markets and global sources—the earlier two phases of globalization—he urged his managers to expand their efforts in "globalizing the intellect of the company." At the same time, he urged his top management group to take strong action to upgrade the quality of their existing employees:

> We're an A-plus company. We want only A players. We can get anyone we want. Shame on any of you who aren't facing into your less-than-the-best. Take care of your best. Reward them. Promote them. Pay them well. Give them a lot of [stock] options and don't spend all that time trying to work plans to get Cs to be Bs. Move them on out early. It's a contribution.[xvi]

EXHIBIT 11

Costs and Benefits of GE's Six Sigma Program
Six Sigma Results: 1996–1999

Source: GE Annual Report, 1998.

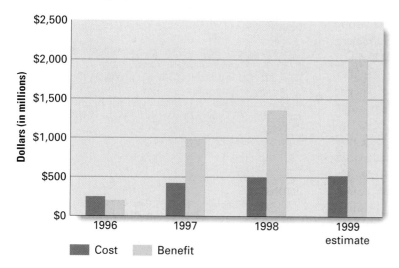

To help clarify those decisions, the company implemented a performance appraisal system that required every manager to rank each of his or her employees into one of five categories based on his or her long-term performance—the "top" 10% as 1s, the "strong" 15% as 2s, the "highly valued" 50% as 3s, the "borderline" 15% as 4s, and the "least effective" 10% as 5s.[3] Every group, even a 10-person team, had to be ranked on this so-called "vitality curve." All 1s and most 2s received stock options but anyone rated a 5 had to go. Welch elaborated on the need to weed out poor performers. "With the 5s it's clear as a bell. I think they know it, and you know it. It's better for everyone. They go on to a new place, a new life, a new start." At the other end of the scale, Welch expected managers to take action on their top performers to develop them: "You send your top 10 on and see how many of them get into the top 10 of the whole business."

Welch knew that nurturing and continuously upgrading the quality of management was one of the main keys to GE's success. He felt that the talent he amassed over 18 years—especially at the senior management levels—was of a significantly higher quality than in past years. "I've got all A players in the Corporate Council. It wasn't like that before. I'm really pleased about that," he said.

Toward Retirement: One More Initiative

Just when the organization felt Welch had put his final stamp on GE, at the 1999 Operating Managers' Meeting in Boca, the 64-year-old CEO introduced his fourth strategic initiative—e-business.[4] Describing the impact of the Internet as "the biggest change I have ever seen," he launched a program he described as "*destroyyourbusiness.com.*" Within two months each unit had a full-time *dyb.com* team focused on the challenge of redefining its business model before someone else did. "Change means opportunity," he told them. "And this is our greatest opportunity yet."

Yet Welch also knew that GE was late to the Internet party. As he acknowledged in his address to shareholders three months after the Boca meeting, "Big companies like us were frightened by the unfamiliarity of the technology. We thought this was

---

[3]Eventually, the five categories were reduced to three—the top 20%, the high-performance 70%, and the bottom 10%. The practice of counseling out the bottom 10% continued under the philosophy of "improve or move."

[4]The three earlier ones were globalization, services, and Six Sigma.

mysterious, Nobel Prize stuff, the province of the wild-eyed and purple haired." But the more he explored the Internet and talked to people about it, the more Welch came to believe that, through processes like Six Sigma, GE had done the really hard work of building the assets needed to support e-business—like strong brands, top ranked product reliability, great fulfillment capability, and excellent service quality. "It's much harder for a dot com startup to challenge us when they don't have the fundamentals down," he said. "They're popcorn stands without a real business or operating capabilities."

As the organization cranked up to push the new initiative through the monthly schedule of reviews that GE operating system required, Welch was impressed by early results from the *dyb.com* teams. "Digitizing the company and developing e-business models is easier—not harder—than we ever imagined," he said. But others were more sanguine. Said David Mark, a partner at McKinsey and Co., "It's going to take a decade for this to play out. I don't think it's a simple transition." If Mark was correct, building GE's e-business would be a long-term challenge for Welch's successor.

SOURCES AND REFERENCES

Byrne, John A., "Jack," *Business Week*, June 8, 1998.

Cosco, Joseph P., "General Electric Works it All Out," *Journal of Business Strategy*, May-June, 1994.

Filipczak, Bob, "CEOs Who Train," *Training*, June, 1996.

Grant, Linda, "GE: The Envelope, Please," *Fortune*, June 26, 1995.

Hodgetts, Richard M., "A Conversation with Steve Kerr, GE's Chief Learning Officer," *Organizational Dynamics*, March 22, 1996.

Kandebo, Stanley, "Engine Services Critical to GE Strategy," *Aviation Week*, February 23, 1998.

Koenig, Peter, "If Europe's Dead, Why is GE Investing Billions There?" *Fortune*, September 9, 1996.

Lorenz, Christopher, "The Alliance-Maker," *Financial Times*, April 14, 1989.

Norman, James R., "A Very Nimble Elephant," *Forbes*, October 10, 1994.

Rifkin, Glenn, "GE: Bringing Good Leaders to Life," *Forbes*, April 8, 1996.

Tichy, M. Noel and Eli Cohen, *The Leadership Engine: How Winning Companies Build Leaders at Every Level* (HarperBusiness, New York, 1997).

Tichy, M. Noel and Eli Cohen, "The Teaching Organization," *Training & Development*, July 1998.

Tichy, M. Noel and Stratford Sherman, *Control Your Destiny or Someone Else Will* (HarperBusiness, New York, 1994).

Tichy, M. Noel and Stratford Sherman, "Walking the Talk at GE," *Training & Development*, June 1996.

Slater, Robert, *Get Better or Get Beaten!* (McGraw-Hill, New York, 1996).

Smart, Tim, "GE's Brave New World," *Business Week*, November 8, 1993.

Stewart, Thomas A., "GE Keeps Those Ideas Coming," *Fortune*, August 12, 1991.

ENDNOTES

i. "General Electric: 1984" (HBS Case No. 385-315), by Professor Francis J. Aguilar and Richard G. Hamermesh and RA Caroline Brainard. © 1985 by the President and Fellows of Harvard College.

ii. Noel Tichy and Ram Charan, "Speed, Simplicity, Self-Confidence: An Interview with Jack Welch," *Harvard Business Review*, September-October 1989.

iii. Anon, "GE Chief Hopes to Shape Agile Giant," *Los Angeles Times*, June 1, 1988.

iv. Tichy and Charan, op. cit., p. 112.

v. Robert Slater, *Jack Welch and the GE Way: Management Insights and Leadership Secrets of the Legendary CEO* (McGraw-Hill), 1998, p. 195.

vi. Tichy and Charan, op. cit., p. 120.

vii. GE Annual Report, 1991.

viii. GE Annual Report, 1989.

ix. GE Annual Report, 1995.

x. GE Annual Report, 1993.

xi. GE Annual Report, 1993.

xii. "Stretch Goals: The Dark Side of Asking for Miracles," Interview excerpts with Steve Kerr, GE's Vice President of Leadership Development. *Fortune*, November 13, 1995.

xiii. GE Annual Report, 1995.

xiv. Tim Smart, "Jack Welch's Encore," *Fortune*, October 28, 1996.

xv. Lewis Edelheit, "GE's R&D Strategy: Be Vital," *Research Technology Management*, March-April, 1998.

xvi. Slater, op. cit., p. 39.

Case 32

Nike's Dispute with the University of Oregon

This case was prepared by Rebecca J. Morris, University of Nebraska at Omaha, and Anne T. Lawrence, San Jose State University.

Nike's Dispute with the University of Oregon[1]

On April 24, 2000, Philip H. Knight, CEO of athletic shoe and apparel maker Nike Inc., publicly announced that he would no longer donate money to the University of Oregon (UO). It was a dramatic and unexpected move for the high-profile executive. A former UO track and field star, Knight had founded Nike's predecessor in 1963 with his former UO coach and mentor, Bill Bowerman. Over the years, Knight had maintained close ties with his alma mater, giving more than $50 million of his personal fortune to the school over a quarter century. In 2000, he was in active discussion with school officials about his biggest donation yet—millions for reno-

vating the football stadium. But suddenly it was all called off. Said Knight in his statement: "[F]or me personally, there will be no further donations of any kind to the University of Oregon. At this time, this is not a situation that can be resolved. The bonds of trust, which allowed me to give at a high level, have been shredded."[2]

At issue was the University of Oregon's intention, announced April 14, 2000, to join the Worker Rights Consortium (WRC). Like many universities, UO was engaged in an internal debate over the ethical responsibilities associated with its role as a purchaser of goods manufactured overseas. Over a period of several months, UO administrators, faculty, and students had been discussing what steps they could take to ensure that products sold in the campus store, especially university-logo apparel, were not manufactured under sweatshop conditions. The university had considered joining two organizations, both of which purported to certify goods as "no sweat." The first, the Fair Labor Association (FLA), had grown out of President Clinton's Apparel Industry Partnership (AIP) initiative and was vigorously backed by Nike, as well as several other leading apparel makers. The second, the Worker Rights Consortium, was supported by student activists and several U.S.-based labor unions that had broken from the AIP after charging it did not go far enough to protect workers. Knight clearly felt that his alma mater had made the wrong choice. "[The] University [has] inserted itself into the new global economy where I make my living," he charged. "And inserted itself on the wrong side, fumbling a teachable moment."

Reprinted by permission from the *Case Research Journal*. Copyright © 2001 by Rebecca J. Morris and Anne T. Lawrence and the North American Case Research Association. All rights reserved. This case was prepared by Rebecca J. Morris, University of Nebraska at Omaha, and Anne T. Lawrence, San Jose State University, as the basis for class discussion rather than to illustrate either effective or ineffective handling of an administrative situation. For the most recent financial results of the company discussed in this case, go to http://finance.yahoo.com, input the company's stock symbol, and download the latest company report from its homepage.

[1]By Rebecca J. Morris, University of Nebraska at Omaha and Anne T. Lawrence, San Jose State University. This case was written on the basis of publicly available information solely for the purpose of stimulating student discussion. All individuals and events are real. An earlier version of this case was presented at the 2000 annual meeting of the North American Case Research Association. The comments of reviewers at that meeting and of three anonymous reviewers for the Case Research Journal are greatly appreciated. All rights reserved jointly to the authors and the North American Case Research Association. Copyright © 2001 by the *Case Research Journal* and Rebecca J. Morris and Anne T. Lawrence.

[2]"Knight's Statement," by Philip H. Knight, via press release, http://www.oregonlive.com.

The dispute between Phil Knight and the University of Oregon captured much of the furor swirling about the issue of the role of multinational corporations in the global economy and the effects of their far-flung operations on their many thousands of workers, communities, and other stakeholders. In part because of its high-profile brand name, Nike had become a lightning rod for activists concerned about worker rights abroad. Like many U.S.-based shoe and apparel makers, Nike had located its manufacturing operations overseas, mainly in Southeast Asia, in search of low wages. Almost all production was carried out by subcontractors rather than by Nike directly. Nike's employees in the United States, by contrast, directed their efforts to the high-end work of research and development, marketing, and retailing. In the context of this global division of labor, what responsibility, if any, did Nike have to ensure adequate working conditions and living standards for the hundreds of thousands of workers, mostly young Asian women, who made its shoes and apparel? If this was not Nike's responsibility, then whose was it? Did organizations like the University of Oregon have any business pressuring companies through their purchasing practices? If so, how should they best do so? In short, what were the lessons of this "teachable moment"?

Nike, Inc.

In 2000, Nike, Inc. was the leading designer and marketer of athletic footwear, apparel, and equipment in the world. Based in Beaverton, Oregon, the company's "swoosh" logo, its "Just Do It!" slogan, and its spokespersons Michael Jordan, Mia Hamm, and Tiger Woods were universally recognized. Nike employed around 20,000 people directly, and *half a million* indirectly in 565 contract factories in 46 countries around the world turning out Nike products.[3] Wholly owned subsidiaries included Bauer Nike Hockey Inc. (hockey equipment), Cole Haan (dress and casual shoes), and Nike Team Sports (licensed team products). Revenues for the 12 months ending November 1999 were almost $9 billion.[4] With a 45 percent global market share, Nike was in a league of its own.[5] Knight owned 34 percent of the

company's stock and was believed to be the sixth richest individual in the United States.[6]

Knight had launched this far-flung global empire shortly after completing his MBA degree at Stanford University in the early 1960s. Drawing on his firsthand knowledge of track and field, he decided to import low-priced track shoes from Japan in partnership with his former college coach. Bowerman would provide design ideas, test the shoes in competition, and endorse the shoes with other coaches; Knight would handle all financial and day-to-day operations of the business. Neither man had much money to offer, so for $500 apiece and a handshake, the company (then called Blue Ribbon Sports) was officially founded in 1963. The company took the name Nike in 1978; two years later, with revenues topping $269 million and 2,700 employees, Nike became a publicly traded company.[7]

From the beginning, marketing had been a critical part of Knight's vision. The founder defined Nike as a "marketing-oriented company." During the 1980s and early 1990s, Nike aggressively sought out endorsements by celebrity athletes to increase brand awareness and foster consumer loyalty. Early Nike endorsers included marathoners Alberto Salazar and Joan Benoit, Olympic gold medalist Carl Lewis, Wimbledon champion Andre Agassi, and six members of the 1992 Olympic basketball "Dream Team." Later Nike endorsers included tennis aces Pete Sampras and Monica Seles, basketball great Michael Jordan, and golf superstar Tiger Woods.

Nike became the world's largest athletic shoe company in 1991 when revenues soared to $3 billion, but that was only the beginning.[8] Continued development of "cool shoes," aggressive geographic expansion, and the world dominance of Nike-endorsing athletes resulted in record-breaking performances year after year. By 1998, Nike's total revenues exceeded $9.5 billion.[9] Although the Asian economic crisis and sluggish U.S. sales caused revenues to dip slightly in 1999, Nike easily led the athletic footwear industry, outpacing the number two firm (Adidas) by 1.5 times.[10] Key events in Nike's history are summarized in Exhibit 1.

[3]Greenhouse, S. (January 26, 2000). "Anti-Sweatshop Movement Is Achieving Gains Overseas," *New York Times*, Section A, p. 10.
[4]Lee, L. (February 21, 2000). "Can Nike Still Do It," *Business Week*, p. 120.
[5]Martinson, J. (July 8, 2000). "Brand Values: Nike: The Sweet Swoosh of Success," *The Guardian* (London), Guardian City Pages, p. 26.

[6]Anonymous. (October 11, 1999). "The Forbes 400: America's Richest People," *Forbes*, p. 296.
[7]*Our History: BRS Becomes Nike.* (n.d). Nike, Inc. Accessed: February 3, 2000. **http://www.nikebiz.com/story/before.shtml.**
[8]*Our History: In Our Own League.* (n.d). Nike, Inc. Accessed: February 3, 2000. **http://www.nikebiz.com/story/chrono.shtml.**
[9]Nike, Inc. (1999, May 31—filing date). Form 10-K. Securities and Exchange Commission. Accessed: February 5, 2000.
[10]Gellene, D. (April 8, 1999). "Ad Reviews: Adidas," *The Los Angeles Times*, Part C, p. 6.

EXHIBIT 1

Key Events in Nike's History

1957	Phil Knight and Coach Bill Bowerman met for the first time at the University of Oregon.
1959	Phil Knight graduated from the University of Oregon with a BBA degree in Accounting.
1962	Knight wrote the marketing research paper outlining the concept that became "Blue Ribbon Sports" (BRS).
1963	The first shipment of 200 Tiger shoes arrived from Japan.
1966	The first retail store was opened.
1969	Knight left the accounting field to devote his full-time efforts to building the company.
1970	Nike's legal dispute with the Japanese supplier resulted in the exploration of manufacturing in Mexico, Puerto Rico, and Canada.
1971	Nike contracted for the production of shoes in Mexico; however, the shoes were a disaster—cracking when used in cold weather.
1972	The first shoes bearing the Nike brand were sold.
1977	Nike contracted with factories in Taiwan and Korea, ending the manufacturing relationship with the Japanese firm.
1978	The split between Blue Ribbon Sports and their Japanese supplier became final. BRS changed to the Nike name for all operations.
1980	Nike sold the first shares of common stock to the public.
1981	Revenues were $457.7 million and Nike had 3,000 employees.
1982	Phil Knight received the Pioneer Award. The Pioneer Award was given annually by the University of Oregon to a person "whose character places him/her in a position of leadership." The award recognized individuals who led in business, philanthropy, communications, government or the arts.
1986	For the first time, Nike revenues surpassed the billion-dollar mark.
1990	Growth in international sales helped Nike reach $2 billion in revenues. Nike employed 5,300 employees in the United States. The Nike World Campus opened in Beaverton, Oregon.
1991	Revenues reached $3 billion with $869 million in international revenues. Michael Jordan wears Nike shoes while leading the Chicago Bulls to their first NBA championship.
1995	Nike's revenues were $4.8 billion. Nike shoes using the patented Nike-Air system were introduced, radically changing shoe design.
1996	Nike's revenues were $6.5 billion. In the Atlanta Olympics, Michael Johnson became the fastest man in the world wearing a pair of specially designed gold metallic Nike's. Phil Knight donated $25 million to the Oregon Campaign. His gift designated $15 million to the creation of endowed chairs. The remaining $10 million helped finance the construction of a new law school building that was named the William W. Knight Law Center after Phil Knight's father. The $25 million gift was the largest single gift to a university in the Pacific Northwest. Knight's earlier gifts to UO totaled $25 million. Knight funds supported athletics and the university library was named for his family in the 1980s.
1998	Nike's revenues were $9.5 billion. Basketball shoes slumped as Michael Jordan retired and the NBA played a shortened season due to a labor dispute. Nike's international trading partner, Nissho Iwai of Japan, donated an undisclosed "generous" amount to the UO Knight Library to "honor Mr. Knight's great commitment to supporting the University of Oregon." Nissho Iwai had made a donation to the renovation of the library in 1990. One floor of the library was named for the Japanese company.
1999	Nike's revenues dipped to $8.8 billion. Revenue decline was attributed to the "brown shoes" movement in the United States and the Asian economic slump.
2000	Phil Knight withdrew his pledge for a $30 million contribution for the University of Oregon's football stadium.

Sources: Our History. (n.d.). Nike, Inc. Accessed: February 3, 2000. **http://www.nikebiz.com/story/chrono.shtml.** Katz, D. R. (1995). *Just Do It: The Nike Spirit in the Corporate World,* Holbrook, MA: Adams Media Corporation. Nike, Inc. (1995–1999). Form 10-K. Securities and Exchange Commission. Accessed: February 5, 2000. The library floor information is based on the following source:"Trading Firm Makes Gift to UO Knight Library endowment." (June 11, 1998). University of Oregon Press Release. Accessed: March 27, 2000. **http://comm.uoregon.edu/newsreleases/official/jun98/G061198_1.html.**

Cutting Edge Products

An important element in Nike's success was its ability to develop cutting-edge products that met the needs of serious athletes, as well as set fashion trends. Research specialists in Nike's Sports Research Labs conducted extensive research and testing to develop new technologies to improve the performance of Nike shoes in a variety of sports. Tom McQuirk, head of the company's Sports Research Labs stated, "Our job here in Sports Research is to define human movement in terms of biomechanics and physiology. Our job is to translate activities into a set of performance-enhancing and injury-reducing needs."[11] For example, research specialists studied the causes of ankle injuries in basketball players to develop shoes that would physically prevent injuries as well as signal information to the user to help him or her resist turning the ankle while in the air. Other specialists developed new polymer materials that would make the shoes lighter, more aerodynamic, or more resistant to the abrasions incurred during normal athletic use.

Findings from the Sports Research Labs were then passed on to design teams that developed the look and styling of the shoes. Drawing heavily from trends in popular culture, shoe designers in the Jordan Building of Nike's Beaverton, Oregon, corporate campus blended the technological with the "romance and imagery and all those subliminal characteristics that make an object important to people in less utilitarian ways."[12] Put more simply, the Nike designers took a technologically sophisticated piece of sporting equipment and gave it attitude.

The Making of Athletic Shoes

Although it was the leading athletic footwear company in the world, Nike never manufactured shoes in any significant number. Rather, from its inception, the company had outsourced production to subcontractors in Southeast Asia, with the company shifting production locations within the region when prevailing wage rates became too high. In the early years, it had imported shoes from Japan. It later shifted production to South Korea and Taiwan, then to Indonesia and Thailand, and later yet to Vietnam and China, as shown in Exhibit 2.[13]

EXHIBIT 2

Location of Shoe Production in Nike Subcontractor Factories, 1995–1999 (Percent of Athletic Shoe Production by Country)

	1995	1996	1997	1998	1999
China	31	34	37	37	40
Indonesia	31	38	37	34	30
South Korea	16	11	5	2	1
Thailand	14	10	10	10	11
Taiwan	8	5	3	2	2
Vietnam		2	8	11	12
Philippines			4	4	2
Italy					2

Source: Nike 10-K statements, 1995–1999.

The reasons for locating shoe production mainly in Southeast Asia were several, but the most important was the cost of labor. The availability of component materials and trade policies were also factors. Modern athletic shoes were composed of mesh, leather, and nylon uppers that were hand-assembled, sewn, and glued to composite soles.[14] Mechanization had not been considered effective for shoe manufacturing due to the fragile materials used and the short life spans of styles of athletic shoes.[15] Therefore, shoe production was highly labor intensive. Developing countries, primarily in Southeast Asia, offered the distinct advantage of considerably lower wage rates. For example, in the early 1990s, when Nike shifted much of its shoe production to Indonesia, daily wages there hovered around $1 a day (compared with wages in the U.S. shoe industry at that time of around $8 an hour).[16]

Along with lower labor costs, Asia provided the additional advantage of access to raw materials suppliers.[17] Very few rubber firms in the United States, for example, produced the sophisticated composite soles demanded in modern athletic shoe designs. Satellite industries necessary for modern shoe production, plentiful in Asia, included tanneries, textiles, and plastic and iron-work moldings.[18]

[11]Katz, D. R. (1995), *Just Do It: The Nike Spirit in the Corporate World* (Holbrook, MA: Adams Media Corporation), p. 132.

[12]Ibid., p. 130.

[13]Although Nike operated shoe factories in New England in the 1970s and 1980s, Nike's annual U.S. production never accounted for more than one week of demand annually. Later, these plants were closed, and Nike stopped producing shoes in the United States, other than prototypes.

[14]Nike, Inc. (1999, May 31—filing date). Form 10-K. Securities and Exchange Commission. Accessed: February 5, 2000.

[15]Vanderbilt, T. (1998). *The Sneaker Book* (New York: New Press), p. 77.

[16]Katz, *Just Do It*, p. 162.

[17]Vanderbilt, *The Sneaker Book*, p. 81.

[18]Ibid., p. 90.

A third factor in determining where to locate production was differential tariffs that applied to athletic shoes. The tariffs were determined by the manner in which the upper was attached to the sole of the shoe. The three types—nonmolded, molded, and fox-banded (where a strip of material was applied over the joint of the sole and upper, as in canvas sneakers)—were assessed different tariffs for importation. Variations in the materials used for the uppers also determined the tariff rate. In general, canvas sneakers were assessed higher tariffs than leather molded footwear, such as basketball or running shoes. As a result, differential tariffs prompted shoe companies to outsource higher margin high-technology athletic shoes while sometimes producing low-margin canvas shoes domestically.[19]

The economic reality for many firms in the athletic footwear industry involved balancing consumer demand for new and innovative styles with pressures to improve the profit picture. Manufacturing new high-technology styles in Southeast Asia permitted the firms to take advantage of lower labor costs, lower tariffs and a better-developed supplier network. Many of Nike's factories in Asia were operated by a small number of Taiwanese and Korean firms that specialized in shoe manufacturing, many owned by some of the wealthiest families in the region. When Nike moved from one location to another, often these companies followed, bringing their managerial expertise with them.

Nike's Subcontractor Factories

In 2000, Nike contracted with over five hundred different footwear and apparel factories around the world to produce its shoes and apparel.[20] Although there was no such thing as a typical Nike plant, a factory operated by the Korean subcontractor Tae Kwang Vina (TKV) in the Bien Hoa City industrial zone near Ho Chi Minh City in Vietnam provided a glimpse into the setting in which many Nike shoes were made.[21]

TKV employed approximately 10,000 workers in the Bien Hoa City factory. The workforce consisted of 200 clerical workers, 355 supervisors, and 9,465 production workers, all making athletic shoes for Nike. Ninety percent of the workers were women between the ages of 18 to 24. Production workers were employed in one of three major areas within the factory: the chemical, stitching, and assembly sections. Production levels at the Bien Hoa City factory reached 400,000 pairs of shoes per month; Nike shoes made at this and other factories made up fully 5 percent of Vietnam's total exports.[22]

A second-generation South Korean shoe worker employed by Nike described the challenges of work in the typical shoe factory as the "three D's." "It's dirty, dangerous, and difficult," explained T. H. Lee. "Making shoes on a production line is something people only do because they see it as an important and lucrative job. Nobody who could do something else for the same wage would be here. It's less dirty, dangerous, and difficult than it was in the past—but it's not an easy way to spend a day."[23]

The Chemical Section[24]

Over one thousand natural and manmade materials were used in the factory to produce shoes from scratch. Workers in the chemical or polyurethane (PU) plant were responsible for producing the high-technology outsoles. Production steps in the chemical division involved stretching and flattening huge blobs of raw rubber on heavy-duty rollers and baking chemical compounds in steel molds to form the innovative three-dimensional outsoles. The chemical composition of the soles changed constantly in response to the cutting-edge formulations developed by the Beaverton, Oregon, design teams, requiring frequent changes in the production process.

The smell of complex polymers, the hot ovens, and the clanging of the steel molds resulted in a working environment that was louder, hotter, and had higher concentrations of chemical fumes than allowed by Vietnamese law.[25] Chemicals used in the section were known to cause eye, skin, and throat

[19]Austen, J. and Barff, R. (1993). "It's Gotta Be da Shoes," *Environment and Planning* 25, pp. 48–52.

[20]Greenhouse, "Anti-Sweatshop Movement Is Achieving Gains Overseas," p. 10.

[21]Descriptions of the Tae Kwang Vina factory in Bien Hoa City were derived from the following: Manning, J. (November 9, 1997). "Nike: Track's Across the Globe" (three-part newspaper series originally appearing in *The Oregonian*), online source http://oregonlive.com/series/nike11091.html. Katz, *Just Do It*; Vanderbilt, *The Sneaker Book*; Ernst & Young (January 13, 1997). *Ernst & Young Environmental and Labor Practice Audit of the Tae Kwang Vina Industrial Ltd. Co., Vietnam.* Copy of the audit available at http://www.corpwatch.org/trac/nike/audit.html.

[22]Greenhouse, S. (November 8, 1997). "Nike Shoe Plant in Vietnam Is Called Unsafe for Workers," *New York Times*, Section A, p. 1.

[23]Katz, *Just Do It*, p. 161.

[24]Manning, J. (November 9, 1997). "Nike: Track's Across the Globe" (three-part newspaper series originally appearing in *The Oregonian*), online source http://oregonlive.com/series/nike11091.html.

[25]Manning, J. (November 11, 1997). "Poverty's Legions Flock to Nike," *The Oregonian*, http://www.oregonlive.com/series/nike11103.html.

irritations; damage to liver and kidneys; nausea; anorexia; and reproductive health hazards through inhalation or in some cases through absorption through the skin.[26] Workers in the chemical section were thought to have high rates of respiratory illnesses, although records kept at the TKV operations did not permit the tracking of illnesses by the factory section.

Workers in the chemical section were issued gloves and surgical-style masks. However, they often discarded the protective gear, complaining that it was too hot and humid to wear them in the plant. Cotton masks and gloves also were ineffective in protecting workers from solvent fumes and exposure to skin-damaging chemicals.[27]

The Stitching Section[28]

In a space the size of three football fields, row after row of sewing machines operated by young women hummed and clattered. One thousand stitchers worked on a single floor of the TKV factory, sewing together nylon, leather, and other fabrics to make the uppers. Other floors of the factory were filled with thousands of additional sewing machines producing different shoe models.

The stitching job required precision and speed. Workers who did not meet the aggressive production goals did not receive a bonus. Failing to meet production goals three times resulted in the worker's dismissal. Workers were sometimes required to work additional hours without pay to meet production quotas.[29] Supervisors were strict, chastising workers for excessive talking or spending too much time in the restrooms. Korean supervisors, often hampered by language and cultural barriers, sometimes resorted to hard-nosed management tactics, hitting or slapping slower workers. Other workers in need of discipline were forced to stand outside the factory for long periods in the tropical sun. The Vietnamese term for this practice was *phoi nang*, or sun-drying.[30]

The Assembly Section[31]

Women worked side by side along an assembly line to join the uppers to the outersoles through the rapid manipulation of sharp knives, skivers,[32] routers, and glue-coated brushes. Women were thought to be better suited for the assembly jobs because their hands were smaller and more capable of the manual dexterity needed to fit the shoe components together precisely. During the assembly process, some 120 pairs of hands touched a single shoe.

A strong, sweet solvent smell was prominent in the assembly area. Ceiling-mounted ventilation fans were ineffective since the heavy fumes settled to the floor. Assembly workers wore cotton surgical masks to protect themselves from the fumes; however, many workers pulled the masks below their noses, saying they were more comfortable that way.[33]

Rows and rows of shoes passed along a conveyor before the sharp eyes of the quality control inspectors. The inspectors examined each of the thousands of shoes produced daily for poor stitching or crooked connections between soles. Defective shoes were discarded. Approved shoes continued on the conveyor to stations where they were laced by assembly workers and finally put into Nike shoeboxes for shipment to the United States.[34]

Despite the dirty, dangerous, and difficult nature of the work inside the Bien Hoa factory, there was no shortage of applicants for positions. Although entry level wages averaged only $1.50 per day (the lowest of all countries where Nike manufactured), many workers viewed factory jobs as better than their other options, such as working in the rice paddies or pedaling a pedicab along the streets of Ho Chi Minh City.[35] With overtime pay at one and a half times the regular rate, workers could double their salaries—generating enough income to purchase a motorscooter or to send money home to impoverished rural relatives. These wages were well above national norms. An independent study by researchers from Dartmouth University showed that the average annual income for workers at two Nike subcontractor factories in Vietnam was

[26]Ernst & Young Audit. (n.d.). Corporate Watch. Accessed: March 26, 2000. **http://www.corpwatch.org/trac/nike/audit.html.**

[27]Ibid.

[28]Manning, J. (November 9, 1997). "Nike: Track's Across the Globe" (three-part newspaper series originally appearing in *The Oregonian*), online source **http://oregonlive.com/series/nike11091.html.**

[29]Manning, J. (November 9, 1997). "Nike's Asian Machine Goes on Trial," (part 1 of a three-part newspaper series originally appearing in *The Oregonian*), online source **http://oregonlive.com/series/nike11091.html.**

[30]Manning, J. (November 10, 1997). "Poverty's Legions Flock to Nike" (part 2 of a three-part newspaper series originally appearing in *The Oregonian*), online source **http://oregonlive.com/series/nike11091.html.**

[31]Vanderbilt, *The Sneaker Book,* p. 84.

[32]Skivers are cutting tools that are used to split leather. In athletic shoe manufacturing, skivers are used to cut away the excess leather when bonding the upper to the sole.

[33]Ernst & Young Audit. **http://www.corpwatch.org/trac/nike/audit.html.**

[34]Katz, *Just Do It,* p. 160.

[35]Lamb, D. (April 18, 1999). "Job Opportunity or Exploitation?" *Los Angeles Times,* Part C, p. 1.

between $545 and $566, compared with the national average of between $250 and $300.[36] Additionally, workers were provided free room and board and access to on-site health care facilities.

Many Vietnamese workers viewed positions in the shoe factory as transitional jobs—a way to earn money for a dowry or to experience living in a larger city. Many returned to their homes after working for Nike for two or three years to marry and begin the next phase of their lives.[37]

The Campaigns Against Nike

In the early 1990s, criticism of Nike's global labor practices began to gather steam. *Harper's Magazine*, for example, published the pay stub of an Indonesian worker, showing that the Nike subcontractor had paid the woman just under 14 cents per hour, and contrasted this with the high retail price of the shoes and the high salaries paid to the company's celebrity endorsers.[38] The Made in the U.S.A. Foundation, a group backed by American unions, used a million dollar ad budget to urge consumers to send their "old, dirty, smelly, worn-out Nikes" to Phil Knight in protest of Nike's Asian manufacturing practices.[39] Human rights groups and Christian organizations joined the labor unions in targeting the labor practices of the athletic shoes firm. Many felt that Nike's anti-authority corporate image ("Just Do It") and message of social betterment through fitness were incompatible with press photos of slight Asian women hunched over sewing machines seventy hours a week, earning just pennies an hour.

By mid-1993, Nike was being regularly pilloried in the press as an imperialist profiteer. A CBS news segment airing on July 2, 1993, opened with images of Michael Jordan and Andre Agassi, two athletes who had multimillion dollar promotion contracts with Nike. Viewers were told to contrast the athletes' pay checks with those of the Chinese and Indonesian workers who made "pennies" so that Nike could "Just Do It."[40]

In 1995, the *Washington Post* reported that a pair of Nike Air Pegasus shoes that retailed for $70 cost Nike only $2.75 in labor costs, or 4 percent of the price paid by consumers. Nike's operating profit on the same pair of shoes was $6.25, while the retailer pocketed $9 in operating profits, as shown in Exhibit 3. Also that year, shareholder activists organized by the Interfaith Center on Corporate Responsibility submitted a shareholder proposal at Nike's annual meeting, calling on the company to review labor practices by its subcontractors; the proposal garnered 3 percent of the shareholder vote.

Things were to get worse. A story in *Life*[41] magazine documented the use of child labor in Pakistan to produce soccer balls for Nike, Adidas, and other companies. The publicity fallout was intense. The public could not ignore the photographs of small children sitting in the dirt, carefully stitching together the panels of a soccer ball that would become the plaything of some American child the same age.[42] Nike moved quickly to work with its Pakistani subcontractor to eliminate the use of child labor, but damage to Nike's image had been done.

In October 1996, CBS News *48 Hours* broadcast a scathing report on Nike's factories in Vietnam. CBS reporter Roberta Baskin focused on low wage rates, extensive overtime, and physical abuse of workers. Several young workers told Baskin how a Korean supervisor had beaten them with a part of a shoe because of problems with production.[43] A journalist in Vietnam told the reporter that the phrase "to Nike someone" was part of the Vietnamese vernacular. It meant to "take out one's frustration on a fellow worker." Vietnamese plant managers refused to be interviewed, covering their faces as they ran inside the factory. CBS news anchor Dan Rather concluded the damaging report by saying, "Nike now says it plans to hire outside observers to talk to employees and examine working conditions in its Vietnam factories, but the company just won't say when that might happen."[44]

The negative publicity was having an effect. In 1996, a marketing research study authorized by Nike reported the perceptions of young people aged thirteen

[36]Baum, B. (August 27, 1999). "Study Concludes That Nike Workers Can More Than Make Ends Meet," *Athenaeum;* online version available at: http://www.athensnewspapers.com/1997/101797/1017.a3nike.html.

[37]Manning, "Poverty's Legions," http://oregonlive.com/series/nike11091.html.

[38]Ballinger, J. (August 1992). "Nike: The New Free Trade Heel," *Harper's,* p. 119.

[39]Katz, *Just Do It,* p. 166.

[40]Katz, *Just Do It,* p. 187.

[41]Schanberg, S. (June 1996). "Six Cents an Hour," *Life Magazine,* pp. 38–47.

[42]Holstein, W.J., Palmer, B., Ur-Rehman, S., and Ito, T. (December 23, 1996). "Santa's Sweatshops," *U.S. News and World Report,* p. 50.

[43]The *48 Hours* report, however, neglected to mention that the supervisor had subsequently been fired and was later criminally convicted in a Vietnamese court (Katz, *Just Do It,* p. 188).

[44]CBS News, *48 Hours* (October 17, 1996), transcript.

EXHIBIT 3

The Cost of a Pair of Nike "Air Pegasus" Shoes

Source: Adapted from *Washington Post* (May 3, 1995). "Why It Costs $70 for a Pair of Athletic Shoes."

A. Cost to Nike		B. Cost to retailer		C. Cost to consumer	
Materials	$9.00	Nike's operating profit	$6.25	Retail sales personnel	$9.50
Tariffs	3.00	Sales, distribution, and administration	5.00	Rent of retail space	9.00
Rent and equipment	3.00	Promotion/advertising	4.00	Retailer's operating profit	9.00
Production labor	2.75	Research and development	0.25	Other expenses	7.00
Subcontractor's operating profit	1.75				
Shipping	0.50				
Cost to Nike	**$20.00**	**Cost to retailer**	**$35.50**	**Cost to consumer**	**$70.00**

to twenty-five of Nike as a company. The top three perceptions, in the order of their response frequency, were athletics, cool, and bad labor practices.[45] Although Nike maintained that its sales were never affected, company executives were clearly concerned about the effect of criticism of its global labor practices on the reputation of the brand they had worked so hard to build.

The Evolution of Nike's Global Labor Practices

In its early years, Nike had maintained that the labor practices of its foreign subcontractors—like TKV—were simply not its responsibility. "When we started Nike," Knight later commented, "it never occurred to us that we should dictate what their factor[ies] should look like, which really didn't matter because we had no idea what a shoe factory should look like anyway."[46] The subcontractors, not Nike, were responsible for

wages and working conditions. Dave Taylor, Nike's vice president of production, explained the company's position: "We don't pay anybody at the factories and we don't set policy within the factories; it is their business to run."[47]

When negative articles first began appearing in the early 1990s, however, Nike managers realized that they needed to take some action to avoid further bad publicity. In 1992, the company drafted its first Code of Conduct (Exhibit 4), which required every subcontractor and supplier in the Nike network to honor all applicable local government labor and environmental regulations, or Nike would terminate the relationship.[48] The subcontractors were also required to allow plant inspections and complete all necessary paperwork. Despite the compliance reports the factories filed every six months, Nike insiders acknowledged that the code of conduct system might not catch all violations. Tony Nava, Nike's country coordinator for Indonesia, told a *Chicago Tribune* reporter, "We can't know if they're actually complying

[45]Manning, "Poverty's Legions," http://wwworegonlive.com/series/nike11101.html.

[46]Philip Knight, Speech to the National Press Club, May 12, 1998.

[47]Katz, *Just Do It*, p. 191.

[48]Ibid.

EXHIBIT 4

Nike's 1992 Code of Conduct

Source: Code of Conduct. (n.d.). Nike, Inc. Accessed: November 18, 2000. **http://www.nikebiz.com/labor/code.shtml.**

NIKE Inc. was founded on a handshake.

Implicit in that act was the determination that we would build our business with all our partners upon trust, teamwork, honesty, and mutual respect. We expect all of our business partners to operate on the same principles.

At the core of the NIKE corporate ethic is the belief that we are a company comprised of many different kinds of people, appreciating individual diversity, and dedicated to equal opportunity for each individual.

NIKE designs, manufactures, and markets sports and fitness products. At each step in that process we are dedicated to minimizing our impact on the environment. We seek to implement to the maximum extent possible the three "R's" of environmental action—reduce, reuse, and recycle.

There is No Finish Line.

MEMORANDUM OF UNDERSTANDING

Wherever NIKE operates around the globe, we are guided by our Code of Conduct and bind our business partners to those principles with a signed Memorandum of Understanding.

Government Regulation of Business (Subcontractor/supplier) certifies compliance with all applicable local government regulations regarding minimum wage; overtime; child labor laws; provisions of pregnancy, menstrual leave; provisions for vacation and holidays; and mandatory retirement benefits.

Safety and Health (Subcontractor/supplier) certifies compliance with all applicable local government regulations regarding occupational health and safety.

Worker Insurance (Subcontractor/supplier) certifies compliance with all applicable local laws providing health insurance, life insurance, and worker's compensation.

Forced Labor (Subcontractor/supplier) certifies that it and its suppliers and contractors do not use any form of forced labor—prison or otherwise.

Environment (Subcontractor/supplier) certifies compliance with all applicable local environmental regulations, and adhere to NIKE's own broader environmental practices, including the prohibition on the use of chloro-flouro-carbons (CFCs), the release of which could contribute to the depletion of the earth's ozone layer.

Equal Opportunity (Subcontractor/supplier) certifies that it does not discriminate in hiring, salary, benefits, advancement, termination, or retirement on the basis of gender, race, religion, age, sexual orientation or ethnic origin.

Documentation and Inspection (Subcontractor/supplier) agrees to maintain on file such documentation as may be needed to demonstrate compliance with the certifications in this Memorandum of Understanding, and further agrees to make these documents available for NIKE's inspection upon request.

with what they put down on paper."[49] In short, Nike required its subcontractors to comply with existing labor laws, but did not feel it was the firm's duty to challenge local policies that suppressed worker rights or kept wages low in order to attract manufacturing.

In 1994, Nike tried to address this problem by hiring Ernst & Young, the accounting firm, to independently monitor worker abuse allegations in Nike's Indonesian factories. Later, Ernst & Young also audited Nike's factories in Thailand and Vietnam. Although these audits were not made public, a copy of the Vietnam audit leaked to the press showed that workers were often unaware of the toxicity of the compounds they were using and ignorant of the need for safety precautions.[50] In 1998, Nike implemented important changes in its Vietnamese plants to reduce exposure to toxins—substituting less harmful chemicals, installing ventilation systems, and training personnel in occupational health and safety issues.

In 1996, Nike established a new Labor Practices Department, headed by Dusty Kidd, formerly a public relations executive for the company. Later that year, Nike hired GoodWorks International, headed by former U.S. ambassador to the United Nations Andrew Young, to investigate conditions in its overseas factories. In January 1997, GoodWorks issued a glossy report, stating that "Nike is doing a good job in the application of its Code of Conduct. But Nike can and should do better." The report was criticized by activists for its failure to look at the issue of wages. Young demurred, saying he did not have expertise in conducting wage surveys. Said one critic, "This was a public relations problem, and the world's largest sneaker company did what it does best: it purchased a celebrity endorsement."[51]

Over the next few years, Nike continued to work to improve labor practices in its overseas subcontractor factories, as well as the public perception of them. In January 1998, Nike formed a Corporate Responsibility Division, combining the Labor Practices, Global Community Affairs, and Environmental Action Teams under the leadership of former Microsoft executive Maria S. Eitel, hired to be Nike's new vice president for corporate and social responsibility. Nike subsequently doubled the staff of this division. In May of that year, Knight gave a speech at the National Press Club, at which he announced several new initiatives. At that time, he committed Nike to raise the minimum age for employment in its shoe factories to eighteen and in its apparel factories to sixteen. He also promised to achieve OSHA standards for indoor air quality in all its factories by the end of the year, mainly by eliminating the use of the solvent toluene; to expand educational programs for workers and its microenterprise loan program; and to fund university research on responsible business practices. Nike also continued its use of external monitors, hiring PricewaterhouseCoopers to join Ernst & Young in a comprehensive program of factory audits, checking them against Nike's code. At the conclusion of his speech Knight said,

> At the end of the day, we don't have all the answers. Nobody has all the answers. We want to be the best corporate citizens we can be. If we continue to improve, and our industry colleagues and people interested in these issues join in our efforts, the workers are the ultimate beneficiaries.[52]

Apparel Industry Partnership

One of Nike's most ambitious social responsibility initiatives was its participation in the Apparel Industry Partnership. It was this involvement that would lead, eventually, to Knight's break with the University of Oregon.

In August 1996, President Clinton launched the White House Apparel Industry Partnership on Workplace Standards (AIP). The initial group was comprised of eighteen organizations. Participants included several leading manufacturers, such as Nike, Reebok, and Liz Claiborne. Also in the group were several labor unions, including the Union of Needletrades, Industrial, and Textile Employees (UNITE) and the Retail, Wholesale and Department Store Union; and several human rights, consumer, and shareholder organizations, including Business for Social Responsibility, the Interfaith Center on Corporate Responsibility, and the National

[49]Goozner, M. (November 7, 1994). "Nike Manager Knows Abuses Do Happen," *Chicago Tribune*, p. 6.

[50]Hammond, K. (November 7, 1997). "Leaked Audit: Nike Factory Violated Worker Laws," *Mother Jones.* http://www.motherjones.com/news_wire/nike.html.

[51]Glass, S. (August 25, 1997). "The Young and the Feckless," *The New Republic*, online source: http://www.corpwatch.org/trac/feature/sweatshops/newprogressive. html. Glass was later fired by *The New Republic,* which charged that Glass had fabricated some of his sources for this and other articles.

[52]Federal News Service. (May 12, 1998). National Press Club Luncheon Address by Philip Knight, Chief Executive Officer, Nike. LEXIS-NEXIS Academic Universe, Category: News. Accessed: August 27, 2000. http://web.lexis-nexis.com/universe.

Consumers League. The goal of the AIP was to develop a set of standards to ensure that apparel and footwear were not made under sweatshop conditions. For companies, it held out the promise of certifying to their customers that their products were "no sweat." For labor and human rights groups, it held out the promise of improving working conditions in overseas factories.[53]

In April 1997, after months of often-fractious meetings, the AIP announced that it had agreed on a Workplace Code of Conduct that sought to define decent and humane working conditions.[54] Companies agreeing to the code would have to pledge not to use forced labor, that is, prisoners or bonded or indentured workers. They could not require more than sixty hours of work a week, including overtime. They could not employ children younger than fifteen years old, or the age for completing compulsory schooling, whichever was older except they could hire fourteen-year-olds if local law allowed. The code also called on signatory companies to treat all workers with respect and dignity; to refrain from discrimination on the basis of gender, race, religion, age, disability, sexual orientation, nationality, political opinion, or social or ethnic origin; and to provide a safe and healthy workplace. Employees' rights to organize and bargain collectively would be respected. In a key provision, the code also required companies to pay at least the local legal minimum wage or the prevailing industry wage, whichever was higher. All standards would apply not only to a company's own facilities but also to their subcontractors or suppliers.

Knight, who prominently joined President Clinton and others at a White House ceremony announcing the code, issued the following statement:

> Nike agreed to participate in this Partnership because it was the first credible attempt, by a diverse group of interests, to address the important issue of improving factories worldwide. It was worth the effort and hard work. The agreement will prove important for several reasons. Not only is our industry stepping up to the plate and taking a giant swing at improving factory conditions, but equally important, we are finally providing consumers some guidance to counter all of the misinformation that has surrounded this issue for far too long.[55]

The Fair Labor Association

But this was not the end of the AIP's work; it also had to agree on a process for monitoring compliance with the code. Although the group hoped to complete its work in six months, over a year later it was still deeply divided on several key matters. Internal documents leaked to the *New York Times* in July 1998 showed that industry representatives had opposed proposals, circulated by labor and human rights members, calling for the monitoring of 30 percent of plants annually by independent auditors. The companies also opposed proposals that would require them to support workers' rights to organize independent unions and to bargain collectively, even in countries like China where workers did not have such rights by law. Said one nonindustry member, "We're teetering on the edge of collapse."[56]

Finally, a subgroup of nine centrist participants, including Nike, began meeting separately in an attempt to move forward. In November 1998, this subgroup announced that it had come to agreement on a monitoring system for overseas factories of U.S.-based companies. The AIP would establish a new organization, the Fair Labor Association (FLA), to oversee compliance with its Workplace Code of Conduct. Companies would be required to monitor their own factories and those of their subcontractors for compliance; all would have to be checked within the first two years. In addition, the FLA would select and certify independent external monitors, who would inspect 10 percent of each firm's factories each year. Most of these monitors were expected to be accounting firms, which had expertise in conducting audits. The monitors' reports would be kept private. If a company were found to be out of compliance, it would be given a chance to correct the problem. Eventually, if it did not, the company would be dropped from the FLA and its termination announced to the public. Companies would pay for most of their own monitoring.[57]

The Clinton administration quickly endorsed the plan. Secretary of Labor Alexis Herman said, "[We are] convinced this agreement lays the foundation to eliminate sweatshop labor, here and abroad. It is workable for business and creates a credible system

[53]"Companies Agree to Meet on Sweatshops," *Washington Post,* August 3, 1996.

[54]For the full text of the Fair Labor Association Workplace Code of Conduct, see **http://www.fairlabor.org/html/amendctr.html#workplace**.

[55]Philip H. Knight, statement released to the press, April 14, 1997.

[56]Steven Greenhouse, "Anti-Sweatshop Coalition Finds Itself at Odds on Garment Factory Code," *New York Times,* July 3, 1998.

[57]For a description of the monitoring process, see: **http://www.fairlabor .org/html/amendctr.html#monitoringprocess**.

that will let consumers know the garments they buy are not produced by exploited workers."[58]

Both manufacturers and institutional buyers stood to benefit from participation in the Fair Labor Association. Companies, once certified for three years, could place an FLA service mark on their brands, signaling both to individual consumers and institutional buyers that their products were "sweatshop-free." It was expected that the FLA would also serve the needs of institutional buyers, particularly universities. By joining the FLA and agreeing to contract only with certified companies, universities could warrant to their students and others that their logo apparel and athletic gear were manufactured under conditions conforming with an established code of fair labor standards.[59] Both parties would pay for these benefits. The FLA was to be funded by dues from participating companies ($5,000 to $100,000 annually, depending on revenue) and by payments from affiliated colleges and universities (based on 1 percent of their licensing income from logo products, up to a $50,000 annual cap).

Criticism of the Fair Labor Association

Although many welcomed the agreement—and some new companies signed on with the FLA soon after it was announced—others did not. Warnaco, a leading apparel maker that had participated in the AIP, quit, saying that the monitoring process would require it to turn over competitive information to outsiders. The American Apparel Manufacturing Association (AAMA), an industry group representing three hundred fifty companies, scoffed at the whole idea of monitoring. "Who is going to do the monitoring?" asked a spokesperson for the AAMA, apparently sarcastically. "Accountants or Jesuit priests?" The FLA monitoring scheme was also attacked as insufficient by some Partnership participants that had not been part of the subgroup. In their view, companies simply could not be relied upon to monitor themselves objectively. Said Jay Mazur, president of UNITE, "The fox cannot watch the chickens. If they want the monitoring to be independent, it can't be controlled by the companies."[60] FLA critics believed that a visit from an external monitor once every ten years would not prevent abuses. And in any case, as a practical matter, they stated that most monitors would be drawn from the major accounting firms that did business with the companies they were monitoring and were therefore unlikely to seek out lapses. Companies would not be required to publish a list of their factories, and any problems uncovered by the monitoring process could be kept from the public under the rules governing nondisclosure of proprietary information.

One of the issues most troubling to critics was the code's position on wages. The code called on companies to pay the minimum wage or prevailing wage, whichever was higher. But in many of the countries of Southeast Asia, these wages fell well below the minimum considered necessary for a decent standard of living for an individual or family. For example, the *Economist*[61] reported that Indonesia's average minimum wage—paid by Nike subcontractors—was only two-thirds of what a person needed for basic subsistence. An alternative view was that a code of conduct should require that companies pay a *living wage*, that is, compensation for a normal workweek adequate to provide for the basic needs of an average family, adjusted for the average number of adult wage earners per family. One problem with this approach, however, was that many countries did not systematically study the cost of living, relative to wages, so defining a living wage was difficult. The Partnership asked the U.S. Department of Labor to conduct a preliminary study of these issues; the results were published in 2000 (Exhibit 5).

The code also called on companies to respect workers' rights to organize and bargain collectively. Yet a number of FLA companies outsourced production to nondemocratic countries, such as China and Vietnam, where workers had no such rights. Finally, some criticized the agreement on the grounds it provided companies, as one put it, "a piece of paper to use as a fig leaf." Commented a representative of the needle trades unions, "The problem with the partnership plan is that it tinkers at the margins of the sweatshop system but creates the impression that it is doing much more. This is potentially helpful to companies stung by public condemnation of their labor practices, but it hurts millions of workers and undermines the growing antisweatshop movement."[62]

[58]"Plan to Curtain Sweatshops Rejected by Union," *New York Times*, November 5, 1998.

[59]For a list of signatory companies, universities, and other organizations, see: http://www.fairlabor.org/html/affiliat.html.

[60]*New York Times*, November 21, 1997.

[61]Anonymous. (June 15, 1991). "Indonesia: Staying Alive," *The Economist*, p. 38.

[62]Alan Howard, "Partners in Sweat," *The Nation*, December 29, 1998.

EXHIBIT 5

Wages, Minimum Wages, and Poverty Lines for Selected Countries (in U.S. Dollars)

Country	Year (Latest Available)	National Poverty Line	Minimum Wage	Prevailing Wage in Apparel and Footwear Industries
China	1997	$21–$27/cap/mo*	$12–$39/mo	$115–$191/mo
Indonesia	1999	$5–$6/cap/mo	$15–$34/mo	$15–$42/mo
South Korea	1999	$182/mo	$265/mo	$727–$932/mo
Thailand	1999	$22/cap/mo	$93–$109/mo	$106/mo
Taiwan	1998	$214–$344/mo	$476/mo	$690–$742/mo
Vietnam	1997	$27–$29/mo	$35–$45/mo	$47–$56/mo
Philippines	1999	$26/cap/mo	$150/mo	$150/mo
Italy	1998	$390/cap/mo	$949–$1,445/mo	$1,280–$1,285/mo
United States	1998	$693/cap/mo	$858/mo–$1,083/mo	$1,420–$1,488/mo

National Poverty Line: Poverty measures reflect an estimate of absolute poverty thresholds based on some specified set of basic needs. Opinions differ as to whether the poverty line should reflect mere physical subsistence levels or sufficient income to provide for a nutritious diet, safe drinking water, suitable housing, energy, transportation, health care, child care, education, savings and discretionary income. Comparability between countries is difficult because the basis for establishing the poverty level usually differs across countries.

Minimum Wage: The minimum wage fixing system differs according to the country's objectives and criteria. It is usually set by striking a balance between the needs of the worker and what employers can afford or what economic conditions will permit. A range for minimum wage indicates that the country has differential minimums based on the region, often differing for urban and rural regions.

Prevailing Wage: The prevailing wage reflects the "going rate" or average level of wages paid by employers for workers in the apparel or footwear industries. Positions requiring greater skills, supervisory responsibilities or workers with longer years of employment typically earn more than the wage reported. Nonwage benefits such as access to health care, paid vacations, supplementary pay or training are not included in the prevailing wage.

Sources: The wages, minimum wages, and poverty lines for selected countries are from the U.S. Department of Labor (February 2000). "Wages, Benefits, Poverty Line and Meeting Workers' Needs in the Apparel and Footwear Industries of Selected Countries." **http://www.dol.gov/ilab/public/media/reports/oiea/main.htm.** The information on Vietnam is from Canada NewsWire (October 16, 1997). "Nike Factory Workers in SE Asia Help Support Their Families and Have Discretionary Income, According to Preliminary Findings of Study by MBA Team From Dartmouth's Tuck School."

*Per capita per month.

The Worker Rights Consortium

Some activists in the antisweatshop movement decided to chart their own course, independent of the FLA. On October 20, 1999, students from more than one hundred colleges held a press conference to announce formation of the Worker Rights Consortium (WRC), and called on their schools to withdraw from, or not to join, the FLA. The organization would be formally launched at a founding convention in April, 2000.[63]

[63] The website for the WRC is http://www.workersrights.org. Further material on disagreements within the FLA that led to the WRC's founding may be found at http://www.sweatshopwatch.org.

The Worker Rights Consortium differed radically in its approach to eliminating sweatshops. First, the WRC did not permit corporations to join; it was comprised exclusively of universities and colleges, with unions and human rights organizations playing an advisory role. In joining the WRC, universities would agree to "require decent working conditions in factories producing their licensed products." Unlike the FLA, the WCA did not endorse a single, comprehensive set of fair labor standards. Rather, it called on its affiliated universities to develop their own codes. However, it did establish minimum standards that such codes should meet ones that were, in some respects, stricter than the FLA's. Perhaps most significantly, companies would have to pay a living wage. Companies were also required to publish the names and addresses of all of their manufacturing facilities, in contrast to FLA rules. Universities could refuse to license goods made in countries where compliance with fair labor standards was "deemed impossible," whatever efforts companies had made to enforce their own codes in factories there.

By contrast with the FLA, monitoring would be carried out by "a network of local organizations in regions where licensed goods are produced," generally nongovernmental organizations, independent human rights groups, and unions. These organizations would conduct unannounced "spot investigations," usually in response to worker complaints; WRC organizers called this the "fire alarm" method of uncovering code violations. Systematic monitoring would not be attempted.

The consortium's governance structure reflected its mission of being an organization by and for colleges and universities. Its 12-person board was composed of 3 representatives of United Students Against Sweatshops, 3 university administrators from participating schools, and 6 members drawn from an Advisory Board of persons with "expertise in the issues surrounding worker abuses in the apparel industry and independent verification of labor standards in apparel factories." No seats at the table were reserved for industry representatives. The group would be financed by 1 percent of licensing revenue from participating universities, as well as foundation grants.

The Universities Take Sides

Over the course of the spring semester 2000, student protests were held on a number of campuses, including the University of Oregon, to demand that their schools join the WRC. By April, around forty-five schools had done so. At UO, the administration encouraged an open debate on the issue so that all sides could be heard on how to ensure that UO products were made under humane conditions. Over a period of several months, the Academic Senate passed a resolution in support of the WRC. In a referendum sponsored by the student government, three-quarters of voters supported a proposal to join the WRC. A committee of faculty, students, administrators, and alumni appointed by the president voted unanimously to join the consortium.[64] Finally, after concluding that all constituents had had an opportunity to be heard, on April 12, 2000, University of Oregon president David Frohnmayer announced that UO would join the WRC for one year. Its membership would be conditional, he said, on the Consortium's agreement to give companies a voice in its operations and universities more power in governance. Shortly after the University's decision was announced in the press, Phil Knight withdrew his philanthropic contribution. In his public announcement, he stated his main disagreements with the Worker Rights Consortium:

> Frankly, we are frustrated that factory monitoring is badly misconstrued. For us one of the great hurdles and real handicaps in the dialogue has been the complexity of the issue. For real progress to be made, all key participants have to be at the table. That's why the FLA has taken so long to get going. The WRC is supported by the AFL-CIO and its affiliated apparel workers' union, UNITE. Their main aim, logically and understandably, however misguided, is to bring apparel jobs back to the U.S. Among WRC rules, no company can participate in setting standards, or monitoring. It has an unrealistic living wage provision. And its "gotcha" approach to monitoring doesn't do what monitoring should—measure conditions and make improvements.[65]

[64]Sarah Edith Jacobson, "Nike's Power Game" [editorial page letter], *New York Times*, May 16, 2000.
[65]"Knight's Statement," by Philip H. Knight, via press release, **http://www.oregonlive.com**.

Case 33

Etch-A-Sketch Ethics

This case was prepared by Charles W. L. Hill, the University of Washington.

The Ohio Art Company is perhaps best known as the producer on one of the top selling toys of all time, the venerable Etch-A-Sketch. More than 100 million of the familiar red rectangular drawing toys have been sold since 1960 when it was invented. The late 1990s, however, was a troubled time for the toy's maker. Confronted with sluggish toy sales, the Ohio Art Company lost money for two years running. In December 2000, it took the strategic decision to outsource production of the Etch-A-Sketch toys to Kin Ki Industrial, a leading Chinese toy maker, laying off one hundred U.S. workers in the process.

The closure of the Etch-A-Sketch line was not unexpected among employees. The company had already moved the production of other toy lines to China, and most employees knew it was just a matter of time before Etch-A-Sketch went too. Still, the decision was a tough one for the company, which did most of its manufacturing in its home base, the small Ohio town of Bryan (population eight thousand). As William Killgallon, the CEO of the Ohio Art Company noted, the employees who made the product "were like family. It was a necessary financial decision we saw coming for some time, and we did it gradually, product by product. But that doesn't mean it's emotionally easy."

In a small town like Bryan, the cumulative effect of outsourcing to China has been significant. The tax base is eroding from a loss of manufacturing and a population decline. The local paper is full of notices of home foreclosures and auctions. According to former employees, the biggest hole in their lives after Etch-A-Sketch moved came from the death of a community. For many workers, the company was their family, and now that family was gone.

The rationale for the outsourcing was simple enough. Pressured to keep the cost of Etch-A-Sketch under $10 by such big retailers as Wal-Mart and Toys "R" Us, the Ohio Art Company had to get its costs down or lose money. In this case, unionized workers making $1,500 a month were replaced by Chinese factory workers who made $75 a month. However, according to Killgallon, the main savings came not from lower wages, but from lower overhead costs for plant, maintenance, electricity, payroll, and the ability to get out from the soaring costs of providing health benefits to U.S. manufacturing employees.

The choice of Kin Ki as manufacturer for Etch-A-Sketch was easy enough—the company had been making pocket-sized Etch-A-Sketch toys for nearly a decade and always delivered on cost. To help Kin Ki, the Ohio Art Company shipped some of its best equipment to the company, and it continues to send crucial raw materials to Kin Ki, such as aluminum powder, which is hard to get in China.

The story would have ended there had it not been for an exposé run in the *New York Times* in December 2003. The *Times* reporter painted a dismal picture of working conditions at the Kin Ki factory that manufactured the Etch-A-Sketch. According to official Kin Ki publications: "Workers at Kin Ki make a decent salary, rarely work nights or weekends and often 'hang out along the streets, playing Ping Pong and watching TV.' They all have work contracts, pensions and medical benefits. The factory canteen offers tasty

Copyright © 2005 by Charles W. L. Hill. This case was prepared by Charles W. L. Hill, the University of Washington, as the basis for class discussion rather than to illustrate either effective or ineffective handling of an administrative situation. Reprinted by permission of Charles W. L. Hill. All rights reserved. For the most recent financial results of the company discussed in this case, go to **http://finance .yahoo.com,** input the company's stock symbol, and download the latest company report from its homepage.

food. The dormitories are comfortable." Not so according to Joseph Kahn, the *Times* reporter. He alleged that real world Kin Ki employees, mostly teenage migrants from internal Chinese provinces, work long hours for 40 percent less than the company claims. They are paid 24 cents per hour, below the legal minimum wage (33 cents an hour) in Shenzhen province where Kin Ki is located. Most do not have pensions, medical benefits, or employment contracts. Production starts at 7:30 A.M. and continues until 10 P.M., with breaks only for lunch and dinner. Saturdays and Sundays are treated as normal workdays. This translates into a work week of seven 12-hour days, or 84 hours a week, well above the standard 40-hour week set by authorities in Shenzhen. Moreover, local rules allow for no more than 32 hours of overtime and stipulate that the employees must be paid 1.5 times the standard hourly wage, but Kin Ki's overtime rate is just 1.3 times base pay.

As for the "comfortable dormitories," the workers sleep head to toe in tiny rooms with windows that are covered with chicken wires. To get into and out of the factories, which are surrounded by high walls, workers must enter and leave through a guarded gate. As for the tasty food, it is apparently a mix of boiled vegetables, beans, and rice with meat or fish served only twice a month.

The workers at Kin Ki have apparently become restless. They went on strike twice in 2003, demanding higher wages and better working conditions. The company responded by raising wages a few cents and allotting an extra dish of food to each worker per day (but still no more meat)! However, Kin Ki simultaneously made "fried squid" of two workers who were ring leaders of the strike (fried squid is apparently a popular term for dismissal). Johnson Tao, a senior executive at the company, denies that the two ring leaders were dismissed for organizing the strikes. Rather, he noted that they were well-known troublemakers who left the factory of their own accord. Tao also acknowledges the low wages at the company, stating, "I know that I need to increase wages to comply with the law. I have the intention of doing this and will raise all wages in 2004."

Meanwhile, back in Ohio, William Killgallon, Ohio's CEO, stated to the *Times* reporter that he considered Kin Ki's executives to be honest and that he had no knowledge of labor problems there. But he said that he intended to make a visit to China soon to make sure that "they understand what we expect."

REFERENCES

Carol Hymowitz. "Toy Maker Survives by Moving an Icon From Ohio to China," *Wall Street Journal*, October 21, 2003, page B1.

Joseph Kahn. "An Ohio Town Is Hard Hit as Leading Industry Moves to China," New York Times, December 7, 2003, page A8.

Joseph Kahn. "Ruse in Toyland: Chinese Workers Hidden Woe," *New York Times*, December 7, 2003, pages A1, A8.

John Seewer. "Etch A Sketch Enters Fourth Decade," *Columbian*, November 22, 2001, page E3.

Case 34

Western Drug Companies and the AIDS Epidemic in South Africa

This case was prepared by Charles W. L. Hill, the University of Washington.

In December 1997, the government of South Africa passed a law that authorized two controversial practices. One, called parallel importing, allowed importers in South Africa to purchase drugs from the cheapest source available, regardless of whether the patent holders had given their approval. Thus, South Africa asserted its right to import "generic versions" of drugs that are still patent protected. The government did this because it claimed to be unable to afford the high cost of medicines that were patent protected. The other practice, called compulsory licensing, permitted the South African government to license local companies to produce cheaper versions of drugs whose patents are held by foreign companies, irrespective of whether the patent holder agreed.

The law seemed to be in violation of international agreements to protect property rights, including World Trade Organization agreements on patents to which South Africa is a signatory. South Africa, however, insisted that the law was necessary given its own health crisis and the high cost of patented medicines. By 1997, South Africa was wrestling with an AIDS crisis of enormous proportions. It was estimated that over 3 million of the country's 45 million people were infected with the virus at the time, more than in any other country. However, although the AIDS epidemic in South Africa was seen as the primary reason for the new law, the law itself was applied to "communicable diseases" (of which AIDS is just one, albeit a devastating one).

Foreign drug manufacturers saw the law as an unbridled attempt to expropriate their intellectual property rights, and thirty-nine foreign companies quickly filed a lawsuit in the country to try to block implementation of the law. Drug manufacturers were particularly concerned about the applicability of the law to all "communicable diseases." They feared that South Africa was the thin end of the wedge, and if the law was allowed to stand, other countries would follow suit. Many Western companies also feared that if poor countries such as South Africa were allowed to buy low-priced generic versions of patent protected drugs, in violation of intellectual property laws, American and European consumers would soon demand the same.

In defense of their patents, the drug companies argued that because drug development is a very expensive, time-consuming, and risky process, they need the protection of intellectual property laws to maintain the incentive to innovate. It can take $800 million and twelve years to develop a drug and bring it to market. Less than one in five compounds that enter clinical trials actually become marketed drugs—the rest fail in trials due to poor efficacy or unfavorable side effects—and of those that make it to market, only three out of ten earn profits that exceed their costs of capital. If drug companies could not count on high prices for their few successful products, the drug development process would dry up.

Copyright © 2005 by Charles W. L. Hill. This case was prepared by Charles W. L. Hill, the University of Washington, as the basis for class discussion rather than to illustrate either effective or ineffective handling of an administrative situation. Reprinted by permission of Charles W. L. Hill. All rights reserved.

The drug companies have long recognized that countries such as South Africa face special health challenges and lack the money to pay developed world prices. Accordingly, there is a history in the industry of pricing drugs low in the developing world or giving them away. For example, many AIDS drugs were already being sold to developing nations at large discounts to their prices in the United States. The South African government thought this was not good enough. The government was quickly supported by various human rights and AIDS organizations, which cast the case as an attempt by the prosperous multinational drug companies of the West to maintain their intellectual property rights in the face of desperate attempts by an impoverished government to stem a deadly crisis. For their part, the drug companies stated that the case had little to do with AIDS and was really about the right of South Africa to break international law.

While the drug companies may have had international law on their side, the tie-in with the AIDS epidemic clearly put them on the public relations defensive. After a blizzard of negative publicity, and little support from Western governments who were keen not to touch this political "hot potato," several leading manufacturers of AIDS drugs, while still opposing the South African law, started to change their policies. In May 2000, five large manufacturers of AIDS medicines—Merck, Bristol-Myers Squibb, Roche, Glaxo, and Boehringer Ingelhiem—announced that they would negotiate lower priced AIDS drugs in developing countries, primarily in Sub-Saharan Africa (some 25 million of the 36 million people infected with the HIV virus in 2000 lived in that region). Still the protests continued.

In February 2001, an Indian drug company, Cipla Ltd., offered to sell a cocktail of three AIDS drugs to poor African nations for $600 per patient per year, and for $350 a year to Doctors without Borders (AIDS is commonly treated with a cocktail that combines up to ten different antiviral drugs). The patents for these drugs were held by Western companies, but Indian law allowed local companies to produce generic versions of patent protected drugs.

The Cipla announcement seemed to galvanize Western drug companies into further action. In March 2001, Merck announced that it would cut the prices of its two AIDS drugs, Crixivan and Stocrin. Crixivan, which sold for $6,016 per year in the United States,

would be sold in developing countries for $600 a year. Stocrin, which cost $4,730 a year in the United States, would be sold for $500. Both drugs were often used together as part of an AIDS cocktail. Officials at Doctors without Borders, the Nobel Peace Prize–winning relief agency, welcomed the announcement, but pointed out that in a region where many people lived on less than a dollar a day, the price was still out of reach of many AIDS patients.

A few days later, Bristol-Meyers Squibb went further, announcing that it would sell its AIDS drug Zerit to poor nations in Africa for just $0.15 a day, or $54 a patient per year, which was below Zerit's costs of production. In the United States and Europe, Zerit was selling for $3,589 per patient per year. This was followed by an announcement from Abbot Labs that it would sell two of its AIDS drugs at "no profit" in Sub-Saharan Africa.

None of these moves, however, were enough to satisfy critics. In April 2001, the drug companies seemed to come to the conclusion that they were losing the public relations war, and they agreed to drop their suit against the South African government. This opened the way for South Africa to start importing cheap generic versions of patented medicines from producers such as Cipla of India. The decision to drop the suit was widely interpreted in the media as a defeat for the drug companies and a reaffirmation of the ability of the South African government to enforce compulsory licensing. At the same time, the pharmaceutical companies appear to have gotten assurances from South Africa that locally produced generic versions of patented drugs would only be sold in Sub-Saharan Africa, and not exported to other regions of the world.

In 2003, Aspen Pharmaceuticals, a South African drug maker, took advantage of the 1997 law to introduce a generic version of Stavudine, and it asked the South African authorities' permission to produce up to six more AIDS drugs. Aspen had licensed the rights to produce this drug, and several others, from Bristol-Meyers Squibb and Glaxo, the large British company. Bristol and Glaxo had waved their rights to royalties from sales of the drugs in Sub-Saharan Africa. At the same, the companies noted that Aspen was only able to sell the drugs within the Sub-Saharan Africa region.

Despite these moves, critics still urged Western drug companies to do more to fight the global AIDS epidemic, which by 2003 was estimated to afflict some

50 million people. For example, in a 2003 *New York Times* Op-Ed article, noted playwright and AIDS activist, Larry Kramer, stated, "It is incumbent upon every manufacturer of every HIV drug to contribute its patents or its drugs free for the salvation of these people.... I believe it is evil for drug companies to possess a means of saving lives and then not provide it to the desperate people who need it. What kind of hideous people have we become? It is time to throw out the selfish notion that these companies have the right not to share their patents."

Meanwhile in South Africa, the AIDS epidemic continued on its relentless course. By 2004, some 5.3 million South Africans were estimated to have been infected with HIV, and 600 people a day were dying from AIDS-related complications. In 2003, the South African government had committed itself to offering at low or no cost antiviral drugs to everyone with AIDS. By working with pharmaceutical companies such as Aspen and three Indian producers of generic drugs, the government was able to purchase a cocktail of antiviral HIV drugs for $65 per patient per month. However, by late 2004 only one out of fifty AIDS patients who were ready for the drugs were getting them, according to news reports. The problem now was distribution and particularly a chronic shortage of clinics, doctors, and nurses. Estimates suggested that it would still be years before cheap AIDS drugs were available to all those who needed them in South Africa.

REFERENCES

R. Block, "Big Drug Firms Defend Right to Patent on AIDS Drugs in South African Courts," *Wall Street Journal*, March 6, 2001, p. A3.

H. Cooper, R. Zimmerman, and L. McGinley, "Patents Pending—AIDS Epidemic Traps Drug Firms in a Vise," *Wall Street Journal*, March 2, 2001, p. A1.

J. Jeter, "Trial Opens in South Africa AIDS Drug Suit," *Washington Post*, March 6, 2001, p. A1.

L. Kramer, "The Plague We Can't Escape," *New York Times*, March 15, 2003, p. A17.

J. Nurton, "Overcoming the AIDS Hurdle," *Managing Intellectual Property*, June 2002, pp. 39–40.

T. Smith, "Mixed View of a Pact for Generic Drugs," *New York Times*, August 29, 2003, p. C3.

C. Timberg, "South Africans with AIDS See a Ray of Hope," *Washington Post*, November 30, 2004, p. A1.